Accounting Principles

Accounting Principles

SECOND EDITION

Jack L. Smith, Ph.D., C.P.A.
Professor of Accounting, University of South Florida

Robert M. Keith, Ph.D., C.P.A.
Professor of Accounting, University of South Florida

William L. Stephens, D.B.A., C.P.A.
Professor of Accounting, University of South Florida

McGraw-Hill Book Company

New York   St. Louis   San Francisco   Auckland   Bogotá   Hamburg   Johannesburg
London   Madrid   Mexico   Montreal   New Delhi   Panama   Paris
São Paulo   Singapore   Sydney   Tokyo   Toronto

ACCOUNTING PRINCIPLES

1 2 3 4 5 6 7 8 9 0   V N H V N H   8 9 8 7 6

ISBN 0-07-059120-2

This book was set in Times Roman by Progressive Typographers, Inc.
The editors were Jim DeVoe, Michael Elia, and Peggy Rehberger;
the designer was Elliot Epstein;
the production supervisor was Diane Renda.
Photography by Peter Epstein; photo on p. 735 by Paul Sequeira/Rapho/Photo
Researchers, Inc.; photo on p. 1029 by McGraw-Hill Corporate Affairs.
New drawings were done by J & R Services, Inc.
Von Hoffmann Press, Inc., was printer and binder.

Library of Congress Cataloging-in-Publication Data

Smith, Jack L.
    Accounting principles.

    Includes index.
    1. Accounting.   I. Keith, Robert M.   II. Stephens,
William L.   III. Title.
HF5635.S644   1986   657   85-17080
ISBN 0-07-059120-2

About the Authors

Jack L. Smith is Professor of Accounting in the College of Business Administration at the University of South Florida. He received a Ph.D. in accounting at the University of Mississippi and is a CPA. Professor Smith is a member of the American Accounting Association, the AICPA, the Florida Institute of Certified Public Accountants, the National Association of Accountants, and the Florida Association of Accounting Educators, and has been active in a number of state and local professional organizations, as well as the Delta Gamma Chapter of Beta Alpha Psi. He is also active in various local and national professional development programs and has received awards as an outstanding discussion leader. In addition to *Accounting for Financial Statement Presentation,* an MBA-level introductory financial accounting text coauthored with Robert M. Keith, Professor Smith is the author of a number of articles in the *Journal of Accountancy, The Florida CPA,* and the *Financial Executive,* as well as two award winning articles published in the May and July 1978 issues of *Management Accountant.* In addition to his writing activities, Jack Smith is also an experienced teacher. His 20 years of working closely with students make this edition of the principles book one that actively involves students in the learning process.

Robert M. Keith is Professor of Accounting in the College of Business Administration at the University of South Florida. He received his Ph.D. in accounting from the University of Alabama and holds the CPA certificate. While his research interests center on financial accounting, Professor Keith also has a strong interest in accounting education at both the college and professional levels. He received the first Outstanding Accounting Faculty Award by the Delta Gamma Chapter of Beta Alpha Psi and was voted an outstanding discussion leader four years in a row by CPA participants in continuing professional education seminars sponsored by the Florida Institute of CPAs. In addition to papers presented at regional meetings of the AAA, Professor Keith's research has appeared in the *Journal of Accountancy* and *The Florida CPA.* He was also a coauthor with Jack L. Smith of *Accounting for Financial Statement Presentation,* published in 1979. Professor Keith is a member of the American Accounting Association, the AICPA, and the Florida Institute of Certified Public Accountants, and has served on the editorial board of *The Florida CPA.*

William L. Stephens is Professor of Accounting in the College of Business Administration at the University of South Florida. He has a DBA from Florida State University and is a CPA. His primary research and teaching interests are in the area of managerial and cost accounting. Active in continuing professional education projects, Professor Stephens is also a member of the American Accounting Association, the National Association of Accountants, and the Florida Institute of Certified Public Accountants. For the past eight years, he has been the faculty advisor to the Delta Gamma Chapter of Beta Alpha Psi. Author of numerous articles in *The Journal of Accountancy,* and *The Accounting Review,* Professor Stephens has also coauthored a study guide for a financial accounting text.

To Diane, Kristie, and Scott

To Leanne and Rob

To my mother-in-law, Eunice Barnes Kinsley, whose unwavering faith in the Lord was an inspiration to all who knew and loved her — throughout the good times and the bad, during her life and at her death.

Contents

Preface

The second edition of *Accounting Principles* is designed to be a comprehensive balanced approach to the community college or university student's first exposure to accounting. The text is intended for use in a two-semester or three-quarter sequence by those students who plan to enter the accounting profession, those who plan a business career, and those who have an interest in broadening their business background. Our assumption in writing this edition is that the student's exposure to business has been very limited. Therefore we have carefully explained and illustrated, where appropriate, all business terms and practices as they are first discussed.

We have planned the second edition to be a blend of accounting concepts and procedures. Students are informed why information is accounted for in a certain manner. The *why* is reinforced by illustrating *how* the accounting is accomplished. Students cannot grasp concepts without adequate attention to the procedures.

IMPORTANT FEATURES OF THE SECOND EDITION

Numerous suggestions have been made by the many users of the first edition. We have considered these suggestions very carefully and adopted those that we feel will contribute to increasing the effectiveness of the text. We have incorporated in this edition numerous pedagogical devices and techniques to which we would like to call your attention. These are classified in the preface as general or specific. In the general category we include those items that are presented in all chapters of the text, while in the second category we highlight those features that are found only in specific chapters.

GENERAL

Retained in the second edition is the informal writing style that makes the material more real, more interesting, and certainly more helpful to the student. We have

- attempted to give the students a feeling that the instructor is with them while they are reading the text.

- A new feature added for the second edition is the short cases appearing with each chapter. These cases are extracted from sources such as *Fortune, Forbes, Harvard Business Review,* securities and exchange releases, and *The Wall Street Journal.* The cases provide the student with an opportunity to see how principles of accounting are embedded within the realities of the business world.

- Each of the six parts of the text is introduced by a section explaining the overall purpose of that part and briefly describing its contents.

- Attractively arranged at the start of each chapter are the chapter objectives that serve to enhance student learning.

- Extensively used throughout each chapter are marginal notes to describe the text material and indicate the purpose of each exercise and problem.

- The text contains an abundance of well illustrated charts, diagrams, and figures designed to help the student easily and quickly visualize concepts, and relationships, and establish perspectives underlying the material as it is explained.

- Summaries and important terms are presented at the end of each chapter.

- Check figures are located with the exercises and problems, not on the end covers nor in a separate list.

SPECIFIC

The focus of the first half of the text is on asset, liability, expense, and revenue accounting. However, at the suggestion of many users we have introduced the
- corporate model in Chapter 4 and use it exclusively commencing in Chapter 5 and thereafter.

- Accounting principles and concepts are discussed and developed fully as they are introduced in the various chapters.

- An interlude in the form of a major section entitled GAAP: Generally Accepted Accounting Principles is located between Chapters 11 and 12 and presents a comprehensive discussion of generally accepted accounting principles. Many users separate the end of Principles I and the start of Principles II at this point.

- A second interlude has been added to the second edition. This is between Chapters 18 and 19 and it serves to provide a smooth transition from financial accounting to management accounting.

- The accounting cycle is reviewed by means of a detailed flowchart at the end of Chapters 3, 4, and 6; the chart is expanded as new procedures are presented.

- A full discussion of reversing entries for accruals and transactions initially recorded in nominal accounts is developed in Chapter 4.

- An extended discussion of the difference between the accrual and cash basis of accounting is located in Chapter 3.

- Chapter 5 from the first edition has been divided into two chapters. The new Chapter 5 deals with accounting for merchandise and includes a discussion of the periodic and perpetual inventory systems.

- A new Chapter 6 has been added. This chapter has an extensive section on the important topic of internal control (and the E. F. Hutton case) and covers the use of special journals.

- The chapter on cash, Chapter 7, has been revised, eliminating the discussion of bank-to-book reconciliations and providing realistic bank reconciliations in the problem material. The lower-of-cost-or-market technique has been expanded in the discussion of marketable securities.

- Chapter 8 on Receivables has been pruned to eliminate duplication of material on control and subsidiary ledgers.

- Included in Chapter 10, "Long-Lived Assets," is a discussion of the impact of income tax depreciation. Material from the first edition on changing prices is transferred to Chapter 18 where the topic is developed more fully.

- Chapter 11, "Current Liabilities and Payroll," has undergone substantial change. Material located in this chapter from the first edition has been shifted to Chapter 27, "Income Taxes." In addition, the material from the first edition found in a separate chapter on payrolls has been consolidated with the other current liability items and arranged in a more logical manner.

- Chapter 15, "Corporations: Long-Term Liabilities," has been included in the corporation section in the second edition because of the input of many of the first edition adopters. This material is viewed as somewhat more difficult than the other material found in the first course and many users felt it would be more appropriate in the second course as well as more logically located with the corporate material. The discussion of the effective-interest method of amortizing premiums and discounts has been expanded to make it easier for the student to understand.

- At the suggestion of first edition users, the discussion of consolidations has been substantially modified in Chapter 16, "Corporations: Investments and Consolidations." While the philosophy of both the purchase and pooling of interest methods is discussed, the procedural explanation is limited to the purchase method at the date of acquisition.

- Chapter 20, "Job Order Costing," and Chapter 21, "Process Costing," are two new chapters. In the first edition these topics were covered in one chapter. A major change from the first edition is that the second edition covers both the weighted-average and FIFO methods of process costing. The coverage of the two methods is completely independent; it is not necessary to understand one in order to cover the other method.

- Chapter 23 contains a comprehensive master budget that is fully discussed and illustrated. The example for the master budget is carried over to the chapter on flexible budgeting (Chapter 24) which compares and contrasts these two types of budgets. A clear, concise development of the relationship between the flexible budget and standard costing is given, contrasting the planning and control functions.

- Chapter 25 on relevant costing is logically placed after cost-volume-profit analysis, so that the contribution approach is a familiar tool, and prior to capital budgeting, so that short-run special decisions are discussed before long-run decisions.

SUPPLEMENTARY MATERIALS

Accompanying the text are the following supplementary materials:

For the Instructor

Solutions Manual. Answers to all the questions, exercises, and problems are contained in this comprehensive manual. The type is extra large so that any transparen-
- cies made from the manual will be clearly seen by the students in the last row of the classroom.

    The questions, exercises, and problems follow closely the textual material. Time estimates, difficulty levels, and descriptions of all exercises and problems are provided as an aid to the instructor in selecting material appropriate for the level of course being taught.

- *Teacher's Manual.* Designed to aid primarily graduate teaching assistants, adjuncts, and other part-time instructors, the teacher's manual contains comments, notes, illustrations, and examples that the authors have found useful in teaching the principles course.

- *Tests and Exams.* Two completely different sets (Set A and Set B) are available to provide the instructor with a number of testing options. Each package contains 20 of each test and exam. Each test covers two or three chapters. The four final exams cover Chapters 1–11, Chapters 12–27, Chapters 12–18, and Overview to Chapter 27.

- *Solutions for Practice Sets.* Contains all the answers for both print practice sets.
- *Test Bank.* For those instructors who wish to construct their own examinations, a manual containing over 2,250 true/false, multiple choice, and short problem test questions arranged by chapter is available. These questions are also available in a computerized test-generation system.
- *Overhead Transparencies.* The publisher has prepared for the instructor a complete set of exercise and problem solution transparencies for classroom use. These are available upon request to adopters of the text.
- *Teacher's Transparencies.* An extensive set of teaching transparencies is available for classroom use as an aid in illustrating many of the concepts discussed in the text.

For the Student

- *Study Guide.* A comprehensive study guide, prepared by Joseph Icerman of Florida State University and Paul Williams of North Carolina State University, contains chapter-by-chapter reviews together with an abundance of multiple-choice, fill-in, and true or false questions as well as numerous problems. Solutions to all items are displayed in the back of the *Study Guide.*
- *Practice Sets.* Two manual practice sets accompany the text. Both sets are prepared by the authors. The first set is to be used after the first six chapters and illustrates the basic system using a periodic inventory method and the special journals. The set is unique because it contains two beginning trial balances and two sets of amounts for each transaction, thus providing the instructor with the opportunity to assign effectively any one of four practice sets although the student purchases only one set.

  The second manual practice set contains various source documents, business forms, and cancelled checks for the student to analyze and process.
- *Computerized Practice Set.* This practice set utilizes microcomputers to process data inputed by the student for a 2-month period of time.
- *Computerized Tutorial.* Reinforcing the text presentation through topic-specific exercises and short problems, this self-paced software is available for both semesters of principles.
- *Working Papers.* Partially filled-in working papers for all problems of the text are preprinted with the problem headings and preliminary data to help students save time and concentrate their energies on the essence of each problem.

ACKNOWLEDGMENTS

We wish to express our sincere appreciation to the many individuals who contributed their efforts to this project. Constructive criticism was gratefully received from

Professor John Armstrong, Suffolk University
Professor Terry Bill, Kaskaskia Community College
Professor Michael S. Blay, Florida Junior College
Professor Ronald E. Brunk, Bethel College, Kansas
Professor Kenneth Coffey, Johnson Community College
Professor John Cucka, Northwestern State University

Professor Philip S. Dole, Rock Valley Community College

Professor Wanda Hill, Valdosta State College

Professor Sandra F. Knecht, Florida Junior College

Professor Kenneth A. Koerber, Bucks County Community College

Professor Christine L. McKeag, University of Evansville

Professor Wayne E. Pfingsten, Belleville Area College

Professor Sharyll A. B. Plato, Central State University

Professor Thomas A. Warren, Florida Junior College

Professor Marilyn Zarzeski, Barry University

We are indebted to our students Diana Ellswich, Kelly Underhill, Tina Pennachio of Arthur Andersen & Company, Kyle Kilian, Diane Miksch, and Debra Abbott, as well as to Professor Alison C. Drews of Clemson University and Professor Blanca Gonzales of Miami-Dade Community College, who checked and rechecked the text and *Solutions Manual* for accuracy. We are most grateful.

We wish to pay special tribute to Peg Zimmerman, John Hartwick, Tom Zaher, Morrie Davidson, Jane Lopresti, and Nancy Sheridan, all of Bucks County Community College, as well as Tom Warren, Mickey Blay, and Sandy Knecht, of Florida Junior College, and John Sargent, St. Joseph's University, for their interest in our project and their time spent with us exchanging ideas. We feel we gained a significant learning experience from our association with these concerned and committed teachers.

We appreciate the help and encouragement of our colleagues at the University of South Florida. Special thanks go to Bob West for his contribution on the effective-interest method and his support as department chairperson, to Jim Lasseter for his comments on the Tax chapter; and to Celina Jozsi for her numerous creative ideas on management accounting.

Once again Florida Steel Corporation provided the financial statements that are illustrated in the text. We appreciate the efforts of Thomas G. Creed, Vice-President, Structural Steel for obtaining permission to use the statements.

From among an enthusiastic McGraw-Hill field staff, we feel especially obligated to Scott Stratford and Frank Flynn for their comprehensive reports which helped us to shape this second edition.

We were again fortunate to have the assistance of two outstanding individuals from the McGraw-Hill editorial staff to guide us in this project. We deeply appreciate the creative abilities of Peggy Rehberger and Mike Elia and hope that we will work together on many more projects. Over the years our relationship with Mike Elia has developed from master and apprentices to a valued friendship.

Jack L. Smith
Robert M. Keith
William L. Stephens

, 1909 - 1910.

Gain or loss (-)

4,501.14	
1,563.60	
81.11	
6,135.85	
692.68	
440.94	
57.22	
124.67	
3.62	
1,319.13	
3,360.99	
711.24	
1,867.67	
254.83	
263.89	
3,037.63	
1,136.16	
- 47.44	
- 216.23	
872.49	
683.65	
585.34	
302.83	

Balance Sheet.

Assets:
   Cash on hand   5, 9
   Book accounts   6, 1
   Notes receivable   2
   Furniture & fixture acct   3
   Misc. suspense   4
   Good will   5, 0
   Stocks & bonds
   Paper stock   2
      Deficit 1910
               $ 18, 32

Liabilities:
   Capital stock   15, 00
   Accounts payable   1, 78
     Net assets 1909   1, 54
               $ 18, 32

```
1910
1,106.35
6,135.67
47.84
642.20
14.54
5,000.00
2,985.42

355.74
$16,285.76


15,000.00
1,285.76

$16,285.76
```

Part One

Financial Accounting: Its Structure and Environment

For many years to come you are going to make economic decisions. These decisions may be required of you in your role as a taxpayer, a voter, an employee, a church member, a business manager, and a husband or wife. To make the best economic decisions, you need the appropriate financial facts. Accounting is a service that provides these facts in the form of financial reports. But before you can use financial reports you need to know how accounting information is generated, processed, and presented. You should also have a basic understanding of accounting principles, be familiar with the terms used by accountants, and understand the limitations of financial reports. Part One of *Accounting Principles* is designed to provide you with this information.

In Part One you will learn that there are many kinds of accounting activities and what each of these activities involves. For the first two-thirds of this text you will be studying just one of these activities—general financial accounting—which is concerned with recording business transactions and preparing financial reports. You will learn how to record transactions for a business entity. And you will learn how to prepare three financial reports—the income statement, the statement of owners' equity, and the balance sheet.

Financial reports are useful to us only when they are reliable and comparable. Certain ground rules called generally accepted accounting principles have been developed over the years to assure us that business entities prepare financial reports that are reliable and comparable. We will tell you in Part One how these generally accepted accounting principles are developed and discuss with you five important principles that you will need to know even at this early stage in your course of study.

Chapter 1

Introduction:
Some Basic Concepts
and the Accounting Model

Through studying this chapter you will learn the following:

- What *accounting information* is, who needs to know it, and why
- What an *economic entity* is
- What the three types of *business entities* are
- What the various types of *accounting activities* are
- The basic purpose of the principal *financial statements* and the type of information contained in each
- How the CPA provides credibility to the financial statements
- The meaning of the term *generally accepted accounting principles*
- What institutions influenced the development of accounting principles, and how they influenced it
- What the basic *accounting concepts and principles* are and what they mean
- How business transactions affect the basic accounting model
- How to record business transactions on a financial transaction worksheet
- How to prepare the financial statements

If you are alive, alert, and an active and interested citizen of the free world, you will be expected to make decisions about how you feel your country's economy should operate and how it should affect the economies of other countries. Depending on which hat you wear in your society, and your attitudes, your interests, and your job, you will have to make some decisions like the following:

Economic decisions require accounting information

Taxpayers Should you support your local government's proposed bond issue to finance increased community services?

Church members Should you support the proposed church operating budget for the forthcoming year?

Finance manager of an international company Should you invest funds for a new plant to be located in France?

Investment manager for a large insurance company Should you buy the stocks or bonds of a particular company?

Loan officer of a local bank Should you grant credit to an applicant for an auto loan?

Representative of a labor union Should demands be made on the company for a 6% pay increase? Or a 10% pay increase?

Executive of an appliance manufacturer Should you buy steel from a Japanese firm?

Member of a corporation's board of directors Should you increase the dividends you pay to your stockholders?

Director of a governmental program Should you request additional funding to carry out the program?

These are all economic decisions, and you need to have information in order to make them. Accounting is a service that provides managers, taxpayers, directors, or whomever, with the financial information they need to make informed decisions.

Financial reports are based on accounting concepts

Like any other discipline, accounting has its own terms and concepts. Financial reports are based on these concepts, and the information in the reports is expressed in accounting terms.

Many beginning students of accounting are surprised to learn that financial reports may not always be a precise measure of actual activity. For example, values presented on financial reports may reflect prices paid several years ago or current prices. Furthermore, accounting involves estimates and estimates preclude precision.

To make informed decisions among economic alternatives, you must have a basic understanding of accounting concepts and terms; you must know how accounting information is generated, processed, and presented; and you must both realize the limitations of financial reports and know how to deal with them.

USERS OF ACCOUNTING INFORMATION

Accounting principles are basically the same for all economic entities

There are many different users of accounting information. Financial reports are used by investors, creditors, managers, taxpayers, union representatives, regulatory agencies, potential investors and creditors, and many others. Broadly speaking, the principles underlying the gathering and presenting of accounting information are basically similar for all economic entities. *Economic entities* are separate, distinct organizations you encounter in our society. Banks, retail stores, state governments, automobile companies, student organizations, and charitable organizations are economic entities you see or hear of daily.

There are two types of economic entities: ***profit-motivated*** entities such as General Motors, Sears, and McDonald's; and ***non-profit-motivated*** entities such as the City of New York, the First Methodist Church, the University of Texas, and Mount Sinai Hospital. Entities of the first type are referred to as **business entities,** the second, **not-for-profit entities.** The term *economic entities* refers to both types.

Business entities and not-for-profit entities are the two types of economic entities

FIGURE 1-1
Economic entities can be either business or not-for-profit entities.

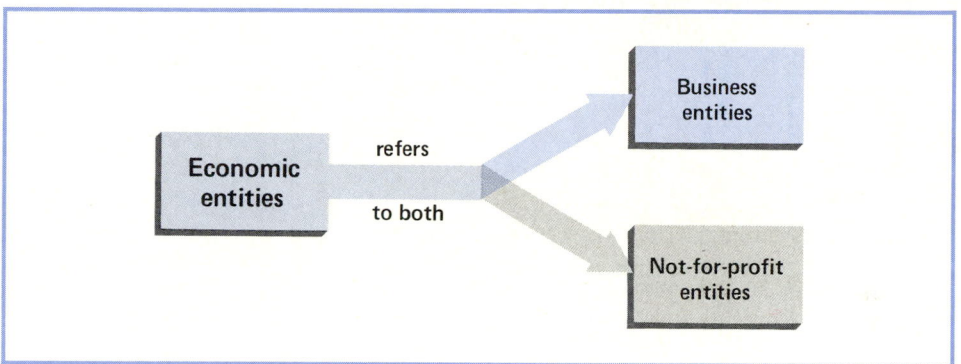

This text will focus on accounting for business entities. After you have achieved an understanding of the principles of accounting as applied to business entities, it will be relatively easy for you to apply the same principles to not-for-profit entities.

Financial reports are used by "inside" and "outside" people

A business entity has "inside" and "outside" people. The inside people are the ones who manage or control the operations and hence the destiny of the business entity. The outside people, who have provided the money to operate the business, are affected in some way by what happens to the business entity or by what it does.

External financial reports provide information needed by users who do not have direct access to the business entity's records. Some users of a business entity's information have the power to generate and enforce laws about what information is made available to them and how such information is to be submitted. As you might well imagine, these users are the Internal Revenue Service, the Securities and Exchange Commission, and the public utility commissions, among others. These agencies prescribe the exact manner in which the financial information is to be reported, what type of information is to be reported, and when and where it is to be reported.

General-purpose financial statements are prepared for investors and creditors

There are also users who need financial information but have neither direct access to a business entity's records nor legislative power to require a business entity to report to them in a specified manner. These users are investors, potential investors, creditors, and potential creditors. Management of business entities meets the needs of these users by preparing general-purpose financial statements covering for specified periods the results of business activities and listing the economic resources entrusted to the entity and the obligations incurred by the entity.

The area of accounting concerned with the preparation and presentation of general-purpose financial statements is referred to as ***financial accounting*** and is the subject of Chapters 1 to 18 of this text.

Internal financial reports are prepared for management

Internal financial reports are prepared exclusively for the inside users—the management of the business entity. These reports provide management with information that will help carry out its objectives and its responsibilities.

Examples of internal reports include:

- Reports contrasting the cost of leasing a new computer with the costs of buying a new one
- Reports showing the results that can be expected from eliminating a department
- Reports showing the cost to produce a certain product

Management accounting is concerned with internal reporting

The area of accounting concerned with internal reporting is referred to as ***management accounting*** and is the subject of Chapters 19 to 27 of this text.

FIGURE 1-2
Users of financial reports can be inside or outside people.

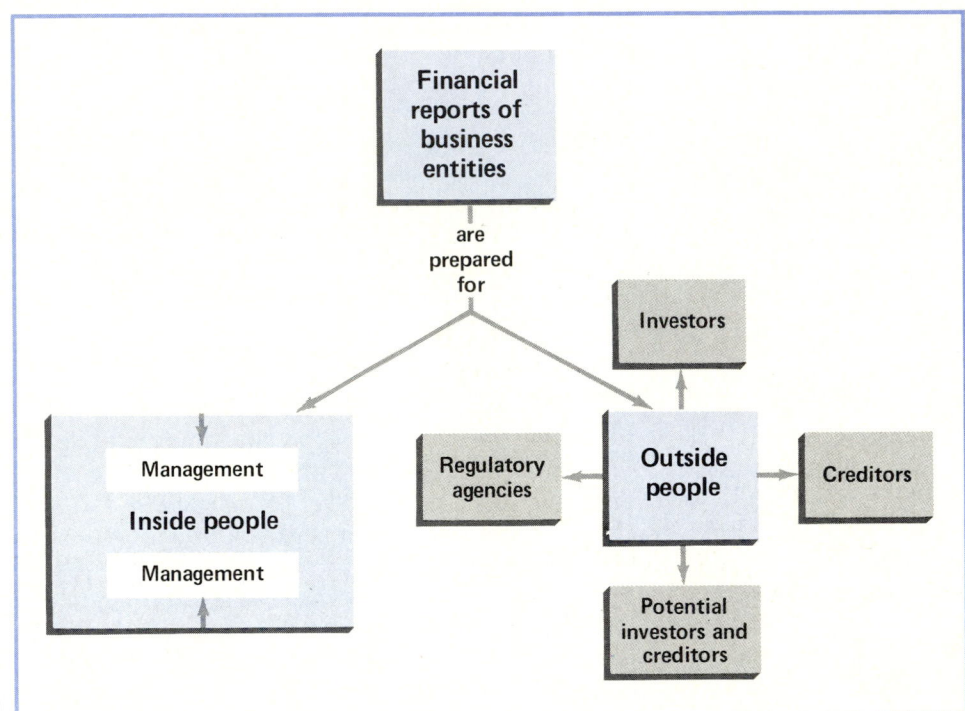

PREPARERS OF ACCOUNTING INFORMATION

The responsibility for the accounting information contained in the financial reports of business and not-for-profit entities ultimately rests with the entity's ***chief executive officer.*** The chief executive officer is the president or chairman of the board of directors of a business entity, or the director, head, mayor, president, or some other designee of a not-for-profit entity. Financial reports, however, are generally prepared not by chief executive officers but by accountants engaged or employed by the economic entity. Both business entities and not-for-profit entities employ accountants.

Business Entities

The executive officer of a business entity in charge of the accounting activity is called the ***controller.*** As you may infer from the title, the controller is responsible for the control of the operations of the business. The controller may have a staff of several hundred accounting and finance employees, as in the case of a large international corporation such as Mobil Oil Company, or a relatively small staff, as with a small enterprise such as a local retail store.

Some small companies operate with only one or two executive officers who, in addition to their other responsibilities, also perform the function of a controller, thus eliminating the need for a separate one. They may employ a full- or part-time accountant to prepare financial reports.

Accounting Activities of Business Entities

In the next few pages, we will describe the following accounting activities of business entities:

- General financial accounting
- Accounting systems design
- Cost accounting
- Budgeting
- Taxation
- Internal auditing
- Data processing

Large international corporations may divide their accounting staffs into departments according to accounting activity. Small departments may perform some of the accounting activities with accountants employed as staff or may hire the services of independent *certified public accountants (CPAs)* for whatever accounting activities management deems necessary.

The descriptions of the accounting activities that follow will provide you with some insight into the important role accountants play in our society.

General Financial Accounting   Business entities are involved daily with numerous business transactions, such as the purchase and sale of goods and services. General financial accounting is concerned with recording these business transactions and preparing financial reports to be used internally by management and externally by investors and creditors as well as by potential investors and creditors. Accountants working in the general financial accounting area are also responsible for preparing financial reports required by most governmental agencies. These reports must be prepared in compliance with the particular governmental agency's regulations, which are referred to as *compliance requirements.*

General financial accounting is concerned with recording business transactions and preparing financial reports

Accounting Systems Design   The numerous business transactions that must be processed and recorded by the general financial accounting staff must first be *classified* before financial reports can be issued. By classifying we mean grouping together related financial transactions. For example, all sales transactions must be grouped together and classified as *sales.* Likewise, all transactions involving the purchase of inventory must be grouped together and classified as *purchases.*

In simplest terms, the classifying process is this: Sales are recorded on a sales form, purchases are recorded on a purchase order form, and each of the many other business transactions is recorded on forms designed to convey the nature and purpose of the financial transaction. One of the functions of accounting systems design is to design the forms that record business activities, thus enabling the classifying process to work smoothly and efficiently. The result is that the mass of accounting data can be summarized in a meaningful manner in the financial reports. Systems design is also concerned with specifying the procedures for how an accounting system should be operated, for implementing these procedures, and for investigating new means of processing the mass of accounting data.

Those working in accounting systems help design forms that summarize accounting data; they also develop and implement accounting procedures

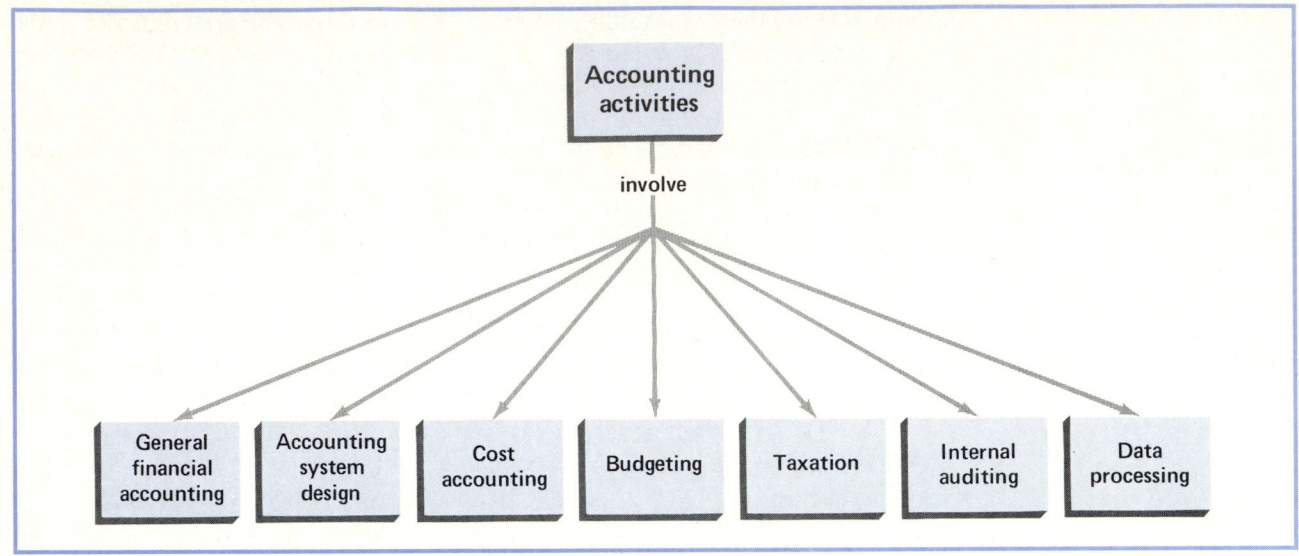

FIGURE 1-3   Accounting involves numerous activities.

Cost Accounting   The accounting activity concerned with gathering accounting information for the purpose of planning and controlling and to determine the cost of a product is referred to as ***cost accounting.*** Not only is it essential to know the cost of a product or a service, but it is even more important to control such costs. It is the responsibility of the cost accounting function to provide management with relevant information to help achieve control over cost.

Budgeting   Business entities can be managed efficiently if they have determined what their objectives are. Expressing these objectives in monetary terms is what the budgeting activity is all about. Budgets covering specific periods of time are prepared. Upon the completion of operating activities for these specific periods of time, what actually happened—the actual results—is compared to what was "budgeted" to happen—the budget. Any differences are analyzed carefully by management with the view toward improving and closing the gap between actual and budget performance in future periods.

Taxation   You are well aware that individuals must pay taxes to the federal government. Business entities are also subject to taxes. A business entity must comply with the requirements of not only the Internal Revenue Service (IRS), but also state, local, and foreign tax laws. The various tax laws to which business entities are subject are very complex. Large corporations have separate tax departments staffed by specialists in tax compliance and tax planning. By the term ***tax compliance*** we mean following the many detailed and specific rules of the taxing authorities in preparing tax returns. The term ***tax planning*** refers to the study of the possible tax effects of various proposed financial transactions in which management may wish to engage. Small firms may have their general accountants prepare the required tax returns. By now you may get the idea that accountants in small firms do just about everything. They do. Small firms may also use the services of a CPA for tax return preparation and tax planning.

Internal auditors review the accounting records and procedures

Internal Auditing   In order to ensure that transactions are recorded, classified, and summarized properly, the records for each of these accounting activities must be reviewed regularly. Internal auditing is that area of accounting concerned with this review of the records. However, the scope of internal auditing extends beyond a review of the company's records. Internal auditing also encompasses a responsibility to ensure that accounting and operating policies and procedures are being properly and consistently followed. The internal auditing function cannot report to an accounting or financial officer. To do so would destroy the independent nature of the work.

Data processing is the physical activity of recording accounting data

Data Processing   Although general financial accounting is the activity responsible for recording business transactions, the actual physical activity of recording the mass of accounting data is not done by general financial accounting. It is done as a separate activity by the data processing department. The data processing department simply provides the service necessary to record the thousands upon thousands of business transactions the entity enters into during the year. Small firms may not have a computer installation of their own. These firms often use the services of data processing companies to meet their needs.

Not-for-Profit Entities

Operating activities of not-for-profit entities are much the same as those of business entities

Although they don't make a profit, not-for-profit entities buy and sell goods and services and require many of the same kinds of transactions as business entities. Thus, the operating activities, the economic resources (things the entity owns), and the obligations of not-for-profit entities can be described and summarized in financial reports in much the same way that they are described and summarized in the financial reports of business entities.

Executive officers of hospitals, directors of governmental agencies, taxpayers, elected schoolboard officials, county commissioners, and investors in municipal bonds all need reliable accounting information on which to base decisions. These needs are met by the same accounting activities as are found in accounting for business entities.

CERTIFIED PUBLIC ACCOUNTANTS (CPAs)

Like physicians and lawyers, CPAs are licensed by the state

Certified public accountants (CPAs) are independent professional accountants, licensed by the state, who provide accounting services to clients for a fee in much the same way that other professionals such as physicians and lawyers provide their services to the public. In order to obtain a license, physicians, lawyers, and CPAs must fulfill educational standards and pass certain tests. This assures the public of a high degree of competence in the practice of medicine, law, or accounting. CPAs, like other professionals, are highly regarded by their clients for two basic reasons: the rigorous training that is necessary to become a member of the profession and the self-imposed high degree of ethics involved.

Requirements for the CPA License

In order to become a CPA, an applicant must pass the comprehensive CPA examination. The CPA exam is a uniform examination prepared by the American Institute of Certified Public Accountants (AICPA). The four-part examination is administered over a $2\frac{1}{2}$-day period every May and November on the same dates in all states.

Although all applicants in every state must pass the same test, there are also a number of other requirements, which can vary from state to state. A candidate must fulfill the appropriate requirements of a specific state to be granted a CPA license. The most common requirements are that an individual must be a U.S. citizen, must be of legal age as defined by the state, must be a college graduate with the equivalent of an accounting major, and, of course, must have a passing grade (75%) on all parts of the CPA exam.

The Role of the CPA

Most of the work done by CPAs is auditing, although a majority of all CPAs also provide tax and management advisory services.

Auditing

> The CPA is a trusted link between inside people and outside people

The major function of the CPA is to serve as a link between the preparers of financial statements and the people who use them. Like most people, most officers of business entities and directors of not-for-profit entities are ethical and honest people. The financial reports they represent to users are prepared with the highest degree of integrity. However, two different officers or directors, given exactly the same information and the same circumstances, may not produce identical reports. You might be inclined to think that one of them must have cheated. Most likely, however, your assumption would prove to be incorrect. Differences of this type result because in accounting there are alternative ways, all of them quite legal, to treat many kinds of business transactions. Of course, and unfortunately, there always have been and always will be cheaters who give inexact and dishonest reports. But, although it may take some time, they are usually discovered.

Users of financial statements do not have access to the financial records of the economic entity in which they are interested. They cannot assure for themselves that proper choices of accounting alternatives have been made. Users also need assurance that the statements fairly and honestly represent the results of operating activities as well as resources and obligations. Because users cannot establish these assurances for themselves, they must rely on assurances from someone else.

FIGURE 1-4
The CPA reviews a business entity's financial statements to provide assurance to outside people.

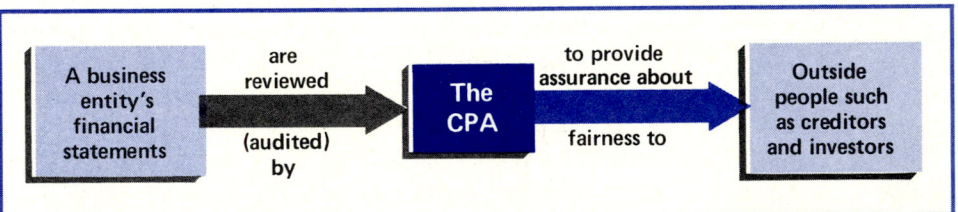

The CPA provides that assurance by performing an independent audit of the economic entity and issuing an audit report that is an integral part of the financial statements issued by the economic entity. By the term *independent audit* we mean a check of the accounting records of an economic entity by someone who is not an employee of the entity or a relation to an officer of the entity. (The check is not made of 100% of the accounting records. That's not necessary. A statistically selected sample of the records is used.) The audit report is a statement of the CPA saying that the financial reports issued by the economic entity are fair and prepared in accordance with approved accounting rules. An audit report usually must accompany the financial reports issued by a business entity.

> The CPA assures the public that financial statements are fair

Tax Services

> CPAs play a major role in any business entity's tax planning

Tax services provided to a client by the CPA include preparing and filing tax returns and, perhaps of greater importance, tax planning. Tax planning directly affects the prime objective of business entities, which is to make profits. Any business decision about how to make those profits involves another decision about how much taxes will have to be paid. With proper tax planning, decisions can be made to reduce taxes that would affect increased profits. CPAs are uniquely qualified to render service in this area because of their knowledge of the tax laws, tax regulations, and various court decisions regarding taxes.

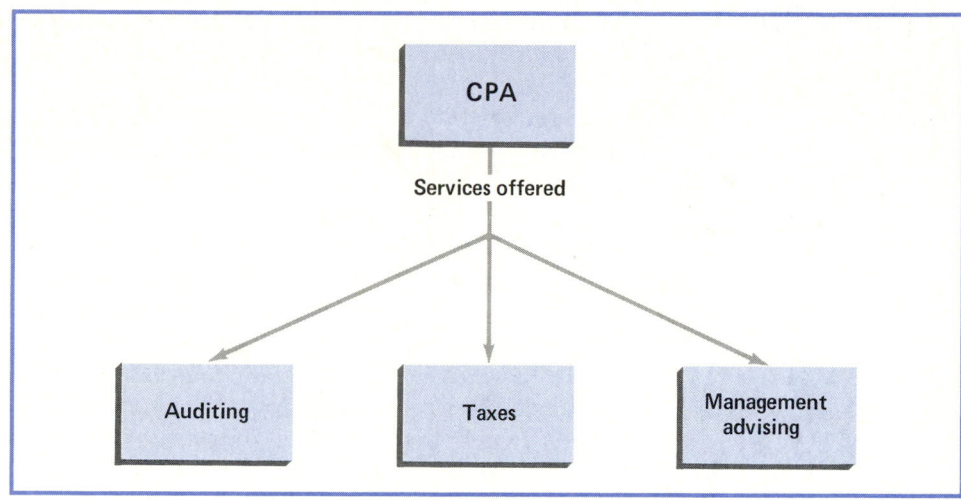

Management Advisory Services

Management advisory services are often a by-product of an audit engagement

Management advisory services are offered by CPAs in addition to auditing and tax services. A CPA, in the course of auditing many different clients, observes many different accounting systems. This experience enables the CPA to analyze any particular client's strengths and weaknesses. Thus, as a CPA audits a business entity, a natural by-product of the audit is suggestions for improving the performance of the business to make profits. Management has come to expect these suggestions as part of the audit. Moreover, management may often want further help, engaging the CPA for specific management services, such as establishing an accounting system for determining costs, or designing a new payroll system, or designing a system for the firm to help estimate future performance. It is not at all uncommon to find mathematicians, statisticians, and engineers on the management services staff of many large CPA firms.

FINANCIAL STATEMENTS FOR BUSINESS ENTITIES

Financial statements are the end product of the general financial accounting activity

Earning profits and paying debts are two important objectives of business entities

Business entities communicate their financial information to interested users through published financial statements. By *published* we mean reports prepared in a manner similar to a glossy-covered magazine such as *Sports Illustrated.* You would find in these reports not only the financial statements but also color pictures of the companies' products and facilities. The reports are usually 30 to 40 pages long. These statements represent the end product of the general financial accounting activity. The main objective of general financial accounting is to communicate a description of the financial condition and operation of a business entity, and that is done through financial statements. The financial statements, the last step in the accounting process, are the starting point in the study of accounting. As with most other things, by understanding what the ultimate goal is, it is easier to understand the concepts and procedures used to achieve it.

While many of the concepts and procedures of accounting are equally applicable to both business entities and not-for-profit entities, this text will be concerned mainly with business entities, whose objective is to earn a profit. To earn a profit, a business entity must sell its service or product at a price that exceeds its cost. In addition, sufficient funds must be generated to pay debts as they become due and to acquire productive resources when needed. Only then can profits become available to those who have invested in the business entity. There are other objectives of business entities, but earning profits and paying debts when due are the two most important.

If a business entity fails to earn sufficient profits, its owners may dispose of the business and invest their funds in more promising alternatives.

A business entity unable to pay its debts as they become due is said to be *insolvent.* When a business entity becomes insolvent, its creditors (the people and firms owed money) can seek payment through legal recourse, which may involve closing the business and selling its equipment and buildings to get some money to pay creditors.

The inability of an entity to pay its current maturing debts is called insolvency

Financial statements are designed to provide users with information concerning the profitability and solvency—the capacity to pay debts—of business enterprises. The *income statement* and the *balance sheet* are the two principal financial statements that contain this information. The income statement tells us about the entity's profitability, while the balance sheet tells us about its solvency. After recording, classifying, and summarizing thousands of business transactions, an accountant represents all that work on an income statement and a balance sheet. These two statements are prepared for managers, owners, creditors, and other users of accounting information for business entities.

The income statement provides information on profitability while the balance sheet provides information on solvency

FIGURE 1-6
Information provided by the financial statements.

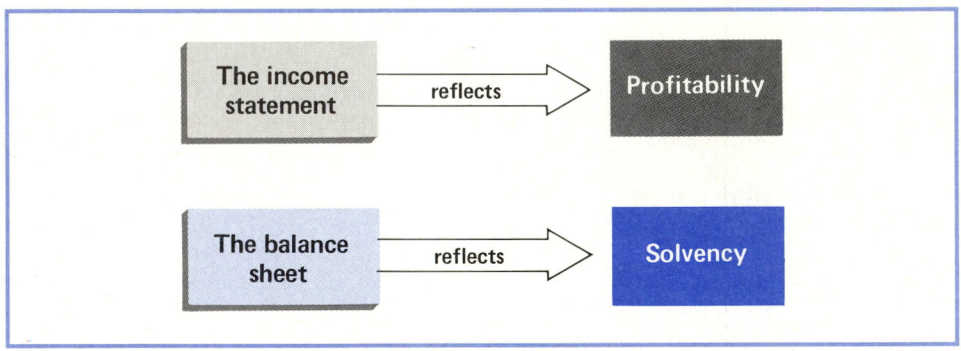

THE THREE TYPES OF BUSINESS ENTITIES

There are three main types of business entities: *proprietorships, partnerships,* and *corporations.* Although there are minor differences in the way each type of business entity reports information, all of them use basically the same type of financial statements. These minor differences will be brought to your attention in Part Four, *Accounting for Partnerships and Corporations.*

Proprietorship

A proprietorship is a business entity owned by one person

A business entity that is owned by one person is called a *proprietorship.* Many attorneys, accountants, and physicians do their professional work as individual practitioners, and thus are proprietorships. The proprietorship form of business is also common for small retail enterprises. The main characteristic of a proprietorship is that it can be formed so easily. You simply decide to start a business, obtain an operating license (if necessary), and there it is—the business exists. There are no other requirements.

No legal distinction exists between a proprietorship and its owner, but a distinction is made for accounting purposes

Legally, the owner of a business entity—the proprietor—and the business entity itself—the proprietorship—are considered to be one and the same. If the proprietor were to die, the proprietorship would cease to exist. However, for accounting purposes a distinction must be made between the two. The following example should clarify this for you.

There is this chap, Louis Garcia, who is a physician and who also owns a sporting

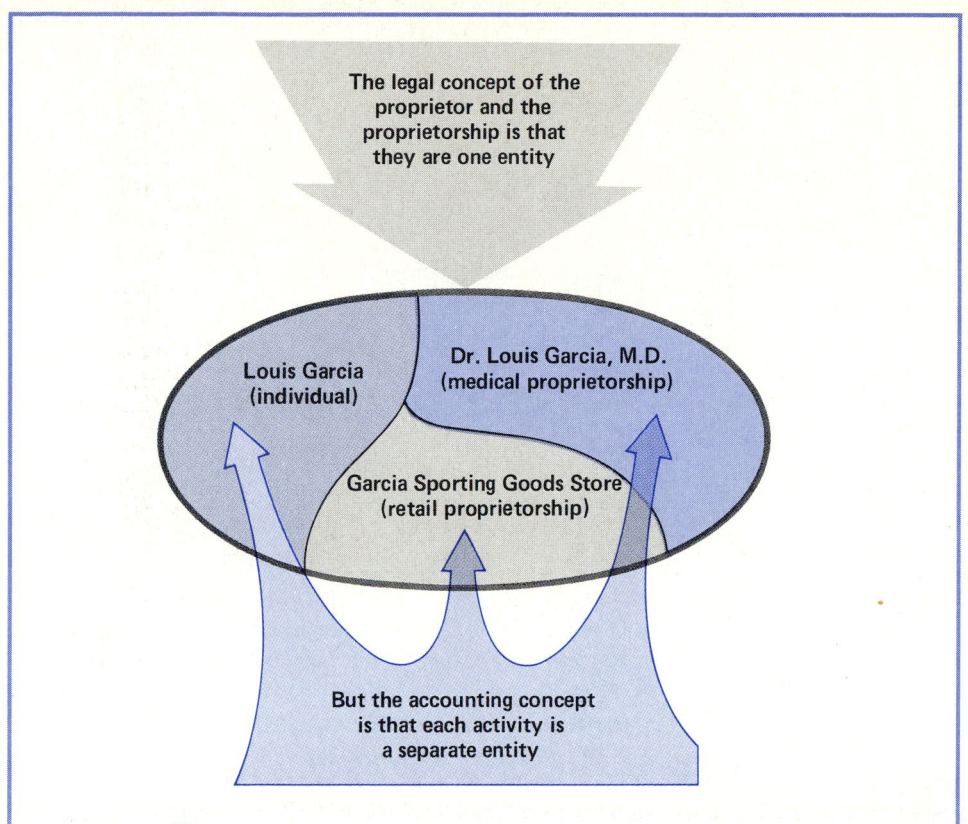

The legal concept of the proprietor and the proprietorship is that they are one entity

Louis Garcia (individual)

Dr. Louis Garcia, M.D. (medical proprietorship)

Garcia Sporting Goods Store (retail proprietorship)

But the accounting concept is that each activity is a separate entity

FIGURE 1-7
Legal and accounting concepts of a proprietorship.

goods store. That is, he owns the medical proprietorship, Louis Garcia, M.D., and the proprietorship, Garcia Sporting Goods Store. Dr. Garcia needs financial information on three separate entities: his medical practice, the sporting goods store, and his own personal affairs. Since there is no legal distinction among these three entities, income taxes are imposed on him only as an individual. Of course, all the income earned from his medical practice as Dr. Garcia and the income earned from his store must be included together as Louis Garcia's personal income.

Partnership

A partnership is a business entity owned by two or more persons

A business entity that is owned by two or more persons is called a ***partnership.*** Most small businesses and professional service groups are partnerships. For example, there are several CPA firms that have more than 1,000 partners. Like a proprietorship, a partnership is easy to form. The various partners simply agree (preferably in writing) to conduct a business entity as co-owners. The agreement typically specifies how the profits will be shared among partners and provides arrangements for settlements to be made to withdrawing partners or upon the death of a partner. Legally, the owners of a partnership and the partnership itself are not considered to be separate. As you may have guessed, the accounting concept is that they are separate. Financial statements are prepared for the business entity and for the partnership, and may also be prepared for each of the individual partners.

No legal distinction is made between a partnership and its partners, but an accounting distinction exists

Corporation

A business entity organized as a corporation is considered by law to be an artificial person. By the term ***artificial person*** we mean that the corporation itself has many of the rights and obligations that a person does. It can be sued and can sue, it can borrow money, it can enter into contracts, and it must pay income taxes. Persons wishing to form a corporation must request state officials to grant that privilege. The request is in the form of an application for a corporate charter. The charter is a document issued by the state, if the request is granted, providing legal evidence that the corporation is created. Upon creation, the corporation issues shares of stock to its owners, who are referred to as **shareholders** or **stockholders.** The shareholders receive stock certificates as evidence of their ownership interests. Most large corporations have many thousands of shareholders.

A corporation is a legal entity, distinct from its owners

The basic concepts and procedures of accounting apply to all three forms of business entities. So, in the first several chapters we'll simply refer to the business entity in general. There are distinctions in accounting among the three forms, as we mentioned previously, and we will get into them later, in Part Four.

THE PRINCIPAL FINANCIAL STATEMENTS

The principal financial statements are the **income statement,** the **balance sheet,** and the **statement of owner's equity.**

The Income Statement

The income statement compares revenue with expenses

The financial statement designed to report the profitability of a business entity is the **income statement.** It is generally considered more important than the balance sheet because the first question asked by most users is whether or not the business entity achieved its first objective. Did the business earn a profit? The answer to that question is the main purpose of an income statement. The income statement compares the *revenue* earned during a specified period of time with the *expenses* incurred during that same period of time, as seen in the following income statement:

The income statement compares revenues and expenses for a period of time

TOM'S REPAIRS AND RENTALS
Income Statement
Year Ended December 31, 1987

Revenues:		
Service Fees.		$ 72,375
Equipment Rental Fees		36,100
Total Revenues		$108,475
Expenses:		
Salaries Expense.	$51,000	
Repairs Expense.	12,450	
Advertising Expense	3,500	
Utilities Expense	1,360	
Total Expenses.		68,310
Net Income		$ 40,165

Revenue

Revenue is the amount charged for goods sold or services rendered

The amount charged for goods sold or services rendered is called **revenue.** Examples of revenue are sales, commissions earned, rental fees, and fees for professional services rendered.

Total revenue earned by Tom's Repairs and Rentals is $108,475. This revenue resulted from two activities: service fees, $72,375, and equipment rental fees, $36,100.

Expenses

Expenses are the costs of goods sold or the services rendered in the process of generating revenues

Expenses are the cost of goods sold by a business entity or the services rendered to it in the process of generating revenue. Examples of expenses are salaries, delivery expenses, utilities expense, and travel expenses. Tom's Repairs and Rentals incurred $68,310 of expenses in generating revenue. If revenue earned exceeds expenses incurred, the difference is *net income.* As illustrated in the Tom's Repairs and Rentals example, revenue exceeds expenses by $40,165, which is the net income. On the other hand, if expenses exceed revenue, the result is a *net loss* for the period.

The Heading

The heading consists of the name of the company, the type of statement, and the time period covered

Notice that the income statement is identified by a heading and that the heading consists of three lines:

1. The first line specifies the name of the company.

2. The second line specifies the type of financial statement it is—this financial statement is an income statement.

3. The third line specifies the period of time covered by the financial statement.

The last item is very important. Revenue and expenses are *time concepts.* Revenue is earned and expenses are incurred over a period of time. When we tell you that Tom's Repairs and Rentals had revenue of $9,500 in January, you will know that we mean Tom's Repairs and Rentals has accumulated revenue of $9,500 from January 1 to January 31. If we say that Tom's Repairs and Rentals incurred $17,000 of expenses in the second quarter, you will know that this amount was incurred from April 1 to June 30. And if we say that Tom's Repairs and Rentals had revenue of $108,475 for the year, you will know that is the amount of revenue earned from January 1 to December 31. Users of the financial statements need to know if the revenue earned and expenses incurred represent amounts for one month, two quarters, or a year. Without knowing what period of time the statement covers, users cannot interpret the financial data reported, nor can they compare them with previous financial statements or financial statements of other firms.

The Balance Sheet

The financial statement designed to show a business entity's financial position—what it owns and what it owes—on a particular date is called the *balance sheet.* By reviewing a firm's balance sheet—comparing what it owns with what it owes—users can make judgments about whether or not and how easily the firm pays its bills—and this, we have already learned, is called the *solvency* of the firm.

See the balance sheet for Tom's Repairs and Rentals at the top of page 14. For the moment, don't be too concerned about the technical terms listed in it. What we want you to be concerned about is that the balance sheet consists of two sides. The left side represents what the firm owns, its *assets;* the right side represents what the firm owes, its *liabilities,* and the amount the owner has invested in the business, the *owner's equity.* In a sense, the business owes the amount shown under owner's equity to the owner. If the business were sold or dissolved and all the liabilities paid, the remaining money would be paid to the owner.

The total of the assets, $108,000, on the left side of Tom's Repairs and Rentals balance sheet is indeed equal to the sum of the liabilities, $24,300, and the owner's equity, $83,700, on the right side—hence the term *balance sheet.*

Like the income statement, the balance sheet has a heading with three important parts: first, the name of the company; second, what type of financial statement it is; and third, the date of the balance sheet. Unlike the income statement, which covers a

---

TOM'S REPAIRS AND RENTALS
Balance Sheet
December 31, 1987

Assets		Liabilities and Owner's Equity	
Cash	$ 6,300	Liabilities:	
Accounts Receivable	9,050	Notes Payable	$ 10,000
Supplies on Hand	2,100	Accounts Payable	14,300
Land	18,000	Total Liabilities	$ 24,300
Building	45,300		
Equipment	27,250	Owner's Equity:	
		Tom Jefferson, Capital	83,700
Total Assets	$108,000	Total Liabilities and Owner's Equity	$108,000

The balance sheet lists what a company owns and what it owes.

The balance sheet covers a point in time

specified *period of time,* the balance sheet is a listing of assets, liabilities, and owner's equity at a *point in time.* That point in time for Tom's Repairs and Rentals is the close of business on December 31, 1987.

The Statement of Owner's Equity

This third financial statement is designed to show how the owner's capital has changed from the start of a period to the end of a period. It is a connecting link between the income statement and the balance sheet. For Tom's Repair and Rentals the statement of owner's equity looks like this:

TOM'S REPAIRS AND RENTALS
Statement of Owner's Equity
Year Ended December 31, 1987

Tom Jefferson, Capital, January 1, 1987	$ 63,535
Add: Net Income	40,165
Total	$103,700
Less: Withdrawals	(20,000)
Tom Jefferson, Capital, December 31, 1987	$ 83,700

The statement of owner's equity explains how the owner's equity has been increased or decreased during the period

---

Again, as with the other two statements, the heading is important. It has three parts: the name of the company, the name of the statement, and the period of time covered. This statement is like the income statement in that it too covers a period of time, from January 1, 1987, to December 31, 1987. The statement tells us that Tom started the year with capital of $63,535. During the year he increased his capital by $40,165; the net income we saw on the income statement. And he took $20,000 from the business; that's the withdrawals. He ended up with capital of $83,700 on December 31, 1987, which was also the figure we saw on the balance sheet in the owner's equity section.

Assets

Assets are owned economic resources that provide future benefits

The **assets** of an economic entity are the economic resources that are owned by the entity and that are expected to provide future benefits. They may be *physical* in nature, such as cash, merchandise, supplies, equipment, trucks, machines, buildings, and land. Or they may not exist in a tangible or physical form.

Nonphysical assets can be legal claims, such as payments due from customers (called *accounts receivable*) or legal rights, such as patents or copyrights. These nonphysical assets produce future benefits. For example, when we sell a product for $10 to one of our customers, the customer may not pay the amount due today. He or she may charge it, and pay at the end of the month. We have sold our product *on account,* earning revenue of $10, and we have a nonphysical asset — an account receivable of $10 — which we anticipate will be collected shortly. The future benefit is the cash we will receive at the end of the month.

To be included on the balance sheet as an asset, an economic resource must be measurable; if it is not measurable, it is not an asset. For example, the managerial ability of the company's president is an economic resource that will provide future benefit, but it is not susceptible to measurement.

Liabilities

Debts of an entity are called liabilities

The *liabilities* of an economic entity are its debts. The debts may be represented as *formal* claims or *informal* claims. A formal claim is a written contract, such as a written promise to repay a borrowed sum of money plus interest at a specified future date; this is called a *note payable.* Or a debt may be represented as an informal claim such as an amount due to a creditor for goods and services acquired but not yet paid for; this is called an *account payable.*

Owner's Equity

Owner's equity is the difference between an entity's assets and its liabilities

To convey to you the meaning of owner's equity, an example is needed. Assume that several of us decide to go into business and we get up $40,000 of our own money to buy an empty factory building. Next, we borrow from a bank $60,000 and buy machines to put in the factory. That's it. We need nothing else; we are ready to operate. At this point we could prepare a balance sheet. If we did, it would look like this:

Assets	Liabilities and Owner's Equity
Assets $100,000	Liabilities $60,000
	Owners' Equity 40,000

The bank has a claim on our assets amounting to $60,000. This is a liability. There are no other creditors' claims on our assets. The difference between the assets and the creditors' claims on those assets, the liabilities, represents the owner's interest in the business. In our business we have a $40,000 interest. This is the *owner's equity* or *capital.* Since the creditors' claim on a business entity's assets take precedence over owner's claims, owner's equity represents a residual amount equal to the difference between assets and liabilities.

Prior to lending money to a business entity, creditors will study the relationship between the resources provided by other creditors and the resources provided by the owner. Generally, the greater the amount of resources provided by creditors compared to that provided by the owner, the greater the risk to be taken by any new creditors considering lending additional funds.

GENERALLY ACCEPTED ACCOUNTING PRINCIPLES

Consider the situation presented by the following facts: Red Company, White Company, and Blue Company are competitors in the data processing industry. Several years ago, each of the three companies acquired identical computers for $100,000. Inflation is such that $100,000 several years ago, when the computers were acquired, is equivalent to $120,000 today. The computer industry is characterized by rapid technological advances such that new computers equivalent in capacity to the older ones acquired by Red, White, and Blue could be purchased today for $75,000. At the end of the current year, when the balance sheets are presented, the value of the computer is listed among the assets of Red Company at $100,000; Blue Company reports the computer as an asset valued at $120,000; and White Company values it at $75,000. Obviously there exists a need for some type of ground rules that all companies will follow when presenting financial statements. Otherwise the statements will not provide information that is useful to investors and creditors.

Generally accepted accounting principles (GAAP) are the ground rules of accounting

The ground rules used by business entities in presenting financial information are called *generally accepted accounting principles (GAAP).* These principles have been developed by the accounting profession over the years in an attempt to provide a consistent system of financial reporting in a constantly changing business environment. Unlike the physical sciences, where natural laws are universally and eternally true, accounting principles may change to meet the needs of emerging and changing financial situations. What may have provided adequate financial information several years ago may not be adequate today.

The authority of accounting principles rests on their general acceptance by the accounting profession. Generally accepted accounting principles encompass not only accounting principles, but various procedures for applying these principles. For example, one accounting principle tells us that the price we paid for a machine must be spread over the period of time, the *life,* we expect to use the machine. We have several accepted procedures for applying this principle. We could spread the cost over the life in equal amounts per year; we could spread the costs based on the number of hours the machine was used each year; or we could spread the cost based on the number of units the machine produced each year.

Accounting principles develop as members of the accounting profession think about various issues in accounting in an attempt to seek solutions to those issues. What may be a theoretically sound solution to a particular accounting problem may have certain practical limitations. The experience of the members of the accounting profession will determine when a practical rather than a conceptual solution to a problem is required. Thus, generally accepted accounting principles are a blend of theoretical principles and practical considerations.

Development of Accounting Principles: Major Institutions

Several groups have been influential in the development of generally accepted accounting principles for the entire accounting profession: the Financial Accounting Standards Board, the American Institute of Certified Public Accountants, the Securities and Exchange Commission, the American Accounting Association, and the National Association of Accountants.

Financial Accounting Standards Board

A major portion of GAAP is developed by the FASB

The group responsible for developing generally accepted accounting principles today is the *Financial Accounting Standards Board,* commonly referred to as the *FASB.* These generally accepted accounting principles are called *Statements* of the Financial Accounting Standards Board and, in effect, must be followed by all business entities issuing financial statements to investors or creditors. The FASB consists of seven full-time members. The FASB members spend a considerable amount of time and effort in developing a standard. *Discussion memorandums,* which are pamphlets explaining the basic issues of the topic under consideration, are prepared; *public hearings,* where accountants and others can express their views orally and in writing, are held; and *exposure drafts,* which are the FASB's planned solutions to the problem, are written. After all this the FASB members vote on the standards, and if four of the seven approve, it is issued to the accounting profession as a new standard.

FIGURE 1-8
The FASB, which is the prime source of GAAP, receives input from several organizations.

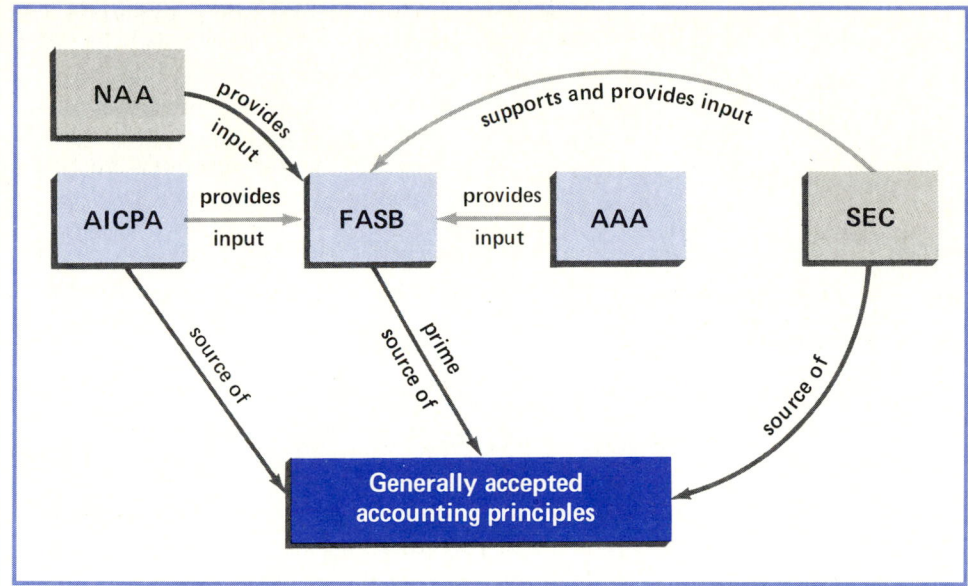

Securities and Exchange Commission

The SEC provides strong support for the FASB

The Securities and Exchange Act of 1934 created an independent quasi-judicial agency of the federal government to administer the various acts concerning the distribution and sale of publicly held securities. This agency is called the *Securities and Exchange Commission (SEC).* Legal authority is vested in the SEC to require whatever specific accounting practices it deems necessary to protect the public. However, the SEC has taken the position that accounting principles are best set in the private sector rather than the public sector. As a consequence the SEC has looked to the FASB to establish generally accepted accounting principles, and thus far most of the FASB statements have been accepted by the SEC as its own requirements for how financial and accounting data must be reported. On occasion the SEC may differ with the FASB over certain accounting principles, and when that happens the SEC may issue its own ruling requiring whatever additional accounting information it believes must be reported to the SEC and perhaps also presented in the annual reports to stockholders. While the SEC could exist without the FASB, most certainly the FASB could not exist without the support of its friendly partner, the SEC, and its power to legislate accounting principles.

American Institute of Certified Public Accountants

As the American Bar Association is to the legal profession and the American Medical Association is to the medical profession, so the *American Institute of Certified Public Accountants (AICPA)* is to the accounting profession. The AICPA is the professional organization representing accountants on a national basis.

Here are some of the ways the AICPA contributes to or affects the generally accepted accounting principles:

The AICPA provides input to the FASB and the SEC

- The AICPA collects reactions of its members to accounting issues and furnishes them to the FASB which considers them in developing new standards.
- The AICPA represents the views of the profession in cases of congressional investigations.
- The AICPA publishes a monthly magazine called the *Journal of Accountancy.*

The APB was the predecessor of the FASB

Prior to the establishment of the FASB in 1973, the AICPA was very directly involved with developing generally accepted accounting principles. The predecessor to the FASB, the Accounting Principles Board (APB), was a committee within the AICPA responsible for issuing statements on accounting principles. These statements were called APB *Opinions* and, unless superseded by a later *Opinion* of the APB, or a *Standard* of the FASB, are still in effect today.

American Accounting Association

The AAA provides indirect and long-range influence on GAAP

The *American Accounting Association (AAA)* is an organization of accounting professors. As such, its influence on establishing accounting principles is somewhat indirect and long-range. The research done by AAA members leans a little more toward the theoretical rather than the practical. The AAA is in continual search for the way accounting issues should be solved. The theoretical solution offered by the AAA today often finds its way into accounting a number of years later. For example, the present concept of the income statement was expressed 20 years ago by the AAA. Articles in the *Accounting Review,* the AAA's quarterly publication, and AAA committee reports will help establish accounting principles 20 years hence.

National Association of Accountants

The *National Association of Accountants* is an organization of private accountants concerned with managerial accounting issues. Their publication, *Management Accounting,* is issued monthly. The organization conducts research on current topics and develops an extensive educational program.

Certain Basic Principles

Now that you have some idea about why generally accepted accounting principles are needed and how and who sets these principles, we'll take a look at some specific and very important accounting principles and the concepts behind them. The principles are the basis for how financial statements are prepared. Of course, there are many principles, and as we take up further topics, we'll also discuss the principles related to those topics. But at this early point, we'll begin with principles that relate to preparing financial statements. As we proceed in this chapter, as well as throughout the entire text, we will regularly refer to the principles relating to the topic under discussion. This will help your awareness and increase your understanding of the reasons why the financial statements are presented as they are.

Five concepts and principles are presented in this section:

1. The cost principle
2. The objectivity principle
3. The business entity concept
4. The going concern concept
5. The stable-dollar concept

The Cost Principle

The cost principle requires that assets be recorded at their exchange price

Assets acquired by a business entity are to be recorded at the exchange price paid for them. The price the buyer pays in exchange for an asset is known as the *historical cost.* It is called a historical cost because once recorded the cost of the asset remains unchanged.

Applying this cost principle to the situation of the Red Company, White Company, and Blue Company discussed on page 16 would require that the identical computers purchased by each company all be recorded at their historical cost, $100,000. Neither the current market value of $75,000, nor the cost adjusted for inflation of $120,000, would be recorded. Neither value is in accordance with this generally accepted accounting principle.

It is important to realize at this early stage that the *assets listed on the balance sheet are measured in dollar amounts that represent the* historical cost *of those assets* not *what presently could be obtained from their sale.*

The Objectivity Principle

The cost of an asset is established by an exchange transaction between an informed buyer and an informed seller. Evidence of the exchange price agreed upon and transacted by both parties can be found in documents such as purchase invoices, sales invoices, property deeds, transfers of title, and other similar documents. This exchange price — the historical cost — can be confirmed by any independent party by simply reviewing the information in the documents that describes the transaction. By the term **independent party** we mean a person who is not related to, nor has a financial interest in the business affairs of, either the buyer or seller. The evidence supplies facts on which assets are measured.

> The objectivity principle requires that values be determined by verifiable objective evidence

The **objectivity principle** establishes the reason for recording assets at cost. Any value other than cost could not be agreed upon by independent parties who are experts in determining values of assets. Estimated market values are not based on fact and are not objective; they are subjective. **Subjective** means that they rest on the opinion of the one making the estimate.

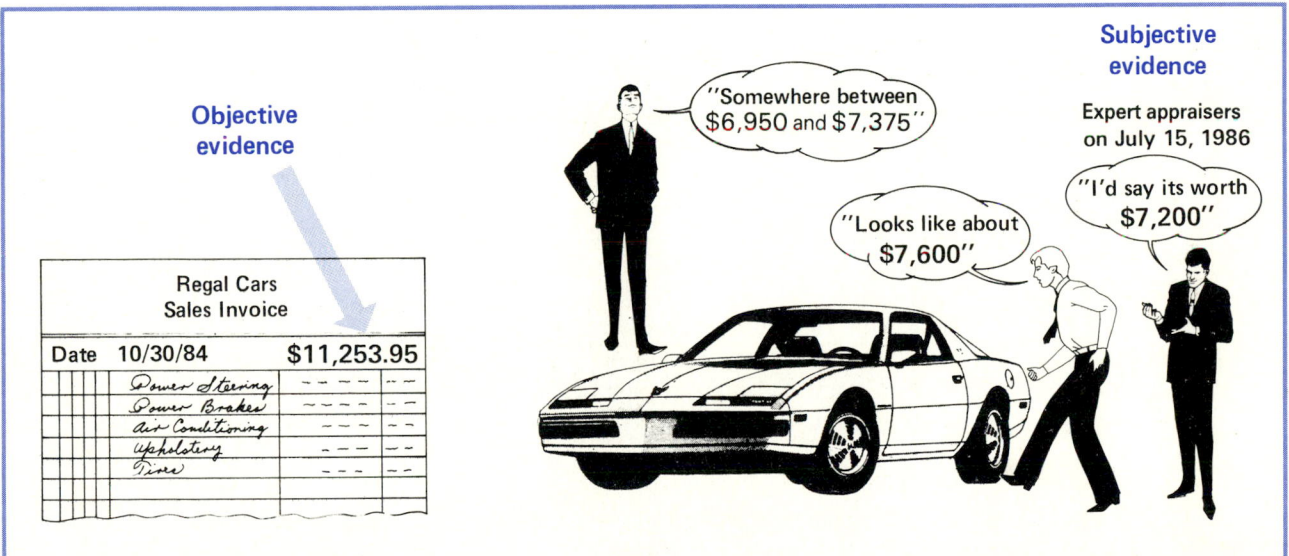

FIGURE 1-9   Objective vs. subjective evidence.
To determine the value of the car on July 15, 1986, for financial reporting the accountant will look to the objective evidence provided by the sales invoice rather than the subjective evidence provided by appraisals.

The Business Entity Concept

> The business entity concept requires that an entity is to be considered separate and distinct from its owners

For accounting purposes financial statements are prepared for each individual business entity, as we discussed previously with the Louis Garcia example on page 11. A business entity is considered to be separate and distinct from its owner or owners. Similarly, when a travel agency and a dry cleaning store are operated by the same person but as two separate proprietorships, the business transactions of each must be recorded, summarized, and reported separately, resulting in an income statement and a balance sheet for each enterprise. The purchase of an automobile by the owner of these two establishments for his or her personal use could not be considered as relating to either business entity. Thus, accounting treats each business entity as generating its own revenue, incurring its own expenses, owning its own assets, and owing its own debts. As seen previously, this is not legally true for a proprietorship or a partnership.

The Going Concern Concept

The assumption that a business will be in existence to complete its objectives is called the going concern concept

Business entities are established with the basic assumption of continued existence. Even though occasionally the entity may incur a loss, so long as the owners can reasonably expect future earnings that will yield profits, a business entity will continue to operate. Thus, it is assumed that a business entity will be in existence for as far into the future as is necessary to complete any projects the business entity plans to undertake. This is the *going concern* concept. It is because of this concept that assets are considered to have future economic benefits. Since the business entity will be in existence long enough to complete any project it is now working on, or plans to work on in the future, any assets that will not be used up in 1 year are recorded on the balance sheet. If we did not have this going concern concept we would be forced to record all assets as expenses on the income statement. We would not know if any future benefit would be received from the asset, since the business entity might not be in operation next year.

For example, a building typically has an estimated useful life of 40 years but its full cost is not recorded as an expense when acquired. Instead, because the business entity expects to be in existence 40 years hence, the cost of the building will be allocated to each of 40 successive annual income statements as an expense. The market value of the building today, as well as most other assets acquired by the business entity, is not considered relevant to the users of the financial statements since the entity does not plan to sell those assets it needs to operate the business. There is considerable disagreement on this last point.

The Stable-Dollar Concept

The stable-dollar concept assumes that the value of the dollar remains the same over time

The mile and the kilometer are standard units that enable us to measure distances. If we know the distance between two cities, we can use that information to estimate the time to travel between them or how much gasoline is needed to make the trip.

Money is the unit of measure employed in recording financial transactions. Knowing the money values assigned to financial transactions enables the users of financial statements to estimate the profitability or solvency of a business enterprise. The mile and the kilometer are precise units of measure. Every mile or kilometer will measure exactly the same distance. Unfortunately the same precision is not true for money. A dollar of 1980 is not the same as a dollar of today. As we know, this is due to inflation.

Accountants do not recognize that the value of the dollar changes over time. They prepare financial statements based on the *stable-dollar concept.*

We use this term *stable dollar* to mean that the dollar of a past year is equal in value to a current dollar. When we compare revenues of 1980 to revenues of 1987, the same dollar is used to measure the revenues from each year. The accounting dollar is thus assumed to be "stable"—it does not change in value over time. This we know is not true! The dollar does change in value over time. We could buy 1 gallon of gasoline for $.34 in 1972. How much is a gallon of gasoline today? The gallon stayed the same, but the dollar certainly didn't.

It is possible to present financial statements adjusted for current values, but to do so would require subjective judgments on the part of those preparing such statements. We could adjust the $40,000 cost of a building acquired several years ago to a current value by the use of the ***Consumer Price Index (CPI).*** If the CPI was 100 when the building was acquired and it is now 250, we would simply multiply the $40,000 by $\frac{250}{100}$ to obtain a current value of $100,000. But is that the true value of the building today? It may cost $125,000 in materials to replace the building today. And why did we use the CPI; why not the wholesale price index or some other index?

While such information concerning current values is useful, accountants generally feel that objectivity in determining historical cost is more important. The FASB has in recent years, however, considered the problem of inflation and has required that the basic financial statements of the largest corporations be supplemented with information concerning changing prices.

THE BASIC ACCOUNTING MODEL

The basic accounting model must always be in balance

The end result of the accounting activity for a business entity is the financial statements that describe the entity. These statements cannot be prepared until the financial transactions of the business entity have been recorded, classified, and summarized. The framework of the financial statements rests on a basic relationship, referred to as the accounting model, as expressed by the balance sheet equation:

$$\text{Assets} = \text{Liabilities} + \text{Owner's Equity}$$

This fundamental equality is always true because the left side of the equation is simply another view of the right side. Assets represent resources owned by the business entity; liabilities and owner's equity represent the claims of those who supplied the assets.

Financial transactions represent the exchange of goods and services between economic entities. Each financial transaction will affect the balance sheet equation. Consider, for example, the acquisition of an asset. We can list only three ways the asset can be acquired:

1. It could be acquired by paying cash — *giving up an asset already owned.* Buying an office desk for cash would be an example.

2. It could be acquired today with a promise to pay the amount due at some future date — *incurring a liability.* Buying an office desk, but not paying for it until next month would illustrate incurring a liability.

3. It could be acquired from the owner of the business entity — *increasing the owner's equity* in the business. If the owner of a business used his or her own personal desk in the business, the business would have acquired the desk from the owner.

Can you see that each of these financial transactions has two parts?

On the one hand, acquiring the office desk by paying cash would increase the total assets owned by the business entity by the cost of the desk. But on the other hand, the cash would be reduced by a like amount.

Acquiring the desk by incurring a liability would increase the total assets, but also increase the liabilities.

Acquiring the desk from the owner would increase the total assets, but also increase the owner's equity.

Since the transaction has two parts, the term ***double-entry accounting*** is used to refer to the recording of financial transactions.

Remember: The ultimate result of the accounting activity for an entity is its financial statements. The first step required to produce financial statements is to record the financial transactions within the framework of the basic accounting model.

Effects of Financial Transactions on the Accounting Model

Every financial transaction, whether very simple or extremely complex, can be analyzed by or expressed in terms of its effect on the balance sheet equation. Every business entity, whether it's General Meat Market or General Motors, analyzes and reflects financial transactions by the effect of each transaction on the balance sheet equation.

It is essential for you to understand the basic accounting model and the effects on the financial transactions upon the model. To help you begin to understand the model, we'll show you an example of how transactions affect the model.

RON'S RENTALS

Ron Sanchez, after working two decades for an international car rental agency, decides to establish his own car rental business. He plans to buy several used cars and trucks, which he will rent to customers on a daily or weekly basis. During the month of July 1987, the first month of Ron's Rentals operations, various financial transactions take place; they are analyzed on the following pages.

Transaction 1   Ron invests $5,000 from his personal savings in the new business entity by depositing a check drawn on his bank account at the Austin National Bank into an account, "Ron's Rentals," established at the Lone Star State Bank.

Let's look at what Ron has done. With this small financial transaction, he has given us a few very important and fundamental things to learn about.

■ A business entity separate and distinct from Ron's personal financial affairs has been created.

■ An economic resource — the $5,000 that is the asset Cash — has been invested in the business entity. The source of this resource is the contribution made by the owner that represents owner's equity, which we shall refer to as Sanchez Capital.

■ The dual nature of the transaction is that cash has been invested and owner's equity created. The effect of this transaction on the basic accounting model — the balance sheet equation — is to increase an asset (Cash) from zero to $5,000 and also to increase owner's equity, Sanchez, Capital, from zero to $5,000.

In this chapter we will analyze financial transactions like these by means of a *financial transaction worksheet.* The financial transaction worksheet is a form used to analyze increases and decreases in the assets, liabilities, or owner's equity of a business entity. When a specific asset, liability, or owner's equity item is created by a financial transaction it is listed on the financial transaction worksheet under the appropriate heading. These are called *accounts* and are used to accumulate money amounts. For example, when Ron contributed the $5,000 asset Cash, it is simply listed under the heading *Asset.*

The following is an illustration of the first transaction for Ron's Rentals. The amounts of assets, liabilities, and owner's equity are all zero before this first transaction, since the business entity did not exist prior to transaction 1.

The owner of the business makes an investment in the business

	RON'S RENTALS Financial Transaction Worksheet Month of July, 1987					
	Assets	**=**	**Liabilities**	**+**	**Owner's Equity**	
Transaction Number	**Cash**				**Sanchez, Capital**	**Owner's Equity Explanation**
(1)	$5,000	=		+	$5,000	Initial investment

Transaction 2   Several used trucks and cars costing $3,000 are acquired by paying a check in that amount to the vendor.

This exchange transaction results in the decrease in one asset — Cash — but a corresponding increase in another asset — Trucks and Cars. Notice that while the value of total assets is unchanged after this transaction, the composition of the assets has changed.

Several used trucks and cars are acquired by paying cash

	RON'S RENTALS Financial Transaction Worksheet Month of July, 1987						
	Assets		**=**	**Liabilities**	**+**	**Owner's Equity**	
Transaction Number	**Cash**	**Trucks and Cars**				**Sanchez, Capital**	**Owner's Equity Explanation**
(1)	+ $5,000					+ $5,000	Initial investment
(2)	− 3,000	+ $3,000					
Totals	$2,000 +	$3,000	=		+	$5,000	

Transaction 3   A used panel truck is purchased on account for $750.

In this case an asset — Trucks and Cars — is increased. However, the truck was obtained not by reducing another asset — Cash — but by incurring a liability. This is what we mean by the term *on account,* acquiring the truck with a promise to pay the amount due at a later date. We may also say *on credit* or *for credit* to mean the same thing. When we buy something in this manner we call the amount we owe the creditor an *account payable.* The dual nature of this transaction is to offset the increase in assets—Trucks and Cars—by a corresponding increase in the liability—Accounts Payable. Of course after this exchange transaction the total of the assets ($2,000 + $3,750 = $5,750) is exactly equal to the total of the liabilities and capital ($750 + $5,000 = $5,750).

A used panel truck is acquired on account

		RON'S RENTALS Financial Transaction Worksheet Month of July, 1987				
		Assets		= Liabilities +	Owner's Equity	
Transaction Number	Cash	Trucks and Cars	Accounts Payable	Sanchez, Capital	Owner's Equity Explanation
(1)	+ $5,000				+ $5,000	Initial investment
(2)	− 3,000	+ $3,000				
(3)		+ 750	+ $750			
Totals	$2,000 +	$3,750	=	$750 +	$5,000	

Transaction 4   Office and certain other necessary supplies in the amount of $650 are acquired on account.

As a result of this transaction, a new asset account called Supplies on Hand is created. Whenever the business entity engages in activities that result in the need to establish new accounts, accountants simply do that: They create new accounts. The new account is given a name that describes that account in as few words as possible. The account *Supplies on Hand* is so-called to distinguish it as an asset. The term *Supplies* might lead to some confusion since it is not clear whether the supplies are "on hand" or "used." *Supplies Used* is an expense, not an asset. This transaction results in an increase in assets—Supplies on Hand—and an increase in the liability Accounts Payable.

Supplies are acquired on account.

			RON'S RENTALS Financial Transaction Worksheet Month of July, 1987				
		Assets			= Liabilities +	Owner's Equity	
Transaction Number	Cash	Supplies on Hand	Trucks and Cars	Accounts Payable	Sanchez, Capital	Owner's Equity Explanation
(1)	+ $5,000				+ $5,000	Initial investment
(2)	− 3,000		+ $3,000			
(3)			+ 750	+ $ 750		
(4)		+ $650		+ 650		
Totals	$2,000 +	$650 +	$3,750	= $1,400 +	$5,000	

Transaction 5 During the month of July Ron collects $1,600 in cash for car rentals.

The rendering of services for a fee was a prime motivating factor in establishing the business entity. Ron hopes to receive more money from his car rentals than he has to spend in providing those car rentals. The excess is ***profit*** or ***net income.*** The $1,600 collected for the car rentals represents revenues and as such reflects an increase in Ron's ownership interest in the business entity. ***Revenue*** is an inflow of cash or other properties in exchange for goods sold or services rendered. When the inflow of cash or other properties is recorded, another asset is not reduced. Nor is a liability incurred. The owner is better off than he was before; this is why owner's equity is increased. The effect of this transaction—$1,600 cash revenue—on the basic accounting equation is to increase the asset Cash and to increase owner's equity, Sanchez, Capital, each by $1,600.

Cash is received for car rentals.

RON'S RENTALS
Financial Transaction Worksheet
Month of July, 1987

Transaction Number	Cash		Supplies on Hand		Trucks and Cars	=	Accounts Payable	+	Sanchez, Capital	Owner's Equity Explanation
(1)	+ $5,000								+ $5,000	Initial investment
(2)	− 3,000				+ $3,000					
(3)					+ 750		+ $ 750			
(4)			+ $650				+ 650			
(5)	+ 1,600								+ 1,600	Car rentals
Totals	$3,600	+	$650	+	$3,750	=	$1,400	+	$6,600	

Transaction 6 Ron paid the Longhorn Gas Station $450 rent for parking the vehicles for the month of July. In addition he paid $250 to a high school student for washing the cars and helping with the office work.

These two items are expenses. They represent an outflow of resources and a reduction of owner's equity. Thus, the asset Cash is decreased by $700 and the owner's equity account—Sanchez, Capital—is decreased by $450 for Rent and $250 for Wages.

RON'S RENTALS
Financial Transaction Worksheet
Month of July, 1987

| Transaction Number | Cash | Assets | | = | Liabilities | + | Owner's Equity | Owner's Equity Explanation |
		Supplies on Hand	Trucks and Cars		Accounts Payable		Sanchez, Capital	
(1)	+ $5,000						+ $5,000	Initial investment
(2)	− 3,000		+ $3,000					
(3)			+ 750		+ $ 750			
(4)		+ $650			+ 650			
(5)	+ 1,600						+ 1,600	Car rentals
(6)	− 700						− 450	Rent
							− 250	Wages
Totals	$2,900	+	$650	+	$3,750	=	$1,400	+	$5,900

Rent and wages are paid.

Transaction 7   Several construction companies rent Ron's trucks from time to time during the month. Ron bills these customers $1,000.

Even though he has not received cash, Ron has earned revenue. He has performed his services and is entitled to payment. Once his services are performed, an economic resource is created. This economic resource is the amount owed to him and is called *accounts receivable.* As seen in transaction 5, revenue is an increase in owner's equity. Thus, this revenue transaction results in an increase in an asset—Accounts Receivable—and a like increase in owner's equity—Sanchez, Capital, in the amount of $1,000.

Several customers are billed.

RON'S RENTALS
Financial Transaction Worksheet
Month of July, 1987

| Transaction Number | Cash | Assets | | | | = | Liabilities | + | Owner's Equity | Owner's Equity Explanation |
		Accounts Receivable	Supplies on Hand	Trucks and Cars			Accounts Payable		Sanchez, Capital	
(1)	+ $5,000								+ $5,000	Initial investment
(2)	− 3,000			+ $3,000						
(3)				+ 750			+ $ 750			
(4)			+ $650				+ 650			
(5)	+ 1,600								+ 1,600	Car rentals
(6)	− 700								− 450	Rent
									− 250	Wages
(7)		+ $1,000							+ 1,000	Truck rentals
Totals	$2,900	+	$1,000	+	$650	+	$3,750	=	$1,400	+	$6,900

Transaction 8   On July 31, Ron pays the $650 bill for the purchase of supplies. He will pay the bill for the used panel truck on August 15.

The payment of the $650 is an outflow of resources, as evidenced by the cash expenditure and the reduction of a liability—Accounts Payable. This payment transaction reduces both cash and accounts payable by $650.

RON'S RENTALS
Financial Transaction Worksheet
Month of July, 1987

	Assets				=	Liabilities	+	Owner's Equity	
Transaction Number	Cash	Accounts Receivable	Supplies on Hand	Trucks and Cars		Accounts Payable		Sanchez, Capital	Owner's Equity Explanation
(1)	+$5,000							+$5,000	Initial investment
(2)	− 3,000			+$3,000					
(3)				+ 750		+$750			
(4)			+$650			+ 650			
(5)	+ 1,600							+ 1,600	Car rentals
(6)	− 700							− 450	Rent
								− 250	Wages
(7)		+$1,000						+ 1,000	Truck rentals
(8)	− 650					− 650			
Totals	$2,250 +	$1,000 +	$650 +	$3,750 =		$750 +		$6,900	

An account payable for supplies is paid.

Transaction 9   A check in the amount of $400 is received from a construction company for truck rentals billed in transaction 7.

While the total assets remain unchanged, their composition does change. The asset *Cash* is increased by $400 and the asset *Accounts Receivable* is decreased by a like amount. The collection of receivables and the payment of accounts payable are two of the most common business transactions.

RON'S RENTALS
Financial Transaction Worksheet
Month of July, 1987

Transaction Number	Cash	Accounts Receivable	Supplies on Hand	Trucks and Cars	=	Accounts Payable	+	Sanchez, Capital	Owner's Equity Explanation
		Assets			**= Liabilities +**			**Owner's Equity**	
(1)	+$5,000							+$5,000	Initial investment
(2)	− 3,000			+$3,000					
(3)				+ 750		+$750			
(4)			+$650			+ 650			
(5)	+ 1,600							+ 1,600	Car rentals
(6)	− 700							− 450	Rent
								− 250	Wages
(7)		+$1,000						+ 1,000	Truck rentals
(8)	− 650					− 650			
(9)	+ 400	− 400							
Totals	$2,650 +	$ 600 +	$650 +	$3,750	=	$750	+	$6,900	

An account receivable is received.

Transaction 10 Ron withdraws $900 from the business for his personal use.

This is the means by which owners of business entities receive a distribution of the profits. Remember transaction 1 in which Ron invested $5,000? At that time we increased cash by $5,000 and also increased owner's equity by a like amount. This was an investment by the owner. It was *not* revenue. Ron simply transferred funds from his personal account to the checking account of the business. A cash withdrawal, such as we have in transaction 10, is exactly the opposite. Funds are simply transferred from the checking account of the business to Ron's personal account. This is not an expense. When an owner of a business removes funds for personal use we call this a ***withdrawal.*** The $900 cash withdrawal transaction results in a reduction of both cash and owner's equity.

Owner's withdrawal is made.

RON'S RENTALS
Financial Transaction Worksheet
Month of July, 1987

Transaction Number	Cash	Accounts Receivable	Supplies on Hand	Trucks and Cars	=	Accounts Payable	+	Sanchez, Capital	Owner's Equity Explanation
		Assets			**= Liabilities +**			**Owner's Equity**	
(1)	+$5,000							+$5,000	Initial investment
(2)	− 3,000			+$3,000					
(3)				+ 750		+$750			
(4)			+$650			+ 650			
(5)	+ 1,600							+ 1,600	Car rentals
(6)	− 700							− 450	Rent
								− 250	Wages
(7)		+$1,000						+ 1,000	Truck rentals
(8)	− 650					− 650			
(9)	+ 400	− 400							
(10)	− 900							− 900	Withdrawal
Totals	$1,750 +	$ 600 +	$650 +	$3,750	=	$750	+	$6,000	

Transaction 11   On the last day of July, Ron counts the various supplies and determines that $150 worth of supplies remain on hand. Since he purchased $650 of supplies at the start of the month, $500 of supplies must have been used during the month.

This $500 represents an expense, Supplies Used, and as such reflects a reduction in owner's equity. This transaction represents supplies used and is recorded as a reduction in Supplies on Hand and a reduction in Sanchez, Capital.

RON'S RENTALS
Financial Transaction Worksheet
Month of July, 1987

Transaction Number	Cash	Accounts Receivable	Supplies on Hand	Trucks and Cars	=	Accounts Payable	+	Sanchez, Capital	Owner's Equity Explanation
		Assets			=	Liabilities	+	Owner's Equity	
(1)	+$5,000							+$5,000	Initial investment
(2)	− 3,000			+$3,000					
(3)				+ 750		+$750			
(4)			+$650			+ 650			
(5)	+ 1,600							+ 1,600	Car rentals
(6)	− 700							− 450	Rent
								− 250	Wages
(7)		+$1,000						+ 1,000	Truck rentals
(8)	− 650					− 650			
(9)	+ 400	− 400							
(10)	− 900							− 900	Withdrawal
(11)			− 500					− 500	Supplies used
Totals	$1,750 +	$ 600 +	$150 +	$3,750	=	$750	+	$5,500	

Supplies used during the period are recorded.

Preparing the Financial Statements

At the end of the month after the last transaction has been recorded on the financial transaction worksheet and each of the columns totaled, it is a relatively simple matter to prepare the financial statements—the income statement, the statement of owner's equity, and the balance sheet. These three statements are presented in Exhibit 1-1 shown at the top of the following page.

Income Statement

The income statement is prepared first. The data for the income statement are contained under the Sanchez, Capital account, since revenues are increases in capital and expenses represent decreases in capital. Only revenue and expenses are shown on the income statement. The initial investment and the withdrawals are not shown on the income statement, since they are neither revenues nor expenses.

Statement of Owner's Equity

Before the balance sheet is prepared, a statement of owner's equity is developed. This statement reflects the increases in capital due to investments and net income—the excess of revenues over expenses and the decreases in capital due to withdrawals.

EXHIBIT 1-1
The Three Financial Statements.

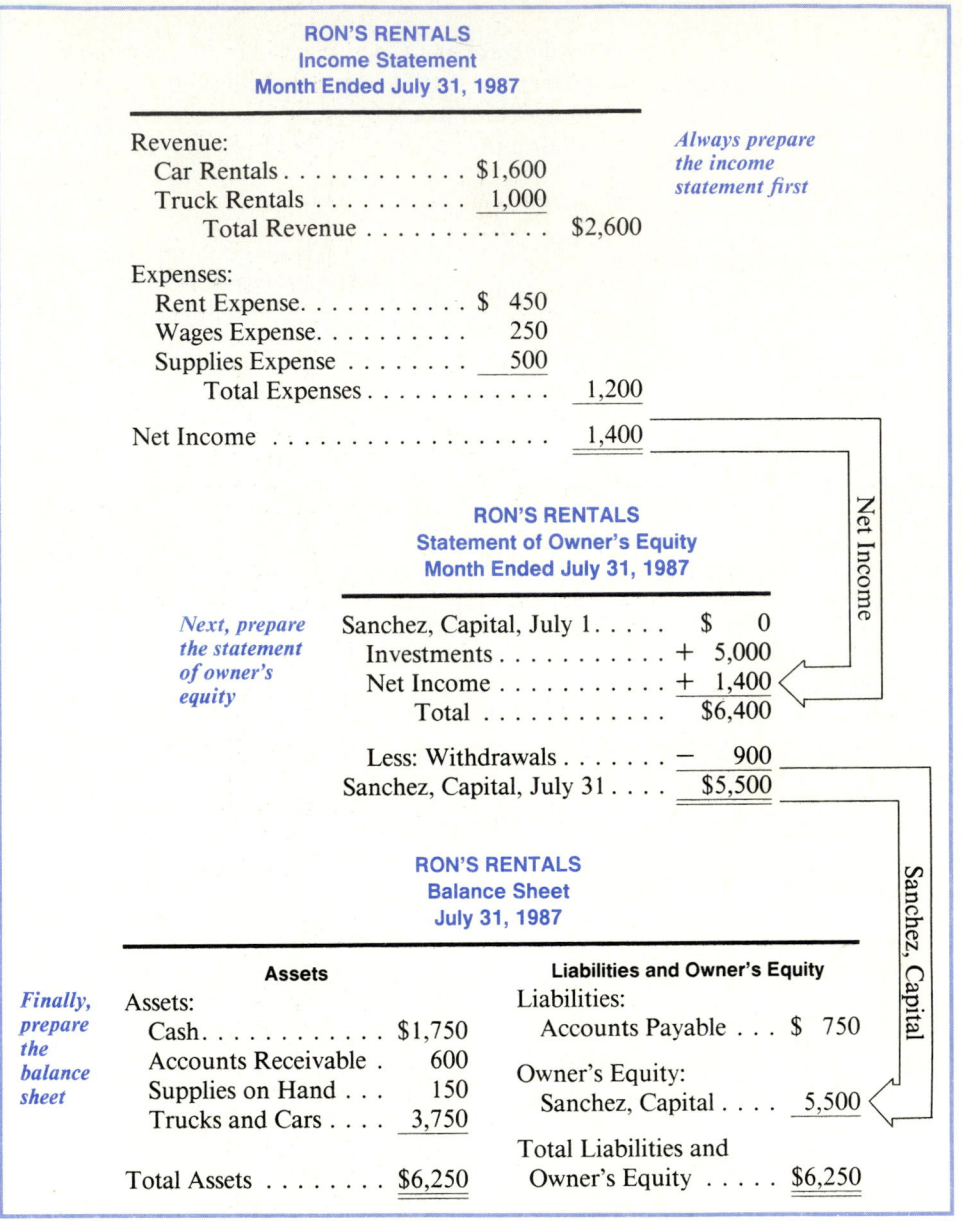

RON'S RENTALS
Income Statement
Month Ended July 31, 1987

Revenue:
  Car Rentals . . . . $1,600   *Always prepare*
  Truck Rentals 1,000   *the income*
     Total Revenue . . . . $2,600   *statement first*

Expenses:
  Rent Expense. . . . . $ 450
  Wages Expense. 250
  Supplies Expense 500
     Total Expenses 1,200

Net Income 1,400

RON'S RENTALS
Statement of Owner's Equity
Month Ended July 31, 1987

Next, prepare   Sanchez, Capital, July 1 . . . . . $ 0
the statement   Investments . . . . + 5,000
of owner's   Net Income . . . . + 1,400
equity   Total $6,400

                     Less: Withdrawals . . . . −   900
                     Sanchez, Capital, July 31 . . . . $5,500

RON'S RENTALS
Balance Sheet
July 31, 1987

	Assets	**Liabilities and Owner's Equity**

Finally,   Assets: Liabilities:
prepare   Cash. . . . . $1,750   Accounts Payable . . . $ 750
the   Accounts Receivable .   600
balance   Supplies on Hand . . .   150   Owner's Equity:
sheet   Trucks and Cars 3,750   Sanchez, Capital   5,500

                                                 Total Liabilities and
              Total Assets . . . . $6,250   Owner's Equity $6,250

This statement explains how Sanchez, Capital increased from a zero balance on July 1 to a $5,500 balance on July 31. The data for this statement are contained on the financial transaction worksheet for the investment and withdrawal information and the income statement for the net income.

Balance Sheet   After completion of the statement of owner's equity, the balance sheet is prepared. The balance sheet is simply the totals of the left side of the financial transaction worksheet—the asset accounts—and the right side—the liability and owner's equity accounts.

THE BUCS BALANCE SHEET
Tampa Tribune confuses balance sheet with income statement

An article appearing in the Tampa Tribune on October 30, 1983, contained the following information:

The on-field misfortunes of the stumble-footed Tampa Bay Buccaneers have local fans reaching for the collective neck of coach John McKay and owner Hugh Culverhouse.

But any frowns you see on the face of multimillionaire attorney Culverhouse are from the Buccaneer's dismal 0 – 8 playing ledger, not their flourishing balance sheet.

Even an 0 – 16 season could not prevent the Buccaneer franchise from showing a profit for the 1983 season, several sources indicate.

Financial figures gathered from five primary National Football sources project a $4.73 million pre-tax profit for the hapless

Buccaneers. A balance sheet compiled by the Tribune showed $23.53 million in revenue and $18.8 million in expenses.

Bucs Balance Sheet '83	
Projected Home Revenue	$ 3,825,300
Projected Road Revenue	2,378,572
Preseason Gate Revenue	1,139,000
Projected Playoff Revenue	500,000
Projected Lounge Box Revenue	578,000
Network Television Revenue	13,400,000
Home Television/Radio Revenue	250,000
Projected Concession/Parking	162,500
Projected Misc. Revenue	1,300,000
Total Projected Revenue	$23,533,372
Total Projected Expenses	18,800,000
Total Projected Net Income	$ 4,733,372

Source: Tampa Tribune-Times, Oct. 30, 1983 by Jeff Smith. Reprinted by permission.

The various types of financial statements are often confused with each other. For example, in the article above, there is a financial statement identified as a *balance sheet.*

Recall that a balance sheet shows an entity's financial position on a particular date. Balance sheets are prepared at the end of the year or, sometimes, at the end of each quarter or month. Balance sheets include assets, liabilities, and owner's equity. Individual accounts are classified under these three main categories.

On the other hand, an income statement shows revenue, expenses, and net income or loss for a specific period of time. The difference between the revenue and the expenses will later be shown in the owner's equity section of the balance sheet.

The financial statement in the article above is, as you will no doubt recognize, an *income statement.*

CHAPTER SUMMARY

Accounting is a service that provides financial reports on which informed economic decisions are based.

Financial reports are prepared for two distinct user groups. Internal financial reports are prepared for management of economic entities — this area of accounting is referred to as *management accounting.* External financial reports are prepared for those who do not have direct access to the entity's records — this area of accounting is referred to as *financial accounting.*

There are many different kinds of accounting activities. Principal among them:

- *General financial accounting* is concerned with recording business transactions and preparing financial reports.
- *Accounting systems design* is concerned with the development of business forms and records, with writing and implementing operating procedures, and with investigating new means of processing accounting data.
- *Cost accounting* involves the gathering of accounting information to determine the cost of a product or service.
- *Budgeting* expresses predetermined business objectives in monetary terms.
- *Taxation* is concerned with the preparation of various tax returns in compliance with the taxing authority's requirements and with tax planning to minimize the impact of taxes on the business entity.

- *Internal auditing* provides a continual review of the accounting records, reports, policies, and procedures.
- *Data processing* is responsible for recording the mass of business transactions generated by a business entity.

Users of external financial statements need assurance that the financial statements have been prepared in a manner that fairly represents the results of activities for the period. Such assurance is provided by the *certified public accountant (CPA),* who issues an audit report based on an independent review of the business transactions underlying the financial report. CPAs are licensed by the various states only after passing the CPA examination. Generally a CPA candidate must have a college degree with a major in accounting to be eligible to take the CPA exam.

The *income statement,* the *statement of owner's equity,* and the *balance sheet* are the principal financial statements generated by the general financial accounting activity.

There are three main types of entities:

1. *Proprietorship*   A business entity owned by one person
2. *Partnership*   A non-incorporated business entity owned by two or more persons
3. *Corporation*   A business entity incorporated under the laws of one of the states

The *income statement* compares *revenues* (the inflow of cash or other properties) earned during a specified period of time, with *expenses,* the cost of goods sold or services rendered during the same period of time.

The *balance sheet* shows the financial position of a business entity at a particular date. The total of the *assets* — the economic resources owned by the entity that are expected to provide future benefits — of a business entity will always equal the sum of its liabilities — its debts — and the *owner's equity* — the owner's interest in the business entity.

Generally accepted accounting principles (GAAP) have been developed over the years in an attempt to provide a rational system of financial reporting. These principles can be considered the ground rules of financial accounting. The most influential groups in the development of generally accepted accounting principles are the *Financial Accounting Standards Board (FASB)* and the *Securities and Exchange Commission (SEC).* The *American Institute of Certified Public Accountants (AICPA),* the *American Accounting Association (AAA),* and the *National Association of Accountants (NAA),* also provide input into the development of GAAP.

Five generally accepted accounting principles need to be considered as you begin to develop your understanding of accounting:

1. The *historical cost principle* states that assets acquired by a business entity are to be recorded at the exchange price paid for such assets and this cost, once recorded, will remain unchanged.
2. The *objectivity principle* provides that objective evidence be established for recording business transactions where the exchange price can be verified by invoice, deeds, transfers of title, or other business documents.
3. The *business entity concept* considers the business to be separate and distinct from its owners.
4. The *going concern concept* assumes that the entity will be in existence for as far into the future as it is reasonable to foresee.
5. Finally, the *stable-dollar concept* assumes that the basic unit of measure employed in recording financial transactions — the dollar — does not change in value over time.

The financial statements of economic entities cannot be prepared until the business transactions have been recorded, classified, and summarized within the framework of the ***basic accounting model.***

The basic accounting model is simply expressed by the balance sheet equation:

$$\textbf{Assets} = \textbf{Liabilities} + \textbf{Owner's Equity}$$

Each transaction will require two elements to be considered that will result in increases or decreases in assets, liabilities, or owner's equity. This dual nature of business transactions gives rise to the term ***double-entry accounting.***

After all business transactions have been recorded and summarized, the financial statements can be prepared. The income statement is prepared first because it yields the net income for the period, and the net income is used to compute the owner's equity that will appear on the balance sheet. This computation is often presented in a ***statement of owner's equity.***

IMPORTANT TERMS USED IN THIS CHAPTER

Account   A specific asset, liability, owner's equity, revenue, or expense used to accumulate money amounts. (page 22)

American Accounting Association   The organization of professional accounting educators. (page 18)

American Institute of Certified Public Accountants   The professional organization of CPAs. (page 17)

Assets   The economic resources that are owned by an economic entity and that are expected to provide future benefits. (page 14)

Balance sheet   The financial statement of a business entity that lists the assets owned, liabilities owed, and owner's equity at a specific point in time. (page 13)

Basic accounting model   The algebraic expression depicting the balance sheet relationship between assets and the sum of liabilities plus owner's equity:

$$\textbf{Assets} = \textbf{Liabilities} + \textbf{Owner's Equity}$$

(page 21)

Budgeting   The accounting activity concerned with expressing predetermined management objectives in monetary terms. (page 6)

Business entity concept   The basic generally accepted accounting principle stating that a business entity is considered to be separate and distinct from its owners for accounting purposes. (page 19)

Capital   A term often used in accounting to mean owner's equity. *Jones, Capital,* for example, is an owners' equity account. (page 15)

Certified Public Accountant   An individual who has met the educational and experience requirements as prescribed by state law and has passed the uniform CPA exam. A CPA performs an independent review of business entities' financial transactions (called an audit) and expresses his or her professional opinion on the fairness of the financial statements issued by the business entity. (page 7)

Controller   The executive officer of a business entity in charge of its accounting activity. (page 4)

Corporation   A business entity that is incorporated under the laws of one of the states. (page 11)

Cost accounting   The accounting activity concerned with determining the cost of producing a product or service. (page 6)

Data processing   The accounting activity concerned with the physical act of recording the mass of accounting data. (page 7)

Double-entry accounting   The process of recording each business transaction by affecting two elements within the basic accounting model. (page 21)

Expenses   The cost of goods sold or services rendered in the process of generating revenues. (page 13)

External financial reports   Reports—the income statement, the statement of owner's equity, and the balance sheet—prepared to meet the informational needs of those who do not have direct access to the business entity's records. (page 3)

Financial accounting   The area of accounting concerned with the preparation and presentation of general-purpose financial statements. (page 3)

Financial Accounting Standards Board   The independent public board, comprising seven full-time members, which is responsible for the development of generally accepted accounting principles. (page 16)

Generally accepted accounting principles (GAAP)   The ground rules used by economic entities in presenting financial information. (page 15)

Going concern concept   The assumption that a business entity will be in existence for as far into the future as it is reasonable to foresee. (page 20)

Historical cost principle   The principle whereby assets acquired by a business entity are to be recorded at the price paid in exchange for such assets. (page 18)

Income statement   The external financial statement designed to report the profitability of a business entity over a period of time by contrasting revenue earned with expenses incurred in the determination of net income. (page 12)

Internal auditing   The area of accounting concerned with checking and reviewing the entity's records, reporting policies, and procedures. (page 7)

Internal financial reports   Reports prepared exclusively for management of business entities. (page 3)

Liabilities   Debts of economic entities. (page 15)

Management accounting   The area of accounting concerned with internal reporting. (page 4)

National Association of Accountants   The professional organization of management accountants. (page 18)

Objectivity principle   The principle requiring objective verifiable evidence as a basis for recording of business transactions. (page 19)

Owner's equity   The financial interest of the owners in a business entity. (page 15)

Partnership   A non-incorporated business entity that is owned by two or more persons. (page 11)

Proprietorship   A business entity that is owned by one person. (page 10)

Revenue   The inflow of cash or other properties in exchange for goods sold or services rendered. (page 12)

Securities and Exchange Commission   An independent quasi-judicial agency of the federal government responsible for administering the various acts concerning the distribution and sale of publicly held securities. (page 17)

Stable-dollar concept   The assumption used in accounting that the unit of measure —the dollar—does not change in value over time. (page 20)

Taxation   The area of accounting concerned with preparation of various tax returns and with tax planning to minimize the impact of taxes on the business entity. (page 6)

QUESTIONS

1. To make informed economic decisions, a knowledge of accounting is essential. Why?

2. The terms *economic entities, business entities,* and *not-for-profit entities* are often used by business persons and accountants. Distinguish among these terms. Are the accounting needs of one different from the others?

3. Distinguish between *internal financial reports* and *external financial reports.*

4. The financial reports of business entities are prepared by and the responsibility of the accountants. Comment.

5. Describe the various areas of accounting activity.

6. What role does the independent certified public accountant play in the issuing of external financial statements?

7. Describe briefly the requirements to become a certified public accountant.

8. Investors are interested in the profitability and solvency of business entities. How does the accountant provide information concerning these two conditions?

9. What is the main objective of financial accounting?

10. There are three types of business entities. What are they? Describe them.

11. The terms *revenue* and *expense* are used often in accounting. Explain each term.

12. What information is contained on an income statement?

13. The balance sheet is a major financial report. What information does it contain?

14. *Assets, liabilities,* and *owner's equity* are all terms found on a balance sheet. What are the meanings of these terms?

15. *Generally accepted accounting principles* (GAAP) is a term used often by accountants. What does it mean?

16. Why are generally accepted accounting principles necessary?

17. *Statements* of the Financial Accounting Standards Board and *Opinions* of the Accounting Principles Board are deemed important to business entities. Why?

18. Explain the function of the Securities and Exchange Commission and its relationship to the FASB.

19. List and explain the five basic concepts and principles discussed in the chapter.

20. What is the basic accounting model? Why is it important?

21. Why does each business transaction have two elements?

22. Describe a business transaction that would:
    a. Decrease an asset and increase a second asset.
    b. Increase an asset and increase owner's equity.
    c. Increase an asset and increase a liability.

23. The James Company reported in December cash sales of $40,000, and sales on account of $95,000; and expenses incurred of $56,000, of which $14,000 was paid in cash. Determine the amount of revenue, expenses, and net income for the month.

24. The capital account of Brown Bakery amounted to $3,000 on January 1 of the current year. By year-end the capital account amounted to $9,000. If Brown withdrew $4,000 during the year, what was the net income for the year?

EXERCISES

Exercise 1-1
Transactions that change the basic accounting model

Listed below are five situations. Describe a transaction for each situation that wll result in the indicated change in the elements of the basic accounting model.
a. Increase an asset and increase a liability.
b. Decrease an asset and decrease a liability.
c. Increase one asset and decrease another asset.
d. Increase an asset and increase owner's equity.
e. Increase an asset, decrease a second asset, and increase a liability.

Exercise 1-2
Computing the missing elements in the basic accounting model

For each of the following, determine the requested item.
a. The liabilities of a business entity having assets of $15,000 and owner's equity of $9,500.
b. The assets of a business entity having liabilities of $74,000 and owner's equity of $126,000.
c. The owner's equity of a business entity having assets of $42,500 and liabilities of $26,250.
d. The revenues of a business entity having expenses of $16,300 and net income of $3,700.
e. The expenses of a business entity having revenues of $36,250 and a net loss of $14,750.

Exercise 1-3
Determining the effect of transactions on the basic elements of the balance sheet equation

During the current month the Atlas Company engaged in the transactions listed below. For each of the transactions, indicate the effect on the basic elements of the balance sheet equation using (+) for increase, (−) for decrease, and (0) for no change. Use the following headings to record your answers.

Transaction Letter	Assets	Liabilities	Owner's Equity

a. Collected accounts receivable.
b. Invested additional funds in the business.
c. Acquired supplies on account.
d. Acquired equipment for cash.
e. Paid a liability.
f. Acquired land, paying 10% in cash.
g. Withdrew cash from the business for personal use.
h. Received cash for services rendered.
i. Billed a customer for services rendered.
j. Received a bill for utilities expense used this month.
k. Returned supplies acquired in transaction c. The supplies had not been paid for as of this date.

Exercise 1-4
Violations of GAAP

Indicate which of the five generally accepted accounting principles or concepts has been violated by each of the situations listed below.
a. Office equipment costing $13,257 was recorded as an expense on the date it was acquired.
b. Listed among the assets of the Brown Paint Company is Mr. Brown's golf cart, valued at $2,500, which is used exclusively by Mr. Brown for golf. Mr. Brown always plays golf alone.
c. The owner of a machine shop acquires a machine from his brother-in-law by exchanging for the machine a second-hand truck used in the business. Since no monetary consideration exchanged hands, the owner used his best judgment in placing a value on the machine, recording it at $4,750.

d. Due to the effect of inflation, Johnson writes up the value of land reflected on his company's balance sheet. (List three principles.)

Exercise 1-5
Preparing a balance sheet from an alphabetical listing of accounts

Listed below in alphabetical order are several items of the Delta Company. Using this information, prepare a proper balance sheet to be dated October 31, 1987.

Accounts Payable	$ 9,500	Land	$ 2,650
Accounts Receivable	6,000	Machines	14,200
Building	10,150	Notes Payable	?
Cash	1,500	Office Supplies on Hand	750
Delta, Capital	22,750	Rental Fees Earned	26,710

(Check figure: Total assets = $35,250)

Exercise 1-6
Identifying transactions in a completed worksheet

The July financial transaction worksheet, containing nine transactions, for Gonzales Service Company is presented below. Describe each of the nine transactions. Transaction (i) is the only transaction affecting the capital account that does not affect net income.

	Cash	Accounts Receivable	Office Supplies	Office Machines	=	Accounts Payable	+	Gonzales Capital
July 1								
Bal.	+$4,000	+$16,000	+$1,500	+$32,000		+$ 7,500		+$46,000
(a)	− 750		+ 750					
(b)	+ 1,575	− 1,575						
(c)		+ 4,200						+ 4,200
(d)	− 1,000			+ 4,000		+ 3,000		
(e)			− 300					− 300
(f)	− 250					− 250		
(g)			+ 700			+ 700		
(h)	− 500							− 500
(i)	− 300							− 300
July 31								
Bal.	$2,775 +	$18,625 +	$2,650 +	$36,000	=	$10,950	+	$49,100

Exercise 1-7
Preparing an income statement from an alphabetical listing of accounts

Presented below are several items for the California Cleaning Company. From this information, prepare an income statement for the year ended December 31, 1987.

California, Withdrawals	$ 2,050	Laundry Revenue	$26,750
Cleaning Supplies Expense	18,150	Rent Expense	12,000
Cleaning Supplies on Hand	2,650	Salaries Expense	21,250
Dry Cleaning Revenue	42,300		

(Check figure: Net income = $17,650)

Exercise 1-8
Preparing a statement of owner's equity

The Edison Company reported $36,000 net income for the year 1987. At the beginning of the business year, May 1, 1986, Mr. Edison's capital had a $42,350 balance; Edison made additional capital investments totaling $16,500 and withdrew $4,300 from the business. Using this information, prepare a statement of owner's equity for the year ended April 30, 1987.

(Check figure: Ending capital = $90,550)

Exercise 1-9

Identifying missing amounts
from a series of related accounts

For each of the four independent cases listed below you are to determine the missing amount:

	A	B	C	D
Assets, July 1	7,000	?	25,000	17,000
Liabilities, July 1	3,000	5,000	13,000	11,000
July capital investment	2,000	3,000	5,000	4,000
July revenues	5,000	7,000	11,000	15,000
July withdrawals	1,000	2,000	?	3,000
July expenses	?	4,000	8,000	10,000
Assets, July 31	9,000	12,000	27,000	19,000
Liabilities, July 31	2,000	4,000	11,000	?

PROBLEMS
Set A

Problem A1-1

Preparing an income statement
and a statement of owner's
equity from a list of accounts
and other data

Listed below are several revenue and expense accounts from the records of Rodney Rodent Pest Control Company for the month of May 1987.

House Service Fees Earned	$48,200	Rent Expense	$ 1,000
Insurance Expense	700	Salaries Expense	37,500
Lawn Service Fees Earned	55,300	Utilities Expense	400
Pesticide Supplies Used	28,200		

Required

1. Prepare an income statement for the month ended May 31, 1987.
2. On May 1, 1987, Mr. Rodent had a $55,000 balance in his capital account. No capital investments were made during the month of May, but Mr. Rodent withdrew $7,500 on May 15 and a like amount again on May 30.
   Prepare a statement of owner's equity for the month ended May 31, 1987.

(Check figure: Rodney Rodent, Capital, May 31, 1987 = $75,700)

Problem A1-2

Preparing a balance sheet from
a list of accounts

The 10 balance sheet accounts of the Sally Sales Real Estate Agency as of October 31, 1987, are listed below.

Sally Sales, Capital	$26,350	Office Building	$15,700
Land	8,250	Accounts Receivable	5,300
Accounts Payable	3,150	Office Equipment	4,200
Cash	2,500	Notes Payable	6,000
Salaries Payable	740	Supplies on Hand	290

Required

Prepare a balance sheet as of October 31, 1987.

(Check figure: Total assets = $36,240)

Problem A1-3

Identifying violations in GAAP

On January 1 of the current year, three identical companies commenced business. During the year each company entered into identical transactions. At year-end the three companies presented the following balance sheets:

BALANCE SHEETS
December 31, 1987

Assets	Red Company	White Company	Blue Company
Assets:			
Cash	$ 5,000	$ 7,000	$ 5,000
Accounts Receivable.	12,000	12,000	12,000
Prepaid Rent.	1,000	–0–	–0–
Office Equipment.	15,000	18,000	12,000
Shop Equipment	8,000	8,000	9,000
Goodwill	–0–	10,000	–0–
Total Assets	$41,000	$55,000	$38,000
Liabilities and Owner's Equity			
Liabilities:			
Accounts Payable.	$ 4,500	$ 4,500	$ 4,500
Notes Payable	6,000	6,000	6,000
Total Liabilities	$10,500	$10,500	$10,500
Owner's Equity:			
Capital.	30,500	44,500	27,500
Total Liabilities and Owner's Equity	$41,000	$55,000	$38,000

A review of the underlying data revealed:

a. The White Company included $2,000 in its Cash account from a personal investment made by Mr. White in a savings and loan account with Freedom Exchange Savings & Loan.

b. Rent in the amount of $3,000 was paid in cash by all three companies on September 1 for the next 6 months rent.

c. At year-end equipment costing $15,000 was valued by the White Company at $18,000, an amount reflecting the effects of inflation on the U.S. economy. Blue Company, however, valued the equipment at $12,000, the amount it would cost at year-end to replace the equipment.

d. Shop equipment costing $8,000 was valued by the Blue Company at $9,000, representing the amount offered to the Blue Company if it decided to sell the equipment.

e. The White Company recorded $10,000 of goodwill on October 1. This amount represents Mr. White's best estimate of his superior managerial talent.

Required   Describe the violations of generally accepting accounting principles made by the three companies.

Problem A1-4
Recording transactions in a financial transaction worksheet

Alice Baker worked for several years as an advertising manager for the Harrisburg Advertising Company. Early in 1987 Ms. Baker decided to establish her own business, Alice Baker Advertising. Ms. Baker opened an account in the business name by depositing $1,500 cash. During her first month of operations, February 1987, the following transactions occurred:

a. Acquired office supplies in the amount of $510 on open account.

b. Received $1,700 cash for advertising services.

c. Paid $270 rent for the month of February.

d. Ms. Baker provided an automobile for the exclusive use of the advertising company. The fair market value of the car on February 1, 1987, was $6,300.

e. Paid the telephone bill of $190.

f. Provided advertising services amounting to $2,000 for the Clean Soap Company; cash was not received.

g. Paid $310 of the amount due for the office supplies previously acquired.

h. Withdrew $1,000 for personal use.

i. Collected $920 of the amount due from the Clean Soap Company.

j. Paid salaries of $1,860.

k. Auto repairs in the amount of $430 were incurred but not yet paid.

Required

1. Establish the following accounts in a financial transaction worksheet: Cash; Accounts Receivable; Supplies on Hand; Automobile; Accounts Payable; Baker, Capital.

    Record the transactions of Alice Baker Advertising for the month of February 1987.

(Check figure: Total assets = $8,380)

2. Compute the amount of net income for the month.

Problem A1-5

Recording transactions in a financial transaction worksheet and preparing the financial statement

On August 1, 1987, John Carleo withdrew $6,500 from his personal savings account and opened a checking account at the Middle National Bank in the name of Carleo Answering Service. The business started by Mr. Carleo provides telephone answering service to clients as well as typing services. During the first month of operations the following activities took place:

a. Acquired answering service equipment for $4,000, paying $1,000 cash, the remainder on a note payable due February 1, 1988.

b. Acquired $925 of typing supplies on account from Miggans Office Supply Company.

c. Billed clients for $2,750 for answering services rendered.

d. Mr. Carleo invested an additional $1,250 in the business.

e. Received $1,375 from clients billed in transaction (c).

f. Billed clients $560 for typing services rendered.

g. Paid telephone bill of $70.

h. Paid salaries of $290.

i. Received $170 cash for additional typing services rendered.

j. Paid rent of $250.

k. Paid Miggans Office Supply Company [see transaction (b)] $500.

Required

1. Using a financial transaction worksheet, record the transactions listed above. Establish the following accounts: Cash; Accounts Receivable; Typing Supplies on Hand; Answering Service Equipment; Notes Payable; Accounts Payable; Carleo, Capital.

(Check figure: Total assets = $14,045)

2. Prepare the following three financial statements:

    a. An income statement for the month ended August 31, 1987.

    b. A statement of owner's equity for the month of August 1987.

    c. A balance sheet as of August 31, 1987.

Problem A1-6

Recording initial account balances and transactions in a financial transaction worksheet and preparing the financial statements

Joan Gomez, after working several years as a master mechanic for Quality Auto Repair and Parts, received an offer from the owner of the company to acquire the company for a cash payment of $29,600. Ms. Gomez accepted the offer on October 1, 1987. The assets she received consisted of Accounts Receivable, $14,500; Auto Parts on Hand, $7,300; Land, $8,900; Shop Building, $32,000; and Shop Equipment, $26,400. The land and building were subject to a $30,000 mortgage payable. In addition, two other liabilities existed, Notes Payable and Accounts Payable, $25,000 and $4,500, respectively. Ms. Gomez invested $5,000 cash as operating capital in the business. The company name is to remain the same.

    During the last quarter of 1987 the following transactions took place:

a. Acquired $3,600 of auto parts from Wilson Manufacturing Company on account.

b. Acquired additional shop equipment costing $5,200 by issuing a note payable in the amount of $4,000 and paying cash for the difference.

c. Collected $9,500 accounts receivable due.
d. Paid $2,500 due on accounts payable.
e. Billed customers $21,500 for auto repair work performed.
f. Paid salaries of $6,700.
g. Received $11,200 cash payments from customers for repair work performed.
h. Paid utilities expense of $2,700.
i. Withdrew $3,200 from the business.
j. Received $5,000 cash for auto parts sales.
k. Reduced auto parts on hand by $4,300, and recorded auto parts expense for parts sold in transaction (j).
l. Collected $7,100 accounts receivable due.

Required

1. Record the initial account balances in a financial transaction worksheet. Then record the transactions for the last quarter of 1987.

(Check figure: Total assets = $120,000)

2. Prepare the following statements:
a. An income statement
b. A statement of owner's equity
c. A balance sheet

Problem A1-7
Preparing the financial statements from a list of accounts in decreasing order of dollar amount

Listed below are the accounts of Adam Anton, Attorney, summarizing his business activity for the month of March 1987.

Anton, Capital, March 1, 1987	$105,000	Office Supplies Used	$7,240
Legal Services Rendered	83,400	Entertainment Expenses	5,300
Office Building	80,000	Cash	3,730
Staff Salaries	61,750	Accounts Payable	3,200
Tax Services Rendered	42,700	Insurance Expense	3,100
Mortgage Payable	25,000	Advertising Expense	2,600
Clerical Salaries	19,620	Additional Investment by Anton	2,500
Office Furniture	19,300	Notes Receivable	2,500
Travel Expense	14,300	Salaries Payable	1,800
Land	12,500	Utilities Expense	1,730
Accounts Receivable	9,990	Office Supplies on Hand	1,230
Professional Development Expense	9,200	Prepaid Insurance	750
Withdrawals	8,150	Miscellaneous Expense	610

Required

1. Prepare an income statement for the month of March 1987.

(Check figure: Net income = $650)

2. Prepare a statement of owner's equity for the month ended March 31, 1987.
3. Prepare a balance sheet as of March 31, 1987.

(Check figure: Total assets = $130,000)

Set B

Problem B1-1
Preparing an income statement and a statement of owner's equity from a list of accounts and other data

Frank Flynn operates an auto repair and paint shop in St. Louis, Missouri, under the name of Flynn's Body and Paint Shop. Listed below are 10 accounts representing activities for the 6-month period ending June 30, 1987.

Auto Repair Fees Earned	$50,800	Frank Flynn, Capital, January 1, 1987	$28,600
Salaries Expense	47,000		
Painting Fees Earned	38,600	Repair Parts Used	10,800

Withdrawals.	$6,000	Additional Capital Investment . . .	$3,000
Equipment Rent Expense	6,000	Utilities Expense	2,800
Paint Expense.	5,600		

Required

1. Prepare an income statement for the 6-month period ended June 30, 1987.

(Check figure: Net income = $17,200)

2. Prepare a statement of owner's equity for the 6-month period ended June 30, 1987.

(Check figure: Flynn, Capital, June 30, 1987 = $42,800)

Problem B1-2
Preparing a balance sheet from a list of accounts

Listed below are the accounts that are to appear on the May 31, 1987, balance sheet of Karen Jackson Consulting Company.

Accounts Payable	$12,675	Jackson, Capital	$25,000
Accounts Receivable	3,750	Land	6,300
Building	27,500	Notes Payable	6,000
Cash	1,800	Office Supplies on Hand.	625
Equipment	9,200	Salaries Payable	5,500

Required

Prepare a balance sheet as of May 31, 1987.

(Check figure: Total assets = $49,175)

Problem B1-3
Identifying violations in GAAP

During the current year the Baker Company, a newly organized service business, entered into the five transactions described below. Mr. Baker has had no previous business education or experience and is consequently ignorant of current accounting practices.

a. Equipment acquired on January 15 for $10,000 is recorded on the December 31 balance sheet at $11,300. Mr. Baker explains that since at the date of acquisition the Consumer Price Index was 100 and had increased to 113 by year-end, the appropriate value for financial statement presentation would accordingly be $11,300.

b. A calculator purchased in early March for $560 can be purchased at year-end for $395. Mr. Baker has used the latter value on the balance sheet.

c. Land bought on July 1 for $25,000 is valued on the December 31 balance sheet at $42,000, a value obtained by considering recent land sales in the vicinity.

d. A lawnmower used by Mr. Baker for his residence is included among the December 31 assets.

e. Included among the expenses is $750 of office rent paid 3 months in advance on December 31 of the current year.

Required

For each of the transactions, list the appropriate generally accepted accounting concept violated, and explain why the treatment of the Baker Company is inappropriate.

Problem B1-4
Recording transactions in a financial transaction worksheet

Pam Ware commenced operating her mildew service, spraying houses with chlorine to clean off mildew, on October 1, 1987. As an initial capital investment she deposited $1,000 in the First Local Bank of Chicago and made available to the business for its exclusive use her 1981 pickup truck, which had a fair value on October 1, 1987, of $3,000. During the month of October the following transactions occurred:

a. Made $450 of repairs to the truck. The $450 was not paid at this time.

b. Acquired supplies in the amount of $300 paying cash.

c. Received $700 cash from customers for mildew service.
d. Paid rent, $250.
e. Billed customers $1,600 for mildew service.
f. Paid $125 of the amount owed in transaction (a).
g. Withdrew $275 from the business.
h. Collected $700 from customers.
i. Paid $50 utilities expense.

Required

1. Record the transactions of Pam Ware Mildew Service for the month of October 1987, using a financial transaction worksheet as illustrated in the chapter. Use the following accounts: Cash; Accounts Receivable; Supplies on Hand; Truck; Accounts Payable; Ware, Capital.

(Check figure: Total assets = $5,600)

2. Determine the amount of net income for the month.

(Check figure: net income = $1,550)

Problem B1-5
Recording transactions in a financial transaction worksheet and prepare the financial statements

On July 1, 1987, Kathy Prosser purchased a beauty shop from its previous owner. Ms. Prosser paid $3,500 cash from her personal savings account for the assets consisting of Beauty Supplies, $1,850; and Beauty Equipment, $2,800. The difference between the cash paid and total assets received was borrowed from the Chicago Trust Bank as a note payable. The company is to be operated under the name of Kathy Prosser Beauty Shop. Subsequent to the acquisition the following transactions occurred during the month of July:
  a. Ms. Prosser invested an additional $1,000 in the business.
  b. Hairstyling for customers was done on account, $190.
  c. Beauty supplies were acquired on account, $350.
  d. Beauty equipment costing $650 was acquired; $300 was paid in cash.
  e. Hairstyling for customers was done, cash in the amount of $750 received.
  f. Repairs to the equipment were made, $150.
  g. Paid $200 cash on account due for beauty supplies acquired in transaction (c).
  h. Paid $100 due on the note payable, and in addition $10 interest expense.
  i. Hairstyling for customers on account, $290.
  j. Paid for utilities, $40.
  k. Paid $240 in wages.
  l. Withdrew $300 for personal use.
  m. Collected $50 for hairstyling done in transaction (b).

Required

1. Record the transactions in a financial transaction worksheet. The following accounts will be needed: Cash; Accounts Receivable; Beauty Supplies on Hand; Beauty Equipment; Notes Payable; Accounts Payable; and Prosser, Capital.

(Check figure: Total assets = $6,540)

2. Prepare the following statements:
  a. An income statement
  b. A statement of owner's equity
  c. A balance sheet

Problem B1-6
Recording accounts found on a balance sheet and transactions on a financial transaction worksheet and preparing the financial statements

The December 31, 1986, balance sheet for the Dave Carter Carpet-Cleaning Service is presented on page 44. Mr. Carter operates his business in Des Moines, Iowa, providing service to office buildings in the downtown area and selling cleaning supplies to apartment buildings in the outlying areas. During the month of January 1987, the following transactions took place:
  a. Billed Des Moines Business Plaza for cleaning services rendered, $750.

DAVE CARTER CARPET-CLEANING SERVICE
Balance Sheet
December 31, 1986

Assets		Liabilities and Owner's Equity	
Cash	$ 1,700	Liabilities:	
Accounts Receivable	3,200	Notes Payable	$ 3,000
Cleaning Supplies on Hand	1,500	Accounts Payable	900
Cleaning Equipment	3,700	Total Liabilities	$ 3,900
Truck	4,200		
		Owner's Equity:	
		Carter, Capital	10,400
Total Assets	$14,300	Total Liabilities and Owner's Equity	$14,300

b. Collected $1,600 from accounts receivable due.

c. Acquired carpet-cleaning supplies on account, $850.

d. Acquired carpet-cleaning equipment for $1,100, issuing a note payable for $900 and paying $200 cash.

e. Sold cleaning supplies to the Hawkeye Apartments for $700.

f. In connection with transaction (e), recorded a reduction in carpet-cleaning supplies on hand by $450 for the cost of the supplies and correspondingly recorded $450 of cleaning supplies expense.

g. Received $540 from the Wheat Exchange Center for cleaning services rendered.

h. Mr. Carter withdrew $1,400 from the business for personal use.

i. Paid $1,000 note payable due; in addition, $125 interest on the note was paid.

j. Paid for gasoline used by the truck $135.

k. Paid salaries of $650.

Required

1. Record the amounts from the December 31, 1986, balance sheet in a financial transaction worksheet, then record the transactions for the month of January 1987.

(Check figure: Total assets = $14,280)

2. Prepare the following statements:
   a. An income statement
   b. A statement of owner's equity
   c. A balance sheet

Problem B1-7
Preparing the financial statements from an alphabetical listing of accounts

The accounts from the balance sheet, statement of owner's equity, and income statement of Alan Alperin, CPA, are:

Accounts Payable	$ 13,000	Auditing Fees Earned	$170,400
Accounts Receivable	19,400	Building	60,000
Alperin, Capital, 1/1/87	87,000	Cash	7,200

Insurance Expense	$ 8,400		Rent Expense.	$ 12,000
Investment by Owner.	5,000		Salaries Payable	5,400
Land	12,000		Salary Expense	125,000
Notes Receivable	6,600		Tax Fees Earned	35,400
Office Equipment	16,200		Taxes Payable	10,000
Office Supplies Expense	16,400		Travel Expense.	9,200
Office Supplies on Hand.	5,600		Utilities Expense.	2,800
Professional Development Expense	11,400		Withdrawals.	14,000

Required   Prepare the three statements from this data for the year ended December 31, 1987.

(Check figure: Total assets, 12/31/87 = $127,000)

Part Two

The Accounting System

The basic objective of the financial accounting activity is the preparation of the principal financial statements — the income statement, the statement of owners' equity, and the balance sheet. In Part Two we will show you how accountants gather, classify, summarize, and communicate accounting information.

You will learn that accounting information is gathered in accounts — the basic elements of financial accounting. Business transactions are first recorded as they occur in various journals and then later transferred to the accounts. We will show you how the accounts are conveniently arranged to facilitate the preparation of the financial statements and how worksheets are used to help in this process.

In order for the financial statements to be useful to you in making decisions, you must have the statements in time to make those decisions. You will see how this forces the accountant to divide the life of a business into short time frames called accounting periods — years, quarters, and months. And this causes the accountant to make estimates as to future events and to make other necessary adjustments to the accounts so that the statements can be issued at the end of the accounting periods.

Chapter 2

Analyzing and Recording Business Transactions

You will learn the following through studying this chapter:

- The nature and meaning of the *account*
- The distinction between a *ledger* and a *journal* and how each is used in the accounting system
- The rules of *debits* and *credits*
- How business transactions are recorded using the *double-entry accounting system*
- How to determine the *balance* for any account
- How to *prepare financial statements* from the ledger accounts

The primary objective of
financial accounting is the
preparation of the financial
statements

The balance sheet, the income statement, and the statement of owner's equity may all be prepared from the information generated by recording business transactions on financial transaction worksheets. We illustrated how to prepare financial statements from transactions worksheets in the previous chapter. But preparing financial statements in that way for any but the simplest of business entities would be extremely cumbersome and impractical. Consequently a simpler, more efficient system has been developed. This system is the basis for all accounting systems, from the small retail store employing a part-time bookkeeper to the giant multinational corporation using the latest computer technology.

The system, which is referred to by accountants as the ***pen-and-ink–double-entry accounting system,*** is the substance of this and the following four chapters. As its name implies, the pen-and-ink system is entirely manual and has been in use for several hundred years. Of course, anything that can be done manually can also be done by a computer faster and more accurately. Computer systems use machines to record, compile, classify, summarize, and prepare the financial statements. But the programmed instructions for the machines are based on the concepts of the pen-and-ink system. Thus, the study of manual pen-and-ink accounting systems is essential in order to understand a computerized accounting system. And all of you will come into contact with computerized systems. The systems may be on large computers, called ***mainframes;*** or the systems may be on microcomputers. But the system is in concept what we will study in the next several chapters.

The "pen-and-ink" system is
basic to computer systems

THE ACCOUNT

The basic element of the
accounting system is the account

The account is the basic building block of any accounting system. A separate record, ***the account,*** is established for each of the individual items that appear on the three financial statements. An account exists, therefore, for each asset, liability, owner's equity, revenue, and expense. The account is used to record increases and decreases resulting from business transactions. When cash is received, the transaction is reflected in the Cash account as an increase. When cash is paid, the Cash account is decreased. Thus, a record is available on a day-by-day basis that will provide management with information concerning a particular item. Questions such as, "What is the amount of accounts payable due? Is the inventory level sufficient to meet this week's demand? Is there adequate cash on hand to pay wages due today?" can each be answered by information contained in one of the accounts.

The account is used to record
increases and decreases in
assets, liabilities, owner's equity,
and revenue and expense items

In its most elementary form, *the account has three parts:*

A title, a place for increases,
and a place for decreases are the
three components of an account

1. ***The account title,*** which is the name of a particular accounting element, such as Cash

2. *A place to record increases in the monetary amounts* in the account

3. *A place to record decreases in the monetary amounts* in the account

An example of the elementary form of the account is shown at the top of page 49.

The title of the account in this example is Cash. On the left side of the account there are three accounting entries representing increases to this account. On the right side there are two accounting entries representing decreases to this account.

The total of the three left side entries amounts to $8,380, which is indicated by the italicized ***footing.*** The term *footing* refers to the addition of a column of figures. The total of the entries on the right side of the account is $2,100, also indicated by the italicized footing. You perhaps have noticed in the account that plus (+) and minus

The elementary form of the account, a T-account

Cash	
Increases in Cash	**Decreases in Cash**
Oct. 1 Owner's Investment 4,350	Oct. 15 Salaries Paid 1,400
12 Cash Received	30 Rent Paid 700
for Services 2,670	
25 Accounts Receivable. . . . 1,360	
8,380	*2,100*
Bal. 6,280	

These amounts are *footings:* the total of a column of figures

(−) signs are not needed. This is because only increases are entered on one side of the account and only decreases are entered on the other side. All increases are added together to obtain the $8,380 and all decreases are added together to obtain the $2,100.

The balance of an account is the difference between the increases and decreases

The net difference between increases and decreases in the Cash account is an increase, and that's why the balance of $6,280 is located on the increases in cash side. Of course total decreases in cash could not have exceeded total increases; as much as we would like this to happen, we cannot spend more cash than we have!

In a textbook we can use italics to show footings. Using a pen-and-ink system in real life, footings and balances are shown in pencil, whereas the entries are recorded in ink.

T-accounts are used to analyze accounting problems

Notice that the elementary form of the account looks like the letter *T*. For this reason it is referred to as a ***T-account.*** The T-account is used by accountants to analyze accounting problems and by instructors in teaching accounting. It is not used by economic entities to record business transactions. In the classroom we can easily write a dozen T-accounts on the chalkboard to demonstrate an accounting problem. The same can be done on the back of an envelope by a practicing accountant.

THE LEDGER

The general ledger contains all the accounts that appear on the financial statements

A *ledger* is simply a group of accounts.

The ***general ledger*** is a book containing all the accounts of an economic entity that appear on the financial statements. In a pen-and-ink system each account would have a separate page in the general ledger. Accounts that have substantial activity, such as the Cash account, may have more than one page. The pages are typically loose-leaf and of heavy construction so that they may be inserted and removed from the ledger as the need arises.

In some cases, a general ledger is sufficient to report all the transactions of an organization. In other cases, more detail is needed. For example, each account of the general ledger may be *too* general, recording only summary information. Certain transactions can be more fully described with more detail in a separate ledger of their own.

An account such as the Accounts Receivable account contains information that comes from each of the detailed accounts in the subsidiary ledger account. The general ledger Accounts Receivable account provides information on the amount of total accounts receivable but does not show the specific amounts owed by individual customers. The ***accounts receivable ledger*** would contain this information since it is a ledger of the individual accounts receivable. The accounts receivable ledger is re-

Accounts Receivable is the general ledger account for the accounts receivable subsidiary ledger

ferred to as a ***subsidiary ledger*** and the Accounts Receivable account of the general ledger is referred to as a ***control account.*** The general ledger account "controls" the subsidiary ledger. By this we mean that the balance in the general ledger account is the amount that the accounts in the subsidiary ledger, when added up, must equal.

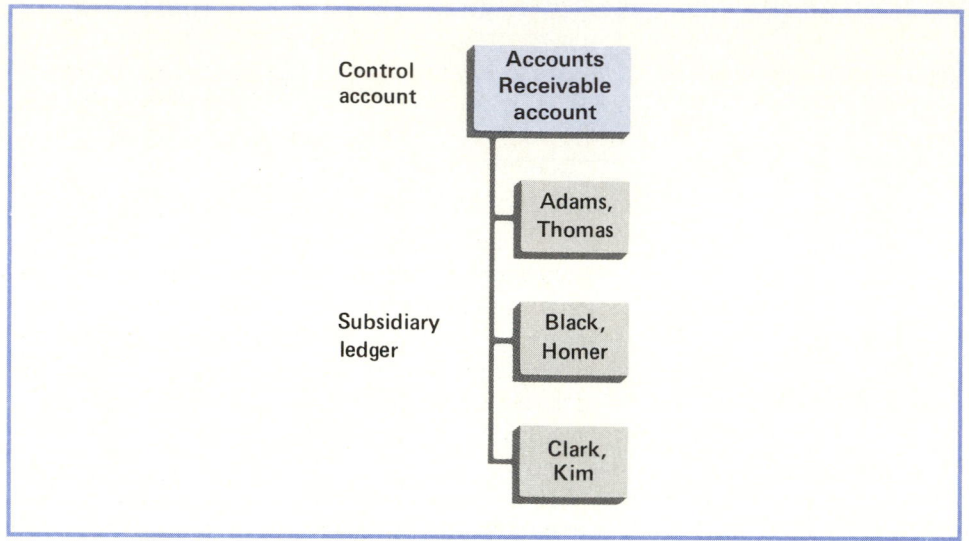

HOW ACCOUNTS ARE CLASSIFIED IN THE GENERAL LEDGER

Accounts in the general ledger are arranged in a certain order

The accounts in the general ledger are arranged in the same order that they would appear in the financial statements. Balance sheet accounts are placed first followed by the income statement accounts.

Do you remember the financial statements we prepared for Ron's Rentals in Chapter 1? Well, in Ron's general ledger we would show the balance sheet accounts first starting with Cash and ending with Sanchez, Capital and Ron Sanchez, Withdrawals. The income statement accounts would follow, starting with the revenue account Car Rentals and ending with the expense account Supplies Expense.

Assets

Assets are divided into current and noncurrent classifications

Assets are commonly subdivided into two major classifications: current assets and noncurrent assets. ***Current assets*** are generally those that can be expected to provide benefits in the near future (within 1 year). ***Noncurrent assets*** are those that are used to provide the business entity with benefits over a number of years.

Current Assets

Typical accounts found under the current asset classification are described below in the order in which they would appear in the general ledger.

Cash You all know that cash is the medium of exchange in a civilized society. A company's Cash account includes not only cash on hand (coins, currency, checks, and money orders), but also checking accounts (demand deposits) and savings accounts (time deposits).

Notes Receivable Occasionally an economic entity may loan money or provide goods or services to another entity, receiving in return in each case a ***note receivable.*** A note receivable is a written agreement between the maker of the note and an economic entity in which the maker promises to pay to the economic entity a specific amount of money on a specified date in the future.

Accounts Receivable Upon accepting goods or services from an economic entity, a customer implies that he or she will pay the agreed price for the goods sold or services rendered. Payment may be made immediately or the customer may be billed, payment to follow within 30 days. The expectation of this future payment is an ***account receivable.***

Inventory Retail stores, wholesale companies, and manufacturing concerns all sell a product rather than a service. The price paid by these entities for the product they plan to sell is recorded in the general ledger account Inventory.

Prepaid Expenses Insurance, rent, and supplies are usually paid for in advance. These prepaid items represent future economic benefits—*assets*—until the time they start to contribute to the earning process. They then become expenses. Prepaid rent becomes rent expense day by day as the business entity occupies the space rented. For example, assume that $900 in rent is paid on June 1 for office space. The following chart reflects how the $900 asset of June 1 reverts to a $900 expense for the month of June.

	June 1	June 2	June 3		June 29	June 30
Prepaid Rent.	$900	$870	$840		$30	$0
Rent Expense	$0	$30	$60		$870	$900

Noncurrent Assets

The common noncurrent assets are:

Equipment This account records the acquisition and disposition of office machines, desks, autos, trucks, file cabinets, and similar items. These assets have useful lives exceeding 1 year. Since their useful lives exceed 1 year, the cost of these items should not be assigned to just the year they were acquired. Rather, it makes sense to allocate their cost over their useful lives in some reasonable way. This allocation process is called ***depreciation.*** Thus, the cost of equipment becomes depreciation expense on a year-by-year basis. Monthly depreciation is typically computed by dividing the yearly depreciation by 12.

Allocating the cost of an asset over its useful life is called depreciation

Buildings Included in this account are retail and wholesale stores, factories, warehouses, and office buildings. These structures typically have useful lives up to 40 or more years and, like equipment, must be depreciated over their useful lives.

Land Land owned and used by the business entity is recorded in the Land account. Since land has an infinite life, no depreciation is recorded.

Liabilities

Liabilities are divided into two classifications: current and long-term

The second group of general ledger accounts is the liability accounts. They too typically fall into two major groups: ***current liabilities*** and ***long-term liabilities.*** The basic distinction between current and long-term liabilities is that current liabilities are due within 1 year. The long-term classification reflects liabilities that will be paid later than 1 year after the balance sheet date.

Current Liabilities

The common current liability accounts are:

Notes Payable   A note payable is like a note receivable but in the reverse direction. In the case of a note payable, the business entity is the maker of the note; that is, the business entity is the party doing the promising, and promises to pay the other party to the agreement a specified amount of money on a specified future date.

Accounts Payable   This account represents the reverse relationship of the accounts receivable. By accepting the goods or services, the buyer agrees to pay for them in the near future.

Salaries Payable   On the date for which a balance sheet is prepared it is very likely that a number of employees have earned salaries that haven't yet been paid. Unpaid earnings represent a liability to the business entity and are recorded in the Salaries Payable account.

Unearned Revenues   When a business entity receives payment before providing its customers with goods or services, the amounts received are recorded in the *Unearned Revenue* account. When the goods or services are provided to the customer, the Unearned Revenue account is reduced and revenue is recognized. If you understand the concept of prepaid expenses, then you may already have wondered about how the business entities receiving the prepaid expense amounts characterize and record those receipts. They characterize them as revenues received but not yet earned. Unearned insurance premiums and unearned rent represent the reverse relationship of prepaid insurance and prepaid rent. The Unearned Revenue account represents a liability because the business entity has an obligation to provide goods or services in the future.

> **Unearned revenues are the opposite of prepaid expenses**

Long-Term Liabilities

The common long-term liability accounts are:

Mortgage Payable   The Mortgage Payable account records long-term debt of the business entity for which the business entity has pledged certain assets as security to the creditor. In the event that the debt payments are not paid, the creditor can force the sale of the mortgaged asset to settle the claim.

Bonds Payable   Corporations often obtain substantial sums of money from lenders to finance the acquisition of inventories, equipment, and other assets. They obtain these funds by issuing *bonds.* The bond is a contract between the issuer and the lender specifying the terms of repayment and the interest to be charged. Bonds, like mortgage payables, represent a long-term liability, since they will be paid after 1 year from the balance sheet date.

Owner's Equity

This third group of general ledger accounts includes the Capital account and the Withdrawals account.

Capital Account

> **The Capital account reflects the owner's contributions, withdrawals, revenues, and expenses**

The Capital account is used to record the amount the owner of the business entity has invested in the entity. The owner's investment includes not only assets contributed to the business by the owner but also the net income earned by the business. This account is reduced by cash or other assets the owner may withdraw from the business. The Capital account is increased by the amount of net income earned during the year. If a loss was incurred, the Capital account would be reduced by the amount of the loss.

Withdrawals Account

When cash or other assets are withdrawn by the owner of a business entity, such withdrawals are recorded in the Withdrawals account rather than directly reducing the Capital account. The Withdrawals account is often called the Drawing account.

Revenue

The fourth group of general ledger accounts is the revenue accounts. These accounts represent earnings during the year. A revenue account is established in the general ledger for each source of revenue. The account titles generally supply an adequate description of the nature of each revenue account. Sales, Commissions Earned, Interest Income, and Fees from Services Rendered are all examples of revenue accounts.

Expenses

Expenses are the fifth and last group of general ledger accounts. Again, the account titles are descriptive of the nature of the account. Typical expenses are: Cost of Goods Sold, Depreciation Expense, Rent Expense, Supplies Expense, Insurance Expense, and Salaries Expense.

THE CHART OF ACCOUNTS

The accounts in the general ledger for one business entity may be different from the accounts found in the general ledger for another entity. The accounts in the general ledger for any business entity depend on several things: the nature of the business and the way it operates; the size of the business entity; the amount of detail needed for management to make its decisions; and, for business entities that must comply with them, rulings of federal or state (or both) regulatory agencies (e.g., the Internal Revenue Service, the Securities and Exchange Commission, and the Federal Power Commission). The amount of detail needed to fulfill compliance with these agencies will also affect the kinds of accounts in the general ledger.

The chart of accounts is a system of organizing and numbering the accounts in the general ledger

To facilitate the recordkeeping process, the accounts in the general ledger are numbered. The use of numbers to identify accounts in business documents is much easier than the use of account titles. Each business entity will normally devise its own numbering system. Numbering the accounts consecutively presents problems in cases where new accounts may have to be added, as often happens with most business entities. So, what is needed is a numbering system that is not necessarily consecutive but is successive and allows for new numbers to be inserted within the succession. For example, a typical numbering system will use a series of multi-digit numbers, the first digit in each number indicating the major classification of the general ledger. Assets may be 1000, liabilities may be 2000, owner's equity accounts 3000, revenues 4000, and expenses 5000.

The second digit will be used to represent subclassifications of each major account. For example, within the assets, 1100 may be used to indicate current assets, 1200 to indicate noncurrent assets, and so on.

Specific general ledger accounts can then be identified by the third digit. For example, Cash would be 1110, Notes Receivable 1120, etc.

Finally, the fourth digit can be used to achieve a more detailed classification, such as 1112 — Cash in Savings Account; or 1113 — Cash on Hand.

With the type of system described above it would be relatively easy to add new accounts as the need arises. For example, if the current asset account Notes Receivable from Officers were to be added, it would be assigned the account number 1121. The use of account numbers is very important in using computerized accounting systems.

Presented below is a typical chart of accounts:

**A list of accounts with their
account numbers is called a
*chart of accounts***

Assets		Liabilities	
Current assets:		Current liabilities:	
1110	Cash	2110	Notes Payable
	1111 Cash in Checking Account	2120	Accounts Payable
	1112 Cash in Savings Account	2130	Salaries Payable
	1113 Cash on Hand	2140	Unearned Rent Revenue
1120	Notes Receivable		
1130	Accounts Receivable	Long-term liabilities:	
1140	Inventory	2210	Mortgage Payable
1150	Prepaid Rent	2220	Bonds Payable
1160	Prepaid Insurance		
1170	Supplies on Hand	Owner's Equity	
		3100	Bill Jones, Capital
Noncurrent assets:		3200	Bill Jones, Withdrawals
1210	Equipment		
1211	Accumulated Depreciation: Equipment	Revenue	
1220	Buildings	4100	Sales
1221	Accumulated Depreciation: Buildings	4200	Commissions Earned
1230	Land	4300	Rent Income
		4400	Interest Income
		Expenses	
		5100	Cost of Sales
		5200	Salaries Expense
		5300	Depreciation Expense
		5400	Rent Expense
		5500	Interest Expense
		5600	Supplies Expense

DEBIT AND CREDIT

Many students come to this part of their study of accounting with preconceived notions about debits and credits. For the moment, forget what you think you know about these two basic terms. Start from the beginning with us.

And in the beginning, when the accounting profession developed, it was arbitrarily decided that entries recorded on the left side of any account should be called ***debits*** and entries recorded on the right side of any account should be called ***credits.*** And that's the way it's been ever since — debits on the left and credits on the right.

**Debits are recorded on the left
side of any account, credits on
the right**

Accounts are the basic building blocks of the accounting system. The account must be capable of reflecting increases and decreases in monetary amounts resulting from business transactions. But which side of the account should be used to show increases? Which side should show decreases? Let's think this through together.

We know that the objective of our accounting system is to provide financial statements — an income statement, a statement of owner's equity, and a balance sheet. We also know that the accounting system must be based on the basic balance sheet equation, *Assets = Liabilities + Owner's Equity.* We used this equation as a basis for the financial transaction worksheet in Chapter 1. We now know that a separate account must be maintained for each item listed in the financial statements. And each account will show increases and decreases.

We have to start somewhere, so why not with the first accounts — assets. It would seem logical to start with increases first, for we cannot decrease something we do not yet have. And it would also seem logical to start with the left side rather than the right because that is the way we read — from left to right.

So we decide that to record an increase in an asset account we will show this on the debit side of the account. Once this decision is made, then the credit side of an asset account must be used for decreases.

Assets are increased by debits; decreased by credits

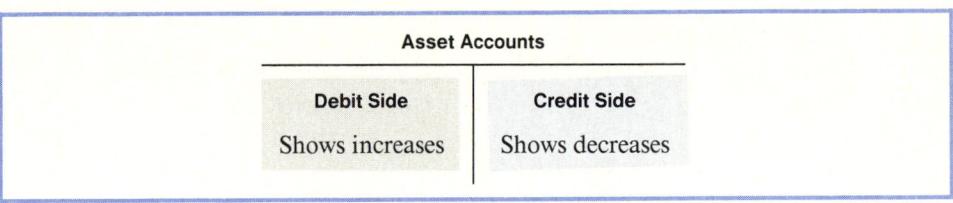

Now, we realize that each financial transaction has two parts as we observed in Chapter 1. If an asset is increased, then if the basic model is to remain in balance something else must happen—namely, one of the following:

1. *Another asset must decrease,* or

2. *A liability must increase,* or

3. *Owner's equity must increase.*

Since we selected the debit side of the asset account to show increases resulting in the credit side to show decreases, the first alternative can be solved when one asset is increased—*debited*—and a second asset is decreased—*credited*—by a like amount. The debit equals the credit; the basic equation remains in balance.

If the increase in the asset resulted from an increase in a liability or an owner's equity account, we would realize that we must use the credit side of those two accounts to record increases. Why? The basic equation must balance. Liabilities and owner's equity accounts are on the opposite side of the basic equation from assets. If debits are used to increase assets, then the opposite, credits, must be used to increase those accounts on the opposite side of the equation to maintain equality, as seen below:

Liabilities and owner's equity are increased by credits; decreased by debits

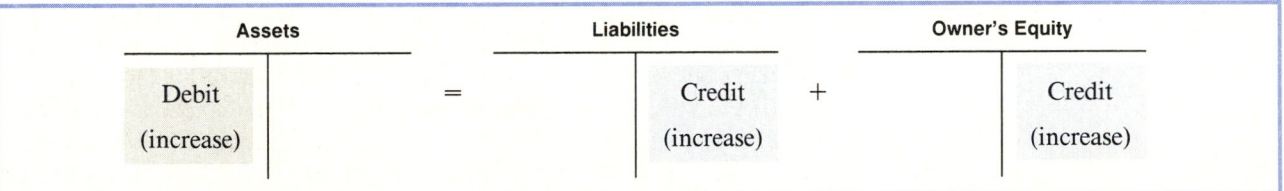

And, if credits increase liabilities and owner's equity accounts, then debits must be used to decrease these accounts.

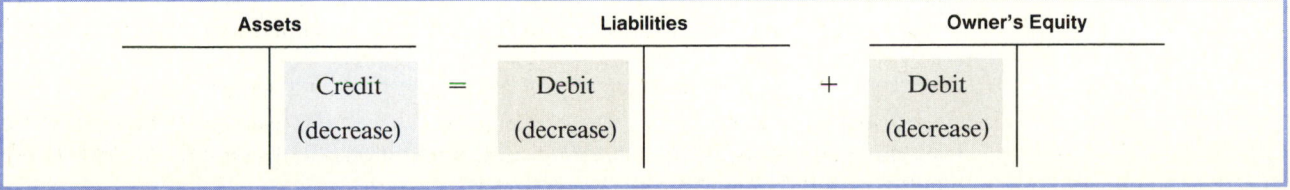

All this, referred to as the ***rules of debit and credit,*** flowed from the initial decision to select debits to record increases in asset accounts.

Now let's summarize and expand on what we have developed.

An account is debited (sometimes the word ***charged*** is used) when an amount is entered on the left side. An account is credited when an amount is entered on the right side. The word *debit* is abbreviated ***Dr,*** and similarly, the word *credit* is abbreviated ***Cr.*** The difference between the sum of the debits in an account and the sum of its credits is the ***account balance.*** A ***debit balance*** results when the sum of the debits exceeds the sum of its credits. If the sum of the credits exceeds the sum of the debits, a ***credit balance*** results.

Debits and credits by themselves do not indicate increases or decreases. Reference must be made to a specific account to determine if the debits or credits represent increases or decreases. This is illustrated in the following chart:

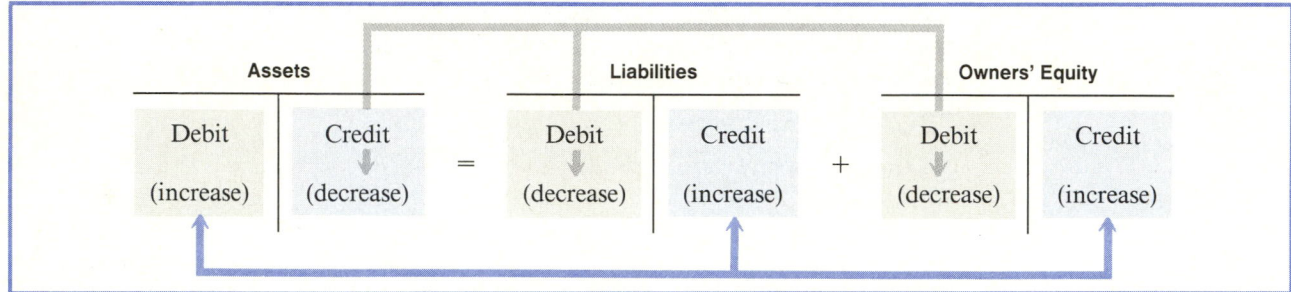

Every single financial transaction affects at least two accounts in the general ledger—an account in which a debit is recorded and an account in which a credit is recorded. The amount recorded in the debit account must equal the amount recorded in the credit account. If one debit account affects more than one credit account, the sum of the credit accounts affected must, of course, equal the amount of the corresponding debit account. Conversely, if one credit account affects more than one debit account, the sum of the debit accounts must equal the amount of the credit account.

This ***law of accounting***—that for every transaction, the sum of the debits must always equal the sum of the credits—is as basic to accounting as Newton's laws of motion (for every action there is an equal and opposite reaction) is to physics.

Let's record a transaction in the new accounting system we have just developed to reinforce our understanding. Assume that a Mr. Brown puts up $1,000 cash in his new business. An asset, Cash, is increased, and owner's equity, Brown, Capital, is also increased as shown below.

Cash		Brown, Capital	
Debit			Credit
1,000			1,000

Assets are increased by debits, owner's equity is increased by credits. Debits of $1,000 equal credits of a like amount.

Income Statement Accounts

Go back to the financial transaction worksheet prepared in Chapter 1 after transaction (11). There you can see that *revenues increase the owner's equity account,* Sanchez, Capital, and *expenses decrease that account.* Withdrawals (drawings) are also part of the owner's equity account.

When we prepared the income statement for Ron's Rentals, we used a financial transaction worksheet. All revenue and expense accounts were listed as plus (+) or minus (−) under the owner's equity account. In your homework from Chapter 1 you spent considerable time after the transactions had been recorded identifying all revenue and expense accounts listed under the owner's equity account.

What do you think? Would it not be much easier if we listed each revenue and expense account separately? Of course it would, and that is what we do.

Revenue, expense, and withdrawals accounts are part of the owner's equity account

But keep in mind that *revenue, expense, and withdrawals accounts are still part of the owner's equity account* and as such are part of the basic balance sheet equation, Assets = Liabilities + Owner's Equity.

Increases and decreases in asset and liability accounts are recorded directly into those accounts, but other than additional investments made by the owner, *increases and decreases in the owner's equity account are recorded in the revenue, expense, and withdrawals accounts.*

The relationship of revenue, expense, and withdrawals accounts to the basic accounting model can be illustrated by the following diagram:

This is how the revenue, expense, and withdrawals accounts relate to the basic accounting equation

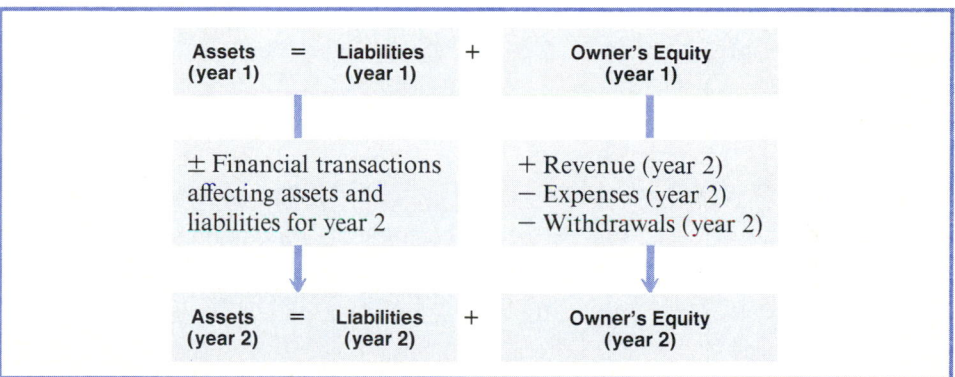

Since revenue, expenses, and the withdrawals account are part of the owner's equity account, the rules of debit and credit as applied to the owner's equity account also apply to these three component accounts within the owner's equity account.

Revenues are increased by credits

If we wish to increase a revenue account, which in turn will increase the owner's equity account, the revenue account must be credited. This is so because the owner's equity account is increased by credits. Notice in the diagram at the top of page 58 that the revenue account is represented as part of the owner's equity account. Specifically, it is represented as part of the credit side. Can you see why? Revenues will always have credit balances. We either earn some revenue or we earn zero revenue. We do not earn "negative" revenue.

Expenses and withdrawals increased by debits

Expenses and withdrawals decrease owner's equity. If we wish *to record a decrease to the owner's equity account, we must debit the account. To increase expenses and withdrawals is to decrease owner's equity;* consequently, *expenses and withdrawals are increased by debits.* Like revenues, expenses and withdrawals either exist or they

Owner's Equity

Debit	Credit
(decrease)	(increase)

Revenue

Debit	Credit
(decrease)	(increase)

Revenues are part of owner's equity

do not. And if they exist they must have debit balances, which explains why they are shown on the debit side of the following diagram:

Owner's Equity

Debit	Credit
(decrease)	(increase)

Expenses

Debit	Credit
(increase)	(decrease)

Withdrawals

Debit	Credit
(increase)	(decrease)

Expenses and withdrawals are part of owner's equity

We have now determined how to record increases and decreases for each of the six basic accounts. These rules of increases and decreases are summarized as follows:

		To Increase	To Decrease
	Assets must be	Debited	Credited
	Liabilities must be	Credited	Debited
	Owner's equity must be	Credited	Debited
Part of Owner's Equity	Revenues must be	Credited	Debited
	Expenses must be	Debited	Credited
	Withdrawals must be	Debited	Credited

Normal Balances

For any account, the normal situation is for the sum of the increases to the account to exceed the sum of the decreases to the account. The resulting balance is a positive balance rather than a negative balance. The positive balance of an account is referred

The normal balance of any account is the excess of that accounts increases over its decreases

to as its ***normal balance.*** Asset accounts typically have total debits in excess of total credits and consequently have a normal debit balance.

For example, consider the Office Supplies on Hand account. When office supplies are acquired, the Office Supplies on Hand account is debited representing the normal balance. When office supplies are used, the Office Supplies on Hand account must be decreased, and this is done by crediting the account. We cannot use more office supplies than we have. We can credit the Office Supplies on Hand account only to the extent of previous debits, resulting in a zero balance. All supplies have been used. The Office Supplies on Hand account cannot have a credit balance. It must have a debit balance, which is its normal balance.

The normal balance of each type of account is always the "Increase" side of the account, as illustrated below:

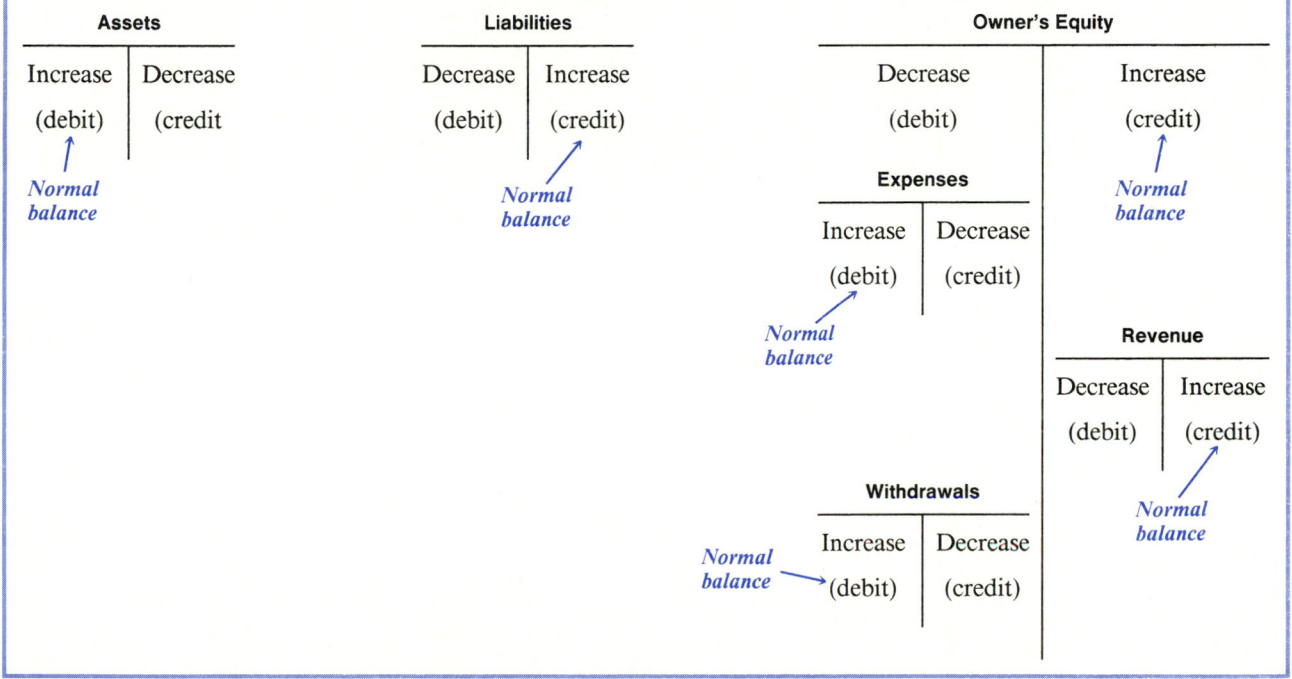

An Illustration

In order to illustrate the application of the rules of debit and credit and how transactions are recorded in the accounts, we will take you through some transactions and analyze them as we apply the rules and record them in the accounts. Prior to being recorded, a transaction must be analyzed to determine which accounts must be increased or decreased. After this has been determined, the rules of debit and credit are applied to effect the appropriate increases and decreases to the accounts.

ADAMS REAL ESTATE

Transaction 1 Amy Adams invests $5,000 of her personal funds in a new business entity entitled Adams Real Estate.

Asset (increase) Cash			=	Owner's Equity (increase) Amy Adams, Capital		
	Debit	Credit			Debit	Credit
(1)	5,000				(1)	5,000

PACIOLI ON ACCOUNTING

Our present double-entry accounting system can be traced back some 500 years to the writings of Fra Luca Pacioli of Venice, Italy. Here's what he had to say about investing funds in a business entity.

In the name of God enter in the Journal the first item of your Inventory, which is the quantity of money that you possess. In

Source: R. Gene Brown and Kenneth S. Johnston, *Pacioli on Accounting,* McGraw-Hill Book Company, New York, 1963, p. 45. Reprinted by permission.

order to know how to enter this Inventory in the Journal and Ledger, you must make use of two other terms; one is called Cash, and the other Capital. Cash means the money on hand. Capital means the entire amount of what you now possess.

At the beginning of all business Journals and Ledgers, Capital must always be en-

tered as a credit and Cash always as a debit. In the management of any type of business, Cash may never have a credit balance, but only debit (unless it balances). If, in balancing your book, you find that Cash has a credit balance, an error in the book is indicated. Cash must always be entered in the Journal in the following way:

Examples for Making Journal Entries.

8th day of November, MCCCCLXXXXIII, in Venice.

First
1   *Debit Cash, credit Capital of myself, Mr. Businessman. At present I have cash in a certain place, consisting of gold, coin, silver, and copper of various coinage as shown on the first sheet of the Inventory, in total so many gold ducats and so many ducats in coin. In our Venetian money all is valued in gold, that is, 24 grossi for each ducat and*
2   *32 picioli for each grosso, and so many gold lire.*

Value:

L. . (lire) S. . (solidi) G. . (grossi) P. . (picioli)

---

* Pacioli suggests that when the debit entry is posted to the Ledger, a vertical line be drawn to the left of the journal entry. When the credit is posted, a "credit posting line" be drawn to the right of the journal entry. The two numbers at the left of the debit posting line are the folio references giving respectively, the Ledger page number of the debit and credit entry.

This transaction increases the economic resource, the asset Cash, and also the owner's equity account, *Amy Adams, Capital.* According to the rules of debit and credit, debits will increase assets and credits will increase owner's equity accounts. Thus the transaction is debit Cash and credit Amy Adams, Capital. Notice that the figure (1) is placed by the $5,000 debit and the $5,000 credit. This is a ***posting reference*** and is used to identify the source [transaction (1) in this case] of the debit or credit in the account.

Transaction 2 Adams Real Estate purchased the following assets for cash: supplies, $500; office equipment, $600; and advertising signs, $300.

Assets (increase) Supplies on Hand		=	Asset (decrease) Cash	
Debit	Credit		Debit	Credit
(2) 500			(1) 5,000	(2) 1,400

Office Equipment	
Debit	Credit
(2) 600	

Advertising Signs	
Debit	Credit
(2) 300	

Three assets are increased by this transaction: Supplies on Hand, Office Equipment, and Advertising Signs, in the total amount of $1,400. These assets were acquired by payment of $1,400 in cash, reducing the asset Cash by $1,400. Assets are increased by debits and reduced by credits. Therefore Supplies on Hand, Office Equipment, and Advertising Signs are debited, each for its appropriate amount, and Cash is credited for the total $1,400.

Transaction 3   Amy acquired an office computer for $4,500, paying $1,000 in cash and issuing a note payable for the difference.

Asset (increase, decrease) Cash		=		Liability (increase) Notes Payable	
Debit	Credit			Debit	Credit
(1) 5,000	(2) 1,400				(3) 3,500
	(3) 1,000				

Office Equipment	
Debit	Credit
(2) 600	
(3) 4,500	

The asset Office Equipment is increased by $4,500 by this transaction. At the same time the asset Cash is decreased and the liability Notes Payable is created and starts off with an increase. Increases in assets are recorded by debits. Decreases in assets are recorded by credits and increases in liabilities are recorded by credits. Thus, this transaction is recorded by debiting the account Office Equipment for $4,500, crediting the account Cash for $1,000, and crediting Notes Payable for $3,500.

Transaction 4   Three months' rent is paid in advance, $750.

Asset (increase) Prepaid Rent		=		Asset (decrease) Cash	
Debit	Credit			Debit	Credit
(4) 750				(1) 5,000	(2) 1,400
					(3) 1,000
					(4) 750

Prepaid Rent, a resource having future economic benefit, has been acquired for the cash payment of $750. The future economic benefit is the right to occupy the rented property. (As each month goes by, $250 of Prepaid Rent will be transferred to the Rent Expense account.) Increases in assets are recorded by debits and decreases in assets are recorded by credits. The transaction is recorded by debiting Prepaid Rent for $750 and crediting Cash for $750.

Transaction 5   Cash is received in the amount of $1,050 as payment of real estate commissions.

Asset (increase) Cash				=	Owner's Equity (increase) Real Estate Commissions		
Debit		Credit			Debit	Credit	
(1)	5,000	(2)	1,400			(5)	1,050
(5)	1,050	(3)	1,000				
		(4)	750				

This transaction increases the asset Cash and Owner's Equity by the revenue received as payment for real estate commissions. Assets are increased by debits and revenues are increased by credits. A debit of $1,050 to Cash and a credit of $1,050 to Real Estate Commissions records the transaction.

Transaction 6   Real estate commissions of $1,600 are earned; the customer is billed and will pay later.

Assets (increase) Accounts Receivable			=	Owner's Equity (increase) Real Estate Commissions		
Debit		Credit		Debit	Credit	
(6)	1,600				(5)	1,050
					(6)	1,600

Services have been performed entitling Adams Real Estate to receive a $1,600 payment that will be paid in the future. Since the service has been completed, revenue is earned. A future economic benefit has been received, the asset Accounts Receivable, in exchange for the service rendered. Assets are increased by debits. Revenues are increased by credits. Debit Accounts Receivable and credit Real Estate Commissions $1,600.

Transaction 7   The first of five payments in the amount of $700 is made for the office computer acquired in transaction (3).

Assets (decrease) Cash			=	Liabilities (decrease) Notes Payable			
Debit		Credit		Debit		Credit	
(1)	5,000	(2)	1,400	(7)	700	(3)	3,500
(5)	1,050	(3)	1,000				
		(4)	750				
		(7)	700				

The asset Cash and the liability Notes Payable are reduced by $700 by this transaction. Assets are decreased by credits; liabilities are decreased by debits. The transaction is recorded by debiting Notes Payable and crediting Cash.

Transaction 8   Additional advertising signs are acquired on account, $150.

Assets (increase) Advertising Signs			=	Liabilities (increase) Accounts Payable			
Debit		Credit		Debit		Credit	
(2)	300					(8)	150
(8)	150						

This transaction increases the asset Advertising Signs and also the liability Accounts Payable each by $150. Assets are increased by debits. Liabilities are increased by credits. Debit Advertising Signs in the amount of $150 and credit Accounts Payable in the amount of $150.

Transaction 9   Paid utilities expense of $50.

Assets (decrease) Cash			=	Owner's Equity (decrease) Utilities Expense			
Debit		Credit		Debit		Credit	
(1)	5,000	(2)	1,400	(9)	50		
(5)	1,050	(3)	1,000				
		(4)	750				
		(7)	700				
		(9)	50				

As in the revenue transactions [(5) and (6)], a separate expense account must be established for each expense item. This transaction increases the expense Utilities, and reduces the asset Cash by $50. Expenses are increased by debits and assets are decreased by credits. Debit Utilities Expense in the amount of $50 and credit Cash in the amount of $50.

Transaction 10   Received $800 in cash from the client for whom service was rendered in transaction (6).

Asset (increase) Cash				=	Asset (decrease) Accounts Receivable			
Debit		Credit			Debit		Credit	
(1)	5,000	(2)	1,400	(6)	1,600	(10)	800
(5)	1,050	(3)	1,000				
(10)	800	(4)	750				
		(7)	700				
		(9)	50				

Payments by customers reduce the asset Accounts Receivable and increase the asset Cash. Assets are increased by debits and decreased by credits. Debit Cash for $800 and credit Accounts Receivable for $800.

Transaction 11   Amy Adams withdraws $250 for personal use.

Assets (decrease) Cash				=	Owner's Equity (decrease) Amy Adams, Withdrawals		
Debit		Credit			Debit		Credit
(1)	5,000	(2)	1,400	(11)	250		
(5)	1,050	(3)	1,000				
(10)	800	(4)	750				
		(7)	700				
		(9)	50				
		(11)	250				

Withdrawals are a reduction of owner's equity but are not an expense of the business entity. Nevertheless, they are recorded separately from the owner's equity account. This transaction increases the Amy Adams, Withdrawals account and reduces cash. Debits record increases in the Withdrawals account and credits record decreases in asset accounts. The transaction is recorded by a debit in the amount of $250 to the Amy Adams, Withdrawals account and a credit of $250 to Cash.

Transaction 12   Salaries in the amount of $450 are paid.

Owner's Equity (decrease) Salaries Expense		=	Assets (decrease) Cash	
Debit	Credit		Debit	Credit
(12) 450			(1) 5,000 (5) 1,050 (10) 800	(2) 1,400 (3) 1,000 (4) 750 (9) 50 (11) 250 (12) 450

The salaries expense transaction is recorded by increasing an expense and reducing an asset. To record the transaction, Salaries Expense is debited in the amount of $450 and Cash is credited in the amount of $450.

The 12 transactions of this illustration are shown in the accounts of the general ledger shown on page 66. Notice that the accounts are organized under the basic elements of the financial statements. Also notice that the number identifying each of the transactions provides a cross reference between the accounts debited and the accounts credited. The $50 credit in the Cash account from transaction (9) can be located in the Utilities Expense account by reference to the *posting reference* (9).

The Trial Balance

A trial balance is a listing of all the accounts and their respective balances

Our objective in using an accounting system is to prepare financial statements more efficiently than we could by use of a financial transaction worksheet. In our example, we have reached a stage where all the transactions for a period of time have been recorded. What next?

Before the statements can be prepared, the balance in each account must be determined. Once this is done (and it was done in the general ledger shown on page 66), we may wish to prove that we have recorded all transactions accurately. How? Well, we know that every transaction is recorded by equal debits and credits, and that the total of the debits must equal the total of the credits in the general ledger. Why not make a list of all the account balances, showing which ones have debit balances and which ones have credit balances? Now, let's *try* to see if the total of the debit accounts will equal, *balance,* the total of the credit accounts. We have prepared a ***trial balance.***

Again, to prepare a trial balance we must first compute the balance of each account in the general ledger. Next, the balance from each account of the general ledger is listed on a two-column work paper in the same order as the accounts appear in the general ledger. The accounts in the general ledger having a debit balance are entered in the first column. The accounts having credit balances are entered in the second column. The debit column is added up and the credit column is added up. The sums of each column should be equal.

The trial balance of Adams Real Estate is presented on page 67. The total of the debit column equals $10,600, which is equal to the total of $10,600 for the credit columns. The trial balance does in fact balance.

Now, once the trial balance is prepared and it balances, it should be relatively easy to prepare the financial statements from the trial balance. Just copy the income statement accounts on an income statement, the statement of owner's equity ac-

ADAMS REAL ESTATE
General Ledger

Assets = **Liabilities** + **Owner's Equity**

Cash

(1)	5,000	(2)	1,400
(5)	1,050	(3)	1,000
(10)	800	(4)	750
		(7)	700
		(9)	50
		(11)	250
		(12)	450
	6,850		*4,600*
Bal.	2,250		

Accounts Receivable

(6)	1,600	(10)	800
Bal.	800		

Prepaid Rent

(4)	750
Bal.	750

Supplies on Hand

(2)	500
Bal.	500

Office Equipment

(2)	600
(3)	4,500
Bal.	5,100

Advertising Signs

(2)	300
(8)	150
Bal.	450

Notes Payable

(7)	700	(3)	3,500
		Bal.	2,800

Accounts Payable

		(8)	150
		Bal.	150

Amy Adams, Capital

		(1)	5,000
		Bal.	5,000

Amy Adams, Withdrawals

(11)	250
Bal.	250

Revenues
Real Estate Commissions

		(5)	1,050
		(6)	1,600
		Bal.	2,650

Expenses
Utilities Expense

(9)	50
Bal.	50

Salaries Expense

(12)	450
Bal.	450

counts, on the statement of owner's equity, and the balance sheet accounts on a balance sheet.

ADAMS REAL ESTATE Trial Balance October 31, 1987	Debits	Credits
Cash.	$ 2,250	
Accounts Receivable	800	
Prepaid Rent	750	
Supplies on Hand	500	
Office Equipment	5,100	
Advertising Signs	450	
Notes Payable.		$ 2,800
Accounts Payable		150
Amy Adams, Capital		5,000
Amy Adams, Withdrawals	250	
Real Estate Commissions		2,650
Utilities Expense.	50	
Salaries Expense	450	
Totals.	$10,600	$10,600

These accounts together with the ending capital account will be used to prepare the balance sheet

These accounts together with the net income, will be used to prepare the statement of owner's equity

And these accounts will be used to prepare the income statement

The trial balance provides proof that the general ledger is in balance. This means that the accountant can be sure of three things:

1. For each transaction, the debits and credits were recorded in equal amounts.

2. The balance (debit balances and credit balances) for each account was calculated correctly.

3. The balances of the various debit and credit accounts have been correctly added together to arrive at the total equality of the debits and credits.

If the trial balance does not balance, the accountant knows that an error, or perhaps several errors, exist. When errors do occur, they are usually one of the three following types:

1. Transaction Errors

Recording an incorrect amount in a general ledger account is a transaction error

When a transaction is recorded, an error might occur through recording an incorrect amount to the general ledger account. One of the most typical errors is to record a debit entry incorrectly as a credit, or a credit as a debit. Another common transaction error is to record only one portion of the transaction, say, the debit, but forget to record the other portion of the transaction, the credit; or to record the credit but not the debit.

2. Account Balance Errors

Errors can occur in calculating the balance of a specific account. Another account balance error is simply to misplace a debit balance in the credit column or a credit balance in the debit column.

3. Trial Balance Errors

Trial balance errors can occur by transferring incorrectly the amount of an account

Transferring an incorrect amount from a general ledger account to the trial balance is a trial balance error

balance to the trial balance. They can also occur by incorrectly recording a debit account balance as a credit on the trial balance, or a credit as a debit. The most simple trial balance error is incorrectly adding the debit or credit columns.

Caution: You cannot automatically assume that because the trial balance balances, the accounts are correct. You must realize that it is possible to have errors in the accounts and that errors may be such that all the debits still equal all the credits. Some ways this can happen are as follows:

Errors may exist even if the trial balance balances

- If an incorrect amount was recorded as both a debit and a credit to the proper accounts, the trial balance will balance.

- Either omitting an entire transaction or recording a transaction two times, the second time in error, would be an error but would cause the trial balance to balance.

- The correct amounts may be recorded to the incorrect accounts; for example, a debit to Cash may be recorded as a debit to Accounts Receivable.

THE JOURNAL

The accounting system does not start with the recording of a transaction in the general ledger accounts. A little reflection will reveal the need for a record of each transaction listed in chronological order — day by day, day after day. If an error is made in recording a transaction, it will more than likely come to light when the trial balance does not balance. At this point the accountant knows that there is an error but does not know where to start looking for it. Look back to the general ledger for Adams Real Estate on page 66, and assume that the transaction numbers were not recorded in the T-accounts as posting references. Suppose you wish to know the source of the $700 credit to the Cash account. How would you find the corresponding debit? A *chronological listing of each transaction together with the use of posting references* solves this problem. Such a record is called a ***journal.***

In the pen-and-ink system transactions are first recorded in the journal and later transferred to the general ledger, a process referred to by accountants as ***posting.*** The journal provides a complete record of each transaction. Most errors in the trial balance can be found by reviewing the postings from the journal to the ledger and the ledger to the trial balance.

A journal is a book of original entry; it records transactions in chronological order

Because transactions are initially recorded in the journal, it is referred to as a ***book of original entry.*** A business enterprise will design a journal to suit its own particular needs. Some entities may use only a few different types of journals; others may use more. Common to most entities, however, is the ***general journal.*** The general journal is the simplest of the journals, and it provides the most flexibility. (Four other specific types of journals are typically used; they will be the subject of Chapter 6.)

Journalizing

Journalizing is the act of recording transactions in the journal

Recording transactions in the journal is called ***journalizing.*** In the general journal, information such as the date, the account to be debited, the amount to be debited, the account to be credited, the amount to be credited, and an explanation of the business transaction are all recorded in appropriate places. A typical general journal page for the first several transactions of the Adams Real Estate illustration is shown on page 69.

1. The Date

The year is recorded at the top of the date column of each journal page. The month is written on the first line of the date column. Neither the month nor the year is repeated on the page unless the month or year changes. The date of each transaction is recorded in the journal. Notice that the dates correspond to the transaction numbers of the illustration.

2. Account Titles and Explanation

The title of the account to be debited is listed at the left of the description column.

The title of the account to be credited is listed on the line below the account debited and the title of the credit is indented.

The explanation of the transaction is recorded below the account credited. The explanation should be brief but adequate to explain the transaction.

3. Amounts Debited and Credited

The debit amount is recorded in the debit column opposite the title of the account debited. The credit amount is recorded in the credit column opposite the title of the account credited.

The posting reference column (Post. Ref.) is not used at the time transactions are recorded in the general journal. When the debits and credits are posted to the general ledger accounts, this column is used to indicate that the posting has been done by placing the account number of the account posted in the posting reference column of the general journal. Only account titles used in general ledgers can be used to record entries in the general journal. If new accounts are needed, they must be added to the general ledger before entries can be recorded under them in the general journal.

	General Journal				Page 1
Date	Description	Post. Ref.	Debit		Credit
1987 Oct. 1	Cash		5000		
	Amy Adams, Capital				5000
	To record initial investment by				
	Amy Adams				
2	Supplies on Hand		500		
	Office Equipment		600		
	Advertising Signs		300		
	Cash				1400
	To record the acquisition of assets				
	as listed.				
3	Office Equipment		4500		
	Cash				1000
	Notes Payable				3500
	To record the acquisition of				
	computer equipment, paying				
	$1,000 down and a $3,500 note.				
	The note is to be repaid in 5 equal				
	monthly installments of $700 each.				
4	Prepaid Rent		750		
	Cash				750
	To record the payment of 3				
	months' rent in advance.				

Debit titles

Credit titles

Explanation of transaction

Standard Ledger Account Format

T-accounts are used for classroom demonstration on the chalkboard. They are representations of actual general ledger accounts.

General ledger accounts of a business entity are not maintained in the form of T-accounts. Illustrated below is an example of the kind of account format that is used. This type of account format is called a *balance column account* since it contains not only columns for both debits and credits but also a column for the account balance.

Date	Explanation	Post. Ref.	Debit	Credit	Balance
			Cash in Checking Account		Account No. 1111
1987 Oct. 1		GJ-1	5000		5000
2		GJ-1		1400	3600
3		GJ-1		1000	2600
4		GJ-1		750	1850
5		GJ-2	1050		2900
7		GJ-2		700	2200

Posting

Posting is the act of transferring a journal entry from the journal to the ledger

Transferring the journal entry debits and credits to their appropriate ledger accounts is referred to as *posting.* In many accounting systems this process is done mechanically or electronically with the aid of equipment designed to accomplish this task. In a pen-and-ink system, it is done manually. Periodically, at the end of each day or week, the transactions recorded in the general journal since the last posting date are posted to the general ledger. Posting consists of recording in the general ledger accounts the debit and credit items already recorded as debit and credit entries in the general journal.

Thus, the general journal is the place where transactions are entered day by day, as they occur; they are not classified by categories. That comes later in the general ledger, where the accountant doesn't need to know about the date of the transactions but does find it more convenient to begin to look at transactions grouped together by category. And the process of putting transactions in a place where they can be identified by the type of transaction is called *posting.*

The posting process is illustrated on page 71. To get an idea of the posting process, refer to this table as we explain it in the following discussion.

Steps in the Posting Process	Explanation
(A)	Locate in the general ledger the account named in the debit portion of the general journal entry.
(B)	Record the date of the transaction in that account in the general ledger.
(C)	Enter the dollar amount of the debit from the journal into the debit column of that particular account in the ledger.

(continued)

Steps in the Posting Process	Explanation
(D)	Record the general journal page number in the posting reference column of the account debited in the general ledger.
(E)	Enter the account number of the ledger account debited in the posting reference column of the journal on the line of the debit portion of the transaction.
(F)	Repeat the steps above for the credit portion of the journal entry.

An illustration of the posting process

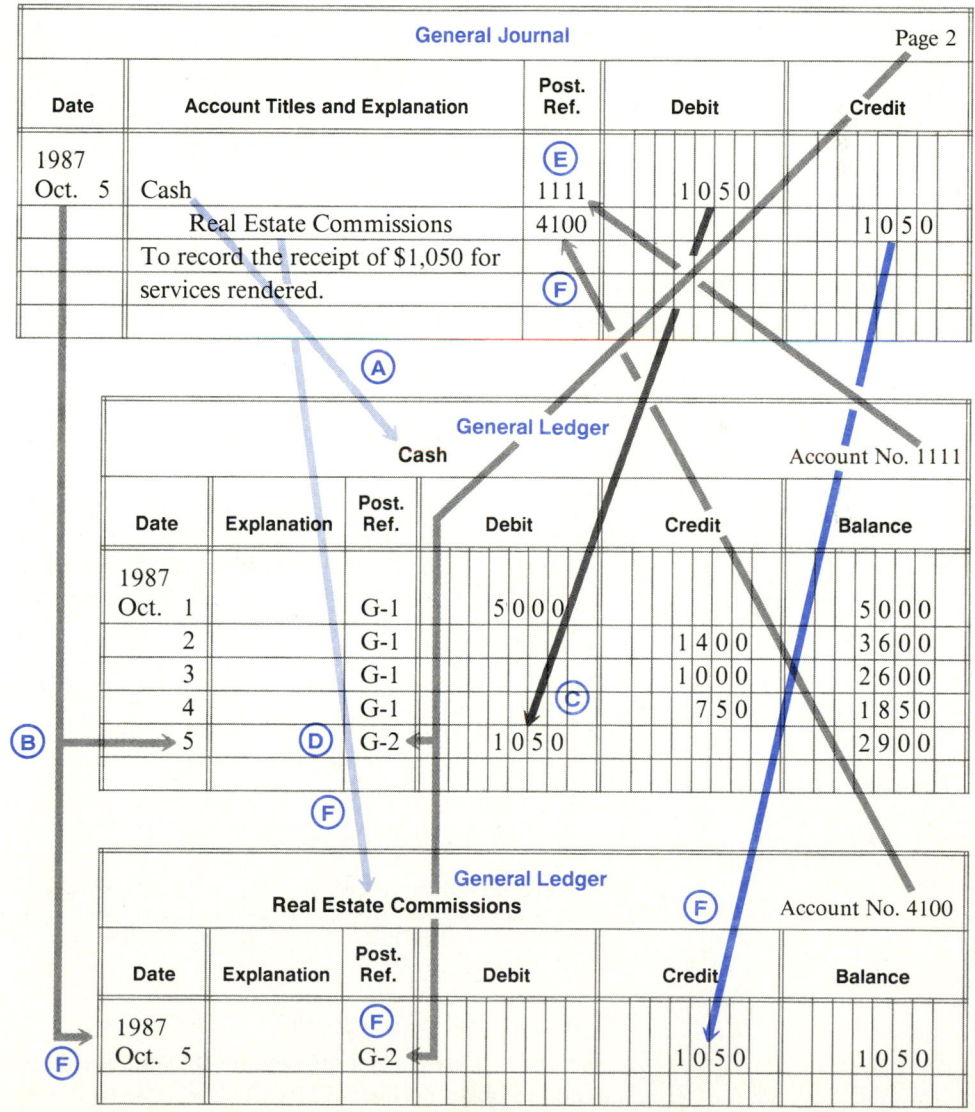

The posting reference columns in both the journal and the ledger serves two purposes. First, a valuable cross reference is achieved. In the event that a question arises concerning an amount in a particular ledger account, the posting reference refers to the journal page where the transaction, the amount, the account titles, and the explanation can be found.

Second, it provides evidence that the accounts have in fact been posted.

Finding Errors

The founding father of accounting once said:

> Who does nothing
> makes no mistakes;
>
> Who makes no mistakes
> Learns nothing

—FRA LUCA PACIOLI (1445–1520)

As you will shortly realize, it is very easy to make errors in working accounting problems. You will also learn, alas, that it is not so easy to find your errors. You can determine an error through chance discovery. More likely, you will learn of errors when the trial balance does not balance.

If your trial balance doesn't balance, subtract the smaller column from the larger column

If an error is discovered because the trial balance did not balance, the difference between the total debit balance and total credit balance should be determined. Often this difference will reveal the nature or location of the error. For example, assume that the debit totals of a trial balance amount to $13,384 and the credit totals $13,700. The difference of $316 might have resulted from the omission of a debit posting of that amount or from a debit of $158 having been posted as a credit. This would cause the credits to be $158 larger than they should be and the debits to be $158 less than they should be, a difference of $316.

If the difference is 10,100, or 1,000, this may be the result of adding the columns incorrectly

Errors of 10, 100, or 1,000 often indicate that the addition of the trial balance columns is in error.

If the difference is divisible by 9, it might be the result of a slide or transposition

If the error is divisible by 9, it is an indication that either a *slide* or a *transposition* has occurred. Moving an entire number either to the right or left is a slide — for example, recording $36 as $360 or $3.60. Reversing the digits in a number is referred to as a transposition. Writing $36 as $63 is an example of a transposition.

The first step to be taken in the process of locating errors is to determine the difference in the trial balance totals. If this does not reveal the error, then each of the various steps in the recording process must be checked, as follows:

Compare the balances in the general ledger to the trial balance. Check the postings from the general journal

- Check the addition of the trial balance.
- Check the transfer of amounts from the general ledger to the trial balance.
- Recompute the account balances.
- Check the posting from the general journal to the general ledger.
- Examine the original transaction to determine if the entry was journalized correctly.

As you proceed through this sequence of steps you will discover the error that causes the trial balance not to balance. Simply retrace your steps starting with the trial balance imbalance.

If an error was made and the trial balance still balances, you will not know the error exists. Discovery then rests on chance or perhaps on hearing from an irate customer who is billed too much for services rendered or goods sold.

Correcting Errors

Errors must be corrected. If an error is discovered in the general journal before the posting is made, it is corrected by drawing a line through the error, such as an inappropriate account title or incorrect amount, and writing the correct account title or correct amount above the error. For example, the entry below was journalized but not posted.

July 14   Cash 375
        Accounts Receivable.   375
        To record payment from customers.

The amount of the entry is determined to be incorrect; it should have been $425. The entry is corrected as follows:

                                                                  425
July 14   Cash . . . . ~~375~~
                                                    425
        Accounts Receivable. . . . .   ~~375~~
        To record payment from customers.

If the error was not discovered until after the posting had taken place and the error was in the *amount* posted, it would be corrected in a similar fashion in the ledger account. However, if the error involves the wrong account, then a correcting journal entry is required. For example, assume that the acquisition of office equipment for cash was incorrectly recorded as a credit to Accounts Payable, as seen below.

Jan. 26   Office Equipment. 218
        Accounts Payable.   218
        To record the acquisition of office equipment.

To correct this error the following entry is needed.

Jan. 31   Accounts Payable. 218
        Cash   218
        To correct an error in the entry of January 26 in which office equipment purchased for cash was erroneously recorded as an acquisition on account.

Some Minor Points

- When recording entries in the journals or postings to the ledgers, dollar signs are not used.

- Commas to indicate thousands of dollars and decimal points to indicate cents are omitted because the rule lines accomplish the purpose served by these items.

- For even dollar amounts, the cents column may be left blank, or zeros or dashes may be used.

- When financial reports are prepared, dollar signs are always used. They are placed only before the first amount at the top of each column of figures and also before amounts representing subtotals and totals.

- Commas and decimal points are required on financial statements prepared on unruled paper.

REVIEW OF THE STEPS IN THE ACCOUNTING PROCESS

At this point, it's a good idea for you to review the steps involved in the accounting process:

1. First, the business entity enters into a transaction with a second party. A business document, such as a sales invoice, is prepared. This business document provides evidence that a transaction has in fact transpired. The transaction is analyzed and journalized in the general journal.

2. At frequent intervals the entries in the general journal are posted to the accounts in the general ledger.

3. Typically, at the end of each month, the balances of the general ledger accounts are determined and a trial balance is prepared.

4. The financial statements are then prepared from the information contained in the trial balance—first the income statement, followed by the statement of owner's equity, and finally the balance sheet.

You should keep clearly in mind that the ultimate objective of the accounting system is to prepare the financial statements. The objective is not the accounting system. Some students become so captivated by the logic of the accounting system that the system itself dominates their attention and activity. Do not fall into this trap. The chairman of the board of directors of General Motors could care less if the system is on the back of an envelope, a pen-and-ink system, or a computer system; or if two-column or three-column journals are used and if accounts are balanced daily or weekly. What is of concern to him is that *the system provides a timely, efficient method that will result in the preparation of financial statements that will reflect fairly the results of operations and the financial position* (the income statement and balance sheet) of General Motors *for the period of time specified.*

CHAPTER SUMMARY

The objective of general financial accounting activity is to prepare the balance sheet, the statement of owner's equity, and the income statement. This objective is achieved through the ***pen-and-ink – double-entry accounting system.*** The pen-and-ink system is actually used by small business entities. Large business entities use high-speed computer techniques to handle massive quantities of data, but they are based on the basic concepts of the pen-and-ink system.

The basic building block of any accounting system is the account. For each individual asset, liability, owner's equity, revenue, and expense item encountered in an entity's financial activities, an account is established. An account consists of three elements: the account title, a location to record increases in the account, and a location to record decreases in the account. Accounts used by business entities appear in balance column form. However, ***T-accounts,*** which are representative of the actual accounts, are used by accountants and students when analyzing accounting problems.

All the accounts that appear in the financial statements of a business entity are contained in a book called the ***general ledger.*** Certain general ledger accounts, such as Accounts Receivable, require that a separate book be maintained listing the individual subparts that constitute the whole. The separate book containing the individual accounts is called a ***subsidiary ledger,*** whereas the related general ledger account is referred to as the ***control account.***

Financial transactions increase or decrease specific general ledger accounts. These increases or decreases in the accounts are recorded with the use of the arbitrary ***rules*** *of debits and credits.* Debits refer to the left side of any account and credits refer to the right side. Since each financial transaction consists of two parts in the double-entry accounting system, for every account debited there must be another account (or accounts) credited. Debits must always equal credits.

Since we have arbitrarily decided that debits will be used to increase asset accounts, it follows that credits must be used to increase liability and owner's equity (including revenue) accounts. This is so because the basic accounting equation, *Assets = Liabilities + Owner's Equity,* must always remain in balance. If debits increase asset accounts, then credits must decrease asset accounts. It then follows that debits must decrease liability and owners' equity (including expense and withdrawal) accounts.

For any specific account the sum of the increases will either exceed or be less than the sum of the decreases. The result is the *account balance.* If the sum of the debits exceeds the sum of the credits, the account is said to have a *debit balance.* Conversely, when credits exceed debits, a *credit balance* results. The typical balance of an account is called its *normal balance* and is *determined by whichever, the debit or the credit, causes the account to increase.*

Thus, *assets, expenses, and withdrawals accounts have normal debit balances, whereas liabilities, owner's equity, and revenue* have normal credit balances.

The accounts are arranged in the general ledger in the order that they would appear in the financial statements, balance sheet accounts first, followed by income statement accounts. Balance sheet accounts are grouped together according to the following classifications: *current assets, noncurrent assets, current liabilities, long-term liabilities,* and *owner's equity.* These classifications will appear as headings on balance sheets. The income statement accounts are listed in the general ledger with the revenue accounts appearing first, followed by the expense accounts.

The recordkeeping process is greatly facilitated when the accounts are numbered. The system of numbered accounts for any business entity is called its *chart of accounts.*

The recordkeeping process begins with the recording of business transactions in a book of original entry called a *journal.* Transactions are listed in the journal in chronological order. Periodically the journal-entry debits and credits are transferred to the appropriate general ledger accounts. This process is referred to as *posting.* After the last entries are journalized and posted a *trial balance* is prepared, typically at the end of every month. The trial balance simply lists all the balances of the general journal ledger accounts and totals all accounts having debit balances and all accounts having credit balances. The sum of the debits in the trial balance must equal the sum of the credits.

Upon completion of the trial balance, the financial statements are prepared.

IMPORTANT TERMS USED IN THIS CHAPTER

Book of original entry   The record used by accountants to initially enter transactions. It is called a *journal.* Transactions are recorded as they occur chronologically. (page 68)

Chart of accounts   The system of numbered general ledger accounts for an economic entity. (page 53)

Control account   A general ledger account, the detail of which is maintained in another book called a *subsidiary ledger.* (page 50)

Credit   The right side of an account, which reflects increases to liability, owner's equity, and revenue accounts and decreases to asset, expense, and withdrawals accounts. (page 54)

Debit   The left side of an account, which reflects increases to asset, expense, and withdrawals accounts and decreases to liability, owner's equity, and revenue accounts. (page 54)

Footing   The addition of a column of figures. (page 48)

Journal   A book of original entry listing financial transactions affecting general ledger accounts in chronological order in terms of their debit and credit amounts. (page 68)

Journalizing   The process of recording financial transactions in a journal. (page 68)

Ledger   A book containing the individual accounts of a business entity. (page 49)

Normal balance   The typical debit or credit balances found in the individual ledger accounts. (page 59)

Posting   The act of transferring the debit and credit entries in a journal to the appropriate ledger accounts. (page 70)

Subsidiary ledger   A book containing the detailed information of a general ledger account called a control account. (page 50)

Trial balance   A schedule reflecting the balances of the individual general ledger accounts. (page 65)

Withdrawals account   The account used to record withdrawals of assets by the owner of a business entity. (page 53)

QUESTIONS

1. One of the most important things to understand about an accounting system is that the system itself is not the most important thing. Explain.

2. What is the difference between an *account* and a *ledger?*

3. What is the purpose of *journals,* and how do they relate to *ledgers?*

4. Explain the meaning of the terms *debit* and *credit.*

5. What are the rules of debit and credit for the balance sheet and income statement accounts?

6. Debits and credits are used to increase and decrease accounts. How is it possible for one of these items, say, debits, to be able to both increase and decrease accounts?

7. What are normal balances? How are they determined?

8. What type of errors could cause a trial balance not to balance?

9. What purpose does the trial balance serve?

10. A trial balance may be in balance but the accounts may be incorrect. How is this possible?

11. How are business transactions entered in the general journal?

12. What is a *T-account?*

13. Of what purpose is a chart of accounts?

14. Listed below are several accounts. Assuming that the business entity has experienced substantial activity during the year, indicate for each account whether or not it will have debit entries and/or credit entries, and the normal balance.

   a. Cash   **e.** Glenda Powell, Capital
   b. Interest Expense   **f.** Office Equipment
   c. Fees Earned   **g.** Accounts Receivable
   d. Accounts Payable   **h.** Rent Expense

15. Cash deposited in a bank is reflected as a debit in the ledger account Cash. However, the bank refers to this transaction as "We have credited your account." Explain this apparent inconsistency.

16. In reviewing the accounts listed in a trial balance it is observed that Accounts Receivable has a $50 credit balance and yet the trial balance balances. Explain.

17. Listed below are the total debits and credits from three trial balances that do not balance. For each case, indicate the type of error you would initially attempt to locate.

	Debit Total	Credit Total
a.	$18,700	$18,600
b.	13,470	13,230
c.	87,614	87,974

18. A number of events common to the accounting function of a business entity are presented below. Prepare a list of these events as they would occur in their logical order.

  a. Determining ledger account balances
  b. Analyzing the transaction
  c. Preparing a balance sheet
  d. Preparing a trial balance
  e. Occurrence of a business transaction
  f. Posting from the journal to the ledger
  g. Preparing a business document
  h. Preparing an income statement
  i. Journalizing transactions
  j. Preparing a statement of owner's equity

19. A business entity performed services in the amount of $450 for a customer. The entry was recorded in the general journal as a debit to Accounts Receivable and a credit to Revenue in the amount of $540. How will this error be discovered?

20. Listed below are several errors. For each error, determine if the trial balance totals would be equal or unequal.

  a. The Able Company paid $1,400 for office supplies. The transaction was recorded as a debit to Office Equipment and a credit to Cash for $1,400.
  b. The Baker Company collected $275 from an account receivable. The entry was recorded as a debit to Cash for $275 and a credit to Accounts Receivable of $257.
  c. Charlie Company purchased office supplies on account in the amount of $400. The entry was not recorded.
  d. Dog Company entered a debit of $50 to the Accounts Receivable account in the general ledger as a $50 credit on the trial balance.
  e. Easy Company recorded rental of office equipment of $150 as a debit to Office Equipment and a credit to Cash.

EXERCISES

Exercise 2-1

Identifying and journalizing transactions found in ledger accounts

Jane Berry operates an industrial equipment repair service that commenced operations in October, 1987. Listed in the T-accounts at the top of page 78 are the first eight transactions of the new business, Berry Repair Service. Using this information, prepare the general journal entries corresponding to these eight transactions.

Cash				Accounts Payable			
(1)	4,000	(2)	890	(6)	500	(3)	300
(8)	900	(4)	1,000			(4)	1,500
		(6)	500				
		(7)	350				

Accounts Receivable				Jane Berry, Capital			
(5)	1,700	(8)	900			(1)	4,000

Office Supplies on Hand				Repair Fees Earned			
(3)	300					(5)	1,700

Office Equipment				Salary Expense			
(2)	890			(7)	350		

Truck			
(4)	2,500		

Exercise 2-2
Journalizing transactions

The following transactions for the month of April 1987 were completed by the Pear Company. Record the transactions in a general journal.

Apr.	4	Acquired office supplies on account, $150.
	6	Paid rent for the month, $320.
	11	Billed customers for advertising fees, $1,500.
	12	Paid for telephone service, $37.
	18	Acquired office equipment, $440, paying one-half in cash and the remainder on account.
	27	Received $700 from customers in payment from the April 11 transaction.

Exercise 2-3
Preparing a trial balance

Robert Dane has operated a furniture repair and refinishing service in Sarasota, Florida, for a number of years. Listed below are the accounts of Dane of Sarasota reflecting activity for the first 6 months of 1987. The accounts are arranged in alphabetical order. From this information, prepare a trial balance as of June 30, 1987, listing the accounts in the proper order.

(Check figure: Total of trial balance = $78,680)

Accounts Payable	$ 970	Rent Expense.	$ 2,400
Accounts Receivable	8,750	Repairing Fees Earned	42,570
Cash	1,500	Salaries Expense	39,700
Dane, Capital	7,310	Salaries Payable	510
Equipment	10,300	Supplies on Hand	2,630
Refinishing Fees Earned.	27,320	Supplies Used	13,400

Exercise 2-4

Preparing a corrected trial balance

The accountant for Sunlight Vision Center has prepared the following trial balance:

SUNLIGHT VISION CENTER
Trial Balance
October 31, 1987

Cash.	$ 3,109	
Accounts Receivable	4,190	
Optical Supplies on Hand	650	
Optical Equipment	3,650	
Accounts Payable		$ 2,760
Notes Payable.		850
Sally Sunlight, Capital		7,120
Sally Sunlight, Withdrawals.		600
Prescription Revenues		1,270
Contact Lens Revenues		1,000
Rent Expense.	600	
Utilities Expense.	100	
Totals.	$12,299	$13,600

As you can see, the trial balance does not balance. Upon investigating the general journal entries and the general ledger accounts, the following information is obtained:

a. In transferring the balance in the Cash account from the general ledger to the trial balance, the last two digits were transposed.

b. The total debits in the Accounts Receivable ledger account were $8,725. The credits totaled $4,575.

c. An entry found in the general journal for a $150 debit to Accounts Receivable and a credit to Prescription Revenues of a like amount was not posted to the general ledger accounts.

d. A debit of $60 to Accounts Payable was not posted to the general ledger. The corresponding credit of $60 was posted correctly to the Cash account.

Prepare a corrected trial balance.

(Check figure: Total of trial balance = $13,090)

Exercise 2-5

Describing the effects of errors on the trial balance

During the month of May 1987, the Green Company made several errors in their accounting records:

a. The general ledger account Accounts Receivable had total debits of $1,750 and total credits of $1,705. The balance of the Accounts Receivable in the trial balance was $95.

b. The acquisition of office supplies for $743 was posted to the general ledger accounts as a debit to Office Supplies on Hand for $473 and a credit to Accounts Payable for $743.

c. Shop Tools were acquired for $362 and recorded as a debit to Office Furniture and a credit to Cash for $362.

d. Services were rendered to the White Company amounting to $675. The entry was recorded as a debit to Accounts Receivable for $765 and a credit to Revenue for Services Rendered $765.

For each of these errors:

1. Indicate whether or not the trial balance will balance;

2. If the trial balance does not balance, identify the debit or credit column as being the larger amount; and

3. Tell the most likely reason for the error's discovery.

Exercise 2-6

Identifying the source of debits and credits

As you become more familiar with the relationship between business transactions and the accounting system, you should see that the accounts are increased and decreased by numerous repetitive transactions. And you should see that individual accounts are usually increased or decreased by very common transactions. For example, we have seen that cash is increased by debits and the most common sources of those debits are investment by owners, cash received when services are rendered, and collections of accounts receivable.

For the accounts listed below, identify the most common reasons for increasing or decreasing the account balances by listing those reasons under the column headings **Sources of Debits** or **Sources of Credits.**

Account	Sources of Debits	Sources of Credits
Cash		
Accounts Receivable.		
Supplies on Hand.		
Accounts Payable.		

PROBLEMS
Set A

Problem A2-1
Recording transactions in T-accounts and preparing a trial balance

Alice Woodard retired from professional bowling in the fall of 1987 to establish her own business—Woodard Lanes. During the month of November the following transactions were completed:

Nov. 1 Deposited $7,550 in the First National Bank of Tulsa in the name of Woodard Lanes.

3 Bought the old Van Winkle Lanes for $82,000. The price included $20,000 for land and $62,000 for the building. Paid $5,000 cash and financed $77,000 by a mortgage payable to First National Bank.

5 Acquired $2,750 of office equipment from Sooner Furniture on account.

6 Bought $1,570 of bowling supplies on account from Strike Bowling Supply Company.

11 Received $3,620 cash from customers for bowling.

16 Paid amount due to Sooner Furniture.

18 Received a bill for $310 from the *Tulsa Daily News* for advertising.

21 The Tulsa Electric Company established a bowling league at company expense for their employees. Billed Tulsa Electric $1,570 for bowling to date.

22 Paid salaries of employees $1,065.

24 Received $750 in partial payment from Tulsa Electric.

28 Paid utilities expense $120.

29 Paid $500 to Strike Bowling Supply Company.

Required

1. Establish the following T-accounts: Cash; Accounts Receivable; Bowling Supplies on Hand; Land; Building; Office Equipment; Accounts Payable; Mortgage Payable; Alice Woodard, Capital; Bowling Fees Earned; Salaries Expense; Advertising Expense; Utilities Expense.

Record the transactions directly into T-accounts using the dates of the transactions to identify each transaction.
2. Prepare a trial balance on November 30, 1987.

(Check figure: Total of trial balance = $91,120)

Problem A2-2
Journalizing and posting; preparing a trial balance

After working for two decades as a computer systems analyst, Donald Yeates left the Big Corporation to establish his own consulting business. Yeates Computer Consulting began business in August 1987 and had the following transactions:

Aug.	1	Donald Yeates transferred $10,300 from his personal savings account to the Clifton National Bank in the name of the new business.
	4	Bought a used computer for $75,000. Yeates paid 10% in cash and the rest was financed by a $67,500, 10% note payable due to the Clifton National Bank.
	5	Acquired office equipment ($4,750) and office supplies ($518) on account from Essex Supply Company.
	7	Paid rent for the month $350.
	10	Received cash of $14,716 for consulting services.
	11	Paid Essex Office Supply Company.
	12	Billed customers $17,313 for consulting services.
	15	Paid employees wages of $9,251.
	17	Bought $1,627 of office supplies from Garden State Office Supply Company on account.
	19	Received $6,500 in payment from customers billed on the 12th.
	24	Paid $1,563 to the Clifton National Bank, $1,000 to reduce the note payable and $563 interest expense.
	31	Yeates withdrew $3,000 for personal use.

Required

1. Prepare general journal entries for the transactions listed above.
2. Post the entries to the ledger accounts using account numbers for cross reference. The following accounts will be required:

Account Number	Account	Account Number	Account
10	Cash	30	Donald Yeates, Capital
11	Accounts Receivable	31	Donald Yeates, Withdrawals
12	Office Supplies on Hand	40	Consulting Fees Earned
13	Office Equipment	50	Salary Expense
14	Computer Equipment	51	Rent Expense
20	Notes Payable	52	Interest Expense
21	Accounts Payable		

3. Prepare a trial balance.

(Check figure: Trial balance totals = $110,456)

Problem A2-3

Preparing a classified balance sheet

The balance sheet accounts of the Little Company for January 31, 1987, are listed below:

Little, Capital.	$71,575	Accounts Receivable	$21,317
Mortgage Payable	65,000	Salaries Payable	16,307
Buildings	50,000	Notes Receivable	15,000
Equipment	42,516	Unearned Revenue	9,200
Accounts Payable	37,519	Cash	6,256
Inventory	37,512	Notes Payable	6,000
Land	30,000	Prepaid Rent	3,000

Required

Prepare a balance sheet classifying the accounts as current assets, noncurrent assets, current liabilities, long-term liabilities, or owner's equity.

(Check figure: Total assets = $205,601)

Problem A2-4

Preparing journal entries from two trial balances

The Doony Company buys all its goods and services on account, paying cash only for salaries and, of course, withdrawals. Payments are made only after appropriate billings are received and accounts payable established. Revenues are recorded when services are rendered. Past experience reveals that 30% of the revenues are cash sales, the remainder being recorded as accounts receivable. The trial balances for the months ended August 31 and September 30, 1987, are presented below:

	August 31		September 30	
Cash	$ 320		$3,120	
Accounts Receivable	680		400	
Repair Parts on Hand	160		280	
Machinery	1,640		1,800	
Accounts Payable		$ 240		$ 120
Richard Doony, Capital		800		800
Richard Doony, Withdrawals	520		560	
Repair Fees Earned		3,200		6,400
Salaries Expense	600		750	
Advertising Expense	200		250	
Telephone Expense	120		160	
Totals	$4,240	$4,240	$7,320	$7,320

Required

By analyzing the information contained in the two trial balances, prepare general journal entries that will reflect the transactions that occurred during the month of September. Omit the explanations to the general journal entries. You will need to establish T-accounts for Accounts Receivable, Accounts Payable, and Cash to determine the collection of accounts receivable and the payment of accounts payable.

Problem A2-5

Correcting a trial balance

The trial balance of Allen Lawn Service does not balance. Unfortunately, the trial balance, presented below, was prepared by Mr. Allen, who does not have any experience in book-keeping.

ALLEN LAWN SERVICE
Trial Balance
February 28, 1987

Cash	$ 382	
Accounts Receivable	1,309	
Lawn Service Supplies on Hand	386	
Lawn Mowers	1,807	
Accounts Payable		$2,151
Salaries Payable		210
Allen, Capital		1,566
Allen, Withdrawals		150
Lawn Service Revenues		2,247
Salaries Expense	440	
Repair Expense	145	
Utilities Expense	25	
Totals	$4,594	$6,324

As a personal friend of Mr. Allen you have been asked to determine why the trial balance does not balance. You do several things.

First you review the trial balance and the process of transferring the amounts from the ledger accounts to the trial balance and you find that:

a. The debit column in the trial balance was incorrectly footed.

b. The balance in the accounts payable general ledger account of $1,251 was transferred as $2,151. [This was discovered before the error in (f) was discovered.]

Next you recompute the balances in each of the general ledger accounts and find:

c. Repair Expenses were overfooted by $18.

d. The total debits in the Cash account amounted to $1,873 and the credits totaled $1,591.

Finally you retrace the postings from the general journal to the general ledger and discover that:

e. A debit posting of $312 to Accounts Receivable was missing.

f. A credit posting of $520 to Accounts Payable should have been $52.

g. A credit posting of $68 to Lawn Service Revenues was missing.

h. A debit of $37 was posted to salaries expense rather than the correct amount $73.

Required | Prepare a corrected trial balance

(Check figure: Trial balance totals $4,874)

Problem A2-6
Journalizing and posting transactions; preparing a trial balance and financial statements

Presented below is the October 1, 1987, balance sheet of Sally Levy Real Estate Agency:

SALLY LEVY REAL ESTATE AGENCY
Balance Sheet
October 1, 1987

Assets		Liabilities and Owner's Equity	
Assets:		Liabilities:	
Cash	$ 4,126	Notes Payable	$ 0
Accounts Receivable.	3,785	Accounts Payable.	4,708
Prepaid Insurance	900	Total Liabilities	$ 4,708
Office Supplies on Hand . . .	736		
Office Equipment.	5,350	Owner's Equity:	
Automobile	9,675	Sally Levy, Capital	19,864
		Total Liabilities and Owner's	
Total Assets	$24,572	Equity.	$24,572

During the month of October 1987, the real estate agency completed the following transactions:

Oct. 2 Sold a residence on the eastside and billed client for commissions earned, $3,720.

4 Paid $681 to Atlas Supply for office supplies previously acquired on account.

6 Paid $307 for advertising in the *Doyletown Daily* for the month of October.

8 Bought office supplies on account from the White Office Supply Company, $417.

13 Collected $1,120 on accounts receivable.

14 Acquired office equipment, paying $350 cash to Allan Furniture Company.

15 Paid salaries, $731.

18 Acquired an automobile for use in the agency for $8,629. Paid $2,500 cash, financing the rest with a $6,129 note payable to Doyletown Exchange Bank.

21 Sold a residence on the southside, receiving a $1,160 commission in cash.

23 Paid $475 rent for the month.

Oct. 24   Received $2,460 collections on accounts receivable.
     29   Sally Levy withdrew $500 for her personal use.
     30   Paid salaries $772.

Required

1. Enter the amounts from the October 1, 1987, balance sheet into the appropriate general ledger accounts using the following account numbers:

110	Cash	160	Automobiles
120	Accounts Receivable	210	Notes Payable
130	Prepaid Insurance	220	Accounts Payable
140	Office Supplies on Hand	310	Sally Levy, Capital
150	Office Equipment		

2. Prepare general journal entries for October transactions.

3. Post the entries to the general ledger using page 18 as the general journal page reference and the following additional account numbers:

320   Sally Levy, Withdrawals
410   Real Estate Commissions
510   Salaries Expense
520   Advertising Expense
530   Rent Expense

4. Prepare a trial balance as of October 31, 1987.

(Check figure: Total trial balance $35,317)

5. Prepare the financial statements (an income statement, a statement of owner's equity, and a balance sheet).

Problem A2-7
Preparing financial statements

On April 1, 1987, Pete Kropotkin invested his personal savings of $16,500 in a checking account at the First National Bank of Siberia, establishing a business that he called Anarchists Consulting Service. Because of his extensive background in terrorism and his astute political insight, Mr. Kropotkin feels that he will be very successful. Mr. Kropotkin desires information on the consulting service's financial status. He engages you to provide this information.

You are able to determine from contracts found in Kropotkin's office that a building and land were acquired on April 3, 1987, for a total of $80,000, land representing one-fourth of this amount. The contract specified that a $10,000 down payment was required and a $70,000 mortgage payable was incurred to satisfy the remaining cost.

A review of Kropotkin's checkbook reveals that checks in the amount of $19,374 were written during the months of April, May, and June. You are able to organize these checks into expenditures for the following items:

Bomb Supplies on Hand	$ 2,131
Prepaid Advertising	650
Mortgage Payable	800
Interest Expense	973
Utilities Expense	251
Lease Expense.	720
Salaries Expense	11,349
Kropotkin, Withdrawals	2,500

Deposits of $30,410 were made during the period, including the amount invested by Kropotkin. The remainder was from collections of fees for consulting. As of June 30, $3,618 of consulting work has been done, but payment has not yet been received.

Several unpaid bills are on hand on June 30; they include $62 for utilities, $140 for lease of a bomb-making machine, and $627 for bomb supplies on hand.

Required   Prepare an income statement, a statement of owner's equity, and a balance sheet. (*Hint:* Use T-accounts to solve this problem. Establish a T-account for each account needed, analyze the transactions, and record the entries directly into the T-accounts.)

(Check figure: Total assets = $88,062)

Set B

Problem B2-1
Recording transactions in T-accounts and preparing a trial balance

After graduating from the University of Arizona Dental School in June 1987, Dr. Pam Ware established an office in her hometown of Chicago, Illinois. During the first month of her new practice, July, the following transactions were completed:

July 1   A checking account in the name of Pam Ware, DDS, was established at the Lincoln State Bank in the amount of $4,250.

3   A dental office was acquired by buying and converting a Pennsylvania Railroad caboose for $25,216. Lincoln State Bank provided a $22,500, 12%, 30-year mortgage, and Dr. Ware paid the difference by issuing her first business check.

5   Dental equipment in the amount of $11,528 was acquired on account from Shockley Dental Supply Company.

6   Dental supplies of $6,250 were acquired from Berger Dental Supply Company on account.

15   Received $2,575 from patients for dental services rendered.

16   Paid salaries, $925.

18   Paid Berger Dental Supply Company $2,250 on account.

20   Received an invoice from the Illinois State Dental Board amounting to $250 for the 1987 state dental license.

21   Billed patients $2,027 for dental services rendered.

24   Paid telephone expense, $57.

27   Withdrew $1,000 for personal use.

30   Received $973 from patients billed July 21.

Required   Record the 12 transactions directly into T-accounts by entering the appropriate debits and credits. Use the dates of the transaction to identify each transaction. You will need the following accounts: Cash; Accounts Receivable; Dental Supplies on Hand; Dental Equipment; Building; Accounts Payable; Mortgage Payable; Pam Ware, Capital; Pam Ware, Withdrawals; Dental Fees Earned; Salaries Expense; License Fee Expense; Telephone Expense.

After recording each transaction, compute the balance in each account and prepare a trial balance dated July 31, 1987.

(Check figure: Total of trial balance = $47,130)

Problem B2-2
Journalizing and posting transactions; preparing a trial balance

Mitzie Mickiff applied for and received from the city of Birmingham, Alabama, an exclusive franchise to provide cable TV to city residents. The franchise was granted on February 1, 1987. The following transactions reflect the business activity of Mickiff Cable TV for the month of February:

Feb. 1   Invested $16,500 of personal funds to open a checking account in the name of Mickiff Cable TV.

2   Paid to the city of Birmingham $5,000 franchise fee. The franchise will be for 10 years. Recorded Franchise Fee Expense for $500 and a noncurrent asset, Prepaid Franchise Fee, $4,500.

Feb.	4	Acquired TV equipment ($4,231) and TV equipment supplies ($826) on account from Harris-Brassfield Supply Company.
	6	Bought four panel trucks for $15,000 each. The trucks were financed by a $10,000 down payment and a $50,000, 6% note payable due to Bessemer Trust Company.
	10	Received cash of $3,092 from customers for cable TV service.
	11	Paid Harris-Brassfield for TV equipment supplies.
	15	Paid employee wages, $2,250.
	18	Billed customers $4,217 for cable TV service.
	19	Bought $326 of TV equipment supplies on account from Hartweck Supply Company.
	23	Received $3,238 from customers billed on the 18th.
	25	Withdrew $4,000 for personal use.

Required

1. Prepare general journal entries for the transactions listed above.
2. Post the entries to the ledger accounts using account numbers for cross reference. The following accounts will be required:

Account Number	Account	Account Number	Account
110	Cash	220	Accounts Payable
120	Accounts Receivable	310	Mitzie Mickiff, Capital
130	TV Equipment Supplies on Hand	320	Mitzie Mickiff, Withdrawals
140	TV Equipment	410	Cable TV Revenue
150	Trucks	510	Salaries Expense
160	Prepaid Franchise Fees	520	Franchise Fee Expense
210	Notes Payable		

3. Prepare a trial balance.

(Check figure: Trial balance totals $78,366)

Problem B2-3
Preparing a classified balance sheet

The balance sheet accounts of the Carleo Company as of October 31, 1987, are listed below:

Accounts Payable	$17,500	Land	$12,500
Accounts Receivable	9,000	Mortgage Payable	25,000
Building	30,000	Notes Payable	2,500
Carleo, Capital	33,500	Notes Receivable	5,000
Cash	1,500	Prepaid Rent	1,000
Equipment	15,000	Prepaid Supplies	2,000
Inventory	10,000	Salaries Payable	7,500

Required

Prepare a classified balance sheet classifying the accounts as current assets, noncurrent assets, current liabilities, long-term liabilities, or owner's equity.

(Check figure: Total assets = $86,000)

Problem B2-4
Preparing journal entries

The comparative balance sheets of Dover Motel for July 1 and July 31, 1987, are presented on page 87, followed by the July 1987 income statement.

DOVER MOTEL
Comparative Balance Sheets

	July 1987 1	July 1987 31		July 1987 1	July 1987 31
Assets:			**Liabilities:**		
Cash....................	$ 593	$ 134	Accounts Payable	$ 2,157	$ 2,381
Accounts Receivable	1,725	1,573	Taxes Payable..............	1,200	500
Linen Supplies on Hand	487	903	Total Liabilities..........	$ 3,357	$ 2,881
Prepaid Insurance	650	600			
Furniture.................	17,660	18,281	**Owner's Equity:**		
Building	40,000	40,000	Dover, Capital	77,758	78,610
Land....................	20,000	20,000	Total Liabilities and		
Total Assets................	$81,115	$81,491	Owner's Equity.............	$81,115	$81,491

DOVER MOTEL
Income Statement
For the Month Ended July 31, 1987

Revenues:		
Room Rental Revenues........................		$13,360
Expenses:		
Salaries Expense..........................	$11,016	
Insurance Expense	50	
Utilities Expense	127	
Laundry Expense..........................	315	11,508
Net Income		$ 1,852

Linen Supplies and Furniture are the only acquisitions Dover Motel ever makes on account. Room rentals are 80% on account and 20% for cash. Mrs. Dover withdrew cash for her personal use during the month.

Required   Using the financial statements and the additional information, prepare the general journal entries (without explanations) that will best reflect the transactions that transpired during the month of July 1987.

Problem B2-5
Correcting a trial balance

The April 1987 trial balance for Chatham Lock Company is presented on page 88. It does not balance. Chatham's regular bookkeeper, Alan Alperin, is on vacation, and Chatham attempted to prepare the trial balance. Unfortunately, Mr. Chatham is a much better locksmith than he is a bookkeeper, for the trial balance does not balance.

Cash.	$ 448	
Accounts Receivable	1,896	
Keys on Hand	716	
Machinery.	2,100	
Truck	3,500	
Accounts Payable		$ 726
Chatham, Capital		5,138
Chatham, Withdrawals.		500
Revenues.		3,716
Salaries Expense	350	
Rent Expense.	100	
Telephone Expense	64	
Totals.	$10,174	$10,080

Mr. Chatham asked the Bowling Green State University for help, and the accounting department chairman sends her brightest student, you, to Mr. Chatham's shop.

Upon reviewing the process of transferring the amounts in the ledger accounts to the trial balance and reviewing the trial balance, you discover two errors:

a. The debit column in the trial balance was incorrectly footed.

b. The balance in the accounts payable general ledger of $627 was transferred as $726.

When you recompute the balances of the general ledger accounts, two more errors are discovered:

c. Telephone Expense was overfooted by $18.

d. The total debits in the Cash account amounted to $1,846 and the credits totaled $1,498.

Four errors were discovered when you retraced the postings from the general journal to the general ledger:

e. A debit posting to Accounts Receivable in the amount of $520 should have been $52.

f. A debit posting to Accounts Payable of $460 was missing.

g. A credit posting to Revenues in the amount of $76 was missing.

h. A credit of $310 was posted to Accounts Payable rather than the correct amount of $301.

Required   Prepare a corrected trial balance.

(Check figure: Trial balance totals $9,088)

Problem B2-6

Journalizing and posting transactions, preparing a trial balance and financial statements

Nelson Black is a highly successful stock car driver. With his 1960 red Corvair he has won many of the races he has entered. Presented at the top of the next page is the September 1, 1987, trial balance of Black Stock Car Company together with account numbers.

While racing in California in September, the following transactions were completed:

Credit Accounts Receivable

Sept.	2	Received $2,500 from Sacramento Speedway for prize money won in August.
	4	Paid Debbie Dennis $526 for a set of tires purchased and billed in August.
	5	Bought $621 of repair parts from Donald Burdin on account.
	7	Won first place at Golden Gate Raceway and received cash of $3,250.
	10	Bought a second 1960 Corvair in San Diego for $1,250, paying $250 down and the remainder on open account.
	11	Paid for gasoline $387.
	14	Finished third at Redwoods Racetrack, the prize money of $750 to be mailed sometime in October.
	15	Paid Pat Mitchell and Bonni Lieberman, the pit crew, $1,500 salaries.

Acct. No.			
1.	Cash	$2,536	
2.	Accounts Receivable.	4,500	
3.	Repair Parts on Hand	718	
4.	Stock Cars	1,800	
5.	Accounts Payable.		$1,307
6.	Nelson Black, Capital		8,247
7.	Nelson Black, Withdrawals.	–0–	
8.	Racing Revenues		–0–
9.	Pit Crew Salaries Expense	–0–	
10.	Gasoline Expense.	–0–	
11.	Travel Expense	–0–	
	Totals	$9,554	$9,554

Sept. 19   Paid travel expenses, $1,071.
22   Placed second in the Westwood Dirt Track, receiving $1,000 cash.
Credit Accounts Receivable   25   Received $500 from Santa Clara Speedway for eighth-place finish in August.
27   Nelson Black withdrew $2,000 for personal use.

Required   **1.** Enter the September 1, 1987, trial balance amounts into the appropriate general ledger accounts.
2. Prepare general journal entries for the transactions for the month of September.
3. Post the transactions to the general ledger (use the general journal page number 7 as the posting reference).
4. Prepare a trial balance.

(Check figure: Trial balance totals $15,649)

5. Prepare an income statement, a statement of owner's equity, and a balance sheet.

Problem B2-7
Preparing financial statements

After two decades of service to the CIA, Special Agent Ed Wyden retired to form his own company, Wyden Information Service. On January 1, 1987, Mr. Wyden deposited $2,500 of personal savings in a checking account in the name of the new company.

For the next 3 months business flourished. Contracts with the CIA led to a number of revenue-producing activities. Mr. Wyden became too active to maintain proper accounting records. At the end of the 3-month period he wishes to know how well the business did financially and requests your help.

From a review of the deposits made to the Princetown National Bank and conversation with Mr. Wyden, you determine that all funds received have been deposited in the bank and total $95,420. Included in that total was the $2,500 initial deposit. You are able to organize the remaining deposits into three categories. The first category, consisting of $25,410, is classified as code deciphering revenue. The second category amounts to $62,710 for information on such things as Russia's current wheat crop and France's progress toward a new laser-equipped jet fighter. You classify this category as Information Revenue. The last category is the proceeds of a note payable to the Princetown National Bank. You are able to account for all checks written during the 3-month period and they total $85,060, consisting of $15,000 in withdrawals; $29,200 for salaries; $26,500 for travel, $12,360 for equipment rental expense; $1,500 repayment of the note payable; and $500 interest expense.

On Mr. Wyden's desk you find a bill from Eastern Airlines amounting to $750 for a business trip and a bill for $337 from Ludlum Electronics for equipmental rental. In addition, Mr. Wyden informs you that he has performed information services for clients amounting to $1,250 for which he has not yet been paid, and one code deciphering contract for $2,500, to be paid by the client on April 15.

Required   Prepare an income statement, a statement of owner's equity, and a balance sheet. (*Hint:* Establish a T-account for each account needed. Analyze the information in the form of business transactions, recording them directly into the T-accounts.)

(Check figure: Total assets = $14,110)

Chapter 3

Periodic Procedures: Adjusting the Accounts

After studying this chapter you should understand the following:

- The distinction between *external* and *internal* transactions
- Why certain accounts require adjustments at the end of an accounting period
- What a *contra*-asset account is
- Why the net income of a business entity is not a precise amount
- The purpose of an adjusted trial balance and how to prepare one
- The various steps involved in the accounting process
- What we mean by *classified* financial statements
- The *cash basis* and the *accrual basis* of accounting
- The *revenue-recognition principle* and the *matching concept*

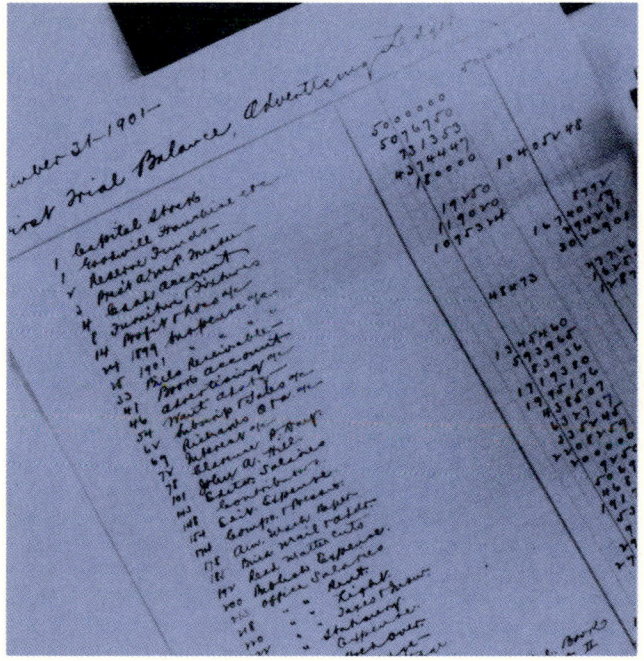

It may come as a surprise to you that the basic elements of the accounting model are not precisely measured on the financial statements of a business enterprise. Only after completing all the business transactions over the *entire life* of a business entity can the exact amount of assets, revenue, expenses, and net income be determined. But that's utterly impractical.

Accounting is not an exact science

To see what we mean, consider a company having a building acquired at a cost of $400,000 on January 1, 1960, when the company first started operations. At that time the company estimated that the building would have a 40-year life, and would be replaced by a new building on January 1, 2000. But 25 years later, January 1, 1985, the building proves to be dysfunctional—meaning that for whatever reason it no longer serves its original purpose—and a new building is acquired on that date.

Accountants must use estimates

At this early point in your accounting education we think you can already see intuitively that the cost of the original building must be assigned to the expense of doing business over the period of time that that building was in use. Very simply, on January 1, 1960, the yearly building expense for the next 40 years was *estimated* at $10,000 per year ($400,000 ÷ 40 years). But since the building was replaced in 1985, the *actual* yearly expense turned out to be $16,000 per year ($400,000 ÷ 25 years). The precise amount of the yearly building expense can be determined only after the full life of the building.

FIGURE 3-1
A comparison of the estimated vs. actual useful life of a building.

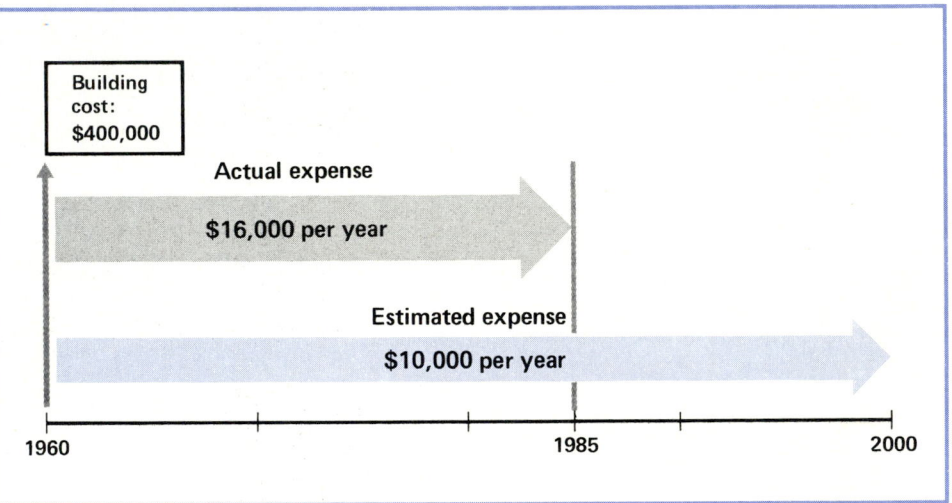

The actual yearly expense is only determined at the end of the asset's life

Annual expense is estimated in 1960 at the beginning of the asset's life

Most business entities remain in business as far into the future as can reasonably be projected

Of course anyone interested in the affairs of a business entity cannot wait until the entity completes all the business transactions over its entire life before receiving financial reports on its financial position and results of operations. It is true that some business entities cease operations after several years, but most remain in business decade after decade and will continue to remain in business as far into the future as can reasonably be projected. This is the basis of the ***going concern*** concept discussed in Chapter 1.

Financial statements are prepared monthly, quarterly, and yearly

To provide timely information in financial statements, accountants break the life of business entities into time frames. At the end of each time frame, accountants prepare financial statements. These time frames are referred to as ***accounting periods*** and are typically a year, a quarter, or a month in length. Parties external to the entity do not receive monthly statements; they do not need such frequent reporting. The contrast between annual and quarterly reports is illustrated in the financial statements shown on page 93.

Financial Statements for External Parties.

Annual reports.

MOON SERVICE COMPANY
Income Statement
Year Ended December 31, 1987

Revenue:
Fees Earned		$105,000
Investment Income		36,000
Total Revenue		$141,000

Expenses:
Salaries	$37,500	
Rent Expense	7,500	
Advertising Expense	12,000	
Total Expenses		57,000

Net Income. . . . . $ 84,000

MOON SERVICE COMPANY
Balance Sheet
December 31, 1987

Assets

Current Assets:
Cash	$ 60,000
Accounts Receivable	240,000
Supplies on Hand	15,000
Total Current Assets	$315,000

Noncurrent Assets:
Truck	45,000

Total Assets $360,000

Liabilities and Owner's Equity

Liabilities

Current Liabilities:
Note Payable	$ 30,000
Accounts Payable	45,000
Total Current Liabilities	$ 75,000

Owner's Equity

Moon, Capital.   285,000

Total Liabilities and Owner's Equity $360,000

Quarterly report.

MOON SERVICE COMPANY
Income Statement
Quarter Ended December 31, 1987

Revenue	$36,000
Expenses	15,500
Net Income	$20,500

Financial statements reflect *fairly,* not *precisely,* the financial position and results of operations of business entities

Notice that the quarterly report is a highly condensed version of the income statement. Sometimes a highly condensed version of the balance sheet is also given. It is the annual report that offers complete financial information to external parties. Although financial statements cannot be regarded as precise, they do reflect fairly the financial position and results of operations for the accounting periods indicated. Business decisions are made with the reliance that financial statements fairly represent what they are supposed to represent. We use the term *fairly* to mean that the financial statements reflect the underlying economic events and transactions within an acceptable range of accuracy; much of the study of accounting has to do with what we mean by "fairly."

One of the advantages of recognizing the life of a business entity as a series of regular, successive accounting periods is ***comparability.*** Comparing between business activities of the current period and those of similar past periods makes it possible to judge how the business performed. Has revenue increased? Have expenses decreased? Has net income improved? Has the entity's financial position been strengthened? These are typical questions that can be answered by comparing financial statements of successive accounting periods.

You will find that preparing financial statements at the end of accounting periods does present some problems. The types of transactions you have learned to record in the accounting records in the first two chapters represent exchange transactions between a business entity and *second parties*—parties external to the entity. These we refer to as *external transactions.*

External transactions are between a business entity and second parties

Consider, for example, an external transaction made on October 1 of the current year for a $1,200, 12-month insurance policy. On that date prepaid insurance would be recorded as an asset measured at $1,200. But 3 months later, on December 31, only 9 months of insurance coverage remain, while 3 months of insurance expense has been incurred. The financial statements prepared at the end of the accounting period *must* reflect these shifts in asset and expense values; the statement must show the following:

1. All assets owned

2. All liabilities owed

3. All revenue earned

4. All expenses incurred

Adjusting entries are internal transactions

To meet this objective, some of the accounts must be *adjusted.* The adjustment is accomplished by means of a general journal entry called an *adjusting entry.* This is referred to as an *internal transaction.*

Figure 3-2 shows the values that should be reflected on the financial statements for Prepaid Insurance and Insurance Expense on October 1 and December 31. Insurance for 12 months was paid for in advance; insurance was "consumed" for 3 months; and 9 months of insurance not yet consumed, a future economic benefit, remain. At $100 per month this would mean that $900 should be the amount of Prepaid Insurance reported on the balance sheet. Further, because 3 months of economic benefits have been received, at $100 per month, $300 of Insurance Expense should be reported on

**FIGURE 3-2
Adjusting entry: Prepaid Insurance becomes Insurance Expense.**

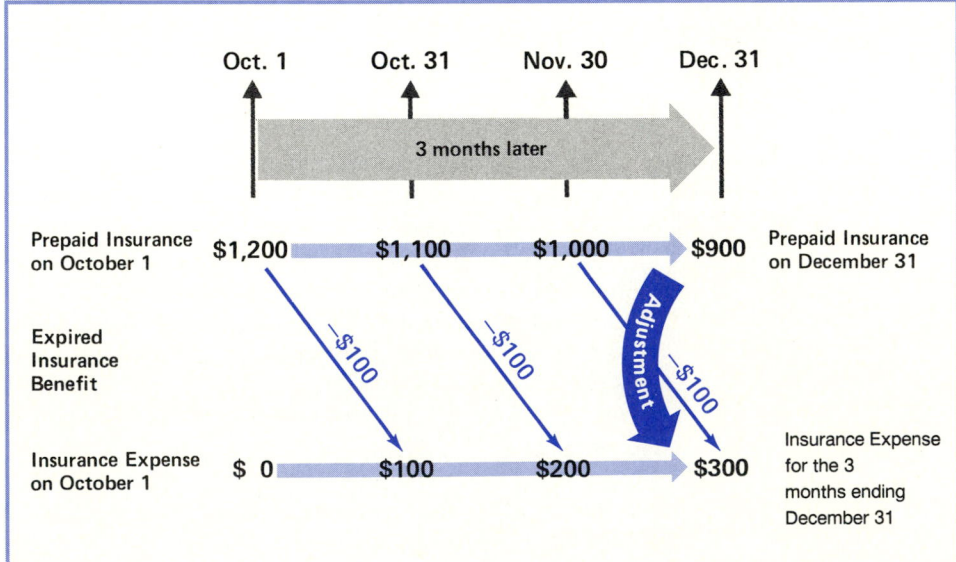

the income statement. Thus, on December 31, an *adjusting entry* is needed that will reduce Prepaid Insurance by $300 and increase Insurance Expense by a like amount.

TYPES OF ADJUSTING ENTRIES

Deferrals and accruals are two types of adjusting entries

There are two broad classifications of adjusting entries:

1. One classification includes goods and services collected or paid for in advance of benefits given or received and would require adjustments of external transactions previously recorded in the general journal and posted to the ledger accounts. These we will call **deferrals.**

2. The other classification of adjusting entries includes revenue already earned and expenses already incurred for which no transaction as yet has been recorded. These we will call **accruals.**

Every adjusting entry affects both the income statement and the balance sheet.

Deferrals

Within the broad classification of deferrals there are three types of adjusting entries: **prepaid expenses, unearned revenue,** and **depreciation.**

Prepaid Expenses

An asset is an unexpired cost

An expense is an expired cost

Items that are paid for before they are used are called prepaid expenses. At the time these items are acquired a cost is incurred. This cost represents an asset and is an **unexpired cost.** As time passes the asset is consumed in part or in total and the consumed amount becomes an expense, which is an **expired cost.** Examples of prepaid expenses are prepaid insurance, prepaid rent, office supplies on hand, repair parts on hand, and, in the broadest sense, buildings and office equipment.

To see how to adjust a prepaid expense, as well as how to make the other adjustments we will introduce in the following pages, consider the trial balance of the Wilma Adams Advertising Agency, shown below, which is prepared at the end of the first month of operations.

THE WILMA ADAMS ADVERTISING AGENCY
Trial Balance
November 30, 1987

Line			
	Cash	$ 244	
(a)	Note Receivable, 12% due Apr. 30	1,500	
	Accounts Receivable	1,251	
(b)	Advertising Supplies on Hand	386	
(c)	Prepaid Rent	450	
(d)	Office Equipment	3,600	
	Accounts Payable		$ 572
(e)	Unearned Advertising Revenue		600
	Wilma Adams, Capital		3,500
(f)	Wilma Adams, Withdrawals	150	
	Advertising Revenue		3,706
(g)	Salary Expense	725	
	Utilities Expense	47	
	Miscellaneous Expense	25	
	Totals	$8,378	$8,378

On November 1, rent at $150 per month for 3 months was paid in advance by the advertising agency and recorded in the general journal by the following entry:

Nov. 1   Prepaid Rent 450
          Cash   450
          To record payment of rent in advance for November, December, and
          January at $150 per month.

At the end of November the advertising agency has received the benefit of occupying space for 1 month and has the right to occupancy for 2 additional months. The accounting record—that is, the Prepaid Rent [the line designated (c)] as seen in the November 30 trial balance—does not reflect this situation. An adjusting entry is required. One month's expired cost, $150, must be recorded as Rent Expense, and 2 months' unexpired costs must remain on the balance sheet as Prepaid Rent of $300. The adjusting entry would be recorded as follows:

Rent Expense adjusting entry

Nov. 30   Rent Expense. 150
            Prepaid Rent   150
          To record rent expense.

In essense, $150 has been transferred from the Prepaid Rent account to the Rent Expense account, as can be seen by the posted T-accounts:

Asset Prepaid Rent				Expense Rent Expense	
Nov. 1	450	Nov. 30	150	Nov. 30	150
Bal.	300				

Notice that the balance in the Prepaid Rent account after the posting of the adjusting entry is $300.

Advertising Supplies on Hand represents another type of prepaid expense. Notice the line designated (b) on the Wilma Adams Advertising Agency trial balance. As of November 30, the trial balance indicates that there is $386 of advertising supplies on hand. These supplies were acquired on November 8 and recorded in the general journal by the following entry:

The advertising supplies were acquired on November 8, but that's not what is on hand at November 30

Nov. 8   Advertising Supplies on Hand 386
          Cash   386
          To record acquisition of advertising supplies.

These supplies represent an asset worth $386 to the agency on November 8. But as the agency uses advertising supplies during the month, the asset is reduced and an expense, Advertising Supplies Used, is incurred. Can you see that no purpose would be served by recording Advertising Supplies Used as an expense each time supplies are consumed? To do so would require extensive bookkeeping efforts with no benefit, since the financial statements are not needed until the *end of the month*. But you should realize that at the end of the month an adjusting entry for the supplies is required to properly reflect the amount consumed—*the expense incurred*—and the amount of supplies remaining—*the value of supplies on hand*. The values to be recorded in the financial statements by means of adjusting the accounts are determined by counting (taking an inventory of) the advertising supplies remaining on hand at the end of the month. By subtracting the supplies on hand at the end of the month from the supplies acquired during the month (plus the supplies on hand at the beginning of the month, if any), the amount of supplies used can be determined.

For example, if the amount of supplies on hand at the end of the month as revealed by the count is $133, then $253 of advertising supplies must have been used during the month, as seen in the following analysis:

Advertising Supplies	
On hand, November 1	$ 0
Acquired, November 8	386
Available	$386
On hand, November 30	133
Used	$253

From this information the appropriate adjusting entry required would be recorded as follows:

The adjusting entry reduces the asset, Advertising Supplies on Hand, and increases the expense, Advertising Supplies Used, to reflect the situation on November 30

Nov. 30   Advertising Supplies Used 253
                    Advertising Supplies on Hand   253
               To record advertising supplies used.

The debit to Advertising Supplies Used establishes in the accounts the fact that a $253 expense has been incurred. The credit to Advertising Supplies on Hand reduces the asset from $386 to $133, the value of the asset at month-end.

Posting the adjusting entry to the ledger accounts would affect the accounts as shown in the following T-accounts:

The T-accounts reflect the transfer of $253 of used advertising supplies from the asset account to the expense account

Asset Advertising Supplies on Hand				Expense Advertising Supplies Used	
Nov. 1	386	Nov. 30	253	Nov. 30	253
Bal.	133				

Unearned Revenue

Unearned revenue is adjusted in much the same way we adjust prepaid expenses. The difference lies only in the accounts involved: Liability and revenue accounts are adjusted rather than asset and expense accounts.

To see what we mean, look at the account Unearned Advertising Revenue of $600 [designated line (e)] on the trial balance of the advertising agency (page 95). This represents a $600 payment made to the agency by a client in advance of the advertising services yet to be rendered. The payment was made on November 1 for 6 months of weekly advertising to be placed in local newspapers. As of November 1, Wilma Adams Advertising Agency has received an asset, Cash, for $600; and incurred an obligation, which accountants refer to as a liability, Unearned Advertising Revenue, to perform a service in the amount of $600 for the client. As the weeks go by and the ads are placed in the newspaper, the obligation is reduced and revenue is earned. Since financial statements are needed as of November 30, an adjusting entry is required on that date to properly reflect all revenue earned during the month and all liabilities owed at month-end. After all, $100 of the $600 paid by the client was indeed spent for the cost of newspaper ads during the month of November. Thus, the agency earned that $100 during November, leaving $500 in Unearned Revenue as of the end of the month. The appropriate adjusting entry reducing the liability Unearned Advertising Revenue by $100 ($600 ÷ 6 months) and recording the Advertising Revenue of $100 is illustrated as follows:

The advertising revenue adjusting entry reduces the liability, Unearned Advertising Revenue, and increases the revenue account, Advertising Revenue

Nov. 30   Unearned Advertising Revenue 100
    Advertising Revenue   100
    To record advertising revenue earned $100.

Posting the adjusting entry to the ledger accounts is illustrated in the following T-accounts:

These T-accounts show the transfer of $100 from the liability account to the revenue account

Liability			Revenue		
Unearned Advertising Revenue			**Advertising Revenue**		
					3,706
Nov. 30	100	Nov. 1 600	Nov. 30		100
		Bal. 500	Bal.		3,806

Depreciation

The cost of such noncurrent assets as buildings, equipment, and vehicles must be allocated as an expense over the periods of time these assets are expected to be used by the company owning them. This expense is called ***depreciation.***

Allocating the cost of buildings and equipment over their useful lives is called depreciation

To illustrate the adjustment necessary to reflect the expiration of fixed assets, refer again to the Wilma Adams Advertising Agency trial balance. Office equipment in the amount of $3,600 was acquired on November 1 [see line (d)]. The equipment is estimated to have a 10-year life, after which it will be considered worthless. Depreciation expense is determined by allocating the $3,600 over 10 years, or $360 per year. One month's depreciation would then be $30 ($360 ÷ 12), and the adjusting entry would be:

A depreciation adjusting entry reduces an asset by using the Accumulated Depreciation account

Nov. 30   Depreciation Expense 30
    Accumulated Depreciation: Office Equipment   30
    To record 1 month's depreciation.

The ledger accounts would reflect the following:

The recording of $30 depreciation expense is illustrated in these T-accounts

Asset			Expense		
Office Equipment			**Depreciation Expense**		
Nov. 1	3,600		Nov. 30	30	
Accumulated Depreciation:					
Office Equipment					
		Nov. 30 30			

A contra-asset account has a credit balance

Unlike the adjustments made for prepaid assets, when the depreciation adjusting entry is recorded the fixed asset is not directly reduced. Rather, the account ***Accumulated Depreciation*** is used. This account is a ***contra account,*** specifically a ***contra-asset account.*** By the term *contra account* we mean an account that has a balance opposite the normal balance. We would expect an asset account to have a debit balance, but a contra-asset account has a credit balance. Thus, a contra-asset account reduces assets—the Accumulated Depreciation account reduces the noncurrent asset accounts. A contra-liability account would have a debit balance.

The book value of a depreciable asset is the difference between its cost and its related accumulated depreciation

On the balance sheet both the Office Equipment account and the Accumulated Depreciation: Office Equipment account would appear. The difference between these two accounts ($3,570) is called the ***book value*** of the asset. It is the value that is recorded in the "firm's books," and it would appear on the balance sheet like this:

Office Equipment	$3,600
Less: Accumulated Depreciation.	30
	$3,570

The reason we use a contra-asset account is to preserve the original cost of the fixed asset. Users of the financial statements can then compare the depreciation recorded to date—that is, the accumulated depreciation—with the original cost found in the asset account. This comparison provides the user with information as to the relative age of the assets. For example, assume that a balance sheet were prepared 7 years from the date the Wilma Adams Advertising Agency started business. The Accumulated Depreciation account would have a balance of $2,520 ($3,600 $\times \frac{7}{10}$) and would appear on the October 31 balance sheet 7 years hence as follows:

Office Equipment	$3,600
Less: Accumulated Depreciation.	2,520
	$1,080

The book value of $1,080, when compared to the cost, would inform investors that the office equipment is nearing the end of its useful life and that the company may need to replace the asset in the near future.

By comparing the relationship of the book value or accumulated depreciation to the asset cost, we can determine roughly if the asset needs to be replaced in the near future

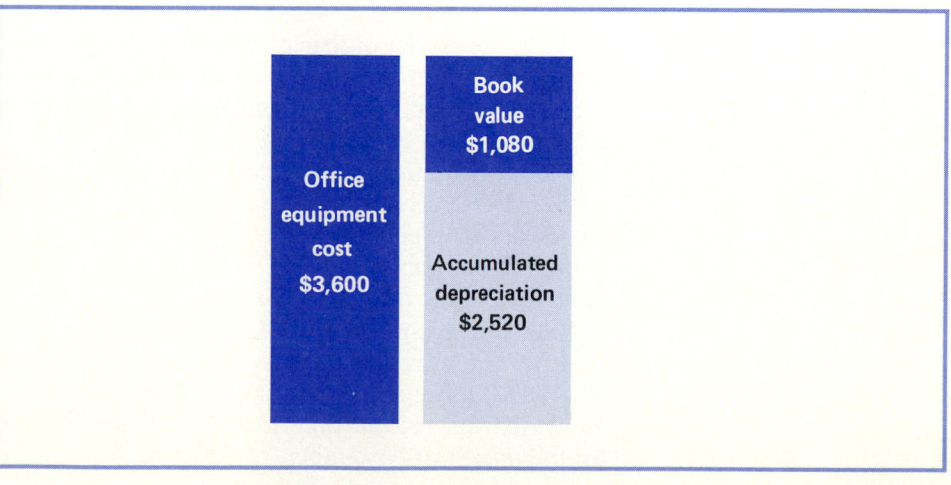

The general ledger account Accumulated Depreciation: Office Equipment would accumulate depreciation of $30 per month for 84 months (7 years × 12 months) as seen below:

Accumulated Depreciation: Office Equipment		
	Nov. 30, 1987	30
	Dec. 31, 1987	30
	Jan. 31, 1988	30
	Sep. 30, 1994	30
	Oct. 31, 1994	30
	Bal.	2,520

Accruals

Accrual adjusting entries record revenues earned and expenses incurred

Adjustments for revenue already earned and expenses already incurred but for which no transaction has been recorded are called ***accruals.*** We will consider two types of adjusting entries as examples of accruals: salaries and interest.

Salaries

Expenses are paid in one of three ways:

1. In advance of the benefits they provide, like the deferrals discussed earlier

2. During the accounting period when the benefits are received—for example, the telephone bill

3. After their benefits have already been received

Accrual adjusting entries are made at period-end

The most recognizable business expenses not paid for until after their benefits have been received are salaries and wages. No one is paid until his or her services have been provided—not the President of the United States, not the production line workers at General Motors, not your instructor, and not you.

Employees earn their salary or wages every hour of the day and every day of the week. However, for practical reasons, employees are paid after they have provided their services, periodically—weekly, biweekly, or monthly. When these payments are made before the end of the accounting period, the expense is recorded by a journal entry debiting Salaries Expense and crediting Cash. A problem occurs when the last day of the acounting period is not the day on which employees are paid—that is, when it is not a payday. In this case the employees have performed a service that represents an expense to the company. The company in turn has a liability to the employees for these services. The financial statements must reflect both the *expense incurred* and the *liability owed.* You can see that an adjusting entry is required.

Referring again to the Wilma Adams Advertising Agency, notice that Salary Expense amounts to $725 [designated line (g)] on the trial balance dated November 30, 1987. This represents the sum of two biweekly payments, one made on Friday, November 10, and one on Friday, November 24, as shown in the following calendar for the month of November.

NOVEMBER

	Working Days				Weekend	
Mon.	Tues.	Wed.	Thurs.	Fri.	Sat.	Sun.
		1	2	3	4	5
6	7	8	9	*PAYDAY $350*	11	12
13	14	15	16	17	18	19
20	21	22	23	*PAYDAY $375*	25	26
27	28	29	30	**DECEMBER 1**	**2**	**3**
4	**5**	**6**	**7**	*PAYDAY $400*	**9**	**10**

During the last week of November there are four additional workdays prior to the end of the month. The next scheduled payday is not until Friday, December 8. Assume that salaries accrue at a rate of $40 a day. Thus, $160 ($40 × 4 days) of additional Salary Expense must be recorded in the general journal on November 30 to properly reflect all the expenses incurred during the month of November. Further, the advertising agency has, as of November 30, a liability of $160 for unpaid salaries that must also be recorded. The adjusting entry to accrue the $160 would be recorded as follows:

Salaries adjusting entry increases an expense, Salary Expense, and records a liability, Salaries Payable

Nov. 30	Salary Expense 160	
	Salaries Payable	160
	To record accrual of salaries, $160.	

After the adjusting entry is recorded, Salary Expense will total $885, representing the proper expense for the month—salaries already paid, $725; plus salaries to be paid, $160. Salaries Payable will be $160, which is the liability as of November 30. The effect of the adjusting entry is illustrated in the T-accounts as follows:

These T-accounts reflect the recording of the accrued salaries adjusting entry

	Expense		Liability	
	Salary Expense		**Salaries Payable**	
Nov. 10	350		Nov. 30	160
Nov. 24	375			
Nov. 30	160			

Care must be taken when the December 8 payroll is recorded. If the entry is made in the usual manner—that is, a debit to Salary Expense and a credit to Cash—Salary Expense for December would be overstated by $160. Assuming that the December 8 payroll amounts to $400, the appropriate entry for the date would be recorded as follows:

IMPROPER ADJUSTING ENTRY

The Securities and Exchange Commission reported on April 5, 1984, that as a result of their investigation of Alpex Computer Corporation's financial statements for the year ended December 31, 1981, they found that the statements were materially false and misleading. Among other improprieties the SEC discovered that Alpex had improperly recorded as income $81,314 of accrued interest on worthless notes receivable. As a result of the improper recording of the item, Alpex's revenues were overstated by 40%; operating losses were understated by 85%; and net income was overstated by 13%.

Source: Securities and Exchange Commission, *Accounting and Auditing Enforcement Release No. 27,* April 5, 1984.

The purpose of the interest income accrual adjusting entry is to properly match revenue earned to the appropriate accounting period. Apparently Alpex Computer Corporation has used this simple adjusting entry to significantly increase revenues on its 1981 income statement.

```
Dec. 8   Salaries Payable . . . . . . . . . . . . . . . . . . . . . . . . . . . . . 160
         Salary Expense . . . . . . . . . . . . . . . . . . . . . . . . . . . . . . 240
             Cash. . . . . . . . . . . . . . . . . . . . . . . . . . . . . . . . . . .        400
         To record payment of salaries.
```

When the December 8 entry is made, Salaries Payable must be debited because that liability was paid. Salary Expense is debited for $240, representing the expense incurred for the 6 working days in December (6 days × $40). The November calendar should help you in understanding this entry. The $400 paid to employees on December 8 consists of $160 paid for work done in November and $240 for work done in December.

Interest

Like salaries, interest is earned day by day. However, accountants do not record it until after it is paid. Thus, if the accounting period ends before the interest is paid, an adjusting entry is required. This adjusting entry will record the amount of the interest income (or interest expense, in the case of borrowed funds) incurred during the period and the corresponding asset for the interest receivable (or liability for the interest payable).

To see how this works, consider the 12% note receivable due to the Wilma Adams Advertising Agency on April 30 [see line (a)]. The note was issued on November 1, 1987, and will be repaid 6 months later, on April 30, 1988. The interest income incurred on this note during the month of November is calculated according to the following formula:

Interest calculation

$$\text{Interest} = \textbf{principal} \times \textbf{rate} \times \textbf{time}$$
$$= \$1,500 \times 12\% \text{ per year} \times \tfrac{1}{12} \text{ year}$$
$$= \$1,500 \times \frac{.12}{\text{year}} \times \frac{1 \text{ year}}{12}$$
$$= \$15$$

The adjusting entry to record the interest income incurred in November is presented below:

Interest income adjusting entry

```
Nov. 30   Interest Receivable . . . . . . . . . . . . . . . . . . . . . . . . . . . . 15
              Interest Income . . . . . . . . . . . . . . . . . . . . . . . . . . . .        15
          To record interest income for the month of November.
```

If Wilma Adams had issued a 12% note payable rather than the note receivable, the adjusting entry would be as follows:

Interest expense adjusting entry

Nov. 30	Interest Expense. 15	
	Interest Payable	15
	To record interest expense for the month of November.	

THE ADJUSTED TRIAL BALANCE

The adjusted trial balance is prepared after the adjusting entries are made

After the adjusting entries are recorded and posted, a second trial balance is prepared. We call this second trial balance the ***adjusted trial balance.*** The first trial balance is called the ***unadjusted trial balance.*** Both trial balances of the Wilma Adams Advertising Agency are presented below. Notice that the adjustments are inserted between the two trial balances to show how the unadjusted trial balance was "adjusted" in determining the adjusted trial balance.

THE WILMA ADAMS ADVERTISING AGENCY

	Unadjusted Trial Balance November 30, 1987		Adjustments	Adjusted Trial Balance November 30, 1987	
Cash.	$ 244			$ 244	
Note Receivable, 12% due Apr. 30	1,500			1,500	
Interest Receivable.			+ 15(a)	15	
Accounts Receivable	1,251			1,251	
Advertising Supplies on Hand	386		− 253(b)	133	
Prepaid Rent	450		− 150(c)	300	
Office Equipment	3,600			3,600	
Accumulated Depreciation: Office Equipment			+ 30(d)		$ 30
Accounts Payable		$ 572			572
Salaries Payable.			+ 160(g)		160
Unearned Advertising Revenue		600	− 100(e)		500
Wilma Adams, Capital		3,500			3,500
Wilma Adams, Withdrawals	150			150	
Advertising Revenue		3,706	+ 100(e)		3,806
Interest Income.			+ 15(a)		15
Salary Expense	725		+ 160(g)	885	
Rent Expense			+ 150(c)	150	
Advertising Supplies Used			+ 253(b)	253	
Depreciation Expense.			+ 30(d)	30	
Utilities Expense.	47			47	
Miscellaneous Expense	25			25	
Totals	$8,378	$8,378		$8,583	$8,583

The financial statements are prepared directly from the adjusted trial balance. We prepare the income statement first because the net income figure is needed when we prepare the statement of owner's equity. The statement of owner's equity then provides the ending capital balance, which we need for the balance sheet. The income statement is relatively easy to prepare once the adjusted trial balance is prepared, as can be seen from the illustration on page 104.

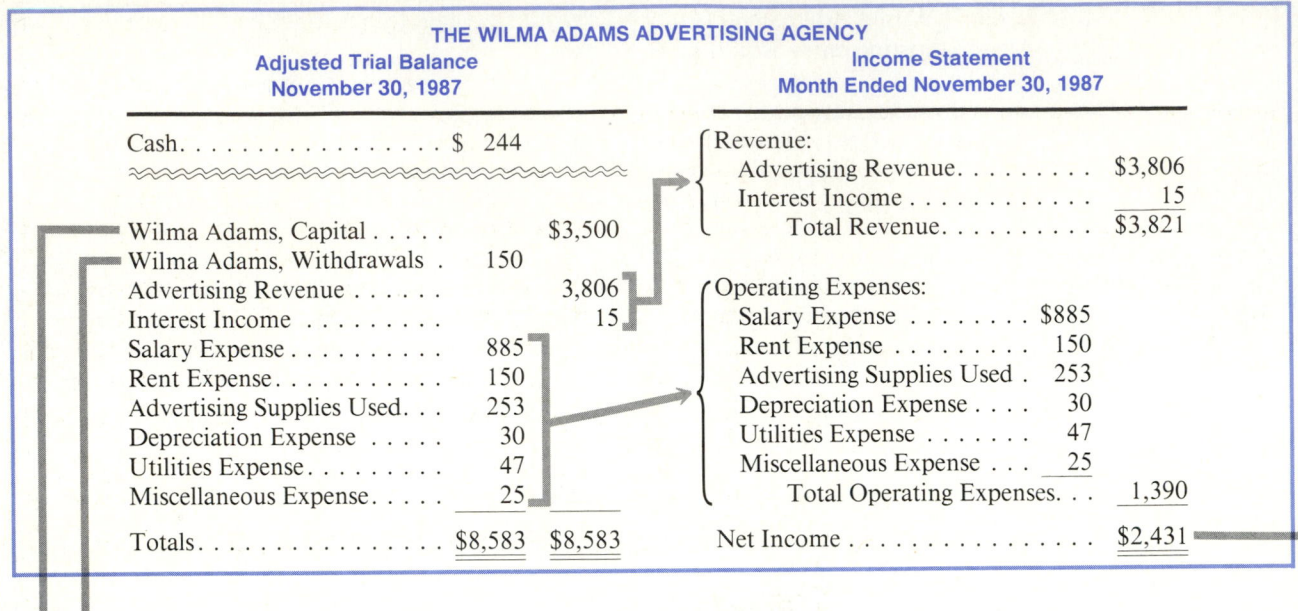

THE WILMA ADAMS ADVERTISING AGENCY

Adjusted Trial Balance November 30, 1987			Income Statement Month Ended November 30, 1987	
Cash	$ 244		Revenue:	
			Advertising Revenue	$3,806
			Interest Income	15
Wilma Adams, Capital		$3,500	Total Revenue	$3,821
Wilma Adams, Withdrawals	150			
Advertising Revenue		3,806	Operating Expenses:	
Interest Income		15	Salary Expense	$885
Salary Expense	885		Rent Expense	150
Rent Expense	150		Advertising Supplies Used	253
Advertising Supplies Used	253		Depreciation Expense	30
Depreciation Expense	30		Utilities Expense	47
Utilities Expense	47		Miscellaneous Expense	25
Miscellaneous Expense	25		Total Operating Expenses	1,390
Totals	$8,583	$8,583	Net Income	$2,431

On the statement of owner's equity we simply add the net income of $2,431 to the beginning balance in the Capital account, and subtract the withdrawals of $150 [line (f), unadjusted trial balance] to arrive at the ending capital balance. There were no additional capital investments during November by the Wilma Adams Advertising Agency. The statement of owner's equity would appear as follows:

THE WILMA ADAMS ADVERTISING AGENCY
Statement of Owner's Equity
Month Ended November 30, 1987

Wilma Adams, Capital, Nov. 1, 1987		$3,500
Net Income	$2,431	
Less: Withdrawals	150	2,281
Wilma Adams, Capital, Nov. 30. 1987		$5,781

Rather than preparing a separate statement of owner's equity, this information may be presented in the owner's equity section of the balance sheet, as we have illustrated in the balance sheet prepared for the Wilma Adams Advertising Agency.

Finally, the balance sheet is prepared using again the adjusted trial balance, as illustrated on page 105.

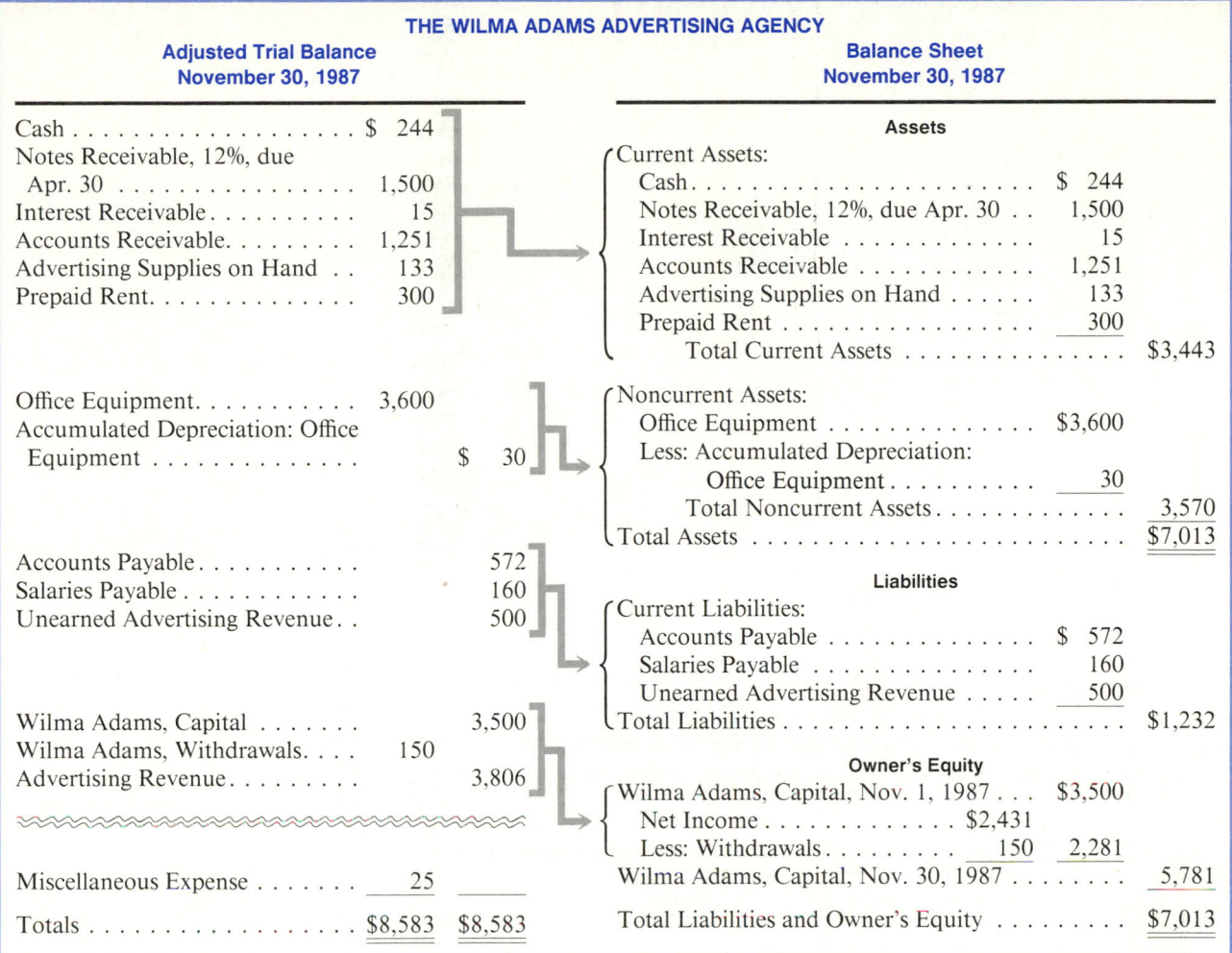

THE WILMA ADAMS ADVERTISING AGENCY

Adjusted Trial Balance
November 30, 1987

Cash	$ 244	
Notes Receivable, 12%, due Apr. 30	1,500	
Interest Receivable.	15	
Accounts Receivable.	1,251	
Advertising Supplies on Hand . .	133	
Prepaid Rent.	300	
Office Equipment.	3,600	
Accumulated Depreciation: Office Equipment		$ 30
Accounts Payable.		572
Salaries Payable		160
Unearned Advertising Revenue. .		500
Wilma Adams, Capital		3,500
Wilma Adams, Withdrawals. . . .	150	
Advertising Revenue.		3,806
Miscellaneous Expense	25	
Totals	$8,583	$8,583

Balance Sheet
November 30, 1987

Assets

Current Assets:		
Cash.	$ 244	
Notes Receivable, 12%, due Apr. 30 . .	1,500	
Interest Receivable	15	
Accounts Receivable	1,251	
Advertising Supplies on Hand	133	
Prepaid Rent	300	
Total Current Assets		$3,443
Noncurrent Assets:		
Office Equipment	$3,600	
Less: Accumulated Depreciation: Office Equipment	30	
Total Noncurrent Assets.		3,570
Total Assets		$7,013

Liabilities

Current Liabilities:		
Accounts Payable	$ 572	
Salaries Payable	160	
Unearned Advertising Revenue	500	
Total Liabilities		$1,232

Owner's Equity

Wilma Adams, Capital, Nov. 1, 1987 . . .	$3,500	
Net Income $2,431		
Less: Withdrawals. 150	2,281	
Wilma Adams, Capital, Nov. 30, 1987		5,781
Total Liabilities and Owner's Equity		$7,013

THE ACCOUNTING PROCESS REVIEWED

Financial statements are the ultimate objective of accounting

The ultimate objective of financial accounting is to prepare financial statements that represent meaningfully and fairly the results of operations of a business entity over a period of time and its financial position at a point in time. The process we have described in this chapter and the preceding chapter is a practical means of achieving that objective. The steps involved in the financial accounting process are shown in Figure 3-3.

FORM AND CONTENT OF FINANCIAL STATEMENTS

Classified financial statements are very useful

Financial statements become more useful when their basic elements — the individual asset accounts, liability accounts, revenue accounts, and expense accounts — are grouped meaningfully. Until now, we have presented only simple financial statements containing relatively few items. With so few items we did not need to present *classified financial statements* — *financial statements with like accounts grouped together.* People who use financial statements find the classification of the assets and liabilities into common groupings very helpful when analyzing and comparing financial statements for lending and investment decisions.

Users of financial statements can readily determine the profitability and solvency

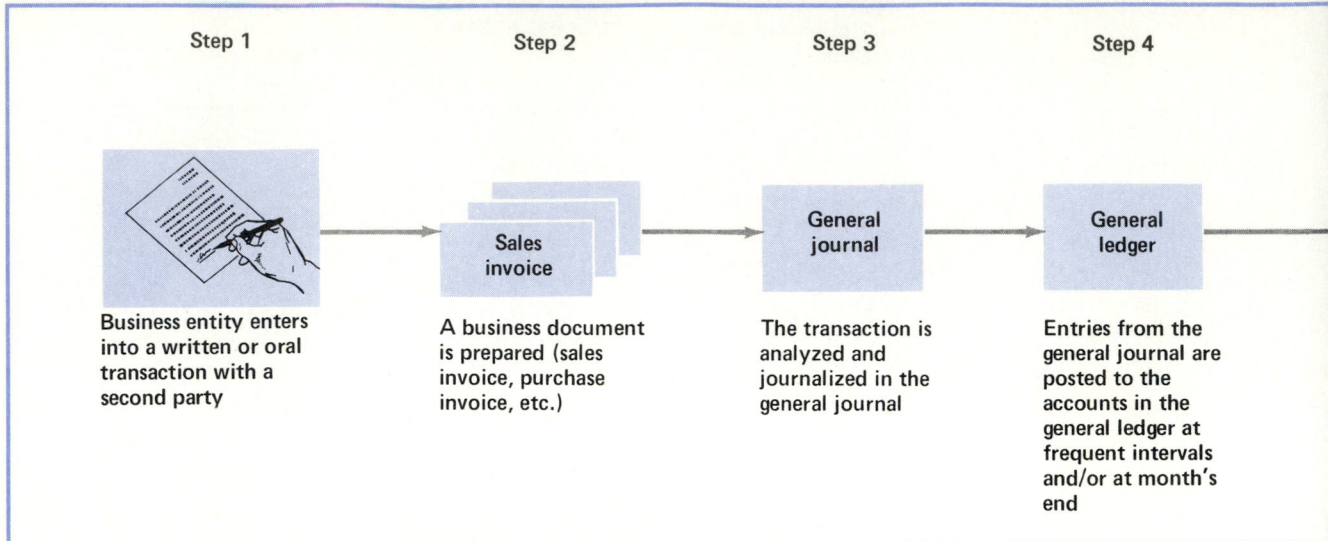

Step 1	Step 2	Step 3	Step 4

Business entity enters into a written or oral transaction with a second party

A business document is prepared (sales invoice, purchase invoice, etc.)

The transaction is analyzed and journalized in the general journal

Entries from the general journal are posted to the accounts in the general ledger at frequent intervals and/or at month's end

FIGURE 3-3   The accounting process.

of a business entity by studying the relationship between significant asset and liability groupings on the balance sheet as well as the relationships between revenue and expense groupings on the income statement. These useful groupings enable the user to compare financial statements of different companies. Can you appreciate the difficulty statement users would have if each company were to use its own system of classification?

The form and content of financial statements evolved over time and continues to evolve in response to changing business practices. What was acceptable presentation in the early 1960s may not be acceptable today. Within the broad framework of financial statement classification, individual business entities will attempt to give a clear, meaningful, and fair presentation of their results of operations and financial position.

The Balance Sheet

Typically, assets on the balance sheet are classified into five major groupings: (1) current assets, (2) investments, (3) property, plant, and equipment, (4) intangibles, and (5) other assets.

Liabilities generally are classified into two groups: (1) current liabilities and (2) long-term liabilities. The classification of the components of owner's equity is dependent on the form of business organization. In the first four chapters of this text the proprietorship is the form used. The owner's equity section of a proprietorship consists of the Capital and Withdrawals accounts.

The balance sheet of the Hillsborough Retail Store, presented on page 108, illustrates these classifications, each of which is discussed in the following sections.

Assets

The operating cycle consists of three phases

Current Assets   Current assets are assets that are *expected to be converted into cash within a year or the normal operation cycle, whichever is longer.* The ***operating cycle*** is the average length of time between the purchase of merchandise inventory and the realization of cash from the sale of the merchandise inventory. It consists of three phases:

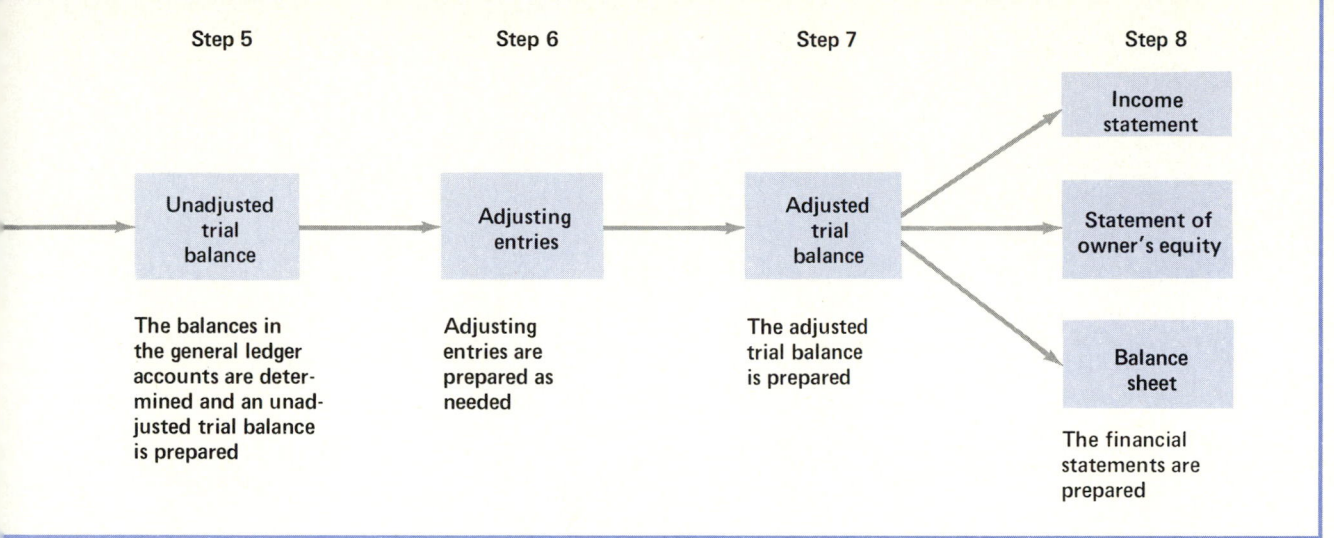

1. The purchase of merchandise inventory
2. The sale of the merchandise inventory on account
3. The collection of cash from the accounts receivable

FIGURE 3-4
The operating cycle.

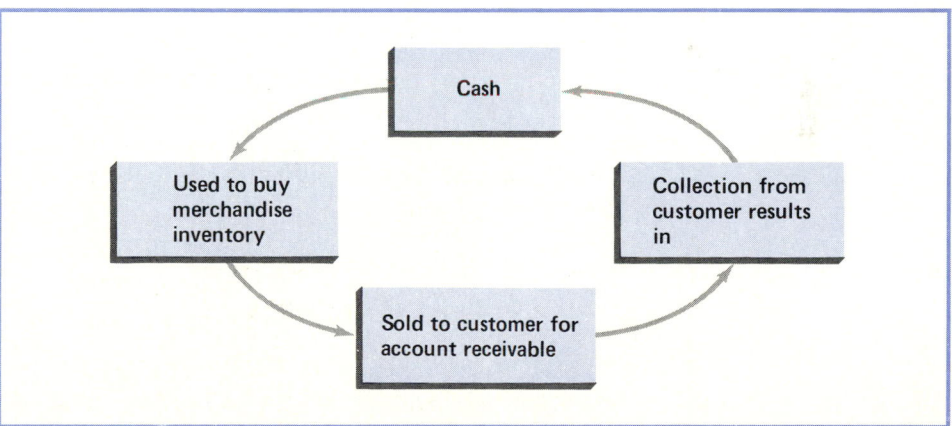

For some entities, such as a grocery store, this period of time — the operating cycle — is only a few weeks. For others, it may extend over a number of years — examples are the distillery industry (it takes years for some liquors to mature into their flavors) and the lumber industry (there are many years between seedling and timber). Most businesses find, however, that their operating cycles are several months in duration, and if not, then commonly less than a year.

Current assets include Cash, Marketable Securities, Notes Receivable, Accounts Receivable, Merchandise Inventory, and Prepaid Expenses. These assets will be converted into cash during the operating cycle.

HILLSBOROUGH RETAIL STORE
Balance Sheet
December 31, 1987

Assets

A classified balance lists the current asset accounts first

Current Assets:

Cash	$ 2,356	
Marketable Securities	6,200	
Notes Receivable	1,500	
Accounts Receivable	8,217	
Merchandise Inventory	29,114	
Prepaid Expenses	1,623	
Total Current Assets		$ 49,010

Investments:

Bonds	$ 3,500	
Stocks	7,250	
Total Investments		10,750

Property, Plant, and Equipment:

Land			$10,700
Buildings	$60,250		
These are contra-asset accounts
Less: Accumulated Depreciation	13,175	47,075	
Equipment	$42,500		
Less: Accumulated Depreciation	10,600	31,900	
Total Property, Plant, and Equipment			89,675

Intangibles:

Goodwill	$ 2,500	
Patents	1,525	
Total Intangibles		4,025
Total Assets		$153,460

Liabilities

Liabilities are classified as either current or long term

Current Liabilities:

Notes Payable	$ 7,000	
Accounts Payable	13,426	
Salaries Payable	2,137	
Federal Income Taxes Payable	4,281	
Unearned Revenue	3,148	
Total Current Liabilities		$29,992

Long-Term Liabilities:

Mortgage Payable $7\frac{1}{4}$%	$45,170	
Bonds Payable, $8\frac{3}{8}$%, due May 1, 1996	20,000	
Total Long-Term Liabilities		65,170
Total Liabilities		$ 95,162

Owner's Equity

The owner's equity section

Jane Hillsborough, Capital, Jan. 1, 1987		$20,425
Net Income for the Year	$61,873	
Less: Withdrawals	24,000	37,873
Jane Hillsborough, Capital, Dec. 31, 1987		58,298
Total Liabilities and Owners' Equity		$153,460

Current assets are listed on the balance sheet in order of their *liquidity.* By the term liquidity we mean the nearness to cash. The most liquid asset is *Cash.* As assets move through the operating cycle from Merchandise Inventory to Accounts Receivable to Cash they become more liquid.

Marketable Securities are classified as current assets because management intends to dispose of them within the year. U.S. Treasury bills, certificates of deposit, and common stocks of other business entities are typical examples. Companies will invest in marketable securities because they have excess cash available for short periods of time — 30, 60, or 90 days. These financial instruments will provide the company with a rate of return that is not available when cash is held in checking accounts.

Notes Receivable expected to be collected within the year are current assets. Notes receivable commonly originate when a customer cannot pay his or her account receivable when it becomes due. The note, which bears interest, is a more formal agreement than the account receivable. It is a written promise to pay a certain amount on some certain future date.

Merchandise Inventory is the product or products acquired by companies from various suppliers that the companies plan to resell to their customers.

Prepaid Expenses consist of Prepaid Rent, Prepaid Insurance, and Supplies on Hand. These items are not typically shown separately but are included in total under the caption Prepaid Expenses since, even in total, they are not generally large in amount. Prepaid Expenses represent current assets because if they were not already owned the business entity would be required to expend current assets to obtain them. They will be consumed during the operating cycle and become expenses.

Investments   Investments are distinguished from marketable securities in that management does not intend to convert investments into cash within the year. Bonds, stocks, and real estate are typical assets classified under the Investment caption.

Property, Plant, and Equipment   Tangible, long-lived assets that are used in the production or sale of inventory or in the providing of services are classified as plant and equipment. Land, Buildings, and Equipment, are the most common plant and equipment accounts. Land does not wear out; consequently, no depreciation is recorded for land.

Buildings and equipment, on the other hand, do wear out, having limited lives, and their cost must be allocated over the period of time they provide usefulness. This, as you already know, is called *depreciation. Accumulated Depreciation* (a contra asset) is reflected under the plant and equipment classification as a subtraction from the related Building or Equipment account.

Intangibles   Intangible assets represent legal rights or certain economic relationships that provide their owners with future economic benefits. Goodwill, patents, franchises, and copyrights are common examples. Intangible assets do not have physical substance.

Other Assets   Occasionally, a business entity will have an asset that cannot be classified within one of the other four classifications. In this situation the classification *other assets* is used.

Liabilities

Current Liabilities   Obligations that require the use of current assets for their payment are classified as current liabilities. Thus, they represent liabilities that will be paid within an operating cycle or a year, whichever is longer. Common current liabilities are Notes Payable, Accounts Payable, Salaries Payable, and Taxes Payable.

Unearned Revenue is advance payments received from customers. These payments represent an obligation to provide future goods or services and are consequently also classified as current liabilities. They may be listed as Advances from Customers, Unearned Revenue (as in the Hillsborough Retail Store illustration), or Prepaid Income. Rent received by property owners in advance and payments received by publishers for magazine subscriptions are two examples of unearned revenue.

Long-Term Liabilities   Simply stated, liabilities that are not current liabilities are long-term liabilities. They represent obligations that will be paid in the future, later than 1 year after the date on the balance sheet. Mortgages Payable and Bonds Payable are the two most common examples.

Owner's Equity

Owner's equity represents the owner's interest in the business entity. The classification of this section is dependent on whether the business is organized as a proprietorship, a partnership, or a corporation. For a proprietorship or a partnership, owners' equity will consist of the Beginning Capital account (a separate capital account is maintained for each partner in a partnership), plus additional investments made during the year, minus withdrawals during the year, resulting in the Ending Capital account. This is, of course, a summary of the activity in the Capital account (or accounts).

Rather than presenting this information on the balance sheet, a statement of owners' equity may be prepared. In this case only the ending capital will be listed on the balance sheet.

While a separate Capital account is maintained for each partner in a partnership, only one account will typically appear on the balance sheet. This account is called *partners' capital.*

The owners' equity section of a corporation's financial statements will have at least three accounts: Capital Stock, Paid-In Capital, and Retained Earnings. These accounts will be discussed in later chapters; hence you need not be concerned about them at this point.

The Income Statement

A classified income statement for the Hillsborough Retail store appears at the top of page 111.

Three major classifications are found on the Hillsborough Retail Store income statement: (1) sales, (2) cost of merchandise sold, and (3) operating expenses. Operating expenses consist of selling expenses and general and administrative expenses.

The sales and cost of merchandise sold sections will be discussed in detail in Chapter 5.

The operating expenses deal with selling expenses and general administrative expenses. If an expense is related to the selling effort, it is classified as a selling expense. If not, it is a general and administrative expense.

CASH VERSUS ACCRUAL ACCOUNTING

At this point you must be made aware of the distinction between accounting on a cash basis and accounting using an accrual basis. The income statement of the Hillsborough Retail Store is prepared under the accrual basis, as are all income statements prepared in accordance with generally accepted accounting principles.

In *cash-basis* accounting, a revenue is reported on the income statement only if that revenue was in fact received in the form of cash. The same goes for expenses on the income statement; an expense is reported only if it was indeed disbursed in cash.

HILLSBOROUGH RETAIL STORE
Income Statement
For the Year Ended December 31, 1987

Sales			$429,480
Cost of Merchandise Sold			253,170
Gross Profit on Sales			$176,310
Operating Expenses:			
Selling Expenses:			
Sales Commissions		$26,321	
Sales Salaries		9,407	
Advertising Expense		3,500	
Insurance Expense		1,250	
Depreciation Expense		1,600	
Total Selling Expenses		$ 42,078	
General and Administrative Expenses:			
Executive Salaries		$52,900	
Clerical Salaries		11,250	
Insurance Expense		450	
Office Supplies Expense		926	
Taxes Expense		4,083	
Depreciation Expense		2,750	
Total General and Administrative Expense		72,359	
Total Operating Expenses			114,437
Net income			$ 61,873

Thus, net income under the cash basis would simply represent the difference between cash receipts and cash disbursements. If the cash basis of accounting were used, none of the adjustments discussed in this chapter would be necessary.

The accounting profession has determined that financial statements prepared under *the cash basis of accounting* do not *fairly represent the results of operations or the financial position of a business entity.* A company using the cash basis could easily increase its net income by encouraging its customers to pay their bills early. Net income could also be significantly increased if the company delayed payment of its own bills. This is referred to as ***profit manipulation.*** The cash basis of accounting is therefore not part of generally accepted accounting principles.

Cash-basis accounting is subject to profit manipulation

Generally accepted accounting principles require that financial statements be prepared under the ***accrual basis*** of accounting. The accrual basis is based on two concepts: the revenue-recognition principle and the matching concept.

According to the ***revenue-recognition principle,*** revenue is reported in the financial statements *in the accounting period in which it is earned, not in the accounting period when the cash representing that revenue is received.* For example, a department store sells a shirt to a credit account customer on December 28. The revenue representing the sale of that shirt is recognized on that date — not when the customer pays for the shirt, which may be sometime later in January or February.

According to the ***matching concept,*** all expenses associated with the generation of revenue must be matched against that revenue in the same period that the revenue was earned. The sale of the shirt in the example above would require that the cost of the shirt, the salaries of the sales people, the depreciation on the display counter, and all the other expenses associated with the sale of the shirt must be expensed when the shirt is sold, whether those expenses were paid for or not.

The following example will help explain the difference between the cash basis and the accrual basis of accounting, as well as clarify what we mean by the revenue-recognition principle and the matching concept.

Assume that the Brown Company entered into a contract on January 18, 1987, with the Green Company to supply Green with a machine for an agreed price of $1,000.

On February 21, 1987, Brown purchases the machine from a wholesaler for $800 on account.

Brown delivers the machine to Green on March 16, 1987, payment to Brown to be made on account.

Green pays Brown $1,000 on April 30, 1987.

Brown pays the wholesaler $800 on May 15, 1987.

Brown's transactions are summarized in Figure 3-5.

FIGURE 3-5
A summary of Brown's transactions.

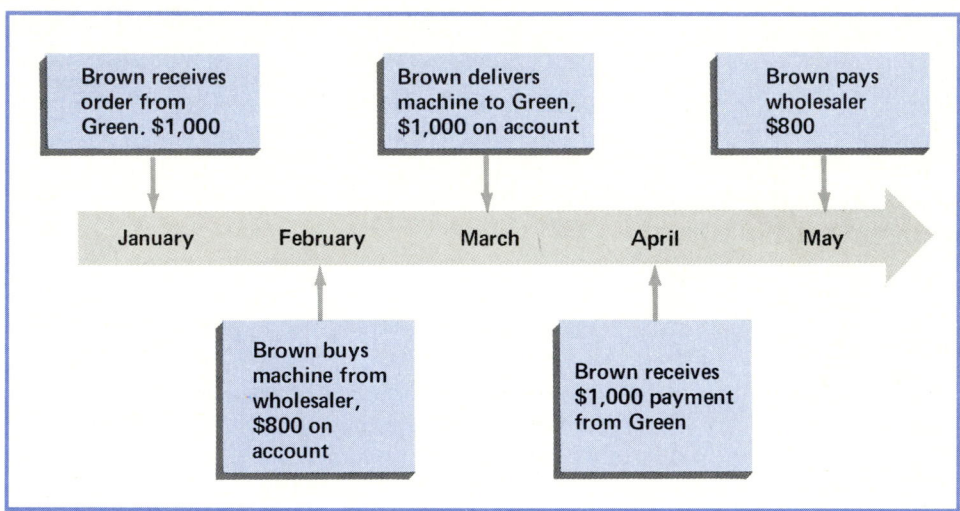

Under the cash basis of accounting, Brown's net income for each of the 5 months would be determined as follows:

Cash basis

	January	February	March	April	May
Revenue	$ 0	$ 0	$ 0	$1,000	$ 0
Expenses	0	0	0	0	800
Net Income	$ 0	$ 0	$ 0	$1,000	$(800)

The accrual basis of accounting would report net income for each of the 5 months according to the following table:

Accrual basis

	January	February	March	April	May
Revenue	$ 0	$ 0	$1,000	$ 0	$ 0
Expenses	0	0	(800)	0	0
Net Income	$ 0	$ 0	$ 200	$ 0	$ 0

It is the accrual basis that best provides the statement user with information concerning future cash flows and that consequently represents fairly the results of operations. In January an *agreement to sell* a machine was made between Brown and Green. This agreement does not constitute a sale, since performance has not been made by either party. Brown must provide the machine and Green must accept it before a sale is effected.

The purchase of the machine by Brown for $800 in February represents the acquisition of an asset, Merchandise Inventory. At this point it is not an expense since it has not yet been delivered to Green.

Income is earned in March because:

1. Revenue is recognized by the delivery of the machine—a sale is made; and

2. An expense is incurred, the machine is sold, and it becomes an expense on the income statement—Cost of Merchandise Sold—to be matched against the sale made this period.

The collection of the $1,000 account receivable in April represents the increase in one asset, Cash, and the reduction of a second, Accounts Receivable.

The payment of $800 in May represents the reduction of Cash and the reduction of a current liability.

Under the cash basis, revenue of $1,000 is not recognized until actually received in April, and expenses of $800 are not recorded until actually paid in May. Clearly, the evidence exists in March that can provide the basis for reporting the economic substance of the transaction to those interested in such information. A legal sale has in fact been made. The subsequent receipt from the sale and payment to the wholesaler follow as a normal consequence that *can be predicted at the point of sale.*

Profit manipulation is difficult under the accrual basis, where there are established criteria for recognizing both revenue and expenses. These criteria specify the time when revenue and expenses are to be recognized; it cannot be manipulated.

CHAPTER SUMMARY

Creditors, potential owners, and other parties outside a business entity are, of course, concerned about its financial resources, its obligations, and the results of its activities. These parties do not have direct access to the accounting records of the entity. Nevertheless, they need to be informed in a timely and regular manner of the economic activity of the business entity.

The life of a business entity is divided into time frames—months, quarters, and years—called *accounting periods.* Accountants prepare financial statements at the end of each time frame—that is, at the end of each month, each quarter, and each year.

The *balance sheet* reports the status as of the close of business on the *last day of a time frame;* the *income statement* reports the activity *during the period of time covered by the time frame.*

A business entity needs and buys assets such as buildings and equipment that are used during many years, covering many accounting periods. Only after an asset was no longer useful would a business entity know exactly how long it served and how to allocate its cost precisely over each of the accounting periods during its useful life. But it is highly impractical to wait for the end of an asset's useful life to account precisely for its cost during each accounting period. The practical solution is to estimate how long it will be useful, and to allocate its total cost over each of the accounting periods of its life — a process called *depreciation,* resulting in an expense called *Depreciation Expense.* Because the calculation of Depreciation Expense depends on an estimate, it is only an approximation of the actual expense. And because Depreciation Expense is not precise, neither is the net income calculated and reported during an accounting period.

During an accounting period a business entity makes exchanges with second parties (buyers, sellers, lenders). These exchanges are called *external transactions.* The economic result of an external transaction is recorded during the accounting period in which it was made even though the actual result may not occur until a later period. That is, the accounts debited or credited by some external transactions may not reflect the actual situation at the end of the accounting period. For example, some assets acquired during a period may have been consumed before the end of that period; interest income may have been earned but not yet received on money loaned; or salary expense may have been incurred for salaries earned by employees but not yet paid. Nevertheless, the financial statements prepared at the end of the accounting period must reflect the following:

1. All assets owned   **3.** All revenue earned
2. All liabilities owed   **4.** All expenses incurred

To meet this objective, certain amounts must be increased or decreased by means of adjusting entries in the general journal — an *internal transaction* — as of the last day of the accounting period.

There are two basic types of adjusting entries: *deferrals,* which require adjustment because the goods and/or services already paid for in full may not have been completely consumed at period-end; and *accruals,* which represent revenue earned and expenses incurred for which no transaction has been recorded during the period.

Prepaid Expenses, Unearned Revenue, and Depreciation are examples of deferrals.

At the moment an asset is acquired, it is represented as a *prepaid expense* — an unexpired cost. A Prepaid Expense becomes an expired cost — representing an expense — as the asset is consumed over time.

Similarly, when *Unearned Revenue* is received, it is represented as a liability. As services are performed or goods are delivered in fulfillment of the Unearned Revenue, the liability is reduced and revenue is represented as earned.

The expenses for buildings and equipment are similar to Prepaid Expenses. Over time, as they are used, they become expired costs — represented as *Depreciation Expenses.* But, unlike Prepaid Expenses, the Building and Equipment accounts are not reduced directly as the expense is recorded. Rather, a *contra-asset* account called *Accumulated Depreciation* is increased. The use of the contra-asset account maintains the Building or Equipment account at its original cost, which provides useful information to statement users.

Salary Expense, Interest Expense, Interest Revenue, and the counterparts of these items — Salaries Payable, Interest Payable, and Interest Receivable — are examples of accruals. These accounts are accrued over time although payment is made or received on specific dates. When the financial statements are prepared on dates other than the date of a payment or a receipt, the accruals must be measured and recorded by adjusting entries to present fairly the results of operations and the financial position.

After all the adjusting entries are, first, recorded in the general journal and, next, posted to each of the appropriate general ledger accounts, then an *adjusted trial balance* can be prepared. The adjusted trial balance is used to prepare the financial statements.

If each of these types of accounts—asset accounts, liability accounts, revenue accounts, and expense accounts—is grouped in some meaningful way, they will provide the basis for easily preparing useful financial statements. Such financial statements are referred to as *classified financial statements.*

The balance sheet is classified into the following groupings:

1. Five major asset groupings:
   a. Current assets
   b. Long-term investments
   c. Property, plant, and equipment
   d. Intangibles
   e. Other assets
2. Two major liability groupings
   a. Current liabilities
   b. Long-term liabilities
3. Owners' equity accounts

The income statement classifications consist of the following:

1. Revenue
2. Cost of merchandise sold
3. Operating expenses
   a. Selling expenses
   b. General and administrative expenses

Generally accepted accounting principles require that financial statements be prepared using the *accrual basis of accounting* rather than the *cash basis.* The underlying concept of the accrual basis of accounting is the *revenue-recognition principle:* Revenue must be reflected on the financial statements in the accounting period in which it is earned. Furthermore, expenses must be also reflected on the financial statements in the accounting period in which they are incurred, and they must be matched against revenue earned. This is called the *matching concept.*

IMPORTANT TERMS USED IN THIS CHAPTER

Accounting period   The length of time for which financial activities are reported on the income statement. An accounting period is typically 1 year. However, income statements are also prepared quarterly, thus covering accounting periods of 3 months' duration. (page 92)

Accrual-basis accounting   The generally accepted accounting principle requiring that revenue be recorded when earned and that expenses be recorded when incurred. (page 110)

Accruals   Expenses that are incurred and whose benefits have been consumed, but that have not yet been paid for; also revenue that is earned and whose benefits have been received but for which payment has not been received. (page 95)

Accumulated Depreciation   A balance sheet account that is shown as a deduction from the related Building or Equipment account. It is a contra asset and accumulates the depreciation taken on the asset over its useful life. (page 98)

Adjusted trial balance   A trial balance prepared after all adjusting entries have been made. (page 103)

Adjusting entries   The entries made at the end of an accounting period to reflect internal changes during the period in all expenses and liabilities incurred, revenue earned, and assets owned. (page 94)

Book value   The difference between the amount shown in a specific fixed asset account and its accumulated depreciation. (page 99)

Cash-basis accounting   The accounting system that records revenue only upon the receipt of cash and records expenses only upon payment. It is not a generally accepted accounting principle. (page 110)

Contra account   An account with a balance opposite the normal balance. A contra-asset account, for example, has a credit balance, whereas an asset account has a debit balance. (page 99)

Current assets   Assets that are expected to be converted into cash within a year or within the normal operating cycle, whichever is longer. (page 106)

Current liabilities   Obligations requiring the use of current assets for their liquidation or payment. (page 109)

Depreciation   The cost of a fixed asset (other than land) that is allocated over the period of time for which benefits are received from the fixed asset. (page 98)

Expired cost   An expense representing the amount of an asset that is considered to have been used up over a period of time. (page 95)

External transactions   Exchange transactions between the business entity and parties outside the entity. (page 94)

Intangibles   Legal rights or certain economic relationships that provide their owners with future economic benefits. (page 109)

Internal transactions   Adjusting entries made by a business entity to reflect more accurately the status of the accounts at the end of a period. (page 94)

Long-term investments   Bonds, stocks, and real estate that a business entity owns and does not intend to sell for cash within the year. (page 109)

Long-term liabilities   Obligations that will be paid at some future time beyond 1 year from the balance sheet date. (page 110)

Matching concept   The generally accepted accounting principle that requires that expenses incurred for providing a product or service during an accounting period be matched against revenue earned by that product or service during the same accounting period. (page 111)

Operating cycle   The time between the purchase of merchandise inventory and the realization of cash from the sale of that merchandise inventory. (page 106)

Prepaid expenses   Expenses that are paid for before they are used; consequently they are classified as current assets. (page 95)

Revenue-recognition principle   The generally accepted accounting principle requiring that revenue be reflected on the income statement in the period in which it is earned. (page 111)

Time-period principle   The generally accepted accounting principle that requires that the economic life of a business entity be divided into time frames called *accounting* periods and that financial statements be prepared at the end of these time frames. (page 92)

Unearned revenue   The liability incurred for cash received in advance of goods or services rendered. (page 97)

Unexpired cost   That part of the cost of an asset representing the economic benefit it has not yet provided or its services not yet consumed. (page 95)

QUESTIONS

1. There are two types of business transactions, *external* transactions and *internal* transactions. How do they differ?

2. At the end of an accounting period, certain accounts are adjusted. Why?

3. What is the meaning of the term *unexpired cost? Expired cost?*

4. Explain the difference between *deferrals* and *accruals* as classifications of adjusting entries.

5. "The net income of a business entity is determined by measuring the amount of revenue generated and subtracting the expenses incurred, appropriately measured. As a consequence the resulting difference, net income, is a precise measure of operating performance for the period under consideration." Comment.

6. What is the nature of the account Accumulated Depreciation?

7. If a company fails to accrue salaries at the end of a month, what will be the effect of this omission on the financial statements?

8. Give examples of three unexpired costs and three related expired costs.

9. If rent is paid monthly in advance on the first day of each month, there is an advantage in debiting rent expense when payment is made. Explain this advantage.

10. Consider a new account that has not been discussed in the chapter, called *Prepaid Income.* What is the nature of this account, and how should it be classified?

11. Explain the difference between *marketable securities* and *investments.*

12. Why are *classified financial statements* prepared?

13. What are current assets? What are *current liabilities?*

14. What is an *operating cycle?*

15. The cash basis of accounting is not considered to be a generally accepted accounting principle. Explain why not.

16. What is the *matching concept?*

17. Explain the *revenue-recognition principle.*

18. What are the steps involved in the accounting process?

EXERCISES

Exercise 3-1
Adjusting salaries

The employees at Whitehall Company are paid on alternate Fridays, the last payday being February 17, 1987. Whitehall employs seven individuals who earn $8.00 per hour each. All seven work 8 hours per day, 5 days per week.

Prepare the adjusting entry needed on Tuesday, February 28, to record the accrual of salaries for the month. Prepare the entry on Friday, March 3, to record the payment of the salaries.

Exercise 3-2
Analyzing accounts:
Determining the missing item

This exercise is designed to test your ability to analyze an account. For each of the four independent cases listed below, determine the amount indicated.

a. Supplies in the amount of $4,700 were acquired during the year. Supplies on hand at the beginning of the year amounted to $1,350, whereas the ending balance was $2,170. What was the amount of supplies used during the year?

b. The supplies on hand at the end of the year were $950. Supplies acquired during the year amounted to $6,600, and supplies used were $7,040. What was the amount of supplies on hand at the beginning of the year?

c. Supplies of $16,570 were consumed during the year. Supplies on hand at the beginning of the year amounted to $3,130, whereas the ending balance was $2,990. What was the amount of supplies acquired?

d. Supplies acquired during the year amounted to $2,300. The ending balance of supplies was two-thirds that of the beginning balance, and the supplies consumed during the year amounted to eight times the beginning balance. What was the ending balance?

Exercise 3-3
Adjusting entries

For each of the four situations described below, prepare the appropriate adjusting entry required at the end of the month.

a. On October 1, 1987, the Maxwell Company paid $1,575 rent in advance for the months of October, November, and December. Prepare the October 31 adjusting entry.

b. A $300,000 note payable was issued by the Datamaster Company to the Dallas State Bank on September 1, 1987. The note was a 180-day, 12% note due on February 1, 1988, together with the interest. Prepare the December 31 adjusting entry for Datamaster Company.

c. Advance ticket sales amounted to $5,280,000 by the time the Lutz Lancers started the 1987 NFL football season. All tickets are priced at $12 for each of the eight home games. By November 30 the Lancers had played five home games. Prepare the November 30 adjusting entry to record the revenue earned for the five home games.

d. A new machine costing $9,000 was acquired by the Reeves Company on July 1, 1987. The machine has an estimated life of 15 years, after which it will be worthless. Prepare the December 31, 1987, adjusting entry.

Exercise 3-4
Error effects on selected accounts

An error of omission is forgetting to do something. If an accountant forgets to record the year-end adjusting entries, that is an error of omission and it will, of course, affect the financial statement.

Using the following chart, indicate the effect of the five omission errors on the financial statement classifications listed. If as a result of the omission a classification is overstated, indicate this by placing a (+) in the appropriate space. An understatement is to be indicated by a (−). If the omisson has no effect on the classification, place (0) in the appropriate space.

	Effect of Omission				
	a	b	c	d	e
Revenue					
Expenses.					
Net Income					
Current Assets					
Noncurrent Assets					
Current Liabilities.					
Long-Term Liabilities					
Capital					

a. Depreciation was not recorded.
b. Unearned revenue was not reduced to reflect revenue earned.
c. Salaries were not accrued.

d. Office supplies on hand was not reduced to reflect office supplies used.
e. Interest income on notes receivable was not accrued.

Exercise 3-5
Adjusting entries

The selected accounts of the Milligan Company reflect December 31, 1987, balances before any adjusting entries have been recorded.

	Debit	Credit
Prepaid Insurance	900	
Office Supplies on Hand	1,865	
Accumulated Depreciation		2,500
Unearned Service Revenue		165

Using the following additional information, prepare the appropriate year-end adjusting entries.
a. The insurance policy was acquired to cover the building and its contents for the 12-month period commencing October 1, 1987.
b. A count of the office supplies remaining on hand on December 31, 1987, amounts to $790.
c. The accumulated depreciation relates to equipment acquired on July 1, 1986.
d. A check in the amount of $165 was received on December 1 for services to be performed over the next 3 months.

Exercise 3-6
Effects of failure to record adjusting entries

Bennie Bookkeeper was too ill to report to work on December 31, 1987, consequently no adjusting entries were made for the following items:
a. Supplies on hand amounted to $375 on December 31; the amount in the general ledger account Supplies on Hand was $1,500.
b. Prepaid insurance had a balance of $1,800 representing an entry made for that amount on November 1, 1987, for a 1-year insurance policy.
c. A balance of $2,400 was in the Unearned Rent Income account as a result of an entry reflecting 4 months' rent paid in advance on October 1, 1987.
d. Salaries in the amount of $495 had accrued and were not paid by December 31, 1987.
For each of these items, tell the effect of the omission of the adjusting entry.

PROBLEMS
Set A

Problem A3-1
Adjusting entries

The information presented below pertains to the 1987 year-end activities of the Fletcher Company, which ends its accounting year on December 31.
a. The general ledger account Shop Supplies on Hand had a $3,725 balance on the last day of the month. A count of the shop supplies amounts to $1,340.
b. As of the last day of the month employees have earned $2,710 of salaries that have not been paid.
c. Fletcher Company rents certain storage warehouses. On October 1, 1987, Fletcher received $7,200 rental fees in cash for the 6-month period October 1, 1987, to April 1, 1988. The amount was recorded as Unearned Rental Income.
d. The depreciation on office equipment amounts to $2,750 for the year.
e. A $1,800 check was mailed to the Madison Advertising Agency on November 1, 1987, for advertising in various trade journals for the months of November, December, and January. The entry was recorded as a debit to prepaid advertising.

Required Prepare the appropriate adjusting entry for each of the five items listed above.

Problem A3-2
Adjusting entries

Described below are a number of independent situations requiring adjusting entries. Analyze each situation carefully and then prepare the appropriate adjusting entry. Assume that the accounting year ends December 31, 1987.

a. On January 1, 1987, the Office Supplies on Hand account in the general ledger had a debit balance of $2,308. Office supplies in the amount of $11,027 were acquired during the year. A physical count of the office supplies on December 31, 1987, totaled $1,476. When office supplies are acquired the company debits the Office Supplies on Hand account.

b. The Big Top Company borrowed $50,000 from the Last State Bank on November 1, 1987, issuing a note payable for that amount. The note is due on May 1, 1988, together with 15% interest. (Interest is expressed at the annual rate.)

c. On October 1, 1987, the Appletree Company acquired a DataMaster Computer for $140,000. It is anticipated that the computer will be used for 10 years; consequently the annual depreciation is $14,000.

d. The Zelko Company insures its building against loss from fire. The policy was acquired on September 1, 1984, by paying $2,400 on that date for 3 years of insurance coverage. On September 1, 1987, the policy was renewed for an additional 3 years and a check was mailed to the insurance company for $2,640 for the 3-year policy. The company debits the Prepaid Insurance account when insurance is acquired.

e. The University Food Center sells meal tickets to students for $3.00 per ticket, but the tickets are sold only in books of 20 ($60 per book). During the fall semester of 1987, 14,500 books were sold, and as of December 31, 1987, 275,173 meal tickets were collected. The fall semester ends on January 25, 1988, and every student will use all of his or her tickets because the Food Center's food is so good. The Food Center records the sale of the meal tickets as Unearned Food Revenue when the cash is received.

f. The University of South Florida pays its faculty every other Friday. The last payday was December 21, 1987. December 31 is on a Monday, so 6 days of salaries have accrued. The salaries accrue even though school is not in session and December 25 is on Tuesday. The pay scale at USF is as follows.

Faculty	Number	Daily Rate
Professor	215	$180
Associate professor	374	125
Assistant professor	513	80
Instructor	341	65

g. On January 1, 1987, the Prepaid Rent account of the Rodgers Company had a balance of $2,800. This balance represents the remaining future service of a 1-year lease paid in advance for the rental of the company autos. The lease was dated June 1, 1986. A new lease was written on June 1, 1987, calling for a 20% increase in the monthly rent. A check was written in the amount equal to 12 months' rent paid in advance on June 4, 1987.

Problem A3-3
Journalizing and posting adjusting entries; preparing an adjusted trial balance

Presented on page 121 is the unadjusted trial balance of Keystone Catering Service for the year ended December 31, 1987.

Required

1. For each of the six items listed below, prepare the appropriate adjusting entry.
   a. On May 1, 1987, the company accepted a $5,000, 18% note from the American Meatpacking Association in payment for catering services performed at the Meatpackers

KEYSTONE CATERING SERVICE
Unadjusted Trial Balance
December 31, 1987

Cash	$ 2,763	
Notes Receivable	5,000	
Interest Receivable	–0–	
Accounts Receivable	7,416	
Prepaid Advertising	900	
Catering Supplies on Hand	12,426	
Land	25,000	
Building	75,000	
Accumulated Depreciation: Building		$ 15,000
Trucks	27,410	
Accumulated Depreciation: Trucks		7,500
Accounts Payable		3,047
Salaries Payable		–0–
Kate Keystone, Capital		100,000
Kate Keystone, Withdrawals	16,750	
Catering Revenue		111,461
Interest Income		–0–
Salary Expense	63,200	
Advertising Expense	–0–	
Catering Supplies Used	–0–	
Depreciation Expense: Buildings	–0–	
Depreciation Expense: Trucks	–0–	
Utilities Expense	1,143	
Totals	$237,008	$237,008

Annual Convention. (The revenue is reflected in the 1987 catering revenue of $111,461.) The note is due on February 1, 1988, together with the total interest.

b. Advertising in the amount of $900 was acquired on November 1, 1987, for 1 year of advertisements to be placed in various publications.

c. The amount of catering supplies on hand on December 31, 1987, is $1,317.

d. The company has computed the depreciation expense to be $1,500 on the building and $2,500 on the trucks.

e. Accrued salaries on December 31, 1987, amount to $3,750.

f. An unpaid utility bill in the amount of $157 has not been recorded.

2. For each account found in the unadjusted trial balance establish a general ledger account. Enter the amount found in the unadjusted trial balance into the general ledger accounts. Post the adjusting entries. Compute the adjusted balances.

3. Prepare an adjusted trial balance.

(Check figure: Totals = $245,515)

Problem A3-4
Journalizing and posting
adjusting entries; preparing an
adjusted trial balance and
financial statements

The unadjusted trial balance of the Hamlet Company for October 31, 1987, appears on page 122:

1. Establish a general ledger account for each item found in the unadjusted trial balance.

2. Additional information is presented below; from this information prepare the necessary adjusting entries, establishing new general ledger accounts as needed.

HAMLET COMPANY
Unadjusted Trial Balance
October 31, 1987

Cash	$ 860	
Accounts Receivable.	2,700	
Office Supplies on Hand	1,340	
Land.	9,000	
Office Building	52,250	
Accumulated Depreciation: Office Building.		$ 21,000
Office Equipment.	12,500	
Accumulated Depreciation: Office Equipment		3,500
Accounts Payable		2,410
Note Payable		20,000
Unearned Revenue		2,300
Hans Hamlet, Capital, Nov. 1, 1986		13,000
Hans Hamlet, Withdrawals	48,600	
Revenue		94,380
Salary Expense	24,500	
Telephone Expense	2,640	
Interest Expense	2,200	
Totals	$156,590	$156,590

a. Office Supplies on Hand on October 31, 1987, is determined to be $570.

b. Depreciation for the year amounts to $1,250 for office equipment and $5,250 for the office building.

c. Salaries in the amount of $950 have accrued by October 31, 1987, and remain unpaid.

d. The interest rate on the note payable is 12% per year. The note was incurred when the building was acquired several years ago. Please note that $2,200 of interest expense has been paid in 1987. The note is due in 1992.

e. By the end of October the entire amount of Unearned Revenue had been earned.

f. A telephone bill in the amount of $300 remains unpaid and unrecorded on October 31, 1987.

3. Prepare an adjusted trial balance.

(Check figure: Trial balance totals $164,540)

4. Prepare an income statement and a classified balance sheet properly dated for the Hamlet Company.

Problem A3-5

Preparing adjusting entries from unadjusted and adjusted trial balances

Two trial balances are presented on page 123. One is unadjusted, the other is the adjusted trial balance of the Aggressive Real Estate Agency. The year-end adjusting entries can be determined by comparing the two trial balances. By this method you are to record the adjusting journal entries made on December 31, 1987.

AGGRESSIVE REAL ESTATE AGENCY
Trial Balances
December 31, 1987

	Unadjusted		Adjusted	
Cash	$ 3,417		$ 3,417	
Notes Receivable	7,500		7,500	
Interest Receivable	–0–		125	
Commissions Receivable	18,900		21,300	
Prepaid Advertising	2,400		600	
Office Supplies on Hand	1,908		243	
Land	30,000		30,000	
Building	80,000		80,000	
Accumulated Depreciation: Building		$ 20,000		$ 21,000
Furniture	15,000		15,000	
Accumulated Depreciation: Furniture		5,000		6,500
Accounts Payable		1,618		1,618
Interest Payable		–0–		600
Salaries Payable		–0–		2,640
Mortgage Payable		50,000		50,000
Susan Sellfast, Capital		65,481		65,481
Susan Sellfast, Withdrawals	24,000		24,000	
Real Estate Commissions Earned		126,750		129,150
Interest Income		–0–		125
Salary Expense	79,324		81,964	
Advertising Expense	–0–		1,800	
Office Supplies Used	–0–		1,665	
Depreciation: Building	–0–		1,000	
Depreciation: Furniture	–0–		1,500	
Interest Expense	6,400		7,000	
Totals	$268,849	$268,849	$277,114	$277,114

Problem A3-6
Preparing a classified balance sheet

Listed below are the accounts of Adam Andrews. From this list you are to prepare a classified balance sheet.

Equipment	$477,500	Note Payable: Current	$8,000
Sales	426,500	Goodwill	5,000
Adam Andrews, Capital,		Prepaid Rent	3,500
Dec. 31, 1987	405,600	Cash	3,500
Adams Andrews, Capital,		New York City Bonds	3,300
Jan. 1, 1987	387,500	Temporary Investments	3,200
Buildings	175,000	IBM Common Stock	2,700
Acc. Depr.: Equip.	125,000	Accounts Receivable	2,500
Mortgage Payable	95,000	Notes Receivable	2,000
Bonds Payable	70,000	Accounts Payable	1,700
Merchandise Inventory	31,500	Unearned Revenue	1,600
Depreciation Expense	26,000	Salaries Payable	1,500
Accumulated Depreciation:		Supplies on Hand	1,200
Building	24,000	Advances to Employees	1,000
Federal Income Taxes Payable	16,500	Interest Income	700
Land Held for Future Plant Site	15,000	Accrued Interest on Note	
Withdrawals	13,000	Payable	500
Patents	12,500	Advertising Expense	400
Land	10,000	Net Income, 1987	X

(Check figure: Total assets = $600,400)

Set B

Problem B3-1
Adjusting entries

The following information is available on December 31, 1987, concerning the activities of the Denver Company:

a. Recorded in the Unearned Lease Income account is $3,600 of lease payments received on December 1, 1987, for the next 12 months.

b. The general ledger account of Shop Supplies on Hand shows a $6,250 debit balance. A count of the shop supplies amounts to $1,070.

c. Salaries in the amount of $2,750 have accrued since the last payday.

d. Prepaid Advertising has a debit balance of $4,800 representing a payment made to Big Sky Advertising Agency on November 1 for 24 months of advertising services.

e. The annual depreciation on the office equipment is $3,750.

Required Record the appropriate adjusting entries.

Problem B3-2
Adjusting entries

For each of the independent items listed below, prepare adjusting entries for the year ended December 31, 1987.

a. On May 1, 1987 the Young Company received $7,200 for subscriptions to its magazine YoungFolks. The subscriptions are for 3 years and are recorded in the Unearned Subscription Revenue account.

b. The Schaefer Company acquired a warehouse on October 1, 1987, at a cost of $168,000. The building has an estimated 40-year useful life; thus the annual depreciation is $4,200.

c. The Prepaid Insurance account had a $420 balance on January 1, 1987, representing the remainder of a 3-year policy acquired on August 1, 1984. On April 1, 1987, a second policy was acquired and a premium of $2,400 was paid in advance for the 2-year policy. A payment of $2,880 was made on August 1, 1987, to renew the first policy for an additional 3 years. The company records insurance in the prepaid account.

d. The Penn Company pays their employees every Friday. The company employs 14 individuals who are paid according to the following union scale:

Job Classification	Number of Employees	Per-Hour Rate
Stock clerk	4	$ 5.50
Forklift operator	5	6.75
Drill press operator	3	8.25
Maintenance person	2	10.50

December 31 is on a Tuesday. All employees worked 8 hours on Monday and Tuesday.

e. During the year acquisitions of office supplies were made totaling $5,068 and recorded as Office Supplies on Hand. A count of office supplies on December 31, 1986, amounted to $2,636. The count on December 31, 1987, was $1,572.

f. On March 1, 1987, the Tampa Company borrowed $25,000 from the First National Bank at 15% (unless stated otherwise, interest is always expressed at the annual rate). The note payable will be repaid on February 28, 1988, together with the interest.

g. The office furniture of the Dallas Company is rented from the Lone Star Furniture Company. On October 1, 1985, Dallas Company paid Lone Star $4,800 in advance for furniture it will rent for 2 years. On October 1, 1987, the agreement was renewed for an additional 2 years at $5,280. Dallas Company records rent paid in advance in an asset account.

Problem B3-3

Journalizing and posting adjusting entries; preparing an adjusted trial balance

The unadjusted trial balance presented below is from the December 31, 1987, general ledger of Wilson's Uniform Supply Service.

WILSONS UNIFORM SUPPLY SERVICE
Unadjusted Trial Balance
December 31, 1987

Cash	$ 5,080	
Accounts Receivable.	6,360	
Prepaid Insurance	1,000	
Uniforms on Hand.	13,270	
Land	11,300	
Building.	30,000	
Accumulated Depreciation: Building		$ 10,000
Cleaning Equipment.	12,000	
Accumulated Depreciation: Cleaning Equipment		3,000
Accounts Payable		4,150
Salaries Payable.		–0–
Unearned Uniform Rentals		–0–
Wilson, Capital, Jan. 1, 1987		56,360
Wilson, Withdrawals	48,000	
Uniform Rentals		193,000
Salary Expense	139,000	
Insurance Expense	–0–	
Uniforms Used	–0–	
Depreciation Expense: Building	–0–	
Depreciation Expense: Cleaning Equipment	–0–	
Utilities Expense	500	
Totals	$266,510	$266,510

Required

1. From the following information, prepare adjusting entries.
   a. Included in Uniform Rentals is $2,300 received from Builtstrong Industries on December 1, 1987, for service for the months of December 1987 and January 1988.
   b. The balance in the Prepaid Insurance account represents insurance premiums for 10 months paid in advance on September 1, 1987.
   c. On December 28, 1987, uniforms were provided to Atlantic Warehouse Corporation. The service was $2,500 but has not yet been recorded or paid.
   d. The company buys uniforms, recording their acquisition in the Uniforms on Hand account, and rents the uniforms to customers. The customers return soiled uniforms twice a week for clean uniforms. Uniforms that are beyond repair are recorded as Uniforms Used. A count of the uniforms on hand on December 31, 1987, amounted to $1,360.
   e. Depreciation expense for the building for the year amounts to $3,000. Depreciation expense for the cleaning equipment amounts to $2,000.
   f. Accrued salaries on December 31, 1987, amount to $1,500.
   g. A utility bill in the amount of $160. is unpaid at year-end.
2. Establish a ledger for each account found in the trial balance, record the amounts from the unadjusted trial balance, post the adjusting entries, and determine the ending balances.
3. Prepare an adjusted trial balance as of December 31, 1987.

(Check figure: Trial balance totals = $275,670)

Problem B3-4

Journalizing and posting adjusting entries; preparing an adjusted trial balance and financial statements

The unadjusted trial balance of Willie's Weight Control Clinic for the year ended July 31, 1987, appears below:

WILLIE'S WEIGHT CONTROL CLINIC
Unadjusted Trial Balance
July 31, 1987

Cash	$ 2,635	
Accounts Receivable.	740	
Prepaid Advertising	150	
Office Supplies on Hand	2,330	
Land.	10,000	
Building.	45,000	
Accumulated Depreciation: Building		$ 15,000
Furniture	12,500	
Accumulated Depreciation: Furniture		2,500
Accounts Payable		460
Unearned Weight Control Revenues		575
Mortgage Payable		30,000
Willie, Capital.		28,515
Willie, Withdrawals	24,000	
Weight Control Revenues		86,745
Salary Expense	60,715	
Telephone Expense	520	
Interest Expense	4,125	
Utilities Expense	1,080	
Totals	$163,795	$163,795

Required

1. For each item found in the trial balance, open a general ledger account.
2. From the information presented below, prepare adjusting entries and post them to the general ledger accounts. Establish new accounts as needed.
   a. The unearned weight control revenues of $575 have been earned by July 31, 1987.
   b. Depreciation for the year amounts to $1,050 for the building and $750 for the furniture.
   c. The prepaid advertising represents 3 months advertising paid in advance on July 1, 1987.
   d. Accrued salaries as of July 31, 1987, amount to $560.
   e. Interest expense on the mortgage in the amount of $375 has accrued as of July 31, 1987.
   f. Office supplies on hand on July 31, 1987, amount to $705.
3. Prepare an adjusted trial balance as of July 31, 1987.

(Check figure: Trial balance totals = $166,530)

4. Prepare an income statement for the year ended July 31, 1987, and a balance sheet as of July 31, 1987.

Problem B3-5

Preparing adjusting entries from unadjusted and adjusted trial balances

Presented on page 127 are the unadjusted and adjusted trial balances of Ridgemont Race Track. By comparing the two trial balances, determine the adjustments that were made and prepare the adjusting entries. You may omit the journal explanations.

RIDGEMONT RACE TRACK
Trial Balances
December 31, 1987

	Unadjusted		Adjusted	
Cash	$ 1,800		$ 1,800	
Accounts Receivable	740		740	
Prepaid Advertising	2,300		800	
Supplies on Hand	–0–		3,600	
Land	28,000		28,000	
Racetrack	74,000		74,000	
Accumulated Depreciation: Racetrack		$ 12,000		$ 18,000
Equipment	12,600		12,600	
Accumulated Depreciation: Equipment		3,800		6,000
Accounts Payable		3,480		3,480
Salaries Payable		–0–		600
Unearned Revenue		–0–		150
Mortgage Payable		30,000		30,000
Ridgemont, Capital		38,360		38,360
Ridgemont, Withdrawals	18,000		18,000	
Racetrack Revenues		145,200		145,050
Salary Expense	90,400		91,000	
Advertising Expense	–0–		1,500	
Supplies Used	5,000		1,400	
Depreciation Expense: Racetrack	–0–		6,000	
Depreciation Expense: Equipment	–0–		2,200	
Totals	$232,840	$232,840	$241,640	$241,640

Problem B3-6

Preparing a classified balance sheet

The list of accounts presented below for the Pasco Company is in alphabetical order. From this list, prepare a classified balance sheet.

Accounts Payable	$ 19,800	Investment in Real Estate	$ 12,600
Accounts Receivable	54,750	Land	21,750
Accumulated Depreciation: Building	28,650	Marketable Securities	20,250
		Merchandise Inventory	34,050
Accumulated Depreciation: Equipment	39,450	Mortgage Payment Due 2013	87,450
		Net Income 1987	108,450
Advertising Expense	20,100	Notes Payable	15,000
Buildings	124,800	Notes Receivable	8,250
Cash	12,000	Pasco, Capital, Jan. 1, 1987	185,550
Copyrights	11,250	Pasco, Capital, Dec. 31, 1987	221,850
Depreciation Expense	40,950	Patents	15,000
Equipment	146,250	Prepaid Advertising	5,400
Equipment Notes Payable Due 1995	60,000	Salaries Payable	8,550
		Sales	543,750
Franchise Cost	9,450	Unearned Revenue	31,800
Goodwill	18,300	Withdrawals	72,150
Investment in Municipal Bonds	18,450		

(Check figure: Total assets = $444,450)

Problem B3-7
Preparing a correct income statement

The statement of profits presented below was prepared by Lance Lovelace and represents the business activity for the year ended December 31, 1987, for Lovelace Language School.

LOVELACE LANGUAGE SCHOOL
Statement of Profits
December 31, 1987

Tuition Fees		$160,875
Operating Expenses Paid:		
Salaries to Professors	$80,425	
Language Lab Equipment	10,500	
Language Lab Supplies	2,775	
Insurance	200	
Interest	800	
Other Items	36,600	
Total Expenses		131,300
Profits for the Year		$ 29,575

Mr. Lovelace wishes to open a second school on the west side of town and is seeking a bank loan. But before going to the bank he asks you to review his statement and supporting records. After reviewing the underlying documents, you find that the $160,875 Tuition Fees was determined by adding the cash received from the language students, $105,425 (including $12,050 from students who were enrolled in the fall semester of 1986 but did not pay until January 1987); $15,000 fees for the fall of 1987 which will be paid in January 1988; and $40,450 fees that students will pay for the spring of 1988 courses (based on a survey of the students enrolled in the fall 1987 classes).

Salaries amounting to $3,400 have been earned by the faculty as of December 31, 1987, but not paid. Included in the $80,425 of salaries to professors were $950 of salaries accrued as of December 31, 1986.

The language lab equipment was acquired on July 1, 1987, and will be used for 5 years, after which it will be worthless. The $2,775 language lab supplies represents the amount paid for supplies during 1987. In addition, $815 of supplies were purchased on account in early December 1987 and not yet paid for by year-end. On January 1, 1987, $1,510 of supplies were on hand. The amount of supplies on hand on December 31, 1987, was $630. On December 1 the insurance policy expired. The previous policy was paid in advance on December 1, 1986, for the 12-month period covering December 1, 1986, to November 30, 1987. The rate was $180 per month. Commencing December 1, 1987, the rate was increased to $200 per month and Mr. Lovelace elected to pay the premiums on a monthly basis.

As of the last day of 1987, $50 of interest has accrued.

Included in other items were the following:

Advertising Expense	$14,000
Utilities Expense	1,500
Rent Expense	5,600
Withdrawals	12,000
Miscellaneous Expense	3,500

Required

Prepare for Mr. Lovelace an income statement that reflects accrual accounting and is in accordance with generally accepted accounting principles.

(Check figure: Net loss = $7,650)

Chapter 4

Periodic Procedures: Closing the Accounts and the Worksheet

After studying this chapter you should be able to:

- Identify which accounts are closed at the end of an accounting period and explain why
- Prepare *closing entries*
- Prepare a *worksheet*
- Use a worksheet to prepare *interim financial statements*
- Prepare a *post-closing trial balance*
- Explain why *reversing* entries are used
- List the steps in the accounting process
- Discuss the differences between the corporate entity and a proprietorship

The accounting process we have described thus far would be adequate for only the smallest of business entities. That is, for a small business like the ones in the examples in the preceding chapters, we could prepare financial statements directly from the adjusted trial balance at the end of each accounting period — monthly, quarterly, and annually. Due to the relatively few accounts, no additional period-end accounting procedures would be required.

Additional periodic procedures are necessary

However, for most business entities additional periodic procedures are necessary. As the number of accounts increases it becomes more difficult to prepare the financial statements and commence a new accounting period without the aid of these additional accounting procedures. Consider for a moment the problem of a company that recorded Salaries Expense in the general ledger totaling $65,000 for the entire year 1987. During the month of January 1988, salaries of $6,000 are incurred. In preparing financial statements for January 1988, we can see that salaries *should be* reported at $6,000. But without some way of identifying the end of the 1987 accounting period and the start of the 1988 period, the journalization of the 1988 salaries would result in a $6,000 posting to the Salaries Expense account in the general ledger, as illustrated below:

This account is not correct because it shows salaries expense for both 1987 and 1988

Salary Expense		
Jan.–Dec. 1987	65,000	
Jan. 1988	6,000	

The result is that in the general ledger, salaries would be reflected at $71,000, representing the total from 1987 plus the first month of 1988.

We must find a way to identify clearly the 1987 salaries and distinguish them from the 1988 salaries. What we need to show is that:

The salary expense account for 1987 should show only 1987 salaries

Salary Expense		
Jan.–Dec. 1987	65,000	

and the 1988 salaries expense account should show only 1988 salaries

Salary Expense		
Jan. 1988	6,000	

The procedure used in accounting to solve this problem is called the **closing process,** which we will discuss and explain in the first half of this chapter.

The greater the number of transactions a company has, the greater the risk that errors can occur at any point where data are recorded — in recording the journal entries, posting from the journals to the ledger, or adjusting the accounts. Not only does a large number of transactions increase the risk of error, but so does the frequency with which the accounts are used. That is, larger companies must prepare financial statements more frequently, usually on a monthly basis, than smaller companies. Thus, a company that prepares financial statements more frequently suffers a greater risk of error in its reporting.

To help deal with the possibility of error, accountants use a tool called a **worksheet.** The worksheet helps in four ways:

1. It organizes the process of preparing the financial statements.

2. It reduces the possibility of introducing errors in that process.

3. It aids in discovering errors that do occur.

4. It provides monthly statements without the formal adjusting and closing process.

In the second half of this chapter, we will introduce the worksheet and explain how to use it.

THE CLOSING PROCESS

To prepare you for what's coming up in this chapter, we will begin by briefly reviewing and expanding on two things introduced earlier: the accounts used to prepare balance sheets — balance sheet accounts — and the accounts used to prepare income statements — income statement accounts.

*Balance sheet accounts represent the balance of an asset, liability, or owner's equity account *at a particular point in time.* For example, business transactions cause increases and decreases in the Cash account regularly throughout the accounting period. But the balance in a Cash account represents the amount of cash on hand at the time the balance is calculated. Balance sheet accounts are sometimes called **permanent accounts** or **real accounts** because, once established, they will generally remain on the books for many years.

Income statement accounts, which comprise *revenue accounts* and *expense accounts,* represent accumulations of revenue and expenses *during a particular period of time.* For example, a Salary account represents the total salary expense incurred between the start of the accounting period and date of the income statement. When we discuss salary expense, we must specify not only the amount of the expense but also the time period during which those salaries were incurred. Are the salaries for the month? The quarter? The year 1987? The year 1988? Because revenue accounts and expense accounts reflect activity only for the period of time they cover, both of these income statement accounts are sometimes referred to as **temporary accounts,** or as **nominal accounts.** *Temporary* describes the nature of these accounts: They exist for only one accounting period. These accounts will show increases over time; they cannot show decreases.

Balance sheet accounts represent an account balance at a particular point in time

Income statement accounts accumulate amounts for particular periods of time

Income statement accounts only increase during the year; they do not decrease

Deriving the Capital Account from the Revenue and Expense Accounts

If we were to rely solely on what we have learned thus far to prepare financial statements, our work would be more difficult than it need be. We would have two problems:

1. At the end of a period the Capital account would reflect a beginning-of-period balance while all other balance sheet accounts would reflect period-end balances. That's because we do not record anything in the Capital account. We use the revenue and expense accounts instead. What we must do is get the Capital account to show an end-of-period balance.

2. The balances in the revenue and expense accounts would not be for the latest accounting period (for example, the year 1987), but rather would be cumulative balances, starting from when the company first commenced operations. That is, revenue and expense account balances, as we now know them, are not *period-end balances, but cumulative balances.* We have to find some way of getting the accounts to show totals for only a single period.

The closing process transfers revenue and expense accounts back to the Capital account

The closing process is a procedure whereby the revenue and expense accounts are "transferred" back to the Capital account. This procedure makes it simpler to end one accounting period and start another. The closing process solves the two problems.

Each revenue and expense account is "closed out" at the end of an accounting period. *By **closed out** we simply mean that at period-end the account is reduced to a zero balance.* If we do that for each of the revenue and expense accounts, then the amount we close out will be a total for the period, for each account, not a cumulative total. A zero balance at the end of one accounting period means, of course, that the account starts with a zero balance at the beginning of the next period.

After closing, all revenue and expense accounts will have a zero balance

Now, an obvious question is, What do we do with the closed-out balances from each of the revenue and expense accounts? The answer is: We transfer them to the Capital account. In doing that, we accomplish the other objective: transferring the period-end balances from each of the revenue and expense accounts to the Capital account, yielding a Capital account that reflects period-end balances.

That's the basic idea behind the closing process. We'll now show you in a step-by-step sequence how it works, using the Graf's Wallpapering and Decorating Service adjusted trial balance, shown below.

GRAF'S WALLPAPERING AND DECORATING SERVICE
Adjusted Trial Balance
December 31, 1987

Cash	$ 1,250		Balance Sheet Accounts
Notes Receivable	2,500		
Accounts Receivable	3,375		
Prepaid Advertising Supplies.	1,625		
Prepaid Rent	1,750		
Equipment	16,250		
Accumulated Depreciation.		$ 7,500	
Salaries Payable		500	
Notes Payable		6,250	
Accounts Payable.		1,125	
Graf, Capital, 1/1/87.		26,250	
Withdrawal Account with Debit Balance {Graf, Withdrawals	42,500		Withdrawal Account }
Revenue Accounts with Credit Balances {Wallpapering Revenue		62,500	
Decorating Revenue		38,750	
Interest Income		250	
Expense Accounts with Debit Balances {Salary Expense.	56,250		Income Statement Accounts
Depreciation Expense	3,750		
Rent Expense	3,750		
Wallpaper Supplies Used	8,375		
Utilities Expense	1,125		
Interest Expense.	625		
Totals	$143,125	$143,125	

Closing the Expense Accounts

In the adjusted trial balance for Graf's Wallpapering and Decorating Service, there are six expense accounts, and, as we already learned, expense accounts accumulate debit balances. The six expense accounts are: Salary Expense, Depreciation Expense,

Rent Expense, Wallpaper Supplies Used, Utilities Expense, and Interest Expense.

Expense accounts are closed by credits equal to the account's debit balance

An expense account is closed by "crediting" it for an amount equal to the debit balance. This results in a zero balance, or to be more consistent and precise, a zero debit balance. Remember: *A zero balance is our objective in closing an expense account at the end of a period.*

But what do we do with the debit balance that was in the expense account before we credited it?

Expense and Revenue Summary is an account that aids in the closing process

For the closing process, we must establish a temporary account called ***Expense and Revenue Summary*** (or ***Income Summary,*** or ***Profit and Loss Summary***). It is so called because it contains a record of the expenses, or debit balances, for the period, and, as we shall see, also the revenue or credit balances for the period.

The sum of the debit balances is recorded as a debit in the Expense and Revenue Summary.

The closing entry recorded in the general journal for Graf's Wallpapering and Decorating Service to close the expense accounts would appear as follows:

Closing the income statement accounts with debit balances by debiting the Expense and Revenue Summary account

1987
Dec. 31 Expense and Revenue Summary 73,875
                    Salary Expense   56,250
                    Depreciation Expense.   3,750
                    Rent Expense.   3,750
                    Wallpaper Supplies Used   8,375
                    Utilities Expense.   1,125
                    Interest Expense   625
           To close the expense accounts.

After posting the closing entry to the general ledger, each expense account will have a zero balance. The sum of the debit balances of the expense accounts is transferred to the Expense and Revenue Summary account as a debit. The effect of the closing process on the expense accounts is illustrated in the diagram below.

Salary Expense			Depreciation Expense			Rent Expense		
		(Closing)			(Closing)			(Closing)
Bal.	56,250	Dec. 31 56,250	Bal.	3,750	Dec. 31 3,750	Bal.	3,750	Dec. 31 3,750
Bal.	-0-		Bal.	-0-		Bal.	-0-	

Wallpaper Supplies Used			Utilities Expense			Interest Expense		
		(Closing)			(Closing)			(Closing)
Bal.	8,375	Dec. 31 8,375	Bal.	1,125	Dec. 31 1,125	Bal.	625	Dec. 31 625
Bal.	-0-		Bal.	-0-		Bal.	-0-	

Expense and Revenue Summary		**General Ledger Accounts after Closing**
Dec. 31 73,875		

Closing the Revenue Accounts

Revenue accounts are closed by debits equal to the account's credit balance

To close the revenue accounts we must debit each revenue account and credit the Expense and Revenue Summary

Graf's Wallpapering and Decorating Service has three revenue accounts which, of course, have credit balances: Wallpapering Revenue, Decorating Revenue, and Interest Income. A revenue account is closed by debiting it by an amount equal to its credit balance. The result, of course, is a zero balance, or more correct, a zero credit balance.

Each credit balance to be closed is recorded in the general journal for Graf's as follows:

```
1987
Dec. 31  Wallpapering Revenue . . . . . . . . . . . . . . . . . . . . . . . 62,500
         Decorating Revenue. . . . . . . . . . . . . . . . . . . . . . . . 38,750
         Interest Income. . . . . . . . . . . . . . . . . . . . . . . .    250
            Expense and Revenue Summary. . . . . . . . . . . . . .           101,500
         To close the revenue accounts.
```

The sum of the three credit balances is transferred as a credit entry to the Expense and Revenue Summary. This is illustrated below.

Wallpapering Revenue		Decorating Revenue		Interest Income	
(Closing)		(Closing)		(Closing)	
Dec. 31 62,500	Bal. 62,500	Dec. 31 38,750	Bal. 38,750	Dec. 31 250	Bal. 250
	Bal. -0-		Bal. -0-		Bal. -0-

Expense and Revenue Summary

Dec. 31 73,875	Dec. 31 101,500
	Bal. 27,625

After all the debit and credit balances have been transferred to the Expense and Revenue Summary, each expense and revenue account is left with a zero balance ready to accumulate the next accounting period's debits and credits.

Closing the Expense and Revenue Summary

The Expense and Revenue Summary is now just that—a summary. The *summary balance* is the difference between the sum of the transferred debits—the expenses—and the sum of the transferred credits—the revenue—which is the net income for the period. In this case, the credit balance is $27,625, or the income for the period. If the debits had exceeded the credits, a net loss would have resulted (expenses would have been larger than revenue).

The balance in the Expense and Revenue Summary account—the $27,625 net income—is now transferred to the Capital account by a closing entry. This will increase the Capital account by the amount of the net income and reduce the Expense and Revenue Summary to a zero balance. Now (1) the Capital account reflects the effects of its component revenue and expense accounts, *and* (2) all revenue and expense accounts from this accounting period have zero balances. Our objective has been accomplished.

A third closing entry transfers the balance in the Expense and Revenue Summary to the Capital account

The general journal entry closing the Expense and Revenue Summary and the effect of posting this entry to the general ledger Capital account for Graf's Wallpapering and Decorating Service are illustrated as follows:

```
1987
Dec. 31  Expense and Revenue Summary ................... 27,625
              Graf, Capital ...............................          27,625
         To close the Expense and Revenue Summary account.
```

Expense and Revenue Summary				Graf, Capital		
Dec. 31	73,875	Dec. 31	101,500		Bal.	26,250
(Closing)					(Closing)	
Dec. 31	27,675	Bal.	27,625		Dec. 31	27,625
		Bal.	-0-			

The last closing entry transfers the Withdrawals account balance to the Capital account

One more step is needed to complete the closing process: We need to close out the Withdrawals account. The Withdrawals account is used whenever the owner of a business entity removes funds from the business for personal use. Withdrawals are not expenses. For this reason the Withdrawals account is not closed when the expense accounts are closed to the Expense and Revenue Summary. Instead, Withdrawals are reductions in the Capital of the business, just as are expenses. Also, Withdrawals accumulate over time just as expenses do.

So for the same two reasons we closed the expense and revenue accounts—to reflect the ending Capital balance and to have a zero balance in the temporary accounts—we also close the Withdrawals account. This is accomplished by the following general ledger entry:

```
1987
Dec. 31  Graf, Capital ............................... 42,500
              Graf, Withdrawals........................          42,500
         To close the Withdrawals account.
```

The Capital account will reflect the ending balance after the Withdrawal debit has been closed, shown as follows:

Graf, Withdrawals				Graf, Capital			
		(Closing)		(Closing)		Bal.	26,250	Beginning Capital Balance
Bal.	42,500	Dec. 31	42,500	Dec. 31	42,500			
Bal.	-0-					(Closing)		
						Dec. 31	27,625	
						Bal.	11,375	Ending Capital Balance

With the closing of the Withdrawals account, the closing process is completed: All expense and revenue accounts and the Withdrawals account have a zero balance, and the Capital account reflects the period-end balance.

THE WORKSHEET

Worksheets are extremely important and helpful, but they are not part of the permanent accounting records of a business entity.

Records such as the general journal, the general ledger, and the financial statements are permanent. These records require that they be permanent so they are maintained in a durable state, by use of ink in a manual system or by printed or typed material in an electronic or mechanical system.

Worksheets are prepared in pencil; they are not part of the permanent accounting records

Worksheets are prepared in pencil so that any detected errors can be easily erased and corrected prior to preparing the period-end financial statements, which are permanent. Accountants prepare worksheets to help organize the period-end accounting procedures in a logical manner.

In the process of recording in the journal and posting in the ledgers, and in adjusting and closing entries, it is not uncommon to make mistakes. To avoid the possibility of advancing those mistakes to the permanent records, it makes sense to first prepare a trial run of the period procedures. The worksheet provides this trial run.

After the worksheet is prepared, it is examined for errors. Any errors found are corrected. It is then an easy matter to prepare the formal—and permanent—financial statements from the corrected, error-free worksheet. Also, because of the way the worksheet is organized, it makes the adjusting and closing processes more straightforward and easier to do.

In the worksheet there are five column headings, each embracing a pair of debit–credit columns, as shown below.

Unadjusted Trial Balance		Adjustments		Adjusted Trial Balance		Income Statement		Balance Sheet	
Debit	Credit	Debit	Credit	Debit	Credit	Debit	Credit	Debit	Credit

Unadjusted Trial Balance Columns

The unadjusted trial balance is entered on the first pair of columns on the worksheet

After all external transactions during the accounting period have been recorded in the general journal and posted to the general ledger, the unadjusted trial balance is prepared and entered on the first pair of columns on the worksheet.

To demonstrate how to use the worksheet, we'll begin with the unadjusted trial balance of the Royal Company, shown in the worksheet at the top of the facing page.

The Royal Company started its first operations on October 1, 1987. At the end of October, in addition to what we see in the unadjusted trial balance, we also know the following facts:

1. Royal's rent is $280 per month.

2. The value of Office Supplies on Hand is $280.

The unadjusted trial balance is recorded on a worksheet

ROYAL COMPANY
Worksheet
Month Ended October 31, 1987

Accounts	Unadjusted Trial Balance		Adjust
	Debit	Credit	Debit
Cash	1,960		
Accounts Receivable	3,080		
Prepaid Rent	2,520		
Office Supplies on Hand	420		
Office Equipment	7,000		
Accounts Payable		2,100	
Unearned Revenue		1,190	
Royal, Capital		9,450	
Royal, Withdrawals	840		
Revenue		7,840	
Salary Expense	4,620		
Utilities Expense	140		
Totals	20,580	20,580	

3. A machine purchased and installed on the first of October is depreciated at the rate of $210 per month.

4. Revenue in the amount of $560 has been earned but not yet recorded, since cash was not received.

5. Unearned Revenue of $420, recorded earlier in the month, has been earned.

6. Salaries in the amount of $350 are owed to Royal's employees.

Adjustments Columns

Adjustments are entered in the second pair of columns on the worksheet

You may have already gotten the idea that for accounts requiring adjustments, the adjustments are not entered into the general journal. Rather, the adjustments are entered on the worksheet in the second pair of columns, labeled Adjustments.

Now, let's see how adjustments are handled on the worksheet. We will consider how to make adjustments for the six items already introduced. Refer to the worksheet on the next page as you go through the steps.

1. The $2,520 Prepaid Rent on the unadjusted trial balance represents rent paid in advance on October 1, 1987, for the next 9 months (Royal's rent is $280 per month) ending June 30, 1988. Since the month of October has expired, we must recognize 1 month's rent expense and reduce the prepaid rent by $280.

   The first step in making this adjustment: On the worksheet enter $280 in the credit column under Adjustments and opposite the Prepaid Rent account.

   The second step: Subtract $280 credit adjustment from the $2,520 debit balance in the unadjusted trial balance. The result yields a $2,240 debit balance remaining,

ROYAL COMPANY
Worksheet
Month Ended October 31, 1987

Accounts	Unadjusted Trial Balance Debit	Unadjusted Trial Balance Credit	Adjustments Debit	Adjustments Credit	Adjus Trial Bal Debit
Cash	1,960				1,960
Accounts Receivable	3,080		(d) 560		3,640
Prepaid Rent	2,520			(a) 280	2,240
Office Supplies on Hand	420			(b) 140	280
Office Equipment	7,000				
Accounts Payable		2,100			
Unearned Revenue		1,190	(e) 420		
Royal, Capital		9,450			
Royal, Withdrawals	840				
Revenue		7,840		(d) 560	
				(e) 420	
Salary Expense	4,620		(f) 350		
Utilities Expense	140				
Totals	20,580	20,580			
Rent Expense			(a) 280		
Office Supplies Used			(b) 140		
Depreciation Expense			(c) 210		
Accumulated Depreciation				(c) 210	
Salaries Payable				(f) 350	
Totals			1,960	1,960	

Rent of $280 has expired. This amount is deducted from Prepaid Rent . . .

. . . and the account Rent Expense is inserted on the worksheet

which will be reflected in the adjusted trial balance column for Prepaid Rent. (To focus on one thing at a time—in this case, how and what to record in the adjustments column—we will forego discussion of this step and the adjusted trial balance as we proceed through the following items, confining our explanation mostly to the adjustments columns. We will, of course, return to the adjusted trial balance as the next topic in explaining how to use the worksheet.)

The third step: The debit portion of the adjustment is to recognize $280 Rent Expense. But this account, Rent Expense, does not appear on the unadjusted trial balance. We must introduce a Rent Expense account to the worksheet. Once we do that, we can enter opposite Rent Expense and under Adjustments a $280 debit, as shown in the illustration.

The fourth step: We have just made one adjustment. Soon, we will have made a number of adjustments in the adjustments column. Remember that one of the purposes of the worksheet is to help us analyze and review all the adjustments for the period, to examine the adjustments for errors (if it turns out that the period-end balance doesn't balance), and to correct them. To do that, we will need some way

The debit and credit portions of an adjusting entry are identified on a worksheet by a reference letter

of quickly and easily identifying the corresponding pairs of debits and credits comprising each adjustment. Thus, we *key* with a reference letter the debit and credit entries that comprise an adjustment. To identify the adjustments originating with the unadjusted Prepaid Rent account, see in the illustration that we use the letter *a* to designate the credit component, the $280 credit adjustment to Prepaid Rent, as well as the debit component, the corresponding $280 debit adjustment to Rent Expense. This letter *a* identifies the debit and credit adjustments that comprise the adjustment to the Prepaid Rent account at the end of the period.

Office supplies of $140 are consumed. The Office Supplies Used account must be inserted on the worksheet.

2. A count of the office supplies on hand on the last day of the month reveals that the value of the supplies on hand at the end of the month is $280. Since the Office Supplies on Hand account had a $420 debit balance on the first of the month, we will need an adjustment of $140. On the worksheet under the adjustments column, a $140 credit is entered for the Office Supplies on Hand account. This $140 credit adjustment results in a $280 debit balance, as shown under the adjusted trial balance column, at the end of the period for the Office Supplies on Hand account.

   Since office supplies were used during the month and since there was no Office Supplies Used account listed in the unadjusted trial balance, we must introduce that account. The $140 expense is then recognized on the worksheet by entering a $140 debit under the adjustments column opposite the newly introduced Office Supplies Used account. The credit and debit are both keyed with *b* to identify this adjustment.

For the depreciation of $210, both the Depreciation Expense and the Accumulated Depreciation accounts must be added

3. Depreciation for the month amounts to $210. However, notice that neither the expense account, Depreciation Expense, nor the contra-asset account, Accumulated Depreciation, appears on the unadjusted trial balance. Because both accounts are needed to account for—that is, *adjust*—the $210 depreciation, we simply introduce them on the worksheet. Under the adjustments column opposite the newly introduced Depreciation Expense account we enter a $210 debit, and corresponding to that, we enter a $210 credit under the adjustments column opposite the newly introduced Accumulated Depreciation account. The letter *c* identifies the debit and the credit corresponding to the depreciation adjustment. (Note: Because this is the first month of the first year of operations, there are no prior-years' activities. Specifically, depreciation is not reflected in an Accumulated Depreciation account. In subsequent periods, the account Accumulated Depreciation will, of course, have a balance.)

4. At the end of the month, $560 of revenue was earned but has not been recorded. For this adjustment, keyed with *d*, we must record a $560 debit opposite Accounts Receivable and a corresponding $560 credit opposite Revenue.

5. Unearned revenue recorded previously in the month in the amount of $420 was earned by the end of the month. The adjustment for this is that a $420 debit is entered for the Unearned Revenue account and a $420 credit is entered for Revenue, each entry keyed *e*. Note that there are two adjustments for Revenue: *d*, $560 credit from Accounts Receivable, and *e*, $420 credit from Unearned Revenue.

6. Accrued salaries on October 31, 1987, amount to $350. By now you should be able to make this adjustment quickly and easily. For the Salary Expense account, enter a $350 debit under the adjustments column; and introduce a new account, Salaries Payable, for which you enter a $350 credit, all of which is keyed *f*.

After the last adjustment has been entered on the worksheet, caution dictates that we check our work at this point before we proceed to the next column. The debit column is totaled and the credit column is totaled. If the sum of the debits equals the sum of the credits, we may proceed. If not, then there is an error somewhere in the adjustments column.

We have seen that there are cases when accounts must be introduced into the worksheet when making adjustments. After you have prepared several worksheets and become more familiar with the adjusting process, you will learn to anticipate the need for additional accounts and what accounts you will need. You will then be able to allow sufficient space in appropriate places on the worksheet for accounts anticipated.

It might be helpful to consider that there are two ways of looking at the entries in the adjustments column: (1) There are those adjustments made to the trial balance accounts already recorded in the first column of the worksheet (see the top of the adjustments column); and (2) there are those adjustments to accounts that are not on the worksheet and that have to be introduced (see the bottom of the adjustments column).

Adjusted Trial Balance Columns

The adjusted trial balance reflects the adjustments to the unadjusted trial balance

The adjusted trial balance column is, like all the headings on the worksheet, exactly what it says it is. The "adjusted" column reflects "adjustments" to the "unadjusted" column.

For each account, the unadjusted trial balance debits and the adjustments debits are added and the sum is recorded in the debit column of the adjusted trial balance. For example, Accounts Receivable has a $3,080 debit in the unadjusted trial balance. This debit is added to the $560 debit adjustment, and the result is the $3,640 debit in the adjusted trial balance. Of course, the same is done for the credits for each account. For accounts that are newly introduced on the worksheet, the adjusted balances — the adjustment debits and credits — are simply carried over into the adjusted trial balance columns.

The first thing we do with the adjusted trial balance is the same thing we just did with the adjustments: We add up all the debits and add up all the credits. If the sum of the debits equals the sum of the credits, then we can be assured that we have not made any arithmetic errors in the amounts in the adjusted trial balance columns. If it turns out that the sums don't balance — aren't equal — then we have some work to do: We must look for the error or errors and correct them. Once we are assured that the sums of the adjusted debits and credits are equal, the adjusted trial balance is ready for us to use in preparing the worksheet income statement and balance sheets, which are the next sequence of worksheet columns.

The worksheet for the Royal Company presented on page 141 has been extended to the point where it illustrates the progress to the adjusted trial balance from the preceding columns.

If you have already observed something about the totals of the columns, you are beginning to think like an accountant: The total of the adjusted debits is $21,700, which is *not* equal to the sum of the totals of the unadjusted debits and the adjustments debits ($20,580 + $1,960 = $22,540). Of course, the same is true for the credits: The credit total of the third column does not equal the sum of the totals of the credits of the first two columns.

If you already understand why, then you are beginning to think like a keen accountant. The reason for the apparent inconsistency can be explained as follows:

ROYAL COMPANY Worksheet Month Ended October 31, 1989							
	Unadjusted Trial Balance		Adjustments		Adjusted Trial Balance		Inco State
Accounts	Debit	Credit	Debit	Credit	Debit	Credit	
Cash	1,960				1,960		
Accounts Receivable	3,080		(d) 560		3,640		
Prepaid Rent	2,520			(a) 280	2,240		
Office Supplies on Hand	420			(b) 140	280		
Office Equipment	7,000				7,000		
Accounts Payable		2,100				2,100	
Unearned Revenue		1,190	(e) 420			770	
Royal, Capital		9,450				9,450	
Royal, Withdrawals	840				840		
Revenue		7,840		(d) 560			
				(e) 420		8,820	
Salary Expense	4,620		(f) 350		4,970		
Utilities Expense	140				140		
Totals	20,580	20,580					
Rent Expense			(a) 280		280		
Office Supplies Used			(b) 140		140		
Depreciation Expense			(c) 210		210		
Accumulated Depreciation				(c) 210		210	
Salaries Payable				(f) 350		350	
Totals			1,960	1,960	21,700	21,700	

While debits in the adjustments column may be added to debits in the unadjusted trial balance column in arriving at the total debits in the adjusted trial balance column — as with the salary expense ($4,620 Dr. + $350 Dr. = $4,970 Dr.) — debits in the adjustments column *may also be subtracted* from credits in the unadjusted trial balance column in arriving at the credit balance in the adjusted trial balance. Unearned revenue provides an example on the Royal Company worksheet — $1,190 Cr. − $420 Dr. = $770 Cr. Of course the same is true when dealing with the credit adjustment — Office Supplies on Hand ($420 Dr. − $140 Cr. = $280 Dr.).

Income Statement and Balance Sheet Columns

Income statement accounts from the adjusted trial balance are transferred to the income statement columns

The next step in using the worksheet is to separate the adjusted trial balance into income statement account balances and balance sheet account balances. The procedure is simply to transfer from the adjusted trial balance columns each debit and credit balance to its proper place in the income statement columns and each debit and credit balance to its proper place in the balance sheet columns. How well you do that depends, of course, on how well you know which are income statement accounts and which are balance sheet accounts. (Refer to the worksheet on page 142 as you proceed through the following discussion.)

	ROYAL COMPANY Worksheet Month Ended October 31, 1989									
	Unadjusted Trial Balance		Adjustments		Adjusted Trial Balance		Income Statement		Balance Sheet	
Accounts	Debit	Credit	Debit	Credit	Debit	Credit	Debit	Credit	Debit	Credit
Cash	1,960				1,960				1,960	
Accounts Receivable	3,080		*d* 560		3,640				3,640	
Prepaid Rent	2,520			*a* 280	2,240				2,240	
Office Supplies on Hand	420			*b* 140	280				280	
Office Equipment	7,000				7,000				7,000	
Accounts Payable		2,100				2,100				2,100
Unearned Revenue		1,190	*e* 420			770				770
Royal, Capital		9,450				9,450				9,450
Royal, Withdrawals	840				840				840	
Revenue		7,840		*d* 560						
				e 420		8,820		8,820		
Salary Expense	4,620		*f* 350		4,970		4,970			
Utilities Expense	140				140		140			
Totals	20,580	20,580								
Rent Expense			*a* 280		280		280			
Office Supplies Used			*b* 140		140		140			
Depreciation Expense			*c* 210		210		210			
Accumulated Depreciation				*c* 210		210				210
Salaries Payable				*f* 350		350				350
Totals			1,960	1,960	21,700	21,700	5,740	8,820	15,960	12,880
Net Income							3,080			3,080
Totals							8,820	8,820	15,960	15,960

Balance sheet accounts are transferred to the balance sheet columns

For example, Cash is a balance sheet account; therefore, we carry the $1,960 debit from the adjusted trial balance forward to the balance sheet debit column. Accounts Receivable is also a balance sheet account, so of course we carry the $3,640 adjusted trial balance debit balance forward to the balance sheet debit column. Revenue and Salary Expense are both income statement accounts; thus the $8,820 Adjusted Revenue credit is carried forward as an income statement credit, and the $4,970 Salary Expense debit is carried forward as a debit on the income statement.

As always, attention to detail is very important. Carrying an account balance forward to the wrong column is a common error, as you will soon discover. Carrying the Salaries Payable balance to the income statement credit column is perhaps the most common student error. This is so because of the location of Salaries Payable on the worksheet. It is not found near the other balance sheet accounts because it was added to the bottom of the worksheet by the Salaries adjusting entry; it is located with the income statement accounts. The tendency is to carry the balance to the income statement credit column because most of the other accounts in this section of the worksheet are carried there. It is a simple, inadvertent error, but it is nevertheless still an error.

After all items from the adjusted trial balance have been carried forward to their proper places, each income statement column is totaled and each balance sheet column is totaled.

The total of the income statement credit column (in this example there is only one income statement credit) is $8,820. The total of the income statement debits is $5,740. The income statement credits exceed the income statement debits by $3,080, which is the *net income* for the month. If the debit column had exceeded the credit column, a *net loss* would have been the result.

The balance sheet debits add up to $15,960. Balance sheet credits add up to $12,880. Balance sheet debits exceed balance sheet credits by $3,080, which is the net income. The balance sheet cannot balance until net income is added to the Capital account. Remember, the Capital account reflects the *beginning* rather than *ending* balance. Net Income must be added (and Withdrawals subtracted) to arrive at the ending Capital balance.

The worksheet may "balance" but still contain an error

If the net income (or loss) determined from the totals of the income statement column debits and credits turns out to be different from the net income (or loss) determined from the totals of the balance sheet column debits and credits, then you can be sure the worksheet contains one or more errors.

But if the net income (or loss) determined from the income statement columns turns out to be the same as the net income (or loss) determined from the balance sheet columns, can you be sure that there are no errors in the worksheet? The answer is no. For example, if Salaries Payable had been incorrectly entered as an income statement credit item rather than a balance sheet credit item, the affected parts of the worksheet would appear as shown below.

Accounts	Una~~s~~ted Trial ~~Bala~~nce Credit	Income Statement Debit	Income Statement Credit	Balance Sheet Debit	Balance Sheet Credit	
Cash				1,960		
						⎤ Because this is in the wrong place
Salaries Payable			350			⎤ this is wrong
		5,740	9,170	15,960	12,530	
Net Income		3,430			3,430	
		9,170	9,170	15,960	15,960	

Caution: This net income is wrong because the Salaries Payable credit balance was entered incorrectly in the income statement credit column

Although Salaries Payable was entered in the wrong place, Net Income is $3,430 as determined by both the income statement columns and the balance sheet columns arithmetic. But $3,430 is not the correct income, because the total credits on both the income statement column and the balance sheet column are wrong. The error would most likely be discovered when we prepare the income statement. We would, hopefully, recognize that Salaries Payable should not be classified as a revenue item.

Preparing the Financial Statements

Keep in mind that the sole purpose of preparing the worksheet is to aid in the preparation of the financial statements. If worksheets didn't serve this purpose, we

The income statement is
prepared first

wouldn't use them. Once a worksheet is prepared, it is easy to prepare the financial statements. The income statement is prepared from the information contained on the worksheet in the income statement columns and for our example, it appears as follows:

ROYAL COMPANY
Income Statement
Month Ended October 31, 1987

Revenue		$8,820
Expenses:		
Salary Expense	$4,970	
Utilities Expense	140	
Rent Expense	280	
Office Supplies Used	140	
Depreciation Expense.	210	
Total Expense		5,740
Net Income		$3,080

The balance sheet is prepared in a similar manner. Remember, however, that the worksheet contains the *beginning* Capital balance, which must be adjusted by the Net Income and Withdrawals to arrive at the ending Capital balance. See the type displayed in color in the owner's equity portion of the Royal Company balance sheet below for the determination of the ending Capital balance.

Next, the ending owner's equity must be determined which may be part of the balance sheet

---

ROYAL COMPANY
Balance Sheet
October 31, 1987

Assets			Liabilities and Owner's Equity		
Current Assets:			Current Liabilities:		
Cash	$1,960		Accounts Payable	$ 2,100	
Accounts Receivable	3,640		Salaries Payable	350	
Prepaid Rent	2,240		Unearned Revenue	770	
Office Supplies on Hand	280		Total Current Liabilities.		$ 3,220
Total Current Assets		$ 8,120			
			Owner's Equity:		
Plant and Equipment:			Royal, Capital 10/1/87	$ 9,450	
Office Equipment	$7,000		Net Income.	3,080	
Less: Accumulated Depreciation . .	210			$12,530	
Total Plant and Equipment.		6,790	Less: Withdrawals.	840	
			Royal, Capital 10/31/87.		11,690
Total Assets		$14,910	Total Liabilities and Owner's Equity		$14,910

Journalizing the Adjusting and Closing Entries

Adjusting and closing entries may be recorded in the general journal and general ledger either at the end of each month, each quarter, or at the end of the year,

The adjusting and closing entries may be recorded at the end of each month, each quarter, or at year-end

depending on the company's policy. The most common period to formally adjust and close the accounts is annually. If it is a company's policy to formally adjust and close at the end of each year, then after the worksheet is completed and financial statements are prepared at the end of each month or quarter, no further periodic procedures are needed. The adjusting and closing entries are not journalized and consequently not posted.

Adjusting Entries.

Adjusting entries are prepared from the worksheet.

			ROYAL COMPANY		
			General Journal		Page 12
Date	Account Titles and Explanation	Post. Ref.	Debit	Credit	
Oct. 31	Rent Expense		2 8 0		
	Prepaid Rent			2 8 0	
	To adjust prepaid rent and				
	recognize rent expense for the				
	month.				
31	Office Supplies Used		1 4 0		
	Office Supplies on Hand			1 4 0	
	To adjust office supplies on hand				
	and recognize office supplies used				
	for the month.				
31	Depreciation Expense		2 1 0		
	Accumulated Depreciation			2 1 0	
	To record depreciation expense				
	for the month.				
31	Accounts Receivable		5 6 0		
	Revenue			5 6 0	
	To record revenue earned but not				
	collected at end of month.				
31	Unearned Revenue		4 2 0		
	Revenue			4 2 0	
	To adjust unearned revenue and to				
	recognize revenue earned for the				
	month.				
31	Salary Expense		3 5 0		
	Salaries Payable			3 5 0	
	To record accrued salaries at the				
	end of the month.				

ROYAL COMPANY
General Ledger

Cash			
Bal.	1,960		

Unearned Revenue			
GJ 12	420	Bal.	1,190
		Bal.	770

Rent Expense			
GJ 12	280	GJ 13	280

Accounts Receivable			
Bal.	3,080		
GJ 12	560		
Bal.	3,640		

Royal, Capital			
		Bal.	9,450
GJ 13	840	GJ 13	3,080
		Bal.	11,690

Office Supplies Used			
GJ 12	140	GJ 13	140

Prepaid Rent			
Bal.	2,520	GJ 12	280
Bal.	2,240		

Royal, Withdrawals			
Bal.	840	GJ 13	840

Depreciation Expense			
GJ 12	210	GJ 13	210

Office Supplies on Hand			
Bal.	420	GJ 12	140
Bal.	280		

Revenue			
		Bal.	7,840
		GJ 12	560
		GJ 12	420
GJ 13	8,820		8,820

Accumulated Depreciation			
		GJ 12	210

Office Equipment			
Bal.	7,000		

Salary Expense			
Bal.	4,620		
GJ 12	350		
	4,970	GJ 13	4,970

Salaries Payable			
		GJ 12	350

Accounts Payable			
		Bal.	2,100

Utilities Expense			
Bal.	140	GJ 13	140

Expense and Revenue Summary			
GJ 13	5,740	GJ 13	8,820
GJ 13	3,080		3,080

The general ledger after the adjusting and closing entries have been posted.

But at year-end, after the worksheet is completed and the financial statements are prepared, the adjusting and closing entries are formally journalized. For adjusting entries this involves merely recording in the general journal information contained in the adjustments columns of the worksheet. Once the adjusting entries are journalized, they are then posted to the general ledger accounts.

Let's see how this works for the Royal Company. After Royal's financial statements have been prepared for the period ended October 31, 1987, the adjusting entries are entered in the general journal as shown on page 145.

The adjusting entries are then posted to the general ledger, as can be seen in the Royal Company general ledger illustrated on page 146.

Closing Entries

The closing entries are also prepared from the information contained on the worksheet. By using the income debit and credit columns on the worksheet and the amount of the Withdrawals in the debit balance sheet column, the closing entries can be prepared.

In the worksheet, the accounts shown in the income statement debit column, all of which are expenses, are credited in the general ledger to reduce them to a zero balance. The expense accounts are now ready for the next accounting period. The total of the debit column, $5,740, which is the total of the expenses, is now debited to the Expense and Revenue Summary account, which as you recall is a new account established just to facilitate the closing process.

Each account in the income statement credit column (in this example there is only one account) is credited to reduce it to a zero balance so that the revenue accounts are ready to be used for the next accounting period. And the Expense and Revenue Summary account is credited for the total of the credit income statement column, $8,820—the total revenue.

The Expense and Revenue Summary account will now have a credit balance of $3,080—the net income ($8,820 Cr. − $5,740 Dr.) for the month. The net income is transferred to the Capital account by a debit of $3,080 to the Expense and Revenue Summary account (reducing this account to a zero balance) and a credit to the Royal, Capital account.

Finally, the Withdrawals are transferred to the Capital account by a debit to the Capital account of $840 and a corresponding credit to the Royal, Withdrawals account (reducing the Withdrawal account to a zero balance).

The closing entries of the Royal Company are presented in the general journal shown at the top of page 148.

Post-Closing Trial Balance

Only asset, liability, and capital accounts appear on a post-closing trial balance

We need a final joint check on the adjusting and closing process. This check is the *post-closing trial balance.* A post-closing trial balance contains only asset, liability, and capital accounts because all revenue, expense, and withdrawal accounts *have been closed,* their balances having been transferred to the Capital account. As the name implies, a post-closing trial balance is prepared from the general ledger after the adjusting and closing entries have been posted. Presented at the bottom of page 148 is the October 31, 1987, post-closing trial balance of the Royal Company.

Interim Statements

Monthly and quarterly financial statements are called interim statements

A principal advantage of the worksheet is that we can prepare financial statements from it directly, and without having to formally adjust and close the general ledger accounts. We may wish to do this for interim periods. By the term *interim periods* we

Closing Entries.

Closing entries are also prepared from the worksheet.

Date	Description	Post. Ref.	Debit	Credit
1987 Oct. 31	Expense and Revenue Summary		5 7 4 0	
	Salary Expense			4 9 7 0
	Utilities Expense			1 4 0
	Rent Expense			2 8 0
	Office Supplies Used			1 4 0
	Depreciation Expense			2 1 0
	To close the expense accounts.			
31	Revenue		8 8 2 0	
	Expense and Revenue			
	Summary			8 8 2 0
	To close the revenue accounts.			
31	Expense and Revenue Summary		3 0 8 0	
	Royal, Capital			3 0 8 0
	To close Expense and Revenue			
	Summary.			
31	Royal, Capital		8 4 0	
	Royal, Withdrawals			8 4 0
	To close Withdrawals account.			

ROYAL COMPANY
General Journal   Page 13

ROYAL COMPANY
Post-Closing Trial Balance
October 31, 1987

Cash.	$ 1,960	
Accounts Receivable	3,640	
Prepaid Rent	2,240	
Office Supplies on Hand.	280	
Office Equipment	7,000	
Accumulated Depreciation		$ 210
Accounts Payable		2,100
Salaries Payable		350
Unearned Revenue		770
Royal, Capital		11,690
Totals.	$15,120	$15,120

mean the accounting periods contained within the annual accounting period— monthly and quarterly accounting periods, as illustrated in the following diagram:

	Accounting Periods							
	Jan.	Feb.	March	Apr.	May		Nov.	Dec.
Monthly	First month	Second month	Third month	Fourth month	Fifth month		Eleventh month	Twelfth month
Quarterly	First quarter			Second quarter			Fourth quarter	
Annual	Year							

(Interim Periods: Monthly, Quarterly; Annual)

Financial statements can be and are prepared informally from the worksheet on a monthly or quarterly basis. Such statements are called ***interim statements.***

For the first month of the year the monthly interim financial statements are prepared directly from the worksheet, just as we described in the previous sections. But the adjusting and closing entries *are not journalized.* At the end of the second month another worksheet is prepared. The adjustments on this second worksheet must be recorded *cumulatively* for the 2 months. For example, since the Royal Company started operations on October 1, 1987, the adjustments on the worksheet as of October 31 represent *only 1 month's activity.*

For the second worksheet, which would be dated November 30, 1987, *2 months'* activity would be reflected by the worksheet adjustments. For example, the Prepaid Rent adjustment for November 30, 1987, would appear as follows:

ROYAL COMPANY
Worksheet
Two Months Ended November 30, 1987

Accounts	Unadjusted Trial Balance		Adjustments		Adjusted Trial Balance		Income Statement		Balance Sheet	
	Debit	Credit	Debit	Credit	Debit	Credit	Debit	Credit	Debit	Credit
Prepaid Rent	2,520			(a) 560	1,960				1,960	
Rent Expense			(a) 560		560		560			

Worksheet adjustments are cumulative

Rent Expense is recorded as a $560 debit representing *2 months'* expense. When the income statement is prepared for the month of November it will represent financial activity for the 2-month period. In order to prepare an income statement solely for the month of November, the income statement items from the month of October must be subtracted from the income statement items for the 2-month period ended November 30, 1987, as illustrated at the top of the next page.

	From the November 30 Worksheet Representing 2 Months	From the October 31 Worksheet Representing 1 Month	Income Statement for the Month of November
Revenue	$19,740	$8,820	$10,920
Expenses:			
Salary Expense	$10,500	$4,970	$ 5,530
Utilities Expense	350	140	210
Rent Expense	560	280	280
Office Supplies Used	490	140	350
Depreciation Expense	420	210	210
Total Expense	$12,320	$5,740	$ 6,580
Net Income	$ 7,420	$3,080	$ 4,340

The balance sheet can be prepared directly from the November 30 worksheet since balance sheet accounts, by their nature, are cumulative anyway.

Quarterly interim income statements are prepared by adding together the monthly income statements comprising the quarter, except the first quarter. Can you see why? At the end of the first quarter the worksheet prepared at that time will reflect 3 months' activity — the quarter's activity. So the figures on the first-quarter worksheet are used for the first-quarter interim income statements.

A company may elect to adjust and close its accounts monthly if it so wishes. But if the company elects to adjust and close its accounts only at the end of the yearly accounting period, the worksheet can be used to provide the necessary information for the preparation of the interim financial statements.

ACCOUNTING FOR THE CORPORATE ENTITY

You must have noticed that all the examples in the text to this point and all the exercises and problems were proprietorships. We chose this form because it is the simplest of the three forms of business organization. It has only one capital account; that's why its so simple. But few of you will ever work for a proprietorship or own your own business. Most of you will end up working for small or large corporations. For that reason we are now going to introduce you to the equity accounts of a corporate entity. The asset and liability accounts of corporate entities are the same accounts that we have been using all along with proprietorships, so there is nothing new to learn there. It's only in the owners' equity accounts that a difference appears in accounting for a corporation. Before we start this section you may wish to reread pages 10 to 12 in Chapter 1, where the three types of business organizations are discussed.

The owners' equity section of a corporation is called stockholders' or shareholders' equity. With a proprietorship only one account was needed in the owner's equity section. We did not have to distinguish between capital invested by the owner and the earnings of the business. But most states do not allow a corporation to distribute dividends unless it has earnings. So corporations must distinguish between invested capital and earnings. Invested capital is the funds that the owners invest in the business; in return, the owners receive shares of stock as evidence of their ownership interest. Hence, they are called **shareholders** or **stockholders.**

When a corporation is formed or when additional capital is invested in the business, the entry to record the investment is similar to what we have seen with the proprietorship, but rather than crediting the capital account we credit the **Common**

Stock account. Here is the entry for a new corporation consisting of 10 stockholders who invest a total of $125,000, receiving 12,500 shares from the corporation.

Oct. 18 Cash 125,000
                 Common Stock   125,000
                 To record the issuance of 12,500 shares of $10-par-value com-
                 mon stock.

(Notice in the explanation that the stock had a $10 par value. The par value is determined when the corporation is organized, but don't worry about that for now. This will be discussed in great detail in Chapter 15.)

As we said, corporations must distinguish between invested capital and earnings. The Common Stock account shows the invested capital. To account for the earnings we will use the *Retained Earnings* account. This account functions like the Capital account in a proprietorship in that it is increased by revenues and decreased by expenses and *dividends* (distributions of earnings to stockholders, like the Withdrawals account of a proprietorship). Like the Capital account, the Retained Earnings account does not change until the closing entries are recorded. Let's use the Royal Company closing entries we made on page 148 to illustrate how these would appear for Royal as a corporation.

						ROYAL CORPORATION General Journal					Page 13	
Date	Description	Post. Ref.		Debit				Credit				
1987 Oct. 31	Expense and Revenue Summary			5 7 4 0								
	Salary Expense							4 9 7 0				
	Utilities Expense							1 4 0				
	Rent Expense							2 8 0				
	Office Supplies Used							1 4 0				
	Depreciation Expense							2 1 0				
	To close the expense accounts.											
31	Revenue			8 8 2 0								
	Expense and Revenue											
	Summary							8 8 2 0				
	To close the revenue accounts.											
31	Expense and Revenue Summary			3 0 8 0								
	Retained Earnings							3 0 8 0				
	To close the Expense and Revenue											
	account.											
31	Retained Earnings			8 4 0								
	Dividends							8 4 0				
	To close the Dividends account.											

Like the Withdrawals account, the Dividends account is used to record the distribution of earnings to the owners' of the business. The entry to record the payment of dividends would look like this:

```
Oct. 18   Dividends ...................................... 840
             Cash .......................................          840
          To record the payment of dividends.
```

The last thing we need to discuss at this stage in our introduction to corporate accounting is how the stockholders' equity section will look on the balance sheet. It will look like this:

Stockholders' Equity	
Common Stock, $10 Par Value, 12,500 Shares Issued	$125,000
Retained Earnings	2,240
Total Stockholders' Equity	$127,240

The Retained Earnings balance of $2,240 was determined by subtracting the $840 dividend from the earnings of $3,080. Can you now see how the term retained earnings originated? It represents the *earnings* that are *retained* in the business.

ACCOUNTING POLICY AND ADJUSTING ENTRIES

Let's return for a moment to the Royal example (page 137) and the account Prepaid Rent. Royal made an advance cash payment for 9 months' rent. We have already described that transaction in academic terms as an external transaction that will provide future economic benefits, and we recorded it in the asset account.

The mirror image of this transaction is the payment received from Royal by the business entity renting the building—or office space or whatever—to Royal. This business entity has incurred an obligation that must be fulfilled over the next 9 months. If we were this company we would record this obligation in a liability account called Unearned Rental Revenue.

On either side of this event—one side is paying for the rent in advance, the other side is receiving rent in advance—the economic substance of the transaction does, in fact, represent an asset (rental fees paid for) and a liability (rental services owed for fees received).

We have used balance sheet accounts to record either side of the transaction (Prepaid Rent or Unearned Rental Revenue). These accounts must be adjusted as each month passes and monthly financial statements are prepared. Royal's Prepaid Rent account will be reduced and the Rent Expense account increased as service is received; the building owner's Unearned Rental Revenue account will be reduced and the Rental Revenue account will be increased as it "delivers" the monthly rental service. The financial statements will reflect the expense incurred or revenue earned, and the remaining future economic benefit or future obligation.

But what would happen if Royal had elected to record the $2,250 advance rental payment for 9 months' rent in the Rent Expense account rather than the Prepaid Rent account? Would there be economic calamity? Would the FASB expel Royal from the business community? Of course not. No one really cares how Royal elects to record its transactions *so long as its financial statements reflect the economic substance of the transactions.* That is why adjusting entries are made: to adjust the accounts so that the financial statements prepared from the accounts—or as we now know, from the worksheet — do in fact reflect the economic substance of the multitude of transactions the business entity entered into during the accounting period.

The question that should now be asked is, *Why?* Why record rent paid in advance as an expense? Here's why. Let's assume that Royal has an accounting year of October 1 to September 30. And that Royal *does not* prepare monthly adjusting and closing entries. Instead, Royal prepares cumulative adjustments on the various monthly worksheets and prepares financial statements directly from those worksheets.

At the end of the first month an adjusting entry is needed on the worksheet that will reduce the Rent Expense from $2,520 to $280 — 1 month's rent. The entry must also establish the asset account Prepaid Rent to reflect 8 months' future economic benefit — $2,240. The entry would appear on the worksheet as follows:

<table>
<tr><td colspan="7" align="center">ROYAL COMPANY
Worksheet
Month Ended October 31, 1987</td></tr>
<tr><td rowspan="2">Accounts</td><td colspan="2" align="center">Unadjusted
Trial Balance</td><td colspan="2" align="center">Adjustments</td><td colspan="2" align="center">Adjusted
Trial Balance</td></tr>
<tr><td>Debit</td><td>Credit</td><td>Debit</td><td>Credit</td><td>Debit</td><td>Credit</td></tr>
<tr><td>Prepaid Rent</td><td></td><td></td><td>(a) 2,240</td><td></td><td>2,240</td><td></td></tr>
<tr><td>Rent Expense</td><td>2,520</td><td></td><td></td><td>(a) 2,240</td><td>280</td><td></td></tr>
<tr><td></td><td></td><td></td><td></td><td></td><td></td><td></td></tr>
</table>

Now, compare the *adjusted trial balance* above with the one on page 142. Prepaid Rent ($2,240) and Rent Expense ($280) are the same in both cases. Thus, the financial statements will reflect the economic substance of the transaction.

Let's move 9 months down the road. Can you see that no adjusting entry is required? As of June 30, Rent Expense for the year is $2,520 and no Prepaid Rent exists. This may be the reason Royal elected to record the transaction initially in an expense account. They know that by the time the year is over — assuming that the rental agreement is not renewed — no *formal* adjusting entry will be required. Remember that we assumed Royal adjusts and closes the books only at year-end.

> Transactions may be recorded initially in expense or revenue accounts

You can see now that *there may be occasions where a business entity may elect to record a transaction in an expense account rather than an asset account. And, the mirror image of the transaction may be recorded in a revenue account rather than a liability account.* This is an *accounting policy decision.* Once the decision is made the accountant will then follow the policy in recording the transaction and make the appropriate adjusting entry based on that policy decision.

In the following two sections, we will show through examples how the accounting policy selected determines the way accounts are adjusted.

Asset versus Expense Classification

> Acquisition of certain assets may be recorded as expenses, then later be adjusted

On October 1, 1987, the Cannon Company acquires a 3-year insurance policy for $1,200 paid in advance. Cannon will record this transaction in one of two ways, depending on which of two possible accounting policies it follows. The $1,200 payment may initially be recorded either as an asset or as an expense; both possibilities are illustrated as follows:

| Date | **Initial Entry Recorded as . . .** | | | |
	. . . An Asset		**. . . or as**	**. . . An Expense**
1987 Prepaid Insurance. 1,200			Insurance Expense 1,200	
Cash		1,200	Cash	1,200

When an insurance policy is acquired, it can be recorded as either an asset or an expense . . .

Financial statements are to be prepared on December 31, 1987. At $1,200 for 3 years, the cost of insurance comes out to $33.33 per month. On December 31, 3 months' insurance has been consumed, or

Insurance expense = $33.33 per month $\times$ 3 months = $100

leaving 33 months' insurance remaining, or

Prepaid insurance = $1,200 − ($33.33 per month $\times$ 3 months) = $1,100

on December 31.

Prepaid Insurance must reflect a $1,100 debit balance and Insurance Expense must be stated at $100. To arrive at these debit balances, an adjusting entry is required. The appropriate adjustment depends on how the initial transaction was recorded. Presented below in general journal entry form are the required adjusting entries.

. . . so long as the appropriate adjusting entry is made.

| Date | **Adjusting Entry Required if Initial Entry Recorded as . . .** | | | |
	. . . An Asset		**. . . or as**	**. . . An Expense**
1987				
Dec. 31 Insurance Expense 100			Prepaid Insurance 1,100	
Prepaid Insurance		100	Insurance Expense	1,100

The effect of the adjusting entries on the general ledger accounts is illustrated below for both accounting policies.

| **General Ledger Accounts after Adjusting Entry if Initial Entry Recorded as . . .** | | | | | |
. . . An Asset			**. . . or as**	**. . . An Expense**	
Prepaid Insurance			**Prepaid Insurance**		
10/1/87	1,200	12/31/87 Adj. 100	12/31/87 Adj.	1,100	
12/31/87	1,100				
Insurance Expense			**Insurance Expense**		
12/31/87 Adj.	100		10/1/87	1,200	12/31/87 Adj. 1,100
			12/31/87 Bal.	100	

Liability versus Revenue Classification

The Morrow Company received a check on July 1, 1987, for $1,600 representing 2 years' rent paid in advance. At this date, Morrow may record a credit in that amount for either Unearned Rental Revenue or Rental Revenue, depending on its accounting policy, as follows:

When cash is received for rent paid in advance, the entry can be recorded as a liability or as revenue . . .

	Initial Entry Recorded as . . .		
Date	. . . A Liability	. . . or as	. . . A Revenue
1987			
July 1 Cash 1,600		Cash 1,600	
Unearned Rental Revenue	1,600	Rental Revenue	1,600

On December 31, 1987, financial statements are required. At $1,600 for 2 years the revenue from rentals will be $66.67 per month. On December 31, 6 months' rental revenue has been earned, or

$$\text{Rental revenue} = \$66.67 \text{ per month} \times 6 \text{ months} = \$400$$

leaving 18 months' unearned rental revenue remaining, or

$$\text{Unearned rental revenue} = \$1,600 - (\$66.67 \text{ per mo.} \times 6 \text{ mos.}) = \$1,200$$

On December 31 Unearned Rental Revenue must reflect a $1,200 credit balance and Rental Revenue must be stated at $400. The adjusting entries required to achieve these balances are presented as follows:

. . . so long as the appropriate adjusting entry is made.

	Adjusting Entry Required if Initial Entry Recorded as . . .		
Date	. . . A Liability	. . . or as	. . . A Revenue
1987			
Dec. 31 Unearned Rental Revenue. 400		Rental Revenue. 1,200	
Rental Revenue.	400	Unearned Rental Revenue.	1,200

Illustrated below are the general ledger accounts after the appropriate adjusting entries have been made.

	General Ledger Accounts after Adjusting Entry if Initial Entry Recorded as . . .		
. . . A Liability		. . . or as . . . A Revenue	
Unearned Rental Revenue		**Unearned Rental Revenue**	
12/31/87 Adj. 400	7/1/87 1,600		12/31/87 Adj. 1,200
	12/31/87 Bal. 1,200		
Rental Revenue		**Rental Revenue**	
	12/31/87 Adj. 400	12/31/87 Adj. 1,200	7/1/87 1,600
			12/31/87 Bal. 400

REVERSING ENTRIES

In the preceding two examples we have seen how the choice of an accounting policy affects the manner in which adjusting entries are recorded. Recording the advance payment for insurance in the Insurance Expense account requires an adjusting entry that establishes the Prepaid Insurance account at year-end and reduces the Insurance Expense account to an amount actually consumed. Likewise, when rent payments are received in advance and recorded as Rental Revenue, the appropriate adjustment at year-end is to establish the Unearned Rental Revenue account and reduce the Rental Revenue to the amount actually earned.

The policy of recording entries in income statement accounts (Insurance Expense and Rental Revenue, for example) that require year-end adjustments presents a bookkeeping problem in subsequent accounting periods.

Refer back to the Cannon example (page 153) of the $1,200 insurance policy acquired on October 1, 1987. Now look ahead to 1988 and assume that Cannon buys a second policy on April 1 for $800. It's a 1-year policy. How will this be recorded? Let's assume that the accounting policy is to use income statement accounts; thus the entry will be:

```
1988
Apr. 1   Insurance Expense. . . . . . . . . . . . . . . . . . . . . . . . . . . . . . . . 800
               Cash. . . . . . . . . . . . . . . . . . . . . . . . . . . . . . . . . . . .        800
```

But wait a minute: Where is the unconsumed insurance from the first policy — the Prepaid Insurance? It's in the Prepaid Insurance account, having been transferred there by the December 31 adjusting entry. Further, the Insurance Expense account for 1987 has been closed out by the December 31 closing entry. The ledger accounts on April 1, 1988, accordingly would appear as follows:

Prepaid Insurance		Insurance Expense			
12/31/87 1,100		10/1/87 1,200	12/31/87 Adj. 1,100
		12/31/87 Bal. 100	12/31/87 Closing 100
		1/1/88 Bal. –0–	
		4/1/88 800	

We now have our eggs in two baskets; they should be in one. We have $1,100 in Prepaid Insurance and $800 in Insurance Expense. What needs to be done is to *transfer* the $1,100 from the Prepaid Insurance account to the Insurance Expense account because it is the Cannon Company's accounting policy to record insurance in the Insurance Expense account. The general journal entry required to accomplish this would be as follows:

```
1988
Jan. 1   Insurance Expense . . . . . . . . . . . . . . . . . . . . . . . . . . . . . . 1,100
               Prepaid Insurance. . . . . . . . . . . . . . . . . . . . . . . . . . . .        1,100
```

Reversing entries are exactly the opposite of adjusting entries

Compare this entry to the adjusting entry recorded on page 154 where the insurance was initially recorded as an expense. It is exactly the opposite, the *reverse*. For this reason it is called a ***reversing entry.***

Reversing entries are prepared as of the first day of a new accounting period. The entry to reverse the Morrow Company's December 31 adjusting entry (assuming the Rental Revenue account was used to record the initial receipt of the $1,600 rent, paid in advance, as on page 155) would be:

1988
Jan. 1   Unearned Rental Revenue 1,200
           Rental Revenue   1,200
           To reverse December 31, 1987, adjusting entry.

Reversing entries maintain internal accounting consistency . . .

We can generalize from these two examples. Whenever a company elects to record a transaction initially in an income statement account, and that transaction must later be adjusted, then the adjusting entry must be reversed. This is done to *achieve internal accounting consistency.*

. . . and simplify the recordkeeping process

There is a second reason for reversing entries. Reversing entries are made to *simplify the recordkeeping process.* We can illustrate this by using salaries as an example. Let's assume that Salary Expense is $500 per day; that December 31, 1987, is on Wednesday; and that the usual payday is on Friday. This would mean that on December 31, $1,500 in salaries has been earned but not yet paid. Thus, the adjusting entry for this accrual is $1,500 and would be recorded as follows:

1987
Dec. 31   Salary Expense. 1,500
           Salaries Payable   1,500
           To record adjustment for accrual of salaries.

Prior to this accrual, from January 1, 1987, to December 26, Salary Expense amounted to $127,700. The general ledger accounts Salary Expense and Salaries Payable would appear as follows after the adjusting entry was posted:

General Ledger

Salary Expense		Salaries Payable	
1/1/87 – 12/26/87			
	127,700	12/31/87	
12/31/87		Adj.	1,500
Adj.	1,500		
12/31/87			
Bal.	129,200		

Salary Expense for the entire year would then be closed by the following closing entry:

1987
Dec. 31   Expense and Revenue Summary 129,200
           Salary Expense   129,200
           To close the Salary Expense account.

Posting the closing entry as a credit to the Salary Expense account in the general ledger would result in a zero balance in that account.

Salary Expense			
1/1/87 – 12/26/87	127,700		
12/31/87 Adj.	1,500		
12/31/87 Bal.	129,200	12/31/87 Closing	129,200
Bal.	–0–		

Thus far there are no problems in the way things were handled in 1987. Now here comes the problem of the adjusting entry needing to be reversed to start the new year 1988.

On Friday, January 2, 1988, $2,500 ($500 × 5) is paid to the employees for their week's service. For each of the past 51 weeks the bookkeeper or the computer has recorded the payroll entry in the following manner:

The first payroll entry in a new year requires special consideration

```
Salary Expense . . . . . . . . . . . . . . . . . . . . . . . . . . . . . . . . . . . . . . 2,500
    Cash . . . . . . . . . . . . . . . . . . . . . . . . . . . . . . . . . . . . . . . . . .        2,500
To record salaries paid.
```

For each of the past 51 weeks, that entry has been correct.

Unfortunately, if the entry is recorded in the same manner on January 2, 1988, it will be incorrect. The $2,500 does not represent Salary Expense for the year 1988. Only $1,000 is Salary Expense for 1988; $1,500 is Salary Expense from 1987, as you can see in the following diagram:

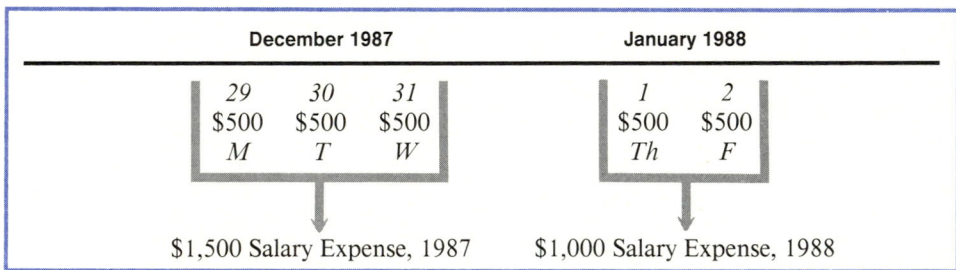

There are two ways to solve this accounting problem.

First, the accountant could make the January 2, 1988, entry for the bookkeeper or the computer. The entry required is:

We could record the first payroll entry in a new year like this . . .

```
1988
Jan. 2   Salaries Payable (1987) . . . . . . . . . . . . . . . . . . . . . . . . . . . 1,500
         Salary Expense (1988) . . . . . . . . . . . . . . . . . . . . . . . . . . . . 1,000
             Cash . . . . . . . . . . . . . . . . . . . . . . . . . . . . . . . . . . . .        2,500
         To record salary expense paid for 1988 and pay accrued salaries
         payable from 1987.
```

Second, a reversing entry could be made as of January 1, 1988. The accrued salaries adjusting entry of December 31, 1987, is reversed as follows:

. . . or we could record a reversing entry

```
1988
Jan. 1   Salaries Payable . . . . . . . . . . . . . . . . . . . . . . . . . . . . . . . . . . 1,500
              Salary Expense. . . . . . . . . . . . . . . . . . . . . . . . . . . . . .          1,500
         To reverse salary adjusting entry of December 31, 1987.
```

The ledger accounts, after the reversing entries are posted, would appear as presented below:

Salary Expense					Salaries Payable			
	127,700				1/1/88		12/31/87	
12/31/87 Adj.	1,500				Reversing	1,500	Adj.	1,500
							Bal.	–0–
12/31/87 Bal.	129,200	12/31/87 Closing	129,200					
		1/1/88 Reversing	1,500					

Notice that the liability account — Salaries Payable — now has a zero balance and that the expense account — Salary Expense — has a $1,500 *credit* balance. The credit in the Salary Expense account is in *anticipation* of the $2,500 debit to be received when the payroll entry of January 2 is made. Now the bookkeeper or the computer can make the January 2 payroll entry in exactly the same way as the entry for each of the other 51 weeks. That is, the January 2, 1988, payroll entry can be made as follows:

The use of a reversing entry enables us to record the payroll entry just as we have done in the past

```
1988
Jan. 2   Salary Expense. . . . . . . . . . . . . . . . . . . . . . . . . . . . . . . . . . 2,500
              Cash . . . . . . . . . . . . . . . . . . . . . . . . . . . . . . . . . . . . . .          2,500
         To record salaries paid.
```

Posting this entry to the Salary Expense account which has been adjusted and closed in 1987 and reversed for $1,500 in 1988 results in a $1,000 debit balance for the year 1988, as shown in the following:

Salary Expense			
	127,700		
12/31/87 Adj.	1,500		
12/31/87 Bal.	129,200	12/31/87 Closing	129,200
1/2/88	2,500	1/1/88 Reversing	1,500
1/2/88 Bal.	1,000		

THE CASE OF AN ACCOUNTANT'S BLIND TRUST

In 1973 a stock loan company called MESCO Broker Services, Inc., was organized in New York City. The company was 70 to 80% owned by Mesirow & Company, which was located in Chicago. The president of MESCO engaged the services of an accountant on a part-time basis to prepare the books of original entry, post to the general ledger, make adjusting entries, and prepare the financial statements that were sent to Mesirow & Company.

From the inception of MESCO the company president began taking salary advances. When the salary advances became excessive, Mesirow officials in Chicago insisted that the practice be stopped and that the advances be treated as a loan to be repaid promptly. In August 1975 the accountant discovered that the president had again taken an advance. The president assured the accountant that the advance would be repaid. Consequently, the accountant recorded the advance as a prepaid expense which was covered by not issuing a paycheck to the president the next pay period.

Shortly thereafter the accountant discovered that the president was again taking advances. The president assured the accountant that they would be repaid. As the accountant discovered the advances in the check book, he would record them as advances in the cash payments journal but cancel them out by a month-end adjusting entry showing the advances as deposits in transit. On the first business day of the following month a reversing entry was made to reestablish the advance account. By this means the advances were not disclosed on the financial statements that were sent to Mesirow in Chicago.

By the end of March 1976 the advances had accumulated to $22,400. Since MESCO's fiscal year-end was March 31, the cash shortage had to be covered. The president accomplished this by borrowing $2,400 from the accountant and $20,000 from two individuals in the stock loan business. The $20,000 was repaid by 12 installments from MESCO by charging the payments to "Stock Loan Fees," a regular expense account. The president repaid the accountant $1,000. (The remaining $1,400 was never repaid.)

Commencing in November 1977 the president began writing checks for fictitious disbursements, entering a fictitious payee on the check stub. The accountant covered these checks by reflecting a transfer of funds between various bank accounts, thus overstating MESCO's cash balance.

Just before the March 31, 1978, year-end the president showed the accountant a deposit slip for $55,000 to cover the missing funds. The deposit slip was a forgery, but when this was discovered the president was missing.

Source: Securities Exchange Act of 1934, Release No. 21135, July 12, 1984.

The MESCO case illustrates the use of reversing entries to hide improper cash advances. The case also illustrates the need for healthy skepticism when dealing with unusual requests from corporate executives.

From this example we can generalize: If a company elects to use reversing entries, then *all accrual adjusting entries must be reversed.* In addition to the Salary Expense/Salaries Payable accrual adjusting entry, we have encountered two other common accruals: the Interest Expense/Interest Payable and the Interest Income/Interest Receivable adjustments. *Accrual adjusting entries are reversed to simplify the record-keeping process.*

A simple way to determine when a reversing entry must be made is this: If the adjusting entry increases a balance sheet account, then that adjusting entry must be reversed. Look at the first adjusting entry we discussed. It's the one dealing with insurance. When insurance was recorded as an expense, the adjusting entry (see page 154) increased the Prepaid Insurance account. And so it was with the second adjusting entry (see page 155). When rental revenue was recorded in a revenue account, the adjusting entry increased the Unearned Revenue account. And when we discussed payroll, the adjusting entry (page 157) increased the Salaries Payable account. All of these accounts—Prepaid Insurance, Unearned Revenue, and Salaries Payable—are balance sheet accounts.

THE ACCOUNTING PROCESS REVIEWED

You must be continually aware that the ultimate objective of financial accounting is to prepare financial statements that represent meaningfully and fairly the results of operations of a business entity over a period of time and its financial position at a point in time. The process we have described in this chapter and the preceding two chapters is a practical means of achieving that objective. The steps involved in the financial accounting process are shown in Figure 4-1, which appears on pages 162 and 163.

CHAPTER SUMMARY

Balance sheet and income statement accounts differ in their basic nature. ***Balance sheet accounts*** — sometimes called ***permanent accounts*** or ***real accounts*** — represent the balance of an account *at a particular point in time.* ***Income statement accounts*** — sometimes called ***temporary accounts*** or ***nominal accounts*** — represent accumulations of revenue and expenses *during a particular period of time.*

The income statement accounts — revenue and expenses — and also the Withdrawals account are extensions of the balance sheet Capital account. They represent increases and decreases to the Capital account, but we do not record these increases and decreases directly in the Capital account. Instead we use the revenue, expenses, and withdrawals accounts because we need the information they contain to prepare the income statement, to determine net income or loss, and to prepare the statement of owners' equity.

Balance sheet accounts can increase or decrease from one accounting period to another, but income statement accounts can only increase.

The use of ***closing entries*** solves two problems for us:

1. Closing entries transfer the revenue, expense, and withdrawal accounts back to the Capital account. This enables us to determine the balance of the Capital account at the end of the accounting period.
2. Closing entries reduce to a zero balance all revenue, expense, and withdrawals or dividends accounts. This enables us to accumulate data in these temporary accounts for the next accounting period. These new accumulations will reflect data *just for the new period.* No data from previous periods will be included, since the accounts started at a zero balance.

Expense accounts are closed by crediting each expense account for an amount equal to the balance in the account. We make the corresponding debit, which will be equal to the sum of the expenses, to a new account which we call ***Expense and Revenue Summary.***

Similarly, we close the revenue accounts by debiting each revenue account for an amount equal to the balance in the account. The corresponding credit for the sum of the revenue accounts is made to the Expense and Revenue Summary.

The balance in the Expense and Revenue Summary, which is the ***net income*** or ***net loss*** for the period, is then transferred to the Capital account by debiting (in the case where net income exists; crediting in the case of a net loss situation) Expense and Revenue Summary and crediting the Capital account.

Finally, we close the Withdrawals or Retained Earnings account by a credit to that account. A debit for a like amount transfers the withdrawals to the Capital account. Now the Capital account will reflect the ending balance, the beginning Capital balance having been increased by the net income — or decreased by a net loss — and decreased by withdrawals.

The ***worksheet,*** which is prepared in pencil, is a tool used by an accountant to organize the adjustments to the accounts and to simplify the process of preparing the monthly, quarterly, and yearly financial statements. The worksheet is used to make adjustments in the trial balance. From the resulting ***adjusted trial balance*** the interim and year-end income statement and balance sheet can be prepared.

Monthly income statements are obtained from the worksheet by simply subtract-

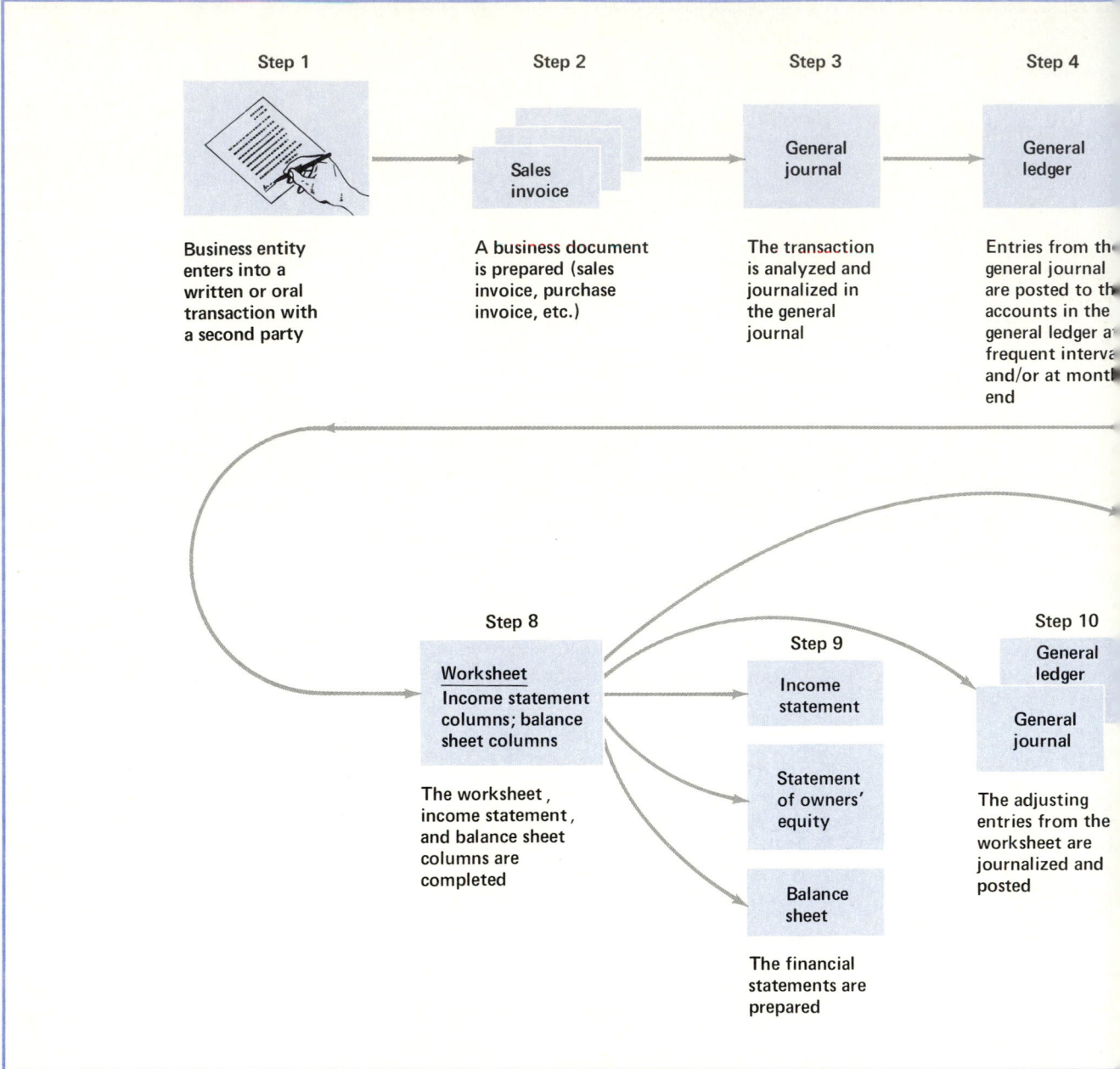

Step 1

Sales invoice

Business entity enters into a written or oral transaction with a second party

Step 2

A business document is prepared (sales invoice, purchase invoice, etc.)

Step 3

General journal

The transaction is analyzed and journalized in the general journal

Step 4

General ledger

Entries from the general journal are posted to the accounts in the general ledger at frequent interval and/or at month end

Step 8

Worksheet
Income statement columns; balance sheet columns

The worksheet, income statement, and balance sheet columns are completed

Step 9

Income statement

Statement of owners' equity

Balance sheet

The financial statements are prepared

Step 10

General ledger

General journal

The adjusting entries from the worksheet are journalized and posted

FIGURE 4-1   Review of the steps in the accounting process.

ing the accumulated amounts in the most recent worksheet income statement columns from the accumulated amounts up through the prior month. The difference represents the current month's income statement because the adjustments made on the worksheet are cumulative from the beginning of the year.

Quarterly income statements are prepared by adding together three monthly income statements representing that particular quarter.

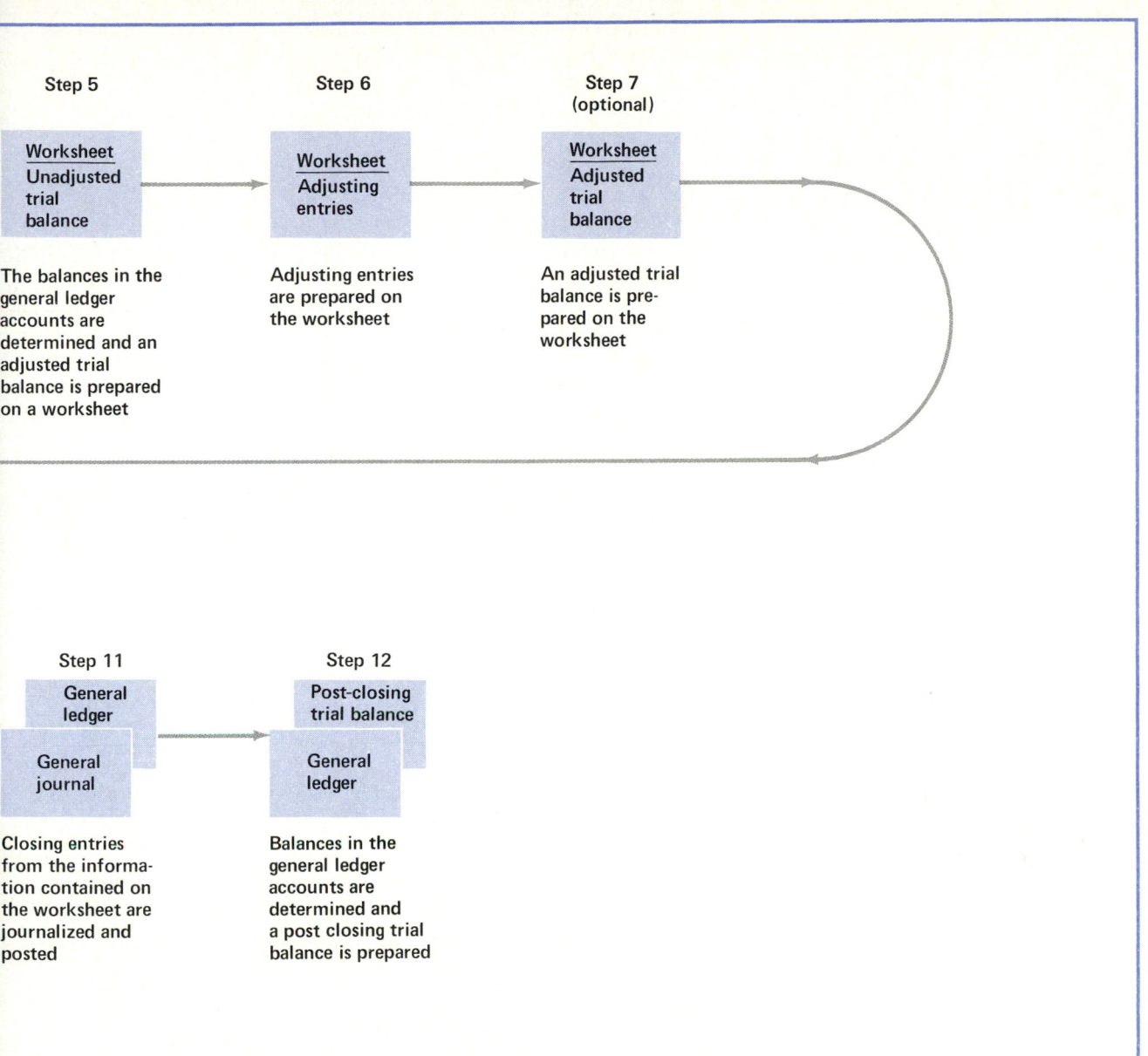

Step 5

Worksheet
Unadjusted
trial
balance

The balances in the
general ledger
accounts are
determined and an
adjusted trial
balance is prepared
on a worksheet

Step 6

Worksheet
Adjusting
entries

Adjusting entries
are prepared on
the worksheet

**Step 7
(optional)**

Worksheet
Adjusted
trial
balance

An adjusted trial
balance is pre-
pared on the
worksheet

Step 11

General
ledger

General
journal

Closing entries
from the informa-
tion contained on
the worksheet are
journalized and
posted

Step 12

Post-closing
trial balance

General
ledger

Balances in the
general ledger
accounts are
determined and
a post closing trial
balance is prepared

A *post-closing trial balance* is prepared after the closing entries have been journalized and posted. The post-closing trial balance contains only balance sheet accounts and is a final check on the adjusting and closing process.

A corporation's equity section is referred to as stockholders' equity, and it contains
an account to reflect the amount invested by the stockholders — Common Stock —
and an account reflecting the earnings and dividend activities — Retained Earnings.

All other accounting activity is the same for a corporation as it is for a proprietorship.

Reversing entries are easy to make. We simply reverse the *appropriate* adjusting entry. The difficulty is knowing which adjusting entry is appropriate. The following rule should help: *If the adjusting entry increases a balance sheet account, it must be reversed.*

IMPORTANT TERMS USED IN THIS CHAPTER

Accounting policy   A business entity's decision on the manner in which accounting alternatives are handled. The decision to record rent paid in advance in the nominal account Rent Expense rather than in the real account Prepaid Rent is an accounting policy decision. (page 152)

Adjusted trial balance   A list of the general ledger accounts after their respective amounts have been updated by the adjustments. The adjusted trial balance is usually prepared on the worksheet. (page 140)

Adjustments   Internal transactions prepared by business entities to bring the accounts up to date prior to the preparation of the financial statements. (page 137)

Balance sheet accounts   Asset, Liability, and Capital accounts. These accounts represent the amount of the particular account at a point in time. They are also called *permanent accounts* or *real accounts.* (page 131)

Closing entries   Internal transactions recorded by business entities to clear all income statement accounts to a zero balance at the end of an accounting period and to transfer these balances to the Capital account. (page 132)

Common Stock   An owners' equity account that reflects the investment made by stockholders. (page 151)

Expense and Revenue Summary   An account used to simplify the closing process. Income statement accounts are first closed to the Expense and Revenue Summary account, which in turn is closed to the Capital account. This account is also called the *Income Summary* account. (page 133)

Income statement accounts   Revenue and Expense accounts. These accounts are extensions of the Capital account and accumulate data for a month, a quarter, or a year, but no longer. They are also called *nominal accounts* or *temporary accounts.* (page 131)

Interim statements   Financial statements prepared on a monthly or quarterly basis directly from the worksheet. (page 147)

Post-closing trial balance   A list of the general ledger accounts after the adjusting and closing entries have been journalized and posted. Only balance sheet accounts will contain balances in a post-closing trial balance. (page 147)

Retained Earnings   An owners' equity account that reflects the earnings and dividends activity of a corporation. (page 151)

Reversing entries   Journal entries that are exactly the opposite of adjusting entries. Where adjusting entries debit an account, the reversing entry will credit that account for the same amount. Reversing entries are used to simplify the record-keeping process and to maintain internal accounting consistency. (page 156)

Unadjusted trial balance   A list of the general ledger accounts after all external transactions have been recorded and posted but prior to consideration for adjustments. (page 136)

Worksheet A multi-column paper used by accountants to organize the period-end accounting procedures in a logical manner. (page 136)

QUESTIONS

1. What is the difference between *closing the books* and *adjusting the accounts?*

2. Why is a *post-closing trial balance* prepared?

3. Explain why the Revenue, Expense, and Withdrawals accounts are called *temporary* or *nominal* accounts.

4. Why are closing entries necessary?

5. What is the difference between the *Expense and Revenue Summary* account and the *Income Summary* account? How are these accounts used?

6. What purpose does the worksheet serve?

7. If the total debits from the unadjusted trial balance are added to the total debits from the adjustments column on a worksheet, the result will be the total debits for the adjusted trial balance. Comment.

8. Depreciation Expense does not appear on an unadjusted trial balance on a worksheet, yet an adjustment requires that depreciation be recorded. How is this situation handled?

9. It is not necessary to prepare an adjusted trial balance on a worksheet. Comment.

10. Explain why some companies may not journalize in the general journal adjustments entered on the worksheet.

11. By using a worksheet accountants are assured that all errors will be found, since a worksheet must balance. Comment.

12. A balance sheet cannot be prepared directly from the information contained in the balance sheet columns of a worksheet. Why not?

13. The income statement debit column on a worksheet will not equal the income statement credit column. Nor will the balance sheet debit column equal the balance sheet credit column. Why not?

14. What advantage does the worksheet offer an accountant when preparing interim financial statements?

15. How does a worksheet facilitate the year-end procedures of journalizing the adjusting and closing entries?

16. Are reversing entries required?

17. A business entity's accounting policy determines how its adjusting entries are made. Explain.

18. What are reversing entries? Why are they necessary?

19. If a company uses reversing entries, how does it determine which adjusting entries to reverse?

20. Summarize briefly the various steps in the accounting process.

EXERCISES

Exercise 4-1
Preparing closing entries

The adjusted trial balance of the Jet Company appears on page 166. From the information contained therein, prepare the appropriate year-end closing entries.

JET COMPANY
Adjusted Trial Balance
December 31, 1987

Cash.	$ 755	
Accounts Receivable	1,486	
Supplies on Hand	341	
Equipment	2,750	
Accumulated Depreciation		$ 975
Accounts Payable		457
Salaries Payable		283
Jet, Capital		2,970
Jet, Withdrawals	650	
Plumbing Revenue		3,784
Carpentry Revenue		1,809
Salary Expense	2,791	
Supplies Used.	877	
Depreciation Expense	270	
Rent Expense.	300	
Miscellaneous Expense.	58	
Totals.	$10,278	$10,278

Exercise 4-2
Preparing closing entries

Presented below is the income statement of the Brandon Company:

BRANDON COMPANY
Income Statement
For the Year Ended August 31, 1981

Revenue:		
Real Estate Commissions Earned.		$75,500
Interest Income		6,300
Total Revenue.		$81,800
Expenses:		
Salary Expense	$42,700	
Advertising Expense	11,300	
Depreciation Expense	1,500	
Rent Expense	4,800	
Office Supplies Used.	3,400	
Utilities Expense	600	
Total Expenses		64,300
Net Income		$17,500

a. During the year Mr. Brandon withdrew $15,000 from the business. The company books are closed annually on August 31. Prepare the year-end closing entries.

b. Assuming that the Brandon Company is a corporation and that $15,000 in dividends were paid, prepare the year-end closing entries.

Exercise 4-3
Completing a worksheet

The worksheet presented below contains a number of missing figures, but there is sufficient information for you to determine the missing figures. Complete the worksheet by supplying the missing figures. *(Check figure: Net income = $6)*

	Unadjusted Trial Balance		Adjustments		Income Statement		Balance Sheet	
	Debit	Credit	Debit	Credit	Debit	Credit	Debit	Credit
Cash							3	
Accounts Receivable	7							
Prepaid Rent	6							
Store Supplies on Hand				4			3	
Store Equipment	10							
Accumulated Depreciation								5
Accounts Payable		2						
Salaries Payable								
Unearned Revenue			2					1
Common Stock		9						
Retained Earnings		4						
Dividends							3	
Revenue						24		
Salary Expense			3		9			
Store Supplies Used								
Rent Expense					2			
Depreciation Expense			1					
Utilities Expense	2							
Net Income								

Exercise 4-4
Preparing a worksheet

The accounts of the Cambridge Company are presented below in descending order:

Consulting Revenue	$30	Accounts Payable	$6
Office Equipment	20	Accounts Receivable	6
Cambridge, Capital	12	Cambridge, Withdrawals.	6
Salary Expense	12	Notes Payable.	4
Office Supplies on Hand.	10	Cash.	2
Accumulated Depreciation	8	Travel Expense.	2
Prepaid Rent	8	Utilities Expense.	2
Unearned Consulting Revenue.	8		

Information available pertaining to the July 31, 1987, year-end adjustments is as follows:

Accrued salaries.	$4	Consulting revenue earned (for which	
Depreciation.	2	cash has already been received)	$6
Expired rent	4	Office supplies on hand	4

From this information prepare and complete a worksheet.

(Check figure: Net income = $4)

Exercise 4-5
Preparing a monthly income statement

The following items appeared on the income statement columns of the Atlanta Company worksheets for the months of June and July 1987. From this information you are to prepare an income statement for the month of July 1987.

(Check figure: Net income for July = $8,865)

ATLANTA COMPANY
Worksheet Income Statement Columns

	June 1987		July 1987	
Dry Cleaning Revenue		$34,050		$50,100
Laundry Revenue		4,410		5,790
Salary Expense	$21,030		$27,525	
Rent Expense	3,000		3,600	
Depreciation Expense	6,600		7,260	
Advertising Expense	750		930	
Laundry Supplies Used	1,260		1,890	
	$32,640	$38,460	$41,205	$55,890
Net Income	5,820		14,685	
	$38,460	$38,460	$55,890	$55,890

Exercise 4-6

Recording adjusting entries

The Buffalo Company entered into the following three transactions during the year 1987:

Mar. 1   Paid $2,400 for advertising for the next 12 months.
June 1   Received $3,600 for rentals property for the next 24 months.
Oct. 1   Acquired store supplies in the amount of $3,230. On December 31, $1,250 of store supplies remain on hand.

a. Assume that the Buffalo Company records these transactions initially in balance sheet accounts. Record the December 31, 1987, adjusting entries.
b. Assume that the Buffalo Company records these transactions initially in income statement accounts. Record the December 31, 1987, adjusting entries.

Exercise 4-7
Identifying reversing entries

Presented below are a number of adjusting entries:

1987			Number
Dec. 31	Consulting Revenue. 1,670		1
	Unearned Consulting Revenue.	1,670	
	To record liability for unearned consulting revenue at year-end.		
31	Prepaid Insurance 600		2
	Insurance Expense.	600	
	To record unexpired insurance at year-end.		

Dec. 31	Depreciation Expense.	1,000		3
	Accumulated Depreciation		1,000	
	To record depreciation for the year.			
31	Salary Expense	1,580		4
	Salaries Payable		1,580	
	To record accrued salaries.			
31	Interest Receivable	500		5
	Interest Income.		500	
	To record accrued interest.			
31	Office Supplies Used	2,630		6
	Office Supplies on Hand		2,630	
	To record office supplies used during the period.			

Some of these adjusting entries will require reversing entries at the start of the new accounting year on January 1, 1988. Identify these adjusting entries.

Exercise 4-8
Adjusting office supplies

At the start of the current year, American, Continental, and National Companies all had $6,700 of office supplies on hand. The three companies have different accounting procedures for recording supplies. American and National show this beginning balance in the Supplies on Hand account, but Continental reflects the beginning balance in the Supplies Used account. American debits the account Supplies on Hand when supplies are acquired, whereas Continental and National follow the policy of debiting Supplies Used upon the acquisition of supplies. All three companies acquired a total of $36,740 of supplies at various times throughout the year, and all three have $2,730 of supplies on hand at the end of the year.
   Prepare the appropriate adjusting entry for each company.

PROBLEMS
Set A

Problem A4-1
Preparing closing entries

Bobby Burk operates a Blood Bank in Burbank. At the end of the current year the accounts listed below appeared in the adjusted trial balance:

Accounts Payable	$ 2,940		Interest Payable	$ 175
Accounts Receivable	17,605		Land	18,900
Accumulated Depreciation	36,715		Miscellaneous Expense.	476
Blood Supplies on Hand.	14,356		Mortgage Payable	42,980
Blood Supplies Used	126,215		Notes Payable	3,500
Building	94,150		Notes Receivable	8,400
Burk, Capital	106,512		Prepaid Rent	840
Burk, Withdrawals	22,000		Rent Expense.	1,680
Cash.	5,348		Revenue from Blood Sales	297,521
Depreciation Expense	7,400		Salaries Expense	130,494
Equipment	61,075		Salaries Payable	1,890
Interest Expense	350		Telephone Expense	1,561
Interest Income	756		Utilities Expense.	2,604

Required Prepare the appropriate year-end closing entries.

(Check figure: Burk, Capital after closing = $112,009)

Problem A4-2
Preparing a worksheet

The unadjusted trial balance below represents activity for the first year of operations of Carla's Clock Repairing Service:

CARLA'S CLOCK REPAIRING SERVICE
Unadjusted Trial Balance
December 31, 1987

Cash.	$ 651	
Accounts Receivable	1,274	
Prepaid Advertising	728	
Prepaid Rent	980	
Clock Supplies on Hand	1,785	
Equipment	3,500	
Accounts Payable		$ 2,100
Carla Clark, Capital		3,108
Carla Clark, Withdrawals	2,800	
Clock Repair Revenue		27,020
Salary Expense	19,460	
Insurance Expense.	700	
Telephone Expense	350	
Totals	$32,228	$32,228

The following information pertains to year-end adjustments:
a. As of December 31, 1987, $525 of salaries has accrued.
b. The equipment, which will have no residual value, is estimated to have a 5-year life.
c. One-fourth of the Prepaid Rent is applicable to 1988.
d. On the last day of December 1987, Carla repaired the clock on the city tower for $294. The revenue has not been recorded, nor has payment been received.
c. A physical count of the clock supplies on hand at year-end amounts to $644.

Required
1. Enter the unadjusted trial balance on a worksheet.
2. Record the adjustments on the worksheet.
3. Complete the worksheet.

(Check figure: Net income = $3,703)

Problem A4-3
Completing a worksheet

The worksheet for Dan's Dating Service (shown at the top of the facing page) is incomplete. A number of items are missing, but by studying the worksheet you can determine the missing figures.

Required
Complete the worksheet.

(Check figure: Net income = $2,020)

DAN'S DATING SERVICE
Worksheet
December 31, 1987

Accounts	Unadjusted Trial Balance Debit	Unadjusted Trial Balance Credit	Adjustment Debit	Adjustment Credit	Income Statement Debit	Income Statement Credit	Balance Sheet Debit	Balance Sheet Credit
Cash	1,700							
Accounts Receivable							2,610	
Prepaid Rent				240			720	
Office Supplies on Hand	1,230						360	
Computer Equipment							7,200	
Accumulated Depreciation:								
Computer Equipment		1,800						2,700
Building	90,000							
Accumulated Depreciation:								
Building		20,000		1,000				
Land	30,000							
Accounts Payable								1,490
Dating Service Revenue								
Received in Advance		340						130
Mortgage Payable								70,000
Dan Darling, Capital		52,500						
Dan Darling, Withdrawals							20,000	
Dating Service Revenue						127,680		
Salary Expense	114,800							
Advertising Expense	2,400							
Utilities Expense					1,800			
Miscellaneous Expense					900			
Rent Expense								
Office Supplies Used								
Depreciation: Computer								
Equipment								
Depreciation: Building								
Salaries Payable								2,750
Net Income								

Problem A4-4

Preparing a worksheet, financial statements, adjusting, and closing entries.

Presented below is the unadjusted trial balance of Ellen's Entertainment Bureau as of December 31, 1987:

Cash	$ 4,710	
Accounts Receivable.	13,400	
Prepaid Advertising	1,800	
Office Supplies on Hand	2,050	
Office Equipment.	19,450	
Accumulated Depreciation: Office Equipment		$ 5,650
Building.	85,500	
Accumulated Depreciation: Building		13,700
Land	27,480	
Accounts Payable		3,250
Unearned Commissions		4,200
Mortgage Payable		65,250
Common Stock.		20,000
Retained Earnings		43,285
Dividends.	25,000	
Commissions Earned		190,360
Salary Expense	147,950	
Equipment Repairs Expense.	4,070	
Utilities Expense	2,690	
Interest Expense	6,525	
Association Dues Expense	1,500	
Telephone Expense	3,570	
Totals	$345,695	$345,695

Additional Data

Information pertaining to the year-end adjustments is presented below:

a. Depreciation for the year is estimated to be $1,750 for the office equipment and $2,200 for the building.

b. Advertising for 36 months was acquired July 1, 1987.

c. Salaries in the amount of $6,350 are accrued at year-end.

d. At year-end, $740 of office supplies remain on hand.

e. Unearned commissions of $3,600 have been earned by year-end.

f. Interest on the mortgage of $650 has been accrued as of December 31, 1987.

Required

1. Record the unadjusted trial balance on the appropriate columns of a worksheet.

2. Prepare the appropriate adjustments on the worksheet and complete the worksheet.

3. Prepare the financial statements.

4. Journalize the adjusting and closing entries.

(Check figure: Net income = $15,095)

Problem A4-5

The complete accounting cycle

During the first month of operations, Tom's Taxidermists entered into the following transactions:

May 1   Tom Tyson acquired equipment valued at $20,000 and supplies amounting to $6,500. Mr. Tyson signed a $26,500 note payable due in 10 years and bearing 12% interest for the equipment and supplies. Land valued at $15,000 and a building valued at $82,500 were acquired by a means of a $60,000 mortgage payable to

	Tulsa First City Bank and $37,500 cash contributed by Mr. Tyson. In addition, Mr. Tyson deposited $4,500 in cash in the name of Tom's Taxidermist for operating funds.
May 3	Advertising in the amount of $450 was acquired from the Sooner Advertising Agency for the next 6 months. A check was issued for that amount. The debit is to be recorded in a balance sheet account.
7	Cash receipts amounting to $3,970 for taxidermy services rendered were deposited.
10	Salaries of $2,560 were paid.
13	Supplies in the amount of $1,790 were acquired on account and are to be recorded in the asset account.
18	Customers were billed $4,080 for taxidermy services rendered.
21	A check in the amount of $1,800 was received from Mr. William Simms for taxidermy services to be rendered over the next few months. This item is to be recorded in a balance sheet account.
24	Collected $3,230 from customers billed on May 18.
28	Paid $1,500 for supplies acquired on the 13th.
29	Paid telephone bill $45.
30	Paid $475 due on the mortgage; of this amount, $300 represents interest expense.
30	Withdrew $1,000 in cash for Mr. Tyson's personal use.

Required   Record the transactions for the month of May in a general journal, post the transactions to general ledger T-accounts, and prepare a trial balance on a worksheet.

Additional Data

The following information pertains to adjustments that are necessary at the end of the month.
a. Interest expense in the amount of $225 has accrued on the note payable.
b. Depreciation on the equipment amounts to $350, and on the building $250.
c. Taxidermy revenue from the Simms transaction (May 21) of $300 is to be recorded.
d. One month of advertising expense is to be recorded.
e. At the end of the month $3,420 of supplies remain on hand.
f. Salaries in the amount of $480 are accrued at the end of the month.

Required   Complete the worksheet, prepare the financial statements, journalize and post the adjusting and closing entries, and prepare a post-closing trial balance.

(Check figure: Net loss = $805)

Problem A4-6
Adjusting and reversing entries

Among the many transactions recorded by the Baltimore Surveying Company during 1987 were the following three:

On August 1, surveying supplies in the amount of $1,575 were acquired. The balance of surveying supplies on January 1, 1987, was $830, and on December 31, 1987, $290 remained.

A check for $2,400 was received on October 1, 1987, for surveying work to be done evenly over the next year.

Accrued salaries amounted to $440 on December 31, 1987. Salaries in the amount of $1,215 were paid on January 3, 1988.

Required   Prepare, without explanations, the transactions on August 1 and October 1 assuming first that balance sheet accounts were used, then assuming that income statement accounts were used. Follow this by recording the appropriate adjusting and reversing entries.

For the accrued salaries, record the January 3, 1988, payment assuming first that no reversing entry was made on January 1, 1987, and then that there was a reversing entry made.

Problem A4-7

Adjusting entries determined from a post-closing trial balance

The trial balance presented below is a little different than a post-closing trial balance. The difference is that in the trial balance below, reversing entries for the new year have been recorded and posted, but no external transactions have yet been recorded. No one would make such a trial balance; it is used here only to test your understanding of the effects of adjusting and reversing entries.

The Fido Pet Grooming Service opened for business on April 1, 1987. The furniture and equipment were acquired on that date and are estimated to have a 10-year life. Also on April 1, $2,400 was paid in advance for a 1-year lease on a building.

The pet grooming supplies on hand on January 1, 1988, represent one-fourth of the amount acquired on April 1, 1987, the only time such supplies were acquired.

FIDO PET GROOMING SERVICE Trial Balance (after Reversing Entries) January 1, 1988		
Cash.	$ 1,015	
Accounts Receivable	870	
Prepaid Rent	600	
Pet Grooming Supplies on Hand	780	
Furniture and Equipment	10,000	
Accumulated Depreciation: Furniture and Equipment		$ 750
Accounts Payable		365
Notes Payable.		4,500
Fido, Capital		7,480
Pet Grooming Revenue		125
Salaries Expense		270
Office Supplies Used	325	
Interest Expense		100
Totals.	$13,590	$13,590

Required

By carefully studying the trial balance and the additional information, you should be able to identify the seven adjusting entries that were made on December 31, 1987. Record these entries in general journal form. (You may omit the journal explanations.)

Set B

Problem B4-1

Closing entries

The following accounts comprise a complete list of all the accounts in the general ledger of Waco Water Company after the year-end adjustments have been made:

Residential Revenue.	$197,310	Notes Payable.	$10,000
Salary Expense	187,040	Supplies on Hand	6,705
Waco, Capital.	150,430	Advertising Expense.	4,750
Equipment.	137,310	Interest Expense	4,250
Commercial Revenue.	110,720	Accounts Payable.	4,065
Building.	93,750	Cash	3,470
Mortgage Payable	85,000	Interest Income.	2,710
Waco, Withdrawals	60,000	Depreciation Expense:	
Land.	50,000	Equipment	2,500
Accumulated Depreciation:		Insurance Expense.	2,400
Building.	36,500	Depreciation Expense: Building .	1,800
Accumulated Depreciation:		Telephone Expense	1,680
Equipment	25,000	Salaries Payable.	1,570
Accounts Receivable.	19,530	Prepaid Insurance	1,400
Supplies Used	18,420	Miscellaneous Expense	520

Required From this information, prepare the appropriate closing entries at year-end, August 31, 1987.

(Check figure: Waco, Capital, August 31, 1987 = $177,810)

Problem B4-2
Completing a worksheet

Presented below is the unadjusted trial balance of Kay Nine Security Service for December 31, 1987:

KAY NINE SECURITY SERVICE Unadjusted Trial Balance December 31, 1987		
Cash	$ 480	
Accounts Receivable	1,850	
Prepaid Insurance	750	
Prepaid Rent	900	
Security Supplies on Hand	855	
Security Equipment	4,360	
Accumulated Depreciation: Security Equipment		$ 1,520
Accounts Payable		380
Kay Nine, Capital		5,710
Kay Nine, Withdrawals	6,200	
Security Service Revenues		26,410
Salaries Expense	17,610	
Advertising Expense	800	
Telephone Expense	215	
Totals	$34,020	$34,020

Information pertaining to the year-end adjustments is as follows:
a. Depreciation on the security equipment for the year is estimated to be $290.
b. Salaries in the amount of $550 have accrued as of December 31, 1987.
c. A total of $315 of security supplies remains on hand on December 31, 1987.
d. Rent in the amount of $200 has expired.
e. The insurance was acquired on December 1, and is a 3-month policy.

Required Enter the unadjusted trial balance on a worksheet, record the required adjustments, and complete the worksheet.

(Check figure: Net income = $5,955)

Problem B4-3
Completing a worksheet

Alice Allan operated an auto repair service. The December 31, 1987, year-end worksheet for the auto repair service is presented on page 176. A number of amounts are missing from the worksheet.

Required From the information contained on the worksheet, determine the missing amounts.

(Check figure: Net income = $24,380)

ALICE AUTO REPAIR SERVICE
Worksheet
December 31, 1987

	Unadjusted Trial Balance		Adjustments		Income Statement		Balance Sheet	
	Debit	Credit	Debit	Credit	Debit	Credit	Debit	Credit
Cash							3,150	
Accounts Receivable	670						2,170	
Prepaid Rent				600			300	
Auto Parts on Hand	1,620						760	
Repair Equipment	4,075						4,075	
Accumulated Depreciation:								
Repair Equipment		2,230						2,745
Office Equipment	2,600						2,600	
Accumulated Depreciation:								
Office Equipment		650						
Accounts Payable				220				1,535
Unearned Repair Revenue			105					105
Alice Allan, Capital		3,000						3,000
Alice Allan, Withdrawals	20,355						20,355	
Repair Revenue						45,165		
Insurance Expense	700				700			
Office Salaries Expense					12,870			
Advertising Expense	1,800				1,800			
Utilities Expense	1,325				1,325			
Tax Expense	1,570				1,570			
Rent Expense								
Auto Parts Used			1,080					
Depreciation: Repair Equipment								
Depreciation: Office Equipment			325					
Office Salaries Payable								670
				5,015				
Net Income								

Problem B4-4

Preparing a worksheet, financial statements, adjusting, and closing entries.

The unadjusted trial balance of the Houston Hydraulic Equipment Repair Service, presented on page 177, was taken from the general ledger on the last day of the accounting year, December 31, 1987.

Cash	$ 1,460	
Notes Receivable	5,000	
Accounts Receivable	8,075	
Prepaid Rent	1,800	
Prepaid Insurance	1,600	
Repair Supplies on Hand	645	
Repair Equipment	31,500	
Accumulated Depreciation: Repair Equipment		$ 8,500
Accounts Payable		2,750
Unearned Repair Revenue		1,860
Common Stock		20,000
Retained Earnings		7,790
Dividends	24,000	
Repair Revenues		96,370
Salary Expense	51,710	
Advertising Expense	7,670	
Travel Expense	2,720	
Utilities Expense	1,090	
Totals	$137,270	$137,270

Additional Data

The following information is available on year-end adjustments.

a. Insurance for 12 months was acquired on April 1, 1987.
b. Salaries in the amount of $3,015 are accrued at year-end.
c. Interest of $250 has accrued on the note receivable.
d. One-fourth of the Unearned Repair Revenue has been earned.
e. Depreciation is estimated to be $750.
f. Repair Supplies used during the year amounts to $395.
g. Rent for 2 years was paid in advance on April 1, 1987.

Required

1. Enter the unadjusted trial balance on a worksheet.
2. Record the appropriate adjusting entries on the worksheets and complete the worksheet.
3. Prepare the financial statements.
4. Journalize the adjusting and closing entries.

(Check figure: Net income = $27,860)

Problem B4-5
The complete accounting cycle

After working two decades as a master die cutter for Hutton Tool and Die Corporation, Martin Fishback resigned and established his own company on April 1, 1987, which he called Fishback Tool and Die. During the month of April the following transactions occurred:

Apr. 1   Fishback deposited the proceeds from his Hutton Tool and Die Corporation Employee Stock Plan — $50,000 — in the First National Bank of Dallas in the name of his new company. On the same date, Fishback acquired land, $10,000; a building, $60,000; and equipment, $30,000; and signed a $55,000 mortgage payable with the bank.

3   Supplies, which are recorded in an asset account, were acquired on account, $4,760.

5   An insurance policy in the amount of $420 was acquired on the building and equipment. The 1-year policy was paid in cash and recorded in an asset account.

9   Completed work on several projects for the Bluebonnet Mfg. Company, billing them $2,790 for the Industrial Revenue earned.

15   Paid salaries, $3,500.

	Apr. 18	Billed Lone Star Medical Equipment Mfg. Company for work completed; Medical Revenue is to be recorded at $4,260.
	19	Paid $125 for advertising for the month of April.
	20	Received $5,000 from Texas Airlines for various projects to be completed within the next 30 days. The credit is to be recorded in the Unearned Industrial Revenue account.
	22	Paid $2,500 on account.
	27	Collected $2,000 from Bluebonnet Mfg. Company.
	29	Paid utilities bill for April, $75.
	30	Mr. Fishback withdrew $3,000 in cash.

Required

1. Record the transactions in a general journal.
2. Post the transactions to the general ledger T-accounts.
3. Prepare an unadjusted trial balance on a worksheet.

Additional Data

The following information pertains to the month-end adjustments.
a. Eighty percent of the Unearned Industrial Revenue has been earned.
b. Accrued salaries amount to $3,500.
c. Supplies on hand on April 30 amount to $530.
d. The insurance expense amounts to $35 per month.
e. Depreciation expense is estimated to be $1,125 for the building and $1,500 for the equipment.

Required

4. Complete the worksheet.
5. Prepare the financial statements.
6. Journalize the monthly adjusting and closing entries; post to the general ledger.
7. Prepare a post-closing trial balance.

(Check figure: Net loss = $3,040)

Problem B4-6
Adjusting and reversing entries

Chicago Color Consultants received a check for $1,800 on April 1, 1987, for consulting services to be rendered evenly over the next 12 months for Windy City Homes. On June 10, 1987, Chicago Color Consultants acquired $1,750 of office supplies on account. On December 31, 1987, $805 of the supplies remain. Accrued salaries on December 31, 1987, amounted to $1,500. Payday was on January 4, 1988, and amounted to $2,400.

Required

Record the receipt of the $1,800 and expenditure of the $1,750, first assuming that Chicago Color Consultants initially use balance sheet accounts to record such transactions, then assuming that income statement accounts are used. Then record the appropriate adjusting entry for each case, followed by the appropriate reversing entry if needed.

In addition, prepare the January 4, 1988, entry to record the payment of salaries assuming first that a reversing entry was not made, then assuming that a reversing entry was made. You may prepare all entries without explanations.

Problem B4-7
Adjusting entries determined from a post-closing trial balance

Altoona Auto Renting Company commenced operations on October 1, 1985. The trial balance presented on page 179 was prepared on January 1, 1988, immediately after the reversing entries were made but prior to recording any external transactions.

The company leases office space, a repair shop, and a parking lot. The lease was signed on October 1, 1987, and a $2,400 payment was made in advance to cover the 12 months' rent.

The automobiles were acquired on October 1, 1985, and are estimated to have a 5-year life.

ALTOONA AUTO RENTING COMPANY
Trial Balance
January 1, 1988

Cash	$ 700	
Accounts Receivable	1,140	
Prepaid Rent	1,800	
Automobiles	3,000	
Accumulated Depreciation: Automobiles		$1,350
Accounts Payable		900
Harrison, Capital		4,515
Auto Renting Revenue		250
Salaries Expense		600
Repair Parts Used	525	
Advertising Expense	300	
Interest Income	150	
Totals	$7,615	$7,615

Required   Seven adjusting entries were made on December 31, 1987. By reviewing carefully the January 1, 1988, trial balance, you will be able to identify these adjustments. Record the adjustments; you may omit the entry explanations.

Chapter 5

Accounting for Merchandise

After you have studied this chapter, you should be able to:

- Calculate the *cost of goods sold* of a merchandising concern
- Explain how a worksheet for a merchandising firm differs from a worksheet for a service business
- Prepare closing entries for a merchandising firm
- Prepare a statement of retained earnings
- Explain the difference between the periodic and perpetual inventory systems

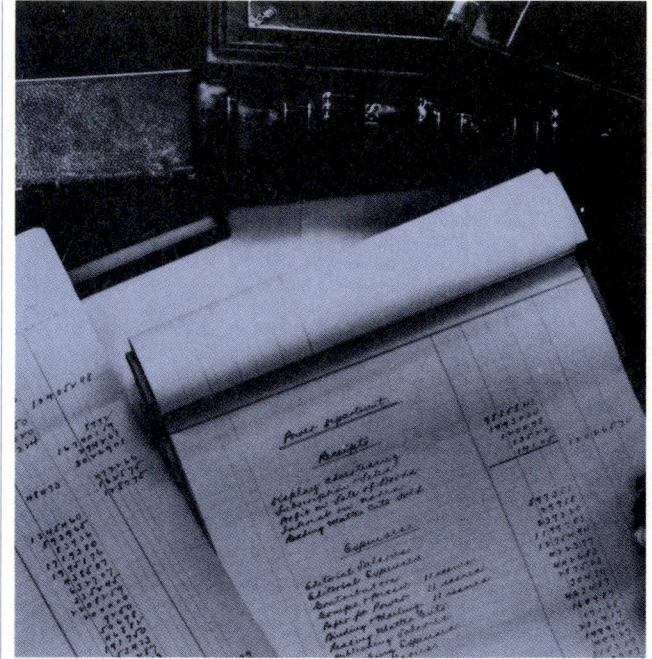

Thus far, we have explained what the accounting process is and how it works: It begins with an economic entity's business transactions (sometimes referred to as external transactions) and ends with the financial statements that depict the entity's financial activity during a period and its financial status at the end of that period. The financial statements prepared by an economic entity can be either formal or informal. *Informal* financial statements covering monthly and quarterly accounting periods are prepared for internal use to help management determine if it is achieving its objectives. *Formal* financial statements are prepared annually; external users can examine them to see how well the entity is performing.

To illustrate the steps of the accounting process, we used in our examples economic entities that are *business,* as opposed to *nonprofit,* entities. Not only did we use business entities, but we used a particular type, a *service* firm whose business activity is to provide, or sell, a service. Real estate agencies, advertising agencies, law firms, and self-employed individuals providing tennis instruction are all examples of service businesses. It is easier to introduce the basic ideas of the accounting process using service entities as examples.

Retailers and wholesalers are merchandising firms that buy and sell products

You are now prepared to understand how the accounting process works for *merchandising firms* (also called *trading firms*), whose business activity is to buy and sell products, either at the *retail* level (the shop from which you, the consumer, buy the product) or at the *wholesale* level (the firm from which the retail shop buys what it sells). The relationship between the merchandising firms and the manufacturer and final consumer is depicted in Figure 5-1 on the following page.

Let's compare and contrast the income statements of a service firm, Mollie's Motel, and a merchandising concern, Sam's Store:

A service firm:

MOLLIE'S MOTEL
Income Statement

Revenue:		
Room Rentals		$36,000
Expenses:		
Salary Expense	$21,000	
Depreciation Expense	4,000	
Cleaning Expense	2,000	
Repairs Expense	1,500	
Linen Used	500	
Total Expenses		29,000
Net Income		$ 7,000

A merchandising concern:

SAM'S STORE
Income Statement

Sales		$120,000
Cost of Goods Sold		80,000
Gross Profit		$ 40,000
Operating Expenses:		
Salary Expense	$25,000	
Depreciation Expense	7,000	
Delivery Expense	3,000	
Insurance Expense	500	
Total Operating Expenses . . .		35,500
Net Income		$ 4,500

The net income for the service company, Mollie's Motel, is simply the difference between revenue earned and total expenses incurred.

For a merchandising concern there are two types of expenses: the cost of goods sold and the operating expenses. The cost of goods sold is the expense of the merchandise sold for the period. And the operating expenses are all the other expenses necessary to run the business.

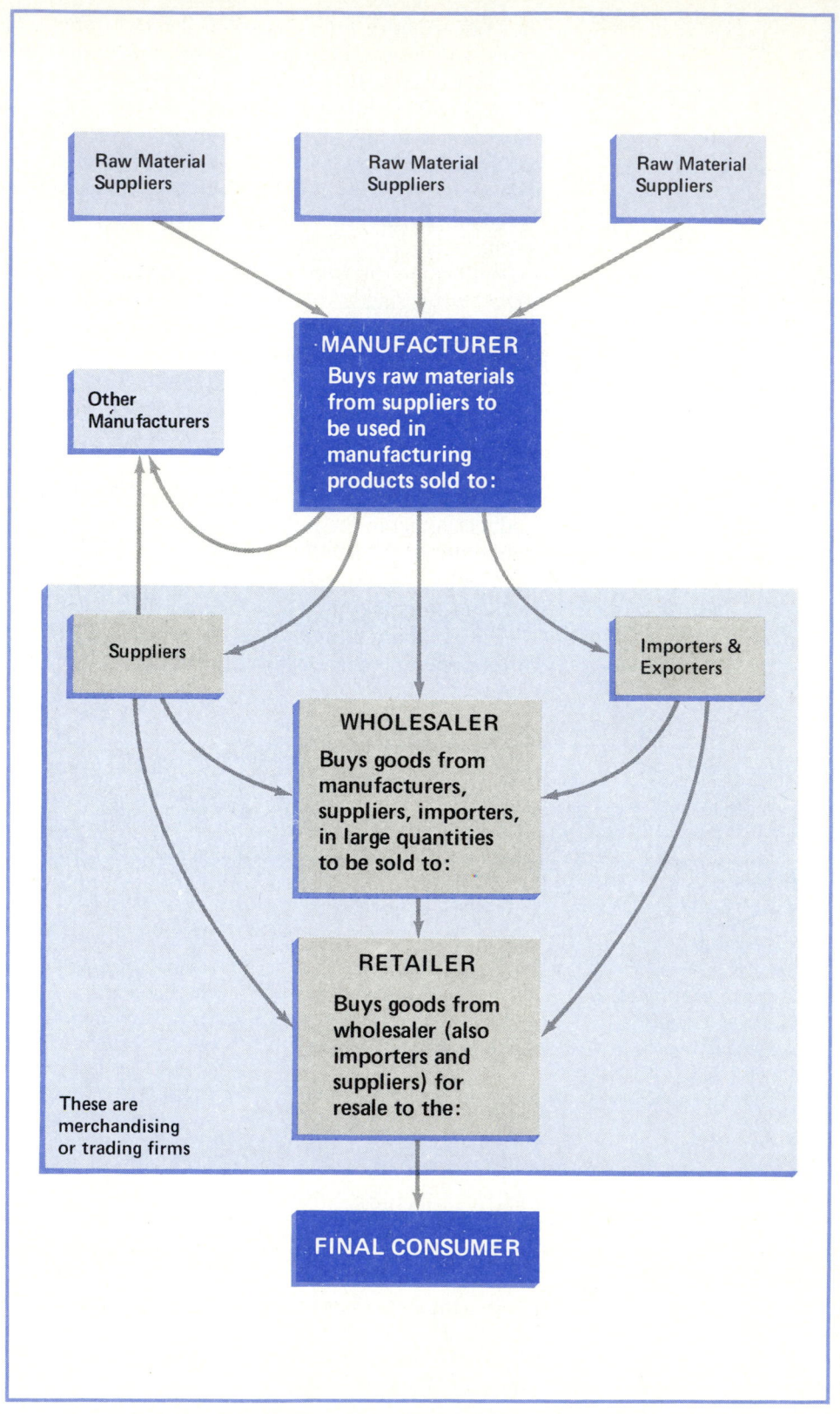

FIGURE 5-1
Relationship between merchandising firms, manufacturer, and final consumer.

The net income of a merchandising concern is determined by subtracting the cost of goods sold from sales to calculate gross profit, and then subtracting the operating expenses from the gross profit to calculate the net income

To determine the net income for a merchandising concern, the cost of goods sold is subtracted from the revenue represented by the sale of that merchandise; the difference is *gross profit* (also called *gross margin*). A service concern does not have gross profit because it does not sell merchandise. From gross profit the operating expenses are deducted to determine the net income. The merchandising concern's operating expenses are similar to the service concern's expenses.

This chapter deals with accounting for a merchandising concern, particularly how to measure the cost of goods sold.

THE INCOME STATEMENT OF A MERCHANDISING CONCERN

The income statement of Micro Discount Supply Company below illustrates how a merchandising firm's income statement is organized. Refer to it as we explain some of the basic details within it. The Micro Discount Supply Company buys microcomputer hardware and software directly from manufacturing companies and sells by direct mail to its customers nationwide.

MICRO DISCOUNT SUPPLY COMPANY
Income Statement
Year Ended December 31, 1987

(a)	Gross Sales.			$177,750
(b)	Less: Sales Returns and Allowances		$ 2,325	
(c)	Sales Discounts.		2,700	(5,025)
	Net Sales			$172,725

The sales section (rows a–c)

	Costs of Goods Sold:				
(d)	Inventory, January 1, 1987			$ 19,050	
(e)	Purchases	$127,875			
(f)	Less: Purchase Returns and Allowances	$ 855			
(g)	Purchase Discounts	2,025	(2,880)		
(h)	Plus: Freight-In.		2,955		
(i)	Net Purchases.			127,950	
(j)	Cost of Goods Available for Sale.			$147,000	
(k)	Less: Inventory, December 31, 1987			23,025	
(l)	Costs of Goods Sold				123,975

The cost of goods sold section

(m)	Gross Profit	$ 48,750

	Operating Expenses:		
	Salary Expense	$ 27,375	
	Advertising Expense.	6,255	
	Rent Expense.	2,700	
	Depreciation Expense: Store Equipment	1,125	
	Insurance Expense.	750	
	Store Supplies Used.	1,920	
	Total Operating Expenses.		40,125

The operating expenses section

Net Income	$ 8,625

A merchandising firm's income statement has three distinct sections

The Micro Discount Supply income statement, like every merchandising firm's income statement, comprises three distinct sections: sales, cost of goods sold, and operating expenses. Some merchandising firms may segregate operating expenses into two subsections — selling expenses and general and administrative expenses. Selling expenses would consist of those expenses related to the marketing function, such as sales salaries or commissions, delivery expenses, and depreciation on store equipment. General and administrative expenses would include all other expenses.

The Sales Section

The primary objective of a merchandising concern is the same as for any business entity: to earn a profit. For a merchandising firm to earn a profit, the amount of its sales revenue must exceed the sum of its cost of goods sold and its operating expenses.

Sales are made either for cash or on account

Merchandise, like services, can be paid in full with cash at the time of the purchase. This is commonly referred to as a *cash sale.* Or, the seller can agree to accept payment at some time after delivery of the merchandise. This is referred to as a *sale on account.*

A cash sale would be recorded in the general journal as shown below:

Cash 42,750
    Sales 42,750

Cash sales and credit sales add up to total sales

To record cash sale of merchandise.

Sales made on account would be recorded in the general journal as follows:

Accounts Receivable 135,000
    Sales. 135,000

To record sale of merchandise on account.

If we were to look into the general journal for the Micro Discount Supply Company, we would see that these two entries add up to total sales of $177,750 as shown on the income statement [line (*a*)]. Of course, we would find hundreds of entries made during the course of the business year, but the total of these hundreds of entries would reflect cash sales of $42,750 and credit sales of $135,000.

Sales Returns and Allowances

After purchasing an item, a customer may find it defective in some way — perhaps it malfunctions, or was identified as the wrong size or the wrong color. The customer returns the item to the seller (the merchandising firm), which acknowledges receipt of the returned item — a transaction that essentially negates the original sale.

Perhaps the defective item is not totally useless (it's merely the wrong color, let's say). As an alternative to returning it, the customer may be allowed to keep it and pay a reduced price, or a part of the original purchase price may be refunded. This allowance on price (also referred to as a *price concession*) helps to avoid the costs of freight, and perhaps storage, which the merchandising firm incurs in accepting returned items.

In either case, the amount of the return or the allowance can be recorded as an entry in the general journal by simply debiting Sales and crediting Cash or Accounts Receivable. But that's not the way it is generally done. First we'll explain why not; then we'll show how returns and allowances are accounted for.

The owners of a merchandising firm will want to know how much merchandise is being returned and why. Is it being returned because it is defective in some way? Merchandise *is* returned for this reason; indeed, a certain amount of returns should be expected in the normal course of business. But returns should not represent a significant percentage of sales.

Merchandise returned because it is defective or the wrong color or size is a common problem of all merchandising concerns

MATTEL, INC., 1971 SALES

Prior to 1971 Mattel, Inc., had recorded half a decade of record sales and earnings, and the company had projected another record year for 1971. The company's fiscal year-end was January 31, by which time management was aware that the projections would not be met; they had miscalculated the market for "Hot Wheels" and "Sizzlers." In order to reflect a sixth straight year of record sales, Mattel's management, among other things, recorded falsely $14.7 million of sales which resulted in overstating the 1971 pretax earnings by $7.8 million.

Sales are recognized under generally accepted accounting principles when the seller has completed all the obligations to the buyer and the risk of ownership has transferred to the buyer.

Mattel recorded sales to 35 customers using 156 invoices under a procedure referred to by Mattel as the "bill and hold" program. This program was a practice where the customer agrees to buy goods but the seller holds the goods until the buyer requests them. In the past Mattel had a limited number of these transactions, all evidenced by written agreement and the physical segregation of the inventory items. Under the January 1971 "bill and hold" program, the merchandise was not shipped by January 31 nor was it physically segregated from Mattel's inventory; the customer did not have to pay for the merchandise until the goods were received and could cancel the order at any time prior to receipt; the risks of ownership remained with Mattel; and in many cases the invoices were prepared without consultation with or participation of the customer.

All the "bill and hold" invoices were recorded in the last 11 days of January 1971.

Since Mattel had adjusted its inventory records to account for the "bill and hold" sales of January 1971, even though the merchandise was not shipped, problems developed in inventory control. The inventory records were unreliable; employees could not tell how much inventory was on hand or whether an order was a fiscal 1972 sale or a 1971 "bill and hold" item.

To compensate for these difficulties Mattel reversed the "bill and hold" sales on its books in May 1972 for $6.3 million of "bill and hold" sales of January 1971 and $6.6 million fiscal 1972 sales. When this reversing entry was recorded in the Accounts Receivable control account, the subsidiary accounts receivable accounts, and the Sales account, another problem was created. The general ledger sales account reflected negative sales for the month of May. To cover the negative sales figure Mattel recorded $11.1 million of fictitious sales, which were posted to its Accounts Receivable account and the Sales account but not to the subsidiary ledgers. Of course that resulted in a difference of $11.1 million between the control account and the subsidiary ledgers. The schedule of accounts receivable for the months May to August all showed a reconciling item of $11.1 million called "May Shipping." By September 1971 normal sales were sufficient to absorb the cancellation of the $11.1 million in fictitious sales and the remaining "bill and hold" sales.

Source: Securities Exchange Act of 1934, Release No. 17878, *Accounting Series Release No. 292,* June 22, 1981.

The Mattel case illustrates the chain of problems that can develop when a company attempts to "adjust" sales figures to reflect higher earnings.

Are there more than expected returns? Is the merchandise being returned because of some failure that is within the control of management? If so, the failure should be corrected. The signal that management action is needed is returns that exceed expected levels.

Sales Returns and Allowances is a contra-revenue account and has a debit balance

How efficiently that signal reaches management depends on the way in which returns and allowances are accounted for. Representing returns and allowances in the general journal by debiting Sales (as suggested earlier) provides no helpful information about the level of returns. To provide information on returns and allowances, a separate account, Sales Returns and Allowances, is established in the general ledger. This is a **contra-revenue account,** which, as you should remember from our discussion in Chapter 3, will have a balance opposite that of a revenue account: The contra-revenue account **Sales Returns and Allowances has a debit balance.**

When merchandise is returned, this transaction is recorded in this contra account by the following general journal entry.

Sales Returns and Allowances 2,325
     Cash (or Accounts Receivable)   2,325
To record returned merchandise.

Again, if we were to look into the general ledger account, we would see that there were a number of returns and allowances during the year and that the $2,325 is the sum of such transactions. The Sales Returns and Allowances are shown on line (*b*) of the Micro Discount Supply Company income statement.

Sales Discounts

Sales Discounts is also a contra-revenue account and has a debit balance

In a sales transaction, the seller and buyer agree to an exchange. The seller agrees to exchange merchandise in return for a specified payment. The exchange agreement —that is, the terms of the sale—will require payment, generally in the form of cash, at either the point of sale or some future date.

Payment in cash at the time of the sale represents no problems for the seller (the merchandising firm) or the accountant. Payment on account represents work for the accountant, and generally represents a disadvantage for the merchandising firm. Before we explain that, you need to know a few things about the timing of a future payment, how it is specified on the bill, and how it is recorded in the ledger accounts.

The arrangement between the seller and the buyer of merchandise concerning the method of payment is usually expressed on the *sales invoice*—the bill. This arrangement is referred to as the *credit terms* of the sale. One common arrangement is to require that the bill be paid 10 days after the end of the month in which the sale was made. This is expressed on the sales invoice as:

The net amount of an invoice is the amount the buyer must pay

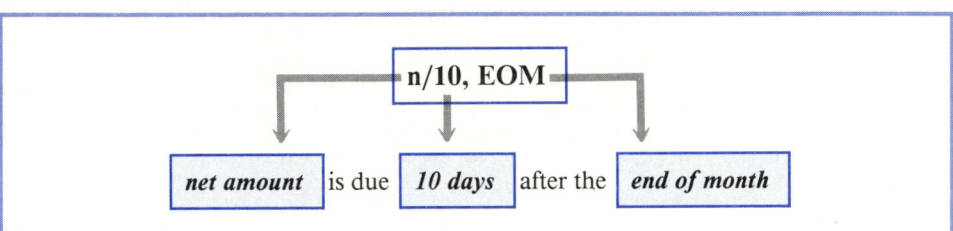

The *net amount* is the cost of the merchandise less any discounts or other price reductions allowed by the seller. It is the amount that the buyer must pay.

Another common credit term is to require payment 30 days after the sale, as evidenced by the date on the sales invoice. The term

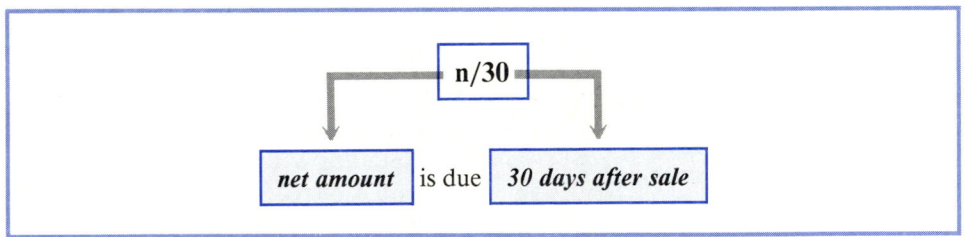

is used to express this arrangement.

Selling merchandise on account has an obvious disadvantage: The seller has already delivered the merchandise but must wait a period of time before cash is received in payment. While waiting for payment, the seller has salaries to pay, new merchandise to acquire, and other obligations that must be paid for. It is in the seller's interest to encourage the buyer to pay promptly. The seller will offer a *cash discount* (a sales discount) if the bill is paid within a specified period of time. For example, it is common practice to offer a 2% discount off the price of the merchandise if it is paid in full within 10 days from the date of the sale. And, of course, if it isn't paid for within 10 days, then it must be paid for within 30 days from the date of the sale. These terms are represented on the sales invoice as:

Sales discounts encourage early payment

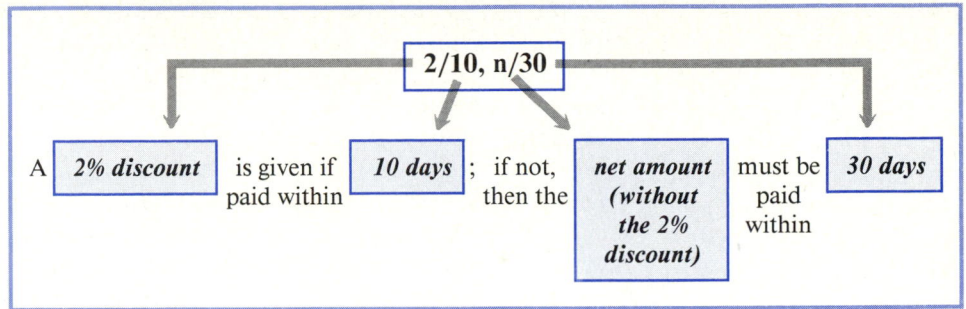

The discount and the period it will be offered are established by the seller. A seller might offer terms 3/10, n/30, meaning a 3% discount if paid within 10 days of the invoice date, or payable in full within 30 days.

To illustrate the accounting for sales discounts, assume that all Micro Discount Supply's credit sales, $135,000, are subject to the credit terms 2/10, n/30, and that all customers on account pay within the 10-day discount period. The entry in the general journal representing the amount of discounts allowed, or *Sales Discounts,* would be calculated by $135,000 \times 2\%$, or:

$$\text{Sales discounts} = \$2,700$$

[See line (*c*) of the Micro Discount income statement on page 183.] And, of course, that discount means that of the $135,000 receivable, only $132,300 ($135,000 − $2,700) in cash is collected.

The entry would appear in the general journal as follows:

Cash. 132,300
Sales Discounts.   2,700
    Accounts Receivable   135,000
To record collection of accounts receivable subject to 2/10, n/30 credit terms.

Sales Discounts, like Sales Returns and Allowances, is a **contra-revenue account,** and as such it also has a **debit balance.** Both accounts are subtracted from gross sales to arrive at net sales. Sales Discounts and Sales Returns and Allowances accounts represent concessions on the sales price given to the buyer, and as such reduce the seller's revenue. Let's look again at the sales section of the Micro Discount Supply Company income statement to reinforce what we have just explained:

The sales section of an income statement lists the revenue account Sales and the two contra-revenue accounts, Sales Returns and Allowances and Sales Discounts

Gross Sales.		$177,750
Less: Sales Returns and Allowances	$2,325	
Sales Discounts	2,700	5,025
Net Sales		$172,725

Trade Discounts

In certain industries some manufacturers and suppliers provide catalogs of their merchandise to their customers. As Figure 5-1 shows, retailers, as well as wholesalers, buy merchandise from manufacturers, suppliers, and importers; wholesalers sell it to retailers; retailers sell it to consumers. We are primarily concerned here about what happens at the manufacturer and supplier level and how it affects the sale at the level between the *retailer,* which we have been referring to as the merchandising firm, and the *consumer,* whom we have referred to as the customer. And what happens is that the manufacturer or supplier may publish a catalog with prices that the retailer can charge its customers. The prices in these catalogs are referred to as **suggested retail prices** or **manufacturer's suggested list prices.** The catalogs do not show the prices the retailers pay. Instead, the catalogs show the discount, commonly referred to as the **trade discount** or the **chain discount** — the amount the retailers deduct from the price listed in the catalog to determine their cost (the price they pay to the manufacturer or supplier). These catalogs and this type of pricing and discounting are common practices in the jewelry and auto-parts industries.

Trade discounts are a means of changing the prices of catalog items

Because these catalogs are expensive to produce, manufacturers and suppliers do not want to revise and publish new catalogs every time they change the prices they charge to retailers. Instead, they keep the manufacturer's suggested list price published in the catalog, but change the trade discount. This is done by simply mailing to the retailers a list of changes in the discount terms. Manufacturers and suppliers may also use trade discounts to make price differentials for several different classes of customers or for different quantities ordered.

Now, let's see what a trade discount or a chain discount is and how it works.

If you look in an auto-parts catalog, you might find the listed price for a carburetor (a necessary part of the system that feeds fuel to the engine) as follows:

$$\textit{\$100, 40-10-5}$$

$100 is the manufacturer's suggested price to the customer.

The retailer figures out the price it pays to the manufacturer in the following way:

A trade discount provides different levels of discount, making it easy to change the price of a product

Suggested list price	$100.00
Less: *40%* trade discount	40.00
	$ 60.00
Less: *10%* trade discount	6.00
	$ 54.00
Less: *5%* trade discount	2.70
Price retailer pays manufacturer or supplier	$ 51.30

Thus, the retailer pays $51.30, which is the equivalent of a total discount of $48.70 off the manufacturer's suggested list price. The manufacturer or supplier will record this sale at $51.30. The retailer will record the acquisition of the merchandise at $51.30, and will in turn sell the merchandise to the customer for $100, or less if he or she so desires.

A manufacturer or supplier who wishes to change the discounted price of a given item — that is, the price he or she receives for it — will change the trade discount. For example, the manufacturer may increase the price by reducing the discount to 40-10 from 40-10-5. Thus the discounted price is effectively increased to $54.00 from $51.30. A manufacturer or supplier may sell directly to retailers at a discount of 40 or 40-10, but the terms to wholesalers might be 40-10-5.

The Cost of Goods Sold Section

The accounting concept of matching requires that the cost incurred in providing goods and services for sale must be matched against the revenue generated by those goods or services in the accounting period they are sold

To determine the net income for any business entity, whether a service business or a merchandising business, you must understand the concept of *matching.* According to this basic principle, the costs incurred in providing goods and services for sale must be matched against the revenue generated by these goods or services in the accounting period they are sold. For example, in the case of a service business—say, Acme Home Cleaning Service—the cost of providing the home-cleaning service to Mrs. Jones may be the $50 wages paid by Acme to their two employees. These wages would be *matched* against the $75 revenue—the fee charged Mrs. Jones—that the expenditure of the labor was able to generate. The idea of matching for a merchandising business proceeds along the same lines. If Tastegood Donuts sells you a dozen creme-filled donuts for $1, the price that Tastegood paid for the donuts—say, $.50 —must be matched against the $1 revenue generated.

For a merchandising firm the cost of the products that the firm offers for sale constitutes a major expenditure. The matching concept requires that only those products sold during an accounting period be matched against the revenue earned. This significant expense is called the *cost of goods sold.* The amount of product not sold—the product on hand at the end of an accounting period—is called the *ending inventory.* Of course, the inventory that is on hand at the end of one accounting period is on hand at the beginning of the next accounting period. In this case it is called *beginning inventory.*

Because cost of goods sold represents the largest expense on the income statement, it deserves special attention. It is placed on the income statement immediately following the revenue section—as illustrated in the case of the Micro Discount Supply Company—so that it can be matched directly with that revenue. The cost of goods sold section represents, or accounts for, all the costs that were incurred to provide the products that were sold during the accounting period. Very briefly, the cost of goods sold is determined by adding together beginning inventory and purchases. This results in the goods that are available for sale. The amount of goods not sold—the ending inventory—is subtracted from the goods that could have been sold—the cost of goods available for sale—to determine what has been sold—the cost of goods sold. Now for the detail.

Beginning Inventory

To calculate the cost of goods sold we begin with the inventory on hand at the start of the accounting period. This year's beginning inventory is simply last year's ending inventory, which was determined by a physical count of each item comprising the inventory at the close of the last business day of the year. The beginning inventory of the Micro Discount Supply Company amounts to $19,050 [line (*d*) on the income statement]. (This process of taking the inventory count and determining its value will be discussed in detail in Chapter 9.)

Purchases

Purchases refer only to merchandise acquired to be resold

The second item we need to calculate cost of goods sold is the cost of the purchases. We use the term *purchases* in accounting to refer to merchandise that is bought for one purpose—to be resold.

We have exercised great care in the previous chapters to avoid the use of the word *purchases* for this very reason. Office supplies, prepaid insurance, buildings, repair parts, automobiles—are all *acquired.*

Only merchandise held for resale is *purchased.* Thus, the general ledger account Purchases records only the inventory obtained during the year for resale.

Like Sales, Purchases may be for cash or on account. The following entry in the general journal illustrates the recording of cash purchases for the Micro Discount Supply Company:

```
Purchases . . . . . . . . . . . . . . . . . . . . . . . . . . . . . . . . . . . . . . . 26,625
    Cash . . . . . . . . . . . . . . . . . . . . . . . . . . . . .                   26,625
To record cash purchases.
```

Purchases on account are recorded in the general journal in the following manner:

```
Purchases . . . . . . . . . . . . . . . . . . . . . . . . . . . . . . . . . . . . 101,250
    Accounts Payable . . . . . . . . . . . . . . . . . . . . . . . . . .           101,250
To record purchases on account.
```

The sum of the cash purchases and purchases on account is $127,875 — the total Purchases [line (*e*)] by Micro Discount for the year 1987. Remember, each of these entries represents the total of hundreds of entries made during the year.

Purchase Returns and Allowances

Before we proceed to this next item, return for a moment to Sales Returns and Allowances. Remember that a merchandising firm — that is, a seller — accepts returns of merchandise (found to be defective for whatever reason) and provides a place in its accounting system to record and account for these sales returns and allowances.

Now, let's look at the other side of this situation. As a purchaser, there is likelihood that you may have to return a certain part of your purchases because of some kind of defect. *Sales returns and allowances* to the seller are at the same time *purchase returns and allowances* to the buyer. Therefore, buyers, such as merchandising firms, must provide a place in their accounting systems to record and account for purchase returns and allowances.

Purchase Returns and Allowances is a contra-expense account and as such has a credit balance

A general ledger account, **Purchase Returns and Allowances,** is established to accumulate this information for management (of a merchandising firm) to review. It provides the same kind of signals to management as the information on Sales Returns and Allowances. Management should expect a normal amount of Purchase Returns and Allowances. But, if the amount suddenly becomes excessive, that indicates to management that its purchasing system and the merchandise need to be examined and analyzed. The relationship of Sales Returns and Allowances and Purchase Returns and Allowances is shown in Figure 5-2.

Purchase Returns and Allowances are recorded in the same way as Sales Returns and Allowances. The summary entry for recording Purchase Returns and Allowances for the Micro Discount Supply Company is as follows:

```
Cash (or Accounts Payable) . . . . . . . . . . . . . . . . . . . . . . . . . . 855
    Purchase Returns and Allowances . . . . . . . . . . . . . . . . . . . . .      855
To record merchandise returned to the seller.
```

Purchase Returns and Allowances represents a transaction in which merchandise is "returned" to the seller and the amount of the price of that merchandise is "returned" to the buyer. Therefore, the amount of Purchase Returns and Allowances appears on the income statement as a subtraction from Purchases. For our example, this is shown as $855 [line (*f*)] subtracted from Purchases in Micro Discount's income statement.

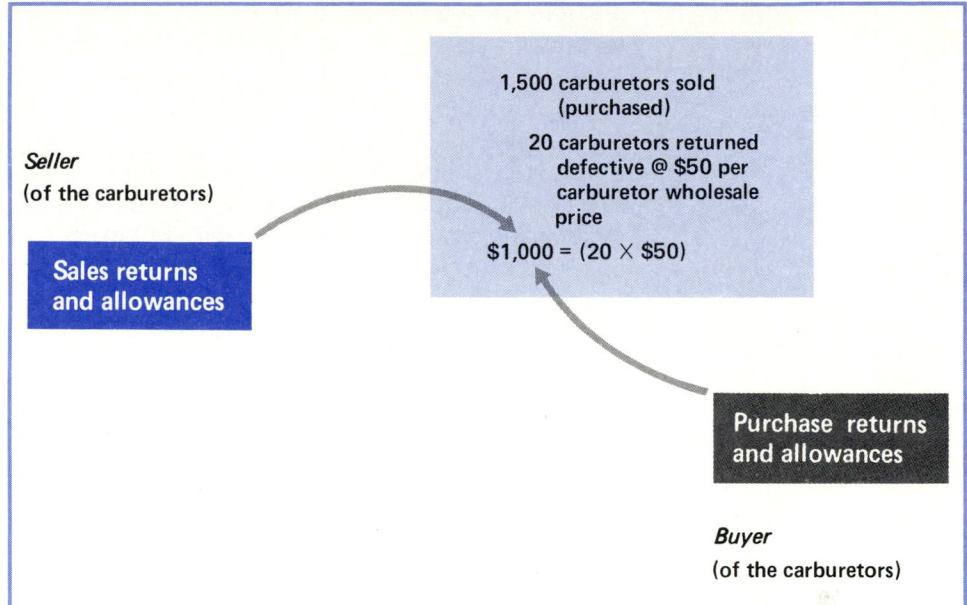

Seller
(of the carburetors)

Sales returns
and allowances

1,500 carburetors sold
(purchased)

20 carburetors returned
defective @ $50 per
carburetor wholesale
price

$1,000 = (20 × $50)

Purchase returns
and allowances

Buyer
(of the carburetors)

FIGURE 5-2
**Relationship of Sales Returns
and Allowances and
Purchases Returns and
Allowances.**

Purchase Discounts

Purchase Discounts is also a
contra-expense account

A seller's sales discounts are at the same time the buyer's purchase discounts. To see how a buyer accounts for and reports purchase discounts on an income statement, let's look back at Micro Discount's purchases on account of $101,250 and assume that the seller's terms are:

$$2/10, \ n/30$$

By now we know this means that the seller will accept as payment in full, 2% less than the amount payable if it is paid within 10 days from the invoice date, or the full amount payable within 30 days. Let's assume that this amount is paid within 10 days, which means that Micro Discount's purchase discount is: 2% × $101,250, or

$$.02 \times \$101{,}250 = \$2{,}025$$

and that the amount paid to the seller is:

$$\$101{,}250 - \$2{,}025 = \$99{,}225$$

This is recorded in the general journal as

Accounts Payable	101,250	
Purchase Discounts		2,025
Cash		99,225

To record payment of accounts subject to credit terms of 2/10, n/30.

Since a purchase discount represents the part of the total purchase amount that does not have to be paid, it is subtracted from total purchases, as shown [line (*g*)] on Micro Discount's income statement.

Freight-In

Thus far, we have discussed some of the basic relationships in an economic transaction between a seller (manufacturer, wholesaler, supplier) and a buyer (retailer or other wholesaler) of merchandise. But we haven't yet discussed a very important relationship, a physical relationship: How will the merchandise be transported from seller to buyer, and who will pay the cost of transportation?

Generally, the terms of the sale will specify who pays the cost of transportation, commonly referred to as the *freight charges.* The term *FOB shipping point* means that the seller agrees to place the merchandise on trucks, railroad cars, or other transportation units *free on board* — at no cost to the buyer — at the shipping point. The cost of transportation from the shipping point to wherever the buyer wants the merchandise delivered is paid for by the buyer. As a convenience the seller may prepay the freight and simply add the cost to the amount of the invoice for the merchandise purchased by the buyer.

> **FOB shipping point means that the seller will pay the freight to the shipping point**

The transportation cost, or freight charged, is usually referred to as *freight-in* by the buyer. A separate account, Freight-In, is established in the general ledger to accumulate these costs.

Although the freight charges are indeed a necessary cost that must be incurred along with the purchase cost, they are segregated from the Purchases account for one specific reason. The Freight-In account provides information to management about the specific costs incurred for transportation. Management uses this information to determine what its transportation needs are, whether or not it is getting its money's worth from its transportation expenses, and whether or not it should buy or lease transportation equipment.

The general journal entry summarizing the total FOB shipping point freight charges paid by Micro Discount Supply Company during the year is as follows:

Freight-In 2,955
   Cash   2,955
To record freight charges on merchandise purchased.

Freight-in is a cost that must be incurred in buying merchandise and is shown [line (*h*)] on Micro Discount's income statement as $2,955.

> **FOB destination means that the seller will pay the freight to the point of destination**

When the seller agrees to pay the cost of transportation, that agreement is referred to as *FOB destination.* FOB destination specifies that the seller will place the merchandise free on board the transportation unit from the shipping point to its destination. There is no freight cost to the buyer. (Of course, you will be safe in assuming that a seller who agrees to FOB destination has already raised the price of the merchandise to cover the cost of transporting it.)

By this point, perhaps you already realize that the amount paid for merchandise — Purchases — does not represent, or fully account for, the value of that merchandise — that is, Net Purchases.

To determine the value of Net Purchases:

1. Add the amount of Purchase Returns and Allowances and the amount of Purchase Discounts.

2. Subtract the sum of Purchase Returns and Allowances and Purchase Discounts from the amount of Purchases.

3. After that subtraction, add the Freight-In costs.

4. The result of that simple arithmetic is Net Purchases.

Net Purchases represents the cost of the merchandise purchased, including all associated costs. Net Purchases [line (*i*)] for the Micro Discount Supply Company is determined as follows:

Purchases		$127,875
Less: Purchase Returns and Allowances	$ 855	
Purchase Discounts.	2,025	(2,880)
Plus: Freight-In		2,955
Net Purchases		$127,950

Cost of Goods Available for Sale

Beginning Inventory plus Net Purchases equal Goods Available for Sale

All the merchandise purchased during the accounting period, as well as all the merchandise in inventory at the beginning of the period, represents the total amount of merchandise that could possibly be sold during the period. This is called the *cost of goods available for sale.* It is the sum of the cost of the merchandise on hand when the period started—the beginning inventory—and the cost of merchandise purchased during the period—net purchases. Cost of goods available for sale for Micro Discount Supply amounts to $147,000 [line (*j*)] determined as follows:

Inventory, January 1, 1987	$ 19,050
Net Purchases	127,950
Cost of Goods Available for Sale	$147,000

Ending Inventory

Of course, a firm will not have sold all its purchases and inventory during an accounting period. The nature of a merchandising business requires that there always be some stock immediately available for sale. After the close of business on the last business day of the year, the amount of merchandise on hand is determined by a physical count of the various items of merchandise in stock at the time. The cost of the ending inventory is then determined by multiplying the unit price of each item by the item quantities and accumulating the total. For example, assume that the count of boxes of $9\frac{1}{2} \times 11$ paper was 27 and the count of So Simple word processing software totaled 9. The unit price paid for each item, assume, was $39.25 and $179.85, respectively. The total cost of these items would be determined as follows:

Item	Quantity	Unit Price Paid	Cost
Boxes of $9\frac{1}{2} \times 11$ paper	27	$ 39.25	$1,059.75
So Simple word processing software	9	179.85	1,618.65
Total cost			$2,678.40

The cost of the entire inventory is calculated in exactly the same manner. A typical merchandising firm could have several thousand items in stock at year-end, so you can see that the process of taking inventory is no small task.

    The cost of the ending inventory, determined as described above, for Micro Discount Supply Company, is $23,025 [line (*k*)]. The ending inventory represents the cost of the merchandise that has not been sold.

Cost of Goods Sold

One of the most important bits of information reported on an income statement of a merchandising concern is gross profit. This figure is used by people who work with financial statements to study the relationship between sales and merchandise sold. To determine gross profit, the cost of goods sold for the period is matched against net sales for the same period. That, of course, brings us to the final item in this discussion of the components of the cost of goods sold section on an income statement — the cost of goods sold.

Goods available for sale less the ending inventory equals the cost of goods sold

The cost of the merchandise sold during a period is determined by subtracting from the cost of the goods available for sale the cost of the goods that were *not* sold. Or, what amounts to the same thing, cost of goods sold is the cost of goods available for sale less the ending inventory. The $123,975 cost of goods sold [line (*l*)] for the Micro Discount Supply Company is calculated as follows:

Cost of Goods Available for Sale	$147,000
Less: Inventory, December 31, 1987	23,025
Cost of Goods Sold	$123,975

To help you obtain a better grasp of this concept, consider the following example. Assume that a sidewalk apple vendor starts the day with 2 apples on hand. During the day he purchases 7 additional apples. So he has a total of 9 apples available for sale. At the end of the day, 3 apples remain unsold. Six apples then must have been sold $(2 + 7 - 3 = 6)$.

Beginning Inventory	2 apples
Plus: Purchases	7 apples
Total Goods Available for Sale	9 apples
Less: Ending Inventory	3 apples
Total Goods Sold	6 apples

Converting this to money terms, assume that the 2 apples of beginning inventory cost $.12 each and the purchases for the day cost $.15 each. The cost of goods sold would be determined as folows:

Beginning Inventory (2 apples × $.12)	$ .24
Purchases (7 apples × $.15)	1.05
Goods Available for Sale	$1.29
Less: Ending Inventory (3 apples × $.15)	.45
Cost of Goods Sold	$ .84

PERIODIC PROCEDURES OF A MERCHANDISING CONCERN

The period-end procedures of a merchandising firm follow the same sequence of steps as a service company:

1. External transactions are recorded in the general journal.

2. The amounts in the general journal are posted to the appropriate general ledger accounts.

3. The trial balance is prepared on the worksheet.

4. Adjustments are entered on the worksheet.

5. The adjusted trial balance is completed on the worksheet.

6. The financial statements are prepared.

Closing, adjusting, and reversing entries are all procedures that a merchandising firm must do periodically, just like a service firm. The types of accounts that are common to both a merchandising business and a service business are recorded and treated in exactly the same way. The accounts that are particular solely to a merchandising business, such as the Inventory account (a service business does not have inventory, hence has no Inventory account), represent new accounts to you and we must explain how they are treated. Let's look at how the accounts particular to a merchandising firm are treated, using the worksheet on page 196 for the Micro Discount Supply Company dated December 31, 1987.

On this worksheet, we have not included the adjusted trial balance columns. Accountants, like other people, don't want to do any more work than necessary, so they proceed directly from the adjustments to the income statement and balance sheet columns. After some practice, you should be able to do the same. So, you may as well start now.

Three adjustments were made as of December 31, 1987.

(a) Depreciation Expense: Store Equipment of $1,125 was recorded.

(b) Store Supplies on Hand was adjusted to reflect $1,920 Store Supplies Used.

(c) Salaries Accrued, $1,875.

The trial balance columns and the adjustments columns are treated in exactly the same way for both service businesses and merchandising businesses. On the worksheet, the distinction between the two is the way the balances in the accounts that distinguish merchandising firms from service firms are carried over to the income statement and the balance sheet columns. These accounts are shown in the shaded areas on Micro Discount's worksheet.

The accounts dealing with sales and purchases, which are income statement accounts, are carried over to the income statement columns in the same manner as any revenue or expense account would be extended, whether for a merchandising firm or service firm. The accounts that pertain to revenue and expenses are illustrated in the large shaded area on the Micro Discount Supply Company worksheet on page 196.

The Inventory Account on the Worksheet

All accounts on the trial balance, except the Inventory and Capital accounts, have period-end balances

Before we proceed to the Inventory account, let's revisit briefly the Capital account. We will review why the Capital account is a beginning balance on the period-end trial balance in the worksheet and how it is closed. And that review will serve as the basis for introducing the Inventory account, which also represents a beginning balance. (All accounts shown on the unadjusted trial balance, except the Capital and Inventory accounts, reflect their end-of-period balances.)

As you may remember, the revenue accounts, the expense accounts, and the Withdrawals account are all *part of* the Capital account. As revenue is earned, the Capital account is increased. As expenses are incurred and withdrawals are made, the Capital account is decreased. The Revenue, Expense, and Withdrawals accounts, although part of the Capital account, are kept separate from the Capital account until the end of the accounting period. The reason for keeping separate

MICRO DISCOUNT SUPPLY COMPANY
Worksheet
December 31, 1987

Accounts	Unadjusted Trial Balance		Adjustments		Income Statement		Balance Sheet	
	Debit	Credit	Debit	Credit	Debit	Credit	Debit	Credit
Cash	17,550						17,550	
Inventory*	19,050				19,050	23,025	23,025	
Store Supplies on Hand	2,625			(b) 1,920			705	
Store Equipment	11,250						11,250	
Accumulated Depreciation:								
Store Equipment		2,250		(a) 1,125				3,375
Notes Payable		4,500						4,500
Common Stock		20,000						20,000
Retained Earnings*		18,655						18,655
Dividends	4,500						4,500	
Sales		177,750				177,750		
Sales Returns and Allowances	2,325				2,325			
Sales Discounts	2,700				2,700			
Purchases	127,875				127,875			
Purchase Returns and Allowances		855				855		
Purchase Discounts		2,025				2,025		
Freight-In	2,955				2,955			
Salary Expense	25,500		(c) 1,875		27,375			
Advertising Expense	6,255				6,255			
Rent Expense	2,700				2,700			
Insurance Expense	750				750			
	226,035	226,035						
Depreciation Expense:								
Store Equipment			(a) 1,125		1,125			
Store Supplies Used			(b) 1,920		1,920			
Salaries Payable				(c) 1,875				1,875
			4,920	4,920	195,030	203,655	57,030	48,405
Net Income					8,625			8,625
					203,655	203,655	57,030	57,030

* All accounts shown on the adjusted trial balance, except the Retained Earnings and Inventory accounts, reflect end-of-period balances.

accounts for revenue, expenses, and withdrawals is to provide information for the preparation of the income statement and the statement of owners' equity.

The Capital account is brought up to date by the closing entries

At the end of the accounting period, after the adjusting entries are recorded in the general journal and posted to the ledger account, the Revenue, Expense, and Withdrawals account balances are transferred to the Capital account by means of the closing entries. This serves two purposes. First, the Revenue, Expense, and Withdrawals accounts are reduced to a zero balance — ready to receive transactions for the new accounting period. And second, the Capital account is brought up to date; it now has a balance that reflects the *end-of-period* position.

You may remember from Chapter 4 that a corporation's Retained Earnings account is like a proprietorship's Capital account. From this point on we will be dealing with corporations. Notice that Micro Discount Supply Company is a corporation. So everything we said about the Capital account now applies to the Retained Earnings account. The Revenue, Expense, and Dividends account balances are transferred to the Retained Earnings account by means of the closing entries. The Retained Earnings account will then reflect the end-of-period balance.

There is a parallel between the way the Retained Earnings and Inventory accounts are handled. Like the Retained Earnings account, the Inventory account represents a beginning balance on the period-end trial balance. That means that although there were many transactions that caused changes in inventory during an accounting period, those changes were not recorded in the Inventory account. The balance we see recorded in the Inventory account at the end of the period is the same balance that was recorded at the beginning of the period.

Of couse, merchandise is purchased during the period. A reasonable question is: Where is that merchandise accounted for, if not in the Inventory account? The answer is that it is accounted for in the Purchases account, which does indeed change as a result of these transactions during the accounting period.

So, there are two basic ideas you must keep in mind as you proceed through this section:

1. *The Inventory account does not change during an accounting period.*
2. *Merchandise purchased during the period is recorded in the Purchases account, which, in effect, represents changes in Inventory.*

The Inventory account is also brought up to date by the closing entries

The ending Inventory balance is obtained in the accounting records via the closing process, just like the ending Retained Earnings balance. To provide the information required for the closing entries, as well as the information for preparing the income statement and balance sheet, both the beginning and ending Inventory balances are reflected on the worksheet. The amount of the ending inventory is determined by physically counting the entire inventory, as we have previously explained.

The beginning inventory is like an expense for the period

The January 1, 1987, beginning inventory — $19,050 in the Micro Discount Supply Company worksheet — is carried over as a debit balance in the income statement (illustrated on the worksheet by the small shaded area). Carrying the Inventory balance to the debit column of the income statement is similar to carrying Purchases or Salary Expense to the debit column under the income statement. That is, the beginning inventory is similar to an expense incurred during the period. This period's beginning inventory was last period's ending inventory, the inventory that was not sold last period. It remains on hand to be sold this period and once sold must be considered as part of the total cost of goods sold — an expense to be matched against this period's revenue.

The ending inventory is an asset

The ending inventory, $23,025 (which Micro Discount has determined by a physical count), is entered in *both* the income statement credit column and the balance sheet debit column. The ending inventory represents those purchases acquired during the year that have not been sold. The ending inventory will be sold next year and, therefore, should not be considered as an expense of the current period. The ending inventory must be subtracted from the total merchandise that is available for sale to determine the proper expense for the current period — the cost of goods sold. That is why the ending inventory is entered as a credit on the worksheet income statement columns: It reflects a reduction of the expenses. Debits *increase* expenses; credits *decrease* expenses. Refer again to the Micro Discount income statement (page 183), specifically the cost of goods sold section. Line (*k*) — the ending inventory — is subtracted from line (*j*) — the cost of goods available for sale — to determine line (*l*), the cost of goods sold. This income statement was prepared from the information contained on the Micro Discount worksheet. Refer to the boxed information in the shaded areas on the worksheet to see the cost of goods sold accounts on the worksheet.

The ending Inventory debit balance of $23,025 on the worksheet balance sheet represents the cost of the inventory on hand at the end of the current period. It is an asset that will become an expense when it is sold. But on December 31, 1987, it is not sold and must be reported on the balance sheet as an asset.

Closing Entries for a Merchandising Concern

Remember in Chapter 4 how we used the worksheet as an aid in preparing the closing entries for a service business? Well, we follow the same basic procedures in using the worksheet of a merchandising business to help us prepare its closing entries.

The closing process

With a service business we first closed all the expense accounts. Remember, in the last chapter we did not yet know about the contra-revenue accounts, Sales Returns and Allowances and Sales Discounts, nor about the contra-expense accounts, Purchase Returns and Allowances and Purchase Discounts.

First close all income statement accounts with a debit balance

It will now be easier for you to first close all income statement accounts with debit balances. On the Micro Discount worksheet these are found in the debit column under the income statement heading. Notice that the total of this column is $195,030. That will be the amount that must be debited to the Expense and Revenue Summary account. Also notice that in addition to the Purchases account, both Sales Returns and Allowances and Sales Discounts have debit balances, as does the *Beginning Inventory.* Here is the first closing entry:

1987
Dec. 31   Expense and Revenue Summary 195,030
                    Inventory   19,050
                    Sales Returns and Allowances.   2,325
                    Sales Discounts   2,700
                    Purchases   127,875
                    Freight-In.   2,955
                    Salary Expense   27,375
                    Advertising Expense   6,255
                    Rent Expense   2,700
                    Insurance Expense   750
                    Depreciation Expense: Store Equipment   1,125
                    Store Supplies Used   1,920
               To close income statement accounts having debit balances
               including beginning inventory.

Now, what has this accomplished? Well, first of all the Purchases account, the

Sales Returns and Allowances account, the Sales Discounts account, and the Freight-In are all "zeroed out."

Second, the cost of the beginning inventory is eliminated from the Inventory general ledger account, which now looks like this:

Inventory			
1987			
Bal. 1/1	19,050	Closing 12/31	19,050

The second closing entry is to close all income statement accounts having a credit balance. (With a service business we closed all revenue accounts, but back in Chapter 4 we did not have Purchase Returns and Allowances, Purchase Discounts, and Ending Inventory.) The second closing entry is shown below.

Next, close income statement accounts with credit balances

1987
Dec. 31   Inventory   23,025
        Sales 177,750
        Purchase Returns and Allowances   855
        Purchase Discounts   2,025
           Expense and Revenue Summary   203,655
        To close income statement accounts having credit balances
        and to establish ending inventory.

The credit of $203,655 to the Expense and Revenue Summary is the total of the credit income statement column on the worksheet. We have closed all the remaining income statement accounts, including our new accounts, Purchase Returns and Allowances and Purchase Discounts. And we have established the ending inventory. Look at the Inventory account now:

Inventory			
1987			
Bal. 1/1	19,050	Closing 12/31	19,050
Closing 12/31	23,025		

The account now reflects the ending balance.

Remember that we are now dealing with a corporation. So to complete the closing process we will close the Expense and Revenue Summary account to the Retained Earnings account as follows:

Dec. 31   Expense and Revenue Summary 8,625
         Retained Earnings   8,625
        To close the Expense and Revenue Summary account.

And finally we will close the Dividends account.

Dec. 31   Retained Earnings 4,500
                  Dividends   4,500
              To close the Dividends account.

THE STATEMENT OF RETAINED EARNINGS

When we discussed proprietorships we explained that a statement of owner's equity is often prepared in addition to the income statement and the balance sheet. Corporations need a similar statement of owners' equity to serve as a connecting link between the income statement and the balance sheet; it is called the *statement of retained earnings.* Its purpose is to explain the changes that have occurred in the retained earnings account for the period. Retained earnings will increase as a result of net income and decrease because of net losses and dividends. The statement of retained earnings for the Micro Discount Supply Company would appear as follows:

MICRO DISCOUNT SUPPLY COMPANY
Statement of Retained Earnings
For the Year Ended December 31, 1987

Retained Earnings, Jan. 1, 1987.	$18,655
Add: Net Income	8,625
Total	$27,280
Less: Dividends	4,500
Retained Earnings, Dec. 31, 1987.	$22,780

Henceforth, whenever you are asked to prepare financial statements you should prepare three statements: an income statement, a statement of retained earnings, and a balance sheet.

PERIODIC AND PERPETUAL INVENTORY SYSTEMS

What we have been describing is a system of gathering information about merchandise inventory and presenting that information on financial statements. This information tells the reader how much merchandise is still on hand at the end of the accounting period and how much merchandise was sold. This system we call the *periodic inventory system.* This particular system has a major disadvantage: We do not know how much merchandise is on hand unless we count it, and we cannot prepare an income statement without knowing the ending merchandise inventory. (We can estimate the ending merchandise inventory using techniques to be explained in Chapter 9, after you have more experience dealing with inventory problems.) There is another inventory system that can tell us how much inventory is on hand without counting the merchandise; this system we call the *perpetual inventory system.* Let's first review the periodic inventory system and then describe the perpetual system.

Periodic Inventory System

When merchandise inventory (notice that we use the terms merchandise and inventory to describe items a wholesaler or retailer buys to resell to others — sometimes we use both terms together, a common redundant expression in accounting) is acquired, an account called Purchases is debited for the cost of the merchandise. If freight charges were incurred, an account called Freight-In is debited. And if some of the merchandise is later returned, an account called Purchase Returns and Allowances is credited. If the merchandise was subject to a cash discount for early payment of the account payable, an account called Purchase Discounts is credited when payment is made. The total cost of all the units available is determined by adding beginning merchandise inventory to the purchases and freight-in and subtracting the returns and allowances and discounts. The cost of goods sold is determined by subtracting the ending inventory (which we must count) from the total cost of all units available.

Perpetual Inventory System

The perpetual inventory system keeps a running balance of the amount of inventory on hand

With a perpetual inventory system the business keeps an up-to-date record of inventory units; in particular cases, inventory costs are kept up to date as well. The most common type of perpetual inventory systems keep track of only the number of units on hand. Many large department and discount stores have cash registers that record the stock number of each item purchased by each customer. These records are then used to determine how many units are on hand at a given time. Management can then reorder on a timely basis to ensure that there is always enough product on the shelves.

Perpetual systems that regularly record both the number of units and the cost of each unit are used mainly by businesses that handle a low volume of high-value articles. For example, an automobile dealership maintains a perpetual inventory system, recording inventory units and the cost of each unit. A drugstore may not. For a drugstore to use a perpetual units and cost system, it would have to keep track of thousands of different products; when one bottle of mouthwash is sold, a record would have to be made of its stock number (brand and size) and its cost (the drug store could have purchased it at any one of a half-dozen different amounts). When the perpetual inventory system is used, the cost of each unit purchased is recorded directly into the Merchandise Inventory account. The Purchases account is not used. When freight charges are incurred, they too are entered directly into the Merchandise Inventory account. The Freight-In account is not used. The same goes for returns and discounts: They are entered as credits to the Merchandise Inventory account and not to Purchase Returns and Allowances nor to Purchase Discounts. When a sale of merchandise is made, an account called Cost of Goods Sold is debited for the cost of the merchandise and the Merchandise Inventory account is credited. By this means the perpetual inventory system can tell us at any time the cost of goods sold and the cost of the units still on hand—the ending inventory. Let's return to the Micro Discount Supply Company as an example to contrast the entries made under a periodic system and under a perpetual system. Remember that Micro Discount had a beginning inventory of $19,050; purchases of $127,875, of which $26,625 were cash purchases; returns of $855; discounts of $2,025; freight charges of $2,955; an ending inventory of $23,025; and the cost of goods sold amounted to $123,975. The general journal entries to record these transactions under both the periodic and perpetual inventory systems would be as at the top of page 202.

Note: The cost of goods sold is the same under either system, $123,975. It is reflected on line (*l*), page 183 in the Micro Discount income statement, which was prepared using the periodic system. And the same amount is now determined under the perpetual system. It is the $127,875 acquisitions, less the $855 returns and the $2,025 discount, plus the $2,955 freight, less the $125,650 cost of merchandise sold (this figure was not given in the Micro Discount example using the periodic system since it was not needed), plus the $1,675 cost of returned merchandise (this figure was also not given in the periodic system since it was on hand when the inventory was counted).

Periodic Inventory System			Perpetual Inventory System		
Purchases.................. 127,875			Inventory................. 127,875		
Accounts Payable	101,250		Accounts Payable	101,250	
Cash.................	26,625		Cash.................	26,625	
To record the acquisition of merchandise for cash and on account.			To record the acquisition of merchandise for cash and on account.		
Cash..................	855		Cash..................	855	
Purchases Returns and Allowances.........		855	Inventory.............		855
To record mdse. returned to seller.			To record mdse. returned to seller.		
Accounts Payable 101,250			Accounts Payable 101,250		
Purchase Discounts	2,025		Inventory.............	2,025	
Cash.................	99,225		Cash.................	99,225	
To record payment of accounts subject to credit terms of 2/10, n/30.			To record payment of accounts subject to credit terms of 2/10, n/30.		
Freight-In	2,955		Inventory.............	2,955	
Cash.................		2,955	Cash.................		2,955
To record freight charges on merchandise purchased.			To record freight charges on merchandise purchased.		
Cash..................	42,750		Cash..................	42,750	
Accounts Receivable 135,000			Accounts Receivable 135,000		
Sales.................		177,750	Sales.................		177,750
To record sale of merchandise for cash and on account.			To record sale of merchandise for cash and on account.		
Note: No entry is made under the periodic system.			Cost of Goods Sold 125,650		
			Inventory.............		125,650
			To record cost of merchandise sold.		
Sales Returns and Allowances ...	2,325		Sales Returns and Allowances ...	2,325	
Cash.................		2,325	Cash.................		2,325
To record return of mdse. sold.			To record return of mdse. sold.		
Note: No entry is made under the periodic system.			Inventory.................	1,675	
			Cost of Goods Sold		1,675
			To record cost of mdse. returned.		

Now let's take a look at the inventory ledger accounts (at the top of page 203) under each system. There is a difference: Under the periodic system the inventory account is **static** — it does not change until the closing entries are made. But under the perpetual system the inventory account is **dynamic** — it changes every time the inventory changes. Please be aware that under the perpetual inventory system we still have to count the ending inventory to ensure the accuracy of our records.

As you study the two methods, notice the following:

1. The perpetual inventory system uses no Purchases account. It records all purchases directly in the Inventory account.

   The periodic system uses a Purchases account.

2. The perpetual inventory system records merchandise returned to suppliers by directly reducing the Inventory account.

   The periodic inventory system uses a Purchase Returns account.

Periodic Inventory Account			
1987			
Bal. 1/1	19,050	Closing	19,050
Closing	23,025		
1986			
Bal. 1/1	23,025		

Perpetual Inventory Account			
1987			
Bal. 1/1	19,050	Returns	855
Purchases	127,875	Discount	2,025
Freight	2,955	Cost of	
Returns	1,675	Sales	125,650
1986			
Bal. 1/1	23,025		

3. The perpetual inventory system records cost of goods sold and reduces inventory when merchandise is sold.

The periodic system calculates cost of goods sold based on the inventory remaining on hand at the end of the period and records cost of goods sold through the closing process.

4. The perpetual inventory system records customer returns by reducing Cost of Goods Sold and increasing the Inventory account.

The periodic system requires no inventory entry; the merchandise is merely returned to stock.

5. The cost of goods sold and the inventory amounts are readily available at any time under the perpetual inventory system.

Cost of goods sold and inventory amounts are usually not available until they are calculated at year-end under the periodic system.

CHAPTER SUMMARY

A merchandising firm sells a product, not a service. The cost of that product, which is referred to as the *cost of goods sold,* is matched against the *net sales* to determine the *gross profit* made on that product. To determine net income, operating expenses are subtracted from the gross profit.

To account for the revenue of a merchandising firm, we have to consider several things that do not exist for the revenue of a service business. The revenue section of an income statement for a merchandising firm contains a Sales revenue account and also two contra-revenue accounts—*Sales Returns and Allowances* and *Sales Discounts.*

To calculate cost of goods sold we have to consider the accounts for *Beginning Inventory* and *Ending Inventory; Purchases,* the two contra accounts *Purchase Returns and Allowances* and *Purchase Discounts,* and *Freight-In.* The sum of beginning inventory and net purchases during the period is equivalent to goods available for sale. Ending inventory is subtracted from goods available for sale to determine the cost of goods sold.

Two types of sales discounts the accountant must be concerned with are as follows:

1. A discount used to encourage a buyer to pay a sale on account promptly. This is a *cash discount,* which is available only if the bill is paid within a specified period.
2. A *trade discount,* or *chain discount,* which is the amount a buyer (wholesaler or retailer) takes off the *list* price of an item to determine the price he or she pays.

A merchandising firm's periodic accounting procedures are not significantly different from those of a service entity. The revenue and expense accounts particular to a merchandising firm are represented in the trial balance on a worksheet just as are any business entity's expense or revenue accounts.

Only the Inventory account is handled differently on a worksheet. The beginning inventory is carried over to the income statement debit column. The ending inventory is placed in both the credit income statement column and the debit balance sheet column.

The beginning inventory is eliminated by the closing entry that credits the beginning inventory. At the same time, Sales Returns and Allowances, Sales Discounts, Purchases, and Freight-In are closed out with all other expense accounts by credits. The corresponding debit is to the Expense and Revenue Summary. The ending inventory is established in the closing entry that debits Ending Inventory, Sales, Purchase Returns and Allowances, and Purchase Discounts. The corresponding credit is to the Expense and Revenue Summary.

Two inventory systems exist that enable companies to determine their ending inventories and the cost of goods sold. The periodic inventory system requires the company to count the ending inventory. Then, by adding the beginning inventory together with the net purchases (purchases less purchase returns and allowances and purchase discounts plus freight-in) and subtracting the ending inventory, the cost of goods sold is determined. The perpetual inventory system records the purchase, returns, freight charges, and cost of the merchandise sold directly in the Inventory account, thus producing an up-to-date record of the inventory on hand and the cost of the goods sold.

IMPORTANT TERMS USED IN THIS CHAPTER

Cost of goods sold   A calculation that determines the amount of merchandise that is sold during a period. It is reflected as a separate section of a merchandising firm's income statement. (page 189)

FOB destination   Terms expressed in a sales contract with respect to shipping merchandise, specifying that the seller is obligated to pay for the freight cost to the buyer's location. (page 192)

FOB shipping point   Terms expressed in a sales contract specifying that the buyer is obligated to pay for the freight cost of shipping merchandise from the seller's location. (page 192)

Freight-In   A general ledger account used to accumulate the cost of transporting merchandise. *Transportation-In* is another title commonly used for this account. (page 191)

Gross profit   The difference between net sales and cost of goods sold. (page 183)

Inventory   Merchandise purchased by a merchandising firm for resale but not yet sold. (page 189)

Periodic inventory system   A system of determining the ending inventory and the cost of goods sold at the end of a period of time by counting the units on hand. (page 200)

Perpetual inventory system   A system for keeping an up-to-date record of the cost of inventory on hand and the cost of goods sold. (page 201)

Purchase Discounts   A general ledger account used to record the reduction from the purchase price that is allowed if payment is made within a specified period of time. (page 191)

Purchase Returns and Allowances   A general ledger account used to accumulate the cost of merchandise returned to the seller as well as the amount of a concession granted by the seller for unsatisfactory goods. (page 190)

Purchases   A general ledger account used to accumulate the cost of merchandise purchased during the period for resale. (page 189)

Sales   A general ledger account used to accumulate the revenue earned from the sale of merchandise. (page 184)

Sales Discounts   A general ledger account used to accumulate the amount allowed as a reduction from the sales price when the invoice is paid within a specified period. (page 186)

Sales Returns and Allowances   A general ledger account used to accumulate the cost of merchandise returned by the buyer as well as the amount of a concession granted to the buyer for unsatisfactory goods. (page 184)

Trade discounts   Deduction allowed to wholesalers and retailers from the price of merchandise listed in catalogs. Also called *chain discounts.* (page 187)

QUESTIONS

1. Income statements are all the same; an income statement from a service company will look just like an income statement from a merchandising concern. Comment.

2. The term *gross profit* appears on the income statement of a merchandising concern. What does this term mean?

3. Often, when merchandise is sold on account, a *cash discount* is given when the bill is paid. Why?

4. What is the purpose of the account *Sales Returns and Allowances?*

5. The account Sales Returns and Allowances is like the following accounts: Sales Discounts, Purchase Returns and Allowances, Purchase Discounts, and Accumulated Depreciation. Explain.

6. Sales agreements often contain terms such as *n/30, EOM; 2/10, n/30;* and *2/10, 1/30, n/60.* What do these terms mean?

7. What is a *trade discount?* How does it differ from a cash discount?

8. Hamlet Company acquired merchandise costing $4,500. The sales agreement called for a 20-10-5 trade discount and a cash discount of 3/10, n/30. If the invoice is paid within 10 days, how much will the merchandise cost?

9. An important figure on an income statement is the *cost of goods sold.* How is this figure determined?

10. Why is *freight-in* considered part of the cost of goods sold?

11. When a trial balance is prepared for a merchandising concern, it includes the *beginning,* not the *ending inventory.* Explain how the worksheet is used to provide the appropriate inventories for the income statement.

12. What do the terms *FOB shipping point* and *FOB destination* mean?

13. How do the closing entries of a merchandising concern differ from the closing entries of a service-type company?

14. The *periodic inventory system* has certain disadvantages. What are they?

15. The Inventory account under the periodic inventory system is a static account, much like the Capital account. Explain this comment.

16. The Inventory account under the *perpetual inventory system* is a dynamic account. Explain.

17. How does the perpetual inventory system handle the sales of merchandise? The return of merchandise sold?

EXERCISES

Exercise 5-1
Computing missing items

In the five following tabulations several items are missing (these missing items are indicated by a dash). You are to compute the missing items and complete the tabulations.

	1	2	3	4	5
Sales	—	200	100	400	—
Beginning Inventory	100	—	20	120	—
Purchases	—	220	70	—	260
Goods Available for Sale	340	—	—	—	300
Ending Inventory	—	180	—	80	80
Cost of Goods Sold	280	—	65	440	—
Gross Profit	320	20	—	—	80

Exercise 5-2
Preparing closing entries

The following accounts appeared in the general ledger of the Emerson Company at the end of 1987:

Sales	$360	Dividends	$45
Purchases	195	Freight-In	40
Inventory, 1/1/87	105	Purchase Returns and Allowances	35
Common Stock	80	Cash	30
Retained Earnings	70	Accounts Payable	25
Accounts Receivable	60	Insurance Expense	20
Inventory, 12/31/87	55	Salaries Payable	15
Salaries Expense	50	Sales Discounts	10

Using this information, prepare the year-end closing entries dated December 31, 1987.

Exercise 5-3
Computing the advantage of borrowing to pay an invoice within the discount period

Dalton Enterprises received an invoice from Big Rock Gravel Company for $3,500 on May 1, 1987. The terms of the invoice were 3/10, n/30, meaning that the invoice must be paid by May 11 if the discount is to be taken. But Dalton will not have the funds available on May 11 to pay the invoice. Dalton can, however, borrow the necessary funds from the United National Federal First Bank of Cutter City at a rate of 12% per year.

If Dalton were to borrow the necessary funds for 20 days (Dalton has a large account receivable to be collected on May 31, which can be used to pay the loan), would Dalton save any money by borrowing the necessary funds on May 11 to pay the invoice within the discount period? How much would they save?

(Check figure: Savings = $82.37)

Exercise 5-4
Computing trade and cash discounts

Alpha Auto Parts purchased $5,400 of auto parts from the Beta Mfg. Company. The invoice had the following trade discount: 40-10-5. In addition a 2% cash discount is available if the invoice is paid within the discount period. If the invoice is paid before the cash discount expires, how much will Alpha pay Beta?

(Check figure: $2,714.80)

Exercise 5-5
Preparing a worksheet

The unadjusted trial balance of the Weston Company as of December 31, 1987 appears at the top of page 207.

WESTON COMPANY
Unadjusted Trial Balance
December 31, 1987

Cash.	$ 10	
Accounts Receivable	30	
Inventory, Jan. 1, 1987.	100	
Shop Supplies on Hand	40	
Shop Equipment.	130	
Accumulated Depreciation		$ 30
Accounts Payable		20
Common Stock		100
Retained Earnings.		80
Dividends	25	
Sales.		395
Sales Returns and Allowances	35	
Purchases	185	
Purchase Discounts		15
Freight-In	20	
Salary Expense	60	
Insurance Expense.	5	
Totals.	$640	$640

Additional Information:

a. Accrued salaries at year-end amount to $15.
b. Shop supplies on hand at year-end amount to $5.
c. Depreciation on the shop equipment is $10.
d. The December 31 inventory amounts to $20.
Prepare a worksheet dated December 31, 1987.

(Check figure: Net loss = $35)

Exercise 5-6
Recording journal entries for returns

The General Sales Company uses the periodic inventory system. During the month of March 1987, the following transactions occurred:

Mar. 3   Purchased merchandise on account, $2,350.
       9   Returned $250 of merchandise purchased on the 3d.
      12   Sold merchandise on account for $1,600.
      17   Merchandise sold for $175 on the 12th is returned.

Prepare the general journal entries for the four dates.

Exercise 5-7
Computing beginning inventory

Using the data presented below for the Attila Company, compute the beginning inventory.

Cost of Goods Sold	$77,900	Purchase Discounts.	$6,500
Ending Inventory	42,700	Purchase Returns and	
Freight-In	3,100	Allowances	2,500
Purchases	105,000		

(Check figure: Beginning inventory = $21,500)

Exercise 5-8
Computing ending inventory

The Jameson Company has sustained a fire loss at their warehouse. Information obtained from the company records reveals the following:

Beginning Inventory.	$17,300	Purchase Discounts	$2,650
Cost of Goods Sold	73,150	Purchase Returns and	
Freight-In	1,700	Allowances.	3,100
Purchases.	95,200		

From this information, calculate the value of the ending inventory so that Jameson may file an insurance claim for the loss.

(Check figure: Ending inventory = $35,300)

Exercise 5-9
Recording inventory transactions under the periodic and perpetual systems

The Thomas Company opened its store on May 1, 1987. During the month of May the following transactions occurred:

May 2   Purchased merchandise on account from the Corner Supply Store, $37,500.
      9   Sold merchandise to Alfred Jones on account, $16,250. The merchandise cost $11,300.
     14   Returned merchandise costing $4,550 to the Corner Supply Store.
     21   Merchandise costing $2,050 was returned by Alfred Jones. The merchandise was sold for $2,730.

Prepare general journal entries for the above transactions, first using the periodic inventory system and then using the perpetual inventory system.

PROBLEMS
Set A

Problem A5-1
Preparing journal entries

The Seattle Cattle Company had the following transactions during the month of June 1987. Record these transactions in a general journal. The company uses the periodic inventory system.

June 3   Sold merchandise on account, $2,100; credit terms 2/10, 1/30, n/60.
      8   Acquired office equipment on account, $5,500; credit terms 2/10, n/30.
      9   Sold office supplies for cash at cost, $350, as an accommodation to Easy Rider Cattle Company.
     10   Received amount due from the June 3 sale.
     11   Purchased merchandise inventory on account, $4,500; credit terms 3/10, n/30.
     12   Returned for credit $1,100 of defective merchandise acquired on June 11.
     14   Purchased $2,570 of merchandise inventory for cash.
     15   Paid for the merchandise acquired on June 11 less the return of June 12.
     17   Paid for the office equipment purchased on June 8.
     18   Sold merchandise on account, $6,500; credit terms 3/10, 1/30, n/60.
     21   Sold merchandise for cash, $2,350.
     23   Paid cash $3,750 for merchandise plus an additional $175 for freight charges.
     29   Received payment due from the sale of June 18.
     30   The customer from the June 18 sale returned $600 of merchandise that he claimed was defective. Seattle Cattle Company paid the customer the amount due.

Problem A5-2
Calculating ending inventory

A fire in downtown Houston on September 29, 1987, destroyed the inventory of the Lone Star Wholesale Company. Lone Star has an insurance policy with the Bluebonnet Insurance Company of Waco. The policy will pay 90% of the amount of the inventory that was lost. But since the inventory was destroyed, the amount is unknown. It can be calculated by using the data available in the company's office.

A relationship between the company's gross profit and net sales can be computed. This relationship (which has been about 43% for the past several years) can then be multiplied times the company's net sales for the first 9 months of 1987. The resulting figure will approximate the gross profit for that period of time. If the gross profit is subtracted from the net sales, the result is the cost of goods sold. And if the cost of goods sold is subtracted from the goods available for sale, the result is an estimate of the value of the destroyed inventory. The insurance company will pay 90% of this value.

Data available from the company records reveals the following:

Freight-In.	$ 13,600	Purchase Returns.	$ 6,430
Jan. 1, 1987, Inventory	196,300	Sales	1,452,600
Purchases.	987,540	Sales Discounts	28,300
Purchase Discounts	16,400	Sales Returns	17,800

Required

Using this information, compute the amount of the insurance claim.

(Check figure: Insurance claim = $335,614.50)

Problem A5-3
Preparing a worksheet and closing entries

Presented below is the unadjusted trial balance of the Davidson Company as of the end of its current business year, March 31, 1987:

DAVIDSON COMPANY
Unadjusted Trial Balance
March 31, 1987

Cash	$ 1,000	
Accounts Receivable.	2,710	
Inventory.	32,200	
Prepaid Insurance	4,450	
Office Supplies on Hand	3,690	
Office Equipment.	21,400	
Accumulated Depreciation:		
Office Equipment.		$ 7,500
Accounts Payable		3,210
Common Stock.		10,000
Retained Earnings		26,000
Dividends.	15,000	
Sales.		193,640
Sales Returns and Allowances.	1,530	
Sales Discounts	2,840	
Purchases.	110,020	
Purchase Returns and Allowances.		1,840
Purchase Discounts		2,310
Freight-In.	2,230	
Salary Expense	38,400	
Rent Expense	5,400	
Advertising Expense.	3,630	
Totals	$244,500	$244,500

The inventory was counted at the close of business on March 31; the count totaled $26,700.

Additional Information:

a. Salaries in the amount of $3,200 are accrued at year-end.
b. Prepaid insurance in the amount of $1,900 expired during the year.
c. Depreciation on the office equipment amounts to $1,500 for the year.
d. Office supplies on hand at year-end are valued at $1,530.

Required

1. Prepare, without the adjusted trial balance columns, a worksheet for the year ended March 31, 1987.
2. Record the appropriate general journal entries to close the accounts for the year ended March 31, 1987.

(Check figure: Net income = $19,480)

Problem A5-4

Preparing a worksheet, financial statements, adjusting and closing entries

The following accounts reflect the business activity of Columbus Company as of December 31, 1987:

Sales	$175,000	Purchase Returns and		
Purchases	115,500	Allowances	$9,050	
Mortgage Payable	60,000	Purchase Discounts.	7,200	
Shop Building	58,000	Accumulated Depreciation:		
Salaries Expense.	55,000	Building	4,000	
Common Stock	51,000	Accounts Receivable	3,750	
Retained Earnings	30,900	Notes Payable	3,000	
Inventory	27,300	Freight-In	2,900	
Land	22,000	Advertising Expense	2,500	
Shop Equipment	20,000	Shop Supplies on Hand	2,300	
Dividends.	15,000	Cash	2,000	
Sales Discounts	13,000	Entertainment Expense	2,000	
Accumulated Depreciation:		Accounts Payable	1,600	
Shop Equipment.	11,500	Prepaid Insurance.	1,500	
Sales Returns and Allowances . . .	10,500			

Additional Information:

a. Depreciation for the year on the shop equipment and the shop building amounts to $1,000 and $1,750, respectively.
b. A count of the shop supplies on hand amounts to $650.
c. Insurance in the amount of $500 has expired.
d. Salaries of $1,050 have accrued as of the last day of the year.
e. A count of the ending inventory amounted to $31,500.

Required

1. Prepare and complete a worksheet for the year.
2. Prepare the financial statements.
3. Journalize the appropriate adjusting and closing entries.

(Check figure: Net loss = $11,900)

Problem A5-5

Preparing journal entries under the periodic and perpetual inventory systems

During the course of business activity, the Great East India Company had the following transactions:

Nov. 1   Purchased merchandise on account from the London Tea Company, $26,000, credit terms, 2/10, n/30.
3   Purchased for cash merchandise from Holland Exports, $15,000.
6   Sold merchandise to Boston Redskins, Inc., on account, credit terms 3/10, n/30, $6,500. The inventory cost $4,800.
9   Returned defective merchandise amounting to $1,500 to the London Tea Company.
10   Received amount due from Boston Redskins, Inc.
10   Paid the London Tea Company the amount due.
14   Sold merchandise to Portland Company, trade terms 40-10-5, credit terms 3/10, n/30, $5,000. The inventory cost $2,000.
16   Portland returned goods that were sold to them for $1,000 (cost $250) before considering the trade and cash discounts.
23   Portland paid the amount due.

Required

1. Prepare the general journal entries to record the transactions assuming that a periodic inventory system is used.
2. Prepare the general journal entries to record the transactions assuming that a perpetual inventory system is used.

3. Assuming that the beginning inventory amounted to $21,500, first prepare the general ledger inventory account under the perpetual inventory system. Then, using the amount of the ending inventory determined under this system, prepare the general ledger inventory account under the periodic inventory system.

(Check figure: Ending inventory = $53,960)

Problem A5-6
Preparing an income statement

The accounts presented below have been selected from the September 30, 1987, year-end trial balance of the Busy Company:

Advertising Expense	$ 8,300	Purchase Returns and	
Depreciation Expense	1,500	Allowances	$ 1,140
Entertainment Expense	2,000	Rent Expense	3,600
Gross Sales	337,000	Salary Expense	36,500
Freight-In	3,900	Sales Discounts	3,600
Insurance Expense	1,000	Sales Returns and Allowances . . .	3,100
Inventory, 10/1/86	25,400	Store Supplies Used	2,560
Inventory, 9/30/87	30,700	Telephone Expense	1,000
Purchases	170,500	Utilities Expense	500
Purchase Discounts	2,700		

Required   Prepare an income statement with three distinct sections: sales, cost of goods sold, and operating expenses. Divide the operating expenses into two sections: selling expenses and general and administrative expenses. The only accounts in the last classification are the telephone and utilities expenses.

(Check figure: Net income = $108,080)

Set B

Problem B5-1
Preparing journal entries

The following transactions occurred in the month of January 1987, and are to be recorded in the general journal of the Baltimore Company. The company uses the periodic inventory system.

Jan. 2   Purchased merchandise inventory on account, credit terms 3/10, n/30, $2,500.
       3   Paid $2,100 for inventory purchased, $150 of which was freight charges. Payment was made in cash.
       4   Purchased office equipment on account, credit terms 3/10, n/30, $1,100.
       6   Sold merchandise on account, 2/10, 1/30, n/60 $1,800.
       8   Returned for credit $700 of merchandise acquired on Jan. 2.
       8   Purchased merchandise inventory on account, credit terms 2/10, n/30, $3,350.
       9   Paid for the inventory purchased on Jan. 2 less the return of Jan. 8 and the appropriate discount.
      11   Paid for the office equipment acquired on Jan. 4.
      14   Sold merchandise for cash $2,750.
      16   Received returned merchandise of $350 from the sales transaction of Jan. 6.
      17   Paid for inventory purchased on Jan. 8.
      21   Received payment for merchandise sold on Jan. 6.
      25   Returned defective inventory amounting to $450 to the vendor from the Jan. 8 transaction. Received cash from the vendor.
      28   Purchased office supplies on account, credit terms 2/10, n/30, $1,250.
      30   Sold office supplies costing $225 for cash to a competitor as an accommodation.

Problem B5-2
Calculating ending inventory

Stan Wholesaler has experienced a very successful year operating his business. He feels that next year will be even better, and he plans to expand his business by 50%. But in order to do that he will need some additional financing from the Local Bank. The bank has asked Stan for an income statement reporting the results of operations for the year. Since last year was Stan's first year in business, Stan did not know that financial statements would be required by the bank. The officials at the bank have informed Stan that if he allows you to prepare an income statement for him, they will grant him the loan.

Reconstructing Stan's records was a difficult job, but you are able to ascertain the following information:

Sales	$350,000	Sales Discounts	$2,300
Purchases	205,000	Purchase Returns and	
Salary Expense	115,000	Allowances	1,950
Inventory, Jan. 1, 1987	22,500	Sales Returns and Allowances	1,570
Rent Expense	6,000	Purchase Discounts	1,240
Advertising Expense	4,000	Supplies Used	890
Freight-In	3,150		

You realize that to prepare the income statement you will need to find the value of the December 31, 1987, inventory. But it is now mid-January, and the ending inventory was not counted. The bank provides you with the following guidelines for determining the ending inventory: "Ending inventories for a wholesale business can be estimated by first multiplying the relationship between gross profit and net sales—traditionally 46% in the wholesale business—times the actual net sales for the period. The resulting figure approximates the actual gross profit. Next subtract the approximate gross profit figure from the net sales to obtain the cost of the goods sold. Finally, the ending inventory is determined by subtracting from the goods available for sale the cost of the goods sold."

Required   Using this technique to find the ending inventory, prepare the income statement.

(Check figure: Net income = $33,330)

Problem B5-3
Preparing a worksheet and closing entries

The unadjusted trial balance of the Delaware Company is presented below:

Cash	$ 1,700	
Accounts Receivable	3,070	
Inventory	26,500	
Prepaid Rent	1,500	
Store Supplies on Hand	2,150	
Store Equipment	15,000	
Accumulated Depreciation: Store Equipment		$ 5,000
Accounts Payable		1,700
Notes Payable		10,000
Common Stock		15,000
Retained Earnings		26,450
Dividends	9,000	
Sales		97,500
Sales Returns and Allowances	1,050	
Sales Discounts	2,750	
Purchases	63,700	
Purchase Returns and Allowances		870
Purchase Discounts		1,430
Freight-In	3,570	
Salary Expense	22,560	
Insurance Expense	3,600	
Travel Expense	1,800	
Totals	$157,950	$157,950

At the end of the business day on December 31, 1987, the inventory was counted and valued at $30,150.

Additional Information:

a. Prepaid rent of $500 expired during the year.
b. Salaries of $1,850 were accrued as of the last day of the year.
c. Store supplies on hand at year-end were $540.
d. Depreciation on the store equipment amounted to $750.
e. The note payable has $650 of accrued interest.

Required

1. Prepare, without the adjusted trial balance columns, a worksheet for the year ended December 31, 1987.
2. Record the year-end closing entries.

(Check figure: Net loss = 940)

Problem B5-4

Preparing a worksheet, financial statements, adjusting and closing entries

Listed in alphabetical order below are the accounts of the New Jersey Company reflecting activity for the year ended March 31, 1987:

Accounts Payable	$ 1,520	Notes Payable	$25,000
Accounts Receivable	3,070	Office Equipment	22,500
Accumulated Depreciation:		Prepaid Rent	900
Building	7,500	Purchase Discounts	1,050
Accumulated Depreciation:		Purchase Returns and	
Office Equipment	2,250	Allowances	770
Building	55,000	Purchases	47,300
Cash	1,600	Retained Earnings	12,000
Common Stock	30,000	Salary Expense	18,400
Dividends	11,000	Sales	83,120
Freight-In	2,250	Sales Discounts	1,430
Inventory	36,700	Sales Returns and Allowances . . .	950
Land	25,000	Telephone Expense	1,010
Miscellaneous Expense	1,050	Utilities Expense	550
Mortgage Payable	65,500		

The accounts do not reflect the results of the year-end adjustments. Information pertaining to these adjustments is presented below:

a. One-third of the rent has expired.
b. Interest on the note payable amounts to $1,250 for the year.
c. Accrued salaries amount to $1,970.
d. Depreciation on the building and office equipment amounts to $1,500 and $1,125, respectively.
e. The ending inventory amounts to $39,900.

Required

1. Prepare a worksheet for the year ended March 31, 1987.
2. Prepare the financial statements for the period.
3. Record the year-end adjusting and closing entries.

(Check figure: Net income = $9,055)

Problem B5-5

Preparing journal entries under the periodic and perpetual inventory systems

Since it first started its business the Wayside Wholesale Company has used the periodic inventory system. Mrs. Wayside, president of the Wayside Wholesale Company, recently read an article in a trade magazine that listed the advantages of the perpetual inventory system. She is now convinced that the company should change to the new system. For the current month, September 1987, she has ordered the accounting department to record all transactions relating to inventory under *both* systems so that she can compare the results at the end of the month. Listed below are the inventory-related transactions.

Sept. 2   Purchased for $25,000 cash merchandise from Underhill Mfg.
       3   Purchased merchandise, $45,000, from Sideview Supplies, credit terms, 2/10, n/30.
       7   Sold merchandise on account to Tailgate Retail Company, credit terms, 3/10, n/30, $15,000. The merchandise cost $12,000.
      10   The merchandise received from Sideview Supplies was partially defective and was returned. The purchase price of this inventory amounted to $1,850.
      11   Paid Sideview the amount due.
      14   Received payment due from Tailgate Retail Company.
      16   Purchased merchandise on account, $20,000, from Downtown Supply Company under the following trade terms: 40-15-5. In addition, credit terms of 2/10, n/30 are available.
      21   Returned $4,000 of goods acquired from Downtown Supply. (The $4,000 amount does not consider either the trade or the cash discounts.)
      24   Paid Downtown Supply the amount due.

Required   **1.** Prepare general journal entries to record the transactions, first using the periodic inventory system and then using the perpetual inventory system.
         2. The beginning inventory amounted to $13,750. First prepare the general ledger inventory account under the perpetual inventory system. With the ending inventory determined by the perpetual system, prepare the inventory account under the periodic system.

(Check figure: Ending inventory = $76,634)

Problem B5-6
Preparing an income statement

A number of selected accounts appear below from the October 31, 1987, year-end trial balance of the Reading Company:

Gross Sales	$275,300	Office Supplies Used	$1,800
Purchases	131,500	Sales Discounts	1,600
Mortgage Payable	75,000	Purchase Returns and	
Inventory, 10/31/87	42,700	Allowances	1,400
Salaries Expense	39,100	Rent Expense	1,200
Inventory, 11/1/86	35,800	Accounts Receivable	800
Advertising Expense	9,500	Entertainment Expense	500
Depreciation Expense	7,500	Insurance Expense	400
Sales Returns and Allowances	2,700	Utilities Expense	300
Freight-In	2,100	Miscellaneous Expenses	100
Purchase Discounts	1,900		

Required   Prepare an income statement classified like the Micro Discount Supply Company example in the text. The statement should have three distinct sections: a section for sales, a section for the cost of goods sold, and a section for operating expenses. The operating expenses should be split into selling expenses and general and administrative expenses. Only the insurance, utilities, and miscellaneous expenses should be in the last classification.

(Check figure: Net income = $87,200)

Chapter 6

Internal Control and Special Journals

When you have completed this chapter you should able to:

- Discuss the nature of an internal control system
- Describe the problems inherent in developing a system of internal control
- Explain why a system of internal control is important
- Explain the purpose of special journals and how to use them
- Explain the posting process of a business entity using special journals
- Describe the relationship between subsidiary and control accounts

"But Mr. Wilson was our most trusted employee," lamented the office manager after the embezzlement was discovered. "Better I should have assigned someone I didn't trust to the funds transfers section, and then I would have watched him like a hawk. Mr. Wilson never even took a day's vacation, such a nice gentleman he was, how could he do this to me?"

An all too familiar scene to those of us in accounting. Look in your local newspaper for the next several months and you will see a similar situation reported. Would we let someone we didn't trust handle our money? And Mr. Wilson never took a vacation. Of course not! If he had, someone else would have had to handle his responsibilities and they would have discovered his "unique" methods of transferring company funds. Mr. Wilson would have been caught. The problem here is that the company evidently did not have any method of providing certain checks and balances in its operations that would prevent this particular fraud. In short, there was no system of *internal control.* That's what this chapter is all about, a discussion of procedures, techniques, and practices designed to provide a dependable and efficient accounting system that will help management plan and control the company's business activities as well as safeguard the company's resources. And part of a dependable and efficient accounting system is the use of special journals, the topic of the last sections of the chapter.

INTERNAL CONTROL

An internal control system can not completely prevent fraud. It can, however, make the perpetration of fraud very difficult

One of the very first things we need to realize about any internal control system, no matter how tightly it is designed, is that it cannot be made 100% foolproof. That's why casualty insurance is carried on company assets and that's why fidelity bonds are carried on employees who handle company funds. But an internal control system can be so designed that no one person is able to perpetrate a fraud. Several dishonest employees will have to coordinate activities (collusion) to do their despicable deeds.

Two types of internal controls are *accounting controls* and *administrative controls.* While we will be most concerned with accounting controls, a brief mention of administrative controls is necessary.

Administrative controls deal with the efficiency of an organization.

Administrative controls are the procedures and methods that are concerned mainly with the operational efficiency of the organization and compliance with the organization's policies. They include such things as time-and-motion studies, performance reports, statistical analyses, and various directives such as requiring company executives to have annual medical examinations. Administrative controls are important to any organization, but accountants are more concerned with controls that affect the reliability of the financial statements and that safeguard the company's resources.

Accounting controls deal with procedures, techniques, and practices that protect a company's assets and provide reliable financial statements

Accounting controls are the procedures, techniques, and practices intended to protect the company's resources and provide for reliable financial statements. We can organize our discussion of internal accounting controls by looking at personnel controls, record controls, and checks and balances.

Personnel Controls

In the selection, training, and assignment of personnel there are several basic considerations needed to develop a strong system of internal control. These considerations are: employee competence, duty assignments, employee responsibility and authority, accountability, and custodianship.

It is essential that employees have the necessary talent, intelligence, and training for their assigned duties

■ *Employee Competence* The organization must make an effort to assure that employees are very carefully selected and that they have the necessary talents, intelligence, and training for the duties assigned to them. And it is equally important that these employees be properly supervised as they perform their duties. Talent and intelligence are wasted if the employee has not been adequately trained to perform assigned tasks. The most important assignment a supervisor has is to train people with the view of having them reach their highest potential within the organization.

■ *Assignment of Responsibility*   Let's picture an accounts receivable section of a large department store; say that we have about 10 employees assigned to this section. A phone call comes in to you from an irate customer complaining about an error in her account. As manager of this section you need to discuss the error with the individual who made the error. Now errors are going to happen; we can't avoid that fact of life. But we can attempt to prevent the same error from happening again. And we have an opportunity to help someone learn from the error. Remember what good old Fra Pacioli once said (page 72): If you don't do anything, you aren't going to make any mistakes; and if you don't make any mistakes, you will not learn. So you ask the group who committed the error, and if the group is like most other groups, 10 fingers will point to 10 different people. The point is that the system must be designed so the responsibility can be pinpointed without question. The group should have been organized so that each employee was assigned a group of customer account numbers over which he or she had responsibility.

A system of internal control must be designed so that responsibility for actions are clearly identified

■ *Division of Work*   Back to Mr. Wilson again. What may have happened was that Mr. Wilson was assigned the responsibilities of depositing customer checks in the bank and also maintaining the accounts receivable records. How easy for him — he just pockets some customer checks and marks their accounts paid with the collections from the next customer or two. As long as he knows where he is in his "system," he can continue this indefinitely. If this was what Mr. Wilson did, we could have prevented it from happening by having someone else handle the responsibility of depositing the checks or maintaining the accounts receivable records. Employee assignments should be divided so that related operations are not performed by the same individual. Where this is the case, it takes several employees conspiring to commit fraud.

Employee assignments should be divided so that related operations are not performed by the same individual

■ *Rotation of Duties*   Rotating the individual assignments within the work unit will serve several purposes. First, it gives the employees training in many of the different areas of the unit, thus providing them with a bigger picture of the unit's role in the organization. Second, it enhances the value of employees, enabling them to understand, appreciate, and perform each other's work should the need arise. Third, it strengthens the system, since departures from standard operating procedures will be discovered when another employee performs the assignment. Fourth, it provides a broader background for the employees, serving as a basis for future promotion.

Rotating employee assignments is essential for training and control

The organization should have a policy that all employees be required to take annual leave. Clearly, such a policy would benefit employees; it can also benefit the firm. How we wish that Mr. Wilson had taken vacations!

Records Controls

Sometimes the activities in records controls may overlap the activities in personnel controls; generally, that's okay. Its just another way of looking at the overall problem of controls. We are going to classify records control into three parts: custodianship, adequacy, and documentation.

Custodianship of assets and record control must be kept separate

■ *Custodianship*   Someone within the firm has to be assigned the responsibility of collecting cash receipts and depositing the cash in the bank. Someone must also be responsible for the company's small tools, parts, and vehicles. If the individual responsible for the tools and parts were also the individual who maintained the records on the tools and parts inventory, a potential would exist for that individual to supply himself and his friends with all the tools and parts they need at company expense. Some fringe benefit! The point is that the individual assigned the custodi-

WHEN E. F. HUTTON KITES, PEOPLE LOSE

Check kiting is the process of covering a shortage in cash by writing a check on one cash account and depositing the check in another cash account. The deposit is reflected in the second cash account but the withdrawal is not shown on the first account. Since it may take several days for the check to be processed by the banking system, the cash shortage can be covered. Accountants generally check for check kiting by requesting that two bank statements be mailed directly from the bank to the accountant: one at month's end and another, called a cutoff statement, 10 days later. All interbank transfers reflected on the second statement are then traced and verified to determine their validity.

The following information was extracted

from an article in the May 2, 1985 business section of the Tampa Tribune:

E. F. Hutton pleaded guilty to 2,000 federal felony charges and was fined $2.75 million in a check kiting scheme that may have involved a total of $10 billion. An estimated 400 banks lost "tens of millions of dollars" in interest payments on money that did not exist. The checks were written on funds of distant banks before money was deposited in those banks to cover the checks. About 10 to 25 people were involved in the scheme and the Justice Department stated that other firms may be doing the same thing.

The 2,000 felony charges represent 2,000 separate counts of mail and wire fraud—each charge representing a single

check. The checks were worth $4.349 billion. Each charge drew a fine of $1,000 and the additional $750,000 levy was to defray the costs of the government investigation.

The Justice Department stated that between July 1, 1980, and February 28, 1982, E. F. Hutton drew against uncollected funds, with daily overdrafts sometimes exceeding $250 million.

The 1981 transactions with the United Virginia Bank in Alexandra, Va. illustrates how the scheme worked. Day after day E. F. Hutton owed the bank about $9 million. Each day new checks were deposited to cover the previous day's checks—but the bank never got the money, only more checks.

Reprinted by permission of the *Tampa Tribune-Times.*

anship of the firm's resources must not have access to the records pertaining to those resources. The individual assigned the responsibility of maintaining the accounts receivable records must not have any access to cash; those preparing the payroll records must not be able to draw checks from the payroll cash account.

Adequate records includes a chart of accounts, control and subsidiary records, and prenumbered paper forms as well as appropriate record-keeping equipment

■ *Adequacy* In order to provide control over the firm's resources as well as to provide timely, accurate, and reliable information to management, adequate records must be maintained. As a matter of fact, all publicly held corporations in the United States are required by law (the Foreign Corrupt Practices Act) to maintain adequate records to assure that the corporation's resources are what and where the corporation says they are. The law requires that a system of internal control must be adequate to assure that the management of the corporation has knowledge of all the entity's business transactions and has approved of them. Adequate records would include a chart of accounts, control accounts and the related subsidiary records, and prenumbered sequential paper forms such as sales orders and checks.

The company's recordkeeping equipment—cash registers, check protectors, bookkeeping machines, and computer hardware and software—must all be adequate to provide the safeguards necessary to achieve proper control as well as to provide timely, accurate, and reliable information to management.

All business transactions must be adequately documented

■ *Documentation* This is another aspect of having adequate records. Each function within the organization must *document* its activity with adequate records. Take the sales function for example. Documentation would include the purchase order from a company wishing to buy our product, the credit approval from our firm's credit department, the sales invoice, the shipping invoice marked "shipped," the accounts receivable subsidiary ledger account for the customer, and whatever other documents, properly authorized with appropriate signatures, are necessary to verify that an order was authorized, filled, sent, received, and paid for. In other words, adequate *documentation* must exist to trace and verify each transaction the corporation enters into from beginning to end. In accounting lingo this is considered to be an "adequate audit trail."

THE E.S.M. AUDIT

"He was bright, charming, and personable, which makes it all the harder to understand," said Howard Groveman, the national director of accounting and auditing for Alexander Grant & Co., about Jose Gomez, a partner involved in an alleged bribery in the alleged E.S.M. fraud. Mr. Gomez was one of the youngest partners in the firm's history.

The E.S.M. Government Securities alleged fraud triggered a panic that resulted in the temporary closing of four score and ten Ohio Saving & Loan institutions. Jose Gomez was the Alexander Grant partner in

charge of the E.S.M. audit. E.S.M. had a negative net worth of $300 million in March, 1985 when it collapsed.

The Securities and Exchange Commission charged Mr. Gomez with accepting $125,000 in payments from E.S.M. for approving false E.S.M. financial statements.

The internal controls of the large CPA firm require that the local office managing partner appoint an "engagement partner" to oversee a specific audit. The engagement partner then recommends a manager and an audit team to perform the engage-

ment. Thus, there should be three responsible individuals for an audit engagement: the audit manager, the engagement partner, and the local office managing partner. This is the internal control feature of separation of duties. But in the E.S.M. case Mr. Gomez was the managing partner of the Fort Lauderdale, Florida office, the engagement partner, and he acted as the manager.

Source: "The Lesson of E.S.M." by Jeffery A. Trachtenberg, *FORBES,* May 6, 1985, page 128.

The internal control features you studied in this section of the chapter apply not only to business entities but to the CPA firms that audit those business entities.

Checks and Balances

The last aspect of internal control we will consider is that of checks and balances. Any good system must provide for a continual review of the recordkeeping functions and the verification of resources. Our discussion is organized into three parts: reconciliations, internal auditing, and external auditing.

Reconciliations are made periodically between a company's assets and the related records

■ *Reconciliations* Every month the company will receive from the bank a statement of the amount of cash the company has on deposit at the bank. The company must then compare the amount reflected on the bank statement with the amount in the general ledger Cash account. This is called a *reconciliation.* Any differences must be explained. We will see how to do this in the next chapter. The Accounts Receivable Control account must be reconciled with the accounts receivable subsidiary ledger (the individual accounts receivable accounts). We will see how to do this in the next section of this chapter. The Inventory account (in a perpetual inventory system) must be reconciled with the physical count of the inventory. And so it goes for all the company's resources. The records are compared with the actual resources to verify that the resource exists and to know how much of it there is.

■ *Internal Auditing* Internal auditing is usually associated with large corporations, but many of the functions of internal auditing departments of large corporations can be carried out by small companies. Basically the function of the internal audit is to review the organization's activities to discover errors or irregularities, to determine if procedures and policies are being followed, and to uncover inefficiency.

■ *External Auditing* Before providing an opinion on a company's financial statements, the CPA must review the company's system of internal control. This outside review offers the company an impartial check of the company's system and often results in many suggestions for improvement.

SPECIAL JOURNALS

Part of a system of good internal control is having adequate records. The system we have developed in the first four chapters has adequate records to handle only the smallest of companies. We need to expand the recordkeeping system to handle a much larger mass of business activities. We need to study the special journals.

The accounting process we have presented up to this point should work well

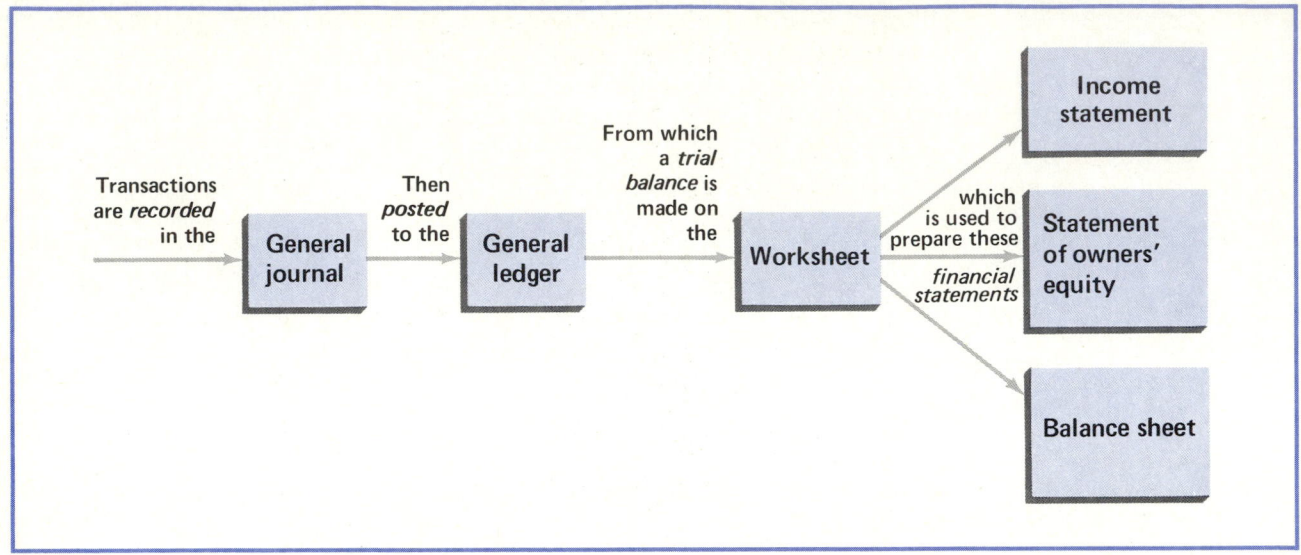

FIGURE 6-1   Manual accounting system.

enough for business entities, service or merchandising, that do not have many transactions or many customers or suppliers. Any transaction, no matter how simple or complex, can be handled by this process. Any *number* of transactions can also be handled, *given an unlimited amount of time.* However, time is limited and expensive, and most business entities have many transactions. Consequently, business entities have developed accounting systems to perform the accounting process. These systems are basically tailor-made for each business entity and range from simple manual accounting systems to expensive and complex electronic systems.

The accounting process you have learned about so far is, basically, the simple manual accounting system, and is illustrated in Figure 6-1. Electronic accounting systems are computer-based and sophisticated, often using the latest and largest of computers and peripheral equipment. The type of system a business entity needs depends on how easily its various types of business transactions can be classified into like groups. For example, a manual system may group together all sales on account for recording. An electronic system may batch all daily customer billings together to update customer files, update inventory stocks, send bills to customers, and compute the amount of the Accounts Receivable balance. All transactions within each group are handled in the same manner.

An electronic accounting system is based on the same principles as a manual accounting system, and it does the same work a manual system does. The difference, of course, is that the electronic system can handle many, many more transactions than a manual system, and can do all of them very much faster. A lot faster!

Accounting textbooks use the basic manual accounting system to describe how transactions are analyzed, classified, and summarized, resulting in the final accounting product—the financial statements. But you should appreciate that even the smallest of firms is today using some electronic systems. And you should also appreciate that the electronic systems are based on the concepts you have learned, and will learn, about a manual system.

Most transactions can be classified into four groups: buying and selling merchandise on account; paying and receiving cash

To begin our discussion of a manual system, let's consider a merchandising firm's transactions. Although an entity engages in many transactions in the normal course of doing its business, almost all of them can be classified in one of four major groups. For example, a merchandising firm sells merchandise on account, purchases merchandise for resale on account, receives cash, and pays cash. For each of these distinct activities a *special journal* is designed. A special journal is a *book of original entry*—a book where transactions are first recorded—designed to record only one class of business transactions. The four most common special journals are the *sales journal,* the *cash receipts journal,* the *purchases journal,* and the *cash payments journal.* The general journal is used only to record transactions that cannot be recorded in one of the special journals.

The Sales Journal

Only sales on account are recorded in the sales journal

Cash sales are recorded in the cash receipts journal

The sales journal is a book of original entry designed to handle only one type of transaction: the sale of merchandise on credit. This transaction requires a debit to Accounts Receivable and a credit to Sales. No other transaction should be recorded in the sales journal. A cash sale, for example, should not be recorded in the sales journal; it should be recorded in the cash receipts journal. The sales journal is a single-column journal, as can be seen in The Jones Company sales journal illustrated in Exhibit 6-1. This is because only one money column is needed—the amount debited to Accounts Receivable is also the amount credited to Sales.

EXHIBIT 6-1

THE JONES COMPANY
Sales Journal
Page 16

Date	Account Debited	Invoice No.	Post. Ref.	Amount
1987				
Aug. 4	Sally Hamm	418	✓	$ 100
6	John Davis	419	✓	85
7	Tom Adams	420	✓	20
15	Linda Jones	421	✓	90
18	Nancy Kantz	422	✓	200
21	William Lennord	423	✓	450
27	Robert Grafton	424	✓	80
30	Ann Knox	425	✓	180
Total				$1,205
				(1130/4100)

The evidence of each sale is a *sales invoice,* which lists the date of the sale, the customer's name, the credit terms, the amount of the sale, and the invoice number. The sales invoice representing the sale to Linda Jones would look like this:

THE JONES COMPANY
1531 Fletcher Avenue
Tampa, Florida   33620

Invoice No. _____ 421 _____

Invoice Date _____ Aug. 15, 1987 _____

Sold to: Linda Jones

3116 Second Street

Brandon, FL   33511

Terms _____ 2/10, n/30 _____

Shipped Via _____ Customer pick-up _____

Date Shipped _____ Aug. 15, 1987 _____

Quantity	Description		Unit Price	Amount
8	13EL7	Fans	$7.50	$60.00
24	20AQ1	Belts	1.25	30.00
				$90.00

A copy of the sales invoice provides the authority and the information to record the transaction in the sales journal.

Notice that the sales journal does not require a description or explanation for a transaction. Because only one type of transaction is recorded, it is obvious what that transaction is—a sale of merchandise on account.

The invoice number provides a reference to the sales invoice. Thus, if any additional information or a review of the original information is needed, the sales invoice can be located by its invoice number.

At the end of each month the total sales on account from the sales journal is posted to the general ledger as a single debit to the Accounts Receivable account and a single credit to the Sales account. In Exhibit 6-1, this is represented by:

$$\underline{\$1,205}$$
$$(1130/4100)$$

where $\$1,205$ = the total of all the sales on account for the month
1130 = the company's account number for Accounts Receivable
4100 = the account number for Sales

Of course, the left/right order of the account numbers indicates that $\$1,205$ is debited to Accounts Receivable (that is, to the account whose reference number is on the left of the slash mark) and $\$1,205$ is credited to Sales (to the account whose number is on the right of the slash).

In this simple illustration, eight sales transactions were recorded but only one posting was required. In a more realistic business situation, there would be several hundred sales transactions during a month's time. No matter how many transactions, only one posting is required. This is the advantage provided by the sales journal in the posting process.

Let's look at the debit side of this entry—Accounts Receivable. We might see a disadvantage in relying solely on the sales journal. The Accounts Receivable account informs management of the amount of total credit outstanding to its customers. The account does not provide any information on the credit of individual customers. Management must know on a daily basis the credit status of the individual customers. Has anyone exceeded his or her credit limit? If so, can additional credit be granted? How long is the account overdue? Answers to these and other related questions are vital to a well-managed company.

The Subsidiary Ledger and the Control Account

The accounts receivable ledger is a subsidiary ledger

Information on the credit of individual customers is recorded in a ***subsidiary ledger,*** which is separate from the general ledger and in which a separate account is maintained for each individual customer. These customer accounts are alphabetized.

The alphabetized ***accounts receivable ledger*** is a subsidiary ledger of the Accounts Receivable account in the general ledger. The Accounts Receivable account in the general ledger is called the ***control account.*** A subsidiary ledger should be established for any general ledger account comprising many individual accounts. For example, if a business entity had 20 different cash accounts, a subsidiary ledger would be established where each of the individual cash accounts could be found, and the general ledger account Cash would be a control account. Subsidiary ledgers are most commonly used for accounts receivable, accounts payable, and equipment.

A subsidiary ledger may contain only 10 or fewer accounts or as many as 10,000 accounts. Figure 6-2 illustrates the relationship between each of five possible general ledger control accounts and the subsidiary ledgers for each control account.

FIGURE 6-2
The Jones Company.
The relationship between
general and subsidiary ledgers.

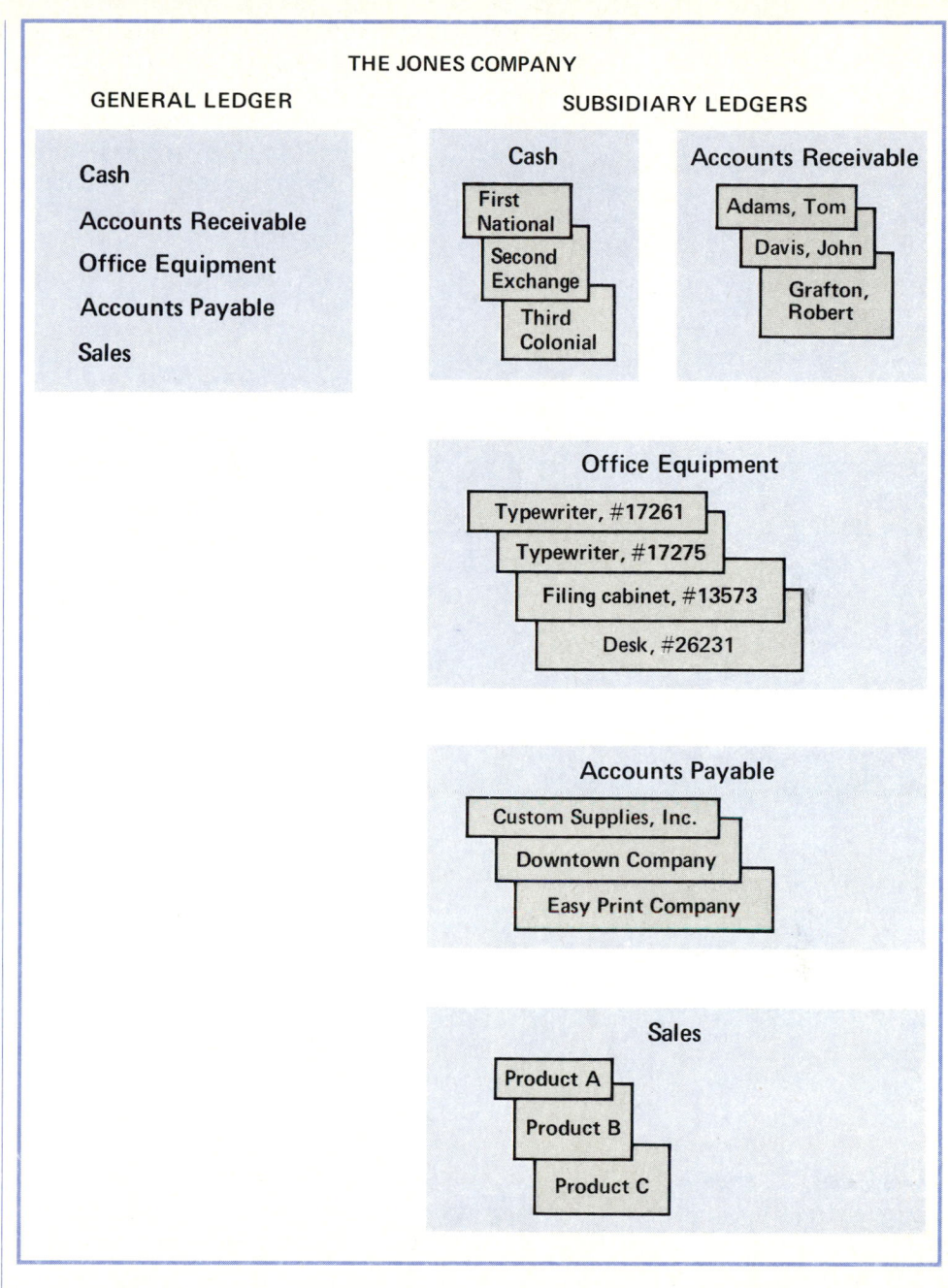

Where there are many individual accounts in a subsidiary ledger, it would be impossible to list each one on a trial balance. However, we don't have to deal with this impossibility because of the control account. The control account reflects the total of the balances of all the individual subsidiary ledger accounts. It takes the place of these numerous accounts in the trial balance.

Let's return to our illustration of the sales journal (page 221) to demonstrate more fully the relationship between the subsidiary ledger and the control account. When The Jones Company makes a sale, such as the $100 credit sale to Sally Hamm on August 4, two things happen: (1) The sale is recorded in the sales journal, and (2) it is also posted as a debit in Sally's Accounts Receivable account in the subsidiary ledger. The fact that the posting has been made is indicated by the check mark (✓) in the posting reference column of the sales journal.

Exhibit 6-2 below illustrates the process of posting from the sales journal to the subsidiary ledger. The subsidiary ledger is posted every day credit sales are made; the general ledger is posted only on the last day of the month.

Let's take a closer look at the posting process. The August 4 entry in the sales

EXHIBIT 6-2   Posting from the Sales Journal to the Subsidiary Ledger and General Ledger.
The subsidiary ledger is posted daily; the general ledger, monthly.

journal represents a sale on account to Sally Hamm for $100. On the date of this transaction a debit is posted to the Accounts Receivable subsidiary account of Sally Hamm. In this subsidiary ledger account the *S16* refers to page 16 of the sales journal, identifying the source of the information recorded. The (✓) in the sales journal indicates that the information it identifies has been posted to the subsidiary ledger.

At the end of the month the total amount of the sales on account, $1,205, is posted to the general ledger accounts. Note that a posting reference, S16, is placed in the control account to identify the source of the information posted.

Before the trial balance is prepared at the end of the month, all the debit balances in the accounts receivable subsidiary ledger are totaled to see if the total agrees with the debit balance in the control account (Accounts Receivable in the general ledger). If no errors occurred, the two will balance.

The Cash Receipts Journal

The cash receipts journal is a multi-column journal

The special journal used to record transactions in which cash is received is called the *cash receipts journal.* Unlike the single-column sales journal, the cash receipts journal contains many columns. There is only one source for data recorded in the sales journal — sales on account — so one column is sufficient. But cash is received from many different sources. Therefore, in the cash receipts journal, a column is needed to record each source of the cash. However, only one column is needed to record the receipt of cash.

Collection of receivables and cash sales are the two most common sources of cash

In designing a cash receipts journal, each business entity must consider all its sources of cash. The two most common regular sources of cash are the collection of accounts receivable and cash sales. Thus, a credit column is established for each of these accounts: Accounts Receivable and Sales. Although there are other sources of cash, they do not occur regularly. So, they are lumped together in one column labeled Sundry Accounts Credit. Nevertheless, for any source that produces more than a few cash transactions each month, a column should be established. The cash receipts journal of The Jones Company is illustrated in Exhibit 6-3.

EXHIBIT 6-3

THE JONES COMPANY
Cash Receipts Journal

Page 9

Date	Account Credited	Explanation	Post. Ref.	Sundry Accounts Cr	Accounts Receivable Cr	Sales Cr	Sales Disc. Dr	Cash Dr
1987								
Aug. 3		Cash sales	—			500		500
5	Common Stock	Issue common stock	3100	1,000				1,000
11	Sally Hamm	Invoice, 8/4 less 2%	✓		100		2	98
15		Cash sales	—			300		300
17	John Davis	Invoice, 8/6 partial	✓		45			45
20	Notes Payable	Bank loan	2110	600				600
21		Cash sales	—			400		400
22	Nancy Kantz	Invoice, 8/18 less 2%	✓		200		4	196
30	Tom Adams	Invoice, 8/7	✓		20			20
				1,600	365	1,200	6	3,159
				(—)	(1130)	(4100)	(4110)	(1110)

Cash sales are recorded in the cash receipts journal by entering the amount of the cash received in the cash debit and the sales credit columns. For example, the amount entered typically represents the total of each day's cash sales as indicated by cash-register tapes. Exhibit 6-3 illustrates three cash sales entries — August 3, August 15, and August 21. Each of these daily totals represent numerous cash sales transactions during the day indicated.

The total of the sales credit column in the cash receipts journal, $1,200 in Exhibit 6-3, is the total cash sales for the month. This amount is posted to the credit column of the Sales account in the general ledger. Thus, a large number of sales transactions have been recorded in the general ledger account by only one posting.

Recall our discussion on sales discounts earlier in Chapter 5. When credit terms are granted and the customer pays the bill within the discount period, a sales discount is given. The general journal entry to record a collection of an account receivable within the discount period would be as follows:

Cash	98	
Sales Discount.	2	
Accounts Receivable.		100

To record collection of accounts receivable subject to 2/10, n/30 credit terms.

To record this in the cash receipts journal two debit money columns are needed, one for cash and one for sales discount.

For example, The Jones Company made a sale on account in the amount of $100 to Sally Hamm on August 4, as reported in the sales journal back in Exhibit 6-1 (page 221). Sally paid in full on August 11, as indicated in the third line of the cash receipts journal (Exhibit 6-3). Therefore, $100 credit is entered for Sally in the accounts receivable column of the cash receipts journal. And, because she paid her bill within 10 days (assuming 2/10, n/30), she gets a discount of 2% (of $100), or $2, which is entered as a debit in the sales discount column.

Notice the check mark (✓) in the posting reference column after the account of Sally Hamm. This indicates that the $100 credit was posted to her Accounts Receivable account in the subsidiary ledger. As with the sales journal, the subsidiary ledger accounts are posted each day.

The total of the accounts receivable column in the cash receipts journal is posted as a credit to the Accounts Receivable control account in the general ledger at the end of the month. In our example, the total was $365. Therefore, a credit of $365 is posted to the Accounts Receivable control account on the last day of the month. To indicate that this has been posted, the Accounts Receivable control account number (1130) is placed under the accounts receivable credit column.

The sundry accounts column is used to handle all sources of cash other than cash sales and collections of receivables

Sources of cash other than cash sales or collections of accounts receivable are entered in the sundry accounts credit column. Two such examples are shown in Exhibit 6-3. On August 5 stockholders invested an additional $1,000 in the business and on August 20 the company borrowed $600 from the bank by issuing a note payable. In each case the general ledger account title must be entered under the caption Account Credited. At the end of the month the amounts found in the sundry column are posted to their respective general ledger accounts. The account numbers of these accounts are entered in the posting reference column to evidence that the posting has been done.

The amounts within each column of the cash receipts journal are added — or as accountants would say, *footed* — at the end of the month. The totals of the credit columns are then added together, or *crossfooted.* Similarly, the debit columns are crossfooted. The purpose of the crossfooting is to prove the equality of the debits and credits. In our example, the crossfooting of the column totals from the cash receipts journal of Exhibit 6-3 appears as follows:

Sundry Accounts Cr		Accounts Receivable Cr		Sales Cr				Sales Discounts Dr		Cash Dr
$1,600	+	$365	+	$1,200	=	$3,165	=	$6	+	$3,159

Upon the assurance that the debits and credits in the cash receipts journal are equal, the totals of each of the columns are posted to their respective accounts in the

EXHIBIT 6-4

THE JONES COMPANY General Ledger	THE JONES COMPANY Accounts Receivable Subsidiary Ledger

Cash   1110

Aug. 31 CR9	3,159	

Accounts Receivable   1130

Aug. 31 S16	1,205	Aug. 31 CR9	365

Notes Payable   2110

	Aug. 20 CR9	600

Common Stock   3100

	Aug. 5 CR9	1,000

Sales   4100

	Aug. 31 S16	1,205
	31 CR9	1,200

Sales Discounts   4110

Aug. 31 CR9	6	

Adams, Tom

Aug. 7 S16	20	Aug. 30 CR9	20

Davis, John

Aug. 6 S16	85	Aug. 17 CR9	45

Grafton, Robert

Aug. 27 S16	80	

Hamm, Sally

Aug. 4 S16	100	Aug. 11 CR9	100

Jones, Linda

Aug. 15 S16	90	

Kantz, Nancy

Aug. 18 S16	200	Aug. 22 CR9	200

Knox, Ann

Aug. 30 S16	180	

Lennord, William

Aug. 21 S16	450	

general journal. The posting is evidenced in the cash receipts journal by annotating under each column total the number that identifies it in the general ledger.

In the sundry accounts credit column, two entries appear. These entries must be posted individually to the general ledger accounts Common Stock, and Notes Payable and the identifying account numbers for each must be entered in the posting reference column.

The total of the sundry accounts credit column is used only in crossfooting to

EXHIBIT 6-5

THE JONES COMPANY
Purchases Journal
Page 11

Date	Account Credited	Invoice Date	Post. Ref.	Amount
1987				
Aug. 2	Easy Print Company	8/2	✓	$ 275
9	Federal Company	8/6	✓	150
14	Custom Supplies, Inc.	8/10	✓	100
19	Downtown Company	8/19	✓	320
22	Federal Company	8/21	✓	15
24	Great Goods, Inc.	8/20	✓	255
				$1,115
				(5100/2120)

monthly posting

daily posting

THE JONES COMPANY
General Ledger

Accounts Payable   2120

	Aug. 31 P11	1,115

Purchases   5100

Aug. 31 P11	1,115	

THE JONES COMPANY
Accounts Payable Subsidiary Ledger

Custom Supplies, Inc.

	Aug. 14 P11	100

Downtown Company

	Aug. 19 P11	320

Easy Print Company

	Aug. 2 P11	275

Federal Company

	Aug. 9 P11	150
	22 P11	15

Great Goods, Inc.

	Aug. 24 P11	255

prove equality of the debits and credits. The total, of course, is not posted because it is a combination of several accounts. This total provides no useful information; it is used simply to aid in proving the equality of the debits and credits. Consequently, no account number is placed under the column total. Instead, the symbol (—) is placed under the column to show it has been considered in the crossfooting.

Presented in Exhibit 6-4 on page 227 are the accounts of the general ledger and the accounts receivable subsidiary ledger after both the sales journal and the cash receipts journal have been posted.

Notice that the source of each of the postings is referenced by the journal page numbers. The posting from the sales journal page 16 is referenced as S16, while the posting from the cash receipts journal page 9 is referenced as CR9.

The Purchases Journal

Only purchases on account are recorded in the purchases journal

Like the sales journal, the ***purchases journal*** is a book of original entry designed to record just one type of business transaction—the purchase of merchandise on account. It is a one-column journal in which each entry is a debit to Purchases and a credit to Accounts Payable. This single-column journal is illustrated in Exhibit 6-5.

Each transaction is recorded in the purchases journal by entering the date of the transaction, the vendor's (creditor's) name, the date of the invoice, and the amount of the purchase. The vendor's accounts are posted each day to their accounts payable in the subsidiary ledger. For example, see the posting of the Easy Print Company account of August 2 in Exhibit 6-5. The procedure is much the same as posting from the sales journal to the subsidiary and general ledgers. The purchases journal page number P11 is recorded as a posting reference in the subsidiary ledger account of the Easy Print Company as the source of authority for the posting.

At the end of the month the purchases journal is footed and the total is posted as a debit to Purchases and also as a credit to Accounts Payable in the general ledger. The account numbers of these two accounts—5100 and 2120, respectively—are annotated under the total of the amount column, indicating that the total has been posted to both accounts. The journal page number is recorded as a posting reference in the general ledger account as authority for the posting.

The Cash Payments Journal

The cash payments journal is a multi-column journal

The payment of cash is recorded in the ***cash payments journal.*** A cash payments journal is structured in much the same way as a cash receipts journal. Because cash is paid out for at least several different purposes, each many times during a month, there are at least several columns in a cash payments journal. Accounts Payable, Purchases, and Sundry are column headings for the typical debits recorded; Purchase Discounts and Cash are the column headings for recording the credits. The cash payments journal of The Jones Company is illustrated in Exhibit 6-6 on page 230.

You are most likely aware that a business entity does not make cash payments in currency, but rather by check. The reason, of course, is that payment by check provides security and control—that is, it provides information that the payments were paid and were received by the payee, as well as a record of the payment amounts, dates paid, and related information. Thus, the format of a cash payments journal differs from a cash receipts journal in one respect: Rather than a column for explaining the nature of cash received, it has a column for simply recording the number of the check used for the cash payment. Of course, should it be necessary to know the nature of the payment, that information can be found for that check in the checkbook records.

There is one exception to the rule that cash payments must be made in check, not currency: Petty cash payments, of course, are made in currency. The reason is

EXHIBIT 6-6

THE JONES COMPANY
Cash Payments Journal   Page 24

Date	Check No.	Account Debited	Post. Ref.	Sundry Accounts Dr	Accounts Payable Dr	Purchases Dr	Purchase Discounts Cr	Cash Cr
1987								
Aug. 3	316	Rent Expense	5400	175				175
9	317	Purchases	—			135		135
11	318	Federal Company	✓		150		3	147
16	319	Salary Expense	5200	200				200
17	320	Easy Print Co.	✓		175			175
22	321	Purchases	—			400		400
24	322	Custom Supplies	✓		100		2	98
26	323	Freight-In	5120	10				10
				385	425	535	5	1,340
				(—)	(2120)	(5100)	(5115)	(1110)

practicability and expediency. We'll discuss petty cash disbursements further in Chapter 7.

Each cash payment is posted from the cash payments journal to the appropriate general and subsidiary ledger accounts in the same way that each cash receipt was posted from the cash receipts journal. Transactions with vendors are posted each day to appropriate accounts in the accounts payable subsidiary ledger. When a transaction is posted from the journal to the subsidiary ledger, a check mark (✓) is entered in the posting reference column. In Exhibit 6-6 the check marks for the entries to Federal Company, Easy Print Company, and Custom Supplies serve as examples that each has been posted.

At the end of the month, each individual entry in the sundry accounts debit column is posted to its appropriate account in the general ledger. Instead of a check mark the account number of the general ledger account is entered in the posting reference column of the cash payments journal to indicate that the transaction has been posted. Examples of these cash payments are Rent Expense, Salary Expense, and Freight-In, as shown in the sundry accounts debit column in Exhibit 6-6.

The cash payments journal is footed and crossfooted to prove the equality of the debits and credits, as was done for the cash receipts journal. Finally, the totals of the columns to be posted in the general ledger are posted in their respective accounts, and to indicate that this had been done, the account numbers are entered under the column totals of the cash payments journal.

The General Journal

Only a few transactions will now be recorded in the general journal

With these four special journals, relatively few transactions are recorded in the general journal. Only transactions that do not involve cash receipts or cash payments, or the purchase or sale of merchandise on credit, are entered as original entries in the general journal. *Adjusting, closing,* and *reversing* entries are examples of such entries.

Two transactions that must be recorded in the general journal are illustrated on page 231. The first, dated August 20, is the acquisition of office equipment on account. This entry cannot be recorded in the purchases journal because that journal records only *purchases of merchandise* on account.

The second transaction is the return of items previously sold to a customer. Because this entry involves neither cash nor a purchase nor a sale, the only place for this entry is in the general journal.

	General Journal			Page 3
Date	**Account Titles and Explanation**	**Post. Ref.**	**Debit**	**Credit**
Aug. 20	Office Equipment	1210	575	
	Accounts Payable *NAME*	2120/✓		575
	To record the acquisition of office equipment from Tate Office Supplies Company, terms 3/10, n/30.			
23	Sales Returns and Allowances	4120	50	
	Accounts Receivable *NAME*	1130/✓		50
	To record the return of items previously sold to Linda Jones on account.			

Since the acquisition of office equipment on account is not a purchase, it must be recorded in the general journal

We post the general journal entries to the appropriate general ledger accounts just as we always have. Evidence that an entry from the journal was posted to the general ledger is signified by the number of the general ledger accounts marked opposite the account posted in the posting reference column. Note in the two general journal entries above that the general ledger accounts—Office Equipment (1210), Accounts Payable (2120), Sales Returns and Allowances (4120), and Accounts Receivable (1130)—have been posted to the general ledger accounts. Also notice that the subsidiary ledger accounts—Tate Office Supplies Company (Accounts Payable) and Linda Jones (Accounts Receivable)—have also been posted. The postings are evidenced by the check marks (✓) after the account numbers in the posting reference column.

Proving the Control Accounts

Exhibit 6-7 (pages 232–233) shows the general ledger and subsidiary ledger for The Jones Company after all the journals have been posted at the end of the month. A trial balance (see Exhibit 6-8) is prepared from the general ledger to test that the sum of its debits equals the sum of its credits. In Exhibit 6-8 the sum of the debits, $5,275, equals the sum of the credits, $5,275. Before continuing with the period-end procedures—preparing the adjusting entries, the closing entries, and the financial statements—we prepare a *schedule* (list) of the subsidiary ledgers to prove that the total of the accounts in a subsidiary ledger equals the balance in the control account. Schedules of accounts receivable and accounts payable appear at the bottom of Exhibit 6-7. The schedule of accounts receivable does not include the accounts of Tom Adams, Sally Hamm, or Nancy Krantz. They all have zero balances, and consequently do not owe The Jones Company anything on the last day of the month. Likewise, in the schedule of accounts payable the Custom Suppliers, Inc., account, which has a zero balance, is not listed.

A schedule of accounts receivable or accounts payable is a list of all the balances in the subsidiary ledger accounts

EXHIBIT 6-7   General and Subsidiary Ledgers after Posting.

THE JONES COMPANY
General Ledger

Cash			1110
Aug. 31 CR9	3,159	Aug. 31 CP24	1,340
Bal.	1,819		

Accounts Receivable			1130
Aug. 31 S16	1,205	Aug. 23 G3	50
		31 CR9	365
Bal.	790		

Office Equipment			1210
Aug. 20 G3	575		

Notes Payable			2110
		Aug. 20 CR9	600

Accounts Payable			2120
Aug. 31 CP24	425	Aug. 20 G3	575
		31 P11	1,115
		Bal.	1,265

Common Stock			3100
		Aug. 5 CR9	1,000

Sales			4100
		Aug. 31 S16	1,205
		31 CR9	1,200
		Bal.	2,405

Sales Discounts			4110
Aug. 31 CR9	6		

Sales Returns and Allowances			4120
Aug. 23 G3	50		

Purchases			5100
Aug. 31 P11	1,115		
31 CP24	535		
Bal.	1,650		

Purchase Discounts			5115
		Aug. 31 CP24	5

Freight-In			5120
Aug. 31 CP24	10		

Salary Expense			5200
Aug. 31 CP24	200		

Rent Expense			5400
Aug. 31 CP24	175		

Accounts Receivable Schedule

Adams, Tom

Aug. 7	S16	20	Aug. 30	CR9	20
Bal.		0			

Davis, John

Aug. 6	S16	85	Aug. 17	CR9	45
Bal.		40			

Grafton, Robert

| Aug. 27 | S16 | 80 | | | |

Hamm, Sally

Aug. 4	S16	100	Aug. 11	CR9	100
Bal.		0			

Jones, Linda

Aug. 15	S16	90	Aug. 23	G3	50
Bal.		40			

Krantz, Nancy

Aug. 18	S16	200	Aug. 22	CR9	200
Bal.		0			

Knox, Ann

| Aug. 21 | S16 | 180 | | | |

Lennord, William

Aug. 31	S16	450			
Bal.		450			

Accounts Payable Schedule

Custom Supplies, Inc.

Aug. 24	CP24	100	Aug. 14	P11	100
			Bal.		0

Downtown Company

| | | | Aug. 19 | P11 | 320 |

Easy Print Company

Aug. 17	CP24	175	Aug. 2	P11	275
			Bal.		100

Federal Company

Aug. 11	CP24	150	Aug. 9	P11	150
			Aug. 22	P11	15
			Bal.		15

Great Goods, Inc.

| | | | Aug. 24 | P11 | 255 |

Tate Office Supplies Co.

| | | | Aug. 20 | G3 | 575 |

**THE JONES COMPANY
Schedule of Accounts Receivable
August 31, 1987**

Davis, John	$ 40
Grafton, Robert	80
Jones, Linda	40
Knox, Ann	180
Lennord, William	450
Total	$790

**THE JONES COMPANY
Schedule of Accounts Payable
August 31, 1987**

Downtown Company	$ 320
Easy Print Company	100
Federal Company	15
Great Goods, Inc.	255
Tate Office Supplies Company	575
Total	$1,265

EXHIBIT 6-8

THE JONES COMPANY Trial Balance August 31, 1987		
	Debit	**Credit**
Cash	$1,819	
Accounts Receivable	790	
Office Equipment	575	
Notes Payable		$ 600
Accounts Payable		1,265
Common Stock		1,000
Sales		2,405
Sales Discounts	6	
Sales Returns and Allowances	50	
Purchases	1,650	
Purchase Discounts		5
Freight-In	10	
Salary Expense	200	
Rent Expense	175	
Totals	$5,275	$5,275

The schedule of accounts receivable amounts to $790, which is the balance found in the Accounts Receivable general ledger account. The subsidiary ledger and control accounts are in agreement. The same is true for the $1,265 total of the accounts payable subsidiary ledger and its control account.

With the proving of the control accounts we have described the last of the new things we need to do in our expanded accounting system. Our manual accounting system now includes five journals, subsidiary ledgers, and the worksheet, and is illustrated in Figure 6-3.

CHAPTER SUMMARY

A system of internal control contains procedures, techniques, and practices to provide a dependable, efficient accounting system that will help management plan and control the company's business activities as well as safeguard its resources. There are two types of internal controls: *accounting controls* and *administrative controls.* Accounting controls protect the company's resources and provide for reliable financial statements; administrative controls are concerned with the operational efficiency of the organization and compliance with its policies.

Accounting controls can be considered to comprise *personnel controls, record controls,* and *checks and balances.* Personnel controls are concerned with employee competence, assignment of responsibilities, division of work, and rotation of duties. The organization should select and train employees who have the necessary talents and intelligence for the duties assigned. And the employees should be assigned duties that are clearly identifiable so that responsibility can be pinpointed. It is important to divide employee assignments so that related operations are not performed by the same individual. Employees should be rotated among the duty assignments. This effects not only training but system control as well, since each employee will realize that at any time someone else may be reassigned to perform his or her duties.

Records controls consist of custodianship, adequacy, and documentation. The employee assigned the responsibility of custodianship of certain resources should

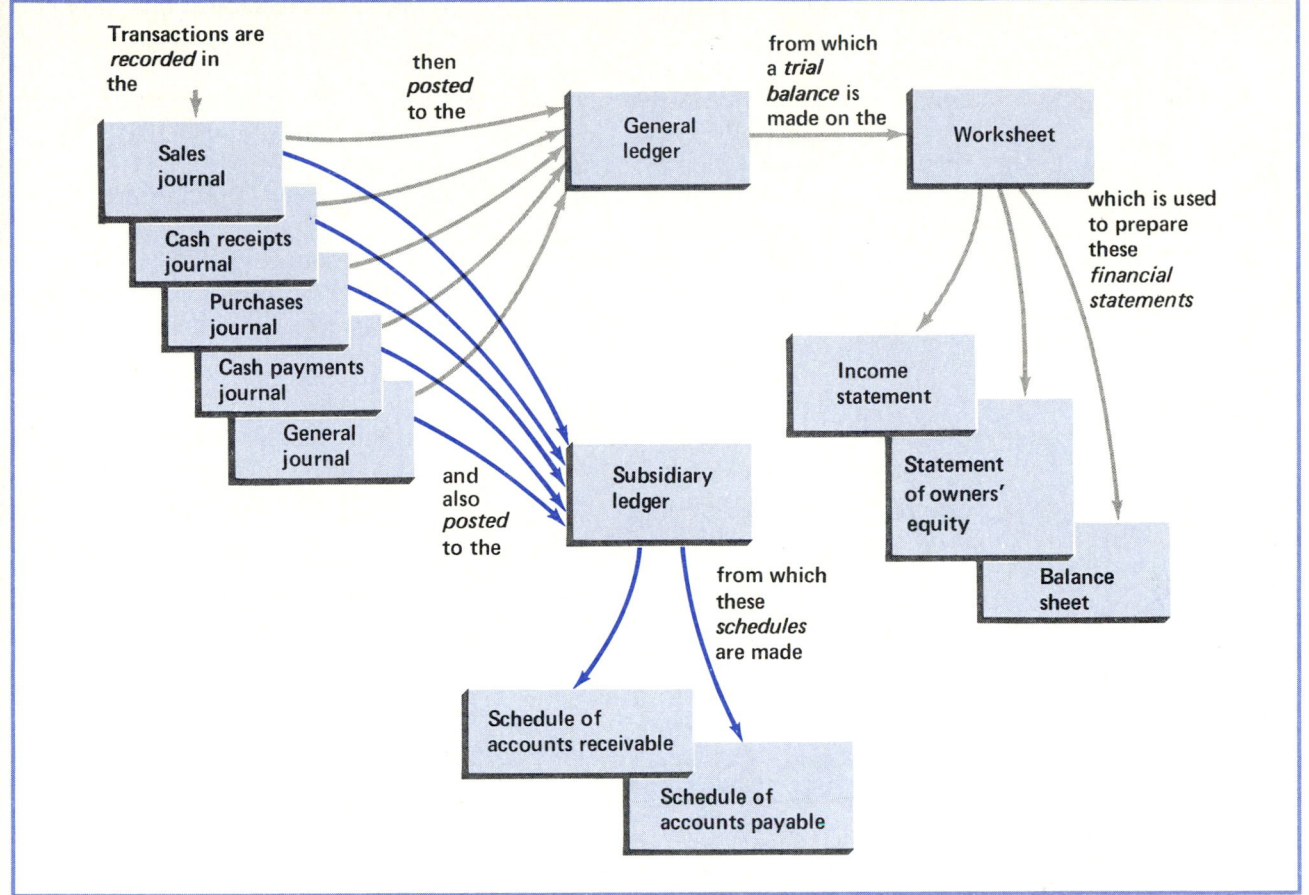

FIGURE 6-3 The accounting system.

never be allowed to have access to the records pertaining to those resources. Records and the recordkeeping equipment should be adequate to provide timely, accurate, and reliable information. And each function within the organization must provide properly documented evidence to verify that it fulfills an appropriate business activity and has been approved at all stages of the transaction.

Checks and balances consist of reconciliations, internal auditing, and external auditing. Reconciliations are required periodically to compare the actual resources to company records to see that the resources in fact do exist and that their proper value is reflected on the company books. The internal auditing function will review the organization's activities to discover errors or irregularities, to determine if company procedures and policies are being followed, and to uncover inefficiencies. The external audit performed by a certified public accountant provides an impartial review of the company records and may result in suggestions for improvement.

Each business activity can be represented in a special journal which is part of a system of internal control. Moreover, a special journal saves time in recording many of the same kinds of business transactions.

There are four types of special journals. The *sales journal* is designed to record all sales of merchandise on account; the *purchases journal* records merchandise bought on account. All transactions involving cash receipts are recorded in the *cash receipts journal;* and all transactions involving cash payments are recorded in the *cash payments journal.* Sales journals and purchases journals are typically one-column journals. The amount of the Accounts Receivable debit is identical to the amount of the Sales credit; similarly, the Purchases debit is identical to the Accounts Payable credit. The cash receipts and the cash payments journals are multi-column journals that are typically tailor-made for the business entity using them.

Transactions that cannot be handled in one of the special journals must be recorded in the general journal.

Posting the special journals to the general ledger accounts involves posting only the column totals to the appropriate account. However, postings from the special journals must also be made to the individual subsidiary ledger accounts in the case of accounts receivable and accounts payable.

IMPORTANT TERMS USED IN THIS CHAPTER

Accounting controls   The procedures, techniques, and practices that will protect the company's resources and provide for reliable financial statements. (page 216)

Administrative controls   The procedures and methods that are concerned mainly with the operational efficiency of the organization and compliance with its policies. (page 216)

Cash payments journal   A book of original entry designed for recording those transactions involving expenditures of cash. (page 229)

Cash receipts journal   A book of original entry designed only for recording business transactions involving receipt of cash. (page 225)

Control account   A general ledger account, such as Accounts Receivable, which is supported by a subsidiary ledger containing the detail of the control account. (page 222)

Documentation   The providing of adequate records to trace and verify each transaction from its beginning to its end. (page 218)

Internal auditing   The function of reviewing the organization's activities to discover errors or irregularities, to determine if the procedures and policies of the company are being followed, and to uncover inefficiencies. (page 219)

Internal control   The procedures, techniques, and practices designed to provide a dependable efficient accounting system that will help management plan and control the company's activities as well as safeguard the company's resources. (page 216)

Purchases journal   A book of original entry used only to record purchases on account. (page 229)

Sales journal   A book of original entry used only to record sales on account. (page 221)

Special Journals   Books of original entry designed to record only one class of business transactions. (page 219)

Subsidiary ledger   A group of accounts, such as the accounts payable subsidiary ledger, which provide the detail of a general ledger control account, in this case Accounts Payable. (page 222)

QUESTIONS

1. Two types of internal controls exist: What are they? Explain each.

2. A company with a strong system of internal control will never have to worry about fraud. Evaluate this statement.

3. What is internal control?

4. Describe the factors an internal control system must consider regarding personnel.

5. Custodianship, adequacy, and documentation are all part of records control; describe each of these functions.

6. In any good system of internal control, checks and balances exist. List and describe three such checks and balances.

7. Internal auditing has the same objectives as external auditing. Evaluate this statement.

8. The Wilson Company bills its customers monthly and receives payments the following month by check. The receptionist opens the daily mail, makes a list of the checks, and gives this list to the bookkeeper, then the receptionist deposits the checks in the bank. At the end of the month a bank statement is sent by the bank to the office manager, who reconciles the bank's balance with the cash reflected on the bookkeeper's general ledger cash account. Evaluate this system.

9. Explain the relationship that exists between a *control account* and its *subsidiary ledger.*

10. What is the purpose of establishing special journals when any transaction, no matter how complex, can be entered in the general journal?

11. The sales journal and the cash receipts journal are posted once a month to the general ledger, yet the individual entries contained in those journals affecting accounts receivable are posted daily to the subsidiary ledger. Explain.

12. The general journal is not needed when companies use special journals. Evaluate this statement.

13. The sales journal of the Welker Company has 326 entries for the month of October. How many posting entries must be made to the sales account for the month of October, assuming that no cash sales were made? Under the same assumption, how many postings must be made to the accounts receivable subsidiary ledger?

14. What purpose do the posting references have in the journals and ledgers?

15. What do the terms *foot* and *crossfoot* mean? Why is it necessary to crossfoot the cash payments journal?

EXERCISES

Exercise 6-1
Analyzing internal control

As the new office manager of the Eastside Branch of Stardust Sales Company, you receive a phone call from a very disturbed customer. It seems that the customer claims that he paid his bill for $157.54 more than 2 months ago, yet for the past 2 months he has received an invoice for that amount from your office. As you investigate the complaint, you discover that the office procedure is for Mr. Todsen, the assistant office manager, to receive all daily receipts and deposit them in the bank. His wife, who is the office bookkeeper, records the receipts directly from the bank deposit slips.

   What action should you now take?

Exercise 6-2
Analyzing internal control

When the stock of inventory appears to be low at the Great Atlanta Dry Goods Store, it is the responsibility of the salesperson who first notices the situation to reorder the needed inventory.

   Comment on this practice.

Exercise 6-3
Analyzing internal control

The Houston Development Company is expanding very rapidly. The current computer operator has just received a promotion and is transferred to the Dallas branch office. As a result, a bright young graduate from the University of Houston's excellent computer science department is hired, given the operating manual to read over the weekend, and will commence duties on the following Monday.

    Comment on this practice.

Exercise 6-4
Analyzing internal control

The Adams Sales Company just installed their first computer. All company records are maintained on the new MBI 4760. Since the system is so "user friendly," the company follows the policy of training individuals in each of the departments to use the computer, thus eliminating the need for a separate computer department.

    Comment on this practice.

Exercise 6-5
Analyzing internal control

Cash sales at the Big Store are brisk every working day. The store employs 8 to 10 cashiers, all of whom work out of the central cash register, which contains one cash drawer.

    Comment on this practice.

Exercise 6-6
Identifying the appropriate journal

Ten transactions are listed below. For each transaction, indicate which of the five basic journals should be used to record the transaction. Use the following symbols for the basic journals:

Journal	Symbol
Cash Receipts	CR
Cash Payments	CP
Sales	S
Purchases	P
General	G

a. Payment of account payable.
b. Sales on account.
c. Adjusting entry for office supplies.
d. Collection of accounts receivable.
e. Receipt of office equipment from the owner of the business. The equipment is to be used in the business.
f. Acquisition of inventory on account.
g. Cash sales.
h. Return of inventory previously purchased, but not yet paid for.
i. Acquisition of office supplies on account.
j. Acquisition of inventory for cash.

Exercise 6-7
Discovering errors

Engle Enterprise has several errors in their accounting system. They request your help in explaining how the system will eventually (if at all) uncover these errors.

a. A posting of $456 appears in the general ledger account, Accounts Receivable. However, the total of the accounts receivable column in the cash receipts journal is correctly footed (added) to $546.
b. The total of the purchases journal amounts to $26,350. It is posted as a debit to Purchases and a credit to Accounts Payable as $26,530.
c. A sales invoice of $575 is entered in the sales journal as $755.
d. The accounts payable column of the cash payments journal is incorrectly totaled to $15,678. It should be $15,876.

Exercise 6-8

Identifying the source of debits and credits

This exercise is designed to test your knowledge of the relationship between the journals and the accounts. For each of the accounts listed, indicate the journal source of the most common debit and credit entries.

	Journal Source	
Account	**Debit**	**Credit**
Cash	Cash Receipts	
Accounts Receivable.		
Prepaid Rent.		
Accounts Payable.		
Sales		
Sales Returns and Allowances.		
Sales Discounts		
Purchases		
Purchase Returns and Allowances		
Purchase Discounts.		
Salaries Expense.		

Exercise 6-9

Completing the journals and posting to the ledger

The sales and cash receipts journals of the James Company for the first month of operations, July 1987, are presented below:

Sales Journal				Page 7
Date	**Account Debited**	**Invoice No.**	**Post. Ref.**	**Amount**
July 5	Sally Anderson	1001		$450
8	Albert Baines	1002		700
11	Nancy Carlson	1003		560
17	Sam Dunlap	1004		975
21	John Eastman	1005		400

Cash Receipts Journal								Page 5
Date	**Account Credited**	**Explanation**	**Post. Ref.**	**Sundry Accounts Credit**	**Accounts Receivable Credit**	**Sales Credit**	**Sales Discount Debit**	**Cash Debit**
July 3		Cash sales				400		400
10	Sally Anderson	Invoice no. 1001, less 2%			450		9	441
14	Notes Payable			500				500
19	Albert Baines	Invoice no. 1002			700			700
23	John Eastman	Invoice no. 1005, less 2%			400		8	392
27		Cash sales				750		750
30	Common Stock	Issue common stock		675				675

Notice that the journals have not been footed, crossfooted, or posted to the ledger accounts. Complete the journals and post to the general and subsidiary ledger accounts using the following account numbers:

Account	Number
Cash	101
Accounts Receivable.	110
Notes Payable	220
Common Stock	310
Sales	410
Sales Discounts	420

Exercise 6-10
Determining cash sales

The Samson Company has the following debit and credit totals for the selected accounts listed below:

Account	Debit	Credit
Cash.	$1,600	$600
Accounts Receivable	3,200	?
Sales Returns and Allowances	100	–0–
Sales Discounts.	180	–0–

Cash and Accounts Receivable had balances of $400 and $600, respectively, at the beginning of the period. You are able to determine that included in the cash debits is $200 from the sale of certain fixed assets. Credit sales amounted to $2,600. Accounts Receivable has an ending balance of $2,000.

From this information, compute the amount of cash sales made during the period.

(Check figure: = $80)

PROBLEMS
Set A

Problem A6-1
Evaluating intenal controls

Upon graduating from the State University you are employed by Devoe Industries as an administrative assistant. Your first assignment is to visit the company's Gluck Division, located in Portland, Maine, in order to evaluate their system of internal control.

Gluck is mailed directly from the Portland plant to customers throughout the Northeast. All sales are made on 30-day credit. Sales invoices are typed and posted to the Accounts Receivable account by Ms. Hansen, who performs this task from 8:00 a.m. to 9:00 a.m. each day prior to opening the office for the business day. From 9:00 a.m. to 5:00 p.m., Ms. Hansen serves as the receptionist.

The mail arrives at 10:30 a.m. and is received by Ms. Hansen, who opens the mail, removes the payments together with the number 2 copy of the sales invoice returned by the customer. She puts the payments in her desk drawer with the rest of the week's receipts and locks the drawer. All other mail is given to the plant manager's secretary, Ms. Whipple.

Ms. Hansen comes into the office on Saturday mornings to post the receipts to the accounts receivable ledger and the Cash account, and prepares the receipts for the weekly deposit, which is made on Monday morning at 10:00 a.m. The sales invoices are placed on Ms. Whipple's desk for her to file during the week.

Once a month Ms. Hansen receives the bank statement from the Exchange Bank of Portland, and she reconciles the bank statement with the cash balance in the company's general ledger. She also, once a month, bills the customers.

Required Evaluate the system of internal control, providing suggestions for its improvement.

Problem A6-2
Developing a system of internal control

Mike Linebacker, a professional football player for the St. Louis Blues, owns a bar in State College, Pennsylvania, called the Nittany Lion Drinking Establishment. The bar caters to the Penn State student body, selling mostly Blue and White beer on tap and some mixed drinks. In the past Mike has had problems with some dishonest employees. Some would sell drinks without ringing up the sale and pocket the price of the drink. On one occasion an employee even brought in his own cash register so the customers could see him ring up the drinks; he would keep the money in his cash register and return to Mike the money in Mike's cash register.

Required Provide some suggestions to develop a system of internal control for Mike's bar. Mike is an absentee owner, visiting State College only once or twice a month.

Problem A6-3
Identifying possible abuses of an internal control system

Southeast Homes, Inc., is a large regional residential builder of medium-priced homes. Subdivisions of homes are constructed under the direction of project managers in many of the major metropolitan areas of Georgia and Florida. The project manager is responsible for engaging all the subcontractors and hiring numerous local individuals to perform the necessary tasks associated with construction of this magnitude. When hiring new employees, the project manager completes all the necessary paperwork and forwards it to the Atlanta main office. If employees prove satisfactory, the project manager initiates the paperwork for pay raises. If the employees are not satisfactory, the project manager terminates their employment.

The project manager weekly prepares the payroll for all the individuals who report to him, sending the appropriate paperwork to Atlanta, and pays the employees from a special fund established for that purpose by the main office. The monies in the fund are deposited weekly from Atlanta after the project manager determines the total payroll and calls the amount to the disbursing department of the home office.

Required Describe the possible abuses that may arise using this system.

Problem A6-4
Recording transactions in sales, purchases and general journals posting to the general and subsidiary ledgers

The Deacon Corporation had the following transactions relating to the purchase and sale of merchandise during its first month of operation, July 1987. All purchases and sales are on account.

July 2 Purchased merchandise from Holland Company, $4,500; invoice dated July 1.
4 Purchased merchandise from French Imports, $6,000; dated July 4.
5 Sold merchandise to Alpha Company for $3,000; invoice number 101.
9 Returned $500 of merchandise to the Holland Company; the merchandise was the wrong color.
12 Purchased $13,550 of merchandise from the German Export Group; invoice dated July 10.
13 Received merchandise amounting to $300 returned by the Alpha Company; the merchandise was defective.
18 Sold to the New York Company merchandise amounting to $7,500; invoice number 102.
23 Sold $5,000 on merchandise to Texas, Inc.; invoice number 103.
26 Purchased $21,000 of merchandise from Canton Company; invoice dated July 25.
29 Sold $750 of merchandise to Alpha Company, invoice number 104.

Required
1. Using a single-column sales journal, a single-column purchases journal, and a general journal, record the transactions listed above.
2. Post to the general and subsidiary ledger accounts. Use the following general ledger account numbers:

Accounts Receivable 120   Sales Returns and Allowances 610
Accounts Payable 240   Purchases 700
Sales 600   Purchase Returns and Allowances . . 710

Use Page 1 for the sales journal, Page 2 for the purchases journal, and Page 3 for the general journal.

Problem A6-5
Recording transactions in the cash receipts and cash payments journals

The cash transactions for the month of November 1987 for Tellson and Company are described below. The company uses multi-column cash receipts and cash payments journals as described in the chapter.

Nov. 1 Acquired office furniture, $5,300.
2 Purchased merchandise for cash from Lorry, Inc., $4,500.
4 Paid freight charges for the merchandise purchased from Lorry, Inc., $250.
6 Sold merchandise for cash, $2,100.
8 Paid Manette Company invoice of $5,000 less 2% discount.
10 Acquired a delivery truck from Antoine Motors, paying a down payment of $4,000 and issuing a note payable for $10,500.
10 Cash sales of merchandise amounted to $3,200.
12 Paid rent on the office for the month of November, $1,250.
13 Received payment from Cruncher Company for merchandise, $4,500 less 3% discount.
14 Mr. Tellson invested an additional $5,000 in the business.
15 Paid semimonthly salaries amounting to $15,000.
18 Paid Pross Company invoice of $6,500 less 2% discount.
20 Purchased merchandise, $2,100.
22 Paid General Telephone Company, $350.
23 Received $7,500 from the Shooter's Hill Bank on note payable due 6 months hence.
25 Paid Defrage Company $2,000 on a past-due invoice.
26 Cash sales of merchandise, $5,100.
28 Received payment from Sydney Carton, $4,000 less a 3% discount.
29 Received payment from Charles Darnay, $5,500. The payment is made past the discount date.
30 Paid semimonthly salaries amounting to $15,000.

Required
Record the transactions in the cash receipts and cash payments journals. Foot and crossfoot the journals.

Problem A6-6
Preparing entries and posting; sales, cash receipts, and general journals

The Danko Company completed the following transactions relating to sales and collection of cash during the month of August 1987. All credit sales have terms of 2/10, n/30, and invoices are dated the transaction date.

Aug. 2 William Danko, the owner, invested $1,000 in the company.
3 Sold on invoice no. 717, $900 of merchandise to G. Peters on account.
5 Sold to R. Otto merchandise on account amounting to $1,600; invoice no. 718.
9 Sold to J. Moon on credit $2,100 of merchandise; invoice no. 719.
10 Received payment from G. Peters.
13 Borrowed $2,500 from the First National Bank on a 10% note payable due in 1 year.

Aug. 17   Received amount due from R. Otto.

17   J. Moon returned $300 of defective merchandise from Aug. 9 sale.

19   Sold to G. Peters on account merchandise in the amount of $3,200; invoice no. 720.

19   Received amount due from J. Moon.

22   Sold merchandise on account to J. Moon, $800; invoice no. 721.

25   G. Peters returned as defective $400 of merchandise sold on Aug. 3.

25   Sold on account to R. Otto merchandise in the amount of $1,500; invoice no. 722.

30   Cash sales, $900.

Required   **1.** Record the transactions in the appropriate journal. Use a single-column sales journal, a cash receipts journal similar to the one illustrated in Exhibit 6-3, and a general journal.

2. Total the sales and cash receipts journals; crossfoot the cash receipts journal.

3. Using the following account and journal page numbers, post to the general and accounts receivable ledgers:

Account	No.	Journal	Page No.
Cash.	10	Sales	27
Accounts Receivable	11	Cash Receipts	19
Notes Payable	20	General	8
William Danko, Capital	30		
Sales.	50		
Sales Discounts.	51		
Sales Returns and Allowances	52		

4. Prepare a schedule of accounts receivable as of the end of the month to prove the balance in the Accounts Receivable control account.

(Check figure: Accounts Receivable balance = $5,108)

Problem A6-7

Preparing entries and posting; purchases, cash payments, and general journals

Listed below are the transactions completed by the Taylor Supply Company for the month of October 1987 relating to purchases and cash payments. Assume that all merchandise purchased for credit have terms of 2/10, n/30.

Oct. 1   Purchased $2,600 of merchandise from the Scranton Merchandise Corporation on account. Invoice dated Oct. 1.

1   Merchandise on account in the amount of $3,500 was acquired from Quentin Wholesale. Invoice dated Oct. 1.

4   Paid Quentin Wholesale amount due by issuing check no. 125.

5   Returned defective merchandise to Scranton Merchandise Corporation for credit, $250.

8   Issued check no. 126 in the amount of $1,200 for salary expense.

8   Issued check no. 127 to James Taylor, the owner, for $500 withdrawals.

10   Purchased from Scranton Merchandise Corporation $1,750 merchandise on account. Invoice dated Oct. 8.

10   Paid Scranton Merchandise Corporation amount due from Oct. 1 purchase. Issued check no. 128.

14   Purchased merchandise on account from Thomas, Inc., $800, invoice dated this date. Freight charges on this merchandise amounted to $55. Issued check no. 129 in payment of freight.

Oct. 15   Returned $1,350 of defective merchandise acquired from Quentin Wholesale on Oct. 1. Quentin credited Taylor's account.

18   Issued check no. 130 to Scranton Merchandise Corporation for amount due.

19   Purchased on account $4,250 of merchandise from Quentin Wholesale. Invoice dated this date.

21   Issued check no. 131 for $170 cash purchases.

26   Issued check no. 132 for partial payment of $2,500 of merchandise acquired on Oct. 19.

Required

1. Record the transactions in a single-column purchases journal, a cash payments journal, or the general journal.

2. Total the purchases and cash payments journals. Crossfoot the cash payments journal.

3. Using the posting reference numbers below, post to the general and accounts payable ledgers:

Account	No.	Journal	Page No.
Cash	110	Purchases	71
Accounts Payable	210	Cash Payments	56
James Taylor, Withdrawals	320	General	24
Purchases	510		
Purchase Discounts	520		
Purchase Returns and Allowances	530		
Freight-In	540		
Salary Expense	610		

4. Prepare a schedule of accounts payable outstanding as of October 31, 1987, to prove the Accounts Payable control account.

(Check figure: Accounts Payable balance = $1,227)

Problem A6-8
Comprehensive problem

(*Note:* This problem is to be used as a mini-practice set.)

The following transactions were completed by the Mary Whitehall Company during the month of June 1987.

Journal Notation

June 1   Received $2,500 cash from the First National Bank; issued a note payable for that amount due in 60 days.   CR _____

1   Purchased office supplies for $1,000 cash. Issued check no. 115.   CP _____

2   Sold merchandise on account to Mary Berstein and Tom Adams; $1,200 and $2,700 respectively.   S _____

3   Purchased merchandise from the Xact Supply Company on account amounting to $1,000, invoice dated June 2.   P _____

5   Mary Berstein returned merchandise acquired on June 2, $300.   G _____

6   Sold merchandise on account to Lucy Carter, $950.   S _____

9   Paid Xact Supply amount due. Issued check no. 118.   CP _____

June 10   Sold $200 of office supplies on hand for cash to a competitor as an accommodation.   CR _____

12   Received payments from Tom Adams and Mary Berstein.   CR _____

13   Purchased on account merchandise costing $1,750 from Tyler Commercial Company.   P _____

14   Sold merchandise on account to Norma Elder, $1,300.   S _____

15   Cash sales, $850.   CR _____

15   Paid salaries, $500. Issued check no. 120.   CP _____

19   Sold merchandise on account to John Davis, $3,200.   S _____

19   Purchased from Xact Supply Company $250 of merchandise.   P _____

19   Paid Tyler Commercial amount due. Issued check no. 121.   CP _____

20   Received payment due from Lucy Carter.   CR _____

21   Returned to Tyler Commercial for credit defective merchandise costing $1,000. The merchandise was paid for on June 19.   G _____

21   Sold merchandise on account to Nancy Foxworth, $250.   S _____

23   Purchased $2,100 of merchandise on account from Tyler Commercial.   P _____

25   Received $600 partial payment from Norma Elder.   CR _____

25   Purchased office equipment on account from Vitenwyk Corporation, $500.   G _____

26   Sold Mary Berstein merchandise on account, $2,150.   S _____

26   Mary Whitehall invested $1,000 cash in the company.   CR _____

29   Purchased merchandise costing $1,350 on account from Villanson and Company.   P _____

30   Issued check no. 122 for cash purchases amounting to $500.   CP _____

30   Mary Berstein paid amount due.   CR _____

Required   **1.** Using single-column sales and purchases journals, a cash receipts and a cash payments journal, and a general journal, record the transactions listed above. You may wish to use the journal notation column to classify the transactions according to the journal they will be entered to.

2. Foot and crossfoot the journals.

3. Post to the general and subsidiary ledgers, using the following account numbers for posting references:

Cash	110	Sales	410
Accounts Receivable.	120	Sales Returns and Allowances.	420
Inventory.	130	Sales Discounts	430
Office Supplies on Hand	140	Purchases.	510
Office Equipment.	150	Purchase Returns and Allowances . .	520
Accumulated Depreciation:		Purchase Discounts	530
Office Equipment.	155	Salary Expense	610
Accounts Payable.	210	Office Supplies Used.	620
Notes Payable	220	Depreciation: Office Equipment . . .	630
Mary Whitehall, Capital	310	Expense & Revenue Sum.	710

Use the following page numbers for the journal posting references:

Sales	32	Cash Payments	41
Cash Receipts	17	General	9
Purchases.	21		

The beginning inventory is $7,000. To balance this, place a $7,000 credit in Mary Whitehall, Capital as a beginning balance. Ending inventory amounts to $7,500.

    Assume that all credit sales and purchases are under 2/10, n/30 terms. The first sales invoice is no. 624.

4. Prepare an unadjusted trial balance on a worksheet and record the following adjustments on the worksheet:

    a. Supplies Used, $250.

    b. Depreciation: Office Equipment, $50.

    Complete the worksheet.

5. Record adjusting and closing entries in the general journal and post to the general ledger.

6. Prepare a schedule of accounts receivable and accounts payable.

7. PREPARE INCOME STATEMENT + BALANCE SHEET   *(Check figure: Net income = $5,970)*

Set B

Problem B6-1
Analyzing internal control

Mr. Bumble operates a retail store in a certain town to which we will assign no fictitious name. For the first time in many years, Mrs. Corney failed to report to work. Her responsibilities include maintaining the general and subsidiary ledgers as well as handling all cash receipts. Mr. Bumble himself controls all cash disbursements. Late in the morning of Mrs. Corney's most unusual absence, a Mr. Sowerberry, the parochial undertaker, appeared at the Bumble establishment to acquire material for his business. Since Mrs. Corney was unavailable, Mr. Bumble processed the order. As Mr. Bumble removed Mr. Sowerberry's subsidiary accounts receivable ledger card, Mr. Bumble remarked that Mr. Sowerberry had made only a partial payment on his last invoice. This astounded Mr. Sowerberry, and he informed Mr. Bumble that he had indeed paid the invoice in full by check delivered himself to Mrs. Corney on Thursday last. Perplexed, Mr. Bumble asked young Oliver to review the accounts receivable subsidiary ledger. After several hours Oliver reported back to Mr. Bumble that most customers are current on their accounts but that many had made two or more payments on individual invoices.

Required   Explain the possible reason for the partial payments being posted to the accounts.

Problem B6-2
Analyzing internal control

Several items of inventory were missing from the Appomattox Warehouse on December 31, 1987. The inventory records reflected that the items had been placed in stock and had not yet been sold. But a careful count of the inventory on the last day of the year revealed that the items were nowhere to be found. The items, while small in size, were rather expensive, ranging from $750 to $2,200 each. Bob Lee, the company general manager, requests the warehouse supervisor, Jim Longstreet, to describe the operating procedures followed at the warehouse.

    Longstreet reports that as merchandise is received it is counted by George Pickett, who then completes the Count Form and forwards it together with the supplier's invoice to Jubal Early in the purchasing department. Jubal prepares a purchase order from this information, and compares the order with the Request for Inventory Form (a form prepared by the retail stores and sent directly to the vendors). If a difference exists in the amount received and the amount requested, Jubal calls George Pickett to reaffirm the count. If the count is confirmed, the purchase order is signed by Jubal and sent to the payment department, where Joe Johnston prepares a check to be mailed to the supplier.

    Merchandise is removed from stock only when a Send Inventory Form is received. These forms are prepared by the salespeople in the retail outlets of the company and are processed daily.

Required   Evaluate the procedures used by this company to control its inventory.

Problem B6-3
Designing a system of internal control

You have been appointed Athletic Director of Big Time University. Big Time has just completed a new facility for its basketball program. The Hoops Hood, as the new facility is called, has a capacity of 25,578 seats. Since the Big Time Bruisers have always been a national powerhouse in basketball, near-capacity crowds can be expected in the new facility.

Your responsibility is to design a system of internal control to assure the university that all monies for the basketball games are collected and accounted for. Season tickets are sold at $40 to students (about 7,500 are expected to be sold), at $90 to faculty (about 500), at $140 to Blue Jacket Club Members (about 9,300), and at $180 to White Jacket Club Members (about 1,500). The remaining tickets are sold on a game-by-game basis at local retail stores, at the Hoops Hood box office, and at the four gates on game nights. The remaining tickets sell for $6 each.

This year's schedule includes 12 home games.

Required

Design a system for distributing, accounting for, and controlling the tickets and controlling cash receipts.

Problem B6-4
Recording transactions in sales, purchases, and general journals. Posting to general and subsidiary ledgers

Transactions relating to the purchase and sales of merchandise during the month of January 1987, for the Bulldog Company appear below. All purchases and sales are on account.

Jan. 3   Purchased merchandise in the amount of $6,700 from Gator, Inc.; invoice dated Jan. 2.
     4   Sold to the War Eagle Company merchandise amounting to $3,550; invoice number 342.
     6   Returned $300 of merchandise acquired from Gator, Inc.
     9   Purchased from Wildcat Enterprises $10,250 of merchandise; invoice dated Jan. 9.
    11   Sold merchandise to Rebel, Inc., on invoice number 343, amounting to $3,750
    14   Purchased $7,350 of merchandise from the Tide Company. Invoice dated Jan. 12.
    17   Received $400 of merchandise returned by the War Eagle Company.
    22   Sold to the Maroon Bulldog $22,500 of merchandise on invoice number 344.
    25   Purchased $5,700 of merchandise from Tiger, Ltd.; invoice dated Jan. 24.
    29   Merchandise was sold to Rebel, Inc., amounting to $11,200; invoice number 345.
    30   Purchased $15,000 of merchandise from the Tide Company; invoice dated Jan. 29.

Required

Record the transactions in a single-column sales journal, a single-column purchases journal, and a general journal. Post to the general and subsidiary ledger accounts using the following account numbers:

Accounts Receivable	110	Sales Returns and Allowances	520
Accounts Payable	210	Purchases	600
Sales	500	Purchase Returns and Allowances . .	610

Use Page 11 for the sales journal, Page 23 for the purchases journal, and Page 5 for the general journal.

Problem B6-5
Recording transactions in cash receipts and cash payments journals

The Epson Company uses multi-column cash receipts and cash payments journals like those described in the chapter. Listed below are all the cash transactions for the month of August 1987.

Aug. 1   Purchased merchandise from IBM, $5,600.
     2   Sold merchandise for cash, $14,500.
     4   Paid Datamax invoice of $8,500 less 2% discount.
     5   Acquired office supplies from Apple Company, $450.
     7   Paid freight on the IBM merchandise, $125.

Aug. 10   Received payment from Digital Company for merchandise of $6,200 less 3% discount.

12   Received $5,000 from the First National Bank on a note payable due 6 months hence.

12   Acquired office furniture amounting to $15,000, paying $5,000 in cash and issuing a note payable for the balance.

14   Cash sales amounted to $9,500.

16   Paid $350 to Trasheighty for repairs on auto.

17   Paid Texas Instruments invoice of $3,000 less 2% discount.

19   Epson invested $2,700 in the business.

21   Received $7,500 from Commodare less 3% discount.

22   Paid Continental Telephone $250.

22   Paid $5,000 cash for merchandise received this date.

24   Paid $1,550 sales commissions to James Smoothtalker.

25   Received from Victwenty $4,000 on an invoice past the discount date.

27   Cash in the amount of $450 is received for merchandise returned to the vendor from the transaction on Aug. 22.

30   Paid monthly salaries amounting to $7,370.

Required   Record the transactions in the cash receipts and cash payments journals. Foot and crossfoot the journals.

Problem B6-6
Preparing entries and posting; sales, cash, receipts, and general journals

During the month of February 1987, General Company had the following transactions relating to the sales of merchandise and the collection of cash. All invoices are dated the transaction date.

Feb. 2   Sold merchandise to Zara Company for $2,500; credit terms 2/10, n/30 (invoice no. 310).

3   Sold merchandise to Yanko Brothers at a cost of $4,300; credit terms 2/10, n/30 (invoice no. 311).

7   Yanko Brothers returned defective merchandise having a sale price of $1,300.

10   Sold merchandise to Wallace Supply, terms 2/10, n/30; $15,200 (invoice no. 312).

11   Received amount due from Zara Company from Feb. 2 sale.

13   Received amount due from Yanko Brothers less returned merchandise of Feb. 7.

14   Received $20,000 from the First National Bank. Issued a 6-month, 10% note payable in that amount to the bank.

15   Sold merchandise for cash, $15,070.

22   Received amount due from Wallace Supply.

23   Sold mechandise to Zara Company, $1,900; credit terms 2/10, n/30 (invoice no. 313).

24   Paid $1,550 sales commissions to James Smoothtalker.

25   Zara Company returned for credit defective merchandise having a sales price of $1,400. Original invoice no. 310.

28   Sold merchandise on account to United Feed Company, $870; terms 2/10, n/30 (invoice no. 314).

Required   1. Using a single-column sales journal, a cash receipts journal similar to the one illustrated in Exhibit 6-3, and a general journal, record the transactions.
2. Foot the sales journal; foot and crossfoot the cash receipts journal.
3. Post to the general ledger accounts and the accounts receivable subsidiary ledger. Use the following account numbers for posting references:

Cash	110	Sales	500
Accounts Receivable	120	Sales Returns and Allowances	510
Notes Payable	210	Sales Discounts	520
Jim General, Capital	300		

Use Page 26 for the sales journal, Page 31 for the cash receipts journal, and Page 18 for the general journal.
4. Prove the control account for Accounts Receivable by preparing a schedule of accounts receivable.

(Check figure: Accounts Receivable balance = $1,398)

Problem B6-7
Preparing entries and posting; purchases, cash payments, and general journals

The following transactions occurred during the month of May 1987, relating to the purchase of merchandise and the payment of cash for the John Atlas Company. All merchandise acquired for credit have 2/10, n/30 terms.

May 1   Paid advertising expense $150, check no. 514.
   2   Purchased merchandise from Eagan Supply Company, $1,550. Invoice dated May 1.
   3   Purchased merchandise from Foxworth Hardware; invoice price $1,900, dated May 1.
   5   Returned for credit $900 of goods purchased from Foxworth Hardware on invoice dated May 1.
   7   Paid Eagan Supply Company amount due less discount; check no. 515.
   9   Issued check no. 516 for amount due to Foxworth Hardware less returns and discounts.
   12   Issued check no. 517 for salaries amounting to $2,500.
   16   Paid freight on merchandise purchased from Eagan, $25. Issued check no. 518.
   25   Issued check no. 519 for cash purchases amounting to $600.
   26   Returned defective merchandise costing $400 to Eagan Supply Company. The merchandise was acquired on May 1.
   27   Purchased merchandise costing $400 from Foxworth Hardware. Invoice date May 25.
   29   Purchased office equipment on account from Kato Company, $850.
   29   Purchased merchandise from Grossman Services, $1,350. Invoice date May 29.

Required

1. Using a single-column purchases journal, a cash payments journal similar to the one illustrated in the chapter, and a general journal, record the transactions.
2. Foot the purchases journal; foot and crossfoot the cash payments journal.
3. Post to the general ledger accounts and the accounts payable subsidiary ledger. Use the following account numbers for posting references:

Cash	101	Purchase Returns and Allowances	552
Office Equipment	161	Freight-In	553
Accounts Payable	201	Advertising Expense	610
Purchases	550	Salary Expense	640
Purchase Discounts	551		

Use Page 42 for the purchases journal, Page 73 for the cash payments journal, and Page 16 for the general journal.
4. Prove the control account for Accounts Payable by preparing a schedule of accounts payable.

(Check figure: Accounts Payable balance = $2,208)

Problem B6-8
Comprehensive problem

(*Note:* This problem is to be used as a mini-practice set.)
At the close of business on August 31, 1987, the Thomas Biddle Store had the following account balances: Cash, $2,000; Inventory, $4,500; Store Equipment, $5,000; Accumulated Depreciation: Store Equipment, $100; and Thomas Biddle, Capital, $11,400.

The Thomas Biddle Store buys and sells merchandise on account under 2/10, n/30 credit terms. During the month of September 1987, the following transactions took place:

			Journal Notation
Sept.	1	Thomas Biddle invested $1,500 cash in the store.	CR
	2	Purchased $1,950 merchandise on account from Otto Products, Inc. Invoice date Sept. 1.	P
	2	Paid freight charges of $180 in cash. Check no. 418.	CP
	3	Sold to William Lancaster merchandise on account, $800. Invoice no. 136.	S
	5	Returned $700 defective merchandise to Otto Products, Inc.	G
	7	Purchased an additional $700 of merchandise from Otto Products, Inc., on account. Invoice dated this date.	P
	8	Sold $1,650 of merchandise to Tony Mundale on account. Invoice no. 137.	S
	8	Received amount due from William Lancaster.	CR
	10	Cash sales, $2,310.	CR
	11	Issued check no. 419 to Otto Products for amount due from Sept. 2 purchase (note the returned merchandise on Sept. 5).	CP
	12	Sold to William Lancaster $900 of merchandise on account. Invoice no. 138.	S
	13	Purchased from Nance Wholesale merchandise costing $2,200. Invoice date Sept. 12.	P
	15	Purchased $320 merchandise for cash from Pearson Supply Company. Issued check no. 420.	CP
	15	Purchased from Pearson Supply Company $1,400 of merchandise on account. Invoice dated Sept. 14.	P
	15	Purchased from Pearson Supply Company $400 of store supplies on account. Invoice dated Sept. 15.	G
	16	Sold $1,700 of merchandise to William Lancaster on account. Invoice no. 139.	S
	17	Received amount due from Tony Mundale.	CR
	18	Paid salaries, $645. Issued check no. 421.	CP
	19	Paid Otto Products, Inc., amount due from Sept. 7 purchase. Issued check no. 422.	CP
	21	Sold to Terri Keller $500 of merchandise on account. Invoice no. 140.	S
	21	Issued check no. 423 to Thomas Biddle for $400 withdrawal.	CP
	22	Purchased $500 merchandise on account from Otto Products, Inc. Invoice dated Sept. 22.	P
	22	Paid Nance Wholesale amount due. Issued check no. 424.	CP
	26	Received payment from Terri Keller for amount due.	CR

Sept. 28   William Lancaster returned defective merchandise amounting to $200 which he acquired on Sept. 3. He paid for this merchandise on Sept. 8.

G _____

28   Purchased on account from Pearson Supply Company merchandise costing $2,750. Invoice dated Sept. 27.

P _____

29   Sold Tony Mundale (invoice no. 141) $2,450 merchandise on account.

S _____

30   Received payment from William Lancaster for merchandise sold on invoice no. 139.

CR _____

Required

1. Record the September transactions in the appropriate journal, using single-column sales and purchases journals, multi-column cash receipts and payments journals, and a general journal. You may wish to use the journal notation column to classify the transactions according to the journal they will be entered to.
2. Foot and crossfoot the journals.
3. Using the following account and journal page numbers, post the general and subsidiary ledgers:

Account	Number	Account	Number	Journal	Page Numbers
Cash	110	Sales Returns and Allowances	430	Sales	14
Accounts Receivable	120	Purchases	510	Cash Receipts	21
Inventory	130	Purchase Discounts	520	Purchases	32
Store Supplies on Hand	140	Purchase Returns and Allowances	530	Cash Payments	9
Store Equipment	150	Freight-In	540	General	4
Accumulated Depreciation: Store Equipment	155	Salary Expense	610		
Accounts Payable	210	Store Supplies Used	620		
Salaries Payable	220	Depreciation Expense: Store Equipment	630		
Thomas Biddle, Capital	310	Expense and Revenue Summary	800		
Thomas Biddle, Withdrawals	320				
Sales	410				
Sales Discounts	420				

4. Prepare an unadjusted trial balance on a worksheet and record the following adjustments on the worksheet:
   a. Store Supplies Used, $150.
   b. Depreciation Expense: Store Equipment, $50.
   Complete the worksheet.
   c. Accrued Salaries, $75.
   d. Ending Inventory, $4,000.
5. Record adjusting and closing entries in the general journal and post to the general ledger.
6. Prepare schedules of accounts receivable and accounts payable.

(Check figure: Net loss = $596)

Part Three

Accounting for Assets, Current Liabilities, and Related Revenue and Expenses

By now you know that the resources a company uses in its operations are called assets. You have already had some experience in recording assets, adjusting asset accounts, and placing them on simple financial statements. In the first three chapters of Part Three we will take a close look at the major assets found on the balance sheets of most businesses.

As assets are used up they become expenses. You will learn how to measure the amount of an asset that has been used up and how to transfer these amounts to expense accounts.

Cash and marketable securities are said to be the most liquid assets because they can be readily used to buy things that the business needs in its operations. You will learn the elaborate internal control measures that a business must take to ensure that cash is not stolen or misused. These measures are a part of the internal control system you have already studied.

When a company sells something on credit or loans someone money, it has a right to receive future payment. You will learn about the two major types of receivables—accounts receivable and notes receivable. You will also learn how to account for receivables that we expect not to collect—our bad debts.

Merchandise inventory is perhaps the most important asset for most businesses. It is this asset that is sold to earn revenues. You already know one way to calculate cost of goods sold expense. In Chapter 9, you will learn four different methods that may be used to determine the amounts assigned to ending inventory and cost of goods sold. You will also learn how you can estimate the amount of inventory when you can't count it because it has been stolen or destroyed.

The long-lived assets that a company has may be tangible or intangible. You will learn how to calculate the cost of these assets and how to allocate their costs to expense accounts.

In Chapter 11 we will switch to the liability side of the balance sheet. You will learn about current liabilities — those obligations that a company must pay within 1 year. Salaries and wages are one of the major current liabilities. We will show you how employers develop a payroll system that provides information to appropriate taxing authorities and efficiently records and distributes payroll to employees.

Chapter 7

Cash and Marketable Securities

Some of the things you should learn from studying this chapter are:

- What cash means to the accountant
- Why internal control over cash is needed
- What a *voucher system* is and how it provides internal control
- What a *bank reconciliation* is, why it is necessary, and how to prepare it
- How a *petty cash fund* works, and how it fits within an internal control system
- What *surplus cash* means, and why it is invested in temporary investments (marketable securities)
- How to record the purchase, sale, and income from marketable securities

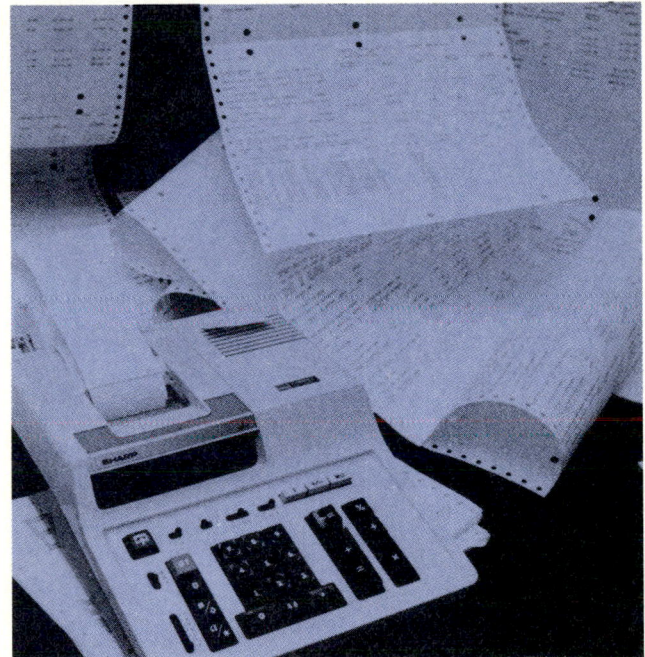

ACCOUNTING FOR CASH

The Nature of Cash

For accounting purposes, "cash" represents more than money in the form of paper currency and coins that we use in simple, everyday financial transactions. The accountant's "cash" appearing on the balance sheet includes money in other forms as well, although not all other forms. For example, many people consider savings accounts, travelers' checks, checking accounts, money orders, U.S. government savings bonds, and postage stamps to be money. Not all of these, however, are cash. *Cash,* as the term is used by accountants, means:

Accountant's definition of cash

1. A current asset on deposit in a bank that can be withdrawn immediately and used for any business purpose, *or*

2. A current asset that a bank will readily accept for deposit.

According to the accountant's definition, cash includes: paper currency and coins; the money in checking accounts; a check written on a checking account (also called a *demand deposit account*); the money in certain savings accounts (the money in some types of savings accounts cannot be withdrawn without penalty); money orders (a form of check usually issued at a bank, post office, or convenience store); and travelers' checks (a form of check requiring the user to sign at the time the check is issued and again at the time it is used to pay for something).

Cash does not include postage stamps, U.S. government savings bonds, or promissory notes (which are simply formal IOUs), whether from individuals or companies. None of these forms of money is considered cash, because they cannot be deposited directly in a bank account. Nor is money held in a special bank account that can be used for only one purpose, such as to retire long-term debt or pay retirement benefits. This money would not be represented as cash on the balance sheet because its use is restricted. Management could not legally use it to pay employees for their services or to purchase merchandise. Items not included in Cash do appear elsewhere on the balance sheet, under such headings as Temporary Investments, Prepaid Postage, or Long-Term Investments.

Internal Control over Cash

Cash, in any form, can be converted to its simplest, most acceptable form—commonly referred to as *money,* which everyone wants. Because it is so easily convertible into money, everyone wants cash in any form. And because everyone wants it, it must be protected.

If not protected or controlled, cash in the form of money may be lost to pilfering; cash in other forms may be lost in enormous sums to clever schemes of theft. Of course, cash is also lost through honest mistakes. For these reasons the cash flowing through an economic entity must be protected or controlled.

Internal control of cash

In Chapter 6 you learned about the system of internal control. In this chapter we will see how this system can be used to protect the company's cash. We will focus on two parts of the system:

1. *Custodianship,* in this case the controls used to protect the currency, coins, checks, and other physical forms that cash may take; and

2. *Other records controls,* in this case the various recordkeeping controls that assure the ready availability of reliable information about the flow of cash in all forms. (This information includes the reasons why cash is received and the purposes for which it is spent.)

In even the smallest merchandising firm, you can readily observe an example of the most basic form of internal control of the cash system — the ***cash register.*** A cash register provides physical control — protection for cash in its physical form — as well as recordkeeping control — gathering information about where cash has come from. A cash register makes an instant record of cash received, provides a receipt for the customer, and serves as a place to temporarily secure the cash received. The record of money received is a copy of the customer's receipt. It is preserved on a paper tape (or sometimes a magnetic tape) locked in the cash register, and is used to verify that the amount of money received by a sales clerk is the same amount that is placed in the cash register.

Cash registers and company safes are not as secure as a bank vault. Cash received during the day should not be kept at the business overnight. To minimize opportunities for theft it should be deposited in the firm's checking account each day.

Cash registers and safes are obvious controls over cash. Other controls are not so obvious. For example, the cash receipts journal and the cash payments journal are used to provide recordkeeping control and to make cash theft schemes more difficult to carry out. In all but the smallest businesses these journals make it possible to isolate the handling and recording of the inflow of cash from writing checks and recording the outflow of cash to pay bills. This separation makes it difficult for the theft of cash between its being received and deposited in a checking account and the writing of checks on that account to go undetected.

In very small firms with only a few employees it is not always possible to have one person in charge of recording cash inflows and another handling cash outflows. In these businesses it is best for the owner or manager to perform as many of the cash-related chores as possible.

Other internal controls over cash include:

- Using checks to pay for all expenditures
- Requiring written authorization, called a ***voucher,*** before any check can be issued
- Requiring the signatures of two or more of the firm's managers on all checks greater than a certain amount
- Reconciling the monthly bank statement, performed by someone who doesn't ordinarily handle cash
- Using a carefully controlled fund, called a ***petty cash fund,*** for payments in small amounts that make a check impractical or unacceptable

The Voucher System

As you know, an internal control system extends beyond cash; it includes physical and recordkeeping controls over all the assets of the business. One part of this system assures that appropriate planned acquisitions are made, received in good condition, billed at correct amounts, and paid for on time. In a small business, the owner is usually involved directly in each of these activities. Thus, in safeguarding his or her interests, the owner effects an informal system of internal control.

However, owners of large businesses cannot be closely involved in all the activities of the business. The activities are organized into many separate functions, and different groups of employees are delegated the authority to perform each function. For example, one group of employees orders goods and services, another group receives and inspects them, a third group decides the proper amount and timing of payment, and still another group actually writes and mails the checks. In large firms it is necessary to have a formal system of internal control to assure that the activity of incurring obligations (acquiring goods and services) is separated from the activity of paying for them. Of course, the purpose of separating these activities is to have different individuals performing them. Nevertheless, there must be a written form of communication (what to pay, how much, when, etc.) linking the various activities of the employees, to allow management to control and monitor what goes on. This is what the voucher system is all about.

The Voucher

To explain what a voucher is and the internal control purpose it serves, we must begin at the earliest point in the process of acquiring goods or services or purchasing merchandise for resale. As we explain this process we will describe each of the written communication links in the system.

First, you should understand that a large firm is organized into different departments, each performing a particular function. To perform their functions, the departments need goods and services that must be acquired (bought) from other firms. These goods and services may be used up in operating the business—e.g., typing paper and paper bags—or may be sold to customers—e.g., merchandise inventory. Rather than give each department the authority to buy its goods and services, a large firm will give that authority to a single department—the ***purchasing department***—which does the buying for all departments. In this way, the firm can more effectively exert control over all acquisitions. A central purchasing department not only offers a means of internal control, it also offers the opportunity to combine acquisitions of identical goods required by different departments, and thus to obtain discounts that might not be available for acquisitions in smaller quantities.

Steps in acquiring goods and services

Let's follow a typical purchase of merchandise through the system from beginning to end. The audio department of Mozart Electronics Company needs more stereo

---

PURCHASE REQUISITION

MOZART ELECTRONICS COMPANY

From _____ Audio Department _____   **Date** _____ May 15, 1988 _____

Suggested Vendor Blair and Rumble Speaker Company

St. Louis, MO

Purchase the Following

Quantity	Number	Description
100	SE-21406	stereo speakers

Reason for Request Resupply
inventory of speakers.

To be completed by purchasing department:

Date Ordered _____ 5-18-88 _____

Authorized by _____ J.L. Johnson _____   **P.O. Number** _____ G-134 _____

STEP 1: Purchase requisition is prepared

The manager of the audio department of Mozart Electronics requests that more stereo speakers be acquired by sending this purchase requisition to the purchasing department

speakers to sell. The manager of this department has already received permission to spend a certain amount for merchandise during the year. Now the need for speakers must be communicated to the central purchasing department in writing, using a standard form called a ***purchase requisition.*** This purchase requisition is used only to communicate needs to the central purchasing department; it never goes outside the firm. Its internal control function is to limit the purchase of goods and services to those managers who have authority to acquire them. The audio department's requisition for speakers might look something like the one at the bottom of the facing page.

When the central purchasing department receives the purchase requisition, it will check to be sure that the audio department hasn't already spent all that was authorized for the year. If the department has not spent its total authorization, the purchasing department will order the speakers from a manufacturer or wholesaler by sending them a purchase order. A ***purchase order*** is a written request for an outside vendor to supply goods or services. Look at the purchase order for the speakers shown below.

STEP 2: Purchase order is prepared

The purchasing department approves the request for stereo speakers and sends this purchase order to the supplier

---

PURCHASE ORDER

No. _____ G-134 _____

MOZART ELECTRONICS COMPANY
1691 Lanier Drive
Columbus, WV   22305

To Blair and Rumble Speaker Co. _____   Date _____ May 18, 1988 _____

2530 Jefferson Ave _____

St. Louis, MO   44620 _____

Shipping Instructions Ship to Mozart Electronics Company at above address _____

FOB destination _____

Ship Via _Truck_   Date needed _____ 6/20/88 _____

Terms Requested __2/10, n/30__

Please Accept Our Order for the Following:

Quantity	✓	Number	Description	Price Each	Amount
100		SE-21406	stereo speakers	$240	$24,000

Purchase order number must appear on all invoices.

Ordered by ___R.J.Wood___

Blair and Rumble Speaker Co. will fill the order and ship the speakers to Mozart Electronics Company. At the same time they will mail Mozart a bill, called a ***sales invoice,*** for the goods shipped. The sales invoice gives the quantity and description of the goods shipped and terms of payment (see page 258, top).

SALES INVOICE

BLAIR AND RUMBLE SPEAKER COMPANY
2530 Jefferson Ave
St. Louis, MO 44620

No. B10-1173

Date June 15, 1988

Your Order No. G-134

STEP 3: Outside supplier fills order; sends goods and sales invoice

The supplier sends this sales invoice to let Mozart know that the speakers were shipped and also as a request for payment

Sold to Mozart Electronics Company

1691 Lanier Drive

Columbus, WV   22305

Shipping Instructions

Ship to same

Quantity	Description	Price Each	Amount
100	SE-21406 stereo speakers	$240	$24,000

Shipped Via

Ajax Express

Date Shipped 6/15/88   Terms 2/10, n/30

FOB delivered

When the speakers reach Mozart Electronics, someone must inspect them to be sure that the merchandise received was in fact ordered, that the correct quantity was received, and that it is in good condition. Large businesses have a *receiving department* that specializes in performing these internal control tasks. The receiving department is separate from the purchasing department to prevent someone in the purchasing department from placing an unauthorized order and stealing the goods as soon as they arrive. The receiving department prepares an internal document called a *receiving report* to verify that these tasks have been accomplished. Mozart Electronics' receiving report is shown below.

RECEIVING REPORT

MOZART ELECTRONICS COMPANY

Date June 18, 1988

P.O. No. G-134

Vendor Blair and Rumble Speaker Co.

Carrier Ajax Express

STEP 4: Receiving department checks goods and prepares receiving report

Mozart's receiving department verifies that the speakers were received in good condition and sends this receiving report to the accounting department to confirm that the speakers were received

The Following Was Received:

Quantity	Description	Condition
100	#SE-21406 Speakers	Good

Received and Checked by Herman Carlisle

We have been careful to point out that the system we have been describing is one that would be used by large businesses. Smaller firms would combine many of the functions—the department needing the goods might also place the order and in some cases even receive and inspect the goods. The internal control in the smaller business is weakened by this lack of separation and by not having one group of employees check on the actions of another. Again, this weakness is overcome to some degree by having the owner actively involved in all phases of the operation.

Copies of all four of the documents we have described—the purchase requisition, the purchase order, the sales invoice, and the receiving report—are sent to the *accounting department,* which is responsible for the following functions:

STEP 5: Accounting department receives and checks documents, prepares voucher, records in voucher register

1. Comparing the purchase requisition and purchase order with the sales invoice to verify the quantities, prices, and terms of the goods or services ordered

2. Comparing the sales invoice with the receiving report to verify that the goods or services have been received

3. Verifying that an authorized person has signed the purchase requisition, the purchase order, and the receiving report

4. Verifying the arithmetical accuracy of the sales invoice to ensure that the company is not paying too much

We've finally reached the point in our system when we can describe a *voucher.* A voucher is an authorization in writing, usually on a preprinted standard form, on which the particular details characterizing a liability are inserted. The accounting department will prepare a voucher to verify that it has performed the comparisons and verifications described above. The accounting department prepares a voucher for each check that is to be written, no matter whether the check is to pay for goods purchased, to pay salaries to employees, to pay back a loan, to pay for advertising, or to pay for any other business acquisitions.

An example of a typical voucher (front and back) is shown in Exhibit 7-1. The front of the voucher simply contains the information from the sales invoice. This information is used in preparing and mailing the check to pay the liability. The back of the voucher shows that the comparisons and verifications have been completed. As each task is accomplished, the clerk responsible for the verification indicates this with his or her initials. (See the upper left corner of the voucher back.) Also on the back of the voucher is the section called *Accounting Distribution.* This section contains (1) the name of the account or accounts debited, (2) the amount credited to Vouchers Payable (Vouchers Payable is the liability account that is used for all obligations in the voucher system), and (3) the signature of the accounting department person responsible for deciding which accounts should be debited. The information in the accounting distribution section is recorded as an entry in a journal called a *voucher register.*

The accounting department representative "vouches for"—accepts responsibility for the truthfulness and accuracy of—the information on the voucher and that the voucher represents a liability properly incurred. That signature at the lower right-hand corner of the back of the voucher indicates that all is well with the information on the voucher and that approval is given to issue a check in payment. The purchase requisition, purchase order, sales invoice, and receiving report are stapled to the voucher. Now the authorization for payment (the voucher) and all of the supporting documents are together in one neat package. This package is sent to the cashier, who issues a check to pay the liability.

STEP 6: Cashier receives voucher package, issues check, records in check register

EXHIBIT 7-1
A Voucher Illustrated.

Voucher no. 317

MOZART ELECTRONICS COMPANY
1691 Lanier Drive
Columbus WV   22305

Payee __Blair and Rumble Speaker Co.__   Date _____ June 20, 1988 _____

__2530 Jefferson Ave.__

__St. Louis, MO   44620__

Attach supporting documents

Invoice Date	Terms	Details	Amount
June 15, 1988	2/10, n/30	Invoice no. B10-1173	
		FOB Columbus	$24,000
		Less: Cash discount	480
		Net amount due	$23,520

Approved for Payment _____ R. G. Adams _____

(Accounting Department)

(a) Voucher Front.

Invoice Approval				Accounting Distribution	
	Date	By		Debit	Amount
Credit terms	6/20	CR		Purchases	$24,000
Amounts	6/20	CR		Freight-In	
Arithmetic	6/20	CR		Office Supplies	
Quantities	6/20	CR		Office Salaries	
Authorizations	6/20	CR		Advertising Expense	
				_____	
				_____	
				Credit	**Amount**
				Vouchers Payable	$24,000
Payment:					

Check No. _____ 4304 _____

Check Date _____ June 24, 1988 _____

Check Amount _____ $23,520 _____   Distribution Approved _____ J.L. Battle _____

(Accounting Department)

(b) Voucher Back.

When payment is made, the check number, date, and amount are entered on the voucher in the spaces provided. This information is needed to resolve any questions that might arise in the future concerning settlement of the liability.

After payment is made:

■ The number identifying the voucher is marked on an extra copy of the sales invoice (remember, one copy is stapled to the voucher).

STEP 7: Accounting department files documents	■ The voucher (with attached documents) is filed in numerical order with the other vouchers that have already been paid.

- ■ The extra sales invoice is filed alphabetically according to the name of the supplier or vendor. Marking the number of the voucher on the extra sales invoice provides a system of cross-referencing between the two.

The system that you have just learned about is illustrated in Figure 7-1 (shown on pages 262–263). Review this diagram carefully and be sure that all the steps in the system are clear to you.

The Voucher Register

In a voucher system a voucher is prepared for each expenditure, so each voucher represents a specific liability. Payment of the liabilities is made only by check and only after the supporting documents indicating authorizations are attached. (The supporting documents for the purchase of goods were the purchase requisition, purchase order, receiving report, and sales invoice.) Information from the voucher is recorded in the *voucher register,* a journal that combines features of the purchases journal and the cash payments journal (both were discussed in Chapter 6). An example of a typical voucher register is shown in Exhibit 7-2 below.

EXHIBIT 7-2

MOZART ELECTRONICS COMPANY
Voucher Register
Page 43

Date	Vou. No.	Payee	Payment Date	Ck. No.	Vou. Pay-able Credit	Pur-chases Debit	Freight-In Debit	Salary Ex-pense Debit	Other Accounts Debited Title	Post. Ref.	Am't.
1988											
June 5	315	ABC Warehouse	6/7	4297	600	600					
13	316	Payroll	6/15	4298	5,200			5,200			
20	317	Blair and Rumble Co.	6/24	4304	24,000	24,000					
21	318	Jones Transport	6/25	4307	50		50				
30	335	Lutz Bank	6/30	4346	100				Interest Expense	710	100
30	336	Brown Co.			3,400	3,400					
30	337	Payroll	6/30	4347	4,800			4,800			
30	338	Don's Furniture			3,850				Office Furniture	250	3,850
					53,020	33,500	1,220	10,000			8,300
					(220)	(510)	(604)	(610)			

Recording in voucher register	The voucher register is similar to the purchases journal in that it records purchases made on account. For example, the purchase of stereo speakers from Blair and Rumble Co. that we have been discussing is the third item on the Mozart voucher register in Exhibit 7-2. The voucher register is similar to the cash payments journal in

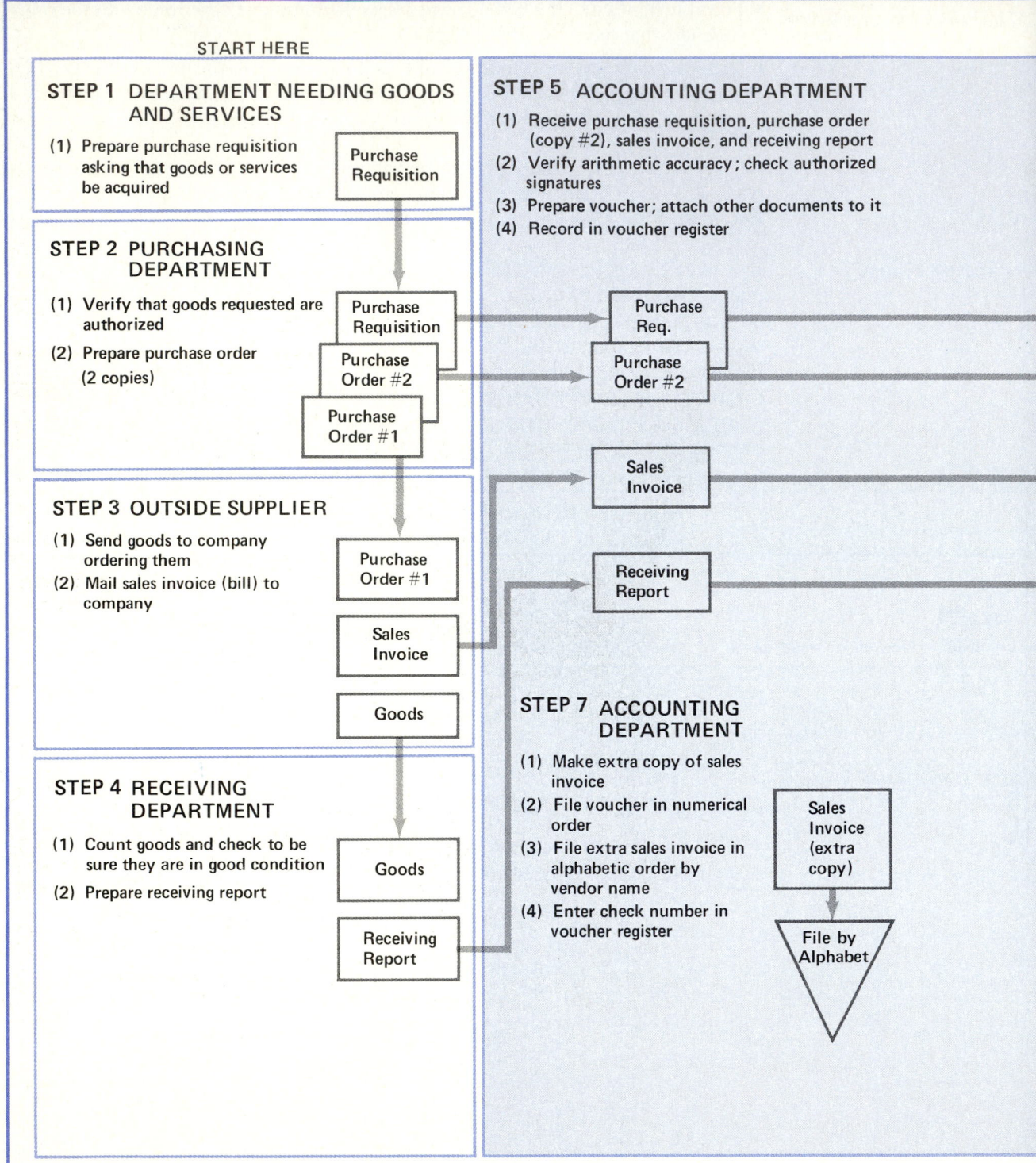

FIGURE 7-1   Diagram of goods acquisition and voucher system.

Follow the flow step by step and be sure you understand how the business documents we have discussed fit into this system.

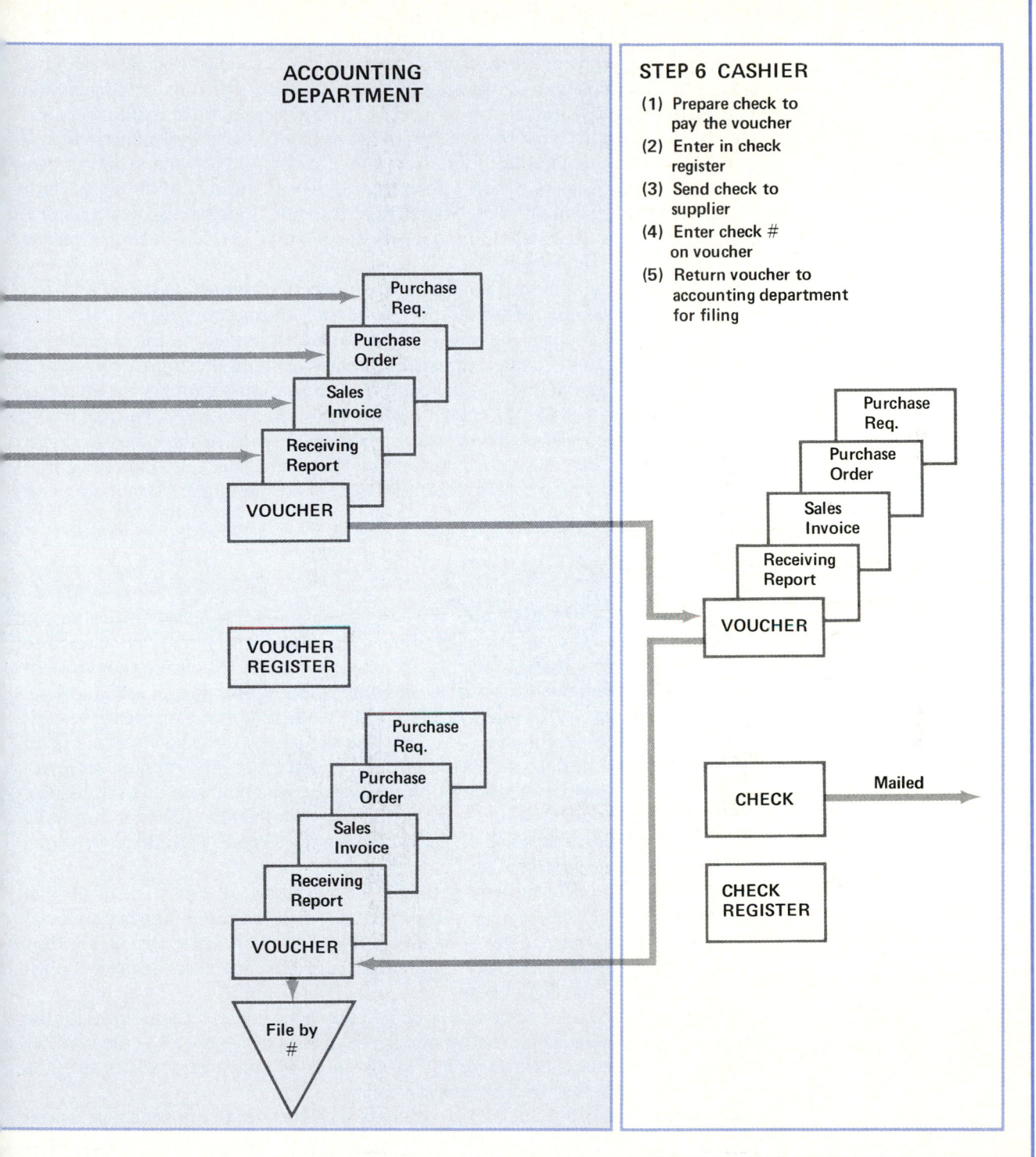

ACCOUNTING
DEPARTMENT

STEP 6 CASHIER

(1) Prepare check to
    pay the voucher
(2) Enter in check
    register
(3) Send check to
    supplier
(4) Enter check #
    on voucher
(5) Return voucher to
    accounting department
    for filing

Purchase Req.
Purchase Order
Sales Invoice
Receiving Report
VOUCHER

VOUCHER REGISTER

Purchase Req.
Purchase Order
Sales Invoice
Receiving Report
VOUCHER

File by #

Purchase Req.
Purchase Order
Sales Invoice
Receiving Report
VOUCHER

CHECK — Mailed

CHECK REGISTER

that it has many columns—one for each particular expenditure that occurs frequently and one to handle all other types of expenditures. Mozart Electronics has special columns for Purchases, Freight-In, and Salary Expense.

The information from every voucher is entered in the voucher register, even for a voucher that authorizes an immediate issuance of a check. The vouchers are entered in numerical order as illustrated in column 2 of the register shown in Exhibit 7-2. The date of the voucher, the voucher number, the payee, the Vouchers Payable credit and the account(s) to be debited are all entered when recording the voucher in the register. When the voucher is paid, the date (fourth column) and number of the check (fifth column) issued in payment of the voucher are entered. Notice in this example that this information is not entered for vouchers no. 336 and 338, which simply means that they have not yet been paid.

The amounts from the voucher register are transferred *(posted)* to the accounts in the same manner as the amounts from the special journals you learned about in Chapter 6. Before posting, the arithmetic accuracy is verified by footing (adding down the columns) and crossfooting (adding across the lines). Postings are indicated by placing the account number at the bottom of an account column—for example, (220)—indicating that $53,020 credit has been posted to Vouchers Payable in the general ledger. A special posting reference column is used in the other accounts debited section of the register, as illustrated with voucher no. 335, indicating that $100 has been posted as a debit to Interest Expense (account no. 710) in the general ledger.

The Check Register

Recording in check register

After the voucher has been approved in the accounting department and entered in the voucher register, it is sent to the cashier for payment. The accounting department representative's signature on a voucher represents the authority to the cashier to issue a check. As the cashier receives each voucher, he or she inspects it to see if immediate payment is required. If a check is not required immediately, the unpaid voucher is filed by the date that payment is to be made. This filing system serves an internal control purpose by assuring that payment will be made in time to take advantage of purchase discounts—the deduction from the sales price the company gets for paying within a specified time. (Remember the terms 2/10, n/30 on Mozart's purchase from Blair and Rumble.)

When the cashier determines that the day for payment has arrived, he or she will write a check. This disbursement of cash is recorded in the *check register,* a special journal consisting of three debit or credit columns—Vouchers Payable Debit, Purchase Discounts Credit, and Cash Credit. Mozart Electronics' check register is illustrated at the top of the facing page.

In addition to the debit and credit columns, the check register has columns for the date the check was issued, the check number, and the payee, as well as the voucher number paid by the check. Payment of vouchers is indicated by recording the voucher number in the voucher number column.

The process of posting the check register is similar to that of posting any special journal. For example, posting the debit to Vouchers Payable in Mozart's check register is indicated by the account number (220) placed at the bottom of the Vouchers Payable Debit column.

You may find it helpful to trace voucher no. 317 illustrated in Exhibit 7-1 (page 260) to the Mozart Electronics voucher register and check register.

MOZART ELECTRONICS COMPANY
Check Register

Date	Check No.	Payee	Voucher No.	Vouchers Payable Debit	Purchase Discounts Credit	Cash Credit
1988 June 7	4297	ABC Warehouse	315	600		600
24	4304	Blair and Rumble Co.	317	24,000	480	23,520
24	4305	B & R Supply Co.	310	250		250
24	4306	Quality Plumbing Co.	305	150		150
25	4307	Jones Transport	318	50		50
30	4347	Payroll	337	4,800		4,800
				42,550	1,250	41,300
				(220)	(512)	(110)

Bank Reconciliation

Checks written to employees, vendors, and others are presented to your bank for payment. Your bank sends you a bank statement, usually once each month, which summarizes your checks that have been presented for payment as well as your deposits and service charges for the period. Exhibit 7-3 on page 266 shows what a typical monthly bank statement looks like. Notice that the check numbers and amounts of all checks processed by the bank during the month are shown. Deposits and service charges are identified by the date they were added or deducted from your account.

It is not at all uncommon to find that the ending balance in the monthly statement compiled by the bank does not agree with the ending balance that appears in the checkbook. When this happens, someone in the business must determine the reasons for the difference between the two ending balances. A complete and satisfactory explanation of the differences between the bank's records and the company's is called a *reconciliation.*

Some differences may be expected routinely every month. For example, the amount of checks written by the business but not received by the bank before it prepares the monthly bank statement will appear as a deduction in the checkbook but not in the bank's records. Similarly, deposits mailed but not yet received by the bank will appear in the business's records but not on the bank's monthly statement.

Other differences may result from errors or embezzlement by an employee. The bank may have incorrectly deducted the amount of a check, or the business may have entered an amount incorrectly in its checkbook. An employee may have stolen a blank check, forged it, and cashed it. Since the check was never entered in the checkbook, a difference will exist between the bank balance and the checkbook balance.

Bank reconciliations are an important part of the internal control system. They help us locate errors in the recordkeeping system and assist us in discovering employee schemes to defraud the company. The bank reconciliation should always be prepared by an individual who is not involved with preparing and approving

EXHIBIT 7-3

MERCHANTS NATIONAL BANK

Direct Inquiries to:

Merchants National Bank of Texas
PO Box 35907
Temple, Texas   76501
(817) 555-4444

Statement Date
11/30/87

Account Number
1098674399

HILL STREET HARDWARE
478 Hill Street
Temple, Texas   76501

Balance Last Statement	Deposits and Credits		Checks and Debits		Balance This Statement
	No.	Total Amount	No.	Total Amount	
3,993.62	7	4,925.54	15	3,458.36	5,460.80

Date	Amount Credited	Description
11/2	1,385.56	Deposit
11/7	347.78	Deposit
11/9	1,244.56	Deposit
11/13	527.91	Deposit
11/18	876.30	Deposit
11/24	462.87	Deposit
11/29	80.56	Deposit

Checks:

Date	Check No.	Amount	Date	Check No.	Amount
11/2	1862	188.95	11/2	1875	222.77
11/4	1876	160.73	11/5	1884	88.33
11/7	1896	100.00	11/9	1899	275.75
11/10	1900	25.79	11/10	1901	341.07
11/14	1902	890.50	11/17	1903	84.19
11/19	1905	308.61	11/22	1906	170.87
11/26	1907	400.80	11/30	1909	178.64

Other Debits:

Date	Amount	Description
11/30	21.36	Service charge

MEMBER FDIC

NOTICE: SEE REVERSE SIDE FOR INFORMATION.

vouchers or writing checks. We want an *independent* party verifying that the work of the other employees was accurate and proper.

Most businesses use the bank-and-books-to-correct-cash reconciliation to trace the differences between the bank statement and checking account. This method allows us to show corrections needed in the checkbook (and accounting records) and still derive a correct ending cash balance. Using the Ward Company as an example, we will illustrate how to reconcile both the ending balance on the bank statement and the ending balance in the checkbook to the same correct cash balance.

WARD COMPANY
Bank Reconciliation:
Bank-and-Books-to-Correct-Cash Method

Ron Dollar, an accountant employed by the Ward Company, is responsible for preparing the monthly bank reconciliation. The bank statement showed an ending balance for November 30, 1988, of $34,173.80, whereas the checkbook balance was $30,388.60. The idea with this method is to adjust each of the balances to reflect the correct end-of-month balance, and in doing so, to reconcile the two with one another. Adjusting the bank balance begins with the ending balance from the bank statement; adjusting the checkbook balance begins with the ending balance in the checkbook. Each is adjusted independently; the resulting corrected balance for each should be identical.

The reconciliation process disclosed the following items. After reading each, refer to Exhibit 7-4 (page 268) to see how it appears on the reconciliation.

1. In comparing the checkbook stubs with the canceled checks, Ron discovered that 15 checks totaling $5,854.80 had not yet been processed by the bank. The $5,854.80 must be deducted from the $34,173.80 balance reported by the bank, since Ward Company no longer has control over this amount of cash. From Ward's point of view the cash is spent; only the mechanical process of presenting the checks to Ward's bank remains.

2. Cash in the amount of $1,970 was deposited in the night depository on November 30 and did not appear on the bank statement, since it was processed by the bank on December 2. This $1,970 must be added to the ending balance, since it is cash that was still at Ward's disposal on November 30. A correct November 30 cash balance must include this amount.

3. An error was discovered in the checkbook. In comparing the canceled checks with the check stubs, Ron noticed that check no. 1140, written in the amount of $120, had been deducted from the checkbook as $210. The checkbook balance is incorrect. It is too low by the amount of $90 ($210 − $120). This error must be corrected by adding $90 to the November 30 checkbook balance.

4. A bank error was also found in comparing canceled checks with check stubs. The bank had deducted check no. 1131 from Ward's account as $346. The actual amount of the check was $364. The bank should be notified at once so that its records can be corrected. In order for the correct cash balance to be derived on the bank reconciliation, the $18 error ($364 − $346) must be deducted from the balance according to the bank.

5. A check stamped NOT SUFFICIENT FUNDS (NSF) was returned with the bank statement. J. Hays, a customer, had given Ward the check to pay for merchandise. Ward thought that Hays' check was cash at the time it was received. The bank clearing process revealed that it was in fact nothing more than a written promise to pay cash. Ward has less cash than the checkbook balance represents. So Hays' check for $182.60 must be deducted from the balance

shown in Ward's checkbook to reflect the correct cash balance. Until Ward collects from Hays, the check represents not cash but simply an IOU.

6. The November bank statement shows a $25.00 service charge. Bank service charges are fees levied by the bank for printing and processing the company's checks, returning NSF checks, and providing other banking services. These service charges have not been deducted from Ward's checkbook because the amount was unknown until the bank statement was received. This deduction must appear on the reconciliation in calculating the correct cash balance.

Since no other errors or differences can be detected, the 11/30/88 balances and adjustments are totaled, each total producing a correct ending cash balance of $30,271. This amount should apear as Cash in Bank on Ward's balance sheet on November 30, 1988, despite the fact that it appears neither in Ward's checkbook nor on the November 30 bank statement. Exhibit 7-4 shows how the completed reconciliation would appear.

Recording Unrecorded Transactions and Correcting Errors

As you have just seen, the reconciliation process often uncovers transactions that by their nature haven't been recorded in the checkbook records, as well as errors in some of the transactions that have been recorded. From the Ward Company reconciliation,

EXHIBIT 7-4   Bank Reconciliation.
Bank and book balances reconciled to correct cash amount.

WARD COMPANY
Bank Reconciliation
November 30, 1988

Balance per bank statement 11/30/88		$34,173.80	Balance per checkbook 11/30/88		$30,388.60
Add:			Add:		
Deposits in transit on 11/30/88		1,970.00	Check no. 1140 for $120 deducted from checkbook		
Total.		$36,143.80	as $210		90.00
			Total		$30,478.60
Deduct:			Deduct:		
Checks outstanding on 11/30/88	$5,854.80		NSF check of J. Hays.	$182.60	
Check no. 1131 for $364 deducted from account			Bank service fees	25.00	(207.60)
as $346	18.00	(5,872.80)			
Correct ending balance, 11/30/1988		$30,271.00	Correct ending balance, 11/30/1988		$30,271.00

If correct amounts are identical after all adjustments
have been made, your reconciliation is complete.

an example of a typical unrecorded transaction is the check in the amount of $182.60 that was returned because it wasn't represented by sufficient cash in the checking account of the individual who wrote it (J. Hays). All unrecorded transactions and errors detected—whether uncovered in the bank balance reconciliation or the firm's checkbook balance reconciliation—must be accounted for and recorded in the bank's records as well as in the firm's accounting records. The firm is responsible for correcting errors and recording corrections and unrecorded transactions in its records; the bank is responsible for the same in its records.

The company must analyze each adjustment in the checkbook section of the reconciliation and determine which accounts are correct and which are in error. There are few general rules for deciding how unrecorded transactions and errors should be recorded in the accounting records; each adjustment must be considered independently. Let's analyze the adjustments, which are typical, shown for the Ward Company in the preceding illustration.

Adjustment

Check no. 1140 in the amount of $120 erroneously deducted from the
checkbook as $210 . . . . $90

Correcting an error in recording a check

Analysis   When this transaction was originally recorded in a journal, some account was debited for $210 and Cash was credited for $210. We must discover which account was debited so we can correct it. Inspection of the book of original journal entry (cash disbursements journal or general journal) will reveal which account was debited for a greater amount than it should have been. Assume that the account was Advertising Expense. We have determined by inspecting the original journal entry, then, that too much Advertising Expense was recorded and that too much was deducted from Cash.

Correcting Entry

Cash 90
    Advertising Expense   90
To correct an error in recording check no. 1140 ($210 − $120 = $90).

Adjustment

NSF check of J. Hays $182.60

Recording an NSF check

Analysis   When the check was received from Hays, Ward debited Cash and credited another account, let's say Sales. The book of original entry (cash receipts journal or general journal) will show the credit to the Sales account. The only account in error in the original entry is Cash, since a sale was made and recorded in the correct amount. The problem is that cash was not received from the customer; the check represents not cash but an IOU. Proper recording of this transaction will involve debiting Accounts Receivable to record the IOU from the customer, and crediting Cash, reducing it by the amount of Hays' check, which turned out not to represent cash after all.

Correcting Entry

Accounts Receivable: J. Hays 182.60
    Cash 182.60
To record an NSF check received with the November bank statement.

Adjustment

Bank service fees $25.00

Recording bank service fees

Analysis Since the amount of bank service charges may vary with the number of checks processed and the number and types of other services a firm uses, Ward first learned the amount of the bank service charges for November by seeing the amount on the bank statement. Ward must record the fees by debiting an expense and reducing cash.

Correcting Entry

Bank Service Charge Expense 25.00
    Cash 25.00
To record November bank service charge.

One fact you should have noticed from the above examples: When a correction or unrecorded transaction requires that an amount must be *added* to the checkbook balance on the reconciliation, there is a corresponding entry that includes a *debit (increase) to Cash* in the same amount. Similarly, for adjustments requiring a *deduction* from the checkbook balance on the reconciliation, there is a corresponding general journal entry requiring *a credit (decrease) to Cash.*

Petty Cash

Most cash payments made by businesses are in the form of checks. The fact that each check must be individually prepared and signed provides a measure of control over the outflow of cash. The canceled checks provide proof that payment was made.

Reason for petty cash fund

However, in spite of these advantages, there are instances where payment by check is impractical. In these instances, payment is made in the form of currency and coin. A small amount of currency and coin set aside for this purpose is called a ***petty cash fund.*** Examples of proper uses of petty cash include payment of taxi fare for an employee to deliver personally and immediately business documents across town, payment for delivery charges on a part for a typewriter that was shipped collect, and purchase of a small number of postage stamps.

Setting up a petty cash fund

The petty cash fund is established by transferring a small amount of cash from the checking account, say, $50, in the form of currency, to a person who is designated to be responsible for it — the ***petty cashier.*** This person may be a receptionist, a secre-

HERMETITE'S LOOSE CASH CONTROLS RESULT IN EMBEZZLEMENT

Hermetite Corp. manufactures hermetic seals, an electrical component, for sale to the electronics industry. The company's stock is owned by the public. Hermetite's size may be judged by its sales and income. Sales and income for 1980 were approximately $11 million and $500,000, respectively. During 1981 the company earned about $500,000 on $9.5 million of sales.

Hermetite doesn't know exactly when Samson Gilman, the bookkeeper and office manager, began to embezzle from the company; but it was determined that between September 1975 and October 1980, he stole approximately $240,000. In 1978 his theft was about 34% of Hermetite's income before income taxes!

How can a trusted employee steal from a relatively large company over an extended period of time? We need only look at Hermetite's internal controls over cash to see how Gilman perpetrated his fraud.

Gilman obtained blank Hermetite checks and made them payable to a local bank. He "signed" the checks using a signature plate embossed with the company president's signature. He endorsed and cashed the checks at the local bank. Gilman has the cash as easy as this! Now to cover up the theft to avoid detection.

Since Gilman kept the company books, he simply did not record the fake checks in the cash payments journal—but he did include the amount in the totals of the journal columns. (That takes care of the credit to Cash.) The fake purchase reports that he made out resulted in a debit to Raw Materials Purchases. (Now both the debit and credit are "buried" in the books.)

Gilman would have been caught, however, if someone else had reconciled the bank statement with the cash account each month. The checks endorsed by Gilman would have raised the suspicions of even

the office boy. Unfortunately for Hermetite, another of Samson Gilman's duties was to reconcile the bank account. It was a very easy matter for him to destroy the incriminating checks before anyone learned of them.

Hermetite's lack of meaningful internal controls enabled Gilman to steal virtually at will. He had complete control over the blank company checks, facsimile signature plates, check-writing machines, journals, bank statements, and canceled checks. Moreover, Gilman personally prepared Hermetite's cash payments journal, corporate checks, bank reconciliations, and forms used to input data into the data processing system that compiled the general ledger and other records.

Source: Securities Exchange Act of 1934 Release No. 18976, Administrative Proceeding File No. 3-6162, August 18, 1982.

Hermetite should have been aware of Gilman's theft long before he had the opportunity to steal as much as he did. The CPA who audited Hermetite's financial statements each year should have noticed the lax control over cash and informed the company management of the problems. If more rigorous procedures had been established, perhaps Mr. Gilman would not have been tempted to embezzle funds.

Based on what you have learned about internal control in Chapters 6 and 7, what controls can you suggest to Hermetite to ensure that the new bookkeeper does not repeat Gilman's theft?

tary, a bookkeeper, or any employee considered responsible and reliable and in a position to disburse it effectively. The petty cash fund is set up by a check made payable to Petty Cash. The petty cashier then cashes this check and keeps the money in a container he or she is responsible for safeguarding.

The accounting entry to establish the petty cash fund is as follows:

Petty Cash 50
   Cash 50
To establish a petty cash fund.

This entry merely transfers cash from a cash-in-bank (checking) account to a cash-on-hand account. The total cash of the business at this point remains unchanged.

Petty cash voucher explained
    Just as for payments by check, payments from the petty cash fund can be made only with authorization in writing. This written authorization is also a voucher, although it is much simpler than the one we discussed at the beginning of the chapter, and may look something like this:

RIVERBEND CORP.
Petty Cash Disbursement Voucher

Date *December 28, 1987*   Voucher No. *104*

                    Amount of Payment $ *14.35*

Reason for Payment *To pay for office machine part*
received on C.O.D. shipment

Signature of Person Receiving Payment *J.P. Hall*

Approved by *Andrea Johnson*

Usually the petty cashier fills out the voucher and has the person requesting the cash sign it. The petty cashier then files the voucher in the petty cash container and disburses money from the container in the amount of the voucher. The total of the money and the amounts represented by the vouchers must at all times equal the original total of the petty cash fund. That is, the petty cashier must have either the money or approved vouchers showing what it was used for.

Petty cash disbursement vouchers are similar to the vouchers used in the voucher system described earlier. Both vouchers are written authorizations to pay cash. Petty cash vouchers differ in that they are usually not recorded in a formal register.

Replenishing the petty cash fund

When the money in the petty cash fund is running low, the petty cashier will present the vouchers to the manager at a higher level of responsibility who has the authority to replenish it.

Assume that the following vouchers were presented for reimbursement:

Petty Cash Voucher Number	Reason for Disbursement	Amount
101	Paid messenger to deliver package	$ 5.25
102	Purchased postage stamps	1.50
103	Purchased office supplies	6.40
104	Paid for office machine part which was shipped COD	14.35
105	Purchased office supplies	4.40
	Total	$31.90

A check would be made out to Petty Cash for $31.90 and the various expenses represented by each of the vouchers would be recorded. The following entry would be made:

```
Delivery Expense. . . . . . . . . . . . . . . . . . . . . . . . . . . . .    5.25
Office Supplies Expense . . . . . . . . . . . . . . . . . . . . . . . .   10.80
Postage Expense . . . . . . . . . . . . . . . . . . . . . . . . . . . .    1.50
Repairs Expense . . . . . . . . . . . . . . . . . . . . . . . . . . . .   14.35
    Cash . . . . . . . . . . . . . . . . . . . . . . . . . . . . . . . .           31.90
To replenish petty cash fund and record expenses.
```

The replenishment entry made no debit to Petty Cash since we did not increase the petty cash fund. The petty cash fund asset shows a total of $50 before and after the reimbursement. Before reimbursement the asset Petty Cash was, of course, overstated by $31.90 because some of the money had been spent. The replenishment entry formally records the disbursements of money for expenses that have already taken place. The petty cashier now has $50 in money in the cash box and no paid vouchers. The process of petty cash outlays and fund reimbursement can begin again.

The asset Petty Cash is debited only when the fund is originally established or when it is increased. Expenses are debited when the fund is replenished. The fund is replenished whenever it is running low and at the end of the accounting cycle. When cash is running low, replenishment is necessary to ensure that an adequate amount is always on hand to meet day-to-day petty cash needs. At the end of the accounting cycle, replenishment is necessary to record all previously unrecorded expenses in accordance with the matching principle.

Cash Over and Short

Treatment of small mistakes in cash

In spite of the safeguards designed to control the inflows and outflows of money, small mistakes do occur. For example, assume that in the previous petty cash fund illustration the petty cash vouchers total $31.90 and the currency and coins in the petty cash box total $16.70. The petty cash fund, which should total $50, now totals only $48.60 ($31.90 + $16.70). The $1.40 shortage in the petty cash fund was due to a petty cashier mistake — probably paying out more than a petty cash voucher authorized.

The entry to replenish the petty cash fund must also record the cash shortage:

Delivery Expense	5.25	
Office Supplies Expense	10.80	
Postage Expense	1.50	
Repairs Expense	14.35	
Cash Over and Short	1.40	
Cash		33.30

To replenish a petty cash fund, record expenses and a $1.40 cash shortage.

The Cash Over and Short account was debited for $1.40 to record the shortage. If there has been an overage, the same account would be credited for the amount of the overage. If Cash Over and Short has a debit balance at the end of the accounting period, it would be reported as a Miscellaneous Expense on the income statement. A credit balance in the account would be reported as Miscellaneous Income.

The Cash Over and Short account is also used when the money in a cash register drawer (say, $530) does not total to the same amount that is recorded on the cash register tape (say, $528). In this case the entry to record the cash sales must also record the cash overage or shortage:

Cash	530	
Sales		528
Cash Over and Short		2

To record cash sales for the day and a cash overage of $2.

Management will monitor the amount and frequency of cash overages and shortages from a particular petty cash fund or cash register. Frequent overages and shortages may indicate that employees are being careless. Repeated shortages may mean that employees are stealing.

ACCOUNTING FOR MARKETABLE SECURITIES

The Nature of Marketable Securities

Many businesses experience widely fluctuating cash balances during the year. During some seasons of the year, most of their cash may be invested in merchandise inventory; during other seasons most of the goods may be sold, inventory may be low, and there will be a surplus of cash in the company's checking account. A toy manufacturer, for example, probably has an overabundance of cash during the fall months when the Christmas season shipments have been completed and payments are received from customers. This abundance of cash will be needed later next spring and summer when the company will again invest in the toys for the following Christmas.

Surplus cash is the cash that is not needed for the current day-to-day operation of the business. What should a company do with a temporary cash surplus? One alternative would be to leave the funds in the checking account until needed. A better option would be to use this extra cash in some way to earn a return. If the surplus cash can be put to work for a short time, any profit earned will be more than if the cash is left idle in a checking account which earns little or no interest. The investments that a company makes with a temporary cash surplus are called *marketable securities,* or *temporary investments.*

To be classified as a marketable security, or temporary investment, on the balance sheet, two tests must be met:

Marketable security classification tests

1. Management must intend to hold the investment for a short time, usually less than 1 year.

2. The investment must be readily marketable; i.e., management must be able to sell the investment very quickly.

The Composition of Marketable Securities

Bonds, stocks, and short-term notes issued by corporations and by the U.S. government are common types of securities that may be purchased and held for short periods.

Bonds are issued by corporations as a way of borrowing money. By acquiring a bond you are really lending cash to the corporation selling it. Once purchased, bonds may be traded on the securities exchanges just as stocks are. Bond prices are quoted on the securities exchanges as a percentage of their maturity value. A $1,000 bond quoted at 100 would sell for 100% of its maturity value, or $1,000. The same bond quoted at 96 would sell for 96% of its maturity value, or $960. No matter what you pay for a bond, you will receive the maturity value ($1,000) at the end of the bond's life. The income from a bond is the interest paid to the investor — the lender — for the use of his or her cash. Of course, management will purchase bonds of companies in sound financial condition to minimize the risk of not receiving interest when it is due.

Stock is a document that represents evidence of ownership, or a share of ownership, in another company. Individuals and corporations may readily invest in a share of ownership through a broker who buys it at a stock exchange such as the New York Stock Exchange or the American Stock Exchange. Stock prices are quoted in dollars per share of stock. A stock quoted at $12\frac{1}{2}$ would sell for $12.50 per share; one quoted at $378\frac{3}{4}$ would sell for $378.75 per share. By purchasing shares of stock, management hopes to profit by receiving dividends or by selling the stock for more than its original cost. Management will, of course, be very careful to buy a relatively safe stock because the cash invested will be needed in a short time. Investing in speculative, high-risk stocks could result in a loss of a significant part of the cash used in the investment — the price of these shares could quickly decline considerably below the original purchase price.

Management may also elect to purchase bonds and stocks as long-term investments. These investments ordinarily involve the use of cash that will not be needed in the future. Long-term investments are not included as marketable securities; we will discuss this more fully in Chapter 16.

Accounting for Temporary Investments in Bonds

When bonds are purchased they are recorded in the Marketable Securities account at the cost of the bond. As interest is earned, it is recorded as Interest Income. When the bonds are sold, any difference between the selling price and the cost is recorded in the journal as a gain or loss. These procedures are demonstrated in the Murdock Mower Company illustration that follows.

MURDOCK MOWER COMPANY

Purchase of temporary bond investment

Transaction On October 1, 1987, the Murdock Mower Company purchased from a broker 100 Gulf Coast Telephone bonds, each of the $1,000 bonds paying 8% annual interest. The $100,000 (100 bonds × $1,000 each) cost includes all brokerage fees related to the transaction. The bonds pay interest semiannually on September 30 and on March 31.

Analysis Murdock Mower's management invested some extra cash in Gulf Coast Telephone bonds. Management intends to hold the bonds and earn interest until the cash is needed the following spring.

Journal Entry

```
1987
Oct. 1   Marketable Securities ........................ 100,000
              Cash .................................            100,000
         To record the purchse of one hundred $1,000 Gulf Coast
         Telephone bonds bearing interest at 8% annually.
```

Accrual of interest earned on bonds

Adjustment By December 31, 1987, Murdock's year-end, interest for 3 months has been earned. Three months' interest would be calculated as follows:

$$(.08)(\$100,000)(\tfrac{3}{12}) = \$2,000$$

Analysis Since 3 months' interest was earned in 1987 but will not be received until March 31, 1988, it must be recorded on December 31, 1987, the accounting year-end, by means of an adjusting entry.

Adjusting Entry

```
1987
Dec. 31   Interest Receivable ........................... 2,000
               Interest Income ..........................         2,000
          To record 3 months' interest earned on a temporary investment
          in bonds.
```

Cash interest received on bonds

Transaction March 31, 1988, Murdock received $4,000 for 6 months' interest on the Gulf Coast Telephone Bonds:

$$(.08)(\$100,000)(\tfrac{6}{12}) = \$4,000$$

Analysis Murdock received $2,000 in interest that was earned in 1987 and $2,000 that was earned in 1988. The amount earned in 1987 has already been recorded as income; the receivable remains to be collected. The amount earned in 1988 must be recorded as income.

Journal Entry

1988
Mar. 31   Cash 4,000
           Interest Receivable 2,000
           Interest Income 2,000
           To record receipt of 6 months' interest on Gulf Coast Telephone bonds.

Sale of temporary bond investment

Transaction April 1, 1988, Murdock sold the Gulf Coast Telephone bonds for $100,500.

Analysis Murdock needs the cash to pay for salaries, purchases of inventory, advertising, and other operating expenses. A broker sold the bonds on one of the security exchanges.

Journal Entry

1988
Apr. 1   Cash 100,500
           Marketable Securities 100,000
           Gain on Sale of Marketable Securities 500
           To record the sale of one hundred $1,000 Gulf Coast Telephone bonds.

Murdock Mower management used $100,000 of surplus cash to earn $4,500—$4,000 interest plus $500 increase in value of the bonds—during the 6-month period. Had the funds been left in the checking account, they would have produced little or no income for the company.

Accounting for Temporary Investments in Stock

Stock purchased as a temporary investment is recorded in the journal at cost, including all brokerage fees. Dividends, which are not guaranteed, are recorded as Dividend Income when distributed to shareholders. A marketable security sold for more than its original cost results in a gain. If sold for less than original cost, it results in a loss.

Entries to record these types of transactions are shown in the following illustration.

FINEGIN FENCE COMPANY

Purchase of temporary stock
investment

Transaction   Finegin Fence Company purchased 1,000 shares of Mammoth Motor Co. stock on December 1, 1987, when the stock was selling for $38 per share. A $1,900 commission was paid to a broker to handle the transaction.

Analysis   Finegin Fence decided to invest some seasonally idle cash in a relatively safe stock. Mammoth Motors stock has a stable market price and the company has consistently paid each year a $4 dividend on each share. A stockbroker was contacted who purchased the shares on the New York Stock Exchange in Finegin's behalf. The total cost of the shares is calculated as shown below:

$$(1{,}000 \text{ shares})(\$38 \text{ per share}) + \$1{,}900 \text{ (commission)} = \$38{,}000 + \$1{,}900$$
$$= \$39{,}900$$

Journal Entry

1987
Dec. 1   Marketable Securities. 39,900
        Cash 39,900
        To record the purchase of 1,000 shares of Mammoth Motor
        Company stock.

Cash dividend received on stock
investment

Transaction   January 15, 1988, Mammoth declared and paid its quarterly dividend—$1 per share.

Analysis   Finegin Fence received $1,000 from Mammoth Motors. Note that Finegin does not accrue dividends at the accounting year-end in the same way that Murdock Mower accrued interest in the previous illustration. Dividends are not earned with the passage of time as interest is. Mammoth Motors is not obligated to pay its owners dividends. It makes that evaluation four times a year. A firm is obligated to its bondholders to pay interest at set times.

Journal Entry

1988
Jan. 15   Cash. 1,000
        Dividend Income 1,000
        To record dividend received from Mammoth Motors.

Sale of temporary stock
investment

Transaction   March 30, 1988, Finegin sold the Mammoth stock for $43.50 per share and paid a broker $2,000 to handle the transaction.

Analysis   Since Finegin needed the cash for its day-to-day operations, the Mammoth stock was sold. A broker's commission must be paid when stock is sold, just as when stock is purchased. The amount received is as follows:

Selling price.	$ 43.50 per share
Number of shares sold	1,000 shares
Total.	$43,500
Less: Broker's commission	2,000
Net cash received	$41,500

The net cash received of $41,500 less the cost of $39,900 yields a gain of $1,600.

Journal Entry

1988
Mar. 30   Cash 41,500
                  Marketable Securities.   39,900
                  Gain on Sale of Marketable Securities   1,600
            To record the sale of Mammoth Motors Company stock.

Like any asset, the value of stock changes with time. But, unlike most other assets, the change in value of stock, can be determined easily — the prices of shares of stock are quoted continuously. This value is reliable as an unbiased measure because it is set by many buyers and sellers trading stock on the stock exchange. At what value is the stock to be reported on a balance sheet at the end of an accounting period?

Temporary investments on balance sheet at lower of cost or market

Generally accepted accounting principles dictate that temporary investments in stock be shown on the balance sheet at either the original cost or the market value, whichever is lower. Thus on December 31, 1987, if the Mammoth stock had been selling for $37 per share, Finegin would have shown Marketable Securities at $37,000 and recorded a $2,900 loss. This value is less than the original cost — the idea behind reporting the lower value is to show a more conservative financial picture to the readers of Finegin's financial statements.

Finegin would prepare the following entry to record the loss:

1987
Dec. 31   Loss to Reduce Marketable Securities to Market Value. 2,900
                  Allowance to Reduce Marketable Securities
                     to Market Value   2,900
            To reduce marketable securities to market value, which is lower
            than cost

The loss would be shown on the income statement as a nonoperating loss. The allowance account would be shown as a contra asset deducted from Marketable Securities.

Finegin's December 31, 1987, balance sheet, then, would have shown the following:

Marketable Securities (cost)	$39,900	
Less: Allowance to Reduce Marketable Securities		
to Market Value.	(2,900)	$37,000

If the value of stock has increased above the original cost, the stock is shown on the balance sheet at original cost. No gain is recognized until the stock is sold. Again, this rule against showing increases in value presents a conservative financial picture to the statement readers.

You should have a good grasp of why we feel that lower-of-cost-or-market procedures are important. We will leave a complete discussion of the complex rules governing the application of this technique to a more advanced accounting course.

BALANCE SHEET CLASSIFICATIONS

Current assets, the first category of accounts appearing in the asset section of any balance sheet, includes all assets that will be converted into cash or used up in the operation of the business during the next year. The current asset accounts are arranged in order of liquidity—first is the asset most readily converted into cash and last is the asset least readily converted into cash. The top of this list is, of course, Cash, followed by Marketable Securities. Various types of receivables would appear next. A listing of typical current assets in order of liquidity follows:

Current Assets:

Cash

Marketable Securities

Less: Allowance to Reduce Marketable Securities to Market Value

Notes Receivable

Accounts Receivable

Less: Allowance for Uncollectible Accounts

Other Receivables

Merchandise Inventory

Supplies Inventory

Prepaid Assets

Receivables and Inventories will be discussed in detail in the next two chapters.

CHAPTER SUMMARY

Because cash is the most liquid and most readily acceptable asset, it is universally desirable. For that reason, special internal controls must be established to protect it from theft. Among these safeguards are *cash registers, printed receipts, safes, separate recording of cash receipts and cash payments,* a *voucher system* to control cash payments, *reconciliation of bank statements,* and *petty cash funds.*

Under a voucher system, (1) all expenditures must be authorized; (2) the goods or services must be received, inspected, and reported; and (3) the proper amount must be paid in a timely fashion.

A *voucher* is an internal document on which is recorded the verifications that authorized goods and services were acquired as well as authorizations for payment. Information from vouchers is recorded in a special journal called the *voucher register.*

When a check is written to pay a liability, it is recorded in the check register and also in the voucher register.

Bank reconciliations are prepared to explain the differences between the cash balance shown on the bank statement and the cash amount in the company's checkbook. An important part of the system of internal control, bank reconciliations help locate errors made by the company and by the bank. The *bank-and-books-to-*

correct-cash reconciliation illustrated in the chapter is the technique used by most businesses. The reconciliation will reveal unrecorded transactions, which will have to be recorded in the journals; and errors, which will have to be corrected by making an entry in the general journal.

A *petty cash fund* contains a small amount of cash money to be used for payments where a check is impractical.

Marketable securities are short-term investments purchased with cash temporarily in excess of the cash needed for the operation of the company.

Current assets are listed on the balance sheet in order of liquidity.

IMPORTANT TERMS USED IN THIS CHAPTER

Bank reconciliation An analysis of the differences between the ending cash balance as reported by the bank and the ending cash balance as recorded in the company's records. (page 265)

Bond A security issued, or sold, by a corporation as a means of borrowing money, which means that a bond is really a loan from the bondholder. (page 274)

Cash All money on deposit in banks that can be obtained immediately and used at the discretion of the management of the company, and all items on hand that will be accepted by a bank for deposit. (page 254)

Check register A three-column journal of original entry used to record the disbursement of cash by check. It has a minimum of two columns to record a debit to Vouchers Payable and a credit to Cash. A Purchase Discounts credit column is commonly added when the company's suppliers offer cash discounts. (page 264)

Current assets All assets that will be converted into cash or used up in the operation of the business during the next year. The current asset accounts are usually the first category in the asset section of a balance sheet. (page 279)

Deposit in transit Cash sent to the bank — sent through the mail or placed in a night depository — for deposit but not received in time to be included in the ending balance and listed on the bank statement. (page 267)

Dividend A corporation's earnings distributed in the form of cash or other assets, to its shareholders. (page 276)

Internal control The system of safeguards intended to protect assets from theft and to ensure proper financial recordkeeping. (page 254)

Marketable securities Investments that can be readily sold and that management intends to keep for less than 1 year. Also known as *temporary investments* or *short-term investments.* (page 274)

NSF check (Not Sufficient Funds check) A check presented for payment to the bank and rejected because the depositor's account does not contain sufficient cash to represent the amount of the check. (page 267)

Petty cash fund A small amount of cash used for payments when a check is impractical. The contents of the fund must always total the same amount. The fund may contain cash or cash and paid vouchers. (page 270)

Purchase order A business document that reaches outside the firm — an external business document — recognized as having the power and authority to specify an order for goods or services to suppliers and vendors and the commitment to pay for them. (page 257)

Purchase requisition An internal business document, that is, a document that originates and remains within the firm, specifying goods or services needed and requesting the firm to acquire them. (page 257)

Receiving report   An internal business document to indicate the quantity and condition of goods or services that have been received. (page 258)

Sales invoice   A business document prepared by the vendor, or supplier, itemizing the goods or services ordered and delivered. The sales invoice usually constitutes a request for payment. (page 257)

Stock   A certificate issued by a corporation, representing the share of ownership in it. (page 274)

Vendor   A seller of goods or services. (page 257)

Voucher   A written authorization to pay. Vouchers usually contain the name of the individual or company to be paid, the amount of the payment, the reason for the payment, a signature authorizing payment, and the accounts to be debited or credited as a result of the payment. (page 259)

Voucher register   A multi-column journal of original entry used to record transactions authorized by vouchers. It has one credit column to record Vouchers Payable and debit columns for Purchases, Freight-In, Salary Expense, and any other expense that must be recorded often. It also has an other accounts debited section to record debits to accounts that occur less frequently. (page 259)

Voucher system   The system used by a business to ensure that all expenditures are authorized; that the goods or services ordered are received; and that only the goods or services received are paid for, and within a time period that allows the firm to take advantage of cash discounts. (page 255)

Vouchers payable   A general ledger account used in place of Accounts Payable in a voucher system. (page 259)

QUESTIONS

1. Explain why a travelers' check for $1,000 is cash according to the accountant's definition, whereas a U.S. government savings bond is not cash.

2. List at least six internal controls over cash that would be used by a large department store.

3. Separation of duties is a common internal control technique. Separation of duties may not be possible in a small business with only a few employees. Explain how a small business may attempt to compensate for not having many employees.

4. What internal control system assures that appropriate planned acquisitions are made, received in good condition, billed at correct amounts, and paid for on time?

5. What is the purpose of each of the business documents listed below?

   a. Purchase requisition   **c.** Sales invoice
   b. Purchase order   **d.** Receiving report

6. Two special journals discussed in Chapter 6 are replaced by the voucher register and the check register when a voucher system is used. Which special journals are replaced? Explain why they are replaced.

7. In which business department are each of the following documents prepared?

   a. Purchase requisition   **d.** Voucher
   b. Purchase order   **e.** Check
   c. Receiving report

8. Why do businesses prepare bank reconciliations?

9. What are outstanding checks? Why are they subtracted from the bank statement cash balance on bank reconciliations?

10. Green Co. received a check with its bank statement marked "NSF." What is an NSF check? How will it appear on a bank-and-books-to-correct-cash reconciliation?

11. Which of the following items on a bank reconciliation require the company to make a journal entry:

Outstanding checks	Deposits in transit
Bank service fees	NSF checks
Checkbook errors	Bank errors

12. What are petty cash funds? Why are they used?

13. "The contents of a $50 petty cash fund must always equal $50 even if $38 has been paid from it." Explain what is meant by this statement.

14. How are petty cash vouchers like vouchers used in the voucher system? How do they differ?

15. Where will Cash Over and Short appear on an income statement? Explain.

16. What two tests must an investment meet in order to be classified as a marketable security?

17. Why do companies purchase marketable securities?

18. Iris Co. purchased a bond maturing in 20 years. Can this bond be classified as a marketable security? Explain.

19. What rule is used to determine the order of current assets on a balance sheet?

EXERCISES

Exercise 7-1
Determining items to include in Cash

Victoria Nursery's balance sheet shows cash in the amount of $8,456. The following items were used in arriving at this amount:

Currency and coin on hand	$ 107.40
Postage stamps on hand	18.60
Checking account balance	7,680.00
Petty cash fund balance	50.00
U.S. government savings bond	100.00
Passbook savings account at Union Savings	450.00
Travelers' checks received from customers	20.00
A promissory note from Abe Rosen, a customer	30.00

What is the correct amount of cash that Victoria Nursery should report on its balance sheet?

(Check figure: Correct cash = $8,307.40)

Exercise 7-2
Selecting the proper journal to use

Buford's Plumbing Supply uses an accounting system that includes the following journals and other books of original entry:

Sales journal	Check register
Cash receipts journal	General journal
Voucher register	

Which journal or register would be used to record each of the transactions listed below? You may need to list more than one journal or register to record a transaction completely.

a. A cash sale of $350 was made to Bill Jones.
b. An invoice for $1,230 was received from China Supply Co. All supporting documentation (purchase requisition, purchase order, and receiving report) are on file.
c. A sale of $489 was made to R&J Plumbing Contractors. Terms of the sale were 2/10, n/30.
d. Check no. 5672 was written to pay the China Supply invoice.
e. The month's telephone bill for $97.80 was received from Mountain Standard Phone Company.
f. $57.30 was collected from Bruce Jennings, a customer.
g. The week's payroll was paid by cashing check no. 5673 and placing cash in the employee pay envelopes.

h. A bill for $369 was received from Landry Roofing for repair work completed earlier in the month.

i. An invoice for $962 was received from Reliable Pipe Co. All supporting documentation is on file.

j. An adjusting entry was made to record the amount of prepaid insurance used up during the month.

Exercise 7-3

Evaluating bank-and-books-to-correct-cash reconciliation items

A bank reconciliation is being prepared that reconciles the bank and book balances to the correct cash balance. Indicate the proper treatment for each of the items below by placing an "X" in the appropriate column(s) on your solutions paper.

	Add to Bank Balance	Deduct from Bank Balance	Add to Book Balance	Deduct from Book Balance
Outstanding checks	_____	_____	_____	_____
Bank service charges	_____	_____	_____	_____
A check for $28 entered in the checkbook as $82	_____	_____	_____	_____
Deposits in transit	_____	_____	_____	_____
A customer's NSF check returned with the bank statement	_____	_____	_____	_____

Exercise 7-4

Explaining entries made from a bank reconciliation

Vance Wright prepared the following journal entries based on items on the May 1988 bank reconciliation:

a. 1988
   May 31   Bank Service Charge Expense.   40
                  Cash   40

b. 1988
   May 31   Accounts Receivable—J. Tomm   125
                  Cash   125

c. 1988
   May 31   Cash   36
                  Supplies Expense.   36

Explain the type of adjustment on the bank reconciliation that would have resulted in each of the entries.

Exercise 7-5

Recording petty cash reimbursement

On June 1, 1988, McLane Co. established a $50 petty cash fund. On June 30, the petty cash box contained the following:

Voucher Number	Purpose of Disbursement	Amount of Disbursement
101	Office supplies	$ 7.00
102	Postage	3.00
103	Merchandise	10.00
104	Computer floppy disks	18.00
105	Freight-In	3.00

$8.00 in currency and coins.

Prepare the appropriate entries to establish the petty cash fund on June 1 and to reimburse the fund on June 30.

(Check figure: June 30 entry includes a $42 credit to Cash)

Exercise 7-6
Calculating interest earned on temporary bond investment

Athens Co. purchased a $20,000 Lorton, Inc., bond on May 1, 1988. The bond pays 12% interest on April 30 and October 31 each year. Calculate the amount of interest income from this temporary investment that would appear on Athens' December 31, 1988, income statement.

(Check figure: Interest income for 1988 = $1,600)

Exercise 7-7
Recording temporary investment in stock

Schultz Music invests seasonally idle cash in common stock. Prepare journal entries to record the following transactions relating to Schultz's marketable securities during 1987:

June 1   Purchased 500 shares of General Computer, Inc., stock for $42 per share. A broker's commission of $1,000 was paid.

     30   Received a cash dividend of $.80 per share.

Sept. 1   Sold 200 shares for $9,500 less a broker's commission of $450.

Dec. 31   The market value of the stock was $43 per share. If the lower-of-cost-or-market method is used, at what amount should the marketable securities appear on the balance sheet?

(Check figure: Gain on sale of General Computer stock Sept. 1 = $250)

Exercise 7-8
Preparing current assets section of balance sheet

Lopez Art Supply has the following assets on December 31, 1986:

Building	$ 89,000
Office supplies	6,500
Cash on hand	2,200
Accounts receivable	164,000
Prepaid insurance	3,800
Trucks	38,900
Accumulated depreciation: Building	6,400
Cash in checking account	58,200
Merchandise inventory	492,800
Accumulated depreciation: Trucks	13,000
Marketable securities	6,600

Select the current asset accounts from the list above and prepare the current assets section of Lopez's balance sheet in good form.

(Check figure: Total current assets = $734,100)

PROBLEMS
Set A

Problem A7-1
Recording transactions in a voucher register, check register, and general journal

Ruskin Supply Company uses a voucher system to help control expenditures. During July 1988, the following transactions occurred:

July 1   Purchased merchandise from Empire Wholesale Co., $1,800, terms 2/10, n/30. Recorded voucher no. 456 payable to Empire.

July 3   Recorded voucher no. 457 payable to Pioneer Freight in the amount of $120 for shipping charges on the merchandise acquired from Empire.

8   Issued check no. 2980 in payment of voucher no. 456.

9   Recorded voucher no. 458 payable to Payroll, $3,100. Issued check no. 2981 in payment of the voucher.

11   Recorded voucher no. 459 payable to Koolaire, Inc., in the amount of $1,200 for routine maintenance on Ruskin's heating and air conditioning system. The work had been completed on June 5.

12   Purchased merchandise from Ross, Inc., in the amount of $2,400, terms 3/20, n/45. Recorded voucher no. 460 payable to Ross.

18   Issued check no. 2982 in payment of voucher no. 459.

21   Purchased a microcomputer from Pace Office Equipment Company in the amount of $4,690. Recorded voucher no. 461 payable to Pace.

21   Returned defective merchandise to Ross. List price $500.

22   Issued check no. 2983 in payment of voucher no. 461.

27   Recorded voucher no. 462 payable to Payroll, $3,440. Issued check no. 2984 in payment of the voucher.

Required   Using a voucher register, a check register, and a general journal, record the Ruskin Supply Company transactions.

(Check figure: Total of vouchers payable from voucher register = $16,750)

Problem A7-2
Preparing a bank reconciliation

You have been assigned the task of preparing the February 28, 1987, bank reconciliation for Tracy's Hardware. During the process of completing the reconciliation you discover the following facts:

a. The balance in the checkbook on February 28, 1987, was $2,257.60.

b. Checks written prior to February 28 that have not yet cleared the bank total $932.50.

c. A deposit of $425.10 was placed in the night depository on February 28. This deposit was recorded by the bank on March 1, so it does not appear on the bank statement.

d. The balance on the February 28 bank statement was $2,731.25.

e. A bank service charge of $6.75 appeared on the bank statement but has not been deducted in the checkbook.

f. Check no. 231 was deducted in the checkbook as $47.00. The actual amount of the check was $74.00.

Required   Prepare a bank-and-books-to-correct-cash reconciliation.

(Check figure: Correct cash = $2,223.85)

Problem A7-3
Preparing a bank reconciliation and journal entries

Jay Watson owns and operates a small business. Each month when the bank statement arrives in the mail, Jay compares the balance the bank says he has with the balance in his books; they are never the same. Jay has asked you to review his records and prepare a schedule that reconciles the balance on the bank statement with the balance in the company's books.

Watson provides you with the following information:

MOUNTAIN NATIONAL BANK
Cedar, GA

J. Watson Co.
212 Parsons Blvd.
Cedar, GA

Statement Date: February 28, 1986

Balance Last Statement	Deposits and Credits		Checks and Debits		Balance This Statement
	No.	Total Amount	No.	Total Amount	
968.30	4	5,836.79	12	4,344.81	2,460.28

Date	Amount Credited	Description
2/6	1,177.99	Deposit
2/13	2,230.64	Deposit
2/20	1,428.16	Deposit
2/27	1,000.00	Loan proceeds

Checks:

Date	Check No.	Amount	Date	Check No.	Amount
2/2	676	143.30	2/19	689	255.82
2/5	684	61.50	2/21	690	478.85
2/8	686	694.25	2/24	691	424.16
2/10	687	1,238.50	2/24	692	910.82
2/17	688	54.61			

Other Debits:

Date	Amount	Description
2/28	40.00	Safe deposit box rental (1 year)
2/28	15.00	Check printing
2/28	28.00	Monthly service charge

From Cash Receipts Journal
(All cash receipts are deposited):

Date	Cash (Dr.)
2/6	1,177.99
2/12	2,230.64
2/20	1,428.16
2/28	492.56
Total	5,329.35

From Cash Payments Journal
(All cash payments are made by check):

Date	Check No.	Cash (Cr.)
2/3	684	61.50
2/4	685	308.10
2/4	686	694.25
2/9	687	1,238.50
2/17	688	45.61
2/18	689	255.82
2/19	690	478.85
2/20	691	424.16
2/22	692	910.82
2/26	693	5.88
2/27	694	278.12
2/27	695	23.90
Total		4,725.51

From the General Ledger:

Date	Explanation	P/R	Dr.	Cr.	Balance
Jan. 31	Balance	✓			730.70
Feb. 28		C/R-4	5,329.35		6,060.05
Feb. 28		C/P-6		4,725.51	1,334.54

a. In reviewing the January bank statement, you discover that checks no. 619 ($94.30) and no. 676 ($143.30) were outstanding on January 31.

b. Watson did not order or receive any new checks this month. The check printing charge is an error.

c. In paying the $54.61 monthly phone bill, Watson wrote the correct amount on check no. 688, but entered $45.61 in the checkbook and cash payments journal.

d. Watson had applied for a $1,000, 6-month loan from the bank. The loan was approved on February 27 and the amount added to the bank account. Watson has made no entry to record the loan.

Required

1. Prepare a bank reconciliation that reconciles Watson's bank statement balance and his cash book balance to a correct cash amount.

2. Prepare any journal entries needed on Watson's books as indicated by the reconciliation.

(Check figure: Correct cash balance = $2,257.54)

Problem A7-4
Recording temporary investment in bonds

Sands Company regularly invests idle cash in corporate bonds. Sands' investment transactions for 1986 and 1987 are shown below:

1986

Apr.   1   Sands purchased twenty $1,000 bonds of Lake Enterprises for $20,000. The bonds have an annual interest rate of 12%. The interest is paid semiannually on March 31 and September 30.

Sept. 30   Received the semiannual interest.

Oct.   1   Sold three-fourths of the bonds for $14,600 net of brokerage fees and commissions.

Dec. 31   Accrued 3 month's interest receivable on the Lake Enterprises bonds.

    31   Closed all temporary accounts relating to the bond investment.

1987

Mar. 31   Received the semiannual interest on the bonds.

Apr.   1   Sold the remaining Lake Enterprises bonds for $5,250 net of brokerage fees and commissions.

Required

Prepare journal entries to record the transactions and events listed above. Your entries should be supported by clearly labeled calculations.

(Check figure: Total interest income for 1986 = $1,350)

Problem A7-5
Recording temporary investment in stock

San Juan Equipment routinely invests seasonally idle cash in common stocks. The following transactions took place in 1988:

Jan.   5   San Juan purchased 100 shares of Garcia Tools Co. for $15 per share. A $75 broker's commission was paid.

Mar.   4   San Juan bought 250 shares of Juarez Steel for $45 per share plus a broker's commission of $1,200.

Apr. 15   A $.50-per-share quarterly dividend was received on the Garcia stock.

June 12   Thirty shares of the Garcia stock were sold. The net cash received after deducting broker's fees was $480.

July 15   A $.50-per-share quarterly dividend was received on the Garcia stock.

Sept. 14   Fifty shares of Juarez stock were sold for $56 per share. A brokerage commission of $2 per share must be deducted from the sales price in determining the amount received by San Juan.

Oct. 15   A $.50-per-share quarterly dividend was received on the Garcia stock.

Dec. 31   A $2-per-share annual dividend was received on the Juarez stock.

    31   Entries were made to close all temporary accounts.

Required

1. Prepare journal entries to record the transactions and events listed above. Your entries should be supported by clearly labeled calculations.

2. Assume that on December 31, 1988, the market price of the Garcia stock was $16 per share and the market price of the Juarez stock was $55 per share. At what amount will the marketable securities appear on the December 31, 1988, balance sheet? Explain.

(Check figure: Total dividend income during 1988 = $520)

Problem A7-6
Preparing a bank reconciliation

The following bank reconciliation was prepared by the accountant for Bernard's Book Bindery:

BERNARD'S BOOK BINDERY
Bank Reconciliation
April 30, 1988

Balance per bank statement 4/30/88.		$ 6,785
Add: Deposits in transit.		950
Deduct: Outstanding checks.		(2,390)
Correct cash balance 4/30/88		$ 5,345
Balance per checkbook 4/30/88.		$ 5,974
Add: Check no. 1329 for $35 was deducted in the checkbook as $53. The check was issued to pay for an ad in the local college newspaper		18
Deduct: Bank service charges for April	$ 45	
NSF check from Corner Bookstore	135	
Check no. 1354 for $467 was not deducted in the checkbook or entered in the financial records. The check was issued to pay for April's rent on warehouse space	467	(647)
Correct cash balance 4/30/88		$ 5,345

Required Prepare journal entries for Bernard's Book Bindery that would be indicated as a result of the April bank reconciliation.

(Check figure: Cash is credited for a net of $629 in the journal entry or entries)

Problem A7-7
Reimbursing a petty cash fund that has been misused

Peacock Paint Co. has a $50 petty cash fund that is kept by George Painman. When Painman failed to report for work for several days, the company investigated. Painman's landlady reported that he had vacated his apartment and left no forwarding address. Peacock's office manager, Linda Legion, decided to audit Painman's petty cash box. When the box was opened, the following items were found:

A receipt for a typewriter ribbon.	$ 6.75
Invoices for purchases of merchandise paid out of petty cash	450.00
Sales invoices. Merchandise was sold to customers and the cash put in the petty cash fund.	4,986.00
A receipt for postage stamps	20.00
Currency and coin.	1.25

Required 1. In what ways did G. Painman misuse the Peacock petty cash fund?
2. Prepare a schedule showing the amount of cash that should be in Painman's petty cash box.
3. Prepare the entry required to reimburse the petty cash fund. The $50 fund is to be the responsibility of Durwood Doright. (Hint: You will need to record the purchases and sales that Painman processed through petty cash.)

(Check figure: Cash that should be in petty cash box = $4,559.25)

Problem A7-8
Recording temporary investments in bonds

Magic Trailers, Inc., regularly invests seasonally idle cash in corporate bonds. The following transactions and events relate to these investments. (Assume that Magic's fiscal year ends on September 30.)

1987

Aug. 1   Magic purchased five $1,000 Mercer Shipping Co. bonds. The bonds pay 15% interest on January 31 and July 31 each year. The $5,000 cost includes all brokerage fees and commissions.

Sept. 1   Magic purchased five $5,000 Pioneer Engineering Co. bonds. The bonds pay 12% interest on February 28 and August 31 each year. The $25,000 cost includes all brokerage fees and commissions.

       30   Magic accrued interest on the Mercer Shipping and Pioneer Engineering bonds.

1988

Jan. 31   Magic received the semiannual interest on the Mercer bonds.
Feb.   1   Magic sold three of the Mercer bonds. The net cash proceeds were $2,650.
       28   Magic received the semiannual interest on the Pioneer bonds.
July 31   Magic received the semiannual interest on the Mercer bonds.
Aug. 31   Magic received the semiannual interest on the Pioneer bonds.
Sept. 1   Magic sold the Pioneer bonds for $25,750 net of all fees and commissions.
       30   Magic accrued all appropriate interest.

Required

1. Prepare all entries needed on the above dates. (Include any appropriate closing entries.)
2. How much interest income will Magic Trailers show on its income statement for the year ended September 30, 1988?

(Check figure: 1988 interest income = $3,200)

Set B

Problem B7-1
Recording transactions in a voucher register, check register, and general journal

To help control expenditures, Metro Rock Co. uses a voucher system. During the month of October 1988, the following transactions occurred:

Oct. 1   Inventory in the amount of $1,000 was purchased on account from Stein Gravel Co. with credit terms of 2/10, n/30. Recorded voucher no. 356.
       4   Purchased inventory on account in the amount of $800 on account from Sam's Marble, Inc. Credit terms 3/15, n/45. Recorded voucher no. 357.
       8   Paid voucher no. 356 by issuing check no. 6540.
      15   Recorded voucher no. 358 payable to Payroll in the amount of $1,800. Issued check no. 6541 in payment of the voucher.
      16   Issued check no. 6542 in payment of voucher no. 357.
      21   Issued voucher no. 359 payable to Sampson Equipment in the amount of $18,500 for a new piece of loading equipment. Issued check no. 6543 in payment of this voucher.
      24   Purchased inventory on account from Redman Quarry, $2,000, terms 2/10, n/30. Recorded voucher no. 360.
      26   Returned $500 of inventory to Redman Quarry. The stone was unsatisfactory.
      27   Recorded voucher no. 361 payable to Reams Freight in the amount of $200 for freight on inventory purchased from Redman.
      28   Recorded voucher no. 362 for $432 payable to Gothom Electric Co. for the monthly electric bill. Issued check no. 6544 in payment of this voucher.
      31   Recorded voucher no. 363 payable to Payroll in the amount of $1500. Issued check no. 6545 in payment of the voucher.

Required

Using a voucher register, a check register, and a general journal, record the Metro Rock Co. transactions listed above.

(Check figure: Total of vouchers payable from voucher register = $26,232)

Problem B7-2
Preparing a bank reconciliation

As an accountant for Horizon Brothers, Inc., one of your responsibilities is to prepare the monthly bank reconciliation. In preparing to complete the November 30, 1986, reconciliation, you have assembled the following facts:

a. The balance on the November 30 bank statement was $14,342.80.

b. The balance in the checkbook on November 30 was $10,097.70.

c. Check no. 5102 was deducted in the checkbook as $2,100. The actual amount of the check was $1,200.

d. A deposit of $2,467 was placed in the night depository on November 30. The deposit was not recorded by the bank until December 1, so it does not appear on the November bank statement.

e. Bank service charges for the month total $62.50. This charge has not been deducted in the checkbook.

f. Checks written prior to November 30 that have not yet cleared the bank total $5,874.60.

Required

Prepare a reconciliation of bank and book balances to the correct cash amount.

(Check figure: Correct cash = $10,935.20)

Problem B7-3
Preparing a bank reconciliation and journal entries

Grace Pawloski owns and operates a real estate office. You have been hired to prepare a reconciliation of Pawloski's cash balance on the bank statement with the amount that appears in her company books. You are also to determine the correct cash amount. Pawloski provides you with the following information:

FARM & HOME NATIONAL BANK
Palmira, NY

Pawloski Real Estate
4130 Vista Drive
Palmira, NY   *Statement Date: May 31, 1987*

Balance Last Statement	Deposits and Credits		Checks and Debits		Balance This Statement
	No.	Total Amount	No.	Total Amount	
1,936.60	4	11,673.58	12	8,689.62	4,920.56

Date	Amount Credited	Description
5/3	2,355.98	Deposit
5/15	4,461.28	Deposit
5/22	2,856.32	Deposit
5/25	2,000.00	Deposit

Checks:

Date	Check No.	Amount	Date	Check No.	Amount
5/4	2376	286.80	5/19	2489	511.64
5/7	2484	123.00	5/21	2490	957.75
5/8	2486	1,388.55	5/25	2491	848.32
5/10	2487	2,477.00	5/29	2492	1,821.64
5/17	2488	109.22			

Other Debits:

Date	Amount	Description
5/31	40.00	Safe deposit box rental (1 year)
5/31	75.70	NSF check (R. Prado)
5/31	50.00	Monthly service charge

From Cash Receipts Journal
(All cash receipts are deposited):

Date	Cash (Dr.)
5/5	2,355.98
5/15	4,461.28
5/22	2,856.32
5/25	2,000.00
5/31	859.12
Total	12,532.70

From Cash Payments Journal
(All cash payments are made by check):

Date	Check No.	Cash (Cr.)
5/5	2484	213.00
5/6	2485	616.20
5/7	2486	1,388.55
5/7	2487	2,477.00
5/12	2488	109.22
5/15	2489	511.64
5/18	2490	957.75
5/21	2491	848.32
5/23	2492	1,821.64
5/25	2493	11.76
5/28	2494	556.24
5/31	2495	47.80
Total		9,559.12

From the General Ledger:

Date	Explanation	P/R	Dr.	Cr.	Balance
Apr. 31	Balance	✓			1,601.30
May 31		C/R-2	12,532.70		14,098.30
May 31		C/P-5		9,559.12	4,574.88

a. In reviewing the April bank statement, you discover that checks no. 2370 ($48.50) and no. 2376 ($286.80) were outstanding on April 30.

b. The $40 charge for safe deposit box rental was incorrect. Pawloski had applied for a safe deposit box but canceled the order when none were available.

c. Check no. 2484 was written to pay for an advertisement in the local newspaper. An incorrect amount was entered in the checkbook and cash payments journal. $123, the correct amount, appears on the check.

d. The bank returned a customer's check marked NSF. Pawloski believes that she will collect from R. Prado, the customer.

Required

1. Prepare a bank reconciliation that reconciles Pawloski's bank statement balance and her cash book balance to a correct cash amount.

2. Prepare any journal entries needed on Pawloski's books as indicated by the reconciliation.

(Check figure: Correct cash balance = $4,539.18)

Problem B7-4
Recording temporary investment in bonds

On January 1, 1988, Harte Co., adopted a policy of investing seasonally idle cash in corporate bonds. The 1988 and 1989 transactions relating to these investments are shown below:

1988

Jan. 1   Harte purchased ten $1,000 bonds of Chase, Inc. The cost of the 12% bonds including brokerage fees is $10,000. The bonds pay interest semiannually on June 30 and December 31.

June 30   Received the semiannual interest.

July 1   Sold four of the Chase bonds for $4,250 net of brokerage fees and commissions.

Dec. 31   Received the semiannual interest.

  31   Closed all temporary accounts relating to the bond investment.

1989

Jan. 1   Sold the remainder of the Chase, Inc., bonds for $5,800 net of brokerage fees and commissions.

Required   Prepare journal entries to record the transactions and events listed above. Your entries should be supported by clearly labeled calculations.

(Check figure: Total interest earned during 1988 = $960)

Problem B7-5
Recording temporary investment in stock

Cone Appliances, Inc., routinely invests seasonally idle cash in common stocks. The following transactions took place during 1987:

Jan. 1   Cone purchased 1,000 shares of Dependable Steel Co. for $5 per share. A $250 commission was paid to the broker who handled the purchase.

Feb. 16   Cone bought 400 shares of Liberty Publishing Co. for $25 per share. A broker's commission of $500 was paid on the transaction.

Mar. 31   Received a quarterly dividend of $.50 per share on the Liberty stock.

May 18   One hundred shares of Liberty stock were sold. $2,675 cash was received after all brokerage commissions were paid.

June 30   Received a $.50-per-share quarterly dividend on the Liberty stock and a $.25-per-share semiannual dividend on the Dependable stock.

Sept. 30   Received a $.50-per-share quarterly dividend on the Liberty stock.

Nov. 8   One hundred shares of the Dependable stock were sold for $6 per share. A commission of $.30 per share must be deducted from the sales price in determining the amount received by Cone.

Dec. 31   A $.25-per-share dividend was received on the Dependable stock. No fourth-quarter dividend was received on the Liberty stock.

  31   Entries were made to close all temporary accounts.

Required   1. Prepare journal entries to record the transactions and events listed above. Your entries should be supported by clearly labeled calculations.
2. Assume that on December 31, 1987, the market price of the Dependable stock was $4.75 per share; the market price of the Liberty stock was $26 per share. At what amount will the marketable securities appear on the December 31, 1987, balance sheet? Explain.

(Check figure: Total dividend income during 1987 = $975)

Problem B7-6
Preparing a bank reconciliation

The following bank reconciliation was prepared by the accountant for Rainbow Cleaners:

RAINBOW CLEANERS
Bank Reconciliation
January 31, 1986

Balance per bank statement 1/31/86	$4,607.50
Add: Deposits in transit	240.00
Deduct: Outstanding checks.	(674.50)
Correct cash balance 1/31/86	$4,173.00
Balance per checkbook 1/31/86	$4,378.50

Add: Check no. 619 for $20.50 was deducted in the checkbook
        as $205. The check was issued to pay for changing the
        oil in the delivery truck 184.50

Deduct: Bank service charge for Jan.   . . . . $ 20.00
        Check no. 640 for $365 was deducted in the checkbook
        and entered in the financial records as $3.65. The check
        was issued to pay for cleaning fluid. 361.35
        NSF check from customer: John Davit. 8.65   (390.00)

Correct cash balance. $4,173.00

Required   Prepare journal entries for Rainbow Cleaners that would be indicated as a result of the January bank reconciliation.

(Check figure: Cash is credited for a net of $205.50 in the journal entry or entries)

Problem B7-7
Reimbursing a petty cash fund
that has been misused

Toddler Togs, Inc., has a $100 petty cash fund that is kept by Thelma Spendthrift. When Spendthrift failed to report to work for several days, Toddler investigated. Spendthrift's roommate said that Thelma had moved to Los Angeles to work in the movies. The Toddler internal audit department decided that an audit of Thelma's petty cash box would be appropriate. The petty cash box contained the following:

Sales invoices. Merchandise was sold to customers and the cash put in the petty cash fund	$9,678.00
A receipt for mailing a package via Express Mail	11.40
Invoices for merchandise paid for out of petty cash	565.00
A receipt for a package that arrived postage due.	4.65
An IOU from the Toddler company president.	25.00
Currency and coin.	1.20

Required   1. In what ways did Thelma Spendthrift misuse the petty cash fund?
2. Prepare a schedule showing the amount of cash that should be in Thelma's petty cash box.
3. Prepare the entry required to reimburse the petty cash fund. The $100 fund is to be the responsibility of Selma Safeman. (Hint: You will need to record the purchases and sales that Thelma processed through petty cash.)

(Check figure: Cash that should be in the petty cash box = $9,171.95)

Problem B7-8
Recording temporary
investments in bonds

Wilson Foods Co. invests seasonally idle cash in corporate bonds. The following transactions and events relate to these investments. (Assume that Wilson's fiscal year ends on August 31.)

1987

May 1   Purchased ten $1,000 Burma Imports Company bonds. The bonds pay 15% interest on April 30 and October 31. The $10,000 cost includes all brokerage fees and commissions.

July 1   Purchased fifteen $1,000 bonds of Sewell Enterprises. These bonds pay 18% interest on June 30 and December 31 each year. The $15,000 cost includes all brokerage fees and commissions.

Aug. 31   Wilson accrued interest on the Burma Imports and Sewell Enterprises bonds.

Oct. 31   Received the semiannual interest on the Burma Imports bonds.

Nov. 1   Sold three of the Burma Imports bonds. The net cash proceeds from the sale were $2,942.

Dec. 31   Received the semiannual interest on the Sewell Enterprises bonds.

1988

Jan. 1   Sold 10 of the Sewell bonds. The net cash proceeds from the sale were $10,425.

Apr. 30   Received the semiannual interest on the Burma Imports bonds.

June 30   Received the semiannual interest on the Sewell bonds.

July 1   Sold the five remaining Sewell bonds. $5,315 was received after all commissions and fees were deducted.

Aug. 31   Wilson accrued all appropriate interest.

Required

1. Prepare all entries needed on the above dates. (Include any appropriate closing entries.)
2. How much interest income will Wilson show on its income statement for the year ended August 31, 1988?

(Check figure: 1988 interest income = $2,475)

Chapter 8   Receivables

Some of the things you will learn by studying this chapter are:

- What is meant by an *account receivable* and an *uncollectible account*

- The direct write-off method of accounting for uncollectible accounts, and why it is simple to use but doesn't adequately match losses from uncollectibles with credit sales

- What is meant by the *Allowance for Uncollectible Accounts* and *Bad Debts Expense*

- How to use the *percentage of credit sales method* and the *aging of receivables method* to calculate Bad Debts Expense

- How to prepare journal entries for an account receivable; how to write off an account receivable thought to be uncollectible; and how to reinstate an account previously written off but later collected

- What a *note receivable* is

- The difference between *interest-bearing* and *non-interest-bearing* notes receivable

- How to calculate the proceeds from a discounted note and prepare the journal entries associated with the discounting process

- How to account for credit provided by credit card companies

- How receivables are disclosed on a balance sheet

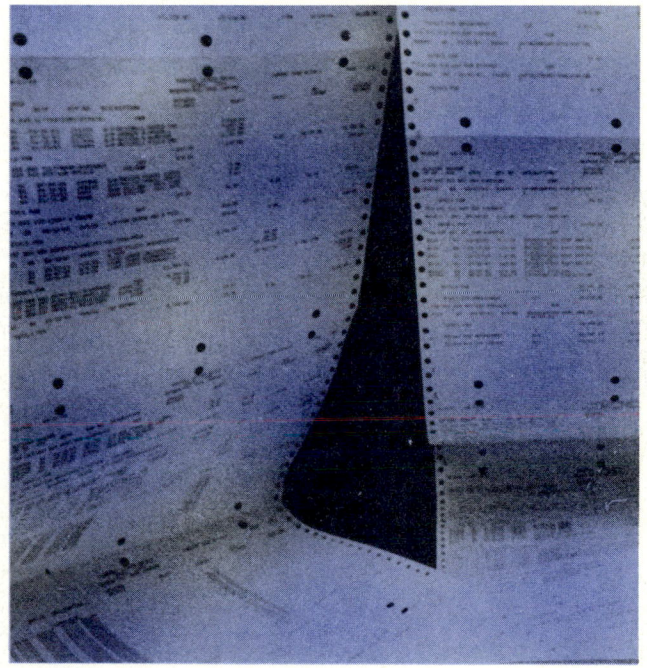

ACCOUNTS RECEIVABLE

Purchasers, either individuals or large organizations, usually don't give a stack of cash money to the accounting department of the seller the moment they receive the goods or services ordered. Nor do they pay at that precise moment with cash in the form of a check. They pay later, *after* having received the goods or services.

There are two reasons for credit purchases: (1) Buyers need goods and services that they can't (or may prefer not to) pay for immediately—e.g., it would be inconvenient to pay each truck driver as soon as a shipment of goods is unloaded—and (2) sellers can sell more through credit sales than if they were to insist on immediate cash payments. And this brings us to accounts receivable.

To an accountant, a credit sale is an ***account receivable,*** which is also called an ***open account*** or a ***trade receivable.*** In a credit sale, the seller and buyer enter into a contract, written or oral, in which the buyer agrees to pay the seller for all goods and services purchased within a specified time—typically 30, 60, or 90 days—after the buyer is

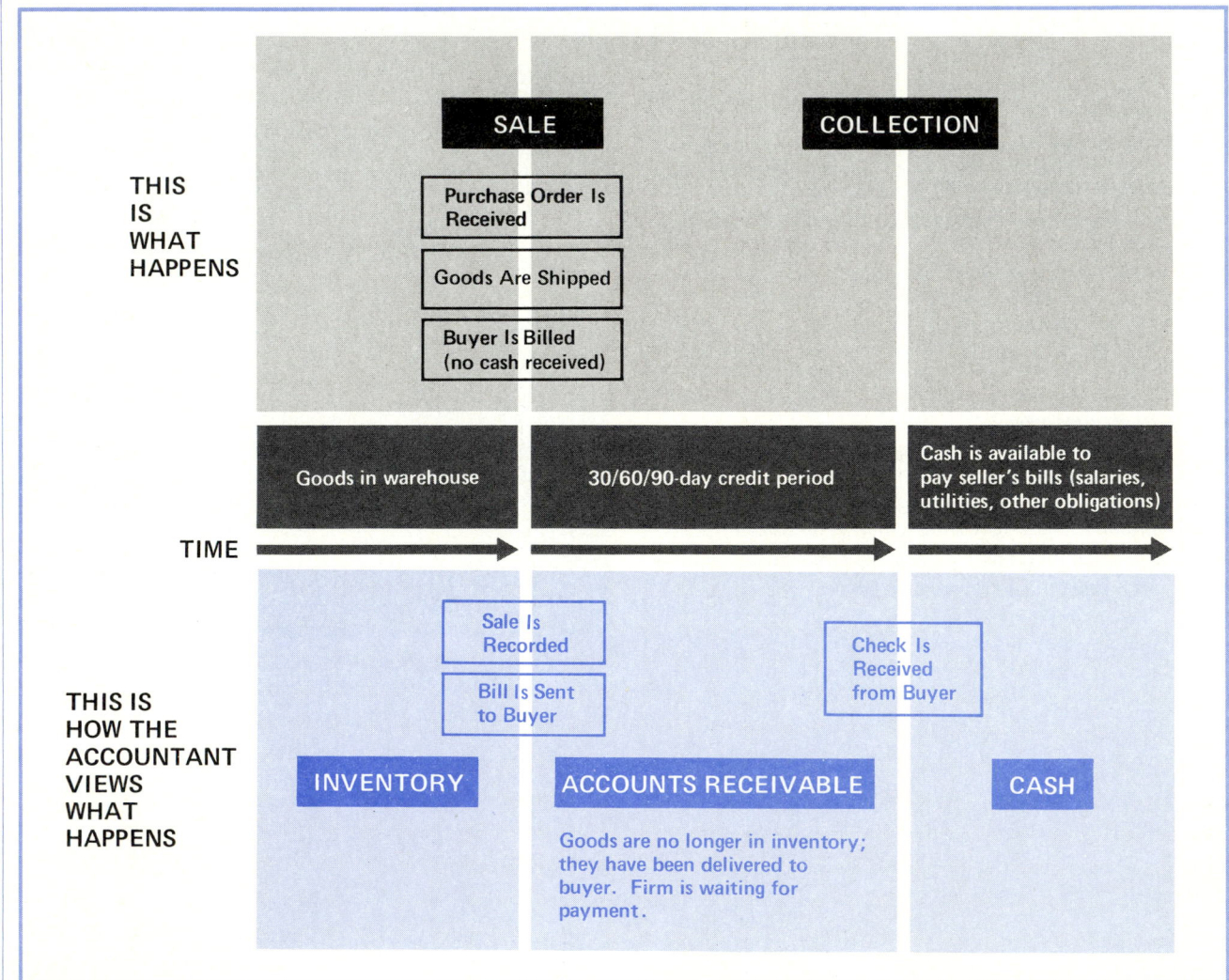

FIGURE 8-1   The Credit Sales Process.
The credit sales process involves selling goods, shipping them to customers, and waiting to receive cash. The accountant sees this as a flow from inventory to accounts receivable and finally to cash.

Accounts receivable are claims against customers for goods or services sold on credit

billed. From the time the seller records the sale until the time the cash is collected, the seller has a claim against the buyer for the value of the goods or services delivered. This claim is carried in the seller's records as an Account Receivable. Figure 8-1 shows this credit sales process.

Sales on account are recorded in the sales journal and then posted to the general ledger Account Receivable and the subsidiary ledger Account Receivable for each individual customer. Remember from your study of the sales journal in Chapter 6 that the column total of the sales journal is posted to the general ledger and each individual sale is posted to the subsidiary ledger. Thus, when you look at the balance sheet for any accounting period, you will see one line listing Accounts Receivable, which might be in the amount of, say, $57,385. That amount, of course, is the sum of perhaps thousands of individual Accounts Receivable, all recorded in individual ledger accounts. These ledger accounts might be recorded in the form of hand-printed notations on ledger sheets, or in the more modern medium of machine-printed cards, or perhaps even on a computer memory device. The total of all the Accounts Receivable ledger accounts in the subsidiary ledger and the total of the Accounts Receivable account in the general ledger must, of course, agree at all times.

As an example, consider the following. Button Company made a sale of $500 to L. Padgett on account. The entry to record this sale in general journal form[1] is as follows:

The entry to record a sale on account

```
1988
Dec. 30   Accounts Receivable: L. Padgett. . . . . . . . . . . . . . . . . . . . . . . 500
               Sales. . . . . . . . . . . . . . . . . . . . . . . . . . . . . . . . . . . . . . .        500
          To record sale on account.
```

All of Button's accounts receivable on December 3, 1988, are listed in the reconciliation below. This schedule proves that the total of the accounts receivable in the subsidiary ledger equals the balance of the Accounts Receivable control account in the general ledger.

The total of the subsidiary ledger Accounts Receivable must equal the total of the general ledger Accounts Receivable

---

BUTTON COMPANY
Reconciliation of General and Subsidiary Accounts Receivable Ledgers
December 31, 1988

Accounts Receivable general ledger account balance $2,830

Subsidiary ledger Accounts Receivable:
D. Carmack	$420
F. Grindle	150
H. Hollingsworth	810
R. Luttrell	120
S. Marcus	405
J. Oswald	175
L. Padgett	500
A. Wright	250

Total $2,830

---

[1] All our journal entries in the examples throughout the rest of the book are in general journal form even though the entry may actually be made in a special journal. This will make illustrations much easier because we won't have to construct special journals each time we make an entry.

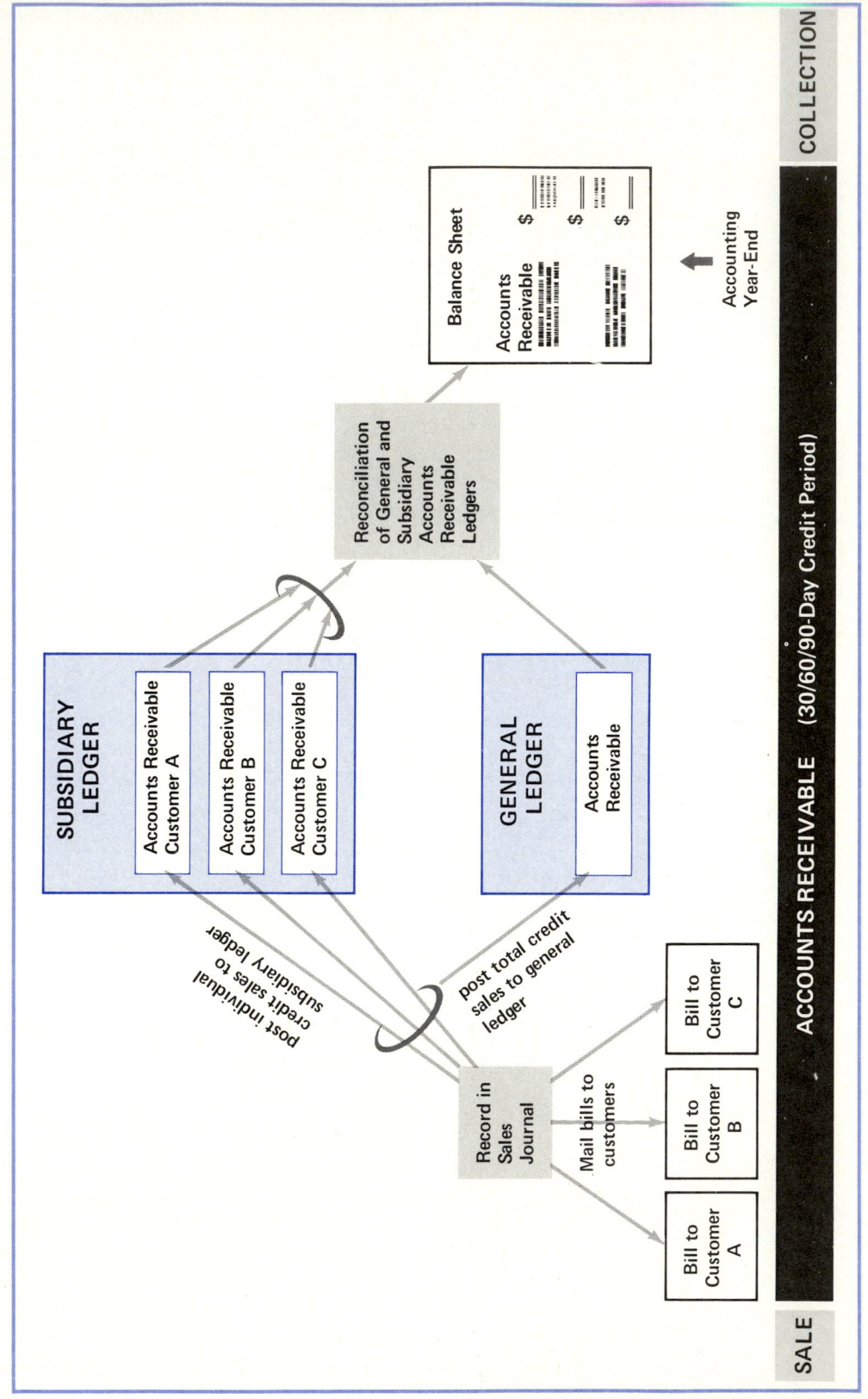

FIGURE 8-2   The Accounts Receivable Accounting Process.

When a credit sale is made, it is recorded in the sales journal and posted to the general and subsidiary accounts receivable ledger accounts. At the end of the period, general and subsidiary ledgers are reconciled. Accounts Receivable appears as a single amount on the balance sheet.

When L. Padgett paid his account on January 5, 1989, the following entry was made in the general journal:

The entry to record a payment on account

```
1989
Jan. 5  Cash . . . . . . . . . . . . . . . . . . . . . . . . . . . . . . . . . . . 500
            Accounts Receivable: L. Padgett . . . . . . . . . . . . . . . . . . . . . .      500
        To record receipt of payment on account.
```

The accounting process for accounts receivable is shown in Figure 8-2. This illustration assumes that the accounting year (fiscal year) ends before the account receivable is collected.

Accounting for Uncollectible Accounts

Any business firm will carefully evaluate a customer's current financial condition and credit history before selling to that customer on account. In spite of the care taken before granting credit, there occasionally will be those customers who, for whatever reasons, cannot or will not pay their accounts.

How does the accountant treat an account receivable that is not paid and in all probability will never be paid? To understand how to represent in the accounting records an account receivable that will not be paid, consider the following:

1. The firm used resources in providing the goods or services sold on account.

2. Revenue was recorded at the time of the sale.

3. Goods or services were delivered.

4. Until those goods or services are paid for, the amount of the unpaid bill is much like a loan to the buyer.

5. The seller may give up hope that the buyer will pay, but the seller does not simply forget about the costs represented in the value of goods or services delivered and not paid for.

All that adds up to a *bad debt,* which is regarded as a cost of doing business, or more specifically, as a cost of granting credit to do business. The amount that will not be collected is usually called *uncollectible accounts expense* or *bad debts expense.*

The two most common ways of accounting for bad debts expense are: (1) the direct write-off method, in which the accountant recognizes bad debts expense when a specific customer's account is determined to be uncollectible; and (2) the percentage of credit sales and the aging of receivables methods, in which the accountant estimates total uncollectible accounts and records bad debts expense before knowing which specific customer's accounts will be uncollectible.

Direct Write-Off Method

As an example of the direct write-off method, assume that during 1987, Retail, Inc., made sales on account to several thousand customers. One of them, J. Doe, declared bankruptcy, having no cash available to satisfy creditors' demands. Upon learning of Doe's bankruptcy, Retail determined that Doe's account was uncollectible and at the same time recognized it as a bad debts expense. Retail, Inc., made the following entry to write off Doe's account:

The entry to write off an account using the direct write-off method

```
1987
Feb. 20   Bad Debts Expense . . . . . . . . . . . . . . . . . . . . . . . . . . . . 290
              Accounts Receivable: J. Doe . . . . . . . . . . . . . . . . . . . . . .      290
          To write off account of J. Doe that is uncollectible.
```

Bad Debts Expense will appear as an operating expense on Retail's income statement. The credit will be posted to Retail's Accounts Receivable general ledger account and to the Accounts Receivable: J. Doe subsidiary ledger account. The write-off effectively removed Doe's account receivable from our books; it now has a zero balance.

Accounting theory limits the use of the direct write-off method because of two major objections to it: (1) It violates the matching principle and (2) it distorts the amount of Accounts Receivable on the balance sheet. The violation of the matching principle distorts what is reported on the income statement. Remember: According to the matching principle, the expenses incurred in earning revenue during a period of time should be matched with the revenue earned during that period.

For example, assume that a sale on account is made in 1987. This sale is recorded as an account receivable and a 1987 revenue. This revenue appears on the 1987 income statement. Now, assume that 1988 comes along but not the customer's payment. It is 1 year later and the company has not yet been paid. The company finally gives up hope that payment will ever be received. The account is declared uncollectible and becomes Bad Debts Expense. The Sales Revenue appeared on the 1987 income statement. Some of the expenses—that Bad Debt Expense—that contributed to 1987 income appear on the 1988 income statement, not on the 1987 income statement. The result of this mismatching is that both 1987 and 1988 incomes are distorted.

Continuing with our example, let us turn to the other major objection to the direct write-off method: that it distorts Accounts Receivable on the balance sheet. If, in 1987, the company reasonably expects to collect all the accounts, there is no distortion. However, the company knows that some accounts will later prove uncollectible. Failure to recognize this fact and to estimate these uncollectibles blissfully implies that every cent of every sale on account will be received in payment. Thus, the direct write-off method will result in a 1987 balance sheet Accounts Receivable amount that is greater than the amount that the company expects to collect.

The direct write-off method offers two advantages—it is simple and accurate. It is simple because the company does not have to develop a means of estimating uncollectibles—no estimate is needed. It is accurate because no estimation errors are made—there are no estimates.

Publicly held companies must abide by the rules of accounting theory, so they cannot use the direct write-off method. Owners of small businesses often ignore the major objections to the direct write-off method and use it because it is so simple to apply. The Internal Revenue Service also allows its use on income tax returns.

Percentage of Credit Sales Method

Unlike the direct write-off method, the percentage of credit sales method records bad debts expense before we know which specific customers' accounts will be uncollectible. The percentage of credit sales method requires that an estimate of uncollectibles be made at the end of each year by multiplying sales made on credit by a percentage. The percentage reflects management's estimate of the portion of the current year's credit sales that will ultimately prove uncollectible.

Management makes this estimate by examining the past experience of its collections, as well as the collection experience of similar companies having similar credit-granting policies. For example:

Sylvan, Inc., had total sales of $2,800,000 during 1987; $300,000 were cash sales and $2,500,000 were on credit. Sylvan's management determined that approximately $1\frac{1}{2}\%$ of the total credit sales would eventually prove uncollectible. That is, at

Direct write-off violates matching and distorts Accounts Receivable

Direct write-off method is simple and accurate

Percentage of credit sales method estimates uncollectible accounts

the end of 1987, management estimates that $1\frac{1}{2}$% of all the credit sales made during 1987 will never be collected.

Based on this estimate, the amount of the 1987 bad debts expense is calculated as follows:

Total sales.	$2,800,000
Less: Cash sales	−300,000
Credit sales	$2,500,000
Bad debts percentage, $1\frac{1}{2}$%, or	×.015
1987 Bad debts expense	$ 37,500

The following is the adjusting entry to record this estimate:

The entry to record an estimate of bad debts expense using the percentage of credit sales method

1987			
Dec. 31	Bad Debts Expense	37,500	
	Allowance for Uncollectible Accounts		37,500
	To record an estimate of the 1987 credit sales that are expected to be uncollectible.		

Bad Debts Expense is classified on the income statement as an operating expense — it's a cost of doing business. Allowance for Uncollectible Accounts is a contra account to the current asset Accounts Receivable. Remember: A contra asset is an asset account with a negative (credit) balance. It is subtracted from another asset account — in this case, Accounts Receivable.

The Allowance for Uncollectible Accounts is used:
(1) To show the reader the portion of receivables we expect *not* to collect

In the direct write-off method our debit was to Bad Debts Expense and our credit was to Accounts Receivable. Why did we credit a contra account in the percentage of credit sales method rather than crediting Accounts Receivable? The contra asset, Allowance for Uncollectible Accounts, is used for two reasons. First, use of this account allows the balance sheet to show the total accounts receivable and the portion of this total that the company expects not to collect. If Sylvan collects none of the $2,500,000 credit sales by the end of 1987, Accounts Receivable is disclosed on the 1987 balance sheet as follows:

Accounts Receivable.	$2,500,000	
Less: Allowance for Uncollectible Accounts.	(37,500)	$2,462,500

If we had credited Accounts Receivable, only the $2,462,500 amount could be disclosed. The balance sheet reader needs to know what part of the accounts receivable probably won't be collected.

(2) Because we can't credit Accounts Receivable subsidiary ledger accounts

A second, and more practical, reason that a contra asset was used is that it is impossible to properly post the credit to Accounts Receivable. Remember, whenever this account is debited or credited, we must post the amount to the general ledger account and to the subsidiary ledger account(s). At the time we estimate our bad debts we know the total amount of our uncollectibles, but we don't know which specific customers will not pay. We can't post to subsidiary ledger accounts because we don't know whose account to post. We use Allowance for Uncollectible Accounts until we determine which customers' accounts are bad.

For example, on January 15, 1988, Sylvan, Inc., determined that the $1,230 account of K. Wood could not be collected. The following entry is made to write off the account:

Entry to write off a customer's account when bad debts were estimated

```
1988
Jan. 15   Allowance for Uncollectible Accounts. . . . . . . . . . . . . . . . . . 1,230
              Accounts Receivable: K. Wood  . . . . . . . . . . . . . . . . . . .          1,230
          To write off the account of K. Wood that is determined to be
          uncollectible.
```

Now we can post the credit to the Accounts Receivable general ledger account and to K. Wood's Accounts Receivable subsidiary ledger account. Notice that no expense is recorded when the account is written off. The expense was estimated in advance as part of the $37,500 Bad Debts Expense calculated and recorded in the general journal on December 31, 1987.

The sequence of events thus far is this:

The percentage of credit sales procedure

1. Credit sales for the year are totaled.

2. Based on past experience, a percentage of the credit sales that will not be collected is estimated.

3. At the end of the year the amount of bad debts expense is calculated and recorded in the general journal by a debit to Bad Debts Expense and a credit to Allowance for Uncollectible Accounts. Notice that we have recorded the sales revenue and the bad debts expense in the same year — good matching.

4. Later, as an individual customer hasn't paid and it is determined that he or she won't pay, that customer's account is written off, reduced to zero, by debiting (reducing) the Allowance for Uncollectible Accounts, and by crediting (reducing) Accounts Receivable in both the general ledger and the subsidiary ledger.

There are cases where a particular account is identified and written off as uncollectible, and then that customer finally pays up. To follow the accounting procedures in this kind of case, let's continue with our example.

On January 20, 1988, Sylvan, Inc., wrote off M. Rose's $475 account, which was believed to be uncollectible. On January 31, a check was received from Rose to pay the account in full. The following journal entries are necessary to record these events:

Entries:
(1) To write off a customer's account

```
1988
Jan. 20   Allowance for Uncollectible Accounts . . . . . . . . . . . . . . . . . . 475
              Accounts Receivable: M. Rose . . . . . . . . . . . . . . . . . . . .          475
          To write off uncollectible account of M. Rose.
```

(2) To reinstate the account

```
       31   Accounts Receivable: M. Rose . . . . . . . . . . . . . . . . . . . . . . 475
              Allowance for Uncollectible Accounts . . . . . . . . . . . . . . . .          475
          To reinstate M. Rose's account previously written off.
```

(3) To record receipt of payment

```
       31   Cash . . . . . . . . . . . . . . . . . . . . . . . . . . . . . . . . . . . . 475
              Accounts Receivable: M. Rose . . . . . . . . . . . . . . . . . . . .          475
          To record payment of account in full.
```

The entry on January 31 to reinstate Rose's account does just that — it restores his account to where it was before the January 20 write-off entry. Rose's account is reinstated in Sylvan's general and subsidiary ledgers, showing that it is no longer considered a write-off; rather it is a paid-up account. The subsidiary ledger accounts provide a credit history for each customer. Reinstating Rose's account puts his credit history in a favorable position for him to ask for credit again in the future.

Let's return for a moment to the Allowance for Uncollectible Accounts, or the ***Allowance for Bad Debts,*** as it is sometimes called. Remember: We estimated, based on an accurate picture of past credit experience, that $37,500 in Accounts Receivable would not be paid. If Rose just paid his $475; what does that payment do to our estimate of uncollectibles? It does nothing. A total of $37,500 will eventually still not be paid. Instead of Rose, someone else, not yet identified, will turn out to be a nonpaying culprit.

Aging of Receivables Method

The aging of receivables method estimates uncollectible amounts

Like the percentage of credit sales method, the aging of receivables method of determining the amount of receivables that will not be collected involves recording bad debts expense before we know which specific customers' accounts will be uncollectible. It is more accurate than the percentage of credit sales method, but it requires a bit more work.

Instead of looking at the total credit sales made during a period, this method looks at how old an account receivable is at the end of a period. The older a particular account receivable is, the greater the likelihood that it will never be collected. For accounts receivable that are just past due, there is less certainty that they will not be collected.

The *aging of receivables method* entails performing three steps at the end of each period:

The aging of receivables procedure

1. Receivables are grouped by age. For example, a 2-month-past-due $10,000 account receivable and a 2-month-old $50 receivable are grouped together, while a 1-year, $1,000 receivable and a $100, year-old receivable are grouped together.

2. A percentage reflecting an estimate of how much will never be collected is applied to the total amount of receivables in each age group — perhaps 5% of the fresh (2-month-old) receivables is estimated to be uncollectible. This means that of the $10,050 total ($10,000 + $50), $502.50 (.05 × $10,050) is expected not to be collected. For the year-old receivables, let's say that 90% is estimated to be uncollectible. Of the $1,100 ($1,000 + $100) of receivables in this group, $990 (.90 × $1,100) are expected to be bad.

3. And finally, the amounts of the uncollectibles for each age group are added to get the total amount of uncollectibles estimated for the period. In our simple example, $502.50 + $990.00 = $1,492.50 total uncollectibles.

The estimates for the percentages to apply in each age group are determined from past experience, and generally in much the same way as the estimates for the percentage of credit sales method.

The example that appears below will illustrate the aging of receivables technique.

Murphy Company began operations on January 1, 1988. On December 31, 1988, the following aging schedule was prepared:

Accounts Receivable Aging Schedule
December 31, 1988

Customer's Name	Not Yet Due	1–30 Days Past Due	31–60 Days Past Due	61–90 Days Past Due	Over 90 Days Past Due
C. Abel	$ 250				
B. Barker	348				
A. Carwile			$ 615		
K. Dennis					$ 100
T. Eagleton				$ 78	
F. Farmer		$ 198			
H. Whitley		491			
R. Zifer	90				
Totals	$160,000	$45,000	$14,000	$2,500	$1,000

An aging schedule groups accounts by how old they are

Based on this schedule and after carefully considering the collection experience of similar companies in the industry, Murphy's management then prepared the following estimate of uncollectible accounts:

1988 estimate of uncollectible accounts based on the aging of receivables method

Estimate of Uncollectible Accounts
December 31, 1988

Age Category	Amount in the Age Category	Percentage Expected to Be Uncollectible	Amount Expected to Be Uncollectible
Not yet due	$160,000	2%	$3,200
1–30 days past due	45,000	5	2,250
31–60 days past due	14,000	15	2,100
61–90 days past due	2,500	40	1,000
Over 90 days past due	1,000	80	800
Totals	$222,500		$9,350

Since this is Murphy's first year of operations, the following entry would be prepared to record Bad Debts Expense for 1988:

The entry to record an estimate of Bad Debts Expense using the aging of receivables method

```
1988
Dec. 31   Bad Debts Expense............................. 9,350
              Allowance for Uncollectible Accounts..............        9,350
          To record bad debts expense for 1988.
```

During 1989, a number of individual accounts remained uncollected for so long that Murphy finally gave up expecting them to be paid. Murphy identified each account, declared it to be uncollectible, and wrote it off. The total amount written off for these uncollectible accounts was $7,150. The Allowance for Uncollectible Accounts was estimated to be $9,350. Thus, the difference between the allowance originally estimated and the write-offs, $9,350 − $7,150, leaves $2,200 remaining in the allowance account from 1988. We still expect $2,200 in 1988 receivables to be uncollectible, but we still haven't identified the individual customers' accounts.

As of December 31, 1989, new credit sales have been added to Accounts Receivable and collections and write-offs have been deducted; write-offs have been deducted from Allowance for Uncollectibles but 1989 Bad Debts Expense has not yet been added. The accounts, then, have the following balances:

Accounts Receivable..	$394,000
Allowance for Uncollectible Accounts	(2,200)

At the end of 1989, another schedule of 1989 accounts receivable grouped by age is prepared. The following estimate of uncollectible accounts is then made:

1989 estimate of uncollectible accounts using the aging of receivables method

Estimate of Uncollectible Accounts
December 31, 1989

Age Category	Amount in the Age Category	Percentage Expected to Be Uncollectible	Amount Expected to Be Uncollectible
Not yet due	$298,000	2%	$ 5,960
1–30 days past due	64,000	5	3,200
31–60 days past due	25,000	15	3,750
61–90 days past due	4,500	40	1,800
Over 90 days past due	2,500	80	2,000
Totals	$394,000		$16,710

We have estimated that $16,710 of accounts receivable on hand on December 31, 1989, will be uncollectible. Some of these are carried over from 1988 and were provided for in the bad debts entry on December 31, 1988. To be specific, the $2,200 balance in the allowance account applies to 1988 receivables. We don't want to record this $2,200 as Bad Debts Expense *again*—we already took care of this amount in 1988. We must deduct this amount, then, in calculating our 1989 Bad Debts Expense, as the following calculation shows:

The balance of Allowance for Uncollectible Accounts must be deducted when calculating Bad Debts Expense using the aging of receivables method

Bad Debts Expense for 1989:	
Total accounts estimated to be uncollectible on 12/31/89.............	$16,710
Less: Balance in Allowance for Uncollectible Accounts before 1989 Bad	
Debts Expense is recorded	2,200
Bad debts provision needed in 1989	$14,510

The following general journal entry is made:

```
1989
Dec. 31   Bad Debts Expense ...............................  14,510
                Allowance for Uncollectible Accounts .............        14,510
          To record bad debts expense for 1989.
```

The Allowance for Uncollectible Accounts appears in the general ledger as follows:

The Allowance for Uncollectible Accounts showing 1988 and 1989 transactions

Allowance for Uncollectible Accounts			
Total of specific accounts written off during 1989	7,150	1988 provision for uncollectible accounts	9,350
Total debits	7,150	Total credits	9,350
		Balance 12/31/89 before 1989 bad debts are recorded	2,200
		1989 provision for uncollectible accounts	14,510
		Balance 12/31/89 after 1989 bad debts are recorded	16,710

Sometimes the Allowance for Uncollectibles account may have a debit balance. This happens when we have written off more accounts than we estimated would go bad. When this happens the aging of receivables method requires that we add enough to the allowance account to produce the credit balance that the aging schedule indicates it should have. For example, assume in our previous illustration that the Allowance for Uncollectibles had a *debit* balance of $1,000 (we wrote off $10,350 of uncollectibles instead of $7,150). The calculation of bad debts expense would be as follows:

Bad Debts Expense for 1989:	
Total accounts estimated to be uncollectible on 12/31/89.	$16,710
Add: Debit balance in Allowance for Uncollectible Accounts before 1989 Bad Debts Expense is recorded	1,000
Bad debts provision needed in 1989.	$17,710

The Allowance for Uncollectibles would end up with a credit balance of $16,710 ($1,000 debit + $17,710 credit = $16,710 credit). This is exactly the amount that the aging schedule predicts will be uncollectible.

Remember, the aging schedule tells you the balance you will need in the allowance account. If the allowance already has a credit balance, deduct the credit balance from the aging schedule amount to derive bad debts expense. If the allowance has a debit balance, add the debit balance to the aging schedule amount to derive bad debts expense.

Inaccurate Estimates

The objectives of accounting for uncollectibles are: (1) to determine, as accurately as possible, the amount of accounts that will indeed be collected; and (2) to match the expense associated with not collecting, Bad Debts Expense, with the revenue that it helped to generate.

The direct write-off method accomplishes the first objective but ignores the second. The percentage of credit sales and the aging of receivables methods attempt to fulfill both objectives. In making this attempt these methods use estimates of future uncollectibles. Like any prediction of future events, these estimates are sometimes inaccurate. We adjust for—correct—the inaccurate estimates periodically (say, every 2 years or every 5 years). The accounting department of the company will be asked to do an analysis of the company's collections and write-offs to determine the amount that should be in the Allowance for Uncollectible Accounts. The techniques they use in making this determination are beyond the scope of this text. While we won't focus on how the analysis is made, we will discuss how the adjustment is recorded. Let's look at an example to see how the adjustment is made.

The accounting department prepares an analysis to calculate the error in estimating Bad Debts Expense

Salkward Co. has used the percentage of credit sales method to estimate bad debts for the past 5 years. On December 31, 1988, *after* Bad Debts Expense has been recorded for 1988, the receivables, allowance, and expense accounts have the following balances:

Accounts Receivable	$612,300
Allowance for Uncollectible Accounts.	12,200
Bad Debts Expense (1988)	5,000

Salkward's accounting department conducted an analysis which showed that a total of $14,800 is expected to be uncollectible. Salkward has accumulated an inaccuracy—an error—in its estimated bad debts over the last 5 years of $2,600 ($14,800 − $12,200). In fact, Salkward's Bad Debts Expense has been too low by a total of $2,600 over the 5 years:

Amount needed in Allowance for Uncollectible Accounts on 12/31/88.	$14,800
Less: Amount actually in Allowance for Uncollectible Accounts on 12/31/88.	(12,200)
Amount by which allowance must be increased (decreased)	$ 2,600

Inaccurate estimates are corrected by adjusting the current year's Bad Debts Expense and by correcting the balance of the Allowance for Uncollectible Accounts. Salkward needs to increase the allowance account and increase the expense account by making the following journal entry:

The entry to correct inaccurate estimate of Bad Debts Expense

1988			
Dec. 31	Bad Debts Expense (1988)	2,600	
	Allowance for Uncollectible Accounts.		2,600
	To correct for inaccurate estimates in bad debts over the past 5 years.		

If Salkward's estimated bad debts has been too high, the expense would have been credited and the allowance debited.

Account balances before and after the correcting entry are:

	Balance before Correction	Balance after Correction
Accounts Receivable.	$612,300	$612,300
Allowance for Uncollectible Accounts.	12,200	14,800
Bad Debts Expense (1988)	5,000	7,600

.W. T. GRANT BANKRUPTCY—CREDIT POLICY A CONTRIBUTING FACTOR

By Stanley H. Slom

When W. T. Grant Co. went into bankruptcy on Oct. 2, 1975, the giant retailer's downfall was widely regarded as a classic example of a company that overreached itself and failed to attract a large and loyal clientele.

Now as a court-appointed trustee probes into the reasons for the biggest retailing failure in history, another picture of Grant is beginning to emerge from thousands of pages of testimony by former executives and other employees. It shows a company that was suffering from a host of internal problems and lacking budget and credit controls.

John E. Sundman, Grant's senior vice-president and treasurer, described credit controls as a disaster area. Before he joined Grant, consumer credit was approved at the store level, he said, and the rejection rate was 20%. That responsibility was transferred to headquarters in October 1974, and rejections of consumer applications soared to 80%.

Mr. Sundman gave an illustration of Grant's credit reputation before he joined the company. "My son-in-law, who was an officer in the Army post (Fort Monmouth, N.J.) at that time, told me that it was common knowledge among the enlisted men that the best way to furnish a house when they moved to a new post was to get it on credit from Grant, because they were fairly confident that they wouldn't have to pay for it if they didn't want to," he said.

In fact, Grant headquarters encouraged the stores to promote consumer credit even though it was costing the company somewhere between 15% and 19% of its sales, he said. As of the year ended Jan. 30, 1975, Grant's sales were $1.7 billion.

Mr. Sundman said that prior to Feb. 1, 1975, he couldn't rely with confidence upon any credit information figures coming out of Grant's stores in the Southeast. There was,

he said, improper reporting of delinquent customer accounts, and often merchandise was repossessed without the delinquent customer's account being credited or the merchandise entered on the store records.

Also, he said, important information was lacking concerning the aging of accounts receivable throughout the Grant chain. Aging is the amount of time an account is unpaid. At one point, he said he found that someone had changed the time of writing off bad debts, which averaged $2 million a month, to nine months from six months.

Based on the information he had, Mr. Sundman said, he reached the conclusion that Grant's profit for the year ended Jan. 31, 1974—the period in which the bad-debts time was lengthened—had been overstated to make the company look better.

Source: *The Wall Street Journal*, February 4, 1977, page 6.

Someone in the W. T. Grant organization was "improving" profits by $2 million per month by delaying the write-off of uncollectible accounts. You know that the entry to write off an account usually does not affect bad debts expense or any revenue accounts; how, then, did the delay benefit Grant? We can only guess exactly how the delay helped. The most likely explanation goes something like this:

Since Grant was using the aging of receivables method, bad debts could have been manipulated by changing the aging categories—some accounts could thereby be moved from a category with a high percentage of uncollectibility to a category with a lower percentage of uncollectibility. Thus, the monthly estimate of bad debts expense would be lower and net income would be higher—by $2 million per month—than it would have been if the receivables had been aged properly.

1988 Bad Debts Expense now contains $5,000 that applies directly to 1988 credit sales and $2,600 that is a correction of inaccurate estimates over the past 5 years. Generally accepted accounting principles require that we correct errors in estimates in this way even though we introduce some mismatching—the $2,600 is shown as a 1988 expense even though it applies to 1984, 1985, 1986, 1987, and 1988.

Salkward's management will adjust the percentage applied to each year's credit sales in the future to calculate a more accurate estimate of uncollectibles. Instead of using, say, $1\frac{1}{4}$% of credit sales, it may determine that $1\frac{1}{2}$% of credit sales is a better estimate.

Uncollectible Accounts — Some Practical Considerations

The concepts and methods that you learn from any accounting textbook often are modified to meet the needs of actual operating companies. In our examples we have shown bad debts estimated on December 31, the last day of the accounting period. In practice a company may prepare an income statement each month. Monthly statements require monthly estimates of bad debts expense. The procedures you have learned for the year-end also can be used at the end of a month, a quarter, or a semiannual period. To simplify the process of estimating, a company may choose to use the percentage of credit sales method at the end of each month and the more accurate aging of receivables method at year-end.

Receivables with Credit Balances

Receivables with credit balances are shown on the balance sheet as current liabilities

A credit balance may appear in the account receivable for a particular customer when credits in excess of the account balance are entered in that customer's account. These credits typically result from payments in excess of the amount owed, or from returns of merchandise. An account receivable with a credit balance means that the company has an obligation to that customer. The accountant recognizes and makes known this obligation by classifying any account receivable having a credit balance under the classification current liabilities on the balance sheet.

Balance Sheet Presentation of Accounts Receivable

The following schedule was taken from the accounts receivable subsidiary ledger of Evans Company on December 31, 1988:

Customer's Name	Accounts Receivable Account Balance Debit (Credit)
R. Luttrell	$ 290
G. Jennings	120
K. Kaiser	(300)
W. Lucas	68
B. Miller	415
I. Natoli	172
L. Oswald	350
Total	$1,115

Assume that the Allowance for Uncollectible Accounts has a balance of $65, after providing for 1988 bad debts expense. Accounts Receivable would be disclosed as follows on the 1988 balance sheet (note that the total accounts with debit balances, $1,415, is shown as an asset, while the account with a credit balance is classified as a liability):

EVANS COMPANY
Partial Balance Sheet
December 31, 1988

Assets

Current Assets:
Cash. . . . . $xxxxx
Marketable Securities. xxxxx
Accounts Receivable. $1,415
Less: Allowance for Uncollectible
    Accounts. . . . . (65) $1,350

Liabilities and Owner's Equity

Current Liabilities:
Accounts Payable . . . . $xxxxx
Payable to Customers. 300

NOTES RECEIVABLE

A *promissory note* is a written promise to a person or organization to pay a specific sum of money either on demand or at a specified future date. The person or organization promised payment regards this note as a *note receivable.* The note is signed by the *maker* and is usually payable to the *payee* or the payee's agent. The *maturity value* of a note is the total amount that must be paid by the payee on the future date named in the note. Notes may be *interest-bearing* or *non-interest-bearing.* An interest-bearing note (see example shown below) requires the maker to pay the face amount of the note *plus* interest. This interest is usually paid on the maturity date of the note. A non-interest-bearing note (see example shown on page 313) requires the maker to pay only the face amount of the note at maturity.

Interest-Bearing Promissory Note.
An interest-bearing note is a promise to pay a specific amount plus interest on a certain future date.

| $10,000 | Dover, Florida | June 19, 1987 |

sixty days _____ after date _____ I ____ promise to pay to

the order of _____ Louise Riffle _____

Ten Thousand and 00/100-- dollars

for value received with interest at _____ 9% _____

payable at Creekside National Bank. _____

_____ Amy Selman

The note above does not name a specific maturity date but states that it is due 60 days after the date appearing on the note. You can easily find the maturity date by remembering a simple rule: ***Don't count the first day*** — *June 19* (the day the note was signed), ***but count the last day*** — *August 18.* This rule will come in handy when you're calculating interest a little later — remember it.

Accounts Receivable and Notes Receivable Compared

Some companies prefer to sell on credit to customers, accepting a promissory note rather than maintaining an open account receivable for the customer. The promissory note is considered a note receivable by the company and a note payable by the customer. (Accounting for notes payable will be discussed in Chapter 11.) Let's examine the differences between notes and accounts receivable and see why one might be preferred over the other.

Remember: An account receivable comes from an open credit arrangement in which the seller and buyer have a contract providing that the buyer will pay the seller for any goods and services purchased within a specified time — typically 30, 60, or 90 days. The buyer hasn't agreed to pay any specific amount but to pay for whatever is purchased. The buyer may later refuse to pay, claiming that no goods or services were received, that the quantity received was not that billed by the seller, that some goods were returned but his or her account was not credited, or that the quality was so poor that some adjustment should be made to the sales price. In short, there are many grounds for argument about the amount due to the seller.

Notes are preferable because: (1) They contain specific terms of payment . . .

A note receivable, on the other hand, is preferable because it is a written instrument defining specific terms of payment, signed by the buyer. The buyer must pay the amount shown on the face of the note — there can be no argument about conditions existing outside of what appears on the note itself. Of course, if the buyer has been wronged by the seller, the buyer may sue the seller for relief. This suit, however, is separate from the question of the payment of the note.

(2) They are negotiable . . .

Another feature of a note receivable that makes it a preferable method of payment for credit sales is that it is a ***negotiable instrument.*** This means the holder of the promised payment can sell that promise to someone else willing to buy it—though the original holder will receive less than the amount promised in the note. Selling a note is called ***discounting a note,*** a process we will get into a bit later in this chapter. Accounts receivable are not negotiable instruments; although they may be sold, the process is cumbersome and is usually done only for very large amounts.

(3) And they are for longer periods and bear interest

Finally, notes are preferable because they are usually for a longer period and because they bear interest. Accounts receivable are normally used where the credit period is relatively short—30, 60, or 90 days—and no interest charge is made.

Notes, then, are preferable because they represent a stronger claim, are negotiable instruments, are for longer terms, and bear interest. For these reasons many companies will accept a note receivable in payment of a past-due account receivable.

Determining Interest on Notes

Interest formula

Interest earned on notes receivable can be calculated by the simple interest formula:

$$\textbf{Interest} = \textbf{principal} \times \textbf{rate} \times \textbf{time}$$
$$I = P \times R \times T$$

where Principal = the maturity value of the note excluding interest

Rate = the annual interest rate specified on the face of the note

Time = the number of days for which interest is calculated divided by 360 days (We are using 360 days for simplicity; most financial institutions use 365 days.)

The interest due for the interest-bearing note payable to Louise Riffle, illustrated on page 310, is calculated as follows:

Interest for the full 60 days

$$\text{Interest} = \$10,000 \times .09 \times \tfrac{60}{360}$$
$$= \$900 \times \tfrac{1}{6}$$
$$= \$150$$

If Louise Riffle's accounting year ended on July 31, she would need to prepare an adjusting entry to record interest earned up until that date. This calculation would be as follows:

Interest accrued after 42 days (Remember—Don't count the day the note was signed.)

$$\text{Interest} = \$10,000 \times .09 \times \text{time}$$
$$\text{Time} = 11 \text{ days in June (June 20–30)}$$
$$+ \underline{31} \text{ days in July (July 1–31)}$$
$$= \underline{\underline{42}} \text{ days (June 20–July 31)}$$

Counting of days begins on June 20 since the first full day is assumed to have elapsed by that date.

$$\text{Interest} = \$10,000 \times .09 \times \tfrac{42}{360}$$
$$= \$900 \times \tfrac{42}{360}$$
$$= \$105$$

| **Recording Notes and Interest** | Louise Riffle would record the note received from Amy Selman as follows: |

Entries to record:

(1) Receipt of note

1987

June 19	Notes Receivable	10,000	
	Sales.		10,000
	To record sale, 60-day, 9% note received.		

(2) Accrual of interest

July 31	Interest Receivable	105	
	Interest Income		105
	To record interest earned on Selman note.		

(3) Receipt of payment at maturity

Aug. 18	Cash.	10,150	
	Notes Receivable		10,000
	Interest Receivable		105
	Interest Income		45
	To record receipt of principal and interest on Selman note at maturity.		

Comments about the Preceding Entries

June 19   The assumption was made that the $10,000 note was received in a sale transaction. If the note had been received in payment of an account receivable, the credit in the entry would have been to Accounts Receivable: Selman. No interest is recorded on the note until it is earned (until the note has been held for a period of time). Interest is earned as time passes.

July 31   Since Riffle's fiscal year ends July 31, interest earned through that day, $105, was accrued. Interest Receivable, $105, appears along with the Notes Receivable, $10,000, under current assets on the July 31 balance sheet. The Interest Receivable account is carried forward into the next accounting year, when it will be collected. Interest income, $105, would be shown under other income and expense on the income statement for the year ended July 31, 1987. Interest Income is closed to Expense and Revenue Summary on July 31. No reversing entry is made on August 1, 1987.

August 18   The full amount of the principal and interest were collected. The remaining $45 ($10,000 $\times$ .09 $\times \frac{18}{360}$) interest earned was recorded. Note that Riffle earned 42 days of interest, $105, before July 31; and 18 days of interest, $45, after July 31. The full $150 interest was collected on August 18.

Dishonored Notes

A note that is not paid at maturity is a *dishonored note*

A note that is not paid at maturity is a ***dishonored note.*** Notes receivable that have not yet matured are recorded in the Notes Receivable account. When a note passes its maturity date but has not been paid, the note becomes dishonored and the holder transfers the record of it to Accounts Receivable. For example, assume that the Kintigh Co. received a $2,000, 6% note due in 90 days from Helms, Inc., in payment of a past-due account receivable. At maturity Helms failed to pay the $2,000 plus $30 interest due.

Day 1	Notes Receivable	2,000	
	Accounts Receivable: Helms		2,000
	To record receipt of $2,000, 6%, 90-day note in settlement of an account receivable.		

Day 90	Accounts Receivable	2,030	
	Interest Income		30
	Notes Receivable		2,000

To record interest earned ($2,000 × .06 × $\frac{90}{360}$) and dishonoring of note by Helms.

Kintigh recorded the $30 interest earned even though Helms did not pay. Kintigh has allowed Helms the use of the $2,000 for 90 days and is entitled to the $30 interest charge for the 90 days of credit extended to Helms. Kintigh's claim on day 90 is $2,030, not just the $2,000 face value of the note. Interest will continue to accrue on the past-due receivable. Some state laws allow the rate to increase to the maximum legal limit. The longer the maker of the note delays paying, the more he or she will owe the payee of the note.

The probability of collecting Helm's account receivable may be very low. This fact should be considered by Kintigh's management in calculating the estimate of Bad Debts Expense at the end of the current year.

Non-Interest-Bearing Notes

Maturity value of non-interest-bearing notes includes principal and interest

A ***non-interest-bearing promissory note*** contains all of the characteristics of an interest-bearing note except that the maturity value includes principal *and* interest. It would be accurate to say that these notes *include* interest in the face of the note. The holder of a non-interest-bearing note does earn interest. The interest is *included in* the amount written on the face of the note *rather than added to* the face value of the note.

Assume that Tim Brooks, Inc., received a note from Doug Davis to settle a $5,000 account receivable. Brooks agreed to accept from Davis a note for $5,200 maturing in 6 months. An illustration of this type of note appears below.

Non-Interest-Bearing Note.

This non-interest-bearing note is for $5,200—$5,000 principal; $200 interest.

$5,200   Old Town, Maine   January 1, 1986

six months   after date   I   promise to pay to

the order of   Tim Brooks, Inc.

Five Thousand Two Hundred and 00/100--- dollars

for value received.

Payable at Valley National Bank.

Doug Davis

The $200 above the amount of the $5,000 account receivable represents the interest that will be paid to Brooks for his having to wait 6 months to receive payment. On the day Brooks receives the note, no interest has been earned. Brooks will earn the interest as the 6-month period passes.

Brooks would prepare the following entries to account for this note:

Entries to record:
(1) Receipt of non-interest-bearing note

1986			
Jan. 1	Notes Receivable	5,200	
	Accounts Receivable: Davis		5,000
	Discount on Notes Receivable		200

To record receipt of $5,200, 6-month note in settlement of $5,000 account.

(2) Accrual of interest for the full term of the note

June 30   Discount on Notes Receivable 200
                    Interest Income   200
                    To record interest earned on Davis note.

(3) Receipt of payment at maturity

    30   Cash 5,200
                    Notes Receivable   5,200
                    To record receipt of payment on Davis note.

Discount on notes receivable is a contra-asset account showing the unearned interest on the non-interest-bearing note

Discount on Notes Receivable reflects the *unearned* interest on the note. It is a contra-current-asset account which is shown as a deduction from notes receivable on the balance sheet.

If Brooks' fiscal year had ended during the 6-month period, say, March 31, the amount of interest earned as of the last day of the year would have been transferred from the Discount on Notes Receivable account to the Interest Income account. On the date the note is due, the remainder of the amount in the discount account would be transferred to Interest Income. This process is illustrated below:

The discount is transferred to Interest Income as it is earned over time

January 1		March 31		June 30	
$5,200	Note Receivable	$5,200	Note Receivable	$5,200	Note Receivable
(200)	Discount	(100)	Discount	0	Discount
$5,000	Note Receivable (net)	$5,100	Note Receivable (net)	$5,200	Note Receivable (net)
$ 0	Interest Income	$ 100	Interest Income	$ 100	Interest Income (Jan. 1–Mar. 31)
				$ 100	Interest Income (Apr. 1–June 30)

Notice that as the amount of the discount decreases the amount that Brooks has "earned" increases. The $5,000 was earned when Brooks sold merchandise to Davis on account sometime before January 1; the $200 interest was earned as the 6-month period passed—$100 over the first 3 months and $100 over the last 3 months. By June 30, then, Brooks has earned the entire $5,200.

Discounting Notes Receivable

"Selling" a note receivable to a bank is called *discounting the note*

A holder of a note who needs cash before the note matures may take the note to a bank, which ***discounts*** it. This simply means that the bank "buys" the note from the holder, paying the holder an amount of cash that is normally less than the maturity value of the note, and then collects the maturity value from the maker at the maturity date. The difference between the amount that the payee receives from the bank and the maturity value of the note is the bank's fee for discounting the note. In effect, this difference is the interest the bank will earn instead of the payee.

The bank calculates its fee for accepting the note from the holder, the ***discount,*** by applying a discount rate to the maturity value of the note. This ***discount rate*** is really an interest rate charged by the bank for holding the note for the remainder of its life.

Notes may be discounted with recourse or without recourse

What happens if the maker of the note fails to pay the bank at maturity? If the note was discounted ***with recourse,*** the bank will demand payment from the original payee. Discounting with recourse means that the bank requires the payee on the note to agree to pay the amount of the note if the maker won't pay it at maturity. If the note was discounted ***without recourse,*** the bank is stuck with the loss, unable to commit the original payee to pay the amount the maker fails to pay. So you can be sure that almost no bank discounts without recourse.

Both interest-bearing and non-interest-bearing notes may be discounted. We will demonstrate the calculations and entries associated with discounting interest-bearing notes. Discounting non-interest-bearing notes will be left for a more advanced accounting course.

Calculating the Proceeds upon Discounting an Interest-Bearing Note

When discounting an interest-bearing note, the following formula can be used to calculate the amount of cash received — commonly referred to as the *proceeds:*

Formula for calculating the amount of cash received when a note is discounted

$$\text{Proceeds} \quad \text{equals} \quad \left(\begin{array}{l}\text{maturity value} \\ \text{of note}\end{array} \quad \text{less} \quad \begin{array}{l}\text{discount} \\ \text{amount}\end{array}\right)$$

$$\begin{array}{l}\text{Discount} \\ \text{amount}\end{array} \quad \text{equals} \quad \left(\begin{array}{l}\text{maturity value} \\ \text{of note}\end{array} \times \begin{array}{l}\text{discount} \\ \text{rate}\end{array} \times \begin{array}{l}\text{time remaining} \\ \text{until maturity}\end{array}\right)$$

Therefore,

$$\text{Proceeds} \quad \text{equals} \quad \left(\begin{array}{l}\text{maturity} \\ \text{value}\end{array}\right) \quad \text{less} \quad \left(\begin{array}{l}\text{maturity} \\ \text{value}\end{array} \times \begin{array}{l}\text{discount} \\ \text{rate}\end{array} \times \begin{array}{l}\text{time remaining} \\ \text{until maturity}\end{array}\right)$$

Victory Co. received a 6-month, 6%, $5,000 note from Langston, Inc., on January 1, 1988. Victory discounted the note with recourse at the Eastside National Bank on May 1, 1988. Eastside charged a 7% discount rate. The maturity value of the note and the proceeds received by Victory are calculated as follows:

Maturity value of the note:
Face value $5,000
Add: Interest for life of note ($5,000) (.06) ($\frac{1}{2}$ year)   150
Maturity value $5,150

Proceeds of the discounting:
Maturity value. $5,150.00
Less: Discount charged by Eastside ($5,150) (.07) ($\frac{2}{12}$ year) . . . .   (60.08)
Proceeds received by Victory $5,089.92

Recording the Discounting of an Interest-Bearing Note

Victory's entries related to this note would be as follows:

Entries to record:
(1) Receipt of note

1988			
Jan. 1	Notes Receivable	5,000	
	Sales		5,000
	To record sale to Langston, Inc., and receipt of 6-month, 6% note.		

(2) Accrual of interest earned as of discounting date

May 1	Interest Receivable	100	
	Interest Income		100
	To accrue the interest earned from the day the note was received until it was discounted. $5,000 $\times$ .06 $\times \frac{1}{12}$ = $25 per month; $25 per month $\times$ 4 months = $100 interest for 4 months (1/1–5/1).		

(3) The proceeds received, financing fee, and contingent obligation

May 1	Cash 5,089.92	
	Financing Expense 10.08	
	Interest Receivable	100.00
	Notes Receivable Discounted	5,000.00

To record discounting of Langston, Inc., note with recourse at Eastside Bank. Financing fee ($10.08) equals face value ($5,000) plus interest earned to date ($100) less proceeds ($5,089.92).

(4) Removal of note and contingent obligation when maker pays bank at maturity

June 30	Notes Receivable Discounted 5,000	
	Notes Receivable	5,000

To remove the Langston note from the books. The maker paid the bank at maturity.

Before the note was discounted, that is, up through April 30, Victory accrued and recorded the interest that had been earned at the original 6% interest rate. This entry is exactly the same type of entry as is made at the end of the company's fiscal year to accrue interest earned.

The May 1 entry to record the discounting of the note contains two items that need special attention and explanation. First, the Financing Expense ($10.08) amounts to the difference between what Victory would have gotten if the principal plus the full amount of interest earned to date had been paid ($5,100) and the amount actually received ($5,089.92). The Financing Expense, $5,100 − $5,089.92 = $10.08, eventually appears on Victory's income statement in the other income and expense category.

Noted Receivable Discounted is a contra asset representing a contingent obligation

Second, since the note was discounted with recourse, the Notes Receivable Discounted account was credited to reflect the fact that Victory has a *contingent obligation,* a potential responsibility, to pay the note if Langston fails to settle with the bank at maturity. If the note had been discounted without recourse, the credit would simply have been to Notes Receivable.

Immediately following the discounting, Victory has two accounts in its books:

1. Notes Receivable . . . . $5,000   Debit balance

2. Notes Receivable Discounted . . . . ($5,000)   Credit balance

Both of these accounts would appear under current assets on a balance sheet prepared at this time. Notes Receivable Discounted is a contra account to Notes Receivable.

You should take care not to confuse Notes Receivable Discounted with Discount on Notes Receivable. Notes Receivable Discounted is a contra asset indicating a contingent obligation. Discount on Notes Receivable is a contra asset reflecting the unearned interest included in the face amount of a non-interest-bearing note.

Discounting an Interest-Bearing Note: Maker Dishonors

Let's do a second illustration of the discounting process to ensure that you are familiar with the calculations and entries. In this example the maker of the note will not pay the bank at maturity. Pay close attention to the entries used to record this fact.

Dill Company received an $8,000, 9% note from Stewart, Inc. The 120-day note was received on October 31 and discounted at the West End Bank on December 30, 1986, with recourse. The bank's discount rate was 10%.

1986
Oct. 31 Notes Receivable 8,000
        Accounts Receivable: Stewart   8,000
        To record receipt of a 120-day, 9% note from Stewart in
        settlement of an open account.

Dec. 30 Interest Receivable   120
        Interest Income   120
        To accrue interest earned for 60 days ($8,000 $\times$ .09 $\times \frac{60}{360}$).

   30 Cash 8,102.67
        Financing Expense 17.33
        Interest Receivable 120.00
        Notes Receivable Discounted 8,000.00
        To record discounting Stewart note at West End Bank with
        recourse.

Computations	
Proceeds:	
Face value.	$8,000.00
Add: Total interest during life of note ($8,000 $\times$ .09 $\times \frac{120}{360}$)	240.00
Maturity value	$8,240.00
Less: Discount ($8,240 $\times$ .10 $\times \frac{60}{360}$).	(137.33)
Total proceeds.	$8,102.67
Financing expense;	
Face value.	$8,000.00
Add: Interest earned to date ($8,000 $\times$ .09 $\times \frac{60}{360}$)	120.00
Less: Proceeds	(8,102.67)
Total financing expense.	$ 17.33

1987

Entries made when the maker dishonors his or her discounted note

Feb. 28 Accounts Receivable: Stewart 8,240
        Cash   8,240
        To record payment to West End Bank to settle Stewart's note plus
        interest. Stewart dishonored the note.

   28 Notes Receivable Discounted 8,000
        Notes Receivable   8,000
        To remove Stewart's note and the associated contingent obliga-
        tion.

Notice that Dill was required to pay the bank $8,240, the same amount that Stewart should have paid. Also observe that Dill removed the $8,000 note and the contingent obligation from the records. The claim that Dill has against Stewart now amounts to $8,240, which is carried as an account receivable.

Receivables from Officers and Owners

Receivables from officers and owners should be separately disclosed on the balance sheet

Occasionally a business firm will lend available cash to its owners or to its managers who need loans for their personal use. After all, if a firm has surplus cash and is expected to put it to use earning income, it can accomplish this by making interest-earning loans to its owners and managers. In some cases these loans are represented by formal instruments, such as promissory notes; in other cases, they exist only in the form of verbal agreements. Most accountants believe that while these agreements may be entirely proper, it is best to identify such receivables separately on the balance sheet—specifying them as loans to owners, managers, or officers of the firm. This disclosure will highlight the fact that the business has entered into a transaction with a party who is closely related to it. Readers of the balance sheet will then be fully informed of the loan and may investigate the circumstances surrounding the transaction if they so desire.

External Credit: Credit Card Sales

External credit is used when a company accepts VISA, MasterCard, and similar charge cards

Most retailers today make sales to customers accepting credit cards such as VISA, MasterCard, American Express, and Diners Card. Each of these credit cards represents credit provided by an organization external to the customer and retailer. Thus, this form of credit is sometimes referred to as *external credit.*

A customer making a purchase through use of a credit card signs a standard form agreeing to pay to the credit card company the amount of the sale. The retailer sends this form to the credit card company, which in turn pays the amount of the credit sale to the retailer.

The credit card company charges the retailer a fee for providing credit to the customer. The fee is commonly a percentage of the amount of credit—the sales price of the product or service—provided. For this fee, the credit card company not only provides the credit, but in doing so, assumes the costs of providing credit—credit investigation, recordkeeping, billing, and bad debt losses.

The following is an example showing how a retailer using the external credit of a credit card company records its transactions.

Buckeye Stores has an agreement with Plastic Money Charge cards which provides that Buckeye will remit charge tickets to Plastic Money and receive cash within 10 days. Plastic Money will charge Buckeye 8% of the gross sales for which it provides credit for this service. On August 1, Buckeye had charge sales of $10,000 and made the following journal entry.

Entries to record:
(1) Sales on external credit cards

```
1988
Aug. 1   Receivable from Plastic Money . . . . . . . . . . . . . . . . . . . . . . .   9,200
         Financing Expense . . . . . . . . . . . . . . . . . . . . . . . . . . . . .     800
              Sales . . . . . . . . . . . . . . . . . . . . . . . . . . . . . . . . . . . .         10,000
         To record sales less financing expense of $800 ($10,000 × .08)
         remitted to Plastic Money for reimbursement.
```

The following entry would be made to record the receipt of cash from Plastic Money:

(2) Collection from credit card company

```
1988
Aug. 5   Cash . . . . . . . . . . . . . . . . . . . . . . . . . . . . . . . . . . . . . . .   9,200
              Receivable from Plastic Money . . . . . . . . . . . . . . . . . . .           9,200
         To record cash received from credit card company.
```

Receivables on the Balance Sheet

The partial balance sheet illustrated on page 319 shows the disclosure of all receivables and related accounts discussed in this chapter.

```
                          HARTE COMPANY
                        Partial Balance Sheet
                         December 31, 1987
───────────────────────────────────────────────────────────────────────
                               Assets
Current assets:
    Cash . . . . . . . . . . . . . . . . . . . . . . . . . . .    $ 30,000
    Marketable Securities . . . . . . . . . . . . . . . . . .        5,000
    Receivable from Credit Card Company. . . . . . . . . . .       130,200
    Notes Receivable. . . . . . . . . . . . . . . . . . .   $25,000
    Less: Discount on Notes Receivable . . . . . . . . . . . .  (1,200)
          Notes Receivable Discounted . . . . . . . . . . . .   (4,000)    19,800

    Accounts Receivable . . . . . . . . . . . . . . . . . .   $62,000
    Less: Allowance for Uncollectible
          Accounts . . . . . . . . . . . . . . . . . . . .   (2,635)     59,365
    Receivable from Officers . . . . . . . . . . . . . . . . .      2,500
    Interest Receivable . . . . . . . . . . . . . . . . . . . .      1,435
```

```
                             Liabilities
Current liabilities:
    Accounts Payable. . . . . . . . . . . . . . . . . . . . . .   $140,000
    Payable to Customers . . . . . . . . . . . . . . . . . . . .      1,850
```

CHAPTER SUMMARY

When customers buy on credit, the seller's accounting records show this transaction as an account receivable, commonly referred to as an ***open account.*** An ***account receivable*** indicates the buyer's agreement to pay the seller for goods or services purchased. Accounts receivable that are not expected to be collected after a reasonable length of time are recognized by the seller as ***bad debts expense*** — one of the costs of providing credit to customers.

The ***direct write-off method*** delays the recognition of a bad debts expense until a specific account is identified as uncollectible. This method is not in accord with good accounting practice because it does not properly match expenses and revenues and because it distorts the measurement of the amount of Accounts Receivable. The ***percentage of credit sales method*** and the ***aging of receivables method*** both estimate Bad Debts Expense prior to identifying a specific uncollectible account. These methods do a better job of matching and of measuring Accounts Receivable. Errors resulting from inaccurate estimates are corrected in future periods based on analyses by the firm's accounting department.

Estimates of accounts receivable that won't be collected are recorded by debiting Bad Debts Expense and crediting Allowance for Uncollectible Accounts. A specific customer's account is written off by debiting Allowance for Uncollectible Accounts and crediting Accounts Receivable. If a customer later pays an account that was written off, the account is reinstated by debiting Accounts Receivable and crediting Allowance for Uncollectible Accounts; payment is then recorded by debiting Cash and crediting Accounts Receivable.

Accounts Receivable and Allowance for Uncollectible Accounts are classified as current assets on the firm's balance sheet. A customer's account receivable with a credit balance is reported as a current liability for the firm.

Promissory notes — recorded as notes receivable — are often used as a way of offering credit when a sale is made or as a way of formally extending the length of the credit period when an account receivable is past due. Promissory notes are written promises to pay. The promise may specify a face amount — the *principal* — and interest separately payable. Or the promise may specify only a face amount that includes principal and interest, payable together.

Promissory notes may be held until maturity or they may be discounted at a bank prior to maturity. When a note is *discounted with recourse,* and if the maker fails to pay at maturity, then the payee is responsible for paying the bank at maturity. A note *discounted without recourse* carries no such obligation.

When the maker of a note fails to pay at maturity, the payee changes the account from a note receivable to an account receivable and, of course, continues to try to collect.

Interest income is recognized on notes as it is earned. Journal entries are made to formally record the interest income earned either when a note is discounted, when an income statement is prepared, or at the maturity date of the note. In many cases part of the interest earned may be recognized at more than one of these dates.

Receivables from officers and owners — a firm's loans to its officers or owners — are identified on the balance sheet separately from other receivables. This is done to inform readers that transactions have occurred between the business and individuals closely related to it.

Many retailers rely on *external credit* — credit card plans — to provide credit for their sales. The credit card company normally charges a fee that is a percentage of the sales price for providing credit for the retailer.

IMPORTANT TERMS USED IN THIS CHAPTER

Accounts receivable Claims against customers for goods or services sold on credit. These claims are not supported by formal written promises to pay specific amounts, but rather are based on an agreement by the buyer to pay for goods or services purchased. (page 296)

Aging of receivables method A method of calculating the amount of uncollectible accounts and bad debts expense based on the age of the account. The older the uncollectible account, the higher the percentage of the amount of the account that is estimated to be uncollectible. (page 303)

Contingent obligation An obligation that does not currently exist but that may exist in the future if certain events occur. A company discounting a note with recourse at a bank will have a liability to pay the maturity value to the bank if the maker fails to do so. The company's obligation is contingent on the maker's failure to pay the bank. (page 316)

Direct write-off method The method of accounting for uncollectible receivables that requires no estimate of bad debts expense. When a specific individual account is deemed uncollectible, an entry is prepared debiting Bad Debts Expense and crediting Accounts Receivable. This method is not generally accepted practice because it fails to match expenses and revenues and to properly measure the amount of receivables. (page 299)

Discount on Notes Receivable An account used in accounting for non-interest-bearing notes. The balance of this account represents the amount of unearned interest that is included in the face amount of the note. This account has a credit balance and is disclosed as a contra current asset — subtracted from Notes Receivable. (page 314)

Discounting a note receivable The process of "selling" a note receivable before its maturity date. The note is sold for a cash value less than its maturity value—hence, the term *discounting*. (page 314)

Dishonored note receivable A promissory note that the maker fails to pay on the maturity date. (page 316)

Maker of promissory note An individual who signs a promissory note promising to pay a specified amount at maturity. (page 310)

Matching principle An underlying assumption of the income measurement process which states that expenses should be recognized in the same period as the revenues they helped to produce. (page 300)

Maturity value The amount payable on the date at which a promissory note is due. (page 310)

Notes Receivable Discounted An account used to record the face value of notes that have been discounted. It is disclosed as a contra account to Notes Receivable and represents a contingent obligation of the payee to remit the maturity value of the note should the maker fail to do so. (page 316)

Payee of promissory note The individual or company specified to receive payment at the maturity date of the promissory note. (page 310)

Percentage of credit sales method A method of calculating bad debts expense, based on the total credit sales made during a year. Based on past experience from collecting payment for credit sales, a percentage of the total credit sales is estimated never to be collected. (page 300)

Proceeds The amount of cash received from discounting a promissory note at a bank. The proceeds will be less than the maturity value of the note; the difference is the discount (see "Discounting a note receivable"). (page 315)

Promissory note A written promise to pay a specific sum of money on demand or at a certain future date. (page 310)

Promissory note—interest-bearing A promissory note that provides for repayment of principal plus interest at an annual rate specified in the note. (page 310)

Promissory note—non-interest-bearing A promissory note that includes interest in the amount specified on the face of the note as its maturity value. (page 313)

Reinstate an account receivable An accounting procedure of putting back on the books as an account receivable an account previously written off as uncollectible. Accounts are reinstated when payment is (unexpectedly) received. (page 302)

With recourse A stipulation in the discounting of a note receivable which provides that the individual discounting the note will be responsible for paying the maturity value should the maker fail to pay. (page 314)

Without recourse A stipulation in the discounting of a note receivable which provides that only the maker is responsible for paying the maturity value of the note. (page 314)

QUESTIONS

1. What is an account receivable? How does an account receivable differ from a trade receivable or open account?

2. When an entry is made involving accounts receivable, it must be posted to two ledgers. Why are two postings necessary? What two ledgers are involved?

3. What is the purpose of reconciling general and subsidiary accounts receivable ledgers?

4. What are the two major objections to the use of the direct write-off method of accounting for uncollectible accounts?

5. Does the percentage of credit sales method of estimating uncollectible accounts violate the matching principle? Explain.

6. When bad debts expense is estimated, a contra asset, Allowance for Uncollectible Accounts, is credited. Why isn't Accounts Receivable credited instead?

7. Under what circumstances is it necessary to reinstate a customer's account?

8. What is the purpose of aging receivables?

9. When the aging of receivables method is used, why is it necessary to consider the balance in Allowance for Uncollectible Accounts in determining the current Bad Debts Expense?

10. Lewis Co.'s accounting department determined that over the past 5 years Bad Debts Expense has been too high by $4,200. What will Lewis do to correct this error in estimating?

11. Wash Engines, Inc., has several customers' accounts with credit balances. What things could have occurred to cause these credit balances?

12. What is the difference between an account receivable and a note receivable?

13. Why might a company rather hold a note receivable from a customer than an account receivable?

14. What is a dishonored note receivable?

15. Is it true that no interest is earned when a non-interest-bearing note is held?

16. What does the balance of Discount on Notes Receivable represent? Where does this account appear on a balance sheet?

17. Rulco, Inc., can discount a customer's note at the bank "with recourse" or "without recourse." What is the difference between these two? Which will Rulco prefer?

18. Tower Co. discounted a customer's note receivable with recourse. How is the contingent obligation on this note shown on the balance sheet?

19. What special treatment is given receivables from officers and owners of a company? Why is this special treatment necessary?

EXERCISES

Exercise 8-1
Determining and recording bad debts expense using the percentage of credit sales method

Java, Inc., uses the percentage of credit sales method to estimate uncollectible accounts. During 1988 Java's sales totaled $675,000; 92% of this amount was on credit. Java's management estimates that about $1\frac{1}{2}$% of credit sales will eventually prove uncollectible. Prepare the journal entry to record Bad Debts Expense for 1988.

(Check figure: Estimated Bad Debts Expense = $9,315)

Exercise 8-2
Calculating bad debts expense using the percentage of credit sales method and the direct write-off method

During the 2 years that Missing Links Gold Supplies has been in business, credit sales have amounted to $200,000 in year 1 and $400,000 in year 2. Missing Links wrote off customer accounts amounting to $1,800 in year 1 and $4,500 in year 2. Calculate Missing Links' Bad Debts Expense for each year assuming that (**a**) the percentage of credit sales method is used and management estimates that 2% of credit sales will prove uncollectible; and (**b**) the direct write-off method is used. Which method is considered preferable? Why?

(Check figure: Year 2 Bad Debts Expense using percentage of credit sales = $8,000)

Exercise 8-3

Writing off an uncollectible account; reinstating the account when the customer pays

Western Grain Co. sold $3,200 of wheat to Bagels Ltd., during 1987. When Bagels had not paid by October 5, 1988, Western decided to write off the account as uncollectible. On November 2, 1988, a check arrived from Bagels paying the account in full. Prepare the entries to write off the account, to reinstate the account, and to record the receipt of the $3,200. Western uses the percentage of credit sales method to account for uncollectible accounts.

Exercise 8-4

Determining bad debts expense by analyzing Allowance for Uncollectible Accounts

Winde Tea Co. uses the percentage of credit sales method to estimate uncollectible accounts. On January 1, 1986, the Allowance for Uncollectible Accounts had a credit balance of $6,400. During 1986 customer accounts amounting to $5,300 were written off as uncollectible. The balance of the allowance account on December 31, 1986, was $8,640 after the entry to record Bad Debts Expense had been posted. Calculate the amount that was recorded as Bad Debts Expense for the year.

(Check figure: Bad Debts Expense for 1986 = $7,540)

Exercise 8-5

Selecting accounts to be included in Accounts Receivable

On December 31, 1988, Stewart Jewelers has receivables from the following individuals:

Name	Description	Balance Dr. (Cr.)
M. Blay	From sale of merchandise	$1,250
T. Warren	From sale of merchandise	(620)
S. Knecht	From cash loan (Knecht is President of Stewart)	4,000
W. Goode	From sale of merchandise	1,680
B. Purks	From sale of old cash register; Purks gave Stewart a note	500
C. Marshall	From sale of merchandise	2,360
O. Smith	From sale of merchandise	980

Calculate the total accounts receivable that should appear on Stewart's December 31, 1988, balance sheet. State how each amount you omitted from the above total would be disclosed on the balance sheet.

(Check figure: Total accounts receivable = $6,270)

Exercises 8-6

Calculating accrued interest earned on notes

Yates Electric received the following notes during 1987:

$8,000, 60-day, 6% note from Linder Homes, Inc. The note was received on November 16, 1987.
$6,000, 90-day, 10% note from Hunt Construction. The note matures on Feb. 29, 1988.
$4,992, 120-day note from Swank Condominiums. The non-interest-bearing note includes $192 interest in its face amount. The note was received on December 1, 1987.

Calculate the interest income that should be recognized on December 31, 1987, for each note.

(Check figure: $60 interest income on Linder Homes note)

Exercise 8-7

Recording transactions related to interest-bearing note

During 1986 Robbins Furniture Manufacturing entered into the following transactions with Kilbride Furniture Sales:

June 15   Robbins received a $24,000, 10%, 90-day note from Kilbride for an assortment of patio furniture.
     30   Robbins' accounting year ends.
Sept. 13 Robbins receives payment in full from Kilbride.

Prepare the proper journal entry for Robbins on each of the three dates. Show supporting calculations.

(Check figure: Interest income recorded on June 30 = $100)

Exercise 8-8
Calculating the proceeds upon discounting a note

Harris Wholesale Flowers accepted a $10,000 note from a customer in settlement of a past-due account receivable. The 120-day note bears interest at 18%. Needing cash desperately, Harris immediately took the note to Providence Bank and discounted it with recourse. The bank charged a 21% discount rate.

Calculate the proceeds—the amount of cash that Harris received upon discounting the note.

(Check figure: Cash proceeds received by Harris = $9,858)

PROBLEMS
Set A

Problem A8-1
Calculating bad debts expense using direct write-off, percentage of credit sales, and aging of receivables

The following facts relate to Hunter Farm Equipment Company:
a. January 1, 1988, balance of Allowance for Uncollectible Accounts, $5,650 (credit).
b. Total of customer accounts written off during 1988, $4,230.
c. Total sales during 1988, $405,000; 90% of sales are on credit.

Required

Calculate Hunter's Bad Debts Expense for 1988:
1. Assuming that the direct write-off method is used.
2. Assuming that the percentage of credit sales method is used; Hunter uses $2\frac{1}{2}$% to estimate.
3. Assuming that the aging of receivables method is used. An aging schedule shows that accounts totaling $9,620 are estimated to be uncollectible.

(Check figure: Bad Debts Expense using percentage of credit sales = $9,112.50)

Problem A8-2
Recording transactions relating to Accounts Receivable and bad debts

Selected transactions of McGee Security Co. for the years 1986 and 1987 are shown below:

1986

Jan.–Dec.	Total cash sales were $300,000; total credit sales were $1,200,000. (Prepare a summary entry.)
Jan.–Dec.	Collections on accounts amounted to $930,000. (Prepare a summary entry.)
Dec. 31	McGee estimated that uncollectible accounts would amount to about $1\frac{1}{2}$% of credit sales.

1987

Jan. 20	McGee wrote off the $870 account of Samantha Shiftless as uncollectible.
Mar. 4	The $2,660 account of D. Ed Beat was written off as uncollectible.
Apr. 30	A check was received from Samantha Shiftless in full settlement of her account, $870.
Jan.–Dec.	Various other individual accounts amounting to $28,550 were written off.
Jan.–Dec.	Total sales were $1,800,000; 8% of sales were for cash; the remaining sales were on account.
Jan.–Dec.	Total other cash collections were $1,364,000.
Dec. 31	McGee estimated Bad Debts Expense for 1987 using the same percentage as in the prior year.

Required

1. Prepare general journal entries to record the transactions described above. Calculations should be included as part of your journal entry explanation where appropriate.
2. Calculate the balance of Accounts Receivable and Allowance for Uncollectible Accounts on December 31, 1987.

(Check figure: Bad Debts Expense for 1987 = $24,840)

Problem A8-3
Preparing an aging schedule and entries to record bad debts expense

On June 30, 1986, Berry Office Supply has uncollected accounts receivable as shown at the top of page 325. Berry uses an aging schedule to prepare an estimate of uncollectible accounts for the year. Estimates of the percentage uncollectible in each category follow:

Customer Name	Amount	Collection Status
N. Julian	$1,240	Not yet due
J. Cleland	500	20 days past due
R. Hennessy	900	51 days past due
O. Juarez	440	Not yet due
T. Barnard	1,460	63 days past due
T. Fay	400	105 days past due
J. Upchurch	1,320	Not yet due
J. Earnhardt	820	Not yet due
R. Henry	700	35 days past due
D. Clayton	1,120	30 days past due
J. Durham	200	Not yet due
H. Perry	180	45 days past due
R. Rasco	2,400	Not yet due
F. Connell	560	74 days past due
H. Kinnan	980	Not yet due
B. Humphries	340	95 days past due
J. Davis	1,680	29 days past due

Not yet due	1%	61–90 days past due	50%
1–30 days past due	4%	Over 90 days past due.	75%
31–60 days past due	10%		

Required

1. Prepare an aging schedule and an estimate of the total amount expected to be uncollectible.
2. Prepare an adjusting entry to record Bad Debts Expense on June 30, 1986, assuming that the Allowance for Uncollectible Accounts has a credit balance before adjustment of $730.
3. Prepare an adjusting entry to record Bad Debts Expense on June 30, 1986, assuming that the Allowance for Uncollectible Accounts has a debit balance before adjustment of $350.

(Check figure: Balance of Allowance for Uncollectible Accounts after adjustment = $1,949)

Problem A8-4
Recording entries relating to interest-bearing and non-interest-bearing notes

Chatham Fixture, Inc., has an account receivable from Handy Stop Co. in the amount of $4,000. Since Handy is temporarily short of cash, it proposes to give Chatham a 90-day note to settle the account. Chatham agrees and the note is signed on March 31, 1988. Chatham's accounting year ends on April 30. Handy pays the note on June 30, 1988.

Required

1. Prepare Chatham's journal entries on March 31, April 30, and June 30, assuming that Handy gave Chatham a $4,000 note bearing 18% interest. Show supporting calculations.
2. Prepare Chatham's journal entries on March 31, April 30, and June 30, assuming that Handy gave Chatham a $4,180, non-interest-bearing note. Show supporting calculations.

(Check figure: Interest income recorded on April 30 for each note = $60)

Problem A8-5
Calculating proceeds from discounting three notes

On June 1, 1988, Kansas Industrial Tools discounted the three notes described below at the Plains National Bank. The bank charged an 18% discount rate on each note.

Note A, a $4,000, 60-day, 18% note received May 2, 1988
Note B, a $30,000, 6-month, 15% note maturing in 4 months
Note C, a $10,000, 1-year, 20% note received on June 1, 1988

Required

Calculate the amount of cash that would be received by Kansas from discounting each of the three notes. Your calculations should be clearly labeled.

(Check figure: Cash received from discounting note A = $4,058.20)

Problem A8-6
Recording the receipt, discounting, and payment of a dishonored note

Barr Distributors experienced the following transactions relating to a note receivable:

1987
July 1   Received a $24,000 note from Odessa Lamps in payment of an overdue account. The note bears interest at 15% and matures in 9 months.

1988
Jan. 1   After holding the note for 6 months, Barr discounted it at the Fairfax Bank with recourse. The bank charged an 18% discount rate.
Apr. 1   Barr received notice from the bank that Odessa failed to pay the note when due. Barr paid the maturity value of the note to Fairfax Bank.

Required

Prepare the appropriate journal entries relating to each of the transactions above. Barr's accounting year ends on June 30. Show clearly labeled calculations to support your entries.

(Check figure: Proceeds from discounting the note = $25,498.50)

Problem A8-7
Recording transactions relating to notes receivable

Freeman Equipment Company sells forklifts to wholesalers, retailers, and manufacturers. These machines are normally sold on 60-day open accounts, but occasionally Freeman will accept a longer-term note. The transactions below relate to three such notes that were received in 1987.

Feb. 1   Freeman received a 12-month, 18%, $12,000 note from Pilgrim Foods in exchange for a forklift with a total retail price of $12,000.
May 1   Freeman sold Bellaire Battery Co. two forklifts with a total sales price of $30,000. Bellaire gave Freeman a 9-month, non-interest-bearing note for $33,375.
      1   Freeman discounted the Pilgrim Foods note at the Liberty Bank with recourse. The bank charged a discount rate of 20%.
Aug. 1   Freeman sold Du-Gro Chemical Company a forklift for $24,000. Du-Gro gave Freeman a 6-month, 10% note.
Dec. 31   Freeman discounted the Du-Gro note at the Franklin Finance Company without recourse. Franklin charged a 12% discount rate.
Dec. 31   Freeman's accounting year ends.

Required

1. Prepare the appropriate journal entries to record each of the transactions above. Show supporting calculations as part of your journal entry explanations.
2. Prepare Freeman's December 31, 1987, balance sheet disclosure that relates to notes receivable.
3. What is the total interest earned during 1987 by Freeman on these three notes?

(Check figure: Interest earned during 1987 = $4,540)

Problem A8-8
Recording accounts receivable and external credit card transactions

Sandra's Sportswear sells a full line of ladies clothing. Sandra sells to customers for cash, on a 30-day Sandra's charge account, or through two national credit cards: Passport and Mister Charge. Sandra remits charge tickets to the national credit card companies weekly. Passport assesses a fee of 6% of gross sales, whereas Mister Charge charges 8% of gross sales. Both credit card companies remit cash to Sandra within 10 days.

    Sandra has the following sales and collections during January 1988:

	Jan. 1–7	Jan. 8–14	Jan. 15–21	Jan. 22–31
Cash sales	$ 500	$ 840	$1,050	$ 620
Sandra's charge sales	800	1,260	3,080	2,460
Passport sales.	2,000	2,900	2,600	1,000
Mister Charge sales	1,300	2,200	1,600	2,400
Collected on Sandra's accounts		690	1,480	1,830
Collected from Passport		1,880	2,726	2,444
Collected from Mister Charge		1,196	2,024	1,472

On January 31 Sandra provided for estimated uncollectible accounts using the percentage of credit sales method. Sandra estimates that 2% of credit sales will prove uncollectible.

Required
1. Prepare summary entries to record sales and collections for *each* of the four weeks.
2. Prepare the entry to record Bad Debts Expense on January 31.
3. What receivable amounts will appear on the January 31, 1988, balance sheet?

(Check figure: Bad Debts Expense = $152)

Problem A8-9
Determining correct balance sheet disclosures of receivables accounts

Marlin, Inc., reports the following receivables on its tentative September 30, 1988, balance sheet:

Accounts Receivable	$87,900	
Less: Allowance for Uncollectibles	(1,978)	$ 85,922
Receivable from Credit Card Companies		142,700
Interest Receivable.		1,625
Notes Receivable	$41,450	
Less: Discount on Notes Receivable	(4,050)	
Notes Receivable Discounted.	(11,000)	26,400
Net Receivables.		$256,647

Upon investigation you discover the following additional facts:
a. The balance of Accounts Receivable includes customer accounts of $800 with credit balances and a receivable from the president of Marlin in the amount of $2,000.
b. Notes Receivable includes all notes, some of which have been discounted. Notes totaling $8,250 were discounted with recourse and $2,750 without recourse.
c. The $11,000 Notes Receivable Discounted includes all notes discounted—with and without recourse.

Required
1. Determine the current balance that should be disclosed for each of the accounts on the balance sheet shown above. Add any accounts that you believe are necessary.
2. Prepare a corrected receivables section of the September 30, 1988, balance sheet.

(Check figure: Gross Accounts Receivable from Trade Customers = $86,700)

Set B

Problem B8-1
Calculating bad debts expense using direct write-off, percentage of credit sales, and aging of receivables

An examination of the financial records of Eastern Tool and Die Co. reveals the following facts:
a. Sales for 1987 were $650,000; 98% of sales were on credit.
b. Allowance for Uncollectible Accounts had a credit balance of $9,990 on January 1, 1987.
c. During 1987, Eastern wrote off $8,800 of customer accounts as uncollectible.

Required

Calculate Eastern's 1987 Bad Debts Expense under each of the following assumptions:
1. The direct write-off method is used.
2. The percentage of credit sales method is used. Management estimates that 2% of credit sales will prove uncollectible.
3. The aging of receivables method is used. An aging schedule prepared on December 31 indicates that accounts totaling $11,750 will be uncollectible.

(Check figure: Bad Debts Expense using percentage of credit sales method = $12,740)

Problem B8-2
Recording transactions relating to Accounts Receivable and bad debts

Levine Wholesale Foods opened on November 1, 1987. The information below describes selected transactions that occurred during 1987 and 1988:

1987
Nov. 1–Dec. 31   Levine's cash sales amounted to $20,000; credit sales totaled $60,000. (Prepare a summary entry.)
Nov. 1–Dec. 31   Levine collected 60% of the total sales on account. (Prepare a summary entry.)
Dec. 31   Levine estimated that uncollectible accounts would amount to about 2% of credit sales.

1988
Jan. 19   Levine wrote off the $71 account of Dee Ceased as uncollectible.
Mar. 30   The $37 account of B. Hank Rupp was written off as uncollectible.
Apr. 15   A check was received from Rupp in full settlement of his account.
Jan.–Dec. Various other individual accounts amounting to $618 were written off.
Jan.–Dec. Total sales were $240,000; 88% of sales were on account, the remaining sales were for cash.
Jan.–Dec. Total other cash collections were $160,000.
Dec. 31   Levine estimated Bad Debts Expense for 1988 using the same percentage as in the prior year.

Required

1. Prepare general journal entries to record the transactions described above. Calculations should be included as part of your journal entry explanation where appropriate.
2. Calculate the balance of Accounts Receivable and Allowance for Uncollectible Accounts on December 31, 1988.

(Check figure: Bad Debts Expense for 1988 = $4,224)

Problem B8-3
Preparing an aging schedule and entries to record bad debts expense

On September 30, 1986, Davis Electronics has uncollected accounts receivable, as shown at the top of page 329. Davis uses an aging schedule to prepare an estimate of Bad Debts Expense for the year. Estimates of the percentage uncollectible in each category follow:

Customer Name	Amount	Collection Status
Mosley Stereo	$ 9,100	15 days past due
Buckner Systems Inc.	22,400	Not yet due
Stevens T.V.	17,850	Not yet due
Spivey Sounds Co.	2,400	130 days past due
Murphy Department Store	20,050	45 days past due
Waters Appliances	650	98 days past due
Ezelle T.V. & Stereo	7,750	Not yet due
Jacob Stores	3,050	103 days past due
Geiger Sales Co.	17,200	75 days past due
Bidwell Hi-Fi	21,050	Not yet due
Van Zant Stereo Town	14,500	105 days past due
Hutson Speaker World	7,250	8 days past due
Eller Stereo, Inc.	5,100	240 days past due
Cooke Boutique	12,400	Not yet due
Parsons Electronics	4,200	90 days past due
Moore Audio, Inc.	1,250	80 days past due
Knipe Sound Systems	2,500	Not yet due
Pricher Bargain Center	10,000	40 days past due

Not yet due	2%	91–120 days past due	40%
1–60 days past due	5%	Over 120 days past due	85%
61–90 days past due	10%		

Required

1. Prepare an aging schedule and an estimate of the total amount expected to be uncollectible.
2. Prepare an adjusting entry to record Bad Debts Expense on September 30, 1986. The Allowance for Uncollectible Accounts has a credit balance before adjustment of $4,750.
3. Prepare an adjusting entry to record Bad Debts Expense on September 30, 1986, assuming that the Allowance for Uncollectible Accounts has a debit balance before adjustment of $331.

(Check figure: Balance of Allowance for Uncollectible Accounts after adjustment = $19,919)

Problem B8-4

Recording entries relating to interest-bearing and non-interest-bearing notes

Amstrap Co. has an account receivable from Spartan Tools in the amount of $10,000. Spartan is having some short-run cash flow problems and proposes to settle the account by giving Amstrap a 120-day note. Amstrap accepts the note on August 31, 1987. Amstrap's accounting year ends on September 30. Spartan pays the note on its due date, December 29, 1987.

Required

1. Prepare Amstrap's journal entries on August 31, September 30, and December 29, 1987, assuming that Spartan gave Amstrap a $10,000 note bearing interest at an annual rate of 12%. Show supporting calculations.
2. Prepare Amstrap's journal entries on August 31, September 30, and December 29, assuming that Spartan gave Amstrap a $10,400, non-interest-bearing note. Show supporting calculations.

(Check figure: Interest income recorded on September 30 for each note = $100)

Problem B8-5
Calculating proceeds from discounting three notes

On November 1, 1987, Aero Cable Co. discounted the three notes described below at the Jefferson Fidelity Bank. The bank charged a 15% discount rate on each note.

Note 1, a $2,000, 120-day, 12% note received on September 2, 1987
Note 2, a $30,000, 60-day, 18% note maturing in 30 days
Note 3, a $8,000, 90-day, 15% note received on November 1, 1987

Required

Calculate the amount of cash that would be received by Aero from discounting each of the three notes. Your calculations should be clearly labeled.

(Check figure: Cash received from discounting note 1 = $2,028)

Problem B8-6
Recording the receipt, discounting, and payment of a dishonored note

The following transactions relate to a note received by Solar Systems from A. Gonzalez:

1987
Aug. 1   Received an $18,000 note from Gonzalez in settlement of an overdue account. The note bears interest at 12% and matures in 6 months.
Oct. 1   After holding the note for 2 months, Solar discounted the note at the Parkside Bank. The bank charged a 15% discount rate.

1988
Feb. 1   Received notice from the bank that Gonzalez had failed to pay the note when due. Solar paid the maturity value of the note to the Parkside Bank.

Required

Prepare the appropriate journal entries relating to each of the transactions above. Show clearly labeled calculations to support your entries.

(Check figure: Proceeds from discounting the note = $18,126)

Problem B8-7
Recording transactions relating to notes receivable

Summers Mowers sells large industrial mowers to businesses, government agencies, and large estates. Normally, these sales are on 30-day open accounts, but occasionally Summers will accept a longer-term note. The transactions below relate to three such notes that were received in 1988:

Sept. 1   Summers received a 6-month, 9%, $8,000 note from Wimbley School in exchange for two large mowers with a total retail price of $8,000.
Oct. 1   Summers sold the City of Mulberry several mowers with a total sales price of $12,000. The City of Mulberry gave Summers a 1-year, non-interest-bearing note for $13,200.
Nov. 1   Summers discounted the Wimbley School note at the Fortune National Bank with recourse. The bank charged a discount rate of 12%.
1   Summers sold Morey's Nursery a tractor for $30,000. Morey gave Summers a 3-month, 10% note.
Dec. 1   Summers discounted Morey's note without recourse at the Dakota Bank and Trust Company. The bank charged a 12% discount rate.
31   Summers' accounting year ends.

Required

1. Prepare the appropriate journal entries to record each of the transactions above. Show supporting calculations as part of your journal entry explanations.
2. Prepare Summers' December 31, 1988, balance sheet disclosure that relates to notes receivable.
3. What is the total interest earned during 1988 by Summers on these three notes?

(Check figure: Total interest earned during 1988 = $670)

Problem B8-8
Recording accounts receivable and external credit card transactions

Cawthon's Men's Wear sells men's clothing. Cawthon accepts cash, a 30-day Cawthon charge account, or one of two national credit cards: National Express and Instant Money. Cawthon remits charge tickets to the national firms weekly. National Express assesses a fee of 5% of gross sales for its credit card services, whereas Instant Money charges 6% of gross sales. Both credit card companies remit cash to Cawthon within 10 days.

Cawthon has the following sales and collections during December 1987:

	Dec. 1–7	Dec. 8–14	Dec. 15–21	Dec. 22–31
Cash sales	$1,000	$1,600	$2,240	$ 600
Cawthon's charge sales.	400	1,240	1,750	300
National Express sales	2,400	4,800	6,000	1,800
Instant Money sales	1,600	2,800	3,600	1,400
Collected on Cawthon's accounts.		160	600	870
Collected from National Express		2,280	4,560	5,700
Collected from Instant Money.		1,504	2,632	3,384

On December 31 Cawthon provided for estimated uncollectible accounts using the percentage of credit sales method. Cawthon estimates that 3% of credit sales will prove uncollectible.

Required

1. Prepare summary entries to record sales and collections for *each* of the four weeks.
2. Prepare the entry to record Bad Debts Expense on December 31.
3. What receivable amounts will appear on the December 31, 1987, balance sheet?

(Check figure: Bad Debts Expense = $110.70)

Problem B8-9

Determining correct balance sheet disclosures of receivables accounts

Central Processing Co. reports the following receivables on its tentative October 31, 1988, balance sheet:

Accounts Receivable	$247,800	
Less: Allowance for Uncollectibles	(11,000)	$236,800
Receivable from Credit Card Companies		408,000
Interest Receivable.		3,600
Notes Receivable	$ 52,600	
Less: Discount on Notes Receivable	(3,440)	
Notes Receivable Discounted.	(14,600)	34,560
Net Receivables.		$682,960

Upon investigation you discover the following additional facts:

a. The balance of Accounts Receivable includes customer accounts of $4,200 with credit balances and a receivable from Central's vice president of production in the amount of $15,000.

b. Notes Receivable includes all notes, some of which have been discounted. Notes totaling $12,000 were discounted with recourse and $2,600 without recourse.

c. The $14,600 Notes Receivable Discounted includes all notes discounted—with and without recourse.

Required

1. Determine the current balance that should be disclosed for each of the accounts on the balance sheet shown above. Add any accounts that you believe are necessary.
2. Prepare a corrected receivables section of the October 31, 1988, balance sheet.

(Check figure: Gross Accounts Receivable from Trade Customers = $237,000)

Chapter 9

Accounting for Merchandise Inventory

You will learn these things from studying this chapter:

- What merchandise inventory is and how to determine the cost of inventory purchased
- The gross and net methods of recording purchase discounts
- The structure of the cost of goods sold section of the income statement
- What *cost flow* means and how it corresponds to physical units flow
- How to use the *first-in, first-out; weighted average; last-in, first-out;* and *specific identification* periodic inventory cost methods
- The *lower-of-cost-or-market* method for valuing inventory
- The *gross profit* and *retail inventory* methods for estimating ending inventory costs
- How an error in inventory accounting affects income
- How to use the first-in, first-out and last-in, first-out perpetual inventory cost methods

Merchandise inventory is finished goods held for sale by retailers and wholesalers. Completed goods held for sale by manufacturers is called *finished goods inventory.* Since accounting for merchandise inventory and finished goods inventory is the same, we will use the term merchandise inventory to refer to both in this chapter.

Some goods are purchased in finished condition ready to sell—no work is performed on them before they are sold. For example, retailers such as hardware stores purchase hammers and nails, and screwdrivers and screws, all of which are immediately ready for resale. Another example is shirts and blouses that your local clothing shop buys and places on the shelves for immediate resale.

Other goods are purchased that require some minor finishing or assembly before they are ready for sale. Examples are bicycles that are shipped unassembled and put together by your local bicycle shop, and that are then ready for sale; and some furniture that must be assembled before it is sold. Since such finishing activities are minor, goods such as these are included in merchandise inventory.

There are firms that purchase raw materials that require considerable work to convert into finished products. For example, a furniture manufacturer buys wood, plastic, glue, nails, and other raw materials and converts them into tables, desks, and bookcases. The wood, plastic, glue, and nails are *raw materials inventory.* The completed—except perhaps for minor assembly—tables, desks, and bookcases are merchandise inventory, or finished goods inventory.

To be included in merchandise inventory the finished goods must be held for sale. Thus, the same assets represented by one firm as merchandise inventory may be considered differently by another firm. Consider this simple example: Byron Office Supply Company has desks and file cabinets in its warehouses ready for sale—these are assets that Byron represents as merchandise inventory. The Culbreath Plumbing Supply Company buys some of these desks and file cabinets—these assets are represented by Culbreath's accountants as office equipment, because that's what they are. Culbreath "consumes" desks and file cabinets; it doesn't sell them. Culbreath sells pipes, valves, bathtubs, and sinks—these things are Culbreath's merchandise inventory.

Any good, whether it is iron ore or vacant lots or toy trains, if it is a finished good and held ready for sale, is the merchandise inventory of the firm owning it.

In this chapter, we are going to be concerned only with merchandise that is completely finished or that requires only minor assembly. That will keep manufacturing costs out of our discussion of accounting for merchandise inventory. (We'll take those up later in Chapter 19, where you will be prepared for it.) Accounting for merchandise inventory involves two problems:

1. Determining the total cost of inventory acquired

2. Allocating those costs between the goods that were sold (cost of goods sold) and those that remain (ending inventory)

DETERMINING THE COST OF MERCHANDISE PURCHASED

General rule for finding the cost of merchandise

The following is a general rule for determining the cost of merchandise:

The cost of merchandise includes the invoice price and all reasonable and necessary costs incurred in getting it to a condition and place where it is ready for sale.

This rule means that the merchandise inventory's cost includes not only its invoice price but also the costs of freight, insurance during shipment, handling, and storage—all reasonable costs incurred in getting the asset to the point where it becomes merchandise inventory on the shelf ready for the consumer to purchase. Most firms have many different products on their shelves for sale. Yet some of the costs, such as fire insurance, handling, and storage, represent costs that cover all merchandise. In reality, a firm's accounting system does not carefully trace each of these costs to each item in inventory. To do so would prove unnecessarily expensive in comparison to the value of the information obtained. For example, to apply the cost rule literally would mean that the salary of a receiving clerk in a department store must be divided among all the various items of inventory in proportion to the time spent unloading each one. The cost of allocating the clerk's salary, typically around $15,000 per year, among $5,000,000 of inventory, would contribute little to the profitability of the department store. Nor would it provide relevant information on the income statement.

Nevertheless, all of the basic costs are accounted for in one way or another; some are accounted for very carefully, as we shall see.

Invoice Price

The first thing we have to consider in determining the cost of inventory is the price paid to the seller for it. The amount paid is often less than the price listed in the seller's catalog. In other words, the seller has *discounted* the catalog (or list) price. Sellers offer three different types of discounts: trade discounts, quantity discounts, and cash discounts (purchase discounts).

Trade Discounts

You learned in Chapter 5 that trade discounts are deductions allowed to wholesalers and retailers from the price of merchandise listed in catalogs. Trade discounts may be specified as a single percentage or a chain of percentages. The following example will remind you how trade discounts work. Chiefland Wholesale sells to retailers at a 20-20 trade discount. If the total list price of the merchandise purchased is $100,000, the price after trade discounts is calculated as follows:

Total list price	$100,000
Less 20% (.2) ($100,000)	(20,000)
Total after first 20%	$ 80,000
Less 20% (.2) ($80,000)	(16,000)
Price after trade discounts	$ 64,000

If you're still unsure about your understanding of trade discounts, review pages 187–188 in Chapter 5.

Quantity Discounts

Quantity discounts reduce the price for customers buying large quantities

To customers buying a large quantity of the same item, a wholesaler may offer not only a trade discount but also a quantity discount. Usually, the manufacturer or wholesaler includes in his or her catalog or price list this additional *quantity discount* and the quantity at which it becomes applicable.

The invoice price on the customer's bill is the list price less the trade discount and any quantity discounts. For example, Dusty's Sports World receives a 20% trade discount on purchases from Jox Wholesale Sporting Goods. Jox also offers an additional 5% quantity discount if a gross (12 dozen) of softballs is purchased. The invoice price of 15 dozen softballs at a list price of $40 per dozen is:

Calculation of invoice price with trade and quantity discounts

List price, 15 dozen @ $40	$ 600
Less: Trade discount (.20 × $600)	(120)
Subtotal.	$ 480
Less: Quantity discount (.05 × $480)	(24)
Invoice price	$ 456

Dusty would prepare the following entry to record the purchase:

Purchases	456	
Accounts Payable		456
To record the purchase of 15 dozen softballs on account.		

Cash Discounts

Cash discounts are offered to encourage customers to pay quickly

The purpose of cash discounts is to encourage buyers to pay for their purchases in a short period of time. As we already explained in Chapter 5, these discounts are usually expressed by abbreviations such as 2/10, n/30. This means that the buyer may deduct 2% from the invoice price if payment is made within 10 days of receiving the invoice, or that the net invoice price is due in full within 30 days.

In the preceding example, if Dusty were offered terms of 2/10, n/30, he could deduct an additional $9.12 [(.02) ($456)] — if he pays within 10 days of the invoice date. Dusty may choose to record the purchase in one of two ways—at the gross invoice price, $456, or at the net invoice price, $446.88 ($456.00 − $9.12). Let's look closely at these two alternatives, the gross method and the net method.

The Gross Method   If Dusty elects to use the gross method, he would make the following entry on the date of purchase:

Purchases	456.00	
Accounts Payable		456.00
To record the purchase of merchandise.		

If Dusty pays within 10 days, he receives the $9.12 discount and records the payment like this:

Accounts Payable	456.00	
Purchase Discounts.		9.12
Cash		446.88
To record cash payment within the discount period.		

If Dusty fails to pay within the 10-day period, no discount is recorded. Accounts Payable would be debited and Cash credited for $456.

Remember, the Purchase Discounts account is deducted from Purchases when we prepare the cost of goods sold section of the income statement.

The Net Method   If Dusty had followed the net method rather than the gross method, he would have recorded the purchase initially at the list price less trade, quantity, *and cash discounts*—$446.88. The *anticipated* cash discount is deducted; remember, Dusty must pay within 10 days to be entitled to this discount.

Here are the purchase and payment entries assuming that Dusty takes advantage of the cash discount:

On the date of the purchase:

Purchases	446.88	
Accounts Payable		446.88
To record purchase of merchandise.		

On the date of payment 9 days later:

Accounts Payable	446.88	
Cash		446.88
To record payment within the discount period.		

If Dusty fails to pay within the 10-day discount period, he must pay the full $456, but Accounts Payable has a balance of only $446.88. When he pays the $446.88, Dusty no longer owes Jox Wholesale, so he simply eliminates the account payable with a debit equal to the balance in the account. He credits Cash for the amount of the payment. The $9.12 difference is recorded in a new account called Purchase Discounts Lost. Here is Dusty's entry if he *does not* pay within the discount period:

Accounts Payable	446.88	
Purchase Discounts Lost	9.12	
Cash		456.00
To record payment of account after the discount period has expired.		

This new account, Purchase Discounts Lost, is a red flag to management, indicating a failure in the company's operating procedure to take all discounts allowed. Purchase Discounts Lost is not used in the calculation of cost of goods sold. Since it is really an interest charge for waiting to pay for the merchandise, Purchase Discounts Lost is shown on the income statement as a nonoperating expense, just as Interest Expense would be.

The partial income statements at the top of page 337 will illustrate the *location* of Purchase Discounts and Purchase Discounts Lost. These statements are for two different companies—a single company will use *either* the gross *or* the net method but not both.

Purchase Returns and Allowances

When merchandise is received, it is routinely inspected by the purchaser to ensure that it is of the quality ordered and not defective. Merchandise that does not pass this inspection is returned to the seller and an entry like the following is made in the buyer's general journal:

Buyer's entry to record returned merchandise

Nov. 15 Accounts Payable	588	
Purchase Returns and Allowances		588
To record the return of 20 defective units of merchandise.		

Purchase Returns and Allowances is a contra account that is deducted from Purchases in calculating cost of goods sold on the income statement.

The amount of the debit to Accounts Payable and the credit to Purchase Returns and Allowances is determined by whether the gross or the net method has been used

GROSS PRICE METHOD COMPANY Partial Income Statement			NET PRICE METHOD COMPANY Partial Income Statement		
Sales		$10,000	Sales		$26,000
Cost of Goods Sold:			Cost of Goods Sold:		
Merchandise Inventory (beginning)	$4,000		Merchandise Inventory (beginning)	$ 9,000	
Add: Purchases.	$3,200		Add: Purchases.	6,800	
			Goods Available for Sale	$15,800	
Deduct: Purchase Discounts . . .	(64)		Less: Merchandise Inventory (ending). . .	(8,300)	
Net Purchases	3,136		Cost of Goods Sold		(7,500)
Goods Available for Sale	$7,136		Gross Profit on Sales.		$18,500
Less: Merchandise Inventory (ending). . .	(2,500)				
Cost of Goods Sold		(4,636)	Operating Expenses:		
Gross Profit on Sales		$ 5,364	Selling Expenses	$ 2,200	
			General and Administrative Expenses. . .	1,400	
Operating Expenses:			Total Operating Expenses		(3,600)
Selling Expenses	$ 850				
General and Administrative Expenses. . .	614	(1,464)	Income from Primary Operations		$14,900
Total Operating Expenses					
			Other Income and Expenses:		
Income from Primary Operations.		$ 3,900	Interest Expense	$ 1,380	
			Purchase Discounts Lost	510	
Other Income and Expenses:					
Interest Expense		(1,380)	Total Other Expenses		(1,890)
Net Income		$ 2,520	Net Income		$13,010

to record purchases. If the gross method has been used, the amount in the entry will be before cash discounts. If the net method has been used, the amount in the entry will be after cash discounts.

Freight-In

If the buyer of merchandise is required to pay the cost of transporting that merchandise, the transportation cost becomes a part of the total inventory cost. The transportation cost is charged to a Freight-In account and is added to the cost of merchandise purchased in determining total cost in the cost of goods sold section of the income statement. The entry to record a $38 payment for freight would look like this:

Entry to record freight paid by the buyer

```
June 25   Freight-In . . . . . . . . . . . . . . . . . . . . . . . . . . . . . . . . . . . 38
              Cash . . . . . . . . . . . . . . . . . . . . . . . . . . . . . . . . . . . . . . . . . . . .        38
          To record payment of shipping costs on merchandise purchased.
```

THE COST OF GOODS SOLD SECTION

Two steps are required to calculate the cost of goods sold as shown on the income statement:

1. Find the cost of *all* the merchandise that the company had available for sale during the period.

2. Subtract from it the cost of the merchandise that was not sold at the end of the period.

An example of this calculation is shown at the top of page 338.

The key to this calculation is, of course, the cost of merchandise inventory at the

Observe that Freight-In is
added to Purchases while
Purchase Discounts and
Purchase Returns
are subtracted

FARLEY, INC.
Schedule of Cost of Goods Sold
Month Ended March 31, 1988

Merchandise Inventory, March 1		$ 74,200
Add: Merchandise Purchased during March:		
Purchases	$184,500	
+Freight-In	5,100	
−Purchase Discounts	(3,500)	
−Purchase Returns and Allowances	(7,600)	
Net Cost of Merchandise Purchased		178,500
Goods Available for Sale during March		$252,700
Less: Merchandise Inventory, March 31		(87,100)
Cost of Goods Sold Expense		$165,600

end of the period. We know how to calculate the net cost of merchandise purchased. The merchandise inventory at the beginning of the period is merely the preceding period's ending inventory. Thus, the purpose of this chapter is to determine the costs represented by merchandise inventory at the end of the period so that we can report the cost of goods sold during the period and have the beginning inventory for the next period.

DETERMINING ENDING INVENTORY — PHYSICAL UNITS

To determine the cost represented in Ending Inventory, you must: (1) measure, or count, the number of physical units of merchandise owned by the firm, that is, the units available for sale but not yet sold; and (2) then determine the total cost represented by those unsold units.

As we shall see, the number of units to be physically counted in inventory include:

Physical units included in
ending inventory

1. The units in the firm's warehouses, stockrooms, shelves, and even in the windows and showcases for display

2. The units ordered and owned by the firm, but not yet received

3. The units that may be on their way to a customer or sales agent but are still owned by the firm

4. The units in the hands of a sales agent but still owned by the firm

All businesses that own inventory should count it at least once each year. Even firms with sophisticated computer systems or complex hand-kept records of each item entering and leaving the firm need to count the inventory to be sure that no recordkeeping errors were made and to discover the amount of any inventory stolen or spoiled.

The Physical Count

A reliable ending inventory cost depends on an accurate count of all the merchandise in inventory. The best way to do that is through a visual inspection and a physical count of all the merchandise not sold at the end of the period. Teams of employees are assigned to count all units on the shelves, in the stockrooms, and in other storage areas. Their count totals are entered on tally sheets similar to the one shown on page 339. Note that no costs are entered on the tally sheet at the time of the physical count. The costs are supplied later by the accounting department. To ensure the accuracy of the total inventory, the original counter's totals are checked and verified on a random basis by another counter.

Inventory Tally Sheet

Department _____ Air Conditioners _____   Date _____ December 31, 1988 _____

Location _____ Stockroom _____

Counter's Signature _____ I. M. Accurate _____

Verified by _____

Stock No.	Description	Number of Units	Unit Cost	Total Cost
85-1291	4,000 Btu portable	4		
85-1292	5,000 Btu portable	2		
85-0796	12,800 Btu window unit	6		
85-0798	11,700 Btu window unit	10		

The number of units counted are entered on an inventory tally sheet

The physical count covers the units found on the firm's premises. But as we began to explain, that's only one part of measuring the physical units for the purposes of ending inventory. There may also be units owned by the firm but not available on the firm's premises to be counted. These units may be *in transit,* meaning on the way to the firm, or *out on consignment,* meaning that the firm owns them but someone else has them to sell for the firm. Some of the units on the firm's premises should be excluded from ending inventory. These units may be *in on consignment,* meaning that the firm has them but doesn't own them—it's keeping them to sell for someone else. In any case, the important thing to realize is that goods owned by the firm, whatever their physical location, are the ones to be included in ending inventory.

Goods in Transit

Goods we buy FOB shipping point we own while in shipment

When goods are purchased from a supplier, the terms of shipment are either FOB (free on board) shipping point, or FOB destination. These terms specify who pays the freight and the point at which legal title to the goods passes from buyer to seller.

FOB shipping point means that the seller pays freight to the shipping point, usually the seller's plant or warehouse, and that title passes to the buyer at the shipping point. In this case, the buyer owns the goods while in shipment and is responsible for all freight charges. A company purchasing goods FOB shipping point must include these units in its Ending Inventory account and its Purchases account even though the goods have not been received.

FOB destination means that the seller pays the freight to the destination, usually the buyer's place of business, and that title to the goods passes at the point of destination. A company purchasing goods FOB destination does not own the goods in transit, is not responsible for freight charges, and does not include these goods in Ending Inventory or Purchases.

Goods on Consignment

Under certain conditions a firm may choose to market its goods through an agent. The agent doesn't own the goods even though they may be in his or her possession; the firm owns the goods until the agent sells them. The owner of the merchandise is called the *consignor;* the agent is called the *consignee,* who acts on behalf of the owner in selling the goods. Although the consignee never actually owns the merchandise, he or

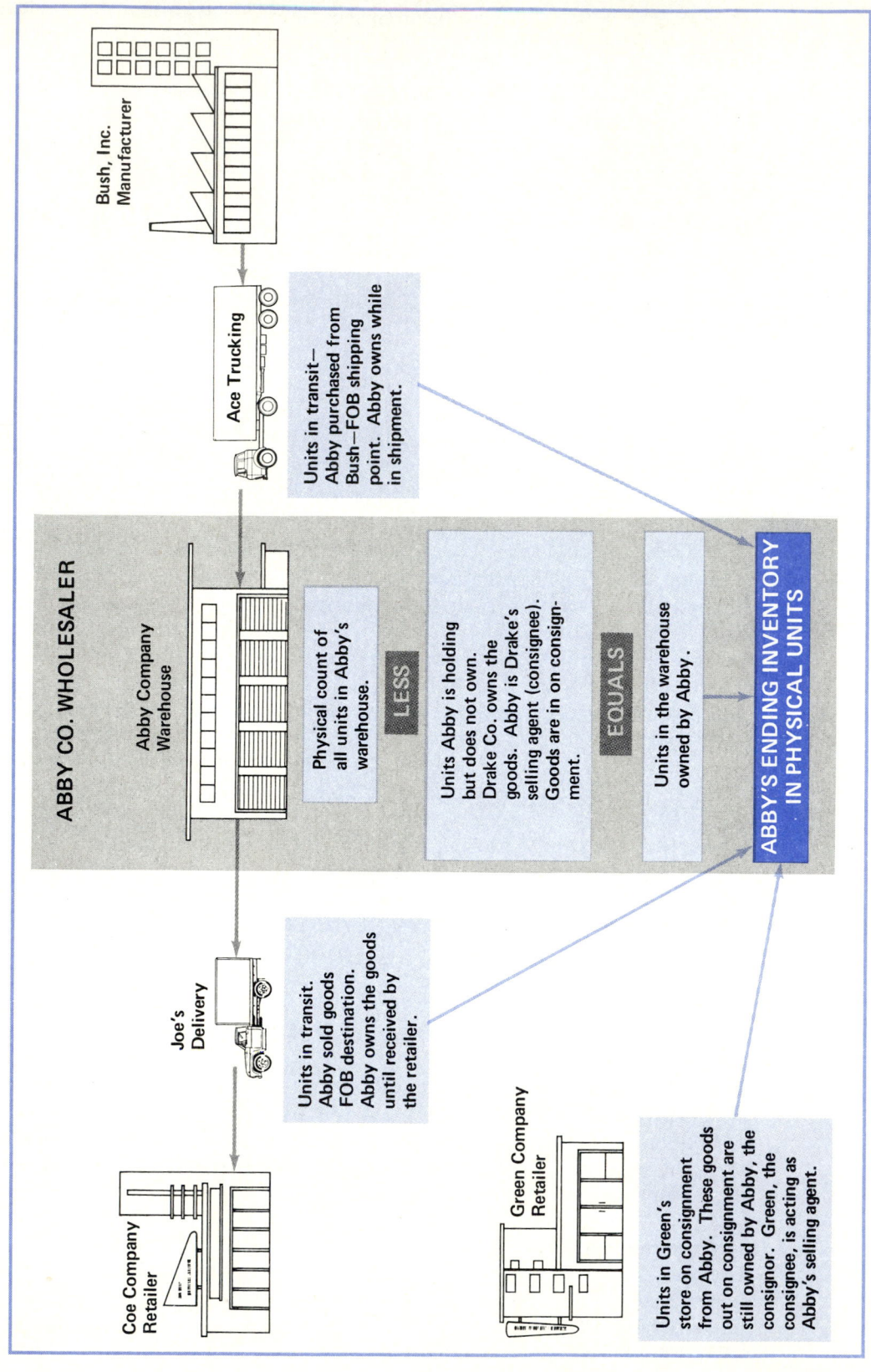

Bush, Inc. Manufacturer

Ace Trucking

Units in transit—Abby purchased from Bush—FOB shipping point. Abby owns while in shipment.

ABBY CO. WHOLESALER

Abby Company Warehouse

Physical count of all units in Abby's warehouse.

LESS

Units Abby is holding but does not own. Drake Co. owns the goods. Abby is Drake's selling agent (consignee). Goods are in on consignment.

EQUALS

Units in the warehouse owned by Abby.

ABBY'S ENDING INVENTORY IN PHYSICAL UNITS

Joe's Delivery

Units in transit. Abby sold goods FOB destination. Abby owns the goods until received by the retailer.

Coe Company Retailer

Green Company Retailer

Units in Green's store on consignment from Abby. These goods out on consignment are still owned by Abby, the consignor. Green, the consignee, is acting as Abby's selling agent.

FIGURE 9-1   Physical Units Included in Ending Inventory.

(1) Units on the way to us shipped FOB shipping point
(2) Units in our warehouse that we own (excluding goods in on consignment)
(3) Units on the way to our customers shipped FOB destination
(4) Our goods in the hands of a selling agent — out on consignment

she agrees to exercise due care over it until sold. After the sale, the consignee deducts from the proceeds of the sale a selling commission and expenses incurred in carrying out the sale, and sends the balance to the consignor.

Our goods out on consignment must be included in ending inventory

The consignor — a company that has goods *out* to an agent on consignment — must include these goods in its ending inventory; the consignor owns the goods.

The consignee — an agent that has goods *in* on consignment — excludes these goods from its ending inventory count; the goods are the property of the consignor, not the consignee.

Figure 9-1 illustrates the determination of physical ending inventory for the Abby Company.

DETERMINING ENDING INVENTORY — COST

To begin to get some understanding of how to determine the cost represented in Ending Inventory, consider this situation:

It is June 30, and the Grow Well Garden Supply Company has determined by physical count that it has 89 bags of fertilizer in stock. On June 2, Grow Well purchased from the wholesaler 200 bags of fertilizer for a total cost of $400; on June 12, 100 bags were purchased for $220; and on June 20, 50 bags were purchased for $120. In other words, three batches were purchased during the month, and, if you are swift at simple arithmetic, you will realize that the cost per bag of fertilizer was different with the purchase of each batch.

What, then, should Grow Well use as the unit cost for the 89 unsold units on June 30 to calculate the total cost represented in Ending Inventory?

There are several ways to assign a unit cost to the units in ending inventory: the *first-in, first-out method,* called ***FIFO;*** the ***weighted average method;*** the ***last-in, first-out,*** or ***LIFO, method;*** and the ***specific identification method.*** Each method is based on the idea that *costs flow through* the accounts. We will explain what that means and how to use each method to determine the costs tied up in Ending Inventory.

The data shown in Exhibit 9-1 will be used to demonstrate the calculations involved in each method.

EXHIBIT 9-1
Data to Be Used in Calculating Ending Inventory and Cost of Goods Sold under FIFO, LIFO, Weighted Average, and Specific Identification Methods.

LENOX CO.
Inventory Data
Month Ended January 31, 1988

	Units	×	Cost Each	=	Total
Goods available for sale:					
Beginning inventory	0	×	0	=	0
January 5 purchase	50	×	$1.00	=	$ 50.00
January 12 purchase	100	×	1.50	=	150.00
January 18 purchase	200	×	2.00	=	400.00
January 20 purchase	100	×	2.50	=	250.00
January 27 purchase	50	×	3.00	=	150.00
Total available	500 units				$1,000.00

Units remaining at end of month:
  By physical count . . . . 220 units remaining

Units sold during the month:
  Total units available − total units remaining: 500 − 220 = 280 units sold

We are interested here in the flow of costs, *not* the flow of physical units

Caution: You must keep in mind, as we explain each method, that each is based on the *flow of costs,* not *the flow of physical units* through the firm. To be sure you realize the difference between the two flows, consider the following:

1. *Physical flow* may be understood by visualizing the bags of fertilizer, or other goods, "marching" from the receiving dock, to the stockroom, to the display counter, to the customer's car. The goods have no cost amount indelibly printed on them — and each bag is exactly alike.

2. *Cash flow* is the "march" of the unit costs from the Purchases account to either Ending Inventory or Cost of Goods Sold. Whereas physical flows are determined by the actual movement of goods, cost flows are controlled by the accountant's pencil.

Cost flows and physical flows do not have to be the same, as we shall see.

First In, First Out (FIFO)

FIFO:
(1) First (earliest) costs go to Cost of Goods Sold
(2) Last (most recent) costs go to Ending Inventory

Here's how the FIFO method works. Keep your eye on Exhibit 9-1 and let's begin unrealistically but simply.

If Lenox sold only one unit during the month, the cost of goods sold would be recorded as $1.00 (from the January 5 purchase). The remaining costs (the remaining January 5 purchase and all other January purchases) would be in ending inventory.

Now let's assume that Lenox sold 51 units. The unit cost of these 51 units sold would be the cost of the first 51 units purchased — 50 units from the January 5 batch and 1 unit from the January 12 batch. The cost of ending inventory would include the remaining costs of 99 units from the January 12 purchase and the costs of all other units purchased during the month.

According to FIFO, the cost of the earliest (first) purchases go to cost of goods sold. The remaining costs (the latest costs) are assigned to ending inventory.

Using the data in Exhibit 9-1, the Lenox Company calculates its cost of goods sold and its ending inventory cost using the FIFO method as follows:

FIFO Cost of Goods Sold during January 1988

	Units Sold	×	Unit Cost	=	Total Cost
From January 5 purchase.	50	×	$1.00	=	$ 50.00
From January 12 purchase.	100	×	1.50	=	150.00
From January 18 purchase.	130	×	2.00	=	260.00
FIFO cost of goods sold.	280 total units sold				$460.00

Lenox's FIFO cost of goods sold

FIFO Ending Inventory, January 31, 1988

	Units Unsold	×	Unit Cost	=	Total Cost
From January 18 purchase	70	×	$2.00	=	$140.00
From January 20 purchase	100	×	2.50	=	250.00
From January 27 purchase	50	×	3.00	=	150.00
FIFO ending inventory cost.	220 total units unsold				$540.00

Lenox's FIFO ending inventory

There are several things to observe from these calculations:

The total number of units purchased during the month was 500 units; the total number sold was 280. That means 280 units ÷ 500 units, or 56% of all units purchased, physically "flowed" through the firm.

Now let's take a look at what we mean by *cost flow.* The total cost for all the units was $1,000; the cost of goods sold, as we saw, was $460. That means, based on the total cost of all goods purchased, there was a cost flow of $460 ÷ $1,000 or 46% of total costs through the firm.

Here is a case where the flow of physical units and the flow of costs are certainly and clearly not the same. The reason should also be clear: the pattern of rising prices for each subsequent batch of units during the month. The lower unit costs from purchases at the beginning of the month were charged to the cost of the units sold. That left the higher unit costs from the purchases toward the end of the month to be assigned to the units in the ending inventory.

Weighted Average (WA)

Before we look at the weighted average inventory method, let's see how a weighted average differs from a simple average. Consider the following greatly simplified example:

Moon's Office Supplies purchased one desk for $40 and later bought 10 more identical ones for $1,500 ($150 each). The simple average cost would be:

$$\frac{\text{Unit cost in each batch purchased}}{\text{Number of batches purchased}} = \frac{\$40 + \$150}{2} = \frac{\$190}{2} = \frac{\$95 \text{ simple average}}{\text{cost per unit}}$$

The size of the two batches purchased was clearly different, but the simple average calculation considered them to be the same. Thus the simple average gives us an inaccurate cost per unit of $95. We know that this cost is not accurate because the simple average cost per unit, $95, multiplied by the number of units, 11, equals $1,045 — not the $1,540 ($40 + $1,500) that we know to be the total cost.

The weighted average cost takes into consideration not only the cost per unit in each batch but also the number of units purchased at each cost. More weight is given to the second batch than the first — in fact, 10 times more weight, since 10 times more units were purchased. Moon's weighted average cost would be:

$$\frac{\text{Total cost for all units purchased}}{\text{Total number of units purchased}} = \frac{\$1,540}{11} = \underline{\underline{\$140}} \text{ weighted average cost per unit}$$

Weighted average assigns the same *per-unit* costs to goods sold and goods unsold

A weighted average weights each batch purchased by including the total cost of the batch and the number of units in the batch. Less weight is given to smaller and/or lower-cost batches than to larger and/or higher-cost batches. The weighted average gives us an accurate average cost per unit, since $140 weighted average cost per unit × 11 units = $1,540.

In the weighted average inventory method, the cost of each unit of inventory is considered to be the weighted average cost of all goods available for sale during the period. This means that the weighted average cost per unit is used to calculate cost of goods sold, as well as the cost of ending inventory.

Lenox Company's cost of goods sold and the cost of ending inventory using the weighted average method would be determined as follows:

$$\text{Weighted average cost per unit of goods available} = \frac{\text{total cost of all units available for sale}}{\text{total units available for sale}}$$

$$\text{Weighted average cost} = \frac{\$1,000}{500 \text{ units}}$$

$$= \$2.00 \text{ per unit}$$

Lenox's weighted average cost of goods sold

Cost of goods sold using weighted average:

$2.00 per unit $\times$ 280 units sold = $\underline{\$560}$ **Cost of goods sold**

Lenox's weighted average ending inventory

Ending inventory cost using weighted average:

$2.00 per unit $\times$ 220 units left unsold = $\underline{\$440}$ **Ending inventory**

Last In, First Out (LIFO)

LIFO:
(1) Last costs go to Cost of Goods Sold
(2) First costs to Ending Inventory

The last-in, first-out method assigns costs in reverse order to that of the FIFO method. *With LIFO, as the name implies, the last costs incurred are assigned to Cost of Goods Sold and the earlier costs are assigned to Ending Inventory.*

Lenox Company cost calculations under LIFO are shown below:

LIFO Cost of Goods Sold Expense

	Units Sold	$\times$	Unit Cost	=	Total Cost
Lenox's LIFO cost of goods sold					
From January 27 purchase	50	$\times$	$3.00	=	$150.00
From January 20 purchase	100	$\times$	2.50	=	250.00
From January 18 purchase	130	$\times$	2.00	=	260.00
LIFO cost of goods sold	280 units				$660.00

LIFO Ending Inventory

	Units Unsold	$\times$	Unit Cost	=	Total Cost
Lenox's LIFO ending inventory					
From January 5 purchase	50	$\times$	$1.00	=	$ 50.00
From January 12 purchase	100	$\times$	1.50	=	150.00
From January 18 purchase	70	$\times$	2.00	=	140.00
LIFO ending inventory	220 units				$340.00

Of course, by this point, you have noticed that there are startling differences for costs of goods sold and costs of ending inventory among the three methods. Let's cover the final inventory cost method, and then we'll explain which methods will yield the most representative inventory costs for various situations.

Specific Identification (SI)

The specific identification method is based on the assumption that each unit purchased, sold, or in inventory has its own identity, that it is separate and distinguishable from any other unit. If this is possible, then certainly it is simple enough to specify the particular cost of each unit. Each unit sold or remaining in inventory is identified, and its specific unit cost is used in calculating cost of goods sold or ending inventory cost.

Specific identification is used when each unit is clearly different

Of course, the specific identification method does not work for large volumes of identical, low-cost items. This method is appropriate for companies that handle a relatively low volume of physical units, each having a high cost. Of course, each unit must be clearly different from the others, as would be the case with original oil paintings, antiques, diamonds, and automobiles.

The specific identification method is *not* appropriate where each unit is the same in appearance but is differentiated from other units through serial numbers, such as the same model of washers, refrigerators, or televisions.

Specific identification: Cost flows and physical flows are the same

Of course, it is highly unlikely that the situation for Lenox as described in Exhibit 9-1 would be suitable for the specific identification method. Nevertheless, let's assume that it is suitable, for the purpose of demonstrating how to calculate cost of goods sold and ending inventory cost using this method.

For purposes of this illustration of specific identification, the units and costs shown below were selected arbitrarily. Management in a real-world situation would

Specific Identification Cost of Goods Sold

	Units Sold	×	Unit Cost	=	Total Cost
From January 5 purchase	30	×	$1.00	=	$ 30.00
From January 12 purchase	60	×	1.50	=	90.00
From January 18 purchase	130	×	2.00	=	260.00
From January 20 purchase	60	×	2.50	=	150.00
From January 27 purchase	0	×	3.00	=	0
Specific identification cost of goods sold	280 units				$530.00

Lenox's specific identification cost of goods sold

Specific Identification Ending Inventory

	Units Unsold	×	Unit Cost	=	Total Cost
From January 5 purchase	20	×	$1.00	=	$ 20.00
From January 12 purchase	40	×	1.50	=	60.00
From January 18 purchase	70	×	2.00	=	140.00
From January 20 purchase	40	×	2.50	=	100.00
From January 27 purchase	50	×	3.00	=	150.00
Specific identification ending inventory	220 units				$470.00

Lenox's specific identification ending inventory

be required to trace each unit to the purchase invoice to determine the unit cost. You should have noticed that unlike the other three methods, the specific identification method has no regular cost flow pattern.

A Shortcut

In each of the four methods illustrated, the total 500 units and the total $1,000 cost were accounted for. That is, using each method, we showed that all of the units and all of the cost were included either in cost of goods sold or in ending inventory. This fact is summarized below:

	FIFO		Weighted Average		LIFO		Specific Identification	
	Units	$	Units	$	Units	$	Units	$
Cost of goods sold	280	460	280	560	280	660	280	530
Ending inventory	220	540	220	440	220	340	220	470
Total goods available	500	1,000	500	1,000	500	1,000	500	1,000

Cost of goods sold = cost of goods available less cost (FIFO, WA, LIFO, SI) of ending inventory

Since we know the total costs of all units on hand during the period, it is possible to calculate ending inventory cost and then determine cost of goods sold by subtracting it from the total cost of all goods available. Likewise, we could calculate cost of goods sold and then determine ending inventory by subtracting it from the total cost of all goods available. For example, assume that only ending inventory costs were calculated for Lenox Company. The cost of goods sold could be determined by simply subtracting ending inventory costs from total cost, as follows:

	FIFO	Weighted Average	LIFO	Specific Identification
Total cost of goods available	$1,000	$1,000	$1,000	$1,000
Computed ending inventory cost	−540	−440	−340	−470
Assumed cost of goods sold	$ 460	$ 560	$ 660	$ 530

This shortcut approach is the way that cost of goods sold is calculated in real businesses. The FIFO, weighted average, LIFO, and specific identification methods are really ending inventory methods. Now you realize that once we find the ending inventory, using one of these methods, cost of goods sold may be determined by a simple subtraction of ending inventory from total cost of goods available.

You will understand the inventory methods better at first if you calculate the ending inventory and cost of goods sold amounts separately. Then, you can check your answers by adding the two to see if you get the total cost of goods available.

Before we go any further, look at Figure 9-2 (pages 348–349) for one more illustration of how these four cost flow methods work.

Comparing Inventory Cost Methods

You should have observed thus far that for the same number of units sold, each method yields a different cost of goods sold. That means that for the same selling price per unit, each method provides a different profit. This fact is shown in the table on page 347 comparing different gross profits under the four different methods for calculating ending inventory and cost of goods sold. In each case, we assume that the selling price is $5.00 per unit for each of the 280 units sold during January.

		Weighted		**Specific**

LENOX COMPANY
Gross Profits under Four Inventory Methods
Month Ended January 31, 1988

	FIFO	Weighted Average	LIFO	Specific Identification
Sales (280 × $5).	$1,400	$1,400	$1,400	$1,400
Cost of goods sold:				
1/1/88 inventory.	0	0	0	0
Purchases	$1,000	$1,000	$1,000	$1,000
Goods available for sale	$1,000	$1,000	$1,000	$1,000
1/31/88 inventory	540	440	340	470
Cost of goods sold	$ 460	$ 560	$ 660	$ 530
Gross profit.	$ 940	$ 840	$ 740	$ 870

Each inventory method yields a different gross profit

Depending on which inventory cost method Lenox uses, the company can show profits ranging from $740 to $940. Yet in each case sales and purchases are exactly the same. The only difference lies in the method used to calculate ending inventory costs.

Why are so many different inventory cost methods available? Why is it possible to report the *same* events, using different methods, and produce different results?

These questions are difficult, perhaps impossible, to answer satisfactorily. Nevertheless, let's try to answer them by examining some of the advantages and disadvantages of each method.

The underlying characteristics of each method are shown in Exhibit 9-2 (page 350) as well as the advantages and disadvantages that we are about to discuss. An assumption underlying our conclusions is that inventory costs are rising; that is, a period of inflation exists.

FIFO

The ending inventory calculated using the FIFO method contains the more recent, highest costs. That implies that the units sold were assigned the older, lower costs. Thus FIFO calculates the highest ending inventory costs and the lowest cost of goods sold among the three inventory methods.

Ending inventory is reported as a current asset on the balance sheet. If you believe that the balance sheet should report the most recent costs possible, you would use the FIFO method for inventory costs.

FIFO advantages

The main advantage of FIFO is that it is a simple method to use. Also, for most merchandising businesses, the flow of costs approximates the flow of physical units. Some business people believe that this logical relationship between cost and physical flow is important in choosing an inventory method. Accounting theory, you remember, does not emphasize the flow relationship, so this advantage is largely a personal one for those business people who feel it is important.

FIFO disadvantages

The disadvantages of FIFO are that it does not match current costs with current revenue, certainly not as well as does LIFO. (Remember: Using FIFO, the cost of goods sold is based on older, hence lower, unit costs.) In periods of rapidly rising prices, this mismatch will produce an artificially high income, causing the firm to pay higher income taxes than if the LIFO method were used.

Weighted Average

This method considers that each unit of inventory of a particular type is identical and can be sold for the same price, and therefore has equal economic significance to the

FIGURE 9-2
Four Inventory Cost Flow Methods.

Assumptions: The company has five identical units. The units were acquired in the order shown—the $2 unit first, the $4 unit second, etc. The cost of each unit is shown on the unit. Three units are sold; two units are left.

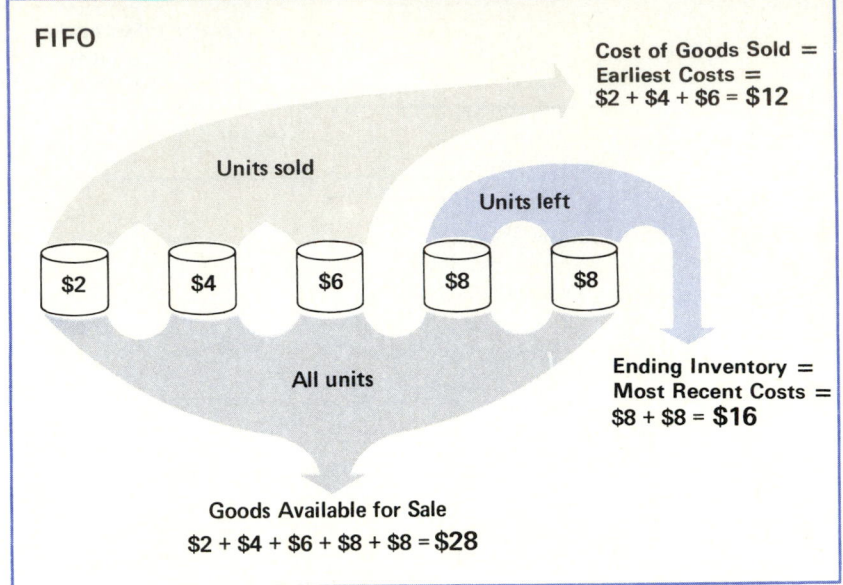

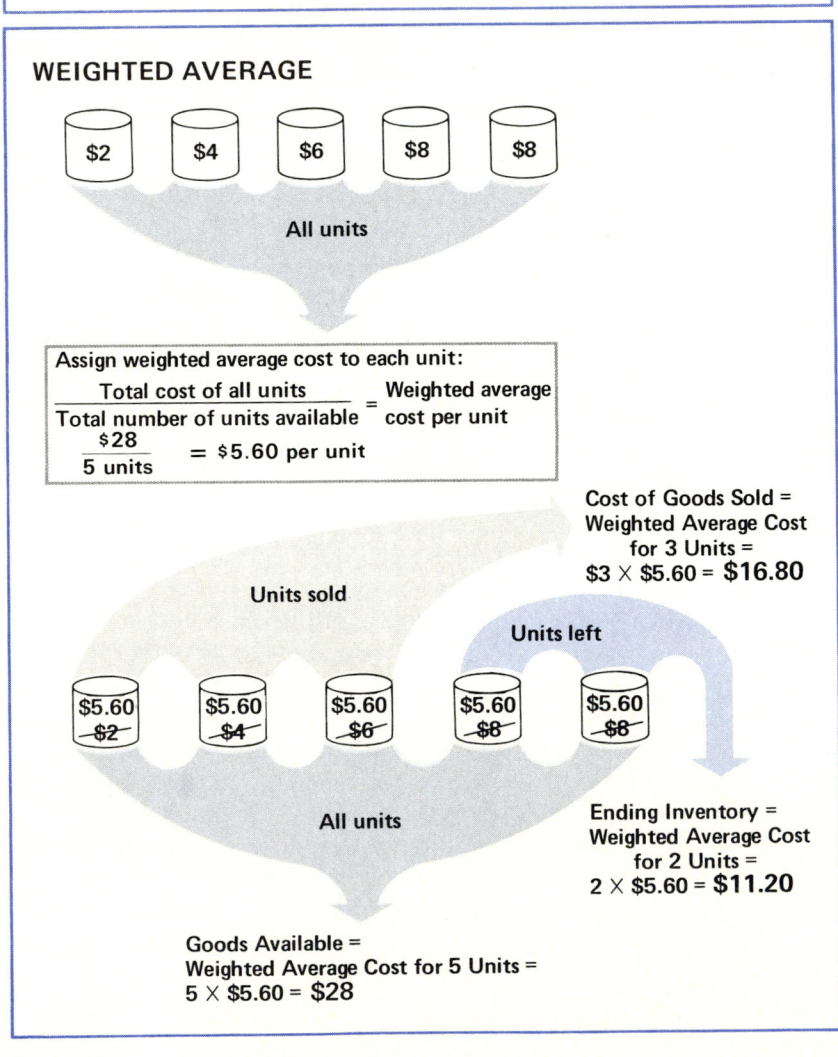

The flows in these diagrams are intended to show cost flows, not physical flows—remember that the units are identical, so physical flow is not important.

Cost of Goods Sold plus Ending Inventory equals Cost of Goods Available ($28) for each method.

Cost of Ending Inventory is: FIFO = Most Recent Costs; Weighted Average = Weighted Average Cost per Unit × Number of Units Unsold; LIFO = Earliest Costs; Specific Identification = Actual Cost of Physical Units Left.

Cost of Goods Sold is: FIFO = Earliest Costs; Weighted Average = Weighted Average Cost per Unit × Number of Units Sold; LIFO = Most Recent Costs; Specific Identification = Actual Cost of Physical Units Sold.

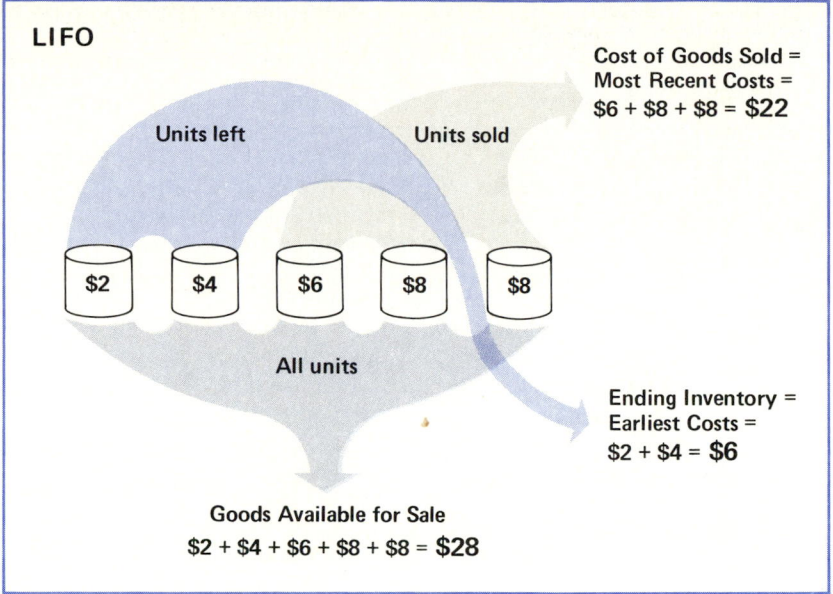

LIFO

Units left   Units sold

Cost of Goods Sold = Most Recent Costs = $6 + $8 + $8 = **$22**

$2 $4 $6 $8 $8

All units

Ending Inventory = Earliest Costs = $2 + $4 = **$6**

Goods Available for Sale
$2 + $4 + $6 + $8 + $8 = **$28**

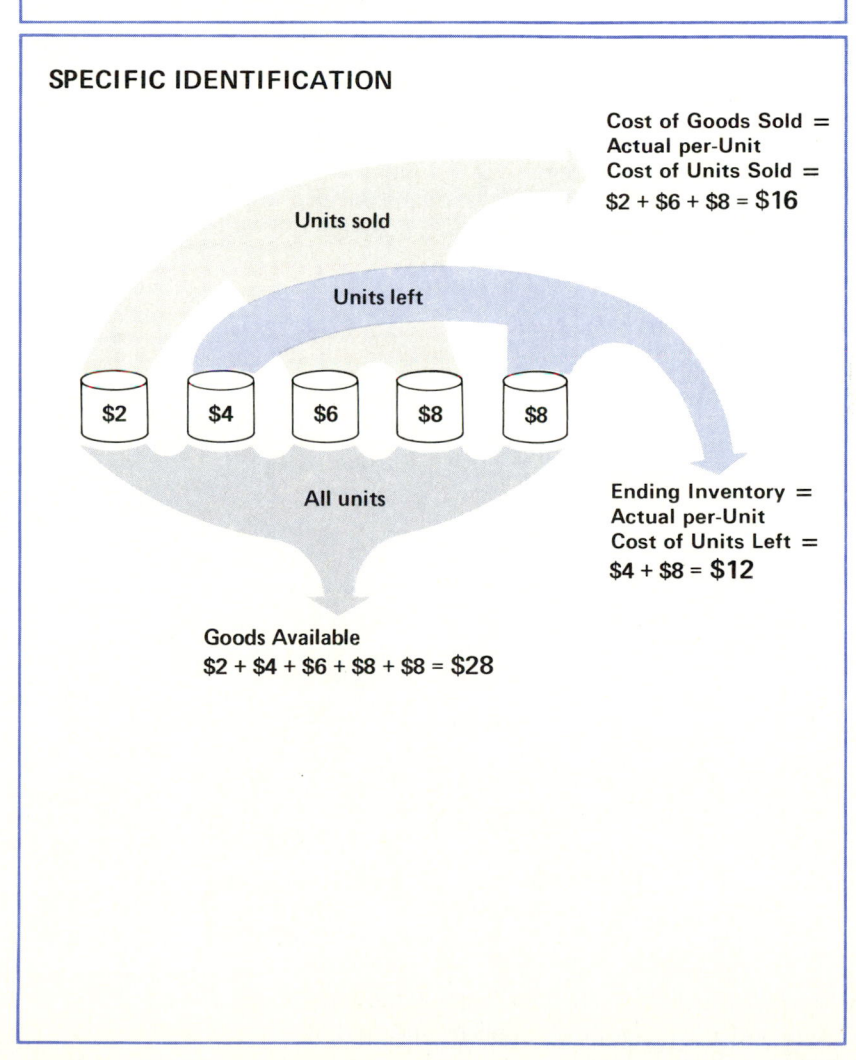

SPECIFIC IDENTIFICATION

Units sold

Units left

Cost of Goods Sold = Actual per-Unit Cost of Units Sold = $2 + $6 + $8 = **$16**

$2 $4 $6 $8 $8

All units

Ending Inventory = Actual per-Unit Cost of Units Left = $4 + $8 = **$12**

Goods Available
$2 + $4 + $6 + $8 + $8 = **$28**

EXHIBIT 9-2
Characteristics of Four Inventory Costing Methods.

	FIFO	Weighted Average	LIFO	Specific Identification
Ending inventory costs	The more recent unit costs are assigned to the units not sold—those in ending inventory.	The same unit costs—the weighted average cost per unit—are assigned to units not sold and to units sold.	The earliest unit costs are assigned to the units not sold—those in ending inventory.	The actual per-unit cost of each unit unsold is assigned to ending inventory.
Cost of goods sold	Earliest unit costs are assigned to units sold—those in cost of goods sold expense.	The same unit costs—the weighted average cost per unit—are assigned to units sold and unsold.	The more recent unit costs are assigned to the units sold—those in cost of goods sold expense.	The actual per-unit cost of each unit sold is assigned to cost of goods sold expense.
Advantages (strengths)	1. Simple method to use 2. Yields ending inventory amount on the balance sheet comprising more current costs than if weighted average or LIFO is used 3. Produces cost flow approximating physical flow better than weighted average or LIFO	1. Assigns equal unit cost to each unit of inventory 2. Does not produce widely fluctuating profits when inventory costs are fluctuating as FIFO and LIFO do	1. Matches more recent costs with current revenue better than FIFO or weighted average 2. Yields the lowest income, thus the lowest income tax obligation during periods of inflation	1. Simple method to use 2. Cost flows and physical flows are the same 3. Matches each unit cost with the revenue it helped produce
Disadvantages (weaknesses)	1. Does not match recent costs with current revenue as well as LIFO does 2. Yields a higher taxable income than LIFO or weighted average during periods of inflation	1. Does not match recent costs with current revenue as well as LIFO does 2. Does not produce an ending inventory amount containing costs that are as recent as under FIFO	1. Does not produce an ending inventory amount containing costs that are as recent as under FIFO or weighted average 2. Complicated to use by a firm with many products	1. Use is limited to those firms having small quantity of high-cost, unique goods

firm. Units having equal economic significance should be assigned equal costs. The weighted average method assigns an equal cost to each unit, sold or unsold, unlike the FIFO or LIFO method.

Weighted average advantages   An advantage of the weighted average method is that it produces costs of goods sold, and thus profits, that fluctuate less sharply than FIFO and LIFO. A substantial increase or decrease in inventory cost will cause FIFO and LIFO incomes suddenly to increase or decrease. Weighted average will combine these new costs with old costs in calculating the average cost per unit. Charging these average unit costs to cost of goods sold will result in a less dramatic change in income.

Weighted average disadvantages

Disadvantages of the weighted average method are: (1) It fails to match current costs with current revenue as well as LIFO does; and (2) it does not produce an ending inventory cost that approximates current inventory costs as well as FIFO.

LIFO

LIFO advantages

One advantage of LIFO is that it matches most recent costs with most current revenue. (Remember that under LIFO the costs of the units most recently purchased are assigned to cost of goods sold.) Because of this better matching, LIFO provides a better measure of income than either FIFO or weighted average.

Furthermore, in periods of rising costs LIFO produces a lower income than the income calculated by either FIFO or weighted average. The Lenox Company illustration (page 347) clearly shows this. Why would a company want to show a lower income? The lower a firm's taxable income, the lower the income taxes the firm has to pay. The Internal Revenue Service requires that if a company adopts LIFO, it must use LIFO for both income statement reporting and for the income tax return. In the 1970s many corporations switched to the LIFO method of calculating ending inventory and cost of goods sold to gain this income tax advantage.

LIFO disadvantages

The disadvantages of LIFO are: (1) It may be rather complicated to implement in companies having a large number of different types of inventory; and (2) it may result in very old and currently unrealistic ending inventory costs, and thus, an unrealistic measure of current assets on the balance sheet.

Specific Identification

The specific identification cost method matches specific costs of identified units with specific revenue earned by selling those units. Thus, the cost flows follow exactly the physical flow of goods through the firm.

This method would be impractical for companies with extremely large numbers of units of inventory and undesirable for companies dealing in units that are not clearly different from each other. Because it is not based on orderly patterns of costs flowing through the accounts, there is no point in comparing it with the other cost flow methods.

Consistency of Inventory Method

Consistency requires using the same inventory method each year

The *consistency* principle of accounting requires that the same accounting method should be applied from period to period. This means that when a company selects an inventory method, such as FIFO, it must use that method each year. The method used is disclosed in the footnotes to the financial statements or as a parenthetical note alongside the merchandise inventory on the balance sheet. Readers of the income statement and the balance sheet will be able to follow trends in cost of goods sold and ending inventory costs over a period of time, because they will know that any change in income or asset valuation will be caused by a change in actual costs, not by a change in the method of determining inventory costs.

The consistency principle doesn't prohibit a firm from ever changing accounting methods. A firm can change methods if it has a good reason to do so. The effects of the change on income and asset measurement are disclosed in the financial statement footnotes.

LOWER OF COST OR MARKET

There may be cases where there is plenty of an item in inventory but the demand for it suddenly falls off. Two things will then happen:

NO FREE LIFO

Everybody knows that LIFO inventory accounting helps minimize the effect of inflation on an income statement by using the most recent inventory cost. The latest additions to inventory (last in), with the highest costs, are counted as being the first shipped (first out). This eliminates the lag effect of the more traditional first-in, first-out method in which oldest costs are matched first against most recent prices, thus inflating earnings continuously until prices stop rising.

But there is a price for having a more realistic income statement, à la LIFO: an increasingly less realistic balance sheet. It works like this: Usually, when a company switches from FIFO to LIFO, its existing stock of raw materials, work in progress and finished goods stay on the books at costs prevalent at the time of the switch, which is generally much less than their current value. The difference between that ever older stock of goods with its frozen values and current market value is the "LIFO cush-

ion." That cushion can grow in periods of rising prices as inventory grows—the difference between this year's larger stock of goods and last year's then becomes another layer of the cushion. But the cushion doesn't show on the balance sheet, thus owners' equity is understated.

When a company pares inventory and cuts into the cushion, it gets a major and misleading shot in the arm from matching frozen older costs against current prices. That's what a number of oil companies have been doing since last year [1981]. But until that happens the LIFO cushion is not transferred to owners' equity.

Just how distorted those equity figures can be for a company with a lot of capital tied up in inventory was underscored recently in a survey of the chemical industry done by Norman Weinger of Oppenheimer & CO., the brokerage house. Weinger calculated that Union Carbide's net worth was understated by about 18% just because of its aging LIFO cushion.

* * *

The LIFO news is not all bad, of course. A big LIFO cushion can be a very pleasant surprise for stockholders. According to Weinger, many steel companies' LIFO cushions equal or exceed the companies' total stock market value. National Steel's LIFO cushion at the end of 1981 totaled $742 million—towering over its recent market value of $322 million.

What happens now that inflation is slowing down? To the extent that it continues to slow, the LIFO cushions will cease growing; but they'll still be there—unless real deflation sets in. But here's another complication: This year, with so many companies cutting inventories, a good part of those cushions are helping to pad earnings, making them look better than they are. That's the fascinating thing about accounting: The more you strive to make it reflect the real world, the more complex it becomes.

Source: FORBES, December 6, 1982, pages 168, 171.

A growing company is going to have a growing amount of ending inventory each year. The greater quantities of inventory will be necessary for the company to meet increased customer demands. When using LIFO, these greater and greater quantities of ending inventory build upon one another much like a layer cake. The oldest costs are in the bottom layer, with newer and newer costs added each year. If these old costs were to appear on the income statement, they would be matched with recent, much higher selling prices, yielding abnormally high profit margins. The difference between these lower costs and more recent higher inventory costs is called a "LIFO cushion" in the article you have just read. A strike, an interrupted source of inventory supply, a decrease in demand for the company's products, or some other situation might cause a company to use up its LIFO cushion by reducing the quantity of its ending inventory. The result is to show much higher profits on the income statement—and a much higher tax bill due to the IRS.

1. At the wholesale or supplier level, the replacement cost of those items will decline. This replacement cost is what we will call the *market price of inventory.*

2. At the level of merchandising firm, the selling price will have to be lowered to get rid of—that is, to be competitive in selling—what remains in inventory.

Thus the firm is caught in a squeeze between lower selling price and higher inventory cost.

The firm's inventory isn't valued at the lower replacement cost because it hasn't bought any at that price. Indeed, it is loaded with inventory purchased at the older, higher price, which is the cost of that inventory.

Further, since the firm must sell it at a lower selling price, the company's ability to generate the normal gross profit on its sales is impaired—its cost of goods sold will be at the old, higher costs while its sales will be at the new, lower selling price. Such a loss in profit is measurable. The loss—and the reduction in the inventory's value—should be recognized in the period when the drop in replacement cost—the event causing the loss—occurs, not in a later period when the items are sold.

The lower-of-cost-or-market method measures the drop in the replacement cost of inventory

The loss in value resulting from a reduction in the replacement cost of inventory is calculated by the *lower-of-cost-or-market* method, simply called *LCM.* LCM is calculated by comparing inventory cost, as determined by one of the methods discussed earlier in the chapter, with market, which is the current replacement cost of the goods. LCM can be applied to each item of inventory, to various subgroupings of inventory, or to the inventory as a whole, as is shown below:

Inventory Item No.	Description	Quantity	Cost (FIFO)	Market (Replacement Cost)	LCM Item by Item
101	Hose	10	$ 20	$ 18	$ 18
102	Bracket	40	40	42	40
103	Clamp	5	20	15	15
206	Motor	100	125	100	100
208	Mount	60	180	165	165
210	Generator	250	188	208	188
Totals			$573	$548	$526

The LCM item-by-item column amounts are determined by comparing the cost and market for each item and choosing the lower of the two in each case—the cost is lower for items no. 102 and no. 210; market is lower for all the others. These LCM item-by-item amounts are totaled and this amount, $526, is used to calculate the loss as follows:

LCM item by item

Cost (FIFO).	$573
LCM (item by item)	526
Loss.	$ 47

The loss in value can be estimated also by comparing the total cost of all the inventory with the total market of all the inventory:

LCM total inventory basis

Cost (FIFO).	$573
LCM (total inventory)	548
Loss.	$ 25

A firm will choose the one of these methods—item by item, or total inventory—that is easiest for it to use. Either method of estimating the loss is acceptable, provided that it is used consistently from period to period.

Conservatism means we use the methods that are least likely to overstate assets and income

The principle of *conservatism* is the justification for the LCM rule. Conservatism in accounting means that we should choose accounting methods that are least likely to overstate assets and income. Valuing inventory at cost when its replacement cost is lower overstates the asset Merchandise Inventory. Thus, we apply the conservatism principle and use LCM to reduce Inventory to a more realistic amount and, at the same time, recognize the loss in value that has occurred.

We have demonstrated the basic idea behind LCM. For further consideration of the more complex refinements of this technique, consult a more advanced accounting text.

ESTIMATING INVENTORY AMOUNTS

There may be situations where it is inconvenient or impossible to count inventory for the purpose of preparing an income statement. For most firms, the time and expense involved in counting inventory once each month would make it too costly to prepare monthly income statements. Also, a catastrophe, such as a fire, could destroy inventory, making it impossible to count. Thus, it would be impossible to prepare a meaningful income statement—we wouldn't know how much of the inventory purchased had been sold before the fire and how much had been destroyed. To overcome these problems, two methods have been devised as ways of estimating ending inventory without actually taking a physical count: the ***gross profit method*** and the ***retail inventory method.***

Gross Profit Method

The ***gross profit method*** relies on the relationship among sales, cost of goods sold, and gross profit to derive an estimate of ending inventory cost. The following illustration demonstrates how this method works.

A partial income statement (we have left out operating expenses and income taxes) for the year 1987 for Colonist Company follows:

COLONIST COMPANY
Partial Income Statement
Year Ended December 31, 1987

Sales.		$100,000	100%
Cost of Goods Sold:			
Beginning Inventory.	$16,000		
Purchases	74,000		
Goods Available for Sale	$90,000		
Ending Inventory.	10,000	80,000	80%
Gross Profit on Sales		$ 20,000	20%

On April 4, 1988, the Colonist Company warehouse was completely destroyed by fire. The accounting records were stored in a fireproof vault, making available the information about sales revenue, beginning inventory cost, and purchases for the period January 1–April 4, 1988.

We have added percentages on the 1987 Colonist income statement so that you can see the relationship between sales, cost of goods sold, and gross profit. Cost of goods sold is 80% of sales ($80,000 ÷ $100,000), and gross profit is 20% of sales ($20,000 ÷ $100,000). There were no changes in inventory costs or selling prices that would have altered these percentages during the first part of 1988. We assume, then, that the same percentage relationships existed until the date of the fire. The salvaged 1988 accounting records provide these data:

Sales (Jan. 1–Apr. 4, 1988).	$24,000
Purchases (Jan. 1–Apr. 4, 1988)	16,200
Beginning Inventory (Jan. 1, 1988).	10,000

Ending inventory can be calculated as follows:

Goods available for sale:		
Beginning inventory (known) (Jan. 1)...............		$10,000
Purchases (known) (Jan. 1–Apr. 4)...............		16,200
Goods available for sale...............		$26,200
Less: Cost of goods sold:		
Sales (known) (Jan. 1–Apr. 4)...............	$24,000	
× Cost of goods sold % (estimated)...............	80%	19,200
Estimated ending inventory, April 4, 1988...............		$ 7,000

You should be aware of two things when you consider using the gross profit method:

To use the gross profit method we must know sales, a gross profit %, beginning inventory, and purchases

1. Accounting records are normally protected against fire and theft. So it is not unrealistic to expect that sales, beginning inventory, and purchases figures would be available.

2. Percentages expressing the relationship between past gross profit and sales, and cost of goods sold and sales, should not be used blindly. Consideration should always be given to modifying these percentages to reflect any recent changes in costs or selling prices.

Retail Inventory Method

The retail inventory method estimates ending inventory by relying on the relationship between the cost of inventory and its selling price

The *retail inventory method* is based on the percentage relationship between the cost of inventory and its selling price. As its name implies, this method was developed for use by retail establishments to estimate ending inventory cost.

You will need to understand three terms to follow how to use this method:

1. *Original markup*   The amount added to the cost of merchandise to arrive at its original selling price

2. *Additional markup*   An addition to the original selling price yielding an even higher selling price

3. *Markdown*   A deduction from the original selling price resulting in a lower selling price

FAIRBURN FASHIONS
Calculation of Ending Inventory
Using Retail Inventory Method
June 30, 1987

	Cost	Retail
Beginning inventory...............	$ 38,000	$ 51,000
Purchases (net)...............	92,500	115,000
Additional markups...............		10,000
Markdowns...............		(2,000)
Total cost and selling price of goods available.......	$130,500	$174,000
Less: Sales (net)...............		(114,000)
Ending inventory at retail...............		$ 60,000
× Cost-to-retail ratio ($130,500 ÷ $174,000)...............		75%
Ending inventory at cost...............		$ 45,000

For all goods available for sale during the period, Fairburn first accumulated the total cost, $130,500, and the total selling price, $174,000, of all goods available during the period. These amounts were used to compute a ***cost-to-retail ratio,*** which is the ratio of the cost of goods available to the selling price of goods available ($130,500 ÷ $174,000 = 75%). This ratio simply states that the cost of the goods on hand was 75% of their retail selling price.

Next, actual sales *at the retail price* are deducted from the total selling price of all goods available for sale.

This calculation yields an ending inventory at its retail selling value.

Ending inventory at cost is derived by multiplying ending inventory at retail by the cost-to-retail ratio.

We have used the retail inventory method to estimate the cost of ending inventory. In actual practice the retail inventory method may be used to estimate ending inventory at lower-of-cost-or-market or at replacement cost, depending on how the markups and markdowns are treated in the computation. Further modifications are required if an estimate of LIFO ending inventory is desired. The complexities of these applications are beyond the scope of an introductory text.

INVENTORY ERRORS

Errors can happen in the process of calculating ending inventory costs. After all, it is a complex process that includes counting inventory, determining which units to include or exclude based on FOB and consignment terms, and applying one of the cost flow methods.

To understand how an error in the calculation of ending inventory cost affects the income statement, consider the illustration at the bottom of page 357.

Note that an error in ending inventory for year 1 also affects the next year because the ending inventory cost in year 1 becomes the beginning inventory cost for year 2. If the ending inventory cost of year 2 is correct, there will be no additional effect on year 3 because the beginning inventory for year 3 will be correct. Thus the impact of the error is confined to a 2-year period, and the error is said to ***self-correct*** or ***counterbalance*** over the 2 years. In our illustration the understatement of ending inventory in year 1 causes an understatement of year 1 gross profit. This is counterbalanced in year 2 by the understatement of beginning inventory, which causes an overstatement of year 2 gross profit.

A quick way to determine the effects of inventory errors

There is a quick way to determine the effects of errors in inventory cost without constructing a cost of goods sold section. Simply visualize the Expense and Revenue Summary account after all revenue, expenses, and inventory items have been closed:

Revenue appears on the credit side of Expense and Revenue Summary (the closing entry is to debit the revenue account and credit Expense and Revenue Summary).

Expenses appear on the debit side (the closing entry is to debit Expense and Revenue Summary and credit the expense account).

Since Beginning Inventory and Purchases have debit balances, the closing entry will be to debit Expense and Revenue Summary and credit these two accounts.

MARK COMPANY
Correct Gross Profit Computation
Years 1 and 2

	Year 1		Year 2	
Sales.		$100		$160
Cost of goods sold:				
Beginning inventory	$ 20		$ 50	
Purchases	90		120	
Goods available for sale.	$110		$170	
Ending inventory	50	60	70	100
Gross profit (correct)		$ 40		$ 60

MARK COMPANY
Inventory Error in Gross Profit Computation
Years 1 and 2

	Year 1		Year 2	
Sales.		$100		$160
Cost of goods sold:				
Beginning inventory (erroneous in year 2)	$ 20		$ 30	
Purchases	90		120	
Goods available for sale.	$110		$150	
Ending inventory (erroneous in year 1)	30	80	70	80
Gross profit (erroneous)		$ 20		$ 80

Effect of Inventory Error

	Year 1	Year 2	Total
Correct gross profit	$40	$60	$100
Erroneous gross profit	20	80	100
Effect of error	$20	$20	$–0–
	↑	↑	↑
	Gross profit understated by $20	Gross profit overstated by $20	No effect for 2-year period

Inventory errors affect income in each of 2 years

The effect of an inventory error on a combined 2-year period is zero

Ending Inventory is then established by debiting Merchandise Inventory and crediting Expense and Revenue Summary.

The above items, then, would appear as follows:

Expense and Revenue Summary

Expenses	Revenue
Beginning inventory	Ending inventory
Purchases	

Now observe that an error in either Beginning Inventory or Purchases will have the *same effect* as an error in an expense account. For example, an understatement of Beginning Inventory will have the same effect as understating an expense — to overstate income. An error in Ending Inventory will have the *same effect* as an error in a revenue account. For example, an understatement of Ending Inventory will have the same effect as understating revenue — to understate income.

Use this mental shortcut to review the Mark Company illustration presented on page 357.

PERPETUAL FIFO AND PERPETUAL LIFO

By now you have probably become aware that throughout this chapter we have been using the periodic inventory system for determining ending inventory and cost of goods sold. You should remember from Chapter 5 that when the *periodic inventory system* is used, ending inventory units, ending inventory cost, and cost of goods sold are determined at the *end* of each time period. No doubt you also remember from Chapter 5 that there is another method called the perpetual inventory system. Under the *perpetual inventory system,* we keep track of inventory on hand and cost of goods sold on a continuing basis. In Chapter 5 we demonstrated the accounting entries that would be made under the periodic and perpetual systems and discussed the differences in applying these two methods. You may want to refresh your memory by quickly reviewing pages 200–203.

In order to demonstrate perpetual inventory entries in Chapter 5, we assumed that the cost of each unit of inventory sold was known; that is, we used the specific identification method. Now you know that the specific identification method is not always appropriate or even possible to use (remember the bags of fertilizer). FIFO, LIFO, and weighted average may also be used in the perpetual inventory system. The journal entries are the same, only the way of calculating the cost of goods sold and ending inventory differs. We'll demonstrate perpetual FIFO and LIFO and leave the more complex weighted average for a more advanced accounting course.

Remember, when we use the periodic system, we wait until the end of the period to decide what costs to assign to ending inventory and what costs to assign to cost of goods sold. With the perpetual system, we must decide what cost to assign to cost of goods sold at the time each sale is made. Each time we make a sale, we record the sale in one entry and the cost of goods sold in another. The following simple example illustrates perpetual FIFO and perpetual LIFO.

The purchase and sales data for September are shown below:

Date	Description	Units	Cost Each	Total Cost
Sept. 1	Purchase	10	$8.00	$ 80
Sept. 10	Purchase	12	8.50	102
Sept. 12	Sale	8		
Sept. 18	Purchase	5	9.00	45
Sept. 25	Sale	10		
			Total cost of goods available	$227

Cost of goods sold for perpetual FIFO and perpetual LIFO would be calculated at the time of each sale as shown on page 359.

You should notice that:

1. Perpetual FIFO assigns the earliest costs to cost of goods sold each time a sale is made.
   Perpetual LIFO assigns the most recent costs to cost of goods sold each time a sale is made.

Perpetual FIFO

Date of Purchase or Sale		Cost of Goods Sold	Number of Units and Costs Remaining in Inventory
Sept. 1	Purchase	—	10 units @ $8.00
Sept. 10	Purchase	—	10 units @ $8.00 12 units @ $8.50
Sept. 12	Sale	8 units × $8.00 = $64	2 units @ $8.00 12 units @ $8.50
Sept. 18	Purchase	—	2 units @ $8.00 12 units @ $8.50 5 units @ $9.00
Sept. 25	Sale	2 units × $8.00 = $16 +8 units × $8.50 = 68 $84	4 units @ $8.50 5 units @ $9.00

(Left margin: Calculations using perpetual FIFO)

Total cost of goods sold—Perpetual FIFO:
Sept. 12 Sale . . . . $ 64
+Sept. 25 Sale 84
Total cost of goods sold. $148

Total ending inventory—Perpetual FIFO:
4 units × $8.50 =. . . . . $ 34
+5 units × $9.00 =. 45
Total ending inventory. . . . . $ 79

Perpetual LIFO

Date of Purchase or Sale		Cost of Goods Sold	Number of Units and Costs Remaining in Inventory
Sept. 1	Purchase	—	10 units @ $8.00
Sept. 10	Purchase	—	10 units @ $8.00 12 units @ $8.50
Sept. 12	Sale	8 units × $8.50 = $68	10 units @ $8.00 4 units @ $8.50
Sept. 18	Purchase	—	10 units @ $8.00 4 units @ $8.50 5 units @ $9.00
Sept. 25	Sale	5 units × $9.00 = $45 +4 units × $8.50 = 34 +1 unit × $8.00 = 8 $87	9 units @ $8.00

(Left margin: Calculations using perpetual LIFO)

Total cost of goods sold—Perpetual LIFO:
Sept. 12 Sale . . . . $ 68
+Sept. 25 Sale 87
Total cost of goods sold. $155

Total ending inventory—Perpetual LIFO:
9 units × $8.00 =. . . . . $ 72

2. Perpetual FIFO assigns the most recent costs to ending inventory.
Perpetual LIFO assigns the earliest costs to ending inventory.

A final observation: Perpetual and periodic FIFO yield the same cost of goods sold and ending inventory amounts. Perpetual and periodic LIFO usually yield different results.

CHAPTER SUMMARY

Merchandise inventory — the goods held for sale — is a major part of the total assets of retailers and wholesalers. Merchandise inventory for a manufacturer is usually called finished goods inventory.

Accounting for merchandise inventory involves three tasks: (1) calculating the cost of units purchased; (2) determining the number of physical units on hand; and (3) allocating cost between those units on hand and those that were sold.

The cost of units purchased usually includes three items: (1) the list price of the goods; (2) less any trade, quantity, and cash discounts; (3) plus the cost of freight paid in bringing the inventory to the seller's place of business. Purchases may be recorded using the *gross method* or the *net method.* The cost of units returned is not considered part of the purchase cost.

To determine the physical units on hand, they must be physically counted and consideration must be given to goods in transit and consignment arrangements. Units purchased *FOB shipping point* must be included in ending inventory even though not yet received. Goods purchased *FOB destination* are not included; they are included only after they have been received. *Goods in on consignment* are excluded from ending inventory because they are the legal property of another company, the *consignor. Goods out on consignment* must be included in ending inventory because they belong to the firm even though they are not physically present.

There are four methods of assigning cost to the units in ending inventory: (1) *first in, first out;* (2) *weighted average;* (3) *last in, first out;* and (4) *specific identification.* Under identical starting, operating, and ending conditions, each method will produce a different gross profit. The inventory method chosen must be used consistently year after year unless a change in method can be justified. When there is a change in inventory method, it must be disclosed on the financial statements.

If the demand for an item falls off at the retail level, the value of the inventory of those items will similarly decline. And at the wholesale level, their replacement cost will also decline. When this happens, the problem is what to use as inventory "cost" — the actual cost already paid? Or the current replacement cost (also referred to as *market cost*)? A solution to this problem is *lower of cost* (actual cost paid) *or market* (current replacement cost), or *LCM.* LCM recognizes a loss in the period in which the value of the inventory declined, not in the period in which the inventory is sold.

When a physical count of inventory is inconvenient, impractical, or impossible, the cost of ending inventory may be estimated by the *gross profit method* or the *retail inventory method.*

An error in the ending inventory of one year will automatically cause an error in the beginning inventory of the next period. Errors in ending inventory amounts are said to be *self-correcting,* or *counterbalancing,* over a 2-year period.

Any of the four methods of determining ending inventory cost may be applied in a *perpetual* or a *periodic* inventory system. Under a complete perpetual inventory system both the cost and the number of units on hand are known at all times. In a periodic system the ending inventory is determined by physical count and costs are assigned based on this count. The periodic system determines ending inventory only at the end of a period.

IMPORTANT TERMS USED IN THIS CHAPTER

Additional markup   The incremental increase in price above the original selling price of inventory. (page 355)

Cash discount   A reduction in the invoice price for paying cash within a specified period. The payment terms are abbreviated in the general form 2/10, n/30, where 2/10 means 2% discount if paid within 10 days and n/30 means that the total invoice price is due within 30 days if no discount is taken. Any terms may be specified. (page 335)

Consignment   An arrangement in which one business, the consignee, sells goods owned by another business, the consignor. At no time does the consignee own the goods. The consignee receives a commission for selling the consignor's goods and has a responsibility for caring for them while they are in his or her possession. (page 339)

Consistency principle   The assumption that the accounting methods used in a current time period have already been used in past periods and will continue to be used in future periods. (page 351)

Finished goods inventory   The name that manufacturers use for merchandise inventory. (page 333)

First in, first out (FIFO)   The method of accounting for inventory costs that assumes that the first, or earliest, costs incurred are the first costs that will be charged to Cost of Goods Sold Expense and the most recent costs will be assigned to Ending Inventory. (page 342)

FOB destination   Terms of shipping inventory that specify: (1) that the seller pays the freight to the point of destination; and (2) that title, the ownership, to the inventory passes from the seller to the buyer at the destination point. (page 339)

FOB shipping point   Terms of shipping inventory that specify: (1) that the seller does not pay the freight beyond the shipping point; and (2) that title passes from the seller to the buyer at the shipping point. The shipping point is usually considered to be the seller's place of business. (page 339)

Freight-in   Transportation cost paid by the buyer. (page 337)

Gross method   A method of recording purchases on credit at the gross invoice price — after trade and quantity discounts but before cash discounts. When cash discounts are taken, Purchase Discounts is credited for the amount of the discount. (page 335)

Gross profit method   A method of estimating the cost of inventory based on past records of sales, cost of goods sold, and gross profit and the relationships among these amounts. (page 354)

Last in, first out (LIFO)   The method of accounting for inventory costs that assumes that the most recent costs incurred are the first costs that will be charged to Cost of Goods Sold Expense, and the first costs, the oldest costs, will be assigned to Ending Inventory. (page 344)

Lower of cost or market (LCM)   A comparison of the cost of inventory with the replacement cost of the same inventory to determine if there has been a loss in the value of inventory that should be recorded. When replacement cost is lower than cost, a loss is recorded. (page 353)

Markdown   The incremental decrease in the selling price below the original selling price. (page 355)

Merchandise inventory   Goods held for sale. In manufacturing concerns, merchandise inventory is usually called finished goods inventory. (page 333)

Net method   A method of recording purchases on credit at the net invoice price anticipating that cash discounts will be taken. If the cash discount is not taken, Purchase Discounts Lost is debited at the time of payment. (page 335)

Original markup   The amount by which the original selling price exceeds its purchase price. See also *additional markup.* (page 355)

Periodic inventory method   A system of determining the ending inventory units, ending inventory cost, and cost of goods sold at the end of a period of time. (page 358)

Perpetual inventory method   A system for keeping an up-to-date record of the cost of inventory on hand and the cost of goods sold. (page 358)

Quantity discount   A reduction in the list price for purchasing a large number of units. (page 334)

Retail inventory method   A system for estimating the cost of ending inventory based on the relationship between the retail price of goods available for sale and the cost of those same goods. (page 355)

Specific identification   The method of accounting for inventory costs that identifies each specific unit of inventory and its cost. When the inventory is sold, its cost is assigned to Cost of Goods Sold; otherwise the cost remains in Ending Inventory. This method can be used only in those instances where each item is clearly different from the others. (page 344)

Trade discount   A variable reduction in the listed selling price; the reduction allowed is at the discretion of the seller. Hence, a way of adjusting the price for different classes of customers. (page 334)

Weighted average method   The method of accounting for inventory costs that assigns the same cost to each unit sold and each unit remaining in inventory. The weighted average cost for each unit equals the total cost of goods available for sale divided by the total number of units available for sale. (page 343)

QUESTIONS

1. How is raw materials inventory different from merchandise inventory?

2. Are dump trucks merchandise inventory? Explain.

3. Conner Co. has an account called Purchase Discounts on its books. Is Conner using the gross or net method of recording purchases? Explain.

4. Howard Co. received a trade discount, a quantity discount, and a cash discount on merchandise recently purchased. Howard uses the net method of recording purchases. Which of these discounts will be recorded in a separate account? Explain.

5. Where do Purchase Discounts and Purchase Discounts Lost appear on a company's income statement? Will a single company have both of these accounts on the same income statement? Explain.

6. Lee Co. buys all of its inventory FOB shipping point, whereas Key Co. buys all of its inventory FOB destination. Which company will have a Freight-In account? Explain.

7. Should goods out on consignment be included in ending inventory? Explain.

8. FIFO, LIFO, and weighted average are said to be inventory cost flow assumptions. Does cost flow differ from physical flow? Explain.

9. Which inventory method has the same cost flow and physical flow? Explain why.

10. List the strengths, or advantages, of the FIFO inventory method.

11. Merchandise inventory may be purchased at several different prices during a period and yet the weighted average method assigns the same amount to each unit in ending inventory. What is the justification for this weighted average procedure?

12. List the strengths, or advantages, of the LIFO inventory method.

13. The consistency principle means that the same accounting principles (or methods) used this period were also used last period. Does this mean that once a company decides to use FIFO, it can never switch to LIFO or weighted average?

14. How are *cost* and *market* determined in the lower-of-cost-or-market application?

15. What are two methods of determining an estimated ending inventory amount? Under what circumstances might a company want to estimate ending inventory?

16. When the gross profit method is used, two assumptions are made. What are they?

17. What estimation method makes use of a cost-to-retail ratio? How is this ratio calculated?

18. Why does an error in the ending inventory of year 1 also cause an error in year 2 income?

19. Errors in ending inventory are said to be *self-correcting*. Explain what this means.

20. What is the primary difference between a periodic inventory system and a perpetual inventory system?

EXERCISES

Exercise 9-1
Calculating the cost of inventory purchased by using trade, quantity, and cash discounts.

On April 1, Murphy Co. purchased 200 tires from the Radial Tire Co. The tires have a list price in Radial's catalog of $40 each. Radial allows a 20-10 trade discount and a quantity discount of 2% on orders of 100 or more tires. The terms of the purchase are 2/15, n/45. Murphy paid for the order on April 12. What was the cost of the tires to Murphy?

(Check figure: Net cost of inventory = $5,531.90)

Exercise 9-2
Recording the purchase of and payment for goods using the gross method

On October 1, Rameriz, Inc., purchased 30 beds from Hickory Furniture Manufacturing for $60 each. Terms of the purchase were 3/10, n/30; there were no trade or quantity discounts. Rameriz uses the *gross method* of recording purchases.
a. Assuming that Rameriz paid on October 9, prepare entries for October 1 and October 9.
b. Assuming that Rameriz paid on October 31, prepare entries for October 1 and October 31.

(Check figure: Purchase Discounts recorded on October 9 = $54.)

Exercise 9-3
Recording the purchase of and payment for goods using the net method

On June 1, Washington Stores purchased 20 toasters from Consumer Electric Products for $5.50 each. There were no trade or quantity discounts offered, but a cash discount is available with terms of 2/10, n/30. Washington uses the *net method* of recording purchases.
a. Assuming that Washington paid on June 5, prepare entries for June 1 and June 5.
b. Assuming that Washington paid on June 28, prepare entries for June 1 and June 28.

(Check figure: Purchase Discounts Lost recorded on June 28 = $2.20)

Exercise 9-4

Preparing the cost of goods sold section on an income statement

The following information was taken from the records of Hubbard, Inc., on December 31, 1986:

Merchandise Inventory (Jan. 1, 1986)	$ 60,000
Purchase Discounts	8,000
Purchases	368,000
Freight-In	32,000
Merchandise Inventory (Dec. 31, 1986)	90,000
Purchase Returns and Allowances	22,000

Calculate the cost of goods sold for the year ended December 31, 1986.

(Check figure: Cost of goods sold = $340,000)

Exercise 9-5

Determining the number of physical units in ending inventory

Perez Wholesale Supply is in the process of determining the number of physical units that should be in ending merchandise inventory. Using the information below, calculate the proper total physical units in ending inventory. Give a reason for omitting any item that you do not believe should be included in ending inventory.

Disposition	Number of Units
In stockroom	60,000
In shipment from suppliers (purchased FOB shipping point)	4,500
In shipment from suppliers (purchased FOB destination)	18,400
Out on consignment	13,600
On loading platform awaiting shipment to customers (legal title has not yet passed to customers)	2,800
In on consignment	1,800
In shipment to customers (merchandise was sold FOB shipping point)	4,400

(Check figure: 80,900 units in ending inventory)

Exercise 9-6

Calculating the ending inventory and cost of goods sold using periodic FIFO, LIFO, and weighted average

Jason Torre, President of Torre's Ball Bearings, wants you to prepare a comparison of ending inventory and cost of goods sold using three different periodic inventory methods. Data from the company's records follow:

	Units	Purchase Price Per Unit
Beginning inventory	40	$ 8.00
Mar. 5 purchase	60	12.00
Mar. 14 purchase	120	13.00
Mar. 25 purchase	100	14.00

80 units were on hand at the end of March.

Calculate the amount of ending inventory and cost of goods sold using periodic FIFO, weighted average, and LIFO.

(Check figure: Cost of goods sold using FIFO = $2,880)

Exercise 9-7

Using the gross profit method to estimate inventory lost

Forster Furniture lost all of its inventory in a recent tornado. Since the company uses the periodic inventory method, there is no record of exactly how much inventory was on hand at the time of the disaster. The controller asks you to provide an estimate of the amount that was on hand. The following information is available:

Purchases (net)	$450,000
Sales	600,000
Beginning inventory	100,000
Gross profit percent for the prior period	40%

(Check figure: Estimated inventory on hand = $190,000)

Exercise 9-8
Using the retail inventory method to estimate ending inventory

Gibson Men's Apparel wants to determine its approximate quarterly income without going to the expense and bother of counting ending inventory. The following information has been gathered for the quarter:

	Cost	Retail
Sales	—	$300,000
Beginning inventory	$ 60,000	84,000
Additional markups	—	14,000
Purchases (net)	245,600	290,000
Markdowns	—	6,000

Prepare an estimate of Gibson's gross profit for the quarter. (Use the retail inventory method to determine ending inventory.)

(Check figure: Estimated gross profit = $60,000)

Exercise 9-9
Calculating the effects of inventory errors on income of two years

Barker's Lighting Supplies sells light fixtures. At the end of 1987, the bookkeeper omitted some units from ending inventory. The units were out on consignment. The cost of the fixtures omitted was $6,000. The error was discovered on December 31, 1988. Income statements prepared *before* the error was discovered follow:

BARKER'S LIGHTING SUPPLIES Income Statements Years Ended December 31				
	1987		**1988**	
Sales	$75,000		$135,000	
Cost of Goods Sold:				
Beginning Inventory	$ 9,000		$12,000	
Purchases	39,000		70,000	
Goods Available for Sale	$48,000		$82,000	
Ending Inventory	12,000	36,000	21,000	61,000
Gross Profit		$39,000		$ 74,000
Operating Expenses		14,000		27,000
Net Income		$25,000		$ 47,000

Ending inventory on December 31, 1988, was correct. What effect will the bookkeeper's error have on 1987 and 1988 income? Prepare calculations to support your answer.

(Check figure: 1988 income is overstated by $6,000)

Calculating ending inventory and cost of goods sold using perpetual LIFO

Chambliss Sales provides you with the following purchases and sales data:

Date	Description	Units	Cost Each	Total Cost
Dec. 1	Purchase	8	$20	$160
8	Purchase	12	22	264
14	Sale	6		
22	Purchase	10	24	240
31	Sale	7		
Total cost of goods available				$664

Calculate the cost of goods sold and ending inventory using perpetual FIFO and perpetual LIFO.   *(Check figure: Cost of goods sold using perpetual LIFO = $300)*

PROBLEMS
Set A

Problem A9-1
Calculating the cost of inventory using the gross method

Wanda's Watercraft made three purchases of inventory during its first month of operations:

Mar. 5   Purchased 10 canoes from New City Boats. New City gave Wanda a 25% trade discount and terms of 4/20, n/30. The list price per canoe was $200. The inventory was shipped FOB destination; the total freight bill was $88. Wanda paid for the inventory on March 23.

7   Purchased three Fiberglas fishing boats listing for $720 each from Whopper Craft. Whopper gave Wanda a 30-10 trade discount and terms of 2/20, n/60. The boats were sent FOB shipping point and arrived at the store on March 20. The freight on the shipment was $115. Wanda paid Whopper on April 15.

10   Purchased two speed boats from Pro-Ski Boats. The boats listed for $4,500 each. Wanda received a 15% trade discount, a 5% quantity discount, and terms of 3/15, n/30. The boats, shipped FOB shipping point, were received on July 20. Freight charges amounted to $210. Wanda paid Pro-Ski on April 19.

Required   Assuming that Wanda uses the gross method of recording purchases, prepare clearly labeled schedules showing the calculation of the cost of **(1)** the canoes, **(2)** the fishing boats, and **(3)** the speed boats. Assume that the cash discount period begins on the purchase date, that is, March 5, March 7, and March 10. Note: Journal entries are not required.

(Check figure: Cost of the speed boats = $7,477.50)

Problem A9-2
Preparing entries to record purchases under the gross and net methods

Dial Art Supplies made the following purchases and payments during the month of November 1988:

Nov. 3   Purchased assorted paints and brushes from Rainbow Supplies for $3,600. Terms of the purchase were 2/10, n/30.

6   Purchased easels and canvases from Art Goods, Inc. Terms of the purchase were 3/15, n/45. The gross invoice amount was $1,260.

12   Dial paid Rainbow for the November 3 purchase.
30   Dial paid Art Goods for the easels and canvases.

Required   Assuming that the discount period begins on the date of purchase, prepare entries to record Dial's November purchases and payments using **(1)** the gross method of recording purchases; **(2)** the net method of recording purchases. Supporting calculations should be included as part of your journal entry explanations.

(Check figure: Purchase Discounts Lost using the net method = $37.80)

Problem A9-3

Calculating ending inventory and cost of goods sold using FIFO, LIFO, and weighted average

Stallings Company began business in June. The following purchases were made during the month:

Date	Units	Cost per Unit	Total Cost
June 3	40	$6.00	$240
10	20	6.40	128
14	110	6.60	726
24	50	6.80	340
28	10	7.00	70

Stalling's stock clerk reported that 80 units were on hand at the end of the month.

Required   Calculate the ending inventory and cost of goods sold under the periodic FIFO, LIFO, and weighted average methods. Do not use the shortcut. (Round the weighted average cost per unit to the nearest cent.)

(Check figure: Ending inventory under the weighted average method = $523.20)

Problem A9-4

Calculating ending inventory and cost of goods sold using FIFO, LIFO, and weighted average

Fountain Power Tools received the following schedules from the purchasing department manager and the marketing director:

FOUNTAIN POWER TOOLS
Summary of Purchasing Activity
Quarter Ended March 31, 1986

Date	Description	Units	Cost per Unit
Jan. 1	Inventory on hand	8,800	$ 9.60
Jan. 10	Purchase	2,000	9.90
Jan. 12	Return of defective units	500	9.90
Feb. 18	Purchase	3,000	10.20
Feb. 21	Purchase	6,000	10.50
Feb. 28	Purchase	1,500	10.40
Mar. 14	Purchase	4,500	10.80
Mar. 28	Return of defective units	800	10.80

FOUNTAIN POWER TOOLS
Summary of Sales
Quarter Ended March 31, 1986

Period Covered	Description	Units	Sales Price per Unit
Jan. 1–15	Sales	2,300	$24.00
Jan. 1–15	Customer returns	30	24.00
Jan. 16–31	Sales	4,200	24.60
Jan. 16–31	Customer returns	20	24.60
Feb. 1–15	Sales	2,100	25.00
Feb. 16–28	Sales	1,400	25.50
Feb. 16–28	Customer returns	50	25.50
Mar. 1–31	Sales	4,000	25.60

Required   Compute the ending inventory and cost of goods sold for Fountain Power Tools for the first quarter of 1986 under the periodic FIFO, LIFO, and weighted average methods. Use the shortcut. Round the weighted average cost per unit to the nearest cent.

(Check figure: Ending inventory under the periodic LIFO method = $102,390)

Problem A9-5
Applying LCM on an item-by-item basis, and to inventory as a whole

Plato's Paint Store uses lower of cost or market to value ending inventory. The following inventory summary was prepared on October 31, Plato's year-end:

Inventory Group	Inventory Stock Number	Quantity	Cost (FIFO)	Market (Replacement Cost)
Paint	A401	40 cases	$1,600	$1,525
	A415	10 cases	450	400
	A420	45 cases	2,340	2,400
Brushes	B101	10 cases	135	145
	B115	50 cases	945	963
	B117	20 cases	194	205
	B119	5 cases	64	44
Ladders	C940	20 each	446	400
	C945	100 each	2,560	2,300
	C948	3 each	90	99

Required   Calculate the amount of inventory that Plato should disclose on the October 31 balance sheet, assuming that lower of cost or market is applied:
1. On an item-by-item basis
2. To the inventory as a whole

(Check figure: LCM applied on an item-by-item basis = $8,373)

Problem A9-6
Using gross profit method to estimate inventory lost in a storm

On September 13, 1988, a tornado destroyed much of the inventory of Toy Heaven. Toy Heaven managed to salvage only $750 of merchandise. The insurance adjuster needs an estimate of the total inventory on hand at the time of the storm in order to pay Toy Heaven for its losses. The toy store manager has put together the following information:

TOY HEAVEN		
Income Statement		
Year Ended June 30, 1988		
Sales (net)		$210,000
Cost of Goods Sold:		
Merchandise Inventory 7/1/87.	$ 12,250	
Purchases (net).	156,000	
Goods Available for Sale	$168,250	
Merchandise Inventory 6/30/88.	21,250	147,000
Gross Profit on Sales		$ 63,000
Operating Expenses		40,000
Net Income		$ 23,000
Sales (July 1 – Sept. 13, 1988).		$ 89,500
Purchases (July 1 – Sept. 13, 1988).		64,375

Required | Calculate the amount of inventory Toy Heaven lost in the storm.

(Check figure: Cost of inventory lost = $22,225)

Problem A9-7

Using retail inventory method to estimate inventory; preparing an income statement and a balance sheet

Arnold Foster, owner of Arnold's Camera, is considering selling a part of the business to Gail Marshall. Gail has asked to see an up-to-date set of financial statements. Arnold is upset because his fiscal year doesn't end for another 2 months and he believes it will be expensive and time-consuming to count physical inventory. You volunteer to help Arnold in the preparation of his financial statements. You suggest that the retail inventory method be used to estimate ending inventory. Arnold provides the information shown below:

ARNOLD'S CAMERA Adjusted Trial Balance April 30, 1987		
	Debit	**Credit**
Cash	$ 32,000	
Merchandise Inventory (July 1, 1986)	17,000	
Supplies on Hand	1,600	
Store Fixtures	64,000	
Accumulated Depreciation: Store Fixtures		$ 16,800
Accounts Payable.		23,000
Common Stock ($10 par)		50,000
Retained Earnings		17,200
Sales		290,000
Sales Returns	7,000	
Purchases.	252,800	
Purchase Returns and Allowances		8,000
Freight-In.	5,000	
Depreciation Expense	5,600	
Other Operating Expenses	20,000	
Total.	$405,000	$405,000

Other Information

Merchandise on hand July 1, 1986, had a retail price of:	$ 21,200
Net purchases were marked to sell for:	312,200
Net additional markups amounted to:	9,100
Net markdowns amounted to:	9,000

Required | 1. Prepare a schedule calculating your estimate of the cost of ending inventory.
2. Prepare an income statement for the period July 1, 1986, through April 30, 1987.
3. Prepare a balance sheet for Arnold on April 30, 1987.

(Check figure: Estimated ending inventory = $40,400)

Problem A9-8

Calculating the effects of inventory errors on incomes of four years

You have been hired as the inventory accounting clerk for Drew, Inc. Your first task is to review the inventory records for the past 4 years and determine if there were any mistakes. You discovered the following errors:

a. 1985 ending inventory was overstated because goods shipped to customers FOB shipping point were included. The overstatement amounted to $8,400.

b. 1985 sales were understated by $20,000 because sales of goods described in **a** were also omitted. These sales were erroneously recorded in 1986.

c. 1986 ending inventory was understated by $13,000 because goods out on consignment were omitted.

d. 1987 ending inventory was understated by $35,000. Employees neglected to count the inventory in a basement room.

e. 1988 purchases totaling $5,000 were not recorded. The bookkeeper had overlooked the invoice. The goods were included in ending inventory.

f. 1988 ending inventory was overstated by $2,160 because of an error in addition.

Required

Prepare a schedule showing the calculation of the correct net income for each of the 4 years. The reported net income for each year is shown below. Hint: Set up your solution paper as follows:

Description	1985	1986	1987	1988
Net income (loss) reported	$69,000	$38,400	($8,000)	$30,000

Add or subtract the effects of each error in the appropriate columns; total each column to find corrected net income.

(Check figure: 1987 corrected net income = $14,000)

Problem A9-9

Calculating ending inventory using periodic and perpetual FIFO and LIFO

Atlantic Co. has the following record of purchases and sales for its first month of operations, June 1987:

Purchases			
Date	Units	Cost per Unit	Total Cost
June 2	200	$3.00	$ 600
10	80	3.25	260
17	240	3.50	840
23	80	3.75	300
30	40	4.00	160
Totals	640		$2,160

Sales	
Date	Units
June 13	100
20	160
27	40

Required

1. Calculate ending inventory and cost of goods sold using periodic FIFO and periodic LIFO.
2. Calculate ending inventory and cost of goods sold using perpetual FIFO and perpetual LIFO.

(Check figure: Cost of goods sold, perpetual LIFO = $1,030)

Set B

Problem B9-1

Calculating the cost of inventory using the gross method

Percival's Personal Computers acquired the following computers during its first month of operations:

Aug. 2   Purchased four Desk Top Computers from Big Blu Computers, Inc. The list price
           of each computer was $2,000. Big Blu offered Percival a 10% trade discount and
           terms of 3/15, n/30. The computers were shipped FOB shipping point; the total
           freight bill was $500. Percival paid for the inventory on August 30.

      5   Purchased two Einstein Portable Computers from Einstein Electronics. The
           computers listed for $1,500 each. The terms of the purchase were 2/10, n/60,
           20-10 trade discount, and FOB destination. Freight charges totaled $600. Percival
           had not paid Einstein on August 31.

     20   Purchased 20 Homegame Computers from Abacus Computers. The computers
           listed for $300 each and were shipped to Percival FOB shipping point. Percival
           received a 10% trade discount, a 5% quantity discount, and terms of 1/10, n/30.
           The computers were received on August 25. Freight charges amounted to $375.
           Percival paid for the purchase on August 28.

Required   Assuming that Percival used the gross method of recording purchases, prepare clearly labeled
              schedules showing calculations of the cost of **(1)** the Desk Top Computers, **(2)** the Einstein
              Portable Computers, and **(3)** the Homegame Computers. Assume that the cash discount
              period begins on the purchase date, that is, August 2, August 5, and August 20. (Note: Journal
              entries are not required.)

(Check figure: Cost of the Homegame Computers = $5,453.70)

Problem B9-2

**Preparing entries to record
purchases under the gross and
net methods**

Kinetic Communications made the following purchases and payments for inventory during
December 1987:

Dec. 4   Purchased 500 push-button telephones from Sound Transmission, Inc.; terms of
           the purchase were 2/10, n/30. The phones have a list price of $20 each.

      8   Purchased an assortment of desk- and wall-model rotary dial phones from East-
           ern Equipment Co. for $2,250. Terms of the purchase were 5/10, n/30.

     15   Paid Eastern Equipment the amount due.

     30   Paid Sound Transmission for the December 4 purchase.

Required   Prepare journal entries to record Kinetic's purchases and payments assuming that **(1)** the gross
              method is used to record purchases; **(2)** the net method is used to record purchases. Supporting
              calculations should be part of your journal entry explanations.

(Check figure: Purchase Discounts on the gross method will have a credit balance of $112.50)

Problem B9-3

**Calculating ending inventory
and cost of goods sold using
FIFO, LIFO, and weighted
average**

Armando Mart has the following inventory record for the month of January:

	Units	Cost per Unit	Total Cost
Inventory Jan. 1	10	$10.00	$100.00
Purchase Jan. 5	4	11.00	44.00
Purchase Jan. 10	9	12.00	108.00
Purchase Jan. 16	10	13.00	130.00
Purchase Jan. 24	7	14.00	98.00

A count of the inventory on hand on January 31 revealed that 18 units remained.

Required   Calculate ending inventory and cost of goods sold under the periodic FIFO, LIFO, and
              weighted average methods. Do not use the shortcut.

(Check figure: Ending inventory under the FIFO method = $240)

Problem B9-4

Calculating ending inventory and cost of goods sold using FIFO, LIFO, and weighted average

Kern Fire and Safety Equipment Co. experienced the following inventory-related transactions during the first quarter of 1987:

		Units	$ per Unit
Jan. 1	Inventory on hand	2,250	3.20
Jan. 1–15	Sales of inventory	750	8.00
Jan. 16	Purchase	500	3.30
Jan. 20	Defective inventory returned to vendor	100	3.30
Jan. 16–31	Sales of inventory	1,400	8.20
Feb. 4	Purchase	1,000	3.40
Feb. 13	Purchase	2,000	3.50
Feb. 1–15	Sales of inventory	700	8.50
Feb. 27	Purchase	500	3.48
Feb. 16–28	Sales of inventory	450	8.55
Mar. 17	Purchase	1,500	3.60
Mar. 25	Defective inventory returned to vendor	250	3.60
Mar. 1–31	Sales of inventory	1,300	8.60

Required

Prepare a schedule calculating the ending inventory and cost of goods sold for Kern for the first quarter of 1987 using the periodic FIFO, LIFO, and weighted average methods. Use the shortcut.

(Check figure: Weighted average cost per unit = $3.40)

Problem B9-5

Applying LCM on an item-by-item basis, and to inventory as a whole

Karl's Cold Appliances is preparing financial statements for the year ended June 30, 1988. Karl wants to use lower of cost or market to value ending inventory. The following inventory summary has been prepared:

Inventory Group	Inventory Item No.	Quantity	Cost (FIFO)	Market (Replacement Cost)
Freezers	1001	2	$ 140	$ 145
	1002	3	1,350	1,260
	1003	2	960	920
	1004	5	2,100	2,120
Refrigerators	2021	1	196	200
	2022	5	1,170	1,120
	2023	2	639	630
Ice makers	3041	1	150	142
	3042	4	896	920
	3043	2	368	360

Required

Calculate the amount of inventory that Karl will show on the June 30, 1988, balance sheet, assuming that the lower of cost or market is applied:
1. On an item-by-item basis
2. To the inventory as a whole

(Check figure: LCM applied to inventory as a whole = $7,817)

Problem B9-6

Using the gross profit method to estimate inventory lost in a flood

On February 18, 1988, a flood destroyed much of the inventory of Ranger Hardware Store. The total amount of merchandise that was salvaged amounts to $8,000. Ranger has asked you to help prepare an estimate of the loss in order to file a claim with the insurance company. You are handed the following schedule of data that has been gathered:

RANGER HARDWARE STORE **Income Statement** **Year Ended November 30, 1987**		
Sales (net)		$250,000
Cost of Goods Sold:		
Merchandise Inventory 12/1/86.	$ 34,000	
Purchases (net).	152,000	
Goods Available for Sale	$186,000	
Merchandise Inventory 11/30/87	36,000	150,000
Gross Profit on Sales		$100,000
Operating Expenses		27,000
Net Income		$ 73,000
Sales (Dec. 1, 1987–Feb. 18, 1988)		$ 44,000
Purchases (Dec. 1, 1987–Feb. 18, 1988).		22,000

Required   Calculate the cost of the inventory lost in the flood.

(Check figure: Cost of inventory lost = $23,600)

Problem B9-7
Using the retail inventory method to estimate inventory; preparing an income statement and a balance sheet

Vera's Pool and Patio Store is applying for a loan at the Community National Bank. The bank has asked to see up-to-date financial statements. Vera Tinsley, owner of the store, explains to you that she isn't due to count her inventory for another 2 months—the end of the fiscal year. You volunteer to help prepare an income statement for her using the retail inventory method to estimate her ending inventory. Vera provides you with the following trial balance and additional information:

VERA'S POOL AND PATIO STORE **Adjusted Trial Balance** **June 30, 1987**		
	Debit	**Credit**
Cash.	$ 83,000	
Merchandise Inventory (Sept. 1, 1986)	54,000	
Supplies on Hand	3,000	
Equipment	580,000	
Accumulated Depreciation: Equipment		$ 96,000
Accounts Payable		34,000
Common Stock ($1 par).		450,000
Retained Earnings.		18,000
Sales.		420,000
Sales Returns	20,000	
Purchases	120,000	
Purchase Discounts		4,000
Freight-In	14,000	
Depreciation Expense	48,000	
Other Operating Expenses.	100,000	
Total	$1,022,000	$1,022,000

Other Information

Merchandise on hand on 9/1/86 had a retail price of:	$108,000
Net purchases were marked to sell for:	372,000
Net additional markups amounted to:	10,000
Net markdowns amounted to:	30,000

Required

1. Prepare a schedule calculating your estimate of ending inventory.
2. Prepare an income statement for the period September 1, 1986 to June 30, 1987.
3. Prepare a balance sheet for Vera as of June 30, 1987.

(Check figure: Estimated ending inventory = $24,000)

Problem B9-8

Calculating the effects of inventory errors on incomes of four years

You have been reviewing the inventory records of Powell, Inc., for the last 4 years. Your investigation revealed the following errors:

a. 1986 ending inventory was understated by $6,300 because goods purchased FOB shipping point were omitted.

b. 1987 sales were overstated by $5,000 because sales shipped to customers FOB destination were included. (These goods had not been included in cost of goods sold for 1987.) The sales should have been recorded in 1988. (The goods were included in cost of goods sold for 1988.)

c. 1987 ending inventory was overstated by $1,500. The cost of goods in on consignment was inadvertently included in ending inventory.

d. 1988 ending inventory was overstated by $2,250. Employees counted one bin of merchandise twice.

e. 1989 ending inventory was understated by $1,000. Goods out on consignment were not included.

Reported income (loss) in each of the last four years was: 1986 = $30,000; 1987 = $17,800; 1988 = $9,000; 1989 = ($1,000).

Required

Prepare a schedule showing the calculation of corrected net income for each of the 4 years. Hint: Set up your solution paper as illustrated below:

Description	1986	1987	1988	1989
Net income reported	$30,000	$17,800	$9,000	$(1,000)

Add or subtract the effects of each error in the appropriate columns; total each column to find corrected net income.

(Check figure: 1988 corrected net income = $13,250)

Problem B9-9

Calculating the ending inventory using periodic and perpetual FIFO and LIFO

Pacific Imports provides you with the following data about its purchases and sales for the month of April 1988, its first month of operations:

Purchases			
Date	Units	Cost per Unit	Total Cost
Apr. 1	100	$2.50	$250
5	40	2.55	102
15	120	2.70	324
24	40	2.80	112
30	20	2.85	57
Totals	320		$845

Sales	
Date	Units
Apr. 8	50
17	80
29	20

Required

1. Calculate ending inventory and cost of goods sold using periodic FIFO and periodic LIFO.
2. Calculate ending inventory and cost of goods sold using perpetual FIFO and perpetual LIFO.

(Check figure: Cost of goods sold, perpetual LIFO = $399)

Chapter 10   Long-Lived Assets

Some of the things you should learn from studying this chapter are:

- How to recognize *long-lived assets* and distinguish between the two types, *tangible* and *intangible*
- Which assets are normally classified as *property, plant,* and *equipment* and why
- How to determine the cost of a property, plant, and equipment asset
- To distinguish between a *capital expenditure* and a *revenue expenditure*
- How to calculate *depreciation* using the *straight-line, units-of-production, sum-of-the-years'-digits,* and *double declining-balance* methods
- To *record acquisition, depreciation,* and *disposal* of *property, plant,* and *equipment* assets
- To *calculate depletion* and prepare journal entries to *record depletion*
- The difference between *depreciation for financial accounting purposes* and *depreciation for income tax purposes (ACRS depreciation)*
- Which assets are normally classified as *intangibles* and why
- To calculate and prepare entries for *amortization* of intangible assets

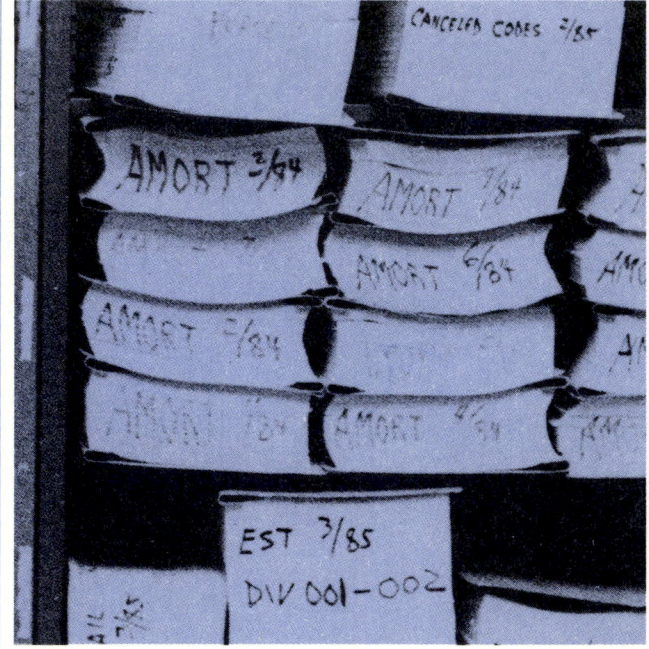

We have already explained that all a firm's assets can be classified as either current assets or long-lived assets. Assets that will be used up in a firm's operations or are soon to be converted into cash (within 1 year or one operating cycle, whichever is longer) are current assets. All other assets, then, are long-lived assets. Long-lived assets provide benefits for more than 1 year or one operating cycle. Classifications of long-lived assets typically found on a balance sheet are investments; property, plant, and equipment; and intangibles. In this chapter we will cover two of these long-lived assets — property, plant, and equipment; and intangibles. Investments, that is, long-term investments representing long-lived assets, will be discussed in Chapter 16.

PROPERTY, PLANT, AND EQUIPMENT

Property, plant, and equipment assets are tangible long-lived assets owned by the business and used in its operations

Typical assets included in *property, plant, and equipment* are land, building, machinery, office equipment, delivery equipment, and natural resources — all tangible long-lived assets owned by a business and used in its operations.

Assets not considered as property, plant, and equipment, are, for example: investments in stocks and bonds of other companies; patents (these are not tangible); land held for investment purposes (this asset is not used in the firm's operations); and buildings under construction (these are not yet used in the operations of the business).

Acquisition Cost

As you might well imagine, the cost of a long-lived asset that fits the category of property, plant, and equipment is more than the price tag on the asset itself. There will be many other costs that must be either necessarily or reasonably incurred to acquire the asset. There will also be some costs associated with the acquisition that may seem necessary or reasonable, but upon close examination, will be determined to be expenses that are chargeable elsewhere. Of course, it's the accountant's job to determine which costs are to become part of the total cost of the asset and which costs are not.

The general rule for determining the cost of inventory, cited in Chapter 9, applies equally to the cost of property, plant, and equipment assets:

General rule for determining acquisition cost

All reasonable and necessary costs to get an asset in position and condition ready for use may be included as part of the cost of the asset.

An example will illustrate how to determine what costs are part of the asset cost and which are not. Print-It Company incurred the following costs when it acquired a printing press:

1. Catalog list price $30,000
2. Trade discount 20%
3. Cash discount (terms 4/20, n/60) . . . .
4. Freight cost (terms FOB shipping point) . . . . $ 900
5. Insurance while in shipment   150
6. Repair cost. (Forklift operator dropped machine while clowning around during unloading. Repair was necessary before the machine could be placed in service. Because the damage occurred after receipt, the shipment insurance does not cover cost of repairs. Print-It must pay for repairs.).   2,500
7. Rewiring cost. (Accessible power was inadequate to supply the requirements of the new machine.)   250
8. Concrete slab cost. (It was necessary to pour a slab with bolts embed-

ded in it. The machine was bolted to the slab to prevent excessive vibration.) $100

9. Consulting engineer's fee. (A consulting engineer was called in to thoroughly test the machine and demonstrate its operation.). 500

10. Materials used in testing. (Cost of materials used by consulting engineer to test machine and demonstrate its operation.). 80

11. Maintenance cost. (Cost of materials needed during first month of operations.) 25

12. Operator's salary. (Salary during the first month of operations.). . . 800

The following analysis reflects the decisions made in applying the acquisition cost rule:

Description/Justification	Cost of Machinery: Charge to Machinery Account — Amount	Not Cost of Machinery: Charge to Other Accounts — Account Title	Not Cost of Machinery: Charge to Other Accounts — Amount
1 and 2. Catalog Price Less Trade Discount $30,000 less (.20) ($30,000) = $30,000 less $6,000 =	$24,000		
3. Cash Discount ($24,000) (.04) = The cash price of the machine is $23,040 ($24,000 − $960). This amount is included in the cost of the machine. If Print-It chooses not to pay the cash price within the first 20 days— remember, the terms are 4/20, n/60—$24,000 will be due at the end of 60 days. Print-It will have borrowed the $23,040 from the seller for 40 days and paid $960 interest. *The cost of financing an asset is not part of the cost of the asset.* If Print-It elects to wait until the end of 60 days to pay, $23,040 will be charged to Machinery and $960 will be charged to Interest Expense. *The amount of the cash discount is always deducted, even if the buyer chooses not to take advantage of it.*	(960)		
4. Freight Cost Because the purchase was FOB shipping point, Print-It must pay the freight cost.	900		
5. Insurance While in Shipment Insurance paid to protect the asset while in shipment is a reasonable cost.	150		
6. Repair Cost The cost of these repairs are not covered by insurance. Although it is a necessary cost to get the machine into working order, *it is not a reasonable and necessary* cost in acquiring assets. Properly trained and supervised employees are expected to be careful in handling the company's assets.		Loss Due to Employee Negligence	$2,500

(continued)

Description/Justification	Cost of Machinery: Charge to Machinery Account	Not Cost of Machinery: Charge to Other Accounts	
	Amount	Account Title	Amount
7. Rewiring Cost The cost of installing a special electric power line to supply the power needs of the machine is considered a reasonable and necessary cost. This cost is not considered part of the cost of the building, because the installation is designed to serve only this one machine. There is no assurance that it will be useful to others in the future.	250		
8. Concrete Slab The logic for adding this cost to the machine is the same as for the cost of the specially installed power line.	100		
9. Consulting Engineer's Fee Setting the machine to perform to Print-It's special needs is a reasonable cost incurred in getting the machine into initial operation.	500		
10. Materials Used in Testing This is a cost necessary to the consulting engineer's task. Materials used in normal production after the machine is operational become part of the expense of operations.	80		
11 and 12. Maintenance Cost and Operator's Salary These costs were incurred after the machine became operational; therefore they are operating costs, *not* acquisition costs.		Maintenance Expense Salary Expense	25 800
Total cost of machine	$25,020		

The following entry records all of Print-It's costs. It summarizes the total costs of acquiring the machine, and identifies each of the other costs associated with but not part of the total machine cost.

```
Dec. 1–31   Machinery..................................  25,020
            Loss Due to Employee Negligence .............   2,500
            Maintenance Expense .......................       25
            Salary Expense ............................      800
                Cash..................................            28,345
            To record the cost of the printing press, costs incidental to its
            acquisition, and costs of operating it during December.
```

The Print-It Company example shows many of the common costs incurred in acquiring long-lived assets such as machinery and equipment. The following are some of the common acquisition costs for other property, plant, and equipment assets:

Common acquisition costs associated with various property, plant, and equipment assets

Land   Land is an asset that is considered to have an unlimited useful life. Costs of surveying to determine the boundaries of the land, costs incurred in removing old buildings, title insurance and legal fees, and other costs of a permanent nature such as draining swampy land or filling to level land, all are considered part of the cost of land.

Land improvement   The cost of driveways, sidewalks, shrubbery, sprinkler systems, and parking lots are all recorded in one account called Land Improvements. These items differ from land in that each has a limited useful life.

Buildings   The cost of a building includes construction costs, architectural fees, insurance (for fire, theft of materials, and natural disasters) while under construction, building permit fees, cost of surveying for the purpose of locating the building on the land, and the cost of grading associated with the construction of a basement or providing adequate drainage of surface water.

Natural resources   Mineral deposits, oil wells, and timberland are material resources that exist in a natural state (natural resources). The cost of these natural resources includes the costs associated with acquiring land, including the natural resource borne by the land, as well as, for example, the cost of building access roads, sinking mine shafts, laying rail tracks into the mine, and other costs incurred in getting ready to extract the resource.

Leased assets   Businesses often sign contracts to rent assets for a long period of time (5, 10, 25, or more years). These contracts are called leases. Certain lease contracts are considered to be equivalent to buying the asset — if a firm leased an automobile for 5 years, and if the expected useful life of the car is 5 years, the company can be said to have obtained all of the benefits of owning the asset. These kinds of leased assets are recorded just as if the company actually owned them. (This subject is discussed more fully in Chapter 15.)

Thus far, we have kept the discussion simple: Either we haven't indicated how property, plant, and equipment assets are paid for, or we tended to suggest that they were acquired with cash or on short-term credit. In the real world, long-lived assets are extremely costly and, of course, are also acquired in exchange for other assets, on long-term credit, or in exchange for an ownership interest in the business. Or they may be acquired through a combination of all these possibilities.

No matter what the arrangement for acquiring the asset, it should be recorded at its market value — the cash price specified — on the date it is formally acquired. The total cost of the asset includes all reasonable and necessary costs to get an asset in position and condition ready for use.

Lump-Sum Acquisitions

Cost is allocated to each asset acquired in a group purchase by the relative-value allocation method

Occasionally, a business may acquire several assets for one price. In such cases it is necessary to allocate the one lump-sum cost among the several assets. Normally, this is done by a *relative-value allocation,* such as the one illustrated as follows.

Delta, Inc., acquired land, a building, and machinery from Calamity Company for $1,000,000. A professional appraiser valued each of the assets at the following amounts: land $800,000, building $560,000, and machinery $240,000. The $1,000,000 is allocated among the assets as follows:

Asset	Appraised Value	Percent of Total Appraised Value	×	Total Cost	=	Cost Allocated to Asset
Land	$ 800,000	$800,000/$1,600,000 = 50%	×	$1,000,000	=	$ 500,000
Building	560,000	$560,000/$1,600,000 = 35%	×	1,000,000	=	350,000
Machinery	240,000	$240,000/$1,600,000 = 15%	×	1,000,000	=	150,000
Totals	$1,600,000			100%		$1,000,000

The following entry would be made to record the acquisition:

Mar. 15	Land	500,000	
	Building	350,000	
	Machinery.............................	150,000	
	Cash.................................		1,000,000
	To record acquisition of land, building, and machinery.		

Observe that the appraised value is $1,600,000 and the actual cost is $1,000,000. Although the assets were appraised at $600,000 over actual cost, they are recorded at cost. They are not recorded at the value someone says they are worth. Recording them at cost is objective and verifiable.

Capital versus Revenue Expenditures

Capital expenditures benefit several periods; revenue expenditures benefit only one period

Cost incurred for, or associated with, assets that will provide economic benefits over several accounting periods are called *capital expenditures.* All capital expenditures associated with a particular asset are added to the cost of that asset.

Costs incurred that will provide economic benefits only during the current accounting period are called *revenue expenditures.* Revenue expenditures are recorded in expense accounts.

At the time an asset is acquired, all of the costs meeting the requirements of the general acquisition-cost rule are considered capital expenditures. For example, in the Print-It Company illustration, the invoice price less discounts, plus the costs of freight, insurance during shipment, rewiring, concrete slab, consulting engineer's fee, and materials used in testing are all proper acquisition costs and are therefore capital expenditures.

Some expenditures incurred after the asset is acquired and placed in service may also be considered capital expenditures, for example, the cost of replacing a truck engine with a more fuel-efficient one; the cost of adding a solar-powered heating unit to a building; the cost of overhauling a machine's motor; and the cost of resurfacing a parking lot.

Revenue expenditures consist primarily of the costs of regular maintenance, cleaning, and minor repairs. Examples of revenue expenditures include the costs of oil, grease and other lubricants, light bulbs, window panes, oil filters, tires, and the salary of custodians and mechanics who perform regular maintenance functions.

It is important to distinguish between capital expenditures and revenue expenditures because they affect the measurement of income differently.

Capital expenditures are allocated to income over the several years during which they provide benefits (i.e., the single capital expenditure is spread out over a number of years). If a capital expenditure is erroneously treated as a revenue expenditure and entirely expensed during the current period, current expenses will be too high and therefore income will be too low. In subsequent years, when part of the capital expenditure should have been expensed, expenses will be too low and income will be too high. There will be a mismatching between expenses and revenues.

Revenue expenditures incorrectly charged to an asset account will also mismatch expenses and revenues, in this case causing the opposite effect: Expenses on the current income statement will be understated and thus current income will be overstated.

Depreciation

Depreciation is the allocation of a tangible asset's cost over its useful life

When someone says something like, "My new car is now one year old and it has depreciated $2,000," what they are talking about is a decrease in the market value of the asset. This is *not* what accountants mean by depreciation. In accounting, ***depreciation*** means the allocation of the cost of a tangible asset over its useful economic life.

When a company purchases a tangible long-lived asset, it is really buying a large bundle of service benefits that will be provided by that asset over time in the future. These future service benefits enable the asset's owner to earn revenue by providing a place (buildings) in which to manufacture, store, and sell the products, by furnishing a means (machines) of fashioning and packaging the product, or by providing a way (trucks) to deliver goods. As an asset is used over time, the bundle of future service benefits available from it becomes smaller and smaller. The part of the original cost of the asset that is assigned to the bundle of service benefits that have been used up is called depreciation.

An example of how depreciation expense is recorded is shown by the following entry:

Dec. 31	Depreciation Expense.	10,000	
	Accumulated Depreciation		10,000
	To record depreciation for the year.		

What Causes Depreciation?

Physical wear-and-tear and obsolescence are the two causes of depreciation

The common causes of depreciation are physical wear-and-tear and obsolescence. In today's rapidly developing technological economy, obsolescence is a more important consideration than physical deterioration. For example, Pitch Company purchases a computer for $800,000. In evaluating how to depreciate that cost, Pitch Company first has to decide how many years the machine will last. Management observes that, with proper maintenance, it will continue processing information for a period of 20 years. But management also knows that the computer industry will probably develop a more efficient machine that will handle Pitch's increased information needs more efficiently within 5 years. For the current computer, the useful life to Pitch will be 5, *not* 20, years. At the end of the 5 years, Pitch will probably be able to sell its computer to a smaller company whose information needs it can adequately serve. The asset will not have deteriorated much at all, but it will be obsolete for Pitch's purposes. For other businesses it will not be obsolete.

Management's estimate of an asset's useful economic life is an essential ingredient in calculating depreciation.

How Much Depreciation Should Be Recorded?

There are several methods of determining how to depreciate the cost of an asset over its useful economic lifetime. That is, there are different ways of determining the cost to be allocated to each year of its life. We will demonstrate how to use each of these different methods using the same basic information:

Acquisition cost of asset. $125,000

Estimated salvage value (what we can sell the asset for at the end of
its useful life). $15,000

Estimated useful life in years. . . . . 10 years

Estimated useful life in units of output (the total units we can expect the machine to produce during its useful life) . . . . 220,000 units

Straight-Line Depreciation

Straight-line depreciation assumes that we receive equal benefits from an asset each day of the asset's life. Straight-line, then, allocates an equal part of the total cost to each day of an asset's useful life. We usually record depreciation on a monthly or annual basis rather than daily. The basic idea is that straight-line recognizes the same

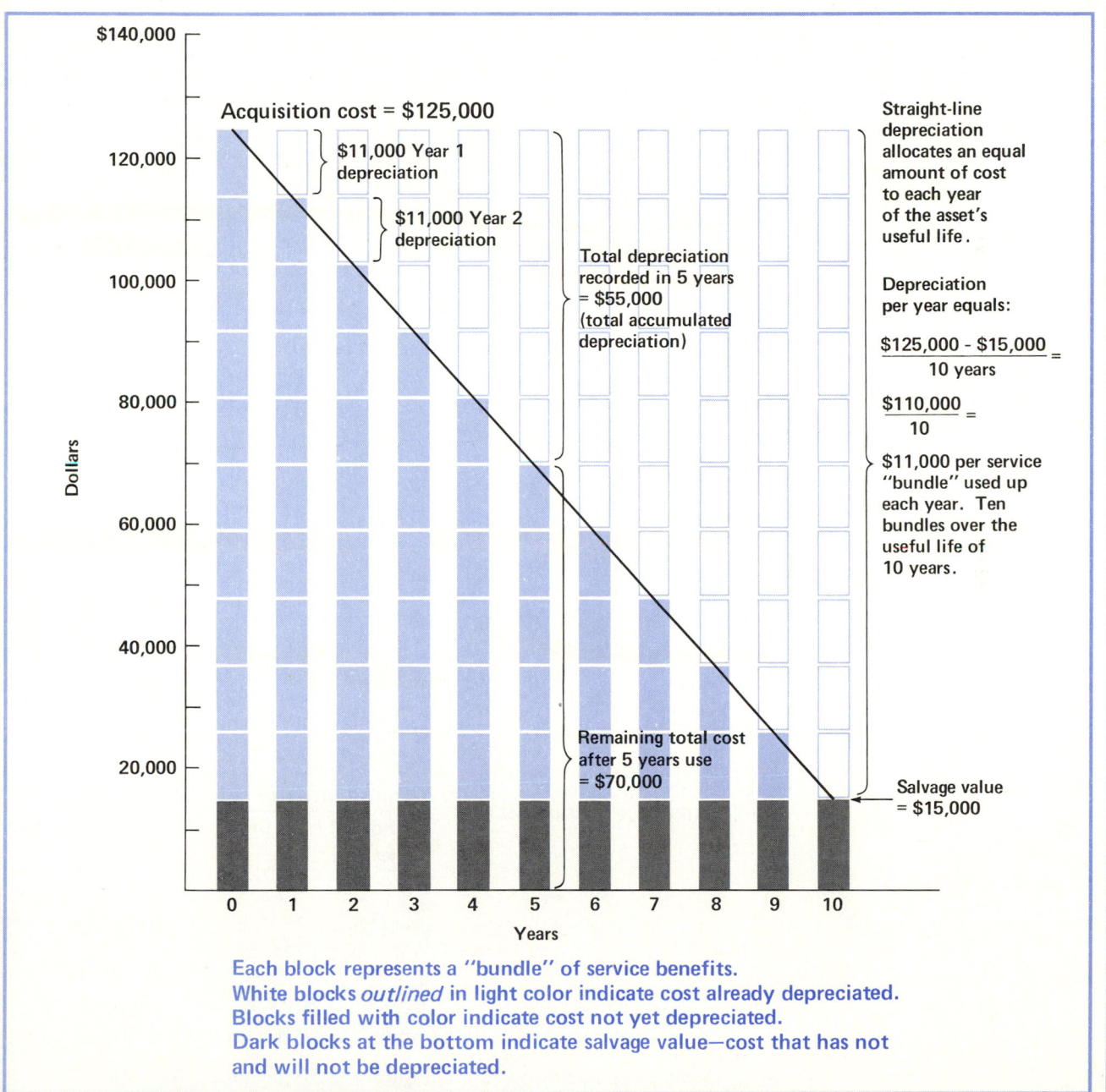

FIGURE 10-1   Straight-Line Depreciation.

Within the figure:

Acquisition cost = $125,000

$11,000 Year 1 depreciation

$11,000 Year 2 depreciation

Total depreciation recorded in 5 years = $55,000 (total accumulated depreciation)

Remaining total cost after 5 years use = $70,000

Salvage value = $15,000

Straight-line depreciation allocates an equal amount of cost to each year of the asset's useful life.

Depreciation per year equals:

$$\frac{\$125{,}000 - \$15{,}000}{10 \text{ years}} =$$

$$\frac{\$110{,}000}{10} =$$

$11,000 per service "bundle" used up each year. Ten bundles over the useful life of 10 years.

(Dollars axis: $140,000, 120,000, 100,000, 80,000, 60,000, 40,000, 20,000; Years axis: 0 1 2 3 4 5 6 7 8 9 10)

Each block represents a "bundle" of service benefits.
White blocks *outlined* in light color indicate cost already depreciated.
Blocks filled with color indicate cost not yet depreciated.
Dark blocks at the bottom indicate salvage value—cost that has not and will not be depreciated.

amount of depreciation per unit of time—whatever that unit of time is. Here is the straight-line depreciation formula and the yearly depreciation for our $125,000 asset:

The straight-line method relates depreciation to the passage of time

$$\text{Straight-line depreciation per year} = \frac{\text{acquisition cost} - \text{estimated salvage value}}{\text{estimated useful life in years}}$$

$$= \frac{\$125,000 - \$15,000}{10 \text{ years}}$$

$$= \frac{\$110,000}{10 \text{ years}}$$

$$= \underline{\$11,000 \text{ per year}}$$

Depreciation will be the same amount, $11,000, for each full year of the asset's life. The straight-line method assumes that an equal amount of the asset's total service benefits are used up each year.

Figure 10-1 on page 383 shows graphically how the straight-line method works.

Units-of-Output Depreciation

The units-of-output method relates depreciation to the using up of service benefits

The units-of-output method is used for assets whose useful life is limited by physical wear-and-tear rather than obsolescence. This method is used for assets that are physically worn out before they become obsolete. According to the units-of-output method, as an asset produces a unit of output, it also uses up some of the service benefits available from the asset. Each unit produced uses up the same amount of the asset's service benefits. The more units the asset produces in a period, the greater the service benefits it uses up in that period. What all this simply means is that the part of the asset's total cost to be depreciated in a period depends directly on the number of units the asset produces in that period.

The units-of-output method would be appropriate for a delivery truck. The truck will not become obsolete; it will deliver products year after year until it is worn out. The more it is used, the quicker it will be worn out, and the greater the depreciation. The units of output for a delivery truck are tons of goods delivered per mile per period. The service benefits used would be measured in miles driven per period.

To use the units-of-output depreciation method, it is essential to have some way of measuring the asset's output during a particular period of time. For our delivery truck an odometer measures the miles driven. Automatic counters are used on production line machinery, and devices measuring flying hours are used for company airplanes.

Returning to our basic example. Assume that 10,000 units are produced in year 1 and 24,000 units in year 2. The depreciation for each of these years is calculated as follows:

$$\text{Units-of-output depreciation per unit} = \frac{\text{acquisition cost} - \text{estimated salvage value}}{\text{estimated total lifetime units of production}}$$

$$= \frac{\$125,000 - \$15,000}{220,000 \text{ units}}$$

$$= \frac{\$110,000}{220,000 \text{ units}}$$

$$= \underline{\$.50 \text{ per unit}}$$

Year 1 depreciation = 10,000 units × $.50 per unit = $\underline{\$\ 5,000}$

Year 2 depreciation = 24,000 units × $.50 per unit = $\underline{\$12,000}$

Sum-of-the-Years'-Digits Depreciation

The sum-of-the-years'-digits method allocates more depreciation to early years of an asset's life and less to the later years

The basic idea behind the sum-of-the-years'-digits method is that more service benefits are received in the early years of an asset's life when it is new, and fewer benefits are received each year as the asset grows older.

The sum-of-the-years'-digits (SYD) method assigns more depreciation expense to the early years of the asset's life and less to later ones. It is a method of "accelerated depreciation."

The procedure for calculating SYD depreciation for our basic example is outlined in the following steps:

STEP 1: Determine the sum of the digits of the years of the asset's useful life.

$$1 + 2 + 3 + 4 + 5 + 6 + 7 + 8 + 9 + 10 = 55$$

An easy way to determine the sum of the digits

Of course, you can see how cumbersome this process would be for an asset with say a 15-, 20-, or 25-year life. A shortcut formula that yields the same results as the more tedious addition process is:

$$\text{Sum of the digits} = n\left(\frac{n+1}{2}\right)$$

where n = number of years in the asset's life.

$$\text{10-year sum of the digits} = 10\left(\frac{10+1}{2}\right)$$

$$= 10(5.5)$$

$$= 55$$

STEP 2: Determine the asset's acquisition cost and salvage value, and the difference between these two amounts. In the example these are given as $125,000 and $15,000, respectively, and the difference is $110,000.

STEP 3: Multiply the difference between cost and salvage by a fraction composed of a numerator representing the number of years of life remaining at the beginning of the current year and a denominator representing the sum of the digits determined in step 1. The largest fraction represents the largest proportion of the cost to be depreciated in year 1. The lowest fraction represents the smallest proportion of the cost to be depreciated in year 10, the last year.

Year of Asset's Life	Years Remaining in Asset's Life	Fraction = $\dfrac{\text{Years Remaining}}{\text{Sum of the Years' Digits}}$	
1	10	Highest proportion depreciated	$\frac{10}{55}$
2	9		$\frac{9}{55}$
3	8		$\frac{8}{55}$
4	7		$\frac{7}{55}$
5	6		$\frac{6}{55}$
6	5		$\frac{5}{55}$
7	4		$\frac{4}{55}$
8	3		$\frac{3}{55}$
9	2	Lowest proportion depreciated	$\frac{2}{55}$
10	1		$\frac{1}{55}$
$\overline{55}$ = Sum of the years' digits			$\frac{55}{55}$ = 100%

Depreciation expense under sum-of-the-years'-digits method for each of the 10 years would be:

Year	Fraction	×	Cost — Salvage ($125,000 − $15,000)	=	Depreciation Expense
1	$\frac{10}{55}$		$110,000		$ 20,000
2	$\frac{9}{55}$		110,000		18,000
3	$\frac{8}{55}$		110,000		16,000
4	$\frac{7}{55}$		110,000		14,000
5	$\frac{6}{55}$		110,000		12,000
6	$\frac{5}{55}$		110,000		10,000
7	$\frac{4}{55}$		110,000		8,000
8	$\frac{3}{55}$		110,000		6,000
9	$\frac{2}{55}$		110,000		4,000
10	$\frac{1}{55}$		110,000		2,000

Total depreciated $110,000

SYD depreciation decreases by a constant amount each year

Note that after the depreciation for the first few years has been calculated, you can see that the depreciation expense decreases by a constant amount ($2,000) each year. Subsequent years' depreciation may be determined merely by deducting this constant amount. For example, year 3 depreciation = $16,000, year 4 depreciation = $16,000 less the constant $2,000 = $14,000.

Sum-of-the-years'-digits is an appropriate method for assets that provide more service benefits in the early years of their lives and less in later years. Many assets are efficient when first purchased but become less efficient as time passes. This decrease in utility may be caused by technological obsolescence or by increasing maintenance costs that become necessary because of the accumulated effects of physical wear-and-tear. Copying machines and computers are examples of assets that are depreciated by an accelerated depreciation method such as sum-of-the-years'-digits.

Figure 10-2 is a graphic illustration of how the sum-of-the-years'-digits method works.

Double Declining-Balance Depreciation

Double declining-balance depreciation allocates even more depreciation to the early years of an asset's life than SYD

Another method for accelerating the depreciation, even more during the early years than the sum-of-the-years'-digits method, is declining-balance depreciation, or a simplified version commonly referred to as the ***double declining-balance method***. This method is based on the same idea as the sum-of-the-years'-digits method and is used for assets that provide even more consumable service benefits in the early years, therefore requiring more depreciation in those years.

Declining-balance depreciation, like the other depreciation methods, looks at (1) the acquisition cost, (2) an estimate of the life of the asset, and (3) its estimated salvage value. Plugging that information into a complex formula and solving it yields a percentage. Starting with the acquisition cost, this percentage is applied to that cost to determine the depreciation expense for the first year. The same percentage is applied to the remaining cost of the asset after the first year to determine the depreciation expense for the second year. And so on. Applying the same percentage to the remaining cost of the asset in each subsequent year — the declining balance — allocates the depreciation expense each year in such a way that the balance of the cost of the asset

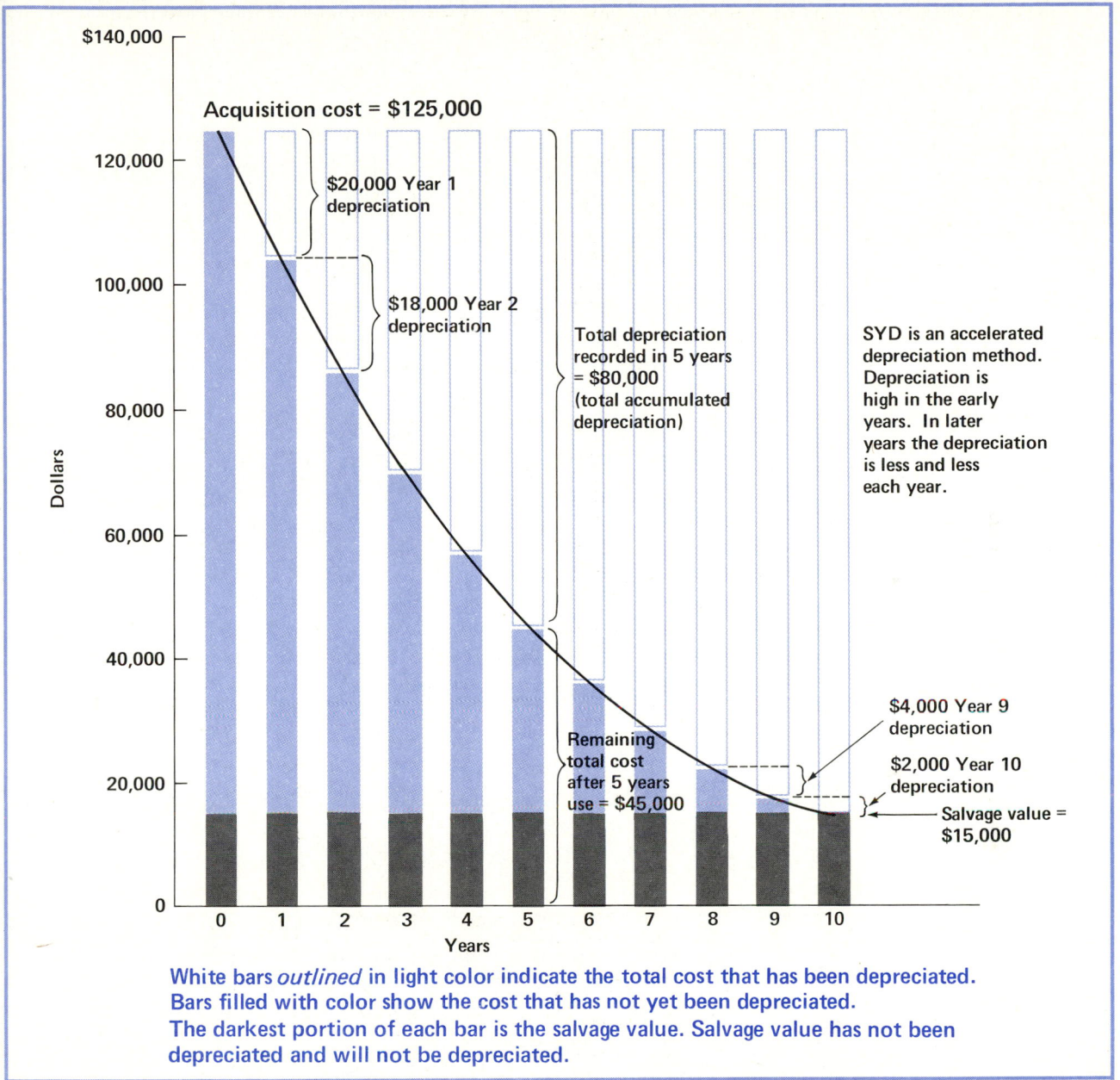

$140,000

Acquisition cost = $125,000

120,000

$20,000 Year 1
depreciation

100,000

$18,000 Year 2
depreciation

Total depreciation
recorded in 5 years
= $80,000
(total accumulated
depreciation)

SYD is an accelerated
depreciation method.
Depreciation is
high in the early
years. In later
years the depreciation
is less and less
each year.

80,000

60,000

40,000

$4,000 Year 9
depreciation

Remaining
total cost
after 5 years
use = $45,000

$2,000 Year 10
depreciation

20,000

Salvage value =
$15,000

0

0   1   2   3   4   5   6   7   8   9   10

Years

Dollars

White bars *outlined* in light color indicate the total cost that has been depreciated.
Bars filled with color show the cost that has not yet been depreciated.
The darkest portion of each bar is the salvage value. Salvage value has not been
depreciated and will not be depreciated.

FIGURE 10-2 Sum-of-the-Year's-Digits Depreciation.

The double declining-balance
method uses twice the straight-
line depreciation rate

declines precisely to the salvage value at the end of the estimated lifetime. Hence, the
name "declining-balance depreciation."

This precise declining-balance method can be replaced with a very simple and
reasonably close approximation, which makes the complex formula unnecessary and
which brings us to what we mean by "double declining-balance depreciation."

Instead of a complex formula, calculate the percentage that would result if you
used the straight-line method—*but* double that percentage and apply it to the remaining balance (book value) each year.

Returning to our basic example to see how this works, consider the following steps:

Double declining-balance procedure

STEP 1: Determine for a straight-line method, the percentage used to calculate the depreciation expense in each year of its useful life. The percentage is the reciprocal of the number of years of useful life, that is,

$$\frac{1}{\text{number of years of useful life}}$$

For example, an asset with a 10-year life has a straight-line depreciation rate, or percentage of $\frac{1}{10}$ or 10% in each year.

STEP 2: Double the percentage rate calculated in step 1.

$$2 \times \tfrac{1}{10} = \tfrac{2}{10} \text{ or } 20\%$$

Hint: Whenever the rate contains a repeating decimal, use the fraction rather than the decimal equivalent. For example, $\frac{1}{3} = .333$ (use $\frac{1}{3}$), $\frac{1}{12} = .0833$ (use $\frac{1}{12}$). Using the fraction will make your calculations easier and more accurate.

STEP 3: Apply this percentage rate to the acquisition cost of the asset (*do not* deduct salvage). This will yield year 1 depreciation expense.

$$\text{Year 1 depreciation expense} = 20\% \times \$125,000$$
$$= \underline{\$25,000}$$

STEP 4: For each succeeding year multiply the percentage calculated in step 2 by the book value at the beginning of that year. (Remember, book value is cost minus all prior depreciation.)

(a) Year 2 depreciation expense = 20% ($125,000 − $25,000) = $20,000

(b) Year 3 depreciation expense = 20%($125,000 − $25,000 − $20,000) = $16,000

(c) And so on

The schedule below shows the depreciation for each of the 10 years. Note that the double declining-balance method will not usually depreciate the cost down to exactly salvage value over the useful life. (Remember, the double declining-balance rate is

Year	Book Value at Beginning of Year (cost − prior depreciation)	× Depreciation Rate =	Double Declining-Balance Depreciation Expense
1	$125,000	.20	$ 25,000
2	100,000	.20	20,000
3	80,000	.20	16,000
4	64,000	.20	12,800
5	51,200	.20	10,240
6	40,960	.20	8,192
7	32,768	.20	6,554
8	26,214	.20	5,243
9	20,971	.20	4,194
10	16,777	*	1,777
			Total depreciated $110,000

* Note: Since salvage is $15,000, the final-year depreciation is limited to $1,777 ($16,777 − $15,000), *not* .20 × $16,777 = $3,355.

Be careful not to depreciate an asset to an amount below its salvage value

just an approximation of the precise declining-balance rate.) It may be necessary, then, to adjust the amount of depreciation in the final year so as not to depreciate below the salvage value. Sometimes it may be necessary to record no depreciation in the final year or years of the asset's useful life. *When using the double declining-balance method, depreciate down to salvage value and then stop depreciating.*

The double declining-balance method of depreciation is reviewed in Figure 10-3.

Depreciation Methods Compared

The straight-line, sum-of-the-years'-digits, and double declining-balance methods produce depreciation expense amounts that follow a pattern. We have shown you

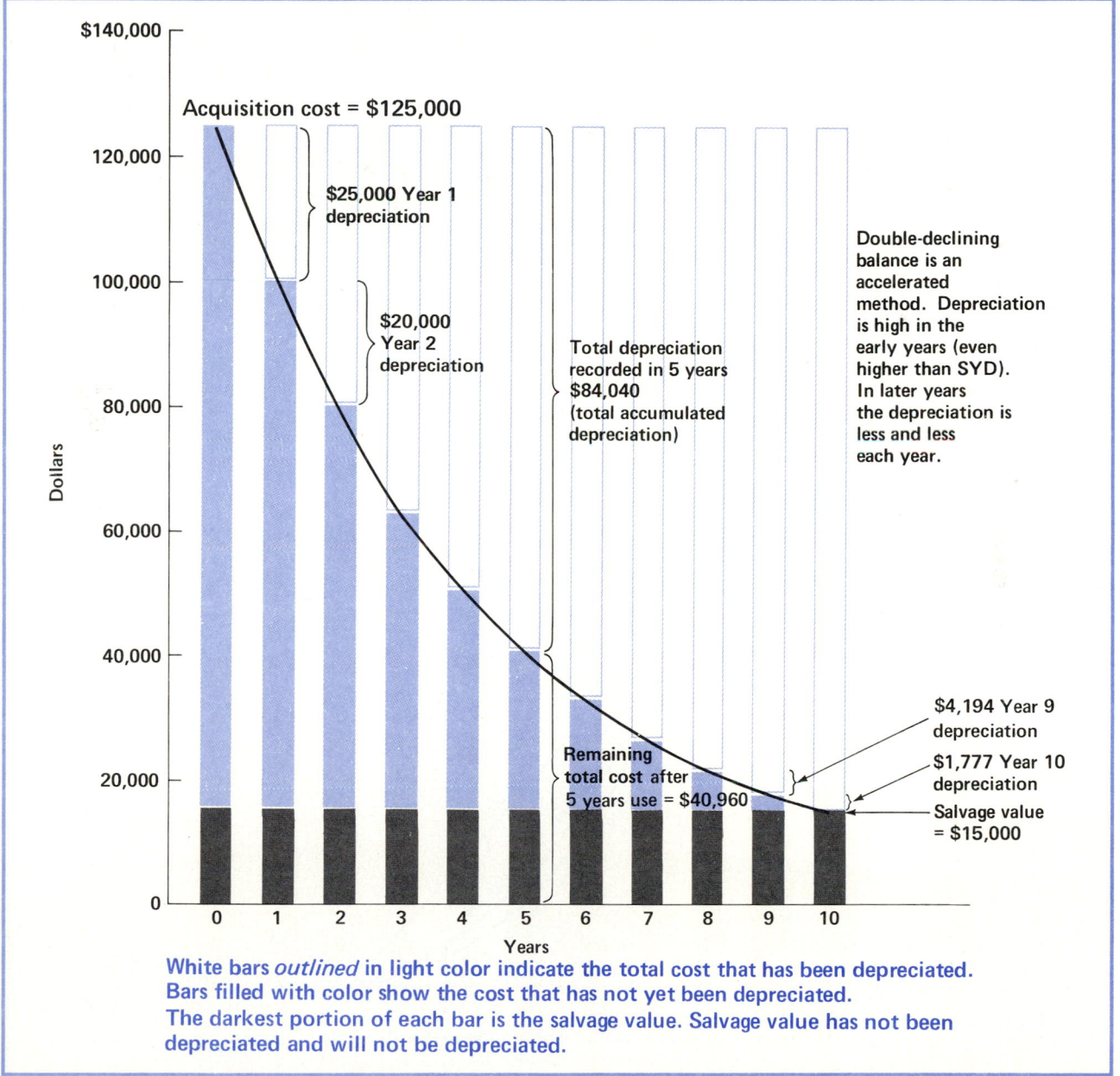

White bars *outlined* in light color indicate the total cost that has been depreciated.
Bars filled with color show the cost that has not yet been depreciated.
The darkest portion of each bar is the salvage value. Salvage value has not been depreciated and will not be depreciated.

FIGURE 10-3   Double Declining-Balance Depreciation.

these patterns for each method numerically and graphically. As a review let's look at all three methods side by side, first in a table and then graphically as illustrated in Figure 10-4.

$$\text{Total amount to be depreciated} = \text{acquisition cost less salvage}$$
$$= \$125{,}000 - \$15{,}000$$
$$= \underline{\$110{,}000}$$

Comparison of the yearly depreciation expense under three methods

Year	Straight Line	Sum of the Years' Digits	Double Declining Balance
1	$ 11,000	$ 20,000	$ 25,000
2	11,000	18,000	20,000
3	11,000	16,000	16,000
4	11,000	14,000	12,800
5	11,000	12,000	10,240
6	11,000	10,000	8,192
7	11,000	8,000	6,554
8	11,000	6,000	5,243
9	11,000	4,000	4,194
10	11,000	2,000	1,777
	$110,000	$110,000	$110,000

FIGURE 10-4
A Comparison of the Straight-Line, Sum-of-the-Years'-Digits, and Double Declining-Balance Methods of Determining Depreciation.
Each depreciation line shows the decline in book value from acquisition cost to salvage value.

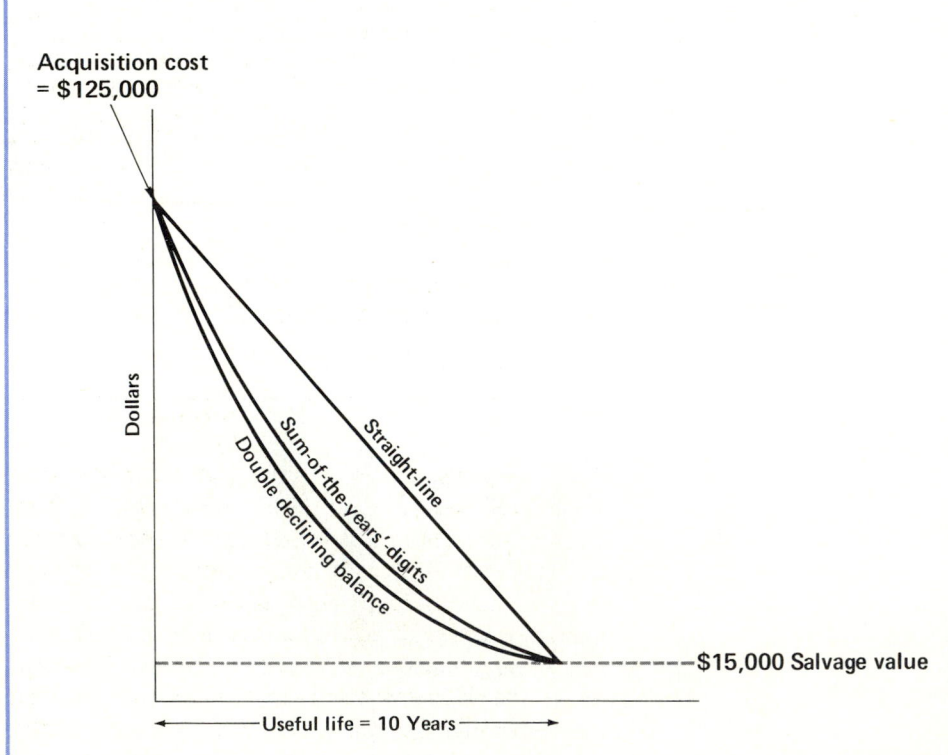

Depreciation—Balance Sheet Disclosure

Earlier, we indicated that depreciation expense is recorded by debiting a Depreciation Expense account and crediting an Accumulated Depreciation account. Because depreciation is a measure of how much of an asset's service benefits have been used, why not just credit the asset account? Why bother with an Accumulated Depreciation account? Perhaps the following illustration will help answer these questions.

Suppose you come across the following disclosure of the property, plant, and equipment section on a balance sheet:

Property, Plant, and Equipment:	
Land	$1,000,000
Building	500,000
Total	$1,500,000

(Note: This is not the correct disclosure of the Building asset.)

Reporting the building in this way doesn't give the balance sheet reader enough information. Any one of a number of underlying factual situations might exist. Let's look at two extreme possibilities for this same disclosure:

Possibility 1

Property, Plant, and Equipment:		
Land		$1,000,000
Building	$15,000,000	
Less: Accumulated Depreciation	14,500,000	500,000
Total		$1,500,000

In this case, the building is nearly fully depreciated.

Possibility 2

Property, Plant, and Equipment:		
Land		$1,000,000
Building	$650,000	
Less: Accumulated Depreciation	150,000	500,000
Total		$1,500,000

In this case, the building is only partially depreciated.

The original disclosure, which we should see as an incorrect way to report a depreciable asset, does show a total of $1,500,000 of property, plant, and equipment assets, but it does not reveal whether the building is almost fully depreciated as is the case in possibility 1, or if it has a large proportion of its cost still to be depreciated as is the case in possibility 2. Specific information about depreciation is very important to the statement reader.

If possibility 1 is the actual situation, it could mean that the company is going to need a new building in the near future. The company, therefore, is either going to have to raise a large sum of money to purchase one or perhaps lease a new building.

If possibility 2 is the actual situation, the company can continue to operate for some time before its present building will be worn out.

Why we use an Accumulated Depreciation contra account

    The disclosure of the Accumulated Depreciation contra account gives the statement reader the information necessary to make a rough approximation of the portion of the asset used up and an idea of how long it will be before the company will have to make a large capital outlay to replace it.

Property, Plant, and Equipment:		
Land		$ 5,000,000
Building	$12,000,000	
Less: Accumulated Depreciation	1,500,000	10,500,000
Machinery.	$ 2,300,000	
Less: Accumulated Depreciation	1,800,000	500,000
Office Equipment	$ 250,000	
Less: Accumulated Depreciation	45,000	205,000
Total		$16,205,000

(Note: This is the correct way to disclose property, plant, and equipment assets.)

    The depreciation method used for each type of asset and its estimated life are indicated in footnotes to the financial statements. Depreciation Expense appears on the income statement.

Depreciation and Cash

Depreciation spreads an asset's cost over its useful life. The accountant accomplishes this by debiting an expense account and crediting a contra-asset account at the end of each period.

    The point we want to make here is that cash is never a part of a depreciation transaction. Any depreciation expense entry clearly shows that Cash is neither debited nor credited.

    Furthermore, an Accumulated Depreciation account shows the total portion of an asset's cost that has been charged to expense through the end of a current period — that is, it represents that part of the asset's total available bundle of services which has been used up. Perhaps that's the best way to think of an Accumulated Depreciation account. It should help to make clear that accumulated depreciation does not repre-

Recording depreciation does not provide cash for replacing an asset

sent accumulated cash. Sometimes students get the idea that Accumulated Depreciation is an account that sets aside cash for replacing the asset. Not so.

    The cost of replacing assets may be financed through borrowing, by leasing, or by using cash that has been set aside for this purpose. None of these transactions has anything to do with depreciation.

Depreciation and Income Taxes

The depreciation methods discussed thus far are those that have been used traditionally to measure depreciation expense for the purpose of preparing income statements and balance sheets. These methods attempt to allocate an asset's cost over its useful life in proportion to the benefits received in each year.

    In preparing financial statements we are bound by the rules of good accounting theory. In preparing income tax returns we are required to use the rules specified in the tax laws. Sometimes tax rules and good accounting theory agree; many times they do not. Depreciation is one area in which we probably use different calculations for financial accounting purposes from those we use for tax purposes. You have learned the financial accounting methods; now let's take a simplified look at the tax rules.

Beginning with the 1981 tax law, depreciable assets were classified as having 3-year, 5-year, 10-year, or 18-year write-off periods. (We will call these tax lives.) Certain types of assets were placed into each of these four classifications. Almost always the actual useful life of an asset is longer than the tax life. For example, the 3-year tax life includes cars and light-duty trucks, the 5-year tax life includes office furniture and equipment, railroad tank cars are placed in the 10-year category, and most buildings are placed in the 18-year category.

In calculating tax depreciation for assets purchased after 1980, you may use the accelerated cost recovery system (ACRS) or a straight-line method. To calculate ACRS depreciation you simply take the cost of the asset (do *not* deduct salvage value) and multiply by a percentage defined by the tax law. The percentage used depends on the tax life of the property and the year of the asset's life. The percentages to be used in each year of a 3- and 5-year tax life asset are shown below:

	3-Year Tax Life	5-Year Tax Life
Year 1	25%	15%
Year 2	38%	22%
Year 3	37%	21%
Year 4		21%
Year 5		21%

To find 1987 tax depreciation for an automobile purchased for $16,000 any time during 1987, you simply multiply 25% × $16,000 and derive $4,000 as your depreciation deduction. In 1988 and 1989 your deductions will be $6,080 (38% × $16,000), and $5,920 (37% × $16,000), respectively.

The tax law still allows you to use straight-line depreciation for tax purposes, but the calculations are a little different from the straight-line method you already know. The differences are:

1. You ignore the actual life and use the 3-, 5-, 10-, or 18-year tax lives.

2. You ignore salvage value.

3. You must take $\frac{1}{2}$ year's depreciation in the first year no matter when during the year the asset was purchased. This also means that you will take $\frac{1}{2}$ year's depreciation in the last year.

Tax straight-line depreciation for our 3-year-life asset automobile would be as follows:

Year 1	$16,000/3 years × $\frac{1}{2}$ year	=	$ 2,667
Year 2	$16,000/3 years	=	5,333
Year 3	$16,000/3 years	=	5,333
Year 4	$16,000/3 years × $\frac{1}{2}$ year	=	2,667
Total tax depreciation			$16,000

DOUBLE STANDARD

by Jill Andresky

One of the old standbys for financial officers when times got tough has always been to try to pick up earnings by slowing depreciation charges.

Last year's Accelerated Cost Recovery System only made that easier by effectively permitting companies to depreciate plant and equipment at different rates for tax and accounting purposes. Says Ronald Murray, Coopers & Lybrand's director of accounting and SEC technical services: "Now you can have a slower book depreciation schedule, which helps financial statements, and yet still stay with fast depreciation for tax purposes, which helps cash flow."

Changing depreciation schedules can make quite a difference for a company. Inland Steel, which recently slowed down its depreciation, will reduce this year's losses by $43 million. (Inland made only $57 million last year.)

The easiest way to lower depreciation charges is to switch from accelerated depreciation to straight-line, where the same sum gets written off every year.

Those companies who want to lower their depreciation even further in hard times can switch to the units-of-output method, where charges are tied not to time but to production volume. In this way a plant running at 40% of capacity generates 60% lower depreciation charges. Ernst & Whinney's Denny Beresford, partner in charge of accounting standards, expects that more companies will follow the lead of Inland Steel by switching to units-of-output depreciation.

For the investor, several questions remain so far unresolved. What about the problem of technological obsolescence, for example? Any slow method of depreciation might well encourage management to keep a piece of machinery in operation long after far superior replacements become available. The risk is great with units of output, especially in slow times.

Beresford raises a related issue: quality of earnings. "Some people would view a company that uses accelerated depreciation as being more conservative in its financial reporting and thus having a higher quality of earnings," he comments. IBM, for example, is still using the so-called sum-of-the-years'-digits method, which raises depreciation charges dramatically in the early years of an asset's life and then slows down as time goes on. As Beresford puts it: "A company changing away from accelerated to straight line might be viewed by some people as reporting at that time lower quality earnings."

Source: Forbes, November 22, 1982, page 178.

Companies may change depreciation methods during an asset's life, if they have good theoretical justification for doing so. This article points out that some companies switch methods for apparently no reason other than to make their income statement income higher.

How does fast tax depreciation "help cash flow"? Use of ACRS depreciation means that taxable income will be lower than income statement income. Thus, the company will pay less income taxes—a cash savings.

The article implies that companies whose assets are not fully depreciated will continue to use them even though technologically superior assets exist. This short-sighted decision making may hurt the company in the long run. You will learn more about using accounting information to make *good* business decisions in the last eight chapters of this text.

ACRS and tax straight-line depreciation usually offer a tax advantage. Since the tax life of an asset is generally shorter than the actual useful life, the depreciation deduction on the tax return is higher in the early years of an asset's life than the depreciation expense on the income statement—the higher the tax deduction, the lower the taxes due in those early years. Of course the time will come when the depreciation deduction on the tax return reaches zero while the depreciation deduction on the income statement continues. When this happens the taxes due will be higher than the tax expense. What all this means is that, by using the tax depreciation methods, we have *postponed* the payment of taxes—a definite advantage when you remember that we have those dollars to invest until the taxes are due in a later year.

Our purpose in introducing you to tax depreciation is to emphasize that financial accounting and tax accounting are often very different and to show you that as a business-person it may be important for you to know the major differences between accounting and tax rules. You will learn more about income taxes in the last chapter of this text.

Depletion

For the purpose of explaining the basic idea behind depreciating an asset, we suggested that the asset might be considered as a total bundle of services that are used up during its lifetime. Depletion is like depreciation, although it is less conceptual and more tangible. You can see the service bundles being used up.

The same idea behind depreciation is applied to the depletion of a natural resource. A natural resource is what its name implies: It is a resource existing naturally — not constructed by humans. Examples of typical natural resources are deposits of coal, oil, iron ore, phosphate, and other minerals. These natural resources are typically used as raw materials in the production of other goods.

A quantity of a natural resource can be considered as consisting of a total bundle of materials — tons of coal, barrels of oil, etc. — available from it. As these materials are removed, a part of the natural resource is used up — depleted. The amount of the materials used up can be measured with a fair amount of accuracy. *Depletion* is the allocation of the cost of the part of a natural resource estimated to be used up in an accounting period. Depletion is calculated in exactly the same way as the units-of-output depreciation is calculated — and it is the only acceptable way to calculate depletion (there are no accelerated ways of calculating depletion).

> Depletion is the allocation of the cost of a natural resource over its life as it is physically used up

The cost and salvage value of the natural resource are determined, along with an estimate of the total number of units (tons, barrels, etc.) that it is capable of producing. The cost less salvage is divided by the estimated total units. The result is depletion per unit produced. The following is an example.

Eureka Mining Co. paid $3,800,000 for a piece of land, including mining rights. Geologists estimated that 15,000,000 tons of uranium could be mined from this plot. Appraisers estimated that the land could be sold for $800,000 after mining is completed. Eureka mined 1,000,000 tons of uranium in year 1 and 3,000,000 tons in year 2.

The calculation of depletion per unit, and the journal entries to record the depletion in each year, are as follows:

$$\text{Depletion per ton} = \frac{\text{cost of property} - \text{salvage value of property}}{\text{total number of tons of uranium}}$$

$$= \frac{\$3,800,000 - \$800,000}{15,000,000 \text{ tons}}$$

$$= \frac{\$3,000,000}{15,000,000 \text{ tons}}$$

$$= \$.20 \text{ per ton}$$

Year 1
Dec. 31 Depletion Expense 200,000
         Uranium Mining Property   200,000
         To record depletion for year 1 ($.20 per ton) ×
         (1,000,000 tons) = $200,000.

Year 2
Dec. 31 Depletion Expense 600,000
         Uranium Mining Property   600,000
         To record depletion for year 2 ($.20 per ton) ×
         (3,000,000 tons) = $600,000.

Observe that the asset was credited in this case rather than a contra-asset account. This is customary, probably because a mineral deposit is not replaceable in the same way that a machine or a building is. Exploration and discovery are necessary, if replacement is possible at all.

Footnotes to the financial statements will provide the reader with information about the number of tons mined in the current period and the total number of tons still in the ground.

Disposal of Property, Plant, and Equipment

As assets wear out, become obsolete, or are no longer needed, the business may decide to sell them or trade them in on new ones.

An asset "depreciates" up to the point in time when it is no longer in use or until it is fully depreciated—whichever comes first. By *fully depreciated* we mean that all of the cost except salvage value has been depreciated. Theoretically, when an asset is fully depreciated, all of those bundles of service benefits have been used up. If a mistake has been made in estimating an asset's useful life, the company may still be using it even though it may be fully depreciated. When this happens, we stop recording depreciation but leave the cost of the asset and its accumulated depreciation on the company's financial records. When the company stops getting benefits from the asset, it is sold, traded, or written off.

Example A: Asset Written off at the End of the Period

Flax Co. owns a machine that had cost $20,000. Accumulated depreciation through December 31, 1987, is $20,000.

The machine is fully depreciated; it doesn't even have a salvage value. (It would cost more to sell it than it would be worth.) Flax takes it to the city dump.

The machine is written off by the following entry:

Writing off a fully depreciated machine

Dec. 31	Accumulated Depreciation: Machine.	20,000	
	Machine		20,000
	To write off a fully depreciated machine removed from service and disposed of.		

Example B: Asset Sold Immediately after the End of the Period

Ogle, Inc., owns a machine that had cost $100,000 and had accumulated depreciation through December 31, 1987, of $45,000. The machine was sold on January 1, 1988, for $70,000.

The gain or loss on the sale is calculated as follows:

Selling price of asset.		$70,000
Less: Book value of asset:		
Cost.	$100,000	
Less: Accumulated depreciation.	45,000	55,000
Gain on sale of asset		$15,000

When we sell an asset for more than its book value, we record a gain

Jan. 1	Cash	70,000	
	Accumulated Depreciation: Machine	45,000	
	Machine		100,000
	Gain on Sale of Machine.		15,000
	To record sale of machine on 1/1/88.		

Observe that the machine was removed from the general ledger by crediting the Machinery account for its *cost*.

Accumulated depreciation on this machine was eliminated by debiting Accumulated Depreciation: Machine for the total recorded through December 31, 1987.

The Gain on Sale of Machine would be shown on the income statement under "Other Gains and Losses." Losses on sales (or exchanges) of assets also would be presented in this section of the income statement.

Example C: Asset Sold during an Accounting Period

Hawke Co. owns a building that originally cost $189,000, has an estimated useful life of 10 years and a $9,000 salvage value. The building was purchased on January 1, 1982, and was used continuously until it was sold on October 1, 1988, for $65,000.

The building was shown on the December 31, 1987, balance sheet as follows:

Building.	$189,000	
Less: Accumulated Depreciation	108,000*	$81,000

* Calculation of accumulated depreciation, using straight-line depreciation:

$$\frac{\$189{,}000 - \$9{,}000}{10 \text{ years}} \times 6 \text{ years } (1982-1987) = \$18{,}000 \text{ per year} \times 6 \text{ years} = \$108{,}000$$

Partial year depreciation must be recorded when an asset is sold during a year

For the year in which the building is sold, the depreciation must be recorded for the part of the year that the asset was used. In this case, the building was used for 9 months, up through September 30, the day before the sale. This adjustment will bring total lifetime accumulated depreciation right up to date prior to recording the sale.

1988			
Oct. 1	Depreciation Expense.	13,500	
	Accumulated Depreciation: Building.		13,500
	To record 9 months depreciation		

$[(\$189{,}000 - \$9{,}000)/10 \text{ years} = \$18{,}000 \text{ per year} \times \frac{9}{12} = \$13{,}500]$.

To calculate the gain or loss on the sale:

When we sell an asset for less than its book value, we record a loss

Selling price of building		$65,000
Less: Book value of building:		
Cost.	$189,000	
Less: Total accumulated depreciation since acquisition		
($108,000 + $13,500).	121,500	67,500
Loss on sale of building		$ (2,500)

The entry to record the sale is:

1988			
Oct. 1	Cash	65,000	
	Accumulated Depreciation: Building	121,500	
	Loss on Sale of Building	2,500	
	Building.		189,000
	To record sale of building.		

When recording sales of long-lived assets, remember:

Guidelines for recording the sale of a long-lived asset

1. Record its depreciation from the date acquired up to the day of the sale.
2. Recognize the gain or loss on the sale.

   A gain is indicated when we receive more for an asset than its book value (book value = original cost less accumulated depreciation).

   A loss is indicated when we receive less for an asset than its book value.

When assets are traded for similar ones, a loss may be recorded, but not a gain

Similarly, when an asset is traded in on a new one, depreciation is recorded up to the date of the trade. Such a trade is commonly a transaction in which the old asset plus some cash is exchanged for a new asset much like the old one. If the old asset is traded for a new one of a *similar type,* the cost of the new asset equals the book value of the old asset (original cost minus its accumulated depreciation) plus the amount of cash given. In no case may the new asset be carried at more than its actual fair market value. This fair market value limitation may result in a *loss* being recorded on the trade. Good accounting theory prohibits the recognition of gains on trades of similar assets when cash is paid out. The following examples will clarify these rules governing trades of similar assets.

Example D: Asset Traded for a Similar One — No Gain or Loss Indicated

Fiske, Inc., traded a delivery van that originally cost $12,500 and has an accumulated depreciation of $8,500 for a new van having a fair market price of $19,000. (The van's list price is $21,500, but it has been selling for $19,000 regularly at dealers in the area.) Fiske agreed to give the old van and $15,000 in exchange for the new one. The cost of the new van is:

The cost of a new asset cannot be higher than its fair market value

Cost of old van.	$12,500
Less: Accumulated depreciation on old van	8,500
= Book value of old van.	$ 4,000
+ Cash paid.	15,000
= Cost of new van	$19,000

In this case the cost of the new van is equal to its fair market price. That is, the book value of the two assets given up (old van, $4,000 plus cash, $15,000) is the same as the fair market price ($19,000 for a new van).

Let's calculate the gain or loss as we did in the previous examples:

No gain or loss is recognized when the book value of the assets given equal the fair market value of the asset received

Exchange value of old van (selling price of old van is the value we receive — the market value of the new van)	$ 19,000
Less book value of all assets given:	
Book value of old van ($12,500 − $8,500)	(4,000)
Book value of cash given.	(15,000)
Gain or (loss).	$ 0

The entry to record the exchange is:

Jan. 2	Delivery Equipment (new van).	19,000	
	Accumulated Depreciation (on old van).	8,500	
	Delivery Equipment (old van)		12,500
	Cash.		15,000
	To record trade of old van for a new one.		

Example E: Asset Traded for a Similar One — Gain Indicated — But Not Recorded

Assume the same facts as in Example D except that Fiske acquires the new van in exchange for the old van and $10,000 cash. The cost of the new van is:

Book value of old van ($12,500 − $8,500)	$ 4,000
+ Cash paid	10,000
= Cost of new van	$14,000

When the fair market value of the asset acquired is higher than the book value of the assets given, the cost of the new asset equals the book value of the assets given

Our gain or loss calculation reveals that a gain is indicated:

Exchange value of old van (selling price of old van is the value we receive — the market value of the new van)	$ 19,000
Less book value of all assets given:	
Book value of old van ($12,500 − $8,500)	(4,000)
Book value of cash given	(10,000)
Gain or (loss)	$ 5,000

No gain is recorded when assets are exchanged

Good accounting theory says that we cannot recognize this gain because we didn't sell the old asset for cash or another current asset. This is said to be an "unrealized" gain because we didn't receive a liquid asset such as cash.

Since we can't recognize the gain, we can't record the new van at its fair market value — $19,000 — we must record it at the book value of the assets we gave for it — $14,000 ($4,000 old van plus $10,000 cash).

The entry to record the exchange is:

Jan. 2	Delivery Equipment (new van)	14,000	
	Accumulated Depreciation (old van)	8,500	
	Delivery Equipment (old van)		12,500
	Cash		10,000
	To record trade of old van for a new one.		

Example F: Asset Traded for a Similar One — Loss Indicated and Recorded

Assume the same facts as in Example D except that Fiske acquires the new van in exchange for the old van and $18,000. The cost of the new van is $19,000. The prior method of calculation would yield a cost of $22,000:

Cost of old van	$12,500
Less: Accumulated depreciation on old van	8,500
= Book value of old van	$ 4,000
+ Cash paid	18,000
= Cost of new van (tentative)	$22,000

When the fair market value of the asset acquired is lower than the book value of the assets given, the cost of the new asset equals the fair market value of the asset acquired

Fiske can't record the new van at $22,000 because this is more than it is worth — it has a fair market value of $19,000. Generally accepted accounting principles will not allow Fiske to record the van at more than its fair market value.

The gain or loss calculation sheds some light on what really happened:

> Exchange value of old van (selling price of old van is the value we receive — the market value of the new van) . . . . $ 19,000
> Less book value of all assets given:
>   Book value of old van ($12,500 − $8,500) . . . . (4,000)
>   Book value of cash given . . . . (18,000)
>
> Gain or (loss) . . . . $(3,000)

Fiske will be required to record a loss on this transaction because the book value of the two assets given up (the old van, $4,000 plus cash, $18,000) is $3,000 more than the value of the asset acquired ($19,000). The entry to record the exchange is:

Jan. 2	Delivery Equipment (new van)	19,000	
	Accumulated Depreciation (old van)	8,500	
	Loss on Trade of Equipment	3,000	
	Delivery Equipment (old van)		12,500
	Cash		18,000
	To record trade of old van for a new one.		

Losses may be recorded when assets are exchanged

The justification for requiring the recognition of a loss but not allowing the recognition of a gain is the principle of conservatism. The ***principle of conservatism*** requires that losses should be recognized when incurred, but gains should be deferred until cash or another liquid asset is received.

Remember to follow these rules when recording an exchange of one long-lived asset for a similar one :

Rules for recording exchanges of similar long-lived assets

1. Cost of the new asset is recognized and recorded as the *lesser* of:
   a. The book value of all assets given to acquire the new one, or
   b. The fair market value of the new one.

2. Gains are not recognized on exchanges of similar assets. (Gains are recognized on sales of assets.)

3. Losses are recognized on exchanges of similar assets.

4. Depreciation of old assets given up must be recorded up to the date of the trade.

INTANGIBLE ASSETS

Intangible assets lack physical substance and are not held for investment

Long-lived assets that (1) lack physical substance and (2) are not held for investment are classified as ***intangible assets.***

Short-lived assets such as accounts receivable and prepaid expenses lack physical substance and are not investments but they are not classified as intangible assets — they are classified as current assets.

Similarly, long-term investments in stocks and bonds are not classified as intangibles — they are classified according to their purpose; they are investments.

Cost of Intangible Assets

The acquisition cost of intangible assets is determined by using the same general rule as for property, plant, and equipment:

The same cost rule is used for intangible and tangible assets

All reasonable and necessary costs to get an asset in position and condition ready for use may be included as part of the cost of the asset.

An intangible can be acquired, such as a patent bought from an inventor, or it can be created internally such as a copyright for an advertising jingle created by an employee of your advertising department. In either case, the cost of acquisition or the cost of development is included as part of an intangible's total cost. Legal fees, costs of filing documents with government agencies and costs of defending ownership, are other costs commonly associated with intangibles.

Because it is sometimes difficult to establish the existence of an asset that lacks physical substance, we must be very careful in the case of internally created intangibles. When we spend money we may be buying future benefits (an asset) or we may be deriving all benefits now (an expense). If we charge an amount to an asset account when an expense should have been used, we have understated expenses on the income statement and overstated net income.

The following are some common intangibles and the problems in measuring their cost and the using up of this cost.

Factors to consider in determining the cost of various intangible assets

Patents are exclusive rights granted by the U.S. government permitting one person or firm to manufacture, use, and sell a certain product. Polaroid film is a good example of a product manufactured under a patent. The owner of a patent may allow others to make and sell the product, usually charging a fee for this right. A patent is granted for a period of 17 years, although the product it protects may become obsolete in a much shorter time. When that happens the patent's useful life may be less than its 17-year legal life.

The costs of bringing successful suits against those who seek to copy a product—patent infringement suits—are considered a part of the cost of the patent. Unsuccessful patent infringement suits mean that the court ruled that the defendants didn't copy your product, or if they did, that they had a right to do so. The result of an unsuccessful suit may be that you no longer have a patent.

Patents can be purchased from their owners. Patents purchased from others are good only until the originally granted 17-year life expires. For example, a 16-year-old patent if purchased will provide rights to the purchaser for only one more year.

Copyrights are rights granted by the U.S. government for the exclusive use of a literary or artistic work for the creator's life plus 50 years. The copyright gives the creator, heirs, or persons to whom the right has been sold the exclusive right to publish or reproduce the work for this period of time.

The cost of obtaining a copyright is very small, only the cost of completing a form and the payment of a small fee to the U.S. Copyright office. The cost of a copyright purchased from an author, however, may be very high. Can you imagine how much it might cost to purchase the copyright to the *Star Wars* movies?

Goodwill represents a number of intangible advantages such as superior operating efficiency, an unusually well-trained sales force, excellent client relations or public relations, an outstanding reputation or image in the marketplace, and an advantageous location. A firm that has all or many of these advantages has *goodwill* and will earn a higher return on its income-producing assets than will a firm having the same assets but not having goodwill.

Goodwill is recorded only when it is purchased

Goodwill is one of those internally created assets that is almost impossible to value, especially with any degree of objectivity. Nevertheless, goodwill can be acquired—but not by itself—it comes along with all the other tangible and intangible assets comprising the firm acquired. And, it is only at acquisition that goodwill can be objectively valued, and that's when it is recorded. The value of goodwill is the part of the total acquisition cost that cannot be assigned to the other assets acquired, as the following example illustrates.

Roof Company agreed to purchase all of the assets of Branch, Inc., for $530,000. The net assets (total assets minus total liabilities) on Branch's balance sheet were $385,000 and their fair market value, the amount for which they could be sold, at the time totaled $505,000. The negotiated price of Branch was higher than the total market value of the individual assets because Branch had consistently been able to earn a much higher rate of return on its assets than other firms in the industry. Roof Company therefore recorded goodwill of $25,000 (acquisition price of total asset package $530,000 less the total market value of the assets acquired $505,000 = $25,000).

Franchises are rights to sell a specific brand of products or services in a certain geographic area. Franchise agreements to operate a fast food restaurant such as McDonalds or Burger King probably come to mind immediately. Many municipalities grant franchises to private firms to provide such services as garbage removal, cable television, and electric power. The cost of the franchise includes payments made in advance of operating the franchised business, and legal fees for preparing contracts specifying the terms of the franchise agreement.

Trademarks are exclusive rights to use a certain name or symbol for an unlimited future period. For a new trademark, the initial cost of these assets may be quite small, consisting of the artist's fee to develop a symbol and a nominal filing fee to register the trademark with a government agency. The cost of acquiring an established and a well-known trademark may involve substantial sums—imagine what it would cost to purchase the name Coke or Pepsi, if this were even possible.

Organization costs are expenditures made in establishing a business. Organization costs include attorney's fees for drawing up a partnership agreement or articles of incorporation (the legal document creating a corporation), and fees paid to state and local governments to register as a business organization. The costs of organizing a business provide benefits for the life of the business. These costs are considered to be an intangible asset.

Amortization of Intangibles

Amortization is the process of allocating the cost of an intangible over its useful life

The process of allocating the cost of an intangible asset over all the periods it provides benefits is called *amortization.* Intangibles are normally amortized on a straight-line basis unless some other system can be shown to be clearly preferable. Straight-line amortization is identical to straight-line depreciation:

$$\text{Amortization per year} = \frac{\text{cost of intangible asset} - \text{salvage value}}{\text{number of years of useful life}}$$

Straight-line amortization is calculated just like straight-line depreciation

The *cost* of specific intangibles is determined by applying the general acquisition-cost rule.

Generally, an intangible asset has no *salvage value.* At the end of an intangible's life there is nothing of value left.

The *useful life* of an intangible may be much less than its legal life; a patent, for example, may provide benefits for 5 years instead of the legal maximum of 17. In any case, authoritative accounting rules establish an arbitrary maximum of 40 years for the amortization of any intangible. A copyright with a possible 90-year life usually loses substantially all of its economic usefulness over a period of 40 years or less. Goodwill has such an indeterminate life that some maximum was needed.

For example, Lee Company purchased a patent from Grant, Inc., for $17,500. The remaining legal life of the patent is 12 years, but Lee believes that it will be useful for only 7 years. The calculation of the amortization and the annual journal entry to record amortization is as follows:

$$\text{Amortization per year} = \frac{\$17,500 - 0}{7 \text{ years}} = \underline{\$2,500 \text{ per year}}$$

Dec. 31   Patent Amortization Expense 2,500
              Patents.   2,500
            To record patent amortization for the year.

Accumulated amortization accounts are not customarily used for intangibles since these assets are difficult if not impossible to replace at the end of their useful lifes. Appropriate footnotes disclose the estimated useful lives of intangibles.

CHAPTER SUMMARY

Property, plant, and equipment is a balance sheet classification that includes all *tangible long-lived assets* owned by a business and used in its operations to help produce revenues. The acquisition cost of a tangible long-lived asset includes all reasonable and necessary costs to get it in position and condition ready for use. Common property, plant, and equipment assets include land, buildings, machinery, equipment, and natural resources.

Expenditures made after the acquisition may be added to the cost of the asset — *capital expenditures* — or charged to expense — *revenue expenditures.* The asset account is increased whenever the expenditure benefits several future accounting periods. An expense account is debited when only the current accounting period is benefited.

Allocating the cost of a property, plant, and equipment asset (other than a natural resource) over its useful life is called *depreciation.* Depreciation results from physical wear-and-tear as well as from technical obsolescence.

Straight-line depreciation allocates an equal cost to each time period; *units-of-output depreciation* allocates an equal cost to each unit produced.

The *sum-of-the-years'-digits* and *double declining-balance* methods recognize higher depreciation amounts in the early years of an asset's life when it is more productive and requires less maintenance; as a result, lower depreciation is recognized in later years when the asset is less efficient.

Property, plant, and equipment assets are disclosed on the balance sheet at original cost. For assets other than land an Accumulated Depreciation account is also shown as a subtraction from the cost amount. The difference between the balances in these two accounts — the asset and the accumulated depreciation — gives the statement reader a rough idea as to how long it will be before the asset must be replaced. This difference is the amount of the undepreciated cost.

Depreciation methods used for income tax calculations are different from those used in financial accounting. Tax laws assign an arbitrary life to assets instead of using their actual useful lives. *Accelerated cost recovery system (ACRS)* and a special form of straight-line depreciation are allowed for calculating tax depreciation.

Depletion is similar to depreciation; depletion is allocation of the cost of a natural resource that has been consumed. An equal cost is assigned to each unit produced.

When a property, plant, and equipment asset is sold, the depreciation must be accrued up until the date of sale. When the selling price exceeds its book value, a gain is recognized. If book value is larger than the selling price, a loss is recorded.

The balance sheet classification *Intangible Assets* includes a firm's long-lived assets that lack physical substance but are used in its operations. The acquisition cost of an intangible is amortized over its useful life, usually on a straight-line basis. A maximum life of 40 years is allowed. Common intangible assets are patents, copyrights, goodwill, and franchises.

IMPORTANT TERMS USED IN THIS CHAPTER

Accelerated Cost Recovery System (ACRS) A method of calculating depreciation for income tax purposes. The method may be used for assets placed in service after 1980. Depreciation each year is calculated by multiplying a prescribed percentage by the asset's cost. (page 393)

Accumulated depreciation The total part of the cost of a property, plant, and equipment asset that is considered to be "consumed" and that has been charged to depreciation expense. (page 391)

Amortization Allocation of the cost of an intangible asset over its useful life. (page 402)

Book value An asset's total cost less its accumulated depreciation. (page 398)

Capital expenditures Costs incurred for assets that provide benefits over several accounting periods. (page 381)

Copyright A right granted by the U.S. government for the exclusive use of a literary or artistic work for the creator's life plus 50 years. (page 401)

Depletion Allocation of a natural resource's cost estimated to be used up in a time period. An equal cost is assigned to each unit of natural resource extracted. (page 395)

Depreciation Allocation of the total cost of a tangible long-lived asset over its useful life. (page 382)

Double declining-balance depreciation A system of allocating an asset's cost over its useful life in decreasing amounts each year. Depreciation per year is calculated by multiplying a fixed percentage (twice the straight-line rate) by the asset's declining book value. (page 386)

Franchise The exclusive right to sell a specific brand of products or services in a certain geographic area. (page 402)

Goodwill If the acquisition price of a business is more than the fair market value of its net assets, the excess is the cost of that business's goodwill. (page 401)

Intangible assets Assets that lack physical substance but that are an important part of a business's operations. (A balance sheet classification.) (page 400)

Organization costs Costs incurred to establish a business. (page 402)

Patent A right granted by the U.S. government for the exclusive manufacture, use, and sale of a certain product for a 17-year period. (page 401)

Property, plant, and equipment Tangible long-lived assets owned by a business and used in its operations. (A balance sheet classification.) (page 377)

Relative-value allocation The allocation of the total cost of a group of assets among each asset based on the value of each asset relative to the value of the whole group. (page 380)

Revenue expenditures Costs incurred that benefit only the current accounting period. (page 381)

Straight-line depreciation A system of depreciating an asset's cost that allocates an equal amount of cost in each time period of the asset's useful life. Depreciation per period = (cost − salvage value) ÷ estimated useful life. (page 383)

Sum-of-the-years'-digits depreciation A system of depreciation that allocates a decreasing cost to each successive period in the asset's life. Depreciation for a period = [number of years left in the asset's life (as of the beginning of the year) ÷ the sum of the digits of the asset's useful life] × (cost − salvage value). (page 385)

Trademark Exclusive right to use a certain name or symbol for an unlimited future period. (page 402)

Units-of-output depreciation A system of depreciation that allocates an equal cost to each unit produced. Depreciation per period = (number of units produced this period) × [(cost − salvage value) ÷ useful life stated in units]. (page 384)

QUESTIONS

1. What is the general rule for determining the cost of a long-lived asset? Give examples of at least four costs that would be included in the cost of a building.

2. Explain why cash discounts are always deducted in determining the cost of a long-lived asset, even if the company doesn't take advantage of the cash discount.

3. Pilot, Inc., purchased a machine for $48,000 cash. When the machine arrived, it had to be stored in a local warehouse because the room to house the new machine was still under construction. Should the storage charges of $550 be added to the cost to the machine or should they be expensed? Explain.

4. The cost of freight on a machine acquired on December 31, 1986, was debited to Miscellaneous Expense rather than Machinery. What effect will this error have on 1986 income? 1987 income?

5. What are the two most common causes of depreciation? Which cause is most crucial in determining the useful life of an asset in the contemporary U.S. economy? Explain.

6. Curlew Co. shows the following on its December 31, 1987, balance sheet:

Building. $250,000
Less: Accumulated Depreciation 75,000 $175,000

Does this tell the statement reader that Curlew's building is worth $250,000? $175,000? Explain.

7. What is meant by the term *accelerated depreciation?* List two accelerated depreciation methods.

8. At times the amount of depreciation indicated by the double declining-balance formula will not be the depreciation recorded. Under what conditions must the amount indicated by the formula be adjusted? Explain.

9. Winger Co. shows a truck with a cost of $23,000 and an accumulated depreciation of $8,700. How much cash has been set aside for the replacement of the truck through the depreciation process? Explain.

10. When an asset's cost and its accumulated depreciation are equal in amount, the asset is said to be fully depreciated. Are the asset and the accumulated depreciation accounts removed from the financial records when this happens? Explain.

11. Baker Co. used straight-line depreciation for financial statements and an accelerated method for income tax returns. This amounts to keeping "two sets of books" and is illegal. Do you agree? Explain.

12. What is ACRS depreciation? For what purpose is ACRS depreciation used?

13. What is the difference between depreciation and depletion? Is accelerated depletion allowed?

14. Under what conditions will a company record a loss on an asset that is traded or sold?

15. Accounts Receivable, Investment in City of Charleston Bonds, and Copyrights are examples of assets that lack physical substance. Which of these will appear under the heading "Intangible Assets" on the balance sheet? Explain why those omitted would not be classified among intangible assets.

16. How does amortization differ from depreciation? What method of amortization is most widely used?

17. Over what time period is an intangible asset amortized?

18. Auden, Inc., has been manufacturing computer furniture for 10 years. Auden has consistently earned a much higher rate of return on its assets than its competitors. Auden is widely recognized as the most successful firm in the industry. Would you expect goodwill to exist in Auden's business? Explain. Where would you expect to find goodwill on Auden's financial statements? Explain.

EXERCISES

Exercise 10-1
Calculate the cost of a computer

Chase Company purchased a new computer from Analog Computers. The following costs were incurred:

List price of the computer	$100,000
Trade discount allowed to Chase	10%
Cash discount allowed for payment within 30 days	3%
Cost of air conditioning the room where the new computer is to be used. The computer requires a certain temperature and humidity to operate properly	$ 1,250
Insurance on the computer. The policy covers damage from vandalism, fire, flood, and certain other natural disasters (3-year premium)	360
Cost of 1-year maintenance contract. The computer will be serviced weekly by Analog technicians	2,080
Cost of rewiring needed to provide proper electric power	420

Prepare a schedule that shows the calculation of the cost of the computer to Chase Company.

(Check figure: Cost of computer = $88,970)

Exercise 10-2
Using relative value allocation

Hamilton, Inc., bought some assets from Gray Construction, which was disposing of its road construction division. The assets purchased and their appraised values appear below:

Asset	Appraised Value
Bulldozers	$ 50,000
Dump trucks	125,000
Scrapers	187,500
Excavators	262,500
Total	$625,000

Assuming that Hamilton paid $500,000 for all of the assets listed, prepare a schedule showing the calculation of the cost that would be assigned to each one. Prepare the entry to record the acquisition.

(Check figure: Cost assigned to excavators = $210,000)

Exercise 10-3
Calculating units-of-output depreciation

Cosmo Co. purchased a company airplane on January 1, 1987, for $204,000. Cosmo expects to use the plane for 5 years, at which time it will have a salvage value of $24,000. Cosmo believes that, with proper maintenance, the plane will fly approximately 7,500 hours during the 5 years. During 1987 and 1988, the plane flew 1,200 and 1,620 hours, respectively.

Prepare the entry to record depreciation for the years ended December 31, 1987 and 1988, using the units-of-output method of depreciation. Present clearly labeled calculations to support your solution.

(Check figure: Units-of-output depreciation for 1987 = $28,800)

Exercise 10-4
Calculating sum-of-the-years'-digits depreciation

Mingo, Inc., purchased equipment on November 1, 1986, for $49,500. The equipment has an expected useful life of 5 years and an estimated salvage value of $4,500.

Calculate the depreciation expense for the years ended October 31, 1987 and 1988, using the sum-of-the-years'-digits method. Prepare the journal entries to record the depreciation.

(Check figure: SYD depreciation for 1987 = $15,000)

Exercise 10-5
Calculating double declining-balance depreciation

On January 1, 1987, Bowen Company purchased a large power generator for $320,000. The generator is expected to last 5 years and have a salvage value of $20,000.

Calculate the depreciation that would be recorded on December 31, 1987 and 1988, using the double declining-balance method. Prepare journal entries to record the depreciation.

(Check figure: DDB depreciation for 1987 = $128,000)

Exercise 10-6
Calculating depletion

Rich Vein Mining Co. purchased and developed a mining site at a total cost of $3,000,000. Geologists estimate that 4,500,000 tons of iron ore are contained in the property. Rich Vein mined and sold 400,000 tons of iron ore during 1988. The sales price was $1.25 per ton. The salvage value of the property is estimated to be $75,000.

Calculate the depletion for 1988. Prepare entries to record depletion and to record the sale of the ore.

(Check figure: Depletion for 1988 = $260,000)

Exercise 10-7
Preparing entries to record sales of equipment

Barclay, Inc., sold a crane on January 1, 1988. The crane had originally cost $600,000. Total depreciation recorded through December 31, 1987, is $420,000.

Prepare the entry to record the sale of equipment at each of the following amounts: **(a)** $200,000; **(b)** $180,000; **(c)** $130,000.

[Check figure: Loss on sale of equipment (c) = $50,000]

Exercise 10-8
Preparing entries to record exchanges of assets

Lynn, Inc., traded a pizza oven having a cost of $3,250 and an accumulated depreciation of $1,500 for a new pizza oven having a fair market value of $4,500.

Prepare the entry to record the acquisition of the new oven, assuming that Lynn was required to pay **(a)** $2,750 in addition to the old oven; **(b)** $2,000 cash in addition to the old oven; and **(c)** $3,100 in addition to the old oven. Show clearly labeled calculations to support your entries.

[Check figure: Cost of oven (b) = $3,750]

Exercise 10-9
Preparing entries to amortize intangibles

Wingate, Inc., purchased two intangible assets on January 1, 1987. A patent was acquired for $27,200, and goodwill was purchased for $128,000, as part of the acquisition of Holmes Corp. The patent is a new one and has its full legal life remaining. The goodwill is expected to last for an indefinite time.

Prepare the amortization entries for Patents and Goodwill on December 31, 1987, assuming that the patent is to be amortized over its legal life (no salvage value) and the goodwill is to be amortized over the maximum period allowed. Your entries should be supported by clearly labeled calculations.

(Check figure: Goodwill amortization expense = $3,200)

Exercise 10-10
Calculating ACRS, tax straight-line, accounting depreciation

On January 1, 1986, Sunset Corp. purchased some office furniture for $12,500. The furniture has a 10-year life for financial accounting purposes, but income tax laws arbitrarily assign it a 5-year life for income tax purposes. The furniture is expected to have a $2,500 salvage value.

Calculate 1986, 1987, and 1988 depreciation expense by each of the following methods: **(a)** ACRS; **(b)** tax straight line; **(c)** financial accounting straight line.

(Check figure: ACRS depreciation for 1987 = $2,750)

PROBLEMS
Set A

Problem A10-1
Calculating the cost of several assets

The management of Tides Corp. has asked for your assistance in determining the cost of their property, plant, and equipment assets. Tides began operations on January 3, 1987. During the year the following transactions that management believes may relate to long-lived assets took place:

a. Paid $300,000 for land, building, and machinery. The land was appraised at $65,000, the building at $162,500, and the machinery at $97,500. Tides was able to acquire the assets at less than their appraised value because the seller was badly in need of cash.
b. $250 was paid for title insurance on the land.
c. $1,000 was paid to drain a portion of the land and to haul in fill dirt so that the land could be used for a parking lot.
d. $500 was paid for a survey to determine the exact location of the driveways and parking lots to be constructed.
e. $11,000 was paid for grading and paving driveways and parking lots.
f. $2,400 was paid to a cleaning service to sweep the driveways and parking lots for the remainder of 1987.
g. $12,000 was paid to have a new roof put on the building. The roof is expected to last 20 years, which is also the remaining life of the building.
h. $7,250 was paid to have the motors in several of the machines overhauled.
i. $60 was paid to replace several window panes that were broken after Tides moved into the building.
j. $250 was paid for a supply of oil, grease, and cleaning compounds that would be needed to assure efficient operation of the machines.

Required   Set up a solutions paper with the following column headings:

Description	Land	Buildings	Other Accounts Name	Amount

For each of the 10 items listed in the problem, place the amount in the column indicating the correct account. If the amount should not be debited to either Land or Buildings, decide which account would be proper and place the account name and amount in the final column.

(Check figure: Buildings = $162,000)

Problem A10-2
Calculating depreciation under four different methods

On January 1, 1985, Pace Systems, Inc., purchased a large truck. Pace estimates the $315,000 truck will last for 6 years, at which time its salvage value will be $52,500. Pace plans to use the truck for the following mileage each year: 1985, 150,000; 1986, 220,000; 1987, 220,000; 1988, 190,000; 1989, 150,000; 1990, 70,000.

Required   Calculate the amount of depreciation in each of the 6 years under **(1)** the straight-line method;

(2) the units-of-output method; (3) the sum-of-the-years'-digits method; and (4) the double declining-balance method. Round to the nearest whole dollar.

(Check figure: Double declining-balance depreciation in 1987 = $46,667)

Problem A10-3
Using different methods to calculate depreciation on various assets

Sonic Manufacturing, Inc., purchased the following new assets on January 1, 1987:

Asset	Cost	Salvage	Estimated Useful Life, Years
Paper shredder	$14,000	$1,500	5
Copying machine	18,500	2,500	4
Waste paper compactor	8,500	100	8

Required For each of the assets listed above, determine:
1. The straight-line depreciation rate
2. The amount of depreciation expense for 1987 and 1988 using the straight-line method
3. The double declining-balance rate
4. The amount of depreciation expense for 1987 and 1988 using the double declining-balance method

(Check figure: Double declining-balance depreciation on the waste paper compactor for 1987 = $2,125)

Problem A10-4
Calculating depreciation under three different methods

Overstreet Corp. has been in business for several years. On December 31, 1988, the following major long-lived assets were on hand:

Buildings purchased June 30, 1978, for $2,800,000. Their estimated useful life and salvage value are 15 years and $130,000, respectively.

Delivery truck purchased January 1, 1985, for $34,000. The truck had an estimated useful life of 5 years and a salvage value of $4,000.

Machinery purchased September 1, 1988, for $144,000. Engineers predict the useful life to be 12 years and the salvage value to be $6,000.

Overstreet uses the straight-line method for buildings, the sum-of-the-years'-digits method for delivery trucks, and the double declining-balance method for machinery.

Required Calculate the depreciation expense that should be recorded for the year ended December 31, 1988, for each of the assets.

(Check figure: 1988 depreciation on machinery = $8,000)

Problem A10-5
Recording sales and exchanges of equipment

On January 1, 1988, Moyer Restaurant Corp.'s balance sheet lists the following equipment:

Baking Oven	$ 9,000	
Less: Accumulated Depreciation	6,800	$ 2,200
Dishwasher	$30,000	
Less: Accumulated Depreciation	6,000	24,000
Deep Fryer	$12,000	
Less: Accumulated Depreciation.	9,000	3,000

The following transactions affecting equipment took place during 1988:
a. The baking oven was sold for $1,500.

b. The old dishwasher was traded in on a similar machine that operated more efficiently. The fair market value of the new washer was $38,000. In addition to giving the old dishwasher, Moyer was required to pay $20,000 cash.

c. The old deep fryer was traded for a new one having a fair market price of $15,000. Moyer was required to pay $10,000 in addition to the old fryer.

Required   Prepare journal entries to record each of the transactions described above. Each entry should be supported by clearly labeled calculations.

(Check figure: Loss on trading dishwasher = $6,000)

Problem A10-6
Recording depreciation and disposals of equipment

During 1987 DeAngelo's Garage disposed of several long-lived assets and acquired several others. Information relating to these transactions follows:

Jan. 1   DeAngelo traded an old wrecker having a cost of $45,000 and an accumulated depreciation of $15,000 for a new one having a fair market value of $68,000. DeAngelo was required to pay $40,000 in addition to the old wrecker.

May 1   DeAngelo sold an old engine diagnostic machine for $1,000. The machine cost $6,500 and had an accumulated depreciation on January 1, 1987, of $4,200. DeAngelo uses the straight-line method of depreciation. The machine has an estimated useful life of 5 years and a $500 salvage value.

Oct. 1   DeAngelo sold an air compressor for $25 as scrap. The machine was purchased on Sept. 30, 1982, for $1,500; it was estimated to have a useful life of 5 years and a salvage value of $240. Depreciation had been correctly recorded through Dec. 31, 1986.

Nov. 1   DeAngelo traded a front-end alignment machine for a new one having a fair market value of $7,500. The old machine had been purchased on Jan. 1, 1980, for $4,500. The estimated useful life of the old machine was 12 years; the estimated salvage value was $180. Accumulated depreciation on Jan. 1, 1987, was $2,520. DeAngelo was required to pay $5,500 in addition to the old machine.

Required   Prepare the entry to record each of the transactions listed above. You may also need an entry to record depreciation for part of the year. Assume that DeAngelo has not recorded any depreciation since December 31, 1986. Your entries should be supported by clearly labeled calculations.

(Check figure: Cost of new alignment machine = $7,180)

Problem A10-7
Recording acquisition and amortization of intangible assets

Pioneer Corp. began business in 1987. The controller has listed the following transactions and events which she is unsure about:

Jan. 1   Paid attorney $1,250 to draw up articles of incorporation and file them with the state government.

May 1   Purchased a franchise to sell Mainsail yachts. $12,000 cash was paid; the balance of $15,000 is due within 1 year.

July 1   Paid $2,000 to a song writer to write the words and music for a theme song for the company's advertising. Pioneer acquired the copyright as a part of the fee.

Oct. 1   Paid $500 to an artist to design a logo for the company. This logo was registered at an additional cost of $50.

Dec. 31   Pioneer has had such a successful first year that management feels that some goodwill has been created. The firm's management team estimates the value of this goodwill to be at least $3,500.

Required   **1.** Analyze each of the transactions and events. Prepare all necessary journal entries. If no entry is required, write "no entry" and give the reason that none is needed.

2. Prepare entries needed on December 31 to amortize the intangible assets. Assume that all the intangibles are to be amortized over a 10-year period.

(Check figure: Franchise amortization expense = $1,800)

Problem A10-8

Answering questions about Property, Plant, & Equipment as presented on a balance sheet

The Lange & Associates, Inc., balance sheet for 1988 shows one column for the current year and another for the previous year. The long-lived assets section is reproduced below:

	Dec. 31, 1988	Dec. 31, 1987
Property, Plant, and Equipment:		
Land	$ 960,000	$1,030,000
Building.	$2,500,000	$2,800,000
Less: Accumulated Depreciation	(360,000)	(400,000)
Net Book Value of Building	$2,140,000	$2,400,000
Equipment	$ 420,000	$ 420,000
Less: Accumulated Depreciation	(150,000)	(120,000)
Net Book Value of Equipment	$ 270,000	$ 300,000
Total Property, Plant, and Equipment	$3,370,000	$3,730,000
Intangibles:		
Franchises	$ 36,000	$ 40,000

Required

Prepare answers to the following questions about Lange's long-lived assets. Your answers should be supported by calculations.

1. What is the most logical explanation for the change in the Land account?

2. One building costing $300,000 and having an accumulated depreciation of $100,000 was sold for $196,000 during 1988. What is the amount of depreciation expense on buildings for 1988?

3. Assuming that no equipment was bought or sold during 1988, what is the amount of depreciation expense on equipment during 1988?

4. Assuming that no franchise was bought or sold during 1988, what is the amount of franchise amortization expense for 1988?

(Check figure: Depreciation expense on buildings = $60,000)

Set B

Problem B10-1

Calculating the cost of several assets

Keene, Inc., debits an account called Long-Lived Assets for the purchase of any asset that is expected to last longer than 1 year. During its first year of operations Keene made the following debits to Long-Lived Assets:

a. $400,000 was paid for a parcel of land.

b. $13,100 was paid for title insurance and legal fees related to the purchase of the land.

c. $28,000 was paid to have the land cleared, filled, and leveled so that it would be suitable for use.

d. $6,400 was paid for a survey to determine the exact placement of a building on the land.

e. $1,000 was paid for a building permit.

f. $300,000 was paid to an architect to design the building and supervise construction.

g. $1,600,000 was paid to a contractor to erect the building.

h. $284,000 was paid for paving parking lots and driveways.

i. $207,000 was paid for landscaping.

j. $32,800 was paid to erect a fence around the property.

Required

Set up a solutions paper with the following headings:

Description	Land	Buildings	Land Improvements

For each of the 10 items listed in the problem, place the amount in the column indicating the correct property, plant, and equipment account.

(Check figure: Cost of Buildings = $1,907,400)

Problem B10-2

Calculating depreciation under four different methods

Webster & Sons, Inc., purchased a machine for $32,000 on January 1, 1985. Webster expects to use the machine for 4 years, at which time its estimated salvage value will be $2,000. Production from the machine over the 4 years is budgeted at the following levels: 1985, 10,000 units; 1986, 20,000 units; 1987, 40,000 units; 1988, 5,000 units.

Required

Calculate the amount of depreciation in each of the four years of the asset's life under **(1)** the straight-line method; **(2)** the units-of-output method; **(3)** the sum-of-the-years'-digits method; and **(4)** the double declining-balance method.

(Check figure: Double declining-balance depreciation for 1987 = $4,000)

Problem B10-3

Using different methods to calculate depreciation on various assets

J. Stone and Daughters, Inc., acquired the following new assets on January 1, 1987:

Asset	Cost	Salvage	Estimated Useful Life
Office furniture	$150,000	$ 15,000	5 years
Telephone system	210,000	30,000	6 years
Building	900,000	100,000	20 years

Required

For each of the assets listed, determine:
1. The straight-line depreciation rate
2. The amount of depreciation expense for 1987 and 1988 using the straight-line method
3. The double declining-balance rate
4. The amount of depreciation expense for 1987 and 1988 using the double declining-balance method

(Check figure: 1988 double declining-balance depreciation for the building = $81,000)

Problem B10-4

Calculating depreciation under three different methods

Garcia, Inc., began operations on January 1, 1987. During the first year of business the following asset purchases were made:

Jan. 1   Equipment was acquired at a cost of $380,000. Engineers predict the useful life of the equipment to be 15 years and the salvage value to be $20,000.

Feb. 1   A building was purchased for $800,000. The building has an expected useful life of 20 years and a salvage value of $50,000.

Mar. 1   A fleet of delivery vans was acquired for $72,000. The vans should last 5 years and have a salvage value of $10,000.

Garcia uses the straight-line method for buildings, the sum-of-the-years'-digits method for equipment, and the double declining-balance method for trucks.

Required

Prepare a schedule showing the 1987 and 1988 depreciation for each of the assets listed above. Clearly labeled calculations should be shown to support your solution.

(Check figure: SYD depreciation on equipment for 1988 = $42,000)

Problem B10-5
Recording sales and exchanges
of various assets

Mulligan, Inc.'s, December 31, 1987, balance sheet includes the following property, plant, and equipment assets:

Land.		$750,000
Building	$1,800,000	
Less: Accumulated Depreciation.	1,600,000	200,000
Refrigeration Equipment.	$ 460,000	
Less: Accumulated Depreciation.	220,000	240,000
Delivery Trucks	$ 125,000	
Less: Accumulated Depreciation.	100,000	25,000

The following transactions affecting property, plant, and equipment assets took place on January 1, 1988:

a. The land and building were sold for $1,175,000. Mulligan has decided to lease space as soon as an acceptable facility can be located.

b. The old refrigeration equipment was traded on similar units with a larger capacity. The fair market price of the new assets was $650,000. Mulligan was required to pay $450,000 in addition to giving the old equipment.

c. The old delivery trucks were traded for new ones. Mulligan was required to pay $150,000 in addition to trading the old trucks. The new trucks have a fair market value of $182,000.

Required   Prepare journal entries to record each of the January 1, 1988, transactions. Each entry should be supported by clearly labeled calculations.

(Check figure: Cost of new trucks = $175,000)

Problem B10-6
Recording depreciation and
disposals of various assets

During 1987, Tryon Airlines engaged in the following transactions relating to property, plant, and equipment assets:

Jan. 1   Tryon traded a computer that had a cost of $400,000 and accumulated depreciation of $140,000 for a new computer having a fair market value of $640,000. Tryon was required to pay $400,000 in addition to the old computer.

Apr. 1   Tryon sold a building for $250,000. The building cost $300,000 and has an accumulated depreciation of $100,000 on January 1, 1987. Tryon uses the straight-line method of depreciation. The building was estimated to have a useful life of 20 years and a salvage value of $20,000.

June 30   Tryon sold old baggage carts for $125 as scrap. The carts were purchased on July 1, 1982, for $3,000; they were estimated to have a useful life of 5 years and a salvage value of $200. Accumulated depreciation on Jan. 1, 1987, was $2,520. The straight-line method is used.

Sept. 30   Tryon traded an old airplane for a new one having a fair market price of $5,000,000. The old airplane had been purchased on Feb. 1, 1978, for $2,000,000, had no salvage value, and was fully depreciated as of January 1, 1987. Tryon was required to pay $4,950,000 in addition to giving the old airplane.

Required   Prepare the entry to record each of the transactions listed above. You may also need an entry to record depreciation for part of the year. Assume that Tryon has not recorded any depreciation since December 31, 1986. Your entries should be supported by clearly labeled calculations.

(Check figure: June 30 entry, loss on disposal of baggage carts = $75)

Problem B10-7
Recording acquisition and
amortization of intangible assets

Discovery Enterprises is a diversified company involved in many different business ventures. Selected Discovery transactions for 1987 are described below:

Jan. 1   Acquired a patent for an artificial sweetener made from mango juice. The patent cost $96,000 and is expected to have an economic life of 16 years.

Apr. 1   Purchased a 5-year franchise to sell popcorn with exotic flavors from Tropicpop, Inc. The franchise price was $18,000; one-third of the price was paid in 1987; the remainder is due within 1 year.

June 30   Purchased an operating deli. Goodwill purchased as a part of the transaction totaled $50,000.

Nov. 1   Purchased a copyright for a play entitled *The Basket Case* for $18,000. The copyright is expected to have a useful life of 10 years.

Required

1. Prepare entries to record each of the transactions listed above.
2. Prepare the appropriate amortization entries on December 31, 1987. Assume that the goodwill is to be amortized over the maximum number of years.

(Check figure: Copyright amortization expense = $300)

Problem B10-8
Answering questions about
Property, Plant, & Equipment
as presented on a balance sheet

Aquatech, Inc.'s, year-end balance sheet shows one column for the current year and another column for the previous year. The long-lived assets appear on Aquatech's 1988 balance sheet as follows:

	Dec. 31, 1988	Dec. 31, 1987
Property, Plant, and Equipment:		
Land	$400,000	$310,000
Building	$500,000	$500,000
Less: Accumulated Depreciation	(125,000)	(87,500)
Net Book Value of Building	$375,000	$412,500
Machinery	$ 75,000	$125,000
Less: Accumulated Depreciation	(30,000)	(40,000)
Net Book Value of Machinery	$ 45,000	$ 85,000
Total Property, Plant, and Equipment	$820,000	$807,500
Intangibles:		
Patents	$100,000	$130,000

Required

Prepare answers to the following questions about Aquatech's long-lived assets. Your answers should be supported by calculations.
1. What is the most logical explanation for the change in the Land account?
2. Assuming that no buildings were bought or sold during 1988, what is the amount of depreciation expense on the buildings during 1988?
3. One piece of machinery costing $50,000 and having an accumulated depreciation of $12,500 was sold for $37,500 during 1988. What is the amount of depreciation expense on machinery during 1988?
4. Assuming that no patents were bought or sold during 1988, what is the amount of patent amortization expense for 1988?

(Check figure: Depreciation expense on buildings = $37,500)

Chapter 11

Current Liabilities and Payroll Accounting

After studying this chapter you should understand:

- Why accounting for current liabilities is important
- The difference between current and long-term liabilities
- The difference between two groups of current liabilities
- How we account for estimated and contingent liabilities
- How to compute the gross earnings for individual employees and how to determine the deductions to be made from those gross earnings
- That payroll taxes and income taxes withheld from employees' salaries are remitted to the governmental agencies
- How to record payroll data in a payroll register and how to prepare from the payroll register the general journal entries to record the payroll

Your ability to borrow money enables you to enjoy many of the things our society makes available. Very few people would own their own homes if they could not borrow money. Nor would many of us have cars, furniture, or a multitude of goods and services (including college educations) without being able to borrow money from various stores, banks, or other sources. In fact the operation of our national and international economies depends on the extension of credit. Without it, or if its cost is too high, goods and services cannot be paid for; plants close, and people are unemployed. The vast majority of our businesses purchase inventories and acquire plant and equipment by incurring liabilities. We, as individuals, have far more purchasing potential when credit is available. Our aggregate purchasing potential has enabled business and industrial firms to expand to the size where large-scale production is possible, thus reducing the costs of goods and services. Extending credit to business entities has provided them with the resources necessary to build plants and acquire or manufacture inventories that we demand.

Extending credit means that someone has incurred a liability. And liabilities must be properly accounted for. What we are particularly concerned about is that all the liabilities of a business entity are recorded in the books of account and find their way to the balance sheet. Unrecorded liabilities such as accrued salaries mean that expenses—in this case salary expense—are also not recorded. This results in an overstatement of net income.

When liabilities are not recorded, there are often expenses that are not recorded

Our basic problem in accounting for liabilities is to assure ourselves that all the liabilities are recorded. We must search for unpaid invoices, examine credit agreements, and review customers' advance payments and our company payrolls to be sure all liabilities are recorded.

Liabilities are the result of past transactions. They are legal obligations for the future payment of assets or the future performance of services. When we prepare financial statements we classify liabilities as either current or long-term. You may recall from Chapter 3 that we said *current liabilities* are obligations that require the use of current assets for their payment. They are liabilities that will be paid within an operating cycle or a year, whichever is longer. Payment can be made by expending a current asset or by incurring another current liability.

Current liabilities are paid with current assets or by incurring another current liability

Most companies have several operating cycles within a year. Liabilities of these companies maturing within 1 year would be classified as current. But consider such industries as liquor, forest products, and tobacco. Their operating cycles exceed 1 year. Liabilities incurred by these companies for inventories and related items, even though they exceed 1 year, we will classify as current.

Salaries and wages and their related taxes represent major current liabilities that will be discussed in the second half of this chapter, which deals with payroll accounting.

Liabilities that do not meet the criteria for the current liability classification we will classify as *long-term.* Bonds payable, mortgages payable, and long-term notes payable are all examples of long-term liabilities. We will consider the problems of accounting for long-term liabilities in Chapter 15.

What we will be concerned about in the first half of the chapter is a discussion of the accounting problems relating to current liabilities. Notes payable, accounts payable, interest payable, accrued salaries, and unearned revenues are all examples of current liabilities. For purposes of organization we have found it convenient to divide current liabilities into two groups. Group A will consist of those liabilities we know for sure exist on the balance sheet date, and we know exactly how much is owed.

One group of current liabilities is definite as to existence and amount

A second group is indefinite as to existence or amount

Group B current liabilities are a little different. They may or *may not* exist. Not only that, but we may or may not know the amount owed. Group A current liabilities are definite as to existence and amount. Group B current liabilities may be definite as to existence but not amount, or indefinite as to existence and amount.

GROUP A CURRENT LIABILITIES

By far the vast majority of current liabilities fall into Group A. Contractual relationships between the business entity and its lending institutions, vendors, employees, and customers provide evidence of the existence of the current liability and specify the amount of the obligation. Group A current liabilities that we will discuss in this chapter are notes payable, interest payable, and accounts payable. Two other Group A current liabilities, salaries payable and unearned revenue, were discussed in Chapter 3.

Notes Payable

There are a number of reasons why a note payable is issued

A written promise to pay a definite sum of money on demand or at a definite date is called a promissory note. To the maker of the note it is a note payable. To the payee of the note it is a note receivable. An example of an interest-bearing promissory note is illustrated in Chapter 8 on page 310. Notes payable are issued for a variety of reasons. Perhaps someone is unable to pay an account payable when due and wishes an extension of time. Or perhaps we wish to take advantage of a cash discount, paying the invoice early with funds borrowed. A note may be issued for the acquisition of inventory or other assets. The need of cash for payment of other maturing obligations may prompt the incurrence of a note payable. Each of these examples is considered in the following sections.

Extension of Time

Suppose that someone is unable to pay a bill when due. What can be done? Well, one solution is to request the creditor to grant an extension of time to pay the bill. If granted, the creditor will require that, in addition to the amount due, interest be charged on this amount for the length of the extension. This is, of course, a reasonable request, since the use of money has a cost (interest) just as does the use of office space (rent).

Let's consider an example to illustrate the accounting for a note payable issued to extend an account payable. Evergreen Shop has an obligation to Back Bay Supplies on an account payable in the amount of $1,800. The account is due on May 31. Back Bay Supplies agrees to accept a 60-day, 10% note payable in that amount from Evergreen Shop as an extension of the account payable. Evergreen Shop will record the note as follows:

An account payable is paid by incurring another current liability—a note payable

May 31	Accounts Payable: Back Bay Supplies	1,800	
	Notes Payable		1,800
	To record the issuance of a 60-day, 10% note due July 30 as an extension of account due.		

In the event any legal proceedings are necessary to obtain payment from Evergreen Shop, the note payable places Back Bay Supplies in a stronger legal position than does the account payable. The note payable is a formal written promise to pay a certain sum at a definite time. The account payable may have been simply an oral agreement.

On July 30, the due date of the note payable, Evergreen Shop will pay to Back Bay Supplies $1,830. To the $1,800 original amount due is added $30 of interest ($1,800 × 10% × $\frac{60}{360}$).

Unless you are told otherwise, interest rates are always expressed as annual rates. For periods of time less than a year we will use 360 days, as this is the most common practice.

To record the payment to Back Bay Supplies, Evergreen Shop will make the following entry:

A note payable is paid and interest expense recorded

July 30	Notes Payable	1,800	
	Interest Expense	30	
	Cash		1,830
	To record payment of amount due to Back Bay Supplies on note issued May 31.		

Cash Discount

It may surprise you to know that we can save money by borrowing money. If merchandise is sold to us with credit terms including a cash discount for early payment, a wise decision if we are short of cash would be to borrow money to pay the invoice within the discount period rather than letting the discount lapse and paying the bill in full on the due date.

Let's see how this works. Assume that on April 1, company A sells company B goods costing $1,000 under credit terms of 2/10, n/30. Company B is entitled to a $20 discount if the invoice is paid within 10 days; it must pay the invoice within 30 days. But company B does not have $980 on April 10, 10 days from the invoice date, so

Sometimes we can save money by borrowing money

company B borrows that amount from a bank on April 10 at 12% interest for the remaining 20 days until April 30. The $980 obtained from the bank is paid to company A in full settlement of the account on April 10. Twenty days later company B will pay the bank $986.53, which we can determine like this:

$$\$980 \times .12 \times \tfrac{20}{360} = \quad \$6.53 \qquad \text{(Interest for 20 days)}$$

$$\$980 + \quad \$6.53 = \$986.53 \qquad \text{(Principal plus interest)}$$

Company B would record the following entries relating to the payment to company A and the note payable to the bank:

Apr. 1	Purchases	1,000.00	
	Accounts Payable		1,000.00
	To record the purchase of merchandise on account, credit terms 2/10, n/30.		
10	Cash	980.00	
	Notes Payable		980.00
	To record the issuance of a 20-day, 12% note to the bank. Proceeds of the note are to be used for the payment of amount due.		
10	Accounts Payable	1,000.00	
	Purchase Discounts		20.00
	Cash		980.00
	To record payment of amount due to company A.		
30	Notes Payable	980.00	
	Interest Expense	6.53	
	Cash		986.53
	To record payment of amount due to bank plus interest.		

By paying the invoice on time with money borrowed from the bank and repaying the bank when due, company A was able to save $13.47, the difference between the gross purchases and the amount paid to the bank on April 30 ($1,000.00 − $986.53) or the cash discount and the interest expense ($20.00 − $6.53). Company A has saved money by borrowing money.

Borrowed Funds

We can borrow money by issuing a note payable

If a business is short of cash it may borrow money from the bank by issuing a note payable. This is a common practice for many companies during those periods of the year when their cash inflow falls below a certain level. The note is repaid when cash inflow exceeds a level necessary to maintain current operations.

The bank may lend money in one of two manners. First, the bank may prepare a ***promissory note*** for the borrower's signature requiring that the requested funds be repaid at a specified future date together with interest. The note will state:

A note payable plus interest

One hundred eighty days after April 1, 1987, the undersigned promises to pay the sum of $6,000 with interest of 9% per annum.

A note payable which includes interest

The second manner in which a bank may lend money we call ***discounting.*** Under this procedure the bank will deduct the interest on the date the note is issued. Thus, the interest charge is included in the *face amount* of the promissory note. The note will read:

One hundred eighty days after April 1, 1987, the undersigned promises to pay the sum of $6,000.

In the first case the bank will give the borrower $6,000 — called the ***proceeds*** — on the date the note is signed.

But not in the second case. The proceeds will only be $5,730 assuming 9% *discount* rate. The discount of $270 is subtracted from the face of the note in determining the proceeds. Here's how we arrived at the $270 discount:

$$\$6,000 \times .09 \times \tfrac{180}{360} = \$270$$

The first note would be recorded like this:

An interest-bearing note is issued . . .

```
1987
Apr. 1   Cash . . . . . . . . . . . . . . . . . . . . . . . . . . . . . . . . . . . . .   6,000
             Notes Payable . . . . . . . . . . . . . . . . . . . . . . . . . . . . . .          6,000
         To record 180-day promissory note in the amount of $6,000, inter-
         est rate 9%.
```

When payment is made on September 30, we would record the entry as:

. . . and paid

```
1987
Sept. 30   Notes Payable . . . . . . . . . . . . . . . . . . . . . . . . . . . . . .   6,000
           Interest Expense . . . . . . . . . . . . . . . . . . . . . . . . . . . . .    270
               Cash . . . . . . . . . . . . . . . . . . . . . . . . . . . . . . . . . .          6,270
           To record payment of note plus interest ($6,000 × 9% × 180/360).
```

But if the note were discounted, the April 1 entry would be recorded like this:

A discounted note is issued . . .

```
1987
Apr. 1   Cash . . . . . . . . . . . . . . . . . . . . . . . . . . . . . . . . . . . . .   5,730
         Discount on Notes Payable . . . . . . . . . . . . . . . . . . . . . . .    270
             Notes Payable . . . . . . . . . . . . . . . . . . . . . . . . . . . . .          6,000
         To record 180-day promissory note in the amount of $6,000, dis-
         count rate 9%.
```

Upon payment we would make these entries:

. . . and paid

```
1987
Sept. 30   Notes Payable . . . . . . . . . . . . . . . . . . . . . . . . . . . . . . . . .   6,000
                 Cash . . . . . . . . . . . . . . . . . . . . . . . . . . . . . . . . . . .          6,000
           To record payment of note.

      30   Interest Expense  . . . . . . . . . . . . . . . . . . . . . . . . . . . . . .     270
                 Discount on Notes Payable . . . . . . . . . . . . . . . . . . . . .             270
           To record interest expense incurred and to eliminate discount on
           notes payable.
```

Under the discounting procedure the contra-liability account Discount on Notes Payable is established on the date funds are borrowed, April 1. If a balance sheet were prepared at this time the note payable would be presented as follows:

A discounted note payable on the balance sheet

Current Liabilities
Notes Payable. $6,000
Less: Discount on Notes Payable 270 $5,730

This presentation reflects that the liability as of April 1 amounts to only $5,730. The $270 discount on notes payable represents the amount of interest cost that will be incurred over the life of the note. For this reason a second entry is required on the payment date, September 30. The second entry records the interest expense and eliminates the discount on notes payable.

If we were to prepare financial statements monthly, interest expense of $45 per month ($270 ÷ 6 months) would have to be reflected on each income statement. On the balance sheet the contra-liability account Discount on Notes Payable would have to be reduced by $45 each month. This reduction of the contra liability would result in an increase in the net liability by a like amount until September 30 when the liability will have grown to $6,000.

A 9% interest rate is not the same as a 9% discount

In the examples above, money was borrowed first by issuing a $6,000, 9% interest-bearing note and second by discounting at 9% a $6,000 note. You should realize that a 9% interest rate is not equivalent to a 9% discount rate. We can show you this by use of the simple interest formula $I = PRT$. Let's express the formula in terms of the rate, $R = I/PT$. Interest for the discounted note amounted to $270, the amount borrowed was $5,730, and the time was one-half of a year. Thus:

$$R = \frac{\$270}{\$5,730 \times \frac{1}{2}} = 9.42\%$$

The discount rate of 9% on a $6,000, $\frac{1}{2}$-year note is equivalent to a 9.42% interest rate.

Acquisition of Assets

Notes payable are sometimes issued to acquire assets

We often find in business that companies will acquire inventory or other assets by issuing a note payable. The note is generally written for the total amount due at maturity. For example, if merchandise were acquired by issuing a note payable due in 9 months, the note would be written for, say, $21,500, the amount due 9 months hence. But that is not what the merchandise is worth today. Our problem is that we must separate the $21,500 into two components. One component is the fair value of the merchandise on the date the merchandise was acquired — the cost of the merchandise if we paid cash rather than issuing a note. Let's say that this would be $20,000. The second component is the cost of using borrowed money for 9 months, $1,500 in this case. Let's put these facts in an example and see how the transactions will be recorded.

Assume that we entered into this transaction on April 1 of the current year issuing the note rather than paying cash for merchandise we plan to sell our customers. Using a periodic inventory system we would record the purchase on April 1 like this:

Merchandise inventory is acquired and recorded at its fair value	Apr. 1 Purchases	20,000	
	Discount on Notes Payable	1,500	
	Notes Payable		21,500
	To record the purchase of merchandise by the issuance of a 9-month note payable.		

Notice that we did not record interest expense for $1,500. Instead we used the Discount on Notes Payable account—a contra-liability account. Now when we pay the note on the last day of December, 9 months later, we record two entries, the first to pay the note and the second to record the interest expense. Here they are:

A note payable is paid and interest expense is recorded	Dec. 31 Notes Payable.	21,500	
	Cash.		21,500
	To record payment of note payable.		
	Interest Expense	1,500	
	Discount on Notes Payable		1,500
	To adjust discount on note payable to reflect interest incurred.		

We could not record the purchases at $21,500 on April 1 because they were worth only $20,000. And we must show that we have incurred an expense, interest expense, of $1,500 for the privilege of postponing for 9 months the payment of the money borrowed.

Interest Payable

In all of our previous examples concerning notes payable the notes were issued and repaid within the same accounting period. But when notes are issued in one accounting period and repaid in another, an adjusting entry is required at year-end to record the interest expense and the existence of an additional liability, interest payable.

For example, assume that the Boyette Company issues a 90-day, $10,000, 10% interest-bearing note on November 1, 1987, maturing on January 30, 1988. At year-end, December 31, the Boyette Company has had the use of the $10,000 for 60 days. The cost of the use of these funds, the interest expense, must be included on the income statement to be matched against revenues for the year 1987. In addition, a liability exists for the future payment of the interest expense incurred to date. This liability must be reflected among the current liabilities on the balance sheet.

The necessary entries to reflect the accrued interest and payment of the Boyette Company note are presented at the top of page 422, first assuming that a reversing entry is not recorded, then assuming that a reversing entry is recorded.

On January 30, 1988, when the note matures, we must exercise care in recording the payment when a reversing entry is not used. Only 30 days' interest must be reflected in the new year (1988). This amounts to $83.33 [($10,000)(.10)(30/360)]. In addition, the obligation for the interest payable, $166.67, must be eliminated. If a

No Reversing Entry Is Made		A Reversing Entry Is Made	

The Adjusting Entry

1987

Dec. 31 Interest Expense. 166.67

   Interest Payable 166.67

To record accrued interest on $10,000, 90-day, 10% note payable issued Nov. 1 ($10,000)(.10)(60/360).

Interest Expense. 166.67

   Interest Payable 166.67

To record accrued interest on $10,000, 90-day, 10% note payable issued Nov. 1 ($10,000)(.10)(60/360).

The Closing Entry

Dec. 31 Expense and Revenue

   Summary 166.67

      Interest Expense. . . . 166.67

To close the Interest Expense account.

Expense and Revenue

   Summary 166.67

      Interest Expense. . . . 166.67

To close the Interest Expense account.

The Reversing Entry

1988

Jan. 1 No entry

Interest Payable 166.67

   Interest Expense. . . . 166.67

To reverse the interest accrual adjusting entry.

The Payment Entry

Jan. 30 Notes Payable 10,000.00

   Interest Payable 166.67

   Interest Expense. 83.33

      Cash 10,250.00

To record the payment of the maturing note.

Note Payable. 10,000.00

Interest Expense. 250.00

   Cash 10,250.00

To record the payment of the maturing note.

reversing entry had been used, the proper interest expense for 1988 would be reflected in the Interest Expense account:

Interest Expense 1988			
Jan. 30 Payment	250.00	Jan. 1 Reversing entry	166.67
Bal.	83.33		

Accounts Payable

Business firms most often acquire merchandise, supplies, equipment, and services on credit. When this happens there is an oral or implied promise to pay for the goods or services acquired. This promise to pay is an ***account payable.*** While a claim against the acquiring company's asset does exist, the account payable is less formal than a note payable. In the event a business were forced into bankruptcy, the claims of those holding notes payable would receive priority over the holders of accounts payable.

In dealing with accounts payable, a company must establish accounting policies concerning the method of recording purchase discounts, control over a large number of vendor accounts, and control over disbursements. We have discussed each of these items in previous chapters. Cash or purchase discounts were discussed in Chapter 5, control and subsidiary accounts were discussed in Chapter 6, and control over disbursements was discussed in Chapter 7.

GROUP B CURRENT LIABILITIES

Warranties

Some liabilities exist but we don't know how much they are. We have to estimate the amounts

We may find that there are certain liabilities that we know exist at the time financial statements are prepared but unfortunately we do not know the amount of these liabilities. An example of this type of liability is the obligation incurred when goods are sold with warranties. Appliances are typically sold with the guarantee that in the event of a malfunction within a reasonable period of time after acquisition, the seller will repair the appliance at no cost to the buyer.

Our job here is to estimate the amount of the liability and reflect this on the balance sheet. When we estimate the liability we are, of course, also estimating the related expense that will be reflected on the income statement. The expense is incurred in the period the sale of the appliance was made, not in a subsequent period when the repairs are performed. This is the basis of the matching principle.

When the repairs are made, the liability is eliminated. Let's see how this works. Assume Coal Township Appliance Company sold 400 appliances during the year 1987. From past experience they can estimate that 10% of the appliances will prove to be defective. They also estimate that the typical repair will cost $20. During 1987, 15 appliances require service calls at a total cost of $315. In 1988, 27 additional service calls are made at a total cost of $490. Coal Township Appliance Company would make these entries in 1987:

```
1987
Various   Warranty Expense.................................. 315
dates           Cash, Parts, Labor............................        315
          To record expenditures amounting to $315 for repair services on 15
          appliances that were sold in 1987.


1987
Dec. 31   Warranty Expense.................................. 500
                Estimated Liability under Warranty Obligations ..........        500
          To record estimated liability under warranty obligations for repair
          services to be performed on appliances sold in 1987. (400 appliances
          sold)(10%) = 40 appliances estimated to be repaired. 40 − 15 repaired
          1987 = 25 appliances sold in 1987 that are estimated will be repaired
          in 1988 at $20 each = $500.
```

The income statement prepared for the year ended December 31, 1987, would reflect warranty expenses in the amount of $815 matched against appliance sale revenues. Expenditures in 1987 amounted to $315 on 15 actual repairs, which are recorded as 1987 expenses. In addition it is estimated that 25 more repairs must be made, [(400)(10%) − 15], at an estimated cost of $500, (25)($20), and this amount is also expensed in 1987, resulting in a total of $815.

The December 31, 1987, balance sheet would show the estimated liability of $500 representing the estimate of the obligation for future repair services that relate to 1987 sales.

In 1988 the entry to record the expenditure of $490 relating to the 27 actual appliances serviced that were from 1987 sales would be:

```
1988
Various
dates    Estimated Liability under Warranty Obligations . . . . . . . . . . . .  490
                Cash, Parts, Labor . . . . . . . . . . . . . . . . . . . . . . . . . .          490
            To record expenditures amounting to $490 relating to 1987 sales.
```

At this point the balance in the liability account is a $10 credit. If the company had perfect knowledge, the liability would have been established for $490, the estimate made at the end of 1987. But no one possesses perfect knowledge; hence, actual experience will differ from the estimate and a debit or credit balance in the liability account will result. No adjustment of the liability account is required unless a trend develops where it becomes obvious that the estimate is either too high or too low. A revision of the estimating process is then in order.

Premiums

A very similar situation occurs when companies offer premiums to stimulate sales of certain products. You all have seen the cereal companies offer dishes, knives, plates, and other prizes when you send in a certain number of cereal box tops and perhaps some money. This is an advertising tool to increase the sale of the product. The accounting for the advertising expense or promotional expense is just like that for the warranties. The expense of the advertising must be recorded in the year the product was sold, but not all the box tops will be returned in that year. So the accountant must estimate the amount of premium claims that are outstanding at year-end. And this amount is recorded as an estimated liability on the balance sheet.

For example, assume that in 1987 General Food Store offers their customers a coupon for every $10 of grocery purchases. The coupons can be exchanged for a dish of the customer's choice, on a basis of one coupon plus $1 for one dish. Past experience indicates that 80% of the coupons will be redeemed. During 1987 General Food Store purchased 25,000 dishes at an average cost of $1.40 per dish and 22,000 coupons were redeemed. The entries to record the acquisition of the dishes and the redemption of the coupons would appear as follows:

```
1987    Inventory of Dishes (25,000)(1.40) . . . . . . . . . . . . . . . . . . .  35,000
                Accounts Payable . . . . . . . . . . . . . . . . . . . . . . . . . . .        35,000
            To record the acquisition of 25,000 dishes at $1.40 each.

        Advertising Expense . . . . . . . . . . . . . . . . . . . . . . . . . . . .    8,800
        Cash  . . . . . . . . . . . . . . . . . . . . . . . . . . . . . . . . . . . . .   22,000
                Inventory of Dishes (22,000)(1.40) . . . . . . . . . . . . . . . .        30,800
            To record the redemption of 22,000 coupons for dishes.
```

If total sales for the year amounted to $300,000, General Food Store would have to estimate the amount of coupons that remain outstanding at the end of the year. This estimate would be determined by considering that, based on sales of $300,000, there would be 30,000 coupons ($300,000 ÷ $10) issued during the year and that 24,000 would be redeemed (30,000)(.8). Since 22,000 have already been turned in, that would leave 2,000 outstanding, so the December 31, 1987, journal entry would be:

```
1987
Dec. 31   Advertising Expense. . . . . . . . . . . . . . . . . . . . . . . . . . . . 800
              Estimated Liability for Coupons Outstanding . . . . . . . . . . .        800
          To record the estimated liability for coupons outstanding
          ($1.40 − $1.00)(2,000).
```

Contingencies

Certain current liabilities are indefinite as to existence and amount. These are referred to as ***contingent liabilities.*** Some future event must take place (or not take place) that will determine if the liability will require payment and the amount of such a payment. Examples of such liabilities are litigation, expropriation, and accommodation endorsement of indebtedness of others. Litigation refers to lawsuits in progress. Expropriation is the act of a country taking control of businesses operating within its jurisdiction. An accommodation endorsement is the co-signing of a note for someone to provide the creditor with additional security. If the maker of the note fails to pay the note, the cosigner must.

Accounting for contingent liabilities requires a decision to be made regarding the chance or likelihood of the specific future event taking place. This "likelihood" is classified into three categories: *probable, reasonably possible,* and *remote*.

Only in the case of a contingency classified as probable will we record a liability and the corresponding loss. Even if the liability is classified as probable, the amount of the loss must be capable of reasonable estimation before the entry can be recorded.

To illustrate, assume that Phills Phosphate Company operates a branch in Bartow, Florida. A recent lower-level court decision has awarded an employee $100,000 in an injury damage suit. Although the company will appeal the ruling, legal counsel is of the opinion that it is *probable* the company will lose the appeal. The entry to record the contingent liability is:

A contingent liability is recorded

```
Loss Due to Litigation . . . . . . . . . . . . . . . . . . . . . . . . . . . . . . 100,000
      Contingent Liability for Litigation . . . . . . . . . . . . . . . . . . .        100,000
To record loss in period sustained and to establish contingent liability in
the amount of $100,000.
```

If the contingent liability is classified as reasonably possible or if it is probable but the amount cannot be estimated, a footnote to the financial statements is prepared describing the contingency. If the contingent liability is classified as remote, in most cases no accounting is necessary. Remember that only *material* contingent items would be reported on the financial statements or disclosed in the footnotes.

PAYROLL ACCOUNTING

Most of you have worked at one time or other—summer jobs, part-time jobs while attending school, or full-time jobs before starting or returning to school. Some of you were paid weekly—probably those who worked in factories, small retail stores, and some offices. Some of you were paid biweekly—those of you who were clerical workers for larger retail stores and larger businesses, including work-study programs at most universities. A few of you were paid semimonthly—those who were considered middle management by some employers or who were office workers where this mode of payment is common. Even fewer of you were paid monthly, as is the common mode of payment for executives. Some of you have experience with companies where everyone is paid weekly. Others have worked for companies that pay different employee groups weekly, biweekly, semimonthly, and monthly. That's a lot of payroll activity.

No matter where you worked, your paycheck—together with all the other paychecks—constituted a significant cost to your employer. For many companies the cost of labor often exceeds 40 to 50% of the company's total operating costs. When we consider the frequency of payrolls and their size, it's no wonder that payroll accounting is a major activity for most companies.

Many of you are aware that federal, state, and local legislation has increased your employer's burden with regard to payroll. Your employer must pay taxes on his or her total payroll. He or she must withhold taxes from your pay and remit them to the proper taxing authorities. Your employer must maintain payroll records for each of you. And he or she must prepare various periodic reports to be submitted to the appropriate governmental bodies. All of this increases considerably your employer's cost of labor and the related cost of recordkeeping.

Most of you are not particularly concerned with your employer's payroll problems. What you are concerned about is that you receive your correct pay at the time it was promised to you. Your employer recognizes your concern and his or her legal responsibilities. Consequently, most companies will design a payroll system that will generate for you, and all other employees, an accurate, timely paycheck. The payroll system your employer designs must be responsive to other needs as well. It must be able to accumulate payroll information on each employee as required by the various governmental agencies, and to provide the appropriate reports to those agencies together with timely remittances of taxes due. Also, the system must be so designed so that safeguards are provided against payments to nonexistent employees, overpayment of employees, payments to employees who have been terminated, and other fraudulent activities.

The Payroll System

Before we start our discussion of the mechanics of payroll accounting, look at Figure 11-1, pages 428–429, which provides a broad overview of the payroll system. Study the figure carefully but do not become overly concerned if you have questions concerning the detail of the payroll register, the employee individual earnings records, W-4's, and any other new item you may see. All of these will be explained in detail in this chapter. What we want you to have at this point is a general idea of what is involved in paying employees.

You will observe from the figure that many different people are involved. This is a key to achieving strong internal control over payrolls. Of course, a small company where the owner prepares the payroll would have no need for such a system. The owner would know all the employees and who had or had not worked during the pay period. But for larger companies, separation of duties is essential.

Notice that employee attendance is recorded in the various departments by *time cards* or *attendance reports.* If time cards are used, department heads must still prepare an absentee report to compare with the time cards. This prevents an employee from punching in a friend's time card.

When you were first hired by your company, a ***personnel record*** was established for you. Your address, Social Security number, birth date, relatives, work experience, education, and military experience were all recorded on this document. As time went on, additional information was added to your personnel file: positions you held with the company, your salary, termination date, leaves of absence, performance evaluations, accidents, and insurance plans. For large companies the personnel file is

---

Margin notes:

Company payrolls represent a frequent and sizable expenditure

Federal, state, and local legislation has imposed burdens on payroll accounting

Separation of duties is essential for strong internal control over payrolls

A personnel file is established for each employee

maintained by the personnel department. Usually each piece of new information to be added to your personnel file must be authorized by a change-of-status report. Your personnel record will also contain authorization from you directing the company to withhold certain amounts from your paycheck for various deductions such as medical insurance, union dues, and savings bonds.

The time cards, together with information from your personnel records, provide the basis for the accounting department payroll division to update your *employee earnings record.* This record, together with the records of all other employees, is used to prepare the *payroll register,* paychecks, and also the many reports required by governmental bodies.

The totals of the payroll register are used by the accounts payable division to prepare a voucher authorizing the cash disbursements division of the treasurer's department to issue a check for the total payroll. This check transfers cash from the company's general funds to a special payroll cash account.

The voucher also serves as authority for the general ledger division to record the payroll. When the cash disbursements division issues the check, it also records it in the cash disbursements journal, which in turn is recorded by the general ledger division in the general ledger.

The individual paychecks prepared by the payroll division are signed by the treasurer, reviewed, and co-signed by the internal auditor. The checks are then distributed to the various departments to be given to you and the other employees.

The internal auditor must be constantly on guard against errors, both unintentional and intentional. Various payroll schemes have been attempted by unscrupulous employees to defraud the company of money. The following are examples of such schemes:

Payroll frauds

1. Listing fictitious employees

2. Listing former employees

3. Increasing certain employees' pay rates

4. Listing incorrect totals on the payroll register

5. Not deducting employees' absent time

6. Preparing payroll cash account deposit greater than payroll

7. Making duplicate paychecks

The separation of duties described by the payroll flow chart makes it very difficult, *but not impossible,* for employees to commit a payroll fraud. The people in personnel have no authority to prepare payrolls or write checks. Those in accounting cannot increase or decrease payroll deductions on individual employees, nor can they sign the payroll checks. The treasurer can write checks, but only those authorized, and he or she cannot record entries in the general ledger.

With this overview of the payroll system, let's now get into the detail of preparing the payroll and the related payroll accounting problems.

Computing Gross Pay

Salaries are paid to clerical and managerial employees; wages are paid to skilled and unskilled laborers

We begin our discussion of the payroll system with the determination of the salary or wage to be paid to each individual employee. The term *salary* refers to the renumeration given to clerical and managerial employees. Payments to employees for skilled and unskilled labor are typically called *wages.* If you work in an office you receive a salary; if you work in a factory or shop you receive wages. The salary or wages you are

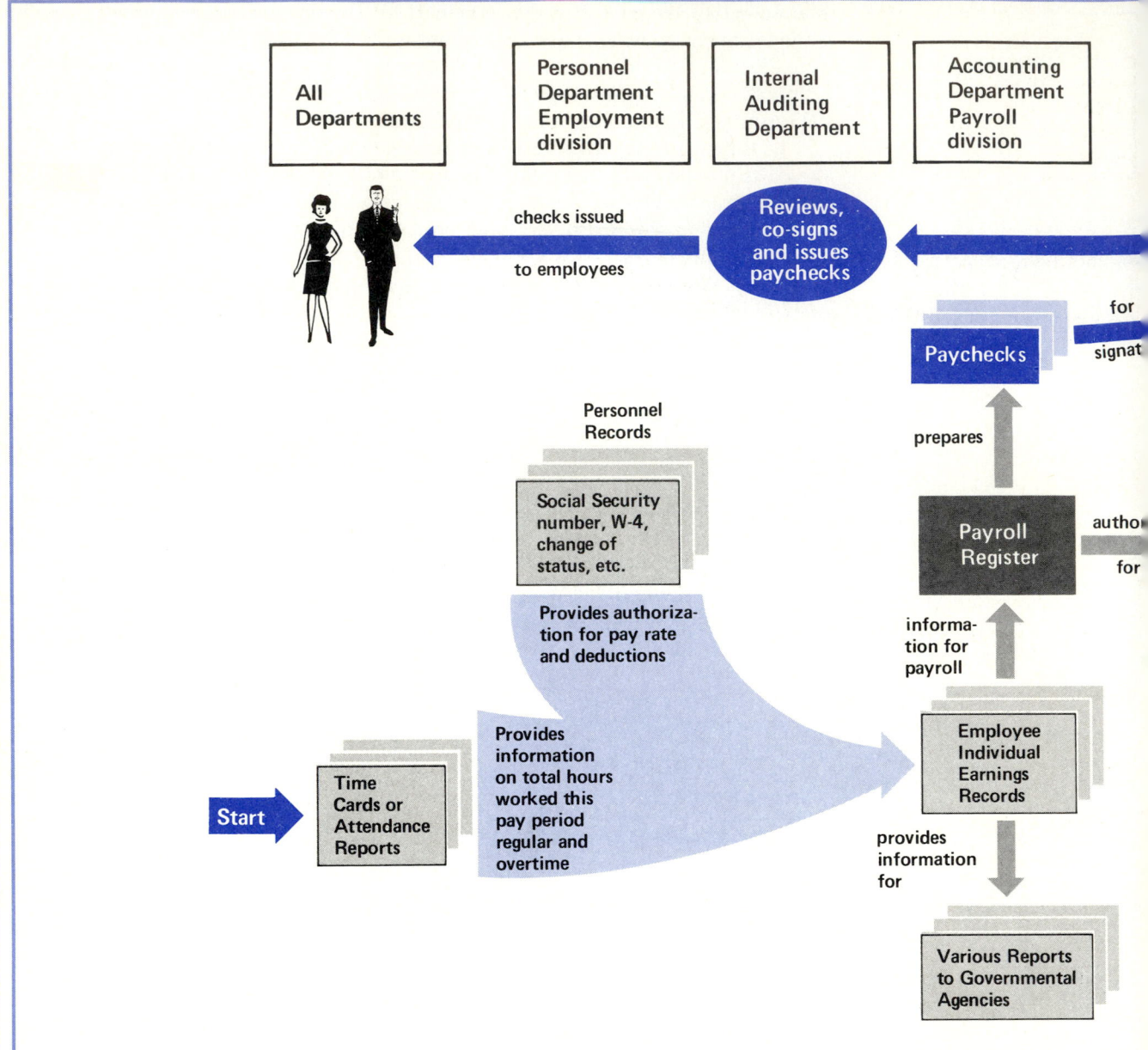

FIGURE 11-1   Payroll Flow Chart
For large companies, paying employees involves many departments and activities.

paid may be determined by mutual agreement between you and your employer subject to, of course, market conditions for the position you are filling. Sometimes union contracts determine your pay.

Before we go any further we must distinguish between those who perform services as employees and those who perform services as independent contractors. An *employee* is one who is subject to the control and direction of the company for which he or she works. An *independent contractor* is not subject to such control and direction. We can illustrate this important difference by contrasting the difference be-

The director of accounting and finance is an employee; a certified public accountant is an independent contractor

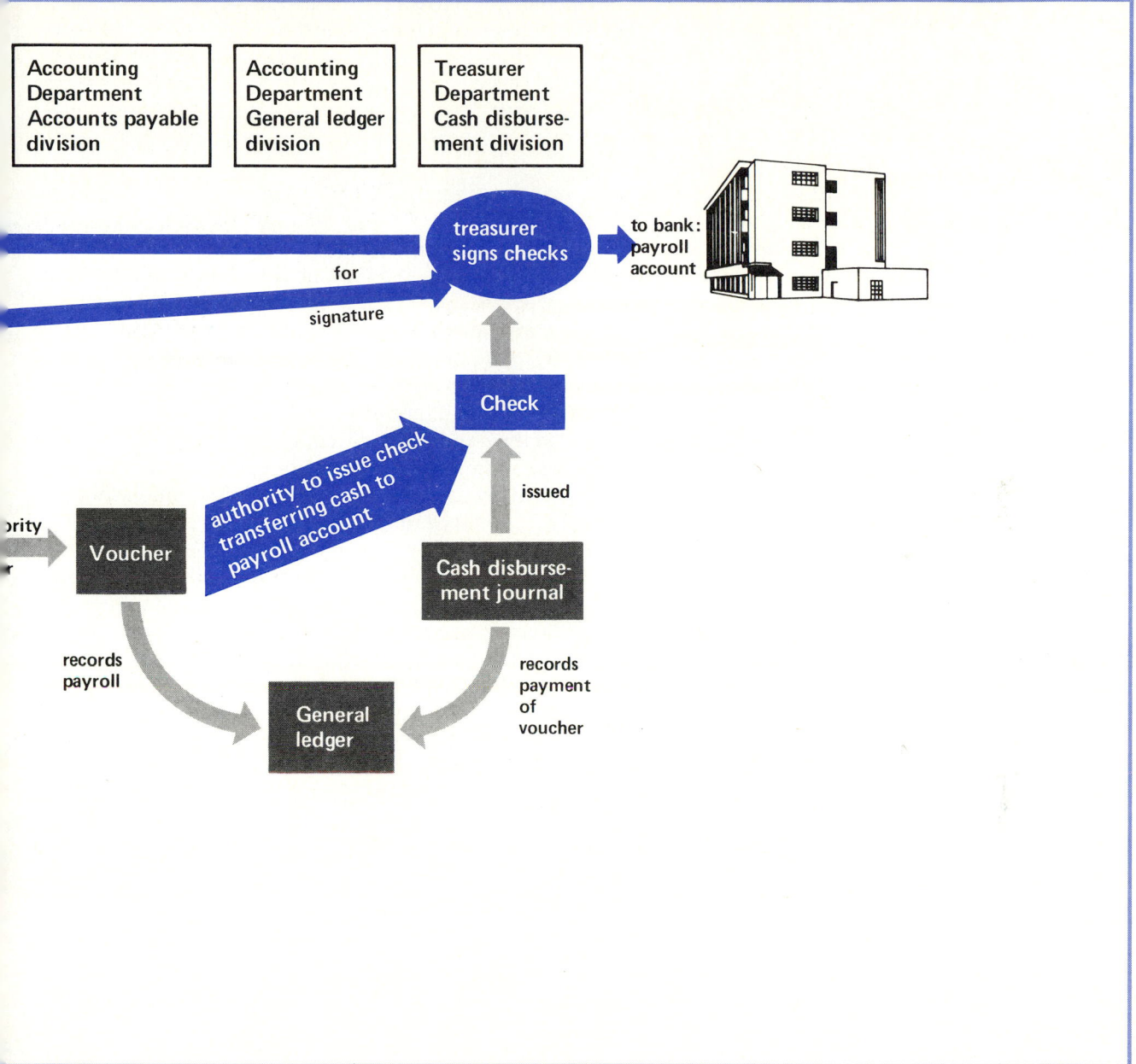

tween the director of accounting and finance of a large company and the company's certified public accountant. The director of accounting and finance may have a considerable degree of freedom in the exercise of his or her authority, but is still an employee responsible to, controlled, and directed by the vice president, president, and board of directors of the company. The CPA performing an audit of the accounting records of the company discharges his or her responsibility in accordance with professional standards in the manner he or she thinks is most appropriate. The CPA is not subject to control and direction from the client company. Similarly, a construction company may employ an individual to frame houses under construction or may engage the services of an independent framing contractor.

Fees paid to independent contractors are not subject to payroll taxes

This distinction between an employee and an independent contractor is important because the wages or salary paid to an employee is subject to the employee withholding tax and the related payroll tax requirements imposed by governmental agencies. The amount paid to an independent contractor, the *fee,* is not subject to these requirements.

Gross pay is the amount an employee earns before any deductions are subtracted

Determination of an employee's earnings for a particular pay period results in an amount that we call *gross pay.* This is the amount that the employee has earned before any required or authorized deductions are subtracted. The amount of gross pay depends on the type of work performed and the amount of hours worked. Most business entities are subject to the provisions of the Federal Fair Labor Standards Act (referred to as the Wages and Hours Law). The law generally requires the employer to pay a minimum of $3.35 (1985) per hour and at least one and one-half times the regular hourly rate for all hours worked in excess of a stated number. For many years this number has been 40 hours. Certain administrative, executive, and supervisory employees are exempt from the time-and-one-half requirement.

In addition to the provisions of the Wages and Hours Law, premium rates are common for employees working at nights or on weekends. Of course union contracts may provide pay scales well in excess of the minimum wage and time and one-half for overtime.

Consider the following examples. Helen Troy is employed by the White Insurance Company at an annual salary of $14,560. Her position is covered by the Wages and Hours Law; consequently all hours worked in excess of 40 hours per week are to be compensated at the rate of one and one-half times the regular hourly rate. The number of hours in a year is considered to be 2,080 (40 hours per week × 52 weeks per year). Ms. Troy has worked 86 hours during the current biweekly pay period. Her regular biweekly pay is $560 ($14,560 ÷ 26 biweekly periods). She will be paid that amount even if she works less than 80 hours, since she is a salaried employee and the White Insurance Company has provided her with this benefit. On an hourly basis Ms. Troy is paid at a rate of $7.00 per hour ($14,560 ÷ 2,080 hours). Overtime is then paid at a rate of $10.50 per hour ($7.00 × $1\frac{1}{2}$). Ms. Troy's gross earnings are computed as follows:

Base biweekly salary	$560.00
Overtime earnings (6 hr × $10.50)	63.00
Total earnings	$623.00

The determination of the amount of hours worked during the week is a function of the payroll system. Each company will establish its own method for compiling such information. In the case of a small office, the system may require the office manager to note the hours worked in a simple log book. Many of you have worked in a large office or factory and have seen a more formalized timekeeping system whereby the direct supervisor prepares a weekly report on a specified form accounting for each hour of each employee's work time. Most common in many large companies is the time clock. A time clock is placed at the entrance to a work area together with a rack for holding individual employee time cards. A new card is provided each employee at the beginning of each pay period. When the employees arrive at work they remove their card from the rack and insert it in the time clock to record the time of arrival, and then replace the card in the rack. The process is repeated upon the completion of the workday to record the time of departure. At the end of the pay period the time card provides a record of the hours each individual worked and serves as a basis for computing gross pay.

In certain high-security areas within some companies time clocks serve as a security device for controlling admittance. The time clock is combined with a computer that will open the door to the work area when the time card is inserted. The time card will appear like a plastic credit card and is carried at all times by the employee. When the card is inserted not only will the door open but the time of arrival is recorded on the computer.

When time clocks are combined with computers, the process of recording the payroll, accumulating the necessary payroll information for governmental agencies, and computing the amount of net pay to be disbursed to each employee is all done by the computer.

Computers are now combined with time clocks to provide security and generate payroll information

Deductions from Gross Pay

Some deductions from gross pay are required by law and some may be voluntary

What you *take home* is usually a far cry from your gross pay. That is because several deductions are subtracted from your gross pay in arriving at your *net pay.* For the most part these deductions are required by law or union contracts. You may also authorize deductions for such items as medical and health insurance, life insurance, U.S. savings bonds, and stock purchase plans. Deductions required by law are federal income taxes, Social Security taxes, state and city income taxes where applicable, and state unemployment compensation tax on employees, where applicable.

Federal Income Taxes

The federal government requires your company and all other employers to act as a tax-collecting agent for the receipt of your and all other employees' income taxes. Employers are required to compute the amount of income taxes to be withheld from each employee and to collect and deposit that amount to the account of the federal government. This is a pay-as-you-go system and assures the government that the majority of taxes due will be collected in a timely manner.

The amount that is deducted from your gross earnings for federal income taxes is dependent on the amount of your gross earnings for the pay period and the number of allowances you claimed. Every new employee is required to prepare an Employee's Withholding Allowance Certificate (Form W-4, illustrated in Exhibit 11-1, page 432), which provides the employer with the authorization to compute the amount of taxes to be withheld.

All employees are required to complete a W-4 when they are first employed by a company

An allowance of $1,000 for each dependent is deducted from the employee's estimated annual earnings in determining the amount of federal income taxes to be withheld for the pay period. One exemption is allowed for each dependent of the employee, including the employee. Further, if the employee or the employee's spouse is over 65 or blind, additional allowances are allowed.

The amount of taxes withheld from your salary is calculated such that given your pay rate and allowances, the total withheld during the year will be approximately equal to your tax liability at the end of the year. The system of income tax used in the United States is a graduated tax system. The more you earn under a graduated tax system the greater the tax rate used in determining the amount of taxes that must be paid. Thus, those earning larger salaries and wages can expect proportionately larger amounts to be withheld.

Federal income taxes withheld from your paycheck each payday should approximate your tax liability at year-end

The determination of the amount of federal income taxes to be withheld from your gross earnings is generally accomplished with the aid of a *wage bracket withholding table,* found in the federal government tax publication entitled *Circular E,* as shown

A wage bracket withholding table is used to determine the amount of taxes to be withheld from your paycheck

Form **W-4** (Rev. January 1985)	Department of the Treasury—Internal Revenue Service **Employee's Withholding Allowance Certificate**	OMB No. 1545-0010 Expires: 11-30-87

1 Type or print your full name
HELEN PARIS TROY

2 Your social security number
195-36-2805

Home address (number and street or rural route)
151 Main Street

City or town, State, and ZIP code
Bethlehem, Florida 33511

3 Marital Status
☐ Single   ☒ Married
☐ Married, but withhold at higher Single rate
Note: If married, but legally separated, or spouse is a nonresident alien, check the Single box.

4 Total number of allowances you are claiming (from line F of the worksheet on page 2) **3**

5 Additional amount, if any, you want deducted from each pay . . . . $

6 I claim exemption from withholding because (see instructions and check boxes below that apply):
  a ☐ Last year I did not owe any Federal income tax and had a right to a full refund of **ALL** income tax withheld, **AND**
  b ☐ This year I do not expect to owe any Federal income tax and expect to have a right to a full refund of **ALL** income tax withheld. If both a and b apply, enter the year effective and "EXEMPT" here . . . ▶   Year
  c If you entered "EXEMPT" on line 6b, are you a full-time student? . . . . ☐ Yes ☐ No

Under penalties of perjury, I certify that I am entitled to the number of withholding allowances claimed on this certificate, or if claiming exemption from withholding, that I am entitled to claim the exempt status.
Employee's signature ▶ *Helen Paris Troy*   Date ▶ **March 4** , 19 **87**

7 Employer's name and address **(Employer: Complete 7, 8, and 9 only if sending to IRS)**
White Insurance Company
625 Fourth Street
Bethlehem, Fl

8 Office code

9 Employer identification number
17 121648

EXHIBIT 11-1   Employee's Withholding Allowance Certificate.

in Exhibit 11-2 (page 433). These tables are prepared for weekly, biweekly, semimonthly, and monthly pay periods and for single, married, and head-of-household taxpayers. The table in Exhibit 11-2 is for married persons paid biweekly.

Let's see how this wage bracket withholding table works. Assume that Helen Troy of the White Insurance Company earned $623 for the current biweekly pay period. Ms. Troy has claimed three withholding allowances. To find the amount of income taxes to be withheld, simply locate the wage bracket line on the table that brackets $623, which is the $620–$640 bracket. Next locate the column for three withholding allowances. Where the $620–$640 line intersects the three withholding allowances column is found $57.90, which is the amount of income taxes to be withheld.

Federal Insurance Contributions Act (FICA)

FICA taxes provide for retirement and Medicare benefits

The funds necessary to provide monthly retirement payments and Medicare benefits for qualified retired workers are obtained by payroll deductions authorized by the Federal Insurance Contributions Act. The retirement and medical benefits are provided for qualified workers under the provisions of the Social Security Act. Retirement benefits are based on the age at retirement and the average earnings of the retiree. You can retire at age 62 but you will not receive full retirement benefits. Full retirement benefits are provided only for those who retire at age 65. In addition to retirement and Medicare benefits, the Social Security Act provides death and disability benefits.

The required funds to operate the Social Security programs are collected by employers through the means of withholding contributions by each employee from the employee's gross earnings. In 1985 FICA taxes are contributed at a rate of 7% on the first $37,800 of earned wages. In addition to the employee's contribution, the employer must contribute a like amount, as we will explain later.

Since the limit and percent increases frequently, a rate of 7% on $40,000 will be used in all problems in this text. Consequently, Ms. Helen Troy's amount of FICA taxes to be withheld from her $623 for the current pay period would be $43.61 ($623 × .07), assuming that she has not exceeded the $40,000 limit.

Currently a great deal of controversy exists concerning the financing of our Social Security system. With an increasing proportion of the total population reaching retirement age, a question exists as to the ability of the FICA contributions to finance the Social Security benefits promised. Considerable support is being generated for using general tax revenue to finance the Social Security programs, as is done in many other countries. The alternative is to reduce the amount of benefits provided.

Additional Payroll Deductions

All states have unemployment insurance programs in which the federal government participates. Most states finance this program by taxes imposed only on the employer. In a few states the tax is imposed on employees as well. These states require employers to withhold such taxes from employees' earnings.

In addition to federal income taxes, FICA taxes, and in some states state unemployment compensation taxes, many states require employers to withhold state income taxes, and in some cities a city wage tax withholding is also required. Also deducted from employees' gross earnings may be union dues (which may or may not be voluntary), health and life insurance premiums, amounts authorized by the em-

EXHIBIT 11-2   Withholding Table.

And the Wages Are —		And the Number of Withholding Allowances Claimed Is —										
At Least	But Less Than	0	1	2	3	4	5	6	7	8	9	10 or More
		The Amount of Income Tax to Be Withheld Shall Be —										
$ 600	$ 620	$ 74.20	$ 67.60	$ 61.10	$ 54.50	$ 48.00	$ 41.50	$ 34.90	$ 29.80	$ 25.20	$ 20.60	$ 16.00
620	640	77.60	71.00	64.50	57.90	51.40	44.90	38.30	32.20	27.60	23.00	18.40
640	660	81.00	74.40	67.90	61.30	54.80	48.30	41.70	35.20	30.00	25.40	20.80
660	680	84.40	77.80	71.30	64.70	58.20	51.70	45.10	38.60	32.40	27.80	23.20
680	700	87.80	81.20	74.70	68.10	61.60	55.10	48.50	42.00	35.50	30.20	25.60
$ 700	$ 720	$ 91.20	$ 84.60	$ 78.10	$ 71.50	$ 65.00	$ 58.50	$ 51.90	$ 45.40	$ 38.90	$ 32.60	$ 28.00
720	740	94.60	88.00	81.50	74.90	68.40	61.90	55.30	48.80	42.30	35.70	30.40
740	760	98.60	91.40	84.90	78.30	71.80	65.30	58.70	52.20	45.70	39.10	32.80
760	780	103.00	94.80	88.30	81.70	75.20	68.70	62.10	55.60	49.10	42.50	36.00
780	800	107.40	98.90	91.70	85.10	78.60	72.10	65.50	59.00	52.50	45.90	39.40
$ 800	$ 820	$111.80	$103.30	$ 95.10	$ 88.50	$ 82.00	$ 75.50	$ 68.90	$ 62.40	$ 55.90	$ 49.30	$ 42.80
820	840	116.20	107.70	99.30	91.90	85.40	78.90	72.30	65.80	59.30	52.70	46.20
840	860	120.60	112.10	103.70	95.30	88.80	82.30	75.70	69.20	62.70	56.10	49.60
860	880	125.00	116.50	108.10	99.60	92.20	85.70	79.10	72.60	66.10	59.50	53.00
880	900	129.40	120.90	112.50	104.00	95.60	89.10	82.50	76.00	69.50	62.90	56.40
$1,600	$1,620	$338.50	$325.80	$313.10	$300.50	$287.80	$275.10	$262.40	$249.70	$237.60	$226.90	$216.10
1,620	1,640	345.10	332.40	319.70	307.10	294.40	281.70	269.00	256.30	243.60	232.50	221.70
1,640	1,660	351.70	339.00	326.30	313.70	301.00	288.30	275.60	262.90	250.20	238.10	227.30
1,660	1,680	358.30	345.60	332.90	320.30	307.60	294.90	282.20	269.50	256.80	244.10	232.90
1,680	1,700	364.90	352.20	339.50	326.90	314.20	301.50	288.80	276.10	263.40	250.70	238.50

Biweekly Payroll Period — Employee Married — In Effect January 1, 1984

ployee for savings bonds, stock purchase plans, and repayments of loans from the employer.

Assuming that Ms. Helen Troy has authorized a deduction of $23.15 for hospitalization insurance, the amount of net pay she would receive for the current biweekly pay period would be determined as follows:

Gross earnings		$623.00
Deductions:		
Federal income taxes withheld	$57.90	
FICA tax withheld	43.61	
Hospitalization insurance premium	23.15	
Total deductions		124.66
Net earnings.		$498.34

Payment of Taxes Withheld

The Federal Income Tax Laws and the Federal Insurance Contribution Act require that employers maintain adequate records. These records must be kept for 4 years, and provide information on each employee, showing the amount of federal income taxes withheld and the amount of wages subject to FICA taxes.

The amounts withheld from employees' gross earnings, together with the employer's portion of the FICA taxes, must be remitted to the Internal Revenue Service as prescribed by law. If the combined withheld taxes and employer-employee Social Security taxes are $3,000 or more for an *eighth-monthy period* (that means one-eighth of a month), a deposit is required within 3 banking days after the end of the period. An eighth-monthly period is a period that ends on the 3d, 7th, 11th, 15th, 19th, 22d, 25th, or last day of the month. The combined withheld taxes and employer-employee Social Security taxes are deposited in a bank authorized by the U.S. Treasury Department to accept these deposits. Upon receipt of the deposit the bank mails a punched card indicating the amount deposited to the Internal Revenue Service. If the combined taxes are less than $500 at the end of the calendar quarter, payment is due at the end of the next month. If the combined taxes are more than $500 but less than $3,000 at the end of any month, they must be deposited within 15 days after the end of the month.

An Employer's Quarterly Federal Tax Return (Form 941) and any payments due are required to be filed by the last day of the month after the end of each calendar quarter. The form shows the total income tax withheld, the amount of wages subject to FICA taxes, the amount of FICA taxes paid (both employee and employer portions), the deposits made during previous periods of the quarter, and the amount due with the return.

Employer Payroll Taxes

What we have said so far about payrolls has been limited to the amounts that have been withheld from you. Your employer is also subject to payroll taxes. These taxes are based on the amount of gross earnings up to prescribed limits earned by the employer's employees. Just as real estate taxes or occupational licenses are an operating expense of doing business, so are payroll taxes. They are recorded as debits to expense accounts just as any other expense would be.

FICA Taxes

FICA taxes are imposed on employers as well as employees

The amount that you contribute to the Social Security program is matched by your employer. The FICA tax expense and corresponding liability for your employer is determined by multiplying the total amount of wages subject to FICA tax by the appropriate tax rate. As with the employee portion, we will use a rate of 7% on the first $40,000 to estimate the actual rate.

Federal and State Unemployment Compensation Tax

Payrolls are subject to federal and state unemployment compensation taxes

Unemployment compensation taxes may be reduced by state merit-rating plans

Unemployment funds are provided by the Social Security System under a joint federal-state program. These funds are administered by the state governments and are used for the relief of those qualified persons who are temporarily unemployed. The Federal Unemployment Compensation Tax (FUC tax) and the State Unemployment Compensation Tax (SUC tax) are levied on the employers and are not deducted from the employee's gross earnings. (Some states do require an employee contribution to be withheld from the employee by the employer.) The FUC tax is 3.5% on the first $7,000 of wages paid to each employee. The employer may reduce his or her FUC tax, however, by contributions to the SUC tax up to 2.7%. Thus, a total tax of 3.5% is levied with .8% going to the federal government for approving the state programs and for paying a portion of the state's administrative expenses. The state's portion, 2.7%, is used to pay unemployment compensation.

In order to encourage employers to maintain a stable work force and thus reduce unemployment, a merit-rating plan is used by many states. For those employers within the state who have maintained a stable work force, that is, whose employees have applied for relatively little or no unemployment compensation, the SUC tax rate is reduced from the 2.7% to a rate as little as .8% in some states.

Here is how we could calculate payroll taxes. Assume that the White Insurance Company has a total biweekly payroll for the current period of $36,750. Of this amount $21,380 are subject to FICA taxes at the 7.0% rate and $14,620 are subject to unemployment compensation taxes of .7% FUC and 1.6% SUC. Remember, once an employee has earned more than $40,000, his or her wages are no longer subject to FICA taxes. And once the $7,000 limit is passed, wages are not subject to the FUC or SUC taxes. That's why the full payroll of $36,750 is not used to determine these taxes. The total amount of payroll taxes expense is computed like this:

FICA taxes ($21,380 × .07)	$1,496.60
FUC taxes ($14,620 × .007)	102.34
SUC taxes ($14,620 × .016)	233.92
Total payroll taxes	$1,832.86

We have already discussed the payment of the employer's portion of the FICA taxes. Payment of the FUC tax must be made quarterly if the unpaid taxes exceed $100 for the quarter. An annual return—Employer's Annual Federal Unemployment Tax Return (Form 940)—is required to be filed by January 31 of the following year. The states generally require a quarterly tax report and payment within 1 month after the end of the calendar quarter.

The White Insurance Company would record the payroll taxes in the general journal as follows:

```
Payroll Taxes Expense . . . . . . . . . . . . . . . . . . . . . . . . . . . . . .   1,832.86
    FICA Taxes Payable. . . . . . . . . . . . . . . . . . . . . . . . . .              1,496.60
    FUC Taxes Payable . . . . . . . . . . . . . . . . . . . . . . . . . .               102.34
    SUC Taxes Payable . . . . . . . . . . . . . . . . . . . . . . . . . .               233.92
To record payroll taxes.
```

White Insurance Company would make a similar entry every pay period.

The Payroll Register

Your employer, like most others, will summarize the hours you and your coworkers worked — as evidenced by your time cards — in a payroll register. This multi-column form is used to assemble the necessary data for preparing the payroll for the period and for recording the employer's payroll taxes. The design of the payroll register will suit the needs of the particular company using the register. The biweekly payroll register of the White Insurance Company is shown in Exhibit 11-3. This type of register is satisfactory for a pen-and-ink system or one that uses a bookkeeping machine.

Most of the data that appears on the White Insurance Company Payroll Register are self-evident. The total hours worked during the biweekly period, and the regular, overtime, and total earnings are inserted in the appropriate columns. The two columns under the heading taxable earnings provide information for determining the payroll taxes. Data for these columns are obtained from the *employee's earnings record,* discussed in the next section.

Deductions from total earnings are recorded in their appropriate columns. The total deductions and net pay are determined next. Upon payment the check number is recorded in the payroll register. The last two columns are used to distribute the salaries to the proper expense account. In the case of the White Insurance Company these accounts are the Underwriting Department Salary Expense and the Claims Department Salary Expense. Typical distributions are to Sales Salary Expense, Office Salary Expense, and Shop Salary Expense.

Checking the payroll register

Once the register is complete, it is verified for arithmetic accuracy before the checks are issued and the payroll is entered in the books of account. The cross-verification process can be summarized by the tabulation at the top of the facing page:

EXHIBIT 11-3 White Insurance Company Biweekly Payroll Period Ending June 23, 1987.
Payroll registers are designed to meet the needs of each individual company.

Employee	Total Hours	Earnings			Taxable Earnings	
		Regular	Overtime	Total	FICA	Unemployment Compensation
Abbott, Henry	80	$ 1,500.00		$ 1,500.00		
Adams, Mary	80	650.00		650.00	$ 650.00	
Bussman, John	87	480.00	$ 63.00	543.00	543.00	$ 543.00
Fox, Fanny	80	975.00		975.00	975.00	
Troy, Helen	86	560.00	63.00	623.00	623.00	623.00
Zako, Ruth	80	1,200.00		1,200.00	1,200.00	
		$34,300.00	$2,450.00	$36,750.00	$21,380.00	$14,620.00

Earnings:
Regular $34,300.00
Overtime 2,450.00

Total $36,750.00

Deductions:
FIT . . . . $ 7,923.30
FICA 1,496.60
Union dues 785.00
Health ins. 573.75
U.S. savings bonds 225.00
Total $11,003.65
Net pay 25,746.35

Total $36,750.00

Distribution:
Underwriting Dept.
Salary Expense $21,370.00
Claims Dept.
Salary Expense 15,380.00

Total $36,750.00

Once the payroll register is completed and checked, the payroll general journal entries can be made. Here are White Insurance Company's two payroll entries:

Payroll general journal entries

1987
June 23   Underwriting Department Salary Expense 21,370.00
Claims Department Salary Expense 15,380.00
Federal Income Tax Payable:
Employees 7,923.30
FICA Tax Payable 1,496.60
Union Dues Payable 785.00
Health Insurance Premiums Payable 573.75
U.S. Savings Bonds Deductions Payable 225.00
Salaries Payable 25,746.35
To record biweekly payroll from the payroll register.

	Deductions					Payment		Distribution	
FIT	FICA	Union Dues	Health Ins.	U.S. Savings Bonds	Total	Net Pay	Check No.	Underwriting Dept. Salaries	Claims Dept. Salaries
$ 343.20			$ 28.50	$ 25.00	$ 396.70	$ 1,103.30	2607	$ 1,500.00	
86.30	$ 45.50	$ 15.00	14.25		161.05	488.95	2608		$ 650.00
73.40	38.01	10.00	23.15		144.56	398.44	2609		543.00
193.20	68.25		28.50	25.00	314.95	660.05	2610	975.00	
57.90	43.61		23.15		124.66	498.34	2693	623.00	
208.50	84.00		28.50		321.00	879.00	2694		1,200.00
$7,923.30	$1,496.60	$785.00	$573.75	$225.00	$11,003.65	$25,746.35		$21,370.00	$15,380.00

June 23	Payroll Taxes Expense 1,832.86	
	FICA Taxes Payable	1,496.60
	FUC Taxes Payable	102.34
	SUC Taxes Payable	233.92
	To record payroll taxes.	

The payroll taxes were previously computed when we discussed employer payroll taxes in the last section.

The Payroll Bank Account

Typically, payroll checks are written against a special payroll bank account. When the payroll register is complete and the general journal entries relating to the payroll are recorded, a check drawn against the regular bank account in the amount of the total net pay ($25,746.35 in the example) is deposited in the payroll account. Now individual payroll checks are prepared and issued to the employees. When all the employees cash their checks, the payroll account will be reduced to a zero balance.

Payroll bank accounts are used to help control payrolls and to simplify the preparation of the bank reconciliation

This process simplifies the reconciliation of the regular bank account and serves as a control over payrolls. Since only one check is written for the entire payroll, the problem of payroll checks outstanding is eliminated when reconciling the regular

EXHIBIT 11-4   Employee's Earnings Record.

Name ___Troy, Helen___   Telephone ___689-3571___   Social Security number ___195-36-2805___

Address ___151 Main Street___   Date Employed ___March 4, 1987___   Date of Birth ___Oct. 4, 1942___

___Bethlehem, Florida 33511___

Date Terminated _____   Reason _____

Married   (xx)   Pay Rate   ___$14,560___

Single   ( )   Equivalent Hourly Rate ___$7.00___

Head of Household ( )   Number of Exemptions (3)

Department ___Underwriting___

	Earnings					Deductions							
Period Ending	Total Hours	Regular	Over-time	Total	Cumulative	FIT	FICA	Union Dues	Health Insurance	U.S. Savings Bonds	Total	Net Pay	Check No.
Mar. 18	80	$ 560		$ 560	$ 560	$ 61.40	$ 34.33		$ 23.15		$118.88	$ 441.12	651
1st quarter		560		560	560	61.40	34.33		23.15		118.88	441.12	
Apr. 1	80	560		560	1,120	61.40	34.33		23.15		118.88	441.12	816
Apr. 15	88	560	84	644	1,764	78.20	39.48		23.15		140.83	503.17	1128
June 23	86	560	63	623	4,067	57.90	43.61		23.15		124.66	498.34	2693
2d quarter		3,360	147	3,507	4,067	397.70	215.09		138.90		751.69	2,755.31	
3d quarter													
4th quarter													
Yearly total													

1 Control number	22222	OMB No. 1545-0008		
2 Employer's name, address, and ZIP code White Insurance Company 625 Fourth Street Bethlehem, Florida 33511		**3** Employer's identification number 17 121648		**4** Employer's State number 463-571

| | | **5** Stat. employee ☐   Deceased ☐   Legal rep. ☐   942 emp. ☐   Subtotal ☐   Void ☐ | | |

| | | **6** Allocated tips | **7** Advance EIC payment | |

8 Employee's social security number 195-36-2805	**9** Federal income tax withheld $2,056.17	**10** Wages, tips, other compensation $11,517.56	**11** Social security tax withheld $806.23
12 Employee's name, address, and ZIP code Helen Paris Troy 151 Main Street Bethlehem, Florida 33511		**13** Social security wages $11,517.56	**14** Social security tips
		16	
		17 State income tax	**18** State wages, tips, etc.	**19** Name of State
		20 Local income tax	**21** Local wages, tips, etc.	**22** Name of locality

Form **W-2 Wage and Tax Statement**   **1984**   Copy B To be filed with employee's Federal tax return   Department of the Treasury
This information is being furnished to the Internal Revenue Service.   Internal Revenue Service

EXHIBIT 11-5   Wage and Tax Statement.

cash account. When reconciling the payroll account only payroll checks are involved, simplifying this process.

When the payroll checks are written, it is most common to provide the details of the net pay computation to the individual employees. This may be in the form of a detachable portion of the check, or it may be a separate form given to the employee when the check is issued. Both the current period's and the year-to-date earnings and deductions are generally provided.

The Employee's Earnings Record

The cumulative amount of your and all other employee's earnings and other payroll data is recorded on a form referred to as the *employee's earnings record.* This form provides information as to when you have reached the earnings limit of $7,000 for imposing the employer unemployment taxes and when you have reached the FICA tax limit. Thus, the employee's earnings record provides the basis for recording the amount of taxable FICA and unemployment compensation earnings in the payroll register. It provides the basis for preparing the federal and state payroll tax returns. Helen Troy's employee's earnings record is shown in Exhibit 11-4.

Information from the employee's earnings record provides the basis for recording entries in the payroll register

The employee's earnings record provides the basis for the entries made in the payroll register. The information in the employee's earnings record is cumulated by quarter and totaled at year-end. The year-end totals provide the necessary data for the Form W-2 Wage and Tax Statement (see Exhibit 11-5 above) employers are required to give to each employee by January 31 of the year following the tax year. Additional copies of the W-2 are sent to the Internal Revenue Service and the Social Security Administration. Entries 9 and 10 of Form W-2 provide the IRS with the amount of income taxes withheld and the total wages paid to the employee. Entries 11 and 13 provide the Social Security Administration with the amount of FICA employee taxes withheld and the total wages that were subject to FICA taxes. This information is credited to the individual's account with the Social Security Administration.

CHAPTER SUMMARY

We have divided *current liabilities* into two groups. The first, which we call group A, are those which we know for sure exist at the balance sheet date. And we know the exact amount of each of these liabilities. In the second group — group B — we include those liabilities that may or may not exist and we may or may not know how much they are.

Notes payable, interest payable, accounts payable, salaries payable, and *unearned revenues* are examples of accounts we would include in the first group of current liabilities.

Accounting for notes payable reveals two methods of obtaining funds from the bank. We can borrow funds by either discounting a note or by issuing a note at its face value. When discounting, the interest is deducted from the proceeds of the note. If a note is issued at face value, the interest is paid at the maturity date of the note.

Estimated liabilities such as product warranties and corporate income taxes payable and *contingent liabilities* such as litigation are examples of what we would classify as group B liabilities. These liabilities and their related expenses must be estimated and recorded. We classify contingent liabilities as to probable, reasonable possible, or remote in order to determine the appropriate accounting treatment.

Accounting for the cost of labor begins with the establishment of a *payroll system* designed to process the basic payroll information, generate employee paychecks in a timely manner, generate appropriate reports and remittances as required by various governmental agencies, and safeguard the entity against improper payments. The computation of each individual's gross earnings commences the process that culminates with the issuance of a paycheck to the employee. In computing *gross earnings,* consideration is given to the employee's rate of pay, regular hours worked, and overtime hours worked.

Deductions are subtracted from an employee's gross pay in arriving at his or her net take-home pay. The deductions are of two types: those required by law or contract and those that are voluntary. *Deductions required by law* are federal income taxes withheld, Federal Insurance Contributions Act withholdings, state and city income taxes where appropriate, and union dues where appropriae. *Voluntary deductions* are those the employee authorizes the employer to withhold from his or her gross earnings, such as health insurance premiums and U.S. savings bonds payments. In addition to the requirements to withhold income tax and FICA taxes from employees, employers are required to pay certain taxes based on employee earnings. Employers must pay FICA, Federal Unemployment Compensation, and state Unemployment Compensation taxes.

Payroll registers provide an important vehicle for summarizing individual payroll information needed for the preparation of general journal entries required to record the payroll in the accounts. *Employee earnings records* provide basic data for determining appropriate payroll deductions and recording the individual employee's gross earnings, deductions, and net earnings in the payroll register.

IMPORTANT TERMS USED IN THIS CHAPTER

Contingent liability   A liability that is indefinite as to existence or amount. (page 425)

Current liabilities   Liabilities that will be liquidated by the expenditure of current assets or the incurrence of another current liability within 1 year or one operating cycle, whichever is longer. (page 416)

Discount on notes payable   A contra-liability account reflecting the amount of unincurred interest expense remaining until the maturity of a discounted note payable. (page 420)

Discount rate   The rate used to calculate the amount of interest that must be deducted from the face of a note to determine the proceeds of a discounted note. (page 419)

Discounting   Borrowing money from a bank where the bank deducts the interest from the amount borrowed before the money is advanced to the borrower. (page 419)

Employee   An individual who is subject to the control and direction of the business entity for which he or she works. (page 428)

Employee's earnings record   A form maintained by an employer for each employee providing a record of the employee's cumulative earnings, deductions, net pay, and other payroll data. (page 439)

Employee's Withholding Allowance Certificate   A form used by the employer to determine the amount of federal income tax to withhold from an employee. The employee prepares the form stating his or her marital status and the number of withholding allowances claimed. (page 432)

Employer's Quarterly Federal Tax Return   A form required by the last day of the month after the end of each calendar quarter showing the total income tax withheld from employees, the amount of wages subject to FICA taxes, the amount of FICA taxes paid (both employee and employer portions), the deposits made during previous periods of the quarter, and the amount due with the tax return. (page 434)

Estimated liability   A liability that is known to exist but the amount is not known. (page 423)

FICA taxes   Taxes imposed by the Federal Insurance Contributions Act to finance the Social Security Program. Equal FICA tax amounts are paid by the employer and the employee. (page 432)

Gross earnings   The total amount of an employee's pay before deductions. (page 430)

Independent contractor   An individual who performs services for an economic entity. This person is not subject to the economic entity's control and direction. (page 428)

Net pay   The amount of pay left after deducting such items as FICA taxes, federal income taxes, and union dues. (page 431)

Payroll register   A record maintained by an employer showing the amount of gross pay, deductions, and net pay for each employee and the total for all employees. (page 436)

Payroll taxes   Taxes generally levied on the employers based on the gross wages (subject to certain limits) of their employees. (page 434)

Proceeds of discounted note   The amount of money received from a bank upon discounting a note. (page 419)

Promissory note   A written promise to pay a definite sum of money on demand or at a definite future date. (page 419)

Salary   Consideration given to employees for professional, administrative, managerial, or clerical services performed for an economic entity. (page 427)

Unemployment compensation taxes   Federal and state taxes levied on an economic entity's payroll that provide funds for the payment of unemployment benefits. (page 435)

Wage bracket withholding table   A table provided by the government used to determine the amount of income tax to withhold from employees. (page 431)

Wages   Consideration given to employees who provide their services for an hourly rate. (page 427)

QUESTIONS

1. What is the difference between a current liability and a long-term liability?

2. Why is accounting for current liabilities important?

3. Why is it important that liabilities be classified as either current or long-term?

4. Liabilities can be organized into two groups. Categorize each group and give examples of typical liabilities found in each group.

5. List four reasons why a business entity might issue a note payable.

6. Distinguish between a note issued at *face value* and a *discounted note.*

7. Describe the accounting problem involved in accounting for the acquisition of an asset by the issuance of a note payable.

8. An interest rate and a discount rate of 10% are not the same. Explain.

9. When notes are discounted, a liability is recorded for the face value of the note and cash is increased by the proceeds. How is the difference between the proceeds and the face value of the note accounted for?

10. If a promissory note were issued in one accounting period and repaid in a second accounting period, an adjusting entry would be required at the end of the first accounting period. Explain.

11. Explain why year-end adjusting entries are needed for estimated liabilities such as product warranties.

12. What is a *contingent liability?*

13. How are the three classes of contingent liabilities accounted for?

14. What is the difference between the terms *wages* and *salaries?*

15. Why is it important to have the status of an individual rendering services clearly established as either an *employee* or an *independent contractor?*

16. How is the amount of gross pay determined for an employee?

17. What are the most common deductions from gross earnings in computing *net pay?*

18. How does an employer determine the amount of federal income taxes to withhold from an employee?

19. How does an employer determine the amount of FICA taxes to withhold from an employee?

20. The employer must remit the taxes withheld from employees to the government. How is this accomplished?

21. Describe the various employer payroll taxes.

22. What is the purpose of a *payroll register?*

23. Generally a company will establish a special checking account for the purpose of writing the payroll checks. Why?

24. What purpose does the *employee's earnings record* serve?

25. Time cards are a common means of recording employee attendance. Still, many companies require department or section heads to prepare an absentee report. Why?

26. What type of information is maintained in an employee's personnel file?

27. What source documents are required in order to prepare paychecks for a company's employees?

28. What is to prevent a dishonest employee in the accounting department from inserting a fictitious or former employee's name into the payroll register, making the paycheck, and then cashing the paycheck?

29. How can a dishonest accounting department employee benefit from overstating the total amount of the net pay column on the payroll register?

30. A company has a certain project it must complete this year that will take 10,000 labor-hours of work. The company can hire, at $5 per hour, either 5 full-time employees or 20 part-time employees to do the job. Discuss the advantage and disadvantages of both alternatives.

EXERCISES

Exercise 11-1
Journal entries for an interest-bearing and a discounted note

On December 1, 1987, Mighty Motors, Inc., issued a promissory note to the Greater Detroit National Bank in the amount of $650,000. The note is a 6-month note and bears interest at the rate of 12%. Prepare general journal entries for the issuance of the note, the December 31, 1987, adjustment, and the May 30, 1988, payment assuming that:
a. The bank pays Mighty Motors $650,000 on December 1, 1987, and collects the face of the note plus interest on May 30, 1988.
b. The bank discounts the note on December 1, 1987, subtracting the total 6 months' interest from the face of the note, and collects the $650,000 borrowed funds on May 30, 1988.

Exercise 11-2
Acquisition of an asset by issuing a note

American Business Machines, Inc., agrees to sell to The Dataservice Company a new model 3725 computer. The terms of the agreement are that Dataservice will pay American Business Machines $40,000 cash and $1,000 per month at the end of each month for the next 5 years. If Dataservice had paid cash for the computer the price would have been $88,000. A note payable for the total of the payments was signed on October 1, 1987. Prepare the general journal entries made by Dataservice on October 1, 1987, and October 31, 1987.

Exercise 11-3
Determining the number of days to borrow money so that discount isn't lost

The Big Spender is a little short of funds. She just acquired a new model 321 PlayThing from Heavy Equipment Company for $40,000 with credit terms of 3/10, n/30. Big Spender can borrow funds from the PinchAPenny Exchange Bank at 12%. For how long a period could Big Spender borrow funds from the bank such that the interest on the borrowed funds does not exceed the purchase discount? (Assume a 360-day year.)

(Check figure: 93 days)

Exercise 11-4
Estimating product warranties

From January 1, 1987, to December 31, 1987, the Temple Terrace Appliance Company sold 3,600 washers and dryers. The appliances are sold under an 18-month warranty plan whereby the company will repair any appliance it sells at no cost to the customer for the first 18 months of service. Repair costs are estimated to be $25 per unit, and 8% of the units are estimated to require repairs. During 1987, 176 units were repaired at a cost of $4,180. An additional 107 units were repaired in 1988 at a cost of $2,810 before the warranties expired.

Record a single entry to summarize the repairs made in 1987, record the December 31 adjusting entry to recognize the remaining liability at that date, and finally record a single entry to summarize the repairs made in 1988.

Exercise 11-5

Accounting for contingent liabilities

Peoples Utility of Pennsylvania operates a nuclear power plant on an island in the Lehigh River. In the month of April 1987 a series of human errors caused the cooling system to malfunction and the nuclear fuel core to overheat as a result. Damage to the fuel core, if any, cannot be determined until the reactor cools down and is safe to inspect, a process that may take several months. Peoples Utility has a year-end of April 30. The power plant is insured for $300,000,000, has a book value of $375,000,000 and a fair value of $780,000,000.

a. Assuming that it is *probable* that the plant is so damaged that it will never operate again, what accounting treatment is required?

b. Assuming that it is *reasonably possible* that some damage occurred, what accounting treatment is required?

Exercise 11-6

Preparing payroll entry from a payroll register

The data presented below have been selected from the payroll register of Gentle Dynamics Corporation. They consist of the column totals for the current biweekly pay period:

Regular Earnings	$85,000	Federal Income Taxes	
Department A Expense	60,000	Withheld	$19,600
Department B Expense	38,000	Overtime Earnings	13,000
FICA Tax Withheld	6,860	Union Dues Withheld	3,000

From this information you are to prepare, without explanation, the general journal entry to record the biweekly payroll.

(Check figure: Salaries and Wages Payable: $68,540)

Exercise 11-7

Computing take home pay

Sweet Sam works the counter at the 56th Street Dairy King. He is paid at the rate of $3.75 per hour. Last week Sweet Sam worked 55 hours. Determine the take-home pay for Sweet Sam assuming the following: Dairy King is subject to the Federal Fair Labor Standards Act, Sweet Sam has federal income taxes withheld amounting to $28.10, and the FICA taxes are 7% on the first $40,000 of earned wages (Sweet Sam has not exceeded this limit). In addition to the above, Sweet Sam has $7.50 withheld for his union dues as a member of the Dairy Dippers Local 17532 and $9.15 withheld for hospitalization insurance.

(Check figure: Net pay = $173.22)

Exercise 11-8

Preparing payroll journal entries

The cumulative earnings of the six employees of Careful Carla's Consulting Company is presented below. The data do not include the current pay period, which is shown in a separate column. All data reflect gross pay. Using this information you are to prepare, without explanation, the general journal entries to record the payroll and the payroll taxes for the current period. Assume the total federal income tax withheld for the current period to be $640; FICA taxes are imposed at the rate of 7% on the first $40,000 of earned income; the federal unemployment tax rate is .8% on the first $7,000 of earned income; and the state unemployment tax rate is 2.7% on the first $7,000 of earned income. No deductions are made from the employee's pay other than those appropriate taxes listed above.

Employee	Earnings to Date Prior to Current Period	Earnings Current Period
Washington, George	$43,500	$1,250
Adams, John	39,700	970
Jefferson, Thomas	16,750	540
Madison, James	7,500	230
Monroe, James	6,950	180
Adams, Quincy	5,100	125

(Check figure: Payroll Tax Expense = $102.38)

Exercise 11-9
Recording payroll tax expense

During the month of November 1987 the payroll of Dayton Dry Goods Store amounts to $120,000. Of this amount three-fifths was not subject to state and federal unemployment taxes and one-fifth was not subject to the FICA tax. Assuming that the state unemployment tax rate is 1.9%, the federal unemployment tax rate is .8%, and the FICA tax rate is 7%, prepare, without explanation, the general journal entry to record the employer payroll taxes for the month of November.

(Check figure: Payroll Tax Expense = $8,016)

Exercise 11-10
Preparing a payroll register and related payroll entries

Jackson Swimming Pool Company employees three people. Last week these three worked 40, 46, and 42 hours. The pay rate for all three employees is $4.50 per hour. The first two employees have earned more than $7,000 prior to last week's pay period. The third employee was hired only 2 weeks ago, consequently he will not exceed $7,000 total earnings for the entire year. All employees had a medical insurance deduction of $12. Federal income taxes withheld were $37, $45, and $40, respectively. Assume that FICA taxes are determined by using a 7% rate on all earnings up to a maximum of $40,000 and federal and state unemployment compensation taxes are .8% and 2.7%, respectively, up to a limit of $7,000. Prepare a payroll register for the week, the general journal entry to record the payroll, and the general journal entry to record the payroll taxes. No employee has exceeded the FICA limit.

(Check figure: Payroll Tax Expense = $48.35)

PROBLEMS
Set A

Problem A11-1
Current liabilities on a balance sheet

A review of the general ledger of the Muhlenburg Corporation reveals the following selected accounts as of December 31, 1987:

Accounts Payable.	$ 47,320
Accumulated Depreciation.	9,500
Allowance for Uncollectible Accounts	3,750
Bonds Payable: Due 1995	200,000
Bonds Payable: Due 1988	50,000
Customer Advances	5,700
Deferred Consulting Revenues	15,000
Discount on Notes Payable	2,300
Dividends Payable	10,000
Estimated Federal Income Taxes Payable	2,500
Estimated Liability for Premium Offers Outstanding	2,150
Estimated Liability under Product Warranties	1,570
Federal Unemployment Tax Payable	590
FICA Taxes Payable.	1,650
Income Taxes Withheld from Employees	3,320
Notes Payable	65,000
Pottsville City Property Taxes Due	3,500
Unearned Advertising Revenue.	1,000
Union Dues Withheld from Employees	1,050
Wages Payable.	31,560

Required

Using the information above, prepare the current liability section of the Muhlenburg Corporation's December 31, 1987, balance sheet.

(Check figure: Total current liabilities: $239,610)

Problem A11-2
Current liabilities on a balance sheet

The following information is available on December 31, 1987, concerning Clay Manufacturing Company's liabilities:

a. Accounts Payable total $215,300.

b. The company received a check in the amount of $14,500 from Polk, Inc., as an advance payment on job no. 1436, which will be completed late in March 1988.

c. Clay Manufacturing's Appliance Division sells direct to customers and the appliances carry a 24-month warranty; 62,000 appliances were sold in 1987. The company estimates that 8% of the appliances sold will require repairs, which will average $20 per unit. During 1987, 2,070 units sold in 1987 were repaired under warranty.

d. Salaries and wages unpaid as of December 31, 1987, amounted to $14,430.

e. Clay Manufacturing received notice on December 21, 1987, that Garner Oil was placed in bankruptcy. Clay had endorsed as a guarantor a $15,000 note payable issued by Garner Oil to the Houston Drilling Supply Company.

f. Two notes payable were outstanding as of the last day of the year. The first was a note issued to the Exchange Bank in the amount of $30,000. The note, which was issued on March 1, 1987, and will mature on February 28, 1988, bears interest at a rate of 12%. Clay received $30,000 from the Exchange Bank on March 1, 1987. The second note was issued to Rayburn Trust on October 1, 1987. This $50,000 note will mature on March 30, 1988, and has an interest rate of 14%. Clay received $46,500 on the day the note was issued.

Required

Prepare the current liabilities section of Clay Manufacturing Company's balance sheet as of December 31, 1987.

(Check figure: Total current liabilities = $398,280)

Problem A11-3
Preparing entries for promotional campaign

Sales have been lagging for Johnson Soap Company, and as a result the company has adopted a promotion campaign in 1987. For its lead product, Lyndon Lime Soap Powder, the company will give each customer a coupon for every box purchased. The coupons can be exchanged for a series of gifts described on the boxes by sending in five coupons for each gift. The company estimates that 60% of the coupons will be redeemed.

For the year 1987 Johnson Soap purchases 15,000 gifts at an average cost of $1.80 each. During the year the company sold 150,000 boxes of Lyndon Lime Soap Powder at $4.25 per box; 57,000 coupons were redeemed. In 1988 sales of the soap powder amounted to 182,000 boxes at $4.30 per box; 72,500 coupons were redeemed, including some coupons from 1987. The company purchased an additional 13,000 gifts at $1.80 each.

Required

Prepare general journal entries for the years 1987 and 1988 relating to the promotion campaign. (Hint: This problem is similar to a product warranty problem.)

(Check figure: Estimated liability for coupons outstanding 1988 = $25,092)

Problem A11-4
Recording entries relating to payrolls in the voucher register, the check register, and the general journal

On July 1, 1987, the trial balance of Stratford Products, Inc., contained the following selected accounts relating to payrolls:

Federal Income Taxes Withheld from Employees.	$2,340
FICA Tax Payable.	870
Federal Unemployment Tax Payable.	115
State Unemployment Tax Payable	360
Medical Insurance Premiums Withheld	1,190

During the month of July the following transactions relating to payrolls occurred:

July 4   Voucher no. 716 was prepared payable to Oxford State Bank in the amount of $3,210. This voucher authorizes payment of federal income taxes withheld and FICA taxes payable. The Oxford State Bank is a federal depository.

4   Check no. 698 was issued in payment of voucher no. 716.

July 15   The bimonthly pay period ends this date. The payroll was recorded in the general journal using the following data:

Gross Earnings	$7,300
Federal Income Taxes Withheld	1,460
FICA Taxes Payable	511
Medical Insurance Premiums Withheld	425

15   Prepared voucher no. 731 for the net amount of the payroll. The voucher is issued payable to Payroll.

16   Issued check no. 712 in payment of voucher no. 731. The check was deposited in the payroll account.

20   Voucher no. 740 was prepared payable to Big Bucks Insurance Company for the amount of medical insurance premiums due to date.

20   Issued check no. 723 in payment of voucher no. 740.

24   Voucher no. 755 was prepared payable to the State of Iowa for the amount of state unemployment tax payable.

24   Issued check no. 733 in payment of voucher no. 755.

30   The bimonthly pay period ended this date. The payroll was recorded in the general journal using the following data:

Gross Earnings	$7,700
Federal Income Taxes Withheld	1,540
FICA Taxes Payable	539
Medical Insurance Premiums Withheld	425

30   Prepared voucher no. 761 for the net amount of the payroll.

30   Check no. 738 was issued in payment of voucher no. 761.

30   A general journal entry was prepared to record the employer's payroll taxes due for the month of July. The following taxes apply:

FICA Taxes	$1,050
State Unemployment Tax	375
Federal Unemployment Tax	105

Required   Record the transactions listed above using a voucher register, a check register, or a general journal, as appropriate.

(Check figure: Total Vouchers Payable = $15,285)

Problem A11-5
Preparing payroll register and related entries

Every Friday is payday for the six employees of Regional Records, Inc. Presented below are the payroll data for the current pay period:

	Hours Worked		Pay Rate	Federal Income Taxes	Medical Insurance	Earnings to End of Previous Period
Employee	Regular	Overtime				
Berwanger, Jay	40	4	$7.75	$ 71.30	$14.00	$ 8,780.00
Kelley, Larry	40	3	4.20	37.20	14.00	6,815.00
Clinton, Francis	40		Salary	195.00	21.50	42,000.00
O'Brien, Denise	40	6	6.50	59.10	14.00	4,587.00
Kinnick, Nile	40	14	Salary	175.00	21.50	39,875.00
Hammon, Tom	40		5.25	42.00	14.00	7,500.00

The two salaried employees, Mrs. Clinton and Mr. Kinnick, receive salaries of $975 and $825, respectively. Both of these individuals work in the office; the other four hourly employees work in the warehouse.

Regional Records is subject to payroll taxes of 7% FICA, .8% Federal Unemployment Compensation Taxes, and 2.3% State Unemployment Compensation Taxes. The FICA tax is imposed on the employees as well and is imposed on all salaries and wages up to a maximum of $40,000. The federal and state unemployment taxes are imposed on the first $7,000 of salaries and wages.

Required

1. Prepare a payroll register for the current pay period; the payroll checks to the employees start with check no. 313.

(Check figure: Total net pay = $2,109.52)

2. Prepare, without explanation, the general journal entries to record the payroll and the employer's payroll taxes.

Problem A11-6
Preparing payroll entries for a 3-month period

Presented below are data relating to the monthly payrolls of International Trade Publications for the second quarter of 1987:

	April	May	June
Total salaries paid	$93,500	$95,200	$91,700
Salaries subject to FICA tax	92,700	64,300	49,800
Salaries subject to unemployment taxes	36,900	19,600	8,400

Federal income taxes withheld from all employees amount to 25% of the total salaries paid. The FICA tax rate is 7%, the federal and state unemployment tax rates are .8% and 2.3%, respectively.

International Trade Publications remits to the Internal Revenue Service on the third day following the end of the month payment for federal income taxes withheld and all FICA taxes due. On the same date payment is made to the State of New York for the state unemployment tax due. The federal unemployment tax is paid in January.

Required

1. Prepare, without explanations, the general journal entries to record the payroll and related taxes for the months of April, May, and June. (Round your answer to the nearest whole dollar.)
2. Prepare, without explanations, the general journal entries to record the remittances made relating to the payroll taxes for the months of April, May, and June. (Total salaries paid in March amounted to $95,000, all of which was subject to FICA taxes and $53,500 was subject to unemployment taxes.)

(Check figure: Total remittance for June = $33,253)

3. List the liability accounts and account balances that relate to payrolls that would appear on the June 30, 1987, balance sheet. FUC Tax Payable as of March 31, 1987 = $1,972.

Problem A11-7
Identifying errors in a payroll register

AroundTown Delivery Service, Inc., employs five individuals to deliver important correspondence among the many offices in downtown Philadelphia. The crew uses roller skates and can provide faster service than the local mail or other express services. The crew is managed by Mrs. Betty Rollalong, who also prepares the payroll, issues the paychecks (which are signed by Mr. AroundTown, the principal stockholder in the business), and draws a check on the general cash account to transfer the payroll cash account to cover the payroll.

Mr. AroundTown has become very concerned over the past few weeks about the company's decreasing cash balance in the regular cash account. He asks for your help with his problem and you consent. One of the items that you ask to review is the most recent payroll register and related payroll information on all six employees. The register appears below:

AROUNDTOWN DELIVERY SERVICE, INC.
Weekly Payroll
Week Ended December 12, 1987

| Employee | Total Hours | Earnings | | | Taxable Earnings | | Deductions | | | | Payment | |
		Regular	Overtime	Total	FICA	UC	FIT	FICA	Union Dues	Total	Net Pay	Check Number
Gonzelas, Speedy	48	$ 200.00	$ 60.00	$ 260.00	$ 260.00	$100.00	$ 52.00	$18.20	$15.00	$ 85.20	$ 174.80	123
Roadrunner, Ron	42	220.00	16.50	236.50	236.50		47.30	16.56	15.00	78.86	157.64	124
Rollalong, Betty	46	240.00	54.00	294.00	294.00	294.00	5.88	2.58	15.00	23.46	270.54	125
Rollalong, Thomas	52	400.00	90.00	490.00			48.00		15.00	63.00	431.00	126
Swiftly, Stanly	44	200.00	30.00	230.00	230.00		46.00	16.10	15.00	77.10	152.90	127
Zip, Tip	42	300.00	22.50	322.50	322.50		64.50	22.58	15.00	101.08	220.42	128
Totals		$1,760.00	$273.00	$2,033.00	$1,343.00	$394.00	$263.08	$94.01	$90.00	$428.70	$1,607.30	

From the related payroll information you ascertain the following:

Employee	Pay Rate	Cumulative Earnings Prior to Dec. 12
Gonzelas, Speedy	$5.00/hr	$ 6,900
Roadrunner, Ron	5.50	7,600
Rollalong, Betty	5.00	3,400
Rollalong, Thomas	6.00	9,200
Swiftly, Stanly	5.00	7,100
Zip, Tip	7.50	10,300

Union dues for each employee amount to $15.00 per week, and each employee is subject to federal income taxes of 20% of gross earnings. Mr. AroundTown informs you that the following individuals worked overtime during the current pay period: Gonzelas, 8 hours; Roadrunner, 2 hours; Swiftly, 4 hours; and Zip, 2 hours.

Required   Analyze carefully the data presented and list the errors you discover. The FICA tax is 7% on the first $40,000.

Problem A11-8
Cost analysis of hiring employees or engaging independent contractors

Continental Motors Company, the world's largest automobile manufacturer, employs several hundred people as inventory counters. These individuals visit the various plant sites and count inventories of parts and supplies on a continual basis.

The company is considering engaging We-Count Inventories, Inc., in lieu of the company counters. We-Count has submitted a proposal to do a pilot program for the Studepacker Division. The proposal estimates that the work will take 102,000 labor-hours to be billed at the following rates:

Labor-Hours	Classification	Billing Rate
90,000	Counters	$ 7.25
8,000	Reviewers	12.00
4,000	Supervisors	20.00

Continental currently employs 50 counters in the Studepacker Division. It currently takes 1 year to count the division's inventory. The counters earn an average wage of $15,000 per year, which is subject to the normal payroll taxes (7% FICA on all wages up to $40,000, Federal Unemployment Compensation .8% up to $7,000; and State Unemployment Compensation 2.7%, up to $7,000). In addition, benefits to the employees amount to 6.25% of the total payroll, and it costs $1.10 per employee per week to process the various payroll and personnel records.

Required Develop for Continental Motors Company an analysis of the cost of taking inventory in the Studepacker Division by the present method and by the proposed pilot program.

(Check figure: If current policy is followed—$864,485)

Set B

Problem B11-1
Current liabilities on a balance sheet

The following account balances from the general ledger of the Montgomery Company as of December 31, 1987, are available for review:

Accounts Payable	$27,500	Accumulated Depreciation	$2,750
Salaries Payable	18,500	Bonus Payable	2,700
Current Maturity of Long-Term		Liability Arising from Purchase	
Debt	15,000	Commitments	2,000
Notes Payable Due in 6 Months	15,000	Discount on Notes Payable Due in	
Income Taxes Payable	13,500	6 Months	1,750
Dividends Payable	10,000	Estimated Liability Under Product	
Income Taxes Withheld from		Warranty	1,630
Employees	6,300	Allowance for Uncollectible	
Notes Payable to Vendors Due in		Accounts	1,500
180 Days	5,000	Hospital Insurance Premiums	
Unearned Service Contract		Payable	1,300
Revenue	3,750	Property Taxes Payable	1,300
Deferred Rent Income	3,600	FICA Taxes Payable	1,200
Estimated Liability for Coupons		Federal Unemployment Tax	
Outstanding	3,250	Payable	220
Advances from Customers	3,000		

Required Prepare the current liabilities section of Montgomery Company's December 31, 1987, balance sheet.

(Check figure: Total current liabilities = $133,000)

Problem B11-2
Current liabilities on a balance sheet

Juneau Corporation obtained the following information relating to its liabilities for the year ended September 30, 1987:

a. The corporation received $12,750 from the Alaska Showshoe Company on September 1, 1987, for consulting services to be rendered from September 1 to November 30, 1987.

b. Salaries in the amount of $3,750 have accrued by September 30, 1987.

c. In addition to its consulting activities, the Juneau Corporation sells a product that carries a 24-month warranty. During the year, 15,000 units were sold. Repairs were made on 615 units in 1987. It is estimated that 7% of the units sold will require repairs at an average cost of $16 each.

d. Accounts payable at year-end amounted to $23,760.

e. The Fairbanks National Bank notified Juneau Corporation that a note in the amount of $7,000 issued by the Spenard Company was past due. Juneau Corporation had co-signed the note as an accommodation for the Spenard Company.

f. A note payable to the Fort Richardson Chemical Exchange Bank in the amount of $50,000 was issued on July 1, 1987. On that date the corporation received $44,000 from the bank. The note matures on January 1, 1988.

g. Another note payable to the Fort Richardson Chemical Exchange Bank in the amount of $25,000 was issued on January 1, 1987. The note is due on January 1, 1988, together with 12% interest.

Required Prepare the current liabilities section of the Juneau Corporation's balance sheet as of September 30, 1987.

(Check figure: Total current liabilities = $124,220)

Problem B11-3
Preparing entries for a promotional campaign

Phoenix Mills Company began a promotional campaign on January 1, 1987, to promote the sales of their line of breakfast cereals, which includes Wheat Wams, Barley Bangs, and O.K. Oats. One of the major features of the campaign is that customers buying the cereal products will be able to obtain a valuable set of original Yuma glassware by sending in to Phoenix Mills $10 and five box tops from any of the three cereals. The advertising consultant advises Phoenix Mills that for every 10,000 boxes of cereal sold, 650 box tops will be returned.

For the years 1987 and 1988 the following transactions relating to the campaign occurred:

1987

a. Purchased 5,000 sets of glasses from Yuma Glass Company at $18.75 per set. An asset Promotional Glassware Inventory was debited and Accounts Payable was credited.

b. Sold 400,000 boxes of the three types of cereal for an average price of $3.75 per box.

c. Customers returned 23,000 box tops together with the proper amount of cash. Phoenix Mills distributed the appropriate number of sets of glassware. The account Promotional Expense is used to record the related expense.

d. The year-end adjusting entry is recorded to reflect the estimated expense.

1988

e. Acquired 5,700 sets of glassware on account from Yuma Glass Company at $18.75 per set.

f. 500,000 boxes of cereal were sold at an average price of $3.90.

g. Customers returned 29,000 box tops and paid the appropriate amount for the glassware. The company issued the proper number of sets of glassware to the customers.

h. Recorded the appropriate year-end adjusting entry.

Required Prepare the general journal entries relating to the transactions listed above.

(Check figure: Estimated liability for promotional campaign, 1988 = $11,375)

Problem B11-4
Recording payroll entries in the voucher register, cash register, and general journal

The five employees of San Antonio Steel Company are paid bimonthly on the 15th and again on the 30th. The general ledger accounts relating to payroll that appear below were taken from the October 31, 1987, trial balance:

Federal Income Taxes Withheld	$580	SUC Tax Payable	$97
FICA Tax Payable	275	Union Dues Withheld	75
FUC Tax Payable	125		

The following transactions relating to payrolls were completed during the month of November 1987:

Nov. 8   Voucher no. 723 payable to the Steelworkers of America was prepared for union dues withheld to date.

   8   Check no. 698 was issued in payment of voucher no. 723.

  15   The first bimonthly payroll was prepared and recorded in the general journal. Gross earnings amount to $2,450. The following deductions were taken:

Federal Income Taxes	$610	FICA Taxes	$153
Union Dues	75		

Nov. 15	Voucher no. 742 payable to Payroll Account was prepared for the net amount of the payroll.
15	Check no. 712 was issued in payment of voucher no. 742.
17	Prepared voucher no. 753 payable to the State of Texas for State Unemployment Compensation Tax Payable.
17	Check no. 719 was issued in payment of voucher no. 753.
19	Prepared voucher no. 761 payable to the Alamo Exchange Bank for federal income taxes withheld and the FICA tax payable as of October 31, 1987.
19	Issued check no. 726 in payment of voucher no. 761. The check was made payable to Alamo Exchange Bank.
30	Recorded the payroll due this date in the general journal. The gross earnings amounted to $2,670 and the following deductions were taken:

Federal Income Taxes . . . . . . $670   FICA Taxes. $125
Union Dues   75

30	Recorded in the general journal the employer's payroll taxes for the month of November. The employer's FICA taxes amount to $278, the SUC tax is $81, and the FUC tax is $41
30	Prepared voucher no. 773 for the net amount of the payroll.
30	Issued check no. 737 in payment of voucher no. 773.

Required   Record the transactions in the voucher register, check register, or general journal as appropriate.

(Check figure: Vouchers Payable total = $4,439)

Problem B11-5
Preparing payroll and related entries

Presented below is information pertaining to the weekly payroll of the California Cotton Company:

	Hours Worked		Pay Rate	Federal Income Taxes	Union Dues	Earnings to End of Previous Period
Employee	Regular	Overtime				
Baldridge, Malcoln	40		$7.75	$ 46.00	$11.50	$ 8,970.00
Block, John R.	40	8	6.25	65.00	11.50	10,237.50
Donovan, Raymond	40	4	4.50	41.40	11.50	6,915.75
Regan, Donald T.	40		Salary	240.00		38,910.00
Smith, William	40	10	Salary	280.00		54,600.00
Weinberger, Casper	40	2	3.75	32.25	11.50	6,288.75

Mr. Smith, the company president, is paid a weekly salary of $1,400. Mr. Regan, the vice president, is paid a weekly salary of $1,200. The officers' salaries are charged to the Administrative Salaries account; all other wages are charged to the Showroom Wages account.

The following payroll taxes apply: FICA taxes, 7% up to a maximum of $40,000; federal unemployment tax, 0.8% up to the first $7,000; state unemployment tax, 2.7% up to the first $7,000.

Required   1. Prepare a payroll register for the week. Start with check no. 214.

(Check figure: Total net pay = $2,706.07)

2. Prepare the general journal entries, without explanation, to record the payroll and the payroll taxes.

Problem B11-6

Preparing payroll entries for a 3-month period

The employees of Abbott Homes, Inc., are paid monthly on the last day of the month. The data presented below reflect activity concerning the payroll for the third quarter of 1987:

	Total Salaries Paid	Salaries Subject to FICA Tax	Salaries Subject to Unemployment Compensation Taxes
July	$248,000	$248,000	$190,000
Aug.	261,000	235,000	130,000
Sept.	255,000	187,000	98,000

Income taxes are withheld at a rate of 25% on all salaries. A 7% FICA tax applies to earnings up to a maximum of $40,000, and federal and state unemployment taxes are applied at rates of .8% and 2.7%, respectively, on earnings up to $7,000. Remittances are made to the Internal Revenue Service and the State Unemployment Agency on the third day following the end of the month. The federal unemployment tax is paid in January.

Required

1. Prepare, without explanations, the general journal entries to record the payroll and related taxes for the months of July, August, and September.
2. In June total salaries amounted to $230,000, all of which was subject to FICA taxes and $195,000 of which was subject to unemployment taxes. Using this information and the information contained in the problem, prepare the general journal entries, without explanation, to record the remittances made relating to the payroll taxes for the months of July, August, and September.

(Check figure: Total remittance for July = $94,965)

3. List the liability accounts that would appear on the July 31, 1987, balance sheet. Total salaries subject to federal unemployment taxes from January 1 to June 30 amount to $695,000.

Problem B11-7

Identifying errors in a payroll register

The Fallstaff Fabricating Company recently created a personnel division and assigned you to be the new personnel manager. Among your other duties you are now responsible for the company payroll. In preparing for the pay period ending Friday, November 27, 1987, you are reviewing the payroll register prepared for Friday, November 20, 1987, for the welding section. The register is presented below:

FALLSTAFF FABRICATING COMPANY
Welding Section
Weekly Payroll
Week Ended November 20, 1987

Employee	Total Hours	Earnings Regular	Earnings Overtime	Earnings Total	Taxable Earnings FICA	Taxable Earnings UC	Deductions FIT	Deductions FICA	Deductions Union Dues	Deductions Total	Payment Net Pay	Payment Check Number
Ballentine, Nancy	46	$ 240.00	$ 54.00	$ 294.00	$ 294.00		$ 44.10	$20.58	$ 6.75	$ 71.43	$ 222.57	916
Carling, Thomas	54	300.00	157.50	457.50			22.88		6.75	29.63	427.87	917
Miller, William	40	240.00		240.00	240.00		36.00	16.80	6.75	59.55	180.45	918
Pabst, Marylin	48	350.00	105.00	405.00			20.25		6.75	27.00	378.00	919
Slitz, Joseph	40	350.00		350.00	350.00		52.50	24.50	6.75	83.75	266.25	920
Strol, Randy	44	300.00	45.00	345.00	345.00		51.75	24.15	6.75	82.65	262.35	921
Totals		$2,780.00	$361.50	$3,091.50	$1,229.00		$227.48	$86.03	$40.50	$354.01	$2,737.49	

In reviewing the employee personnel files of the welding section you find the following information:

a. All employees in the welding section are subject to federal income tax withholding of 15% of gross earnings.

b. All employees are subject to union dues of $6.75 a week.

c. Pay rates are: Pabst and Slitz, $8.75 per hour; Carling and Strol, $7.50 per hour; Ballentine and Miller, $6.00 per hour.

d. Slitz has earned $15,300 prior to the November 20 pay period and this the highest of any employee. Miller has earned $6,880 and Strol $4,180. All others have earned more than $7,000 but less than $15,300.

e. The section's attendance report reveals that both Ballentine and Strol worked overtime during the week of November 20. Ballentine worked 46 hours and Strol worked 44 hours.

Prior to your assuming the responsibility for the payroll, this task was handled by Terry Carling, Thomas' brother. FICA Taxes are imposed at the rate of 7% on the first $40,000 and the unemployment taxes at .8% federal and 2.7% state on the first $7,000.

Required

After carefully reviewing the data, list the errors you discover.

Problem B11-8
Cost analysis of hiring employees or engaging independent contractors

Ann Knowles is a real estate broker and is considering starting her own agency. With 20 individuals selling for her she thinks she can sell $12,500,000 worth of real estate a year.

If she employs the 20 individuals she must pay them an average salary of $25,000 plus provide for pension and medical benefits that will amount to 5% of the total payroll. In addition she will have the normal payroll taxes of 7% FICA (up to a $30,000 limit) and federal and state unemployment compensation of .8% and 2.7%, respectively (up to a $7,000 limit).

Ms. Knowles will receive an 8% broker's commission on the real estate sold; however if she does not employ 20 individuals, but rather engages them as agents—independent contractors—she will have to split the commission equally with them: 4% for her, 4% for the agent.

Required

Prepare an analysis that will show Ms. Knowles which of the two alternatives she should select.

(Check Figure: Total income if the 20 individuals are employed = $435,100)

GAAP
Generally Accepted Accounting Principles Reviewed and Expanded

Some of the things you will learn about when studying this section are:

- Why generally accepted accounting principles are necessary
- Who is responsible for developing generally accepted accounting principles and how they are developed
- How generally accepted accounting principles are enforced
- What the *conceptual framework study* is and how it will affect accounting principles
- What the objectives of financial reporting are
- How financial reporting meets certain qualitative characteristics
- What the basic underlying assumptions of accounting are

Over the past 11 chapters we have introduced you to a number of generally accepted accounting principles—GAAP. We haven't provided you with an overall picture of generally accepted accounting principles until now because you weren't ready for it. Now you are—you have a good grasp of the financial accounting model and its purpose. You now have the background that you need to understand why we do what we do in accounting, that is, how the principles relate to the accounting process.

THE NEED FOR GAAP

Generally accepted accounting principles are the ground rules of accounting

In Chapter 1, we briefly introduced generally accepted accounting principles, suggesting that they are the ground rules of accounting. They assure us that similar economic events will be reported in the same manner by everyone. And when several acceptable alternatives exist for recording an economic event—say, inventory cost flows or depreciation—these ground rules require us to disclose which alternative was used in the financial statements. Since everyone must follow GAAP, the result is a consistent system of financial reporting that provides users of financial statements with information that is reliable, understandable, and comparable to prior years and among companies. Without these ground rules there would be chaos in financial reporting. General Motors might use the FIFO inventory method, Ford might use LIFO, and neither might tell us which it used. How could we meaningfully compare the two companies? We couldn't. And that's the point. That's why we need GAAP.

AUTHORITATIVE SUPPORT FOR GAAP

Who tells us what GAAP are? Even more important, who tells us that we must follow GAAP? What happens if we don't?

Back in Chapter 1 we said that the authority of GAAP rests on their acceptance by the accounting profession. And that's true, but it's not quite the whole story.

You know that the independent auditor—the CPA—provides statement users with an assurance that the statements represent fairly the results of operations and the financial condition of the company. The auditor gives this assurance, which is really an objective opinion, after examining the accounting records. And the auditor's opinion of the statements' fairness is an integral part of the statements themselves.

In that opinion the auditor must say whether or not the financial statements are presented fairly and prepared in accordance with GAAP. Why? Because the auditor must follow the pronouncements of the accounting profession to remain and practice in it. Failure to follow the pronouncements is cause for expulsion—the state board of accountancy could remove the CPA's license to practice public accounting.

One of the pronouncements is found in the American Institute of Certified Public Accountants (AICPA) *Statements on Auditing Standards.* It says that the auditor's report must state whether the financial statements are presented in accordance with GAAP. Another pronouncement, found in the AICPA Code of Professional Ethics, states that the CPA must not express an opinion that financial statements are in conformity with GAAP if the statements contain any departure from an accounting principle issued by the Financial Accounting Standards Board (FASB) or the old Accounting Principles Board (APB). The CPA may not issue an opinion stating that a set of financial statements is in conformity with GAAP when it is not. And without that opinion from the CPA, users cannot rely on the fairness of the financial statements.

The pronouncements of the public accounting profession and the regulations of the SEC provide authoritative support for GAAP

Many companies fall under the regulations of the Securities and Exchange Commission (SEC). And the SEC has direct legal power to force these companies to follow its accounting rules—failure to comply could mean a trip to jail. Most of the SEC's accounting rules are the same as those of the FASB and APB because the SEC has adopted them as their rules. The SEC normally looks to the FASB to establish accepted accounting principles.

GAAP, then, has authoritative support from two sources:

1. Indirectly, from the CPAs who must follow professional accounting pronouncements

2. From the SEC, which has legal authority to enforce compliance with these same pronouncements

THE MEANING AND DEVELOPMENT OF GAAP

Let's look more closely at the meaning of GAAP. Yes, they are the ground rules of accounting. But let's be more specific.

Generally accepted accounting principles is a technical accounting term. It includes conventions, concepts, standards, rules, principles, and procedures that are necessary to define accepted accounting practice at a particular time. That's how the profession itself explains GAAP in one of its pronouncements. Furthermore, generally accepted accounting principles are principles that have *substantial authoritative support*. The APB *Opinions* and FASB *Standards* constitute substantial authoritative support. But there is substantial authoritative support from outside the APB and FASB. Other authoritative support comes from the following:

- APB and FASB interpretations of *Opinions* and *Standards*
- Industry audit guides
- Industry accounting practices
- APB *Statements*
- AICPA statements of position
- Pronouncements of the SEC
- Accounting textbook and articles

There is no one single source for GAAP

Unfortunately, there isn't just one single source of generally accepted accounting principles. There have been a number of attempts, all unsuccessful thus far, to develop a single source. However, the FASB has recently completed a major project — called the **conceptual framework study** — that holds great promise. Several parts of the study are discussed in the following sections.

THE CONCEPTUAL FRAMEWORK STUDY

The Objectives of Financial Statements

The first part of the conceptual framework study is concerned with the objectives of financial reporting. Why are financial statements needed? Who needs them? What are the backgrounds of the people who need the financial statements? And what information do they need and how should it be presented so that they can understand it? This part of the study was completed in 1978.

Useful Information for Decisions

Financial reporting should provide useful information to investors and creditors

Financial reporting should provide information that is useful to present and potential investors and creditors. That's the first objective of a financial statement. The FASB listed only present and potential investors and creditors as users. Why? There are many more users — the IRS, the SEC, and management, to name a few. But is there any question in your mind about the ability of these groups to get whatever financial information they need concerning the company? Of course not. The IRS and the SEC have legal authority to get what they want—you either provide the requested information or go to jail. And management can get what they want: Employees provide the requested information or they are fired. Only investors and creditors do not have this direct access, so it is for these groups that financial statements are prepared.

The financial statements are the end product of the accounting activity. They represent the classification and summarization of many financial transactions, some of which are very complex. There simply isn't any way these activities can be presented in the financial statements so that everyone—we mean everyone from a skilled financial analyst to the unskilled small investor—can understand what they mean. The FASB assumes that readers of financial statements have a basic background in business and economics and will take the time and effort to study the statements and related notes. This, by the way, includes you.

Useful Information for Assessing Cash Flows

Financial reporting should provide useful information for assessing cash flows

The second objective of financial statements is that financial reporting should provide information that is useful in assessing cash flows. What we're concerned with is the amounts, timing, and uncertainty of the net cash inflow to the company. We're interested because people invest to increase their cash. The final test investors look at is whether or not they received more cash from an investment than they spent on it. And they want information that will help them choose between receiving cash now (selling their stock) or at some future date. They need information that will help them assess the risk that the amounts and timing of future cash receipts will not be as expected.

Useful Information about Balance Sheet Items and Changes in Them

Financial reports should help investors and creditors assess strengths and weaknesses of business entities

The third and last objective of financial statements is that financial reporting should provide information about the economic resources (assets); the claims to those resources (liabilities and owners' equity); and the effects of transactions, events, and circumstances that change resources and claims to those resources. That's the way the FASB puts it. Investors want this information to help them assess the company's strengths and weaknesses; to assess the company's liquidity (ability to convert assets to cash) and solvency (ability to pay its bills); and to evaluate information about the company's performance during the period.

Qualitative Characteristics

The second part of the conceptual framework study is concerned with examining the characteristics that make accounting information useful. This part of the study was completed in the spring of 1980.

1. Usefulness

Financial information must be useful to those who want it, but not too costly for those who prepare it

Usefulness, of course, is the most important characteristic of any reported information. People want accounting information that's useful—but what's useful to one user may not be as useful to another. Accounting standards must be set to require that just the right amount of information is reported in a financial statement. Well, now, exactly what does "just the right amount of information" mean? It doesn't mean *exactly* anything. What it does mean generally is that (1) the information must be useful to most of the people who want to use it, and (2) preparing that useful information won't be a burdensome (cost, time, complexity) task for those who have to prepare it.

2. Understandability

To be useful, financial information must be understandable

If you can't understand the accounting information given to you, it isn't useful even though it may be relevant to whatever decision you want to make. Let's expand on an example used by the FASB when they explain the term *understandability*. Suppose you're a vegetarian on a summer trip to Paris. Ordering a meal from a menu will present you with a problem. The waiter provides you with useful information relevant to your decision — the information is there on the menu in French. But if you can't understand it, it's useless.

Accounting information must be presented in a manner that investors and creditors understand. But, as we said before, it is assumed that investors and creditors have a basic knowledge of business and economics and that they will spend time and effort in studying the financial statements.

3. Relevance

To be useful, financial information must be relevant

For information to be relevant it must have a bearing on a decision to be made — it must make a difference in that decision. Return to the vegetarian example. Assume that you ask the waiter for a menu printed in English. He returns with an English menu of meat dishes. Now you have information that is understandable, but not useful or relevant. Finally, the waiter brings an English vegetable menu — this is both relevant and useful for your decision. You can now select whatever dish suits your vegetarian fancy.

4. Reliability

Reliable financial information must be free from error and bias. And it must be verifiable

Accounting information should be reliable. That means it should be free from error. And it should be free from any bias of those who are providing it. For information to be reliable we must be able to prove — to *verify* — that it is free from error and bias. If different accountants working independently but using the same accounting methods arrive at the same results, the information is verified and proved to be reliable. Accounting information must always be able to stand the test of independent verification.

Be careful what conclusions you draw from the reliability characteristic. You can be sure that the tablets in a bottle of aspirin conform to the formula written on the side of the bottle. And you can be sure that the amounts reported on a set of financial statements are reliable. But the reason that you relied on the aspirin was the claim that two tablets would cure your headache — that was *relevant* information. The reliability of the formula was irrelevant. Accounting information does not claim to cure your financial headaches; it just claims that the information in the accounting bottle conforms to the accounting measurement formulas.

5. Timeliness

We must receive financial information in time to make decisions, otherwise the information is irrelevant and useless

Accounting information will be irrelevant and useless if we don't have it in time to make decisions. We must have accounting information before it loses its capacity to influence decisions. How fast information loses this capacity depends on the decision to be made. Accounting information needed for a corporate takeover bid (such as U.S. Steel buying Marathon Oil) may have value for only a few days or even hours. Information needed for the annual report would have value over a much longer period of time.

Sometimes we have to sacrifice precision for timeliness because approximate information now is more useful than precise information later. For example, isn't that what we do with the estimate of uncollectible accounts? We could know the exact amount of accounts that prove uncollectible if we just waited awhile. But by then the information would no longer be useful.

6. Verifiability

Financial information must be verifiable in order to be reliable

Accounting information must be susceptible of being reviewed by others. And when others can review independently the information contained in purchase invoices, sales invoices, property deeds, transfers of title, and other similar documents and arrive at the same values reported in the financial statements, the information is said to be verified. It's the ability to review the underlying documents that the verifiability characteristic is concerned with, not the results of the review. If the underlying documents are not available, the information reported on the financial statements can't be verified. And that means it can't be relied upon.

7. Neutrality

Financial information cannot favor one group over another group

Accounting information should not favor one group of users or preparers over another group. It should be free from bias. Both in making and in using accounting standards, the major concern should be the relevance and reliability of the information, not how that information affects one group or another.

Postponing the recording of purchases made in the last week of December until January would be reflected on the income statement by higher reported earnings for the current year. The higher reported earnings would reflect favorably on management this year. Neutrality would require that purchases be recorded when acquired, regardless of the effect on management's reported performance.

8. Comparability

Accounting information is useful if it is comparable

Usefulness is enhanced if accounting information can be compared with similar information for the same company through time, and similar information among companies at the same time. The principal reason for developing accounting standards is to reduce the use of different accounting methods. The use of many different accounting methods is what makes comparisons difficult.

Comparisons enable users to detect and explain similarities and differences among companies, and to evaluate the performance of each over time.

9. Completeness

In order to be reliable, financial information must be complete

For accounting information to be reliable, of course, it must be complete. Completeness implies that nothing material is left out that would be vital to investors or creditors in assessing the underlying events and conditions of the business. Of course, we have to consider what is material and what is the additional cost of getting additional information. Materiality and costs are limiting factors on completeness. Relevance determines what the limit is. A map for buried treasure may be complete in every detail but two—the name of the person making the map and the approximate value of the treasure. The irrelevance of the first omission and the cost of getting that information preclude obtaining it. But certainly the relevance of the second omission dictates that some effort should be made to obtain that missing information before investing substantial time and money to recover the treasure.

THE STRUCTURE OF GAAP

Remember what we said before about generally accepted accounting principles: They are conventions, concepts, standards, rules, principles, and procedures that are necessary to define accepted accounting practice at a particular time. About a dozen of these form a structure from which all the rest are derived. We can organize these into three areas: basic assumptions, basic principles, and basic modifiers.

Basic Assumptions

GAAP rests on four basic assumptions or concepts.

1. The business entity concept

2. The accounting period concept

3. The going concern concept

4. The stable-dollar concept

The Business Entity Concept

Accountants consider business entities as separate and distinct from their owners

A business entity is considered for accounting purposes as separate and distinct from its owners. Each business entity is treated for accounting purposes as generating its own revenue, incurring its own expenses, owning its own assets, and owing its own liabilities. Now that's not legally true if the entity is a proprietorship or a partnership. Accountants report on the economic substance of activities, and that may not always reflect the legal form.

EXHIBIT 1
Business Entities.
Illustrated here are a number of different business entities and the periods of time financial statements are prepared for those entities.

Year			1985				1986				1987				1988	
Quarter	1	2	3	4	1	2	3	4	1	2	3	4	1	2	3	
Individual:																
Alex Himself																
Proprietorship:																
Alex Real Estate Agency																
Partnership:																
Alex and Zack, Consulting																
Corporations:																
Alex Motor Company																
Alex Body Company																
Alex Glass Company																
Alexmobile Company																

    Exhibit 1 depicts what we mean by the business entity concept. The exhibit shows the business activities of Joe Alex, who is very successful.

    Joe operates a real estate agency. It's a proprietorship, which means that the agency doesn't have a legal existence. Its assets are Joe's assets as far as the law is concerned. The Alex Real Estate Agency assets are available to Joe's personal creditors if they can't be satisfied from his individual assets, and vice versa. If Joe can't pay his personal creditors, they can go to court to sue, if necessary, to be paid out of the Alex Real Estate Agency assets. The same goes for the real estate agency creditors. If they aren't paid, they can sue to be paid out of Joe's personal assets.

Accountants emphasize economic substance over legal form when preparing financial information for business entities

For accounting purposes, however, we ignore the legal form and, as Joe's accountants, prepare separate sets of financial statements for Joe the individual and the Alex Real Estate Agency.

Joe Alex and Barbara Zack are partners in a consulting firm. That's a business entity and we would prepare a set of financial statements for it also. Legally, of course, the assets of the partnership are available to *both* Joe's personal creditors and Barbara's personal creditors, just as Joe's assets are available for the proprietorship.

Several years ago Joe developed a fuel-efficient automobile that he calls the Alexmobile. Joe now owns a business that manufactures the Alexmobile. He organized it as a corporation. What he actually did was first to organize the Alex Motor Company, whose objective was providing financial and marketing activities for the Alexmobile. He became the principal stockholder but sold 40% of the stock to 1,000 interested investors. Then he set up three other corporations. The stock of these companies is all owned by the Alex Motor Company. The Alex Body Company provides auto frames, the Alex Glass Company provides windows, and the Alexmobile Company manufactures the car. Each of the four corporations is a legal entity. Each owns its own assets and owes its own debts. Each generates its own revenue and incurs its own expenses. Each prepares its own set of financial statements.

But Alex Motor Company owns 100% of the other three. Investors and creditors are interested in what the group as a whole has done. So when financial statements are prepared for the investors and creditors, the four sets of statements are combined — we call it *consolidated* — and only one set of statements is issued. The business entity is the whole group, even though there are four corporations. Economic substance is emphasized over legal form.

The Accounting Period Concept

We would know exactly how well all of Joe Alex's business ventures did from the time he started each if we waited until he sold his last real estate, consulted with his last client, and manufactured and sold the last Alexmobile. We could then precisely measure the revenue and expenses, the assets and liabilities. But of course we can't wait — Joe wants to know how he is doing *now* and at *frequent intervals* as long as he is in business. So do his creditors and the investors in Alex Motor Company.

Unfortunately for us accountants, Joe's business ventures don't stop operating when Joe wants financial statements. (Joe is very happy about that; he doesn't want anything to stop.) So we have to stop Joe's business artificially at frequent intervals to make the financial statements. And, as you know, we will stop the business *on paper* at the end of selected time intervals — years and quarters for Joe, his creditors, and investors; and monthly for Joe. These periods, although artificial, are timely and provide a consistent frame of reference to measure Joe's activities and to compare those measurements with previous periods and other companies.

The life of a business entity is broken up into frequent segments (years, quarters, and months) for accounting purposes

When we divide the life of a business entity into short segments, we are going to lose exactness. But it is the timeliness qualitative characteristic that makes accounting information useful, even if we have to approximate some of that information.

We prepare annually a complete set of financial statements with related footnotes for investors and creditors. However, only the major items of the income statement are reported to investors and creditors on interim statements — that means quarterly (or monthly, but we don't give investors and creditors montly statements).

Refer back to Exhibit 1. This time look at the column headings 1985, 1986, and 1987. The years ended 1985, 1986, and 1987 represent the periods of time for which we will issue complete financial statements for each of Joe's business entities. Notice in the exhibit that each year is divided into four quarters, representing the periods of time for which we will issue interim statements for the businesses. We probably won't issue a fourth-quarter report because at the end of that quarter it's time to make the annual report.

The Going Concern Concept

Accountants assume that business entities will remain in business long enough to allocate the cost of assets over the periods of time that entities expect to use these assets

Joe established his various business ventures assuming that they would have a long life. He fully expects each of them to continue in business as far in the future as he can see — through good times and bad, profits and losses — and that over their continued existence, there will be mostly good times and profits.

Accountants similarly assume that a business entity will continue in existence for a long time. They call this assumption the ***going concern assumption,*** which is the rationale behind recording probable future economic benefits as assets rather than as expenses. For example, we record a building or a patent as an asset because we assume that we will be in business long enough to allocate the cost of the item to the periods of time we use it. If we did not make this assumption we would charge off the building and patent as expenses in the year we bought them. And that would really mess up the income statement. We would be matching this year's revenue with this year's expenditures — not expenses — with a resulting figure that would not provide us with much meaning.

The Stable-Dollar Concept

When preparing the basic financial reports, accountants ignore the changing value of the dollar

Money is a common unit of measure that we can use to record economic transactions and prepare financial statements. Everybody understands money — it's universally available, it's certainly relevant to financial transactions, and it's easy to use. Imagine trying to see how well Xerox did this year if the unit of measure were chickens or automobiles or wheat. These last three items have value, and as such can certainly be used to measure other goods. But they are not *common* economic denominators — only money is.

But money — the dollar — as a measure of economic activity does not have a constant value over time. Actually, the value of a dollar has decreased over time, especially in recent years. It is not time that causes the change in the value of money, but economic events. The dollar is not constant like units of physical measure. A mile or a quart always measure exactly the same; they are precise. These measures will not change when there is a shortage of oil, a surplus of corn, a Democratic majority in the House, or a military crisis in the Middle East. But the value of the dollar will.

Several ways have been proposed to deal with the change in the value of the dollar, so that financial reports today can be meaningfully related to financial reports in the past. The alternatives are to adjust the values on the financial statements for replacement values or price-level changes or both. But there are problems with these approaches. Adjusting for replacement values causes us concern because we would be leaving the comfortable area of objective verifiable evidence to support statement values. And adjusting for price-level changes causes us concern about the appropriateness of one index for measuring many different factors that cause changes in prices.

Certain very large corporations are required to disclose information about replacement costs and price-level-adjusted data. But that's a topic we'll get to later in the course, in Chapter 18.

Basic Principles

The six principles that form the framework for the practice of accounting rest on the four basic assumptions. These principles are as follows:

1. The cost principle

2. The matching principle

3. The revenue-recognition principle

4. The expense-recognition principle

5. The full disclosure principle

6. The consistency principle

1. The Cost Principle

The cost principle is based on objective verifiable evidence

Exchange prices offer us objective, verifiable evidence of values for the goods and services we may exchange with others. On the day that exchanges are made we record the exchange prices in our accounting records. We call these prices *historical costs.* As time goes on, the values for the items we acquired may increase. But we will not record these increases in values, for several reasons.

One major reason is that we no longer have that objective verifiable evidence as to the item's new value. Yes, we know it's worth more and some expert can tell us what he or she thinks it's worth. So can another expert, whose valuations will not be the same as the first expert's. You see, their opinions are subjective, not objective. Therefore, the increase in value cannot be verified by independent parties. And that's very important, because the values on the financial statements must be capable of being verified so that investors and creditors can rely on the financial statements. Independent auditors will insist on verifying items in the accounting records before they issue their opinion. In verifying values, the auditors will look to various source documents for their objective evidence—purchase invoices, titles of ownership, property deeds, brokers' advices, and such items.

A second reason we use historical costs is that we have acquired goods and services for use in our operations, and once acquired the price we paid for them is relevant—not what they're worth today. We will assign the *costs* we paid to those periods of time that have received the benefit of the goods or services we acquired. There is substantial disagreement over this point. Some say that the values today are relevant and should be measured and disclosed (as mentioned previously, this topic of replacement costs and price-level-adjusted data will be discussed later in the text).

Very simply, what we mean by the cost principle is that we will record goods and services at the prices we paid for them and will not change those values at a later date when prices increase.

2. The Matching Principle

Revenue and expenses are matched to measure net income

How well did we do? That's a question often asked by management, investors, and creditors. (The answer is on the income statement.) It's asked more often than the question, What resources do we have? (The answer is on the balance sheet.) For this reason, the income statement is considered more important than the balance sheet—

not that the balance sheet isn't important; it is. But the income statement is more important. It measures a company's earnings by comparing revenue with expenses. Expenses incurred in a particular time period are compared—matched—with the revenue earned during the same time period. Expenses are incurred because they directly or indirectly are responsible for generating revenue.

3. The Revenue-Recognition Principle

Earning revenue is a process that takes place over an extended period of time

Revenue is the inflow of assets that results from producing goods or rendering services. But exactly when do we record revenue? The earning of revenue does not take place all at one point in time—the *earning process* extends over a considerable length of time.

For example, let's look at Joe Alex Real Estate Agency. Joe has to do a number of things to earn revenue. He has to advertise, he has to take clients to see houses, he has to obtain clients who wish to sell houses, he has to help his clients finance the sale or purchase of the houses—he has a host of things to do. But specifically when should Joe recognize revenue?

Accountants answer this question by saying that revenue should be recognized when both of the following conditions are met:

a. The earning process is essentially complete, and

b. An exchange has taken place.

We can usually recognize revenue when title passes

For most companies these conditions are met at the time the goods are sold or services are rendered. This is called the ***point-of-sale method of recognizing revenue.*** For Joe Alex Real Estate Agency, revenue is recognized at the point in time when the title to the house passes from one client to the other.

But there are some exceptions to the general rule—and for good reasons.

Consider first the problem of the ***installment sales method of recognizing revenue.*** Many things are sold on an installment sales basis. We sell a $600 appliance to a customer today and receive a down payment of $100. The appliance is delivered and the $500 balance will be paid in installments over the next 36 months (plus interest, of course). Since the sale was made today, we should recognize $600 of revenue. We should also recognize the expenses of selling the appliance, and that would include an estimate of the bad debts expense (based on all the appliances we sold this year).

Revenue is sometimes not recognized until cash is received

But what if we can't estimate the amount of accounts that will not pay us? Then we *will not* recognize revenue when the sale is made. What we will do is to recognize revenue a little bit at a time as the cash payments are received. This is a very conservative approach, and the reason we use it is because we are not sure that the receivables we booked when the sale was made are ever going to be collected.

Another exception concerns contract projects—very common in the construction industry. Let's look at a new business Joe Alex just started. It's a construction company, and Joe has a contract to build a nuclear aircraft carrier for the U.S. government for $4 billion. It will take about 6 years to build the carrier. Now, if we follow the point-of-sale method, Joe's construction company will show no profits for the first 5 years. But in year 6, when the sale takes place, the company will show a profit. And what a profit!! Don't you think the economic facts are really distorted? Was the construction company doing poorly for the first 5 years? Certainly not, with the contract it has. Do you think Joe will have any problem selling the aircraft carrier?

Of course not—the U.S. government must buy it for the agreed price when it's complete according to the specifications. It's all spelled out in the contract Joe and Uncle Sam signed before the work started.

Sometimes revenue is recognized as a long-term project is being constructed

What the construction company will do is to recognize revenue over the 6-year life of the project. How? Based on reasonable estimates of the project's progress. The amount of revenue to be recognized in any year is determined by comparing the costs incurred that year to the total estimated costs for the entire project. The resulting percentage is applied against the total revenue for the project, and that tells us how much revenue to recognize. This is called the ***percentage-of-completion method of recognizing revenue.***

And sometimes revenue is recognized when production is complete

One more exception to recognizing revenue at the point of sale is called the ***production method of recognizing revenue.*** Here revenue is recognized when production is complete even though a sale hasn't been made. We can use this method only when we are dealing with businesses where we are sure products will be sold—businesses that produce things like precious metals (gold, silver, uranium), or certain government-supported farm products (corn, wheat, soybeans).

4. The Expense-Recognition Principle

Here we are concerned with the point in time when a cost becomes an expense. Everything we acquire is a cost before it becomes an expense. We show costs on the balance sheet as assets—they are ***unexpired costs,*** meaning we have paid them but we haven't yet gotten any economic benefits from them. We show expenses on the income statement—they are ***expired costs,*** meaning we paid for them and have received the economic benefits represented by the cost. But when do we move costs from the balance sheet to show them as expenses on the income statement?

We recognize expenses in three ways:

Expenses are recognized by direct association, by rational allocation, and by immediate recognition

a. Certain costs become expenses because we can ***associate*** them ***directly*** with revenue. When Joe Alex sells an Alexmobile, at that time the costs of the car—which are reflected as inventory on the company's balance sheet—become expenses, recorded under cost of goods sold on the income statement.

b. Certain costs become expenses by ***systematic and rational allocation.*** If we can't associate costs directly with revenue, the next best approach is to assign the costs to expenses over time periods in some reasonable manner. That's basically the idea behind the depreciation of buildings and equipment and the amortization of intangibles.

c. Some costs don't fit the first method and are too elusive to apply the second—these costs we recognize as expenses ***immediately,*** as soon as incurred. Joe Alex's salary is a good example. As the president of Alex Motor Company, Joe's salary should be allocated to those periods of time that receive the benefits of his efforts. Now, if Joe is really concerned about his ongoing concern, he spends some of his time on this year's activities, but probably more of his time planning future years' activities. It would be impossible to track Joe's current salary and activity to results to come in future years. For example, while singing in the shower, Joe thinks of a jingle to advertise the 1988 Alexmobiles. Time expired: 2 minutes. Two minutes of Joe's time this year is worth $15.75. To allocate that to 1988 is impossible. (Well, nothing is impossible. It's just not practical to try to determine this information.) The practical solution is to expense Joe's salary in total this year.

5. The Full Disclosure Principle

Information relevant to users must be disclosed in the statements or in the footnotes

Investors and creditors have every right to expect that the financial statements they are using contain all the significant economic and financial information that is relevant to their understanding of the entity's financial status. That's what we mean by full disclosure. This information can be communicated in the financial statements or in the notes that supplement them.

Full disclosure does not mean that everything must be disclosed. That would be too costly. A balance must be maintained between the cost of disclosing information and its relevance to users. Basically, if the information will make a difference in investor or creditor decisions, it should be disclosed.

6. The Consistency Principle

Consistency requires that the same generally accepted accounting principles are used period after period for the same accounting events

Accounting information is useful if it can be compared with similar information for the same company through time and with similar information between companies at the same time. But you have seen in the first 11 chapters that there are alternative generally accepted accounting principles for a number of areas — inventories, depreciation, and uncollectibles, for example. For accountants, the consistency principle means that the same accounting method will be applied to accounting events from period to period. If we choose LIFO inventory, we would expect to continue using LIFO year after year. We can't use FIFO in year 2 and average cost in year 3.

Does that mean that a company can never switch to another accounting method? No, companies can and in fact do change accounting methods — but only if they can demonstrate that the new method is preferable to the old one. Of course, if a change is made, the full disclosure principle would require that the nature and effect of the accounting change and the reason for the change must be disclosed in the financial statements when the change is made.

Basic Modifiers

We can't always follow the basic principles blindly. Sometimes practical considerations force us to modify our basic principles. The following are three basic modifiers:

1. Materiality
2. Conservatism
3. Industry practices

Materiality

The concept of materiality is relative — what is material to one company may be immaterial to another

Let's consider a few examples to develop the idea of materiality. In the first one, we'll go back to the Alexmobile Company. The engineering department has recommended — and the idea is accepted — to install an additional part on one of the engine assembly machines. This is not a repair; it's a new part. The cost is $14.11. Now, the cost principle requires us to record the part as an asset and allocate its cost over the 12-year remaining life of the machine. But do you think it's worth the effort to record as an asset the $14.11 and then depreciate it? Of course not. It would probably cost more in accounting effort to capitalize the part than the part is worth.

Also in the Alexmobile Company, at year-end the accounts receivable subsidiary ledger has a balance that is $150,000 greater than the control account. That's pretty big — or is it? We can't tell until we know the size of the accounts receivable. Let's say that the control account has a balance of $1,500,000. So the $150,000 difference is 10% and that's material. But now let's say the general ledger control account is $150,000,000. Now the $150,000 difference is only .1%, and when compared to the $150,000,000 it's small — it's not material.

Materiality is a relative thing. The way accountants apply the materiality principle is to determine whether or not they think the item in question will affect decisions of users of the financial statements. If it does, then it's material and must be reported in accordance with generally accepted accounting principles.

We may sometimes find that while an individual transaction is immaterial, a series of related immaterial transactions are material in the aggregate.

Conservatism

Conservatism to accountants means that when they cannot decide between two alternatives they will select the alternative that will understate net assets and net income

In recording business transactions, we look to GAAP for guidance. We often find several alternative ways we can record the transactions, and we select the alternative that we feel most fairly represents the economic substance of the transaction. That method is preferable, based on our considerable experience and judgment in selecting accounting alternatives.

But there are times when there is no clear-cut alternative. When this happens we will then select the most conservative alternative. By *conservative* we generally mean least likely to overstate net assets and net income. If we are uncertain, it's better to err by understating rather than overstating these items.

Industry Practices

Almost every major industry has some peculiarity about it that requires careful consideration when determining how to report the economic affairs of the companies in that industry in accordance with GAAP. Most often we can reconcile the peculiarity with generally accepted accounting principles. But in some cases we can't, and then we have to rely on what is generally accepted within the industry and work within that as the modifier to GAAP.

Perhaps the best example of an industry practice is found in the meatpacking industry, where market values are used to measure inventories of the various cuts of meat. It's just impossible to allocate the costs of a steer to the various by-products in any meaningful way.

QUESTIONS

1. Why do we need generally accepted accounting principles?

2. How are generally accepted accounting principles enforced?

3. Specifically what does the term *generally accepted accounting principles* mean?

4. What is the *conceptual framework study?*

5. What are the basic objectives of financial statements?

6. "General-purpose financial statements are prepared so that the general public should be able to understand them." Evaluate this statement.

7. The second project of the conceptual framework study is called "Qualitative Characteristics of Accounting Information." What was the purpose of the project? List the qualitative characteristics.

8. The most important characteristic of accounting information is usefulness. How do the other characteristics relate to usefulness?

9. About a dozen generally accepted accounting principles form a structure from which all the other generally accepted accounting principles are derived. Explain this structure.

10. The Buick automobile is a popular domestic automobile, and its manufacture is financed by numerous investors and creditors. But these investors and creditors never see Buick's balance sheet and income statement. Why not?

11. "Financial statements do not precisely measure revenue, expenses, assets, and liabilities." Explain this statement.

12. "Basic accounting principles rest on the basic assumptions of accounting. For example, the cost principle rests upon the going concern concept." Explain.

13. "The stable-dollar concept prohibits companies from providing investors and creditors with important relevant information." Evaluate this statement.

14. Revenue is recognized when the earning process is essentially complete and an exchange has taken place. Generally, this is at the point of sale, but there are three exceptions to this general rule. Why?

15. The matching principle requires that revenue earned in a particular time period be compared with those expenses incurred during the same time period that were directly or indirectly responsible for generating the revenue. Specifically how are expenses recognized?

16. What does the full disclosure principle mean to investors and creditors?

17. "Atlas Company adopted the FIFO method of inventory costing in 1954 when it first started business. The company wishes to switch to the LIFO method this year but can't because it would violate the consistency principle." Evaluate this statement.

18. "Sometimes practical considerations cause the basic principles to be modifed." Explain.

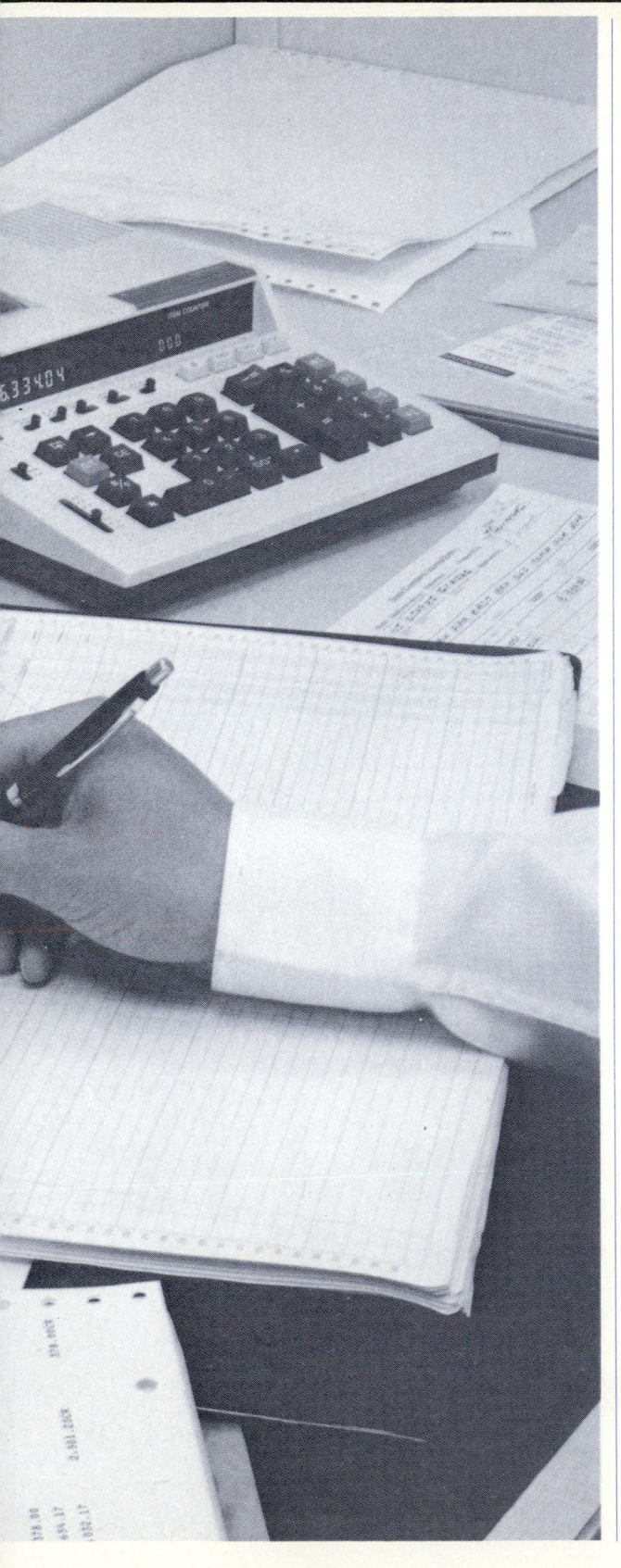

Part Four

Accounting for Partnerships and Corporations

Throughout our study of the first eleven chapters, we have not been overly concerned with the form of business ownership. From Chapter 1 to Chapter 4 we worked with proprietorships. Towards the end of Chapter 4 we introduced the corporate form and from Chapter 5 on we used this form of business organization. But we never really dealt with the owners' equity topic because we had enough to do studying assets and liabilities. In Part Four of *Accounting Principles* it is time to learn about accounting for partnerships and corporations.

The assets, liabilities, revenues, and expenses are accounted for in the same way for each of the three forms of business organization. What you've learned thus far about these items doesn't change. What does change is the way we account for owners' equity. The next three chapters will focus on accounting for the owners' equity of partnerships and corporations. The last two chapters of Part Four will show how to account for corporate long-term liabilities and investments, and how two corporations may be combined into one.

A partnership is a voluntary business association of two or more individuals. The partners must decide how they are going to share profits and losses, what procedures to follow when a new partner enters or an old partner withdraws, and what to do if the partnership is liquidated. You will learn the accounting procedures needed to record these events in the accounting records.

A corporation is an artificial being created by law. Corporations sell common stock and sometimes preferred stock to acquire assets to use in their operations. You will learn the various ways that corporations sell stock, how they borrow money, how they distribute earnings to stockholders as dividends, and how they report the various ownership claims in the Stockholders' Equity section of the balance sheet.

One corporation may buy the stock of another corporation. If it purchases enough stock, it owns the other company. You will learn how to account for these investments and how we may put the financial statements of two corporations together and report them as one business entity.

Chapter 12

Partnerships

We wrote this chapter for you to learn the following things by studying it:

■ The reasons individuals may wish to form partnerships and the characteristics of partnerships

■ Why assets are recorded at their fair value upon partnership formation

■ The various methods of determining how partnership profits and losses are distributed

■ The distinction between admitting a new partner by the purchase of an interest or by an investment, and the accounting treatment required under each method

■ The accounting problems involved in a partnership liquidation

Up to this point we have concentrated on certain limited objectives. First, we introduced the principal financial statements, the income statement, statement of retained earnings, and balance sheet. Next, we discussed the manner in which business transactions are recorded and summarized to generate these financial statements. Following this we considered the basic elements of the financial statements. So far we have studied assets, liabilities, and their related revenues and expenses. Now it's time to complete the study of the basic elements by a discussion of the capital accounts.

Remember that in Chapter 1 we discussed the three main types of business entities: proprietorships, partnerships, and corporations. So far we have not found it necessary to distinguish among these three types of entities. Accounting for assets and liabilities is *not* dependent on the form of a business organization. Consequently, we used proprietorships and very simple corporations in the first 11 chapters. In this chapter we are concerned with a study of the second type of business entity, the partnership. We will complete the study of capital accounts in the following two chapters by discussing the third type of business entity, the corporation.

If three members of your class decide to form together as a group to wash cars for $5 per car, that's a partnership. It's a partnership because the Uniform Partnership Act—which most states have adopted—says it is. The act defines a *partnership* as "an association of two or more persons to carry on, as co-owners, a business for profit." This act governs the formation and operation of partnerships.

You have all come into contact with businesses formed as partnerships. Perhaps your first exposure to a partnership was your visit to your medical doctor and your dentist. If these professionals did not conduct their businesses alone, they conducted them as partnerships. The partnership form of business is common to the professions. So we see public accounting and law firms, as well as medical and dental practices, operated as partnerships. Many small manufacturing, assemblying, wholesale, retail, and service companies are also organized as partnerships.

People join together to form partnerships for a number of reasons. Some of us have more organizational and managerial ability than others. Some of us have more knowledge and experience than others. Some of us have more money than others. A partnership utilizes the combined abilities, experiences, and capital of the partners to make the business stronger than if only one individual owned it. Perhaps the prime reason individuals seek partners is to obtain additional capital.

For the professions, until recently, the corporate form of organization was denied in many states. Since a personal service was rendered, it was felt that the corporate form generated a feeling of impersonality and provided protection against lawsuits for poor quality work. In a corporation only the money invested in the corporation by the stockholders is subject to attack in a lawsuit. That's not true for the partners in a partnership. Not only is the money they invested in the partnership subject to attack, but also their personal and other business assets. Many states have recently enacted legislation allowing professional organizations to incorporate. Even so, the largest of the partnerships, the international certified public accounting firms, have not elected to become corporations. Most of these firms have in excess of 1,500 partners, and several have more than 2,000 partners.

Partnerships will present us with a number of interesting accounting problems, but before we can get you started in partnership accounting, there are a number of things you need to know about partnerships.

PARTNERSHIP CHARACTERISTICS

A partnership is like a proprietorship in that it is not considered to be a separate legal entity. The partners are the individual legal entities. And the characteristics of partnerships all relate to this fact.

Sidebar notes:

Accounting for assets and liabilities does not depend on the form of business organization

A partnership is a voluntary association of individuals to operate a business for profit

Most professional associations are organized as partnerships

Partnerships are formed to utilize the combined abilities, experiences, and capital of the partners

Ease of Formation

It's easy to form a partnership

As we said before, if two or more of us agree to start a business, any business, with the object of earning a profit, we have created a partnership. We don't need to have permission from the county commissioners, nor the IRS, nor the SEC, nor the state attorney general, nor anyone else to form a partnership. We just do it. In fact we don't even need a written contract between the partners. An oral agreement is all that is needed. It's very easy to form a partnership, just do it.

Voluntary Association

Partnerships are voluntary associations of individuals

No one can force us into a partnership. A partnership is a voluntary association. We are legally responsible for the business acts of our partners, and that legal responsibility extends beyond whatever funds we may have invested in the partnership. It extends to our personal and other business assets. So you can see it would be unfair and unreasonable to force us into partnerships with people we don't like or trust. We should *and do* have the right to select those people we wish to associate with in a partnership.

Articles of Partnership

A partner's written agreement is called the articles of partnership

All we need to form a partnership is an oral agreement. But we would be well advised to formalize the partner relationship by a written agreement. This is called the ***articles of partnership.*** Some of the things we would need to include in this document would be:

- The manner in which we share profits or losses
- The amount each of us is to invest
- The amount each of us may withdraw
- How new partners are to be admitted
- How old partners are allowed to withdraw

Mutual Agency

Each partner can act for the partnership. That's mutual agency.

If you do business with a partnership you have a right to assume that the partner you are talking to has the authority to bind the partnership to whatever legal business transaction the two of you are talking about. Unless, of course, you are told or notified otherwise. The partners are all agents for the partnership. That means that each partner can act for the partnership. That's where the term ***mutual agency*** comes from. Here's how this concept works. The city of Bethlehem, Pennsylvania, may enter into an agreement with Mr. Garcia of Weinstein, Garcia, and Trovanivich for an audit of the city's general fund knowing that Mr. Garcia has full authority to bind his CPA firm to a contract. But if the city were to enter into a contract with Mr. Garcia for the sale of sewerage pipes to the city, the city would not expect this to be binding on the CPA firm, since the transaction is not within the scope of an accounting firm's business. (Of course, Mr. Garcia would not enter into the second transaction, since he would not be considered independent in his relationship with the city when performing the audit to fulfill the first contract.)

So you can see that it is very important to select your partners carefully. Mutual agency coupled with unlimited liability could cause you a good deal of grief if you select an irresponsible or unethical partner.

Unlimited Liability

Unlimited liability makes each partner personally responsible for the partnership obligations

Suppose things don't go well for your partnership and you can't pay your bills. What then? Well, your creditors can look to the partnership assets for the settlement of their claims and if the assets aren't enough, what then? Your individual assets—that's what. Creditors can seek satisfaction from the personal assets of the individual partners. This is the ***unlimited liability*** characteristic of a partnership. If the personal assets of some of your partners are exhausted, the creditors can come to you and the remaining partners to settle whatever debts are still unpaid.

Limited Life

A partnership is dissolved whenever a new partner is admitted, a partner withdraws, dies, is incapacitated, or bankrupt. It has a limited life

The life of a partnership is limited. A partnership dissolves when one of the partners withdraws, dies, is forced into personal bankruptcy, or becomes incapacitated. A partnership is also dissolved when the specific objective for which the partnership was formed is achieved. If the articles of partnership specify the life of the partnership to be for a certain period of time, when that time has expired the partnership is dissolved. Of course the partnership may be dissolved by the decision of any one of the partners. The admission of a new partner also dissolves the old partnership.

You should realize that the dissolution of a partnership does not mean that the business operations are interrupted. Large partnerships, such as the regional and national CPA firms and certain law firms, provide in the partnership agreement for the manner in which the admission of new partners and the retirement of old partners is to be handled. You and I are generally unaware of the retirement, withdrawal, or admission of partners to the partnership of these firms.

Co-Ownership of Property

Partnership assets are owned jointly by all the partners

When a partnership is formed, some of you may invest cash, some may invest office equipment or other assets, some may simply invest their talents. But whatever assets are invested become the property of all the partners. The partner contributing the asset no longer retains any personal right to that asset. The assets are jointly owned by all of you so when a partnership is terminated, the individual partners may not receive back the same assets they contributed. Of course, if it is agreeable to all the partners, the assets may be given back to those who contributed them. Often, however, the partners settle their claims against the partnership by the distribution of cash.

Income Participation

Profits and losses are distributed equally unless specified otherwise

It's important that you specify in the articles of partnership how the profits and losses are to be shared between the partners. How this is done is a matter of mutual consent between all the partners. But if you don't have an agreement, profits and losses will be distributed equally.

ADVANTAGES AND DISADVANTAGES

The partnership form of business organization offers a number of advantages

The partnership form of organization may offer you certain advantages over operating by yourself as a proprietorship or even operating with other individuals as owners organized as a corporation. These are some of the advantages:

1. *Capitalization* The amount of money invested by the owners of the business is called its *capitalization.* The more owners, the more capital. This is one of the main reasons you may wish to have a partner—for his or her money, to help finance your business activities.

2. *Talent* The more partners you have, the more talent you have. Of course, that also means more people will share the profits. The advantage of having more talent is that you can utilize the unique skills and abilities of several people. Each of you can specialize in an area of the business that can best use your talents.

3. *Ease of formation* It's so easy for you to form a partnership. You and the other partners just say you are a partnership and you are. That's not the case if you want to operate as a corporation. You must go through a formal legal process to be incorporated.

4. *Cost of organization* The only cost you will have in becoming a partnership is the legal fee to have the articles of partnership drawn up. If you choose not to do this, then you have no costs at all. Becoming a corporation will require cash outlays for the application to the state in which you wish to be incorporated plus legal fees to file the application and preparation of the corporate charter and bylaws.

5. *Tax advantages* Your partnership is not a legal entity. And that means it doesn't have to pay income taxes. You pay income taxes on your personal income including your share of the partnership income. However, certain corporations can elect to be taxed as if they were partnerships. That's called the Subchapter S option, which we will talk about in Chapter 27.

6. *Informality* Corporations require formal legal procedures to do many of the things that you can do as a partnership without such rigidity. For example, in a corporation the distribution of income requires a board of directors' meeting to declare a dividend before payment can be made to the stockholders. In a partnership, you and the other partners may withdraw funds without such legal action.

7. *Less government supervision* Generally partnerships have less government supervision than corporations.

Operating as a partnership has some disadvantages

Organizing as a partnership does have advantages, but it also has a number of disadvantages. They are:

1. *Loss of freedom* You can't run a partnership as you would a proprietorship. As a sole owner of a business you answer to no one. But with a partnership you must answer to your partners, and they to you. You have mutual agency and unlimited liability. This requires mutual agreement on the affairs of the partnership.

2. *Limited life* If one of your partners dies or withdraws, the partnership is dissolved. That does not mean, however, that your business is over. You have most likely provided for this situation in the articles of partnership.

3. *Unlimited liability* Corporations are legal entities and as a result are legally responsible for their actions, but only to the extent of their capitalization. Partnerships are not legal entities, so you and the other partners are legally responsible for your partnership's actions. As you now know, once the partnership assets are used to settle creditors' claims, your personal assets and those personal assets of your partners, may be required to settle any unsatisfied creditors' claims.

4. *Mutual agency* Let's put it this way: A fool is one who has a fool as a partner. You're responsible for his acts, and with unlimited liability if he acts the fool, you pay for it.

5. *Capitalization* If you need large sums of money to operate your business, the corporate form of organization is a much better vehicle for raising what you need. That's because you can sell shares of stock to a *large number of people* who are interested in a good investment for their money but don't want to become involved in the operations of the business.

6. *Tax disadvantages* Depending on your income, it might be that you pay more income taxes organized as a partnership than if you organized as a corporation. Since this is subject to whatever tax laws and tax rates are currently in effect, we can't give any hard-and-fast rule. Each partnership has to look at its own situation.

PARTNERSHIP ACCOUNTING

Accounting for business transactions with external parties for a partnership is the same as we learned for a proprietorship or for that matter for a corporation. Assets, liabilities, revenues, and expenses are all recorded according to the generally accepted accounting principles discussed in the first 11 chapters. It is in the owners' equity section that we see differences.

Partnership accounting requires that we establish a separate capital and a separate withdrawal account for each partner. The manner in which we distribute the net income or loss between the partners is unique for partnerships and differentiates a partnership from a corporation.

In the rest of this chapter we are going to introduce you to the following problems of partnership accounting: partnership formation, income distribution of a partnership, partnership financial statements, partnership dissolution, and partnership liquidation.

Partnership Formation

When a partnership is formed, a journal entry is made to record the assets contributed by each partner and the liabilities of each partner that are assumed by the partnership. If only cash is contributed and no liabilities are assumed, the problem of valuation is simple. The entry we would make to record the formation of a partnership in this situation would be simply to debit cash and credit the two partners' capital accounts like this:

A separate capital account is needed for each partner

Cash	25,000	
Jones, Capital		10,000
Smith, Capital		15,000

To record cash investments by Smith and Jones.

But what if, in addition to cash, other assets are contributed? Then we have a valuation problem. At what value should we record the assets? The original cost? The book value of the assets on the individual partner's books? The fair value today? Some other value?

Our generally accepted accounting principles tell us what to do. Specifically, the historical cost concept would require that assets contributed by individual partners be valued at their fair value on the date they are transferred to the partnership. What constitutes a fair value is, of course, subject to the mutual agreement of the partners.

Assets are valued at their fair values on the day they are contributed to the partnership

Let's look at the firm of Ortiz and Mervine to see how we would account for the formation of a new partnership when cash and other assets are contributed. On July 1 of the current year Mary Ortiz and Bill Mervine agree to combine their competing sporting goods stores and form a partnership. The partners are to contribute the assets of their previous stores. It is agreed that the liabilities of the proprietorships will be assumed by the partnership. A capital account is established for each partner with a credit balance equal to the total assets less the total liabilities contributed by that partner. These are the journal entries to open the accounts of the partnership:

Contribution of cash and other assets in forming a partnership

July 1	Cash	3,500	
	Accounts Receivable	6,200	
	Merchandise Inventory	12,700	
	Store Supplies on Hand	900	
	Accounts Payable		2,400
	Mary Ortiz, Capital		20,900

To record investment of Mary Ortiz.

```
July 1   Cash. . . . . . . . . . . . . . . . . . . . . . . . . . . . . . . . . . . . . . . .    1,700
         Accounts Receivable . . . . . . . . . . . . . . . . . . . . . . . . . . .    7,300
         Merchandise Inventory. . . . . . . . . . . . . . . . . . . . . . . . . .    9,100
         Store Equipment. . . . . . . . . . . . . . . . . . . . . . . . . . . . . . .    6,500
         Building  . . . . . . . . . . . . . . . . . . . . . . . . . . . . . . . . . .   25,200
         Land. . . . . . . . . . . . . . . . . . . . . . . . . . . . . . . . . . . . . .   10,000
             Accounts Payable . . . . . . . . . . . . . . . . . . . . . . . . .                4,500
             Mortgage Payable . . . . . . . . . . . . . . . . . . . . . . . . .               26,200
             Bill Mervine, Capital . . . . . . . . . . . . . . . . . . . . . . .               29,100
         To record investment of Bill Mervine.
```

The values of the assets, other than cash, are the amounts both Mary and Bill agreed upon. The amounts represent the fair values as of July 1 of the store supplies, inventories, equipment, building, and land. The Accounts Receivable balance represents the face amount of only those receivables from the proprietorships that can reasonably be expected to be collected. Accounts that have only a small chance of collectibility are not transferred to the partnership.

The values of the assets other than cash will not agree with the amounts recorded in the books of the two proprietorships. That's because the values have increased (or perhaps decreased) since they were first acquired by Mary or Bill. That's what happened with the land Bill contributed. He paid $8,000 for it 5 years ago. And the building cost him $17,000 to build shortly after he puchased the land. Those were the values recorded on the books of Bill Mervine's Sporting Goods Store. The building has $4,200 of accumulated depreciation recorded also. But the fair value of the building today is $25,200 and that's what goes on the partnership books — not the original cost of $17,000, nor the book value of $12,800 ($17,000 − $4,200) — but the fair value today. Since the building has increased in value over the past 5 years, Bill is the one who should receive the credit for the increase. And he does this by recording the building at $25,200 and crediting his capital account for a similar amount.

Income Distribution of a Partnership

Salaries and interest allowances are a means of equitably distributing partnership profit

You and your partners can distribute your partnership income any way you want. What you will most likely consider is the services performed by each partner, the talent and capital contributed, and perhaps the length of time in the partnership.

You can adjust for differences in time devoted to the business and managerial or technical ability by providing *allowances* for salaries. Partnership salaries are merely a means to distribute partnership profits in an equitable manner; they are not salaries in the legal sense of the word. You and the other partners are owners of the business entity, not employees.

You can adjust for differences in capital contributions by *allowing* interest on the capital balances. Interest allowed in this manner is not interest expense on borrowed funds; it is again a *means to achieve an equitable distribution* of profits.

Most often you will find that partners share earnings (or losses) in one of these three general ways:

1. An established ratio

2. The capital investment relationship

3. Salary and interest allowances, the remainder in an established ratio

Established Ratio

Remember that if the articles of partnership are silent as to the manner of profit distribution, profits and losses are to be distributed equally. Any other ratio must be established by the partnership agreement. Whatever ratio you agree upon is an attempt to adjust for service and capital contributions.

For example, when Mary Ortiz and Bill Mervine formed their sporting goods partnership they agreed to share profits in the ratio of 75% for Ortiz and 25% for Mervine ($\frac{3}{4}$ and $\frac{1}{4}$ or a 3 : 1 ratio). The income for their first one-half year of operation was $8,000. Here is how it was distributed:

Profit distribution by a fixed ratio

	Division of Profit
Mary Ortiz ($8,000 × .75)	$6,000
Bill Mervine ($8,000 × .25)	2,000
Net income	$8,000

The net income of $8,000 appeared as a credit balance in the Expense and Revenue Summary account after the normal closing entries were made. Then the Expense and Revenue Summary account was closed like this:

Recording partnership profit

```
Dec. 31   Expense and Revenue Summary . . . . . . . . . . . . . . . . . . . . . 8,000
                Mary Ortiz, Capital. . . . . . . . . . . . . . . . . . . . . . . . . . .      6,000
                Bill Mervine, Capital. . . . . . . . . . . . . . . . . . . . . . . . . .      2,000
          To close the expense and revenue summary account and distribute
          partnership profits.
```

If Mary or Bill had made any withdrawals during the year, an entry debiting their respective withdrawal accounts would have been made. Then the withdrawal accounts would have been closed to their capital accounts, just like proprietorship accounting.

Capital Investment Relationship

Maybe the reason your partnership makes a profit is closely related to the amount of capital you and your partners have invested. If that's true, you should consider sharing those profits based on the partners' beginning or average capital balances.

The firm of Adams and Hancock share profits that way, let's see how it works. Adams and Hancock have beginning capital account balances of $20,000 and $40,000, respectively. During the year Adams invested an additional $10,000 on April 1 and withdrew $5,000 on October 1. Hancock withdrew $5,000 on July 1 and invested $25,000 additional capital on October 1. Their capital accounts look like this:

Adams, Capital				Hancock, Capital			
Oct. 1	5,000	Bal. Apr. 1	20,000 10,000	July 1	5,000	Bal. Oct. 1	40,000 25,000
		Bal.	25,000			Bal.	60,000

Beginning Ratio   The partnership earned $21,000 this year and if profits were to be divided according to the beginning capital account relationship, Adams would get one-third. That's because his beginning capital ($20,000) is one-third of the total beginning capital ($20,000 + $40,000). Hancock would then receive two-thirds ($40,000 ÷ $60,000). The journal entry the firm would have to make to record the profits would be:

<table>
<tr><td>Dec. 31</td><td>Expense and Revenue Summary . . . .</td><td>21,000</td><td></td></tr>
<tr><td></td><td>   Adams, Capital. . . . .</td><td></td><td>7,000</td></tr>
<tr><td></td><td>   Hancock, Capital . . . .</td><td></td><td>14,000</td></tr>
<tr><td></td><td>To close the expense and revenue summary account and to distribute profits.</td><td></td><td></td></tr>
</table>

Profit distribution based on beginning capital account ratios

Average Capital Balances Ratio   But Adams and Hancock elected not to distribute their profits based on the beginning capital account ratio. Instead they chose to use the *average* capital balance ratio. That's because they think it is more equitable since they make material investments and withdrawals during the year. The calculation of the average capital balance is a little more complex than one may think at first glance. Adding the beginning and ending balances and dividing by 2 will not properly state the average capital balance. We can show you this by a simple example.

Tom and Jane are partners. On January 1 Tom has a zero balance in his capital account while Jane has $10. Eleven months go by with no change. Then on December 1 Tom invests $10 and Jane withdraws $10. So at year-end, December 31, Tom has a $10 balance in his capital account and Jane has zero. When we add the beginning and ending balances for both Tom and Jane and divide each by 2, the result is a $5 average for each of them. But Jane had her $10 invested for 11 months of the year while Tom had $10 invested for only 1 month. The point is that we must consider the length of time that capital is invested in the partnership.

The way we consider time is by calculating something called *dollar-months.* Dollar-months is the result obtained by multiplying the dollar investment by the length of time those dollars are invested. That's the way Adams and Hancock did it. Adams had $20,000 invested from January 1 to April 1; then he invested an additional $10,000, bringing his capital balance to $30,000. On October 1 he withdrew $5,000, reducing his account to $25,000. His total dollar-months were determined by this calculation:

Calculation of a partner's total dollar-months, which is divided by 12 to determine the average capital balance

Dollars	Months	Dollar-Months
$20,000	3	$ 60,000
30,000	6	180,000
25,000	3	75,000
Total		$315,000

Average capital balance = $315,000 ÷ 12 months = $26,250

The $20,000 invested from January 1 to April 1 (3 months) is equivalent to $60,000 dollar-months ($20,000 × 3). From April 1 to October 1 (6 months) he had $30,000 invested, equivalent to $180,000 dollar-months ($30,000 × 6). And during the last 3 months (October 1 to December 31) he had $25,000 invested or $75,000 dollar-months ($25,000 × 3).

Adams' average capital balance for the year was determined by dividing his total $315,000 dollar-months by the 12 months of the year—$26,250.

For Hancock the total dollar-months were:

Dollar-months calculation for the second partner

Dollars	Months	Dollar-Months
$40,000	6	$240,000
35,000	3	105,000
60,000	3	180,000
Total		$525,000

Average capital balance = $525,000 ÷ 12 months = $43,750

His beginning balance of $40,000 remained in the partnership for 6 months (January 1 to July 1), resulting in $240,000 dollar-months. Then on July 1 he withdrew $5,000, reducing his capital balance to $35,000 until October 1. This was another $105,000 dollar-months ($35,000 × 3), and finally, on October 1 he invested $25,000, bringing his capital balance up to $60,000 for the last 3 months of the year—that meant still another $180,000 dollar-months ($60,000 × 3). So his average capital balance was $43,750—the total $525,000 dollar-months divided by 12 months.

The firm's profits of $21,000 were distributed to Adams and Hancock based on the ratio of their average capital balances. Adams' portion of the $70,000 total average capital balance ($26,250 + $43,750) was 37.5% ($26,250 ÷ $70,000) and Hancock's was 62.5% ($43,750 ÷ $70,000). So Adams got $7,875 ($21,000 × .375) and Hancock $13,125 ($21,000 × .625) which was distributed to the partners by this entry:

Profit distribution based on average capital balances

```
Dec. 31   Expense and Revenue Summary ................... 21,000
               Adams, Capital.............................        7,875
               Hancock, Capital .........................       13,125
           To close the expense and revenue summary account and distrib-
           ute profits.
```

Allowance for Salaries and Interest

The differences in partner's capital, time, and talent can be compensated for by allowing for salaries and interest in the partnership distribution agreement

Perhaps your partnership has partners who contribute different things. Joe may provide the money you need to start up. You are going to spend all your waking hours on the partnership business, and Melissa is the smart one. We can set up an arrangement to compensate each of you fairly for your unique contribution. We can give credit for salaries to you and Melissa for your time and her talent. And we can give credit to Joe for interest on his money. Remember, you and Melissa are not being paid salaries, nor is Joe being paid interest. This is just a way of distributing profits (hopefully there are some) to each of you in an equitable manner. Any profits left over after allowing for salaries and interest are to be distributed to the three of you equally because we have already adjusted for differences in your capital, time, and talents.

Let's look at the partnership of Tinker, Chance, and Evans to see how this arrangement works. The partnership earned $100,000 this year. Tinker devotes full time to the partnership affairs and is allowed a salary of $22,000 for his managerial ability. Chance spends only 30 hours per week in the business and is therefore given credit for only $15,000 of salary. Evans also spends 30 hours per week in the business, but it's his technical know-how that makes the partnership go. He is given credit for a salary of $25,000. Interest of 10% is allowed on the partners' beginning capital balances—

$40,000, $50,000, and $20,000, respectively—and the remaining profits are split equally. Here is how the $100,000 partnership net income is distributed:

Calculation of profit distribution allowing for interest and salaries

TINKER, CHANCE, and EVANS
Income Distribution Schedule
Year Ended December 31, 1987

Allowance	Tinker	Chance	Evans	Totals
Interest	$ 4,000	$ 5,000	$ 2,000	$ 11,000
Salary	22,000	15,000	25,000	62,000
Totals	$26,000	$20,000	$27,000	$ 73,000
Remainder	9,000	9,000	9,000	27,000
Net income	$35,000	$29,000	$36,000	$100,000

After the credit of $11,000 is allowed for interest and the $62,000 for salaries, a balance of $27,000 ($100,000 − $11,000 − $62,000) remains to be distributed equally to the three partners ($9,000 each).

The general journal entry to record the profit distribution would look like this:

Profit distribution based on allowances for interest and salaries

Dec. 31	Expense and Revenue Summary.	100,000	
	Tinker, Capital		35,000
	Chance, Capital.		29,000
	Evans, Capital.		36,000
	To close the expense and revenue summary account and distribute partnership profits.		

Don't forget that interest and salaries *have not* been paid to the partners. The allowances for interest and salaries are only a means of determining how the net income for the period should be distributed.

What happens if the interest and salary allowances exceed net income? It doesn't matter; the income distribution is done the same way. Let's say that in 1988 Tinker, Chance, and Evans had a partnership income of $46,000 and it is distributed as follows:

Calculation of profit distribution when interest and salary allowances exceed net income

TINKER, CHANCE, and EVANS
Income Distribution Schedule
Year Ended December 31, 1988

Allowance	Tinker	Chance	Evans	Totals
Interest	$ 4,000	$ 5,000	$ 2,000	$11,000
Salary	22,000	15,000	25,000	62,000
Totals	$26,000	$20,000	$27,000	$73,000
Remainder	(9,000)	(9,000)	(9,000)	(27,000)
Net income	$17,000	$11,000	$18,000	$46,000

Notice that the total allowances for interest and salaries exceeds net income by $27,000 ($73,000 − $46,000) and that this negative excess is distributed equally to the individual partners in the same manner as the positive excess was last year. The result is a reduction of $9,000 for each partner after allowing for interest and salary. The profit distribution journal entry would be:

<table>
<tr><td>Dec. 31</td><td>Expense and Revenue Summary . . . .</td><td>46,000</td><td></td></tr>
<tr><td></td><td>Tinker, Capital . . . .</td><td></td><td>17,000</td></tr>
<tr><td></td><td>Chance, Capital . . . .</td><td></td><td>11,000</td></tr>
<tr><td></td><td>Evans, Capital . . . .</td><td></td><td>18,000</td></tr>
<tr><td></td><td>To close the expense and revenue summary account and distribute partnership profits.</td><td></td><td></td></tr>
</table>

Profit distribution based on allowances for interest and salaries which exceed net income

Partnership Financial Statements

The financial statements of a partnership and a proprietorship are similar. The income statements are identical in format except that on the partnership income statement the income distribution may be presented on the bottom portion of the statement. This is shown for the Tinker, Chance, and Evans partnership like this:

The income distribution may be shown on a partnership income statement

TINKER, CHANCE, AND EVANS
Income Statement
Year Ended December 31, 1987

Sales		$787,000
Less: Sales Discounts	$11,400	

〰〰〰〰〰〰〰〰〰〰〰〰〰〰〰〰〰〰〰〰〰〰〰〰〰〰〰〰

Net Income		$100,000
Income Distribution:		
Tinker	$35,000	
Chance.	29,000	
Evans.	36,000	$100,000

We are also going to need a statement of partners' capital accounts. This statement provides the partners with summarized information that shows the increases and decreases in their respective capital accounts during the year as well as the beginning and ending balances. It looks like this:

The statement of partners' capital accounts shows the investment, income distributions, and withdrawals of each partner

TINKER, CHANCE, AND EVANS
Statement of Partners' Capital Accounts
Year Ended December 31, 1987

	Tinker	Chance	Evans	Totals
Capital, Jan. 1, 1987	$ 40,000	$50,000	$20,000	$110,000
Add: Investments	60,000			60,000
Net Income	35,000	29,000	36,000	100,000
	$135,000	$79,000	$56,000	$270,000
Less: Withdrawals	22,000	18,000	27,000	67,000
Capital, Dec. 31, 1987	$113,000	$61,000	$29,000	$203,000

The balance sheet of a partnership differs from that of a proprietorship only in the capital section. A partnership with few partners will have a capital account for each partner reflecting the partner's ending capital balance. But one with many partners will show only one account — Partners' Capital — which is the total of all the individual partners' accounts.

Partnership Dissolution

A partnership may dissolve but the business may continue

One of the partnership characteristics we discussed earlier was that a partnership is dissolved whenever a new partner is admitted or an old partner withdraws. Either way the *business* can continue, but the *partnership* is dissolved. It is the legal arrangement between the partners that ceases to exist, not the business. When the partnership is dissolved, new articles of partnership should be prepared, or the original articles of partnership should contain provisions for the admission of new partners or the withdrawal of old partners. Both of these possibilities require special accounting treatment, which we are now going to tell you about.

Admission of a New Partner

You could admit a new partner to your partnership in one of two ways. The new partner could either **purchase an interest** from one or more of the old partners, or the new partner could **invest in the partnership.** Of course, the admission of a new partner is contingent upon your consent as well as the consent of all of the other partners.

Purchase of an Interest

If one of your partners sells his interest in the partnership to someone, and that person is accepted by all the remaining partners, the transaction is a private one between the retiring partner and the new partner. It is called a **purchase of an interest.** The amount paid to the retiring partner does not affect your capital account or that of the other partners. The transaction is shown on the partnership's books by transferring the retiring partner's capital account to the new partner. Let's see how this works.

Assume that the partnership of Donnis, Edwards, and Findley is dissolved when Donnis sells his interest in the partnership to Gillete. Both Edwards and Findley agree to accept Gillete as a partner. Just before the dissolution, the partners had these capital balances:

Donnis	Edwards	Findley	Total
$10,000	$30,000	$20,000	$60,000

The partnership has been very successful, and all indications are that it will continue to be so. Gillete has evaluated the partnership very carefully and considers Donnis' asking price of $14,000 for his interest in the partnership to be reasonable. Gillete pays Donnis $14,000 and is admitted to the partnership of Edwards, Findley, and Gillete. Here is how we would record the admission of Gillete by a purchase of an interest:

Admission of a new partner by purchase of an interest from a retiring partner

Donnis, Capital 10,000
    Gillete, Capital. 10,000
To record admission of Gillete by a transfer of Donnis' capital.

An important point is that the price paid for the partnership interest, $14,000, is not recorded. That is a private transaction between Donnis and Gillete. The cash is paid by Gillete to Donnis and is not entered in the partnership records. Edwards and Findley may never know the amount Donnis received.

Let's change the example. This time let's assume that rather than buying an interest from Donnis, Gillete gains admission by the purchase of a 20% interest from each partner. Gillete would pay the three partners whatever price they individually negotiated with him. And his admission would be like this:

Admission of a new partner by purchase of a 20% interest from each of the old partners

Donnis, Capital	2,000	
Edwards, Capital	6,000	
Findley, Capital	4,000	
Gillete, Capital		12,000

To record admission of Gillete by a transfer of a 20% interest of each partner.

Again, the price that Gillete paid to the individual partners is not recorded. What is recorded is a reduction of each of the old partners' capital by 20%, and Gillete's capital is established for the sum of the three debits.

Investment in the Partnership

You could admit a new partner by requiring an investment of assets. If assets other than cash are to be invested, everyone must agree on their values. This time assets are invested directly into the partnership and not given to the individual partners. The investment will increase the partnership's total assets and as a result the total owners' equity. Let's look again at the partnership of Donnis, Edwards, and Findley. They agree to accept Gillete to a 25% interest in the partnership with the investment of $20,000 cash. After the investment, total assets will have increased by $20,000, as will partners' equity. Specifically, the partners' equity will equal $80,000, consisting of the following:

Total partners' equity after a $20,000 investment of cash by a new partner

Donnis, Capital	$10,000
Edwards, Capital	30,000
Findley, Capital	20,000
Investment by Gillete	20,000
Total	$80,000

Since Gillete is to receive a 25% interest of the $80,000, his capital account will be established for $20,000 ($80,000 × .25), the amount of his investment. Gillete's admission would be recorded in the general journal as follows:

Admission of a partner by an investment

Cash	20,000	
Gillete, Capital		20,000

To record admission of Gillete to a 25% interest in the firm.

Once Gillete is admitted, new articles of partnership will be prepared specifying how profits and losses are to be shared. While Gillete has a 25% interest in the net assets of the partnership, it does not necessarily follow that he shall receive 25% of all profits and losses. His share of profits and losses will be established by the new articles of partnership.

SURVIVAL OF THE FITTEST

While there are many types of partnerships in the United States, CPA and law firms are the most numerous. They generally have the most employees and the most partners. Every year thousands of accounting and law graduates enter their profession's most prestigious firms. And 8 to 10 years later only a few remain and are admitted to partnership. Writing in the January 3, 1983, Wall Street Journal, Barbara Rosen points out that "making partner at a top New York law firm isn't easy. Not making it is tougher."

For those prestigious New York law firms partnership consideration comes up about seven years after graduation. For CPA firms it's a little longer. Data from Columbia University shows that of 246 lawyers entering 10 New York law firms in 1972 only 33 be-

came partners. What happened to the rest? Well most leave before seven years. Many entry level accountants and lawyers view the prestigious firms as a necessary training ground for their careers. They receive excellent training and exposure. This in turn provides them with many lucrative and challenging employment opportunities with their firm's clients. A number of individuals leave to set up their own CPA or law firms. And some stay, aspiring to partnership.

Still, of those remaining only a few will make partner. Technical ability is *not* the reason for rejection. These are all highly intelligent, highly motivated people, all top students in their graduating class. Further, if a staff member did not demonstrate technical ability they would have been dismissed

many years before. So what determines who is in and who is out?

Several factors could be the answer. Perhaps it's leadership ability, perhaps the ability to get along with colleagues, perhaps the ability to attract new clients. Or perhaps too many talented people are up for partnership at the same time. It could also be that bad economic times resulted in a poor financial year for the firm. Whatever the reason, for those rejected it is most likely the first time they have experienced failure and it is most certainly a situation for which coping is most difficult.

Source: The Wall Street Journal, January 3, 1983, page 1.

Not everyone who enters a CPA or law firm will become a partner.

A bonus may be the price of admission to a partnership

Investment with Bonus to Old Partners Sometimes a new partner must pay a premium for admission into an existing partnership. When Gillete purchased a 25% interest in the Donnis, Edwards, Findley partnership for $20,000, he got what he paid for (25% of the total capital of $80,000 equals $20,000), and the capital accounts of the old partners remained unchanged. But why charge a premium? That's the charge for the privilege of participating in the profits of a successful partnership. We call it a *bonus* and it's shared by the old partners—in their old profit-and-loss ratio—because they made the partnership successful.

Let's change our example and assume that Gillete's $20,000 bought him a 20% interest in the partnership, instead of a 25% interest. Also we need to know how Donnis, Edwards, and Findley shared profits—it was 25%, 25%, and 50%.

Gillete will receive credit in his capital account for 20% ($16,000) of the total net assets of the new partnership, which amounts to $80,000. The $80,000 is the sum of the three old partners' capital accounts and the $20,000 cash invested by Gillete.

Total net partnership assets after investment by new partner

Net assets prior to admission of Gillete (equal to the sum of the capital accounts of Donnis, $10,000; Edwards, $30,000; and Findley, $20,000)	$60,000
Cash invested by Gillete	20,000
Net assets after admission of Gillete	$80,000
Gillete's equity of 20% ($80,000 × .20)	$16,000

The bonus is the difference between the cash Gillete invested and the credit he is allowed in his capital account. It is $4,000 ($20,000 − $16,000). It is allocated to the old partners in their old profit-and-loss ratio like this:

Donnis ($4,000 × .25)...	$1,000
Edwards ($4,000 × .25)...	1,000
Findley ($4,000 × .50)...	2,000
Total..	$4,000

Admission of new partner by investment, bonus to old partners

We record Gillete's admission by this general journal entry:

Cash	20,000	
Donnis, Capital		1,000
Edwards, Capital		1,000
Findley, Capital		2,000
Gillete, Capital		16,000
To record admission of Gillete to a 20% interest in the firm.		

Investment with Goodwill Recorded for Old Partners   Gillete may object to the recording of his $20,000 cash investment as only a $16,000 credit to his capital account. What he would like is to invest $20,000 and receive a $20,000 credit in his capital account. We can do this by recording ***goodwill*** instead of the bonus. Goodwill is an intangible asset. It is a measure of the value of the successful partnership. It is an objective measure because Gillete is willing to pay $20,000 for a 20% interest, which means that the value of the partnership must be $100,000, determined as follows:

Determining the value of a partnership

$$.20X = \$20,000$$
$$X = \$100,000$$

But the total recorded net assets after Gillete's $20,000 investment was $80,000, which is $20,000 less than the $100,000 value we just calculated. The $20,000 must be the value of an asset that has not been recorded. That asset is goodwill. The goodwill is a result of the successful efforts of the old partners, and we have to record this goodwill before we admit Gillete. The goodwill is allocated to the old partners in their old profit-and-loss ratio like this:

Recording partnership goodwill

Goodwill	20,000	
Donnis, Capital ($20,000 × .25)		5,000
Edwards, Capital ($20,000 × .25).....................		5,000
Findley, Capital ($20,000 × .50)		10,000
To record goodwill based on value determined by admission of Gillete.		

Admission of a partner by an investment after goodwill is recorded

Gillete is now admitted by an entry that records his capital account equal to his investment:

Cash	20,000	
Gillete, Capital		20,000
To record the admission of Gillete to the firm.		

Investment with Bonus to New Partner   But what if the old partnership wasn't very successful and they need Gillete's managerial ability or his capital? Now Donnis, Edwards, and Findley are willing to give Gillete a premium to join their firm. The premium, a bonus, would be charged to each of the old partners in their old profit-and-loss ratio. Let's change the example once more to show how we account for a bonus for the new partner. This time Gillete is admitted to the partnership by investing $20,000 in cash and receiving a 30% interest.

We can determine the amount to be credited to Gillete's capital account and the allocation of the bonus against the old partners by the following calculation:

Net assets prior to admission of Gillete	$60,000
Cash invested by Gillete	20,000
Net assets after admission of Gillete	$80,000
Gillete's equity of 30% ($80,000 × .30)	$24,000

The $4,000 ($24,000 − $20,000) bonus to Gillete is allocated to the old partners according to the old partnership profit-and-loss ratio of 25%, 25%, 50%. So Donnis and Edwards each will be charged $1,000 ($4,000 × .25) and Findley will be charged $2,000 ($4,000 × .50). Here is the entry to record Gillete's admission:

Admission of new partner by purchase of an interest, bonus to new partner		
Cash	20,000	
Donnis, Capital	1,000	
Edwards, Capital	1,000	
Findley, Capital	2,000	
Gillete, Capital		24,000
To record admission of Gillete to a 30% interest in the firm.		

Investment with Goodwill Recorded for New Partner   Now it's the old partners who may not wish to have their capital accounts reduced as a result of Gillete's admission. If it is agreeable to everybody, goodwill may be recorded. This time it's Gillete who is responsible for the goodwill, and we compute its value by starting with the $60,000 net assets of the partnership prior to Gillete's admission. Since the capital accounts are not going to change after Gillete invests $20,000, it follows that the old partners will have 70% (Gillete will have 30%) of the total net assets. So we can determine the total net assets by stating that 70% of the total net assets must equal $60,000:

Determination of net assets after admission of new partner who brings in goodwill

$$.70X = \$60,000$$

$$X = \$85,714 \qquad \text{Total net assets}$$

and the amount of goodwill is computed like this:

Determination of goodwill brought in by new partner

Total net assets		$85,714
Net assets prior to Gillete's admission	$60,000	
Investment by Gillete	20,000	
Tangible net assets		80,000
Goodwill		$ 5,714

Gillete's admission is then recorded by this journal entry:

Admission of new partner bringing in goodwill

```
Cash .......................................  20,000
Goodwill ...................................   5,714
    Gillete, Capital. ...................................      25,714
To record the admission of Gillete to a 30% interest in the firm.
```

Withdrawal of a Partner

Something you want to be sure to do if you withdraw from a partnership is to have the accounting records audited and the partnership assets revalued. Why? Well, when you withdraw you will remove assets—most likely cash—from the partnership equal to the balance in your capital account. So you want your capital account to reflect what those assets are worth today, not 5 years ago when you were admitted to the partnership. You helped make the partnership what it is today, and you should share in the increase in value.

To show you how this works, consider the partnership of Tom, Dick, and Harry, who share profits 40%, 40%, and 20% (2:2:1). The partners have the following balances in their capital accounts: $25,000, $20,000, and $30,000. On July 1, Dick plans to withdraw from the partnership. Prior to the withdrawal an audit is performed and the assets are revalued at their fair values. This results in a $10,000 increase in the value of land and a writedown of inventory amounting to $4,000. The adjustment is recorded by this general journal entry:

Revaluing the partnership assets

```
Land ....................................... 10,000
    Inventory .......................................        4,000
    Tom, Capital (⅖ × $6,000) ............................        2,400
    Dick, Capital (⅖ × $6,000) ...........................        2,400
    Harry, Capital (⅕ × $6,000)  .........................        1,200
To record the revaluation of land and inventory.
```

Now Dick's capital account has a balance of $22,400 ($20,000 + $2,400) and his withdrawal is recorded like this:

Withdrawal of a partner

```
Dick, Capital. ................................... 22,400
    Cash (or other assets) ...........................       22,400
To record the withdrawal of Dick.
```

Notice in the entry that Dick may take cash or any other assets mutually agreeable that equal $22,400.

Partnership Liquidation

Remember that the dissolution of a partnership does not mean the business is terminated. When that happens, it is called a *liquidation* and the partnership assets are distributed to the creditors and the individual partners. A liquidation may be a voluntary agreement by the partners, or it may be the result of legal action initiated by the partnership creditors.

A dissolution is the end of a partnership. A liquidation is the end of a partnership's business

Whether voluntary or involuntary, the liquidation typically has three phases. First we sell the assets; then we pay the creditors; and finally we distribute cash to the partners. Usually we can't sell all the assets at one time. We sell them over an extended period of time. As cash becomes available, creditors are paid and we can make some distribution of cash to the partners. We call this a *liquidation by installments* and it is beyond the scope of our text. What we will do is to consider the liquidation as being accomplished all in one period of time.

Let's start with the partnership of Alice, Betty, and Carol. Their partnership agreement calls for profits and losses to be shared in a 2:2:1 ratio. On the date of the liquidation the partnership balance sheet looks like this:

ALICE, BETTY, AND CAROL
Balance Sheet
July 15, 1987

Assets	Liabilities and Owners' Equity
Cash. $10,000	Accounts Payable $20,000
Other Assets. 60,000	Alice, Capital 5,000
	Betty, Capital 20,000
	Carol, Capital. 25,000
	Total Liabilities and Owners'
Total Assets $70,000	Equity. $70,000

Gain on Sale of Partnership Assets

If we can sell the partnership assets for $75,000, we'll have a gain of $15,000 ($75,000 − $60,000). We then distribute the gain to the partners in their agreed profit-and-loss ratio of 2:2:1 or $6,000 each to Alice and Betty, and $3,000 to Carol. We record the sale of the assets and the distribution of the gain in this general journal entry:

Distribution of a gain on the sale of partnership assets

Cash	75,000	
Other Assets		60,000
Alice, Capital.		6,000
Betty, Capital		6,000
Carol, Capital		3,000

To record the sale of other assets and the distribution of the resulting gain in the profit-and-loss ratio.

Next we pay the creditors the $20,000 owed to them:

Payment of partnership creditors

Accounts Payable.	20,000	
Cash		20,000

To record the payment of Accounts Payable.

The partnership now has a $65,000 cash balance ($10,000 + $75,000 − $20,000), no other assets, and no liabilities. We now distribute the cash to the partners in accordance with their *respective capital balances.* So Alice will get $11,000 ($5,000 + $6,000); Betty, $26,000 ($20,000 + $6,000); and Carol, $28,000 ($25,000 + $3,000). The final distribution is *not* determined by the profit-and-loss ratio, but by the balances in the respective capital accounts at that time. We record the distribution of the $65,000 cash to the individual partners this way:

Distribution of cash to the partners

Alice, Capital.	11,000	
Betty, Capital	26,000	
Carol, Capital	28,000	
Cash		65,000

To record the distribution of cash to the individual partners.

We find it very useful to use a partnership liquidation schedule to summarize the liquidation process. The schedule works like the transaction analysis worksheet you used in Chapter 1. Each transaction is recorded on a single line and the appropriate accounts are either increased or decreased. This way we always know the balance in each account. Just like the transaction analysis worksheet, the liquidation schedule should balance after each transaction. Since we have a running record of each account, we will know how much is in each capital account after the assets are sold and the creditors are paid. And the total of the capital accounts must equal the cash balance, because that's all that's left. When the cash is distributed to the partners according to their capital balances, all accounts will have a zero balance.

A partnership liquidation schedule summarizes the liquidation process.

ALICE, BETTY, AND CAROL
Partnership Liquidation Schedule
July 15, 1987

	Cash	+	Other Assets	=	Accounts Payable	+	Alice, Capital	+	Betty, Capital	+	Carol, Capital
	$10,000		$60,000		$20,000		$ 5,000		$20,000		$25,000
Sale of assets for gain	75,000		(60,000)				6,000		6,000		3,000
	$85,000		–0–		$20,000		$11,000		$26,000		$28,000
Payment of liabilities	(20,000)				(20,000)						
	$65,000		–0–		–0–		$11,000		$26,000		$28,000
Cash distribution	(65,000)						(11,000)		(26,000)		(28,000)
	–0–		–0–		–0–		–0–		–0–		–0–

Loss on Sale of Partnership Assets: Capital Accounts Sufficient to Absorb Loss

It may be that we will have to sell the partnership assets at a loss. If the individual partners' capital accounts are sufficient to absorb the loss, we go through the procedures just like we did in the last example. To show you this, let's assume that the assets of the Alice, Betty, and Carol partnership are sold for $50,000 rather than $75,000. We would recognize a loss of $10,000 ($60,000 − $50,000) and distribute it $4,000 ($10,000 × .40) to Alice, $4,000 ($10,000 × .40) to Betty, and $2,000 ($10,000 × .20) to Carol. The $20,000 of Accounts Payable would be paid and the remaining $40,000 cash ($10,000 + $50,000 − $20,000) distributed in accordance with the balances in the capital accounts: $1,000 for Alice ($5,000 − $4,000), $16,000 for Betty ($20,000 − $4,000), and $23,000 for Carol ($25,000 − $2,000). Here is the partnership liquidation schedule summarizing the sale of the partnership assets at a loss:

Liquidation schedule where assets are sold at a loss.

ALICE, BETTY, AND CAROL
Partnership Liquidation Schedule
July 15, 1987

	Cash	+	Other Assets	=	Accounts Payable	+	Alice, Capital	+	Betty, Capital	+	Carol, Capital
	$10,000		$60,000		$20,000		$5,000		$20,000		$25,000
Sale of assets for loss	50,000		(60,000)				(4,000)		(4,000)		(2,000)
	$60,000		–0–		$20,000		$1,000		$16,000		$23,000
Payment of liabilities	(20,000)				(20,000)						
	$40,000		–0–		–0–		$1,000		$16,000		$23,000
Cash distribution	(40,000)						(1,000)		(16,000)		(23,000)
	–0–		–0–		–0–		–0–		–0–		–0–

The general journal entries to record the three phases of the liquidation are made like this:

Journal entries for a partnership liquidation where the assets are sold at a loss

Cash	50,000	
Alice, Capital.	4,000	
Betty, Capital	4,000	
Carol, Capital	2,000	
Other Assets		60,000

To record sale of other assets.

Accounts Payable.	20,000	
Cash		20,000

To record payment of Accounts Payable.

Alice, Capital.	1,000	
Betty, Capital	16,000	
Carol, Capital	23,000	
Cash		40,000

To record distribution of cash to partners upon liquidation of partnership.

Sometimes when the partnership assets are sold for a loss, one or more of the partner's capital accounts may end up with a debit balance. If that happens, and the partner with a debit balance in her capital account cannot provide personal assets to the partnership to eliminate the deficit, the remaining partners must absorb the deficit between them in their *remaining profit-and-loss ratio.*

Now what does all this mean? Let's go back to our example and this time sell the assets for only $40,000. This time a $20,000 loss ($60,000 − $40,000) must be absorbed — $8,000 by Alice ($20,000 × .40), $8,000 by Betty ($20,000 × .40), and $4,000 by Carol ($20,000 × .20). Alice ends up with a $3,000 deficit ($5,000 − $8,000), which must be absorbed by Betty and Carol in their remaining profit-and-loss ratio, 40% for Betty and 20% for Carol or 2 : 1. So Betty will pick up another $2,000 loss ($3,000 × ⅔), and Carol will absorb $1,000 ($3,000 × ⅓). That leaves Betty with a $10,000 credit in her capital account ($20,000 − $8,000 − $2,000) and Carol with $20,000 ($25,000 − $4,000 − $1,000), all of which is summarized in this partnership liquidation schedule:

Liquidation schedule where assets are sold at a loss and a partner's deficit must be absorbed.

	Cash	+	Other Assets	=	Accounts Payable	+	Alice, Capital	+	Betty, Capital	+	Carol, Capital
	$10,000		$60,000		$20,000		$ 5,000		$20,000		$25,000
Sale of assets for loss	40,000		(60,000)				(8,000)		(8,000)		(4,000)
	$50,000		–0–		$20,000		$(3,000)		$12,000		$21,000
Payment of liabilities	(20,000)				(20,000)						
	$30,000		–0–		–0–		$(3,000)		$12,000		$21,000
Deficit absorbed							3,000		(2,000)		(1,000)
	$30,000		–0–		–0–		–0–		$10,000		$20,000
Cash distribution	(30,000)								(10,000)		(20,000)
	–0–		–0–		–0–		–0–		–0–		–0–

ALICE, BETTY, AND CAROL
Partnership Liquidation Schedule
July 15, 1987

Here are the general journal entries to record this liquidation:

```
Cash . . . . . . . . . . . . . . . . . . . . . . . . . . . . . . . . . . . . . . . . .   40,000
Alice, Capital. . . . . . . . . . . . . . . . . . . . . . . . . . . . . . . . . . .    8,000
Betty, Capital . . . . . . . . . . . . . . . . . . . . . . . . . . . . . . . . . . .    8,000
Carol, Capital . . . . . . . . . . . . . . . . . . . . . . . . . . . . . . . . . . .    4,000
    Other Assets . . . . . . . . . . . . . . . . . . . . . . . . . . . . . . . . .             60,000
To record sale of partnership assets.


Accounts Payable. . . . . . . . . . . . . . . . . . . . . . . . . . . . . . .   20,000
    Cash . . . . . . . . . . . . . . . . . . . . . . . . . . . . . . . . . . . . . . .             20,000
To record payment of partnership liabilities.


Betty, Capital . . . . . . . . . . . . . . . . . . . . . . . . . . . . . . . . . .    2,000
Carol, Capital . . . . . . . . . . . . . . . . . . . . . . . . . . . . . . . . . . .    1,000
    Alice, Capital. . . . . . . . . . . . . . . . . . . . . . . . . . . . . . . . .              3,000
To record absorption of deficit in Alice's capital account by Betty and
Carol.


Betty, Capital . . . . . . . . . . . . . . . . . . . . . . . . . . . . . . . . . .   10,000
Carol, Capital . . . . . . . . . . . . . . . . . . . . . . . . . . . . . . . . . .   20,000
    Cash . . . . . . . . . . . . . . . . . . . . . . . . . . . . . . . . . . . . . . .             30,000
To record distribution of cash to Betty and Carol in accordance with
capital balances upon partnership liquidation.
```

CHAPTER SUMMARY

Our discussion of the principles of accounting has reached a point where it is essential that the three major types of business entities be distinguished. A study of the capital accounts cannot be undertaken without understanding the differences between proprietorships, partnerships, and corporations.

Partnerships, the subject of this chapter, are defined as "an association of two or more persons to carry on, as co-owners, a business for profit." They are a very common form of business organization for the professions, that is, law, medicine, and accounting. Small business entities in the wholesale and retail trades as well as in manufacturing also use the partnership form of organization.

A major reason for an individual businessperson to seek a partner is to obtain additional capital. Individuals also find it advantageous to combine their experience, knowledge, organizational, and managerial abilities.

When choosing the appropriate form of business organization, whether to incorporate or to be a partnership, individuals must consider the characteristics of each form and the advantages and disadvantages resulting from these characteristics. Advantages of the partnership are: the ability to generate more capital than proprietorships, the combination of talents, the ease of formation, the low cost of organizing, certain tax advantages, its informality, and relatively less government regulation than corporations.

The disadvantages of partnerships are: the loss of freedom of action, its limited life, its unlimited liability to the partners, the fact that each partner is a mutual agent for all other partners, the limited amount of capital that can be raised comparative to a corporation, and certain tax disadvantages.

The problems relating to partnership accounting can be organized into the following areas: formation, income distribution, dissolution, and liquidation. Problems of asset and liability measurement and disclosure are not dependent on the form of business organization.

When a partnership is formed, a separate capital account must be established for each partner. Assets contributed by the partners are to be valued at their fair value on the date the partnership is formed. This is the historical cost concept. All partners must agree on the valuations assigned to the various assets.

Profits and losses of a partnership are distributed to the individual partners in accordance with the provisions contained in the ***articles of partnership.*** If no such provision exists, profits and losses are distributed equally. Provisions generally attempt to consider differences in services performed and capital contributed. Provisions for profit and loss distribution may provide for distribution in certain ***fixed ratios,*** by ***capital balance relationships,*** or by considering ***salary or interest equivalents.***

Partnership dissolution occurs whenever there is a change in the number of individuals in the partnership. The business entity does not terminate, but the legal relationship does. Admitting a new partner requires mutual consent of the old partners. The admission may be accomplished by the ***purchase of an interest*** of an old partner or partners for a mutually agreeable consideration. The amount of consideration is not reflected on the partnership's books, only the transfer of the ownership interest being recorded.

Admission may be gained by an ***investment of assets.*** In this case a new partner contributes assets directly into the partnership, receiving a credit in a newly established capital account less than, equal to, or greater than the fair value of the contributed assets. The difference between the fair value of the assets and the capital account credit is reflected on the partnership books as either a bonus or goodwill.

Withdrawal of a partner typically calls for a ***revaluation*** of the partnership assets with a corresponding increase or decrease in the partners' capital accounts. The withdrawing partner is then given cash equal to the balance in his capital account.

The termination of a partnership's business activities, the sale of partnership assets, the resulting payment of all liabilities, and the distribution of partnership assets to the partners is called ***partnership liquidation.***

Gains or losses on the sale of partnership assets are distributed to the individual partners in accordance with the profit-and-loss ratios when a partnership is liquidated. After the liabilities are paid, all remaining cash (or other assets) is distributed to the individual partners in accordance with the balance in their respective capital accounts. If a deficit appears in a capital account as a result of a loss on the sale of partnership assets, that partner must contribute cash to the partnership equal to the deficit. If he or she is unable to do so, the remaining partners must absorb the deficit in their remaining profit-and-loss ratios.

IMPORTANT TERMS USED IN THIS CHAPTER

Articles of partnership A formal written contract between the partners in a partnership that establishes responsibilities, commitments, and the manner in which profits and losses are to be distributed. (page 457)

Dissolution of a partnership The termination of a partnership relationship as a result of a change in the number of partners. The relationship terminates but the business entity does not. (page 467)

Income distribution The manner in which partnership profits and losses are allocated to the individual partners. (page 461)

Limited life   The characteristic of a partnership that dissolves the partnership with the admission of a new partner, the withdrawal of a partner, or the death of a partner. (page 458)

Liquidation   The termination of a business entity by selling its assets and distributing the resulting cash to the creditors and owners. (page 472)

Mutual agency   The authority of each partner in a partnership to legally bind all other partners to contracts. (page 457)

Partnership   An association of two or more persons to carry on, as co-owners, a business for profit. (page 456)

Purchase of an interest   A business transaction involving the transfer of an ownership interest between an existing partner or partners and a new partner. (page 467)

Unlimited liability   The legal obligation making each partner in a partnership personally responsible for the partnership's obligations. (page 457)

QUESTIONS

1. Over the past several years Martha Jones and Rapheal Garcia have operated a profitable flower shop. They are currently thinking of admitting Peter Knowles into their partnership. Explain why this action is under consideration.

2. What does the term *articles of partnership* refer to? Why is it considered necessary?

3. Distinguish between the terms *limited life* and *unlimited liability.*

4. Define the term *mutual agency.*

5. What is a partnership?

6. When forming a partnership, why is it necessary to value assets contributed by the partners at their fair value on the date of formation?

7. Partners are not paid salaries but rather are *allowed* a salary. Explain.

8. How can a partnership agreement provide for an equitable distribution of profits and losses when the individual partners have different amounts of capital invested in the partnership?

9. When a new partner is admitted to a partnership, he or she may be admitted by a *purchase of an interest* or by an *investment in the partnership.* Distinguish between these two approaches.

10. Brown has a 25% interest in the partnership of Brown and Clark. His capital account has a credit balance of $25,000 and Clark has a credit balance of $75,000. Brown sells his 25% interest to Ellenton, Clark agrees, for $33,000. Comment on the appropriate accounting treatment for this transaction.

11. Moon, Night, Owl, and Peter share profits according to the following ratio: 4:3:2:2. If profits for the current year are $88,000, how much will Owl's share be?

12. The partnership of E, F, and G is liquidated on October 31 of the current year. After the assets are sold for cash and the creditors paid, F has a deficit in his capital account. Must he contribute cash to the partnership equal to the deficit? Why? Assume he cannot contribute cash; what must next be done? If he cannot contribute cash now but at a later date acquires cash equal to the deficit, must he contribute cash then to E and G?

13. Atlas is an audit partner of Foot, Tie, and Company, CPAs. He contracts with Johnson Supply Company for five 15-horsepower tractors to be delivered in 2 weeks. The CPA firm refuses to accept delivery at that time. Does Johnson Supply Company have an enforceable legal claim against the CPA firm?

14. In a partnership liquidation, gains and losses are distributed in the profit-and-loss ratio, but the final cash settlement is made to the partners in accordance with the balances in their capital accounts. Explain.

15. Carter, a partner in the law firm of Allen, Burke, and Carter, withdrew as a salary $43,000 during the current year. At year-end it is determined that Carter's share of the profits amounted to only $38,000. If Carter's beginning capital account had a balance of $25,000, what will be the ending balance? Explain.

16. Miller and Ortiz agree to admit DeSear into their partnership for a cash contribution of $10,000, giving him a one-fourth interest. Net assets prior to DeSear's admission total $20,000. Based on this arrangement, DeSear will receive $7,500 in his capital account, the remaining $2,500 being a bonus that Miller and Ortiz will share. Why would DeSear agree to this arrangement?

EXERCISES

Exercise 12-1
Formation of a partnership

Effective April 1, 1987, Tom and Jerry agree to form a partnership from their two respective proprietorships. The balance sheets presented below reflect the financial position of each proprietorship as of March 31, 1987:

	Tom	Jerry
Assets		
Cash.	$ 400	$ 1,000
Accounts Receivable	2,400	1,400
Merchandise Inventory.	6,600	8,400
Prepaid Rent	—	800
Store Equipment.	8,000	6,000
Accumulated Depreciation	(3,000)	(3,600)
Building	25,000	—
Accumulated Depreciation	(5,000)	—
Land	12,000	
Totals	$46,400	$14,000
Liabilities and Owners' Equity		
Accounts Payable	$1,500	$ 600
Mortgage Payable	12,000	—
Tom, Capital	32,900	—
Jerry, Capital	—	13,400
Totals	$46,400	$14,000

As of April 1, 1987, the fair value of Tom's assets are: merchandise inventory, $5,400; store equipment, $3,000; building, $50,000; and land $20,000.

For Jerry the fair value of the assets on the same date are: merchandise inventory, $9,000; store equipment, $1,300; and prepaid rent $0.

All other items on the two balance sheets are stated at fair values.

From this information, present general journal entries to record the opening of the partnership accounts.

(Check figure: Tom, Capital, $67,700)

Exercise 12-2

Determining the partners' share of profits

The East Bay Hardware Company is owned by Phil and Alice. This year the hardware Company reported a $75,000 profit. Determine each partner's share of the profits under each of the following assumptions:
a. Nothing is mentioned in the partnership agreement concerning the sharing of profits.
b. Phil is to receive two-fifths of the profits, Alice three-fifths.
c. Profits are to be shared by Phil and Alice in a 3:1 ratio.

(Check figure part b: Alice, $45,000)

Exercise 12-3

Calculating average capital balances

From the information presented below concerning George and Gracie's capital accounts, determine the average capital balance of each partner:

George, Capital		Gracie, Capital	
Balance, Jan. 1	$20,000	Balance, Jan. 1	$70,000
Investment, Apr. 1	40,000	Withdrawal, Mar. 1	30,000
Withdrawal, Oct. 1	20,000	Withdrawal, July 1	10,000

(Check figure: George: $45,000)

Exercise 12-4

Distribution of partnership profits

The partnership agreement among Hart, Jackson, and Mondale provides that the distribution of profits and losses shall be determined allowing a 20% rate of return on average capital balances, salary allowances of $34,000, $50,000, and $46,000, respectively, and the remainder equally. Average capital balances for the current year were: Hart, $60,000; Jackson, $100,000; and Mondale, $40,000.
a. Prepare an income distribution schedule assuming that the income for the year was $185,000.

(Check figure: Hart income: $51,000)

b. Prepare an income distribution schedule assuming that the income for the year was $155,000.

(Check figure: Mondale income: $49,000)

Exercise 12-5

Purchase of an interest

The Three S Food Place is owned and operated as a partnership by Sally, Sam, and Saul. As of October 1, the capital accounts of the three partners were as follows: Sally, $120,000; Sam, $70,000; and Saul, $30,000. Sam has arranged to sell his interest in the partnership to Susan. (The other two partners agree to accept Susan as a partner.) Susan is to pay $80,000 (fair value); and $2,000 per month for the next 10 months. Record the general journal entry on the partnership books to admit Susan.

Exercise 12-6

Admitting a new partner: bonus and goodwill to old partners

White has been accepted into the partnership of Black, Brown, and Green with a 25% interest for an investment of $90,000. The old partners share profits in a 2:1:1 ratio and had capital accounts prior to White's admission of $80,000, $100,000, and $60,000, respectively.
a. Record the general journal entry to admit White, assuming that a bonus is to be given to the old partners.

(Check figure: Bonus to Brown, $1,875)

b. Record the general journal entry to admit White assuming that goodwill is to be recorded.

(Check figure: Goodwill = $30,000)

Exercise 12-7

Withdrawal of a partner

Pete is planning to retire from the partnership of Pete, Whetstone, and Andersen. At the date of retirement Pete's capital account has a $66,000 credit balance before any revaluations.

An audit of the partnership accounts is performed and the assets are revalued at their fair values. As a result, inventory and land are increased by $6,000 and $10,000, respectively. Assuming that the partners share profits in a 3:3:2 ratio, prepare the general journal entries required for the revaluation and the withdrawal of Pete.

(Check figure: Pete, ending capital = $72,000)

Exercise 12-8
Partnership liquidation

The partnership of Marty, Martha, and Mary is being liquidated. All liabilities have been paid and all assets have been sold for cash. The capital accounts of the partners have the following balances:

Marty	$20,000 credit
Martha	8,000 debit
Mary	12,000 credit

Profits are shared equally. Assuming that Martha has no personal assets, how is the $24,000 remaining cash balance to be distributed?

(Check figure: Marty to receive $16,000)

PROBLEMS
Set A

Problem A12-1
Partnership formation

Adams and Baker are competitors selling heavy equipment. They believe that they can increase their business and reduce their costs by combining the two proprietorships into a partnership. An agreement is reached between the two to form a partnership commencing May 1 of the current year. Adams will work full-time, Baker only 20 hours per week. Consequently, the partners agree to share profits and losses in a 2:1 ratio and to contribute and maintain capital in a corresponding ratio. This is accomplished by Baker withdrawing cash.

The balance sheets of the two proprietorships as of April 31 are presented at the top of page 482.

The partners agree that the name of the partnership will be Adams and Baker Equipment Company. They also agree to the following:
a. Concerning the transfer of Adams' assets and liabilities:
(1) The Accounts Receivable are to be valued at $151,200 and the Allowance for Doubtful Accounts stated at a zero balance to commence the new partnership.
(2) Merchandise Inventory is to be reduced by $52,600.
(3) Office Supplies are to remain as stated.
(4) Land is to be established at its fair value of $54,000.
(5) Fixed assets are to be recorded as follows: Office Equipment, $8,000; Building, $96,000; and Repair Equipment, $62,000
(6) One-half of the Notes Payable are to be considered personal notes of Adams. All other liabilities are accepted by the partnership.
b. Concerning the transfer of Baker's assets and liabilities:
(1) A write-off of $16,200 of Accounts Receivable is required. As with Adams, Baker's Allowance for Doubtful Accounts is to be stated at a zero balance.
(2) Merchandise Inventory is to be increased by $3,600.
(3) The Prepaid Rent is for the building Baker occupies. The partnership plans to build a new structure in the near future and will continue to rent, occupying two locations, until the new building is complete.
(4) Office Supplies are to be as stated.
(5) Office Equipment is to be valued at $20,000.
(6) Accounts Payable are accepted as stated.

Required 1. Prepare the general journal entries to record the formation of the new partnership.

(Check figure: Baker withdraws $21,300, leaving a $185,300 capital balance)

Balance Sheets
April 31, 1987

	Adams	Baker
Assets		
Cash	$ 21,000	$ 15,000
Accounts Receivable.	194,600	84,600
Less: Allowance for Doubtful Accounts	(11,200)	(7,200)
Merchandise Inventory	230,800	150,400
Prepaid Rent.	—	3,000
Office Supplies	15,200	2,000
Land	20,000	—
Building.	64,000	—
Less: Accumulated Depreciation	(16,000)	—
Office Equipment.	12,000	31,000
Less: Accumulated Depreciation	(3,000)	(6,600)
Repair Equipment	86,000	—
Less: Accumulated Depreciation	(34,000)	—
Total Assets	$579,400	$272,200
Liabilities and Owners' Equity		
Notes Payable	$ 60,000	—
Accounts Payable.	85,000	55,800
Mortgage Payable	100,000	—
Adams, Capital	334,400	—
Baker, Capital	—	216,400
Total Liabilities and Owners' Equity	$579,400	$272,200

2. For the 8 months ending December 31, the partnership reports a profit of $300,000. During this period Adams has withdrawn $75,000 and Baker $37,500. Prepare a statement of the partners' capital accounts.

(Check figure: Total capital December 31, $743,400)

Problem A12-2
Profit distribution, different partnership arrangements

During the year 1987 the accounting firm of Paton, Hatfield, and Montgomery earned a profit of $416,250. Paton had a capital balance on January 1 of $75,000; he invested an additional $15,000 on March 31; withdrew $30,000 on September 30; and invested $22,500 on October 31.

Hatfield's balance on January 1 was $90,000. This was increased by $45,000 on February 28 and reduced to $81,000 on July 31, remaining at $81,000 until year-end.

Montgomery had a capital investment amounting to $60,000 on January 1. This was doubled on April 30 and reduced by $30,000 on August 31.

Required

Determine the profit distribution for each of the five different assumptions listed below:
1. Profits are distributed to the partners equally.
2. Profits are distributed in an 8:4:3 ratio.
3. Profits are distributed in the ratio of the January 1, 1987, capital balances.
4. Profits are distributed in the ratio of the average capital balances.
5. Profits are distributed allowing 12% interest on the average capital balances; salaries of $39,000, $27,000, and $33,000, respectively; and the remainder is shared equally.

[Check figure: Paton's share of profits: (1) $138,750; (2) $222,000 (3) $138,750; (4) $123,750; (5) $143,550]

Problem A12-3
Profit distribution, different
profit levels

The partnership agreement among Baldwin, Coleman, and Eaton provides the following:
a. An allowance of 15% on the average partner's capital shall be provided for interest equiva-
    lents. The average capital balances for 1987 are $240,000, $300,000, and $180,000, respec-
    tively.
b. Salary equivalents shall be $105,000 for Baldwin, $90,000 for Coleman, and $120,000 for
    Eaton.
c. A bonus of 10% of any profits is to be allowed for Baldwin.
d. The remainder is to be distributed equally.

Required

Prepare an income distribution schedule for each of the following levels: **(1)** $600,000 profit;
(2) $450,000 profit; **(3)** $45,000 loss.

[Check figure: Baldwin's share of profits: (1) $240,000; (2) $180,000; (3) $15,000 loss]

Problem A12-4
Admission of a new partner,
bonus or goodwill recorded

Williams and Wilson agree to admit Washington into their partnership for a 30% interest with
a $30,000 cash investment. Prior to the admission of Washington the two partners shared
profits in a 2:1 ratio and had capital accounts in the amounts of $24,000 and $36,000,
respectively.

Required

1. Assuming that a bonus is to be recorded for the old partners, prepare the general journal
   entry necessary to reflect the admission of Washington.

   (Check figure: Washington, Capital = $27,000)

2. Washington wants his capital account to reflect a credit equal to his investment. Record the
   journal entry to admit Washington assuming that goodwill is recorded.

   (Check figure: Goodwill = $10,000)

3. Assume that Washington is to be given a 40% interest in the partnership rather than a 30%
   interest. Record the general journal entry to admit Washington assuming that a bonus is
   given to Washington.

   (Check figure: Washington, Capital = $36,000)

4. Record the entry to admit Washington reflecting the goodwill he is contributing.

   (Check figure: Goodwill = $10,000)

Problem A12-5
Withdrawal from a partnership

The Riverhills Industrial Park is operated by the partnership of Mullens, Nole, and Oleson.
Nole turned 65 on November 1, 1987, and is required by the partnership agreement to retire.
Presented at the top of page 484 is the company's balance sheet as of October 31, 1987. Prior
to the withdrawal of Nole, the partners shared profits and losses in a 4:3:3 ratio.

Required

Prepare the general entries necessary to record the retirement of Nole under each of the
following independent situations:
1. Nole sells one-fourth of his interest to Mullens for $15,000, another one-fourth interest to
   Oleson for $15,000, and the remaining one-half to Peters for $27,500. Mullens and Oleson
   agree to Peters' admission into the new partnership.
2. The assets and liabilities are restated at their fair values as of November 1. Nole is to receive
   real estate equal in value to $15,000 and cash for the remainder due him. The following
   adjustments are made: Accounts Receivable are reduced by $3,250; the Allowance for
   Doubtful Accounts is decreased by $750; Inventory of Real Estate is reduced by $7,400;
   Office Supplies are increased by $550; Office Equipment is reduced to book value of
   $10,000 by increasing Accumulated Depreciation by $2,500; and the Accounts Payable are
   reduced by $1,850.

   (Check figure: Cash received by Nole = $27,000)

THE RIVERHILLS INDUSTRIAL PARK
Balance Sheet
October 31, 1987

Assets		Liabilities and Owners' Equity	
Cash.	$ 31,500	Notes Payable	$ 25,150
Accounts Receivable	64,600	Accounts Payable	47,350
Allowance for Doubtful		Mullens, Capital	60,000
Accounts	(6,750)	Nole, Capital	45,000
Inventory of Real Estate	105,400	Oleson, Capital.	38,500
Office Supplies	7,250		
Prepaid Rent	1,500		
Office Equipment	16,150		
Accumulated Depreciation . . .	(3,650)		
		Total Liabilities and Owners'	
Total Assets	$216,000	Equity.	$216,000

3. Cash of $48,500 is to be paid to Nole. The bonus is absorbed by Mullens and Oleson in a 4 : 3 ratio.

4. Cash of $38,000 is to be paid to Nole. The difference between the credit in Nole's capital account and the cash received is to be credited to the remaining partners in a 4 : 3 ratio.

Problem A12-6
General journal entries for a partnership liquidation

The partnership of Garcia, Johnson, and Steinberg has experienced financial difficulties over the past several years. As a result, the partners, who share profits and losses in a 2 : 1 : 1 ratio, decide to liquidate the firm. The trial balance of the partnership as of October 1, 1987, is presented below:

GARCIA, JOHNSON, AND STEINBERG
Trial Balance
October 1, 1987

Cash	$ 28,000	
Accounts Receivable.	126,400	
Allowance for Doubtful Accounts		$ 7,400
Merchandise Inventory	195,400	
Prepaid Insurance	6,000	
Office Equipment.	21,000	
Accumulated Depreciation: Office Equipment		7,000
Machinery	54,400	
Accumulated Depreciation: Machinery		21,400
Building.	250,000	
Accumulated Depreciation: Building		75,000
Land	80,000	
Notes Payable.		80,000
Accounts Payable		147,000
Mortgage Payable		160,000
Garcia, Capital		90,000
Johnson, Capital		40,000
Steinberg, Capital.		133,400
Totals	$761,200	$761,200

Required   The following transactions occurred in the month of October, resulting in the liquidation of the partnership. No partner has any personal assets that can be contributed to the partnership. Prepare general journal entries for each transaction.

Oct. 6   Accounts Receivable in the amount of $25,400 are written off. The remainder are collected. The Allowance for Doubtful Accounts is also written off. Use an account entitled Loss on Liquidation to record all gains and losses resulting from the liquidation.
      9   The merchandise inventory is sold to a competitor for $107,000.
     11   A refund of $2,000 is received on the prepaid insurance.
     14   The office equipment, machinery, building, and land were sold to Hartley Corporation for $74,000. The mortgage payable was transferred to Hartley Corporation.
     15   The notes payable and accounts payable are settled by paying creditors $220,600.
     15   The Loss on Liquidation account is closed to the partner's capital accounts in the profit-and-loss ratio.
     15   The deficit in Johnson's capital account is absorbed in the remaining profit-and-loss ratio by Garcia and Steinberg.
     15   Cash is distributed to Garcia and Steinberg.

(Check figure: Cash distributed to Steinberg = $89,400)

Problem A12-7
A partnership liquidation schedule

For several years the partnership of Babson, Clark, and Dunn has reported losses. Prospects for a recovery of their business appear slim, and on December 31, 1987, the partners agree to liquidate their partnership.

On the date of liquidation, partnership assets total $337,500, of which $22,500 is cash. Liabilities total $135,000, and the partners' capital accounts reflect $43,875, $135,000, and $23,625, respectively.

The partners share profits and losses in a 3:2:1 ratio. No partner has personal assets that can be contributed to the partnership.

Required   Prepare partnership liquidation schedules assuming that other assets were sold for:
1. $247,500
2. $213,750
3. $193,500

*[Check figure; Cash distributed to Clark: **(1)** $112,500; **(2)** $96,750; **(3)** $81,000]*

Set B

Problem B12-1
Partnership formation

The feed and supply store operated by Betty White has been very successful. As a result she feels it is an appropriate time to expand operations. Betty contacts Jim DeVoe, who owns a warehouse and the land it stands on, and offers to form a partnersip to be called White and DeVoe Feed and Supply Store. DeVoe accepts and the partnership is formed on July 1, 1987.

Presented on page 486 is the trial balance of White Feed and Supply Store as of June 30, 1987.

The partners agree to share profits and losses equally and decide that each will invest an equal amount in the partnership. White and DeVoe agree that DeVoe's land is worth $90,000 and his building $300,000. DeVoe is to contribute cash in an amount to bring his capital account equal to White.

Agreement is reached by the two partners on the following items concerning the transfer of White Feed and Supply Store to the partnership:
a. Accounts Receivable in the amount of $61,200 are to be written off and the Allowance for Doubtful Accounts eliminated.
b. Merchandise inventory is to be decreased by $26,400.
c. The prepaid rent is for the warehouse used by White. All merchandise will be transferred to DeVoe's building. No refund will be received on the unused rent paid in advance.

Cash	$ 45,900	
Accounts Receivable.	420,600	
Allowance for Doubtful Accounts		$ 23,400
Merchandise Inventory	202,500	
Prepaid Rent.	5,850	
Store Equipment	78,000	
Accumulated Depreciation		19,500
Notes Payable.		66,000
Accounts Payable		101,100
White, Capital.		542,850
Totals	$752,850	$752,850

d. The store equipment has a fair value of $60,000.
e. All other items, assets and liabilities, are to be transferred at their book values.

Required   **1.** Prepare the general journal entries to record the formation of the new partnership.

(Check figure: DeVoe's cash contribution = $84,300)

2. At the end of the year, December 31, 1987, a profit of $178,000 is shown. Each partner has made withdrawals of $49,000. Prepare a statement of the partners' capital accounts.

(Check figure: Total capital, December 31, 1987 = $1,028,600)

Problem B12-2
Profit distribution, different partnership arrangements

During their first year of operations, the partnership of Ferris, Getty, and Holland earned $45,450. Summarized below is the activity of the individual partner's capital accounts:

	Ferris	Getty	Holland
Capital, Jan. 1.	$10,000	$15,000	$20,000
Mar. 31, Investment.	10,000		
May 31, Withdrawal		(2,500)	
June 30, Investment.			2,500
July 31, Withdrawal.		(2,500)	
Oct. 31, Investment		3,000	
Oct. 31, Withdrawal.			(7,500)
Capital, Dec. 31	$20,000	$13,000	$15,000

Required   Determine the partners' share of the partnership profits under the assumption that profits are shared:
1. Equally
2. In a 5:2:2 ratio
3. In the ratio of the January 1 capital balances
4. In the ratio of the average capital balances
5. Allowing for 10% interest on the average capital balances; salaries of $9,650, $7,600, and $8,150, respectively; and the remainder equally

[Check figure: Holland's share of profits = (1) $15,150; (2) $10,100; (3) $20,200; (4) $18,000; (5) $15,150]

Problem B12-3
Profit distribution, different profit levels

The partnership agreement of Orthello, Hamlet, and MacBeth provides for the following: Profits and losses shall be distributed by allowing 10% interest on average capital balances and salaries of $37,500, $67,500, and $22,500, respectively; MacBeth is entitled to a bonus of 5% of reported profits (if any); any remainder is to be shared equally.

Average capital balances for 1987 are: Orthello, $300,000; Hamlet, $225,000; and Mac-Beth, $450,000.

Required   Prepare income distribution schedules for each of the following levels of income: **(1)** $270,000; **(2)** $225,000; **(3)** $(22,520) loss

[Check figure: MacBeth's share of income: (1) $91,500; (2) $75,000; (3) ($15,000) loss]

Problem B12-4
Admission of a new partner, bonus or goodwill recorded

Johnson and Kelly operate a profitable bingo and beer concession at Golden Oaks Retirement Village. In order to expand their business to other retirement communities, an additional $25,000 cash is needed. The partners contact Landon and find him willing to contribute the required funds. A new partnership is formed with Landon receiving a 20% interest.

Prior to the admission of Landon, Johnson had a $25,000 capital account balance and Kelly had a $50,000 balance. The old partners shared profits in a 3:2 ratio.

Required   **1.** Record the general journal entry to admit Landon, assuming that a bonus is given to the old partners.

(Check figure: Landon, Capital = $20,000)

2. Record the general journal entry to admit Landon, assuming that goodwill is to be recorded.

(Check figure: Goodwill = $25,000)

Rather than receiving a 20% interest, assume that Landon receives a 30% interest.

3. Record the general journal entry to admit Landon, assuming that a bonus is given to Landon.

4. Record the general journal entry to admit Landon, assuming that goodwill is recorded.

(Check figure: Goodwill = $7,143)

5. Assume that Landon does not invest in the partnership but purchases an interest instead. Specifically, Landon purchases a 20% interest, paying Johnson $5,500 and Kelly $11,000. Record the general journal entry to admit Landon under this assumption.

Problem B12-5
Withdrawal from a partnership

Albright, Benson, and Cooley share profits and losses in a 3:2:1 ratio. On May 1, 1987, Benson withdraws from the partnership. The partners' trial balance on that date is presented below:

Cash	$ 58,200	
Accounts Receivable.	38,760	
Allowance for Doubtful Accounts		$ 2,040
Merchandise Inventory	78,600	
Machinery	32,400	
Accumulated Depreciation		12,600
Accounts Payable		61,620
Albright, Capital		65,940
Benson, Capital.		43,956
Cooley, Capital		21,804
Totals	$207,960	$207,960

Required   For each of the following independent situations, prepare the general journal entries necessary to record the retirement of Benson:

1. Benson sells one-half of his interest to Albright and one-half to Cooley for $24,000 each.

2. Benson sells his interest to Dennis for $54,000. Both Albright and Cooley agree to accept Dennis into the new partnership.
3. Benson is paid cash equal to the balance in his capital account after the following adjustments are recorded: Accounts Receivable are revalued to $36,000; the Allowance for Doubtful Accounts is reduced to $1,680; Merchandise Inventory is reduced by $6,600; and Accumulated Depreciation is increased to $18,000.

(Check figure: Cash given to Benson = $39,156)

4. Benson is paid $54,516, the bonus being debited to the remaining partners' capital accounts in a 3:1 ratio.
5. Benson is paid $36,012, the bonus being credited to the remaining partners' capital accounts in a 3:1 ratio.

Problem B12-6

General journal entries for a partnership liquidation

The trial balance presented below was taken from the partnership records of Pint, Quart, and Gallon on October 1, 1987:

Cash	$ 15,000	
Accounts Receivable.	82,200	
Allowance for Doubtful Accounts		$ 4,500
Land	18,000	
Building.	186,000	
Accumulated Depreciation: Building		97,500
Office Equipment.	42,000	
Accumulated Depreciation: Office Equipment		9,000
Accounts Payable		51,000
Mortgage Payable		60,000
Pint, Capital		61,200
Quart, Capital		15,000
Gallon, Capital		45,000
Totals	$343,200	$343,200

The partners share profits and losses in a 2:2:1 ratio. During the month of October 1987, the partnership is liquidated.

Required

Prepare the general journal entries to record the following October transactions:

Oct. 2   Accounts Receivable in the amount of $69,600 are collected. The remaining accounts and the Allowance for Doubtful Accounts are written off to an account entitled Loss on Liquidation. This account is to be used to record all gains and losses resulting from the liquidation.

4   The office equipment is sold to the Atlanta Company for $19,500.

9   The land and building are sold to Such Crust Bakery for $8,100 cash. The mortgage payable is transferred to the bakery in this transaction.

14   The accounts payable are paid.

15   The Loss on Liquidation account is closed to the partners' capital accounts in the profit-and-loss ratio.

15   Quart contributes cash necessary to remove the deficit in his capital account.

15   Cash is distributed to Pint and Gallon equal to the credit balances in their respective capital accounts.

(Check figure: Cash distributed to Pint = $37,200)

Problem B12-7

A partnership liquidation schedule

The investment firm of Thomas, Tally, and Toth is being liquidated. The partners share profits in a 5 : 3 : 2 ratio. On December 12, 1987, the date of liquidation, the partnership had $50,000 cash and $160,000 of other assets. Outstanding liabilities amounted to $90,000 and the capital accounts had credit balances of $60,000, $20,000, and $40,000, respectively. None of the partners had any personal assets that could be contributed to the partnership.

Required

Prepare a partnership liquidation schedule assuming that the other assets are sold for **(1)** $100,000; **(2)** $70,000; **(3)** $49,000.

*(Check figure: Cash distributed to Toth = **(1)** $28,000; **(2)** $20,000; **(3)** $9,000)*

Chapter 13

Corporations: Formation and Common Stock Transactions

Some of the things you will learn by studying this chapter are:

- What a corporation is, how its management is structured, and the advantages and disadvantages of being organized as a corporation
- The general steps that are followed in organizing a new corporation
- What *common* stock is, and the rights of a common stockholder
- How to prepare journal entries to record issuing common stock on a *subscription basis,* for cash, and for assets other than cash
- What we mean by *treasury stock* and how to prepare journal entries to record the acquisition and sale of treasury stock
- What *donated capital* is
- What is meant by *par value, stated value, market value,* and *book value* of stock.

DESCRIPTION OF THE CORPORATION

A corporation is an artificial legal being

A *corporation* is an artificial legal being created by a government charter that endows it with certain powers. A corporation exists in the eyes of the law as though it were a person separate and distinct from the people who own it. It has many of the rights that a natural person possesses. It may own property, borrow money, sue and be sued, and in a sense it may even get "married" to another corporation through a merger. Corporations do not possess a natural citizen's rights to vote or to be elected to public office.

Corporations are the dominant form of business organization in the United States. While proprietorships and partnerships are probably more numerous, corporations own the largest amount of resources, produce and sell the most products, and employ the greatest number of individuals.

Some corporations are established by the federal government to operate in the public interest. An example is the Federal Deposit Insurance Corporation (FDIC), which insures the safety of many deposits in banks. The corporations you are most familiar with, those in business to make and sell products and services, are created under the laws of the various states. A corporation must meet the requirements set forth by the state in which it is incorporated. A company may incorporate in one state, have its main office in another state, and operate in many states. The Coca-Cola Company, for instance, is incorporated in Delaware, has its primary executive offices in Georgia, and operates in all 50 states (and in many foreign countries).

Articles of Incorporation

The articles of incorporation are written documents giving the state basic information about a proposed corporation

When you decide you want to do business as a corporation, you must apply to a state government for permission to be a corporation—to *incorporate.*

You begin the incorporation process by filing proposed articles of incorporation together with the required fee with the appropriate state office. A lawyer should be consulted in writing the proposed articles so that they will be in the proper form and will include all information required by state law. When these *articles of incorporation* are approved, they become a part of the *charter* creating the corporation. The charter is the document issued by a state government giving a business the legal right to begin operating as a corporation.

Since each state has its own laws governing what should be included in the articles of incorporation, the contents of the articles will vary from state to state. Here are some of the things that are commonly included:

Corporations may have almost any name and any legal purpose

1. *Name and purpose of the corporation*   Within certain limits you can choose almost any name for your corporation. You cannot, of course, call yourself the Ford Motor Corporation—another group has already picked that one.

   You may state your purpose narrowly—for example, you could say that you are establishing a corporation to sell peanuts at high school football games in Michigan. Or you may state your purpose broadly, so that you can diversify into many types of business without having to form a new corporation each time you want to begin a new type of business. For example, your purpose might be to enter into any lawful business activity permitted by the state of Michigan.

Capital stock is certificates of ownership in a corporation

2. *Capital stock*   Ownership of a corporation is represented by shares of stock. Every corporation must have one type of stock, called *common stock.* In addition, other types, or classes, of stock may be sold.

   The charter must state the classes of stock that your corporation has permission to sell, the number of shares of each type that you are authorized to sell, what rights or special preferences are granted to each type of stock, and what restrictions are imposed upon each class.

The amount of assets contributed by owners at the beginning of the new business must also be specified.

We will discuss the various classes of stock and their rights and restrictions later in this chapter and the next.

The corporation must have an official address

3. *Place of business* You must specify the location of your principal office or place of business, so that an official address will be registered with the state. Your tax bills, lawsuits filed against you, and other legal correspondence will be sent to this legal address.

A corporation's life may be unending

4. *Duration* The life of your corporation must be defined. Although you may select a short life, such as 10 years, most corporations elect a perpetual — unending — life.

A corporation's governing body is its board of directors

5. *Directors and officers* You must list the names and addresses of the first governing body of your corporation, the board of directors, and its operating managers, the officers. After the corporation begins operations, the stockholders (owners) will meet and elect new members to the board of directors.

The people forming a new corporation are called incorporators

6. *Incorporators* The names and addresses of the individuals filing the articles of incorporation, the *incorporators,* must be listed. You must also disclose the number of shares of stock that each incorporator has agreed to buy and how the shares are to be paid for. Cash or some other asset — building, land, equipment — may be used to pay for shares.

If all the required information is properly presented, the state will issue a certificate of incorporation, or *charter.* Once you receive the charter, you may begin selling stock and operating your business.

Before we explain how to account for issuing stock, let's examine why the incorporators might have chosen the corporate form of business instead of a partnership, and how the management structure of a corporation appears.

Advantages of Corporations

Several characteristics of corporations may make this form of organization more desirable than either a partnership or a proprietorship:

1. *Greater amounts of capital can be raised* Large numbers of individuals and institutions can more easily and efficiently acquire and dispose of ownership interests in a corporation than in a partnership. Many corporations have several million stockholders who have cumulatively invested more than $100 million.

2. *Owners' liability is limited* Liability of the owners is limited to the amount invested in the corporation — the amount that each stockholder paid for his or her stock. Creditors having a claim against the corporation must be paid only from the assets of the corporation; personal assets of the stockholders are not available to creditors. In a partnership one or more partners must have unlimited liability, thus risking personal as well as business assets.

3. *Ownership shares are easily transferred* After the initial sale of stock, shares may be transferred in private sale transactions, traded (sold) on established securities markets such as the New York Stock Exchange, or given away. The only involvement of the corporation in these transactions is in keeping an up-to-date list of the names and addresses of the stockholders.

The billions of dollars changing hands daily through sales of stock on the New York Stock Exchange and the American Stock Exchange do not flow into the coffers of the corporations whose stock is being traded. Corporations acquire capital, cash, and other assets only upon a new issuance of stock or upon the sale of stock previously reacquired. Of course, corporations may also borrow money by issuing bonds or by getting a loan from a bank or other financial institution.

Sale of a partnership interest is usually a much more complex affair. Remember, each new partner must be acceptable to all of the old partners.

4. ***Continuity of existence*** Continuity of existence refers to the unlimited life of a corporation. The transfer of ownership shares does not affect the corporation's ability to operate routinely over decades. In contrast, a partnership's life ends each time a new partner enters or an old one retires. Continuity of existence makes long-term borrowing easier for a corporation than for partnerships and proprietorships.

**Disadvantages
of Corporations**

If the corporate form were preferable in every way, there would be little reason for proprietorships and partnerships to exist. Anyone thinking of forming a corporation should also consider its negative characteristics:

1. ***Double taxation exists*** The income of a corporation is taxed twice. Corporate income is taxed for the first time when it is earned by the entity. As an artificial person the corporation enjoys the natural citizen's obligation to pay income taxes. We will discuss some of the many special rules that apply to corporate tax returns in Chapter 27. In 1984, the maximum income tax rate that must be paid by a corporation was 46%.

Corporate income is taxed a second time when it is distributed to shareholders. After an initial $100 exclusion ($200 for a married person filing a joint return), all dividends are taxed to individuals at a rate dependent on their level of income. Thus, the corporate income is taxed twice—once when the corporation earns it, and a second time when the stockholder receives it as dividends. Only after this double tax is paid is the corporate income available for the individual owner to spend.

Income is taxed only once in a partnership. Individual partners pay income taxes at personal income tax rates when the income is earned. The partnership entity is not required to pay income taxes. Some small corporations may avoid double taxation by electing to be taxed as partnerships. These ***Subchapter S corporations*** will be discussed in Chapter 27.

Let's look at the example on the next page and compare the amounts that an individual owner of a corporation and of a partnership will have to spend after taxes.

We have made some simplifying assumptions in this example. The point is still valid, however: Corporate income is taxed twice and ultimately provides less spendable cash for its owners than if the business were operated as a partnership.

2. ***Government regulation is extensive*** Corporations are subject to more government regulations than either proprietorships or partnerships. One federal agency that regulates all publicly owned corporations is the Securities and Exchange Commission. It has influence over the activities of only a very few partnerships.

**The SEC regulates publicly held
corporations**

The Securities and Exchange Commission (SEC) has the responsibility for seeing that truthful information is presented to potential investors in corporate stocks. Subject to certain minimum size limitations, a corporation planning to sell stock to the public must file extensive information about its business activities, directors, operating performance (income), and financial position (balance sheet). After careful review by SEC staff members, this factual information can be made

The Facts Assumed for Our Example:

This example shows the effect of double taxation on corporate owners

	The Corporation	The Partnership
Number of owners	10 stockholders	10 partners
Net income (assume all of it is taxable)	$200,000	$200,000
Tax rate for the business	46%	0%
Tax rate for the owners	16%	16%

The Comparison:

	The Corporation	The Partnership
Tax paid by each business:		
Net income	$200,000	$200,000
Tax rate	× 46%	× 0
Tax paid	$ 92,000	$ 0
Amount distributed to each owner:		
Income before tax	$200,000	$200,000
Income tax	(92,000)	0
Income after tax	$108,000	$200,000
Divide by number of owners	÷ 10	÷ 10
Amount received by each owner	$ 10,800	$ 20,000
Tax paid by each owner:		
Amount received by the owner	$ 10,800	$ 20,000
Less: Dividend exclusion (assume this is a joint return)	(200)	0
Taxable amount	$ 10,600	$ 20,000
Income tax rate	× .16	× .16
Tax paid	$ 1,696	$ 3,200
Amount available to spend:		
Amount received	$ 10,800	$ 20,000
Less: Income taxes paid	(1,696)	(3,200)
Amount the owner can spend	$ 9,104	$ 16,800

public by the corporation. The public can then study the data and decide whether to purchase stock from the corporation. The corporation must also file quarterly financial reports (called *10Q's*) and annual financial reports (called *10K's*) with the SEC. These reports are also available to stockholders and other interested parties.

Compliance with the regulations of the SEC and the various other federal, state, and local agencies is often an expensive and time-consuming activity.

THIS CONCERN OFFERS STOCKHOLDERS A LITTLE TASTE OF THEIR INVESTMENTS

by Matt O'Connor

Tired of reading annual reports? George M. Chester thought he had a solution, but he ran into a problem.

Mr. Chester is president of Wisconsin Securities Co. of Delaware, a Milwaukee investment company with $40 million in assets and 231 stockholders.

In a recent letter to shareholders Mr. Chester wrote, "Each printed annual report costs the company $5. In our opinion no annual report is worth a fraction of this amount." Instead, he offered all 231 holders "a sample from one of our investments," urging them to "think of all the time and expense this will save you and us and the Securities and Exchange Commission."

Enclosed with the letter was a reply post card offering shareholders the choice of the company's annual report or a $5 10-ounce can of ginger cookies made by a company Wisconsin Securities invested $80,000 in last December.

"A DISASTER"

Mr. Chester, a wealthy 61-year-old lawyer who raises llamas as a hobby, likes to quip that he came up with the cookie scheme to "divert" stockholders from worrying about Wisconsin Securities' investment in Armco, Inc., the Ohio steel company, an investment he describes as "a disaster." Wisconsin Securities holds 400,000 shares in Armco. (Over several years, Armco's stock price dropped to $14 a share from $40 a share on the New York Stock Exchange, but it is up to about $19 currently.)

Early returns were running 2 to 1 in favor of the cookies, although Frederick Ott, a stockholder and friend of Mr. Chester, said he wanted a report because Mr. Chester usually includes Mr. Ott's name, along with a quote from Mr. Ott saying, "something stupid."

REMEMBER RULE 30d-1

But Mr. Chester had also sent a copy of his shareholder letter to the SEC. And last week he had a call from its Chicago office informing him that under Rule 30d-1 of the Investment Company Act of 1940 he must send every shareholder an annual report.

Mr. Chester doesn't dispute the findings. "They said I could send the cookies too, and shareholders could eat the cookies while they read the report," he says. Undeterred, he's sending shareholders both the report and the cookies.

And he has big plans for 1988. Wisconsin Securities has a $7.4 million investment in an Ohio foundry with a plant in Scotland. The plant is next door to a whisky distillery So Mr. Chester will be sending shareholders — along with the annual report, of course — a $25 bottle of Scotch single-malt whisky call Glenturret.

Source: The Wall Street Journal, March 12, 1984, page 31.

In this chapter extensive government regulation is discussed as a disadvantage of the corporate form of business. As this humorous article shows, the regulations were created for the protection of the investing public. A single stockholder holding a small number of shares has very little power in a corporation. The Securities and Exchange Commission has the authority to enforce the various securities laws, which are designed, in part, to make sure that publicly owned corporations provide owners and prospective owners with factual information about corporate activities.

Compliance with the regulations of the SEC may be expensive and time-consuming, but it is the price corporations must pay to protect the investing public from unsavory or misguided corporate managers.

Corporate Organization Structure

The organization structure of most large corporations follows the same basic pattern. You will find that this pattern is modified somewhat to fit the needs of specific organizations. But, if you understand this basic structure, you will have a good grasp of the various parts of the corporate structure.

Figure 13-1 at the top of page 496 shows the basic corporate organization structure and an explanation of the function of each group in the structure.

Stockholders

The stockholders are the owners of the corporation. Most state corporation laws give the stockholders certain rights. These stockholder rights usually include the following:

A list of stockholder rights

1. The right to receive a certificate as evidence of ownership interest, and to transfer such shares as they choose through either sale or gift.

2. The right to vote at stockholders' meetings for the election of directors and on other such matters as may be brought before the stockholders for action.

3. The right to purchase a portion of any new shares issued such that they will own the same percentage of the total shares after the new issuance of stock as before. This

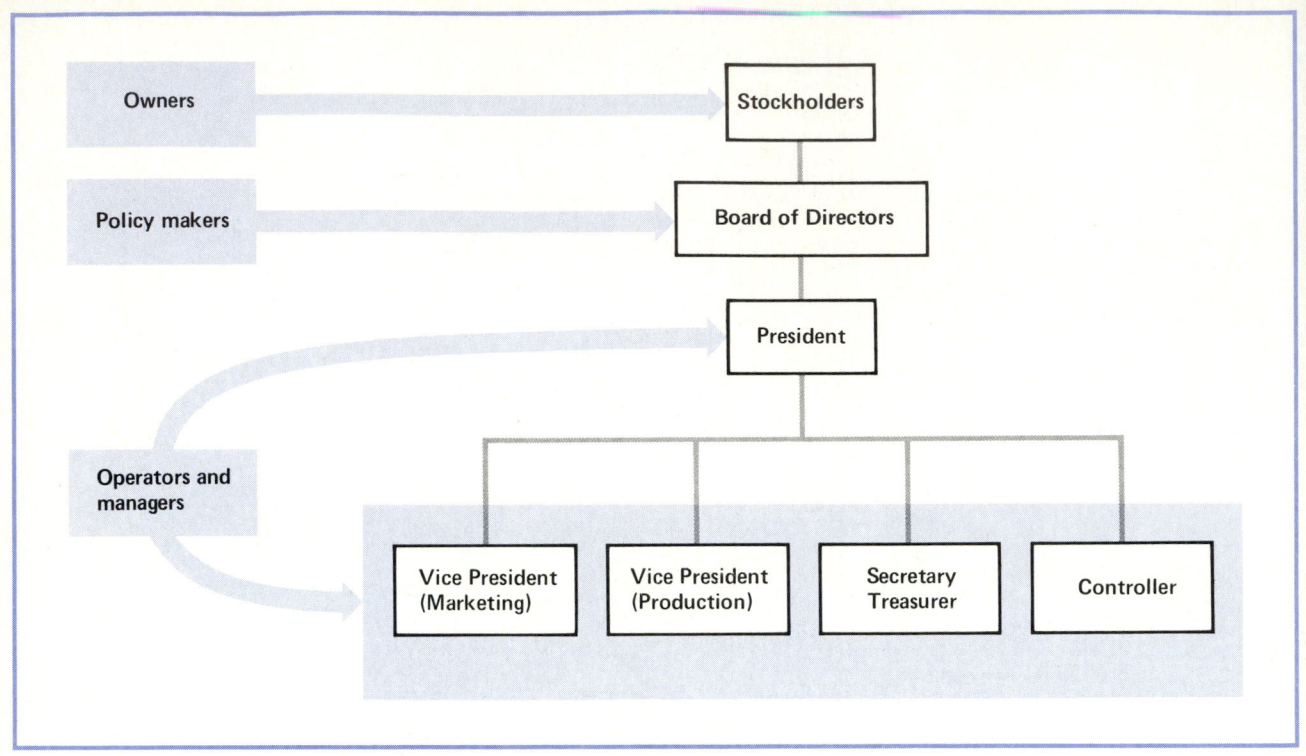

FIGURE 13-1   Corporate Organization Structure.

preemptive right may be given up in some cases by a vote of the stockholders. One such case may exist when a special stock purchase plan (stock option plan) is initiated to reward top-level executives.

4. The right to receive dividends declared by the board of directors. This distribution of profits usually takes the form of cash, but other assets may be distributed as well.

5. The right to receive assets upon dissolution of the corporation if any remain after the creditors have been paid.

Stockholders normally acquire one of two basic types of stock as evidence of their ownership interest: common or preferred.

Common stock represents the primary ownership of the corporation. Common stockholders possess all of the rights listed above. More than any other security holders, they reap the rewards or suffer the consequences of a volatile stock market. If only one class of stock is issued, it is common stock.

When stock is sold and paid for in full, the owner is sent a stock certificate showing how many shares he or she owns. At this point the stock is said to be *issued.*

Figure 13-2 shows a common stock certificate.

Preferred stock is issued by many corporations to appeal to investors who are unwilling to take all the risks involved in common stock ownership. The rights of the common stockholder are modified to provide the preferred stockholder with certain advantages not available to common stockholders; e.g., dividends are paid to preferred stockholders before any are paid to the common stockholders. At the same time, preferred stockholders give up some of the privileges accorded to common stockholders, e.g., the right to vote for members of the board of directors. We will take a closer look at preferred stock in Chapter 14.

Common stockholders are the primary owners of a corporation

Preferred stock is a less risky investment than common stock because preferred stockholders have special privileges

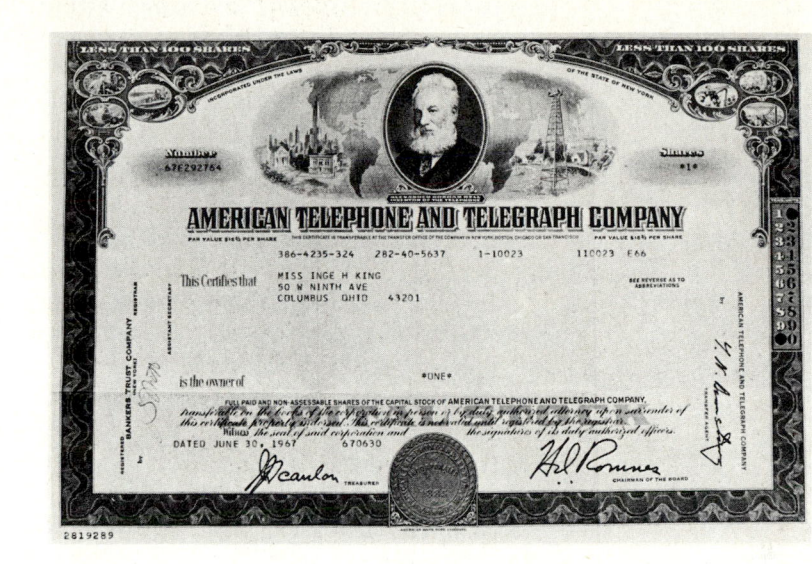

FIGURE 13-2
Common Stock Certificate.

Board of Directors

> The board of directors (1) makes policy, (2) evaluates managers, and (3) makes other decisions they are required by law to make

The board of directors, elected by the stockholders, is responsible for the management of the corporation. The board usually delegates the power to make operating decisions and to run the day-to-day activities of the business to a professional management team.

The board normally confines its attention to making policy, reviewing management performance, and acting on matters that can legally be decided only by the board. Decisions to expand the business by introducing a new product or by opening operations in a new geographic area are examples of major policy decisions. Declaring that dividends will be paid to stockholders is an action that can be taken legally only by the board.

President and Other Operating Officers

> The president and other officers operate the corporation

The president, various vice presidents, the secretary-treasurer, and the controller are responsible for carrying out the policies set by the board.

They operate the corporation by supervising the purchase (or manufacture) of the product, and by selling and distributing the product. They hire employees, prepare budgets, arrange short-term borrowing, and attend to all the other details necessary to run a business.

ORGANIZING A CORPORATION AND SELLING STOCK

As we discuss accounting problems relating to organizing a corporation and selling stock, we follow the experiences of Bill and Betsy Prince and two of their friends in establishing a computer store.

PC CITY, INC.

Bill and Betsy Prince and two of their friends decide to go into the business of selling personal computers, software, and computer supplies. After discussing the merits of various types of business organizations, they elect to incorporate as PC CITY, Inc. A lawyer and a CPA are hired to prepare the necessary articles of incorporation, to set up the accounting system, and to advise them regarding the various tax forms they will need to file. Within a short time the articles of incorporation are approved and the charter is received. The corporation is ready to sell stock.

The charter of incorporation authorizes PC CITY to issue 100,000 shares of $10-par stock.

Par versus No-Par Stock

A par or stated value may be set at the time stock is authorized

Many state laws require that stock have a par value. **Par value** is an amount determined arbitrarily and in no way is intended to reflect the actual market value of the stock. In some states par value defines an amount of **legal capital** that must be retained in the business. The amount represented as legal capital cannot be distributed to stockholders except when the corporation is liquidated. A corporation is liquidated when it goes out of business, pays all its debts, and gives any remaining assets to the stockholders.

Par and stated values are arbitrary—they do not reflect what the stock is worth

Due to the confusion among investors as to the actual meaning of par value, many states now permit the issuance of **no-par** stock. Some of these states allow the board of directors to arbitrarily select a **stated value.** If this is done, the stock is said to be **no-par with a stated value.** A stated value serves the same purpose as par value. But since stated value is not printed on the stock certificates, there is less risk of confusing investors.

In accounting for the issuance of stock, the par or stated value, if any, is recorded in the Common Stock account. This method preserves the legal capital in a separate account and makes balance sheet disclosure easier. Any amount received over and above par or stated value is credited to Paid-In Capital in Excess of Par (or Stated Value). Since par or stated value is usually set at a nominal amount, common stock is rarely sold for less than that value. No-par stock without a stated value is accounted for simply by crediting Common Stock for its sale price.

We've shown you how to record stock sold for its par value—just debit Cash and credit Common Stock—see page 151 in Chapter 4. Since stock is seldom sold for its nominal par value, we will assume that PC CITY sells its stock above par.

Selling Stock for Cash

Common Stock is credited for the par or stated value of the stock sold

Each of the four PC CITY incorporators agree to purchase 5,000 shares for $15 per share. The entry to record this sale on January 5, 1987—20,000 shares (4 × 5,000)—of stock is as follows:

```
Jan. 5   Cash . . . . . . . . . . . . . . . . . . . . . . . . . . . . . . . . . . . . 300,000
                Common Stock . . . . . . . . . . . . . . . . . . . . . . . . .         200,000
                Paid-In Capital in Excess of Par. . . . . . . . . . . . . .         100,000
         To record the sale of 20,000 shares of $10-par stock for $15
         per share to the incorporators. (20,000 shares × $15 =
         $300,000)
```

If the PC CITY, Inc., stock had been no par with no stated value, the sale would have been recorded by debiting Cash and crediting Common Stock for $300,000.

Selling Stock by Subscription

Corporations wishing to sell stock to the public may choose to sell the shares on subscription. In a **subscription sale,** a subscriber agrees to purchase a specified number of shares at an agreed price. The subscriber makes a down payment when he or

Stock sold on subscription is paid for in installments

she signs the subscription contract; the balance is paid in installments. The subscriber receives no shares until he or she pays the contract price in full.

On January 30, 1987, PC CITY, Inc., sells subscriptions to 5,000 shares of stock at $18 per share. A 20% down payment is received at the time the subscription contract is signed. The remainder is due in two equal installments on March 1 and April 1, 1987.

Jan. 30	Stock Subscriptions Receivable	72,000	
	Cash	18,000	
	Common Stock Subscribed		50,000
	Paid-In Capital in Excess of Par		40,000

To record the sale of subscriptions to 5,000 shares of $10-par common stock and the receipt of a 20% down payment: $(5,000 \times \$18) = \$90,000 \times 20\% = \$18,000$.

A current asset, Stock Subscriptions Receivable, is debited for the unpaid balance of the subscription contract. A temporary stockholders' equity account, Common Stock Subscribed, is credited for the par or stated value of the shares subscribed. This account will remain only until the shares are paid in full and certificates are issued. Common Stock Subscribed is shown in the stockholders' equity section immediately below the Common Stock account. Paid-In Capital in Excess of Par is credited for the difference between the subscription price and the par value.

PC CITY, Inc., receives the two subscription installments.

Mar. 1	Cash	36,000	
	Stock Subscriptions Receivable		36,000
	To record receipt of first installment.		
Apr. 1	Cash	36,000	
	Stock Subscriptions Receivable		36,000
	To record receipt of second intallment.		

When subscribers pay the installments due, the entry is similar to that which is made when customers pay on account: Cash is debited, and the receivable is credited.

When the subscription price is paid in full, the stock is issued

PC CITY, Inc., issues the shares for the fully paid subscriptions.

Apr. 1	Common Stock Subscribed	50,000	
	Common Stock		50,000
	To record the issuance of 5,000 shares of $10-par common stock.		

When subscriptions have been paid in full, we remove the temporary account, Common Stock Subscribed, and credit Common Stock. Remember that Common

Stock Subscribed, was originally credited for the *par value* of the subscribed shares. Par value, then, is the amount we transfer to the Common Stock account.

Selling Stock for Noncash Consideration

Stock sold for noncash assets is valued at either the market value of the stock or the market value of the asset

Occasionally stock is issued in exchange for services or assets. Transactions of this type are especially common in small corporations.

The selling price of the stock in this type of transaction is considered to be either the fair market value of the stock or the fair market value of the service or asset, whichever can be determined more objectively.

The fair market value of the stock being sold is usually more objective when the stock is actively traded on a stock exchange. To find the market value, you would simply call a stockbroker or check *The Wall Street Journal* for a stock price quotation. This quotation will provide an objective measure of the values exchanged in your noncash transaction.

Appraisal values of the services or assets received for the stock are more reliable when stocks are inactively traded. Stock in small, closely held corporations may change hands rarely, if at all. No current, bargained market value will be available for these shares.

The par or stated value of the stock should never be used as a measure of the selling price. Remember, these amounts are nominal and are arbitrarily determined when the corporation is formed. Par or stated value rarely reflects the current value of either the stock issued or the asset received.

Issuing Stock in Exchange for Services

A corporation may issue shares in exchange for legal, accounting, architectural, or other services.

PC CITY, Inc., issues 100 shares of stock to J. Barrister in exchange for legal services rendered in drawing up the articles of incorporation.

Apr. 2	Organization Cost	1,800	
	Common Stock		1,000
	Paid-In Capital in Excess of Par.		800
	To record issuance of 100 shares of stock in exchange for legal services: $18 \times 100 = \$1,800$.		

The amount we used in the preceding entry could have been determined in two ways:

1. The current market price of the stock issued could be used as a measure of the value of the services received. Since PC CITY stock is not actively traded on a stock exchange, and since no sale of the stock has been negotiated since January, we will look for another measure of value.

2. The normal fee for performing this type of legal service could be used if this fee is well known. We will assume for this example that PC CITY's articles are not complex and that lawyers have a fairly standard fee of $1,800 for preparing simple articles of incorporation. We will also want to check to see if this value seems reasonable based on earlier selling prices of the stock. The stock sold in January for $18 per share and this stock also is being valued at $18 per share; this amount is certainly reasonable. If the value in this transaction were $50 per share, we would want to reconsider the method of choosing our stock value.

$1,800 is a well-known, standard fee for the type of service PC CITY received, and the amount is reasonable. We used $1,800 to record the value of the services received and the stock issued.

Organization Cost is debited for the costs of organizing a new corporation

Organization Cost is debited. This intangible asset is charged for legal fees, amounts paid to the chartering state, costs of printing the stock certificates, and other amounts expended in organizing a new corporation.

Organization Cost, like all intangible assets, must be amortized over its useful life, subject to a maximum of 40 years. Many corporations amortize organization costs over 5 years because this is the life they use on their income tax return. Since the amount of the amortization per year is relatively small (not material), no serious mismatching problems are created by using this short life.

Issuing Stock in Exchange for Assets

Often in smaller corporations a prospective stockholder will contribute assets that the corporation needs in its operations in exchange for stock.

PC CITY issues 500 shares of stock to Rods and Plots for 1 acre of land.

Sept. 1	Land	12,000	
	Common Stock		5,000
	Paid-In Capital in Excess of Par		7,000
	To record issuance of 500 shares of stock in exchange for 1 acre of land. (Land appraised at $12,000.)		

Approximately 5 months have elapsed since PC CITY last issued stock, on April 2, 1987. Since the stock is not actively traded, the old market value may not accurately reflect the current worth of the stock. In most cases no standard price is available for land because each piece is unique. In such instances we use one or more independent appraisals to establish an estimate of the asset's market value. We use this appraised value as the selling price of the stock and the acquisition price of the land.

TREASURY STOCK

Treasury stock is the corporation's own stock that it has reacquired

A corporation may reacquire its own stock by purchasing it on a stock exchange (through a stockbroker) or by a private transaction with an individual stockholder. This repurchased stock is called *treasury stock.*

Treasury stock may be purchased for later issuance to executives or employees under a stock option or stock purchase plan, for the purpose of buying out a disgruntled shareholder, or for a variety of other reasons.

While shares are held in the treasury, they do not possess the rights of outstanding shares—they cannot vote or receive dividends.

Purchase of Treasury Stock for Cash

PC CITY, Inc., repurchases 50 shares of stock at $25 per share.

Sept. 15	Treasury Stock	1,250	
	Cash		1,250
	To record acquisition of 50 shares of stock at $25 per share.		

Treasury Stock is a negative stockholders' equity account

Treasury Stock is debited for the cost of the reacquired shares. Since these shares are to be held for only a short time and not retired, the transaction reflects a temporary reduction in total stockholders' equity. We show this temporary reduction by reporting Treasury Stock on the balance sheet as a contra- (negative) stockholders' equity account. Remember, the par value and any amounts originally received in excess of par still appear in the Common Stock and Paid-In Capital in Excess of Par accounts.

At the end of this chapter we will show you exactly how treasury stock is shown in the stockholders' equity section.

Purchase of Treasury Stock for Noncash Assets

The cost of treasury stock is either the fair value of assets given or the fair value of the stock acquired

The corporation may give some asset other than cash for the stock it is buying back. The cost of the treasury stock in these transactions is the fair value of the assets given or the fair value of the stock being purchased, whichever is more objectively determinable. This rule should sound familiar. We used it for deciding the selling price of stock for noncash assets or services.

The corporation's assets are carried in the accounting records at cost. Or, sometimes they are carried at cost less accumulated depreciation, depletion, or amortization. They do not appear on the corporation's books at their market value.

When we use these assets to buy treasury stock, we must make two journal entries: one to revalue the asset—increase it or decrease it to its fair value—and a second to record the purchase of the treasury stock. The effect of these two entries will be the same as if we had sold the asset for cash and then used the cash to purchase treasury stock.

PC CITY exchanges one-half of the acre of land acquired on September 1 for 300 shares of stock. The half acre of land is appraised at $7,500.

Sept. 20	Land		1,500	
	Gain from Increasing Land to Fair Value			1,500
	To increase ½ acre of land from $6,000 cost to $7,500 fair value.			
20	Treasury Stock		7,500	
	Land			7,500
	To record exchange of land for 300 shares of common stock.			
	Cost basis per share = $7,500 ÷ 300 shares = $25 per share.			

When we record the asset revaluation, we will recognize a gain or loss—just as we would if the asset had been sold for cash. This gain or loss account is shown on the income statement under Other Gains and Losses.

The gain or loss we record is a gain or loss on the disposal of an asset, not on the purchase of treasury stock.

Sale of Treasury Stock above Cost

PC CITY sells 20 shares of treasury stock for $30 per share. The treasury stock had been purchased for $25 per share.

Sept. 30	Cash		600	
	Treasury Stock			500
	Paid-In Capital from Treasury Stock			100
	To record sale of 20 shares of treasury stock that originally cost $25 for $30 each.			

Paid-In Capital from Treasury Stock is credited when we sell treasury stock for more than its cost

A corporation may decide to sell treasury stock to an employee or to another person who wants to invest in the business. The treasury stock may be sold for more than the corporation originally paid. In this case we must do the following: (1) Debit Cash to record the asset we receive; (2) credit Treasury Stock to decrease this account — we no longer have the treasury stock; and (3) credit Paid-In Capital from Treasury Stock to record the amount we receive over and above what we originally paid for the treasury stock. Paid-In Capital from Treasury Stock specifically identifies the source of the new paid-in capital.

When we sell an asset for more than its cost, we record a gain. Treasury stock is not an asset. *Corporations are not allowed to recognize gains or losses as a result of buying and selling their own stock.* Corporate income results from carrying on the business of the company, not from speculating in or attempting to manipulate the price of its own stock.

Sale of Treasury Stock below Cost

PC CITY sells 20 shares of treasury stock for $22 per share.

Oct. 31	Cash	440	
	Paid-In Capital from Treasury Stock	60	
	Treasury Stock		500
	To record sale of 20 shares of treasury stock that originally cost $25 for $22 each.		

When treasury shares are sold for less than their cost, we must record a decrease in stockholders' equity. This decrease is charged to:

Treasury stock sold for less than its cost reduces Paid-In Capital from Treasury Stock, then Retained Earnings

1. Paid-In Capital from Treasury stock, until its balance reaches zero; then to
2. Retained Earnings (an account showing the accumulated income of the corporation).

In no case should such decreases be reported on the income statement as a loss.

In our illustration, PC CITY created Paid-In Capital from Treasury Stock when it sold treasury stock on September 30. We then debit that account for the $60 excess of the cost of the treasury stock over the amount PC CITY sold it for on October 31. If the September 30 transaction had not occurred, PC CITY would not have had Paid-In Capital from Treasury Stock. In that case we would have debited the $60 to Retained Earnings.

Notice that in all cases we debit Treasury Stock for the cost of shares acquired and credit it for cost when the shares are resold. When all treasury shares have been disposed of, Treasury Stock will have a zero balance.

We have summarized accounting for treasury stock in Exhibit 13-1 on page 504.

DONATED CAPITAL

Shares of stock or assets may be donated to a corporation

Profit-making corporations may receive donations of assets or of shares of their stock. Stockholders may donate shares in order for the corporation to have stock available to sell to raise additional capital or to use in stock option plans designed to keep or attract outstanding management talent. The cost of these treasury shares is zero; therefore we make no formal journal entry to record the acquisition. A memoran-

EXHIBIT 13-1
Accounting for Treasury Stock.

Rules for buying treasury stock

Rules for selling treasury stock

When Buying Treasury Stock:

For Cash	Record treasury stock at the amount of cash given.
For Noncash Assets	Revalue the asset you give to its fair value. When you increase or decrease the asset, record a gain or loss.
	Record treasury stock at the fair market value of the asset given or the fair market value of the stock. Use the one of these values that is most objectively measured.

When Selling Treasury Stock:

For More Than It Cost	Remove the cost of treasury stock from the accounts.
	Record the extra amount received as Paid-In Capital from Treasury Stock.
For Less Than It Cost	Remove the cost of treasury stock from the accounts.
	Decrease stockholders' equity for the excess of the cost over the selling price of the treasury stock by:
	1. Debiting Paid-In Capital from Treasury Stock. When the balance of this account is reduced to zero,
	2. Debit Retained Earnings.

dum entry is often made in the general journal to officially note the fact that shares were received. This stock is treasury stock with no cost.

PC CITY receives 50 shares of common stock as a donation.

Nov. 5   Memorandum: Received 50 shares of donated common stock.

If donated shares are later sold, Cash is debited and Donated Capital is credited for their sales price.

Cities and counties often donate land and occasionally other assets to attract new industry to operate in their locality. When new industry moves into a geographic area, the area benefits through increased employment and by receiving the taxes that the company pays. The company benefits by having the use of an asset at no cost.

PC CITY receives the donation of an old building from the City of Parrish. The building will be moved by the city from its present site to PC's land. PC CITY will use the building as a retail store and also refurbish the structure and maintain it as a historical landmark. The fair value of the building in its present condition is $15,000.

Dec. 15   Building 15,000
            Donated Capital   15,000
            To record donation of building by the city of Parrish.

Donated Capital is the paid-in capital account used to reflect the value of assets donated

Assets donated to the company are recorded at their fair value when they are received. Donated Capital, a stockholders' equity account, is credited to record the source of the asset entering the pool of resources that management has to use.

STOCKHOLDERS' EQUITY ON THE BALANCE SHEET

A review of the disclosure of the stockholders' equity accounts discussed in this chapter will help you visualize the effect that each stockholders' equity transaction has on the balance sheet. Our discussion is based on the PC CITY, Inc., stockholders' equity section as it appears after the entries illustrated in this chapter.

First, let's look at PC CITY's general ledger (page 506) to see how each stockholders' equity account will appear after we post all the transactions.

When we have posted all of the entries to the general ledger accounts and found the balance of each account, we are ready to prepare financial statements.

Stockholders' equity accounts are shown on the balance sheet. Here is what PC CITY's balance sheet stockholders' equity section looks like:

Stockholders' Equity

Paid-In Capital:
  Common Stock, $10 par, 100,000 shares authorized, 25,600 shares issued,
    25,240 shares outstanding (360 shares are in the treasury) $256,000
  Additional Paid-In Capital:
    Paid-In Capital in Excess of Par $147,800
    Paid-In Capital from Treasury Stock   40
    Donated Capital   15,000
        Total Additional Paid-In Capital   162,840
Total Paid-In Capital $418,840

Earned Capital:
  Retained Earnings (amount assumed)   12,600
Total $431,440
Less: Treasury Stock (360 shares) at cost . . . .   (7,750)

Total Stockholders' Equity $423,690

Balance sheet stockholders' equity reports capital by source: (1) paid-in by owners and others (2) earned by the corporation

The major objective of the stockholders' equity section is to report the capital of the corporation by source—where the assets came from. For this reason we divide stockholders' equity into two basic subsections: paid-in capital and earned capital. *Paid-in capital* measures the resources contributed by owners and others. *Earned capital,* retained earnings, reflects the resources that have been earned by the corporation since it began, minus any earnings paid out as dividends. We will discuss earned capital in Chapter 14.

The paid-in capital subsection is divided into two categories, one showing the par or stated value of stock issued or subscribed and the other disclosing amounts contributed in excess of par, or contributed through other transactions. Observe that we report several important pieces of information for common stock:

Common stock information we report on the balance sheet

1. The *par or stated value,* or the fact that it is no-par stock

2. The number of shares *authorized* by the articles of incorporation

PC CITY, INC.
General Ledger — Stockholders' Equity Accounts
December 31, 1987

Common Stock ($10 par)

		Jan. 5 (20,000 shs)	200,000
		Apr. 1 (5,000 shs)	50,000
		Apr. 2 (100 shs)	1,000
		Sept. 1 (500 shs)	5,000
		Dec. 31 Bal.	
		(25,600 shs)	256,000

Paid-In Capital in Excess of Par

		Jan. 5	100,000
		Jan. 30	40,000
		Apr. 2	800
		Sept. 1	7,000
		Dec. 31 Bal.	147,800

Common Stock Subscribed

Apr. 1 (5,000 shs)	50,000	Jan. 30 (5,000 shs)	50,000
		Dec. 31 Bal.	0

Donated Capital

		Dec. 15	15,000
		Dec. 31 Bal.	15,000

Treasury Stock

Sept. 15 (50 shs)	1,250	Sept. 30 (20 shs)	500
Sept. 20 (300 shs)	7,500	Oct. 31 (20 shs)	500
Nov. 5 (50 shs)	0		
Total (400 shs)	8,750	Total (40 shs)	1,000
Dec. 31 Bal			
(360 shs)	7,750		

Paid-In Capital from Treasury Stock

Oct. 31	60	Sept. 30	100
		Dec. 31 Bal.	40

3. The total number of shares that have been *issued* by the corporation at any time

4. The total number of shares *outstanding*—in the hands of stockholders

5. The number of shares held *in the treasury*

The par or stated value of any stock subscribed but not issued immediately follows common stock. All of PC's subscribed stock has been paid for and issued, so we didn't have Common Stock Subscribed on PC CITY's balance sheet.

The second paid-in capital category, additional paid-in capital, contains a listing of the accounts that arose either as a result of stockholders paying more than par or stated value for their shares, or from other contributed-capital transactions. Donated capital and increases in paid-in capital resulting from treasury stock transactions are examples of additional paid-in capital. Generally accepted accounting principles also allow donated capital to be shown in a separate stockholders' equity section. We're including it with additional paid-in capital for simplicity. This listing of accounts accomplishes our goal of reporting sources of all corporate capital.

The temporary contra-stockholders' equity account, Treasury Stock, is subtracted from the total of paid-in and earned capital.

STOCK VALUE

The word "value" is used in several different ways when applied to common stock. The purpose of this final section of the chapter is to review the concepts of par value, stated value, and market value and to introduce you to two new terms—book value and liquidation value.

Par Value and Stated Value

Par value is an arbitrary amount per share set by the charter of incorporation. Par value is usually a nominal amount and does not reflect the actual value of a share of stock. Some states use par value to set the minimum amount of capital (legal capital) that must be retained in the business. Legal capital cannot be distributed to the stockholders except when the corporation is liquidated.

Stated value is also an arbitrary amount per share, but it is set by the board of directors instead of the charter of incorporation. Unlike par value, stated value is not printed on the stock certificate, so there is less risk of investors mistakenly believing that stated value is the stock's worth. Like par value, some states use stated value to establish the legal capital of the corporation.

Market Value

A stock's market value is the amount that a share of stock is selling for. Market value is determined by investor expectations about the future of the company and future general economic conditions. Such things as expected company earnings, expected dividend payments, the general financial condition of the company, expected future interest rates, and expected changes in tax rates may influence an investor's decision about the worth of a share of stock. In Chapter 18 we will discuss several tools that an investor can use in analyzing the financial condition of a company.

Book Value

The book value per share of stock is the claim against a company's assets represented by one share of stock. Book value per share is calculated by dividing total stock-holders' equity (which is just total assets minus total liabilities) by the total number of shares of stock *outstanding* plus any shares subscribed but not yet issued. Treasury shares are not outstanding, so they are omitted. The book value per share of PC CITY's stock would be calculated as follows:

$$\frac{\text{Total stockholders' equity}}{\text{Total shares outstanding}} = \frac{\$423,690}{25,240 \text{ shs}} = \$16.79 \text{ per share}$$

PC CITY has no subscribed but unissued shares. If it did, the number of these shares would be added to the shares outstanding.

Liquidation Value

The *liquidation value* of a share of stock is the amount that a stockholder will receive if the corporation ceases operations, sells all of its assets, pays off all of its liabilities, and distributes the remaining cash to the stockholders. Since some of the assets will be sold at a gain and others at a loss, the liquidation value cannot be determined in advance of the sale of the assets.

Liquidation value can be higher or lower than book value before the liquidation process begins (remember, stockholders' equity goes up when the company has gains and down when it has losses). If PC CITY sold its assets for $380,000, a $43,690 loss would be incurred:

Selling price	$ 380,000
Less: Book value of net assets	(423,690)
Gain (loss) on sale of net assets	$ (43,690)

When the loss is deducted from retained earnings, total stockholders' equity would be reduced by $43,690. The liquidation value per share would be $15.06 [($423,690 − $43,690) ÷ 25,240 shs]. The book value before this process began was $16.79. The assets had a historical cost value of $16.79 per share, but when they were sold they proved to be worth only $15.06 per share.

CHAPTER SUMMARY

Corporations are the dominant business form in our economy. These legal beings are established by state charters after the incorporators file acceptable articles of incorporation and pay the proper fee. The *articles of incorporation* spell out the corporation's name and purpose for existence; the types of stock that it can issue, including number of shares and par value; the location of the principal corporate office; and the corporation's permitted legal life. In addition, the names and addresses of the first board of directors and the incorporators are listed.

Advantages that corporations have over proprietorships and partnerships are as follows: (1) They can raise greater amounts of capital, (2) their owners have limited liability, (3) their owners can easily transfer ownership shares, and (4) they have almost unlimited lives. Double taxation and extensive government regulation are the two primary disadvantages of corporations.

The corporate organizational structure has the stockholders on top, followed by the board of directors and then the president and other operating officers. Stockholders possess certain legal rights as owners of the corporation. Among the most important of these rights are:

1. The right to receive stock certificates.
2. The right to vote in corporate elections. (They elect the board of directors.)
3. The right to maintain their proportionate ownership (the preemptive right).
4. The right to receive dividends.
5. The right to receive residual assets upon dissolution.

The **board of directors** is responsible for managing the corporation. The board's attention is usually confined to broad matters of policy, reviewing management performance, and other matters that only they can legally perform.

The **management officers** operate the business in conformity with the board of directors' policies.

The gathering of capital needed to operate the corporation begins with the sale of common stock. Common stock may be sold for cash, on a subscription basis, or in exchange for services or noncash assets. The par or stated value, if any, of the issued stock is credited to the Common Stock account. Any amount received in excess of par or stated value is recorded in an additional paid-in capital account.

Stock repurchased by a corporation is called **treasury stock.** Since treasury stock may be acquired for a variety of purposes, it is held in a temporary contra-stock-holders' equity account until it is needed. Reissuance of treasury stock above its cost creates additional paid-in capital. Reissuance below cost decreases paid-in capital and, in some cases, earned capital.

Donated capital may take the form of stock or other assets. Donations of stock are recorded by a memorandum entry; Donated Capital is credited when these shares are subsequently sold. Donations of assets are recorded at the fair value of the asset.

The stockholders' equity section of the balance sheet is divided into categories which are structured like this:

Paid-In Capital:
    Capital Stock
    Additional Paid-In Capital

Earned Capital
Less: Treasury Stock

IMPORTANT TERMS USED IN THIS CHAPTER

Articles of incorporation The written documents filed with a state government outlining basic information about the corporation, including its name, purpose, capital structure, and the names of individuals involved in its beginning. (page 491)

Authorized stock The total capital stock that may be issued by the corporation as stipulated in the articles of incorporation. The classes of stock, par value, and total number of shares are specified. (page 491)

Board of directors The group of individuals elected by the stockholders and entrusted with the responsibility for managing a corporation. (page 497)

Book value per share The claim against a company's assets represented by each share of stock. Book value per share is calculated as follows: (total stockholders' equity ÷ total shares outstanding). (page 507)

Capital stock Certificates of ownership issued by a corporation. Capital stock may refer to common stock or preferred stock or both. (page 491)

Charter The document issued by a state government that gives a business the legal right to begin operating as a corporation. (page 491)

Common stock A class of capital stock that represents the basic ownership of a corporation. Common stock carries the right to vote, share in earnings, maintain proportionate ownership share, and receive residual assets in liquidation. (page 496)

Corporation   An artificial legal being created by government charter and possessing many of the rights of a natural person. (page 491)

Donated capital   The value of assets or shares of capital stock given to a corporation. (page 503)

Earned capital   The total income of the corporation since its incorporation, minus dividends paid to shareholders. (page 505)

Issued stock   Shares of capital stock that have been sold at some point in the corporation's history. See *authorized stock* and *outstanding stock.* (page 496)

Legal capital   An amount of paid-in capital that must be retained in the corporation. Minimum legal capital, defined by state law, usually consists of the par value or stated value of the issued stock. (page 498)

Liquidation value per share   The claim against a company's cash represented by each share of stock. Liquidation value per share can be determined only after all assets have been sold and all liabilities have been paid. (page 508)

Market value per share   The amount that a share of stock is selling for on the open market. (page 507)

Organization cost   An intangible asset consisting of the legal fees, state charter fees, and other costs incurred in creating a corporation. (page 501)

Outstanding stock   Shares of capital stock in the hands of stockholders. (page 507)

Paid-in capital   The amount of resources invested in the corporation by its stockholders, contributed through donation, and received as a result of certain treasury stock transactions. (page 505)

Par value   An arbitrary per-share amount specified in the articles of incorporation (and printed on the face of each stock certificate). Usually defines the legal capital of the corporation. (page 498)

Preferred stock   A class of capital stock that carries certain rights that have priority over those of common stock. Priority rights to dividends and to distributions of assets in liquidation are typical. (page 496)

Stated value   An arbitrary per-share amount specified by official action of the board of directors for no-par stock. May define the legal capital of the corporation. (page 498)

Stock subscription   A method of selling capital stock in which a purchaser signs a contract agreeing to buy a specified number of shares at a negotiated price. The stock is normally paid for in installments. (page 498)

Stockholder   Owner of shares of capital stock. (page 495)

Treasury stock   Shares of capital stock reacquired and held by the issuing corporation. (page 501)

QUESTIONS

1. Briefly explain how a corporation is created. Is it more difficult to create a partnership or a corporation? Explain.

2. How does the liability of a partner differ from the liability of a stockholder? Explain.

3. It is usually easier to transfer ownership interest in a corporation than to transfer ownership interest in a partnership. Explain why this is true.

4. Explain how the income of a corporation is taxed twice.

5. Explain the stockholders' *preemptive right.*

6. What activities are normally engaged in by a corporation's board of directors?

7. One Corp.'s stock has a par value of $1 per share; Two Corp.'s stock has a stated value of $1; Three Corp.'s stock has no par or stated value. Explain how the sale of one share of stock for $5 would be accounted for by each corporation.

8. Corporation A's stock has a par value of $1. Corporation B's stock has a par value of $10. Which stock is worth more? Explain.

9. How does a sale of stock on a subscription basis differ from a sale of stock for immediate cash?

10. How is each of the following shown on a corporation's balance sheet: Stock Subscriptions Receivable, Common Stock Subscribed?

11. What are organization costs? How are organization costs shown on the balance sheet?

12. Recently 100,000 shares of a large corporation's stock traded on the New York Stock Exchange for $50 per share. How much will the corporation receive as a result of this transaction? Explain.

13. Oz Corp. exchanged 100 shares of its $10-par common stock for some office furniture. Explain how Oz should determine the proper amount for this transaction.

14. What is treasury stock? How is treasury stock shown on a corporation's balance sheet?

15. Kermit Corp. purchased treasury stock for $100 and later sold it for $125. How will this $25 "gain" be reported on the financial statements?

16. Squires Corp. received a pickup truck and 100 shares of its own stock as a donation from a stockholder. Explain the amount that would be assigned to Donated Capital in each of these cases.

17. Explain the difference between paid-in capital and earned capital.

18. What is meant by authorized stock, issued stock, and outstanding stock? Explain.

19. Is it possible to have more shares of stock issued than outstanding? Explain.

20. Herix stock has a book value of $38.20 per share. Does this mean that, if the corporation liquidates, each stockholder will receive $38.20 for each share of stock owned?

EXERCISES

Exercise 13-1
Recording the sale of par value stock

Prepare the proper journal entry to record each of the following 1987 transactions and events. If no entry is required, write, "No Entry."

July 1   Lane, Inc., received a charter of incorporation that authorizes the issuance of 500,000 shares of $5-par stock.
       12   Lane, Inc., sold 40,000 shares for $6 per share.
       23   Lane, Inc., sold 3,000 shares for $10 per share.

Exercise 13-2
Recording the sale of stock with a stated value

Hatcher Company was incorporated early in 1988. The following events occurred during January:

Jan. 2   Received a charter of incorporation from the state of Mississippi. The charter authorizes Hatcher to issue 100,000 shares of no-par stock. The Hatcher board of directors votes to set a stated value of $1 on each share.
       7   10,000 shares of stock were sold for $17,800.
       25   10,000 shares of stock were sold for $24,300.

Prepare journal entries to record the transactions and events above. If no entry is required, write, "No Entry."

Exercise 13-3
Recording the sale of no-par stock

Honest Fred Used Cars, Inc., began business in 1987. The following events and transactions occurred during the first month of operations:

Oct. 2   A charter of incorporation was received from the state of West Virginia. The charter authorized the sale of 1 million shares of no-par stock.
10   Fred sold 5,000 shares of stock for $5 per share.
29   Fred sold 3,500 shares of stock for $1 per share.

Prepare journal entries to record the transactions and events above. If no entry is required, write, "No Entry."

Exercise 13-4
Recording stock sold on subscription

Prepare the proper journal entries to record each of the following 1986 transactions:

Feb. 3   Martinez, Inc., sold subscriptions for 600 shares of $2-par common stock. The subscription price of $12 per share is to be paid in three installments, $4 down at the time of the subscription, and $4 at the beginning of March and April.
Mar. 1   Martinez collected the first installment.
Apr. 1   Martinez collected the second installment and issued the stock.

Exercise 13-5
Calculating various paid-in capital amounts for three corporations

Larry, Inc., is authorized by its charter to issue 100,000 shares of no-par stock. During its first year of operations 60,000 shares were sold for $15 per share.

Curly Corp. is authorized by its charter to issue 500,000 shares of $5-par stock. During its first year of operations Curly sold 10,000 shares for $20 per share and 40,000 shares for $17.50 per share.

Moe, Inc., is authorized by its charter to issue 1 million shares of no-par stock. Moe's board of directors adopted a stated value of $1 per share. During Moe's first year of operations 100,000 shares were sold for $500,000 and 80,000 shares were sold for $400,000.

Prepare schedules showing the calculation of common stock, additional paid-in capital, and total paid-in capital for Larry, Curly, and Moe, respectively. Your calculations should be clearly labeled.

(Check figure: Total paid-in capital for Larry = $900,000)

Exercise 13-6
Recording stock sold for cash, for services, and for noncash assets

Landcare, Inc., was authorized by its charter of incorporation to issue 400,000 shares of $1-par common stock. Prepare entries to record each of the following 1988 transactions. Explain why you chose the amount that you did for the account debited.

Aug. 1   Landcare sold 40,000 shares of stock for $15 per share.
2   Landcare issued 400 shares to Used Machinery in exchange for a tractor. The advertised price of the tractor was $6,995.
16   Landcare issued 200 shares to G. Hernandez for services rendered in the process of applying for a charter of incorporation.
Dec. 31   20,000 shares were issued for a plot of land to be used as a plant nursery. The land was appraised by two independent appraisers at $240,000 and $260,000.

(Check figure: Land was debited for $250,000)

Exercise 13-7
Preparing treasury stock entries

Tanner, Inc., has the following stock outstanding on December 31, 1986:

Common Stock, $10 par, 1,000,000 shares authorized,
400,000 shares issued and outstanding. $4,000,000
Paid-In Capital in Excess of Par Value   5,000,000

Prepare journal entries to record the following transactions that took place in 1987:

Mar. 10   Tanner repurchased 1,000 shares for $22.50 per share.
June 19   Tanner sold 600 of the shares purchased on Mar. 10 for $26.00 per share.
Oct. 2   Tanner sold the remaining 400 shares purchased on Mar. 10 for $20 per share.

(Check figure: Paid-In Capital from Treasury Stock June 19 entry = $2,100)

Exercise 13-8

Recording acquisition of treasury stock for noncash assets

Vicar Corp. has offered to exchange some used assets for shares of Vicar common stock. During 1986 the following exchanges took place:

Nov. 2   Vicar traded a forklift with a market value of $9,000 for 200 shares of stock. The forklift had a cost of $15,000 and an accumulated depreciation on the day of the exchange of $8,500.

Dec. 1   Vicar exchanged a trailer having a cost of $37,500 and an accumulated depreciation on the date of the trade of $17,000 for 400 shares of stock. The trailer has a fair value of $19,200.

Prepare entries to revalue each of the assets and to record acquisition of the treasury stock.

(Check figure: Loss from Decreasing Trailer to Fair Value = $1,300)

Exercise 13-9

Calculating book value per share of common stock

The December 31, 1987, McBee Corp.'s stockholders' equity section appears as follows:

Paid-In Capital:
  Common Stock, $10 par, 100,000 shares authorized,
    60,000 shares issued and outstanding $600,000
  Paid-In Capital in Excess of Par   204,000
Total Paid-In Capital $804,000

Earned Capital:
  Retained Earnings   18,000

Total Stockholders' Equity $822,000

Calculate the book value per share of McBee's common stock.

(Check figure: Book value per share = $13.70)

PROBLEMS
Set A

Problem A13-1

Preparing entries related to issuance of stock

Ranon, Inc., was recently chartered by the State of New York. Transactions relating to the issuance of common stock during 1986 are described below:

Aug. 4   Ranon, Inc., received a charter of incorporation from the State of New York. Ranon was authorized to issue 2,000,000 shares of no-par common stock. The board of directors voted to establish a stated value of $5 per share.
      6   Ranon issued 60,000 shares for $540,000 cash.
      7   Ranon issued 1,000 shares to Steinburg and O'Leary, Attorneys at Law, in payment for legal services rendered in preparing the articles of incorporation.
Sept. 1   Ranon issued 2,000 shares to Ramona Chaffin in exchange for a plot of land. The land's value has been established by independent appraisers at $18,500.
     24   10,000 shares of stock were sold for $11 per share cash.
     27   1,500 shares of stock were issued to Vernon Pope in exchange for some office equipment. The equipment will be used in rented offices until a new building can be constructed.

Dec. 10   Polk City donated a building valued at $250,000 to Ranon. Ranon has agreed to move the building and preserve its basic architectural style. The moving is expected to be completed by Dec. 20, 1986.

Required   Prepare journal entries to record each of the transactions described above. If no entry is necessary write, "No Entry." Calculations should be included as part of your journal entry explanation where appropriate.

(Check figure: The August 7 entry includes a debit to Organization Cost of $9,000)

Problem A13-2
Recording stock sold on subscription

Zand Company has been authorized to issue 500,000 shares of $2-par common stock. Zand's 1988 stock issuance transactions are described below:

Apr. 12   Zand sold subscriptions for 150,000 shares of stock. The shares have a subscription price of $10 each. 20% of the subscription price was received as a down payment.

May 6   200,000 shares were sold for $1,200,000.

    12   Subscribers paid an installment amounting to 40% of the subscription price.

June 6   1,000 shares were exchanged for a full-page advertisement in a national magazine. The ad appeared in the June 10 edition. The rate charged for such an advertisement is $65,000.

    12   The final 40% of the subscription price was received and the stock was issued.

Required   Prepare journal entries to record the transactions described above. Calculations should be included as part of your journal entry where appropriate.

Problem A13-3
Recording purchases and sales of treasury stock

The December 31, 1986, stockholders' equity section of Young Corp.'s balance sheet is as follows:

Stockholders' Equity	
Paid-In Capital:	
Common Stock, $5 par, 200,000 shares authorized, 150,000 shares issued and outstanding	$ 750,000
Paid-In Capital in Excess of Par	187,500
Total Paid-In Capital	$ 937,500
Earned Capital:	
Retained Earnings	545,500
Total Stockholders' Equity	$1,483,000

Required   Prepare Young Corp.'s journal entries to record the following transactions that took place during January 1987:

Jan. 4   Purchased 24,000 shares of Young's stock for $168,000.

    15   Sold 4,000 shares of the treasury stock for $8 per share.

    25   Sold 14,000 shares of the treasury stock for $6.50 per share.

    31   Sold the remaining 6,000 shares of treasury stock for $7 per share.

Problem A13-4

Oliver Tires, Inc., was incorporated in 1987. The following events and transactions relate to the company's stockholders' equity accounts during the first year of its existence:

Preparing T-account entries to record stockholders' equity transactions; preparing a stockholders' equity section

Jan.	6	The charter of incorporation was received authorizing Oliver to issue 500,000 shares of $10 par common stock.
	7	50,000 shares of stock were issued to the incorporators for $750,000 cash.
	21	Subscriptions to 50,000 shares were sold. The subscription price of $18 per share is to be received as follows: one-third on January 21, one-third on February 15, and one-third on March 15. The one-third down payment was received.
Feb.	5	200 shares of stock were issued to Rubin and Perot, Attorneys at Law, in payment for legal services received in establishing the corporation. A value of $3,600 was deemed to be proper.
	15	The one-third installment due on the subscribed stock was received.
Mar.	1	Oliver purchased 5,000 shares from one of the incorporators for $18 per share.
	15	The final installment was received on the subscribed shares. The shares were issued.
	31	Oliver sold 2,000 shares of treasury stock for $21 per share.
Apr.	15	Oliver received 2 acres of land adjoining the city dump as a used-tire recycling center. The land, having a fair market value of $20,000, was donated by Twin City.
	30	Oliver traded a patent with a book value of $4,000 and a fair market value of $8,200 for 400 shares of Oliver common stock.
May	27	Oliver sold 1,000 shares of the treasury stock purchased on Mar. 1 for $17 per share.

The balance of the Retained Earnings account after all 1987 entries is $28,000. (Establish an account with this balance.)

Required

1. Prepare T-account entries for each of the events and transactions above. Do not make entries in general journal form. Set up T-accounts and post your entries directly to the T-accounts.
2. Prepare the stockholders' equity section of the Oliver Tire balance sheet. You should include all appropriate disclosures discussed in this chapter.

(Check figure: Total stockholders' equity = $1,662,400)

Problem A13-5
Preparing stockholders' equity section of a balance sheet

The following stockholders' equity accounts were included on the December 31, 1986, trial balance of Leigh, Inc. Each account has a normal balance.

Common Stock Subscribed	$ 10,000
Paid-In Capital from Treasury Stock	48,000
Retained Earnings	144,000
Paid-In Capital in Excess of Par	900,000
Treasury Stock (2,000 shares) at cost	24,000
Common Stock	300,000
Donated Capital	44,000

Leigh was authorized by its charter of incorporation to issue 400,000 shares of $5-par common stock.

Required Prepare the stockholders' equity of Leigh, Inc.'s balance sheet in good form.

(Check figure: Total stockholders' equity = $1,422,000)

Problem A13-6
Calculating missing information from stockholders' equity section

The stockholders' equity section shown at the top of page 516 was prepared by H & D Corp.'s accounting department. The stockholders' equity section omitted several important facts that may be calculated by using the information given.

Stockholders' Equity	
Common Stock, no-par, 20,000 shares issued.	$ 50,000
Common Stock Subscribed	5,000
Paid-In Capital in Excess of Stated Value	47,000
Donated Capital	8,000
Retained Earnings	38,000
Total	$148,000
Less: Treasury Stock (300 shares)	(1,305)
Total Stockholders' Equity.	$146,695

Required

Answer each of the following questions using the data given in the stockholders' equity section above. Show calculations where appropriate.

1. What is the stated value per share of common stock?

2. What is total paid-in capital?

3. How many shares of common stock have been subscribed but not issued?

4. How many shares of common stock are outstanding?

5. How much was paid for each share of treasury stock?

6. What was the average amount paid for the common shares issued and subscribed? (Round your answer to the nearest cent.)

7. What is the book value per share of common stock?

(Check figure: Average amount paid for the shares issued and subscribed = $4.64)

Set B

Problem B13-1
Preparing entries related to issuance of stock

Hamanna Corp. was granted a charter by the state of Nebraska. 1988 transactions related to the issuance of common stock are described below:

Jan. 10   Hamanna Corp. received its charter of incorporation from the state of Nebraska. Hamanna was authorized to issue 200,000 shares of no-par common stock. The board of directors established a stated value of $50 per share.

15   Hamanna sold 30,000 shares for $1,620,000.

21   Hamanna issued 2,000 shares to Barnes, Lopez and Stein, Attorneys at Law, as payment for legal services rendered in preparing the articles of incorporation.

Feb. 15   Hamanna issued 1,000 shares to Robert Cawthon for a piece of land. The land had been appraised by several independent appraisers at an average of $55,000.

Mar. 15   8,000 shares were sold for $56 per share.

18   Hamanna issued 1,000 shares to Olive Griffin in exchange for a portable modular building. The building will be used for office space until a more permanent structure can be built.

Apr. 1   Gothom City donated 50 acres of land appraised at $4,500 per acre to Hamanna Corp. The land is to be used as the site for Hamanna's primary manufacturing facility.

Required

Prepare journal entries to record each of the transactions described above. If no entry is necessary, write, "No Entry." Calculations should be included as part of your journal entry explanation where appropriate.

(Check figure: The January 21 entry included a debit to Organization Cost of $108,000)

Problem B13-2
Recording stock sold on subscription

Auburn, Inc., has been authorized to issue 250,000 shares of $20-par stock. The following 1987 transactions relate to the initial issuance of Auburn stock:

July 1	Auburn sold subscriptions for 50,000 shares of stock. The shares have a subscription price of $30 per share. One-third of the subscription price was received as a down payment.
15	20,000 shares were sold for $640,000.
Aug. 1	An installment amounting to one-third of the subscription price was received.
24	100 shares of stock were exchanged for a new two-way radio system having a fair market value of $3,100.
Sept. 1	The final one-third of the subscription price was received and the stock issued.

Required

Prepare journal entries to record the transactions described above. Calculations should be included as part of your journal entry explanation where appropriate.

Problem B13-3
Recording purchases and sales of treasury stock

Olympic Promotions, Inc., has the following stockholders' equity on the December 31, 1986, balance sheet:

Stockholders' Equity		
Paid-In Capital:		
Common Stock, $10 par, 50,000 shares authorized, 25,000 shares issued and outstanding		$ 250,000
Paid-In Capital in Excess of Par		600,000
Total Paid-In Capital		$ 850,000
Earned Capital:		
Retained Earnings		400,000
Total Stockholders' Equity		$1,250,000

Required

Prepare Olympic Promotions' journal entries to record the following transactions that took place during January 1987:

Jan. 3	Purchased 5,000 shares of Olympic Promotions stock for $40 per share.
6	Sold 1,500 shares of the treasury stock for $44 per share.
10	Sold 2,500 shares of the treasury stock for $36 per share.
20	Sold 1,000 shares of the treasury stock for $40 per share.

Problem B13-4
Preparing T-account entries to record stockholders' equity transactions; preparing a stockholders' equity section

The following events and transactions relate to the stockholders' equity accounts of the Noble Company for 1988:

Jan. 3	The charter of incorporation was received authorizing Noble to issue 200,000 shares of $2.50-par common stock.
5	16,000 shares were sold to the incorporators of the business for a total of $200,000.
15	Subscriptions to 24,000 shares were sold. The subscription price was $15 per share; one-third of the total was received as a down payment.
31	2,000 shares were issued to the firm's attorneys in payment for legal services rendered in drawing up the articles of incorporation. A value of $15 per share was deemed appropriate.
Feb. 1	One-third of the subscription price of the subscribed shares was received.
15	Noble Company purchased 4,000 shares from one of the incorporators for $14 per share.

Mar. 1	The final balance due was received on the subscribed shares. The shares were issued.
20	Noble Company sold 1,000 shares of treasury stock for $17.50 per share.
30	Noble gave a patent with a book value of $2,000 and a fair market value of $11,200 in exchange for 800 shares of Noble common stock.
Apr. 15	Noble sold 1,000 shares of the treasury stock purchased on Feb. 15 for $13.50 per share.
Sept. 30	Noble received 10 acres of land from the City of Hanover. The land has a market value of $25,000.

The balance of the Retained Earnings account after all 1988 entries is $16,400. (Establish an account with this balance.)

Required

1. Prepare T-account entries for each of the events and transactions above. Do not make entries in general journal form. Set up the T-accounts you need and post your entries directly to the T-accounts.
2. Prepare the stockholders' equity section of the Noble Company balance sheet. You should include all appropriate disclosures discussed in this chapter.

(Check figure: Total paid-in capital = $618,000)

Problem B13-5
Preparing stockholders' equity section of a balance sheet

The following stockholders' equity accounts were included in the December 31, 1987, trial balance of Nicklas, Inc.:

	Debit	Credit
Paid-In Capital from Treasury Stock.		$ 25,000
Retained Earnings		175,000
Common Stock Subscribed.		50,000
Paid-In Capital in Excess of Par.		200,000
Common Stock, $5 par		250,000
Donated Capital.		80,000
Treasury Stock (450 shares) at cost.	$11,250	

Nicklas was authorized by its charter of incorporation to issue 100,000 shares of $5-par common stock.

Required

Prepare the stockholders' equity section of Nicklas, Inc.'s balance sheet in good form.

(Check figure: Total stockholders' equity = $768,750)

Problem B13-6
Calculating missing information from stockholders' equity section

The following stockholders' equity section was prepared by the bookkeeper for Public Corp.:

Stockholders' Equity	
Common Stock, $20 par	$ 100,000
Common Stock Subscribed	10,000
Paid-In Capital in Excess of Par	440,000
Donated Capital	85,000
Retained Earnings	365,000
Total	$1,000,000
Less: Treasury Stock (150 shares)	(15,300)
Total Stockholders' Equity	$ 984,700

The stockholders' equity section omitted several important facts that may be calculated by using the information given.

Required   Answer each of the following questions, using the data given in the stockholders' equity section above. Show calculations where appropriate.

1. How many shares of common stock have been issued?
2. What is total paid-in capital?
3. How many shares of common stock have been subscribed but not yet issued?
4. How many shares of common stock are outstanding?
5. How much was paid for each share of treasury stock?
6. What was the average amount paid for the common shares issued and subscribed?
7. What is the book value per share of common stock?

(Check figure: Common stock issued = 5,000 shares)

Chapter 14

Corporations: Retained Earnings, Preferred Stock, and Earnings per Share

After studying this chapter you should understand:

- What retained earnings are
- Why retained earnings are appropriated and the effect of appropriating them
- How to prepare a statement of retained earnings
- Cash, property, stock, and liquidating dividends — what they are, and how they are accounted for
- What special privileges are normally given to preferred stock and how it is accounted for
- How to prepare a complex stockholders' equity section of a balance sheet
- The concepts of primary and fully diluted earnings per share and how earnings per share is shown on the income statement

RETAINED EARNINGS

Retained Earnings shows the income accumulated since the corporation's beginning that is still held by the corporation

In Chapter 4 we introduced retained earnings; you prepared some very simple statements of retained earnings in solving the problems in Chapters 4 and 5. Now its time to review what you already know and to take a much closer look at retained earnings.

Retained Earnings is a stockholders' equity account that shows the income accumulated since the corporation's beginning and still retained in the business. It's the accumulated income that the corporation still has.

When you think of $58 million of retained earnings, visions of large piles of cash may flash through your mind. To understand what retained earnings is, you must forget that vision. Retained earnings is not cash; it is not any specific asset. Retained earnings merely shows where a certain dollar amount of assets originally came from.

The following diagram of a corporation balance sheet helps illustrate this concept:

DUNLAP CORP.
Balance Sheet
December 31, 1987

Assets		Liabilities and Stockholders' Equity	
		Liabilities	
Assets are the *resources* (cash, inventory, land, buildings, patents) that a corporation has to use in earning income.	$587,000	Liabilities show the *source* of some of the assets—those paid for by borrowing money.	$200,000
		Stockholders' Equity	
		Paid-In Capital	
		Paid-In Capital shows a *source* of some assets—those invested by stockholders.	300,000
		Retained Earnings	
		Retained Earnings shows a *source* of assets—those paid for out of the income earned by the corporation.	87,000
Total Assets	$587,000	Total Liabilities and Stockholders' Equity	$587,000

You should see by studying this balance sheet that:

Assets   are   resources

Liabilities and Stockholders' Equity   are   sources of resources

Retained earnings is not an asset; it shows where assets came from

The amount shown as retained earnings doesn't mean that we have that amount of cash on hand. In fact, retained earnings is *not* any asset. It shows where an amount of assets originally came from — the income earned by the corporation.

The Creation of Retained Earnings

Retained Earnings is created as the final step of closing all corporate income accounts. Expenses and revenues are closed into the Expense and Revenue Summary account. The balance of Expense and Revenue Summary is the income (credit balance) or loss (debit balance) for the period. Expense and Revenue Summary is a temporary account showing a single period's operating results. This account is closed into Retained Earnings, a permanent account accumulating the operating results of all periods since the corporation began. The following closing entry establishes a positive Retained Earnings balance:

Retained Earnings is created when Expense and Revenue Summary is closed

Dec. 31   Expense and Revenue Summary 87,400
                    Retained Earnings   87,400
              To close Expense and Revenue Summary into Retained Earnings.

Retained Earnings can have a negative (accumulated debit) balance. This debit balance in Retained Earnings is called *a deficit.* A deficit occurs when accumulated losses are greater than accumulated profits.

Retained Earnings — Appropriations

When a company earns large profits for several years, the Retained Earnings balance will grow rapidly. Stockholders may become restless and begin to wonder why the assets generated through earnings are not being distributed as dividends.

Some of the reasons why management may be accumulating assets are:

■ To expand productive capacity by constructing a new factory building

■ To purchase the assets of another corporation in order to expand into new markets

■ To meet the requirements of a state law requiring that assets be held because the corporation holds a large amount of its own repurchased stock — treasury stock

Reasons for accumulating earnings should be communicated to stockholders

Management needs to communicate the reason for not paying larger dividends to stockholders before they become too irate. This communication may be accomplished by a footnote to the financial statements or by appropriating retained earnings.

An appropriation is accomplished by simply transferring an amount from the unrestricted Retained Earnings account (called *Retained Earnings: Unappropriated*) into a restricted Retained Earnings account (called *Retained Earnings: Appropriated*). The Kimberly Company example illustrates this process.

Kimberly Company plans to build a new warehouse in 5 years. The board of directors decides to appropriate $70,000 of Retained Earnings on December 31, 1986, and each succeeding December 31 through 1990. Construction of the new building is to take place in 1991. The appropriation entry for each December 31 is:

Retained earnings may be appropriated to communicate why they are being accumulated

1986–1990
Dec. 31   Retained Earnings: Unappropriated 70,000
                      Retained Earnings: Appropriated for Plant
                          Expansion   70,000
              To record a restriction placed upon retained earnings.

Appropriating retained earnings does not set aside assets

An appropriation of retained earnings has no effect on assets, and no effect on total retained earnings. Note that the entry in the Kimberly illustration involves two Retained Earnings accounts—no asset account is debited or credited.

Since no specific fund of assets is set aside by appropriating retained earnings, Kimberly Company will have $350,000 ($70,000 × 5 years) of appropriated retained earnings on December 31, 1990, but it may still lack sufficient cash to construct a new building. *Remember, appropriating retained earnings communicates a restriction on retained earnings; it does not set aside a fund of assets.*

Here's how we show an appropriation of retained earnings in the stockholders' equity section of the balance sheet:

KIMBERLY COMPANY
Stockholders' Equity
December 31, 1990

Paid-In Capital:
  Common Stock, $10 par, 100,000 shares authorized, issued,
    and outstanding $1,000,000

Earned Capital:
  Retained Earnings: Unappropriated $540,000
  Retained Earnings: Appropriated for Plant Expansion   350,000
    Total Earned Capital.   890,000

Total Stockholders' Equity $1,890,000

When the restriction on Retained Earnings is no longer needed, we remove the appropriation by debiting the Retained Earnings: Appropriated account and crediting unappropriated retained earnings. When the plant expansion is completed, Kimberly Company removes the restriction by the following entry:

Dec. 31   Retained Earnings: Appropriated for Plant Expansion 350,000
                Retained Earnings: Unappropriated   350,000
           To remove restriction placed upon retained earnings.

Many corporations believe that the disclosure of appropriated retained earnings does more to confuse stockholders than to inform them. These firms disclose retained earnings restrictions by explaining them in a footnote.

Financial statement footnotes often contain important supplemental information not found on the financial statements. Investors should study these notes carefully.

The illustration at the top of page 524 shows how Kimberly's stockholders' equity section and related footnote would look if this method of disclosure is chosen.

Retained Earnings—Prior Period Adjustments

To understand prior period adjustments, we must first understand why an adjustment is needed. Adjustments are needed to correct errors we have made in the past. Let's examine how errors affect the accounts.

An error in an income statement account ends up in Retained Earnings

Assume that an error was made in an income statement account 3 years ago (Salary Expense was understated by $25,000).

The income statement account—Salary Expense—was closed into Expense and

The reason for accumulating retained earnings may also be shown in a footnote

KIMBERLY COMPANY
Stockholders' Equity
December 31, 1990

Paid-In Capital:
    Common Stock, $10 par, 100,000 shares authorized, issued,
        and outstanding. $1,000,000

Earned Capital:
    Retained Earnings: (see Note 3)   890,000

Total Stockholders' Equity $1,890,000

A footnote showing a restriction of retained earnings

Note 3. **Retained earnings restrictions**
The corporation has been limiting the payment of dividends because of a planned plant expansion. Retained earnings restricted for this purpose amount to $350,000.

Revenue Summary at the end of the year. The error is transferred to Expense and Revenue Summary.

Expense and Revenue Summary was then closed into Retained Earnings. The effect of the error is now in Retained Earnings. Retained Earnings is a permanent balance sheet account that is carried forward from year to year—it is not closed.

The correction of Retained Earnings for an error made in a prior year is called a prior period adjustment

The effect of the error, then, must still be in Retained Earnings. More specifically, the current beginning balance of Retained Earnings is wrong if the prior year's error was not corrected. The process of correcting this beginning balance of Retained Earnings we call making a ***prior period adjustment.***

The Hopper Hale illustration shows you how to record a prior period adjustment.

In 1986, Hopper Hale Corporation's bookkeeper debited Advertising Expense and credited Cash when she should have debited Land and credited Cash. The effect of this $25,000 error was to overstate 1986 Advertising Expense and therefore understate 1986 income by $25,000. Land is also understated by $25,000.

The error was discovered in 1987 by an astute auditor. We make the following entry to correct the error:

```
1987
Dec. 31   Land . . . . . . . . . . . . . . . . . . . . . . . . . . . . . . . . . . . 25,000
                  Retained Earnings: Unappropriated . . . . . . . . . . .          25,000
              To correct an error made on the 1986 income statement.
```

Hopper Hale's entry involved a debit to Land and a credit to Retained Earnings because those are the two accounts that are still wrong in 1987. Remember that the 1986 Advertising Expense account was closed to Retained Earnings in 1986, so it is Retained Earnings that is wrong in 1987—not Advertising Expense.

Prior period adjustments may increase or decrease Retained Earnings

Prior period adjustments may increase Retained Earnings, as it did in the Hopper Hale example, or decrease Retained Earnings. You must analyze the effects of each error and decide whether Retained Earnings is too high or too low. Once you make this determination, you will know whether the prior period adjustment requires a debit or a credit to Retained Earnings.

Retained Earnings: A Recap

There are only a few types of transactions that affect Retained Earnings: Unappropriated. We have explained all of them except one—dividends.

When assets are distributed to stockholders as dividends, ==Retained Earnings is debited and an asset is credited.== After we finish looking at Retained Earnings, we will examine dividends in detail. The only thing you need to know now is that Retained Earnings is debited when dividends are declared.

Now you have seen all of the reasons for debiting and crediting Retained Earnings: Unappropriated. We have summarized these reasons for you in the following T-account:

All the reasons why Retained Earnings may increase or decrease

Retained Earnings: Unappropriated	
Decreases	**Increases**
Net loss for the period	Net income for the period
Negative prior period adjustments	Positive prior period adjustments
Dividends declared (cash, property, and stock)	Cancellation of appropriations of retained earnings
Negative effects of certain treasury stock sales (see Chapter 13)	
Additional appropriations of retained earnings	

Statement of Retained Earnings

The statement of retained earnings is one of the four financial statements published by corporations in annual reports to their stockholders.

We have already discussed two of these four statements—the balance sheet and income statement. You will study the third—the statement of changes in financial position—in Chapter 17. Now let's look at the fourth—the statement of retained earnings.

The statement of retained earnings shows what happened to the Retained Earnings account during a period

The statement of retained earnings shows what has happened to the Retained Earnings account during the time period covered by the statement. The 1987 statement of retained earnings for Hopper Hale Corporation shows the disclosure of a prior period adjustment as well as income and dividends for the period:

HOPPER HALE CORPORATION
Statement of Retained Earnings
Year Ended December 31, 1987

Retained Earnings, Jan. 1, 1987	$417,000
Prior Period Adjustment:	
Correction of 1986 Error	25,000
Retained Earnings, Jan. 1, 1987 Corrected	$442,000
Add: Net Income for 1987	62,500
Total	$504,500
Deduct: Dividends Declared during 1987	(82,500)
Retained Earnings, Dec. 31, 1987	$422,000

The ending balance of Retained Earnings shown in the statement of retained earnings is the amount that appears in the stockholders' equity section of the balance sheet.

Corporations with retained earnings appropriations may present a statement of retained earnings which includes a section for unappropriated retained earnings and sections to disclose the changes in each appropriation. The Springdale Company statement below illustrates such a report:

A statement of retained earnings showing unappropriated and appropriated retained earnings

SPRINGDALE COMPANY
Statement of Retained Earnings
Year Ended June 30, 1988

Retained Earnings: Unappropriated:		
Balance, July 1, 1987		$1,450,000
Add: Net Income for the Year	$295,000	
Removal of Contingencies Appropriation	125,000	420,000
Total		$1,870,000
Deduct: Dividends Declared	$148,000	
Appropriation for Plant Expansion	50,000	(198,000)
Balance, June 30, 1988		$1,672,000
Retained Earnings Appropriated for Plant Expansion:		
Balance, July 1, 1987		$ 200,000
Add: Appropriation during the Year		50,000
Deduct: (none)		-0-
Balance, June 30, 1988		$ 250,000
Retained Earnings Appropriated for Contingencies:		
Balance, July 1, 1987		$ 125,000
Add: (none)		-0-
Deduct: Transfer Back to Unappropriated		(125,000)
Balance, June 30, 1988		-0-

Springdale Company has the following earned capital on the June 30, 1988, balance sheet:

Earned Capital:	
Retained Earnings: Unappropriated.	$1,672,000
Retained Earnings: Appropriated for Plant Expansion	250,000
Total Earned Capital	$1,922,000

DIVIDENDS ON COMMON STOCK

Dividends are distributions of earned capital to stockholders

Dividends are distributions of the earned capital of a corporation to its stockholders. These dividends may take the form of cash, assets other than cash, or additional shares of the corporation's stock.

The declaration and payment of dividends is at the discretion of the board of directors. Some corporations have a policy of paying regular, consistent amounts as dividends. Generally, owners of these corporations purchase their stock because they know they can count on the regular receipt of dividends. They use these regular cash inflows from dividends to pay living expenses. Railroads and utilities are examples of industries that pay regular quarterly dividends.

At the other extreme, some corporations seldom, if ever, pay dividends to stockholders. These corporations use all of the assets generated by earnings to expand the business. Stockholders purchase shares in these growth industries primarily to benefit from the increasing market value of the corporation's stock. The electronics industry is an example of a rapidly growing field in which corporations pay few, if any, dividends.

Three points in time are important in the distribution of any dividend: (1) the declaration date, (2) the record date, and (3) the payment date.

The declaration date is the day the board of directors votes to distribute a dividend

The *declaration date* is the day that the board of directors meets and votes to distribute a dividend. The form of the dividend (cash, other assets, or stock), the amount of the dividend, and the record and payment dates are specified at this meeting. At this point the board has legally committed the corporation to pay the dividend. An accounting entry is required on this date to record the obligation.

On the record date a list of stockholders who will receive the dividend is compiled

The *record date* is the day that the list of the names and addresses of the stockholders is compiled. These are the specific owners who will receive the dividend when paid. This date is normally 2 or 3 weeks later than the declaration date. No accounting entry is necessary on the record date because no further financial transaction or commitment has taken place.

On the payment date the dividend is distributed

The *payment date* is the day on which the dividends are sent to the shareholders. An accounting entry is necessary on this date to record the payment of cash, or the distribution of noncash assets or stock.

Cash Dividends

A company must have retained earnings and cash to pay a cash dividend

The majority of dividends paid are cash dividends. These distributions may be made at any time but they typically occur at the end of a quarter or a year. Two items are needed before the board of directors should consider declaring a cash dividend—earned capital and cash.

Most state laws require that dividends be declared out of accumulated earnings, not out of the capital that was invested by owners. The stockholders' equity section in Chapter 13 illustrated that paid-in capital and earned capital are accounted for separately and clearly distinguished on the balance sheet. The board should have little trouble determining whether adequate earned capital exists.

The existence of earned capital does not guarantee that cash exists. The company may have reinvested the assets realized through earnings in inventory or property, plant, and equipment assets. It may have used some of these assets to repay debt.

If the board sees that extra cash will be available after meeting operating needs and that earned capital exists as represented by the balance in Retained Earnings, they may declare a cash dividend.

In Chapter 4, page 152, you saw a simplified example of how dividends are recorded. The following illustration shows what we do on the declaration, record, and payment date.

On May 1, 1987, the board of directors of Clark, Inc., met and declared a cash dividend. The $1.50 per share is to be paid on May 31 to stockholders of record on May 15. Clark has 100,000 shares of common stock outstanding.

May 1   Dividends 150,000
             Dividends Payable   150,000
             To record declaration of cash dividend of $1.50 per share on
             100,000 shares of outstanding stock.

May 15   No entry is required on the record date.

    31   Dividends Payable 150,000
              Cash   150,000
          To record payment of the dividend declared on May 1.

    On May 1 we debited a temporary account called Dividends—just as we did in Chapter 4. Remember, this account is closed into Retained Earnings at the end of the year by the following entry:

Dec. 31   Retained Earnings: Unappropriated 150,000
              Dividends   150,000
          To close Dividends account for all dividends declared during the year.

As you can see, the declaration of the dividend eventually resulted in a reduction of Retained Earnings. Some companies choose not to use a Dividends account; instead, they debit Retained Earnings when the dividend is declared. *In the remaining illustrations and problems for this chapter, we will follow this procedure of debiting Retained Earnings when a dividend is declared.*

The Dividends Payable account that we used is a current liability because we pay the dividend in a short period of time.

The declaration and payment of a cash dividend reduces the total assets and the total equities of the corporation. The decrease in Cash reduces total assets; the decrease in Retained Earnings (either directly, or by closing the Dividends account) reduces stockholders' equity.

Property Dividends

A distribution of assets other than cash is called a property dividend

The amount of a property dividend is the fair market value of the assets distributed

Occasionally we distribute assets other than cash as dividends. Inventory, land, and equipment have all been used for this purpose. The basic requirements of cash dividends also apply to property dividends—we must have adequate earned capital, assets must exist that we can distribute, and the dividend must be declared by the board of directors.

With property dividends we have to solve a problem that we didn't have with cash dividends—at what amount should we record the dividend? Generally accepted accounting principles tell us that the proper amount is the *fair market value* of the assets that will be distributed.

The fact that we carry our assets in the accounting records at cost, or cost less accumulated depreciation, means that we will need to revalue the assets. When we revalue, we will recognize a gain or loss to increase or decrease the asset to its fair value. How do we know what fair value is? We use price quotations, known selling prices, or appraisals.

The effect of revaluing the asset is the same as if we had sold the asset and then distributed the proceeds as a cash dividend.

The Aztec Company example shows you the correct accounting for a property dividend:

The board of directors of Aztec Company declared a property dividend consisting of 10 acres of vacant land costing $10,000 which the company is not using. Since the company has 10 shareholders each of whom owns an equal number of shares, the 10 acres will be divided evenly among them. The dividend was declared on September 15, payable on October 15 to stockholders of record on October 1. Independent appraisals set the current fair value of the property at $16,000.

The entries associated with revaluing an asset and distributing it as a property dividend

Sept. 15	Land		6,000	
	Gain to Increase Land to Fair Market Value.			6,000
	To increase land from cost, $10,000, to market value of $16,000.			
15	Retained Earnings: Unappropriated		16,000	
	Property Dividend Payable			16,000
	To record *declaration* of a property dividend consisting of 10 acres of land with a current appraised value of $16,000.			
Oct. 1	*Record date*—no entry required.			
15	Property Dividend Payable		16,000	
	Land			16,000
	To record *distribution* of the property dividend.			

Aztec did not realize a gain as a result of declaring the dividend but as a result of revaluing the asset. The Gain to Increase Land to Fair Market Value would be shown on the income statement among "other gains and losses."

Property dividends have the same effect on the balance sheet as cash dividends. Total assets decrease because some asset—Land, for example—is paid out. Total stockholders' equity is lower because Retained Earnings is decreased.

Stock Dividends

Remember we said that three things were necessary for a cash or property dividend —an asset to distribute, earned capital, and a declaration by the board of directors. What happens when we have plenty of earned capital and a board willing to declare a dividend but no assets to distribute? The board may declare a stock dividend.

A stock dividend involves issuing additional shares of the corporation's own stock

A *stock dividend* consists of issuing additional shares of the corporation's own stock to its stockholders on a pro rata basis.

For example, Irving Akard owns 10 shares of Tribune Company stock. When the Tribune Company declares and issues a 20% stock dividend, Irving receives two additional shares. Since each other shareholder receives a 20% dividend, the total number of shares increases by 20%. Each shareholder has the same proportionate ownership after the dividend was declared as before:

Each stockholder owns the same percentage of the corporation before and after a stock dividend

Total shares outstanding before dividend	100 shares
Total shares issued in 20% stock dividend	20 shares
Total shares outstanding after dividend	120 shares

Irving owned 10% of the Tribune Company before the dividend was declared (10% × 100 shares = 10 shares) and after the dividend was distributed (10% × 120 shares = 12 shares).

What did Irving gain as a result of the stock dividend? *Nothing!* He owned 10% of the company before and after the dividend. He now has more "pieces of paper" to represent the same ownership. If he desires to realize cash out of the stock dividend, he must sell shares and thus reduce his percentage of ownership in the corporation—something he could have done even before the dividend.

Why, then, do corporations issue stock dividends? The two most commonly given reasons are:

The reasons for issuing a stock dividend

1. To reduce the market price of the stock. When a large number of new shares are issued (over 25% more), the total number of shares of the corporation's stock available in the marketplace is increased to such an extent that the market price of each share drops. The lower market price per share makes the stock more affordable for individuals with small amounts to invest.

2. To distribute something to the shareholders when all cash and noncash assets are needed in the business. In a growing corporation the distribution of a stock dividend is a way of notifying stockholders that these retained earnings have been distributed in the form of additional shares of stock and that they will never be distributed in the form of cash or other assets.

In spite of the questionable value of stock dividends, many corporations issue them and thus we must understand the proper accounting procedures for them. The effect of a stock dividend on the balance sheet is to reduce earned capital and to increase paid-in capital. The amount we record depends on the size of the dividend.

We will use the Hastings Co. information below to illustrate the correct recording of a small stock dividend and a large stock dividend.

HASTINGS COMPANY
Stockholders' Equity before Stock Dividend
June 30, 1988

Paid-In Capital:
  Common Stock, $10 par, 200,000 shares authorized, 120,000 shares
    issued and outstanding $1,200,000
  Paid-In Capital in Excess of Par   300,000
    Total Paid-In Capital $1,500,000

Earned Capital:
  Retained Earnings   940,000

Total Stockholders' Equity $2,440,000

Small Stock Dividends

Small stock dividends: issue fewer than 20–25% new shares

Small stock dividends involve the issuance of new shares amounting to less than 20 to 25% of the shares previously outstanding. In the case of a small stock dividend, we assume that too few new shares are issued to affect the market value of the stock. Each new share, then, has a value equal to the market value of each of the shares previously outstanding. This market value is considered the proper amount to use to account for a small stock dividend.

On July 1, 1988, the Hastings Company board of directors declared a 5% stock dividend to be distributed on August 15 to stockholders of record on July 20. Hastings' stock was trading for $18 per share on July 1.

Small stock dividends are recorded at the market value per share on the declaration date

July 1   Retained Earnings (6,000 shares × $18) 108,000
                Stock Dividend Distributable (6,000 shares × $10) . . .   60,000
                Paid-In Capital in Excess of Par (6,000 shares × $8) . .   48,000
          To record *declaration* of a 5% stock dividend (5% × 120,000
          shares = 6,000 new shares).

Our declaration entry debits Retained Earnings just as we did for property dividends. The amount of the debit is the value of the shares we will issue — the number of new shares we will issue multiplied by the market value of each share.

Stock Dividend Distributable is credited for the par value (or stated value) of the new shares issued. Paid-In Capital in Excess of Par is credited for the amount by which market value of the stock exceeds par (or stated value). Stock Dividend Distributable is a temporary stockholders' equity account that we use until the stock is issued (see August 15 entry below).

We do not credit a liability account in this case because no true liability exists. A liability is an obligation that requires the disbursement of assets or the performance of a service for its satisfaction. We have no such obligation. The board of directors has committed the corporation to issue additional shares of common stock, not to pay out assets or perform services; this commitment, therefore, fails to meet the definition of a liability.

July 20   No journal entry is required on the *record* date.

Aug. 15   Stock Dividend Distributable. 60,000
                Common Stock   60,000
          To record distribution of 6,000 shares of stock as a dividend.

When we issue the dividend, we remove the temporary stockholders' equity account Stock Dividend Distributable and increase Common Stock. We have now replaced the temporary stockholders' equity account with a permanent one.

The effect of this stock dividend was to move $108,000 out of earned capital into paid-in capital. Total assets and total stockholders' equity remain unchanged.

Let's look at Hastings' Stockholders' Equity section before and after the small stock dividend at the top of page 532.

Hastings does have 6,000 more shares of common stock outstanding after the dividend.

Large Stock Dividends

Large stock dividends: issue more than 20–25% new shares

A large stock dividend is a pro rata distribution of new shares amounting to more than 20 to 25% of the stock previously outstanding. When we distribute a large stock dividend, we place so many additional shares into the marketplace that the market price of the stock will probably drop. Since we don't know how large this drop will be, we use the par value of the shares issued as the amount for recording the new shares.

	Before Small Stock Dividend	After Small Stock Dividend
Common stock	$1,200,000	$1,260,000
Paid-in capital in excess of par	300,000	348,000
Total paid-in capital	$1,500,000	$1,608,000
Retained earnings	940,000	832,000
Total stockholders' equity	$2,440,000	$2,440,000

Total paid-in capital increased $108,000.

Total retained earnings decreased $108,000.

Total stockholders' equity is unchanged.

This illustration shows the effect of a small stock dividend on stockholders' equity

Large stock dividends are recorded at the par value of the shares issued

Let's assume that, instead of issuing a 5% stock dividend, Hastings' board declared a 40% stock dividend.

On July 1, 1988, the Hastings Company board of directors declared a 40% stock dividend (*instead* of the 5% dividend in the illustration above). The shares will be distributed on August 31 to stockholders of record on August 1. Hastings' stock was trading for $18 per share on July 1.

```
July  1   Retained Earnings (48,000 shares × $10 par) . . . . . . . .   480,000
              Stock Dividend Distributable . . . . . . . . . . . . . . .          480,000
          To record the declaration of a 40% stock dividend
          (40% × 120,000 shares = 48,000 new shares).

Aug.  1   No journal entry is required on the record date.

     31   Stock Dividend Distributable . . . . . . . . . . . . . . . . . .   480,000
              Common Stock . . . . . . . . . . . . . . . . . . . . . . .          480,000
          To record the distribution of a large stock dividend.
```

Our entries to record a large stock dividend are exactly the same ones we use for a small stock dividend—with one exception. We won't need to credit Paid-In Capital in Excess of Par because there is no excess—the large stock dividend is recorded at par.

The effect of this large stock dividend is to move $480,000 out of earned capital into paid-in capital. Total assets and total stockholders' equity are unchanged.

Again, here is Hastings' stockholders' equity section before and after the dividend:

This illustration shows the effect of a large stock dividend on stockholders' equity

		Before Large Stock Dividend	After Large Stock Dividend
Common stock and total paid-in capital increased by $480,000	Common stock	$1,200,000	$1,680,000
	Paid-in capital in excess of par	300,000	300,000
	Total paid-in capital	$1,500,000	$1,980,000
Retained earnings decreased by $480,000	Retained earnings	940,000	460,000
Total stockholders' equity is unchanged	Total stockholders' equity	$2,440,000	$2,440,000

Hastings now has 48,000 more shares outstanding but the same total stockholders' equity.

Liquidating Dividends

Liquidating dividends are not dividends as we have been using the term. We have been using dividends to mean distributions out of earned capital — giving the owners some of the accumulated income of the corporation.

Liquidating dividends distribute paid-in capital to the stockholders

Liquidating dividends are pro rata distributions of paid-in capital (not earned capital) to the stockholders. We are giving the owners back some of the assets they invested in the company.

Liquidating dividends are paid only when a corporation is permanently reducing its size, or when it is going out of business.

The board of directors must exercise care to declare liquidating dividends only when they are allowed by state statutes. Many of these laws require approval by the stockholders or a court of law. In some states the directors are personally liable for any illegally declared liquidating dividends.

Dividends and Treasury Stock

No dividends are paid on treasury stock. This includes cash dividends, property dividends, stock dividends, and liquidating dividends. When a corporation owns treasury stock, it is holding shares of its own stock. To pay dividends on treasury stock would amount to the corporation paying itself a dividend — a useless exercise.

Stock Splits

In a stock split old shares are replaced with a larger number of new ones

A *stock split* occurs when the board of directors, acting with the permission of the state, reduces the par or stated value of all of its common stock. We accomplish this reduction by issuing additional new shares for each old share held by a stockholder.

Like large stock dividends, the purpose of a stock split is to put many new shares into the marketplace and thus reduce the market price per share.

When we distribute a stock split, the *only* amounts that change on the balance sheet are the number of shares authorized, issued, and outstanding and the par or stated value per share. The dollars assigned to Common Stock, Paid-In Capital in Excess of Par, Retained Earnings, and the other stockholders' equity accounts remain the same.

Because no monetary amounts are involved, we need only a memorandum entry to record a stock split.

The Firebrand Corporation example below and on page 535 demonstrates the effects of a stock split.

FIREBRAND CORPORATION
Stockholders' Equity
September 30, 1988
(before stock split)

Paid-In Capital:
  Common Stock, $1 par, 50,000 shares authorized, issued,
    and outstanding . . . . $ 50,000
  Paid-In Capital in Excess of Par 130,000
      Total Paid-In Capital $180,000

Earned Capital:
  Retained Earnings 315,000

Total Stockholders' Equity $495,000

THE STOCK SPLIT

On October 1,1988, Firebrand received permission to issue a 4 for 1 stock split. Four new shares of $.25-par-value stock are issued for each old share of $1-par stock. 200,000 (50,000 × 4) shares of $.25 ($1 ÷ 4) par stock are now authorized.

Oct. 1   Memorandum. $1-par common stock is split 4 for 1. New par value $.25 per share for 200,000 authorized shares.

FIREBRAND CORPORATION
Stockholders' Equity
October 2, 1988
(after stock split)

Paid-In Capital:
  Common Stock, $.25 par, 200,000 shares authorized, issued,
    and outstanding . . . . $ 50,000
  Paid-In Capital in Excess of Par 130,000
      Total Paid-In Capital $180,000

Earned Capital:
  Retained Earnings 315,000

Total Stockholders' Equity $495,000

The effect of a stock split on stockholders' equity

A stockholder who previously owned 100 shares of Firebrand stock would now own 400 shares. Stock can be split 10 for 1, 2 for 1, or 1½ for 1 or in any other way the corporation desires.

SQUEEZE PLAY

by Robert McGough

Gilbert McDougald played shortstop for the New York Yankees during the 1950s, and in his best year he batted .311. This summer, in a different sort of game, he and a partner went 1 for 3,000, and they shouldn't have any difficulty scoring.

McDougald and Norman Rockwell, who are executive vice president and president of Metropolitan Maintenance Co., took their company private by forcing a 1-for-3000 reverse stock split on their minority shareholders. For every 3,000 old shares, one new share was issued. But anyone who had fewer than 3,000 shares received only cash for his stock, and well below book value at that. Only McDougald and Rockwell owned more than 3,000 shares, so the two of them now own all the stock of the Nutley, N.J., company.

A nice squeeze play. Says Darrell Patrick of S. J. Wolfe & Co., a stockbroker for one of the former shareholders: "That's a ripoff of the shareholders. There's no other way to define it."

Metropolitan Maintenance has a $16 million (1983 sales) business providing maintenance, cleaning, and security services for commercial buildings. But having sold stock in 1972, it found being public wasn't what it wanted, as a languishing price made its shares a poor tool for acquisitions. With only 175 shareholders left this year, it finally decided to get rid of the annoyance. Ousting the outsiders has a tax advantage: It will enable Metropolitan to become a Subchapter S corporation, meaning that McDougald and Rockwell will pay individual income taxes on the profits but no corporate taxes.

"There were very, very few complaints from the stockholders," claims the company's attorney. The company paid $37 per share for fractional shares, scarcely more than half the book value of $72 ($58 excluding goodwill). Earnings per share were up 89% in 1983 to $5.93, and were still climbing at mid-1984. A great time, it would appear, to buy the company.

M. J. Whitman & Co., a New York City financial consulting firm hired by the company for $7,500 to make an appraisal, affirmed that $37 per share was fair. Martin Whitman's defense: "I thought the company was a piece of crap." Noting that Metropolitan at one point appraised its own shares at $26, Whitman says, "My conscience is clear." The proxy did mention that "the opinion of the board of directors must be considered in light of the fact that the board is controlled by Messrs. Rockwell and McDougald, who constitute two of the company's three directors." Nobody can complain about inadequate disclosure.

Warner National Corp., a savings and loan in Ohio, recently did a 1-for-16 reverse split, which will leave only three shareholders. Surgical Appliance Industries, a manufacturer in Cincinnati, is working on a 1-for-50,000 split that will leave only two shareholders. Crystal Tissue, a Middletown, Ohio, wrappings outfit, has proposed a 1-for-4,000 reverse split, but this has been delayed because some outsiders have expressed interest in taking over the entire company. Presumably the minority shareholders will share equally in that reward, although there is no guarantee that the new buyer won't simply pick up the control shares and leave outsiders in the cold.

Great values can frequently be found in thinly traded companies that have been ignored by Wall Street. But securities laws do not offer much protection from reverse splits and other freeze-outs.

Source: Forbes, November 19, 1984, pages 54, 56.

In this chapter you learned that a stock split is a way of putting more shares into the marketplace and thus reducing the market price per share. You now know that a reverse stock split operates in just the opposite manner — it reduces the number of shares in the market and can force stockholders to be "eliminated" by having the corporation buy out old shares that can't be "traded in" for new shares issued in the reverse split. As a result, control of the corporation can be concentrated in the hands of only a few individuals. When only a few people own the corporation's stock, it will cease to be bought and sold on stock exchanges. When this happens, the corporation is said to be private, or closely held.

The steps for calculating the new par or stated value and the new number of shares are:

1. Divide the par value per share by the number of new shares replacing one old share. In the Firebrand example we divided $1 by 4 new shares = $.25 per share.

2. Multiply the number of shares authorized, issued, and outstanding by the number of new shares replacing one old share. In the Firebrand example we multiplied 50,000 old shares by 4 = 200,000 new shares.

If the corporation owns treasury stock at the time of the split, the treasury stock must be split as well. If Firebrand had owned 5,000 shares of treasury stock before the split, it would have 20,000 shares (4 × 5,000) after the split. The par value of this stock is also adjusted to $.25 per share.

The purpose of a stock split is to reduce the market price per share of stock

The purpose of a stock split is to attract a larger number of investors by decreasing the market price of the stock. Stock on the national stock exchanges is normally bought and sold in 100-share lots. Smaller numbers of shares may be traded, but the broker's commission for handling such transactions is relatively high. You would need $9,000 to buy 100 shares of stock priced at $90 per share. A 2 for 1 split would reduce the needed cash to about $4,500 and a 4 for 1 split to $2,250.

Sometimes a large stock dividend is distributed to accomplish the same purpose as a stock split. The advantage of using a stock split rather than a large stock dividend is that more shares may be distributed without affecting retained earnings. Thus we preserve the retained earnings balance for future dividend distributions.

PREFERRED STOCK

We have discussed common stock, the primary ownership shares of a corporation. Now it's time to turn our attention to preferred stock, a second type of equity security sold by many corporations to raise capital.

The authorization to issue preferred stock is included in the articles of incorporation. The authorization provides for:

1. Par value or the stipulation that the stock is to be no par

2. The total number of shares authorized

3. The annual dividend rate or amount

4. The characteristics that the stock is to possess (voting rights, dividend privileges, liquidation preferences, etc.)

Preferred stock offers its owners certain privileges that common stock owners do not have

Preferred stock appeals to a different group of investors than common stock. This is true because preferred stock offers its owners certain privileges (or preferences) not enjoyed by common stockholders.

The corporation offers stock with preferences to reduce the risks of investing. Preferred stock is less risky than common stock. You may be tempted to invest in preferred stock when you wouldn't invest in common. You will understand why preferred stock is less risky when we discuss its characteristics.

Characteristics of Preferred Stock

The characteristics of preferred stock are spelled out in the charter of incorporation. Remember, the charter is the legal document that creates the corporation and specifies the types of equity securities it can issue.

We will discuss characteristics relating to (1) dividends, (2) voting rights, (3) conversion privileges (the stockholders' right to trade preferred stock for another security), (4) callability (the corporation's right to buy back the preferred stock), and (5) liquidation preference.

Dividends

Preferred stockholders receive dividends before common stockholders receive any

Dividends on preferred stock are normally stated as a percentage of par value or a specified number of dollars per year if the stock has no par value. 6% preferred stock with a par value of $100 would pay a $6-per-year dividend—if declared by the board of directors. $3.50 preferred stock would refer to no-par stock paying a dividend of $3.50 annually.

You should understand that dividends on preferred must be declared by the board of directors before they can be paid and, like common dividends, they are not automatic. If the board pays any dividends during a year, however, preferred shareholders will receive their dividends before any are paid to common.

What if the board chooses not to declare a preferred dividend in a given year? If the preferred stock is *cumulative,* the dividends must be paid in a later year before any distributions can be made to common stockholders. Past dividends "owed" to preferred stockholders are called dividends in *arrears.* These obligations are not liabilities until the dividend is declared by the directors. We disclose the existence of this obligation in the footnotes to the financial statements.

Holders of *noncumulative* preferred stock would lose the right to receive dividends not declared in the current year.

<table>
<tr><td> *This illustration shows that cumulative preferred dividends must be paid before common receives any* </td><td>

Arrow, Inc., has 10,000 shares of 8%, $100-par preferred stock and 100,000 shares of $1-par common stock outstanding. The preferred stock is cumulative but no dividends were declared in 1985, 1986, or 1987. The following calculation shows the amount that must be paid to preferred stockholders in 1988 before any dividends can be paid to common:

</td></tr>
</table>

Dividends due each year: (8% × $100 par × 10,000 shares)	$ 80,000
Number of years in arrears: 1985, 1986, 1987	× 3
Total dividends in arrears	$240,000
Add: 1988 dividend	80,000
Total that must be paid before any distribution to common	$320,000

Assuming the same facts except that the preferred stock is noncumulative, Arrow would be required to pay only the $80,000 1988 dividend before distributions could be made to common.

Preferred stockholders are normally limited to receiving the amount of dividends specified — the 8% of $100 in the Arrow example. If this is the case, the stock is referred to as *nonparticipating.*

The corporation may also be authorized to issue participating preferred stock. *Participating preferred* gives the stockholder the right to receive the specified dividend and to receive more when dividends are paid to common stockholders. When all distributions are made, participating preferred will receive the same percentage of par value as the common stockholders for current dividends.

If there are dividends in arrears, cumulative, participating preferred will receive a higher percentage of par value than common stockholders.

To help you in allocating a cash dividend between preferred and common stockholders, we have provided the following step-by-step procedure:

You should use this procedure to allocate dividends between preferred and common stock

1. If preferred is cumulative, give preferred all dividends in arrears. (Noncumulative preferred does not receive dividends in arrears.)

2. Give preferred its current year's dividend percentage or amount.

3. Give common a matching current dividend. (By "matching" we mean the same percentage of its par value as preferred received.)

4. If preferred stock is participating, allocate all remaining dollars in this way:

Additional percentage of par allocated to common and preferred:

$$\frac{\textbf{Number of dollars remaining to be distributed}}{\textbf{Total par value of common and preferred stock}} = \begin{array}{l}\textbf{additional \% of par to give}\\ \textbf{to each}\end{array}$$

Additional % of par × total par value of preferred = amount allocated to preferred

Additional % of par × total par value of common = amount allocated to common

Remember, if preferred is nonparticipating, all remaining dollars go to the common stockholders.

Follow this step-by-step approach as you study the examples we have provided. First an illustration where preferred is noncumulative and participating:

This illustration allocates dividends between common and preferred stockholders assuming that preferred is noncumulative and participating

Mason Company has the following stock outstanding on December 31, 1988:

7% Noncumulative, participating preferred stock, $100 par, 2,000 shares authorized, issued, and outstanding	$ 200,000
Common stock, $10 par, 100,000 shares authorized, issued, and outstanding	1,000,000
Total preferred and common stock	$1,200,000

Mason declared a $108,000 dividend that would be allocated to preferred and common as follows:

	Preferred	Common	Total
Total outstanding stock (par)	$200,000	$1,000,000	$1,200,000
Total dividend declared			$ 108,000
First, regular preferred dividend [(7%)($200,000 par)]	$ 14,000		(14,000)
Amount remaining			$ 94,000
Second, matching common dividend [(7%)($1,000,000)]		$ 70,000	(70,000)
Amount remaining			$ 24,000
Third, remainder allocated to give each the same rate ($24,000 ÷ $1,200,000 = 2%):			
(2%)($200,000)	4,000		(4,000)
(2%)($1,000,000)		20,000	(20,000)
Amount remaining			$ -0-
Total distribution	$ 18,000 + $	90,000 = $	108,000

Each class of stock received a 9% dividend on par value. The $108,000 is a 9% dividend based on total par value of both preferred and common.

Now let's look at a more complex example. In this one the preferred stock is both cumulative (with dividends in arrears) and participating.

This illustration allocates dividends between common and preferred stockholders assuming preferred is cumulative and participating

Elfin Company has the following stock outstanding on December 31, 1986:

8% Cumulative, participating preferred stock, $100 par, 500 shares authorized, issued, and outstanding	$ 50,000
Common stock, $1 par, 150,000 shares authorized, issued, and outstanding	150,000
Total preferred and common stock	$200,000

Elfin did not declare or pay any dividends during 1985; therefore, there are $4,000 (8% × $50,000) preferred dividends in arrears.

Elfin declared a 1986 dividend of $30,000, which would be allocated to preferred and common as follows:

	Preferred	Common	Total
Total outstanding stock (par)	$50,000	$150,000	$200,000
Total dividend declared			$ 30,000
First, preferred dividend in arrears	$ 4,000		(4,000)
Amount remaining			$ 26,000
Second, regular current preferred dividend [(8%)($50,000 par)]	4,000		(4,000)
Amount remaining			$ 22,000
Third, matching common dividend [(8%)($150,000)]		$ 12,000	(12,000)
Amount remaining			$ 10,000
Fourth, remainder allocated to give each the same percentage ($10,000 ÷ $200,000 = 5%):			
(5%)($50,000)	2,500		(2,500)
(5%)($150,000)		7,500	(7,500)
Amount remaining			$ -0-
Total distribution	$10,500 +	$ 19,500 =	$ 30,000

Notice that the matching common dividend only matches the percentage received by preferred shareholders for the current year. Dividends in arrears are not matched.

In this illustration preferred shareholders received a 21% total distribution (8% for 1985 arrears and 13% for 1986). Common stockholders received a 13% total distribution. The current dividend of 13% is the same for both classes of stock.

Voting Rights

Voting rights are not ordinarily given to preferred stockholders. They are not allowed to vote in the election of members to the board of directors, or on other matters that require a vote of the stockholders.

Some state laws may permit us to issue voting preferred stock. Voting, then, is a special privilege that may be included in the characteristics of preferred stock.

Conversion Privilege

An owner of convertible preferred stock has the right to turn in his or her preferred shares to the corporation and receive common shares in their place. The number of common shares to be received is specified on the preferred stock certificate.

For example, K. Houston owns 100 shares of 8% noncumulative preferred stock convertible into common at the rate of one share of preferred for three shares of common. At any time Houston may submit her 100 preferred shares and receive 300 shares of common. The corporation can't make her convert; the decision is hers.

We assume that preferred stock is nonconvertible unless the corporation specifically adds this special feature.

Callability

Callable preferred stock may be retired by the corporation by paying the stockholder a predetermined amount—the ***call price.***

The preferred stock certificate usually provides that the stock will become callable at some future date. The call price typically exceeds the original issue price.

For example, on January 1, 1987, J. Nall purchases 100 shares of 6% cumulative preferred stock for $12 per share. The stock is callable at any time after January 1, 1992, at $25 per share.

Now the corporation has the option. At any time after January 1, 1992, it can retire Nall's stock by paying him $25 per share. Nall can neither force the corporation to retire his stock, nor can he refuse to let the corporation purchase it at the call price.

As you probably observed, the callability provision is not so much a privilege for the preferred stockholder as it is a right for the corporation. The corporation has an easy way of removing the obligations imposed upon it by having preferred stock outstanding. For example, if there is no preferred stock, there are no preferred dividends to pay.

Liquidation Preference

In case of liquidation, creditors receive assets first, then preferred stockholders, and finally common stockholders

All preferred stock includes a liquidation preference. This feature means that, if the corporation decides to cease operations and distribute its assets to creditors and owners, the preferred stockholders will receive assets in settlement of their claims before common stockholders are entitled to any assets.

The liquidation preference doesn't guarantee that preferred shareholders will receive all of the assets to which they are entitled. First the creditors must be paid, then any remaining assets can be used to settle preferred stockholder claims. If any assets are left, they can be distributed to common stockholders.

How much are preferred stockholders entitled to receive? This is a difficult question to answer since the amount depends on state law. In general, preferred shareholders will receive any dividends in arrears (if preferred is cumulative), and the par or stated value per share. Some states also require that the paid-in capital in excess of par (or stated value) be returned to the preferred shareholders on a pro rata basis.

In order to be successful in raising capital by issuing preferred stock, management must put together a "package" of preferences. Their objective will be to offer sufficient appeal to investors without placing an undesirable burden on the corporation or the common stockholders.

All preferred stock will have dividend and liquidation preferences. We must decide whether to add cumulative, participating, convertibility, and voting privileges —or possibly impose a callable restriction.

If we can raise the needed capital by selling nonvoting, noncumulative, nonparticipating preferred, there is no reason to offer voting, cumulative, participating, or convertibility rights.

Accounting for Preferred Stock

We account for preferred stock just like we did common stock

We account for preferred stock just like we did for common stock. The only difference is in the account titles we use. We substitute the accounts Preferred Stock, Paid-In Capital in Excess of Par: Preferred, Preferred Stock Subscribed, and Subscriptions Receivable: Preferred for the corresponding accounts applicable to common stock.

For example, the sale of 100 shares of $10 par preferred stock for $25 per share would be entered in the general journal like this:

Jan. 5	Cash	2,500	
	Preferred Stock.		1,000
	Paid-In Capital in Excess of Par: Preferred		1,500
	To record the sale of 100 shares of $10 par preferred stock.		

We don't usually purchase preferred stock as treasury stock. If we do, we use the same procedures to account for it as we used for common treasury stock in Chapter 13.

THE STOCKHOLDERS' EQUITY SECTION ILLUSTRATED

We have completed our look at the various accounts that may appear in the stockholders' equity section of the balance sheet.

Now we will show you how each of the stockholders' equity accounts we discussed in this chapter and the last look on the balance sheet. In addition, we've added the descriptive information (shares authorized, issued, outstanding, par value, etc.) needed for fair disclosure. See the illustration at the top of page 542.

EARNINGS PER SHARE

Earnings per share is one measure of a corporation's success

If you own stock in a large corporation, you will be interested in how well that corporation is doing. One measure of corporate success is the amount of income it earns. You know, of course, that this information is available on the income statement.

Suppose you looked at the corporate income statement and found a net income of $127,000 reported there. Would that make you happy? You would certainly feel better than if you saw a net loss of $127,000. But in order to decide just how good you should feel, you would need to evaluate this amount in several ways.

We will look at one such evaluation, earnings per share, here. In Chapter 18 we will discuss a number of others.

Earnings per share (EPS), in its simplest form, is the net income earned by a corporation divided by the number of common shares outstanding. If Wise, Inc., earns $127,000 and has 10,000 shares outstanding during the year, the EPS is $12.70 ($127,000 ÷ 10,000). If there are 100,000 shares outstanding, the EPS is $1.27 ($127,000 ÷ 100,000).

You can see that just knowing total net income is not enough. You will also be interested in knowing how much that net income is when spread over all of the shares of stock. The more stock there is outstanding, the less beneficial the income is to each shareholder.

Authoritative financial accounting standards require disclosure of earnings per share on the face of the income statements of all corporations whose stock is publicly traded (sold on a stock exchange or over-the-counter). Closely held corporations, such as those whose stock is owned by the members of a family, are not required to disclose earnings per share amounts. Proprietorships and partnerships do not disclose earnings per share — remember, they do not issue stock so they have no shares.

This stockholders' equity section shows all of the accounts discussed in Chapters 13 and 14

MODEL CORPORATION
Stockholders' Equity
September 30, 1988

Paid-In Capital:

6% Preferred Stock, $100 par, noncumulative, nonvoting, participating, 10,000 shares authorized, 4,000 shs issued and outstanding	$ 400,000	
6% Preferred Stock Subscribed, $100 par, 500 shares.	50,000	
Total Preferred Stock		$ 450,000
Common Stock, no par, stated value $25, 100,000 shs authorized, 60,000 shs issued, 58,500 shs outstanding (1,500 shs in the treasury)	$1,500,000	
Common Stock Subscribed, no par, stated value $25, 1,000 shares	25,000	
Common Stock Dividend Distributable, 5,950 shares, no par, $25 stated value per share	148,750	
Total Common Stock		1,673,750
Additional Paid-In Capital:		
Paid-In Capital in Excess of Par: Preferred	$ 45,000	
Paid-In Capital in Excess of Stated Value: Common	750,000	
Paid-In Capital from Treasury Stock	25,000	
Donated Capital	135,000	
Total Additional Paid-In Capital		955,000
Total Paid-In Capital		$3,078,750
Earned Capital:		
Retained Earnings: Unappropriated	$ 875,000	
Retained Earnings: Appropriated:		
For Plant Expansion	$250,000	
For Contingencies	125,000	
Total Appropriated	375,000	
Total Earned Capital		1,250,000
Total Paid-In and Earned Capital		$4,328,750
Less: Treasury Stock: Common (1,500 shs at cost)		(67,500)
Total Stockholders' Equity		$4,261,250

Historical Earnings per Share

Corporations with simple capital structures report only historical EPS

Corporations with simple capital structures report only historical earnings per share amounts. A ***simple capital structure*** means that the corporation has no convertible preferred stock, convertible bonds, or stock options outstanding that could cause the corporation to issue additional shares of stock. Before we go further, let's be sure you have an idea what convertible securities and stock options are.

Convertible preferred stock and convertible bonds are securities that can be turned in to the corporation by their owners. In return the corporation must give the owners a predetermined number of shares of common stock. Thus, these securities can cause the corporation to issue more shares of common stock.

Stock options are arrangements that allow an individual, usually an executive of the company, to purchase stock at a price lower than she would have to pay if she bought it through a stockbroker. This stock option discount is a reward for the executive's efforts in making the company successful. Stock option plans may also cause the corporation to issue stock. When the executive elects to exercise her option and pay for the stock, the corporation must issue the shares.

Historical earnings per share calculations ignore the potential new shares that the corporation may be required to issue. By definition, in a simple capital structure, the corporation has no convertible securities or stock option plans.

Historical earnings per share is calculated by the following formula:

$$\text{Historical EPS} = \frac{\text{net income} - \text{preferred dividends}}{\text{weighted average common shares outstanding}}$$

Earnings per share is really per *common* share. Preferred dividends must be subtracted from reported net income to derive that portion of the income available to common stockholders. (Remember, preferred dividends must be paid before any distributions may be made to common stockholders.)

We use weighted average common shares outstanding during the year in the calculation in an attempt to equate the shares outstanding with the income produced by the resources received when those shares were sold. We would distort EPS if income on resources available for only 3 months were divided by shares assumed to be outstanding for a full year. The weighted average approach avoids this distortion by dividing income earned on resources used for 3 months by shares outstanding for 3 months.

The Branch, Inc., example shows you how to calculate weighted average shares outstanding. Study it and then we'll discuss the procedure we used.

This illustration shows how to calculate weighted average shares outstanding

Branch, Inc., had 100,000 common shares outstanding on January 1, 1988. The following common stock transactions took place during the year: March 1, sold 12,000 shares; June 30, sold 4,000 shares; November 1, repurchased 6,000 shares as treasury stock:

Date	Number of Shares	×	Fraction of Year Outstanding or Held in Treasury	=	Weighted Average Shares Outstanding
1/1/88	100,000		$\frac{12}{12}$		100,000
3/1/88	12,000		$\frac{10}{12}$		10,000
6/30/88	4,000		$\frac{6}{12}$		2,000
11/1/88	(6,000)		$\frac{2}{12}$		(1,000)
Weighted average common shs outstanding for 1988					111,000 shares

In calculating Branch's weighted average shares, we simply weighted the shares by the number of months that Branch had use of the assets provided from selling those shares:

The 100,000 shares were outstanding the whole year, so we assigned them a weight of 1 ($\frac{12}{12}$).

The shares sold during the year we assigned a weight of less than 1 because we didn't have use of the resources for the whole year. We gave the 12,000 shares sold on March 1 a weight of $\frac{5}{6}$ ($\frac{10}{12}$) because we used the assets they provided for only $\frac{5}{6}$ of a year. Those sold on June 30 were weighted by $\frac{1}{2}$ ($\frac{6}{12}$) for the same reason.

When we bought treasury stock—the 6,000 shares—we used resources. Branch didn't have as many resources at its disposal to earn income because some assets were used to buy treasury stock. We, then, subtracted these shares purchased on November 1 after weighting them by the $\frac{1}{6}$ ($\frac{2}{12}$) of a year that Branch was without the assets used to purchase them.

If Branch's 1988 net income were \$235,320 and no preferred stock was outstanding, the 1988 historical EPS would be:

$$\text{1988 Historical EPS} = \frac{\$235,320 - 0}{111,000 \text{ shares}} = \$2.12 \text{ per share}$$

Primary and Fully Diluted Earnings per Share

Corporations with complex capital structures must report primary and fully diluted EPS

Corporations with complex capital structures are required to report two prospective earnings per share amounts—primary earnings per share and fully diluted earnings per share. A corporation with a *complex capital structure* has securities outstanding that may cause the issuance of additional shares of common stock.

Holders of convertible bonds or convertible preferred stock can submit their securities at any time and receive common shares. Holders of stock options may, at their discretion, pay an exercise price and receive common stock. Earnings per share calculated without considering these potential issuances may present a misleading picture to investors.

For example, suppose that you are evaluating Apex Corporation. Earnings per share is \$4.15 without considering potential issuances. If new shares could be issued and the exercise of stock options is included, earnings per share would be \$2.95. Would you make the same investment decision with the knowledge of the \$2.95 amount as you would if only the \$4.15 figure were available?

To provide investors with knowledge of the potential effects of convertible securities and options, authoritative financial accounting standards require that certain assumptions be made about these possible stock issuances. We must calculate earnings per share *as if* the potential issuance of common stock actually did occur.

Primary EPS includes the most likely issuances of stock

Primary earnings per share is calculated including the effects of securities that are *most likely* to cause issuances of new stock. *Fully diluted earnings per share* considers *all* potential new issuances. Fully diluted EPS thus yields the lowest possible earnings per share amount.

Fully diluted EPS includes all potential issuances of stock

The rules for determining whether potential shares should be included in primary or fully diluted EPS (or both) are complex. A consideration of these detailed requirements is left for the intermediate accounting course.

The following illustration will give you a general idea of the procedures followed in calculating primary and fully diluted EPS.

This illustration shows how primary and fully diluted EPS are calculated

The information below pertains to Valentine, Inc.:

Net income for 1987	\$284,800
Weighted average common stock outstanding	80,000 shares
Preferred dividends paid in 1987.	\$ 8,800
New shares that may be issued if convertible preferred is converted.	9,000 shares
New shares that may be issued if stock options are exercised	12,000 shares

Assume that effects of stock options are included in calculating both primary and fully diluted EPS and that the effect of convertible preferred is included in calculating fully diluted EPS only. The stock options are included in both primary and fully diluted because they are likely to cause issuance of common stock in the future.

The convertible preferred stock is not as likely to be converted; but since the possibility exists, the potential for new shares must be included in calculating fully diluted earnings per share.

$$\textbf{1987 Primary EPS} = \frac{\text{net income} - \text{preferred dividends}}{\substack{\text{wt. avg. common shares outstanding} \\ + \text{ likely new issuances}}}$$

$$= \frac{\$284,800 - \$8,800}{80,000 \text{ shs} + 12,000 \text{ shs}}$$

$$= \frac{\$276,000}{92,000 \text{ shs}}$$

$$= \$3.00 \text{ per share}$$

$$\textbf{1987 Fully diluted EPS} = \frac{\text{net income (see note below)}}{\substack{\text{wt. avg. common shs outstanding} \\ + \text{ all possible new issuances}}}$$

$$= \frac{\$284,800}{80,000 \text{ shs} + 12,000 \text{ shs} + 9,000 \text{ shs}}$$

$$= \frac{\$284,800}{101,000 \text{ shs}}$$

$$= \$2.82 \text{ per share}$$

Note: Preferred dividends are not deducted because this calculation is being made *as if* the preferred stock were converted. If conversion had taken place, no dividends would have been paid.

The bottom of the Valentine income statement would have the following information disclosed:

Net Income	$284,800
Primary Earnings per Common Share	$3.00
Fully Diluted Earnings per Common Share	$2.82

Our calculation of Valentine's primary EPS assumes that:

The convertible preferred stock is unlikely to be converted. We ignore the potential effects of conversion—issuing more shares and not paying preferred dividends.

The options are likely to be exercised. We include the potential effect of issuing

12,000 more shares to the individuals who could exercise these options at any time.

Our assumptions change a little when we calculate Valentine's fully diluted EPS. We now assume that:

The convertible preferred stock may be converted. We include the potential effects of this conversion. If the preferred stock were converted at the beginning of 1987, no preferred dividends would have been paid; so we don't deduct any. If the preferred stock were converted, more common shares (9,000) would be outstanding; so we add these potential new shares to the shares that were outstanding.

The options are still likely to be exercised. We still include the effect of issuing 12,000 more common shares.

CHAPTER SUMMARY

The *Retained Earnings* account is created when the Expense and Revenue Summary account is closed. Retained Earnings, then, accumulates the net income of the corporation from its inception. Reductions in this accumulation occur when dividends are declared and as the result of some treasury stock transactions. Corrections of prior years' errors may cause an increase or decrease in the Retained Earnings balance.

At times the board of directors may restrict a certain amount of retained earnings from distribution as dividends. These restrictions may be communicated by footnote explanation or by appropriating retained earnings.

All changes in retained earnings are shown in a financial statement called the statement of retained earnings. This statement together with the income statement and balance sheet constitute the three major statements we have discussed so far.

Corporations may distribute earned capital in the form of cash, noncash assets, or additional shares of stock. These *dividend distributions* must be declared by the board of directors; a list of eligible stockholders is prepared on the record date; and distribution takes place on the payment date. Adequate retained earnings and distributable assets must exist before a board of directors will consider declaring a dividend.

Liquidating dividends are distributions of paid-in capital of the corporation in the form of assets. These distributions must also be declared by the board of directors. Liquidating dividends are not dividends in the true sense of the word because they are not distributions of earnings.

Preferred stock is a second class of equity security that may be issued to raise capital. Since it carries many privileges not accorded to common stockholders, preferred stock is a lower-risk investment security than common. Among the privileges that may be included are preference in dividend distributions, preference in asset distributions upon liquidation, convertibility, accumulation of undeclared dividends, and participation with common stockholders in extra dividends. A group of privileges will be packaged by the corporation to appeal to a sufficiently large group of investors to raise the needed capital.

Earnings per share amounts must be published in the income statements of corporations whose stock is publicly traded. Corporations with simple capital structures report only historical earnings per share. Corporations that have convertible securities and stock options outstanding are required to issue additional shares of common stock upon demand of these security holders. For this reason these companies must report *primary earnings per share* reflecting the effects of the most likely new share distributions and *fully diluted earnings per share* taking into account all potential common stock issuances.

IMPORTANT TERMS USED IN THIS CHAPTER

Callable preferred stock Preferred stock that may be retired by the issuing corporation by paying the shareholder a predetermined amount—the call price. (page 540)

Complex capital structure A corporate structure that includes securities that may cause the company to issue common stock. Public corporations with complex capital structures must report primary and fully diluted earnings per share at the bottom of their income statements. (page 544)

Convertible securities Preferred stocks or bonds that carry the privilege, at the option of the holder, of being submitted to the corporation in exchange for a specified number of common shares. Preferred stocks and bonds without this privilege are nonconvertible. (page 540)

Cumulative preferred stock Preferred stock on which undeclared dividends of one year become corporate obligations of future years. All prior and current unpaid dividends must be paid before distributions can be made to common stockholders. Preferred stock without this privilege is noncumulative. (page 536)

Declaration date The date on which the board of directors votes to distribute a dividend. (page 527)

Deficit Retained Earnings with a debit (negative) balance. (page 522)

Dividends Pro rata distributions of corporate earned capital in the form of cash, noncash assets, or the corporation's own stock. (page 526)

Earnings per share Net income available to the common stockholder divided by the weighted average common shares outstanding. (page 541)

Fully diluted earnings per share Net income available to the common stockholder divided by actual common shares outstanding and all potential new issuances of common shares. Fully diluted earnings per share is the lowest possible earnings per share amount. (page 544)

Liquidating dividend Distributions of corporate paid-in capital. These distributions are not dividends in the true sense of the word because they do not distribute earnings. (page 533)

Liquidation preference The right of preferred stockholders to receive assets in the liquidation process before common stockholders may receive any assets. (page 540)

Participating preferred stock Preferred stock having the privilege of sharing in dividends with common stockholders after both groups have been paid a specified percentage of par. Preferred stock not having this privilege is nonparticipating. (page 537)

Payment date The date on which previously declared dividends are distributed to stockholders. (page 527)

Primary earnings per share Net income available to common stockholders divided by common shares outstanding plus the most likely issuances of new shares. (page 544)

Prior period adjustment An adjustment of the beginning balance of Retained Earnings as a result of correcting an accounting error committed in an earlier period. (page 524)

Property dividend The pro rata distribution of earned capital to stockholders in the form of assets other than cash. (page 528)

Record date   The date on which owners of stock are identified as those eligible to receive a previously declared dividend. (page 527)

Retained Earnings   A stockholders' equity account representing the accumulated income of a corporation since its beginning. Prior period adjustments, all dividends declared, and certain other adjustments must be deducted in calculating the current balance of this account. (page 521)

Retained Earnings: Appropriated   A stockholders' equity account that reflects a restriction imposed on retained earnings by the board of directors. Appropriated Retained Earnings are not available for dividend distributions. (page 522)

Simple capital structure   A corporate structure that contains no securities that may cause the company to issue common stock. Public corporations with simple capital structures must report historical earnings per share. (page 542)

Stock dividends   A pro rata distribution of earned capital in the form of additional shares of the company's own common stock. (page 529)

Stock split   A reduction of the par or stated value of the authorized stock and a simultaneous increase in the number of shares authorized, issued, and outstanding. (page 533)

QUESTIONS

1. Explain what takes place on the dividend *declaration date, record date,* and *payment date.* On which of these dates is an accounting entry necessary?

2. The board of directors must declare a dividend before one may be distributed. What two additional items must be present before a dividend is paid?

3. What is the effect on assets, liabilities, and stockholders' equity of declaring *and* issuing each of the following types of dividends:

   a. Cash dividend?
   b. Property dividend?
   c. Stock dividend?

4. What is the basic difference in accounting for small and large stock dividends?

5. Liquidating dividends do not result in a reduction of Retained Earnings. Why not?

6. Bolo Corp. stock is currently selling on the stock exchange for $232 per share. Explain two different actions that could be taken by the board of directors to reduce the price of the Bolo shares.

7. Brodgen Co. has a Retained Earnings account with a $35,400 debit balance. Explain how the negative balance could have come about. What is the proper term for negative retained earnings?

8. Mullins Corp. appropriates $25,000 of retained earnings each year to build a new warehouse. After 5 years, how much cash will Mullins have accumulated? Explain.

9. Lamb, Inc., has a total retained earnings of $594,600. $480,600 is appropriated for contingencies. What is the maximum dividend that the Lamb board of directors can declare? Explain.

10. The Zeta Corp. board of directors wishes to place restrictions on retained earnings to limit the amount that can be used for dividends. In what two ways may these restrictions be shown in the corporation's annual report?

11. What are *prior period adjustments?* How are they disclosed in the financial statements?

12. Why do corporations issue both common and preferred stock?

13. From the point of view of an investor, is cumulative or noncumulative preferred stock more desirable?

14. Both callable and convertible preferred stock have provisions that may result in the retirement of preferred stock. What is the primary difference between callable and convertible preferred?

15. The accountant for King, Inc., calculated historical, primary, and fully diluted earnings per share. Which of these would you expect to be the highest? Lowest?

16. Perry Corp. has a complex capital structure. Which earnings per share amounts must Perry report? On which financial statement are earnings per share amounts shown?

EXERCISES

Exercise 14-1
Recording cash dividend

Byte Corp.'s board of directors declared a $50,000 cash dividend on September 1, 1988, payable on October 1, to stockholders of record on September 15. Prepare all appropriate entries needed on the declaration, record, and payment dates.

Exercise 14-2
Recording property dividend

Sunset, Inc.'s board of directors voted to distribute some surplus office equipment to its 10 stockholders as a dividend. Each stockholder will receive a desk, chair, and electric typewriter. The office equipment to be distributed cost $25,000 and has accumulated depreciation at the time of declaration of $3,500. The current value of the equipment is $20,000. The property dividend was declared on March 1, 1987, distributable on April 1, to stockholders of record as of March 15.

Prepare all appropriate entries needed on the declaration, record, and distribution dates.

(Check figure: On March 1, Retained Earnings is debited for $20,000)

Exercise 14-3
Recording small stock dividend

The McDowell, Inc., board of directors voted on June 1, 1986, to declare a 10% stock dividend, distributable on July 1, to stockholders of record on June 15. On June 1, McDowell had 500,000 shares of $1-par common stock authorized. 50,000 shares were issued and outstanding. McDowell stock was selling for $3 per share on June 1.

Prepare the appropriate journal entries needed on June 1, June 15, and July 1.

(Check figure: On July 1, Common Stock is credited for $5,000)

Exercise 14-4
Recording large stock dividend

The Gossage Corp. board of directors voted on November 1, 1987, to declare a 40% stock dividend, distributable on December 31, to stockholders of record on December 1. Gossage's charter authorizes the issuance of 200,000 shares of $5-par common stock. As of November 1 1987, 50,000 shares of common stock are issued and outstanding. The market price of Gossage stock on November 1 is $6.50 per share.

Prepare any entries needed on the declaration, record, and payment dates.

(Check figure: Debit to Retained Earnings on Nov. 1 = $100,000)

Exercise 14-5
Indicating the effect of various transactions on stockholders' equity categories

For each of the independent transactions listed below, indicate the dollar effect on Common Stock, Paid-In Capital in Excess of Par, and Retained Earnings. Indicate increases with a plus (+), decreases with a minus (−), and no effect with a zero (0).

Transaction	Common Stock	Paid-In Capital in Excess of Par	Retained Earnings
Example: $1-par common stock is sold for $5 per share.	+	+	0
a. A cash dividend is declared and paid.			
b. A small stock dividend is declared and paid.			
c. A property dividend is declared and distributed (book value of property = $2,000, fair market value = $1,800).			
d. Retained earnings of $50,000 is appropriated for plant expansion.			
e. A 2 for 1 stock split is implemented.			
f. Expense and Revenue Summary, with a $46,000 credit balance, is closed.			
g. A large stock dividend is declared and distributed.			

Exercise 14-6

Dividing a dividend between preferred and common stockholders

On December 1, 1988, Home Delivery Corp. has 60,000 of 3%, $10-par, cumulative, nonparticipating preferred stock and 75,000 shares of no-par common stock outstanding. The common stock has a stated value of $10 per share.

The Home Delivery board of directors declared a $125,000 cash dividend on December 1, 1988, payable on December 31, to stockholders of record on December 1. Home Delivery did not pay dividends in 1984, 1985, 1986, or 1987.

Prepare a schedule showing how the $125,000 dividend will be split between the preferred and common stockholders.

(Check figure: Common stock gets $35,000 dividend)

Exercise 14-7

Calculating earnings per share

Springer, Inc., reported net income for 1986 of $330,000. 110,000 common shares were outstanding during the entire year. Since Springer is a large, publicly held corporation, it is required to report earnings per share on its income statement each year. The following additional information is available:

a. 1986 cash dividends paid to holders of convertible preferred stock = $22,000.
b. New common shares that may be issued if convertible preferred stock is converted = 40,000.
c. The convertible preferred stock is not likely to be converted, so the new shares are not included in the calculation of primary earnings per share. Since a possibility for conversion exists, they must be included in the calculation of fully diluted earnings per share.

Prepare a schedule showing the calculation of primary and fully diluted earnings per share for 1986.

(Check figure: Primary earnings per share = $2.80)

Exercise 14-8
Calculating the weighted average shares of stock outstanding

Wilmet Corp. compiled the following information about its common stock for the year 1987:

Jan. 1   500,000 shares of common stock were outstanding.
Apr. 1   20,000 previously unissued shares of common stock were sold.
July 1   5,000 shares of common stock were purchased for the treasury.
Oct. 1   5,000 shares of treasury stock were issued for a parcel of land.
Dec. 1   12,000 previously unissued shares of common stock were sold.

Calculate the weighted average number of common shares outstanding during 1987.

(Check figure: Weighted average shares outstanding during 1987 = 514,750)

Exercise 14-9
Calculating earnings per share

Jason Fleece Wool, Inc., reported 1988 income of $434,450. The accountant calculated a weighted average of 364,000 common shares outstanding during the year. The following additional facts are known about Jason:

1. $16,000 of dividends were paid on convertible preferred stock. If the stock is converted, 44,112 new common shares will be issued. It is not likely that this stock will be converted, but it is possible.
2. $10,000 of dividends were paid on nonconvertible preferred stock.
3. Executives of the corporation have the right to acquire 25,000 shares of common stock by exercising stock options. It is considered likely that these options will be exercised.

Calculate Jason Fleece Wool, Inc.'s primary and fully diluted earnings per share for 1988.

(Check figure: Fully diluted earnings per share = $.98)

PROBLEMS
Set A

Problem A14-1
Recording dividends on common and preferred stock

King Corp. had the following stock outstanding on December 31, 1987:

10% Preferred Stock, $40 par, 10,000 shares authorized, issued,
and outstanding . . . . $ 400,000
Common Stock, $10 par, 500,000 shares authorized, 100,000 shares issued
and outstanding 1,000,000

King has traditionally paid the preferred dividend in equal quarterly installments. Common dividends have followed an irregular pattern.

King's board of directors took the following dividend actions during 1988:

Mar. 1   The board declared the quarterly preferred dividend of $1 per share (10% × $40 × ¼).
15   Those owning preferred stock on this date will receive the preferred dividend.
31   The quarterly cash dividend is distributed to preferred shareholders.
Dec. 1   Since King has been having cash flow problems, the board declared no dividends in the second and third quarters. The board voted on Dec. 1 to declare the remaining preferred dividends for the second, third, and fourth quarters of the year. The market price per share of preferred stock was $60 on Dec. 1.
2   The board declared a 15% stock dividend on common stock. The market price per common share was $25 on Dec. 2.
15   Preferred and common stockholders of record on this day will receive dividends. On this day the market price of preferred stock is $62 and the market price of common stock is $27.
30   The common stock dividend was distributed. The market price of common stock was $26 per share on Dec. 30.
31   The cash dividend was distributed to preferred stockholders.

Required Prepare general journal entries to record the transactions and events listed above. If no entry is needed on a particular date, write, "No Entry."

(Check figure: Dec. 1 dividend declared for preferred stockholders = $30,000)

Problem A14-2
Recording retained earnings appropriation, property dividend, and stock split

Imperial, Inc.'s balance sheet stockholders' equity section on December 31, 1987, appears below:

Paid-In Capital:		
Common Stock, $15 par, 200,000 shares authorized, 150,000 shares issued, 145,000 shares outstanding (5,000 shares in treasury)		$2,250,000
Additional Paid-In Capital:		
Paid-In Capital in Excess of Par.	$750,000	
Paid-In Capital from Treasury Stock	50,000	800,000
Total Paid-In Capital.		$3,050,000
Earned Capital:		
Retained Earnings: Unappropriated		4,550,000
Total		$7,600,000
Less: Treasury Stock (5,000 shares), at cost.		(150,000)
Total Stockholders' Equity.		$7,450,000

The following events took place during 1988:
a. During March the Imperial board of directors voted to appropriate $100,000 for future plant expansion.
b. During June a property dividend was declared and distributed. Maize Corp. stock that Imperial had owned as an investment was distributed to the Imperial stockholders. The per-share book value and market value of the Maize stock on the date of declaration were $4.00 and $4.50, respectively. Four shares of Maize stock will be distributed for each share of Imperial stock owned.
c. During August a 3 for 1 stock split was implemented.
d. Income for the year [*excluding* any effect of events (a) through (c) above] was $267,900. [You must adjust the $267,900 for any income statement items in events (a) through (c).]

Required

Prepare Imperial's stockholders' equity section on December 3, 1988, after giving effect to the information in events (a) through (d) above. Your solution should be supported by schedules showing how each amount was derived.

(Check figure: Retained Earnings: Unappropriated = $2,397,900)

Problem A14-3
Recording various transactions and events affecting Retained Earnings

On January 1, 1988, Hood Guitar, Inc., had a Retained Earnings: Unappropriated account with a credit balance of $240,000, and Retained Earnings Appropriated for Contingencies with a credit balance of $40,000. The following events occurred during 1988:

Apr. 15   Since the possibility of a strike has passed, the board of directors voted to remove $20,000 of appropriated retained earnings and return this amount to the unappropriated account.

July 12   The board of directors voted to pay a cash dividend totaling $62,500 on Sept. 1 to stockholders of record on Aug. 1.

Aug. 9   A review of the Land account reveals that $36,000 that was debited to Land in 1986 should have been debited to Property Tax Expense. (Handle the correction as a prior period adjustment.)

Sept. 1   The dividend declared on July 12 was paid.

Oct. 15   The board of directors voted to appropriate retained earnings for plant expansion in the amount of $25,000.

Dec. 31   After closing all revenue and expense accounts for the year, Expense and Revenue Summary has a debit balance of $14,250.

Required

1. Prepare general journal entries to record each of the 1988 events and transactions outlined above.
2. Prepare a statement of retained earnings for the year ended December 31, 1988.

(Check figure: Retained Earnings: Unappropriated 12/31/88 = $122,250)

Problem A14-4

Allocating dividends between preferred and common stockholders under various assumptions

Perez Equipment Corp. has the following capital stock outstanding on December 31, 1988:

8% Preferred Stock, $5 par, 10,000 shares authorized, issued, and outstanding. . . . . $ 50,000

Common Stock, $1 par, 500,000 shares authorized, 450,000 shares issued and outstanding. 450,000

Perez did not declare or pay dividends during 1985, 1986, or 1987.

Required

Prepare schedules showing the amount of 1988 dividends to be received by preferred and by common stockholders under each of the following independent assumptions below:

1. Preferred stock is cumulative and nonparticipating. A $40,000 dividend is declared and paid in 1988.
2. Preferred stock is noncumulative and participating. A $50,000 dividend is declared and paid in 1988.
3. Preferred stock is cumulative and participating. A $72,000 dividend is declared and paid in 1988.

(Check figure: Part 2 total amount received by preferred stockholders = $5,000)

Problem A14-5

Reproducing journal entries affecting Retained Earnings by looking at a statement of retained earnings

R. R. JENKINS, INC.
Statement of Retained Earnings
For Year Ended December 31, 1987

Retained Earnings: Unappropriated:
Balance Jan. 1, 1987 . . . . $370,000
Prior Period Adjustment: To correct a 1985 error in recording insurance expense. Insurance Expense was debited when a cash payment was made; Notes Payable should have been debited 9,250
Balance Jan. 1 as adjusted $379,250

Add: Net Income for the Year $60,000
Reduction of Appropriation for Contingencies 50,000   110,000
Total $489,250

Deduct: Dividend Declared and Paid (cash dividend on preferred stock) $30,000
Dividend Declared and Distributed (small stock dividend on $5-par common stock, 5,000 shares distributed). 47,500   (77,500)

Balance Dec. 31, 1987 . . . . $411,750

Retained Earnings Appropriated for Contingencies:
Balance Jan. 1, 1987 . . . . $125,000
Add: (none) . . . .
Deduct: Appropriation removed during 1987 . . . . (50,000)

Balance Dec. 31, 1987 . . . . $ 75,000

Required

Examine Jenkins' statement of retained earnings for 1987 and prepare in general journal form all of the entries that affected the Retained Earnings account during the year. Dates may be omitted from your entries. (Prepare declaration and distribution entries for any dividends.)

(Check figure: Your solution should contain seven entries)

Problem A14-6
Indicating the effect on balance sheet categories of various events and transactions

For each of the *independent* (unrelated) transactions below, enter the dollar effect in each column of the solutions sheet. Show increases by placing a plus (+) in front of the amount, decreases by placing a minus (−) in front of the amount, and no effect by placing a zero (0) in the column. Headings for the columns and an example are shown on the solutions sheet below:

Description	Total Assets	Total Liabilities	Total Common Stock	Total Additional Paid-In Capital	Total Retained Earnings	Total Stockholders' Equity
Example: Corp. declared a cash dividend of $20,000	0	+$20,000	0	0	−$20,000	−$20,000

a. Corp. sold 2,000 shares of $5-par common stock for $12 per share.
b. Corp. sold 500 shares of $5-par common stock on subscription for $15 per share. A one-third down payment was received.
c. Corp. declared a 10% stock dividend. 100,000 shares of $5-par common stock were outstanding on the declaration date. The market price of the stock is $9 per share.
d. Corp. paid a $10,000 cash dividend, which was declared last year.
e. Corp. collected $500 due on a common stock subscription and issued common stock with a par value of $2,500.
f. Corp. distributed 5,000 shares of $5-par common stock in payment of a stock dividend. (The 30% dividend had been declared in the previous year when the market value of the stock was $12.50 per share.)
g. Corp.'s board of directors implemented a 4 for 1 stock split. Before the split, 10,000 shares of $20-par common stock were outstanding.
h. Corp. purchased 5,000 shares of its own $5-par common stock for $8 per share.
i. Corp.'s board of directors voted to appropriate $50,000 of retained earnings for plant expansion.
j. Corp. corrected a $30,000 error that had been made in a prior year. An entry to record sales had erroneously credited Donated Capital. (Cash was correctly debited.)

Problem A14-7
Recording transactions in stockholders' equity T-accounts, prepare a stockholders' equity section

Spinner Distributing, Inc., has the following stockholders' equity on June 30, 1986:

Common Stock, $10 par, 100,000 shares authorized, 30,000 shares issued and outstanding	$ 300,000
Paid-In Capital in Excess of Par	245,000
Retained Earnings: Unappropriated	555,000
Total Stockholders' Equity	$1,100,000

The following transactions occurred during the following fiscal year:

1986

July 8	Purchased 500 shares of common stock for the treasury, $11,500.
Sept. 21	Declared a cash dividend of $1 per share to stockholders of record on Oct. 15.
Nov. 1	Paid the cash dividend.
26	Sold 10,000 shares of common stock on subscription. The subscription price was $25 per share. A 30% down payment was received.
Dec. 21	Sold the treasury stock for $28 per share. (The stock was originally issued for $17 per share.)

1987

Jan. 26	Collected half of the remaining balance on the stock subscriptions.
Feb. 14	Appropriated $150,000 of retained earnings for plant expansion.
Mar. 26	Collected the balance due on the stock subscriptions and issued the shares.
Apr. 3	Issued 10,000 shares of stock with a market value of $31 per share in exchange for a piece of land. No objective market price is available for the land.
May 4	Declared a 10% stock dividend distributable on July 1 to stockholders of record on June 15. The market price of the stock on May 4 was $32 per share.
June 19	Received a donation of a building that will be moved to the land acquired on April 3. The building was valued at $42,000.
30	Net income for the year was calculated to be $98,800.

Required

1. Set up the following stockholders' equity T-accounts:

   Common Stock
   Paid-In Capital in Excess of Par
   Common Stock Subscribed
   Common Stock Dividend Distributable
   Donated Capital
   Paid-In Capital from Treasury Stock
   Retained Earnings: Unappropriated
   Retained Earnings: Appropriated for Plant Expansion
   Treasury Stock

2. Enter the beginning balances in Common Stock, Paid-In Capital in Excess of Par, and Retained Earnings: Unappropriated.
3. Enter the transactions for the year in the appropriate T-accounts. (You may wish to set up the asset and liability accounts in addition to the stockholders' equity accounts listed above.) Identify each debit and credit by placing the date of the transaction next to the amount.
4. Prepare the stockholders' equity section of Spinners' balance sheet on June 30, 1987, in good form.

(Check figure: Total stockholders' equity = $1,773,800)

Set B

Problem B14-1
Recording dividends on common and preferred stock

Barkley, Incorporated's board of directors took the following actions during 1987 that affected stockholders' equity:

Jan. 1	The board of directors declared the annual cash dividend on the 100,000 shares of 6%, noncumulative, nonparticipating, $1-par preferred stock outstanding. The market price of the preferred stock was $5 on Jan. 1.
1	The board declared a quarterly cash dividend of $1 per share to common stockholders. There were 250,000 shares of $10-par common stock outstanding. The market price per share of stock was $15 on Jan. 1.

Jan. 15	Common stockholders of record on this day will receive the cash dividend.
31	Preferred stockholders of record on this day will receive the cash dividend.
Feb. 15	The cash dividend is distributed to common stockholders.
Mar. 1	The cash dividend is distributed to preferred stockholders.
Oct. 1	Since Barkley's cash position was unfavorable, no dividends on common stock were declared during the second and third quarters of the year. The board of directors voted to declare an 18% stock dividend in lieu of the fourth-quarter cash dividend. The market price per share was $12 on Oct. 1.
Nov. 1	Common stockholders of record on this day will receive the stock dividend. The market price per share of stock was $12.50 on Nov. 1.
Dec. 15	The common stock dividend was distributed. The market price per share of common stock was $14 on Dec. 15.

Required   Prepare the general journal entries to record the transactions and events listed above. If no entry is needed on a particular date, write, "No entry."

(Check figure: Debit to Retained Earnings on Oct. 1 = $540,000)

Problem B14-2
Recording retained earnings appropriation, property dividend, and stock split

The December 31, 1987, stockholders' equity section of Joyner, Inc., appears below:

Paid-In Capital:		
Common Stock, $5 par, 500,000 shares authorized, 100,000 shares issued, 95,000 shares outstanding (5,000 shares in treasury)		$ 500,000
Additional Paid-In Capital:		
Paid-In Capital in Excess of Par.	$200,000	
Donated Capital.	20,000	220,000
Total Paid-In Capital .		720,000
Earned Capital:		
Retained Earnings: Unappropriated		1,750,000
Total		$2,470,000
Less: Treasury Stock (5,000 shares) at cost.		(45,000)
Total Stockholders' Equity.		$2,425,000

The following events took place during 1988:
a. During January a property dividend was declared and distributed. Splash Pool Corp. stock that Joyner, Inc., had owned as an investment was distributed to the Joyner stockholders. The per-share book value and fair market values of the Splash stock on the date of declaration were $1.10 and $1.15, respectively. Two shares of Splash stock will be distributed for each share of Joyner owned.
b. During April, a 2 for 1 stock split was implemented.
c. During December the Joyner board of directors voted to appropriate $40,000 of retained earnings for plant expansion.
d. Income for the year [*excluding* any effect of events (a) through (c) above] was $326,000. [You must adjust the $326,000 for any income statement items contained in events (a) through (c).]

Required   Prepare Joyner's stockholders' equity section on December 31, 1988, after giving effect to the information in events (a) through (d) above. Your solution should be supported by schedules showing how each amount was derived.

(Check figure: Retained Earnings: Unappropriated = $1,827,000)

Problem B14-3
Recording various transactions and events affecting Retained Earnings

Devious Enterprises, Inc., began 1987 with a Retained Earnings: Unappropriated account having a credit balance of $600,000, and Retained Earnings Appropriated for Plant Expansion of $240,000. The following occurred during 1987:

Feb. 15   A review of the Patent account reveals that a patent acquired in 1986 for $300,000 was not amortized. $30,000 Patent Amortization Expense should have been recorded in 1986. (Handle the correction as a prior period adjustment.)

Apr. 21   The board of directors voted to remove $100,000 of appropriated retained earnings and return this amount to the unappropriated account.

May 30   The board of directors voted to pay a cash dividend totaling $360,000 on June 30 to stockholders of record on June 15.

June 30   The dividend declared on May 30 was paid.

Sept. 18   Devious sold 2,000 shares of common stock that had been held in the treasury for $36,000. The treasury stock had cost $40,000. (Devious originally issued all common stock at par and no Paid-In Capital from Treasury Stock account exists.)

Dec. 31   After closing all revenue and expense accounts for the year, Expense and Revenue Summary has a debit balance of $136,000.

Required
1. Prepare general journal entries to record each of the 1987 events and transactions outlined above.
2. Prepare a statement of retained earnings in good form for the year ended December 31, 1987.

(Check figure: Retained Earnings: Unappropriated 12/31/87 = $170,000)

Problem B14-4
Allocating dividends between preferred and common stockholders under various assumptions

Creative Concepts, Inc., has the following capital stock outstanding on December 31, 1987:

6% Preferred Stock, $1 par, 100,000 shares authorized, issued,
and outstanding. $100,000
Common Stock, $5 par, 100,000 shares authorized, 80,000 shares issued
and outstanding.   400,000

Creative Concepts did not declare or pay dividends in 1983, 1984, 1985, or 1986.

Required   Prepare schedules showing the amount of 1987 dividends to be received by preferred and by common stockholders under each of the independent assumptions below:
1. Preferred stock is cumulative and nonparticipating. A $42,000 dividend is declared and paid in 1987.
2. Preferred stock is noncumulative and participating. A $50,000 dividend is declared and paid in 1987.
3. Preferred stock is cumulative and participating. A $100,000 dividend is declared and paid in 1987.

(Check figure: Part 2, total amount received by common stockholders = $40,000)

Problem B14-5
Reproducing journal entries affecting Retained Earnings by looking at a statement of retained earnings

SHOPPER JOY, INC.
Statement of Retained Earnings
For Year Ended December 31, 1986

Retained Earnings: Unappropriated:		
Balance Jan. 1, 1986		$ 684,000
Prior Period Adjustment: To correct a 1984 error in recording sales revenue. Accounts Payable was credited on a cash sale rather than the Sales Revenue account.		5,000
Balance Jan. 1 as adjusted		$ 689,000
Add: Net Income for the Year.		134,000
Total		$ 823,000
Deduct: Dividend Declared and Paid (cash dividend on preferred stock)	$ 56,000	
Dividend Declared and Distributed (small stock dividend on $10-par common stock, 20,000 shares distributed).	480,000	
Appropriated for Self-Insurance	30,000	(566,000)
Balance Dec. 31, 1986		$ 257,000
Retained Earnings Appropriated for Self-Insurance:		
Balance Jan. 1, 1986		$ 120,000
Add: Appropriation during 1986		30,000
Deduct: (none).		
Balance Dec. 31, 1986		$ 150,000

Required

Examine the Shopper Joy statement of retained earnings for 1986 and prepare in general journal form all of the entries that affected the Retained Earnings account for the year. Dates may be omitted from your entries. (Prepare declaration and distribution entries for any dividends.)

(Check figure: Your solution should contain seven entries)

Problem B14-6
Indicating the effect on balance sheet categories of various events and transactions

For each of the *independent* (unrelated) transactions below, enter the dollar effect in each column of the solutions sheet. Show increases by placing a plus (+) in front of the amount, decreases by placing a minus (−) in front of the amount, and no effect by placing a zero (0) in the column. Headings for the columns and an example are shown on the solutions sheet below:

Description	Total Assets	Total Liabilities	Total Common Stock	Total Additional Paid-In Capital	Total Retained Earnings	Total Stockholders' Equity
Example: Inc. declared a cash dividend of $10,000	0	+$10,000	0	0	−$10,000	−$10,000

a. Inc. sold 1,000 shares of $10-par common stock for $18,400.
b. Inc.'s board of directors implemented a 3 for 1 stock split. Before the split, 50,000 shares of $10-par common stock were outstanding.
c. Inc. distributed 10,000 shares of $1-par common stock relating to a stock dividend. (The 40% dividend had been declared in the previous year when the market value of the stock was $2.25 per share.)

d. Inc. collected $2,500 due on a common stock subscription and issued common stock with a par value of $500.

e. Inc. sold 3,000 shares of common stock with a stated value of $2 per share for $12,500.

f. Inc. paid a $4,675 cash dividend that had been declared last year.

g. Inc. purchased 5,000 shares of its $1-par common stock for $5 per share.

h. Inc. sold 100 shares of treasury stock for $2,000. The treasury stock had originally been purchased for $1,200.

i. Inc. declared a 40% stock dividend. 100,000 shares of $1-par common stock is outstanding on the declaration date. The market price of the stock is $2.50 per share.

j. Inc. sold 500 shares of $5-par common stock on subscription for $15 per share. A 10% down payment was received.

Problem B14-7

Recording transactions in stockholders' equity T-accounts, prepare a stockholders' equity section

Scofield Manufacturing Co. has the following stockholders' equity on October 31, 1987:

Common Stock, $5 par, 200,000 shares authorized, 50,000 shares issued and outstanding	$250,000
Paid-In Capital in Excess of Par	150,000
Retained Earnings: Unappropriated	400,000
Total Stockholders' Equity	$800,000

The following transactions occurred during the following fiscal year:

1987
Nov. 5 Purchased 1,000 shares of common stock for the treasury, $10,000.

1988
Jan. 15 Declared a cash dividend of $.50 per share payable Mar. 1 to stockholders of record Feb. 1.

Mar. 1 Paid the cash dividend.

25 Sold 5,000 shares of common stock on subscription. The subscription price was $8 per share. A 20% down payment was received.

Apr. 4 Sold the treasury stock for $12 per share. (The stock was originally issued for $8 per share.)

June 1 Collected half of the remaining balance on the stock subscriptions.

July 31 Appropriated $100,000 of retained earnings for a possible lawsuit loss.

Sept. 1 Collected the balance due on the stock subscription and issued the shares.

15 Issued 5,000 shares of stock in exchange for a forklift. The stock has a market value of $11 per share. No market price was available for the equipment.

30 Declared a 15% stock dividend distributable on Nov. 1 to the stockholders of record on Oct. 15. The market price of the stock on Sept. 30 was $12 per share.

Oct. 20 Received a donation of 10 acres of land valued at $25,000.

31 Calculated net income for the year at $166,000.

Required

1. Set up the following stockholders' equity T-accounts:

> Common Stock
> Paid-In Capital in Excess of Par
> Common Stock Subscribed
> Common Stock Dividend Distributable
> Donated Capital
> Paid-In Capital from Treasury Stock
> Retained Earnings: Unappropriated
> Retained Earnings: Appropriated for Lawsuit Loss
> Treasury Stock

2. Enter the beginning balances in Common Stock, Paid-in Capital in Excess of Par, and Retained Earnings: Unappropriated.

3. Enter the transactions for the year in the appropriate T-accounts. (You may wish to set up the asset and liability accounts in addition to the stockholders' equity accounts listed above.) Identify each debit and credit by placing the date of the transaction next to the amount.

4. Prepare the stockholders' equity section of Scofield's balance sheet on October 31, 1988, in good form.

(Check figure: Total stockholders' equity = $1,063,500)

Chapter 15

Corporations: Long-Term Liabilities

After studying this chapter you should understand the following:

- The comparative advantages and disadvantages of issuing bonds at different earnings levels
- The differences between the various types of bonds
- How to record the entries associated with a bond issue at par
- How the price of bonds can be determined using present value tables
- How to record the entries for a bond issue sold at a premium or discount
- How to amortize premiums or discounts by the *effective-interest* and *straight-line* methods
- How to record the entries associated with the *capitalization of a lease*

Financing the acquisition of plant assets is usually done on a long-term basis

Large expenditures can be financed by the use of internal funds, funds obtained from additional investors, or borrowed funds

Interest on borrowed funds is a tax-deductible item

In Chapter 11 we discussed the financing of the normal recurring operations of business entities. We saw that this was, for the most part, accomplished by the incurrence of current liabilities. Purchases of inventory are made on account; the use of labor is usually paid for weekly, biweekly, or semimonthly; temporary drains on cash are eased by the issuance of short-term notes. These everyday examples show the use of current liabilities in normal, recurring operations. However, situations arise that require substantial cash outlays, and these cannot be financed by the use of current liabilities. The acquisition of additional or replacement equipment or the construction of a new building are examples of such situations. Where do the funds come from to pay for these substantial cash outlays? Let's consider the case of the Lou Jergensen Mail-Order House.

Lou's company has done quite well over the past several years and he is thinking about expanding his business. He needs $250,000 to construct an addition on his building to handle the anticipated increase in the volume of mail orders. One thing Lou could do would be to use cash that he has retained in his business. Of course, in order to accumulate $250,000 Lou would have to severely limit the amount of dividends paid to the company's stockholders. An advantage of this plan is that Lou wouldn't need additional stockholders or creditors to help him. But like most small corporations, Lou's company just doesn't have the $250,000.

Something else Lou might try would be to issue additional stock to interested investors. They could invest the $250,000. But unless profits increase proportionately with the increase in the number of shares, the present stockholders' share of the corporation's earnings will be less than they were before the new stock was issued.

The third thing Lou's corporation could do would be to borrow the $250,000 from creditors on a long-term basis. There are several forms of long-term financing. Proprietorships, partnerships, and corporations may issue long-term notes, or may enter into long-term lease arrangements. In the case of corporations, bonds may be issued. The amount of funds that can be obtained from long-term notes or leases is typically less than that which can be obtained by the issuance of bonds. The reason for this is that long-term notes and leases are typically issued to a single investor or relatively few investors, such as a bank, a leasing company, or an insurance company. Bonds, on the other hand, are sold by underwriters who market them to many investors. But don't become misled into thinking that the amount of funds that can be obtained from notes or leases is insignificant. These instruments are often in the millions of dollars. It is not uncommon, however, for a large corporation to have a bond issue in the hundreds of millions of dollars.

If the $250,000 is obtained from creditors, there is a disadvantage. Interest and principal repayments must be made when due. An advantage of this method is that the present capital structure remains unchanged; that is, Lou and the rest of the present stockholders will not have to share ownership of the corporation with a new group of stockholders. Also, Lou's corporation can deduct the interest on the borrowed money on the corporate tax return.

We cannot establish a single rule that would determine which method of financing would be best for Lou or anyone else. We would have to consider many factors before selecting one means of long-term financing over the others. We can, however, prepare an analysis of the alternatives in a given situation that will help us choose the best alternative available. Such an analysis is presented in the following discussion.

Let us assume that $1 million of additional financing is required to build a new plant. At present there are 100,000 shares of common stock outstanding. The first alternative is to obtain the $1 million from retained earnings (assuming that there is

$1 million in the corporate cash accounts). The second alternative is to find new investors and issue 50,000 additional shares of common stock worth $1 million. Alternative three is to obtain the money from a long-term note, lease, or bond issue requiring a 12% interest expense each year. We assume two earnings levels, $800,000 and $120,000, both before the interest expense and the income tax (assumed to be 45% of earnings before income taxes) have been deducted.

Financing Alternatives for Construction of New Plant.

	From Retained Earnings (100,000 shares outstanding)		From Additional Stockholders (150,000 shares outstanding)		From Long-Term Creditors (100,000 shares outstanding)	
Earnings before interest and income taxes	$800,000	$120,000	$800,000	$120,000	$800,000	$120,000
Interest ($1,000,000 × 12%)					120,000	120,000
Earnings before income taxes	$800,000	$120,000	$800,000	$120,000	$680,000	–0–
Income taxes at 45%	360,000	54,000	360,000	54,000	306,000	–0–
Net income	$440,000	$ 66,000	$440,000	$ 66,000	$374,000	–0–
Earnings per share	$ 4.40	$ 0.66	$ 2.93	$ 0.44	$ 3.74	0.00

If you were a stockholder, *all other conditions being equal,* the first alternative would be the most attractive. Why? Because this alternative provides the highest earnings per share (EPS). At the $800,000 earnings level, EPS is $4.40, which exceeds both the $2.93 EPS projected if the $1 million is obtained from 50,000 new shares and the $3.74 EPS projected if the $1 million is obtained from long-term creditors. Also, the $0.66 EPS at the $120,000 earnings level under the first alternative exceeds the $0.44 and the zero EPS under each of the other alternatives.

BONDS PAYABLE

Once the decision is made to obtain financing by means of issuing bonds, management of the corporation (proprietorships and partnerships do not issue bonds) must next decide what type of bonds to issue. Most corporations do not have the expertise to market their own securities. They usually work with an *investment banker* who provides a service of developing a marketable product — the bonds — and then selling it to the public. This process is called *underwriting* the new issue, which is why investment bankers are often called *underwriters.* The underwriter will help the corporation determine the type of bonds to issue, the interest rate the bonds should carry, the maturity date of the bonds, and other important matters. The bonds are usually sold to the underwriter, or to several underwriters, who in turn sell the bonds to interested investors at a somewhat higher price. Rather than buying the bonds, the underwriter may contract to sell the bonds on a commission basis. Or, the corporation may sell the bonds directly to a large institution such as an insurance company.

Underwriters help corporations issue bonds. They provide advice on the type of bonds to issue, the interest rate to pay, and when the bonds should mature.

The corporation enters into a contract with an agent, called the *trustee,* representing the bondholders. It is the duty of the trustee to assure the bondholders that the

A bond indenture is a contract between the bond trustee and the corporation	corporation is fulfilling its responsibilities under the contract. The contract is referred to as a ***trust indenture*** or ***bond indenture*** and is called the ***deed of trust.*** The trustee is typically a large bank.

In order to make the bond widely marketable so that large sums of money can be generated, bonds are commonly issued in units of $1,000 each. The amount of the bond, $1,000, is called its ***face*** or ***par value.*** The bond indenture will provide for the payment of periodic interest on the face value of the bond. Most bonds pay interest on

Interest on bonds is usually paid twice a year

a semiannual basis. Prices of bonds are expressed for trading purposes per $1,000 of face value. *Priced at 98* means that a $1,000 bond will sell for $980, 98% of $1,000. If a $1,000 bond is quoted at $102\frac{1}{4}$, it will sell for $1,022.50 ($102\frac{1}{4}$% of $1,000).

Bonds can be secured or debenture, term or serial, callable or convertible

A corporation may issue either ***secured*** or ***unsecured bonds.*** A secured bond provides the bondholder with a claim on a specified asset in the event the corporation does not fulfill its responsibilities under the terms of the bond indenture. The pledged or mortgaged assets are typically equipment or buildings. Unsecured bonds are issued on the general credit rating of the issuing corporation and are called ***debenture bonds.*** Only the financially strongest businesses can issue bonds on the basis of their name alone.

Term or ***serial bonds*** may be issued. Term bonds are those in which the entire bond issue matures on a specified date in the future called the ***maturity date.*** Serial bonds mature at various dates over the bond contract. For example, a $50 million serial bond issue dated 1985 might provide for $10 million of bonds to mature commencing in 1996 and each year thereafter through 2000.

Bonds may have a ***callable*** or a ***convertible feature.*** Callable bonds provide the corporation with the right to redeem the bonds prior to their maturity date. When bonds are called, usually the bond indenture provides that a penalty be paid by the issuing entity. This is in the form of a call price, which is slightly higher than the face of the bonds. Convertible bonds provide the bondholder with the right to exchange his or her bonds for an ownership interest in the business entity.

Bonds Issued at Par

After a corporation has decided on the type of bonds to issue, the amount, the interest rate, the interest payment dates, and the maturity date, and the owners of the corporation approve, the trust indenture is prepared and the bonds are printed and issued. Let's use an example at this point to illustrate the accounting for bonds.

Assume that the Karlton Company issues $5 million of 20-year, 12% bonds on May 1, 1987, at par with interest payable semiannually on November 1 and May 1. The entry to record the issuance of the bonds would be as follows:

Bonds sold at par

1987			
May 1	Cash	5,000,000	
	Bonds Payable		5,000,000
	To record the sale of $5,000,000 of 20-year 12% bonds at par.		

On November 1, the first semiannual interest payment is due. This will amount to $300,000, computed as follows: $5,000,000 \times 12\% \times \frac{6}{12}$ year = $300,000. The entry to record the interest payment is recorded as follows:

The first bond interest payment

1987			
Nov. 1	Bond Interest Expense	300,000	
	Cash.		300,000
	To record payment of semiannual interest on bonds payable.		

At the end of the accounting period, December 31, the interest expense applicable to November through December 1987 must be accrued and the liability for interest payable must be recorded. This entry would be recorded as follows:

Bond interest adjusting entry

```
1987
Dec. 31   Bond Interest Expense  . . . . . . . . . . . . . . . . . . . . . .   100,000
                 Bond Interest Payable  . . . . . . . . . . . . . . . . . .              100,000
          To record accrued interest on bonds payable. Interest is com-
          puted as follows: ($5,000,000 × 12% × 2/12 yr).
```

Assuming that the business entity does not use reversing entries, the journal entry to record the May 1, 1988, interest payment would be as follows:

The second bond interest payment

```
1988
May 1    Bond Interest Payable. . . . . . . . . . . . . . . . . . . . . . .   100,000
         Bond Interest Expense  . . . . . . . . . . . . . . . . . . . . . .   200,000
                 Cash . . . . . . . . . . . . . . . . . . . . . . . . . . . .              300,000
         To record payment of semiannual interest on bonds payable.
         Interest expense computed as follows: ($5,000,000 × 12% ×
         4/12 yr).
```

Throughout the life of the bonds, the entries made on November 1, December 31, and May 1 will be repeated year after year until May 1, 2007, when the bonds are finally retired by the following entry:

Retirement of bonds at maturity

```
2007
May 1    Bonds Payable . . . . . . . . . . . . . . . . . . . . . . . . . .   5,000,000
                 Cash  . . . . . . . . . . . . . . . . . . . . . . . . . . .            5,000,000
         To record payment of bonds payable at maturity.
```

Bonds Sold between Interest Payment Dates

According to the trust indenture, bond interest payments are required to be paid on specified dates. These dates are printed on the bond certificates. Bonds may be sold, however, on any date. Thus, it is highly likely that bonds will be sold on a date other than a bond interest payment date. When this occurs, it is necessary to add to the price of the bond the interest accrued on the bond. To illustrate, assume that the Karlton Company bonds from the previous example were sold on July 1, 1987, rather than May 1. The investors must pay, in addition to the $5 million for the bonds, an additional $100,000 for the 2 months' accrued interest ($5,000,000 × .12 × 2/12)—which will be re-earned on the next interest payment date. The entry to record the sale of the bonds on July 1 would be as follows:

Bonds sold 2 months after issue date. Two months' interest must also be sold

```
1987
July 1   Cash. . . . . . . . . . . . . . . . . . . . . . . . . . . . . . . .   5,100,000
                 Bond Interest Payable  . . . . . . . . . . . . . . . .              100,000
                 Bonds Payable  . . . . . . . . . . . . . . . . . . . . .            5,000,000
         To record the sale of $5,000,000 of 20-year, 12% bonds at
         par plus 2 months' accrued interest.
```

Karlton Company is obligated, by the terms of the trust indenture, to make a semiannual interest payment on November 1 in the amount of $300,000. Karlton can pay no other amount but $300,000. When the interest payment is received by the bondholders, they will have been paid effectively for 4 months' interest. They have paid Karlton for 2 months' interest on July 1, but have received 6 months' interest on November 1. The entry to record the interest payment on November 1 is presented below:

The first bond interest payment

1987
Nov. 1   Bond Interest Payable 100,000
         Bond Interest Expense 200,000
           Cash. 300,000
         To record payment of semiannual interest on bonds payable.

Notice that the entry eliminates the Bond Interest Payable established from the July 1 entry and records interest expense for only 4 months.

The entry made on July 1 could have been recorded in a slightly different manner. Rather than crediting the Bond Interest Payable account for the accrued interest, the Bond Interest Expense account could have been credited in *anticipation* of the November 1 debit from the semiannual interest payment. The July 1 entry would then appear as follows:

Bond interest payable could be recorded in Bond Interest Expense account

1987
July 1   Cash. 5,100,000
         Bond Interest Expense 100,000
         Bonds Payable 5,000,000
         To record the sale of $5,000,000 of 20-year, 12% bonds at
         par plus 2 months' accrued interest.

The November 1 entry is then recorded simply as follows:

Recording the first bond interest payment

1987
Nov. 1   Bond Interest Expense 300,000
         Cash. 300,000
         To record payment of semiannual interest on bonds payable.

The result, of course, is that after the November 1 entry is made, the balance in Bond Interest Expense is $200,000, reflecting 4 months' interest expense, as can be seen in the following account:

Bond Interest Expense			
1987 Nov. 1	$300,000	1987 July 1	$100,000
Bal.	$200,000		

Accounting for Bonds Issued at a Discount

More often than not, bonds are sold at a price that differs from their par value. Bonds sold at a price greater than their par value are said to be sold at a *premium.* Bonds sold at a price lower than their par value are said to be sold at a *discount.*

Let's assume that the Karlton bonds that were issued on May 1, 1987, were issued at a price that was less than the $5 million face value. Specifically, let's assume that the bonds were sold for a price of $4,333,413—$666,587 less than the face value. This

$666,587 difference is the ***discount.*** Generally accepted accounting principles require that the liability account Bonds Payable must be recorded at the face value, $5,000,000. A contra-liability account, Discount on Bonds Payable, must then be established to adjust the face value of the bonds to the amount of cash received from selling the bonds. We would record the general journal entry on May 1, 1987, when the bonds are issued, as follows:

Bonds issued at a discount

May 1	Cash	4,333,413	
	Discount on Bonds Payable	666,587	
	Bonds Payable		5,000,000
	To record the sale of $5,000,000 of 20-year, 12% bonds,		
	maturing May 1, 2007.		

If a balance sheet were prepared on this date, the information pertaining to the bonds would be presented in the long-term liabilities section like this:

Long-Term Liabilities:
    12% Bonds Payable Due May 1, 2007 . . . . $5,000,000
    Less: Discount on Bonds Payable 666,587 $4,333,413

The carrying value of a bond is the difference between its face value and the discount

The $4,333,413 representing the difference between the $5,000,000 face value and the $666,587 discount, is called the ***carrying value*** of the bonds.

Now, let's move ahead to May 1, 2007, when the bonds are retired—the $5,000,000 face value of the bonds is paid to the creditors and the bonds are canceled. On that date Karlton Company will issue a check in the amount of $5,000,000 and record this entry:

2007			
May 1	Bonds Payable	5,000,000	
	Cash		5,000,000
	To record the retirement of $5,000,000 of 20-year, 12%		
	bonds due this date.		

What about the Discount on Bonds Payable account? If we no longer have the bonds, we should no longer have the discount! The Discount on Bonds Payable has a debit balance and the account must be credited to eliminate the debit balance. But when the credit is made, what do we debit? Three possibilities exist.

First, let's consider a second entry on May 1, 2007. Karlton has to pay $5,000,000 to retire the bonds, but received only $4,333,413 on May 1, 1987, when the money was borrowed. We could record a loss on the retirement of the bonds. Or perhaps we should not call it a loss but a fee paid for the use of money—interest expense. But was this fee incurred all on one date—May 1, 2007?

Well, what if we made a second entry on the date the bonds were issued—May 1, 1987? We could credit Discount on Bonds Payable and debit a loss on the sale of the bonds for the $666,587. Again, what we are doing is paying for the use of money, and that's interest expense. But was the $666,587 all incurred on May 1, 1987?

Bond discounts must be amortized over the life of the bonds

The $666,587 would seem to have been logically incurred over the period of time Karlton Company used the money—20 years, or 240 months. And that's the third alternative: Allocate the discount over the life of the bonds—in this case, $2,777 per month ($666,587 ÷ 240). This process is called ***amortization.***

You may ask why bonds are sold at a price that is less — or more — than their face value. Well, when bonds are sold — say, the Karlton bonds — they have a stated interest rate in the bond indenture. And that rate is on the face of the bond certificates — 12% for the Karlton bonds. Karlton Company *must* pay 12% interest on the bonds (6% on each of the two semiannual interest payment dates).

What if, when Karlton tries to sell its bonds, the interest rate that other companies are willing to pay on their bonds is 14%? Who would buy Karlton's bonds? Nobody. So Karlton must do something to sell its bonds. It can't change the 12% rate that it must pay as specified by the bond indenture, but it can change the *price* of the bonds — the amount the bonds sell for. Karlton will sell the bonds at a price investors are willing to pay. That price will be such that an investor will earn a 14% return on the investment. Selling the Karlton bonds at $4,333,413, and paying 12% interest a year — actually 6% every 6 months — on the $5,000,000 for 20 years, will give the investor a 14% return. (The section on present value later in this chapter will show you how this was calculated.) So you see the reason bonds are sold at a discount is to adjust the interest rate specified in the bond indenture — which is too low — to the rate of interest investors are willing to pay.

We don't have to amortize the bond discount every month; we can do it on bond interest payment dates and on the year-end closing dates. That's what Karlton will do. So, on the first bond interest payment date — November 1, 1987 — Karlton will record the interest expense as the sum of the cash paid, $300,000 ($5,000,000 × 12% × $\frac{6}{12}$ year), plus 6 months' amortization of the discount, $16,665 ($666,587 × $\frac{6}{240}$). That's a total interest expense for the 6 months of $316,665 ($300,000 + $16,665). Here's the general journal entry:

The first bond interest payment and amortization of the discount

1987			
Nov. 1	Bond Interest Expense 316,665		
	Discount on Bonds Payable..................	16,665	
	Cash......................................	300,000	
	To record payment of semiannual interest on bonds ($5,000,000 × 12% × $\frac{6}{12}$ mo) and amortization of bond discount ($666,587 × $\frac{6}{240}$ mo).		

The December 31 adjusting entry required to accrue the bond interest payable and to amortize the discount would be recorded like this:

The bond interest adjusting entry and amortization of the discount

1987			
Dec. 31	Bond Interest Expense 105,555		
	Discount on Bonds Payable..................	5,555	
	Bond Interest Payable......................	100,000	
	To record accrual of bond interest payable ($5,000,000 × 12% × $\frac{2}{12}$ mo) and amortization of bond discount ($666,587 × $\frac{2}{240}$ mo)		

The December 31 balance sheet would show the carrying value of the bond as follows:

Long-Term Liabilities:		
12% Bonds Payable Due May 1, 2007	$5,000,000	
Less: Discount on Bonds Payable	644,367	$4,355,633

The balance in the discount account has been reduced to $644,367 ($666,587 − $16,665 − $5,555) by the amortization process.

On May 1, 1988, we will pay the semiannual interest payment of $300,000 and amortize 4 months' discount, January 1 to April 30. The following entry will be used to record this payment:

The second bond interest payment and amortization of the discount

```
1988
May 1   Bond Interest Payable. . . . . . . . . . . . . . . . . . . . . . . . . .   100,000
        Bond Interest Expense . . . . . . . . . . . . . . . . . . . . . . . . .   211,110
            Discount on Bonds Payable . . . . . . . . . . . . . . . . . . .              11,110
            Cash . . . . . . . . . . . . . . . . . . . . . . . . . . . . . . . .              300,000
        To record payment of semiannual interest on bonds and amor-
        tize bond discount ($666,587 × $\frac{4}{240}$ mo).
```

Notice that we have debited Bond Interest Payable for $100,000, thus eliminating the liability we accrued on December 31, 1987.

Over the remaining life of the bonds we will make entries on May 1 and November 1 identical to the ones made on May 1, 1988, and November 1, 1987, just illustrated. And on December 31 of each year we will make an accrual identical to the one made on December 31, 1987.

Accounting for Bonds Issued at a Premium

If the market rate of interest is less than the nominal rate, bonds will sell at a premium

Bonds may be sold at a premium, that is, at a price that exceeds par value. The reason for selling bonds at a premium is that the marketplace is reflecting a different market interest rate than that specified in the bond indenture. This is the same reason why bonds are sold at a discount. What determines whether bonds sell at a discount or at a premium is the relationship of the market rate of interest to the rate specified in the bond contract. If the market rate of interest is greater than the rate specified in the bond contract, the *nominal* rate, the bond will sell for a discount. On the other hand, if the market rate of interest is less than the nominal rate, bonds will sell at a *premium.*

Let's now assume the latter to be the case—that the Karlton bonds sell for $5,857,956 on May 1, 1987. A premium of $857,956 results because the market rate of interest must have been less than the nominal rate of 12%. We would record the following entry on May 1, 1987, the bond issue date:

Sale of bonds at a premium

```
1987
May 1   Cash . . . . . . . . . . . . . . . . . . . . . . . . . . . . . . . .   5,857,956
            Premium on Bonds Payable . . . . . . . . . . . . . . .              857,956
            Bonds Payable . . . . . . . . . . . . . . . . . . . . . . .              5,000,000
        To record the sale of $5,000,000 of 20-year, 12% bonds,
        maturing May 1, 2007.
```

On this date the information relating to the bonds would be presented in the long-term liabilities section of the balance sheet as follows:

```
Long-Term Liabilities:
    12% Bonds Payable Due May 1, 2007 . . . . . . . . . . . . .   $5,000,000
    Plus: Premium on Bonds Payable . . . . . . . . . . . . . . . .      857,956   $5,857,956
```

The carrying value of the bond, $5,857,956, is the sum of the $5,000,000 face value and the $857,956 premium.

We will have to amortize the premium over the period of time the bond is outstanding, just as we did with the discount. And we will again do this on bond interest payment dates and at year-end. Consequently, the November 1, 1987, bond interest payment and premium amortization would be recorded as follows:

The first bond interest payment and amortizaton of premium

```
1987
Nov. 1   Bond Interest Expense .........................  278,551
         Premium on Bonds Payable ....................   21,449
             Cash. . . . . . . . . . . . . . . . . . . . . . . . . . . . . . .          300,000
         To record payment of semiannual interest on bonds
         ($5,000,000 × 12% × 6/12 mo) and amortization of bond pre-
         mium ($857,956 × 6/240 mo).
```

This time the interest expense is the difference between the cash paid $300,000, and the $21,449 amortization of the premium ($857,956 × $\frac{6}{240}$). When we had a discount, the interest expense was the sum of the cash and the amortization of the discount.

On December 31, 1987, the bond interest payable must be accrued and the premium must be amortized. The entry to accomplish this would be recorded as follows:

Bond interest adjusting entry and amortization of premium

```
1987
Dec. 31   Bond Interest Expense .........................  92,850
          Premium on Bonds Payable. . . . . . . . . . . . . . . . . . . . .   7,150
              Interest Payable. . . . . . . . . . . . . . . . . . . . . . . . . . .         100,000
          To record accrual of bond interest payable and amortization of
          bond premium ($857,956 × 2/240 mo).
```

The balance sheet on December 31 would reflect the following carrying value of the bond:

> Long-Term Liabilities:
>   12% Bonds Payable Due May 1, 2007 . . . . $5,000,000
>   Plus: Premium on Bonds Payable 829,357 $5,829,357

The premium account of $857,956 on May 1, 1987, has been reduced by the amortization of $21,449 on November 1, 1987, and $7,150 on December 31, 1987.

The interest payment on May 1, 1988, of $300,000 and the 4-month amortization of the premium we will record like this:

The second bond interest payment and amortization of premium

```
1988
May 1   Bond Interest Payable. . . . . . . . . . . . . . . . . . . . . . . . . 100,000
        Bond Interest Expense ......................... 185,701
        Premium on Bonds Payable. . . . . . . . . . . . . . . . . . . . . .  14,299
            Cash . . . . . . . . . . . . . . . . . . . . . . . . . . . . . . . . . . .         300,000
        To record the payment of semiannual interest on bonds and
        amortization of bond premium ($857,956 × 4/240 mo).
```

The bond interest payments on each November 1 and May 1 over the remaining life of the bonds will be identical to the ones made on May 1, 1988, and November 1,

1987. Each December 31 accrual entry each year will be identical to the one made on December 31, 1987.

PRESENT VALUE AND LONG-TERM LIABILITIES

The time value of money considers the relationship among time, money, and interest rates

In our discussion of bonds payable to this point we have ignored a very significant factor: the fact that money has a time value. The promise to pay $5 million 20 years hence is not the same thing as paying $5 million today. Nor is paying $300,000 every 6 months for forty 6-month periods over 20 years equivalent to paying $12 million ($300,000 × 40) today. *Money has a time value.* What is the time value of money? It is the value that equates the $5 million 20 years hence to its *present value* today. It considers the future cash item (the $5 million), the appropriate interest rate, and the length of time between today and the receipt or payment of the future cash item.

Everyone can see that a $5 million deposit made today is worth more than a $5 million deposit made 1 year from today. The deposit made today will earn interest for 1 year, and the interest plus the initial deposit of $5 million will, of course, exceed the $5 million deposited 1 year hence.

If the interest rate was 12%, the $5 million deposit made today would accumulate to $5,600,000 1 year hence — $5,000,000 + (12%) ($5,000,000). The $5,600,000 is called the **amount.** The $5 million deposit made today is called the **present value.** If we know that $5,600,000 is available 1 year hence and money is worth 12%, then we know that the present value today of the $5,600,000 is $5,000,000.

The present value of any amount, for any period of time, at any interest rate, can be found by multiplying the amount by the factor $1/(1 + i)^n$. The value i represents the interest rate *per period.* The value n is the number of periods.

Present value tables have been prepared as an aid to calculating present values. Such a table is illustrated in Table 15-1. We can find the value of the factor $[1/(1 + i)^n]$ for 1 period at 12% by looking in Table 15-1 at the intersection of the $n = 1$ row and the $i = 12\%$ column. The factor is 0.892. To six decimal places the factor is 0.892857. The table (like Table 15-2) has been truncated to three decimal places to facilitate the computations in your homework problems. Multiplying the six-decimal factor 0.892857 times $5,600,000 results in the present value 5,000,000. If we had used the 0.892 truncated figure we would have computed the present value as $4,995,200. For this reason we will use the six-decimal factors in the illustrations, but you can learn the concepts as well by using the truncated three-decimal factors when solving your homework problems.

As an aid in notation for solving present value problems, we will use the lowercase p to mean the present value of a single sum of money. The present value factor is represented by the symbol

$$p_{\overline{n}|i}$$

which we read as

*the present value of a single sum of money for **n** periods at **i** percent*

To express the present value of $5,600,000 at 12% for 1 period we would write:

$$p = \$5,600,000 \, p_{\overline{1}|12\%}$$

Unless we tell you otherwise, interest is expressed at an annual rate. This means that you must take care when using the present value tables to *adjust the interest and the periods* when interest is compounded more frequently than annually. For example, assume that we wish to know the present value of $5,000,000 payable 20 years

TABLE 15-1 Present Value of $1.

$$p_{\overline{n}|1} = \frac{1}{(1+i)^n}$$

n \ i	1%	2%	3%	4%	5%	6%	7%	8%	9%	10%	12%	15%	20%
1	0.990	0.980	0.970	0.961	0.952	0.943	0.934	0.925	0.917	0.909	0.892	0.869	0.833
2	0.980	0.961	0.942	0.924	0.907	0.889	0.873	0.857	0.841	0.826	0.797	0.756	0.694
3	0.970	0.942	0.915	0.888	0.863	0.839	0.816	0.793	0.772	0.751	0.711	0.657	0.578
4	0.960	0.923	0.888	0.854	0.822	0.792	0.762	0.735	0.708	0.683	0.635	0.571	0.482
5	0.951	0.905	0.862	0.821	0.783	0.747	0.712	0.680	0.649	0.620	0.567	0.497	0.401
6	0.942	0.887	0.837	0.790	0.746	0.704	0.666	0.630	0.596	0.564	0.506	0.432	0.334
7	0.932	0.870	0.813	0.759	0.710	0.665	0.622	0.583	0.547	0.513	0.452	0.375	0.279
8	0.923	0.853	0.789	0.730	0.676	0.627	0.582	0.540	0.501	0.466	0.403	0.326	0.232
9	0.914	0.836	0.766	0.702	0.644	0.591	0.543	0.500	0.460	0.424	0.360	0.284	0.193
10	0.905	0.820	0.744	0.675	0.613	0.558	0.508	0.463	0.422	0.385	0.321	0.247	0.161
11	0.896	0.804	0.722	0.649	0.584	0.526	0.475	0.428	0.387	0.350	0.287	0.214	0.134
12	0.887	0.788	0.701	0.624	0.556	0.496	0.444	0.397	0.355	0.318	0.256	0.186	0.112
13	0.878	0.773	0.680	0.600	0.530	0.468	0.414	0.367	0.326	0.289	0.229	0.162	0.093
14	0.869	0.757	0.661	0.577	0.505	0.442	0.387	0.340	0.299	0.263	0.204	0.141	0.077
15	0.861	0.743	0.641	0.555	0.481	0.417	0.362	0.315	0.274	0.239	0.182	0.122	0.064
16	0.852	0.728	0.623	0.533	0.458	0.393	0.338	0.291	0.251	0.217	0.163	0.106	0.054
17	0.844	0.714	0.605	0.513	0.436	0.371	0.316	0.270	0.231	0.197	0.145	0.092	0.045
18	0.836	0.700	0.587	0.493	0.415	0.350	0.295	0.250	0.211	0.179	0.130	0.080	0.037
19	0.827	0.686	0.570	0.474	0.395	0.330	0.276	0.231	0.194	0.163	0.116	0.070	0.031
20	0.819	0.672	0.553	0.456	0.376	0.311	0.258	0.214	0.178	0.148	0.103	0.061	0.026
21	0.811	0.659	0.537	0.438	0.358	0.294	0.241	0.198	0.163	0.135	0.092	0.053	0.021
22	0.803	0.646	0.521	0.421	0.341	0.277	0.225	0.183	0.150	0.122	0.082	0.046	0.018
23	0.795	0.634	0.506	0.405	0.325	0.261	0.210	0.170	0.137	0.111	0.073	0.040	0.015
24	0.787	0.621	0.491	0.390	0.310	0.246	0.197	0.157	0.126	0.101	0.065	0.034	0.012
25	0.779	0.609	0.477	0.375	0.295	0.232	0.184	0.146	0.115	0.092	0.058	0.030	0.010
26	0.772	0.597	0.463	0.360	0.281	0.219	0.172	0.135	0.106	0.083	0.052	0.026	0.008
27	0.764	0.585	0.450	0.346	0.267	0.207	0.160	0.125	0.097	0.076	0.046	0.022	0.007
28	0.756	0.574	0.437	0.333	0.255	0.195	0.150	0.115	0.089	0.069	0.041	0.019	0.006
29	0.749	0.563	0.424	0.320	0.242	0.184	0.140	0.107	0.082	0.063	0.037	0.017	0.005
30	0.741	0.552	0.411	0.308	0.231	0.174	0.131	0.099	0.075	0.057	0.033	0.015	0.004
31	0.734	0.541	0.399	0.296	0.220	0.164	0.122	0.092	0.069	0.052	0.029	0.013	0.003
32	0.727	0.530	0.388	0.285	0.209	0.154	0.114	0.085	0.063	0.047	0.026	0.011	0.002
33	0.720	0.520	0.377	0.274	0.199	0.146	0.107	0.078	0.058	0.043	0.023	0.009	0.002
34	0.712	0.510	0.366	0.263	0.190	0.137	0.100	0.073	0.053	0.039	0.021	0.008	0.002
35	0.705	0.500	0.355	0.253	0.181	0.130	0.093	0.067	0.048	0.035	0.018	0.007	0.001
36	0.698	0.490	0.345	0.243	0.172	0.122	0.087	0.062	0.044	0.032	0.016	0.006	0.001
37	0.692	0.480	0.334	0.234	0.164	0.115	0.081	0.057	0.041	0.029	0.015	0.005	0.001
38	0.685	0.471	0.325	0.225	0.156	0.109	0.076	0.053	0.037	0.026	0.013	0.004	0.001
39	0.678	0.461	0.315	0.216	0.149	0.103	0.071	0.049	0.034	0.024	0.012	0.004	0.001
40	0.671	0.452	0.306	0.208	0.142	0.097	0.066	0.046	0.031	0.022	0.010	0.003	0.000
41	0.665	0.444	0.297	0.200	0.135	0.091	0.062	0.042	0.029	0.020	0.009	0.003	0.000
42	0.658	0.435	0.288	0.192	0.128	0.086	0.058	0.039	0.026	0.018	0.008	0.002	0.000
43	0.651	0.426	0.280	0.185	0.122	0.081	0.054	0.036	0.024	0.016	0.007	0.002	0.000
44	0.645	0.418	0.272	0.178	0.116	0.077	0.050	0.033	0.022	0.015	0.006	0.002	0.000
45	0.639	0.410	0.264	0.171	0.111	0.072	0.047	0.031	0.020	0.013	0.006	0.001	0.000
46	0.632	0.402	0.256	0.164	0.105	0.068	0.044	0.029	0.018	0.012	0.005	0.001	0.000
47	0.626	0.394	0.249	0.158	0.100	0.064	0.041	0.026	0.017	0.011	0.004	0.001	0.000
48	0.620	0.386	0.241	0.152	0.096	0.060	0.038	0.024	0.015	0.010	0.004	0.001	0.000
49	0.614	0.378	0.234	0.146	0.091	0.057	0.036	0.023	0.014	0.009	0.003	0.001	0.000
50	0.608	0.371	0.228	0.140	0.087	0.054	0.033	0.021	0.013	0.008	0.003	0.000	0.000

TABLE 15-2 Present Value of an Ordinary Annuity of $1.

$$P_{\overline{n}|1} = \frac{1 - \dfrac{1}{(1+i)^n}}{i}$$

n \ i	1%	2%	3%	4%	5%	6%	7%	8%	9%	10%	12%	15%	20%
1	0.990	0.980	0.970	0.961	0.952	0.943	0.934	0.925	0.917	0.909	0.892	0.869	0.833
2	1.970	1.941	1.913	1.886	1.850	1.833	1.808	1.783	1.759	1.735	1.690	1.625	1.527
3	2.940	2.883	2.828	2.775	2.723	2.673	2.624	2.577	2.531	2.486	2.401	2.283	2.106
4	3.901	3.807	3.717	3.629	3.545	3.465	3.387	3.312	3.239	3.169	3.037	2.854	2.588
5	4.853	4.713	4.579	4.451	4.329	4.212	4.100	3.992	3.889	3.790	3.604	3.352	2.990
6	5.795	5.601	5.417	5.242	5.075	4.917	4.766	4.622	4.485	4.355	4.111	3.784	3.325
7	6.728	6.471	6.230	6.002	5.786	5.582	5.389	5.206	5.032	4.868	4.563	4.160	3.604
8	7.651	7.325	7.019	6.732	6.463	6.209	5.971	5.746	5.534	5.334	4.967	4.487	3.837
9	8.566	8.162	7.786	7.435	7.107	6.801	6.515	6.246	5.995	5.759	5.328	4.771	4.031
10	9.471	8.982	8.530	8.110	7.721	7.360	7.023	6.710	6.417	6.144	5.650	5.018	4.192
11	10.367	9.786	9.252	8.760	8.306	7.886	7.498	7.138	6.805	6.495	5.937	5.233	4.327
12	11.255	10.575	9.954	9.385	8.863	8.383	7.942	7.536	7.160	6.813	6.194	5.420	4.439
13	12.133	11.348	10.634	9.985	9.393	8.852	8.357	7.903	7.486	7.103	6.423	5.583	4.532
14	13.003	12.106	11.296	10.563	9.898	9.294	8.745	8.244	7.786	7.366	6.628	5.724	4.610
15	13.865	12.849	11.937	11.118	10.379	9.712	9.107	8.559	8.060	7.606	6.810	5.847	4.675
16	14.717	13.577	12.561	11.652	10.837	10.105	9.446	8.851	8.312	7.823	6.973	5.954	4.729
17	15.562	14.291	13.166	12.165	11.274	10.477	9.763	9.121	8.543	8.021	7.119	6.047	4.774
18	16.398	14.992	13.753	12.659	11.689	10.827	10.059	9.371	8.755	8.201	7.249	6.127	4.812
19	17.226	15.678	14.323	13.133	12.058	11.158	10.335	9.603	8.950	8.364	7.365	6.198	4.843
20	18.045	16.351	14.877	13.590	12.462	11.469	10.594	9.818	9.128	8.513	7.469	6.259	4.869
21	18.856	17.011	15.415	14.029	12.821	11.764	10.835	10.016	9.292	8.648	7.562	6.312	4.891
22	19.660	17.658	15.936	14.451	13.163	12.041	11.061	10.200	9.442	8.771	7.644	6.358	4.909
23	20.455	18.292	16.443	14.856	13.488	12.303	11.272	10.371	9.580	8.883	7.718	6.398	4.924
24	21.243	18.913	16.935	15.246	13.798	12.550	11.469	10.528	9.706	8.984	7.784	6.433	4.937
25	22.023	19.523	17.413	15.622	14.093	12.783	11.653	10.674	9.822	9.077	7.843	6.464	4.947
26	22.795	20.121	17.876	15.982	14.375	13.003	11.825	10.809	9.928	9.160	7.895	6.490	4.956
27	23.559	20.706	18.327	16.329	14.643	13.210	11.986	10.935	10.026	9.237	7.942	6.513	4.963
28	24.316	21.281	18.764	16.663	14.898	13.406	12.137	11.051	10.116	9.306	7.984	6.533	4.969
29	25.065	21.844	19.188	16.983	15.141	13.590	12.277	11.158	10.198	9.369	8.021	6.550	4.974
30	25.807	22.396	19.600	17.292	15.372	13.764	12.409	11.257	10.273	9.426	8.055	6.565	4.978
31	26.542	22.937	20.000	17.589	15.592	13.929	12.531	11.349	10.342	9.479	8.084	6.579	4.982
32	27.269	23.468	20.388	17.873	15.802	14.084	12.646	11.434	10.406	9.526	8.111	6.590	4.985
33	27.989	23.988	20.765	18.147	16.002	14.230	12.753	11.513	10.464	9.569	8.135	6.600	4.987
34	28.702	24.498	21.131	18.411	16.192	14.368	12.854	11.586	10.517	9.608	8.156	6.609	4.989
35	29.408	24.998	21.487	18.664	16.374	14.498	12.947	11.654	10.566	9.644	8.175	6.616	4.991
36	30.107	25.488	21.832	18.908	16.546	14.620	13.035	11.717	10.611	9.676	8.192	6.623	4.992
37	30.799	25.969	22.167	19.142	16.711	14.736	13.117	11.775	10.652	9.705	8.207	6.628	4.994
38	31.484	26.440	22.492	19.367	16.867	14.846	13.193	11.828	10.690	9.732	8.220	6.633	4.995
39	32.163	26.902	22.808	19.584	17.071	14.949	13.264	11.878	10.725	9.756	8.233	6.638	4.995
40	32.834	27.355	23.114	19.792	17.159	15.046	13.331	11.924	10.757	9.779	8.243	6.641	4.996
41	33.499	27.799	23.412	19.993	17.294	15.138	13.394	11.967	10.786	9.799	8.253	6.645	4.997
42	34.158	28.234	23.701	20.185	17.423	15.224	13.452	12.006	10.813	9.817	8.261	6.647	4.997
43	34.810	28.661	23.981	20.370	17.545	15.306	13.506	12.043	10.837	9.833	8.269	6.650	4.998
44	35.455	29.079	24.254	20.548	17.662	15.383	13.557	12.077	10.860	9.849	8.276	6.652	4.998
45	36.094	29.490	24.518	20.720	17.774	15.455	13.605	12.108	10.881	9.862	8.282	6.654	4.998
46	36.727	29.892	24.775	20.884	17.880	15.524	13.650	12.137	10.900	9.875	8.287	6.655	4.998
47	37.353	30.286	25.024	21.042	17.981	15.589	13.691	12.164	10.917	9.886	8.292	6.657	4.999
48	37.973	30.673	25.266	21.195	18.077	15.650	13.730	12.189	10.933	9.896	8.297	6.658	4.999
49	38.588	31.052	25.601	21.341	18.168	15.707	13.766	12.212	10.948	9.906	8.301	6.659	4.999
50	39.196	31.423	25.729	21.482	18.255	15.761	13.800	12.233	10.961	9.914	8.304	6.660	4.999

hence if interest is 12% compounded semiannually. Since interest is compounded twice a year and there are 20 years, the number of periods involved is 40. And the interest rate per period is 6%, the annual rate of 12% divided by the number of periods in a year. The present value is expressed as:

The present value of $5,000,000 due 20 years from now. Interest compounded twice a year

$$p = \$5,000,000 \; p_{\overline{40}|6\%}$$
$$= \$5,000,000 \; (\underline{0.097222})$$
$$= \$486,110$$

Note the line under the first three figures to the right of the decimal point. This is the factor you will find in the table.

Let's try another example. This time let's find the present value of $100,000 payable 5 years hence if interest is 16% compounded quarterly. The present value is determined like this:

The present value of the $100,000 due 5 years from now. Interest compounded four times a year

$$p = \$100,000 \; p_{\overline{20}|4\%}$$
$$= \$100,000 \; (\underline{0.456387})$$
$$= \$45,639$$

The Karlton Company incurred two separate obligations when it issued the $5,000,000, 12%, 20-year bonds on May 1, 1987. First, it promised to pay the face amount of the bonds, $5,000,000, twenty years hence. And second, it promised to pay interest of $300,000 ($5,000,000 × 12% × ½ year) every 6 months—on November 1 and May 1—for the life of the bonds, 20 years. These two promises can be expressed on a time line like this:

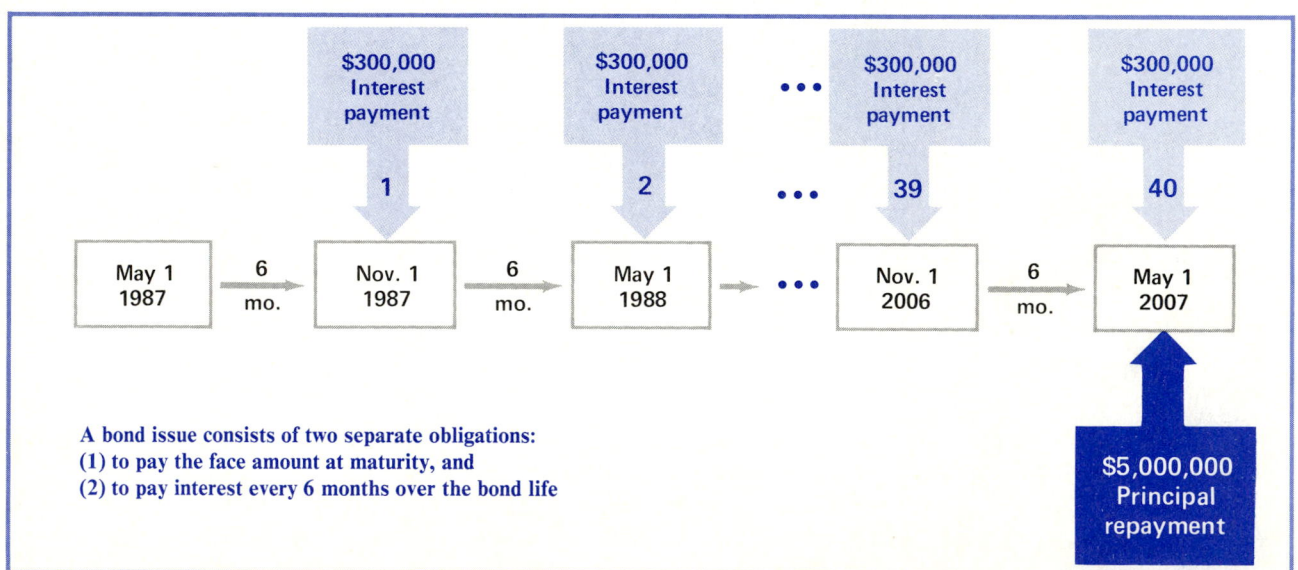

A bond issue consists of two separate obligations:
(1) to pay the face amount at maturity, and
(2) to pay interest every 6 months over the bond life

An ordinary annuity is a series of payments made at the end of each period

The second promise represents a series of payments (40 in number) to be made at the *end of each period.* This is called an **ordinary annuity.** A present value table of ordinary annuity factors is presented in Table 15-2; it works the same way as Table 15-1 did. We use the capital letter *P* to represent the present value of an ordinary annuity and express the fact as:

$$P_{\overline{n}|i}$$

The present value of the $300,000 ordinary annuity of 40 payments at 12% per year (6% per period) would be calculated like this:

$$P = \$300,000 \, P_{\overline{40}|6\%}$$
$$= \$300,000 \, (\underline{15.046297})$$
$$= \$4,513,890$$

Now we can determine the present value of the $5,000,000, 12% 20-year Karlton bonds. It is the sum of the present values of the two separate obligations — the present value of the promise to pay $5,000,000 twenty years hence and the promise to pay $300,000 twice a year for those 20 years. The present value of the bond is:

The present value of a $5,000,000, 20-year, 12% bond when the market rate of interest is 12%

$\$5,000,000 \, p_{\overline{40}|6\%} = \$5,000,000 \, (\underline{0.097222})$	$= \$$	486,110
$300,000 \, P_{\overline{40}|6\%} = $	$300,000 \, (\underline{15.046297}) = $	4,513,890
Present value of the bonds		$\underline{\underline{\$5,000,000}}$

You may be wondering, if the present value of the bonds is $5,000,000, which is also the face value, why bother with all these present value calculations? This is a good question. We have used the 12% interest rate to determine the present value of the bonds. Remember that 12% was the nominal rate — the rate specified in the bond indenture. Using the market rate to determine the present value of bonds when the market rate equals the nominal rate will always result in a present value that will equal the face value. It simply means that the bonds will sell at par.

But remember our discussion several pages back. Bonds will sell at a *discount* if the market rate of interest exceeds the nominal rate. And they will sell at a *premium* if the market rate of interest is less than the nominal rate.

If the market rate of interest equals the nominal rate, bonds will sell at their face value

If the Karlton bonds were issued at a time when the market rate of interest was 14%, the present value of the bonds would be:

The present value of a $5,000,000, 20-year, 12% bond when the market rate is 14%

$\$5,000,000 \, p_{\overline{40}|7\%} = \$5,000,000 \, (\underline{0.066780})$	$= \$$	333,900
$300,000 \, P_{\overline{40}|7\%} = $	$300,000 \, (\underline{13.331709}) = $	3,999,513
Present value of the bonds		$\underline{\$4,333,413}$

This would be, all other economic factors being constant, the price the bonds would sell for. They would sell for a discount of $666,587 ($5,000,000 − $4,333,413).

And if the bonds were issued at a time when the market rate of interest was 10%, the selling price of the bonds would be as follows:

The present value of a $5,000,000, 20-year, 12% bond when the market rate is 10%

$\$5,000,000 \, p_{\overline{40}|5\%} = \$5,000,000 \, (\underline{0.142046})$	$= \$$	710,230
$300,000 \, P_{\overline{40}|5\%} = $	$300,000 \, (\underline{17.159086}) = $	5,147,726
Present value of the bonds		$\underline{\$5,857,956}$

A premium of $857,956 results.

Do you see that in the discount and premium examples the market rate of interest was used to compute the present value? The market rate is called the *effective* rate of interest. The $5,000,000 face of the bond and the $300,000 semiannual interest payment cannot be changed since they are fixed by the terms of the trust indenture. The price the bonds sell for is changed by using the effective rate of interest.

The Effective-Interest Method of Amortizing Bond Discounts and Premiums

When we previously discussed accounting for bonds issued at discounts or premiums we amortized the discount or premium *equally* over the 40 periods. This is called the *straight-line method* of amortization. The amortization is the same for each 6-month period. While this method is easy, it does not reflect the effective interest rate. A method of amortization that does show the effective interest rate, the *effective-interest method,* is the preferred method and must be used unless the difference between the two methods is not material. The straight-line method provides an equal *amount of interest expense* each period. The effective-interest method provides for an equal *rate of interest* each period.

The effective-interest method provides for a constant rate of interest each period

Interest expense is determined by multiplying the bond carrying value by the effective interest rate

Here's how it works. The interest expense for each period is determined by multiplying the carrying value — the face value plus a premium or minus a discount — of the bond at the beginning of the period by the effective rate of interest. The amount of discount to be amortized is the difference between the interest expense and the interest payment for the period.

Let's refer back to the example where the Karlton bonds were sold at a discount to illustrate this process. We would calculate the interest expense for the first interest period ending on November 1, 1987, like this:

Calculating interest expense

($5,000,000 face value − $666,587 discount) × 7% per period effective interest rate
= $303,339 interest expense

Amortizing the discount is accomplished as follows:

Calculating discount amortization

$303,339 interest expense − $300,000 interest payment
= $3,339 discount amortization

TABLE 15-3   KARLTON COMPANY
Effective-Interest Method Bond Discount Amortization Schedule.

Interest Period	A Interest Payment (face value × 6%)	B Interest Expense (Col. E × 7%)	C Discount Amortization (B − A)	D Unamortized Discount (D − C)	E Carrying Value of Bonds (face value − D)
May 1, 1987				$666,587	$4,333,413
Nov. 1, 1987	$300,000	$303,339	$ 3,339	663,248	4,336,752
May 1, 1988	300,000	303,573	3,573	659,675	4,340,325
Nov. 1, 1988	300,000	303,823	3,823	655,852	4,344,148
May 1, 1989	300,000	304,090	4,090	651,762	4,348,238
Nov. 1, 1989	300,000	304,377	4,377	647,385	4,352,615
May 1, 2006	300,000	340,815	40,815	90,400	4,909,600
Nov. 1, 2006	300,000	343,672	43,672	46,728	4,953,272
May 1, 2007	300,000	346,728	46,728	−0−	5,000,000

We now need to determine the amount of discount remaining after the amortization of the $3,339. This unamortized discount is $663,248 ($666,587 − $3,339) and is subtracted from the $5,000,000 face value of the bonds to arrive at the November 1, 1987, carrying value of $4,336,752.

For the next interest period, May 1, 1988, the process is repeated. We take the bond carrying value, $4,336,752, times the 7% per period effective interest rate to arrive at $303,573 interest expense. Subtracting the $300,000 interest payment from the interest expense determines the amount of discount amortization, $3,573, for the second interest period.

A bond discount amortization schedule, such as the one presented in Table 15-3 on page 576 for the Karlton Company bonds, is usually prepared for the life of the bonds when the bonds are issued.

Let's look at the amortization schedule a little differently. Perhaps that will make it easier to understand. On the date that the bonds were issued, two accounts would be created, namely, Bonds Payable for $5,000,000 and Discount on Bonds Payable for $666,587. Presenting these two accounts in T-accounts would look like this:

Bonds Payable		Discount on Bonds Payable	
	5,000,000	666,587	

Now allow us the liberty of combining these two accounts into one *make-believe* account, which we will call Bond Carrying Value, which would look like this:

Bond Carrying Value	
4,333,413	

This is what is happening to the carrying value of the bonds over the first four interest periods:

		Bond Carrying Value	
		4,333,413	
Cash Payment			Interest Expense
(5,000,000)(.06)	300,000	303,339	(4,333,413)(.07)
		4,336,752	
	300,000	303,573	(4,336,752)(.07)
		4,340,325	
	300,000	303,823	(4,340,325)(.07)
		4,344,148	
	300,000	304,090	(4,344,148)(.07)
		4,348,238	

FIGURE 15-1
Bond Discount Amortization.
Effective-interest method.

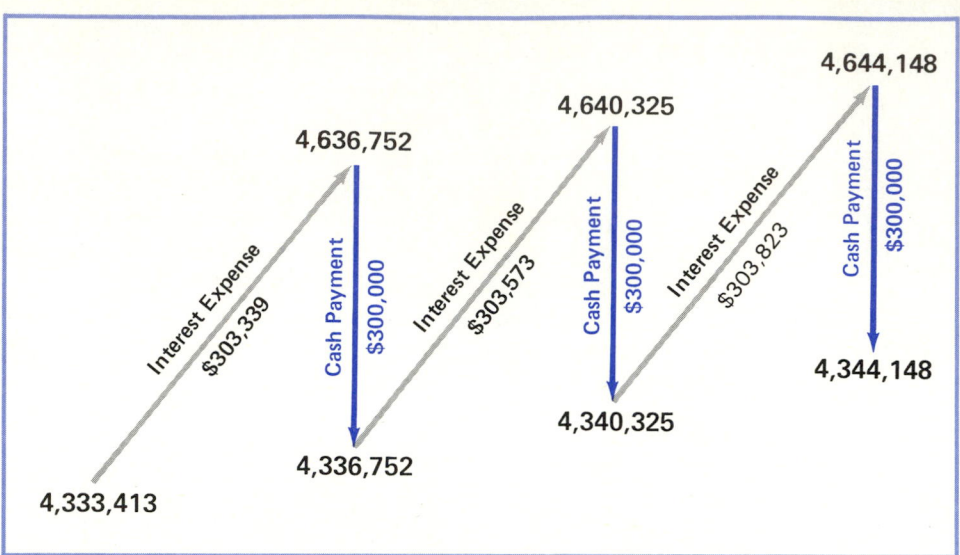

We can look at this concept of amortization using the effective-interest method still another way that may help you. This time let's use a diagram; see Figure 15-1.

What is happening is that the carrying value of the bond is increasing as it earns interest. And it earns interest *every day;* we just record the interest once every 6 months when a cash payment is made. Figure 15-1 shows that the initial carrying value of the bond increases to $4,636,752 ($4,333,413 + the interest of $303,339 for the first 6 months) and then is reduced by the cash payment of $300,000. The cash payment is made all at one time, so the reduction is shown as a straight drop to the new carrying value of $4,336,752. Each successive 6-month period first increases the carrying value by the interest, then reduces the carrying value by the cash payment. But each successive carrying value is a little larger than the previous one—until 20 years pass and the carrying value reaches $5,000,000, the maturity value of the bond.

The first bond interest payment and discount amortization

Using the bond discount amortization schedule, let's compare the general journal entries required under the effective-interest and straight-line methods for the November 1, 1987, interest payment, the December 31, 1987, accrual, and the May 1, 1988, interest payment.

		Method Used	
		Effective-Interest	**Straight-Line**
1987			
Nov. 1	Bond Interest Expense. 303,339		316,665
	Discount on Bonds Payable	3,339	16,665
	Cash	300,000	300,000
	To record payment of semiannual interest on bonds and amortization of bond discount.		

The bond interest adjusting entry and discount amortization

Now compare the Interest Expense under both procedures. A significant difference, $13,326 ($16,665 − $3,339), exists. This is why the effective-interest method is required. It reflects the true interest cost and the straight-line method is only a convenience because it is easy. The December 31 adjusting entry would be recorded like this:

		Method Used	
		Effective-Interest	Straight-Line
1987			
Dec. 31	Bond Interest Expense	101,191	105,555
	Discount on Bonds Payable.	1,191	5,555
	Bond Interest Payable	100,000	100,000
	To record accrual of bond interest payable and amortization of bond discount.		

Can you determine how we arrived at the $1,191 discount amortization under the effective-interest method? Remember that the $5,555 straight-line amortization was calculated by taking $\frac{2}{240}$ of the initial $666,587 discount. This would be the same as taking $\frac{2}{6}$ of the $16,665 semiannual amortization. That's what we did for the effective-interest method, $\frac{2}{6}$ of the $3,573 second-period discount amortization (see Table 15-3). Amortization between interest payment dates under the effective-interest method is done on a straight-line basis.

The second bond interest payment and discount amortization

On May 1, 1988, the semiannual interest payment is recorded like this:

		Method Used	
		Effective-Interest	Straight-Line
1988			
May 1	Bond Interest Payable	100,000	100,000
	Bond Interest Expense.	202,382	211,110
	Discount on Bonds Payable	2,382	11,110
	Cash	300,000	300,000
	To record payment of semiannual interest on bond and amortize bond discount.		

If the Karlton Company bonds were issued on May 1, 1987, at a premium of $857,956, representing a 10% effective interest rate, a bond premium amortization schedule such as the one illustrated in Table 15-4 (page 580) would be prepared. This table is prepared in the identical manner as the bond discount amortization

TABLE 15-4   KARLTON COMPANY
Effective-Interest Method Bond Premium Amortization Schedule

Interest Period	A Interest Payment (face value × 6%)	B Interest Expense (Col. E × 5%)	C Premium Amortization (A − B)	D Unamortized Premium (D − C)	E Carrying Value of Bonds (face value + D)
May 1, 1987				$857,956	$5,857,956
Nov. 1, 1987	$300,000	$292,898	$ 7,102	850,854	5,850,854
May 1, 1988	300,000	292,543	7,457	843,397	5,843,397
Nov. 1, 1988	300,000	292,170	7,830	835,567	5,835,567
May 1, 1989	300,000	291,778	8,222	827,345	5,827,345
Nov. 1, 1989	300,000	291,367	8,633	818,712	5,812,712
May 1, 2006	300,000	256,808	43,192	92,972	5,092,972
Nov. 1, 2006	300,000	254,649	45,351	47,621	5,047,621
May 1, 2007	300,000	252,381	47,621*	—	5,000,000

* Rounding ($2 error due to rounding)

Bond payment and adjusting entries for bonds issued at a premium | schedule. Using this schedule, we would record the comparative entries for November 1, 1987, December 31, 1987, and May 1, 1988, as follows:

		Method Used			
		Effective-Interest		**Straight-Line**	
1987					
Nov. 1	Bond Interest Expense..........................	292,898		278,551	
	Premium on Bonds Payable	7,102		21,449	
	Cash		300,000		300,000
	To record payment of semiannual interest on bonds and amortization of bond discount.				
1987					
Dec. 31	Bond Interest Expense.........................	97,514		92,850	
	Premium on Bonds Payable	2,486		7,150	
	Interest Payable		100,000		100,000
	To record accrual of bond interest payable and amortization of bond premium ($7,457 × $\frac{2}{6}$ for effective-interest method).				
1988					
May 1	Bond Interest Payable	100,000		100,000	
	Bond Interest Expense.........................	195,029		185,701	
	Premium on Bonds Payable	4,971		14,299	
	Cash		300,000		300,000
	To record the payment of semiannual interest on bonds and amortization of bond premium.				

Financial Statement Disclosure of Bonds Payable

Bonds payable must be disclosed at their face values adjusted by separate accounts for unamortized discounts or premiums

Generally accepted accounting principles require that we classify bonds payable on the balance sheet as long-term liabilities. As we have previously illustrated, bonds payable are reported at their face value plus or minus their unamortized discount or premium. In addition, information as to their interest rate, maturity date, interest payment dates, collateral, etc., must be shown either parenthetically next to the account titles on the balance sheet or in a footnote to the financial statements.

If the business entity has several bonds outstanding they may be reflected on the balance sheet as one total, but a supporting schedule providing detailed information on each bond must accompany the financial statements.

Current maturities of bonds payable are transferred to the current liabilities section of the balance sheet *if* they are to be settled by the expenditure of a current asset or creation of a new current liability. However, if settlement is to be made by expending a noncurrent asset or by issuing a new long-term obligation, the current maturity should remain in the long-term liabilities section. A footnote would be required explaining the method of settlement.

LONG-TERM LEASES

There are times when business entities find it more advantageous to lease buildings and equipment on a long-term basis rather than to purchase them. Many of these lease arrangements are fairly simple, requiring the party receiving the right to use the asset, the *lessee,* to record rent expense when the periodic lease payment is made. Upon the completion of the lease term, the lessee has the option of either entering into a new lease, or vacating the building or returning the equipment to the *lessor.*

In recent years, however, leases have become much more flexible and consequently much more complex. Accounting for these new leases has given the accounting profession a very interesting challenge. While legal title to the leased property may remain with the lessor, the terms of the lease may indicate that the *economic substance* of the transaction is in essence a purchase. For instance, the lease may allow the lessee to purchase the asset for a bargain price at the end of the lease term. Under these circumstances the appropriate accounting treatment may not be simply to debit Rent Expense and credit Cash.

Accounting is concerned with the economic substance of a transaction rather than the legal form

Where the economic substance of the lease transaction indicates that the lessee has the rights and benefits of ownership, we must account for the transaction by recognizing the future economic benefits of the asset and by recognizing the obligation of the liability. This is called *capitalizing* the lease.

Let's see how this capitalization works. Pegasus Airline enters into a lease arrangement on January 1, 1987, with the Athens Leasing Company to lease an airplane for 10 years. The terms of the lease requires Pegasus to make payments of $3,655.57 to Athens Leasing at the end of each quarter. Interest is considered to be 8%. The useful life of the aircraft is estimated to be 10 years. We will assume that the terms of this lease arrangement require capitalization of the lease.

We will record the following 1987 entries for Pegasus Airline:

Capitalizing a lease

```
Jan. 1   Leased Equipment . . . . . . . . . . . . . . . . . . . . . . . . . . . . . 100,000
                 Obligation under Capitalized Lease . . . . . . . . . . . . .          100,000
             To record a capitalized lease for an airplane. Lease terms re-
             quire quarterly payments of $3,655.57.
```

On this date Pegasus received an asset, which must be recorded on the books at its fair value. This value is determined by computing the present value of an annuity of

40 quarterly payments at 8% per annum, or 2% per quarter. Using Table 15-2 (page 573), we determine the value as follows:

The present value of a 10-year lease at $3,655.57 per quarter. Interest worth 8%

$$P = \$3,655.57 \, P_{\overline{40}|2\%}$$
$$= \$3,655.57 \, (27.355479)$$
$$= \underline{\underline{\$100,000}}$$

As of January 1, 1987, the $100,000 also represents Pegasus' long-term liability to Athens Leasing.

The first lease payment is to be made on March 31, at which date the following entry is made:

The first lease payment

Obligation under Capitalized Lease	1,655.57	
Interest Expense	2,000.00	
Cash		3,655.57

To record lease payment due this date. Interest is equal to $2,000.00: (.02) ($100,000).

We record Interest Expense in the amount of $2,000, which we can consider interest for the use of the $100,000 "borrowed" funds for the 3-month period. We then reduce the long-term liability by $1,655.57 ($3,655.57 − $2,000.00), representing a repayment of the "principal."

In a similar manner we record the other three payments for the year. The general journal entries for these three payments are summarized below:

	Date					
	June 30		**Sept. 30**		**Dec. 30**	
	Dr	Cr	Dr	Cr	Dr	Cr
Obligation under Capitalized Lease	1,688.68		1,722.45		1,756.90	
Interest Expense	1,966.89		1,933.12		1,898.67	
Cash		3,655.57		3,655.57		3,655.57
To record payment due.						

Lease payment entries

Interest expense is computed as follows:

June 30	($100,000.00 − $1,655.57)(.02)	$1,966.89
Sept. 30	($100,000.00 − $1,655.57 − $1,688.68)(.02)	1,933.12
Dec. 31	($100,000.00 − $1,655.57 − $1,688.68 − $1,722.45)(.02)	1,898.67

At the end of the year, Pegasus must record depreciation on its leased equipment just as it does for equipment that it owns. The depreciation adjusting entry assuming straight-line depreciation would be recorded as follows:

Depreciation Expense on Leased Equipment	10,000	
Accumulated Depreciation on Leased Equipment		10,000

Recording depreciation on lease equipment

To record depreciation on leased equipment of $100,000: ($100,000 ÷ 10).

COMPUTERLAND'S VALUABLE NOTE PAYABLE

ComputerLand is owned by the William H. Millard family. The Oakland, California company operates nearly 800 franchised outlets all over the world. Prior to building the ComputerLand empire, Mr. Millard founded and operated another company called Information Management Science Associates, Inc. (IMS). That company created a manufacturing subsidiary that went bankrupt in 1979. Included among the $1.9 million of liabilities of the subsidiary was a $250,000 promissory note payable due in May of 1981. The note was issued to the Marriner & Co. venture capital group in 1976 to help keep IMS going. The promissory note was originally convertible into shares of IMS but an agreement signed by Mr. Millard granted Marriner the right to convert the note into any other company Millard might establish.

Mr. Millard paid all the scheduled interest payments on the note until May 1981 when he attempted to pay off the principal amount of the note to Marriner & Co. Meanwhile the note was sold to Micro/Vest (for $300,000 plus another $100,000 payable if the note were eventually converted into stock) and this company informed Mr. Millard in March of 1981 that it intended to exercise the conversion provision and convert the note into 20% of ComputerLand's stock. Mr. Millard contended that the agreement was only temporary and that the note could only be converted into shares of IMS. The dispute went to court.

Micro/Vest sold shares in the note to dozens of outsiders including William Agee and Mary Cunningham formerly of the Bendix Corporation. Mr. Millard contended that these individuals had no interest in the case other than to buy shares in the outcome of the lawsuit. Micro/Vest contended that selling the shares in the note was necessary to finance the $1.3 million legal fees.

In early 1985 a jury in Oakland awarded Micro/Vest a 20% interest in ComputerLand plus $115 million in punitive damages.

In addition to bonds and leases, notes payable are often issued on a long-term basis. One such note issued by ComputerLand caused a considerable amount of controversy.

On the December 31, 1987, balance sheet, Pegasus would show the capitalized lease as follows:

Plant, Property, and Equipment:		
Leased Asset	$100,000	
Less: Accumulated Depreciation on Leased Asset	10,000	$90,000

and the obligation would be presented like this:

Long-Term Liabilities:	
Obligations under Capitalized Lease	$93,176.40

This value was computed as follows:

Obligation on January 1, 1987		$100,000.00
Reduction of obligations:		
Mar. 31	$1,655.57	
June 30	1,688.68	
Sept. 30	1,722.45	
Dec. 31	1,756.90	6,823.60
Obligation on December 31, 1987		$ 93,176.40

CHAPTER SUMMARY

In this chapter we were concerned with the measurement and disclosure of, and accounting for, long-term liabilities. The decision to obtain long-term financing rests on many complex interrelated factors, not the least of which is the effect on net income per owner. Since bond interest payments must be paid when due, projected earnings after a bond issue has been made must be sufficient to provide each owner with a greater return than was received prior to the bond issue. If this is not the case, it may be more advantageous to obtain long-term financing by accepting additional owners.

Various types of bonds can be issued by a business entity seeking outside financing. The bonds can be *secured* or *unsecured, term* or *serial, callable* or *convertible.* Market conditions, the relative strength of the business entity at the time the bonds are to be issued, and the purpose for which the requested financing is to be used all are determining factors in selecting the type of bonds to be issued.

When bonds are issued, a contract between the issuing entity and a *trustee,* called a *bond indenture,* is prepared. The trustee, usually a large bank, acts as an agent for the bondholders.

Bonds may be issued at *par,* at a *discount,* or at a *premium.* The price paid for bonds is dependent on the *market rate of interest* at the time the bonds are issued. If the market rate is equal to the nominal rate called for in the bond contract, the bonds are issued at par. If, however, the market rate exceeds the nominal rate, the bonds will sell for a discount. Conversely, if the market rate is less than the nominal rate, the bonds will sell for a premium.

Given the market rate of interest, the price bonds sell for can be determined by the use of *present value techniques.* The price will be the sum of the present value of the face of the bond and the present value of the stream of contractual interest payments, both discounted at the market rate of interest.

The amount of discount or premium involved in the issuance of a bond must be amortized to periodic interest expense over the life of the bonds. Two accounting alternatives accomplish this process: the *effective-interest method* and the *straight-line method.* The straight-line method can be used only when the difference in results obtained under this method and under the effective-interest method is considered to be immaterial.

Bonds are more often than not sold between interest payment dates. In this case the price of the bonds will include the amount of accrued interest from the last interest payment date. At the end of the accounting period, bond interest must be accrued to achieve a proper matching of periodic expense and a recognition of the liability to pay interest due.

An alternative to long-term financing by means of bonds is by leasing. While legal title remains with the lessor, certain types of leases provide in substance the same rights and benefits to the lessee as to the owner of property. In these cases the appropriate accounting treatment requires that the lease be *capitalized.*

IMPORTANT TERMS USED IN THIS CHAPTER

Amortization   The allocation process of writing off bond premiums or discounts to Interest Expense over the life of the bond issue. (page 567)

Bond indenture   A contract between the business entity issuing bonds and the bondholders. Also called **deed of trust.** (page 564)

Callable bonds   Bonds that may be redeemed by the issuing corporation prior to maturity. (page 564)

Convertible bonds   Bonds that may be exchanged at the bondholders' option for an ownership interest in the business entity. (page 564)

Debenture bonds   Bonds that are unsecured; they are issued on the general credit rating of the business entity. (page 564)

Deed of trust   See **bond indenture.**

Effective-interest method   The method used to amortize bond discounts and premiums over the life of the bond issue, by use of the interest rate in effect at the time the bonds were issued. (page 576)

Effective interest rate   The interest rate found in the marketplace at the time bonds are issued. It is this rate that is used to determine the present value of a bond and to amortize bond discount and premiums. (page 576)

Face value of bonds   The amount that will be paid to bondholders at the maturity date of the bonds. (page 564)

Investment banker   An individual or firm that helps market a bond issue. Often known as an **underwriter.** (page 563)

Lease capitalization   The recording of the present value of future lease payments as an asset and liability on the balance sheet. (page 581)

Nominal interest rate   The rate of interest specified in the bond contract. (page 569)

Ordinary annuity   A series of payments commencing 1 period hence and terminating at the end of the last period. (page 574)

Present value techniques   The procedures for finding the value of money today under assumed rates of interest. (page 571)

Secured bonds   Bonds that provide the bondholder with a claim on a specified asset in the event the business entity does not fulfill its responsibilities under the terms of the bond indenture. (page 564)

Serial bonds   Bonds that mature at various successive dates over the life of the bond contract. (page 564)

Straight-line method   A method used to amortize bond discounts or premiums evenly over the life of the bond issue. (page 576)

Term bonds   Bonds that mature in total at the maturity dates specified in the bond contract. (page 564)

Trustee   Typically, a bank acting as an agent for the bondholders that has entered into a contract with a business entity issuing bonds. (page 563)

Underwriter   See **investment banker.**

Unsecured bonds   See **debenture bonds.**

QUESTIONS

1. What are the advantages and disadvantages to the present owners of a business entity of obtaining additional financing by issuing bonds?

2. Distinguish between *term* and *serial* bonds, and between *convertible* and *callable* bonds.

3. When a business entity issues bonds, it incurs two separate liabilities. Explain.

4. How are bond prices determined?

5. What is the difference between accounting for bond premiums and discounts using the effective-interest method and the straight-line method?

6. Why must bond discounts or premiums be amortized?

7. How are bond discounts or premiums reflected on the balance sheet?

8. More often than not, bonds are issued between interest payment dates. What accounting problems does this cause?

9. On June 1 the Dickens Company issues a $1,500,000, 10%, 20-year bond in a 12% market. The bonds are dated April 1 and interest is payable semiannually.

   a. What is the face amount of the bonds?
   b. Did the bond sell for a premium or a discount?
   c. How much is the accrued interest on June 1, the date of issue?
   d. How much interest was paid on the first interest payment date?
   e. What is the nominal interest rate?
   f. What is the effective interest rate?
   g. What is the maturity value of the bond?
   h. Without prejudice to any previous answer, assume that the bond sold for a discount of $70,000. What would be the carrying value on the date of issue?

10. It really does not matter how a company amortizes bond premiums or discounts. The company can select either the effective-interest method or the straight-line method. Comment.

11. What is an *ordinary annuity?*

12. Several years ago the Irving Company issued a $100,000 bond. Interest is payable semiannually. The carrying value of the bond on January 1 of the current year was $98,612. The amount of interest expense recorded for this year was $3,945, while the cash payment of interest was $3,500.

   a. Did the bonds initially sell for a premium or a discount?
   b. What is the carrying value of the bonds at the end of the current year?

13. What does the term *capitalization* mean when discussing a lease contract?

14. Assume that a lease contract requires capitalization of the asset at $100,000 and that an 8% interest factor was used to determine the present value of the lease payment. If the lease requires annual payments of $12,000 and the asset has a 10-year life, determine the amounts that will appear on the financial statements at the end of the first year of the lease.

EXERCISES

Exercise 15-1
Determine earnings per share under different capital structures

Courageous Company and Southern Cross, Ltd., each have bonds payable and stockholders' equity that totals $8,000,000. Courageous has $3,000,000 of bonds payable and Southern Cross has $3,000,000 of stockholders' equity. Courageous has 250,000 shares outstanding and Southern Cross has 200,000. Assuming that the bonds were issued at par and have a 12% interest rate, and that income taxes are 40% of taxable income, determine the amount of earnings per share if income before bond interest expense is first $700,000, then $1,800,000.

(Check figure: At the $700,000 level, earnings per share, Southern Cross, Ltd. = $.30)

Exercise 15-2
Determine bond selling prices

The Intrepid Company issues $4,500,000 of 14%, 20-year bonds on October 1, 1987. Interest is paid on October 1 and April 1. Compute the price the bonds will sell for if the market rate is first 12%, then 16%.

(Check figure: At 16% = $3,963,060)

Exercise 15-3
Journal entries for bonds issued at par

On May 1, 1987, the Constellation Company issued at par a $300,000, 20-year, 12% bond payable. Semiannual interest is paid on May 1 and November 1 of each year. Prepare the general journal entries (without explanation) relating to the bond for the years 1987 and 1988.

Exercise 15-4

Journal entries for bonds issued at a premium

The Columbia Corporation issued on April 1, 1987, $900,000 of 10%, 20-year bonds, receiving $924,000 cash. Interest is paid on April 1 and October 1 of each year. Prepare the general journal entries (without explanation) relating to the bond for the year 1987 using the straight-line method to amortize the premium.

Exercise 15-5

Bond premium amortization schedule and journal entries

The Weatherly Company issued $4,000,000 of $2\frac{1}{2}$-year, 11% bonds on January 1, 1987, at a time when the market interest rate was 12%. The bonds sold for $3,915,753. Interest is payable semiannually. Prepare a bond discount amortization schedule (round to the nearest whole dollar) for the $2\frac{1}{2}$ years and the general journal entry (without explanation) to record the July 1, 1987, interest payment and discount on amortization using the effective-interest method.

Exercise 15-6

Journal entries for bonds issued between interest payment dates

On December 1, 1987, the Ranger Company issued $600,000 of 20-year, 12% bonds at par. The bonds were dated October 1 and pay interest semiannually. Prepare the entry to record the issuance of the bonds, the December 31, 1987, adjusting entry, and the April 1, 1988, interest payment relating to the Ranger bonds.

Exercise 15-7

Journal entries for a capitalized lease

Rainbow Corporation leases certain nautical equipment from Endeavour, Ltd. The lease must be capitalized because of the terms of the lease contract. The lease payments of $550 are to be paid to Endeavour at the end of every month for the next 3 years commencing 30 days from today's date, October 1, 1987. Money is considered to be worth 12% and the equipment has an estimated life of 4 years. Prepare the entry to record the lease, to record the first payment (October 31, 1987), and to record the depreciation of the leased asset on December 31, 1987 (round to the nearest whole dollar). At the end of the lease term the nautical equipment becomes the property of Rainbow Corporation.

(Check figure: Leased equipment = $16,559)

PROBLEMS
Set A

Problem A15-1

Earnings per share for different capital structures

The stockholders of Martin Motors are considering expanding their business. They have decided that they will issue both additional stock and bonds such that their capital structure (the sum of the stockholders' equity and bonds payable) will total $30,000,000. The bonds will be issued at par value. Mr. Martin, the company president, feels that the best arrangement would be to issue $15,000,000 of 10% bonds, $5,000,000 of 12% bonds, and the remainder in stock. Mr. McCormack, the financial vice president, thinks that it would be better to issue only $8,000,000 of the 10% bonds, $7,000,000 of the 12% bonds, and have $15,000,000 in common stock. Under Mr. Martin's plan there would be 200,000 shares of stock outstanding, while Mr. McCormack thinks that there should be 300,000 shares of stock. A 40% tax rate would apply to Martin Motors under either plan.

Required

1. Determine the amount of earnings per share under each plan for earnings before interest and taxes of $2,500,000 and $8,000,000.

(Check figure: At the $8,000,000 level, earnings per share under Mr. McCormack's plan = $12.72)

2. At what income level would the earnings per share be equal under both plans?

(Check figure: $3,020,000)

Problem A15-2

Journal entries for a bond issued between interest payment dates

O'Neil Products received permission from the Securities and Exchange Commission to issue at par $30,000,000 of 16%, 20-year bonds dated November 1, 1987. The bonds were not issued until December 1, 1987. Interest payment dates are November 1 and May 1.

Required

Prepare without explanation all the general journal entries relating to the bond issue for the years 1987 and 1988. Include the year-end adjusting entries and closing entries for the interest expense.

Problem A15-3
Journal entries for a bond
issued at a premium

On June 1, 1987, the Colfax Company issued $4,000,000 of 20-year, 12% bonds. Interest is paid semiannually on June 1 and December 1 of each year. The bonds sold for $4,181,200. The Colfax Company follows the policy of amortizing bond premium and discounts on the straight-line basis and on bond interest payment dates.

Required

Prepare without explanations the general journal entries for the year 1987 relating to the bond transactions.

(Check figure: Premium amortization per month = $755)

Problem A15-4
Journal entries for a bond
issued at a discount

The Pennington Corporation, on May 1, 1987, issued $400,000, 12%, 10-year bonds, receiving $389,200 cash proceeds on that date. Interest is payable semiannually on May 1 and November 1. The bonds are due May 1, 1997.

Required

1. Prepare without explanations the general journal entries for the years 1987 and 1988 relating to the bond transactions, assuming that the straight-line method of amortizing bond discounts is used and that the discount is amortized on bond interest dates.
2. How will the bonds be presented on the December 31, 1988, balance sheet?

(Check figure: Unamortized discount = $9,000)

Problem A15-5
Effective-interest method:
Journal entries for a bond issued
at a discount

The Trumbull Company received $2,200,097 on April 1, 1987, for the issuance of $3,000,000, 20-year, 10% bonds dated April 1, 1987. The bonds were sold in a 14% market and pay interest every 6 months. Trumbull uses the effective-interest method of amortizing bond discounts.

Required

Prepare without explanation the general journal entries for the years 1987 and 1988 relating to the bond issue.

(Check figure: Bond Interest Expense on December 31, 1988 = $77,454)

Problem A15-6
Effective-interest method:
Journal entries for a bond issued
at a premium

Winthrop Wingtip Shoes issued $1,500,000, 13%, 10-year bonds to yield 12% on March 1, 1987, receiving $1,586,024 cash on that date. The bonds pay interest semiannually (March 1 and September 1). Winthrop uses the effective-interest method to amortize bond premiums.

Required

1. Prepare without explanation the general journal entries for 1987 and 1988 relating to the bond transactions.
2. How will the bonds be presented on the December 31, 1988, balance sheet?

(Check figure: Unamortized bond premium = $76,720)

Problem A15-7
Determine bond selling prices

Compute the bond selling prices for each of the following:
1. $4,000,000, 20-year, 11.5% bonds priced to yield 10% interest paid semiannually.
2. $2,500,000, 5-year, 17% bonds priced to yield 16% interest paid quarterly.
3. $4,500,000, 30-year, 13.5% bonds priced to yield 12% interest paid annually.

[Check figures: (1) $4,514,570; (2) $2,583,938; (3) $5,041,913]

Problem A15-8
Journal entries for a capitalized
lease

On September 1, 1987, Bankhead Data Service leased from Longworth Computers a model 720 computer under a lease that requires capitalization. Payments of $2,500 must be made at the end of every month for 3 years. The asset has an estimated economic life of 4 years and will be depreciated over that period of time. Interest of 12% is to be used for the capitalization.

Required

1. Prepare the general journal entries without explanation for the year 1987 pertaining to the lease for Bankhead Data Service. Round your answers to the nearest whole dollar.
2. What accounts pertaining to the lease will appear on the December 31, 1987, financial statements?

(Check figure: Interest Expense = $2,906)

Set B

Problem B15-1
Earnings per share for different capital structures

Due to a large increase in the demand for their product line, Little Rock Business Machines, Inc., is considering expanding their plant capacity by raising additional funds. The funds will come from several sources, a 20-year, 14% bond issue, a 10-year, 16% bond issue, and a common stock issue. The amount of each issue is the subject of the November 15, 1987, board of directors meeting. Mrs. Patterson, the chairperson of the board, feels that $40,000,000 of financing is needed and is of the opinion that $15,000,000 should come from the 14% bonds, $10,000,000 from the 16% bonds, and the remainder from the stock, which would result in a total of 350,000 shares of stock.

   Mr. Williamson, the president of the company, feels that the total capitalization is fine, but the mix is wrong. He would like to see the 14% bonds increased to $20,000,000, the 16% bonds increased to $15,000,000, and only $5,000,000 come from common stock. His plan would result in a total of 200,000 shares of stock.

Required

1. Compute the amount of earnings per share of common stock under each of the two plans, assuming first that earnings before interest and taxes (40%) are first $6,000,000; then assume that the level increases to $20,000,000.

(Check figure: At the $6,000,000 level under Mrs. Patterson's plan, the earnings per share are $3.94)

2. At what income level would the earnings per share be equal under both plans?

(Check figure: $7,200,000)

Problem B15-2
Journal entries for a bond issued between interest payment dates

On March 1, 1987, the Sacramento Company was authorized to issue, at par, $20,000,000 of 18%, 30-year bonds dated March 1, 1987. However, the bonds were not issued until May 1, 1987. Interest is paid semiannually on the bonds on March 1 and September 1.

Required

Record (without explanation) the general journal entries relating to the bond issue for the years 1987 and 1988, including the year-end adjusting and closing entries.

Problem B15-3
Journal entries for a bond issued at a discount

The Denver Corporation issued $9,000,000 of 30-year, 14% bonds on April 1, 1987. Interest is payable semiannually on April 1 and October 1 of each year. The bonds sold for $8,940,000. Bond premium and discounts are amortized on the straight-line basis on bond interest payment dates by the Denver Corporation.

Required

Prepare without explanations the general entries for the year 1987 relating to the bond transactions.

(Check figure: Discount amortization December 31 = $500)

Problem B15-4
Journal entries for bonds issued at a premium

The Hartford Corporation issued $3,000,000 of 16%, 20-year bonds on February 1, 1987, receiving $3,180,000 on that date. Interest is payable on February 1 and August 1 of each year.

Required

1. Prepare without explanation the general journal entries for the years 1987 and 1988 relating to the bond issue, assuming that the straight-line method of amortizing bond premiums is used and that the bond premiums are amortized on interest payment dates.
2. How will the bonds be presented on the December 31, 1988, balance sheet?

(Check figure: Unamortized premium = $162,750)

Problem B15-5
Effective-interest method:
Journal entries for a bond issued
at a discount

Dover Dog Food, Inc., received $627,192 on May 1, 1987, for the issuance of $800,000, 20-year, 14% bonds dated May 1, 1987. The bonds were sold in an 18% market and pay interest semiannually. The company uses the effective-interest method of amortizing bond discounts.

Required

Prepare without explanation the general journal entries for the years 1987 and 1988 relating to the bond issue. Round your answers to the nearest whole dollar.

(Check figure: Bond Interest Expense on December 31, 1988 = $18,860)

Problem B15-6
Effective-interest method:
Journal entries for a bond issued
at a premium

On April 1, 1987, the Tallahassee Times issued $1,000,000 of 10-year, 15% bonds, receiving $1,052,550. The bonds, which were dated April 1, 1987, and pay interest semiannually, have an effective interest of 14%.

Required

1. Prepare the general journal entries without explanation for the years 1987 and 1988 relating to the bonds. Assume that the effective-interest method of amortizing bond premiums is used. Round your answers to the nearest whole dollar.
2. How will the bonds be presented on the December 31, 1988, balance sheet?

(Check figure: Unamortized Bond Premium = $47,493)

Problem B15-7
Determine bond selling prices

For each of the following three independent cases, compute the bond selling prices:
1. $250,000, 5-year, 13% bonds priced to yield 16%; interest is paid quarterly.
2. $450,000, 20-year, 15½% bonds priced to yield 12%; interest is paid semiannually.
3. $800,000, 30-year, 15% bonds priced to yield 15%; interest is paid annually.

[Check figures: (1) $224,419; (2) $568,379; (3) $800,000]

Problem B15-8
Journal entries for a capitalized
lease

Atlanta Airways entered into a lease contract with Honolulu Leasing Company on October 1, 1987, for the lease of several aircraft. According to the terms of the lease, the lease must be capitalized. On the last day of every month, Atlanta Airways is required to pay Honolulu Leasing $1,200,000 for the next 4 years. The aircraft have an estimated economic life of 10 years. Interest of 12% is to be used for the capitalization.

Required

1. Without explanation, prepare the general journal entries for the year 1987 pertaining to the lease for Atlanta Airways.
2. What accounts pertaining to the lease will appear on the December 31, 1987, financial statements?

(Check figure: Interest Expense = $1,344,624)

Chapter 16

Corporations: Investments and Consolidations

Some of the things you should understand after you study this chapter are:

■ The reasons that one corporation invests in stocks and bonds of other corporations

■ How to account for investments in bonds at the time of acquisition, while the corporation owns them, and at the time of sale

■ The cost, lower-of-cost-or-market, and equity methods of accounting for investments in stock

■ The reasons for issuing consolidated financial statements

■ The purchase method of accounting for the acquisition of a subsidiary

■ How to prepare consolidated balance sheets under the purchase method on the date of acquisition

■ What minority interest is and how it is reported on consolidated balance sheets and income statements

Anyone can buy stocks and bonds traded on the securities exchanges — corporations are no exception. Corporations have the right to own property. The word property is just another name for assets. An investment in bonds or stock is an asset just like merchandise inventory, land, or patents.

Corporations buying stocks and bonds through brokers are really buying the stocks and bonds from other investors. These previous owners have held the stocks or bonds for a time, earned dividends or interest on them, and are now selling them because they need cash for some purpose. Corporations may also buy stocks and bonds directly from another corporation that is issuing the securities. It is of no consequence to the investor corporation whether the stocks or bonds are purchased from previous owners or from the issuing corporation; the entries to account for the investment are exactly the same.

In Chapter 7 you learned about short-term investments in stocks and bonds. Excess cash that is expected to be only temporarily available is used to purchase these short-term investments.

In this chapter we will discuss long-term investments in bonds and stocks — the reasons for making these investments and how to account for them.

INVESTMENTS IN BONDS

Reasons for Investing in Bonds

Corporations often accumulate large amounts of cash for future expansion of manufacturing, warehousing, or sales facilities, or for a variety of other reasons. The cash, while it is being accumulated for its intended use, should be put to work earning a return for the corporation. A corporation may decide to invest in bonds for the following reasons:

1. Bonds pay a higher rate of interest over a longer period than do savings accounts or government securities.

2. Bonds are a safer investment than stocks. Interest must be paid to owners of bonds each year. Dividends on stock are paid to stockholders at the discretion of the board of directors of the company issuing the stock. Also, in case of liquidation, an owner of bonds (a creditor of the issuing corporation) will receive a higher priority in the distribution of assets than an owner of stock.

Accounting for Investments in Bonds

Bonds Purchased at Par

Bonds purchased at par value earn the printed rate of interest

When bonds are purchased at their par value, the interest we earn will be at the rate printed on the face of the bond. The interest we earn will also equal the amount of cash interest we receive. The way we record the purchase of bonds and the interest earned is shown in the following example.

KNAVE CUTLERY CO.

Knave Cutlery Co. purchased ten, $1,000, 18% bonds of Fizz Cola, Inc., on January 1, 1987. The bonds pay interest on December 31 and June 30 each year. Knave paid $10,000 for the bonds. Knave purchased the bonds through a securities exchange broker who acquired them from another individual. Knave did not buy the bonds from Fizz Cola.

Jan.	1	Investments in Bonds.	10,000	
		Cash.		10,000
		To record purchase of Fizz Cola bonds as a long-term investment.		

```
June 30   Cash. . . . . . . . . . . . . . . . . . . . . . . . . .   900
              Interest Income . . . . . . . . . . . . . . . . . . . . . . . . .        900
          To record semiannual interest received on Fizz bonds
          ($10,000 × 18% × ½ year = $900).
```

On December 31, Knave will make an identical entry to the June 30 one. In fact, Knave will make this entry each June 30 and December 31 as long as it owns the bonds.

Did you notice that Knave bought the bonds on the day after the interest had been paid to the previous owner of the bonds? This assumption made our illustration simple. Let's make it a little more complex by assuming that Knave buys these same bonds on March 1, 1987.

If we buy bonds between interest dates, we must pay the previous owner the interest he has earned since the last interest payment date.

As the new owner of the bonds on the next interest payment date, we will receive cash for a full 6 months' interest. We must be careful to recognize as income only the amount we earn—the interest income for the time that we have owned the bonds.

Here are Knave's entries for bonds purchased between interest dates:

Entries for bonds bought between interest dates

```
Mar.  1   Investment in Bonds . . . . . . . . . . . . . . . . . . . . . . . . 10,000
          Interest Receivable . . . . . . . . . . . . . . . . . . . . . . . . .    300
              Cash. . . . . . . . . . . . . . . . . . . . . . . . . . . . . .           10,300
          To record purchase of Fizz Cola bonds as a long-term invest-
          ment ($10,000 × 18% × 2/12 = $300).


June 30   Cash. . . . . . . . . . . . . . . . . . . . . . . . . .   900
              Interest Receivable . . . . . . . . . . . . . . . . . . . . . . . .           300
              Interest Income . . . . . . . . . . . . . . . . . . . . . . . . .             600
          To record semiannual interest received on Fizz bonds
          ($10,000 × 18% × 6/12 = $900).
```

On March 1 Knave bought two things: (1) $10,000 of Fizz Cola bonds, and (2) the right to receive $300 earned by the old owner. Knave didn't earn the $300, so Knave must be careful not to record it as income. Knave debited Interest Receivable for the $300 because Knave will receive this amount along with another $600 on June 30.

On June 30 when Knave receives the $900 from Fizz, $300 of it pays back Knave for the amount given to the old owner. $600 is earned by Knave for holding the bonds for 4 months ($10,000 × 18% × 4/12 = $600).

On December 31, 1987, Knave will debit Cash and credit Interest Income for $900. This entry will be made each 6 months for as long as Knave owns the bonds.

The diagram at the top of page 594 will help you visualize the transactions we have illustrated and discussed.

Bonds Purchased at a Discount or Premium

You learned in Chapter 15 that bonds are often issued at amounts below or above their par value. Let's review the reasons for the existence of discounts and premiums.

Bonds sell for less than par (a *discount*) when the interest rate in the market—the rate paid by competing bonds—is higher than the rate printed on the bonds.

Bonds sell at a discount when the market rate of interest is higher than the printed rate

Knave would be foolish to pay the same price for Fizz Cola bonds paying 18% as for Hybrid, Inc.'s bonds paying 20%. To compensate, the Fizz Cola bonds will sell for

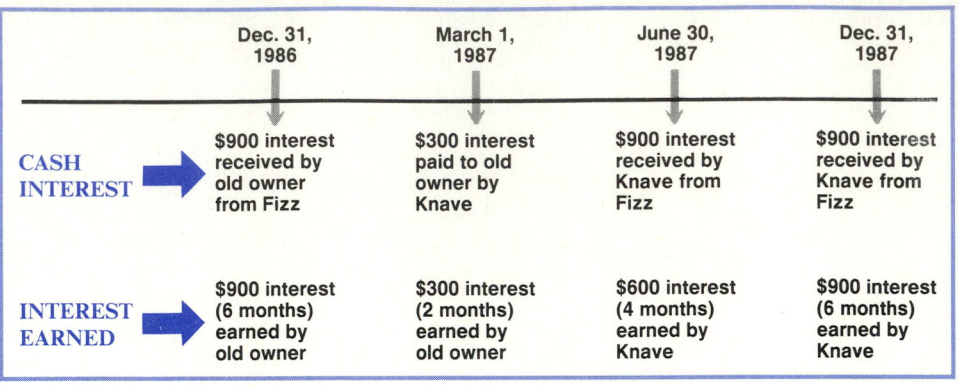

less than par. The buyer of those bonds will still receive the par value when they mature. The difference between par and the selling price is the extra interest income earned by the investor.

Bonds sell for more than par (a *premium*) when the market rate of interest is lower than the rate printed on the bonds.

> **Bonds sell at a premium when the market rate of interest is lower than the printed rate**

Assuming that Knave had bought the bonds when issued by Fizz, you can see that Fizz doesn't want to pay any higher rate than it has to. If the competing interest rate in the market is 16%, that's what Fizz is willing to pay. Since Fizz's printed rate is 18%, Fizz will simply charge the investor more for the bonds. Remember, the investor still receives only the par value at maturity. The extra amount paid by the investor serves to decrease the interest expense for Fizz and decrease the interest income earned by the investor.

Another thing you should remember from Chapter 15 is that we increase or decrease the interest each period by amortizing the discount or premium, respectively. You may also remember that there were two methods of amortization—straight-line and effective-interest.

Now let's use the Knave Cutlery Co. to illustrate accounting for discounts and premiums on investments in bonds.

Straight-Line Amortization of Discounts and Premiums

Assume that Knave Cutlery Co. purchased $300,000 (par value) of Comfort Corp. bonds maturing in 5 years. The bonds have a printed annual interest rate of 18%, which is paid semiannually on June 30 and December 31.

The entries in parallel columns at the top of pages 596 and 597 show how Knave accounts for the bonds using straight-line amortization if they are purchased for $281,388 (a discount) or $320,070 (a premium).

There are some very important things you should learn from studying these entries:

January 1   Knave records the investment in bonds at the amount paid. No separate discount or premium account is established. In Chapter 15 you did use a separate account. There is no theoretical reason for not using separate accounts—it's just customary not to use them for investments.

June 30 and December 31   Knave receives $27,000 in cash because this amount is specified by the bond contract. The fact that the bonds were purchased at an amount other than par makes no difference.

The straight-line method amortizes the same amount of discount or premium each interest period

Knave determines the discount or premium to be amortized each period by dividing the total discount or premium by the number of 6-month periods remaining in the bond's life. The straight-line method amortizes the same amount each period.

Knave records amortization of the discount by debiting the Investment in Bonds account for $1,861.20 each period. Knave keeps doing this until the bonds mature or are sold. If Knave keeps the bonds until maturity, the Investment in Bonds account will be increased to par value—$300,000. Notice that the interest income recorded each period is more than the $27,000 cash received. This is logical—remember that when bonds are purchased at a discount, we earn a higher rate of interest (20%) than the printed rate (18%).

Knave records amortization of the premium by crediting the Investment in Bonds account. The effect of doing this over the 10 remaining periods will be to reduce the Investment account to $300,000. Interest income is less than the $27,000 cash received. This also makes sense—when we buy bonds at a premium we earn less interest (16%) than the printed rate (18%).

Effective Interest Amortization of Discounts and Premiums   The straight-line method amortizes an equal number of dollars each period and recognizes an equal amount of interest income each period. The effective-interest method recognizes interest income at the same rate each period but yields a different number of dollars each period.

You are already familiar with the effective-interest method from Chapter 15. The interest expense you recorded each period was calculated by multiplying the book value of the bonds at the beginning of the period by the effective interest rate. In this chapter you'll do essentially the same thing. To find the interest earned, multiply the balance in the Investment account at the beginning of the period by the effective interest rate.

Let's look at Knave's investment in those same Comfort Corp. bonds to see the effective interest calculations and entries. (See top of pages 598 and 599.)

Again, let's highlight some important things you should learn from studying these entries:

January 1   Knave records the purchase of bonds exactly the same way as when the straight-line method was used.

June 30 and December 31   The $27,000 cash is still received at the end of each 6-month period.

Knave records the discount amortization by debiting the Investment account just as in the straight-line method. The amount is determined by:

1. Calculating interest income

The effective-interest method amortizes a different amount of discount or premium each interest period

$$\frac{\textbf{Balance of investment}}{\textbf{at beginning of period}} \times \textbf{effective interest rate} = \textbf{interest income}$$

2. Subtracting the cash received

$$\textbf{Interest income} - \textbf{cash received} = \textbf{discount amortized}$$

This procedure is repeated on December 31. Remember, though, you must calcu-

Transaction	$300,000 Bonds Purchased at a *Discount* ($281,388) (effective interest rate = 20%)		
Jan. 1, 1988 Knave purchased Comfort bonds ($300,000 par) for cash	Investment in Bonds. . . . . 281,388.00 Cash . . . . To record purchase of Comfort bonds, par value = $300,000.		281,388.00

June 30, 1988 Knave received $27,000 semiannual interest ($300,000 × 18% × $\frac{6}{12}$), and amortized the discount or premium	Cash 27,000.00
	Investment in Bonds. 1,861.20
	   Interest Income . . . .
	To record receipt of semiannual interest and amortization of discount:
	   Discount = $300,000 −
	     $281,388 = $18,612.00
	   Divide by number of periods
	    (5 years × 2 periods per year) ÷ 10
	  Amortization per period $ 1,861.20
			28,861.20

Dec. 31, 1988 Knave received $27,000 semiannual interest and amortized the discount or premium	Cash . . . . 27,000.00 Investment in Bonds. . . . . 1,861.20 Interest Income . . . . To record receipt of semiannual interest and amortization of discount.		28,861.20

late a new Investment account balance before you determine the new interest income and amortization amounts.

Knave records the premium amortization by crediting the Investment account—this was also the same as we did for the straight-line method. The amounts of interest income and premium amortized are determined in the same way that we calculate them for discount amortization.

Knave's amortization of the discount or premium will bring the balance in the Investment account to $300,000 at the end of 5 years. So, the straight-line and effective-interest methods end up at the same place (a $300,000 balance); they just get there differently.

If Knave holds the bonds until they mature in 5 years, $300,000 will be received from Comfort. The following entry records this transaction:

```
1992
Dec. 31   Cash . . . . . . . . . . . . . . . . . . . . . . . . . . . 300,000
              Investment in Bonds. . . . . . . . . . . . . . . . . .          300,000
              To record receipt of maturity value of Comfort Corp. bonds.
              (We are assuming that Knave already recorded the 12/31/92
              interest income and premium amortization.)
```

Sale of Bond Investment

The sale of a bond investment before it matures is recorded by debiting the asset received (usually Cash), crediting Investment in Bonds for their carrying value, and debiting a loss (or crediting a gain).

Let's use Knave again to illustrate. Assume that Knave bought the bonds for

---

$300,000 Bonds Purchased at a *Premium* ($320,070)
(effective interest rate = 16%)

Investment in Bonds.	320,070	
Cash		320,070

To record purchase of Comfort bonds, par value = $300,000.

Cash	27,000	
Investment in Bonds.		2,007
Interest Income		24,993

To record receipt of semiannual interest and amortization of premium:

Premium = $320,070 − $300,000 =	$20,070
Divide by number of periods (5 years × 2 periods per year)	÷ 10
Amortization per period	$ 2,007

Cash	27,000	
Investment in Bonds.		2,007
Interest Income		24,993

To record receipt of semiannual interest and amortization of premium.

$320,070 on January 1, 1988, and sold them for $312,500 on January 1, 1989. The entry to record the sale is:

Bonds sold for more or less than their book value result in a gain or loss

1989			
Jan. 1	Cash	312,500.00	
	Loss on Sale of Bonds	4,669.65	
	Investment in Bonds.		317,169.65

To record sale of Comfort bonds.

Balance of Investment in Bonds on 1/1/89:

Cost 1/1/88	$ 320,070.00
Deduct premium amortized 6/30/88	(1,394.40)
Deduct premium amortized 12/31/88	(1,505.95)
Balance 1/1/89	$ 317,169.65

Loss on sale:

Sales price of investment.	$ 312,500.00
Deduct balance of investment 1/1/89	(317,169.65)
Loss on sale of investment	$ (4,669.65)

    Losses and gains on sales of bonds are shown on the income statement as "Other Gains and Losses." Remember from Chapter 10 that losses and gains on the sale of long-lived assets (buildings, machinery, land) also are disclosed in this section of the income statement.

Transaction	$300,000 Bonds Purchased at a *Discount* ($281,388) (effective interest rate = 20%)		
Jan. 1, 1988 Knave purchased Comfort bonds ($300,000 par) for cash	Investment in Bonds................ 281,388.00 Cash .... To record purchase of Comfort bonds, par value = $300,000.		281,388.00
June 30, 1988 Knave received semiannual interest ($300,000 × 18% × $\frac{6}{12}$), and amortized the discount or premium	Cash .... 27,000.00 Investment in Bonds............... 1,138.80 Interest Income .... To record receipt of semiannual interest and amortization of discount: Balance of investment 1/1/88 .... $281,388.00 Effective interest rate (20% × $\frac{6}{12}$)............ × 10% Interest income .... $ 28,138.80		28,138.80
	Interest income .... $ 28,138.80 Less cash received....... (27,000.00) Discount amortized....... $ 1,138.80		
Balance in the Investment account 7/1/88	Balance 1/1/88 .... $281,388.00 Discount amortized .... + 1,138.80 Balance 7/1/88 .... $282,526.80		
Dec. 31, 1988 Knave received $27,000 semiannual interest and amortized the discount or premium	Cash .... 27,000.00 Investment in Bonds............... 1,252.68 Interest Income .... To record receipt of semiannual interest and amortization of discount: Balance of investment 7/1/88 .... $282,526.80 Effective interest rate .... × 10% Interest income .... $ 28,252.68		28,252.68
	Interest income .... $ 28,252.68 Less cash received....... (27,000.00) Discount amortized....... $ 1,252.68		

INVESTMENTS IN STOCK

Reasons for Investing in Stock

1. Investment

Corporations may decide to purchase stock of other corporations for one or both of the following reasons:

The corporation may wish to invest the cash it's accumulating for plant expansion or other reasons. Further, it may want to earn a higher rate of return than savings accounts, government securities, or even corporate bonds can offer. The corporation is willing to take a little more risk in exchange for higher earnings on its investment.

Common stocks are sometimes selected because their dividend payout rates are high or because their market values are expected to increase. The dividends received plus the increase in market value may be projected to be greater than the interest that could be earned by investing in interest-bearing securities such as bonds.

Investments in Stock

$300,000 Bonds Purchased at a *Premium* ($320,070)
(effective interest rate = 16%)

Investment in Bonds	320,070.00	
Cash		320,070.00

To record purchase of Comfort bonds, par value = $300,000.

Cash	27,000.00	
Investment in Bonds		1,394.40
Interest Income		25,605.60

To record receipt of semiannual interest and amortization
of premium:

Bond investment 1/1/88	$320,070.00
Effective interest rate (16% × $\frac{6}{12}$)	× 8%
Interest income	$ 25,605.60

Interest income	$ 25,605.60
Less cash received	(27,000.00)
Premium amortized	($ 1,394.40)

Balance 1/1/88	$320,070.00
Premium amortized	− 1,394.40
Balance 7/1/88	$318,675.60

Cash	27,000.00	
Investment in Bonds		1,505.95
Interest Income		25,494.05

To record receipt of semiannual interest and amortization
of premium:

Balance of investment 7/1/88	$318,675.60
Effective interest rate	× 8%
Interest income	$ 25,494.05

Interest income	$ 25,494.05
Less cash received	(27,000.00)
Premium amortized	($ 1,505.95)

2. Acquisition

The corporation wants to acquire another corporation by purchasing its stock. Any one individual or entity that acquires enough voting stock of a corporation may elect a sufficient number of directors to significantly influence or even control the actions of the company. The ability to influence another corporation's actions may be especially important if that corporation supplies us with critical materials and supplies, or if it provides a crucial distribution system for our products. If the ownership percentage is high enough, the financial statements of the two corporations may be combined and treated as one entity for reporting purposes.

The next part of this chapter deals with accounting for investments in common stock. The remainder of the chapter is devoted to demonstrating the preparation of consolidated financial statements.

Accounting for Investments in Stock— The Cost Method

When less than 20% of another corporation is owned, the cost method is used

CURRENTLY — OVER 5% ACQUIRED MUST NOTIFY SEC, WITHIN 10 DAYS.

PROPOSED LAW — 24 HOURS NOTICE AND NO ADDITIONAL ACQUISITION FOR 2 BUSINESS DAYS. FOR SHAREHOLDER PROTECTION DURING TAKE-OVER BIDS

When the investor corporation is unable to exert significant influence over the actions of the investee corporation, the *cost method* of accounting, the mechanics of which are explained later, should be used. We presume that no significant influence exists when the investor owns less than 20% of the outstanding voting stock of the investee. The cost method is appropriate in those instances where a company is merely investing accumulated cash without attempting to acquire or control the investee.

The purchase of common stock, the receipt of dividends, and the disposal of the stock are three events typically encountered. The acquisition of stock should be recorded at cost, including brokerage fees and any other costs associated with the purchase. Cash and property dividends are recorded as income when declared by the board of directors of the investee corporation. The difference between the acquisition cost and the sale price of the investment is recognized as a gain or loss on the disposal of the investment. In the following example we will demonstrate the proper entries for each of these events.

Purchase of Stock Investment — Cost Method

The cost method records investments at cost

Robco, Inc., is setting aside $50,000 per year in a special fund for the modernization of its production facilities. The construction is expected to take place at the end of 5 years. In the meantime, the financial managers of Robco decide to invest the funds in common stocks. On June 15, 1988, Robco purchases 5,000 shares of Mammoth Motors Corporation stock, which is selling for $9.25 per share plus a broker's commission of $250. The 5,000 shares constitute 1% of Mammoth's 500,000 shares of outstanding stock. The entry to record the acquisition is:

June 15 Investment in Mammoth Motors Stock 46,500
        Cash   46,500
        To record acquisition of 5,000 shares at $9.25 per share plus a
        broker's commission of $250.

Robco is purchasing stock on the open market (e.g., the New York or American Stock Exchange). The stock is not being acquired from Mammoth Motors but from another investor. Robco records the investment at cost without regard to the stock's par value, original issue price, or any other value.

Income on Stock Investment — Cost Method

The cost method recognizes income when dividends are received

On October 1, the Mammoth board of directors declares a $.25 per share quarterly dividend to stockholders of record on October 15, payable October 31. Robco's entries to record the dividend declaration and the receipt of the cash appear below:

Oct. 1 Dividends Receivable 1,250
        Dividend Income   1,250
        To record Mammoth's declaration of a $.25 per share dividend
        [($.25)(5,000 shares) = $1,250].

   31 Cash 1,250
        Dividends Receivable   1,250
        To record receipt of Mammoth Company dividend.

The dividend income is recorded when the dividend is declared. It is on this date that the Mammoth board incurred a liability to pay the dividend and thus Robco is assured of receiving it.

On November 5, Mammoth declares and issues a 20% stock dividend. Robco prepares a memorandum entry noting that additional shares are received. No income is recognized because no assets are distributed. Robco has more "pieces of paper" to represent the same 1% ownership interest. Robco now owns 6,000 of the 600,000 outstanding shares of Mammoth stock—still 1%. Robco prepares the following memorandum entry:

Nov. 5   Received 1,000 shares of Mammoth Motors common stock as the company's share of a 20% stock dividend.

Robco's total cost of $46,500 or $9.30 per share ($46,500 ÷ 5,000 shares) should now be distributed over 6,000 shares. The average cost of the Mammoth Motors stock is now $7.75 per share ($46,500 ÷ 6,000).

On December 31, 1988, Mammoth Motors reports a net income of $780,000 ($1.30 per share). This information is of interest to Robco since it reflects how well Mammoth is performing. No journal entries are made by Robco to record this information since no income has been received. *The cost method recognizes income only upon the declaration of dividends by the investee.*

Sale of Stock Investment— Cost Method

Shares of stock may be sold for more or less than their cost resulting in a gain or loss

On March 1, 1989, Robco sells 1,200 shares of Mammoth stock at $8 per share less brokerage fees of $115. This disposal is recorded by the following entry:

Mar. 1   Cash [($8 × 1,200 shares) − $115]............... 9,485
　　　　Investment in Mammoth Motors Stock
　　　　　($7.75 × 1,200 shares)...................... 9,300
　　　　Gain on Sale of Mammoth Motors Stock 185
　　　To record the sale of 1,200 shares of Mammoth stock having a book value of $7.75 per share for $8.00 per share.

Remember that following the stock dividend each share of Mammoth now has a cost basis of $7.75; therefore, the sale of 1,200 shares requires a credit to the Investment account of $9,300 (1,200 × $7.75). The difference between the cost and the net proceeds received is recorded as a gain or loss.

Lower-of-Cost-or-Market on Stock Investment—Cost Method

Lower-of-cost-or-market must be applied when the cost method is used

Robco's fiscal year ends on April 30 each year. At this time the *lower-of-cost-or-market procedure* is applied to long-term investments in stocks as well as to the temporary investments in stocks we discussed in Chapter 7. Robco finds the total cost and the total market value of the group of stocks that it owns. If market value is below cost, the investment is reported on the balance sheet at this lower amount. No income statement loss is recognized, however, unless the decline in market value appears to be permanent. Assuming that the 4,800 shares (6,000 bought less 1,200 sold) of Mammoth Motors stock is Robco's only investment, the following entry is appropriate:

Cost of Mammoth shares on hand: 4,800 shares × $7.75 cost basis
　per share.. $37,200
Deduct: Market value of Mammoth shares on hand: 4,800 shares × $7.50
　quoted market price (net of selling commissions) on Apr. 30, 1989 36,000
Unrealized loss.. $ 1,200

Apr. 30   Unrealized Loss on Long-Term Investment in Stock 1,200
             Allowance to Reduce Long-Term Investment in
                Stock to Market Value   1,200
           To record the fact that the market value of long-term investments
           in stock is $1,200 less than cost.

Long-term investments would appear on Robco's balance sheet as follows:

Long-Term Investment:	
Investment in Stock (cost)	$37,200
Less: Allowance to Reduce Investment in Stock to Market Value	(1,200)
Investment in Stock at Lower-of-Cost-or-Market	$36,000

The unrealized loss is reported as a *negative* stockholders' equity account. This account may be shown among the additional paid-in capital accounts (Paid-In Capital in Excess of Par, Donated Capital, etc.) as a deduction.

Accounting for Investments in Stock — The Equity Method

The equity method is used when more than 20% of the stock of another corporation is owned

When an investor corporation exerts significant influence over the investee corporation, the *equity method* of accounting is used. We presume that the investor exerts significant influence when he acquires 20% or more of the investee's stock. If he has sufficient votes to elect members to the investee's board of directors, if he exchanges management personnel with the investee, or if he enters into substantial transactions with the investee, we say that these are further indications of significant influence.

    The equity method accounts for the acquisition of stock at cost; recognizes income (or loss) as it is earned by the investee; reduces the Investment account when dividends are received; and records a gain or loss upon disposal of the stock. The following example will illustrate the equity method.

Purchase of Stock Investment — Equity Method

The equity method records investments at cost

On January 1, 1987, Gracewill Corporation purchases 40,000 of the 100,000 outstanding shares of Sibyll, Inc., for $816,000, including all brokerage fees and taxes. The entry to record the acquisition is:

Jan. 1   Investment in Sibyll, Inc., Stock 816,000
           Cash   816,000
           To record purchase of 40,000 shares (40%) of Sibyll, Inc., stock.

We record the investment at cost just as we would if we were using the cost method.

Income on Stock Investment — Equity Method

The equity method recognizes income as it is earned by the investee

On December 31, 1987, Sibyll reports a net income of $240,000. Under the equity method Gracewill recognizes 40% of these earnings at the time reported by Sibyll — not at the time Sibyll distributes them as dividends. Since the investor may exert significant influence over the investee, the investor may be able to control when dividends are paid and how much is distributed. If income were recognized by the investor at the time dividends were declared, the investor could possibly manipulate his net income by regulating the dividend declarations of the investee. *The equity method eliminates the possibility for manipulation by requiring the investor to recog-*

nize income (or loss) when it is earned by the investee. Gracewill records its share of Sibyll's 1987 income as follows:

```
Dec. 31   Investment in Sibyll, Inc., Stock . . . . . . . . . . . . . . . . . . . 96,000
               Income from Investment in Sibyll, Inc. . . . . . . . . . . . .         96,000
          To record 40% equity in the $240,000 net income of Sibyll, Inc.
```

Since Sibyll earned a $240,000 net income during 1987, its net assets (total assets minus total liabilities) increased by $240,000 and stockholders' equity (retained earnings) increased by $240,000. If Gracewill's Investment account is to continue to reflect a 40% equity in Sibyll's net assets, Gracewill's Investment account must be increased by $96,000 (40% of $240,000).

If a net loss is reported by the investee, the decrease in net assets is recorded by the investor by debiting a loss account and crediting (reducing) the Investment account.

Dividends from Investee — Equity Method

On January 2, 1988, Sibyll, Inc., declares a $.50 per share dividend. The dividend will be paid on January 15 to stockholders of record on January 7. Declaration and distribution of a cash or property dividend reduces the net assets of the investee. The investor, then, reduces the Investment account to record this fact. Also, since Gracewill records income when it is earned by Sibyll, any further income recognition when dividends are distributed would constitute double counting. Gracewill prepares the following entries to record the declaration and receipt of the dividend:

When dividends are declared by an investee, the equity method requires that the Investment account be reduced

```
Jan.  2   Dividends Receivable . . . . . . . . . . . . . . . . . . . . . . . . . 20,000
               Investment in Sibyll, Inc., Stock . . . . . . . . . . . . . . .         20,000
          To record declaration of a $.50 per share dividend by investee
          ($.50 × 40,000 shares = $20,000).

Jan. 15   Cash . . . . . . . . . . . . . . . . . . . . . . . . . . . . . . . . . . 20,000
               Dividends Receivable . . . . . . . . . . . . . . . . . . . . . . .         20,000
          To record receipt of cash dividend from Sibyll, Inc.
```

We handle stock dividends under the equity method exactly as we did under the cost method. A memorandum entry is sufficient to note the fact that additional shares of stock have been received. The ownership percentage and the equity in the net assets of the investee remain unchanged.

Sale of Stock Investment — Equity Method

When stock is sold for more or less than its carrying value, a gain or loss is recorded

An investor may sell some shares of the investee but still have a high enough ownership percentage to exercise significant influence. In such cases we determine the carrying value per share of the investment and record the difference between this carrying value and the selling price of the stock as a gain or loss.

On January 17, 1988, Gracewill disposes of 10,000 shares of Sibyll at $23 per share. This transaction is recorded as follows:

```
Jan. 17   Cash ($23 × 10,000 shares). . . . . . . . . . . . . . . . . . . . . 230,000
               Investment in Sibyll, Inc., Stock . . . . . . . . . . . . . .         223,000
               Gain on Sale of Investment . . . . . . . . . . . . . . . . . .           7,000
          To record the sale of 10,000 shares of Sibyll, Inc.
```

McLOUTH SETTLES EQUITY ACCOUNTING SUIT FILED BY SEC
(Believed the first of its kind)

The Securities and Exchange Commission accused McLouth Steel Corp. of incorrectly using the equity method of accounting in its financial statements. It is believed to be the first suit of its kind.

The SEC also accused the Detroit company of other accounting irregularities that the commission said resulted in overstated earnings and understated losses. The maker of flat-rolled steel products settled the charges by agreeing to a court order barring future violations of antifraud and periodic reporting sections of federal securities law. In settling the charges, the company didn't admit or deny wrongdoing.

The SEC suit, combined with a statement last month by the Financial Accounting Standards Board, will make it tougher for companies to use the equity method. Under that accounting procedure, if a company buys more than 20% of another concern and exercises "significant influence" over that concern, the investment company can include a prorated portion of the other company's earnings in its financial statements.

The SEC charged that although McLouth held 19.87% of Jewell Coal & Coke Co. the company didn't exercise significant influence over Jewell and shouldn't have included any of Jewell's profit in its financial statements between 1974 and 1978.

The commission cited a variety of factors to support its contention. The commission said that McLouth had tried and failed to get representation on Jewell's board and that Jewell had ignored McLouth's wishes on several significant corporate matters.

The FASB, elaborating last month on its 10-year-old equity accounting opinion, said those factors and others should be considered in deciding whether a company could use the equity method.

Companies often file stock-ownership reports with the SEC indicating that they plan to buy 20% of another company and to use the equity accounting method. But the SEC and the FASB are making it clear that the stock ownership alone isn't enough.

Sheldon Goldfarb, an SEC lawyer, said he believed the McLouth case was the first to raise this issue. He added that it was "significant" because companies filing stock-ownership reports will "have to look a little more closely" at whether they can use the equity methods.

The SEC said, for example, that McLouth hadn't been able to persuade Jewell to drop plans to spin off its coal operation from its coke manufacturing business. And it took a suit, which eventually was settled, to get Jewell to increase its dividends, as McLouth wanted, the commission said.

The commission also said that McLouth failed to disclose that after the price of coke rose sharply in 1970, McLouth had to sue to force Jewell to continue to supply coke under a 10-year contract. The suit also was settled.

If McLouth hadn't used the equity accounting method, it could have included in its financial statements only the dividends that Jewell distributed. In 1975, the difference between the two procedures was $3.5 million or 55% of McLouth's pretax earnings, the SEC said.

McLouth sold its Jewell shares in 1978, the SEC said.

As part of the settlement McLouth agreed to have independent directors on its audit committee to review the company's internal accounting controls and accounting methods.

Source: The Wall Street Journal, June 18, 1981, p. 7.

In our discussion of the cost and equity methods we mentioned that the equity method should be used only when the investor company exerts significant influence over the investee company. In this article you can see that the McLouth company management apparently used the equity method to recognize profits for its investment in Jewell Co. even though there was a great deal of tangible evidence that significant influence did not exist. The effect of this misapplication of the equity method was to overstate income.

The SEC felt that McLouth should have been using the more conservative cost method of accounting for its investment in Jewell Co. The cost method would have required McLouth to wait until dividends were declared by Jewell before recognizing profit.

Misapplication of generally accepted accounting principles may result in financial information that can be misleading to the investing public. One of the tasks of the SEC is to enforce the fair presentation of financial information.

The carrying value per share of investment is calculated as follows:

Acquisition cost	$816,000
Portion of 1987 income	96,000
Less dividends received	(20,000)
Balance of Investment account	$892,000
Divide by number of shares owned	÷ 40,000 shs
Carrying value per share owned	$ 22.30
Number of shares sold	× 10,000 shs
Carrying value of shares sold	$223,000

If the ownership drops below 20%, or if significant influence ceases to exist for some other reason, the investor converts to the cost method of accounting for future periods.

The authoritative financial accounting standard covering marketable equity securities states that lower-of-cost-or-market is not appropriate when the investment is accounted for by the equity method. This makes sense—we are not carrying the investment at cost.

The Cost and Equity Methods Contrasted

The table below highlights the similarities and differences in accounting for long-term investments in stock by the cost and equity methods.

The Cost and Equity Methods Compared.

Event	Cost Method	Equity Method
1. Common stock in another corporation is purchased.	Record at cost including brokerage and other fees.	Record at cost including brokerage and other fees.
2. Income (or loss) is reported by the investee.	No entry.	Record a portion of the investee's income or loss. The portion recorded is determined by the percentage of the investee we own.
3. End-of-year market price quotations are available for the investee's stock.	Apply the lower-of-cost-or-market method for the long-term investment.	No action is necessary. Lower-of-cost-or-market is not used.
4. Investee declares a cash or property dividend.	Record dividend income.	Record reduction in Investment account.
5. Investee declares a stock dividend.	Prepare memorandum entry noting the number of shares received.	Prepare memorandum entry noting the number of shares received.
6. Investor sells shares of investee.	Record difference between proceeds and cost per share as a gain or loss.	Record difference between proceeds and carrying value per share as a gain or loss.

CONSOLIDATED FINANCIAL STATEMENTS

The Parent and Subsidiary Relationship

When one corporation owns more than 50% of the stock of another, a parent–subsidiary relationship exists

If Corporation P owns a large enough percentage of the stock of Corporation S, it may not only exert significant influence over Corporation S—it may effectively control the activities of Corporation S. When this situation exists, the controlling corporation is referred to as the ***parent*** and the corporation being controlled is called the ***subsidiary.*** A parent and subsidiary relationship is generally assumed when one corporation owns more than 50% of the outstanding common stock of another.

How does P control S? Remember that each share of common stock we own gives us a vote in the election of the members of the board of directors. If P owns more than 50% of S, P can elect all of the people it wants to S's board. The S board members elected by P (and loyal to P) can then set operating policies and hire the managers to run S. P controls S.

The parent and subsidiary companies are separate legal entities. They may be in different industries, and from all outward appearances they may seem to have no relationship at all to each other. An investor purchasing shares in the parent company is really acquiring indirect ownership interest in one or more subsidiary companies as well. The investor must rely on the financial statements published by the parent to disclose the financial position and operating results of all corporations under the parent's control.

Since the parent owns more than 20% of the stock in each subsidiary corporation, the equity method of accounting is used to account for the investment in the parent company records. The equity method will yield a single amount on P's balance sheet, Investment in Subsidiary Corporation, and a single amount on P's income statement, Income from Investment in Subsidiary Corporation. These two individual amounts do not provide information about the subsidiary's various assets, liabilities, revenues, and expenses.

Investors' decisions may be influenced by the composition of the subsidiary's assets and liabilities. Some of the questions we might ask as investors include: Are the assets composed primarily of cash, receivables, and inventories, or do plant and equipment assets predominate? Are liabilities primarily current or long-term? What assets are pledged as collateral for liabilities?

We may also be curious about the subsidiary's revenues and expenses. Are revenues primarily from merchandise sales, or do disposals of nonoperating assets and miscellaneous income items play a major role? How significant is cost of goods sold expense in relation to administration and selling costs?

Consolidated financial statements provide the investor with more information about the composition of subsidiary and parent financial reports. **Consolidated financial statements** are an attempt to portray the parent and subsidiary companies as a *single economic entity.* A single consolidated balance sheet shows all of the assets and liabilities of the parent and all subsidiary companies. A single consolidated income statement likewise discloses the revenues and expenses of the parent and all subsidiary companies.

The consolidation process may be accomplished by using the purchase or the pooling-of-interests method. The **purchase method** is used when a parent acquires the subsidiary's stock by using cash, other assets, or debt securities. The puchase method is also used if the subsidiary is acquired by exchanging the parent's stock for the subsidiary's stock *and* less than 90% of the subsidiary's stock is acquired. The **pooling method** is used when 90% or more of a subsidiary is acquired by an exchange of parent company stock for subsidiary stock *and* a number of other conditions are satisfied. In the business world, far more consolidations are accomplished using the purchase method.

We will demonstrate the basics of the purchase method in the remainder of this chapter. The pooling method and complex applications of the purchase method will be left for a more advanced accounting course.

> Consolidated financial statements show the parent and subsidiary companies as a single economic entity

Consolidation on the Date of Acquisition — 100% Ownership

> The subsidiary's assets appear on the consolidated balance sheet at their fair market value

There are two important things you must understand about combining financial statements when one company *purchases* another:

1. The subsidiary's assets are placed on the consolidated balance sheet at their cost to the parent corporation. When the parent company buys the assets of the subsidiary, it must pay the fair market value for these assets. This fair market value is the parent's cost.

The parent's cost will probably be different from the carrying value on the books of the subsidiary company. Remember that the subsidiary's asset carrying value is its original cost (or its original cost minus accumulated depreciation). The market value of these assets may have changed substantially since the subsidiary acquired them.

If the parent pays more for the subsidiary's assets than the total of their individual fair market values, the parent has purchased goodwill. This goodwill must also appear on the consolidated balance sheet.

The subsidiary's income earned after acquisition is consolidated

2. The subsidiary's income is combined with the parent's on the consolidated income statement (but only subsidiary income after acquisition). Revenues and expenses incurred by the subsidiary *before* the acquisition date are *not* included in determining the combined net income.

These two points are very logical if you remember that the purchase method assumes that one company is *buying* another at a point in time. The accounting, then, is similar to what we do when we buy any asset — record it at acquisition cost, and recognize profit that it earns only after we buy it.

The following illustration will show you how to prepare a consolidated balance sheet on the day the subsidiary is acquired. We don't have to be concerned with a consolidated income statement on the day of acquisition. A consolidated income statement on the day of acquisition is just a parent company statement, because the subsidiary's earnings up to the day of acquisition are not included.

Parent Company (Company P) acquired all of the outstanding stock of Subsidiary Company (Company S) on January 1, 1988, for $100,000. The individual condensed balance sheets of Company P and Company S immediately after the acquisition are shown in Exhibit 16-1.

What did Company P buy for $100,000? An examination of Company S's balance sheet reveals that the *net assets* (assets minus liabilities) purchased have a carrying value of $85,000 ($125,000 − $40,000). Company P paid $15,000 in excess of the carrying value. We may attribute this $15,000 to the fact that S's carrying value of certain assets may be less than their market value. Or P may have purchased goodwill, an asset possessed by Company S but not listed on its balance sheet. In most cases both undervalued assets and goodwill exist.

EXHIBIT 16-1

COMPANY P AND COMPANY S
Condensed Balance Sheets
January 1, 1988

Company P		Company S	
Assets:		Assets:	
Current Assets (total)	$ 500,000	Current Assets (total)	$ 50,000
Investment in S	100,000	Property, Plant, and	
Property, Plant, and		Equipment Assets (net). . .	75,000
Equipment Assets (net). . .	1,000,000	Total Assets	$125,000
Total Assets	$1,600,000		
Equities:		Equities:	
Current Liabilities	$ 180,000	Current Liabilities	$ 5,000
Long-Term Liabilities	520,000	Long-Term Liabilities	35,000
Common Stock	700,000	Common Stock	60,000
Retained Earnings	200,000	Retained Earnings	25,000
Total Equities.	$1,600,000	Total Equities.	$125,000

Assume that an appraisal of Company S's assets shows land with a market value that is $5,000 higher than its carrying value. All other assets' market and carrying values are the same. We assume that the remaining $10,000 excess payment ($15,000 − $5,000) is for goodwill—we can't identify any other asset that we purchased.

Now that we have determined the market value of the various assets and the amount of goodwill, we can combine the balance sheets. We accomplish this combination by:

Steps in combining balance sheets on the date of acquisition using the purchase method

STEP 1: Eliminating the Investment account found on the parent company's balance sheet and the stockholders' equity accounts on the subsidiary's balance sheet. Any difference between these two amounts will be taken care of by Steps 2 and 3 below.

STEP 2: Adding (or deducting) appropriate amounts to adjust all subsidiary assets and liabilities to their fair values.

STEP 3: Entering goodwill to account for any difference not explained by market value adjustments in Step 2.

The worksheet in Exhibit 16-2 illustrates this procedure.

Intercompany accounts may exist between a parent and a subsidiary. We must

EXHIBIT 16-2

COMPANIES P AND S
Consolidated Balance Sheet—Purchase Method Worksheet
Time of Acquisition—100% Ownership
January 1, 1988

Accounts	Company P	Company S	Adjustments and Eliminations	Consolidated Balance Sheet
Individual Company Balance Sheets				
Assets:				
Current Assets	$ 500,000	$ 50,000		$ 550,000
Investment in S	100,000		(a) (100,000)	
Goodwill			(b) + 10,000	10,000
Property, Plant, & Equip.	1,000,000	75,000	(c) + 5,000	1,080,000
Total Assets	$1,600,000	$125,000	(e) (85,000)	$1,640,000
Equities:				
Current Liabilities	$ 180,000	$ 5,000		$ 185,000
Long-Term Liabilities	520,000	35,000		555,000
Common Stock	700,000	60,000	(d) (60,000)	700,000
Retained Earnings	200,000	25,000	(d) (25,000)	200,000
Total Equities	$1,600,000	$125,000	(e) (85,000)	$1,640,000

(a) The Investment account is eliminated. It is being replaced by S's various assets and liabilities.
(b) Goodwill is added because Company P paid $10,000 more for Company S's assets than their fair market value.
(c) $5,000 must be added because S's land was undervalued. Company P paid fair market value for the land.
(d) Company S's Common Stock and Retained Earnings are eliminated. The stockholders' equity accounts of Company P reflect the ownership of the consolidated entity.
(e) Note that asset adjustment total equals equity adjustment total.

Intercompany accounts are eliminated

eliminate (offset) these against each other in the consolidation process. For example, if Company P had loaned Company S $10,000 during 1987, Company P would have a $10,000 receivable on its balance sheet and Company S would have a $10,000 payable on its balance sheet. This transaction gives the consolidated entity no right to receive cash from an outside party, nor does it create an obligation to pay an outside party. The consolidated entity owes itself $10,000. We take care of this illogical situation by removing both the receivable and payable in preparing the consolidated balance sheet.

Consolidation on the Date of Acquisition — Less than 100% Ownership

When the parent owns less than 100% of a subsidiary, a minority interest exists

When one company buys less than 100% of the stock of another, a *minority interest* exists. In most cases ownership of more than 50% of the subsidiary's stock will give the parent control and necessitate the preparation of consolidated financial statements. The individuals and corporations, other than the parent, who own stock in the subsidiary still have a claim against the subsidiary's assets — a minority interest. We show this minority interest in the stockholders' equity or liabilities section of the consolidated balance sheet. We must also identify part of all future consolidated income as belonging to minority shareholders.

Let's repeat the Company P and Company S illustration assuming that Company P purchased only 90% of Company S stock for $100,000. All other facts of the example are the same. The new worksheet is shown in Exhibit 16-3 below.

EXHIBIT 16-3

COMPANIES P AND S
Consolidated Balance Sheet — Purchase Method Worksheet
Time of Acquisition — 90% Ownership
January 1, 1988

Accounts	Individual Company Balance Sheets Company P	Company S	Adjustments and Eliminations	Consolidated Balance Sheet
Assets:				
Current Assets	$ 500,000	$ 50,000		$ 550,000
Investment in S	100,000		(100,000)	
Goodwill			*(a)* + 19,000	19,000
Property, Plant, & Equip.	1,000,000	75,000	+ 4,500	1,079,500
Total Assets	$1,600,000	$125,000	(76,500)	$1,648,500
Equities:				
Current Liabilities	$ 180,000	$ 5,000		$ 185,000
Long-Term Liabilities	520,000	35,000		555,000
Common Stock	700,000	60,000	*(b)* (60,000)	700,000
Retained Earnings	200,000	25,000	*(b)* (25,000)	200,000
Minority Interest:				
Common Stock			*(b)* + 6,000	6,000
Retained Earnings			*(b)* + 2,500	2,500
Total Equities	$1,600,000	$125,000	(76,500)	$1,648,500

(a) Goodwill is greater than in Exhibit 16-2 because Company P is paying the same amount for a smaller portion of Company S's net assets.

(b) 10% of Company S's Common Stock and Retained Earnings is transferred to minority interest. Minority Interest appears on the published statement as one amount, $8,500.

We now assume that Company P is paying $100,000 for 90% of the $85,000 net assets of Company S. Since the same price is paid for less equity in Company S, Company P must be purchasing more goodwill. The revised calculation of goodwill is shown below:

Calculation of goodwill

Purchase price of 90% of Company S	$100,000
Deduct carrying value of 90% of the net assets of Company S (90% × $85,000)	(76,500)
Difference	$ 23,500
Deduct portion of difference attributable to undervalued Company S land purchased by Company P (90% × $5,000)	(4,500)
Portion of difference attributable to goodwill	$ 19,000

The minority interest on the consolidated balance sheet amounts to 10% of the stockholders' equity of Company S. In the consolidation process we eliminate 90% of Company S's Common Stock and Retained Earnings, leaving the 10% still owned by outside parties. We show minority interest on the consolidated balance sheet as a single amount rather than a separate total for each stockholders' equity account.

CHAPTER SUMMARY

Corporations purchase bonds issued by other corporations to earn interest on cash being accumulated for some future purpose. These bond investments may be purchased on the day they pay interest or at a time between interest payment dates.

Bond investments purchased at par earn interest at the printed rate. Bonds purchased at a discount earn interest at higher than the printed rate; those purchased at a premium earn interest at less than the printed rate. Bond discounts and premiums are not recorded in separate accounts.

Bond premiums and discounts must be amortized over the remaining life of the bonds. We use either the *straight-line* or the *effective-interest method* of amortization.

Bond investments may be held until maturity or sold at any time. If we sell a bond investment, we will recognize a gain or loss if the selling price is above or below the carrying value of the investment.

Corporations purchase stock in other corporations to earn a return on idle funds or to gain influence, and perhaps control, over the actions of other corporations.

The investor corporation uses the *cost method* to account for the common stock investment if no significant influence can be exercised over the investee. The *equity method* is used when significant influence can be exerted. Significant influence is presumed to exist in cases where more than 20% of the investee's stock is owned.

When an investor corporation controls an investee corporation, usually through ownership of more than 50% of the investee's common stock, we prepare *consolidated financial statements.* Consolidated financial statements report the financial position and operating results of the parent corporation and all subsidiaries as if they were one economic entity.

The *purchase method* is used when we acquire controlling interest in a subsidiary by using assets, or stock (if we acquire less than 90% of the subsidiary's stock in exchange for the parent's stock).

Consolidation under the purchase method involves:

1. Recording the subsidiary's assets on the combined balance sheet at their fair market value
2. Recognizing any goodwill purchased
3. Combining revenues and expenses of the parent and subsidiary beginning with the date of acquisition.

The ***pooling method*** is required when we acquire controlling interest in a subsidiary by exchanging parent company stock for 90% or more of the subsidiary's stock.

When less than 100% of a subsidiary is acquired, we must disclose the ***minority interest*** claims against the assets and income of the subsidiary on the balance sheet and income statement respectively.

IMPORTANT TERMS USED IN THIS CHAPTER

Consolidated financial statements   Financial statements that portray a parent and one or more subsidiary companies as a single economic entity. Consolidated statements are prepared when the parent owns more than 50% of the subsidiary's stock. (page 606)

Cost method   A system of accounting used by investors to account for investments in investees over which the investor exerts no significant influence. (page 600)

Effective-interest method   The method used to amortize discounts and premiums on bond investments over the remaining life of the bond by using the interest rate in effect at the time the bonds were purchased. (page 595)

Equity method   A system of accounting used by investors to account for investment in investees over which the investor exerts significant influence. (page 602)

Goodwill   The excess of the purchase price of a business over the total fair market value of the net assets of that business. (page 608)

Intercompany accounts   Accounts arising from transactions between a parent and subsidiary corporation. Intercompany accounts are eliminated in the process of preparing consolidated financial statements. (page 608)

Minority interest   The claim of the minority shareholders against the assets and income of a consolidated entity. (page 609)

Parent corporation   An investor corporation that owns more than 50% of the common stock of an investee corporation. (page 605)

Pooling-of-interests method   A system of preparing consolidated financial statements. This method must be used when the parent corporation exchanges its stock for 90% or more of the subsidiary's common stock and when other defined criteria are satisfied. (page 606)

Purchase method   A system of preparing consolidated financial statements. This method must be used when the parent corporation acquires stock in a subsidiary by giving cash, other assets, or exchanging stock (if less than 90% of the subsidiary's stock is acquired in exchange for the parent's stock). (page 606)

Straight-line method   A method used to amortize discounts or premiums on bond investments. This method amortizes an equal amount of discount or premium each year for the remainder of the bond's life. (page 594)

Subsidiary corporation   A corporation that has more than 50% of its common stock owned by another corporation. (page 605)

QUESTIONS

Note: Questions with * relate to consolidations.

1. Commercial Corp. paid $102,000 for a bond with a par value of $100,000. Why would Commercial be willing to pay more than par value for this bond investment?

2. Allday, Inc., purchased a $10,000-par-value bond for $9,750. Allday did not create a discount account when the investment was recorded. Must Allday still amortize a discount? Explain.

3. On January 1, 1987, Kelly Corp. purchased bonds with a par value of $400,000 and maturing on January 31, 1996. Assuming that Kelly paid $347,000 for the bonds, what will be the balance of the Investment in Bonds account on January 1, 1987, immediately after the purchase, and on December 31, 1996, immediately before they are redeemed by the issuer? Explain each of your answers.

4. Under what circumstances must the purchaser of a bond investment pay interest to the previous owner of the bond?

5. Why do corporations invest in stock of other corporations?

6. What percentage ownership of common stock must investors hold before they are presumed to have significant influence over an investee? Why is the determination of significant influence important?

7. Parrott Corp. acquired 40,000 shares of Sikes, Inc., common stock for $5.75 per share plus an $11,500 brokerage fee. Assuming that Parrott bought 10% of the outstanding Sikes stock, for how much would Parrott debit Investment in Stock? Would your answer be the same if Parrott had bought 40% of the Sikes stock? Explain.

8. Valley received notice of a dividend declaration by Aaron, Inc., an investee. Valley made the following entry:

Dividend Receivable 5,400
    Investment in Aaron Stock   5,400
To record declaration of dividend by Aaron, Inc.

Which method is Valley using to account for the investment in Aaron? Explain.

9. Under what circumstances is the lower-of-cost-or-market method used in accounting for long-term investments in stock? Under what circumstances is this method not appropriate?

*10. Explain how a parent–subsidiary relationship comes into existence.

*11. Why are consolidated financial statements more useful to investors than parent-only financial statements?

*12. Kimco acquired 95% of the common stock of Conrad Co. by giving $2,000,000 cash. Should the purchase or pooling method be used in preparing consolidated financial statements? Explain.

*13. Parent, Inc., purchased all of the common stock of Sub Corp. for cash. The *net* assets of Sub have a book value of $325,000 and a fair market value of $460,000. Assuming the purchase method of consolidation, how much would Parent have to pay in order for $25,000 of goodwill to be reported on the consolidated balance sheet? Explain.

*14. What are intercompany accounts? Why are they eliminated in the consolidation process?

*15. Hugh Corp. owns 95% of the common stock of Smalley, Inc. How is the claim of the owners of the other 5% of Smalley's stock reported on the consolidated financial statements? What is this claim called?

EXERCISES

Note: Exercises and Problems marked with * relate to consolidations.

Exercise 16-1

Recording the purchase of bonds with accrued interest

On August 1, 1988, Thomas Co. purchased Oster Corp. bonds having a $200,000 par value and paying 12% annual interest. Interest is paid semiannually on June 30 and December 31 each year. Thomas purchased the bonds for their par value plus accrued interest.

Prepare the entries Thomas would make on August 1 and December 31, 1988.

(Check figure: Credit to Cash on August 1 = $202,000)

Exercise 16-2

Recording entries for bonds purchased at a discount using straight-line amortization

On March 2, 1987, Hardy Corp. purchased Laurel, Inc., bonds having a par value of $2,000,000. The bonds pay 18% annual interest on March 1 and September 1 and mature in 20 years. Hardy paid $1,928,720 for the bonds.

Prepare entries for Hardy on March 2 and September 1, 1987, assuming that straight-line amortization is used.

(Check figure: Investment in Bonds is debited for $1,782 on September 1, 1987)

Exercise 16-3

Recording entries for bonds purchased at a premium, using effective interest amortization

On March 2, 1986, Young, Inc., purchased 7% Green Co. bonds having a par value of $500,000. The bonds pay interest on March 1 and September 1 each year. Young purchased the bonds for $521,324. At this price the bonds yield an effective interest rate of 6%.

Prepare Young's entries for the purchase on March 2, 1986, and the first interest receipt on September 1, 1986. Use the effective-interest method of amortization.

(Check figure: On September 1, 1986, Investment in Bonds is credited for $1,860.28)

Exercise 16-4

Recording investment in stock events using cost and equity methods

On February 1, 1988, Kiwi, Inc., purchased 20,000 shares of White Corp. common stock for $13.50 per share plus a brokerage commission of $4,000. On June 1, 1988, White declared a $.50 per share dividend to be paid on July 1, to stockholders of record on June 15.

Prepare any journal entries needed on February 1, June 1, June 15, and July 1 to record these events assuming that **(a)** the cost method, and **(b)** the equity method is used. If no entry is required on a given date write, "No Entry."

(Check figure: Dividend income recognized using the cost method = $10,000)

Exercise 16-5

Calculating investment income using cost and equity methods

Castle Corp. owns 10,000 common shares (20%) of Bishop Corp. During 1987 Bishop reported income of $500,000 and declared dividends as follows:

Jan. 1	$.55 per share payable Feb. 1.
Apr. 1	$.65 per share payable May 1.
July 1	A 5,000 share (total) stock dividend distributable Aug. 1.
Sept. 1	$.75 per share dividend payable Oct. 1.

How much income from the investment will Castle report under **(a)** the cost method and **(b)** the equity method?

(Check figure: Income reported using the equity method = $100,000)

Exercise 16-6

Recording entries for investment in stock using the equity method

Owl Oil Co. owns 20,000 shares of Flo-tru Pumps, Inc. The stock, representing 40% ownership of Flo-tru, was purchased for $178,200 on October 1, 1987. Prepare journal entries for each of the following dates, assuming that Owl exerts significant influence over Flo-tru:

1987		
Nov. 1		Flo-tru declares a $.15 per share cash dividend.
Dec. 1		Flo-tru pays the dividend previously declared.
Dec. 31		Flo-tru reports a $9,000 net income for the year. Flo-tru stock is selling for $8.25 per share on the stock exchange.

1988

Jan. 15   Owl sells 5,000 shares of Flo-tru for $8.25 per share less a broker's commission of
           $250. Owl still exerts significant influence.

Dec. 31   Flo-tru reports a $14,000 net income for the year. Flo-tru stock is selling for $8.00
           per share on the stock exchange.

(Check figure: Loss on sale of stock = $3,700)

Exercise 16-7

Making T-account entries for investments on cost and equity methods

Keys, Inc., purchases 1,000 shares (5%) of common stock of Black Corp. and 8,000 shares (25%) of Dome, Inc., as long-term investments. The total cost, including brokerage fees, of the two investments are $233,500 and $793,600, respectively. Keys uses the cost method to account for Black and the equity method to account for Dome. The following transactions and events took place in the year immediately following the purchase of the stocks:

Jan. 15   Dome declared and paid a $2.40 per share cash dividend.
Apr. 1   Black declared and distributed a 10% stock dividend.
June 12   Keys sold 50 shares of Dome for $5,600 after deducting brokerage commissions.
July 31   Dome announced a 2 for 1 stock split.
Sept. 1   Dome declared and paid a $1 per share dividend.
Oct. 1   Keys purchased an additional 1,000 shares of Black for $101,300 plus $2,700
           brokerage fee.
Dec. 31   Black and Dome report income of $86,000 and $320,000 respectively for the
           year. (On Dec. 31, Keys owns 10% of Black and 24.8% of Dome.)

Determine a December 31 balance for Investment in Black and for Investment in Dome. (Hint: Set up a T-account for each investment and enter appropriate increases and decreases. You need not make formal journal entries.)

(Check figure: Balance of Investment in Dome = $833,020)

Exercise 16-8*

Calculating goodwill included in the purchase of subsidiaries

Determine the amount of goodwill, if any, in each of the following acquisitions treated as purchases:

a. Chris Co. purchased 100% of the stock of Harp, Inc., for $300,000. Harp's net assets had a book value of $180,000. Harp's copyrights were undervalued by $8,000, and land was undervalued by $110,000.

b. Star, Inc., purchased 100% of the stock of Angelo Corp. for $750,000. Angelo's net assets have a carrying value of $815,000. Angelo's Accounts Receivable was overvalued by $32,000, Merchandise Inventory was overvalued by $38,000, and Buildings were undervalued by $2,000.

c. Stanco purchased 100% of the stock of Stella Corp. for $1,680,000. Stella's assets have a carrying value of $2,200,000; Stella's liabilities totaled $800,000. The following Stella assets were undervalued: Land by $90,000, Buildings by $126,000, and Equipment by $64,000.

[Check figure: Goodwill in purchase (b) = $3,000]

Exercise 16-9*

Calculating goodwill and minority interest in the purchase of subsidiaries

a. Castro Corp acquired 70% of Riggs, Inc., for $320,000. At the time of the acquisition, Riggs' net assets had a carrying value of $400,000 and a market value of $440,000. Compute the goodwill and the minority interest at the date of acquisition.

b. Chemicals, Inc., acquired 75% of the assets of Plastics Corp. for $240,000. Plastics' net assets had a carrying value of $150,000. Plastics' patents were undervalued by $80,000; land was undervalued by $100,000. Merchandise inventory was overvalued by $18,000. Compute the goodwill and minority interest on the date of acquisition.

[Check figure: Minority interest in part (b) = $37,500]

PROBLEMS
Set A

Problem A16-1
Recording investments in bonds at par and calculating interest income for the year

Quincy Corp. follows a policy of investing the cash it is accumulating to build a new warehouse. The following bond investment transactions took place in 1988:

Jan. 1   Quincy purchased $40,000 of 16% Burr Corp. bonds. The bonds pay interest each year on June 30 and Dec. 31. The bonds were purchased at par.

June 1   Quincy purchased $100,000 of 18% Hamilton,Inc., bonds. The bonds pay interest each year on Feb. 1 and Aug. 1. The bonds were purchased for $100,000 plus accrued interest.

      30   Quincy received the semiannual interest on the Burr bonds.

Aug. 1   Quincy received the semiannual interest on the Hamilton bonds.

Dec. 31   Quincy received the semiannual interest on the Burr bonds.

      31   Quincy accrued 5 months' interest on the Hamilton bonds.

Required

1. Prepare general journal entries to record each of the transactions and events.
2. How much interest income did Quincy earn during 1988? Support your answer with clearly labeled calculations.

(Check figure: Interest income for 1988 = $16,900)

Problem A16-2
Recording investment in bonds at premium using the straight-line and effective-interest methods of amortization

On July 1, 1987, Carthage Corp. purchased Hannibal, Inc., bonds having a par value of $200,000 and paying 14% annual interest. The bonds mature in 10 years and pay interest on June 30 and December 31 each year. Carthage paid $222,766 for the bonds. This purchase price means that Carthage will earn 12% annual effective interest.

Required

1. Assuming that straight-line amortization is used, prepare Carthage's entries on July 1, 1987, December 31, 1987, and June 30, 1988.
2. Assuming effective-interest amortization, prepare Carthage's entries on July 1, 1987, December 31, 1987, and June 30, 1988.

(Check figure: Interest income on June 30, 1988, under the effective-interest method = $13,327.92)

Problem A16-3
Recording investment in bonds at discount using the straight-line and effective-interest methods of amortization

On January 1, 1986, Fairdale Co. purchased Langston Corp. bonds as a long-term investment. The following data relate to these bonds:

Par value. $200,000
Stated interest rate. . . . . 14% annual rate
Interest payment dates . . . . June 30 and Dec. 31
Remaining life of bonds . . . . 10 years
Purchase price $180,252
Effective interest rate earned . . . . 16% annual rate

Required

1. Prepare Fairdale's entries on January 1, June 30, and December 31, 1986, assuming that straight-line amortization is used.
2. Prepare Fairdale's entries on January 1, June 30, and December 31, 1986, assuming that effective-interest amortization is used.

(Check figure: Discount amortized on December 31, 1986, using the effective-interest method = $453.77)

Problem A16-4
Preparing journal entries and balance sheet disclosures for investment in stock using cost and equity methods

Holley, Inc., invests in common stock of other corporations. During 1986 and 1987 the following transactions took place:

1986

Jan. 1   Holley purchased 30,000 shares of Palmetto Co. for $2.50 per share plus $1,500 brokerage commission.

Dec. 1   Palmetto declared a $.10 per share cash dividend payable on January 15, 1987, to stockholders of record on January 1, 1987.

     31   Palmetto reported a net income of $96,000 for the year. Palmetto's stock was trading for $2.75 at the close of the year.

1987

Jan. 15   Holley received the cash dividend from Palmetto.

Apr. 20   Holley sold 6,000 shares of Palmetto for $4.00 per share less a brokerage commission of $1,200.

Sept. 1   Palmetto declared a 20% stock dividend distributable on Oct. 1 to stockholders of record on Sept. 15.

Oct. 1   Holley received the new shares from Palmetto.

Dec. 31   Palmetto reported a net loss of $20,000 for the year. Palmetto stock was trading for $2.00 per share at the close of the year.

Required

1. Prepare general journal entries for Holley, assuming that the cost method is used to account for the investment.
2. Assuming the cost method, show what will appear under Investments on the balance sheet related to Investment in Palmetto on December 31, 1986 and 1987. How much dividend income and other gains or losses will Holley report for 1986 and 1987?
3. Prepare general journal entries for Holley assuming that the equity method is used to account for the investment. (Note: On December 31, 1986, Holley owned 25% of Palmetto; on December 31, 1987, Holley owned 20% of Palmetto.)
4. Assuming the equity method, show what will appear under Investments on the balance sheet related to the Investment in Palmetto on December 31, 1986 and 1987. How much investment income and other gains and losses will Holley report for 1986 and 1987?

(Check figure: Balance of Investment in Holley on December 31, 1987, under the equity method = $74,000)

Problem A16-5
Calculating the beginning balance of stock investment using the equity method when ending balance and transactions for the year are known

On December 31, 1987, Network International has the following long-term investment on the balance sheet:

   Investment in Optics, Inc. $700,250

The following additional information is available:
a. Network exerted significant influence over Optics during the entire year.
b. On Dec. 31, 1987, Network owned 35% (175,000 shares) of Optics' common stock.
c. Optics reported a net income of $620,000 for the year.
d. During August, Optics declared and paid a $.05 per share dividend.
e. During July, Network purchased 25,000 shares of Optics for $81,250 plus a $1,250 brokerage fee. This transaction increased Network's ownership interest from 30% to 35% of Optics.
f. During February, Optics declared and paid a $.05 dividend.
g. During January, Network sold 10,000 shares of Optics, receiving a net of $31,500 after brokerage fees. Network recognized a gain of $3,700 on the sale. This transaction reduced Network's ownership from 32% to 30% of Optics.

Required

Prepare a schedule calculating the balance of Investment in Optics, Inc., on January 1, 1987. (Note: In this problem you must work backward to calculate the beginning-of-the-year amount.)

(Check figure: Balance of Investment on January 1, 1987 = $444,800)

Problem A16-6*

Preparing a consolidation
worksheet on the day of
acquisition

Winston Co. purchased 100% of the stock of Bradey Corp. on January 1, 1988. Immediately following the cash purchase, separate balance sheets of the two companies appeared as follows:

WINSTON CO. and BRADEY CORP.
Balance Sheets
January 1, 1988
(000's omitted)

	Winston	Bradey
Assets		
Current Assets	$ 430	$ 25
Investment in Bradey.	180	
Other Assets.	1,250	85
Total Assets	$1,860	$110
Equities		
Liabilities	$ 290	$ 35
Common Stock	500	50
Retained Earnings.	1,070	25
Total Equities.	$1,860	$110

Required

Prepare a consolidated balance sheet worksheet on the day of the acquisition. Assume that the fair market value of Bradey's current assets was $25,000 and that of other assets was $145,000.

(Check figure: Total consolidated assets = $1,895)

Problem A16-7*

Preparing a consolidation
worksheet on the day of
acquisition when minority
interest is included

Buckeye, Inc., acquired 75% of Keystone Corp. for $600,000 cash. On January 1, 1987, the date of acquisition, Keystone's inventory was undervalued by $100,000; all other assets carrying values and market values were approximately the same. Individual company balance sheets on the acquisition date are shown below:

BUCKEYE, INC., and KEYSTONE CORP.
Balance Sheets
January 1, 1987

	Buckeye	Keystone
Assets		
Current Assets	$2,160,000	$212,500
Investment in Keystone	600,000	
Other Assets.	5,080,000	642,500
Total Assets	$7,840,000	$855,000
Equities		
Current Liabilities	$ 990,000	$ 40,000
Long-Term Liabilities.	1,250,000	125,000
Common Stock.	4,000,000	375,000
Retained Earnings	1,600,000	315,000
Total Equities.	$7,840,000	$855,000

Required

Prepare a worksheet to develop a consolidated balance sheet for Buckeye and Keystone on January 1, 1987.

(Check figure: Minority interest = $172,500)

Set B

Problem B16-1

Recording investments in bonds at par and calculating interest income for the year

The board of directors of Electro Corp. decided to invest in corporate bonds. The following transactions took place in 1986:

Jan.   1   Electro purchased $10,000 of 14% Bull Implements Co. bonds. The bonds pay interest each year on June 30 and Dec. 31. The bonds were purchased at par.

Apr.   1   Electro purchased $100,000 of 12% Team Machine, Inc., bonds. The bonds pay interest each year on Jan. 31 and July 31. The bonds were purchased for $100,000 plus accrued interest.

June 30   Electro received the semiannual interest on the Bull bonds.

July 31   Electro received the semiannual interest on the Team bonds.

Dec. 31   Electro received the semiannual interest on the Bull bonds.

31   Electro accrued 5 months' interest on the Team, Inc., bonds.

Required

1. Prepare general journal entries to record each of the transactions and events.
2. How much interest income did Electro earn during 1986? Support your answer with clearly labeled calculations.

(Check figure: Interest income for 1986 = $10,400)

Problem B16-2

Recording investment in bonds at premium using the straight-line and effective-interest methods of amortization

On July 1, 1986, Bennett Enterprises purchased Olson Co. bonds having a par value of $300,000 and paying 12% annual interest. The bonds mature in 5 years and pay interest on June 30 and December 31 each year. Bennett paid $322,878 for the bonds. This purchase price means that Bennett will earn 10% annual effective interest.

Required

1. Assuming that straight-line amortization is used, prepare Bennett's entries on July 1, 1986, December 31, 1986, and June 30, 1987.
2. Assuming that effective-interest amortization is used, prepare Bennett's entries on July 1, 1986, December 31, 1986, and June 30, 1987.

(Check figure: Interest income on June 30, 1987, under the effective-interest method = $16,051.10)

Problem B16-3

Recording investment in bonds at discount using the straight-line and effective-interest methods of amortization

On January 1, 1988, Reese Construction purchased Coast Concrete bonds as a long-term investment. The following data relate to these bonds:

Par value. $300,000
Stated interest rate. . . . . 12% annual rate
Interest payment dates . . . . June 30 and Dec. 31
Remaining life of bonds . . . . 5 years
Purchase price $278,814
Effective interest rate earned . . . . 14% annual rate

Required

1. Prepare Reese's entries on January 1, June 30, and December 31, 1988, assuming that straight-line amortization is used.
2. Prepare Reese's entries on January 1, June 30, and December 31, 1988, assuming that effective-interest amortization is used.

(Check figure: Discount amortized on December 31, 1988, assuming the effective-interest method = $1,623.17)

Problem B16-4
Preparing journal entries and balance sheet disclosures for investment in stock using cost and equity methods

Terrace Industries invests in common stock of other corporations. The following transactions took place during 1987 and 1988:

1987
Jan. 15   Terrace purchased 6,000 shares of Circle E Corp. for $21.50 per share plus $4,500 brokerage fee.
Dec. 31   Circle E declared a $1.30 per share cash dividend payable on Feb. 1, 1988, to stockholders of record on Jan. 15, 1988.
     31   Circle E reported a net income of $164,000 for the year. Circle E's stock was trading for $22.50 per share at the close of the year.

1988
Feb. 1   Terrace received the cash dividend from Circle E.
May 15   Terrace sold 1,000 shares of Circle E for $28 per share less a brokerage commission of $1,500.
June 30   Circle E declared a 10% stock dividend distributable on Aug. 1 to stockholders of record on July 15.
Aug. 1   Terrace received the new shares from Circle E.
Dec. 31   Circle E reported a net income of $150,000 for the year. Circle E stock was trading for $19 per share at the close of the year.

Required

1. Prepare general journal entries for Terrace, assuming that the cost method is used to account for the investment. (Round any per-share calculations to the nearest cent.)
2. Assuming the cost method, show what will appear under Investments on the balance sheet related to the Investment in Circle E on December 31, 1987 and 1988. How much dividend income and other gains and losses will Terrace report for 1987 and 1988? (Round any per-share calculations to the nearest cent.)
3. Prepare general journal entries for Terrace assuming that the equity method is used to account for the investment. (Note: On December 31, 1987, Terrace owned 30% of Circle E; on December 31, 1988, Terrace owned 25% of Circle E.)
4. Assuming the equity method, show what will appear under Investments on the balance sheet related to the Investment in Circle E on December 31, 1987 and 1988. How much investment income and other gains or losses will Terrace report for 1987 and 1988?

(Check figure: Balance of Investment in Circle E on December 31, 1988, under the equity method = $183,250)

Problem B16-5
Calculating the beginning balance of stock investment using the equity method when ending balance and transactions for the year are known

On December 31, 1988, Tiffany Equipment Co. has the following long-term investment on its balance sheet:

   Investment in Crystal. $1,013,500

The following additional information is available:
a. Tiffany exerted significant influence over Crystal during the entire year.
b. On December 31, 1988, Tiffany owned 45% (225,000 shares) of the Crystal stock.
c. Crystal reported a net income of $850,000 for the year.
d. During November, Crystal declared and paid a $.15 per share cash dividend.
e. During October, Tiffany sold 15,000 shares of Crystal, receiving a net of $51,000 after brokerage fees. Tiffany recognized a $6,750 gain on the sale. This transaction reduced Tiffany's ownership interest from 48% to 45% of Crystal.
f. During May, Crystal declared and paid a $.15 per share cash dividend.
g. During February, Tiffany purchased 5,000 shares of Crystal for a total of $16,500. This purchase increased Tiffany's ownership percentage from 47% to 48% of Crystal.

Required

Prepare a schedule calculating the balance of Investment in Crystal on January 1, 1988. (Note: In this problem you must work backward to compute the beginning-of-the-year amount.)

(Check figure: Balance of Investment on January 1, 1988 = $728,500)

Problem B16-6*

Preparing a consolidation worksheet on the day of acquisition

Britt Co. purchased 100% of the stock of Kory Corp. on January 1, 1987. Immediately after the cash purchase, separate balance sheets of the two companies appeared as follows:

BRITT CO. and KORY CORP.
Balance Sheets
January 1, 1987
(000's omitted)

	Britt	Kory
Assets		
Current Assets	$ 700	$ 80
Investment in Kory.	400	
Other Assets	1,640	300
Total Assets.	$2,740	$380
Equities		
Liabilities	$ 600	$120
Common Stock	1,600	200
Retained Earnings.	540	60
Total Equities	$2,740	$380

Required

Assuming that the fair market value of Kory's current assets was $80,000 and the fair value of its other assets was $360,000 on January 1, 1987, prepare a consolidated balance sheet worksheet on the day of acquisition.

(Check figure: Total consolidated assets = $2,860)

Problem B16-7*

Preparing a consolidation worksheet on the day of acquisition when minority interest is included

Ellis Manufacturing acquired 80% of Pebble Stone Corp. for $475,000 cash. On January 1, 1988, the date of the acquisition, Pebble's inventory was undervalued by $50,000; all other asset book and market values were approximately the same. Individual company balance sheets on the acquisition date are shown at the top of page 621.

Required

Prepare a worksheet to develop a consolidated balance sheet for Ellis and Pebble on January 1, 1988.

(Check figure: Minority interest = $100,000)

ELLIS MANUFACTURING and PEBBLE STONE CORP.
Balance Sheets
January 1, 1988
(000's omitted)

	Ellis	Pebble
Assets		
Current Assets	$ 350	$200
Investment in Pebble	475	
Other Assets	1,225	500
Total Assets	$2,050	$700
Equities		
Current Liabilities	$ 175	$ 50
Long-Term Liabilities	500	150
Common Stock	1,000	425
Retained Earnings	375	75
Total Equities	$2,050	$700

December 31-1901-

First Trial Balance, Advent

1 Capital Stock
1 Goodwill Franchise etc
2 Reserve Funds-
3 Pres't a/n P. Master-
4 Cash account
8 Furniture Fixtures
14 Profit + Loss a/c
24 1899 Suspense a/c
25 1901 " " "
33 Bills Receivable-
41 Bro16 account
46 Advertising a/c
54 Want ad a/c

EPSON

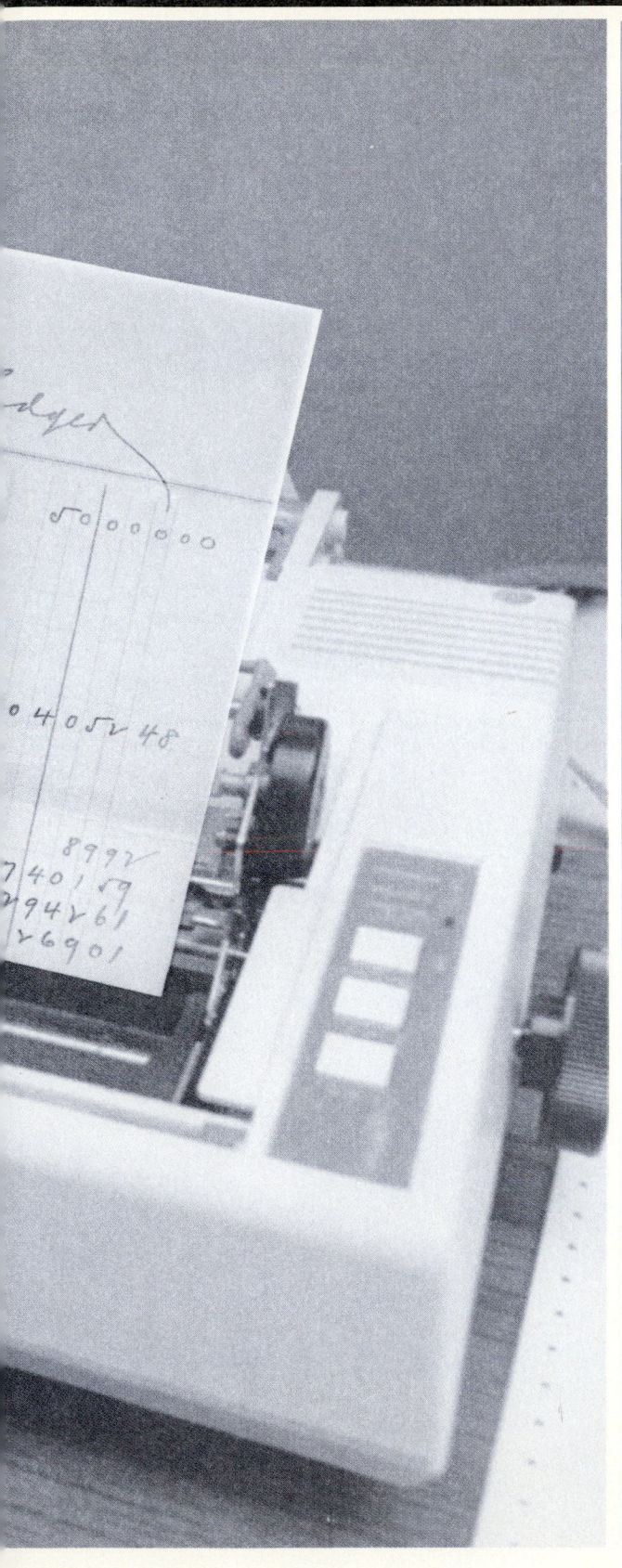

Part Five
Using Financial Statements

You have now learned about the three basic financial statements—the balance sheet, the income statement, and the statement of retained earnings. In Part Five of *Accounting Principles* you will learn to prepare the last major financial statement—the statement of changes in financial position—and to analyze the financial statements that are needed to evaluate a company's financial condition.

Where did the business get the financial resources it needed to operate? How did the business use these financial resources? These are important questions, which can't be answered by studying the balance sheet and income statement. In Chapter 17 you will learn how to prepare a statement of changes in financial position. This new statement is designed to show the inflows and outflows of financial resources during a particular year.

Readers of a company's financial statements may want to know, "Will the company be able to pay its debts when they come due?" or "Does the company have more merchandise inventory than it can sell in a reasonable period of time?" or "Are selling expenses too high?" In Chapter 18 you will learn to analyze the financial statements and calculate various ratios that will help answer these and many other questions. You will also learn about financial statement footnotes, which provide supplemental information. The reader must have these supplemental facts to understand the company's financial condition.

Chapter 17

The Statement of Changes in Financial Position

By studying this chapter, you should learn the following:

- The purpose of the statement of changes in financial position
- The three primary information elements that are included in the statement of changes in financial position
- What funds are and how to calculate funds provided by operations
- How to construct T-account working papers needed to prepare a formal statement of changes in financial position
- How to prepare a formal statement of changes in financial position using a working capital definition and a cash definition of funds
- How to convert an accrual-basis income statement into a cash-basis income statement.

In the previous 16 chapters you have learned about the balance sheet, the income statement, and the statement of changes in owners' equity (the statement of retained earnings for a corporation). You have studied how to measure and record assets, liabilities, owners' equity, revenue, expenses, gains, and losses.

Chapter 17 introduces you to a new financial statement—the statement of changes in financial position. In preparing this statement you will use all of the accounts that you've already learned about. You will learn to analyze these accounts and determine some new information that none of the other statements show.

Generally accepted accounting principles specify that a complete set of annual financial statements must include:

A balance sheet,
An income statement,
A statement of changes in owners' equity accounts, and
A statement of changes in financial position

This requirement applies to all businesses—no matter how large or small.

Before we proceed with our discussion of the statement of changes in financial position, let's briefly review the purposes of other statements.

The purpose of the ***balance sheet*** is to show the resources that a company has—its assets—and where those resources come from: borrowing—liabilities; investments by owners—paid-in capital; and accumulation of earnings—retained earnings. These resources and sources of resources are presented at one instant in time, the end of the accounting period.

The purpose of the ***income statement*** is to show the revenue earned matched with the expenses incurred in earning it. Gains and losses experienced during the time period are also included.

The ***statement of changes in owners' equity*** simply shows the beginning balance of each owner's equity account, the reasons for increases and decreases in each, and its ending balance. For most corporations the only owners' equity account that changes significantly is Retained Earnings. The statement of changes in owners' equity in such cases becomes merely a ***statement of retained earnings.***

We may find it difficult, if not impossible, to learn certain things from studying the three major statements. For example, to discover how a company's growth and expansion was financed, or what amount of liquid resources was generated by operations, we would need to make a detailed analysis of the statements. We would also have to make a number of assumptions before we could even attempt to find out this information. The statement of changes in financial position is designed to fill this information gap left by the other statements.

The objective of the ***statement of changes in financial position*** is to show: (1) significant inflows and outflows of liquid resources during a year; and (2) financing and investing activities not affecting liquid resources during the year. Liquid resources flow into the business from borrowing, from investments by owners, and from operating the business (buying and selling merchandise, for example). Liquid resources flow out of the business when it pays off debts, buys new assets, and pays dividends to owners. A financing and investing activity that doesn't affect liquid resources occurs, for example, when the business issues stock in exchange for a plot of land.

Now that you have a general idea of what the statement is all about, let's see exactly what these liquid resources are and learn how to prepare the statement.

(side notes)
A complete set of financial statements must include a statement of changes in financial position

The statement of changes provides information not shown in the other statements

The statement of changes shows liquid resource flows and financing and investing activities not affecting liquid resources

STATEMENT OF CHANGES: WORKING CAPITAL APPROACH

The Liquid Resource Fund

Liquid resources are defined as cash or working capital

Working capital equals current assets less current liabilities

A major portion of the statement of changes in financial position is devoted to showing the inflows and outflows of liquid resources. We may define *liquid resources* for this purpose in several different ways. The two most widely used definitions are *working capital* and *cash.* Since most large corporations use a working capital definition, we will discuss this one first.

Working capital is net current assets (current assets minus current liabilities). Since all the elements of current assets and current liabilities will be converted into cash, used up, or paid off within the next operating year, we will view these amounts as the liquid resources and obligations over which management will have control in the short term. An increase in working capital during the year indicates that more liquid resources were created than were used during the year. A decrease in working capital indicates that the company is using more liquid resources than it is creating. The statement of changes in financial position shows how working capital was generated during the period and how it was used.

Within the statement of changes we show any business transaction that increases working capital as a source, or an inflow, of funds. Examples of sources include borrowing money from a bank on a long-term note; selling additional capital stock; selling a property, plant, and equipment asset; and selling merchandise inventory. Note that working capital can increase without any inflow of cash. For example, the sale of merchandise on account will increase Accounts Receivable. Since Accounts Receivable is a current asset, working capital will be increased as follows:

Transaction

Merchandise costing $25 was sold on account for $30. The current asset Merchandise Inventory decreased by $25. The current asset Accounts Receivable increased by $30.

An increase in working capital is an inflow of funds

Working Capital before Sale		Working Capital after Sale		
Current Assets (CA)	$ 500	CA	$500 − $25 + $30	$ 505
− Current Liabilities (CL)	(225)	− CL	($225 − $ 0 + $ 0)	(225)
= Working Capital (WC)	$ 275	WC		$ 280

We show transactions that decrease working capital as a use, or an outflow, of funds. Examples of uses of funds include declaring a cash dividend, paying off a long-term liability, and incurring an expense that is to be paid for within the next operating period. Again, a decrease in working capital may involve but does not require an outflow of cash. For example, the purchase of an ad in today's newspaper on credit would increase a current liability, Advertising Payable. An increase in a current liability decreases working capital just as if a cash disbursement had been made:

Transaction

A change in two working capital accounts may have no effect on working capital

An advertisement costing $80 appeared in today's newspaper. The ad must be paid for within 30 days. The current liability Advertising Payable increased by $80. (Advertising Expense is also increased by $80.) See the illustration at top of page 626.

Some transactions involving two working capital accounts may have no effect on

A decrease in working capital is an outflow of funds

Working Capital before Transaction		Working Capital after Transaction		
CA	$ 500	CA	$500 + $ 0	$ 500
− CL	(225)	− CL	($225 + $80)	(305)
WC	$ 275	WC		$ 195

working capital. Examples are collection of a short-term receivable, paying a short-term obligation, and borrowing on a short-term payable:

Transaction

An account payable in the amount of $75 was paid in cash. Both Cash and Accounts Payable were decreased by $75.

Working Capital before Transaction		Working Capital after Transaction		
CA	$ 500	CA	$500 − $75	$ 425
− CL	(225)	− CL	($225 − $75)	(150)
WC	$ 275	WC		$ 275

Now we're ready to prepare a statement of changes showing liquid resource flows. We'll begin with an uncomplicated situation.

Illustration 1—E-Zee Company

Preparing the statement of changes—a simple illustration

We can prepare a statement of changes in an entity having few transactions by analyzing the income statement accounts and determining the causes of changes in noncurrent balance sheet accounts. The E-Zee Company income statement for the year ended December 31, 1988, and comparative balance sheets for 1987 and 1988 are presented on the facing page.

The E-Zee financial statements show data for 2 years in parallel columns. When this is done, it is customary to show the most recent data—1988 in our case—in the first column; the older data is presented in the next column. To make our financial statements more like those of actual companies, we will use this custom in the remainder of this text.

In developing the statement of changes for the E-Zee Company, we will follow this methodical approach:

1. Calculate the increase or decrease in working capital by preparing a schedule of changes in working capital accounts—that is, the current asset and current liability accounts.

2. Examine each noncurrent balance sheet account to discover the cause of any changes in the account balance.

3. Assemble the explanations of changes in account balances and arrange these explanations into a formal statement of changes in financial position.

E-ZEE COMPANY
Income Statement
Year Ended December 31, 1988

Service Revenue		$60,000
Operating Expenses:		
Salaries	$28,000	
Advertising	2,000	
Rent	3,600	
Supplies	15,000	
Depreciation on Trucks	2,400	
Total Expenses		51,000
Income before Tax		$ 9,000
Income Tax Expense		3,600
Net Income		$ 5,400

E-ZEE COMPANY
Comparative Balance Sheets
December 31

	1988	1987
Assets		
Current Assets:		
Cash	$ 4,200	$ 2,800
Accounts Receivable	14,000	10,000
Supplies on Hand	1,000	1,200
Total Current Assets	$19,200	$14,000
Property, Plant, and Equipment:		
Trucks	$22,000	$10,000
Less: Accumulated Depreciation: Trucks	(6,400)	(4,000)
Net Property, Plant, and Equipment	$15,600	$ 6,000
Total Assets	$34,800	$20,000
Liabilities and Stockholders' Equity		
Current Liabilities:		
Accounts Payable	$ 1,800	$ 2,500
Accrued Salaries Payable	600	500
Total Current Liabilities	$ 2,400	$ 3,000
Long-Term Liabilities:		
Notes Payable	10,000	—
Total Liabilities	$12,400	$ 3,000
Stockholders' Equity:		
Common Stock (no par)	$14,000	$14,000
Retained Earnings	8,400	3,000
Total Stockholders' Equity	$22,400	$17,000
Total Liabilities and Stockholders' Equity	$34,800	$20,000

E-ZEE COMPANY
Schedule of Changes in Working Capital Accounts
Year Ended December 31, 1988

	Balance Dec. 31, 1988	Balance Jan. 1, 1988	Effect on Working Capital
Current Assets:			
Cash	$ 4,200	$ 2,800	+ $1,400
Accounts Receivable	14,000	10,000	+ 4,000
Supplies on Hand	1,000	1,200	− 200
Total Current Assets	$19,200	$14,000	
Current Liabilities:			
Accounts Payable	$ 1,800	$ 2,500	+ 700
Accrued Salaries Payable	600	500	− 100
Total Current Liabilities	$ 2,400	$ 3,000	
Working Capital (current assets − current liabilities)	$16,800	$11,000	
Increase in Working Capital			$5,800

A schedule of changes in fund accounts will show the net inflow or outflow of funds

Explanation of the Schedule of Changes in Working Capital Accounts

The working capital at the end of 1988 ($16,800) and the beginning of 1988 ($11,000) is calculated in the first two columns. By comparing these two amounts we can see that working capital increased by $5,800 during the year ($16,800 − $11,000).

The third column shows what effect changes in individual working capital accounts had on the total working capital. For purposes of this analysis we consider each account independently and we assume that all other working capital accounts remained unchanged. Increases in current assets have the effect of increasing working capital. This was the case with Cash and Accounts Receivable. A decrease in a current asset, Supplies on Hand, causes working capital to decrease.

Changes in current liabilities have an opposite effect. Increases in current liability accounts cause working capital to decrease — this liability increase results in a larger amount being deducted from current assets. Accrued Salaries Payable of the E-Zee Company is an example. Decreases in current liability accounts cause working capital to increase. The decrease in Accounts Payable results in a smaller amount being deducted from current assets and thus a larger working capital.

Analysis of Changes in Non-Working-Capital Accounts

Analyzing non-working-capital accounts pinpoints specific inflows and outflows

In our schedule of changes in working capital accounts we discovered that E-Zee Company's liquid resources increased by $5,800 during the year. Where did these liquid resources come from? As we examine the reasons for changes in the noncurrent non-working-capital balance sheet accounts, the answer to this question will become clear.

Before we begin analyzing the non-working-capital balance sheet accounts, you should understand why this approach is a logical one. Every transaction a business enters into eventually affects the balance sheet. You can readily see that debits or credits to assets, liabilities, or owners' equity accounts affect the balance sheet. Remember also that revenue and expenses are closed to Retained Earnings (or Owners' Capital) at the end of the year. Since Retained Earnings is a balance sheet account, all transactions — even those involving revenue and expenses — eventually affect the balance sheet.

Analysis of balance sheet accounts is logical because every financial transaction affects the balance sheet

Since the effect of all transactions is included on the balance sheet, an analysis of the interaction between noncurrent (non-working-capital) and current (working capital) balance sheet accounts will reveal the inflows and outflows of working capital (funds). We don't need to analyze the interaction between two current accounts because, as we illustrated earlier, these transactions will not affect working capital (funds).

Now we're ready to analyze E-Zee Company's non-working-capital balance sheet accounts:

Retained Earnings	Trucks
Common Stock	Accumulated Depreciation: Trucks
Notes Payable	

Retained Earnings   By looking at the comparative balance sheets we can see that Retained Earnings increased by $5,400 ($8,400 − $3,000). We begin our analysis with this non-working-capital account because it contains the effects of all income-oriented operations for the year. In a real business we would look at the general ledger Retained Earnings account and examine each debit and each credit entry. Let's assume that in the E-Zee Company there was only one credit, for $5,400. This credit was to close Expense and Revenue Summary into Retained Earnings. The whole increase in Retained Earnings, then, was due to the income for the year.

Reported net income must be adjusted to derive working capital from operations

We accept $5,400 as our tentative inflow of working capital from operations. If all sales are for cash or on short-term receivables, and if all expenses involve the use of cash, other current assets, or increases in short-term payables, this initial $5,400 inflow assumption would be correct. A net income would represent an inflow from operations and a net loss would represent an outflow from operations.

When we look closely at each revenue and expense on E-Zee's income statement, we find that all revenue did involve inflows of working capital and all expenses—except one—did involve outflows of working capital. The one exception is Depreciation Expense.

Depreciation Expense of $2,400 has the effect of decreasing the book value of Trucks by increasing Accumulated Depreciation: Trucks. Since Trucks is a non-working-capital account, recording depreciation has no effect on any working capital account.

Our $5,400 initial inflow assumption must be increased by $2,400 to eliminate the effect of deducting an expense that uses no working capital.

Working capital provided by E-Zee's income-oriented operations totals $7,800 ($5,400 + $2,400) for 1988.

Common Stock   The comparative balance sheets show that Common Stock did not change during the year. Assume that when we examine the general ledger account, we find no entries. We conclude, then, that there were no inflows or outflows of working capital related to the Common Stock account.

Notes Payable   Again, we look at the comparative balance sheets and calculate that Notes Payable increased by $10,000. When we examine the general ledger account, assume that we discover only one transaction—E-Zee borrowed $10,000 cash from the bank.

Here we have a clear inflow of working capital—the current asset Cash increased. Remember, this is a $10,000 increase in a *long-term note.* If cash had been borrowed on a *short-term* note, working capital would have remained unchanged because both current assets and current liabilities would have increased in the same amount.

Accumulated Depreciation: Trucks   The comparative balance sheets show us that Accumulated Depreciation: Trucks increased by $2,400 ($6,400 − $4,000). We explained the effect of this increase when we examined Retained Earnings and income above.

Trucks   Trucks increased by $12,000 ($22,000 − $10,000). When we look at the general ledger account, assume that we find only one debit entry this year. This entry is for the purchase of a new truck for cash. This acquisition involves an outflow of working capital, since the current asset Cash decreased.

Now we have explained all of the changes in the non-working-capital balance sheet accounts. The information we have gathered can be arranged into the formal statement of changes in financial position shown below.

The basic process that we followed in preparing the E-Zee Company statement of changes in financial position is the same one we'll use in more complex situations. Of course, our analysis will need to be a bit more organized for a company with many different accounts—but we'll still do three basic things:

A review of the basic process used in the E-Zee Company illustration

1. Find out the amount of the change in the liquid resource fund (working capital). We did this by preparing a schedule of changes in working capital accounts.
2. Analyze each nonfund (non-working-capital) account on the balance sheet and determine why its balance increased or decreased.
3. Arrange the information we've gathered into a formal statement of changes in financial position.

Before we proceed to a more complex illustration, let's review some of the concepts we've already studied and introduce some new ones.

E-ZEE COMPANY
Statement of Changes in Financial Position*
Year Ended December 31, 1988

Financial Resources Generated
Working Capital from Operations:
   Net Income . . . . $ 5,400
   Add: Items Not Using Working Capital:
      Depreciation on Trucks 2,400
   Working Capital from Operations . . . . $ 7,800
Other Sources of Working Capital:
   Borrowing on Long-Term Note 10,000
Total Financial Resources Generated $17,800

Financial Resources Used
Working Capital Used:
   To Purchase Truck 12,000

Increase in Working Capital . . . . $ 5,800

* The schedule of changes in working capital accounts is also attached as part of this statement.

Analyzing Funds Flow through the Balance Sheet

In the E-Zee Company we analyzed the changes in each non-working-capital balance sheet account. The purpose of this analysis was to discover inflows and outflows of funds. We've prepared the chart below to help you review this technique and understand why it works.

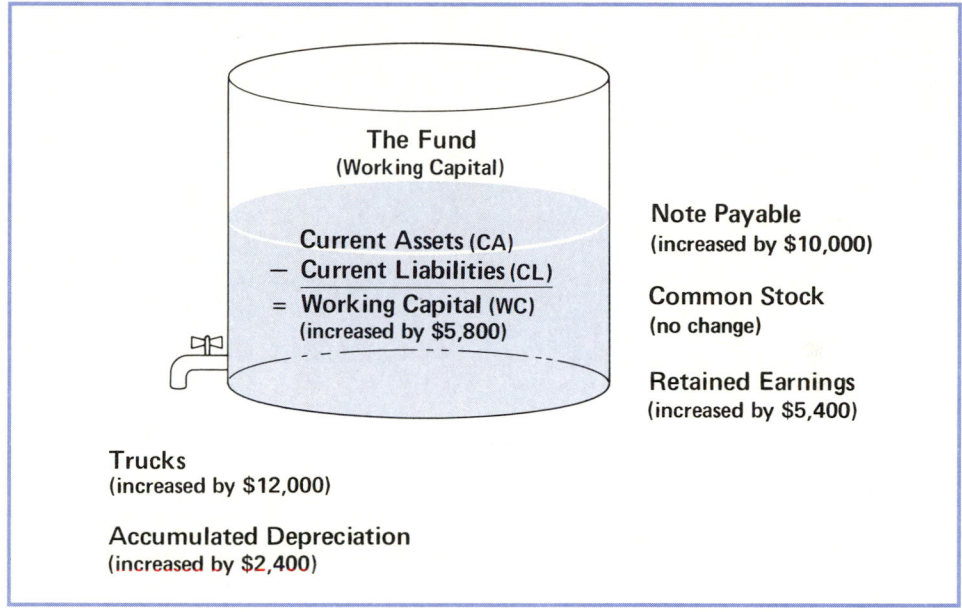

The Fund
(Working Capital)

Current Assets (CA)
− **Current Liabilities** (CL)
= **Working Capital** (WC)
(increased by $5,800)

Note Payable
(increased by $10,000)

Common Stock
(no change)

Retained Earnings
(increased by $5,400)

Trucks
(increased by $12,000)

Accumulated Depreciation
(increased by $2,400)

In this chart we've arranged E-Zee's balance sheet a little differently than you're accustomed to. The current assets and current liabilities are together in a container called "The Fund." The other accounts — nonfund accounts — are positioned as you normally see them on the balance sheet.

Now let's look at the interaction between the fund and nonfund accounts at the top of page 632 to see how liquid resources were poured into or siphoned out of the container during the year.

The level of liquid resources has risen by $5,800 during the year. We calculated this when we prepared our schedule of changes in working capital accounts.

We poured $17,800 into the container of liquid resources ($10,000 from long-term borrowing and $7,800 from income-oriented operations). We siphoned $12,000 out and used it to purchase a truck.

Now that you've seen a simple illustration from beginning to end, you're ready to look more closely at the types of information appearing on the statement of changes.

Working Capital from Operations

The first piece of information that must appear on a statement of changes in financial position is the amount of working capital (funds) provided by the income-directed activities of the business.

We know that the income statement contains data about all of the income-directed activities, so we will want to analyze this document carefully. As you learned earlier, not all of the items on the income statement provide or use working capital. We must adjust net income to remove the effects of these nonfund items when we calculate working capital provided by operations.

We've already seen that depreciation expense must be added back. Here is a more complete list of other items requiring adjustment:

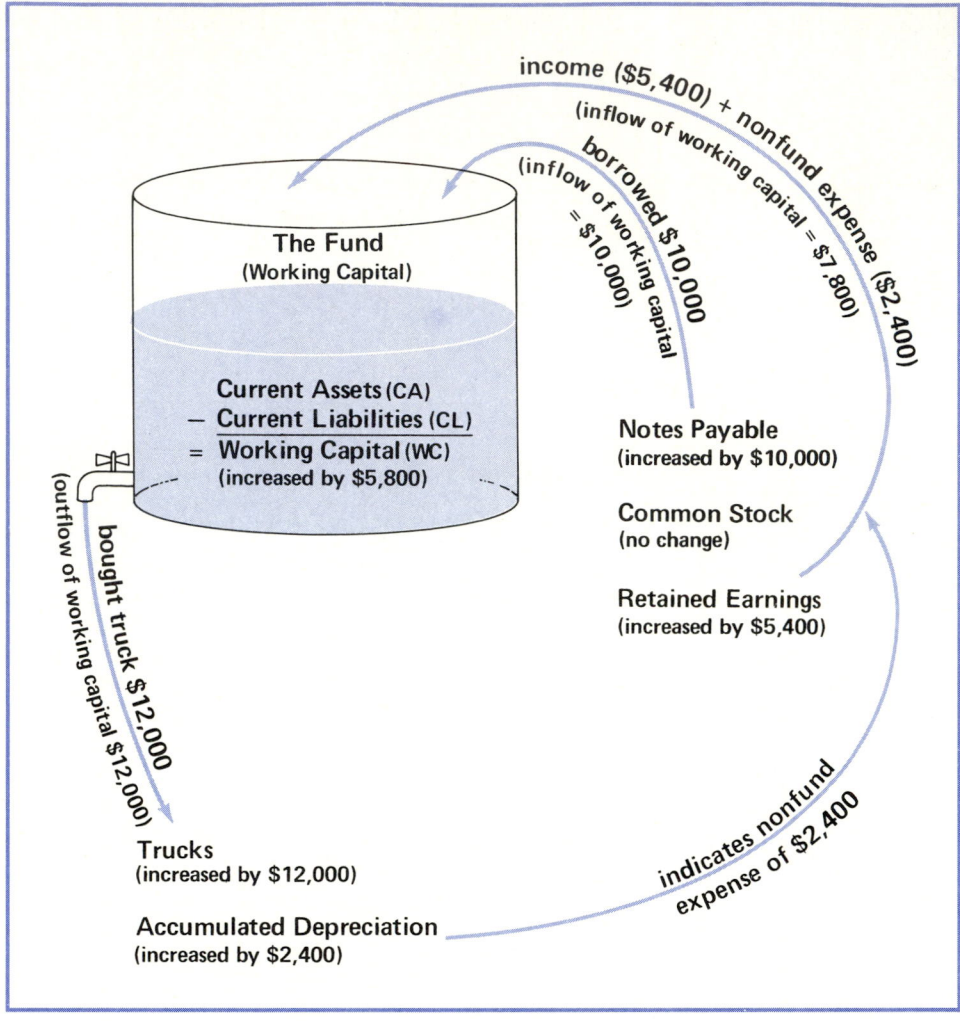

Typical items deducted and added in arriving at working capital from operations

Items deducted on the income statement that do not use working capital — adjust by adding the amounts of these items back to net income:

Depreciation

Amortization of intangible assets

Depletion

Amortization of discount on notes and bonds payable (the amortization originally increased interest expense)

Losses on sales of noncurrent assets (we'll tell you why later)

Items added on the income statement that do not provide working capital — adjust by subtracting the amounts of these items from net income:

Revenue from sales on long-term receivables

Income recognized on investments accounted for by the equity method

Amortization of premium on notes and bonds payable (the amortization originally decreased interest expense)

Gains on sales of noncurrent assets (we'll tell you why later)

Financing and Investing Activities Not Affecting Working Capital

Some significant transactions entered into by a business do not affect working capital but nonetheless should be disclosed on the statement of changes in financial position.

Examples of financing and investing activities not affecting working capital include:

> Some transactions not affecting working capital must be disclosed on the statement of changes

1. Acquiring a noncurrent asset such as a building by incurring a noncurrent liability such as a mortgage bond payable

2. Issuing common stock to retire long-term debt

3. Issuing common stock when convertible bonds or convertible preferred stock is converted

4. Exchanging one noncurrent asset, such as a parcel of land, for another noncurrent asset, such as shares of stock in another corporation

Let's expand our balance sheet flow chart to include some of these financing and investing activities.

You should see from the expanded chart below that these financing and investing activities in no way affected the liquid resource fund. Our flow lines are consistently between nonfund accounts—none of these new flow lines involved the fund container.

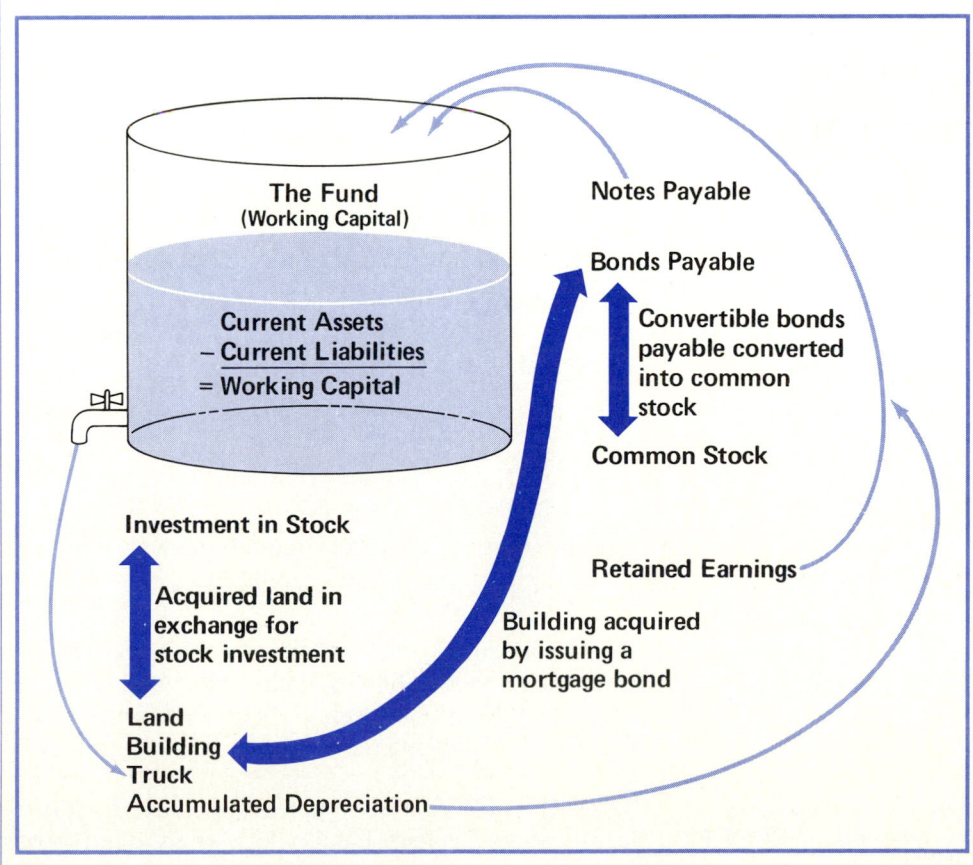

Financing and investing activities are shown on the statement as both a source and a use

In reality there is *no* inflow and *no* outflow of funds when a financing and investing activity takes place. Since generally accepted accounting principles require that we show financing and investing activities on the statement, we must think of a way to disclose them without ending up with a net inflow or a net outflow. One way to accomplish this is to show these financing and investing activities on the statement of changes in *both* the financial resources generated and the financial resources used sections. We must use this counterbalancing disclosure to avoid showing an inflow of funds (which would happen if we disclosed it only in the financial resources generated section) or an outflow of funds (which would occur if we showed it only in the financial resources used section). Dual disclosure as an inflow and an outflow allows us to show the information on the statement without creating the false impression that funds were provided or used by these financing or investing activities.

The all financial resources approach means the statement shows flows of liquid resources and financing and investing activities

The addition of financing and investing activities to our statement of changes means that we are now using the all financial resources approach. Under the ***all financial resources approach*** the statement of changes shows flows of funds *and* financing and investing activities not affecting funds.

The Three Basic Informational Elements

Let's briefly summarize the types of information that must be presented on the statement of changes in financial position. Then we'll move on to a more complex illustration.

The Flow of Funds

A statement of changes prepared in accordance with GAAP includes (1) flows of funds, . . .

Separate information about funds provided by operations, other sources of funds, and uses of funds is required. The fund is usually defined as working capital or cash. Typical *sources* of funds include:

Operations (net income with nonfund additions and deductions)

Selling noncurrent assets (investments, land, buildings, equipment, and intangibles)

Selling stock (common or preferred)

Selling treasury stock (common or preferred)

Borrowing money and issuing long-term debt (bonds payable)

Typical *uses* of funds include:

Purchasing noncurrent assets (investments, land, buildings, equipment, and intangibles)

Paying back long-term debt (bonds and notes)

Purchasing treasury stock (common or preferred)

Paying cash dividends to stockholders

Changes in Individual Fund Accounts

(2) changes in individual fund accounts, and . . .

A schedule showing the impact on working capital of changes in individual current asset and current liability accounts must appear on the statement or in a footnote. This schedule is not necessary when a cash fund is used, because the whole statement is devoted to showing the change in the only fund account—Cash.

Financing and Investing Activities Not Affecting the Fund

The all financial resources approach includes disclosure of those activities that significantly affect the asset, liability, or owners' equity structure of the business without

(3) financing and investing activities not affecting funds

affecting the liquid resource fund. These activities are normally shown in both the resources generated and the resources used sections of the statement.

Examples of financing and investing activities include:

Issuing a long-term debt for a noncurrent asset (issuing mortgage bonds for a building)

Exchanging one noncurrent asset for another (giving shares of stock held as an investment for a plot of land)

Issuing common or preferred stock in exchange for a noncurrent asset (issuing shares of common stock for a machine)

Issuing common or preferred stock to settle a long-term liability (issuing preferred stock to a bondholder in exchange for the bond)

Issuing common stock to retire preferred stock (issuing common stock when convertible preferred stock is converted)

Illustration 2 — Teek Company

Preparing the statement of changes: a complex illustration

The E-Zee Company illustration showed you the concept of the statement of changes. For that purpose we needed a situation where only a few accounts and transactions were involved. Our methodology for E-Zee was an organized, but informal, gathering of facts. That approach was sufficient for such an uncomplicated case where the change in each noncurrent account balance could be explained by one transaction. In reality, even relatively small firms have many more accounts and transactions.

The Teek Company illustration shows you a step-by-step T-account approach for dealing with a mass of accounting data. Study each step carefully and be sure you understand it before moving on to the next one.

Below and on the following page are Teek's income statement and statement of retained earnings for 1987, and the comparative balance sheet for 1986 and 1987:

TEEK COMPANY
Condensed Income Statement
Year Ended December 31, 1987

Sales		$ 290,000
Cost of Goods Sold		(174,000)
Gross Profit on Sales		$ 116,000
Operating Expenses:		
Administrative Expenses	$(45,000)	
Selling Expenses	(20,900)	
Depreciation Expense	(12,000)	
Patent Amortization Expense	(1,000)	(78,900)
Other Income and Expenses:		
Interest Expense	$(15,400)	
Gain on Sale of Land	2,500	(12,900)
Income before Tax		$ 24,200
Income Tax Expense		(9,700)
Net Income		$ 14,500

TEEK COMPANY
Statement of Retained Earnings
Year Ended December 31, 1987

Balance January 1, 1987	$ 88,000
Add: Net Income for the Year.......................	14,500
Deduct: Dividends Declared and Paid during 1987	(10,000)
Balance December 31, 1987	$ 92,500

TEEK COMPANY
Balance Sheet

	December 31, 1987	December 31, 1986	Increase (Decrease) in Account Balance
Assets			
Current Assets:			
Cash...................................	$ 50,000	$ 55,000	$ (5,000)
Accounts Receivable (net)...............	109,000	90,000	19,000
Merchandise Inventory..................	175,000	153,000	22,000
Prepaid Expenses	15,500	17,000	(1,500)
Total Current Assets	$ 349,500	$ 315,000	
Investments:			
Land Held for Investment................	—	$ 27,500	(27,500)
Property, Plant, and Equipment:			
Land Used in Operations	$ 148,400	$ 100,000	48,400
Buildings.............................	465,000	415,000	50,000
Less: Accumulated Depreciation: Building	(217,000)	(205,000)	12,000
Total Property, Plant, and Equipment....	$ 396,400	$ 310,000	
Intangibles:			
Patents	$ 5,000	$ 6,000	(1,000)
Total Assets	$ 750,900	$ 658,500	
Liabilities and Stockholders' Equity			
Current Liabilities:			
Accounts Payable	$ 69,000	$ 75,000	$ (6,000)
Accrued Liabilities	24,500	20,000	4,500
Total Current Liabilities.............	$ 93,500	$ 95,000	
Long-Term Liabilities:			
Bonds Payable	$ 200,000	$ 200,000	–0–
Premium on Bonds Payable	29,400	30,000	(600)
Total Long-Term Liabilities	$ 229,400	$ 230,000	
Total Liabilities........................	$ 322,900	$ 325,000	
Stockholders' Equity:			
Common Stock, no par	$ 335,500	$ 245,500	90,000
Retained Earnings.....................	92,500	88,000	4,500
Total Stockholders' Equity...............	$ 428,000	$ 333,500	
Total Liabilities and Stockholders' Equity	$ 750,900	$ 658,500	

STEP 1: Determine the change in the working capital fund for the year.

One function of the statement of changes in financial position is to show the reasons for an increase or decrease in the working capital fund for the year. Before this can be done the amount of such change must be calculated. Step 1 requires this calculation.

The schedule of changes in working capital accounts is used to accomplish the objective of Step 1. Since this information is also required on the finished statement of changes, we can save effort by attaching the schedule prepared now to the remainder of the statement prepared later. The schedule below is in the same form as we used for the E-Zee Company.

TEEK COMPANY
Schedule of Changes in Working Capital Accounts
Year Ended December 31, 1987

	Balance December 31, 1987	Balance January 1, 1987	Effect on Working Capital
Current Assets:			
Cash.	$ 50,000	$ 55,000	−$ 5,000
Accounts Receivable (net).	109,000	90,000	+ 19,000
Merchandise Inventory.	175,000	153,000	+ 22,000
Prepaid Expenses	15,500	17,000	− 1,500
Total Current Assets	$349,500	$315,000	
Current Liabilities:			
Accounts Payable	$ 69,000	$ 75,000	+ 6,000
Accrued Liabilities	24,500	20,000	− 4,500
Total Current Liabilities	$ 93,500	$ 95,000	
Working Capital	$256,000	$220,000	
Increase in Working Capital.			$36,000

STEP 2: Set up three T-accounts for analysis and additional T-accounts for each non-working-capital asset, liability, and stockholders' equity account on the balance sheet.

Analysis T-accounts are labeled Change in Working Capital, Working Capital from Operations, and Financing and Investing Activities Not Affecting Working Capital. When the analysis is finished these three T-accounts will contain all of the information we need to complete the statement of changes.

Additional T-accounts are set up for each non-working-capital account to make our analysis easier. These T-accounts are illustrated following the explanation of Step 3.

STEP 3: Determine the change (increase or decrease) in each non-working-capital account balance. Enter these changes in each non-working-capital T-ac-

EXHIBIT 17-1

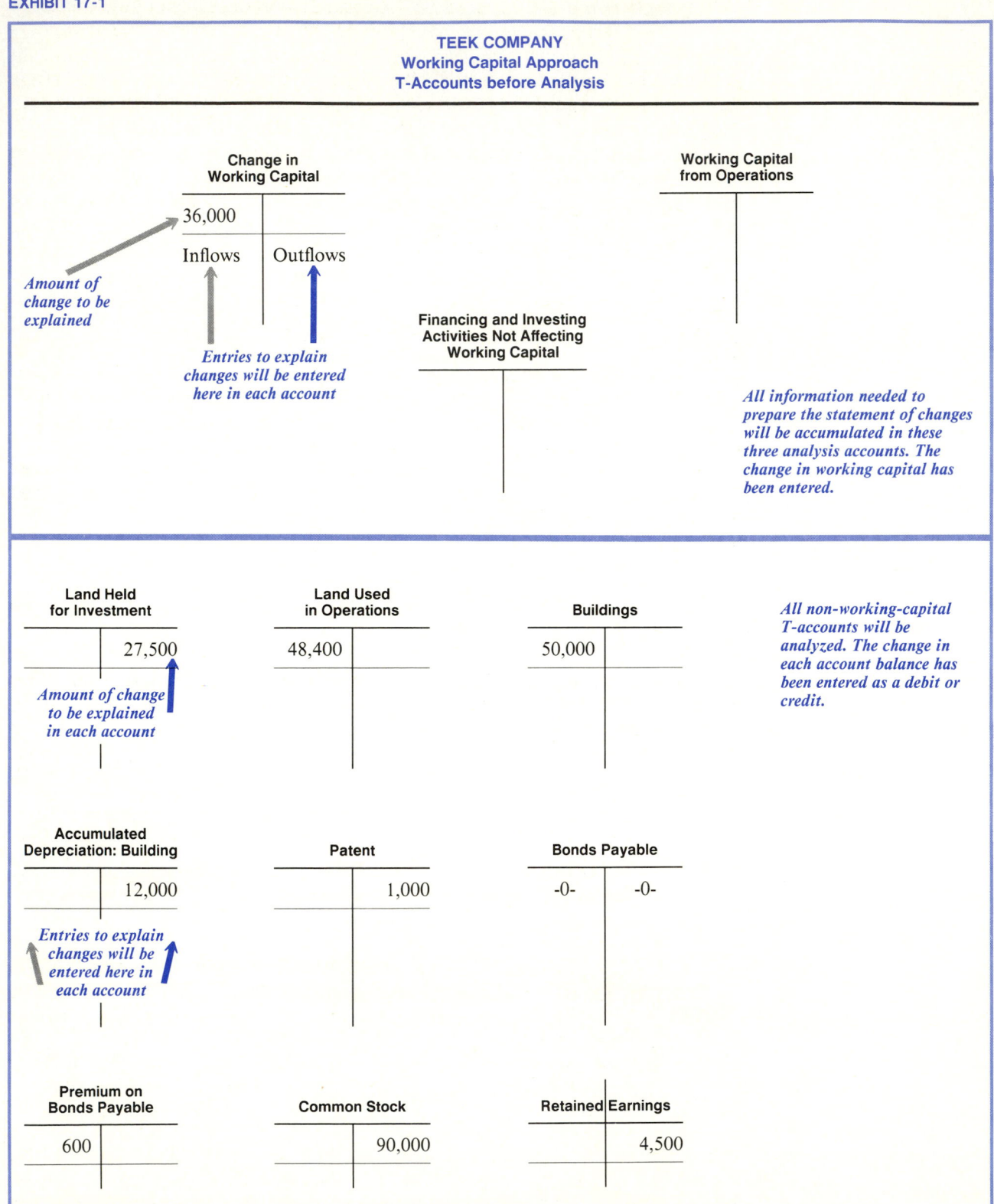

TEEK COMPANY
Working Capital Approach
T-Accounts before Analysis

Change in Working Capital

36,000

Amount of change to be explained

Inflows | Outflows

Entries to explain changes will be entered here in each account

Financing and Investing Activities Not Affecting Working Capital

Working Capital from Operations

All information needed to prepare the statement of changes will be accumulated in these three analysis accounts. The change in working capital has been entered.

Land Held for Investment

27,500

Amount of change to be explained in each account

Land Used in Operations

48,400

Buildings

50,000

All non-working-capital T-accounts will be analyzed. The change in each account balance has been entered as a debit or credit.

Accumulated Depreciation: Building

12,000

Entries to explain changes will be entered here in each account

Patent

1,000

Bonds Payable

-0- | -0-

Premium on Bonds Payable

600

Common Stock

90,000

Retained Earnings

4,500

count. Enter the increase or decrease in working capital in the Change in Working Capital T-account. Draw a line under each change entered.

Changes in non-working-capital accounts are entered on the debit or credit side of the account as required. An increase in a noncurrent asset account balance is entered as a debit since assets are increased by debits. Decreases in noncurrent assets are shown as credits. Noncurrent liabilities, stockholders' equity, and contra assets receive credits to show increases and debits to reflect decreases.

Since working capital represents net current assets (CA − CL), an increase is shown as a debit and a decrease as a credit.

We draw a line across each T-account below the change entered. Each T-account now contains the change that will be explained by our analysis entries that follow in Step 5. No entry is made in Working Capital from Operations or in Financing and Investing Activities Not Affecting Working Capital at this point. These accounts are used for analysis only.

The T-accounts for Teek Company with the changes entered are shown in Exhibit 17-1 on the facing page. Note that these are working paper entries. They will not be included in the formal journals or ledgers of the company. The actual entries were made during the year—they have already been posted to the accounts.

Trace each of the changes entered in T-accounts back to the Teek balance sheet and the schedule of changes in working capital accounts. Do not go on to Step 4 until you understand the first three steps.

STEP 4: Total the debit changes entered and the credit changes entered. These two totals should be equal.

This step is carried out simply to verify that the correct amounts were entered on the proper side of the T-accounts.

This reconciliation for Teek follows:

Debit Changes	=	Credit Changes
36,000 + 48,400 + 50,000 + 600	=	27,500 + 12,000 + 1,000 + 90,000 + 4,500
135,000	=	135,000

STEP 5: Record entries in the T-accounts to reproduce in summary form the transactions that happened during the year.

Use a code letter to key debits and credits in each entry. Include a brief written description of the entry in each of the three analysis T-accounts—Change in Working Capital, Working Capital from Operations, and Financing and Investing Activities Not Affecting Working Capital.

We will now go through the Teek transactions and show you how to enter them in the T-accounts. Beside each transaction we have provided a short version of the T-accounts affected in the margin of the text. The complete T-accounts with all explanations are shown in Exhibit 17-2; you should be careful to examine this exhibit to see where explanations are placed and to see how the completed analysis looks.

Entry Code Letter A

Transaction

Working Capital from Operations 14,500
    Retained Earnings 14,500

Description and Analysis

Reported income was $14,500 for the period. Remember that the initial assumption is that all revenue involved inflows of working capital and that all expenses involved outflows of working capital. Since a positive net income is reported, an inflow is the initial assumption. The entry is to debit Working Capital from Operations to record the increase in working capital and to credit Retained Earnings because this account was credited when Expense and Revenue Summary was originally closed. Look at entry A in Exhibit 17-2 (page 643).

We recommend beginning your T-account analysis with the income for the period and adjustments to this amount.

Working Capital from Operations

A 14,500	

Retained Earnings

	4500
	A 14,500

Entry Code Letter B

Transaction

Working Capital from Operations 12,000
    Accumulated Depreciation: Building 12,000

Description and Analysis

Depreciation expense for the period was recorded by debiting Depreciation Expense and crediting Accumulated Depreciation. The analysis entry debits Working Capital from Operations to accomplish the objective of adding back this nonfund expense to net income. Accumulated Depreciation is credited because this was the original non-working-capital account credited. Look at entry B in Exhibit 17-2.

Working Capital from Operations

A 14,500	
B 12,000	

Accumulated Depreciation: Building

	12,000
	B 12,000

Entry Code Letter C

Transaction

Working Capital from Operations 1,000
    Patents 1,000

Description and Analysis

Patent amortization expense for the period was recorded by debiting the expense account and crediting Patents. Since this too is an expense not using working capital, it must be added back to net income by debiting Working Capital from Operations in the analysis entry. The credit in the analysis entry is to Patents since this was the original non-working-capital credit. Look at entry C in Exhibit 17-2.

Working Capital from Operations

A 14,500	
B 12,000	
C 1,000	

Patents

	1,000
	C 1,000

Entry Code Letter D

Transaction

Premium on Bonds Payable 600
    Working Capital from Operations 600

Description and Analysis

The original entry to record interest was as follows:

Interest Expense 15,400
Premium on Bonds Payable 600
    Cash 16,000

Working Capital from Operations

A 14,500	D 600
B 12,000	
C 1,000	

Premium on Bonds Payable

600	
D 600	

(continued)

The working capital outflow, cash, was $16,000, but the deduction on the income statement was only $15,400 due to the premium amortization. The analysis entry is to debit Premium on Bonds Payable to reproduce the non-working-capital part of the entry and credit Working Capital from Operations to deduct $600 from income to reflect the correct amount of working capital outflow associated with interest. Look at entry D in Exhibit 17-2.

Entry Code Letter

E

Transaction

Change in Working Capital 30,000
    Working Capital from Operations   2,500
    Land Held for Investment 27,500

Description and Analysis

The original entry to record the sale of land was as follows:

Cash 30,000
    Gain on Sale of Land   2,500
    Land Held for Investment 27,500

The total working capital inflow of $30,000 must be shown as Other Sources of Working Capital, not Working Capital from Operations. Presently, $2,500 of this amount is included on the income statement as a gain. The credit to Working Capital from Operations in the analysis entry deducts $2,500 from net income. The debit to Change in Working Capital for $30,000 shows that this amount will be reported under Other Sources. The credit to the Land Held for Investment account for $27,500 reproduces the non-working-capital part of the original entry. Look at entry E in Exhibit 17-2.

Change in Working Capital

	36,000	
E	30,000	

Working Capital from Operations

A	14,500	D		600
B	12,000	E		2,500
C	1,000			

Land Held for Investment

		27,500
	E	27,500

Entry Code Letter

F

Transaction

Change in Working Capital 40,000
    Common Stock   40,000

Description and Analysis

An examination of the journals and ledgers of Teek revealed that no-par common stock was sold for $40,000. This inflow of working capital is not from profit-directed activities, so Working Capital from Operations is unaffected. The analysis entry shows the inflow as a debit to Change in Working Capital; this will be disclosed among Other Sources of Working Capital. The credit to Common Stock takes care of the non-working-capital account involved. Look at entry F in Exhibit 17-2.

Change in Working Capital

	36,000	
E	30,000	
F	40,000	

Common Stock

		90,000
	F	40,000

Entry Code Letter

G

Transaction

Retained Earnings 10,000
    Change in Working Capital   10,000

Description and Analysis

The accounting records indicate that a cash dividend of $10,000 was declared and paid during the period. Retained Earnings is debited to reproduce the non-working-capital part of the entry. Change in Working Capital is credited to reflect the outflow of cash that will be shown under Uses of Working Capital. This transaction does not affect Working Capital from Operations because it is a distribution of income to owners, not an expense incurred in earning income. Look at entry G in Exhibit 17-2.

Change in Working Capital

		36,000		
E		30,000	G	10,000
F		40,000		

Retained Earnings

				4,500
G	10,000		A	14,500

(continued)

Entry Code Letter	Transaction			Change in Working Capital			
H	Land Used in Operations 48,400			36,000			
	Change in Working Capital	48,400		E	30,000	G	10,000
				F	40,000	H	48,400

Description and Analysis

A purchase of land for a parking area was recorded during this year. Land Used in Operations is debited to reproduce the non-working-capital part of the entry. Change in Working Capital is credited to reflect the outflow of cash. This outflow will be shown under Uses of Working Capital. Working Capital from Operations is unaffected since the purchase of land is not reflected on the income statement. Look at entry H in Exhibit 17-2.

Land Used in Operations

48,400	
H 48,400	

Entry Code Letter	Transaction		
I-1	Financing and Investing Activities Not		
	Affecting Working Capital 50,000		
	Common Stock.	50,000	
I-2	Buildings. 50,000		
	Financing and Investing Activities Not		
	Affecting Working Capital	50,000	

Financing and Investing Activities Not Affecting Working Capital

I-1	50,000	I-2	50,000

Description and Analysis

A new building was acquired in exchange for common stock having a market value of $50,000. Working capital is unaffected by this transaction, but since it is a significant activity it must be shown on the statement of changes. This is accomplished by showing the transaction as a financing and investing activity under both Financial Resources Generated and Financial Resources Used.

An entry to reproduce this transaction in the T-accounts would involve merely debiting Building and crediting Common Stock. This method would bury the entry among the non-working-capital accounts and fail to highlight the data needed for preparation of the statement of changes. An alternative procedure is to arbitrarily split the transaction into two parts: (1) issuing the stock and (2) acquiring the building. The two analysis entries above make use of Financing and Investing Activities Not Affecting Working Capital to show the inflow of non-working-capital resources from issuing common stock (entry I-1) and the outflow of non-working-capital resources in acquiring the building (entry I-2). This procedure keeps all information needed to prepare the statement of changes in the three analysis accounts. Look at entries I-1 and I-2 in Exhibit 17-2.

Common Stock

			90,000
		F	40,000
		I-1	50,000

Buildings

50,000	
I-2 50,000	

STEP 6: After all transactions have been reproduced in summary form, verify that the transactions recorded explain the change in each non-working-capital balance sheet account.

Begin the verification process by looking at the debits and credits entered in each non-working-capital balance sheet account in Step 5. If only one transaction has been entered, no further work is necessary. Where more than one transaction was entered, determine the amount of change by adding the debits and credits and ruling the account. For example, see Common Stock and Retained Earnings in Exhibit 17-2. If the amount of change agrees with the change entered at the top of the account in Step

EXHIBIT 17-2

TEEK COMPANY
Working Capital Approach
T-Accounts with Analysis Entries

Change in Working Capital

	36,000		
E Proceeds from Sale of Land	30,000	G Cash Dividend	10,000
F Proceeds from Sale of Common Stock	40,000	H Purchase of Land	48,400
Z Working Capital from Operations	24,400		
Total Debits	94,400	Total Credits	58,400
Balance: Change in Account	36,000 ✓		

Working Capital from Operations

A Net Income	14,500	D Premium on Bonds Payable Amortized	600
B Depr. Exp.	12,000		
C Patent Exp.	1,000	E Gain on Sale Land	2,500
Total Debits	27,500	Total Credits	3,100
Balance	24,400	Z To Close	24,400

Financing and Investing Activities Not Affecting Working Capital

I-1 Non W/C Resources from Issuing Stock	50,000	I-2 Non W/C Resources Used to Acquire Bldg.	50,000

Land Held for Investment

	27,500		
E	27,500		

Land Used in Operations

	48,400		
H	48,400		

Buildings

	50,000		
I-2	50,000		

Accumulated Depreciation: Building

		12,000	
		B 12,000	

Patents

	1,000		
C	1,000		

Bonds Payable

–0–		–0–	

Premium on Bonds Payable

		600	
D	600		

Common Stock

		90,000	
		F	40,000
		I-1	50,000
		Balance of Changes	90,000

Retained Earnings

			4,500
G	10,000	A	14,500
		Balance of Changes	4,500

3, place a check mark on the account. Look at non-working-capital balance sheet T-accounts in Exhibit 17-2.

If the amount of change from the transactions does not agree with the amount of change entered in Step 3, verify that the debits and credits of each entry are equal and that they have been entered on the correct side of the T-account. If the error is not discovered by this process, review the accounting records (or information given) to discover transactions not recorded in the analysis process.

STEP 7: Close Working Capital from Operations into Change in Working Capital. Verify that the amount of change in the Change in Working Capital account has been explained. Verify that the debits equal the credits in the Financing and Investing Activities Not Affecting Working Capital account.

The closing entry for Working Capital from Operations is as follows:

Change in Working Capital 24,400
      Working Capital from Operations   24,400

The balance of the Working Capital from Operations account before closing is the amount that will ultimately appear on the statement of changes as total working capital from operations.

After closing, the Change in Working Capital account includes *all* changes affecting working capital for the period.

STEP 8: Prepare the statement of changes in financial position using the information found in the Change in Working Capital, Working Capital from Operations, and Financing and Investing Activities Not Affecting Working Capital accounts.

Working Capital from Operations is the first section appearing on the statement. The Working Capital from Operations T-account contains the net income, all add-backs (shown as debits), and all deductions (shown as credits). Look at the T-accounts in Exhibit 17-2 and the finished statement in Exhibit 17-3 to see how this information is transferred and presented.

Other Sources of Working Capital is taken from the debit side of the Change in Working Capital T-account. Working Capital Used is taken from the credit side of the same account. Look at Exhibits 17-2 and 17-3 and examine this transfer and presentation.

Financing and investing activities shown as sources are taken from the debit side of Financing and Investing Activities Not Affecting Working Capital. Financing and investing activities shown as uses are taken from the credit side of the same account. Look at Exhibits 17-2 and 17-3 to see how this was accomplished.

STEP 9: Add the schedule of changes in working capital accounts from Step 1 to the part of the statement of changes prepared in Step 8.

The addition of the final information element completes the formal statement of changes in financial position shown in Exhibit 17-3. Study the format of the statement carefully.

EXHIBIT 17-3

TEEK COMPANY
Statement of Changes in Financial Position
(Working Capital Approach)
Year Ended December 31, 1987

Financial Resources Generated

Working Capital Generated:

Net Income			$ 14,500
Add: Depreciation		$12,000	
Amortization of Patent		1,000	13,000
Deduct: Amortization of Premium on Bonds Payable		$ (600)	
Gain on Sale of Land		(2,500)	(3,100)
Working Capital from Operations			$ 24,400
Other Sources of Working Capital:			
Sale of Common Stock		$40,000	
Sale of Land		30,000	70,000
Total Working Capital Generated			$ 94,400
Financing and Investing Activities Not Affecting Working Capital:			
Issued Common Stock in Exchange for Building			50,000
Total Financial Resources Generated			$144,400

Financial Resources Used

Working Capital Used:

To Pay Dividends		$10,000	
To Purchase Land		48,400	
Total Working Capital Used		$58,400	
Financing and Investing Activities Not Affecting Working Capital:			
Acquired Building in Exchange for Common Stock		50,000	
Total Financial Resources Used			108,400
Net Increase in Working Capital			$ 36,000

Schedule of Changes in Working Capital Accounts

	Balance Dec. 31, 1987	Balance Jan. 1, 1987	Effect on Working Capital
Current Assets:			
Cash	$ 50,000	$ 55,000	− $ 5,000
Accounts Receivable (net)	109,000	90,000	+ 19,000
Merchandise Inventory	175,000	153,000	+ 22,000
Prepaid Expenses	15,500	17,000	− 1,500
Total Current Assets	$349,500	$315,000	
Current Liabilities:			
Accounts Payable	$ 69,000	$ 75,000	+ 6,000
Accrued Liabilities	24,500	20,000	− 4,500
Total Current Liabilities	$ 93,500	$ 95,000	
Working Capital	$256,000	$220,000	
Increase in Working Capital			$36,000

The Nine-Step T-Account Method Summarized

The nine steps used in preparing the Teek Company statement are reproduced below without explanation. You will be asked to use these steps in solving some of the problems at the end of this chapter.

A summary of the nine-step T-account method

STEP 1: Determine the change in the working capital fund for the year.

STEP 2: Set up three T-accounts for analysis and additional T-accounts for each non-working-capital asset, liability, and stockholders' equity account on the balance sheet.

STEP 3: Determine the change (increase or decrease) in each non-working-capital account balance. Enter these changes in each non-working-capital T-account. Enter the increase or decrease in working capital in the Change in Working Capital T-account. Draw a line under each change entered.

STEP 4: Total the debit changes entered and the credit changes entered. These two totals should be equal.

STEP 5: Record entries in the T-accounts to reproduce in summary form the transactions that happened during the year.

STEP 6: After all transactions have been reproduced in summary form, verify that the transactions recorded explain the change in each non-working-capital balance sheet account.

STEP 7: Close Working Capital from Operations into Change in Working Capital. Verify that the amount of change in the Change in Working Capital account has been explained. Verify that the debits equal the credits in the Financing and Investing Activities Not Affecting Working Capital account.

STEP 8: Prepare the statement of changes in financial position using the information found in the Change in Working Capital, Working Capital from Operations, and Financing and Investing Activities Not Affecting Working Capital accounts.

STEP 9: Add the schedule of changes in working capital accounts to the part of the statement of changes prepared in Step 8.

STATEMENT OF CHANGES: CASH APPROACH

The liquid resource fund may be defined as cash

The liquid resource fund on the statement of changes may be defined as either working capital or cash. In published financial reports the majority of large businesses use a working capital fund. There is a strong trend in both large and small companies toward more widespread use of a cash liquid resource fund. In fact, the Financial Accounting Standards Board, the group that sets generally accepted accounting principles, has expressed a preference for a statement of cash flows. They may *require* this statement of cash flows in the near future.

Current generally accepted accounting principles require that no matter whether we use a working capital or cash liquid resource fund, we must still show inflows and outflows of liquid resources as well as financing and investing activities not affecting liquid resources—the all financial resources approach.

The balance sheet analysis technique may be used for a cash-basis statement

We still use the balance sheet accounts for analysis, just as we did with the working capital fund, and we will still use the all financial resources approach. Look at the balance sheet flow chart for E-Zee Company's statement of changes on a cash basis below.

All accounts other than Cash are now outside of the container. The accounts are arranged just as they are on E-Zee's balance sheet.

The flow lines for Accounts Receivable, Supplies on Hand, Accumulated Depreciation, Accounts Payable, and Accrued Salaries Payable all intersect the Retained Earnings line. All of these accounts are income statement-oriented and all involve adjusting the reported net income (included in Retained Earnings) to derive Cash from Operations. We'll discuss deriving Cash from Operations a little later.

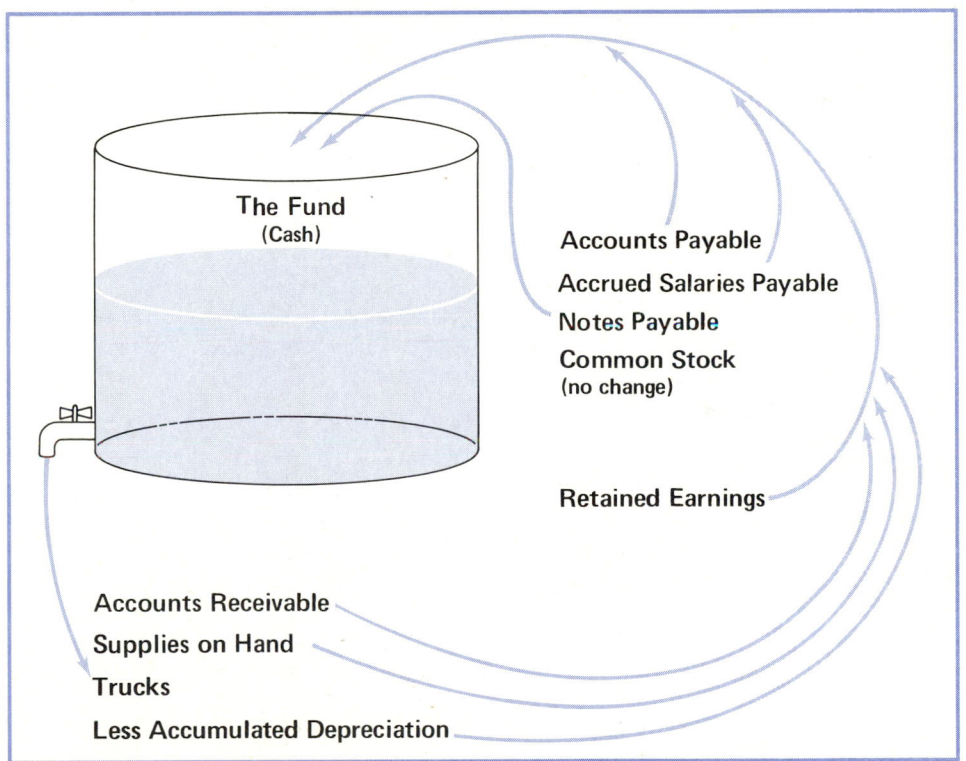

The Fund
(Cash)

Accounts Payable

Accrued Salaries Payable

Notes Payable

Common Stock
(no change)

Retained Earnings

Accounts Receivable

Supplies on Hand

Trucks

Less Accumulated Depreciation

Notes Payable and Trucks are shown in the same way as they were in the working capital statement because they each involved a receipt or payment of cash.

E-Zee had no financing and investing activities not affecting cash. Any transaction affecting two noncash accounts would be a financing and investing activity.

Now that we've taken a general view of the statement of changes—cash basis, let's look at the statement's components in more detail.

Deriving Cash from Operations

In deriving cash from operations we are switching from accrual net income to cash net income

When we calculated working capital from operations, we began with net income and added expenses not using working capital and deducted revenue not providing working capital. We must go through this same process to calculate cash from operations. Our adjustments will convert the company income from an *accrual basis* (which recognizes revenue when earned and matches expenses to derive net income) to a *cash basis* (which recognizes revenue when cash comes in and expenses when cash goes out).

The revenue realization and matching principles so important to accrual-basis income measurement are ignored in preparing a cash-basis income statement. Since generally accepted accounting principles require income statements for external use to be prepared on the accrual basis, cash from operations is normally derived by adjusting accrual-basis net income as follows:

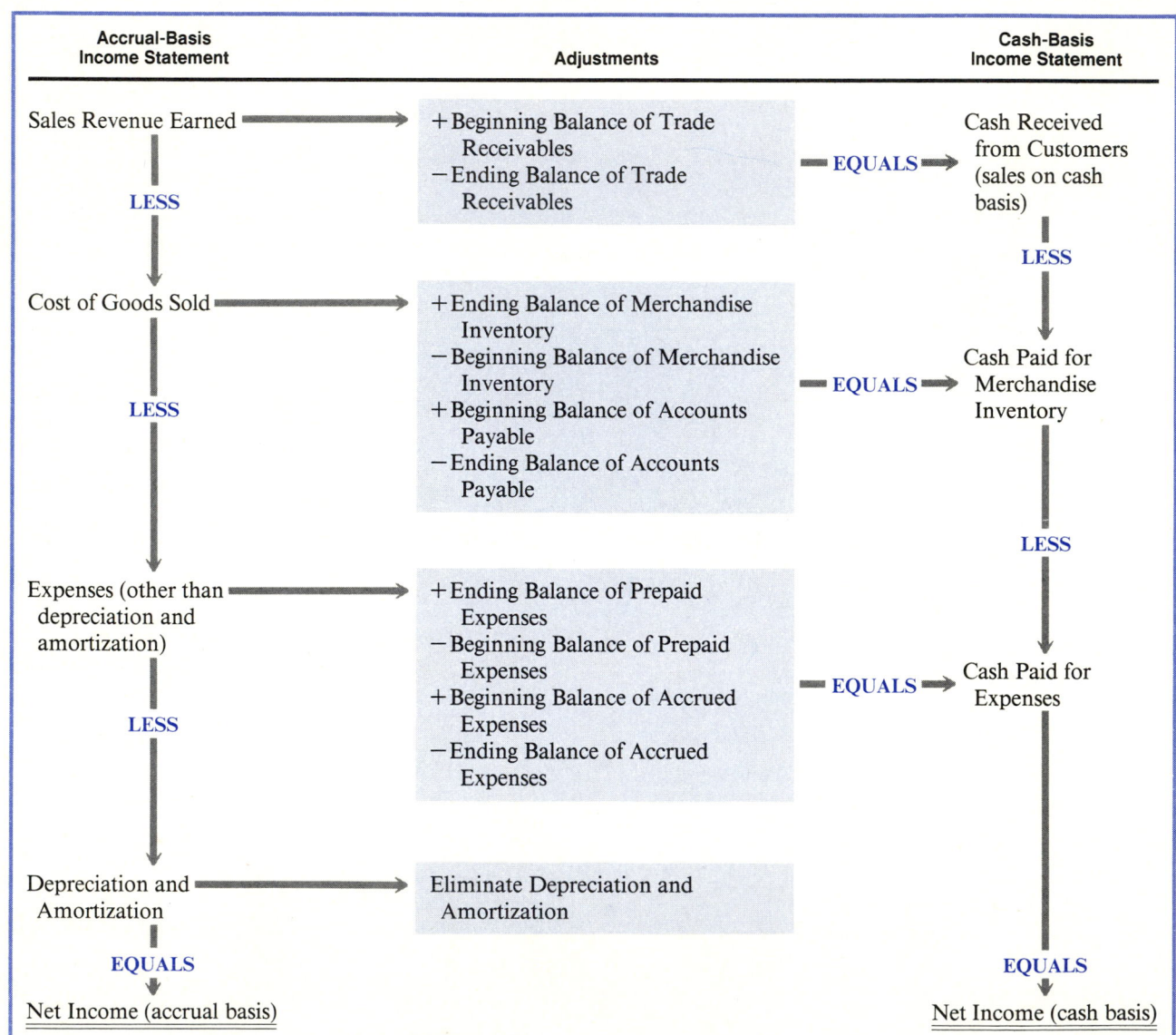

Remember as you look at the logic underlying each of these adjustments that we are interested in calculating cash inflows and cash outflows from income-oriented activities.

Cash Received from Customers

To accrual-basis Sales we add the beginning balance of Accounts Receivable. This will include cash collected on Accounts Receivable during the current year from sales that were reported on the accrual basis in prior years. From accrual-basis Sales we subtract the ending balance of Accounts Receivable. This will exclude credit sales on the current income statement that have not yet been collected.

Cash Paid for Merchandise Inventory

First we calculate net purchases by adding the ending balance of Merchandise Inventory to Cost of Goods Sold and deducting the beginning balance from Cost of Goods Sold.

Now that we know how much merchandise was purchased this year, we must calculate how much was actually paid for. This is accomplished by adding the beginning balance of Accounts Payable—we're assuming that purchases made last year were paid for this year. The process is completed by deducting the ending balance of Accounts Payable—we're removing an amount that is included in purchases this year that won't be paid for until next year.

Cash Paid for Expenses

We must analyze two types of balance sheet accounts in calculating this amount—prepaid expenses (Prepaid Rent, Prepaid Insurance, etc.) and accrued expenses (Salaries Payable, Utilities Payable, etc.).

To accrual income statement expenses we add the ending balance of prepaid expenses—the cash has been paid out this year but the expense won't be reported on the accrual basis until next year. From accrual income statement expenses we deduct the beginning balance of prepaid expenses—we're removing expenses that were included this year but paid for last year.

The beginning balance of accrued expenses is added because we're assuming we paid for these expenses this year even though they were reported on the accrual-basis income statement last year. We deduct the ending balance of accrued expenses—these expenses are on this year's income statement, but they won't be paid until next year.

Depreciation and Amortization

These expenses don't use any cash or any other current asset. We eliminate them in calculating cash from operations just as we did when we were deriving working capital from operations.

Cash from Operations—A Shortcut

We can derive cash from operations a little more quickly by using the following shortcut calculation:

Cash from operations may be derived also by adjusting accrual net income

Accrual-Basis Net Income

Deduct Increase in Accounts Receivable (or *Add* Decrease in Accounts Receivable)

Deduct Increase in Merchandise Inventory (or *Add* Decrease in Merchandise Inventory)

Add Increase in Accounts Payable (or *Deduct* Decrease in Accounts Payable)

Deduct Increase in Prepaid Expenses (or *Add* Decrease in Prepaid Expenses)

Add Increase in Accrued Expenses (or *Deduct* Decrease in Accrued Expenses)

Add Depreciation and Amortization Expenses for the Year

Cash-Basis Net Income

This calculation accomplishes the same thing that we did on page 648. Now we're beginning with net income and adjusting it instead of adjusting each revenue and expense account on the income statement.

Cash from operations on the statement of changes uses this shortcut format.

Other Sources and Uses of Cash

Sources and uses of cash unrelated to income-oriented activities of the company are determined by analyzing the remaining balance sheet accounts—just as Other Sources and Uses of Working Capital were derived earlier. Typical nonoperating sources of cash include selling additional shares of stock, borrowing cash (notes, bonds, etc.), and selling property, plant, and equipment assets or long-term investments. Typical nonoperating uses of cash include paying off short-term or long-term debt, buying treasury stock, and buying property, plant, and equipment assets or long-term investments.

Financing and Investing Activities Not Affecting Cash

Just as we included non-working-capital financial and investing activities, we must also include noncash financing and investing activities. A transaction that is unrelated to income-oriented activities of the company that involves two noncash accounts is a financing and investing activity. Examples include:

Buying a machine and giving a short-term (or long-term) note

Issuing common stock for a building

Trading marketable securities (short-term investments) for a patent

Preparing the Statement of Changes: Cash Basis

The nine-step T-account approach may be used also for the cash basis

The mechanics of preparing the cash-based statement of changes are almost identical to those used for the working capital-based statement. Use the first eight steps of the nine-step process we discussed earlier. Merely substitute the word *cash* for the words *working capital* wherever they appear in the steps. For example, Step 2 would read, "Set up three T-accounts for analysis and additional T-accounts for each noncash asset, liability, and owners' equity account on the balance sheet."

We omit Step 9, involving the schedule of changes in fund accounts, because we have only one liquid fund account—Cash. Our whole statement is devoted to explaining the change in this account; any further schedule would be redundant.

Teek Company: Cash Basis

The Teek illustration is repeated using a cash-basis statement

The Teek Company cash-basis working papers and statement of changes in financial position are shown on pages 651–653. Explanations are provided only for selected entries that are different from the earlier case. Refer back to the Teek financial statements, look at the T-account working papers in Exhibit 17-4, and trace the eight steps through to the statement of changes shown in Exhibit 17-5.

Observations on the Cash-Based Statement

The cash *used* by operations is presented under the general heading Financial Resources *Generated* because generally accepted accounting principles require that this information appear first, whether its amount is positive or negative.

The general format of the cash-based statement is the same as the general format of the statement prepared on a working capital basis. There is no schedule of changes in fund accounts since the only account in the fund is Cash and the entire statement is devoted to showing the reasons for the change in Cash.

EXHIBIT 17-4

TEEK COMPANY
Cash Approach
T-Accounts with Analysis Entries

Change in Cash

			5,000
(10) Cash from Sale of Land	30,000	(12) Cash Dividend Declared and Paid	10,000
(11) Cash from Sale of Common Stock	40,000	(13) Cash Used to Purchase Land	48,400
		(15) Cash Used by Operations	16,600
Total Debits	70,000	Total Credits	75,000
		Net Decrease in Cash	5,000

Cash from Operations

(1) Net Income	14,500	(2) Increase in Accounts Receivable Balance	19,000
(5) Decrease in Prepaid Expenses	1,500	(3) Increase in Merchandise Inventory	22,000
(6) Increase in Accrued Liabilities	4,500	(4) Decrease in Accounts Payable	6,000
(7) Depreciation Expense	12,000	(9) Premium on Bonds Payable Amortized	600
(8) Patent Amortization Expense	1,000	(10) Gain on Sale Land	2,500
Total Debits	33,500	Total Credits	50,100
(15) To Close	16,600	Cash Used by Operations	16,600

Financing and Investing Activities Not Affecting Cash

(14-A) Noncash Resource from Issuing Common Stock	50,000	(14-B) Noncash Resource Used to Acquire New Building	50,000

Accounts Receivable		Merchandise Inventory		Prepaid Expenses		Land Held for Investment	
19,000		22,000			1,500		27,500
(2) 19,000		(3) 22,000		(5) 1,500		(10) 27,500	

(continued)

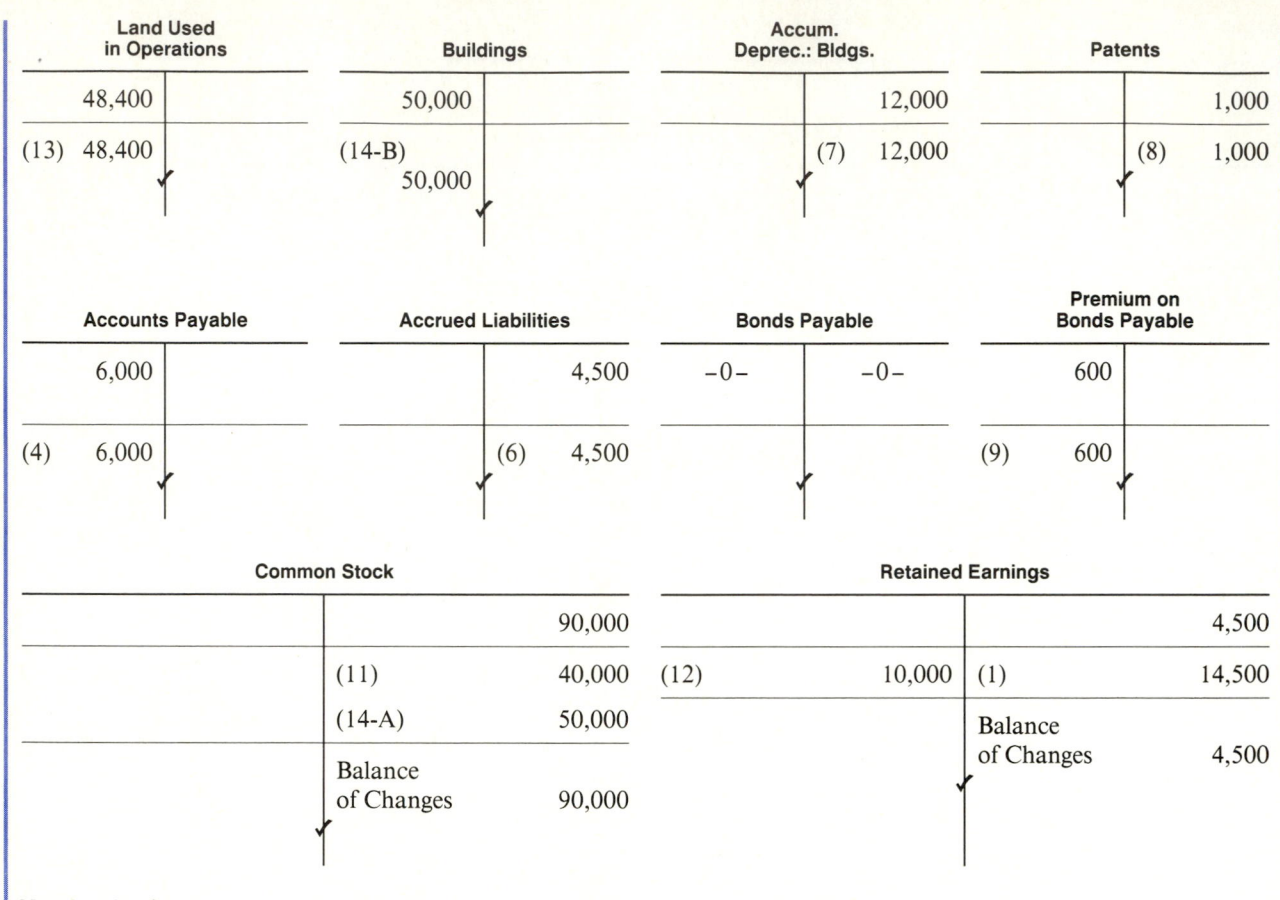

Land Used in Operations		Buildings		Accum. Deprec.: Bldgs.		Patents	
48,400		50,000			12,000		1,000
(13) 48,400		(14-B) 50,000			(7) 12,000		(8) 1,000

Accounts Payable		Accrued Liabilities		Bonds Payable		Premium on Bonds Payable	
6,000			4,500	–0–	–0–		600
(4) 6,000			(6) 4,500				(9) 600

Common Stock		Retained Earnings	
	90,000		4,500
	(11) 40,000	(12) 10,000	(1) 14,500
	(14-A) 50,000	Balance of Changes	4,500
Balance of Changes	90,000		

Note: Numbers in parentheses are worksheet transaction numbers. See the exhibit below.

TEEK COMPANY
Cash Approach Explanation of Selected Worksheet Transactions

Worksheet Transaction Number	Analysis
1	This entry is the same as entry A under the working capital approach. We recommend that you begin with reported net income and then enter adjustments.
2	An increase in Accounts Receivable indicates that more revenue was recorded than the amount of cash received. The increase must be deducted from net income in arriving at Cash from Operations.
3	An increase in Merchandise Inventory indicates that more inventory was purchased this period than was sold. Income must be reduced by the cash paid out in excess of the expense that has been recognized.
4	A decrease in Accounts Payable indicates that cash was paid out this period for purchases made in a prior period. Income must be reduced by this additional cash pay-out that does not appear on the income statement.

(continued)

5   A decrease in Prepaid Expenses means that some expenses on this period's income statement were paid for last period. They are noncash outflows for the current period. The decrease, then, must be added to current net income just as any other noncash expense would be.

6   An increase in Accrued Liabilities means that some accrued expenses on this period's income statement will be paid for in future periods. These expenses that did not require a current use of cash must be added to accrual-basis income.

7–14   These entries are exactly the same as under the working capital approach. The same underlying logic also applies.

15   Cash from Operations is closed into the Change in Cash account. In Teek's case, operations absorbed more cash than they provided, resulting in Net Cash *Used* by Operations rather than Cash Provided by Operations.

EXHIBIT 17-5

TEEK COMPANY
Statement of Changes in Financial Position (cash approach)
Year Ended December 31, 1987

Financial Resources Generated

Cash Generated:

Net Income.		$ 14,500
Add: Decrease in Prepaid Expenses	$ 1,500	
Increase in Accrued Liabilities	4,500	
Depreciation Expense.	12,000	
Amortization of Patent.	1,000	19,000
Deduct: Increase in Accounts Receivable.	$19,000	
Increase in Merchandise Inventory	22,000	
Decrease in Accounts Payable	6,000	
Amortization of Premium on Bonds Payable	600	
Gain on Sale of Land.	2,500	(50,100)
Cash Used by Operations		$ (16,600)
Other Sources of Cash:		
Cash from Sale of Land	$30,000	
Cash from Sale of Common Stock	40,000	70,000
Total Cash Generated		$ 53,400
Financing and Investing Activities Not Affecting Cash:		
Issued Common Stock in Exchange for Building		50,000
Total Financial Resources Generated.		$ 103,400

Financial Resources Used

Cash Used:

To Pay Dividends.	$10,000	
To Purchase Land	48,400	
Total Cash Used.	$58,400	
Financing and Investing Activities Not Affecting Cash:		
Acquired Building in Exchange for Common Stock	50,000	
Total Financial Resources Used		(108,400)
Net Decrease in Cash during the Year		$ (5,000)

EXHIBIT 17-6

<table>
<tr><td colspan="2" align="center">**MODEL COMPANY**
Statement of Changes in Financial Position
Year Ended December 31, 1987</td></tr>
</table>

Financial Resources Generated

Working Capital Generated:

Net Income		$21
+Adjustments Requiring Addition	$16	
−Adjustments Requiring Deduction	(5)	11
Working Capital from Operations		$32

Working capital from operations

Other Sources of Working Capital:

Source Described	$23	
Source Described	13	36
Total Working Capital Generated		$68

Other inflows of working capital

Financing and Investing Activities Not Affecting Working Capital:

F & I Activities Described	15

Financing and investing activities (sources)

Total Financial Resources Generated	$83

Financial Resources Used

Working Capital Used:

Use Described	$44	
Use Described	22	
Total Working Capital Used		$66

Outflows of working capital

Financing and Investing Activities Not Affecting Working Capital:

F & I Activity Described	15

Financing and investing activities (uses)

Total Financial Resources Used	$81
Increase (Decrease) in Working Capital	$ 2

Schedule of Changes in Working Capital Accounts

	Ending Balance	Beginning Balance	Increase (Decrease) in Fund
Current Assets:			
Current Asset	$25	$20	$ 5
Current Asset	8	10	(2)
Total Current Assets	$33	$30	
Current Liabilities:			
Current Liability	$18	$14	(4)
Current Liability	9	12	3
Total Current Liabilities	$27	$26	
Working Capital	$ 6	$ 4	
Increase (Decrease) in Working Capital			$ 2

Schedule of changes in fund accounts

THE STATEMENT FORMAT — A REVIEW

You should have the general format of the statement of changes and the disclosure of the basic informational elements clearly in mind. Review carefully the statement in Exhibit 17-6 before beginning the exercises and problems at the end of the chapter. Informational elements have been highlighted for you.

CHAPTER SUMMARY

The statement of changes in financial position is the fourth major financial statement that must be published for external users. The statement content provides information about the flows of liquid resources, financing and investing activities not affecting liquid resources, and details of changes in the liquid resource accounts. The *liquid resource fund* is defined as either working capital or cash.

The statement of changes must begin with a calculation of *funds provided by operations.* This amount is usually derived by beginning with accrual-basis net income and adding back items that did not use funds and deducting items that did not provide funds.

The *other sources and uses of funds* sections of the statement describe nonoperating inflows and outflows of liquid resources. Borrowing on long-term obligations, issuing capital stock, sale of noncurrent assets, repayment of noncurrent obligations, and purchase of noncurrent assets are examples of common items that would be shown as other sources and uses.

The *all financial resources approach* to the statement stipulates that flows of liquid resources should be supplemented by disclosure of *significant financing and investing activities that do not affect the liquid resource fund.* Acquiring noncurrent assets in exchange for capital stock, retiring noncurrent obligations by giving a noncurrent asset, and issuing new capital stock upon conversion of noncurrent debt are illustrations of financing and investing activities not affecting liquid resources.

Changes in the balances of individual fund accounts must be shown if the fund is defined as working capital. This schedule is not necessary when the fund is defined as cash because the entire statement is devoted to explaining the change in cash.

A nine-step T-account approach is useful in developing working papers needed to analyze the financial records when preparing a statement of changes. This approach uses three major analysis accounts that will contain all the information needed in the preparation of the final statement. Entries are recorded in the T-accounts to reproduce, in summary form, the transactions that took place during the period. Whenever working capital is involved in a transaction, one of the analysis accounts is debited or credited in place of the actual current asset or liability involved. The T-account approach is an orderly, efficient way of handling a large number of transactions in a complex situation.

The format of the statement of changes using a cash fund is substantially the same as one using a working capital approach. The two differences lie in the income adjustments needed, discussed below, and in the omission of the schedule of changes in individual fund accounts mentioned above.

The cash approach to the statement of changes requires the conversion of reported accrual-basis net income into cash flow from operations. This conversion is accomplished by adding or deducting revenue and expenses that did not provide or use cash during the period. Changes in current asset and current liability accounts usually indicate that an adjustment is necessary. An analysis of each of these accounts is made to determine whether an addition or deduction is appropriate and why.

**IMPORTANT TERMS
USED IN THIS CHAPTER**

Accrual-basis income   A measure of income that recognizes revenue as it is earned and matches expenses incurred in earning the revenue reported. (page 647)

All financial resources approach   The statement of changes in financial position that includes financing and investing activities not affecting funds as well as the flow of funds and changes in individual fund accounts. (page 634)

Cash-basis income   A measure of income that recognizes revenue when cash is received and reports expenses when cash is paid out. (page 648)

Financing and investing activities not affecting funds   A transaction that involves only nonfund accounts. (page 633)

Fund   See *liquid resource fund.*

Liquid resource fund   The asset or group of net assets that management may use to meet the operating needs of the business. For purposes of the statement of changes in financial position the liquid resource fund is usually defined as cash or working capital. (page 625)

Nonfund account   A balance sheet account that is not part of the liquid resources being analyzed. If the fund is defined as working capital, all noncurrent assets, noncurrent liability, and stockholders' equity accounts are nonfund accounts. If the fund is defined as cash, all noncash accounts are nonfund accounts. (page 628)

Working capital   Current assets minus current liabilities. A measure of the liquid resources at management's disposal. (page 625)

QUESTIONS

1. Why is the statement of changes in financial position needed when a company already issues a balance sheet, income statement, and statement of retained earnings?

2. In what two ways is the *liquid resource fund* most often defined?

3. Define *working capital* and list at least eight working capital accounts that you have encountered in previous chapters.

4. What three basic informational elements must appear on the statement of changes in financial position?

5. When using a working capital approach to the statement of changes, net income must be adjusted to derive working capital from operations. Why is this adjustment of net income necessary?

6. Why is it logical to analyze balance sheet accounts when preparing to construct a statement of changes in financial position?

7. What is the *all financial resources approach* to the statement of changes in financial position?

8. In the nine-step T-account approach to preparing the statement of changes in financial position, what are the three analysis T-accounts? What is the purpose of each?

9. Where will "other sources of working capital" appear in the analysis T-accounts? (Which T-account, and on which side?) List at least two examples of "other sources of working capital."

10. Where will "uses of working capital" appear in the analysis T-accounts? (Which T-account, and on which side?) List at least two examples of "uses of working capital."

11. In calculating working capital from operations, depreciation expense is added back to net income and amortization of premium on bonds payable is deducted from net income. Where are each of these pieces of information found in the analysis T-accounts? (Which T-account, and on which side?)

12. Why is it necessary in the T-account analysis to split a financing and investing activity not affecting working capital into two parts and analyze it as if it were two transactions?

13. How are financing and investing activities not affecting working capital shown on the statement of changes in financial position?

14. How does calculation of cash-basis income differ from the calculation of accrual-basis income?

15. On December 30, Deal Corp. purchased a desk-top computer, giving a 60-day note for the full purchase price. How is the acquisition shown on the statement of changes if a working capital fund is used? How is the acquisition shown when a cash fund is used?

EXERCISES

Exercises marked with an asterisk * relate to statements of changes with a cash liquid resource fund.

Exercise 17-1
Determining effect on working capital

Rusko, Inc., has current assets of $400,000 and current liabilities of $175,000. Calculate Rusko's working capital. Explain what effect each of the following changes in account balances would have on working capital. Indicate the amount of increase or decrease or state that no change will occur. Each item is to be considered independently.

Example: Cash increases by $16,000.
Effect: Working capital increases by $16,000.

a. Supplies Inventory decreases by $5,690.
b. Accounts Payable decreases by $3,200.
c. Accounts Receivable increases by $24,400.
d. Prepaid Insurance decreases by $1,800.
e. Merchandise Inventory increases by $15,500.
f. Income Taxes Payable increases by $6,100.
g. Allowance for Uncollectibles decreases by $2,800.

(Check figure: Working capital = $225,000)

Exercise 17-2
Calculating working capital

The following accounts were taken from the general ledger of Cruz Corp. Each account has a normal balance.

Cash	$ 60,000
Accounts Payable	136,000
Supplies Inventory	1,150
Land	100,000
Accounts Receivable (net)	79,000
Buildings	265,000
Notes Payable (due in 6 months)	25,000
Merchandise Inventory	210,000
Accumulated Depreciation: Buildings	105,000
Bonds Payable (due in 10 years)	300,000

Calculate Cruz's working capital.

(Check figure: Working capital = $189,150)

Exercise 17-3

Preparing a schedule of changes in working capital accounts

Comparative unclassified balance sheets for Craft Marine are shown below:

CRAFT MARINE
Comparative Balance Sheets (unclassified)
September 30

	1987	1986
Cash	$180,000	$150,000
Marketable Securities (temporary)	68,000	60,000
Accounts Receivable (net)	15,600	21,000
Merchandise Inventory	16,400	17,000
Supplies Inventory	4,200	3,000
Land	100,000	100,000
Buildings	360,000	360,000
Accumulated Depreciation: Buildings	(42,800)	(40,000)
Equipment	204,000	196,000
Accumulated Depreciation: Equipment	(24,000)	(12,000)
Total Assets	$881,400	$855,000
Accounts Payable	$ 62,800	$ 59,000
Notes Payable (due in 6 months)	4,000	10,000
Accrued Wages Payable	9,200	3,500
Accrued Rent Payable	800	500
Interest Payable	—	20,000
Bonds Payable	300,000	300,000
Common Stock	400,000	400,000
Retained Earnings	104,600	62,000
Total Equities	$881,400	$855,000

Prepare a schedule of changes in working capital accounts for the year ended September 30, 1987.

(Check figure: Increase in working capital = $49,400)

Exercise 17-4

Re-creating entries and determining effect on working capital

The following transactions are among those entered into by Champion, Inc., during 1988. Re-create the entry that Champion should have made and determine the effect of the entry on working capital.

Example: Champion borrowed $10,000 from the bank on a long-term note.

Entry: Cash 10,000
                 Notes Payable   10,000

Effect: Working capital increased by $10,000.

a. 100 shares of Texas-T Oil, Inc., was purchased for $21,000 as a long-term investment.

b. An account receivable in the amount of $1,080 was collected.

c. A building was purchased for $170,000. $10,000 cash was paid and a 90-day note was given for the balance.

d. A parcel of land having an original cost of $10,000 was sold for $17,000

e. A customer's account with a $400 balance was written off as uncollectible (the allowance method is used).

f. Champion issued 1,000 shares of $2 par common stock for $2,460.

(Check figure: Two of the transactions did not affect working capital)

Exercise 17-5
Calculating working capital provided by operations

The 1987 income statement of Gull Paper Co. appears below:

GULL PAPER CO.		
Income Statement		
Year Ended December 31, 1987		
Sales.		$240,000
Cost of Goods Sold		90,000
Gross Profit on Sales		$150,000
Operating Expenses:		
Advertising Expense	$14,000	
Depreciation Expense	36,000	
Patent Amortization Expense	5,000	
Salary Expense.	56,000	111,000
Net Income		$ 39,000

Calculate the working capital provided by operations for 1987. (Begin with net income and add back expenses not using working capital.)

(Check figure: Working capital provided by operations = $80,000)

Exercise 17-6
Stating where effect of transactions would appear on statement of changes

Each of the following transactions will result in an Other Source of Working Capital, a Use of Working Capital, or a Financing and Investing Activity Not Affecting Working Capital. Analyze each transaction and state which one of these three categories on the statement of changes will be affected.

a. $400,000 was borrowed by issuing bonds that mature in 20 years.

b. A dump truck with a book value of $3,500 was traded for stationery and other office supplies.

c. A $39,400 cash dividend was declared and paid.

d. A machine was acquired by issuing a 60-day note for the $8,000 purchase price.

e. Land was acquired by exchanging 10,000 shares of common stock for the property. The stock had a market price of $98,000.

f. A patent was sold for $12,500. A 30-day note was accepted for the total amount. (The book value of the patent was also $12,500.)

g. Equipment was purchased for $105,000.

h. Used machinery having a book value of $12,800 was traded for 100 shares of stock in another corporation. The stock acquired is to be held for an extended period.

i. An individual to whom the corporation owed $5,000 on a long-term note accepted a used copying machine in full payment of the debt.

j. 500 shares of common stock were sold on subscription. The subscription payments were due on the first day of each of the 3 months following the subscription sale. The subscription price totaled $75,000.

Exercise 17-7
Preparing working capital from operations section of statement of changes

Turbo Products, Inc., uses the T-account approach to preparing the working papers for the statement of changes in financial position. The following T-account was used to gather information about the working capital generated by operations:

Working Capital from Operations			
(3) Depreciation Expense	50,000	(1) Net Loss for the Year	24,600
(4) Patent Amortization Expense	6,000	(2) Gain on Sale of Land	8,400
(6) Loss on Sale of Equipment	14,600	(6) Amortization of Premium on Bond Payable	19,000

Prepare the Working Capital from Operations portion of the statement of changes in financial position.

(Check figure: Working capital provided by operations = $18,600)

Exercise 17-8*
Converting items from accrual basis to cash basis

Hobbs, Inc., is attempting to convert its accrual-basis income into cash-basis income. For each of the following situations, perform the required conversion:

a. Sales on the accrual-basis income statement amounted to $172,500. Accounts Receivable at the beginning and end of the year totaled $97,500 and $115,000, respectively. Determine cash collected from customers on the cash-basis income statement.

b. Advertising Expense on the accrual-basis income statement was $20,750. Prepaid Advertising increased from $7,000 at the beginning of the year to $8,000 at the end of the year. Determine the cash paid for advertising on the cash-basis income statement.

c. Salary Expense on the accrual-basis income statement was $27,900. Accrued Salaries Payable at the beginning and end of the year amounted to $780 and $1,180, respectively. Determine the cash paid for salaries on the cash-basis income statement.

d. Depreciation Expense on the accrual-basis income statement was $12,500. Accumulated Depreciation increased from $62,500 at the beginning of the year to $75,000 at the end. Calculate the Depreciation Expense on the cash-basis income statement.

(Check figure: Cash collected from customers = $155,000)

PROBLEMS
Set A

Problem A17-1
Calculating working capital from operations for three companies

Note: Problems marked with an asterisk * relate to statements of changes with a cash liquid resource fund.

In each of the three columns below are income statement data for the year ended December 31, 1987:

	Company X	Company Y	Company Z
Sales Revenue	$200,000	$125,000	$60,000
Cost of Goods Sold Expense	80,000	75,000	20,000
Patent Amortization Expense	3,000	6,000	—
Depreciation Expense: Machinery	9,000	10,000	1,750
Organization Cost Amortization Expense	750	—	250
Depreciation Expense: Building.	16,500	9,500	4,200
Income Tax Expense.	26,250	—	12,000
Salary Expense.	25,000	15,500	7,500
Utilities Expense	13,500	7,300	3,800
Gain on Sale of Machine	—	—	2,000
Loss on Sale of Land.	—	2,700	—

Required Prepare the Working Capital from Operations section of the statement of changes in financial position for Companies X, Y, and Z, respectively. (Hint: First calculate net income for each of the three.)

(Check figure: Working Capital from Operations, Company X = $55,250)

Problem A17-2
Preparing statement of changes — T-accounts not required

The 1987 financial statements of Asian Products, Inc., are shown below:

ASIAN PRODUCTS, INC.
Income Statement
Year Ended December 31, 1987
(000s omitted)

Sales.	$2,000
Cost of Goods Sold	(960)
Gross Profit on Sales	$1,040
Operating Expenses:	
Depreciation	(120)
Other.	(440)
Net Income	$ 480

ASIAN PRODUCTS, INC.
Comparative Balance Sheets
December 31,
(000s omitted)

	1987	1986
Assets:		
Current Assets (total)	$1,460	$1,280
Land.	440	416
Building	1,680	1,600
Accumulated Depreciation: Building.	(340)	(220)
Total Assets	$3,240	$3,076
Equities:		
Current Liabilities	$ 384	$ 400
Noncurrent Liabilities	40	420
Common Stock.	1,680	1,600
Retained Earnings.	1,136	656
Total Equities	$3,240	$3,076

Additional information taken from the financial records of Asian Products:
a. Land costing $24,000 was acquired for cash.
b. $380,000 of noncurrent liabilities were paid off with cash.
c. Common stock was issued in exchange for a building with a fair market value of $80,000.

Required Prepare a statement of changes in financial position in good form for the year ended December 31, 1987. You need not prepare T-account working papers. All the information needed to prepare the statement is given in the income statement, balance sheets, and additional information above. (Note: The schedule of changes in individual working capital accounts may be omitted.)

(Check figure: Working Capital from Operations = $600,000)

Problem A17-3
Preparing T-accounts and formal statement of changes

Potter Company condensed balance sheets for December 31, 1986 and 1987, and the condensed income statement for the year ended December 31, 1987, are presented below:

POTTER COMPANY
Income Statement (condensed)
Year Ended December 31, 1987

Sales		$171,000
Cost of Goods Sold Expense		70,650
Gross Profit on Sales		$100,350
Operating Expenses:		
Depreciation Expense: Building	$12,500	
Depreciation Expense: Machinery	3,750	
Patent Amortization Expense	600	
Other Selling and Administrative Expenses	24,000	40,850
Income before Tax		$ 59,500
Income Tax Expense		26,000
Net Income		$ 33,500

POTTER COMPANY
Comparative Balance Sheets (condensed)
December 31

	1987	1986
Assets:		
Current Assets (total)	$ 79,350	$ 57,500
Property, Plant, and Equipment:		
Land	$103,500	$ 73,500
Building	210,000	150,000
Less: Accumulated Depreciation	(45,000)	(32,500)
Machinery	112,500	112,500
Less: Accumulated Depreciation	(21,250)	(17,500)
Total Property, Plant, and Equipment	$359,750	$286,000
Intangible Assets:		
Patent	$ 8,400	$ 9,000
Total Assets	$447,500	$352,500
Liabilities and Stockholders' Equity:		
Current Liabilities (total)	$ 19,000	$ 22,500
Noncurrent Liabilities:		
Bonds Payable (issued at par)	50,000	75,000
Total Liabilities	$ 69,000	$ 97,500
Common Stock (no par)	$290,000	$200,000
Retained Earnings	88,500	55,000
Total Stockholders' Equity	$378,500	$255,000
Total Liabilities and Stockholders' Equity	$447,500	$352,500

In addition, the following information was compiled from the company's financial records:
a. A plot of land was purchased for $30,000 cash.
b. A new building was purchased for cash, $60,000.
c. Additional common stock was issued for $90,000 cash.
d. Bonds with a maturity value of $25,000 were retired when they matured.

Required

1. Prepare working papers to develop a statement of changes in financial position using the working capital approach. Use the nine-step T-account method.
2. Prepare a statement of changes in financial position for the year ended December 31, 1987, in good form. (Note: The schedule of changes in working capital accounts may be omitted.)

(Check figure: Working Capital from Operations = $50,350)

Problem A17-4
Preparing T-accounts and formal statement of changes

Siesta Fashions, Inc., condensed balance sheets for 1987 and 1988 and the income statement for 1988 are shown below:

SIESTA FASHIONS, INC.
Income Statement (condensed)
Year Ended December 31, 1988
(000s omitted)

Sales		$840
Cost of Goods Sold Expense		548
Gross Profit on Sales		$292
Operating Expenses:		
Selling Expenses	$152	
Administrative Expenses	64	
Depreciation Expense: Building	16	
Depreciation Expense: Machinery	10	242
Net Income		$ 50

SIESTA FASHIONS, INC.
Comparative Balance Sheets (Condensed)
December 31
(000s omitted)

	1988	1987
Assets:		
Current Assets (total)	$ 870	$ 840
Property, Plant, and Equipment:		
Land	$ 256	$ 156
Building	242	266
Less: Accumulated Depreciation	(84)	(104)
Machinery	300	140
Less: Accumulated Depreciation	(60)	(50)
Total Property, Plant, and Equipment	$ 654	$ 408
Total Assets	$1,524	$1,248

(continued)

Liabilities and Stockholders' Equity:

Current Liabilities (total)	$ 346	$ 280
Noncurrent Liabilities:		
Bonds Payable (issued at par)	200	200
Total Liabilities.	$ 546	$ 480
Preferred Stock	$ 160	$ —
Common Stock (no par)	600	600
Retained Earnings	218	168
Total Stockholders' Equity	$ 978	$ 768
Total Liabilities and Stockholders' Equity	$1,524	$1,248

In addition, the following information was compiled from the company's records:

a. A building was purchased for $40,000 cash.

b. Machinery for a new assembly line was "purchased" by giving the manufacturer preferred stock. The machinery acquired has a fair market value of $160,000.

c. A building was sold for $28,000. The building had originally cost $64,000 and had accumulated depreciation of $36,000.

d. Land was purchased for $100,000.

Required

1. Prepare working papers to develop a statement of changes in financial position using the working capital approach. Use the nine-step T-account method.

2. Prepare a statement of changes in financial position for the year ended December 31, 1988, in good form. (Note: The schedule of changes in working capital accounts may be omitted.)

(Check figure: Total financial resources generated = $264,000)

Problem A17-5

Preparing formal statement of changes when given three analysis T-accounts

You have just been hired to replace a staff accountant of Carriage, Inc. The staff accountant quit suddenly, and you have been left to finish the statement of changes for the current year. After searching through the papers on the desk, you find a working paper with the following T-accounts:

Change in Working Capital			
			23,000
(E) Proceeds from Issuing		(G) Purchase of Land	123,500
Common Stock	51,850		
(D) Proceeds from Selling			
Building	31,000		
(Z) Working Capital from			
Operations	17,650		
Total Debits	100,500	Total Credits	123,500
		Balance	23,000

(continued)

Working Capital from Operations

(A) Net Income	8,750	(D) Gain on Sale of	
(B) Patent		Building	1,350
Amortization			
Expense	2,250		
(C) Depreciation			
Expense	8,000		
Total Debits	19,000	Total Credits	1,350
W/C from Operations	17,650	(Z) To Close	17,650

Financing and Investing Activities
Not Affecting Working Capital

(F-1) Issued Bonds for		(F-2) Building Acquired	
Building	150,000	by Issuing Bonds	150,000

Required   Using the information found in the three accounts above, prepare a statement of changes for the year ended December 31, 1987, in good form. You may omit the schedule of changes in working capital accounts.

Problem A17-6
Preparing T-accounts and
formal statement of changes

Lott Salt Co. financial statements for 1987 appear below:

LOTT SALT CO.
Income Statement
Year Ended September 30, 1987
(000s omitted)

Sales		$11,892
Cost of Goods Sold.		(8,466)
Gross Profit on Sales.		$ 3,426
Operating Expenses:		
Depreciation Expense: Building	$ (130)	
Depreciation Expense: Equipment.	(46)	
Other Operating Expenses	(2,480)	(2,656)
Income from Primary Operations		$ 770
Other Income and Expense:		
Interest Expense	$ (58)	
Gain on Sale of Building	32	(26)
Income before Tax		$ 744
Income Taxes		(230)
Net Income.		$ 514

LOTT SALT CO.
Statement of Retained Earnings
For Year Ended September 30, 1987
(000s omitted)

Retained Earnings Balance (10/1/86).	$1,024
Add: Net Income for the Year	514
Total	$1,538
Deduct: Dividends Declared and Paid	(194)
Retained Earnings (9/30/87)	$1,344

LOTT SALT CO.
Comparative Balance Sheets
September 30
(000s omitted)

	1987	1986	Increase (Decrease) in Account Balance
Assets:			
Current Assets:			
Cash	$ 676	$ 608	+$ 68
Accounts Receivable (net)	1,280	854	+ 426
Merchandise Inventory	888	1,034	− 146
Total Current Assets.	$ 2,844	$ 2,496	
Property, Plant, and Equipment:			
Land	$ 1,110	$ 860	+ 250
Buildings	2,102	2,050	+ 52
Less: Accumulated Depreciation	(1,010)	(1,032)	− 22
Equipment	1,460	1,460	—
Less: Accumulated Depreciation	(636)	(590)	+ 46
Total Property, Plant, and Equipment	$ 3,026	$ 2,748	
Total Assets.	$ 5,870	$ 5,244	
Liabilities and Stockholders' Equity:			
Current Liabilities:			
Accounts Payable	$ 736	$ 900	−$164
Notes Payable	200	280	− 80
Accrued Payables	132	120	+ 12
Total Current Liabilities	$ 1,068	$ 1,300	
Noncurrent Liabilities:			
Notes Payable (due 6/30/95).	$ 280	—	+ 280
Bonds Payable (due 12/31/99).	600	$ 600	—
Discount on Bonds Payable	(72)	(80)	− 8
Total Noncurrent Liabilities.	$ 808	$ 520	
Total Liabilities	$ 1,876	$ 1,820	
Stockholders' Equity:			
Common Stock (no par)	$ 2,650	$ 2,400	+ 250
Retained Earnings	1,344	1,024	+ 320
Total Stockholders' Equity	$ 3,994	$ 3,424	
Total Liabilities and Stockholders' Equity	$ 5,870	$ 5,244	

An analysis of Lott's financial records revealed the following information:

a. A building costing $248,000 and having an accumulated depreciation of $152,000 was sold for $128,000. The $32,000 gain appears on the income statement.

b. Common stock was issued in exchange for 10 acres of land. The common stock and the land were fairly valued at $250,000.

c. The entry to record interest expense on the bonds was as follows:

Interest Expense 58,000		
Cash.	50,000	
Discount on Bonds Payable.	8,000	

(Fewer liquid resources were used than are reflected in the Interest Expense account.)

d. $280,000 was borrowed from the bank; a note due in 1995 was signed.

e. An addition to the warehouse costing $300,000 was constructed for cash.

f. $194,000 in dividends were declared and paid.

Required

1. Prepare working papers to develop a statement of changes in financial position using a working capital fund. Use the nine-step T-account method.

2. Prepare a statement of changes in financial position for the year ended September 30, 1987, in good form.

(Check figures: Increase in working capital = $580,000
Working capital from operations = $666,000
Total financial resources generated = $1,324,000)

Problem A17-7*
Calculating cash-basis net income

Hamilton Concrete, Inc.'s 1987 income statement and comparative balance sheets for 1986 and 1987 appear below:

HAMILTON CONCRETE, INC.
Comparative Balance Sheets
June 30

	1987	1986
Assets:		
Cash	$ 60,000	$ 40,000
Accounts Receivable (net).	120,000	160,000
Merchandise Inventory	160,000	70,000
Noncurrent Assets (net)	300,000	110,000
Total Assets	$640,000	$380,000
Equities:		
Accounts Payable	$ 80,000	$ 50,000
Accrued Salaries Payable	20,000	80,000
Noncurrent Liabilities	210,000	20,000
Total Liabilities.	$310,000	$150,000
Paid-In Capital.	$200,000	$200,000
Retained Earnings.	130,000	30,000
Total Stockholders' Equity.	$330,000	$230,000
Total Equities	$640,000	$380,000

HAMILTON CONCRETE, INC.
Income Statement
Year Ended June 30, 1987

Sales.	$360,000
Cost of Goods Sold	150,000
Gross Profit on Sales	$210,000

Operating Expenses:

Depreciation Expense	$70,000	
Other Operating Expenses	40,000	110,000

Net Income	$100,000

Required   Calculate Hamilton Concrete's cash-basis net income for the year ended June 30, 1987.

(Check figure: Cash-basis net income = $90,000)

Problem A17-8*
Preparing T-accounts and formal statement of changes using a cash fund

Mainsea Enterprises has decided to prepare a statement of changes in financial position using a cash liquid resource fund. Mainsea's 1987 financial statements appear below:

MAINSEA ENTERPRISES
Income Statement
Year Ended December 31, 1987
(000s omitted)

Sales.	$400
Cost of Goods Sold	225
Gross Profit on Sales	$175

Operating Expenses:

Depreciation.	$33	
Other (including taxes)	92	125

Net Income	$ 50

MAINSEA ENTERPRISES
Balance Sheet
December 31
(000s omitted)

	1987	1986	Increase (Decrease) in Account Balance
Assets:			
Cash.	$ 89	$ 19	+$ 70
Accounts Receivable	108	58	+ 50
Merchandise Inventory.	123	88	+ 35
Prepaid Expenses.	4	5	− 1
Land.	100	70	+ 30
Building	500	400	+ 100
Accumulated Depreciation	(103)	(70)	+ 33
Total Assets.	$ 821	$570	

(continued)

Equities:

Accounts Payable	$ 43	$ 49	–	6
Accrued Payables	16	–	+	16
Bonds Payable (due 1995)	100	–	+	100
Common Stock.	550	450	+	100
Retained Earnings	112	71	+	41
Total Equities	$ 821	$570		

Other Relevant Data

a. Land was purchased for $30,000.
b. Bonds payable in the amount of $100,000 were issued for a new building.
c. A $9,000 cash dividend was declared and paid.
d. Common stock was sold for $100,000 cash.

Required

1. Prepare working papers to develop a statement of changes in financial position using the cash definition of the fund. Use the nine-step T-account method.
2. Prepare a statement of changes in financial position for the year ended December 31, 1987.

(Check figures: Cash from operations = $9,000
Total financial resources generated = $209,000)

Set B

Problem B17-1
Calculating working capital from operations for three companies

In each of the three columns below are income statement data for the year ended December 31, 1987:

	Company A	Company B	Company C
Sales Revenue	$160,000	$300,000	$400,000
Cost of Goods Sold Expense	60,000	180,000	200,000
Advertising Expense	12,000	16,000	40,000
Sales Commission Expense.	6,000	30,000	60,000
Goodwill Amortization Expense	2,000	–	–
Depreciation Expense: Building.	3,000	8,000	72,000
Depreciation Expense: Equipment.	1,000	32,000	24,000
Patent Amortization Expense	3,600	40,000	–
Income Tax Expense.	18,000	–	1,800
Loss on Sale of Machinery	1,600	–	–
Gain on Sale of Land	–	–	20,000

Required

Prepare the working capital from operations section of the statement of changes in financial position for Companies A, B, and C, respectively. (Hint: First calculate net income for each of the three.)

(Check figure: Working capital from operations, Company B = $74,000)

Problem B17-2
Preparing statement of changes — T-accounts not required

The 1987 financial statements of Kord Enterprises, Inc., are shown on page 670. Additional information taken from the financial records of Kord Enterprises:
a. A building costing $140,000 was acquired for cash.

KORD ENTERPRISES
Income Statement
Year Ended December 31, 1987
(000s omitted)

Sales.	$1,600
Cost of Goods Sold	(820)
Gross Profit on Sales	$ 780
Operating Expenses:	
Depreciation	(40)
Other.	(220)
Net Income	$ 520

KORD ENTERPRISES, INC.
Comparative Balance Sheets
December 31
(000s omitted)

	1987	1986
Assets:		
Current Assets (total)	$1,000	$ 840
Land.	280	180
Building	1,640	1,500
Accumulated Depreciation: Building.	(120)	(80)
Total Assets	$2,800	$2,440
Equities:		
Current Liabilities	$ 360	$ 300
Noncurrent Liabilities	80	400
Common Stock.	1,540	1,440
Retained Earnings	820	300
Total Equities	$2,800	$2,440

b. Cash was used to pay off noncurrent liabilities amounting to $320,000.
c. Common stock was issued in exchange for a land with a fair market value of $100,000.

Required Prepare a statement of changes in financial position in good form for the year ended December 31, 1987. You need not prepare T-account working papers. All the information needed to prepare the statement is given in the income statement, balance sheets, and additional information above. (Note: The schedule of changes in individual working capital accounts may be omitted.)

(Check figure: Working capital from operations = $560,000)

Problem B17-3
Preparing T-accounts and
formal statement of changes

Raines, Inc., condensed balance sheets for December 31, 1986 and 1987, and the condensed income statement for the year ended December 31, 1987, are presented on page 671:

RAINES, INC.
Income Statement (condensed)
Year Ended December 31, 1987

Sales.		$970,000
Cost of Goods Sold Expense		630,500
Gross Profit on Sales		$339,500
Operating Expenses:		
Depreciation Expense: Building.	$30,000	
Depreciation Expense: Equipment	28,000	
Copyright Amortization Expense	7,000	
Other Selling and Administrative Expenses	22,500	87,500
Income before Tax.		$252,000
Income Tax Expense		138,500
Net Income		$113,500

RAINES, INC.
Comparative Balance Sheets (condensed)
December 31

	1987	1986
Assets:		
Current Assets (total)	$ 202,500	$ 200,000
Property, Plant, and Equipment:		
Land	$ 196,000	$ 152,000
Building	672,500	610,000
Less: Accumulated Depreciation	(383,000)	(353,000)
Equipment	450,000	450,000
Less: Accumulated Depreciation	(73,000)	(45,000)
Total Property, Plant, and Equipment	$ 862,500	$ 814,000
Intangible Assets:		
Copyright	$ 49,000	$ 56,000
Total Assets.	$1,114,000	$1,070,000
Liabilities and Stockholders' Equity:		
Current Liabilities (total)	$ 80,500	$ 100,000
Noncurrent Liabilities:		
Bonds Payable (issued at par).	200,000	300,000
Total Liabilities	$ 280,500	$ 400,000
Common Stock (no par)	$ 550,000	$ 500,000
Retained Earnings	283,500	170,000
Total Stockholders' Equity.	$ 833,500	$ 670,000
Total Liabilities and Stockholders' Equity	$1,114,000	$1,070,000

In addition, the following information was compiled from the company's financial records:
a. Additional land costing $44,000 was purchased for cash.
b. A new building was purchased for cash, $62,500.
c. Additional common stock was issued for $50,000.
d. $100,000 of outstanding bonds were retired at maturity.

Required

1. Prepare working papers to develop a statement of changes in financial position using the working capital approach. Use the nine-step T-account method.
2. Prepare a statement of changes in financial position for the year ended December 31, 1987, in good form. (Note: The schedule of changes in working capital accounts may be omitted.)

(Check figure: Working capital from operations = $178,500)

Problem B17-4
Preparing T-accounts and formal statement of changes

Advanced Filters, Inc., condensed balance sheets for 1986 and 1987 and the income statement for 1987 are shown below:

ADVANCED FILTERS, INC.
Income Statement (condensed)
Year Ended December 31, 1987
(000s omitted)

Sales.		$700
Cost of Goods Sold Expense		454
Gross Profit on Sales		$246
Operating Expenses:		
Selling Expenses	$70	
Administrative Expenses	40	
Depreciation Expense: Building	80	
Depreciation Expense: Equipment.	30	220
Net Income		$ 26

ADVANCED FILTERS, INC.
Comparative Balance Sheets (condensed)
December 31
(000s omitted)

	1987	1986
Assets:		
Current Assets (total)	$ 212	$ 170
Property, Plant, and Equipment:		
Land	$ 604	$ 428
Building	1,560	1,400
Less: Accumulated Depreciation	(168)	(88)
Equipment	620	660
Less: Accumulated Depreciation	(216)	(200)
Total Property, Plant, and Equipment	$2,400	$2,200
Total Assets	$2,612	$2,370
Liabilities and Stockholders' Equity:		
Current Liabilities (total).	$ 136	$ 80
Noncurrent Liabilities:		
Note Payable.	180	20
Total Liabilities.	$ 316	$ 100
Common Stock (no par)	$2,000	$2,000
Retained Earnings	296	270
Total Stockholders' Equity	$2,296	$2,270
Total Liabilities and Stockholders' Equity	$2,612	$2,370

In addition, the following information was compiled from the company's records:

a. Equipment having a cost of $60,000 and accumulated depreciation of $14,000 was sold for $46,000.

b. A major addition to the building was constructed. The addition was "paid for" by giving the construction company a note for $160,000 due in 3 years.

c. Land was purchased for $176,000.

d. Equipment was purchased for $20,000.

Required

1. Prepare working papers to develop a statement of changes in financial position using the working capital approach. Use the nine-step T-account method.

2. Prepare a statement of changes in financial position for the year ended December 31, 1987, in good form. (Note: The schedule of changes in individual working capital accounts may be omitted.)

(Check figure: Total financial resources generated = $342,000)

Problem B17-5

Preparing formal statement of changes when given three analysis T-accounts

A fire in the office of Wise Corp. destroyed many of the accounting schedules on the desk. A staff accountant had just finished preparing the working papers for a statement of changes in financial position when the fire occurred. All the working papers were destroyed except for a sheet with the following T-accounts:

Change in Working Capital			
			9,000
(E) Proceeds from Issuing Bonds	65,000	(G) Purchase of Patent	120,000
(D) Proceeds from Selling Equipment	39,500		
(Z) Working Capital from Operations	6,500		
Total Debits	111,000	Total Credits	120,000
		Balance	9,000

Working Capital from Operations			
(A) Net Income	1,000		
(B) Depreciation Expense	3,000		
(C) Goodwill Amortization Expense	2,250		
(D) Loss on Sale of Equipment	250		
W/C from Operations	6,500	(Z) To Close	6,500

Financing and Investing Activities Not Affecting Working Capital			
(F-1) Issued Preferred Stock for Land	30,000	(F-2) Land Acquired by Issuing Preferred Stock	30,000

Required

Using the information found in the T-accounts above, prepare a statement of changes for the year ended December 31, 1986, in good form. You may omit the schedule of changes in working capital accounts.

Problem B17-6
Preparing T-accounts and formal statement of changes

Unlimited Products, Inc., financial statements for 1987 appear below:

UNLIMITED PRODUCTS, INC.
Income Statement
Year Ended June 30, 1987
(000s omitted)

Sales			$12,780
Cost of Goods Sold.			(7,668)
Gross Profit on Sales.			$ 5,112
Operating Expenses:			
Depreciation Expense: Building		$ 150	
Depreciation Expense: Equipment		75	
Other Operating Expenses		3,474	(3,699)
Income from Primary Operations			$ 1,413
Other Income and Expense:			
Interest Expense		$ 120	
Loss on Sale of Equipment		45	(165)
Income before Tax			$ 1,248
Income Taxes			(609)
Net Income.			$ 639

UNLIMITED PRODUCTS, INC.
Statement of Retained Earnings
For Year Ended June 30, 1987
(000s omitted)

Retained Earnings Balance (7/1/86)	$ 660
Add: Net Income for the Year	639
Total	$1,299
Deduct: Dividends Declared and Paid	(204)
Retained Earnings (6/30/87)	$1,095

UNLIMITED PRODUCTS, INC.
Comparative Balance Sheets
June 30
(000s omitted)

	1987	1986	Increase (Decrease) in Account Balance
Assets:			
Current Assets:			
Cash.	$ 1,230	$ 1,155	+$ 75
Accounts Receivable (net).	2,520	2,580	− 60
Merchandise Inventory.	975	564	+ 411
Total Current Assets	$ 4,725	$ 4,299	
Property, Plant, and Equipment:			
Land.	$ 1,455	$ 1,155	+ 300
Buildings.	3,210	3,210	—
Less: Accumulated Depreciation.	(570)	(420)	+ 150
Equipment.	2,700	2,565	+ 135
Less: Accumulated Depreciation.	(180)	(240)	− 60
Total Property, Plant, and Equipment	$ 6,615	$ 6,270	
Total Assets	$11,340	$10,569	
Liabilities and Stockholders' Equity:			
Current Liabilities:			
Accounts Payable	$ 615	$ 720	−$105
Bank Loan Payable	—	450	− 450
Accrued Payables	90	129	− 39
Total Current Liabilities	$ 705	$ 1,299	
Noncurrent Liabilities:			
Notes Payable (due 9/30/95)	$ 690	—	+ 690
Bonds Payable (due 12/31/99)	3,000	$ 3,000	—
Premium on Bonds Payable.	600	660	− 60
Total Noncurrent Liabilities	$ 4,290	$ 3,660	
Total Liabilities	$ 4,995	$ 4,959	
Stockholders' Equity:			
Preferred Stock	$ 300	—	+ 300
Common Stock (no par)	4,950	$ 4,950	—
Retained Earnings	1,095	660	+ 435
Total Stockholders' Equity	$ 6,345	$ 5,610	
Total Liabilities and Stockholders' Equity	$11,340	$10,569	

An analysis of Unlimited's financial records revealed the following information:

a. Equipment costing $405,000 and having an accumulated depreciation of $135,000 was sold for $225,000. The $45,000 loss appears on the income statement.

b. Preferred stock with a par vaue of $300,000 was issued for 40 acres of land.
c. The entry to record interest expense on the bonds was as follows:

Interest Expense	75,000	
Premium on Bonds Payable	60,000	
Cash		135,000

(More liquid resources were used than are reflected in the Interest Expense account.)
d. $690,000 was borrowed from the bank; a note due in 1995 was signed.
e. Equipment costing $540,000 was purchased for cash.
f. $204,000 in dividends were declared and paid.

Required

1. Prepare working papers to develop a statement of changes in financial position using a working capital fund. Use the nine-step T-account method.
2. Prepare a statement of changes in financial position for the year ended June 30, 1987, in good form.

(Check figures: Increase in working capital = $1,020,000
Working capital from operations = $849,000
Total financial resources generated = $2,064,000)

Problem B17-7*
Calculating cash-basis net income

Libbey Company's 1987 income statement and comparative balance sheets for 1986 and 1987 are shown below:

LIBBEY COMPANY
Income Statement
Year Ended September 30, 1987

Sales		$180,000
Cost of Goods Sold		75,000
Gross Profit on Sales		$105,000
Operating Expenses:		
Depreciation Expense	$35,000	
Other Operating Expenses	20,000	55,000
Net Income		$ 50,000

LIBBEY COMPANY
Comparative Balance Sheets
September 30

	1987	1986
Assets:		
Cash	$ 30,000	$ 20,000
Accounts Receivable (net)	60,000	80,000
Merchandise Inventory	80,000	35,000
Noncurrent Assets (net)	150,000	55,000
Total Assets	$320,000	$190,000

(continued)

Equities:

Accounts Payable	$ 40,000	$ 25,000
Accrued Salaries Payable	10,000	40,000
Noncurrent Liabilities	105,000	10,000
Total Liabilities.	$155,000	$ 75,000
Paid-In Capital.	$100,000	$100,000
Retained Earnings.	65,000	15,000
Total Stockholders' Equity.	$165,000	$115,000
Total Equities	$320,000	$190,000

Required   Calculate Libbey Company's cash-basis net income for the year ended September 30, 1987.

(Check figure: Cash-basis net income = $45,000)

Problem B17-8*
Preparing T-accounts and
formal statement of changes
using a cash fund

Maxxco, Inc., has elected to prepare a statement of changes in financial position employing a cash liquid resource fund. Maxxco's 1987 financial statements are shown below:

MAXXCO, INC.
Income Statement
Year Ended December 31, 1987
(000s omitted)

Sales.		$800
Cost of Goods Sold		450
Gross Profit on Sales		$350
Operating Expenses:		
Depreciation	$ 65	
Other (including taxes)	185	250
Net Income		$100

MAXXCO, INC.
Balance Sheet
December 31
(000s omitted)

	1987	1986	Increase (Decrease) in Account Balance
Assets:			
Cash	$ 177	$ 38	+$139
Accounts Receivable	217	116	+ 101
Merchandise Inventory.	245	176	+ 69
Prepaid Expenses.	9	11	− 2
Land.	200	140	+ 60
Building	1,000	800	+ 200
Accumulated Depreciation	(205)	(140)	+ 65
Total Assets.	$1,643	$1,141	

(continued)

Equities:

Accounts Payable	....	$ 86	$ 97	− 11
Accrued Payables	....	33	—	+ 33
Bonds Payable (due 1995)	....	200	—	+ 200
Common Stock	....	1,100	900	+ 200
Retained Earnings	....	224	144	+ 80
Total Equities	....	$1,643	$1,141	

Other Relevant Data

a. $60,000 of land was purchased for cash.
b. Bonds payable in the amount of $200,000 were issued for a new building.
c. A $20,000 cash dividend was declared and paid.
d. Common stock was issued for $200,000 cash.

Required

1. Prepare working papers to develop a statement of changes in financial position using the cash definition of the fund. Use the nine-step T-account method.
2. Prepare a statement of changes in financial position for the year ended December 31, 1987.

(Check figure: Cash from operations = $19,000
Total financial resources generated = $419,000)

Chapter 18

Financial Statement Analysis and Interpretation

By studying this chapter, you will learn:

- What *horizontal* and *vertical financial statement analyses* are
- How to prepare *comparative* and *common-size financial statements*
- How to calculate ratios indicating strength of earnings performance: *rate of return on total assets, rate of return on stockholders' equity, earnings per share,* and *price-earnings ratio*
- How to calculate ratios indicating long-term debt-paying ability: *times interest earned* and *debt-to-equity ratio*
- How to calculate ratios indicating the strength of a company's liquid position: *working capital, current ratio, quick ratio, accounts receivable turnover, number of days sales uncollected,* and *inventory turnover*
- The types of information commonly found in financial statement footnotes that assist in evaluating a company's performance and financial strength
- The impact of inflation on the analysis of financial statements

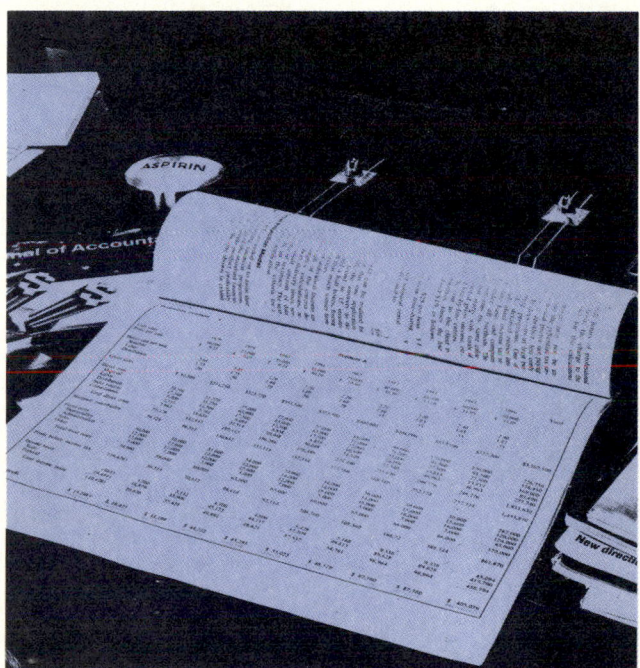

You have studied the structure of financial statements throughout the first 17 chapters. Each component of the four major statements was traced from the original entry recording the data to the point where the item was ultimately disclosed in the appropriate financial statement category. In this chapter we will examine the finished financial statements to discover some of the types of information that can be obtained about the company's earnings performance, its financial structure, and its long- and short-term debt-paying ability.

A company's financial reporting goes beyond just the four financial statements. The auditor's report and the notes to the financial statements also provide valuable sources of information about the company's financial position and results of operations. The *auditor's report* contains the auditor's opinion about whether the presentations on the financial statements are fair within the boundaries of generally accepted accounting principles. Any significant departures from generally accepted accounting principles are noted in the audit report and their effect on the financial statements is quantified wherever possible. The auditor, an independent outside party, gives an opinion on the financial statements only after carefully reviewing and analyzing the statements and the supporting documents. A careful reading of the audit report provides important background information for the analysis of financial statements.

> The auditor's report contains an opinion about whether the financial statement presentations are fair

The notes to the financial statements should not be viewed as an extra bit of data tacked on to the end of the annual report. These notes are an integral part of the statements. They provide significant information found nowhere else in the statements. We will examine the content of some typical notes after we show you how to analyze the financial statements themselves.

COMPARATIVE FINANCIAL STATEMENTS AND TREND ANALYSIS

> Horizontal analysis compares financial data of a company for several years

One approach to financial statement analysis is to compare the financial data of a single company for 2 or more years. This *horizontal analysis* makes it possible to focus attention on items that have changed significantly during the period you are reviewing. Comparison of an item over several periods with a base year may show a trend developing. A *base year* is a year chosen as a beginning point.

Comparative Financial Statements

> Comparative financial statements compare financial data for 2 or more years

Comparative financial statements usually show financial statement data for 2 or more years, the increase or decrease in each item on the statement, and the percentage change as compared with the earliest year reported. Exhibits 18-1 and 18-2 show such comparative balance sheets and income statements for Most, Inc.

On comparative statements the most current year's information is normally presented in the first column. Successive columns show amounts for progressively earlier and earlier years. The Most, Inc., 2-year comparative statements show the amount of change in each statement item. These increases and decreases are calculated simply by subtracting 1986 amounts from 1987 amounts, e.g., Cash: $5,368 − $6,574 = −$1,206. The percentage increase or decrease in each statement amount is also disclosed in the final column. These percentages are calculated by dividing the amount of change by the earliest year amount, e.g., Cash: −$1,206 ÷ $6,574 = −18.3%. The analyst will give most attention to material comparative statement items that show a significant percentage change during the year. Merchandise inventory is an illustration of a material item showing a significant percentage change (24.1%). Marketable securities also had a large percentage increase (96.8%), but this item would be viewed as much less important because of its relatively small dollar amount.

> Material items showing significant changes should be given careful attention

EXHIBIT 18-1

MOST, INC.
Comparative Balance Sheets
(000s omitted)

	December 31, 1987	December 31, 1986	Amount Increase (Decrease)	Percent Increase (Decrease)
Assets				
Current Assets:				
Cash.	$ 5,368	$ 6,574	$ (1,206)	(18.3)%
Marketable Securities.	3,090	1,570	1,520	96.8
Accounts Receivable (less Allowance for Uncollectibles of $710 in 1987 and $814 in 1986)	35,382	32,936	2,446	7.4
Merchandise Inventory.	62,582	50,434	12,148	24.1
Prepaid Expenses	2,870	2,590	280	10.8
Total Current Assets	$109,292	$ 94,104	$15,188	16.1
Investments:				
Investment in Common Stock	$ 6,000	$ 6,000	—	—
Property, Plant, and Equipment:				
Land	$ 4,520	$ 4,300	$ 220	5.1
Building	72,540	72,540	—	—
Less: Accumulated Depreciation.	(30,696)	(29,196)	1,500†	5.1
Equipment.	18,907	16,717	2,190	13.1
Less: Accumulated Depreciation.	(7,980)	(7,840)	140†	1.8
Total Property, Plant, and Equipment	$ 57,291	$ 56,521	$ 770	1.4
Total Assets	$172,583	$156,625	$15,958	10.2 %
Liabilities and Stockholders' Equity				
Current Liabilities:				
Accounts Payable	$ 24,235	$ 30,353	$ (6,118)	(20.2)%
Accrued Payables	9,758	6,137	3,621	59.0
Income Tax Payable	2,040	1,425	615	43.2
Current Portion of Long-Term Debt	3,000	3,000	—	—
Total Current Liabilities	$ 39,033	$ 40,915	$ (1,882)	(4.6)
Long-Term Liabilities:				
8% Mortgage Bonds Payable	$ 25,000	$ 28,000	$ (3,000)	(10.7)
10% Unsecured Note Payable	5,000	—	5,000	*
Total Long-Term Liabilities.	$ 30,000	$ 28,000	$ 2,000	7.1
Total Liabilities	$ 69,033	$ 68,915	$ 118	.2
Stockholders' Equity:				
5% Preferred Stock ($10 par)	$ 500	$ 500	—	—
Common Stock ($1 par)	10,000	9,500	$ 500	5.3
Paid-In Capital in Excess of Par— Common Stock.	35,843	30,053	5,790	19.3
Retained Earnings.	57,207	47,657	9,550	20.0
Total Stockholders' Equity.	$103,550	$ 87,710	$15,840	18.1
Total Liabilities and Stockholders' Equity	$172,583	$156,625	$15,958	10.2 %

* When an amount increases or decreases from zero to another number, the percentage change is infinitely large and therefore meaningless ($\frac{5,000}{0} = \infty$).
† The amounts of the Accumulated Depreciation amounts increased. The effect of these increases is to decrease assets. Remember, Accumulated Depreciation is a contra asset.

EXHIBIT 18-2

MOST, INC.
Comparative Income Statements
(000s omitted)

	For the Year Ended December 31,		Amount Increase (Decrease)	Percent Increase (Decrease)
	1987	1986		
Net Sales	$ 862,915	$ 673,488	$189,427	28.1%
Cost of Goods Sold.	(564,346)	(454,335)	110,011	24.2
Gross Profit on Sales.	$ 298,569	$ 219,153	$ 79,416	36.2
Operating Expenses:				
Selling Expenses	$(212,062)	$(162,571)	$ 49,491	30.4
General and Administrative Expenses	(58,771)	(35,928)	22,843	63.6
Total Operating Expenses	$(270,833)	$(198,499)	$ 72,334	36.4
Other Income and Expenses				
Dividend Income	$ 516	$ 430	$ 86	20.0
Interest Expense	(3,120)	(3,016)	104	3.5
Net Other Income (Expense)	$ (2,604)	$ (2,586)	$ 18	.7
Income before Income Taxes	$ 25,132	$ 18,068	$ 7,064	39.1
Income Tax Expense.	(7,557)	(5,693)	1,864	32.7
Net Income.	$ 17,575	$ 12,375	$ 5,200	42.0%
Earnings per Common Share	$1.80	$1.30		

Generally speaking there were no dramatic shifts in the asset, liability, or stockholders' equity structure of Most. The following observations are among those that may be made:

1. The decrease in cash is accompanied by an increase in marketable securities, indicating that Most may be managing its idle cash better in 1987 by investing a larger part of it.

2. While merchandise inventory has increased significantly (24.1%), there appears to be no cause for alarm because sales have also experienced a large boost (28.1%). It is necessary to have more inventory on hand to meet the growing customer demand.

3. There seems to be a slight shift from using debt to using equity to finance the company. Total liabilities increased only .2% while total stockholders' equity increased 18.1%. These changes occurred while total liabilities and stockholders' equity increased by 10.2%.

Comparative statements provide a means for alerting the analyst to significant shifts that require further attention. He or she will then employ the various techniques we will discuss later in this chapter to analyze those shifts.

Trend Analysis

Trend analysis is another type of horizontal examination that compares proportionate changes in selected financial statement information over time. The time period selected for comparisons is usually at least 5 years and may be as many as 10 or 20.

Trend percentages state selected financial data as a percentage of the same data in a base year

Trend percentages are calculated by selecting a year as a base year and calculating amounts of selected items in following years as percentages of the amount of the same item in the base year. (All amounts in the base year are set equal to 100%.) To illustrate, selected income statement amounts for Most, Inc., for the years 1983 through 1987 are given below:

MOST, INC. Selected Income Statement Amounts for the Years Ended December 31 (000s omitted)					
	1987	1986	1985	1984	1983
Net Sales	$862,915	$673,488	$562,104	$401,982	$388,500
Gross Profit	298,569	219,153	218,181	213,986	209,790
Net Income	17,575	12,375	11,088	10,666	10,560

These amounts are converted into trend percentages by dividing the amount in a given year by the 1983 base year amount, e.g., Sales — 1984: $401,982 ÷ $388,500 = 103%; 1985: $562,104 ÷ $388,500 = 145%, etc. The Most, Inc., trend percentages are tabulated below:

MOST, INC. Selected Income Statement Data Shown as Percentages of 1983 Base Year Years Ended December 31					
	1987	1986	1985	1984	1983
Net Sales	222%	173%	145%	103%	100%
Gross Profit	142	105	104	102	100
Net Income	166	117	105	101	100

Comparisons of dollar amounts over the years indicate that sales, gross profit, and net income are increasing. Comparisons of the trend percentages reveal that gross profit has not increased nearly as rapidly as sales, indicating possibly that the cost of inventory has been increasing more quickly than the sales price. The percentage increase in net income is not nearly as great as the percentage increase in sales, but it generally exceeds the percentage increase in gross profit. One possible explanation for these trend relationships is that management is doing a good job of controlling either selling or general and administrative expenses, or both.

Trend percentages and comparative statements are used to get an overview of a company's performance

Trend percentages, like comparative financial statements, are used to get an overview of an entity's performance. This overview will highlight particular areas where further, more detailed analysis is needed. The analyst of Most, Inc.'s trend percentages, for example, would probably want to look into other ratios and comparisons relating to cost of goods sold and operating expenses.

COMMON-SIZE FINANCIAL STATEMENTS

Relating financial statement items to each other within a single time period is referred to as *vertical analysis.* Common-size financial statements and financial ratios are two

EXHIBIT 18-3

MOST, INC.
Common-Size Income Statements
Years Ended December 31

	1987	1986
Net Sales	100.00%*	100.00%
Cost of Goods Sold	(65.40)	(67.46)
Gross Profit on Sales	34.60	32.54
Operating Expenses:		
Selling Expenses	(24.58)	(24.14)
General and Administrative Expenses	(6.81)	(5.33)
Total Operating Expenses	(31.39)	(29.47)
Other Income and Expense:		
Dividend Income	.06	.06
Interest Expense	(.36)	(.45)
Net Other Income (Expense)	(.30)	(.39)
Income before Income Taxes	2.91	2.68
Income Tax Expense	(.88)	(.85)
Net Income	2.03%	1.83%

* Percentages have been rounded.

Vertical analysis compares financial data within a single year

Common-size financial statements show each item on a statement as a percentage of a key item on that statement

tools employed in vertical analysis. Common-size statements will be discussed in this section and financial ratios in the next.

Common-size financial statements show each item on a statement as a percentage of one key item on that statement. No dollar amounts appear. Each item on an income statement is usually stated as a percentage of net sales. Common-size balance sheets often state all amounts as a percentage of total assets or total equities.

Most, Inc., common-size income statements are shown in Exhibit 18-3. The computational technique is to take each item and divide by Sales of that year, e.g., Cost of Goods Sold 1987: $564,346 ÷ $862,915 = 65.40%; 1986: $454,335 ÷ $673,488 = 67.46%.

Common-size statements are useful for seeing how significant the components of a statement are. Dividend income and interest expense have a very minor effect on Most's net income (they are only .06% and .36% of 1987 sales), while cost of goods sold and selling expenses are of great significance (they are 65.4% and 24.58% of 1987 sales).

The vertical analysis of a single year's statements—common-size statements—may be combined with horizontal analysis—comparative statements—to detect significant changes in financial statement components from year to year. Exhibit 18-3 shows such comparative common-size statements. Perhaps the most notable change occurred in cost of goods sold (which went down from 67.46% to 65.40% of sales) and in operating expenses (which increased from 29.47% to 31.39% of sales). While these changes are not substantial, they bear watching in future periods to see if these trends continue.

Common-size statements can be used to compare companies of differing size

Common-size statements are especially helpful in comparing two companies that differ in size. Imagine comparing Most, Inc.'s income statement with that of the Blaque Company shown below.

BLAQUE COMPANY
Income Statement
Year Ended December 31, 1987
(000s omitted)

Net Sales.	$ 4,535,600
Cost of Goods Sold	(2,585,292)
Gross Profit on Sales	$ 1,950,308
Operating Expenses:	
Selling	$ (689,411)
General and Administrative	(317,492)
Total Operating Expenses	$(1,006,903)
Income before Income Tax	$ 943,405
Income Tax Expense	(452,834)
Net Income	$ 490,571

Blaque is so much larger that a comparison of any number on the two income statements seems meaningless. When Blaque's statement is converted to a common size, comparisons are possible:

BLAQUE COMPANY
Common-Size Income Statement
Year Ended December 31, 1987

Sales	100.0%
Cost of Goods Sold	(57.0)
Gross Profit on Sales	43.0
Operating Expenses	
Selling	(15.2)
General and Administrative	(7.0)
Total Operating Expenses	(22.2)
Income before Income Tax	20.8
Income Tax Expense	(10.0)
Net Income	10.8%

Most, Inc.'s cost of goods sold (see Exhibit 18-3) is a much higher percentage of sales (65.4%) than is Blaque's (57.0%). If the companies are in the same industry, we may question whether the difference is due to volume buying, better inventory management, or possibly just a difference in the inventory costing method (Most may be using LIFO and Blaque FIFO). Blaque's selling expenses are a much lower percentage (15.2%) than Most's (24.58%). The analyst may question what possible efficiencies Blaque has discovered that have eluded Most. Differences in advertising policies, policies on commissions paid to sales representatives, or economies of scale could account for the differences.

Many industry trade associations gather statistics from member firms and produce common-size financial statements based on averages for businesses falling within a predetermined size category. For example, sporting goods stores with annual retail sales under $3 million might submit their income statements in a standardized format to a trade association, which would then compute average cost of goods sold and the other percentages for stores in this size range. These common-size statistics would provide one standard basis for comparisons that could be used to evaluate the relative performance of a company, in much the same way that Most was evaluated in comparison with Blaque.

FINANCIAL RATIO ANALYSIS

A *ratio* is the relationship between two amounts that results from dividing one by the other. The ratio of 1,000 to 500 would be $1,000 \div 500 = 2$, sometimes expressed as $2 : 1$. This means that the first number is twice as large as the second. The ratio of 25 to 50 would be expressed as .5 $(25 \div 50)$ or $.5 : 1$, signifying that the first number is half as large as the second. Ratio analysis can provide additional insights into the operating performance and financial position of Most, Inc.

Analysis of Earnings Performance

Stockholders and potential stockholders employ several ratios to help them evaluate management performance in using the resources of the entity to earn profits. Rate of return on total assets and rate of return on stockholders' equity are two such ratios.

Rate of return (ROR) on total assets is a measure of management's efficiency in using all resources at its disposal. The formula for computing this ratio is as follows:

Rate of return on total assets indicates management's efficiency in using all of the firm's resources

$$\text{Rate of return (ROR) on total assets} = \frac{\text{income before interest expense}}{\text{average total assets}}$$

Income before interest expense is used so that earnings will not be influenced by the manner in which the assets are financed. Interest is a cost of financing the business, not a cost of operating it. Average total assets reflect resources employed throughout the year, not those on hand at the beginning or at the end. This average could be computed by weighting the dollars of assets used by the number of days they are employed and dividing by 365. An approximation of this average may be obtained by adding the beginning and ending asset amounts and dividing by 2. This simplified technique will be used throughout the chapter wherever an average is required.

Most, Inc.'s return on total assets for 1987 is calculated as follows:

$$\text{ROR on total assets} = \frac{\text{net income} + \text{interest expense}}{(\text{total assets, beg. of year} + \text{total assets, end of year}) \div 2}$$

$$\text{ROR on total assets} = \frac{\$17,575,000 + \$3,120,000}{(\$156,625,000 + \$172,583,000) \div 2}$$

$$= \frac{\$20,695,000}{\$164,604,000} = .1257 \text{ or } 12.57\%$$

Most's management earned an average of 12.57% on each dollar of assets invested in the company.

Rate of return on common stockholders' equity indicates management's efficiency in using resources invested by common stockholders

Rate of return (ROR) on common stockholders' equity is a measure of management's effectiveness in using the resources invested by the common stockholders. This rate may be higher or lower than the return on total assets, depending on how judiciously management has combined debt and preferred stock with common stock in financing company's resources. The formula for computing this ratio is as follows:

$$\text{Rate of return (ROR) on common stockholder's equity} = \frac{\text{net income} - \text{preferred dividends}}{\text{average common stockholders' equity}}$$

The earnings amount in the numerator excludes both payments to holders of debt (interest expense) and holders of preferred stock (preferred dividends). Thus the net income less preferred dividends is the net amount earned on the equity of the common stockholders. Average common stockholders' equity is an approximation of the amount invested by this group of owners throughout the year.

The following preliminary computations are made for Most, Inc.:

Preferred dividends:
Par value of preferred stock (at the time dividends are declared). $500,000
Dividend rate paid 5%
Amount of preferred dividends . . . . $ 25,000

Average common stockholders' equity:

Total stockholders' equity	− preferred stockholders' equity	= common stockholders' equity
Jan. 1, 1987 $ 87,710,000	− $500,000	= $ 87,210,000
+ Dec. 31, 1987 103,550,000	− 500,000	= 103,050,000
Total		= $190,260,000
		÷ 2
Average common stockholders' equity for 1987		= $ 95,130,000

The rate of return on Most's common stockholders' equity for 1987 is as follows:

$$\text{ROR on common stockholders' equity} = \frac{\$17,575,000 - \$25,000}{\$95,130,000} = .1845$$

$$= 18.45\%$$

Favorable leverage exists when the company uses assets provided by creditors to earn a higher return for common stockholders

Since the 18.45% return on common stockholders' equity exceeds the 12.57% return on total assets, management has made effective use of *leverage,* or *trading on the equity.* Leverage or trading on the equity involves using the assets invested by common stockholders as collateral for debt financing (borrowing on notes or bonds) and limited-return equity financing (selling preferred stock) in an attempt to earn a higher return for the common stockholder. A simple example will help clarify this concept.

JOHN AND MABEL'S FRUIT STAND

John and Mabel Jones run a fruit and vegetable stand. They have $100 of their own money invested and earn a $5 profit (or 5% return). An additional $100 is borrowed from a friend at 6% interest. In order for John and Mabel to come out ahead on this loan, they must use the borrowed money to earn more than the $6 interest they will have to pay. Assuming that the net income on the $200 of assets is $7, the Jones' have used someone else's money to increase their return from 5% ($5 ÷ $100) to 7% ($7 ÷ $100). Remember, the $7 net income is *after* the interest expense deduction.

Rate of return on John and Mabel's total assets:

$$\frac{\text{Net income} + \text{interest expense}}{\text{Average total assets}} = \frac{\$7 + \$6}{(\$200 + \$200) \div 2} = \frac{\$13}{\$200}$$

$$= .065 \text{ or } 6.5\%$$

Rate of return on John and Mabel's stockholders' equity:

$$\frac{\text{Net income} - \text{preferred dividends}}{\text{Average common stockholders' equity}} = \frac{\$7 - \$0}{(\$100 + \$100) \div 2}$$

$$= \frac{\$7}{\$100} = .07 \text{ or } 7\%$$

Leverage, then, is simply an *attempt* to use funds supplied by nonowners to increase the return to owners. Any time the rate of return on common stockholders' equity exceeds the rate of return on total assets, leverage has been used to the stockholders' advantage.

Leverage may also work to the detriment of common stockholders. If the return on the borrowed and preferred stock capital is not sufficient to pay the interest and preferred dividends on that capital, some of the earnings that would normally be available to common stockholders are absorbed in making up the difference. Any time the rate of return on total assets is more than the rate of return on common stockholders' equity, leverage has been used to the detriment of the stockholders.

Earnings per share of common stock shows the average dollars of income for each share of common stock

Earnings per share of common stock (EPS) is a measure of the income earned on each share of common stock. Calculation of this ratio was discussed in Chapter 14. The formula for a simple capital structure and the calculation of 1987 EPS for Most, Inc., are presented below.

$$\textbf{EPS (simple capital structure)} = \frac{\textbf{net income} - \textbf{preferred dividends}}{\textbf{average number of common shares outstanding}}$$

$$\text{EPS} = \frac{\$17,575,000 - \$25,000}{(9,500,000 \text{ shs} + 10,000,000 \text{ shs}) \div 2}$$

$$= \frac{\$17,550,000}{9,750,000 \text{ shs}} = \underline{\$1.80}$$

Earnings per share amounts must appear on the face of the income statements of public companies. Nonpublic (closely held, or nonpublicly traded) companies are not required to disclose earnings per share amounts. If you review Most, Inc.'s income statement in Exhibit 18-2, you will see that EPS is properly shown for 1987 and 1986.

Price-earnings ratio statistics are one more indicator of the earnings performance of common stock. The formula for calculating the price-earnings ratio is:

$$\textbf{Price-earnings ratio} = \frac{\textbf{market price per share of common stock}}{\textbf{earnings per share of common stock}}$$

Assuming a current market price of $27 for Most, Inc.'s stock, the price-earnings ratio would be as follows:

$$\text{Price-earnings ratio} = \frac{\$27}{\$1.80} = \underline{15} \text{ or } \underline{15:1}$$

The price-earnings ratio reflects the stock market's assessment about the future earnings of the company

This simply means that Most's stock is currently selling for 15 times the amount that each share earned. Price-earnings ratios of 15 are not at all uncommon. A few range as high as 20 or more. The price-earnings ratio is the reflection of the stock market's assessment about the future earnings of the company. Investors have been willing to buy a share of stock for as many as 15 to 20 times the current per-share earnings because they feel that the future income growth of the firm will be sufficient to provide an adequate return on this investment. This return is normally received through a combination of dividends and an increased market value of the stock.

The dividend yield rate indicates the cash payout rate on the common stockholders' investment

Dividend yield rate shows the current year's dividends as a percentage of the current market price of the stock. This indication of the cash payout rate on an investment allows stockholders and potential stockholders to compare interest rates on certificates of deposit, corporate bonds, and other securities with this measure of return on common stock. The investor should be aware that dividend yield rates ignore the potential increase in the market value of common stock. For this reason the dividend yield rate should be combined with other statistics in making investment decisions.

The formula for calculating dividend yield rates and the 1987 dividend yield rate for Most, Inc., assuming that $8,000,000 dividends were paid to common stockholders, follows:

$$\text{Dividend yield rate} = \frac{\text{dividends per share of common stock}}{\text{current market price per share of common stock}}$$

$$\begin{array}{l}\text{1987 dividend yield} \\ \text{rate for Most, Inc.}\end{array} = \frac{\$8,000,000 \div 10,000,000 \text{ shs}}{\$27} = \frac{\$.80}{\$27} = .0296 \text{ or } 2.96\%$$

This relatively low dividend yield rate of 3% on Most, Inc., common stock would not be attractive to investors who count on cash flow from dividends to pay their living expenses. A potential Most, Inc., stockholder would probably be an individual who is more interested in speculating on the growth in the market value of the stock. This type of investor would rely more heavily on growth in earnings per share and recent trends in the market price of the stock than the dividend yield rate.

Analysis of Debt-Paying Ability

Creditors and potential creditors are interested in continuously monitoring a company's ability to pay interest as it comes due and to repay the principal of the debt at maturity. Times interest earned, debt to total assets ratio, and equity to total assets ratio are three statistics that provide information about this debt-paying ability. Later we will discuss several liquid position measures that indicate the ability to meet short-term debt responsibilities.

Times interest earned tells how many times a company could pay its interest expense with assets derived from income

Times interest earned is a ratio that indicates the margin of safety provided by current earnings in meeting the company's interest responsibilities. The formula for calculating this ratio is as follows:

$$\text{Times interest earned} = \frac{\text{income before interest expense and income taxes}}{\text{annual interest expense}}$$

Income before interest expense and income taxes is used because this is the amount that could be used to pay interest—provided it were available in the form of cash. Income taxes are excluded because interest is deductible in calculating income tax.

1987 times interest earned for Most, Inc., is as follows:

$$\text{Times interest earned} = \frac{\$17,575,000 + \$3,120,000 + \$7,557,000}{\$3,120,000}$$

$$= \frac{\$28,252,000}{\$3,120,000} = 9.1 \text{ times}$$

Most's income available to meet its interest responsibilities was about 9 times the amount of its interest expense. Usually if interest is covered several times, long-term creditors consider this an acceptable margin of safety. Most's times interest earned ratio should be quite satisfactory to its creditors.

The ***debt to total assets ratio*** shows the percentage of the firm's assets financed by debt. The higher this percentage, the greater the risk that the company will be unable to meet its obligations when due. The debt to total assets ratio formula and the 1987 calculation for Most, Inc., follow:

The debt to total assets ratio indicates the percentage of a company's assets provided by creditors

$$\text{Debt to total assets ratio} = \frac{\text{total liabilities}}{\text{total assets}}$$

$$\text{Most, Inc., 1987 debt to total assets ratio} = \frac{\$69,033,000}{\$172,583,000} = .399 \text{ or } .40, \text{ or } \underline{40\%}$$

Forty percent of Most's total assets were financed by debt.

The ***stockholders' equity to total assets ratio,*** sometimes called the **equity ratio,** shows the percentage of the firm's assets financed by stockholders. The higher this ratio, the smaller the risk that the company will be unable to meet its obligations when due. After a moment's reflection you should see that the debt to total assets ratio and the stockholders' equity to total assets ratio are complementary, that is, the two percentages should always add to 100%. This is true because all assets are financed by either debt or equity funds. The stockholders' equity to total assets ratio may be found by subtracting the debt to total assets ratio from 100%:

The stockholders' equity to total assets ratio shows the percentage of a company's assets provided by stockholders

$$\text{Stockholders' equity to total assets ratio} = 100\% - \text{debt to total assets ratio}$$

$$\text{1987 Most, Inc., stockholders' equity to total assets ratio} = 100\% - 40\% = \underline{60\%}$$

This ratio may also be calculated by the following formula:

$$\text{Stockholders' equity to total assets ratio} = \frac{\text{total stockholders' equity}}{\text{total assets}}$$

$$\text{1987 Most, Inc., stockholders' equity to total assets ratio} = \frac{\$103,550,000}{\$172,583,000} = .60 \text{ or } \underline{60\%}$$

Sixty percent of Most's assets come from stockholders (including reinvested earnings) and 40% from creditors. This fact, coupled with the favorable leverage and times interest earned statistics, should be satisfactory to long-term creditors. Of course, each analyst will have standards in mind when financial analysis is begun. These standards may vary from analyst to analyst. Statistics satisfactory to one analyst may cause concern to another.

Analysis of Liquid Position

An analysis of a firm's liquid position provides indicators of its short-term debt-paying ability and of management's current operating efficiency. For this reason, *both* investors and creditors are particularly interested in these statistics.

Working capital is a measure of the liquid resources management has to use

Working capital is total current assets minus total current liabilities. This liquid resource fund was discussed extensively in Chapter 17. A strong working capital position can be an advantage to a company attempting to obtain short-term credit at favorable interest rates. Investors and long-term creditors view a strong working capital position as indicating an ability to make expected dividend and interest payments in a timely manner. Most, Inc.'s working capital for 1987 is shown below:

Current assets	$109,292,000
− Current liabilities	39,033,000
= Working capital	$ 70,259,000

The current ratio is one measure of a company's ability to pay its short-term debts

The current ratio is current assets divided by current liabilities. This statistic is often assigned great importance by creditors in making credit-granting decisions. The general formula and 1987 current ratio for Most, Inc., appear below:

$$\text{Current ratio} = \frac{\text{current assets}}{\text{current liabilities}}$$

$$1987 \text{ Most, Inc., current ratio} = \frac{\$109,292,000}{\$39,033,000} = 2.80 \text{ or } 2.8:1$$

This means that for every dollar of current liabilities, Most has $2.80 of current assets. Many creditors feel that a current ratio of 2.0 is satisfactory. Relying too heavily on the current ratio may not be desirable, as the following illustration demonstrates:
The current ratios for Company A and B are calculated as follows:

	Company A	Company B
Current assets:		
Cash	$ 40,000	$175,000
Accounts receivable	60,000	125,000
Merchandise inventory . .	180,000	95,000
Prepaid expenses	20,000	5,000
Total current assets	$300,000	$400,000
Current liabilities	$100,000	$200,000
Current ratio	$300,000 ÷ $100,000 = 3	$400,000 ÷ $200,000 = 2

Company A's current ratio of 3:1 is much better than Company B's 2:1. If we inspect the composition of the current assets, we see that A's cash and accounts receivable are only one-third of total current assets, whereas three-fourths of B's current assets are composed of these two particular liquid resources. In reality, B may be in a position to meet its current obligations as well, if not better, than A.
Company A could further improve its current ratio by merely paying off $40,000 of current liabilities with the $40,000 cash on hand. If this were done, the new current ratio would be:

$$\begin{matrix}\text{Company A current} \\ \text{ratio (revised)}\end{matrix} = \frac{\$300,000 - \$40,000}{\$100,000 - \$40,000} = \frac{\$260,000}{\$60,000} = 4.33$$

This act of manipulating current assets close to the end of the time period can produce a ratio that may satisfy creditors while actually weakening the immediate liquid position of the company.
Limiting your analysis to too few statistics, relying on arbitrary rules of thumb, and not understanding the limitations behind the calculation of a ratio are pitfalls that you must carefully avoid.

The quick ratio is a measure of a company's immediate liquid position

The quick ratio, also known as the *acid-test ratio,* shows the relationship between highly liquid (quick) assets and current liabilities. Quick assets are those that may be converted directly into cash within a short period of time. These include cash, marketable securities, and receivables. Merchandise inventory is omitted because merchandise is normally sold on credit (converted into a receivable) and then the receivable must be collected before cash is realized. Thus inventory is two steps away from cash rather than just one. Prepaid expenses are also omitted because they are usually relatively small in amount and because they are used up in operations rather than converted into cash.

$$\text{Quick ratio} = \frac{\text{quick assets}}{\text{current liabilities}}$$

Most, Inc.'s quick assets ratio on December 31, 1987, is as follows:

Cash.	$ 5,368,000
Marketable securities	3,090,000
Accounts receivable (net)	35,382,000
Total quick assets	$43,840,000

$$\text{1987 Most, Inc., quick ratio} = \frac{\$43,840,000}{\$39,033,000} = 1.12 \text{ or } 1.12:1$$

Creditors generally use the rule of thumb that a quick ratio of 1:1 is satisfactory. Most's quick ratio appears to be acceptable.

The quick ratio, when viewed with the current ratio, gives an idea of the influence of Merchandise Inventory and Prepaid Expenses. Looking at the Company A– Company B illustration again one can see that the quick ratio is a tipoff that Company A's current ratio may be misleading as a sole indicator of debt-paying ability.

	Company A	Company B
Quick assets:		
Cash.	$ 40,000	$175,000
Accounts receivable. . .	60,000	125,000
Total quick assets.	$100,000	$300,000
Quick ratio.	$100,000 ÷ $100,000 = 1	$300,000 ÷ $200,00 = 1.5

Company B has the stronger quick ratio and the weaker current ratio, indicating that Merchandise Inventory and Prepaid Expenses play a less important role in its current position than these assets do in Company A's.

Inventory turnover indicates how quickly a company sells its average investment in inventory

Inventory turnover shows how many times the average dollars invested in merchandise inventory were sold (turned over) during the year. This statistic when compared with the year-end merchandise inventory provides the analyst with a basis for judging whether the company has an excessive investment in merchandise at the end of the year. A too-large ending inventory may indicate that sales volume was not as high as expected near year-end, or possibly that management was inefficient in allowing too much unsold goods to accumulate. On the other hand, a large inventory may be present because of an unusually high sales volume expected near the beginning of the next period. In any case, the analyst will be wise to attempt to discover the reasons for low turnover and excessive ending inventory.

Inventory turnover is calculated by dividing cost of goods sold by average merchandise inventory. Cost of goods sold is used instead of sales because sales includes gross profit, while cost of goods sold, like merchandise inventory, does not. The general formula and the 1987 Most, Inc., inventory turnover follow:

$$\text{Inventory turnover} = \frac{\text{cost of goods sold}}{\text{average merchandise inventory}}$$

$$\text{1987 Most, Inc., inventory turnover} = \frac{\$564,346,000}{(\$50,434,000 + \$62,582,000) \div 2}$$

$$= \frac{\$564,346,000}{\$56,508,000} = \underline{9.99 \text{ times}}$$

Since Most's inventory turns over about 10 times per year, the year-end inventory should be about 10% of cost of goods sold. Most's inventory of $62,582,000 is a little above this amount (10%)($564,346,000) = $56,435,000. This excess is probably explained by Most's increasing sales volume.

Accounts receivable turnover indicates the number of times per year that the average balance of Accounts Receivable is collected. This ratio of sales on credit to average accounts receivable is calculated as follows:

Accounts receivable turnover indicates how quickly a company collects its average Accounts Receivable balance

$$\text{Accounts receivable turnover} = \frac{\text{credit sales}}{\text{average accounts receivable}}$$

Assuming that substantially all of Most, Inc.'s sales are on credit, the firm's 1987 receivables turnover is as follows:

$$\text{1987 Most, Inc., accounts receivable turnover} = \frac{\$862,915,000}{(\$32,936,000 + \$35,382,000) \div 2}$$

$$= \frac{\$862,915,000}{\$34,159,000} = \underline{25.3 \text{ times}}$$

This ratio takes on more meaning when used in the calculation of the statistic discussed next.

Average age of receivables provides a rough approximation of the average time that it takes to collect receivables. Average age of receivables is determined as follows:

Average age of receivables is another measure of how quickly a company collects its Accounts Receivables

$$\text{Average age of receivables} = \frac{365 \text{ days}}{\text{accounts receivable turnover}}$$

$$\text{1987 average age of Most receivables} = \frac{365 \text{ days}}{25.3 \text{ times}} = \underline{14.4 \text{ days}}$$

Most, Inc., takes an average of 14 days to collect its receivables. If Most's credit terms are net 10 days, its collection efforts could be improved. If the credit terms are 15 or 30 days, Most's collection efforts appear to be excellent.

Creditors are interested in receivables turnover and the average age of receivables as indicators of how quickly the company's receivables are converted into the cash required for operations and debt repayment. Investors and creditors use receivables turnover as one more index of management efficiency.

INTERPRETATION OF FINANCIAL RATIOS

Ratios must be compared with some standard to be meaningful

A quick ratio of 1.12, an inventory turnover of 9.99, or a price-earnings ratio of 15 mean very little when considered in a vacuum. Financial ratios become relevant for decision making only when compared with some standards. Each analyst must decide on a set of standards for each ratio that he or she relies on to gauge the performance of the company being analyzed. Some common bases for establishing standards are considered below.

Company History

The company's ratios for past years may be used as a standard

Horizontal analysis has been defined as comparing financial data of a single company for 2 or more years. Comparative financial statements and trend analysis were presented as applications of horizontal analysis. Each of the financial ratios may be computed for a number of years and then compared to form an opinion about whether the company's performance is getting better or worse. If Most's inventory turnover has been 10, 12, and 16 during 1987, 1986, and 1985, respectively, the analyst should be concerned enough to attempt to discover the reason for the deterioration in this ratio. If management inefficiency seems to be the only plausible explanation, the analyst may expect continued problems that could lead to a decision to reject a credit application or not to invest in stock of the corporation.

A major limitation of comparing amounts and ratios for a single company is that there is no basis for a decision about the significance of these statistics. Some external standard is needed against which to measure the company's ratios. For example, if the average inventory turnover in Most's industry is 4, the turnover of 10 may appear excellent. If the industry average is 12, a turnover of 10 may be a cause for concern.

External Standards

Average ratios of other firms in the industry may be used as a standard

Ratio information about other companies is often used as a yardstick against which to compare the statistics of the firm being analyzed. These external data may be obtained by analyzing the financial statements of the other firms; by obtaining copies of industry averages from the publications of trade associations; by examining data on industry norms, average ratios, and credit ratings from credit agencies such as Dun & Bradstreet; or by consulting statistics available in investment service publications such as *Annual Statement Studies* published by Robert Morris Associates.

Care must be taken in deciding which ratios are to be used as standards of comparison. Many companies are so diversified that it is difficult to identify one particular industry in which they operate. A current ratio or inventory turnover ratio for such a conglomerate would be meaningless for comparing with those statistics of another firm operating in only one industry.

In most industries comparability will be affected by size. Larger firms will be able to avail themselves of economies of scale and certain sophisticated quantitative management techniques that may not be practical for smaller ones. Smaller companies may be able to maintain closer client relations and better customer relations than the larger ones. These differences in operating techniques may influence different ratios in different ways. The larger firm, for example, may be expected to have a higher gross profit percentage and inventory turnover, while the smaller one may have a quicker receivables turnover and a lower percentage spent on advertising. Comparisons of similar size entities in the same industry is desirable whenever possible.

The differences in accounting methods employed in generating financial information may also influence the comparability of ratios and other statistics. Among the different principles that firms may employ are different inventory techniques, depreciation methods, estimates of useful lives, methods of accounting for income taxes, and revenue recognition procedures. It is a fairly easy matter to discover which methods a particular company is using. Adjusting the financial information to compensate for differences in accounting methods may prove to be a difficult, if not impossible, task.

Notes to the financial statements, commonly called *footnotes,* provide additional information that may greatly influence your overall judgment about the future potential of the company. Some of the more important footnotes are discussed in this section.

NOTES TO FINANCIAL STATEMENTS

Footnotes provide valuable information about financial statements

Accounting Policies

When a company selects from several acceptable methods, the accounting policy note tells which method was chosen

Authoritative generally accepted accounting principles require that all financial statements contain a note outlining the various accounting methods that the company has elected to use. The accounting policies note explains which accounting method was selected from among several acceptable ones, for example, FIFO or LIFO inventory methods, straight-line or double declining-balance depreciation. The *accounting policies note,* usually the first note to the financial statements, is helpful in deciding how comparable the financial statistics for two different companies are. The following illustration shows a typical accounting policies note:

SUMMARY OF ACCOUNTING POLICIES

Inventories   Inventories are stated generally at cost, which is not in excess of market. The cost of substantially all inventories is determined by the last-in, first-out (LIFO) method.

Depreciation and Depletion   The cost of most manufacturing plant and equipment is depreciated using an accelerated method based primarily on a sum-of-the-years'-digits formula. The cost of mining properties is depreciated or depleted mainly by the units-of-production method.

Consolidation   The financial statements include the consolidation of all wholly and majority-owned subsidiaries except the finance subsidiary. The finance company is so different from the other companies that, even though wholly owned, it is accounted for by the equity method. It appears as an investment on the balance sheet and in "other income" on the income statement.

Methods of accounting for research and development costs, recognition of warranty expenses, and translating foreign subsidiary statements into U.S. currency are not appropriate accounting policy disclosures because only one acceptable method can be used for each of these.

Contingencies

The contingencies note provides information about future events that may occur

Financial statements are analyzed in order to form an opinion about how well a company has performed in the past and to make an estimate about how well it is expected to do in the future. A large potential lawsuit loss could significantly change your forecast about the future of the company. This vital information can be obtained by reading the contingencies note.

A *contingency* is a future event that may occur but whose occurrence is not certain. The *contingencies note* must include a description of all future losses that are probable, reasonably possible, and in some cases even remote. Where an estimate or a range of estimates of the amount of loss can be made, these must also be disclosed.

The following contingencies note is a sample of the typical disclosures that may be made:

NOTE 7 CONTINGENCIES

Early in fiscal 1986, the Federal Trade Commission filed a formal complaint against the Company and two other manufacturers of gudgeon twisters charging them with sharing an unlawful monopoly in violation of the Federal Trade Commission Act. The Commission seeks, among other things, divestiture of certain assets and royalty-free licensing of certain trademarks. The Company denies that it has violated the Act and is vigorously defending its position. Trial is continuing before an Administration Law Judge of the Federal Trade Commission, and it is expected that the litigation will continue for some time at considerable expense.

A lawsuit has been filed against the Company claiming damages from alleged environmental contamination by our Beaver Falls plant. The suit filed on March 30, 1987, in the federal court in Pennsylvania alleges damages of $1,000,000. The State of Pennsylvania has moved to intervene as plaintiff in this case seeking $25,000,000 in compensatory and $1,000,000 in punitive damages. The company will vigorously defend against this lawsuit.

As you learned in Chapter 11, contingencies that are probable in nature and subject to reasonable estimation must be recognized as current period losses. The loss (or expense) must be shown on the income statement and the corresponding liability (or allowance account) must appear on the balance sheet. Bad debts and warranty expenses are illustrations of contingencies considered probable and subject to estimation.

Other Descriptive Notes

Other notes provide descriptive information about balance sheet and income statement items

Some information vital to the understanding of the financial statements is simply too long and detailed to be shown on the statements themselves. This information is usually shown in a descriptive note referenced to a particular item on the income statement or balance sheet. Typical are those providing supplementary information about the following:

Subject of Note	Information Included
Property, plant, and equipment	The types of assets included in this category, their estimated useful lives, and whether they are pledged as collateral for loans
Long-term liabilities	The effective interest rate, maturity dates, repayment terms, collateral for the debt, any restriction imposed by the creditor (such as a limitation on the amount of dividends the company can pay)

Other common descriptive notes relate to pension plans, income taxes, earnings per share calculations, and stock option plans.

OTHER SOURCES OF INFORMATION

Various publications provide general background information

The serious student of financial statement analysis will supplement all of the techniques described thus far with several other sources of financial and nonfinancial information. Magazines such as *Business Week* and *Forbes* and financial newspapers such as *The Wall Street Journal, Barrons,* and the *Commercial and Financial Chron-*

BANK GIVES LOAN TO CONCERN SELLING Xs

This is a true story. Only the bank and the borrower's names have been deleted to protect the innocent and avoid embarrassment.

A Beverly Hills, Calif., accounting firm recently gave a specimen financial statement to a woman business owner who subsequently became a client of the firm.

Months later she called Andrew Hillas, a partner at the CPA firm, Singer, Lewak,

Greenbaum & Goldstein, to complain that her financial statement made no sense. Her Company's name was missing, replaced by a string of Xs, and the numbers were wrong.

"We hadn't done a financial statement for her," Mr. Hillas says. She had looked at the specimen he had given her earlier. And she had given it to her bank — a big one — in applying for a $50,000 loan. Even though the specimen was less than clear about the

company's business (it says the "company is a California corporation engaged in the promotion and sale of xxxxx") and the results didn't jibe with the company's earlier years' results, she got the loan.

Source: The Wall Street Journal, November 14, 1983, page 33.

In the situation explained in this article the bank apparently did not examine a loan applicant's financial statements very carefully in making a large loan. If a closer examination had been made, the banker would have noticed that the statements were merely samples and not intended to represent the financial position of any real company. More rational investing and credit-granting decisions would be made if the techniques you learned in this chapter were used.

icle provide data on prospects for the economy as a whole and for various industries. In addition, articles on management personnel, company strategy, and significant legislation affecting the business community expand the analyst's background knowledge. Up-to-date quarterly operating results and current stock prices also appear in many of these publications.

Several research firms publish financial services that are available on a subscription basis. These are available in most university and large public libraries. We have already mentioned industry trade associations and credit-reporting bureaus as possible sources of information.

Many large corporations provide interview sessions for professional analysts who work for large stock brokerage firms, trust departments of banks, and other institutions that invest vast sums of money. While these sessions do provide an opportunity for the analysts to ask questions that may interest them and to hear management's hopes for the future of the company, they may not act as a means of communicating secret inside information to a chosen few money managers. Such activities would be illegal.

THE IMPACT OF INFLATION

Traditional financial statements ignore the effects of inflation

One of the basic principles of accounting is the assumption that financial statement data are measured by dollars with an unchanging value over time. This *stable measuring unit assumption* is not valid in periods when inflation is causing the dollar to lose buying power at a significant rate. The analyst should realize that the company's traditional financial statements may show results that make little or no allowance for the declining value of the dollar.

Financial statements may be adjusted for changes in the *general price level* — the average price of a large number of goods and services in the economy — or for changes in *specific price levels* — the price of one or a very small number of goods or services. Adjusting for general price level is called *constant-dollar accounting.* Adjusting for specific price levels involves using *current-value accounting.*

The problem of adjusting financial statements to take into account the changing value of the dollar was studied for a number of years before the Financial Accounting Standards Board (FASB) issued an authoritative pronouncement in September 1979, outlining the procedures that large corporations must follow.

Before we discuss the requirements of the FASB relating to constant-dollar and current-value disclosures, we have to introduce the concept of a price index. A *price index* is a measure of the change over time in the average price for a basket of common and necessary goods and services. Let's construct a price index to give you an idea how one works.

Bill and Betsy Dennis decided to construct a Night at the Movies Index (NMI). One evening in 1987 they attended a first-run movie and noted the following prices:

Admission	$5.00
Popcorn (1 buttered, medium)	1.25
Candy (1 box chocolate-covered peanuts)	.90
Soft drink (large)	1.25
Total	$8.40

The $8.40 total they assigned an index number of 1.00 (or 100% of the cost of attending a movie in 1987).

In 1988 Bill and Betsy accumulated a list of prices for the exact same four items and found that they now cost $9.24. The 1988 index number is determined by dividing the new cost by the 1987 base-year cost ($9.24 ÷ $8.40 = 1.10 or 110%). The 110 index means that it costs 10% more to go to the movies in 1988 than it did in 1987.

If this process is repeated year after year, a series of index numbers is created that will measure the changing cost of movie attendance for Bill and Besty over the years. Of course, this index is valid so long as they buy exactly the same items each year.

The *Consumer Price Index* is constructed similarly. The Bureau of Labor Statistics selects a "market basket" of goods that the typical consumer buys. The prices of the goods in this market basket are checked monthly and an index number is calculated. An annual average index number is also published. The base year—the year in which existing prices were assumed to be 100%—used for the Consumer Price Index is 1967. The Consumer Price Index (CPI) for the years 1967 through 1984 appears in Table 18-1 at the top of the facing page. (Note: You'll need these index numbers to solve some of the problems at the end of this chapter.)

As you can see, the consumer had to spend about $2.98 in 1983 to have the same buying power that $1.00 had in 1967. Stated another way, a 1967 dollar will buy only about 33⅓ cents worth of goods in 1983 (100 ÷ 298.4). The buying power of the dollar declined by about $.67 during this period.

Now that you understand the concept of a price index, you're ready to study the FASB requirements on inflation and current values.

Inflation and Financial Statements

You are aware from your study of accounting thus far that financial statements are constructed on a historical cost basis assuming a stable measuring unit. This means that if a building was purchased in 1967 for $500,000, it will appear on a 1983 balance

TABLE 18-1

CONSUMER PRICE INDEX (CPI) 1967–1984			
Year	Consumer Price Index	Year	Consumer Price Index
1967	100.0	1976	170.5
1968	104.2	1977	181.5
1969	109.8	1978	195.4
1970	116.3	1979	217.4
1971	121.3	1980	246.8
1972	125.3	1981	272.4
1973	133.1	1982	289.1
1974	147.7	1983	298.4
1975	161.2	1984	311.1

sheet at $500,000 (less accumulated depreciation). By the same token, depreciation expense on the income statement is calculated by using the $500,000 (less salvage) divided by the useful life. Thus we have 1967 dollars on the balance sheet and income statement. We may also have 1972, 1975, 1978, and 1983 dollars on the same 1983 balance sheet and income statement. We are adding dollars with such widely varying buying power that many accountants believe we are adding apples and oranges and producing totals that are no more meaningful than if we added dollars, francs, and yen.

In 1979, the FASB concluded that financial statement data should be adjusted to reflect constant dollars of the current year using the Consumer Price Index to measure the changing value of the dollar. *Constant-dollar accounting,* then, is the process of converting financial statement amounts into dollars of the same purchasing power. The conversion is done each year, so that in 1983 all financial statement data will be in 1983 dollars, in 1984 all data will be in 1984 dollars, etc. The conversion from historical (old) dollars to constant dollars is accomplished by simply dividing by the old index and multiplying by the new one. The conversion process is demonstrated by the following examples:

Constant-dollar accounting adjusts financial statement data for changes in the general price level

The general formula for converting property, plant, and equipment or intangible assets is:

$$\frac{\text{Cost of asset in historical dollars}}{\text{Index when asset was purchased}} \times \text{current index} = \text{cost of asset in current dollars}$$

A piece of land purchased for $80,000 in 1976 would be converted to 1983 dollars as follows:

$$\frac{\text{Cost of land in 1976 dollars}}{\text{1976 index}} \times \text{1983 index} = \text{cost of land in 1983 dollars}$$

$$\frac{\$80,000}{170.5} \times 298.4 = \$140,012$$

The $500,000 building, its accumulated depreciation, and the depreciation expense conversions are as follows:

	1967 Historical Dollars	Conversion	1983 Constant Dollars
Building	$500,000	$\frac{\$500,000}{100} \times 298.4$	$1,492,000
Accumulated depreciation	425,000	$\frac{\$425,000}{100} \times 298.4$	1,268,200
Net book value	$ 75,000		$ 223,800
1983 depreciation expense*	$ 25,000	$\frac{\$25,000}{100} \times 298.4$	$ 74,600

* Depreciation is calculated on the basis of a 20-year life, with no salvage value, using the straight-line method:
Depreciation expense = $500,000 ÷ 20 years = $25,000 per year
Accumulated depreciation = $25,000 × 17 years = $425,000

A constant-dollar balance sheet would then show Building, $1,492,000; Accumulated Depreciation, $1,268,200; and Land, $140,012. All three are measured in terms of dollars of 1983 buying power.

The building and land assets discussed above are called nonmonetary items. *Nonmonetary items* have values that may move up or down based on the number of dollars they can command in the marketplace. For example, we would expect the value of the building above to be different from its $75,000 historical cost book value. In fact, in a period of inflation we would expect the value to be much higher than $75,000. Likewise, we would expect the land to be worth much more than its $80,000 1976 cost. The adjustment of nonmonetary items to current dollars is a way of recognizing that values of these items in the marketplace are probably at least as much as the adjusted amounts [in our illustration, $223,800 (net) for Building and $140,012 for Land]. Common nonmonetary balance sheet items include merchandise inventory, land, buildings, machinery, equipment, patents, and goodwill.

The value of nonmonetary items changes as the value of the dollar changes

As nonmonetary items are used up and appear on the income statement as expenses, they are likewise nonmonetary expense items; e.g., cost of goods sold expense, depreciation expense, and amortization expense. Conversions of all nonmonetary items are calculated just as we demonstrated for Land, Building, and Building Depreciation Expense earlier.

The holder of nonmonetary items during a period of changing prices would not expect to have any real purchasing power gain or loss. The value of the nonmonetary item is expected to change at least as much as the general purchasing power of the dollar changes.

The value of monetary items cannot change as the value of the dollar changes

Monetary items have future amounts that are fixed either by their nature (cash) or by contract (a receivable or payable). Their values cannot move up and down as the value of the dollar changes. The holder of monetary items is affected much differently than a holder of nonmonetary items. Suppose that in 1976 Company A has $80,000 cash and Company B has land it purchased for $80,000. By 1983 Company A still has $80,000, but because of inflation the cash will buy much less than it would in 1976. Company A suffered a purchasing power loss. Company B, on the other hand, could sell the land and bring much more than $80,000 in the marketplace. If the land can be sold for $140,012, Company B will be exactly as well off in 1983 as it was in 1976. Company B suffered no purchasing power loss.

Cash and receivables are monetary assets. Holding these items during a period of inflation results in purchasing power losses. A loss with cash was illustrated above;

now let's look at a receivable. Suppose that Sam York purchased a machine from Ajax Machinery Sales in 1967 for $100,000 (1967 CPI = 100). York promised to pay for the machine in 1968 (1968 CPI = 104.2). Ajax will receive $100,000 in 1968, the fixed amount York promised to repay; however, Ajax will need $104,200 [($100,000 ÷ 100) × 104.2] in order to be as well off. Ajax lost $4,200 in buying power by agreeing to wait a year to receive payment.

Payables are monetary liabilities. Holding monetary liabilities during a period of inflation results in purchasing power gains. If Fry, Inc., borrows $10,000 in 1967 when the CPI = 100 and repays the $10,000 in 1968 when the CPI is 104.2, Fry will have a purchasing power gain of $420 [($10,000 ÷ 100) × 104.2 minus $10,000; $10,420 − $10,000]. Fry borrowed dollars that had more buying power than those that were repaid.

The calculation of the overall purchasing power gain or loss for a large company is complicated by the fact that cash, receivables, and payables (monetary items) are constantly changing during the year. You understand the basic idea behind what causes purchasing power gains and losses; we will leave the complexities of the complete calculation for a more advanced accounting course.

The financial statement analyst should be aware that constant-dollar income statements can paint quite a different picture from the traditional historical cost statement—especially during periods of high inflation.

Now that we have shown you many of the techniques used to determine constant-dollar net income, let's look at some actual companies' traditional, constant-dollar income, and purchasing power gain or loss for the year ended December 31, 1983:

Company	Income (Loss) as Reported in the Traditional Income Statement (000s omitted)	Constant-Dollar Net Income (Loss) (000s omitted)	Purchasing Power Gain (Loss) (000s omitted)
Anheuser-Busch Companies, Inc.	$ 348,000	$ 279,600	$ 61,800
General Electric Company	2,024,000	1,435,000	(81,000)
General Motors Corporation	3,730,200	3,672,100	258,000

Current-Value Accounting

Current-value accounting uses replacement costs to value assets, liabilities, and some expenses

Current-value accounting involves measuring assets and income in terms of current replacement costs rather than historical costs or historical costs adjusted for changing price levels. A simple illustration will contrast historical cost, constant-dollar, and current-value accounting.

THE SNOPES FAMILY

The Snopes family owns 5 acres of rural land that was acquired in 1967 for $5,000. On a 1983 constant-dollar balance sheet the land would be shown at $14,920 [($5,000 ÷ 100) × 298.4]. This conversion adjusts historical cost for the change in the general price level and states the land in 1983 constant dollars using the CPI. Assume that an interstate highway now passes close to the Snopes's land and the 5 acres fronts on a main access road. The plot is zoned commercial and is considered a prime location for a restaurant, motel, or service station. The Snopes have received a firm offer of $45,000 for the 5 acres. The specific price level of this piece of land has risen much more rapidly than the general price level. Current-value accounting would show the land at $45,000. We have determined the following three values for the land:

Historical cost.	$ 5,000
Constant-dollar based on historical cost	14,920
Current value	45,000

During the period 1967 to 1983, the Snopes family's land increased by $9,920 ($14,920 − $5,000) due to the change in the general price level. Another $30,080 ($45,000 − $14,920) increase was a real value increase due to the change in the specific price level.

Many accountants and financial analysts argue that current-value accounting gives a much more realistic picture of a company's assets and income than does either the historical cost or constant-dollar techniques. They contend that, in order to continue in business, the company will have to purchase inventory, machines, buildings, and various other assets at today's prices (current values) — not at some artificial constant-dollar amount. Current-value income, then, will measure the maximum amount that a company could pay to the stockholders as dividends and still retain its present scale of operations. If we sell a lawn mower for $400 that cost $250, historical accounting would tell us that we have an income of $150. If it costs $300 to buy another lawn mower to sell, however, we could only distribute $100 ($400 − $300) to our stockholders and remain in business. Current-value accounting would report the $100 as income.

You have probably already noticed that a current-value income statement uses replacement costs for cost of goods sold expense, depreciation expense, and other goods and services used up. In most other respects the current-value and constant-dollar income statements are identical.

The FASB *Standard* recognizes the importance of reporting current-value financial information. Large corporations must report the following current-value data:

Current-value information must also be reported by large companies

1. Net income on a current-cost basis.

2. The current-cost amounts of merchandise inventory and of property, plant, and equipment assets at the end of the year.

3. The increase or decrease during the year of the current values of merchandise inventory, and property, plant, and equipment assets. The increase or decrease is to be shown net of inflation.

At the top of the facing page we've added these three pieces of information to the constant-dollar information shown on page 701.

Inflation Reporting — Recent Developments

During the 5-year period, 1979–1983, the FASB required large companies to report five constant-dollar and current-value amounts:

1. Constant-dollar income

2. Purchasing power gains or losses

3. Current-cost income

Company	Income (Loss) as Reported in the Traditional Income Statement (000s omitted)	Constant- Dollar Net Income (Loss) (000s omitted)	Purchasing Power Gain (Loss) (000s omitted)
Anheuser-Busch Companies, Inc.	$ 348,000	$ 279,600	$ 61,800
General Electric Company	2,024,000	1,435,000	(81,000)
General Motors Corporation	3,730,200	3,672,100	258,000

	Current- Cost Income (Loss) (000s omitted)	Total Current Value of Inventory and Properties (000s omitted)	Current-Cost Increase (Decrease) Net of Inflation (000s omitted)
Anheuser-Busch Companies, Inc.	$ 288,000	$ 4,402,700	$ (76,500)
General Electric Company	1,543,000	15,267,000	(568,000)
General Motors Corporation	3,413,700	36,755,200	(233,900)

4. Current-cost amounts of merchandise inventory and property, plant, and equipment

5. The increase or decrease in the current cost of merchandise inventory, and property, plant, and equipment

In 1984 the FASB changed the reporting requirements. Now large companies must report only the last four items listed above. *The FASB now requires that only current-cost information be reported in the financial statement notes.* The Board decided to change the rules because they concluded that:

1. Showing so many different amounts was confusing to statement readers.

2. Calculating all the information costs more than the information was worth.

3. Current-cost information is more useful than constant-dollar amounts.

We have helped you gain an understanding of the general idea behind both the constant-dollar and the current-cost amounts. If the rate of inflation increases to the levels of the mid-to-late 1970s, you will see a great deal of renewed discussion of the effects of inflation on the amounts reported in financial statements.

The analyst should be especially aware of the effects of inflation when comparing two or more companies. The current-cost financial information currently reported will show the combined effect of changes in the general and specific price levels on a company's income and major assets (merchandise inventory, and property, plant, and equipment). In many instances a comparison of the current-value income amounts of different companies will show the analyst how well a company is coping with the effects of inflation.

CHAPTER SUMMARY

The auditor's report, the financial statements, and the notes to the financial statements may be analyzed to provide the reader with insight into a company's earnings performance, the strength of its financial structure, its debt-paying ability, and the effect of inflation on its operations.

The *audit report* contains the auditor's independent opinion about whether the financial statements are presented fairly in conformity with generally accepted accounting principles. A careful study of this report may alert the reader to weaknesses in financial measurement or disclosure.

Financial statements may be analyzed *horizontally* and *vertically.* One horizontal approach compares balance sheets of several years expressed in dollars and percentages. A similar comparison is made of income statements of several years. Another horizontal approach, called *trend analysis,* compares proportionate changes in selected financial information over time. These proportionate changes are expressed as percentages of a designated base year. A third horizontal approach involves comparing financial ratios for several years in order to detect significant changes in them over time.

Vertical financial statement analysis involves comparing items on financial statements of a single period. *Common-size financial statements* state each component of the statements in terms of one other component. A common-size income statement usually states each component as a percentage of sales. A common-size balance sheet presents each item as a percentage of total assets.

Ratio analysis, another form of the vertical approach, may be used to examine earnings performance, debt-paying ability, and liquid position. The following ratios are commonly employed in these evaluations:

Earnings Performance

$$\text{Rate of return on total assets} = \frac{\text{income before interest expense}}{\text{average total assets}}$$

$$\text{Rate of return on common stockholders' equity} = \frac{\text{net income} - \text{preferred dividends}}{\text{average common stockholders' equity}}$$

$$\text{Earnings per share} = \frac{\text{net income} - \text{preferred dividends}}{\text{average number of common shares outstanding}}$$

$$\text{Price-earnings ratio} = \frac{\text{market price per share of common stock}}{\text{earnings per share of common stock}}$$

$$\text{Dividend yield rate} = \frac{\text{dividends per share of common stock}}{\text{current market price per share of common stock}}$$

Debt-Paying Ability

$$\text{Times interest earned} = \frac{\text{income before interest expense and income taxes}}{\text{annual interest expense}}$$

$$\text{Debt to total assets} = \frac{\text{total liabilities}}{\text{total assets}}$$

$$\text{Stockholders' equity to total assets} = \frac{\text{total stockholders' equity}}{\text{total assets}}$$

(continued)

Liquid Position

$$\text{Current ratio} = \frac{\text{current assets}}{\text{current liabilities}}$$

$$\text{Quick ratio} = \frac{\text{quick assets}}{\text{current liabilities}}$$

$$\text{Inventory turnover} = \frac{\text{cost of goods sold}}{\text{average merchandise inventory}}$$

$$\text{Accounts receivable turnover} = \frac{\text{credit sales}}{\text{average accounts receivable}}$$

$$\text{Average age of receivables} = \frac{365 \text{ days}}{\text{accounts receivable turnover}}$$

Ratios take on much more meaning when they can be compared to measures of what they "should be." Standards of comparison are usually obtained by analyzing financial statements of companies in the same industry and averaging the ratios thus determined. Industry averages may also be acquired from trade associations and financial research firms.

Ratio comparisons are most useful when the companies studied are in fact in the same industry, are of approximately the same size, and use similar accounting methods.

Notes to the financial statements are an integral part of the statements. Financial analysis is not complete until the notes have been carefully examined. Each company must disclose choices made from among different accounting methods in an ***accounting policies note.*** The accounting policies note is followed by notes providing detailed information about certain financial statement items such as property, plant, and equipment, and long-term debt. Events that may have a significant effect on future financial statements are disclosed in a ***contingencies note.*** Common contingencies include pending lawsuits and administrative complaints filed by regulatory agencies.

Background information about the firm, its industry, and the economy as a whole may be obtained from business magazines and newspapers, publications of financial research firms, industry trade associations, credit-rating bureaus, and interviews with management.

The effects of inflation may be significant enough to distort the relative performance of different companies. The analyst should realize that traditional financial statements assume no inflation has occurred (i.e., all dollars have a constant value over time). Wherever possible, inflation-adjusted financial statements should be used to obtain a more accurate evaluation of the company's performance and financial position. Large corporations are required to report financial data that take into consideration the combined effect of changes in the general price level, ***constant-dollar accounting,*** and changes in specific price levels, ***current-value accounting.*** The following information is available in the company's footnotes:

1. Purchasing power gain or loss

2. Current-cost net income

3. Current-cost amounts of merchandise inventory, and property, plant, and equipment

4. The increase or decrease in the current cost of Merchandise Inventory, and Property, Plant, and Equipment

Accounting policies note   A description of the various accounting methods that the company has selected to use in preparing its financial statements. Disclosure is made of only those methods selected from among several acceptable ones. (page 695)

Auditor's report   An independent auditor's opinion regarding the fairness of presentation of the financial statements. (page 680)

Common-size financial statement   A financial statement in which each component is stated as a percentage of one other component. A common-size income statement usually states each component as a percentage of sales. A common-size balance sheet presents each item as a percentage of total assets. (page 684)

Comparative financial statements   Presentation of financial statements of more than one period in columnar form. Changes between periods expressed in dollars or percentages may also be included. (page 680)

Constant-dollar accounting   The process of converting traditional financial statement data into dollars with the same purchasing power. Constant-dollar accounting adjusts for changes in the general price level. (page 699)

Consumer Price Index   An index number based on the weighted average of the prices in a market basket of goods that a typical consumer buys. The Consumer Price Index is one measure of the general price level. (page 698)

Contingency   A future event that may occur but whose occurrence is not certain. (page 695)

Current-value accounting   The process of measuring assets in terms of current replacement costs. Current-value accounting adjusts for changes in specific price levels. (page 701)

General price level   The average price of a large number of goods and services in the economy. The Consumer Price Index is one measure of the general price level. (page 697)

Horizontal analysis   Comparing the financial data of a single company for 2 or more years. (page 680)

Inflation   The condition that exists when a larger number of dollars is required to buy the same quantity of goods or services. This decrease in the buying power of the dollar is usually measured by an increase in a price index such as the Consumer Price Index. (page 697)

Leverage   The use of debt or preferred stock financing in an attempt to earn a higher rate of return on common stockholders' equity than would have been possible without this financing. (page 687)

Monetary asset   An asset whose value is fixed at a specified number of dollars regardless of changes in the general purchasing power of the dollar. Cash and accounts receivable are examples. (page 700)

Monetary items   See definitions of *Monetary asset* and *Monetary liability.*

Monetary liability   A liability whose value is fixed at a specified number of dollars regardless of changes in the general purchasing power of the dollar. Accounts payable and bonds payable are examples. (page 701)

Nonmonetary items   Assets or liabilities whose values may move up or down based upon the number of dollars they can command in the marketplace. Merchandise inventory, buildings, and patents are examples of nonmonetary items. (page 700)

Purchasing power gain or loss   The amount of buying power gained from holding monetary liabilities during a period of inflation, or the amount of buying power lost from holding monetary assets during a period of inflation. (page 700)

Ratio   The relationship of one number to another that is determined by dividing the first number by the second. (page 686)

Specific price level   The price of one or a very small number of goods or services. (page 697)

Stable measuring unit assumption   A principle underlying traditional financial statements stating that the purchasing power of the dollar is assumed to remain constant over time. (page 697)

Trading on the equity   See *Leverage.*

Trend analysis   The comparison of proportionate changes in selected financial information over time. These proportionate changes are expressed as a percentage of a designated base year. (page 682)

Vertical analysis   The comparison of items on financial statements of a single period. (page 683)

QUESTIONS

1. Does the auditor's report state that the financial statements present a true and correct picture of the company's financial position? Explain.

2. Can a horizontal analysis be made of a single year's financial statements? Explain.

3. What is the analyst attempting to learn by studying comparative financial statements?

4. Jon Investor is calculating trend percentages for sales and net income of Toco, Inc. If he selects 1985 as his base year, what will the trend percentages be for 1985? How will he calculate the trend percentages for 1986?

5. Explain how vertical analysis differs form horizontal analysis.

6. Which financial statement analysis tool would be most useful in comparing two companies of vastly differing size? Explain how this tool makes the comparison possible.

7. Willco's rate of return on total assets is 11%; explain what this rate tells the analyst.

8. What is meant by favorable leverage? Is favorable leverage present in a company that has a rate of return on total assets of 12% and a rate of return on common stockholders' equity of 10%? Explain.

9. Jarax, Inc., common stock has a dividend yield ratio of 8%; Jarax, Inc., bonds maturing in 20 years offer an effective interest rate of 12%. Explain what the dividend yield rate is. Explain why an investor might prefer the Jarax common stock over the Jarax bonds even though the yield rate on the stock is lower.

10. What does a times interest earned statistic of .95 mean? How would this statistic be evaluated by a long-term creditor? Explain.

11. Why is the quick ratio often a better measure of the very short-term liquid position of a company than the current ratio?

12. Explain how inventory turnover is used to evaluate the amount of inventory on hand at the end of a time period.

13. Clyde Co.'s average age of receivables is 35 days. Explain what additional information is necessary before this average can be evaluated as relatively good or bad.

14. List some external standards against which the performance of a company may be compared.

15. Briefly describe the type of information that you will find in an accounting policies note.

16. The 1967 Consumer Price Index was 100. How many dollars were necessary in 1981 to buy the same amount that $1.00 bought in 1967? By how much did the value of the dollar decline from 1967 through 1981?

17. What are monetary items? How does inflation affect a company holding **(a)** a monetary asset? **(b)** a monetary liability?

18. What are nonmonetary items? Give examples of two nonmonetary assets.

19. How does constant-dollar differ from current-value accounting?

EXERCISES

Exercise 18-1
Preparing common-size income statement

Convert the following income statement into a common-size statement that uses Sales as 100%:

MAYER CORP. Income Statement Year Ended September 30, 1987		
Sales.		$180,000
Cost of Goods Sold		99,000
Gross Profit on Sales		$ 81,000
Operating Expenses:		
Selling Expenses.	$43,200	
General and Administrative Expenses.	16,200	59,400
Income before Income Taxes.		$ 21,600
Income Tax Expense		9,720
Net Income		$ 11,880

(Check figure: Selling Expenses = 24%)

Exercise 18-2
Calculating trend percentages

Pro Foods, Inc., is concerned about the level of its advertising and office salaries expense. Selected income statement data for the past 3 years appear below:

	1988	1987	1986
Sales	$140,000	$60,000	$37,500
Gross profit	89,600	37,200	22,500
Advertising expense	7,000	3,300	2,250
Office salaries expense.	22,400	9,000	4,500
Net income.	30,800	13,800	9,000

Calculate trend percentages for Sales, Advertising Expense, and Office Salaries Expense. Use 1986 as a base year. Round to the nearest percent.

(Check figure: 1988 Advertising Expense = 311%)

Exercise 18-3
Calculating ROR on total assets and on stockholders' equity

The following data have been assembled from the financial statements of Rule, Inc.:

	December 31, 1987	January 1, 1987
Total assets	$180,000	$140,000
Total stockholders' equity.	144,000	112,000
Total preferred stockholders' equity	30,000	30,000
Preferred dividends declared	2,400	—
Net income	20,000	—
Interest expense	5,750	—

Calculate the following ratios:
a. Rate of return on total assets.
b. Rate of return on common stockholders' equity.

(Check figure: Rate of return on common stockholders' equity = 17.96%)

Exercise 18-4
Calculating EPS, P-E ratio, and dividend yield rate

N. Vester is in the process of analyzing the earnings performance of the Boulder Transport Corp. She has gathered the following data from Boulder's financial statements and from a report of the closing market prices of stock:

Net income for 1988	$ 743,000
Preferred dividends declared during 1988	60,000
Common dividends declared Dec. 31, 1988.	620,000
Number of shares of Boulder common stock outstanding:	
Jan. 1, 1988.	1,100,000 shs
Dec. 31, 1988.	1,300,000 shs
Market price per share of common stock on Dec. 31, 1988	$15

Calculate the following ratios relating to the Boulder stock:
a. Earnings per share of common stock
b. The price-earnings ratio
c. The dividend yield rate of common stock

(Check figure: Earnings per share of common stock = $.569)

Exercise 18-5
Calculating times interest earned, debt to total assets ratio, and stockholders' equity to total assets ratio

The president of Tom's Toys, Inc., has asked you to gather some statistics about his company's debt-paying ability. You have compiled the following data:

Net income	$ 900,000
Income tax rate	40%
Interest expense	$ 100,000
Total liabilities.	2,048,000
Total stockholders' equity.	4,352,000

Using the data above, calculate:
a. Times interest earned
b. Debt to total assets ratio
c. Stockholders' equity to total asset ratio

(Check figure: Times interest earned = 16 times)

Exercise 18-6

Calculating working capital, current ratio, and quick ratio

The following information was taken from the balance sheet of Ready Corp.:

Cash	$13,250
Accounts receivable (net)	33,000
Merchandise inventory	40,000
Prepaid expenses	9,950
Accounts payable	25,200
Accrued payables	1,800
Notes payable (due in 6 months)	10,000

Calculate **(a)** working capital, **(b)** current ratio, and **(c)** quick ratio.

(Check figure: Current ratio = 2.6 : 1)

Exercise 18-7

Calculating inventory turnover, accounts receivable turnover, and average age of receivables

You have been assigned the task of evaluating Dorian, Inc.'s management of merchandise and receivables. You decide that inventory turnover, accounts receivable turnover, and average age of receivables statistics will prove valuable in your opinions. The following data are available from Dorian's annual report:

Merchandise inventory:	
Jan. 1.	$ 245,000
Dec. 31	375,000
Accounts receivable:	
Jan. 1.	250,000
Dec. 31	297,000
Cost of goods sold	2,480,000
Cash sales	1,000,000
Total sales	5,100,000
Dorian's credit terms	Net 30 days

a. Calculate inventory turnover, accounts receivable turnover, and average age of receivables.
b. In your opinion, is Dorian doing a good job or a poor job of managing inventory and receivables? Explain.

(Check figure: Accounts receivable turnover = 15 times)

Exercise 18-8
Finding missing balance sheet amounts using ratios

You are given the following ratios and amounts for the Turtle Corp. for 1988:

Current ratio	2.7
Quick ratio	1.17
Inventory turnover	3.4
Accounts receivable turnover.	6.5
Cost of goods sold for 1988	$197,200
Credit sales for 1988	260,000
Accounts receivable, 1/1/88	38,200
Merchandise inventory, 1/1/88	62,000

TURTLE CORP.
Schedule of Current Assets
and Current Liabilities
December 31, 1988

Current assets:		
Cash.		$ 5,000
Accounts receivable.	(2)	
Merchandise inventory.	(3)	
Prepaid insurance		7,200
Total current assets	(1)	$
Current liabilities:		
Accounts payable	(4)	$
Accrued payables		5,000
Total current liabilities.		$40,000

Supply the missing amounts in this schedule. Hint: Solve in numerical order (total current assets first, etc.).

(Check figure: Total current assets = $108,000)

Exercise 18-9
Calculating amount of land adjusted to constant dollars

Build Corp. purchased a plot of land in 1975 for $400,000. Using the Consumer Price Index numbers from Table 18-1, calculate the constant-dollar amount for Land in terms of 1981 dollars, 1982 dollars, and 1983 dollars. (Round to the nearest dollar.)

(Check figure: Land in terms of 1981 dollars = $675,930)

Exercise 18-10
Calculating amount of increase in land attributable to general and specific price level increases

Starr Corporation owns land that was purchased for $800,000 in 1976. At the end of 1983 the land was appraised at $3,320,000. Using the Consumer Price Index numbers in Table 18-1, calculate **(a)** the portion of the increase in value that is due to changes in the general price level, and **(b)** the portion of the increase in value that is a real value increase. (Round to the nearest dollar.)

(Check figure: Real value increase = $1,919,883)

Problem A18-1
Calculating liquid position,
debt-paying ability, and earnings
performance ratios

Poston, Inc.'s income statement and balance sheet for 1987 are presented below:

POSTON, INC.
Income Statement
Year Ended August 31, 1987

Sales.		$150,000
Cost of Goods Sold:		
Merchandise Inventory 9/1/86.	$ 24,000	
Purchases (net).	99,000	
Goods Available for Sale	$123,000	
Merchandise Inventory 8/31/87.	18,000	
Cost of Goods Sold.		105,000
Gross Profit		$ 45,000
Operating Expenses		24,000
Income from Operations.		$ 21,000
Other Income and Expense:		
Interest Expense.		7,000
Income before Tax.		$ 14,000
Income Tax Expense		6,400
Net Income		$ 7,600

POSTON, INC.
Balance Sheet
August 31, 1987

Cash.	$ 6,000
Marketable Securities.	3,000
Accounts Receivable (net).	17,000
Merchandise Inventory	18,000
Property, Plant, and Equipment (net)	160,000
Goodwill.	6,000
Total Assets.	$210,000
Accounts Payable	$ 16,000
Accrued Salaries Payable	2,000
Income Taxes Payable	1,500
Other Accrued Payables	500
10% Note Payable (due in 1998).	70,000
Common Stock ($1 par).	80,000
Retained Earnings.	40,000
Total Liabilities and Stockholders' Equity	$210,000

All sales were on credit. On September 1, 1986, Poston had total assets of $240,000 (including accounts receivable of $13,000 and merchandise inventory of $24,000), total liabilities of $127,600, and total stockholders' equity of $112,400.

Required

1. Calculate the following liquid position ratios: current ratio, quick ratio, inventory turnover, and accounts receivable turnover.
2. Calculate the following ratios indicating debt-paying ability: times interest earned, debt to total assets ratio, and stockholders' equity to total assets ratio.

3. Calculate the following earnings performance statistics: rate of return on total assets, and rate of return on common stockholders' equity.

(Check figure: Debt to total assets ratio = 42.9%)

Problem A18-2
Calculating percentage increase and decrease in comparative balance sheets

The following financial statements are included in the 1988 annual report of Federal Company:

FEDERAL COMPANY
Comparative Balance Sheets
(000s omitted)

	June 30	
	1988	1987
Assets		
Current Assets:		
Cash	$ 31,600	$ 6,000
Accounts Receivable (net of Allowances for Uncollectibles of $560 in 1988 and $192 in 1987)	19,200	9,600
Merchandise Inventory	22,100	20,000
Total Current Assets	$ 72,900	$ 35,600
Property, Plant, and Equipment:		
Land	$ 80,000	$ 90,000
Buildings	20,000	20,000
Less: Accumulated Depreciation	(2,700)	(2,500)
Equipment	15,000	14,000
Less: Accumulated Depreciation	(2,000)	(1,500)
Total Property, Plant, and Equipment	$110,300	$120,000
Intangibles:		
Patents	$ 1,500	$ 1,600
Total Assets	$184,700	$157,200
Liabilities and Stockholders' Equity		
Current Liabilities:		
Accounts Payable	$ 20,000	$ 16,600
Accrued Payables	3,500	3,000
Total Current Liabilities	$ 23,500	$ 19,600
Long-Term Liabilities:		
8% Note Payable (due 1990)	$ 12,000	—
10% Bonds Payable (due 1995)	81,000	$ 81,000
Total Long-Term Liabilities	$ 93,000	$ 81,000
Total Liabilities	$116,500	$100,600
Stockholders' Equity:		
Common Stock, $1 par	$ 10,000	$ 10,000
Paid-In Capital in Excess of Par	26,400	26,400
Retained Earnings	31,800	20,200
Total Stockholders' Equity	$ 68,200	$ 56,600
Total Liabilities and Stockholders' Equity	$184,700	$157,200

FEDERAL COMPANY
Comparative Income Statements
Years Ended June 30,
(000s omitted)

	1988	1987
Net Sales	$160,000	$104,000
Cost of Goods Sold	59,200	37,500
Gross Profit on Sales.	$100,800	$ 66,500
Operating Expenses:		
Sales Salary Expense	$ 25,800	$ 21,600
Utilities Expense.	14,000	11,800
Advertising Expense	27,200	16,800
Other Expenses	5,000	4,200
Total Operating Expenses.	$ 72,000	$ 54,400
Other Income and Expense:		
Interest Expense	$ 10,000	$ 8,600
Income before Income Taxes	$ 18,800	$ 3,500
Income Tax Expense	7,200	1,200
Net Income	$ 11,600	$ 2,300

Required

1. Comparative income statements and balance sheets for 1988 and 1987 are presented above. On your solutions paper, prepare columns showing the amount and percentage increase or decrease for each item on the statements.
2. Based on your solution for requirement (1), answer the following questions:
   a. What are the three balance sheet accounts that experienced the greatest percentage change?
   b. What three revenue or expense accounts on the income statement had the highest percentage change?
   c. Does the large increase in current assets appear to have been generated by profits for the year? Explain.
   d. Sales increased as compared with the prior year. Did expenses seem to increase proportionately also? Comment on any exceptions.

(Check figure: Income statement items with the highest percentage change = Income Tax Expense, Cost of Goods Sold, Advertising Expense)

Problem A18-3
Completing the balance sheet and income statement

The following financial information is available for Dallas Machinery Corp.:
a. All sales were on credit.
b. The debt to total assets ratio is 52%.
c. Working capital is $828.
d. Net income is 14% of sales; gross profit is 65% of sales.
e. The only interest paid was on long-term debt.
f. Inventory turnover = 5. (Beginning inventory = $150.)
g. Accounts receivable turnover = 10. (Beginning accounts receivable = $240.)
h. 46% of the total cost of the building has been depreciated.

Required

Complete the Dallas Machinery Corp. financial statements shown below. Round all calculations to the nearest dollar. (Hint: Determine the amounts in the order indicated by the numbers in parentheses on the statements.)

DALLAS MACHINERY CORP.
Income Statement
Year Ended December 31, 1987

Sales	(1)	$ ____
Cost of Goods Sold	(3)	____
Gross Profit on Sales	(2)	____
Operating Expenses	(15)	____
Interest Expense	(14)	____
Income before Income Taxes	(4)	____
Income Tax Expense (34.67% of income before income taxes)	(5)	____
Net Income		$392

DALLAS MACHINERY CORP.
Balance Sheet
December 31, 1987

Assets:		
Cash		$ 418
Accounts Receivable (net)	(6)	____
Merchandise Inventory	(7)	____
Building	(10)	____
Accumulated Depreciation	(11)	(____)
Total Assets	(9)	$ ____
Liabilities and Stockholders' Equity:		
Accounts Payable	(8)	$ ____
10% Bonds Payable (due 1995)	(12)	____
Common Stock		500
Retained Earnings	(13)	____
Total Equities		$2,600

Problem A18-4
Selecting data needed and calculating five ratios

The following financial data have been assembled for World Coatings, Inc., on December 31, 1988:

Average total assets for 1988	$400,000
Total stockholders' equity (average for 1988)	300,000
Common stock, $2 par	175,000
8% preferred stock, $50 par	75,000
Net income	31,000
Interest expense	3,000
Income tax expense (40% of income before income taxes)	
Market price of common stock, 12/31/88	$2.75
Market price of preferred stock, 12/31/88	$60
Common dividends were paid at the rate of $.10 per share per quarter	
Preferred dividends were declared and paid	
No preferred stock or common stock was issued or reacquired during 1988	

Required | Using whatever data you need from the above list, calculate:
1. Rate of return on total assets
2. Rate of return on common stockholders' equity
3. Earnings per common share
4. Price-earnings ratio
5. Dividend yield rate

(Check figure: Earnings per common share = $.286)

Problem A18-5

Calculating liquidity ratios for two firms and deciding which should receive a short-term loan

Stan, Inc., and Oliver Company both sell irrigation equipment for agricultural use. Both companies have applied for a short-term loan. Data from the December 31, 1987, balance sheets appear below:

	Stan, Inc.	Oliver Company
Cash	$ 27,200	$ 75,000
Marketable securities	1,800	60,000
Accounts receivable (net)	31,000	44,000
Merchandise inventory	180,000	120,000
Property, plant, and equipment (net)	350,000	360,000
Intangibles	1,800	—
Total assets	$591,800	$659,000
Current liabilities	$ 60,000	$100,000
Long-term liabilities	100,000	100,000
Common stock, $10 par	400,000	400,000
Retained earnings	31,800	59,000
Total equities	$591,800	$659,000

Other Information:

	Stan, Inc.	Oliver Company
Accounts receivable, 1/1/87	$ 39,000	$ 35,000
Merchandise inventory, 1/1/87	160,000	130,000
1987 sales:		
Cash	258,000	120,000
Credit	342,000	480,000
1987 cost of goods sold	528,000	360,000

Required | 1. Calculate for each company the current ratio, quick ratio, inventory turnover, accounts receivable turnover, and average age of receivables.
2. Which company would you recommend to receive the short-term loan? Explain.
3. What additional ratios would you consider if the companies were requesting a long-term loan? Explain.

(Check figure: Inventory turnover for Oliver Company = 2.88)

Problem A18-6

Determining the amount at which four assets would appear on a constant-dollar balance sheet

You have been assigned the task of completing the property, plant, and equipment section of a constant-dollar balance sheet that is being prepared for Deats Enterprises, Inc. The following list of property, plant, and equipment assets was taken from the Deats traditional balance sheet on December 31, 1983:

	Year Acquired	Cost	Accumulated Depreciation on 12/31/83
Land	1972	$ 240,000	—
Buildings	1974	1,180,000	$432,000
Machinery	1978	720,000	324,000
Office fixtures	1982	165,000	33,000

Required   Using the Consumer Price Index numbers from Table 18-1, determine the amount at which each of the property, plant, and equipment assets listed above will appear on a constant-dollar balance sheet. You will need to convert both the cost of the asset and any accumulated depreciation. Round to the nearest dollar.

(Check figure: Buildings = $2,383,967)

Set B

Problem B18-1
Calculating liquid position, debt-paying ability, and earnings performance ratios

Milton, Inc.'s income statement and balance sheet for 1988 are presented below:

MILTON, INC.
Income Statement
Year Ended October 31, 1988

Sales.		$300,000
Cost of Goods Sold:		
Merchandise Inventory 11/1/87.	$ 27,500	
Purchases (net).	125,000	
Goods Available for Sale	$152,500	
Merchandise Inventory 10/31/88	32,500	
Cost of Goods Sold.		120,000
Gross Profit		$180,000
Operating Expenses		125,000
Income from Operations.		$ 55,000
Other Income and Expense:		
Interest Expense.		2,000
Income before Tax.		$ 53,000
Income Tax Expense		24,000
Net Income		$ 29,000

MILTON, INC.
Balance Sheet
October 31, 1988

Cash.	$ 3,750
Marketable Securities.	5,400
Accounts Receivable (net).	9,650
Merchandise Inventory	32,500
Property, Plant, and Equipment (net)	80,000
Patents	2,700
Total Assets.	$134,000

(continued)

Accounts Payable	$ 8,100
Accrued Salaries Payable	1,350
Income Taxes Payable	4,800
8% Bonds Payable (due in 1995)	25,000
Common Stock ($10 par)	50,000
Retained Earnings.	44,750
Total Liabilities and Stockholders' Equity	$134,000

All sales were on credit. On November 1, 1987, Milton had total assets of $116,000 (including accounts receivable of $10,350 and merchandise inventory of $27,500), total liabilities of $50,500, and total stockholders' equity of $65,500.

Required

1. Calculate the following liquid position ratios: current ratio, quick ratio, inventory turnover, and accounts receivable turnover.
2. Calculate the following ratios indicating debt-paying ability: times interest earned, debt to total assets ratio, and stockholders' equity to total assets ratio.
3. Calculate the following earnings performance statistics: rate of return on total assets, and rate of return on common stockholders' equity.

(Check figure: Accounts receivable turnover = 30)

Problem B18-2
Calculating percentage increase and decrease in comparative balance sheets

The following financial statements are included in the 1988 annual report of Aspin Company:

ASPIN COMPANY
Comparative Balance Sheets
(000s omitted)

	September 30 1988	1987
Assets		
Current Assets:		
Cash.	$ 7,200	$ 3,600
Accounts Receivable (net of Allowances for Uncollectibles of $120 in 1988 and $40 in 1987).	5,600	3,800
Merchandise Inventory	15,400	11,000
Total Current Assets	$ 28,200	$ 18,400
Property, Plant, and Equipment:		
Land	$ 50,000	$ 44,000
Buildings.	36,000	36,000
Less: Accumulated Depreciation	(600)	(500)
Equipment	7,000	6,000
Less: Accumulated Depreciation	(200)	(100)
Total Property, Plant, and Equipment.	$ 92,200	$ 85,400
Intangibles:		
Copyrights.	$ 2,900	$ 2,800
Total Assets	$123,300	$106,600

(continued)

Liabilities and Stockholders' Equity		
Current Liabilities:		
Accounts Payable	$ 2,000	$ 8,000
Accrued Payables	1,300	1,000
Total Current Liabilities.	$ 3,300	$ 9,000
Long-Term Liabilities:		
6% Note Payable (due 1990)	$ 20,000	$ 20,000
12% Bonds Payable (due 1995)	20,000	—
Total Long-Term Liabilities	$ 40,000	$ 20,000
Total Liabilities.	$ 43,300	$ 29,000
Stockholders' Equity:		
Common Stock, $10 par	$ 20,000	$ 20,000
Paid-In Capital in Excess of Par	8,000	8,000
Retained Earnings.	52,000	49,600
Total Stockholders' Equity	$ 80,000	$ 77,600
Total Liabilities and Stockholders' Equity	$123,300	$106,600

ASPIN COMPANY
Comparative Income Statements
Years Ended September 30,
(000s omitted)

	1988	1987
Net Sales.	$68,400	$76,000
Cost of Goods Sold	24,472	26,600
Gross Profit on Sales	$43,928	$49,400
Operating Expenses:		
Sales Salary Expense.	$10,944	$12,160
Utilities Expense	12,312	9,120
Other Selling Expenses	6,156	6,840
Other General Expenses	2,052	2,280
Total Operating Expenses	$31,464	$30,400
Other Income and Expense:		
Interest Expense.	$ 3,600	$ 1,200
Income before Income Taxes.	$ 8,864	$17,800
Income Tax Expense	3,988	8,010
Net Income	$ 4,876	$ 9,790

Required   **1.** Comparative income statements and balance sheets for 1988 and 1987 are presented above. On your solutions paper, prepare columns showing the amount and percentage increase or decrease for each item on the statements.

2. Based on your solution for requirement (1), answer the following questions:

a. What are the four balance sheet accounts that experienced the greatest percentage change?

b. What three revenue or expense accounts on the income statement had the highest percentage change?

c. Does the large increase in current assets appear to have been generated by profits for the year? Explain.

d. Sales decreased as compared with the prior year. Did expenses seem to decrease proportionately also? Comment on any exceptions.

(Check figure: Income statement items with the highest percentage change = Utilities Expense, Interest Expense, and Income Tax Expense)

Problem B18-3
Completing the balance sheet and income statement

The following financial information is available for Waco Sales, Inc.:
a. All sales were on credit.
b. The debt to total assets ratio is 55%.
c. Working capital is $1,310.
d. Net income is 9.0% of sales; gross profit is 30% of sales.
e. The only interest paid was on long-term debt.
f. Inventory turnover = 6 (beginning inventory = $500).
g. Accounts receivable turnover = 12 (beginning accounts receivable = $300).
h. 45% of the total cost of the building has been depreciated.

Required

Complete the Waco Sales, Inc., financial statements shown below. Round all calculations to the nearest dollar. (Hint: Determine the amounts in the order indicated by the numbers in parentheses on the statements.)

WACO SALES, INC.
Income Statement
Year Ended December 31, 1987

Sales	(1)	$ ___
Cost of Goods Sold	(3)	___
Gross Profit on Sales	(2)	___
Operating Expenses	(15)	___
Interest Expense	(14)	___
Income before Income Taxes	(4)	___
Income Tax Expense (60% of income before income taxes)	(5)	___
Net Income		$540

WACO SALES, INC.
Balance Sheet
December 31, 1987

Assets:		
Cash		$ 310
Accounts Receivable (net)	(6)	___
Merchandise Inventory	(7)	___
Building	(10)	___
Accumulated Depreciation	(11)	(___)
Total Assets	(9)	$ ___
Liabilities and Stockholders' Equity:		
Accounts Payable	(8)	$ ___
6% Bonds Payable (due 1995)	(12)	___
Common Stock		800
Retained Earnings	(13)	___
Total Equities		$4,000

Problem B18-4
Selecting data needed and calculating five ratios

The following financial data have been assembled for Retton Merchandising, Inc., on December 31, 1988:

Average total assets for 1988	$250,000
Total stockholders' equity (average for 1988)	200,000
Common stock, $.25 par	100,000
8% preferred stock, $5 par.	50,000
Net income	15,000
Interest expense	1,000
Income tax expense (40% of income before income taxes)	
Market price of common stock, 12/31/88.	$1.10
Market price of preferred stock, 12/31/88.	$7.50
Common dividends were paid at the rate of $.05 per share per quarter.	
Preferred dividends were declared and paid.	
No preferred stock or common stock was issued or reacquired during 1988.	

Required

Using whatever data you need from the above list, calculate:
1. Rate of return on total assets
2. Rate of return on common stockholders' equity
3. Earnings per common share
4. Price-earnings ratio
5. Dividend yield rate

(Check figure: Rate of return on common stockholders' equity = 7.33%)

Problem B18-5
Calculating liquidity ratios for two firms and deciding which should receive a short-term loan

Front, Inc., and Center Company both sell machinery for washing large trucks. Both companies have applied for a short-term loan. Data from the December 31, 1987, balance sheets appear below:

	Front, Inc.	Center Co.
Cash.	$ 55,000	$ 150,000
Marketable securities	3,600	120,000
Accounts receivable (net)	61,400	90,000
Merchandise inventory.	360,000	240,000
Property, plant, and equipment (net).	700,000	750,000
Intangibles.	3,000	—
Total assets.	$1,183,000	$1,350,000
Current liabilities	$ 120,000	$ 200,000
Long-term liabilities	200,000	200,000
Common stock, $10 par.	800,000	800,000
Retained earnings	63,000	150,000
Total equities	$1,183,000	$1,350,000

Other Information:

	Front, Inc.	Center Co.
Accounts receivable, 1/1/87 . . . . $	78,600	$ 70,000
Merchandise inventory, 1/1/87	320,000	260,000
1987 sales:		
Cash	516,000	240,000
Credit	684,000	960,000
1987 cost of goods sold	1,054,000	700,000

Required

1. Calculate for each company the current ratio, quick ratio, inventory turnover, accounts receivable turnover, and average age of receivables.
2. Which company would you recommend to receive the short-term loan? Explain.
3. What additional ratios would you consider if the companies were requesting a long-term loan? Explain.

(Check figure: Inventory turnover for Center Co. = 2.8)

Problem B18-6
Determining the amount at which four assets would appear on a constant-dollar balance sheet

You have been assigned the task of completing the property, plant, and equipment section of a constant-dollar balance sheet that is being prepared for Target Products Corp. The following list of property, plant, and equipment assets was taken from the Target traditional balance sheet on December 31, 1983:

	Year Acquired	Cost	Accumulated Depreciation on 12/31/83
Land	1971	$ 140,000	—
Buildings	1972	1,500,000	$375,000
Display equipment	1981	230,000	110,000
Delivery equipment	1982	90,000	22,000

Required

Using the Consumer Price Index numbers from Table 18-1, determine the amount at which each of the property, plant, and equipment assets listed above will appear on a constant-dollar balance sheet. You will need to convert both the cost of the asset and any accumulated depreciation. Round to the nearest dollar.

(Check figure: Display equipment = $251,953)

Financial Statements: Florida Steel Corporation

Contained in the following six pages are the financial statements of Florida Steel Corporation, a company listed on the New York Stock Exchange. Ernst and Whinney, an international certified public accounting firm, audited the statements, and their report is found on the last page. Florida Steel's statements were selected because they are relatively free from complicated accounting issues, yet illustrate the principles of accounting and disclosure discussed in the book.

Included with the financial statements are three pages of disclosures entitled *Notes to Financial Statements*. These are an integral part of the statements. Notice in particular that the first note, *Note A,* is a summary of significant accounting policies as required by generally accepted accounting principles.

| | September 30 | |
	1984	1983

ASSETS

CURRENT ASSETS

Cash and cash equivalents—Note D	$ 7,340,119	$ 1,201,557
Accounts receivable, less allowance for possible losses (1984 and 1983—$600,000)—Note B	38,472,017	37,100,178
Inventories—Notes B and C	35,284,638	32,856,977
Prepaid expenses	228,363	274,112
Recoverable and refundable income taxes	277,490	10,800,000
TOTAL CURRENT ASSETS	**81,602,627**	**82,232,824**

PLANT AND EQUIPMENT

Land	9,137,328	2,882,063
Buildings and improvements	17,310,225	17,950,319
Machinery and equipment	149,222,923	150,534,308
Construction in progress (estimated cost to complete: 1984—$13,505,000; 1983—$5,192,000)	2,839,283	1,643,774
	178,509,759	173,010,464
Less allowances for depreciation	59,946,824	54,633,150
	118,562,935	**118,377,314**

OTHER ASSETS	**1,234,320**	**1,836,314**
	$201,399,882	**$202,446,452**

LIABILITIES AND SHAREHOLDERS' EQUITY

CURRENT LIABILITIES

Trade accounts payable	$ 20,627,868	$ 19,943,975
Salaries, wages and employee benefits	6,300,651	6,251,116
Other current liabilities	1,932,575	2,002,825
Federal and state income taxes	348,282	921,551
Current maturities of long-term borrowings	308,000	308,000
Short-term borrowings—Note D	2,000,000	5,000,000
TOTAL CURRENT LIABILITIES	**31,517,376**	**34,427,467**

LONG-TERM BORROWINGS—Note D	**51,545,000**	**58,353,000**
DEFERRED INCOME TAXES—Note E	**28,527,000**	**24,575,000**

SHAREHOLDERS' EQUITY—Notes D and G

Common Stock, par value $1.00 per share—authorized: 1984 and 1983—25,000,000; issued and outstanding: 1984—5,974,863 shares and 1983—5,965,185 shares	5,974,863	5,965,185
Capital in excess of par	2,945,034	2,510,714
Reinvested earnings	80,890,609	76,615,086
TOTAL SHAREHOLDERS' EQUITY	**89,810,506**	**85,090,985**
	$201,399,882	**$202,446,452**

See notes to financial statements.

	Year Ended September 30		
	1984	**1983**	**1982**
NET SALES	$286,108,096	$235,107,846	$248,542,968
OTHER INCOME—Note H	5,405,922	2,247,435	507,120
	291,514,018	237,355,281	249,050,088
COSTS AND EXPENSES			
Cost of sales, excluding depreciation	250,135,673	214,802,296	226,815,710
Selling and administrative	14,757,008	15,781,862	16,460,637
Depreciation	9,166,917	9,362,473	9,249,872
Interest expense	6,429,822	6,685,407	9,654,743
Settlement of litigation—Note I			3,390,000
	280,489,420	246,632,038	265,570,962
INCOME (LOSS) BEFORE INCOME TAXES	11,024,598	(9,276,757)	(16,520,874)
INCOME TAXES (BENEFITS)—Note E	4,363,000	(4,600,000)	(8,200,000)
NET INCOME (LOSS)	$ 6,661,598	$ (4,676,757)	$ (8,320,874)
NET INCOME (LOSS) PER SHARE	$1.12	$(.78)	$(1.40)

See notes to financial statements.

STATEMENTS OF SHAREHOLDERS' EQUITY
FLORIDA STEEL CORPORATION

	Common Stock	Capital in Excess of Par	Reinvested Earnings
Balances at October 1, 1981	$5,925,176	$1,528,309	$95,628,512
Net loss for 1982			(8,320,874)
Cash dividends ($.610 per share)			(3,631,063)
Compensation under employee stock plans—Note G	37,616	847,667	
BALANCES AT SEPTEMBER 30, 1982	5,962,792	2,375,976	83,676,575
Net loss for 1983			(4,676,757)
Cash dividends ($.400 per share)			(2,384,732)
Compensation under employee stock plans—Note G	2,393	134,738	
BALANCES AT SEPTEMBER 30, 1983	5,965,185	2,510,714	76,615,086
Net income for 1984			6,661,598
Cash dividends ($.400 per share)			(2,386,075)
Compensation under employee stock plans—Note G	9,678	434,320	
BALANCES AT SEPTEMBER 30, 1984	$5,974,863	$2,945,034	$80,890,609

See notes to financial statements.

	Year Ended September 30		
	1984	**1983**	**1982**
SOURCE OF WORKING CAPITAL			
From operations:			
Net income (loss)	$ 6,661,598	$ (4,676,757)	$ (8,320,874)
Charges not requiring funds in the current period:			
Depreciation	9,166,917	9,362,473	9,249,872
Deferred income taxes	3,952,000	5,462,000	5,298,200
TOTAL FROM OPERATIONS	**19,780,515**	**10,147,716**	**6,227,198**
Additional long-term borrowings	7,500,000		3,500,000
Proceeds from sale of plant and equipment, less gains included in net income (loss)	2,120,354	1,394,844	15,253
Compensation under employee stock plans	443,998	137,131	885,283
Reduction of noncurrent notes receivable	291,916		
Other items, net	310,078	(117,161)	(241,074)
	30,446,861	**11,562,530**	**10,386,660**
APPLICATION OF WORKING CAPITAL			
Reduction of long-term borrowings	14,308,000	308,000	330,500
Cash dividends	2,386,075	2,384,732	3,631,063
Plant and equipment additions	11,472,892	5,051,803	6,603,103
Noncurrent portion of notes receivable— sales of fixed assets		1,358,583	
	28,166,967	**9,103,118**	**10,564,666**
WORKING CAPITAL INCREASE (DECREASE)	**2,279,894**	**2,459,412**	**(178,006)**
Beginning working capital	47,805,357	45,345,945	45,523,951
ENDING WORKING CAPITAL	**$50,085,251**	**$47,805,357**	**$45,345,945**
CHANGES IN COMPONENTS OF WORKING CAPITAL			
Increase (decrease) in working capital assets:			
Cash	$ 6,138,562	$ 256,100	$ (240,032)
Accounts receivable	1,371,839	6,884,674	(8,468,377)
Inventories	2,427,661	(273,486)	(9,264,641)
Prepaid expenses	(45,749)	(135,045)	124,774
Recoverable and refundable income taxes	(10,522,510)	(2,767,090)	11,757,768
	(630,197)	**3,965,153**	**(6,090,508)**
Increase (decrease) in working capital liabilities:			
Trade accounts payable	683,893	3,503,558	(9,488,384)
Salaries, wages and employee benefits	49,535	(490,632)	387,522
Other current liabilities	(70,250)	(406,236)	(3,965,640)
Federal and state income taxes	(573,269)	921,551	
Current maturities of long-term borrowings		(22,500)	154,000
Short-term borrowings	(3,000,000)	(2,000,000)	7,000,000
	(2,910,091)	**1,505,741**	**(5,912,502)**
WORKING CAPITAL INCREASE (DECREASE)	**$ 2,279,894**	**$ 2,459,412**	**$ (178,006)**

See notes to financial statements.

NOTE A — SUMMARY OF SIGNIFICANT ACCOUNTING POLICIES

Business Segment: The Company is engaged in the manufacture, fabrication and marketing of steel products, primarily for use in construction. Sales made principally to domestic trading corporations for ultimate shipment to overseas destinations, primarily in the Western Hemisphere, amounted to approximately $4,921,000, $12,408,000 and $30,415,000 during 1984, 1983, and 1982, respectively.

Contract Revenue: Sales under contracts are recognized as deliveries of materials are made.

Inventories: Inventories are stated at the lower of cost (determined principally by use of the last-in, first-out method) or market.

Plant and Equipment: Plant and equipment are stated on the basis of cost. Major renewals and betterments are capitalized and depreciated over their estimated useful lives. Maintenance and repairs are charged against operations as incurred. Upon retirement or other disposition of plant and equipment, the cost and related allowances for depreciation are removed from the accounts and any resulting gain or loss is reflected in operations.

Plant start-up and other preoperating costs of new facilities are charged against operations as incurred.

For financial reporting purposes, the Company provides for depreciation of plant and equipment using the straight-line method over the estimated useful lives of 10 to 30 years for buildings and improvements and 3 to 18 years for machinery and equipment.

Income Taxes: The provision for income taxes is based on financial statement income and, therefore, includes deferred income taxes on items reported in different periods for income tax purposes.

The Company uses the flow-through method of recognizing investment tax credits.

Pension Plans: The Company has pension plans covering substantially all employees. Pension cost represents normal cost and amortization of prior service costs principally over 30 years. The Company's policy is to fund accrued pension costs currently.

Net Income Per Share: Net income per share is based on the Company's average number of shares of Common Stock outstanding during each year (5,965,264 in 1984, 5,961,827 in 1983, and 5,953,973 in 1982).

Shares of Common Stock acquired for issuance under the employee stock plans have been excluded from the computation of net earnings per share until issuable to participants.

Reclassifications: Certain 1983 and 1982 amounts have been reclassified to conform with 1984 classifications.

NOTE B — FABRICATION CONTRACTS

Included in trade accounts receivable at September 30, 1984 and 1983, are receivables amounting to approximately $14,409,000 and $15,154,000, respectively, arising from the delivery of fabricated products sold under both short and long-term contracts. Of these amounts, approximately $185,000 and $1,328,000, respectively, represent retainage which is due upon completion of the related contracts and acceptance by the customers. The Company expects such balances to be collected within one year.

Inventories of contract job materials, both in process and awaiting fabrication at September 30, 1984 and 1983, amount to approximately $124,000 and $700,000, respectively (approximately $325,000 and $1,720,000 if stated on a FIFO basis).

NOTE C — INVENTORIES

	September 30 1984	September 30 1983
Finished goods	$22,053,391	$14,644,917
Work in process	3,697,791	4,200,339
Raw materials and operating supplies	9,533,456	14,011,721
	$35,284,638	**$32,856,977**

If the first-in, first-out (FIFO) method of inventory accounting had been used by the Company, inventories would have been $10,587,360 and $11,173,638 higher than reported at September 30, 1984 and 1983, respectively.

During 1984 and 1983, inventory quantities were reduced resulting in the liquidation of LIFO inventory quantities carried at lower costs prevailing in prior years as compared with the cost of 1984 and 1983 purchases. The effect of these liquidations increased net income for 1984 by approximately $1,089,000 and decreased net loss for 1983 by approximately $572,000. The liquidation for 1984 resulted from the sale of two production facilities and is included in other income (see Note H).

Inventories as of September 30, 1983 were reclassified, resulting in increases in finished goods and work-in-process of $3,035,679 and $228,519, respectively, and a decrease in raw materials of $3,264,198.

NOTE D — BORROWINGS

Long-term borrowings consist of the following:

	September 30 1984	September 30 1983
Credit agreement	$41,000,000	$55,000,000
Industrial Revenue Bonds	10,853,000	3,661,000
	51,853,000	58,661,000
Less current maturities	308,000	308,000
	$51,545,000	**$58,353,000**

Effective April 16, 1982, the Company entered into a credit agreement with a bank whereby the Company may borrow a maximum of $70,000,000 on a revolving-credit basis to December 31, 1985, and a term-loan basis for an additional five years. The interest rates are the prime rate during the revolving-credit period, and ¼ of 1% above the prime rate during the term period.

Alternative interest rates, which may at times be less than prime, are available at the Company's discretion. A fee is also payable at a rate ranging from ¼ to ⅜ of 1% per annum on the unused portion of the commitment. The Company has agreed to maintain average compensating balances, which are usually satisfied by balances maintained for normal business operations. Proceeds of the loan were used to retire previous indebtedness at the same bank.

Industrial Revenue Bonds issued in 1981 to partially finance the construction of the steel mill in Jackson, Tennessee, bear interest at 60% of the prime rate. Annual maturities are $308,000, payable in equal quarterly installments, with the final payment of $1,428,000 due on January 1, 1991.

On July 12, 1984, Industrial Revenue Bonds were issued in the amount of $7,500,000 to finance the cost of renovating the rolling facilities at the steel mill in Charlotte, North Carolina, and bear interest at 63% of the prime rate. Annual maturities are $625,000, payable in equal quarterly installments beginning October 1, 1987. As of September 30, 1984, $6,846,000 of the bond proceeds were unexpended and invested in a certificate of deposit at a trustee bank.

Both the credit agreement and Industrial Revenue Bonds contain certain restrictive provisions which relate principally to the payment of cash dividends, acquisition of fixed assets, and incurrence of indebtedness, and which require the maintenance of minimum net current assets to net current liabilities of no less than 1.7 to 1.0 and maintenance of total liabilities to net worth at no greater than 1.8 to 1.0. The amount of reinvested earnings free from restrictions was approximately $1,250,000 at September 30, 1984.

Aggregate maturities of long-term borrowings for the four years subsequent to

September 30, 1985, are as follows: 1986—$6,458,000; 1987—$8,508,000; 1988—$9,133,000; and 1989—$9,133,000.

In addition to the $2,000,000 of short-term borrowing currently outstanding, the Company has another $23,000,000 available under its short-term credit arrangement with banks. The interest rates and restrictive provisions are similar to those of the credit agreement.

NOTE E — INCOME TAXES

The provisions (benefits) for income taxes are comprised of the following amounts:

	1984	1983	1982
Currently payable (recoverable):			
Federal	$ 298,000	$(10,008,000)	$(13,438,000)
State	113,000	(54,000)	(60,000)
	$ 411,000	$(10,062,000)	$(13,498,000)
Deferred:			
Federal	3,952,000	5,462,000	5,273,000
State			25,000
	3,952,000	5,462,000	5,298,000
	$4,363,000	$ (4,600,000)	$ (8,200,000)

A reconciliation of the difference between the effective income tax rate for each year and the statutory Federal income tax rate follows:

	1984	1983	1982
Tax provisions (benefits) at statutory rates	$5,071,000	$ (4,267,000)	$ (7,600,000)
State income taxes, net of Federal income tax effect	61,000	(26,000)	(384,000)
Investment tax credit, net	(432,000)	(365,000)	(918,000)
Lower tax rates on long-term capital gains	(445,000)		
Nondeductible portion of litigation settlement, net			885,000
Other items, net	108,000	58,000	(183,000)
	$4,363,000	$ (4,600,000)	$ (8,200,000)

The sources of timing differences on which deferred income taxes have been provided and the related income tax effect follow:

	1984	1983	1982
Depreciation	$5,043,000	$ 4,862,000	$ 5,456,000
Adjustments for Internal Revenue Service examination		(270,000)	
Investment tax credits, primarily resulting from carryback of net operating losses	(1,331,000)	(474,000)	
Other items, net	240,000	1,344,000	(158,000)
Total deferred income taxes provided	$3,952,000	$ 5,462,000	$ 5,298,000

During 1984, income taxes payable was reduced by approximately $426,000 resulting from an additional tax benefit related to the vesting of shares under a restricted stock plan (see Note G).

During 1983, amounts were reclassified from deferred income taxes to Federal and state income taxes payable as a result of Internal Revenue Service examination of 1979, 1980, 1981 and 1982 Federal income tax returns. The Company is contesting certain additional proposed adjustments. In the opinion of management, the ultimate resolution of these matters will not have a material effect on the financial position of the Company.

NOTE F — EMPLOYEE BENEFIT PLANS

Total pension expense for 1984, 1983 and 1982 was $2,136,000, $2,337,000, and $2,234,000, respectively. Accumulated plan benefit information, as estimated by consulting actuaries, and plan net assets available for benefits are as follows:

	October 1	
	1983	1982
Actuarial present value of accumulated plan benefits:		
Vested	$14,913,000	$13,710,000
Nonvested	2,876,000	2,086,000
	$17,789,000	$15,796,000
Plan net assets available for benefits	$18,152,000	$13,458,000
Assumed rates of return used to determine accumulated plan benefits:		
Active participants	8.0%	8.0%
Inactive participants	12.6%	12.6%

Effective October 1, 1982, a dedicated bond portfolio was established for all inactive plan participants who were receiving benefits or were entitled to receive future benefits from the plan as of October 1, 1982. As of each actuarial valuation date, beginning with October 1, 1982, the effective yield on the dedicated portfolio will be calculated based on the market value of the portfolio as of the valuation date. This rate will be used as the interest assumption for discounting benefits expected to be paid to or on behalf of the dedicated group. As a result of establishing the dedicated bond portfolio, pension expense for 1983 and actuarial present value of accumulated plan benefits as of October 1, 1982 were reduced by $107,000 and $1,296,000, respectively.

The Company also has a voluntary savings plan available to substantially all of its employees. Under this plan, the Company contributes amounts based upon a percentage of the savings paid into the plan by employees. Costs under this plan were $551,000, $547,000 and $519,000 for 1984, 1983 and 1982, respectively.

NOTE G — EMPLOYEE STOCK PLANS

The Company has a restricted stock plan and has reserved 600,000 shares of Common Stock for the purpose of paying incentive compensation to certain officers and key employees based upon the economic performance of the Company. The plan, as administered by the Executive Compensation Committee of the Board of Directors (composed solely of non-management directors), provides that the total fair market value of the aggregate shares transferred annually under the plan shall not exceed 7% of the Company's net income for such year. No participant can receive more than 20% of the shares granted, and stock transferred under the plan shall be forfeited if the participant leaves the employ of the Company within five years from the date of the grant. A participant may request up to 25% of any awards in cash in lieu of stock. No awards under the plan were made in 1984, 1983 or 1982. During 1984, 49,600 shares vested to participants of the plan. Capital in excess of par was increased by $426,000 resulting from an additional tax benefit related to the vesting of the shares.

The Board of Directors established a Tax Reduction Act Stock Ownership Plan (TRASOP) to provide additional retirement benefits to eligible employees who were not included in the restricted stock plan. Contributions to the TRASOP were made by the Company in either cash or the Company's Common Stock in an amount equal to one percent of the Company's qualified investments as defined in the Internal Revenue Code, plus any additional amount which was determined at the discretion of the Board of Directors. Cash contributions were invested in the Company's Common Stock which was held in trust for the benefit of the participants. The portion of the contribution that represented the discretionary amount determined by the Board of Directors vested at the rate of 20% for each year of participation. The remainder of the annual contribution was fully vested at all times.

Effective January 1, 1983, the Company converted the TRASOP to a payroll-based Employee Stock Ownership Plan (PAYSOP). The PAYSOP provides additional retirement benefits to eligible employees, including employees who participate in the restricted stock plan. Contributions to the PAYSOP are made by the Company in either cash or the Company's Common Stock in an amount equal to one-half of 1% of each eligible employee's annual gross compensation paid. A supplemental contribution is made in an amount equal to 4% of the plan year gross compensation paid for each first-year eligible employee, excluding participants in the restricted stock plan. Cash contributions are to be invested in the Company's Common Stock which is to be held in trust for the beneift of the participants. The 4% supplemental contribution amount is vested at the rate of 20% for each year of participation. The remainder of the annual contribution is fully vested at all times.

The Company has provided for contributions to the PAYSOP in 1984 and 1983 of $308,000 and $158,000, respectively, and to the TRASOP in 1982 of $302,000. Income tax expense has been reduced in 1984, 1983 and 1982 by $216,000, $158,000, and $83,500, respectively, for the additional investment tax credit earned by contributing to the respective plans.

The Company acquired shares of its Common Stock for issuance under these plans. In 1983 and 1982, the Company transferred certain shares of this Common Stock, along with 2,393 and 37,616 shares, respectively, of previously unissued Common Stock, to satisfy the requirements of the above plans. The difference between the market value and the cost of this Common Stock, or par value of the previously unissued shares, has been recorded as an adjustment to capital in excess of par.

NOTE H — OTHER INCOME

Other income for 1984 includes $5,257,000 from gains on the sale of two production facilities. The Company sold the Tampa Miscellaneous Fabricating Plant on February 29, 1984 and the Tampa Steel Service Center on March 1, 1984 and recognized a net gain after taxes of $2,823,000 ($.47 per share) after recognizing a charge of $401,000 ($.07 per share) for disposal of certain equipment. The $5,257,000 includes $1,873,000 resulting from liquidation of these facilities' LIFO inventories carried at lower costs prevailing in prior years as compared with the cost of 1984 purchases.

Other income for 1983 includes $1,524,000 from gains on the sale of two production facilities. On December 30, 1982, the Company sold its Jacksonville

Structural Steel Fabricating Plant and recognized a net gain after taxes of $159,500 ($.03 per share). On September 1, 1983, the Company sold its Tampa Metal Culvert Pipe Fabricating Plant and recognized a net gain after taxes of $524,000 ($.09 per share). The non-current portion of the notes received as consideration for these sales is $1,067,000 at September 30, 1984, and is included in other assets.

NOTE I — LITIGATION AND CONTINGENCIES

A consent decree was entered on November 7, 1979, by Final Judgment in United States District Court for the Middle District of Florida, Tampa Division, in the civil action of the United States of America pending since August 1974 against the Company and three other steel companies on alleged combinations and conspiracies in violation of the antitrust laws. The Final Judgment, which does not constitute evidence or an admission against any party, enjoins the companies from violations of the antitrust laws and requires affirmative steps by the companies to ensure compliance with the Final Judgment for a period of five years. On December 10, 1981, the Company paid $3,390,000 related to the settlement of antitrust civil actions that had been pending against the Company for over six years. This settlement increased the 1982 net loss $2,580,000 ($.43 per share), after applicable income taxes of $810,000. All related actions against the Company have been concluded.

During 1983, the Company settled disputes related to the rates of payments to be applied in certain labor disputes and the extent of state sales tax liability. The labor rate settlement increased net loss by $209,000 ($.03 per share), while the sales tax settlement decreased net loss by $389,000 ($.06 per share).

The Company is negotiating with governmental authorities to determine an appropriate method for disposing of certain hazardous wastes generated prior to the enactment of the Federal Hazardous Waste Disposal Laws.

The Company is defending various claims and legal actions which are common to its operations. This includes a suit in the Commonwealth of Puerto Rico against the Company and others for alleged violations of Puerto Rican anti-dumping statutes asking damages in excess of $5,000,000. While it is not feasible to predict or determine the ultimate outcome of these matters, none of them, in the opinion of management, will have a material effect on the Company's financial position or results of operations.

Board of Directors and Shareholders
Florida Steel Corporation
Tampa, Florida

Report of Certified Public Accountants

We have examined the statements of financial position of Florida Steel Corporation as of September 30, 1984 and 1983, and the related statements of operations, shareholders' equity, and changes in financial position for each of the three years in the period ended September 30, 1984. Our examinations were made in accordance with generally accepted auditing standards and, accordingly, included such tests of the accounting records and such other auditing procedures as we considered necessary in the circumstances.

In our opinion, the financial statements referred to above present fairly the financial position of Florida Steel Corporation at September 30, 1984 and 1983, and the results of its operations and changes in its financial position for each of the three years in the period ended September 30, 1984, in conformity with generally accepted accounting principles applied on a consistent basis.

Tampa, Florida
October 31, 1984

Ernst & Whinney

Part Six

Management Accounting: Its Structure and Environment

In the first 18 chapters of this text you studied financial accounting. You learned how to record business transactions and how to prepare the financial reports — reports that are to be issued to users outside the firm, such as investors, creditors, government, and public interest groups.

In the next section of this text you will be studying management accounting. In management accounting you will learn how accountants assist managers in the decision-making process by helping them to plan and control operations. Here the emphasis will be on helping a user inside the firm — the manager — rather than a user who is outside the firm.

You will also learn about the accountant's role in product costing for manufacturers. Product costing involves keeping track of the costs associated with inventories.

We will also discuss numerous tools that accountants use in management accounting. For each of these tools we will: (1) show you how to use it and (2) explain how it helps managers to plan and control.

Overview
Management Accounting:
A Brief Introduction

You will learn the following by studying this transition chapter:

- What *management accounting* is all about
- How management accounting differs from *financial accounting*
- What *cost accounting* is and how it relates to management accounting and financial accounting
- What *planning* and *control* are
- What accounting tools are used to help management plan its objectives and control its activities
- The difference between line responsibility and staff responsibility and what kind of responsibility the accountant has within the organization.
- The different types of costs that management accountants need to be aware of when preparing reports to management

A basic idea you should have gotten by now is that an organization needs quantitative information to function. Management uses the best available quantitative information to make its organization function in the most effective and efficient manner. This information is provided by the accounting system to management, which uses it primarily to accomplish three broad purposes:

1. To provide financial statements to interested external users

2. To plan the operations of the organization in both the short and the long run

3. To control the results of its operations

FINANCIAL ACCOUNTING AND MANAGEMENT ACCOUNTING

Financial accounting

In *financial accounting* the responsibilities of the accountant are to record, classify, analyze, summarize, and report the results of the activities of the organization to creditors, stockholders and prospective investors, governmental bodies, labor unions, environmental organizations, and others. For corporations, the reports to external users are in the form of four general-purpose financial statements—the income statement, the statement of retained earnings, the balance sheet, and the statement of changes in financial position. These financial statements are used by people who are trying to protect or enhance their investments in the organization as well as by others who have a special interest in it.

Management accounting

The remaining chapters in this book deal primarily with *management accounting* (also known as managerial accounting) and its role in the second and third purposes listed above: planning and control.

In management accounting accountants provide information for use by people within the organization—the managers—rather than for use by people outside the organization. Management uses this information for making decisions concerning the internal workings of the organization.

There are many different types of decisions for which managers need accounting information. Listed below are a few examples of typical questions that regularly confront managers:

Decisions that need management accounting information

1. What price should be set for a product line?

2. Should a product line be dropped?

3. Should old equipment be replaced with new equipment?

4. Has an employee performed well enough to warrant a bonus?

5. Should short-term borrowing be arranged to finance current operations?

For managers to make the best decision to resolve each of these questions, the management accountant must provide quantitative information that is timely and relevant. Only with this information can a manager properly plan and control the organization's operations.

Other Differences between Financial Accounting and Management Accounting

The two most basic differences between financial accounting and management accounting are:

Basic differences:
Purposes

1. Financial accounting's purpose is to provide financial statements that will be meaningful to any interested parties; management accounting's purpose is specifically to assist management in planning and control.

Users

2. The people who use financial accounting information are primarily external—that is, outside the organization; the people who use management accounting information are internal—that is, inside the organization.

There are several other differences:

Time orientation

3. The information that financial accountants gather relates primarily to the past; the information that management accountants deal with relates substantially to the future. Whereas financial accounting reports the results of past activities, management accounting often looks to the consequences of current activities on the future.

Availability of information to outsiders

4. Much of the information that management accountants provide managers for making internal decisions is never made available to outside users—they never have any idea of what it entails or how it is prepared. As a result—and thankfully so—we don't have to worry about the same restrictions in the presentation of management accounting information as we do with financial accounting information. That is, what we generate only for internal use does not have to be consistent, nor conservative, nor objective, nor historical. For example, many decisions relate to the proper course of action a manager—and thus the firm—should take. Much of the information the manager needs to make these decisions depends on projections of future revenues and expenses. Since these projections are merely estimates—some would say calculated guesses—they need not be based on the actual recorded amounts of past transactions (i.e., they are not historical). Nor can they usually be verified by third parties (i.e., they are not objective). While it might be desirable that the information used for internal decisions fulfill numerous requirements—for example, managers probably wish that accountants' calculated guesses were more objective—the only requirement that internal information must fulfill is that it help managers make the best decisions on a timely basis.

Accounting system required?

5. Publicly held organizations are required by generally accepted accounting principles to provide financial accounting information to its external users—management has no choice. The users have the right to see the financial statements of the organization. Since the users of financial accounting are outside the organization, the main way they learn about how well management is performing is by studying the financial statements of that organization. No one is going to invest in or lend to an organization that has no financial accounting system or is unwilling to distribute its financial statements to interested parties.

On the other hand, whether or not an organization's accounting system produces management accounting information and makes it available to its managers is completely up to management itself. If management foolishly feels that it can make its many decisions without the help of management accounting information, then it does indeed have the option of doing without this valuable input.

View of organization

6. Financial accounting usually takes a condensed view of the organization as a whole; management accounting takes a detailed view of segments of the organization. The management accountant helps managers at all levels of responsibility within an organization; therefore his or her reports are geared to the appropriate managerial level. The report may be for a division, for a department, for a product line within a department, or for one of several product-line foremen.

THE FINANCIAL ACCOUNTING MENTALITY

The accounting emphasis within many organizations is often placed primarily on the preparation of general-purpose financial statements for external users; much less emphasis is placed on providing information to management to help in the decision-making process. Financial accounting often takes precedence over management accounting.

"In Europe, many companies have one department to collect and analyze data for internal operations and another to prepare external reports. Some companies, like Phillips in the Netherlands, even report to stockholders on the basis used to evaluate internal operations. By contrast, contemporary practice in the United States is to use for internal purposes conventions either developed for external reporting or mandated by such external reporting authorities as the Financial Accounting Standards Board and the SEC."

What some people refer to as the "financial accounting mentality" is the use of financial accounting information for internal purposes, even when that information causes distortions in the internal measurements. For example, when a company measures the performance of one of its divisions with ROI—net income of the division divided by the assets invested in that division—it is very likely that productive assets used by the division but leased from others divisions are included in the denominator only when *Statement #13* of the FASB specifies that they must be capitalized. Naturally, when leased assets are left out of the calculation, the ROI—an internal measurement—will overstate the return that is really being earned by the division. What accountants and financial executives need to do is "redirect their energies—and their thinking—from external reporting to the more effective management of their company's tangible and intangible assets. Internal accounting systems need renovation. . . . Internal accounting practices should be driven by corporate strategy, not by FASB and SEC requirements for external reporting."

Source: Robert S. Kaplan, "Yesterday's Accounting Undermines Production," *Harvard Business Review,* July–August 1984, pp. 95–101. Copyright © 1984 by the President and fellows of Harvard College; all rights reserved. Reprinted by permission of *Harvard Business Review.*

INTERRELATIONSHIP OF FINANCIAL AND MANAGEMENT ACCOUNTING

Financial and management accounting are different, but they are not different

Financial accounting and management accounting are not completely separate disciplines—they are interrelated. For example, the historical information used in financial accounting is often helpful in evaluating future alternative courses of action that management is considering. Management makes a decision about the best future course based on what happened in the past. Later, when the results of that management decision occur, those results become financial information to be integrated into the financial statements. Financial accounting provides information to be used in management accounting decisions; those management decisions, in turn, yield financial results, which, of course, are of interest to people outside the organization.

A good example of the relationship between financial accounting information and management accounting information is the master budget, which we will cover in Chapter 23. The master budget is a basic tool of the management accountant, yet it depends on information from the income statement, the balance sheet, and the statement of retained earnings.

MANAGEMENT ACCOUNTING AND COST ACCOUNTING

One of the responsibilities of a financial accountant is to keep track of all costs related to the product to be sold by the organization. For many organizations the product (inventory) is a significant asset on the balance sheet and results in a significant expense (cost of goods sold) on the income statement. Therefore, it is important that the costs of the product represented as inventory be properly accounted for. The way

Assigning costs to inventory is product costing

an accountant determines the cost of inventory for an organization that produces its own product is first to determine all the costs that went into producing all the units produced. Then, these costs are split up—or, as accountants like to say, *allocated*—between the units sold and the units not yet sold. If we can (1) collect all the costs that went into producing all units, (2) calculate a cost for each unit produced, and (3) determine how many units were sold during a period, and how many were unsold at the end of the period, then (4) we can determine an expense for the units sold—commonly referred to as cost of goods sold—and place that amount on the income statement. The units available for sale, but not yet sold, represent an asset—the ending inventory—and we can similarly determine the costs to assign to the inventory that we place on the balance sheet. This process of determining the costs of the product and then allocating them between the income statement and balance sheet is referred to as *product costing.*

Cost accounting is part management accounting and part financial accounting

The accountant responsible for product costing is the *cost accountant.* The cost accountant's job, however, is not limited to product costing. The cost accountant is part financial accountant and part management accountant, involved in a small part of financial accounting (product costing) plus all of management accounting (assisting management in planning and control). Figure A distinguishes between financial accounting and management accounting and shows how cost accounting relates to the two. The figure shows that *cost accounting* includes all of management accounting plus that part of financial accounting known as product costing.

Nevertheless, the term *management accounting* has gradually come to mean to

FIGURE A
Cost accounting (planning, control, and product costing), which is part financial accounting and part management accounting, is shown in the boxed area.

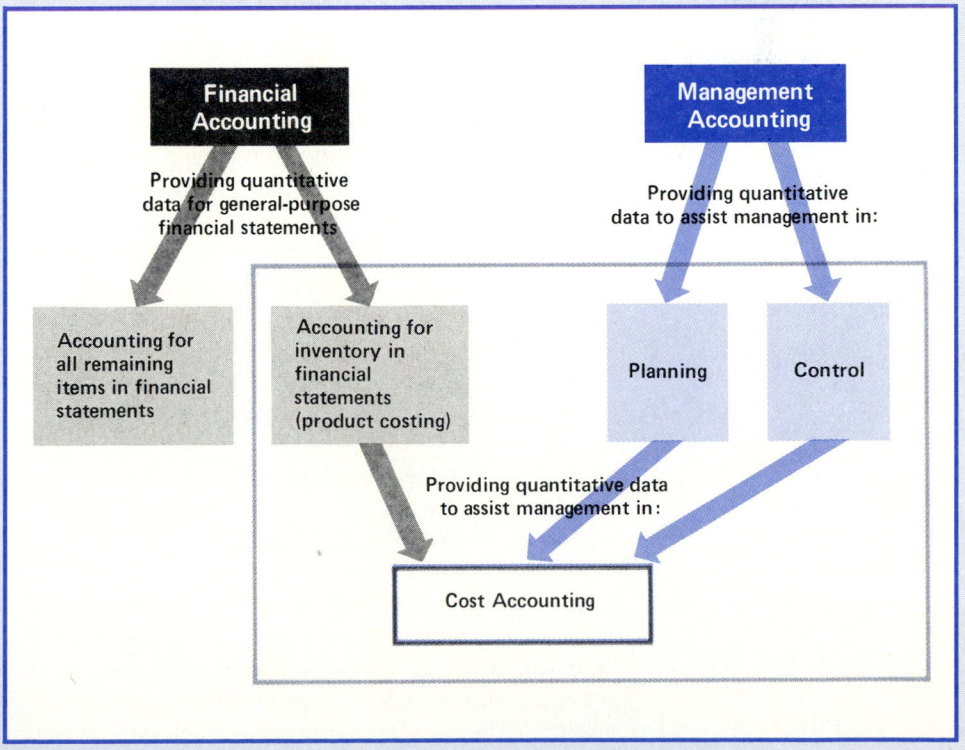

Terminology is not consistent for all users, writers, and teachers. But — when using our text, use our terminology

some people more than we have defined it to be. Some people's definition of management accounting embraces the product costing purpose — that is, they include planning, control, and product costing in the definition of management accounting. We refer to this combination as cost accounting. On the other hand, where we include the product costing purpose as only one of three cost accounting purposes, some people associate cost accounting strictly with product costing.

In addition, the term "management accounting" recently has been used in an even broader sense. The National Association of Accountants, in a recent pronouncement, included in the term "management accounting" *all* accounting functions performed in private organizations — that is, organizations that aren't CPA firms and aren't the government.[1] In this broadest sense, management accounting includes financial accounting, management accounting as we define it, tax accounting, and internal auditing.

Obviously, the terminology is not consistent among all who teach and practice these areas of accounting. For our purposes, *when we refer to management accounting, we mean assisting managers in planning and control. And when we refer to cost accounting, we mean assisting managers in planning, control, and product costing.*

PLANNING

Planning is setting goals and ways to achieve them

Planning in its most basic form involves two things: determining the goals for an organization and determining how to achieve them. Management should know not only where it hopes to be or what it hopes to accomplish during a future period, but also how it expects to reach these ends. Planning should take place at all levels within the organization. Because an organization is typically composed of subunits such as divisions, and each division itself is composed of subunits such as departments, the planning of an overall organization is only as good as the planning within each of the divisions, and for each division within each of its departments. Even the smallest subunit of an organization is involved in the planning process, and its plans must be coordinated with the plans of the overall organization.

Accountants use budgets, to help managers plan

The tool used by the management accountant to assist management in the planning purpose is the *budget.* The budget is a formal quantitative expression of the goals set by management.

Exhibit A is a simple budget for a machine maintenance department for August 1988. It shows, for example, that the maintenance department is expected to spend $43,000 for wages to repair machinery during August, and $15,000 for a foreman to supervise the laborers. In total, the maintenance department is expected to spend $81,400 in August in order to efficiently maintain the machines of the production departments.

Budgets as Tools

In the next eight chapters we will present different types of budgets, each representing a different aspect of the planning process. Examples are:

1. The Master Budget (Chapter 23)

The master budget provides management with an overview of the plans for all operations — sales, production, purchasing, financing, etc. The master budget can warn a company of an impending deficiency of cash, so that arrangements can be made to obtain short-term financing. Or it might indicate an availability of excess cash that can be profitably invested for a short period.

---

[1] National Association of Accountants Management Practices Committee, *Objectives of Management Accounting,* Statements on Management Accounting No. 1B (New York: National Association of Accountants, 1982), p. 1.

EXHIBIT A

During August, $81,400 is
expected to be spent to maintain
machinery

Machine Maintenance Department Budget August 1988	
Supplies	$18,000
Utilities	3,400
Supervision	15,000
Rent	2,000
Wages	43,000
Total	$81,400

**2. Relevant Cost Budgets
for Special Decisions
(Chapter 25)**

This type of budget helps to evaluate nonrecurring decisions, such as whether or not to drop a product line or to accept a special order. To make decisions like these, budgeted income statements must be prepared for each alternative; the alternative that has the most favorable effect on profits is the one exercised.

**3. Capital Budgeting
(Chapter 26)**

Organizations are often faced with the need to purchase additional property, plant, and equipment. To invest in such property will require a substantial commitment of resources. But the result may significantly increase the organization's productive capacity and should improve long-run profits. Capital budgeting analysis offers several methods to assist management in making these decisions.

CONTROL

After the planning process has been completed, that is, goals and the ways to achieve them have been determined, the next thing to do is put the plans to work. And once those plans are at work, it is necessary for managers to monitor the operation in order to see if they are achieving what they are supposed to. In other words, managers need to exert some control over the operations they manage. *Controlling* involves four things:

Control requires
implementation, feedback, and
corrective action

1. Putting the plans to work.

2. Observing those plans at work and gathering information on how well they are performing. The information collected to assess the performance of the organization in reaching its goals is often referred to as *feedback.*

3. If the plans are not on track toward attaining the intended goals, as determined by the feedback, management must determine what action is necessary to get those plans back on track.

4. Taking action to remedy whatever may have caused the plans to go astray.

These steps indicate that the control function picks up where the planning function leaves off. The progression of steps from planning through control is shown in Figure B at the top of page 730.

Once the goals have been set, and the means for attaining them have been determined and the budget representing them has been formulated, it is essential that these plans and the budget be accepted by all personnel within the organization who are affected by them. The personnel affected by the plans should be informed of the purpose of the budget and how the budget can influence the attainment of their own personal goals, their department's goals, as well as the goals of the entire organization.

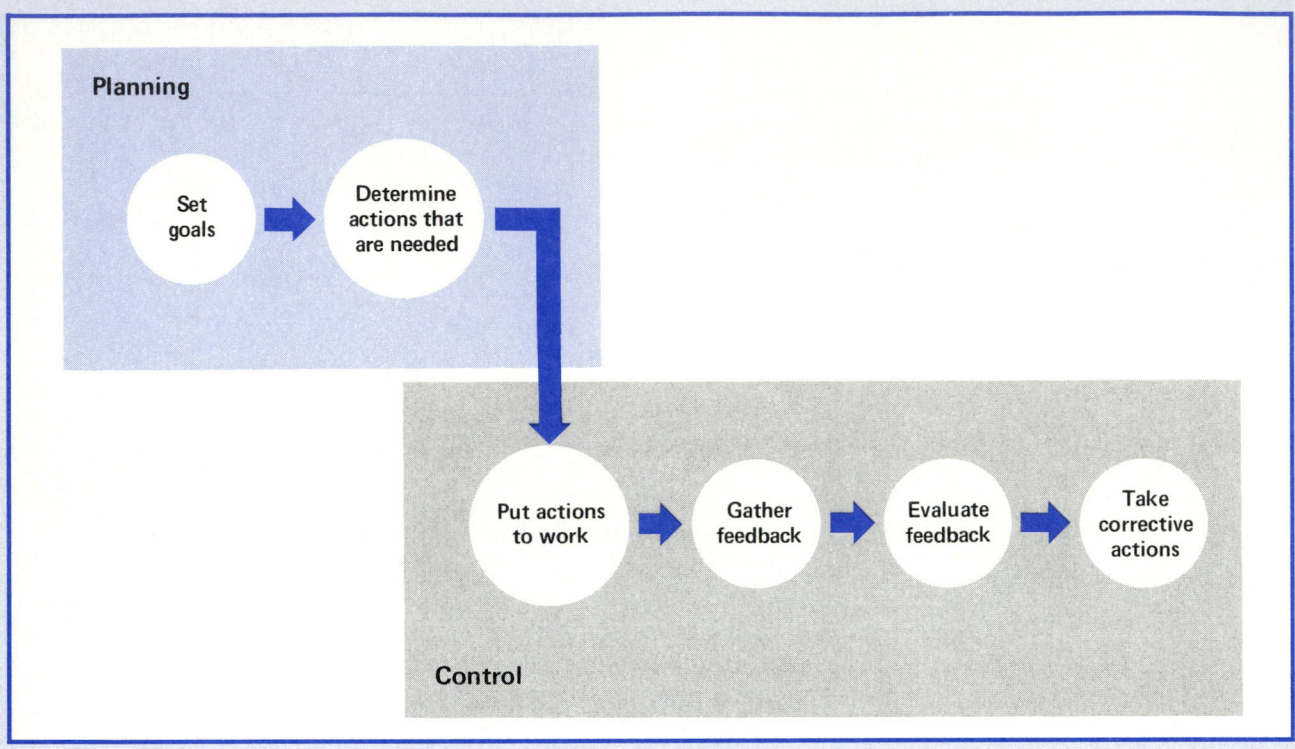

FIGURE B   The Progression of Steps from Planning to Control.

If the personnel who are affected by the plans do not know what they are about or do not accept them, it will be difficult for management to implement the plans. If the plans are implemented by management, but without the support of the affected personnel, it will be difficult, if not impossible, to properly control the ineffective plans.

A basic element of the control process is the accumulation of adequate, timely information — feedback — reflecting how well the plans are working out at all levels within the organization. With this information, an accountant can prepare a ***performance report,*** which is the principal accounting tool for assisting management in controlling operations. A performance report compares a department's actual results with the budget for that department; any differences between actual and budget are listed. Exhibit B portrays a simple version of a performance report for the mainte-

Accountants use performance reports to help managers control

EXHIBIT B

The performance report indicates that $85,550 was actually spent during August 1988, $4,150 in excess of the $81,400 budgeted. The material differences in the third column should be investigated

Machine Maintenance Department Performance Report August 1988			
	Budget	**Actual**	**Differences**
Supplies	$18,000	$20,700	$2,700 over budget
Utilities	3,400	5,000	1,600 over budget
Supervision	15,000	14,800	200 under budget
Rent	2,000	2,000	—
Wages	43,000	43,050	50 over budget
Totals	$81,400	$85,550	$4,150 over budget

nance department. The original budget for this department was shown in Exhibit A.

This performance report offers feedback on how well the maintenance department met its plans — represented by the budget. And this feedback indicates that the department's cost of supplies ($2,700 over budget), utilities ($1,600 over budget), and wages ($50 over budget) were higher than expected; supervision costs ($200 under budget) were lower than expected; and rent was exactly as predicted.

Having received this report from an accountant, a manager can immediately see where the plans are working and where they aren't. It appears from the performance report in Exhibit B that the only item for which the plans are working is the rent. This does not mean, however, that management should devote considerable time and energy to analyzing the causes of the differences for the remaining four items. Usually, only large differences will warrant investigation.

Management by Exception

Should all differences be investigated?

Investigating differences can be time-consuming and costly, requiring careful attention and evaluation by the manager and workers most closely associated with the operation that did not meet the budget. Unless the benefits from knowing the cause of a difference exceed the costs of determining the cause, investigation is not waranted. The costs of investigating a difference are probably about the same regardless of the size of the difference — it shouldn't take any longer to determine the cause of a large difference than it does for a small difference. The potential benefits, however, from investigating a large difference should be much greater than for a small difference. Therefore, the net effect — benefits from investigation less costs of investigation — will probably be positive for large differences (those considered material in amount), but negative for small differences. Since the net effect is positive only for the differences that are large in relation to the amount budgeted — *the material differences* — these are the ones to receive the time and attention needed to determine their causes. The spotlighting of material differences for investigation is referred to as *management by exception.*

Only material differences should be investigated

Although the accounting profession has long been working on a project to determine specifically what is meant by a material amount, no conclusions have as yet been reached, and many accountants doubt if they can be. What is material to one person may not be to another. Each manager must set his or her own guidelines for determining what is material or significant, and use this guide for spotlighting differences to investigate. For example, the manager of the maintenance department whose performance report is shown in Exhibit B may decide that any variance that exceeds 10% of the original budget is material and is to be investigated.

In Exhibit B, the differences for supervision and wages would probably both be considered immaterial, since each one represents a very small variation from the budget. On the other hand, the differences for supplies and utilities each represent a substantial variation from the amounts budgeted. Since these differences are material, they would probably be spotlighted for investigation.

Should we investigate favorable variances too?

Both of the differences spotlighted for investigation were over budget — which accountants commonly refer to as *unfavorable differences.* Does this mean that we only investigate variances that are unfavorable and ignore those that are favorable — that is, under budget? Of course not. Large favorable variances would be examined as well. They might reveal some ways to do things better or for less cost than was originally planned. Once uncovered, they could be instituted as part of the routine.

Responsibility for Differences

It is important that responsibilities are clearly assigned for all activities within an organization. The managers of all departments within the organization need to know

Managers can't control unless responsibilities are assigned

exactly what their responsibilities are, so that they know for which activities they will be held accountable and for which ones they will not be held accountable. It should then come as no surprise if, for example, the manager of the maintenance department is asked to explain why the cost of supplies, shown in Exhibit B, turned out to be $2,700 over budget.

If the maintenance manager was not informed that he was responsible for spending the budgeted amount for supplies of $18,000, several problems may have occurred: (1) He may not have made a complete effort to make sure the budget was attained; (2) he may have felt that it was unfair when he was blamed for the costs being over the budget; or (3) he may have taken no effort to evaluate the cause of the difference or to take corrective action to prevent the recurrence.

Analysis of Differences

Once we have decided which differences are large enough to investigate and who is responsible for them, we need to next determine the cause and corrective action needed for each difference.

For example, referring again to the supplies in Exhibit B, we may learn that the $2,700 difference was due to the following three causes:

1. The purchase price of supplies was higher than anticipated.

2. There was more than normal waste during production because the supplies were of poor quality.

3. The number of times that machines required maintenance was more than usual for the month.

Each of these three causes would be studied to determine if any corrective action need be taken to prevent recurrence. The maintenance department manager may find out from the purchasing agent that the first two causes can be rectified by changing suppliers. A new supplier may agree to sell a better-quality material at a lower price if purchases are made in substantially larger quantities, resulting in significant quantity discounts.

Looking into the third cause, it may be determined that more maintenance was required than was expected because several machines were run on double rather than single shifts, a situation that was not properly anticipated in the budget. In this case, no corrective action is warranted, but the next budget must be adjusted to reflect the increased maintenance required.

In Chapter 24, we will discuss in more detail how to determine, evaluate, and establish corrective actions for differences found in the performance report.

RELATIONSHIP OF PLANNING AND CONTROL

Planning without control is like a ship without a rudder; control without plans is like a ship without a compass

It is essential that planning and control interact with each other for an organization to reach its goals. However, the interaction between planning and control is not quite as simple as we depicted in Figure B. In that diagram we showed a distinct beginning and end — first there was planning, and then there was control. Although we definitely do need to have plans before we can control, the reverse is also true — we need to control before we can do a good job of making new plans. Unless we have the feedback of the control process, it's not possible to revise our expectations for upcoming periods in order to set new goals and the means to attaining them.

A better way to show the interrelationships of planning and control is with the diagram shown in Figure C.

Although the first step for a new organization must be planning, once initial plans

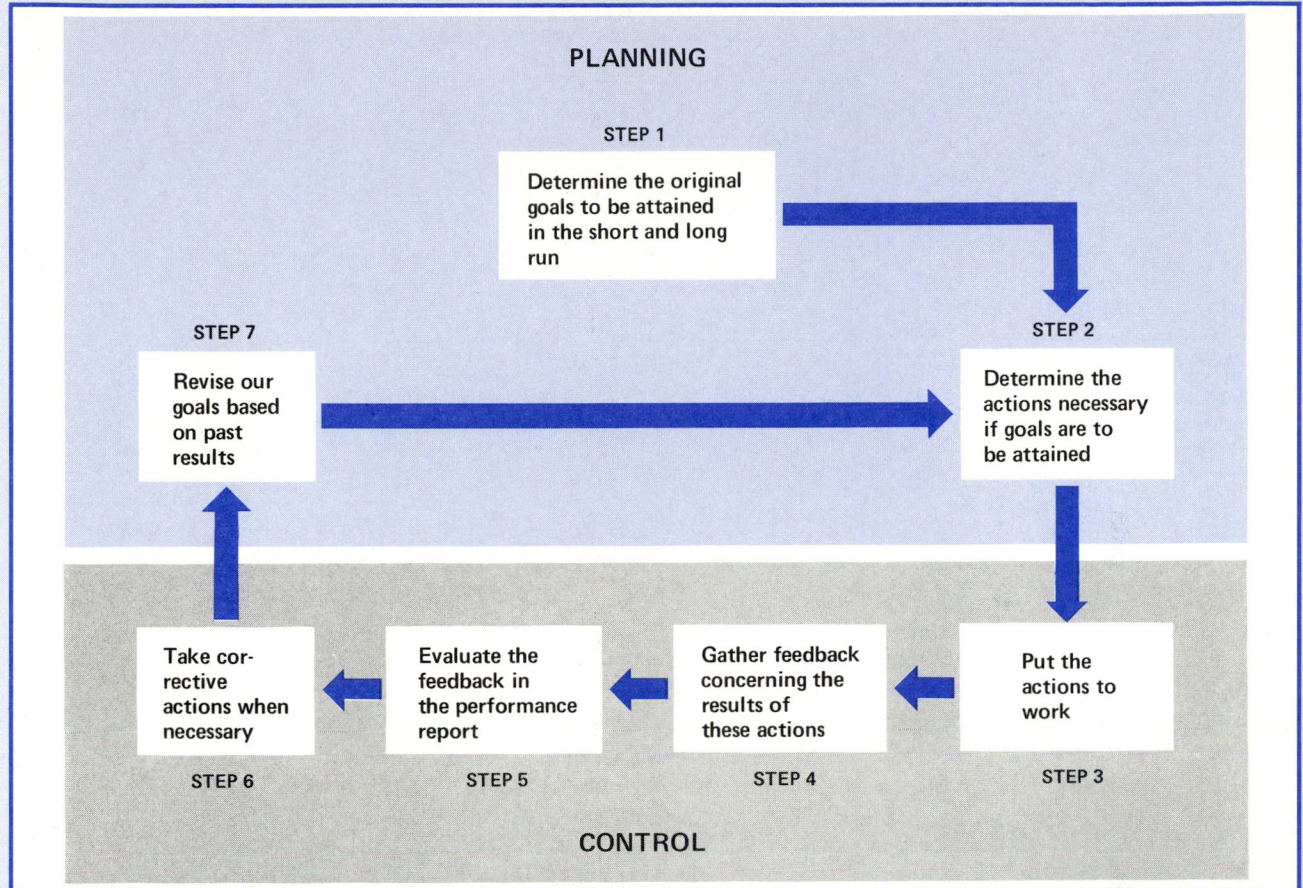

FIGURE C   The Interrelationship of Planning and Control.

have been implemented there will never again be an abrupt beginning, or ending, of this continuous process. Managers do not postpone the control function while planning is taking place and then cease their planning until the control steps are completed. Instead, the planning function is constantly taking place and being improved upon at the same time that the control procedures are being applied.

ROLE OF ACCOUNTING WITHIN THE ORGANIZATION

Accountants give information and advice to managers — they do not make decisions for managers

The role of the accounting department, and the chief accounting executive, the *controller,* is to provide information that managers need in making decisions. The controller gives managers advice that helps them make decisions; he or she does not make the decisions for managers. The controller is in a position of staff responsibility rather than line responsibility. *Staff responsibility* is the responsibility of giving advice, counsel, or service to other departments; *line responsibility* is the responsibility for making decisions and giving directives that guide the activities toward the organization's goals.

Figure D depicts a simplified organization chart for a manufacturer. The figure shows that the controller and the accounting department report directly to the vice president for finance. It also shows that the accounting department assists the selling and manufacturing departments in a staff—advisory—capacity.

The controller is responsible for more than the planning and control aspects of

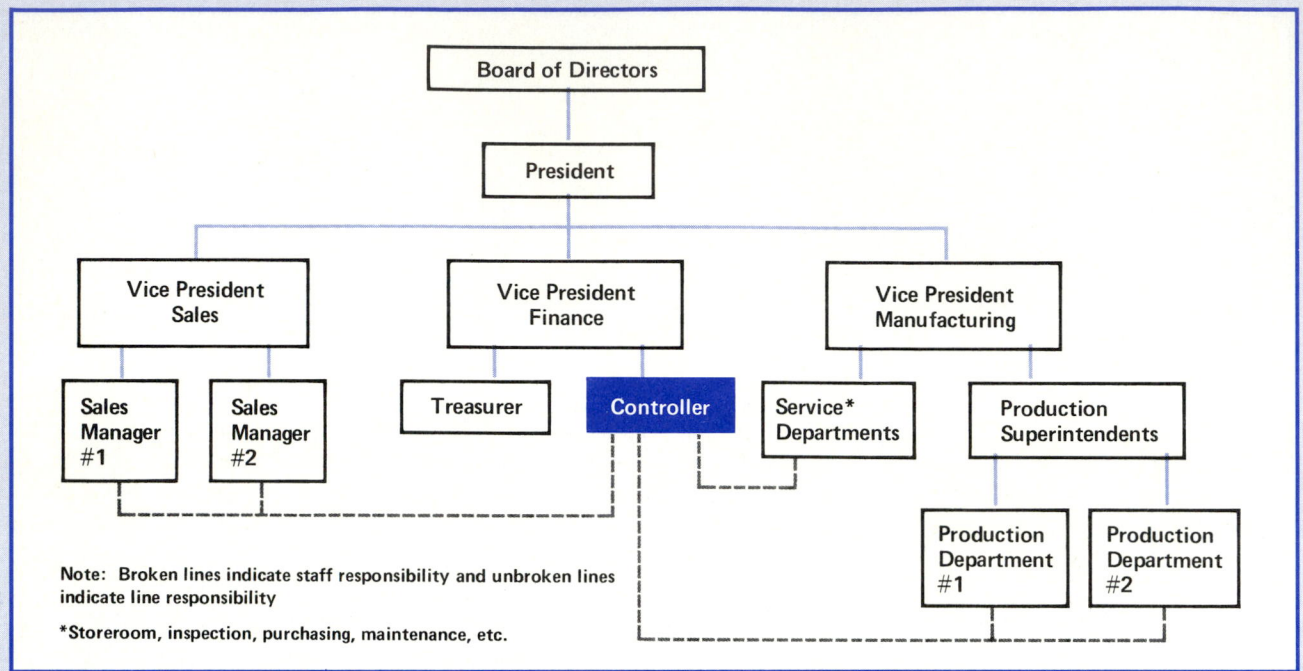

FIGURE D   Organization Chart of a Manufacturer.
The organization chart shows that the controller—the chief accounting executive—reports to the vice president for finance. It also indicates that the controller serves in a staff (advisory) capacity to all other departments: sales, production, and service.

management accounting. The controller's responsibilities also include general accounting, internal audit, and taxes, among others. Although the controller is involved in much more than merely management accounting, we will focus primarily on the role of the controller as a management accountant.

The controller's relationship to department managers typically is a staff relationship. However, the controller has line responsibility over subordinate managers within the accounting department itself. The controller gives directives to the managers of general accounting, taxes, and internal audit departments, advising them how to run their respective departments.

The controller also exerts some line responsibility over the managers of nonaccounting departments. Once the controller has determined the accounting procedures and methods for each department to follow, and has recommended to top management that they be followed by the other departments, the president of the organization then delegates to the controller the authority to implement the accounting system. When the controller gives directives to line managers as to their role in generating quantitative information, the controller acts in a line rather than a staff capacity.

Why would anyone resent the accountant?

Because the accounting department provides much of the information management uses in reaching decisions, sometimes it appears that the controller is doing the actual planning and controlling. This is why managers of other departments sometimes resent the accountants and resist their advice. These managers might feel that the accountants are attempting to run their departments and make their decisions. The accountants' role in the organization must be understood and agreed upon by the managers of other departments and the accountants themselves. Only through good communication and cooperation can they together carry out their functions and strive to achieve the goals of the organization.

In the following chapters we will tell you about the many types of decisions that managers make concerning planning, control, and product costing. For each decision situation we will explain the tools used by accountants to help managers make that decision. You will learn that each of the decisions is based on costs; and for each different type of decision there may be different types of costs that are needed in the accounting tool.

Different costs for different purposes

Management accountants often use the phrase, "different costs for different purposes," meaning that in each decision situation, management has a specific purpose for needing cost information, which differs from the needs for other decisions. And the accountant needs to supply just the right cost information for management to accomplish each purpose.

Because we are going to be concerned with many different kinds of costs, let's begin with the most basic definition of cost:

What is "cost"?

Cost is a measurable sacrifice of resources exchanged for goods or services.

This definition is way too broad to be of any use to us, so we need to tighten it up a bit, and begin to examine different ways that costs can be classified. A cost can be classified depending on how you look at it. To see what we mean, consider the following example:

EXAMPLE: AMY'S LEMONADE STAND

When Amy Carter was a little girl, she used to spend her summer vacation selling lemonade. At the beginning of one summer she paid $2 for a large Styrofoam pitcher and $5 for 150 tiny bags of sugar. In addition, during the summer she paid $10 for lemons and $8.00 for 200 plastic cups. Amy sold 150 cups of lemonade, using all of her lemons and sugar and 180 plastic cups. She also paid some of her friends commissions totaling $4.50 ($.03 per cup sold) to go from house to house selling the lemonade. At the end of her vacation she had only 20 plastic cups remaining, which she planned to keep  until the next summer when she would diversify by selling peanuts as well as lemonade. The Styrofoam pitcher was not reusable.

Now let's look at the various ways of classifying the costs in this example:

Product costs and period costs

1. a. *Product costs* are all the costs incurred and assignable to the units produced and sold. In the example, that amounts to $24.20.

Sugar	$ 5.00
Lemons	10.00
Pitcher	2.00
Cups ($8 ÷ 200 = $.04 per cup × 180 cups)	7.20
Total product costs	$24.20

The 20 unused cups cost $.80 ($.04 per cup × 20 cups) and would be a product cost the next summer when more lemonade would be made.

    b. *Period costs* are expensed when incurred. They are not part of the costs of making the lemonade. For Amy the only period cost was the $4.50 commission paid to her friends to sell the lemonade from house to house.

Variable costs and fixed costs

2. a. *Variable costs* fluctuate in total in response to changes in activity. The cost of lemons, sugar, cups, and commissions are variable costs. They changed with the number of cups made and sold—the changes in activity.

    b. *Fixed costs* remain unchanged in total at all levels of activity. The cost of the Styrofoam pitcher would have been $2 whether Amy had made and sold 10 cups of lemonade or 150 cups.

Controllable costs and noncontrollable costs

3. a. *Controllable costs* are those that can be influenced by a manager during a period of time. Amy should have been able to influence the amount of lemons, sugar, and plastic cups used to sell 150 cups of lemonade. Since she used 180 plastic cups in order to sell 150 cups of lemonade, she did not influence her operation as efficiently as she might have—she wasted 30 cups.

    b. *Noncontrollable costs* are those that cannot be influenced by a manager during a period of time. For example, if Amy was forced to pay the block bully $5 for "protection" during the summer, she would have had little influence over that cost—unless, of course, she told her father. The pitcher would probably have also been a noncontrollable cost.

Relevant costs and irrelevant costs

4. a. *Relevant costs* are those that are different for the alternatives being considered. Assume that Amy's mother suggests using packaged sweetened lemonade rather than fresh-squeezed. If the packaged lemonade is used, there will be no need to purchase lemons and sugar. The cost of the ingredients used to make the lemonade (lemons and sugar versus ready-made packages) would be different—they would be relevant to the decision of how to make the lemonade in the least costly way.

    b. *Irrelevant costs* are those that are the same for the alternatives being considered. No matter which ingredients Amy uses to make the lemonade, the same number of cups will still be needed, the pitcher will still be the container, and the friends are still needed to sell. All of these items will be the same regardless of which ingredients Amy uses in the lemonade—they are irrelevant.

Different costs for different purposes

Depending on the situation to be evaluated, the accountant must decide which type of costs are the ones needed to help a manager make the correct decision. In some cases the accountant must present the costs as product costs or period costs (what is the cost of the lemonade sold during the summer?); the manager may not need to know if the costs are relevant or irrelevant, variable or fixed. In other cases, it may be more helpful for the manager to be aware of which costs are relevant or irrelevant (for

Costs may be classified in many ways

instance, should the lemonade be made with packaged or fresh ingredients?); the manager may not be as concerned with knowing if the costs are product or period, controllable or noncontrollable.

Now, before we finish, let us emphasize one more important point, just in case it isn't clear after our discussion of Amy's lemonade stand. The same cost may be classified in several different ways. For example, a cost may be a product cost, a relevant cost, a controllable cost, and a variable cost—all at the same time. There could be numerous other combinations of cost classifications as well. A cost cannot, of course, at the same time be both variable and fixed, or product and period, or relevant and irrelevant, or controllable and noncontrollable.

For Amy, the cost of lemons was a product cost, a variable cost, a controllable cost, and a relevant cost. The sales commission was a period cost, a variable cost, a controllable cost, and an irrelevant cost. Each other cost would have its own combination of cost classifications.

The list of cost classifications above represents only a portion of the many that will be discussed in the management accounting chapters of this book. Each chapter that follows will discuss, in much greater depth, one or more key cost classifications as a foundation for the development of the specific accounting tool discussed in that chapter.

OVERVIEW SUMMARY

The purpose of *management accounting* is to provide the quantitative information that managers need to plan and control the activities of an organization in reaching its goals. In *planning,* managers do two things: determine the goals for the organization and determine how to achieve them. The tool used by accountants to assist managers in the planning function is the *budget*—the quantitative expression of the goals set by management.

In *controlling,* managers do four things: (1) put the plans to work; (2) observe the plans at work and gather information (*feedback*) on how well they are performing; (3) determine if corrective actions are needed so that final results will be in line with the plans; and (4) take the necessary actions to remedy any problems that may exist. The tool used by accountants to assist managers in the control function is the *performance report.* The performance report compares the actual results to the budget so that the material differences can be spotlighted.

Good planning and control are both essential if an organization is to reach its goals. Neither is more important than the other. Effective planning is not possible without good controls and meaningful control cannot come about without thoughtful planning.

The *controller,* as the chief accounting officer within an organization, is in charge of the accounting department. The accounting department's relationship to other departments involves *staff* rather than *line* responsibilities. By providing information to managers, the accounting department gives advice, counsel, and service to the other departments. It does not make the decisions that affect the activities taken by these departments to reach their goals.

The type of information supplied to management often depends on the type of decision situation itself. For example, there is not merely one set of costs that can be used to make all decisions. Instead, as accountants say, there are "different costs for different purposes." There are product costs and period costs, variable costs and fixed costs, and relevant costs and irrelevant costs—to name just a few.

Budget　The tool used by management accountants to assist management in the planning function. It is a quantitative representation of the goals set by management. (page 728)

Control　A management activity directed toward achieving the organization's goals. It involves the following four steps: (1) putting the plans to work, (2) observing the plans at work and gathering information (feedback) on how well the organization is performing, (3) determining if corrective actions are needed to get the future results back in line with the plans, and (4) taking action to remedy any problems that exist. (page 729)

Controller　The chief accounting executive within an organization. (page 733)

Cost accounting　An accounting system for providing managers with the quantitative information they need in planning and controlling (management accounting), and to determine the cost of a product (a part of financial accounting). (page 727)

Feedback　The information collected to assess the performance of the organization in reaching its goals. (page 729)

Financial accounting　The accounting system for providing managers with the quantitative information they need to prepare financial statements for external users. (page 724)

Line responsibility　The responsibility to make decisions and give commands that directly affect the attainment of an organization's goals. (page 733)

Management accounting　The accounting system for providing the quantitative information managers need in planning and controlling. Also referred to as managerial accounting. (page 724)

Management by exception　Spotlighting the material differences in a performance report as the ones that warrant investigation. (page 731)

Material differences　Those differences in a performance report that are large in relation to the amount budgeted. (page 731)

Performance report　The principal accounting tool for assisting management in the control function. It displays the budget, the actual results, and any differences between budget and actual. (page 730)

Planning　Setting an organization's goals and deciding how to attain them. (page 728)

Product costing　The process of determining the costs of a product and then allocating them between the income statement (as cost of goods sold) and the balance sheet (as inventory). (page 727)

Staff responsibility　The responsibility to give advice, counsel, or service to other departments. (page 733)

QUESTIONS

1. What is meant by the term *planning,* and what is the management accountant's role in this function?

2. Discuss several differences in management accounting and financial accounting.

3. Since financial accounting is required for most organizations, it is a much more important accounting discipline than is management accounting, which is purely voluntary. Discuss.

4. "Management accounting is nothing more than a modern term to describe cost accounting." Comment.

5. Discuss what is meant by the term *product costing.*

6. Explain what is meant by the term *management by exception.*

7. When a manager is evaluating the differences between actual and budgeted results on a performance report, the term *management by exception* means that the manager is concerned with *all unfavorable* differences. Discuss.

8. It should be obvious how a performance report assists management in the control function. But how does it help in the planning function?

9. "Planning is a more vital management function than control." Comment.

10. "Accountants assist management by doing the planning and controlling of management's routine decisions." Do you agree? Explain.

11. "The controller does plan in a special sense." Explain what is meant by this statement.

12. Discuss several different types of routine and nonroutine decisions that managers must make, and for which accountants can generate relevant information.

13. Does a controller within an organization have line responsibility or staff responsibility? Explain.

14. Generally accepted accounting principles provide guidelines for the preparation of general-purpose financial statements. Do the same principles serve as guidelines for the preparation of reports to management for internal decisions?

15. Discuss what is meant by the expression, "different costs for different purposes."

16. The controllers of Companies A and B are discussing how they help management control costs with the aid of performance reports. The controller of Company A says that he examines all variances larger than $500. The controller of Company B (which is much larger than Company A) responds that variances as small as $500 are ignored and only those variances greater than $2,500 are investigated. Which controller is correct in the variances he selects for investigation?

17. A performance report has recently been prepared for one of the production departments of Hi-Tech Company, and the controller and superintendent disagree about which differences to investigate. The superintendent wishes to investigate all unfavorable differences, and the controller expresses apprehension about such a policy. The performance report is shown as follows:

	Budget	Actual	Difference
Materials	$ 50,000	$ 60,000	$(10,000)
Labor	75,000	68,000	7,000
Utilities	6,000	6,100	(100)
Supplies	8,000	7,800	200
Fuel	16,000	16,000	–0–
Totals	$155,000	$157,900	$ (2,900)

As the controller, which differences would you recommend be investigated? Why wouldn't you suggest investigation of all differences? Would you suggest investigating favorable as well as unfavorable differences? Why?

18. How would you react to a production manager's criticism to the controller that the accounting department was attempting to run her operation rather than merely keeping records? Instead of providing information for management's use, it sometimes appeared that the controller was attempting to do the planning and controlling himself.

19. The Andros Company, a retailer, sells a single product, and had the following income statement for 1986:

Sales.	$100,000
Cost of Goods Sold	60,000
Gross Margin	$ 40,000
Operating Costs:	
Salaries. $30,000	
Rent 6,000	
Commissions. 5,000	
Advertising 10,000	51,000
Net Income (Loss).	$ (11,000)

The president of Andros is considering a significant increase in advertising for the following year, 1987, which should double sales. Salaries, which are set by the owner (who is not involved in day-to-day operations) will remain unchanged. Additional space will be rented to accommodate greater storage needs. Commissions will continue to be 5% of sales.

Each cost shown in the income statement above can be classified in several ways:

As a product cost (P) or a period cost (PER)
As a variable cost (V) or a fixed cost (F)
As a relevant cost (R) or an irrelevant cost (I) in the decision of whether or not to stimulate sales with increased advertising
As a controllable cost (C) or a noncontrollable cost (N) for the company president

For each cost listed below, provide the proper classifications by placing the correct letter in the spaces provided.

Item	Product (P) or Period (PER) Cost	Variable (V) or Fixed (F) Cost	Relevant (R) or Irrelevant (I) Cost	Controllable (C) or Noncontrollable (N) Cost
Cost of goods sold	_____	_____	_____	_____
Salaries	_____	_____	_____	_____
Rent	_____	_____	_____	_____
Commissions	_____	_____	_____	_____
Advertising	_____	_____	_____	_____

Chapter 19

An Introduction to Cost Accounting Systems

After studying this chapter you will understand the following:

- What management accountants mean by *activity* and *centers of activity*
- How the concept of activity is used to distinguish between *total costs* and *average costs*
- What a *product cost* is, what a *period cost* is, and how to distinguish them
- How a manufacturing operation basically differs from a retailing operation
- That a retailer has only one type of inventory to be reported, whereas a manufacturer has three types of inventory to be concerned about
- How product costs relate to the inventories for a retailer and for a manufacturer
- How to trace the flow of costs from purchases through to the cost of goods that are sold
- How to prepare an income statement and supporting schedules for a manufacturer

It is the job of the accountant to provide managers with quantitative information. Managers use this information for making a wide variety of decisions. A few examples of the many different decisions regularly confronting managers include:

Different decisions facing managers

■ How much should be recognized as the cost of each unit produced and what is the total amount to be expensed when these units are sold?

■ What should be the sales price for the units awaiting sale to customers?

■ How does a change in the selling price of a product affect the net income generated by that product?

■ How many units need to be sold to generate a desired profit for the organization?

■ Is a particular product generating sufficient profit? If not, should the firm discontinue making that product?

■ Should a special order be accepted?

■ Has a manager adequately controlled the costs of operating his or her department during the previous period?

■ Should the productive capacity of the firm be enlarged?

DIFFERENT WAYS OF REGARDING THE SAME COSTS

As we discussed in the preceding overview to these management accounting chapters, any decision is significantly influenced by the amount of costs involved. Each situation is different, and so may be the cost information needed to make the best decision. Managers describe the situation under analysis to the management accountant. At this point it is up to the management accountant to determine and to provide the particular cost information needed to make the best management decision in that particular situation.

We found out that costs can be product or period costs, variable or fixed costs, controllable or noncontrollable costs, and relevant or irrelevant costs, these examples representing just a few of the types of costs that are used in management accounting. For each decision situation the accountant must decide which type of costs are needed and how to present the costs to the manager in order for this information to be most useful.

In this chapter our primary emphasis will be on the distinction between product costs and period costs. But first we need to have a good understanding of three basic terms—activity, total costs, and average costs. A clear grasp of what they mean is essential to understanding much of the cost terminology that comes later.

TOTAL COSTS, AVERAGE COSTS, AND ACTIVITY

Referring back to Amy's lemonade stand example in the Overview, making lemonade would be considered an *activity.* It is an activity that is measurable—by the number of cups of lemonade produced and sold. It is an activity that has a cost—the dollars incurred to produce that number of cups.

Making video games is an activity—or more specifically, it is the summation of numerous activities needed to produce each of the many different components that make up a computer video game. Each of the activities is measurable in terms of the number of components produced. The costs of each activity can be accumulated and classified as product or period costs, variable or fixed costs, controllable or noncontrollable costs, etc. To properly classify the costs within an organization, you must first develop a good understanding of the term *activity.* We have used this term rather loosely so far, but in such a way that you should have a general feeling of what it means. We will now be more specific.

Activity: a measurement of accomplishment

Management accountants think of activity as something done to produce a result or an output that can be measured. To a management accountant, activity should be a clear indicator of (1) what was done, (2) in a particular place or environment, (3) during a specific period of time, (4) to produce measurable results.

For example, the firm that manufactures computer video games employs trained technicians who assemble components into a complete game. The number of completed games assembled during a month is a rather good indicator of the activity of the assembly shop. The same firm also employs janitors who clean and tidy the assembly shop as well as other areas within the building. The number of square feet cleaned by the janitors would probably be a good way to measure the activity of the janitorial maintenance department, but it would be a poor way to measure the activity of the assembly shop.

Centers of activity: different types for different organizations

Management accountants regard these as two different ***centers of activity*** — subunits within an organization that perform a particular function or produce measurable results. In one case, the center of activity is the assembly department; in the other case, the center of activity is the maintenance department.

A manufacturing firm can be considered to be made up of many or perhaps only a few different centers of activity. For example, the production department could be a center of activity, and/or individual specialized groups could each be centers of activity within the production department. Other centers of activity could be the sales department, or some large division within the firm. The entire firm itself could be considered a center of activity. However, the larger the center of the activity, the more complex it will be for management accountants to deal with and the less helpful will be the information that accountants provide to managers on a daily basis. For a retailer, the center of activity could be a storeroom; for a hospital, the intensive care wing; for a university, the College of Business Administration.

Activity can be measured in different ways

Activity can be measured in many different ways, depending on the type of organization and the types of centers of activity within that organization. For example, within the production department of a manufacturer, a good measure of the activity is the number of units produced or the number of hours worked. For a storeroom, a good measure of activity could be the number of requisitions processed; for an intensive care wing in a hospital, the number of patients treated; for the College of Business Administration, the number of semester hours enrolled by students.

Total Costs and Average Costs

Total costs

The ***total costs*** for a center of activity are simply the sum of all costs related to that center for a specific period of time. For example, for Amy's lemonade production as a center of activity, the total costs were $24.20; for her selling department as a center of activity, the total costs were $4.50.

Average costs = total costs ÷ activity

An ***average cost*** is simply the center of activity's total costs for the period, divided by the activity during the period. For Amy, $24.20, total costs of production, divided by 150 cups produced and sold, results in an average cost of $.16 per cup.

A production department calculates an average cost per unit produced (as in the lemonade example). A hospital might determine an average cost per patient serviced. And a college could compute an average cost per student semester hour enrolled.

The example at the top of page 744 shows how an average cost is calculated for different centers of activity. In each case the total cost is the same but the centers of activity and the measure of activity differ.

Be sure you understand how to measure activity

The point of this simple example is that there is no single measure of activity that is applicable to all centers of activity. A meaningful measure of activity for one center might be meaningless for another. A suitable measure of activity for a center is the one that most logically influences the amount of total cost incurred during a period of time. For example, the number of units produced is a meaningful measure of activity

EXAMPLE 19-1

CENTERS OF ACTIVITY

Assume that the total costs for five different centers of activity are each $100,000. The average cost for each center is found by dividing the $100,000 by the measure of activity for that center.

Average Cost for Different Centers of Activity			
Center of Activity	Possible Measure of Activity	Calculation	Average Cost
Production department	50,000 units produced	$100,000 ÷ 50,000 units	$2 per unit
Sales department	$2 million of sales	$100,000 ÷ $2 million sales	5% of sales dollars
Storeroom	50,000 requisitions filled	$100,000 ÷ 50,000 requisitions	$2 per requisition
Intensive care wing	400 patients treated	$100,000 ÷ 400 patients	$250 per patient
College of Business Administration	20,000 student semester hours	$100,000 ÷ 20,000 hours	$5 per semester hour

for a production department—it has a significant influence on the total costs incurred. On the other hand, the number of units produced would be a silly way to measure the activity of a hospital or a College of Business Administration.

In the following example, notice how Dan Kirby's confusion over the appropriate measure of activity caused him some financial distress.

EXAMPLE 19-2

DAN KIRBY

Dan Kirby, a student, wanted some tutoring prior to his first accounting exam and wondered how much it would cost. A friend who had been tutored the previous week recommended someone who was very good and who charged only $10. Dan contacted this tutor and arranged for an all-night, 10-hour session the night before the exam. At daybreak, Dan was presented a bill for $50. Dumbfounded, he then learned that the rate was $5 per hour, and that his friend needed merely 2 hours at this rate while he needed 10.

If Dan had only thought about it logically, he would have realized that tutoring costs are more closely related to the number of hours tutored at $5/hour than to the number of sessions of unspecified duration, at $10/session. The best measure of activity would have been the number of hours tutored—not the number of sessions.

Basic Definitions and What's to Come

Many of the concepts to follow in this and later chapters are based on the definitions of total costs, average costs, and activity just presented. Thus, a complete understanding of these terms and how to use them is critical before you proceed further.

PRODUCT COSTING

Preparing financial statements and publishing them for interested external parties is the ultimate purpose of financial accounting. For an organization that generates revenue from the sale of a product, the costs of the units to be sold must be fully accounted for and represented in the financial statements.

The Cost of Goods Sold account, found on the income statement, indicates the costs associated with the quantity of units sold during the period. The balance sheet account Inventory represents the costs associated with the quantity of unsold units at the end of a period.

It is the responsibility of the cost accountant to determine the costs to assign to cost of goods sold and the costs to assign to inventory.

Product costing: costing inventory and cost of goods sold

The process of determining the costs of all units that can be sold, and then allocating these costs between the units sold during the period (cost of goods sold) and the units unsold at the end of the period (inventory) is referred to as ***product costing.*** *Only product costs are used in product costing, not period costs.* Let's now take a closer look at the difference between product costs and period costs and some examples.

Product Costs and Period Costs

Product costs are costs that are closely associated with units produced by a manufacturer or purchased for resale by a retailer or wholesaler.

Product costs are inventory costs when incurred

Examples of product costs are the costs of materials and labor used in production by a manufacturer, and the invoice price of merchandise purchased by a retailer. Product costs are assigned to the product when they are incurred and at the same time are classified as an asset, inventory.

Product costs are considered assets when incurred, because they are resources that are expected to provide future economic benefits to the firm. When the units to which product costs are assigned are finally sold, these costs then become an expense, cost of goods sold. For example, the cost of lemons, sugar, and plastic cups used in producing cups of lemonade for Amy are product costs. In addition, if Amy were renting and insuring her sales booth, the related insurance and rental costs would also be product costs. These costs are combined in making the lemonade — an asset — and are considered an asset until the lemonade is sold. Only at the moment of sale do the cost of lemons, sugar, and plastic cups become an expense — as a part of cost of goods sold.

Product costs are assets until the units are sold

Your initial instinct may be to think of these costs as expenses instead of assets — which indeed they will become — but not when they are incurred.

Product costs are assets until the product is sold. At the moment of sale, several things happen:

Product costs are expensed when units are sold

1. The economic benefit, sales revenue, is realized. There is no longer any "future" economic benefit to be realized.

2. Thus, the asset expires.

3. No longer recognizing the product cost as an asset, it is now recognized as an expense, cost of goods sold.

4. The cost of goods sold is matched with the sales revenue on the income statement.

To condense the discussion above, we can merely say that product costs are (1) assigned to inventory when they are incurred, and (2) expensed when the units to which they are assigned are later sold.

Period costs are expensed when incurred; they are not assets

Period costs are costs that are recognized as expenses as soon as they are incurred. *They are not assigned to the product; instead, they are immediately assigned to the income statement as an expense of that period.* For Amy, the commission of $4.50 given to her friends for selling the lemonade is a period cost, not a product cost.

Period costs are not assets, for they are not expected to provide any future economic benefits to the organization. *The benefits provided by period costs are realized fully when the costs are incurred and are recognized in the current period.* Examples of period costs include sales representatives' commissions, administrative salaries, and transportation-out costs for units sold.

The flow diagram in Figure 19-1 gives a general picture of how to determine whether a cost is a product cost or a period cost, and how and when to account for each.

How to distinguish product costs from period costs

FIGURE 19-1
How to Determine Product Costs and Period Costs.

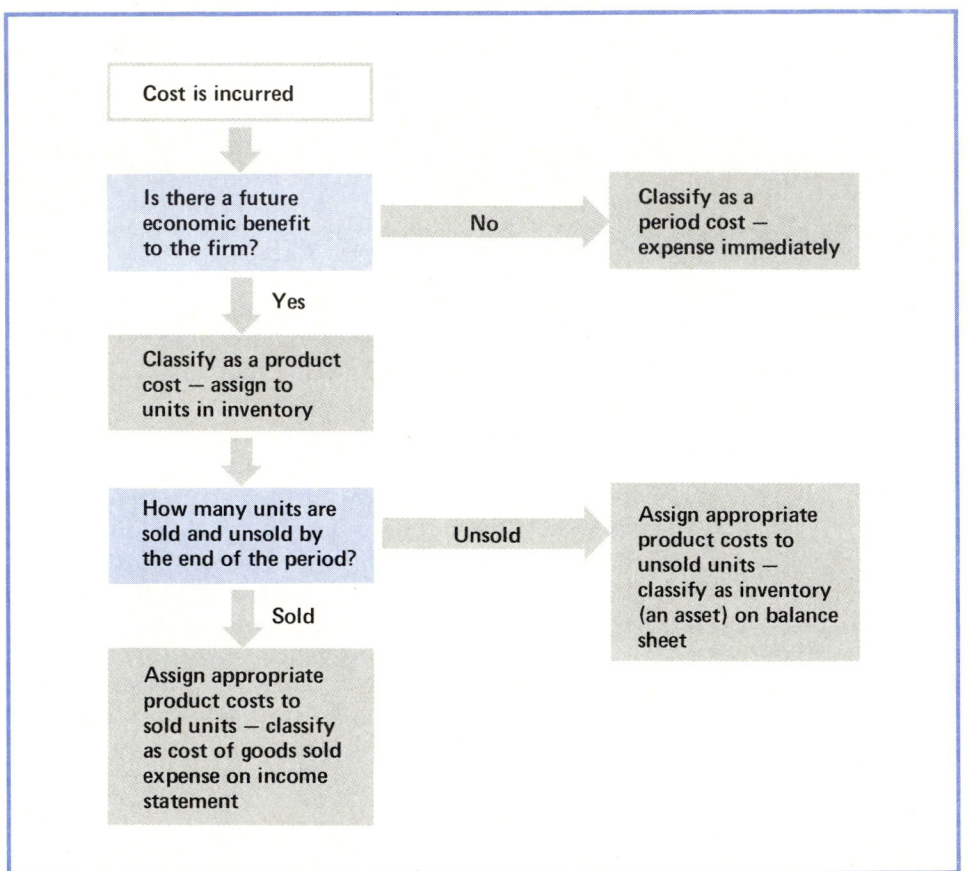

It is important to classify product costs and period costs correctly. If these costs are classified incorrectly, they will be expensed at the wrong time, and the financial statements for the period will be inexact. To see what effect an incorrect product versus period cost classification can have on the income statement as well as the balance sheet, read Example 19-3.

Proper classification is important

EXAMPLE 19-3

THE YODO COMPANY

The Yodo Company completed its first year of operations, 1988. During 1988 Yodo had sales of $50,000 and incurred costs of $75,000. Of the units available for sale, 40% were unsold at year-end. Yodo then prepared two income statements, based on two different cost assumptions:

Assumptions:

1. All costs incurred are product costs.

2. Of the costs incurred, $20,000 are product costs and $55,000 are period costs.

The resulting income statements are shown below.

YODO COMPANY
Income Statement for 1988

	Assumptions	
	1 **All Costs Are** **Product Costs,** **$75,000**	**2** **$20,000 Are Product** **Costs and $55,000 Are** **Period Costs**
Sales Revenue	$50,000	$50,000
Cost of Goods Sold Expense	45,000*	12,000‡
Gross Profit.	$ 5,000	$38,000
Other Expenses (period costs)	–0– †	55,000†
Net Income (Loss)	$ 5,000	($17,000)

* Cost of Goods Sold Expense = total product costs ($75,000) less cost of remaining inventory of unsold units (40% × $75,000 = $30,000) = $45,000.

† Other Expenses = total costs incurred ($75,000) less those that are considered product costs. For assumption 1, $75,000 − $75,000 = $0. For assumption 2, $75,000 − $20,000 = $55,000.

‡ Cost of Goods Sold Expense = total product costs ($20,000) less cost of remaining inventory of unsold units (40% × $20,000 = $8,000) = $12,000.

With assumption 1, the net income was a $5,000 profit; with assumption 2, it was a $17,000 loss — a difference of $22,000 between the two cases. The $22,000 difference in net income can be attributed entirely to the different ways the costs were classified as product and period costs.

If the entire amount of $75,000 is a product cost (assumption 1), the amount expensed in 1988 is only $45,000 (60% × $75,000), because 60% of the units to which the $75,000 was assigned were sold. The remaining $30,000 (40% × $75,000) is assigned to the Inventory account.

In the second case (assumption 2), only $20,000 is considered to be product costs. That means $12,000 (60% × $20,000) is assigned to units sold and therefore is expensed in the current year. As a result, this $12,000 product cost plus the $55,000 period cost, or a total of $67,000, is expensed in the current year.

Let's assume that assumption 2 represents the proper assignment of costs — that is, product costs are indeed $20,000. This being the case, it was improper for Yodo Company to include the full $75,000 as product costs in case 1. Therefore, the $22,000 difference in net incomes represents overstated net income. That is, net income should not be reported as a profit of $5,000; it should be reported as a loss of $17,000. If we were to show the Inventory account on the balance sheet, it should be shown as $8,000, not $30,000; this is also an overstatement of $22,000.

From this example you should see that the accountant cannot accurately measure income and value assets without properly distinguishing between product costs and period costs.

PRODUCT COSTS
The heart and soul of a good cost accounting system

"Increased competition, inflation, and greater attention to interim reporting necessitate the revision of many companys' cost accounting systems. . . . The objective of a new cost accounting system should include accurate product costing, cost control, identifying variances, integrity of inventory accounts, and management information."

The starting point in the development of a useful cost system is with the product costs themselves. "From a study of up-to-date material control and profitability reporting systems in several Fortune 500 companies and many smaller companies, the one overwhelming conclusion that we have is that, in American industry, knowledge of individual product costs is a strategic matter that companies must address to maintain their competitive position. The design and installation of an up-to-date cost system are not trivial undertakings, but if your cost system creaks each time the company moves, action is indicated."

Rather than having an understanding of cost accounting that starts out creaking somewhat, be sure to take all the time you need to completely understand what product costs are, and how they flow through a company's cost accounts. Otherwise the topics of job order costing and process costing, direct costing and absorption costing, and standard costing will be more difficult than they need be.

Source: Robert G. Eiler, Walter K. Goletz, and Daniel P. Keegan, "Is Your Cost Accounting Up to Date?" *Harvard Business Review,* July – August 1982, pp. 132 – end. Copyright © 1982 by the President and Fellows of Harvard College; all rights reserved. Reprinted by permission of *Harvard Business Review.*

Noninventoriable Unexpired Costs

A third type of cost: noninventoriable unexpired

Thus far, we may have given you the impression that all costs are classified as either product costs or period costs. But that's not necessarily so. There is a third group into which costs can be classified when they occur: ***noninventoriable unexpired costs.***

The term ***noninventoriable unexpired costs*** tells you exactly what these costs are. *Noninventoriable unexpired costs represent assets when they are incurred, but they are not costs that can be assigned to inventory* — at least not yet. Examples of noninventoriable unexpired costs include expenditures for prepaid insurance, prepaid rent, machinery, and buildings. Each of these costs is an asset (or unexpired cost) other than inventory. Many of these assets are used up or consumed as time passes. As they expire over time, the amount expired can then be classified as a product cost or a period cost.

For instance, assume that a 3-year insurance policy is acquired for $900. At the time of acquisition, the $900 is an asset, but it is not classified as a product cost — it is classified as prepaid insurance, not inventory. At this moment, the $900 of prepaid insurance is a noninventoriable unexpired cost. After the first year of coverage, $300 worth of insurance has been consumed. This $300 of coverage used up must now be classified as either a product cost or period cost. (The proper classification will depend on the type of organization to which the costs apply, i.e., manufacturer or retailer, as we shall see in the next section.) The remaining $600 is still unexpired after 1 year of the policy; it will continue to be classified as an asset (but not as inventory) in the balance sheet until it expires in the next 2 years. In short, the remaining $600 of insurance cost is still a noninventoriable unexpired cost.

A Way to Simplify

In later sections of this chapter and in most homework problems, for simplicity's sake it will be assumed that all costs can be classified as product costs or period costs. Whenever we introduce noninventoriable unexpired costs, they will be specifically identified.

RETAILERS AND MANUFACTURERS

Before we discuss the different types of product and period costs, we need first to compare the different types of organizations that may have product and period costs. For our purposes, we will classify all organizations as either service organizations, or retailers or manufacturers.

Service organizations are in business to make a profit from the sale of a personal service (accountants, lawyers, advertising agents, etc.) rather than from the sale of inventory. Since service organizations have no inventories, there are no product costs—all of their costs are period costs.

Retailers sell inventory "as is," but manufacturers change the form before sale

Retailing and manufacturing organizations are both in business to make a profit from the sale of inventory. The difference between them is that the *retailer* sells the product in the same form as it is purchased, while the *manufacturer* converts raw materials into the form of a finished product before it can be sold.

Retailing organizations have only one inventory account—Merchandise Inventory. All costs originally assigned to this account are transferred to cost of goods sold expense at time of sale.

Manufacturers must maintain three different inventory accounts—one for each physical form as the product progresses from its raw to finished state:

Inventories for a manufacturer

1. *Raw materials inventory* Materials purchased from a supplier and awaiting use in production

2. *Work-in-process inventory* The unfinished goods in production—the units that are being worked on

3. *Finished goods inventory* The completed product awaiting sale

When materials are acquired, their costs are first placed in the Raw Materials Inventory account until they are needed in production. Once production begins, all production costs, including raw material costs, are accumulated in the Work-in-Process Inventory account and remain there until the product is completed. Once completed, the cost of these units becomes finished goods inventory. As the units are sold, these costs are transferred to cost of goods sold expense.

A simple way to picture in your mind this progression of costs through the inventory accounts is with the following T-accounts:

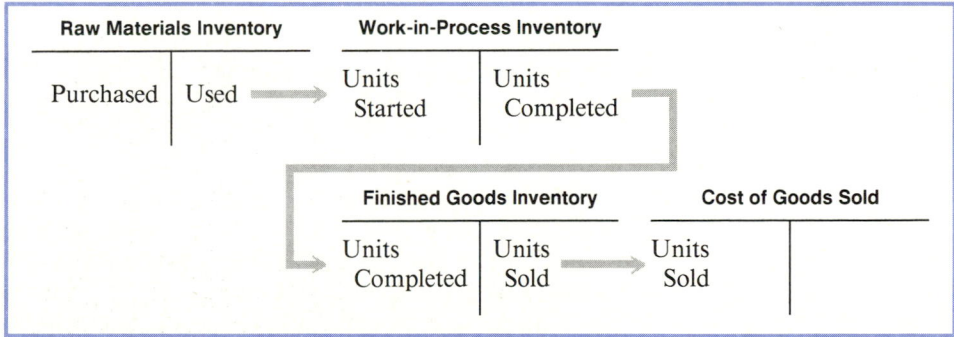

We'll look at this progression of costs in more detail in a few moments.

Now let's see what the different product costs are for the retailer and the manufacturer—that is, what costs are assigned to the respective inventories.

Basic Elements of Product Costs

Product costs for a retailer

Distinguishing product costs from period costs for a retailer is quite simple. Product costs include all costs necessary to get the merchandise inventory from the supplier to the retailer and placed in position for sale. This includes the invoice price of the merchandise and any costs to transport it. Theoretically, there may also be justification for treating the costs of ordering, receiving, and storing the merchandise as product costs. However, since it can be extremely difficult to determine the amount of these costs to assign to different orders purchased, these costs are usually treated as period costs. All other costs for the retailer, such as salaries, expired insurance, expired rent, advertising, utilities, property taxes, and depreciation, are also considered to be related not to the product, but to the period, and are expensed when incurred.

Are all costs for a manufacturer product costs?

The distinction between product costs and period costs is somewhat different for a manufacturer than it is for the retailer. For a manufacturer, the classification of a cost depends on whether it is a cost of a department that is producing a product or of a department that is not producing a product.

To see what we mean, assume that a manufacturing company can be divided into three functional areas: production, sales, and administration. All costs of the selling and administrative departments are period costs; all costs of the production departments are product costs.

Categories of Product Costs

Product costs for a manufacturer fall into one of three main categories:

Direct materials: integral part and easily traceable

1. Direct Materials   ***Direct materials*** are the raw materials that become an integral part of the completed product and that are significant enough to warrant tracing the cost accurately to the finished item. For example, if the production process involves making classroom desks, the direct materials would include wood, formica, and metal legs. Although each desk also includes glue, nails, screws, and varnish, the cost of these raw materials would be insignificant compared to the cost of the major raw materials. The precise cost per desk of each of these minor raw materials might be determinable, but there would be no benefit from having such accurate product costs. You must realize that there is a cost to obtaining information. And as with anything else, you should pay for only as much information as you need.

Nevertheless, we don't forget about the cost of minor raw materials. Such materials as glue, nails, and screws are called ***indirect materials.*** The cost of indirect materials is one of the costs covered under ***factory overhead,*** which we will explain shortly.

One more note on direct materials. The cost of direct materials includes not only the purchase price of the materials, but also whatever freight costs the buyer has to pay for delivery of the materials.

Direct labor: clearly traceable to the product

2. Direct Labor   ***Direct labor*** is the work that directly converts the raw materials into finished goods. Like direct materials, direct labor costs should be clearly traceable to the product being worked on, from the raw to the finished state. For example, the salaries for those laborers who combine the wood, formica, glue, nails, etc., into a finished desk are direct labor costs. But the salaries of workers who bring raw materials to the direct laborers, or of managers who supervise laborers, are examples of ***indirect labor*** costs. Like indirect materials, indirect labor is a component of factory overhead.

Factory overhead: the indirect costs of production

3. Factory Overhead   The simplest way to think of what we mean by ***factory overhead*** costs is this: Combine and add up all the costs of a production department. Then subtract from that total the direct materials costs and the direct labor costs. What remains is the factory overhead costs, which is also called ***manufacturing overhead*** costs. Factory overhead costs represent the indirect costs of production — those that are needed to produce the product, but that cannot be, or for practical reasons (as discussed for indirect materials) shouldn't be, traced directly to the product being worked on. Examples include indirect materials, indirect labor, expired insurance, expired rent, property taxes, maintenance and repairs, utilities, depreciation, idle time, and overtime premium.

Idle time represents the amount paid to laborers for unproductive time. For example, when a machine breaks down, if the laborers stand around waiting for it to be fixed, the wages paid are considered to be idle time. *Overtime premium* is the amount paid to laborers (above the normal hourly rate) for hours worked in excess of the standard hours for a work period.

If factory overhead costs are not traced *directly* to the product being worked on, how do these costs get assigned to the product? That is, how do we determine the factory overhead cost per unit produced? One way is first to determine the total activity for the period—such as the number of desks produced each month—and then to divide that amount into the total overhead costs for that same time period. As a result, each desk is assigned an equal part of the total overhead as its product cost. Additional ways of determining the factory overhead cost per unit produced will be discussed in Chapters 20 and 24.

Sometime accountants find it helpful to combine the terms direct materials and direct labor. This combination of direct costs they call *prime costs.* Similarly, they sometimes find it helpful to combine the terms direct labor and factory overhead, a cost combination referred to as *conversion costs.*

Prime costs represent the direct costs of manufacturing a product.

Conversion costs represent the costs needed to convert raw materials to a finished product (but not including the cost of those raw materials).

You can use Exhibit 19-1 to practice classifying costs as product costs or period costs. To understand how these costs are classified, keep in mind the following:

1. All costs incurred by a retailer are period costs with the exception of the invoice price and transportation costs of merchandise inventory purchased.

2. All costs related to a production department of a manufacturer are product costs.

3. All costs related to nonproduction departments of a manufacturer are period costs.

Prime costs = DM + DL

Conversion costs = DL + FO

**EXHIBIT 19-1
Classifications of Product
Costs and Period Costs.***

	Retailer	Manufacturer		
Type of Cost		Administrative Department Cost	Sales Department Cost	Production Department Cost
Cost of inventory purchases	Pr	†	†	Pr
Transportation-in for inventory purchases	Pr	†	†	Pr
Salaries	P	P	P	Pr
Expired insurance‡	P	P	P	Pr
Expired rent‡	P	P	P	Pr
Utilities	P	P	P	Pr
Property taxes	P	P	P	Pr
Transportation-out for units sold	P	†	P	†
Advertising	P	†	P	†
Depreciation	P	P	P	Pr

* Pr = product costs, P = period costs.

† These costs are not incurred within the respective departments, and their classification would not be applicable.

‡ These are expired insurance and rent, as opposed to the unexpired portions, which are assets in all situations.

EXHIBIT 19-2   T-Accounts for Cost Flow of Retailer.

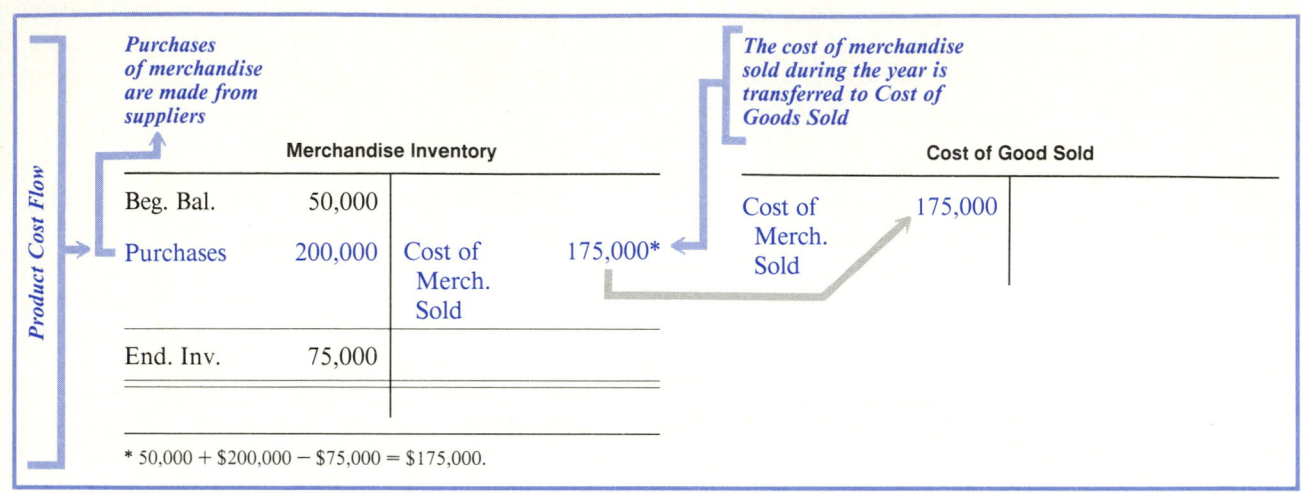

Product Cost Flow

Purchases of merchandise are made from suppliers

The cost of merchandise sold during the year is transferred to Cost of Goods Sold

Merchandise Inventory

Beg. Bal.	50,000		
Purchases	200,000	Cost of Merch. Sold	175,000*
End. Inv.	75,000		

Cost of Good Sold

Cost of Merch. Sold	175,000	

* 50,000 + $200,000 − $75,000 = $175,000.

All Period Costs — Expensed as Incurred

Prepaid Insurance

Beg. Bal.	2,000		
Insurance Paid for during Year	6,000	Insurance Expired during Year	4,000
End. Bal.	4,000		

Insurance Expense

4,000	

Prepaid Rent

Beg. Bal.	5,000		
Prepayments during Year	0	Rent Expired during Year	5,000
End. Bal.	0		

Rent Expense

5,000	

Salaries Payable

		Beg. Bal.	16,000
Salaries Paid during Year	100,000	Salaries Earned during Year	90,000
		End. Bal.	6,000

Salary Expense

90,000	

Flow of Costs

We have just discussed the types of inventories and the types of product costs for both manufacturers and nonmanufacturers. Now we are going to show how the product costs relate to the inventory accounts—that is, how the product costs flow through the inventory accounts from purchase to ultimate sale.

Cost flow of retailer: directly from purchase to sale

Analyzing a retailer's flow of costs is far simpler than analyzing a manufacturer's cost flow. Because the product sold by the retailer is in the same physical form as it was when purchased, there are very few product costs to keep track of. On the other hand, the manufacturing situation involves a large number of costs to convert the raw materials to a finished product.

Exhibit 19-2 shows with the use of separate T-accounts how simply a retailer's product costs flow from the initial purchase (assumed to be $200,000) of merchandise inventory to the cost of goods sold ($175,000). All other costs, such as expired insurance ($4,000), expired rent ($5,000), and salaries ($90,000), are expensed as incurred because they are period costs.

The cost flow for a manufacturer is much longer

The cost flow analysis for the manufacturer is more complex. A manufacturer has many product costs, which flow among three inventories instead of one. We will trace the flow of costs through the three inventory accounts of a manufacturer in a step-by-step manner, using a different exhibit to show each of the following five steps:

1. Purchase and use of raw materials
2. Use of labor
3. Use of factory overhead
4. Transfer of Factory Overhead to Work-in-Process
5. Completion of production
6. Sale of finished goods

Raw materials: first we buy and then we use

STEP 1: Purchase and use of raw materials Exhibit 19-3 on page 754 indicates that the purchases of raw materials are $200,000. When added to the $50,000 on hand at the beginning of the year, there is a total of $250,000 of raw materials available to be used in production during the year. If we find that we still have $75,000 of raw materials on hand at the end of the year, then the amount we must have used during the year is represented as follows:

Total available for use	$250,000
Ending inventory: Raw materials	75,000
Raw materials used during the year	$175,000

Of the $175,000 of raw materials that were used, assume that $165,000 was for direct materials and that the remaining $10,000 was for indirect materials. Notice in Exhibit 19-3 that the direct materials go immediately—directly—to work-in-process inventory, but that the indirect materials go to an account called Factory Overhead Incurred.

The *Factory Overhead Incurred* account accumulates all overhead costs that are incurred during a period; these are represented by debits in the account. Indirect materials is just the first of many. At the end of the period, when the total overhead costs are accounted for, the account is closed to a

EXHIBIT 19-3   Purchase and Use of Raw Materials.

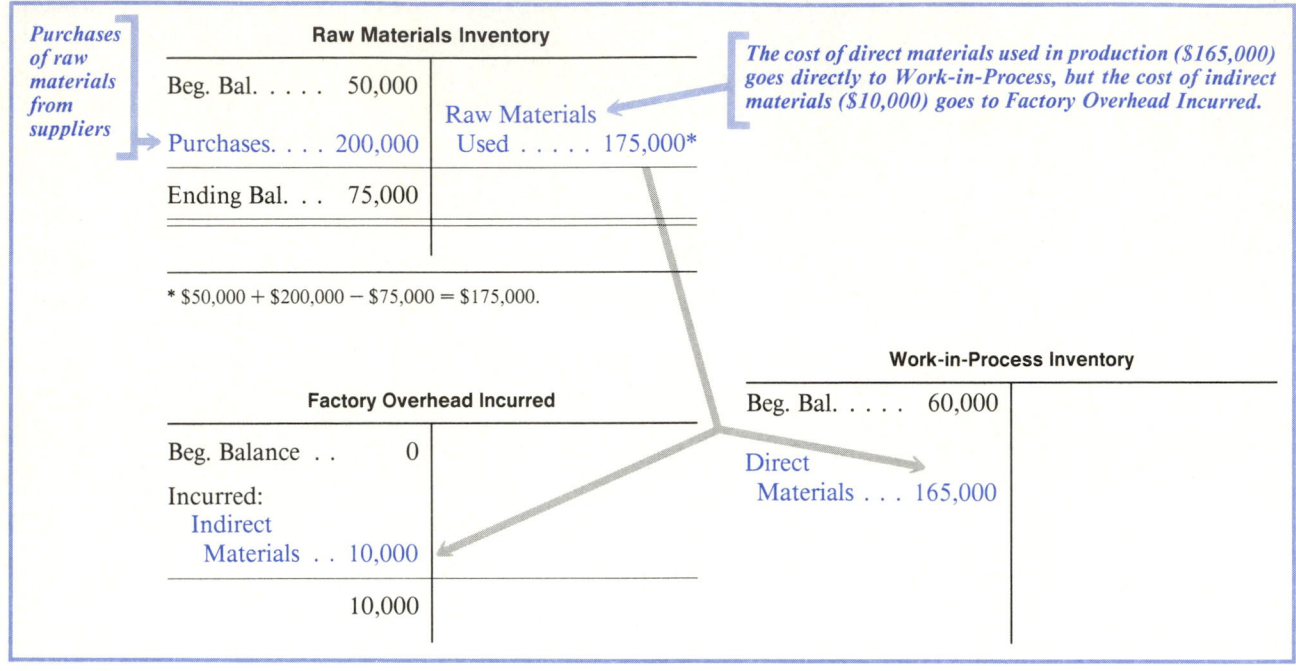

zero balance (which it will still have at the beginning of the next period) with a credit. This total is then transferred in one lump sum to Work-in-Process, with a debit to that account. In this way there will be three debits to Work-in-Process each period — one for direct materials (which we already see in Exhibit 19-3); one for direct labor (which we'll see in Exhibit 19-4); and one for factory overhead (which we'll see in Exhibit 19-6).

What is a beginning balance in Work-in-Process?

We see in Exhibit 19-3 that there is a beginning balance in Work-in-Process Inventory of $60,000. This represents the costs of direct materials, direct labor, and factory overhead incurred during last year, and assigned to those units that were started but not finished by the end of last year. The total costs in Work-in-Process are now merely the beginning balance plus direct materials:

Beginning balance.	$ 60,000
Direct materials	165,000
	$225,000

Salaries: both product and period costs—both direct and indirect costs

STEP 2: Use of labor   During the period the total wages earned by workers are assumed to be $90,000. Of this amount, $70,000 relates to the production department, and $5,000 of these production wages are for indirect laborers. Exhibit 19-4 shows how the payroll is to be distributed. The direct labor ($65,000) goes to Work-in-Process Inventory and the indirect labor ($5,000) goes to Factory Overhead Incurred. Both the direct and the indirect labor costs are product costs, but only the direct labor goes directly to Work-in-Process. Remember from our discussion of direct materials that

EXHIBIT 19-4 Use of Labor.

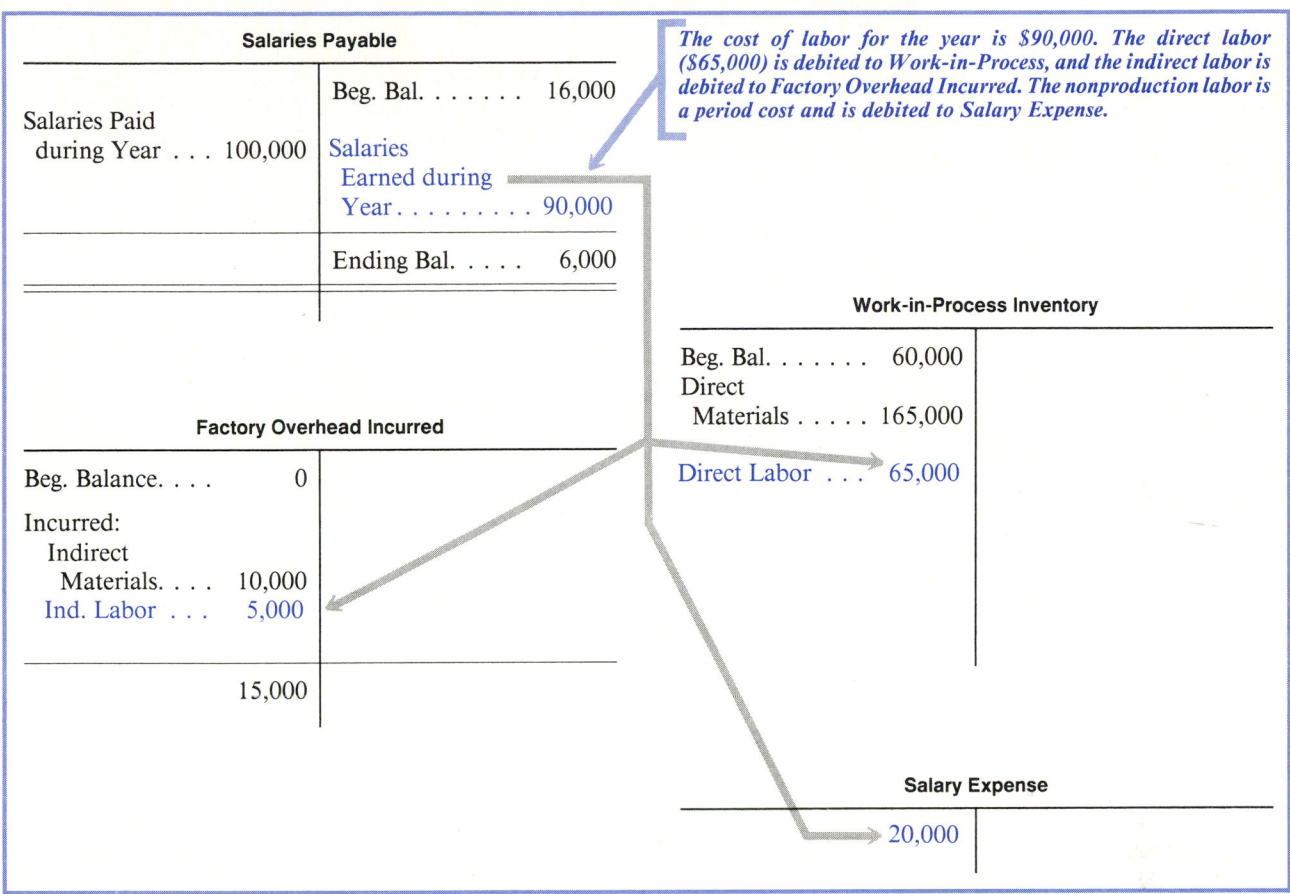

factory overhead costs will eventually get to Work-in-Process, but in a roundabout manner. The rest of the $90,000 ($20,000) goes to Salary Expense—it is a period cost.

The costs accumulated in Work-in-Process Inventory are now as follows:

Beginning balance	$ 60,000
Direct materials	165,000
Direct labor	65,000
	$290,000

STEP 3: Use of factory overhead The total amounts of insurance and rent that expired during the year were as follows:

The remaining factory overhead costs

	Cost of Production Departments	Cost of Nonproducing Departments	Total
Insurance	$3,000	$1,000	$4,000
Rent	4,000	1,000	5,000

EXHIBIT 19-5 Use of Factory Overhead.

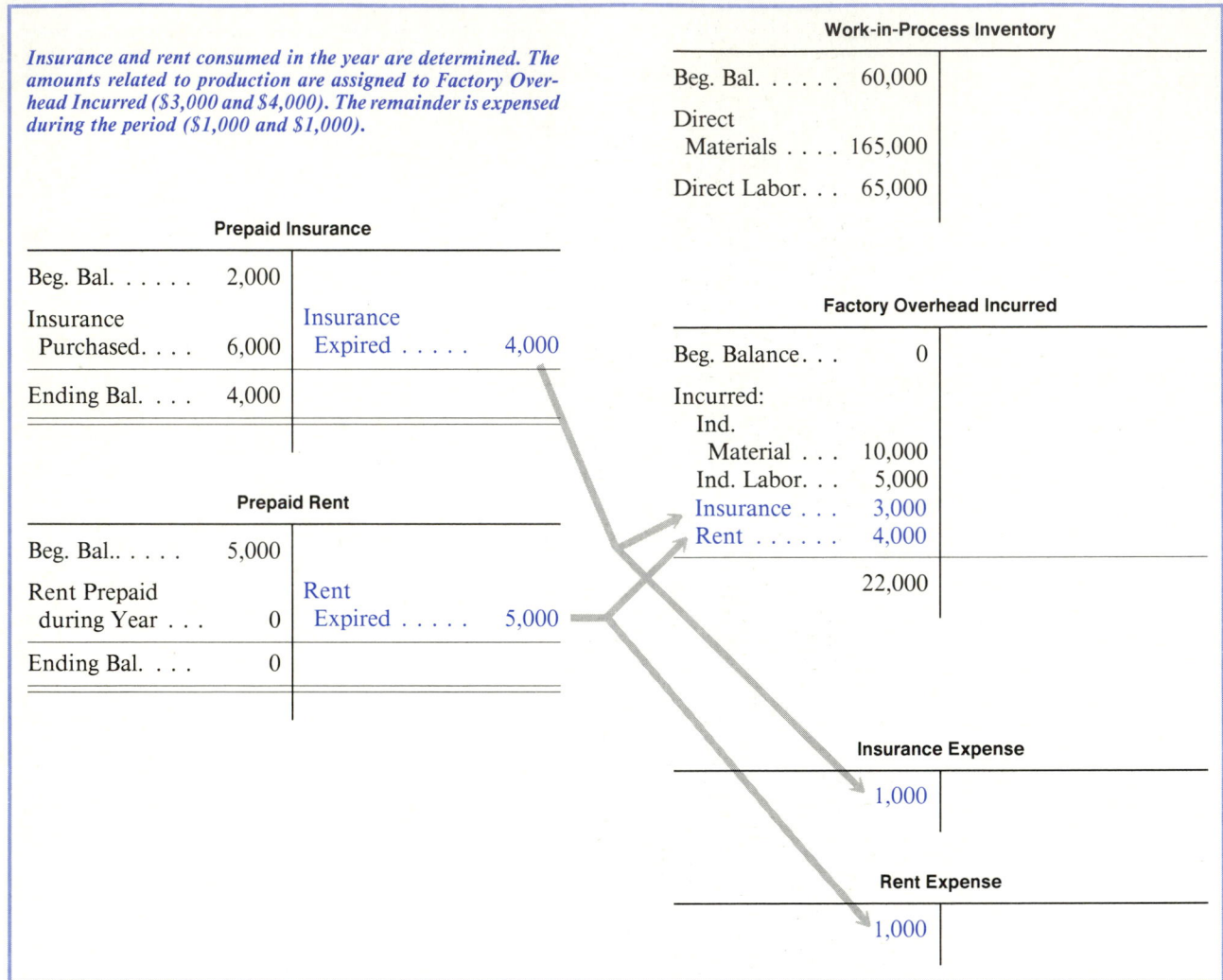

Insurance and rent consumed in the year are determined. The amounts related to production are assigned to Factory Overhead Incurred ($3,000 and $4,000). The remainder is expensed during the period ($1,000 and $1,000).

Work-in-Process Inventory

Beg. Bal.	60,000	
Direct Materials	165,000	
Direct Labor. . .	65,000	

Prepaid Insurance

Beg. Bal.	2,000		
Insurance Purchased. . . .	6,000	Insurance Expired	4,000
Ending Bal. . . .	4,000		

Prepaid Rent

Beg. Bal..	5,000		
Rent Prepaid during Year . . .	0	Rent Expired	5,000
Ending Bal. . . .	0		

Factory Overhead Incurred

Beg. Balance. . .	0	
Incurred:		
Ind. Material . . .	10,000	
Ind. Labor. . .	5,000	
Insurance . . .	3,000	
Rent	4,000	
	22,000	

Insurance Expense

1,000	

Rent Expense

1,000	

As shown in Exhibit 19-5, the insurance and rent related to the production departments ($3,000 and $4,000) are classified as factory overhead costs and are debited to Factory Overhead Incurred. The remaining insurance and rent ($1,000 and $1,000) are expensed as incurred, being debited to Insurance Expense and Rent Expense, respectively.

STEP 4: Transfer of Factory Overhead to Work-in-Process The Work-in-Process account in Exhibit 19-5 is still incomplete. While it is supposed to accumulate all product costs associated with production each period, factory overhead, which is just as much a product cost as direct materials and direct labor, is missing. Remember that the factory overhead costs have been temporarily stored in the Factory Overhead Incurred account, until they are completely accounted for. Since there are no additional factory overhead costs to account for this period, it is now time to transfer the cumulative overhead costs in Factory Overhead Incurred to Work-in-Process. To

EXHIBIT 19-6   Transfer of Factory Overhead to Work-in-Process.

Factory Overhead Incurred			Work-in-Process Inventory		
Beg. Balance. . .	0		Beg. Bal.	60,000	
Incurred:			Direct		
Ind.			Materials	165,000	Total
Material . . .	10,000		Direct		Manuf.
Ind. Labor. . .	5,000		Labor	65,000	Costs
Insurance . . .	3,000		Factory		Incurred = 252,000
Rent	4,000		Overhead	22,000	
	22,000	22,000	Total Manuf.		
			Costs to		
			Account		
			for	312,000	

The factory overhead that has been accumulated in the Factory Overhead Incurred account is now transferred to Work-in-Process — which now has debits for all three product costs

do this we simply credit Factory Overhead Incurred, thus closing the account, and debit Work-in-Process. This is shown in Exhibit 19-6.

Now that there are no additional costs to account for, the total debits to Work-in-Process sum to the following:

Total manufacturing costs to account for

Beginning balance		$ 60,000
Direct materials.	$165,000	
Direct labor	65,000	
Factory overhead.	22,000	252,000
Total manufacturing costs to account for		$312,000

The summation of all debits to Work-in-Process Inventory, $312,000, is referred to as the total manufacturing costs to account for.

A large portion of this total will be assigned to units that are completed during the year; the remainder will be assigned to the units that have been started, and worked on, but are not completed by the end of the year.

In this chapter, we are using an actual cost system of accounting for factory overhead. This means that the *actual* factory overhead costs are assigned to Work-in-Process as a product cost. For several reasons, which we will discuss later, many organizations assign something called **applied factory overhead** (rather than actual factory overhead) to the units. We will discuss applied factory overhead in Chapters 20 and 24.

The units are finally finished

STEP 5: Completion of production   Throughout the year units in process are being completed; the cost of these units is transferred from Work-in-Process to Finished Goods. We assume in Exhibit 19-7 that the cost assigned to units completed during the year is $280,000, and that the amount assigned to the unfinished units remaining in Work-in-Process at year-end is $32,000.

We can see in Exhibit 19-7 that there is a $40,000 beginning balance in Finished Goods Inventory — the amount assigned to units completed last

EXHIBIT 19-7   Completion of Production.

Work-in-Process Inventory

Beg. Bal. 60,000			
Manuf. Costs Incurred during Period. . . 252,000	Cost of Goods Completed during Year . . . 280,000*		
Ending Bal.. 32,000			

The cost of units finished during the year is determined to be $280,000. This amount is transferred from Work-in-Process Inventory to Finished Goods Inventory.

* $60,000 + $252,000 − $32,000 = $280,000.

Finished Goods Inventory

Beg. Bal.. 40,000	
Cost of Goods Completed during Year. . . . 280,000	
Total Available for sale 320,000	

year but not yet sold by the end of the year. When we add this beginning balance ($40,000) to the cost of goods completed in the current period ($280,000), we get $320,000 — the total goods that are available for sale. This means that during the year we had ready for sale finished goods having a cost of $320,000.

STEP 6: Sale of finished goods   The production costs have traveled a long way — starting in raw materials, transferring to work-in-process when the production process began, and coming over to finished goods when production was completed. The costs are still product costs, but they are now in the final stage before they become expenses. All that's left is for the product to be sold.

The finished goods are sold: product costs are finally expensed

The cost of the units sold during the year is $310,000, shown in Exhibit 19-8 — this amount being debited to Cost of Goods Sold and credited to Finished Goods. Finally we have an expense — now and only now do the product costs become expenses.

The production costs associated with the unsold units in finished goods are $10,000. These costs are still part of an asset. They will not be expensed until the units to which they are assigned are sold — probably next year.

The cost accountant has now virtually completed his or her product cost responsibilities for the year:

1. The costs for the manufacturer have been classified as product and period costs.

2. The product costs have been accumulated during production and assigned to the units that were completed during the year and are now awaiting sale.

EXHIBIT 19-8   Sale of Finished Goods.

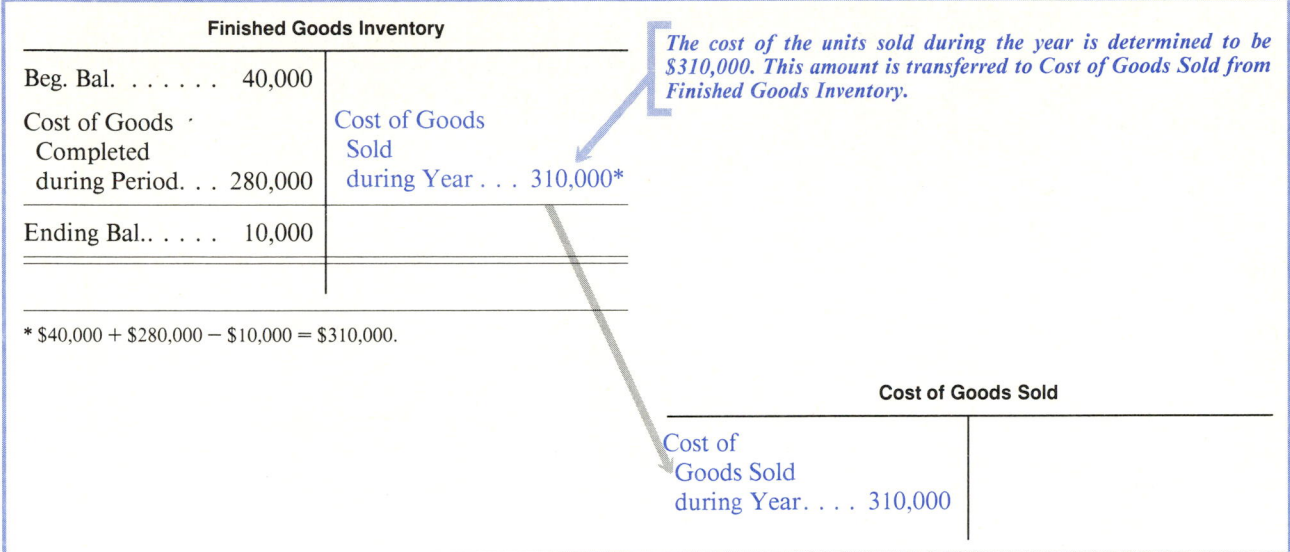

Finished Goods Inventory

Beg. Bal. 40,000		
Cost of Goods Completed during Period. . . 280,000	Cost of Goods Sold during Year . . . 310,000*	
Ending Bal.. 10,000		

The cost of the units sold during the year is determined to be $310,000. This amount is transferred to Cost of Goods Sold from Finished Goods Inventory.

* $40,000 + $280,000 − $10,000 = $310,000.

Cost of Goods Sold

Cost of Goods Sold during Year. . . . 310,000	

3. The cost of the units available for sale has been allocated between the units that were sold — cost of goods sold — and the units that were not sold — finished goods inventory. The financial statements can now be prepared.

Now let's put it all together

But before we go on to the preparation of financial statements, let's take one last look at the cost flow for our manufacturer shown in Exhibits 19-3 through 19-8. Since these exhibits each showed only a small part of the entire flow, and we also want you to see the complete flow, Exhibit 19-9 on pages 760–761 combines the six steps discussed in Exhibits 19-3 through 19-8.

FINANCIAL STATEMENTS

Having traced the flow of product costs through the inventory accounts of both retailing and manufacturing organizations, we now come to the final step in the accounting cycle — the preparation of financial statements. In other words, the effects of the flow of costs depicted in the T-accounts shown in Exhibits 19-2 through 19-9 are eventually represented in the income statement and balance sheet.

The Income Statement

The basic format for the income statement is the same for both a retailer and a manufacturer. Using the same facts that were introduced earlier about the cost flows for the retailer (Exhibit 19-2) and the manufacturer (Exhibit 19-9), condensed income statements are shown below (assume that sales revenue is $400,000, and the year is 1988).

	Retailer	Manufacturer
Sales.	$400,000	$400,000
Less: Cost of Goods Sold.	175,000	310,000
Gross Profit	$225,000	$ 90,000
Less: Selling and Administrative Expenses	99,000	22,000
Net Income	$126,000	$ 68,000

The income statements look alike

EXHIBIT 19-9
Cost Flow of a Manufacturer.

Raw Materials Inventory

Beginning Balance	50,000	Raw Materials
Purchased	200,000*	Used 175,000*
Ending Balance	75,000	

Salaries Payable

Paid 100,000	Beginning Balance 16,000
	Earned for Year .... 90,000†
	Ending Balance 6,000

Prepaid Insurance

Beginning Balance	2,000	Insurance Expired .... 4,000‡
Purchased	6,000	
Ending Balance	4,000	

Prepaid Rent

Beginning Balance	5,000	Rent Expired .... 5,000‡
Prepaid in Year	0	
Ending Balance	0	

* Step 1: Purchase and use of raw materials.
† Step 2: Use of labor.
‡ Step 3: Use of factory overhead.
§ Step 4: Transfer of Factory Overhead to Work-in-Process.
¶ Step 5: Completion of production.
** Step 6: Sale of finished goods.

Cost of goods sold is simple for the retailer

For the retailer, the determination of cost of goods sold, $175,000, is quite simple. The proper form is as follows:

Merchandise Inventory, Jan. 1, 1988	$ 50,000
Plus: Purchases	200,000
Goods Available for Sale	$250,000
Less: Merchandise Inventory, Dec. 31, 1988	75,000
Cost of Goods Sold	$175,000

Now look back at Exhibit 19-2 once again. Notice how the organization of the schedule above for cost of goods sold is nothing more than a formal way to show the flow through the Merchandise Inventory T-account.

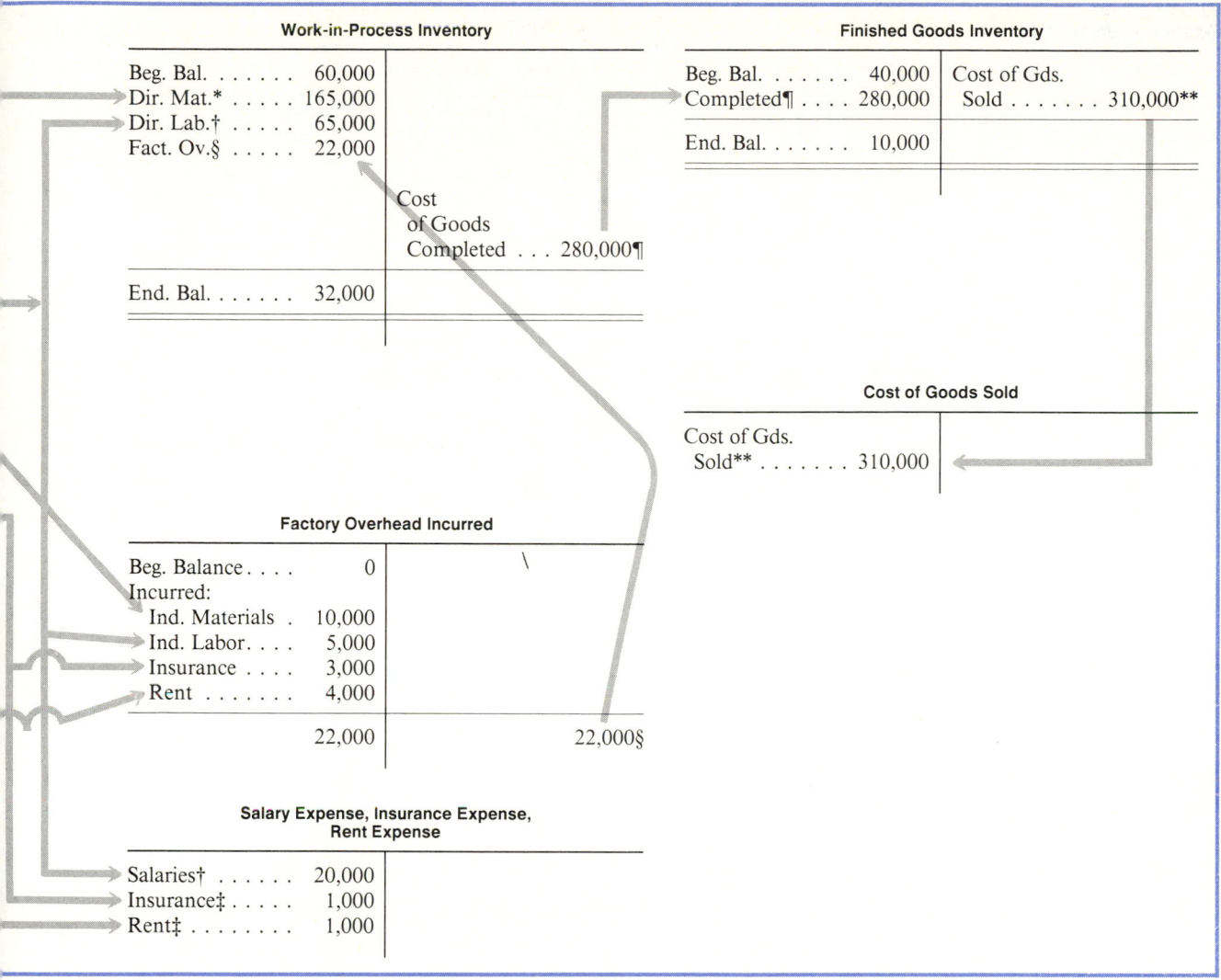

Work-in-Process Inventory

Beg. Bal.	60,000	
Dir. Mat.*	165,000	
Dir. Lab.†	65,000	
Fact. Ov.§	22,000	
		Cost of Goods Completed . . . 280,000¶
End. Bal.	32,000	

Finished Goods Inventory

Beg. Bal.	40,000	Cost of Gds.	
Completed¶	280,000	Sold	310,000**
End. Bal.	10,000		

Cost of Goods Sold

Cost of Gds. Sold**	310,000

Factory Overhead Incurred

Beg. Balance. . . .	0	
Incurred:		
Ind. Materials .	10,000	
Ind. Labor. . . .	5,000	
Insurance	3,000	
Rent	4,000	
	22,000	22,000§

Salary Expense, Insurance Expense, Rent Expense

Salaries†	20,000
Insurance‡	1,000
Rent‡	1,000

There's much more detail for the manufacturer

Determining the cost of goods sold expense for a manufacturer is much more detailed, since it involves the flow of product costs through three inventories rather than one. Often two schedules are used by the cost accountant to calculate the cost of goods sold — these are shown in Exhibit 19-10, which we will explain.

Schedule of Cost of Goods Completed

You should compare the schedules to the T-accounts

The first schedule shows the calculation for cost of goods completed — that is, the cost assigned to all units finished during the year 1988. It is a formal way to show the flow of product costs from raw materials to finished goods. We showed the same flow in a less formal manner with T-accounts in Exhibits 19-3 through 19-7. As you read through schedule 1, it might be a good idea to compare it to the appropriate T-accounts. You will find that the order within the T-accounts and schedule 1 is nearly identical.

It may be helpful to think that there are four basic elements in the calculation of the

EXHIBIT 19-10
Cost of Goods Sold for a
Manufacturer.

Schedule 1
Cost of Goods Completed
Year Ended Dec. 31, 1988

Raw materials inventory, Jan. 1, 1988	$ 50,000
Plus: Purchases	200,000
Raw Materials available for use	$250,000
Less: Raw materials inventory, Dec. 31, 1988.	75,000
Raw materials used.	$175,000*

Direct materials used	$165,000
Plus: Direct labor	65,000
Plus: Factory overhead	22,000
Total manufacturing costs incurred during 1988	$252,000
Plus: Work-in-process inventory, Jan. 1, 1988	60,000
Total manufacturing costs to account for	$312,000
Less: Work-in-process inventory, Dec. 31, 1988	32,000
Cost of goods completed	$280,000

* Of the $175,000 of raw materials used, $165,000 is direct materials and $10,000 is indirect materials (part of the $22,000 of factory overhead).

Schedule 2
Cost of Goods Sold
Year Ended Dec. 31, 1988

Finished goods inventory, Jan. 1, 1988.	$ 40,000
Plus: Cost of goods completed	280,000
Total available for sale	$320,000
Less: Finished goods inventory, Dec. 31, 1988	10,000
Cost of goods sold expense	$310,000

**Cost of goods completed =
DM + DL + FO + WIP −
WIP**

cost of goods completed: (1) direct materials used, (2) direct labor, (3) factory overhead, and (4) the adjustment for the beginning and ending balances in Work-in-Process.

The first three elements add up to $252,000—the total manufacturing costs incurred during 1988:

Direct materials	$165,000
Direct labor	65,000
Factory overhead	22,000
Total manufacturing costs incurred.	$252,000

This is the total of all direct and indirect costs incurred in production, in order to:

1. Complete the units that were unfinished at the beginning of the year,

2. Produce fully completed units during the year, and

3. Start some units that aren't fully completed on the last day of the current year.

With the addition of the beginning balance in Work-in-Process, we now have the total manufacturing costs to account for:

Total manufacturing costs incurred.	$252,000
Work-in-process, Jan. 1, 1988	60,000
Total manufacturing costs to account for	$312,000

When we subtract the ending balance in Work-in-Process ($32,000) we see that the cost of the goods completed is $280,000.

The steps taken to compute the cost of goods completed can also be shown in equation form:

Manufacturing costs incurred (direct material, direct labor, factory overhead)		**beginning inventory of work-in-process**		**total manufacturing costs to account for**	**completed units: transfer costs to finished goods**
	+		=		**unfinished units: costs remain in work-in-process**
$252,000	+	$60,000	=	$312,000	$280,000
					$ 32,000

Schedule of Cost of Goods Sold

The second schedule in Exhibit 19-10 shows how to calculate the cost of goods sold, once we have determined the cost of goods completed. Schedule 2 traces the progression of costs through Finished Goods Inventory in much the same order as we showed in T-account form with Exhibit 19-8.

Cost of goods sold = cost of goods completed + FG − FG

By adding the beginning balance of Finished Goods to the cost of goods completed, we get the cost of goods available for sale, $320,000. Finally, we see that the ending balance in Finished Goods is $10,000; when this amount is subtracted from $320,000 the difference is the cost of goods sold, $310,000.

We can also represent these calculations in equations, as shown below:

Cost of goods completed		**beginning inventory of finished goods**		**goods available for sale**	**sold units: transfer costs to cost of goods sold expense**
	+		=		**unsold units: costs remain in finished goods**
$280,000	+	$40,000	=	$320,000	$310,000
					$ 10,000

As an alternative to computing cost of goods sold with the use of two schedules, it would be perfectly acceptable to combine the two schedules into one. As soon as the cost of goods completed, $280,000, was determined in the first schedule, the begin-

The Balance Sheet

ning and ending inventories of finished goods would be immediately added and subtracted respectively.

Although the retailer's income statement may be considerably different from the manufacturer's income statement, their balance sheets will differ in only one respect —the number of inventory accounts found in the current assets section. For the retailer, the only inventory account is Merchandise Inventory. For the manufacturer there are the three inventory accounts: Raw Materials Inventory, Work-in-Process Inventory, and Finished Goods Inventory.

A COMPREHENSIVE EXAMPLE

We now present a comprehensive example for a manufacturer, which covers most of the key concepts discussed in this chapter. Work through the problem before looking at the solution, as a good test of what you have learned from reading the chapter.

EXAMPLE 19-4

LUOTO PHARMACEUTICAL COMPANY

At the beginning of 1988, the Luoto Pharmaceutical Company had the following inventories:

Raw materials	$10,000
Work-in-process	30,000
Finished goods	50,000

Additional cost and revenue information includes:

Purchases	$ 80,000
Insurance expired	8,000
Rent expired	30,000
Salaries accrued and paid	120,000
Sales	300,000

All of the raw materials used during the year were direct materials. The other costs incurred by production and nonproduction departments are:

	Cost of Production	Cost of Selling and Administration
Insurance expired	$ 4,000	$ 4,000
Rent expired	15,000	15,000
Salaries	60,000	60,000

Of the $60,000 of production salaries, $40,000 was for direct labor and $20,000 was for indirect labor.

At the end of the year the following inventories were on hand:

Raw materials	$20,000
Work-in-process	35,000
Finished goods	40,000

The Luoto Pharmaceutical Company then determines the flow of costs through T-accounts, and prepares a year-end income statement, which includes a detailed section for Cost of Goods Sold Expense. T-accounts are shown in Exhibit 19-11 (on pages 766 and 767), and the income statement and supporting schedules for cost of goods sold are given in Exhibit 19-12 at the top of the next page.

EXHIBIT 19-12
Income Statement and Supporting Schedules — The Cost Flow for Luoto Formally Presented.

Schedule 1
Cost of Goods
Completed

Raw materials inventory, Jan. 1, 1988	$10,000	
Purchases.	80,000	
Total available for use	$90,000	
Raw materials inventory, Dec. 31, 1988	20,000	
Direct materials used		$ 70,000
Direct labor		40,000
Factory overhead:		
Indirect labor.	$20,000	
Insurance	4,000	
Rent	15,000	39,000
Total manufacturing costs incurred		$149,000
Work-in-process inventory, Jan. 1, 1988.		30,000
Total manufacturing costs to account for		$179,000
Work-in-process inventory, Dec. 31, 1988		35,000
Cost of goods completed		$144,000

Schedule 2
Cost of Goods
Sold

Finished goods inventory, Jan. 1, 1988.	$ 50,000
Cost of goods completed	144,000
Goods available for sale	$194,000
Finished goods inventory, Dec. 31, 1988	40,000
Cost of goods sold expense	$154,000

LUOTO PHARMACEUTICAL COMPANY
Income Statement
Year Ended Dec. 31, 1988

Sales.		$300,000
Cost of Goods Sold Expense (see schedules 1 and 2)		154,000
Gross Profit		$146,000
Selling and Administrative Expenses:		
Insurance	$ 4,000	
Rent	15,000	
Salaries.	60,000	79,000
Net Income		$ 67,000

Beginning and Ending Inventories: A Simplifying Assumption

In some examples, exercises, and homework problems, we may state specifically that the cost of the ending work-in-process inventory is equal to the cost of the beginning work-in-process inventory, and also that the cost of the ending finished goods inventory is equal to the cost of the beginning finished goods inventory. For example, let's assume that in the Luoto example, the beginning and ending work-in-process costs are both equal to $30,000, and that the beginning and ending finished goods costs are both equal to $50,000. In that case,

EXHIBIT 19-11   T-Accounts for Luoto Pharmaceutical Company.

The facts from Example 19-5 are shown here in T-account form.

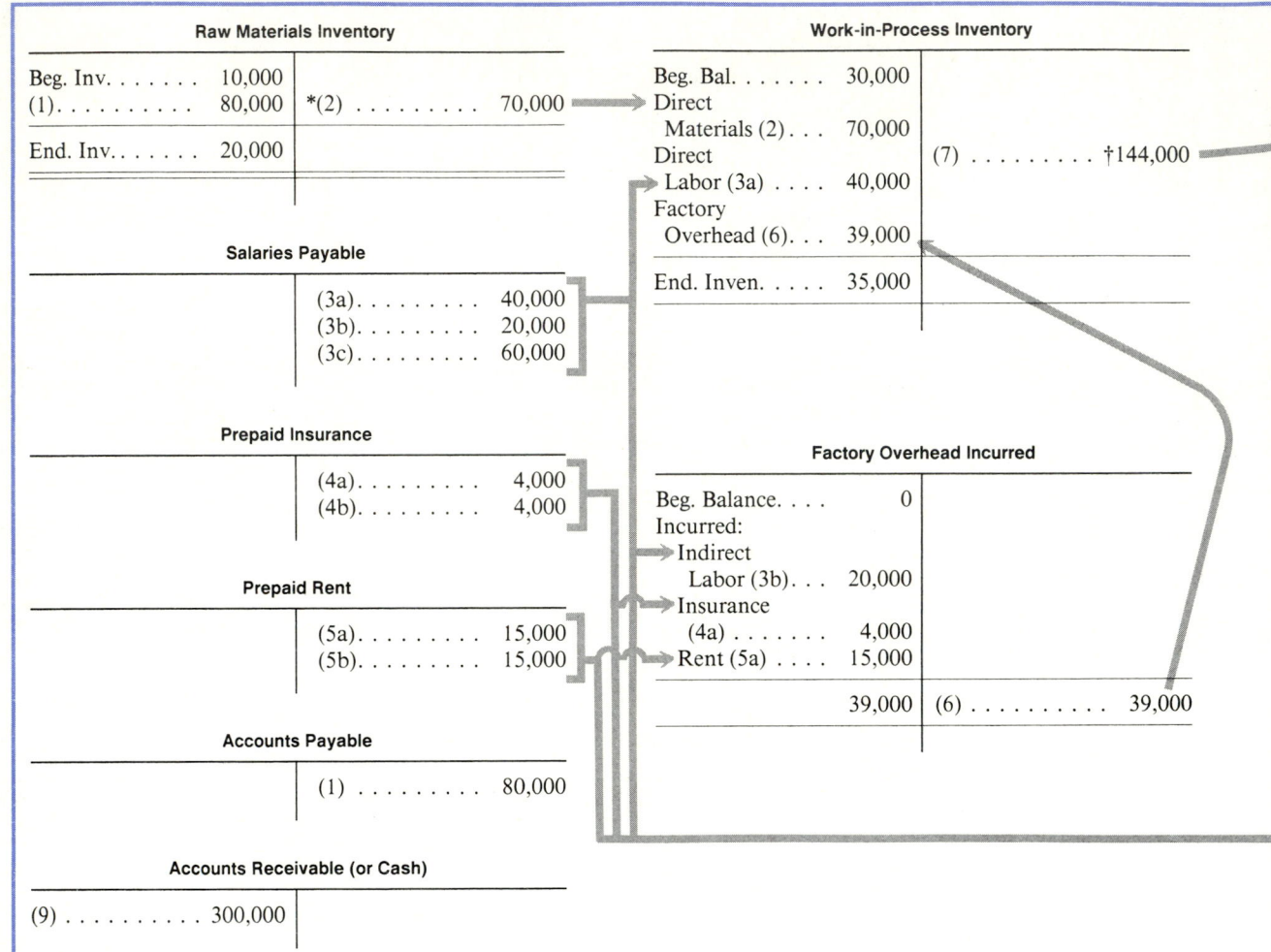

Schedule 1: Cost of Goods Completed

Total manufacturing costs incurred	$149,000
Work-in-process inventory, Jan. 1, 1988 — Beginning	+ 30,000
Total manufacturing costs to account for	$179,000
Work-in-process inventory, Dec. 31, 1988 — Ending	− 30,000
Cost of goods completed	$149,000

Schedule 2: Cost of Goods Sold

Finished goods inventory, Jan. 1, 1988 — Beginning	$ 50,000
Cost of goods completed	+149,000
Goods available for sale.	$199,000
Finished goods inventory, Dec. 31, 1988 — Ending	− 50,000
Cost of goods sold expense.	$149,000

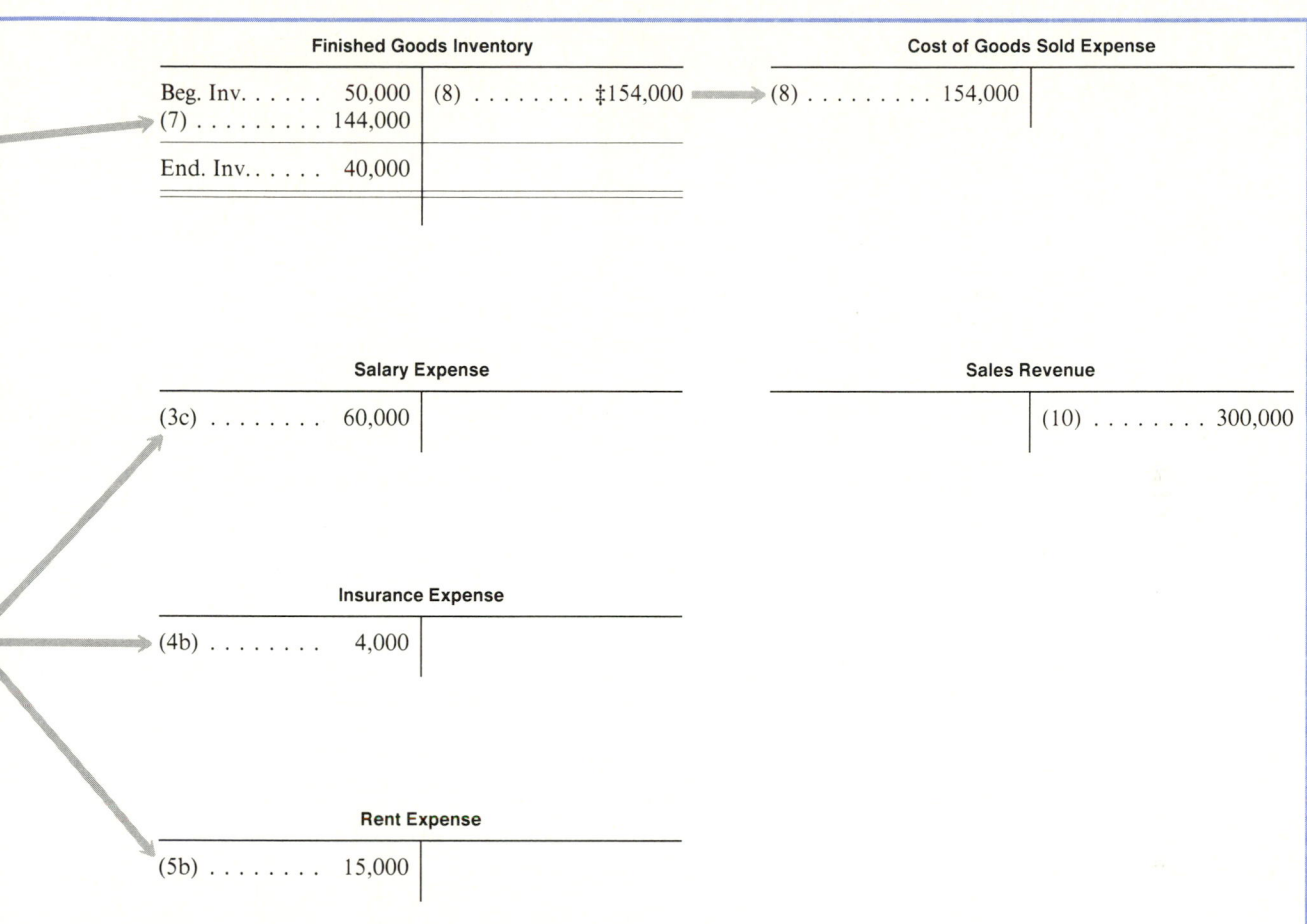

Finished Goods Inventory			Cost of Goods Sold Expense	
Beg. Inv. 50,000	(8) . . . . ‡154,000		(8) 154,000	
(7) 144,000				
End. Inv. 40,000				

Salary Expense		Sales Revenue	
(3c) 60,000			(10) 300,000

Insurance Expense	
(4b) 4,000	

Rent Expense	
(5b) 15,000	

* $10,000 + $80,000 − $20,000 = $70,000.
† $30,000 + $70,000 + $40,000 + $39,000 − $35,000 = $144,000.
‡ $50,000 + $144,000 − $40,000 = $154,000

You can see from these schedules that when the balances for the beginning and ending work-in-process inventories are equal (that is, there is no change in inventory from the beginning to the end of the period), and the balances for the beginning and ending Finished Goods inventories are equal, the Cost of Goods Sold turns out to be equal to the Total Manufacturing Costs Incurred. Or:

Total manufacturing costs incurred			=	cost of goods sold
Direct materials used	+ **direct labor**	+ **factory overhead**	=	**cost of goods sold**
$70,000	+ $40,000	+ $39,000	=	$149,000

Although the assumptions that the beginning and ending inventories are equal may not be realistic, they are often made to simplify the mechanics of computing cost of goods sold. Whenever we want you to make these simplifying assumptions, we will state so quite specifically in the problem.

CHAPTER SUMMARY

It is the job of the management accountant to provide quantitative information to managers to help them make decisions. There are a wide variety of different situations in which managers must make a decision; each situation may require a different type of cost information. It is up to the management accountant to determine and to provide the particular cost information needed to make the best management decision in a particular situation.

Total costs are the sum of all costs incurred within a *center of activity* during a specific period of time. An *average cost* is the total cost for a center of activity during a specific period of time divided by the activity during the period. Management accountants consider *activity* to be something done to produce a result or an output that can be measured. Activity can be measured in many different ways, depending on the type of organization and the types of centers of activity within that organization. For example, within a production department of a manufacturer, activity may be measured by the number of units produced or hours worked. For a storeroom a good measure of activity could be the number of requisitions processed.

In *product costing* we are concerned with determining the cost of the inventory, and with the allocation of these costs to units sold and units unsold. In order to accomplish the product costing purpose we must distinguish between *product costs* and *period costs.* Product costs are assigned to inventory when incurred, and they become an expense when the units to which they are assigned are sold. Period costs are expenses as soon as they are incurred.

There are three types of product costs for a *manufacturer: direct materials, direct labor,* and *factory overhead.* The sum of direct materials and direct labor costs is called *prime costs;* the sum of direct labor and factory overhead costs is referred to as *conversion costs.*

For a manufacturer there are three classifications of inventory—*raw materials, work-in-process,* and *finished goods*—each representing a stage of completion. The flow of product costs through the inventories is as follows. Raw materials are purchased from a supplier and placed in the Raw Materials Inventory account. Direct materials are requisitioned for production and along with direct labor are assigned directly to Work-in-Process. The factory overhead costs (including indirect materials and indirect labor) are first assigned to an account called Factory Overhead Incurred, and the total from that account is then transferred to Work-in-Process. When the units are completed they are transferred to Finished Goods. As completed units are sold, their costs are transferred to Cost of Goods Sold Expense.

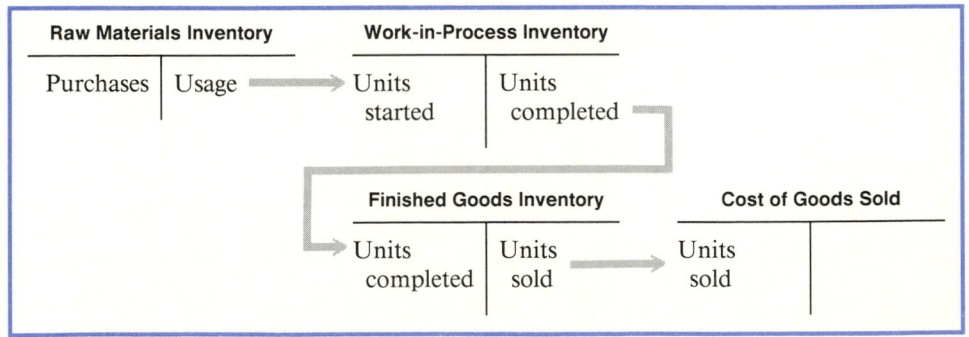

IMPORTANT TERMS USED IN THIS CHAPTER

Activity   A clear indicator of (1) what was done or accomplished, (2) in a particular center of activity, (3) during a specific period of time, (4) to produce measurable results. (page 742)

Average cost   The total costs of a center of activity for a period divided by the activity during the period. (page 743)

Center of activity   A subunit within an organization that performs a particular function or produces measurable results. (page 743)

Conversion costs   The sum of direct labor costs and factory overhead costs. (page 751)

Direct labor   The labor cost that is needed to convert raw materials into a finished product. For a labor cost to be classified as direct labor, it must be clearly and easily traceable to the units that are being produced. (page 750)

Direct materials   The raw materials that become an integral part of the finished product and are significant enough to warrant tracing them from raw materials to finished goods. (page 750)

Factory overhead   The indirect costs of production—total production costs less direct materials and direct labor. Also referred to as *manufacturing overhead.* (page 750)

Factory Overhead Incurred   An account that accumulates the actual factory overhead costs incurred by the production department of a manufacturer. At the end of each period the account is closed to a zero balance, and the total is transferred to Work-in-Process. (page 753)

Finished goods   The units that are completed and awaiting sale. (page 749)

Indirect labor   The labor needed to keep a manufacturing department running, but not involved directly in converting raw materials into a finished product. In other words, indirect labor costs are the labor costs of a production department that are not classified as direct labor. Indirect labor costs are classified as part of factory overhead. (page 750)

Indirect materials   Raw materials that either do not become a physical part of the finished product, or become a physical part of the finished good but are not significant enough in amount to justify tracing the cost to the finished product as a direct material. Indirect materials are classified as factory overhead. (page 750)

Manufacturer   An organization that converts a raw material to a finished product prior to sale. (page 749)

Manufacturing overhead   See *factory overhead.*

Noninventoriable unexpired costs   Costs that are assets when incurred, but not assets that can be immediately assigned to inventory. As the asset expires over time, the amount expired can then be classified as a product or period cost. (page 748)

Period costs   Costs that are expensed when incurred. (page 745)

Prime costs   The sum of direct materials and direct labor costs. (page 751)

Product costing   The process of determining the costs of all units that are to be sold, and then allocating these costs between the units that are sold during the period and the units that are unsold at the end of the period. (page 745)

Product costs   Costs that are closely associated with units produced by a manufacturer or purchased for resale by a retailer. Product costs are assigned to Inventory when incurred and expensed when the units to which they are assigned are sold. (page 745)

Raw materials inventory   The materials purchased from a supplier by a manufacturer to be used in production. When used in production, raw materials will be classified as either direct materials or indirect materials. (page 749)

Retailer   An organization that sells a product in the same physical form in which it was purchased from the supplier. (page 749)

Total costs   The sum of all costs incurred in a center of activity for a specific period of time. (page 743)

Work-in-process   The unfinished goods in production. (page 749)

QUESTIONS

1. Define the term *activity* and list the appropriate measure(s) of activity for the following centers of activity of a manufacturer:
   a. Production department
   b. Storeroom
   c. Sales department
   d. Billing department

2. What is the difference between an average cost and a unit cost?

3. For each center of activity mentioned below, give a possible measure of activity:
   a. A school library
   b. A computer center
   c. A restaurant
   d. A maintenance department
   e. An assembly department
   f. A hospital
   g. A telephone company's installation department
   h. A personnel department

4. Distinguish between *product costs* and *period costs.*

5. Explain what is meant by *noninventoriable unexpired costs.*

6. "All costs that are treated as assets when incurred are considered product costs." Do you agree? Explain.

7. "All costs of a manufacturer are treated alike." Do you agree? Explain.

8. "Period costs can be defined as costs that are expensed in the current period." Do you agree? Why or why not?

9. Are the following items product or period costs: depreciation, salaries, and utilities?

10. What will be the significance for a firm of not making the proper distinction between product and period costs?

11. Distinguish between the operations of a retailer and a manufacturer.

12. What are the three types of inventories for a manufacturer?

13. What is the difference between *raw materials* and *direct materials* for a manufacturer?

14. Why do you suppose that the combination of direct labor and factory overhead is referred to as *conversion costs?*

15. "Prime costs plus conversion costs equal the total manufacturing costs incurred for a period of time." Do you agree? Explain.

16. "Cost of goods sold is equal to the sum of direct materials, direct labor, and factory overhead." Do you agree? Explain.

17. List five examples of factory overhead.

18. Explain why supervisory labor costs are classified as factory overhead rather than direct labor.

19. A small manufacturer, Rinky Dink, generated a $5,000 profit in 1988, determined as follows:

Sales.		$150,000
Cost of goods sold		75,000
Gross profit		$ 75,000
Selling and administrative:		
Salesmen's commissions	$15,000	
President's salary	50,000	
Advertising	5,000	70,000
Net Income		$ 5,000

When a small investor (he was only 4'11″ tall) received his annual report, he made the following comments: "Doesn't Rinky Dink have any depreciable assets or production laborers; or haven't the depreciation and salary expenses been recorded? Shouldn't these expenses also be shown on the income statement?" What reply would you give to the small investor's comment?

EXERCISES

Exercise 19-1
Classification of product costs and period costs

The Oregano Company produces spice racks and needs some help in classifying its costs. It has gathered the following list of costs and asks your help in distinguishing between the product costs and the period costs. Place an X under the proper classification for each cost shown below:

| Cost | Product Cost | | | Period Cost |
	Direct Materials	Direct Labor	Factory Overhead	
Transportation costs on raw materials purchased				
Insurance on factory building				
Property taxes on factory building				
Depreciation on sales representatives' cars				
Salaries of workers putting stools together				
Salaries of machine maintenance personnel				
Sales representatives' commissions				
Transportation costs for units sold				
Screws connecting seats to legs				
Rent on factory building				
Fuel cost to heat administrative offices				

Exercise 19-2

Filling in the unknowns in a raw materials used schedule

Fill in the blanks for the raw materials section of the cost of goods sold schedule of the Grant Manufacturing Company shown below:

	1985	1986	1987
Raw materials inventory, Jan. 1	$ 16,000	$ 14,000	$
Purchases		200,000	
Total available for use	$176,000	$	$250,000
Raw materials inventory, Dec. 31			*
Raw materials used	$162,000	$190,000	$

* The ending inventory is $10,000 higher than the beginning inventory.

(Check figure: Raw materials used = $216,000)

Exercise 19-3

Classifying costs as product costs, period costs, or noninventoriable unexpired costs

The Underhill Company has just completed its first year of operation, 1988, and has gathered the following list of costs incurred during the year. Look over the list and additional facts carefully and then prepare three lists. Classify the costs as: **(a)** product costs, **(b)** period costs, or **(c)** noninventoriable unexpired costs.

Land	$75,000
Prepaid insurance (paid on 1/1 for 3 years)	3,000
Salaries and wages:	
Production	35,000
Salespersons' commissions	27,000
President	40,000
Machinery (10-year life)	90,000
Utilities:	
Production	6,000
Selling and administrative	1,200
Purchases of materials and supplies	80,000

One-fourth of the materials and supplies purchased were used in production in 1988. Another one-fourth was used in the selling and administrative departments. All but $20,000 of the machinery was used in the production department; the remaining machinery was used in the selling and administrative departments.

Two-thirds of the insurance coverage related to production and the remainder to selling and administration.

None of the units were finished by the end of 1988.

Exercise 19-4

The Frazer Company wants to determine an average cost for each of its four departments: production departments P and Q; a storeroom; and a sales office.

Computing averages for different measures of activity

	Department			
	P	**Q**	**Storeroom**	**Sales**
Operating costs	$200,000	$125,000	$25,000	$ 65,000
Units produced (or sold where applicable)	40,000	25,000	N/A	65,000
Direct labor hours	60,000	100,000	N/A	N/A
Number of workers	30	50	6	4
Square feet of space	6,000	9,000	1,000	1,500
Number of requisitions filled	N/A	N/A	250	N/A
Sales revenue	N/A	N/A	N/A	$600,000

Compute average costs for each department, using only those measures of activity that are basically related to the costs of that department.

Exercise 19-5
Cost of goods sold schedule

Based on the list of account balances below for Xanadu Company, prepare a schedule of cost of goods sold. For simplicity, assume that all beginning and ending inventories are zero.

Raw materials added to the physical units produced	$120,000
Supplies used	6,000
Insurance	1,000
Utilities	800
Property taxes	2,500
Labor employed directly in production	67,000
Indirect labor	9,000
Depreciation	2,700
Rent	950
Idle time	150

(Check figure: Cost of goods sold = $210,000)

Exercise 19-6
Determining the cost of direct materials used

Compute the cost of direct materials used for the month of July 1988, based on the following account balances:

Raw materials inventory, July 1, 1988	$ 2,200
Transportation cost of purchases.	1,000
Transportation cost of units sold.	1,200
Invoice cost of units purchased	37,000
Purchase returns	2,700
Raw materials inventory, July 31, 1988	1,500

$1,700 of the raw materials used were classified as factory overhead.

(Check figure: $34,300)

Exercise 19-7
Correcting a schedule of cost of goods sold

Shown below is a schedule of cost of goods sold expense for Error Prone Company for 1987. You are to read it over carefully and make any suggestions that you feel are needed to correct it and/or to make it more presentable.

ERROR PRONE COMPANY
Schedule of Cost of Goods Sold
December 31, 1987

Direct materials, 1/1/87		$ 15,000
Purchases.	$100,000	
Freight-Out	5,000	105,000
Total available for sale		$120,000
Direct materials, 12/31/87.		12,000
Direct materials used (including indirect)		$108,000
Labor:		
Direct.	$ 65,000	
Indirect.	15,000	80,000
Factory expense:		
Utilities	$ 1,200	
Payroll taxes	3,000	
Rent	8,000	
Depreciation	6,000	
President's salary	30,000	48,200
Prime costs plus conversion costs		$236,200
Increase in work-in-process		20,000
Cost of production finished during year		$216,200
Finished goods, 1/1/87		35,000
Total available for sale		$251,200
Finished goods, 12/31/87		31,000
Cost of goods sold expense		$220,200

Exercise 19-8
Determining prime costs and conversion costs

The Axelrod Corporation incurred the following costs during April 1988:

Direct materials.	$220,000
Indirect materials.	$ 54,000
Direct labor	$170,000
Indirect labor	$ 12,000

In addition, the factory overhead costs (exclusive of indirect materials and indirect labor) were $100,000 for the month. Determine the **(a)** prime costs and **(b)** conversion costs for April.

(Check figure: Conversion costs = $336,000)

Exercise 19-9

Incomplete income statements of Kadafy Enterprises are shown below for 3 years. Fill in the missing blanks found in each statement. Beginning and ending inventories are assumed to be zero.

Determining the missing parts in an income statement

	1986	1987	1988
Sales	$200,000	$260,000	$
Cost of goods sold:			
Direct materials. . . $40,000	$ 48,000	$ *	
Direct labor 80,000	100,000	*	
Factory overhead. . 20,000			68,000 $220,000
Gross profit.		$60,000	$ 80,000

* Direct materials are one-half of prime costs during 1988.

[Check figure: Direct Materials (1988) = $76,000]

Exercise 19-10
Preparing an income statement

From the list of accounts shown below, prepare an income statement for the Milburn Company for 1987. There are no beginning or ending inventories for 1987.

Direct materials.	$ 60,000
Factory overhead	75,000
Sales revenue	400,000
Selling and administrative expenses	85,000
Direct labor	100,000

(Check figure: Net income = $80,000)

PROBLEMS
Set A

Problem A19-1
Progression of production costs through T-accounts

The Johnny Fever Company began 1987 with the following balances in inventory:

Raw materials	$ 40,000
Work-in-process	130,000
Finished goods	285,000

During the year the following transactions took place:

Raw materials purchased	$ 56,000
Raw materials used	89,000
Direct labor accrued	130,000
Indirect labor accrued	12,000
Utilities paid	2,700
Accrued rent	4,300
Insurance used	1,400
Cost of goods transferred to finished goods	306,000
Cost of goods sold	511,000

Required
1. Place the beginning balances in T-accounts.
2. Record all transactions that took place in 1987 in T-account form, showing the progression of costs from raw materials to cost of goods sold expense. Indicate the ending balances in the three inventory accounts.

(Check figure: Finished goods inventory = $80,000)

Problem A19-2
Computing cost of goods sold
with and without beginning and
ending inventories

The Radar Company had the following balances in its general ledger accounts for 1987:

Materials used:	
Direct	$140,000
Indirect	14,000
Labor:	
Direct	135,000
Indirect	60,500
Insurance on factory building and machinery	4,000
Property taxes on factory building	2,300
Rent on productive assets	27,000
Utilities on factory building.	20,000
Transportation costs associated with units sold	17,500

Required

1. Assuming no beginning or ending inventories, prepare a schedule of cost of goods sold expense for 1987. How is this schedule simplified by the assumption of zero inventories?
2. Prepare a schedule of cost of goods sold expense for 1987 assuming the following inventories:

> Work-in-process, Jan. 1, 1987 . . . . $52,000
> Work-in-process, Dec. 31, 1987 68,000
> Finished goods, Jan. 1, 1987 95,000
> Finished goods, Dec. 31, 1987 87,000

(Check figure: Cost of goods sold expense = $394,800)

Problem A19-3
Calculating the year-end
inventories for a manufacturer

On December 31, 1987, the Pendulum Swing Company gathered the following information related to 1987:

Materials purchased.	$100,000
Direct materials used (there were no indirect materials used)	80,000
Direct labor	150,000
Factory overhead:	
Indirect labor	23,000
Utilities	1,000
Insurance	1,500
Depreciation	2,000
Cost of units completed and transferred.	250,000
Cost of units sold	280,000

Required

Determine the December 31, 1987, inventories if the January 1, 1987, inventories were as follows:

> Raw materials. $16,000
> Work-in-process 30,000
> Finished goods 60,000

(Check figure: Work-in-process, Dec. 31, 1987 = $37,500)

Problem A19-4
Determining net income for
different assumptions
concerning product costs and
period costs

During 1986, the Coco Manufacturing Company produced 10,000 units, one-half of which were sold at $20 per unit prior to year-end. The direct materials and labor associated with the units produced were $40,000 and $60,000 respectively. The company also incurred an additional $100,000 of costs that had not been classified by year-end. The controller contends that

25% of the costs are for factory overhead and the remainder relate to selling and administration. The vice president for sales argues that 80% of the total relates to production and only 20% is associated with selling and administration. The president says that the income statement for the entire firm will look the same regardless of whom is correct.

Required

1. Do you agree with the assertion made by the president? Explain why or why not.
2. Prepare an income statement for 1986 based on the controller's contention.

(Check figure: net loss = $37,500)

3. Prepare an income statement for 1986 based on the contention of the vice president for sales.

(Check figure: Net loss = $10,000)

4. Explain the difference in the answers to parts (2) and (3).

Problem A19-5
Preparing a detailed income statement for a manufacturer

The Chapman Company is in its first year of operations, 1987, and the head bookkeeper, H. Holman, has gathered the following data for that year:

Sales.	$100,000
Sales returns and allowances	40,000
Wages and salaries:	
Direct laborers.	120,000
Production supervisors	24,000
Maintenance.	16,000
Salespeople.	54,000
Administrators	120,000
Raw materials used:	
Directly associated with units produced	150,000
Indirectly associated with units produced	10,000
Supplies used in administrative offices	4,000
Rentals:	
Factory building	5,000
Selling and administrative building	3,400
Depreciation:	
Production machinery.	3,000
Salespeoples' cars.	2,000
Utilities*.	7,000
Freight-out	50,000

* Allocated on the basis of kilowatthours used in each department. The kilowatthours used were as follows:

Production departments. 24,000
Selling and administrative departments.   4,000

In addition, there were no beginning or ending inventories.

Required

1. Prepare a schedule of cost of goods sold expense for 1987.

(Check figure: Cost of goods sold expense = $334,000)

2. Prepare an income statement for 1987.

Problem A19-6
Preparing a detailed income statement for a manufacturer

The Nellie White Corporation's controller needs to prepare an income statement for the year 1987. She has her head bookkeeper gather the following information for the year:

Revenues

Revenue from the sale of its product totaled $12,000,000, of which $270,000 was returned. Freight costs were $180,000.

Inventory Balances

For 1987 Nellie White had the following inventory balances:

	January 1	December 31
Raw materials and supplies	$450,000	$300,000
Work-in-process	540,000	480,000
Finished goods	660,000	585,000

Materials and Supplies

Purchases of materials and supplies during 1987 were $3,000,000. Of the materials and supplies used, 70% were for raw materials needed for production and 30% were for administrative supplies. Eighty percent of the raw materials issued to production were direct and the remainder were indirect.

Salaries and Wages

The total payroll was distributed as follows:

Production:	
Direct	$3,900,000
Indirect	1,200,000
Selling and administrative	900,000

Rent

The building was rented on January 1, 1987, for 2 years. The rent paid in advance for the 2 years was $90,000. The building was used by the different departments in the following proportions:

Production	four-fifths
Selling and administrative	one-fifth

Depreciation

Machinery having a 10-year life, costing $2,000,000, was purchased on January 1, 1987. All of the machinery is used in production activities.

Required

Prepare, in good form, a detailed income statement for Nellie White Corporation. Also show a supporting schedule for cost of goods sold.

Set B

Problem B19-1
Tracing the flow of product costs through T-accounts of a manufacturer

Mr. Carlson began his company, WARP, Inc., on January 1, 1985. During his second year, 1986, the following events took place:

Raw materials purchased	$30,000
Direct materials used	27,500
Indirect materials used	2,500
Direct labor accrued	32,500
Indirect labor accrued	12,500
Depreciation	1,500
Utilities used	1,000
Property taxes accrued	900
Cost of goods finished during 1986	75,900
Cost of items sold in 1986	95,000

In addition, the controller found the following balances from the general ledger, on January 1, 1986:

Raw materials.	$ 5,000
Work-in-process	12,500
Finished goods	25,000

Required   Place the beginning inventory balances in T-accounts. Record all transactions that took place during 1986 in the T-accounts, showing the progression of costs from raw materials to cost of goods sold expense. Indicate the December 31, 1986, balance in each inventory account.

Problem B19-2

Computing cost of goods sold for a manufacturer with and without beginning and ending inventories

The controller for Cinderella Company has gathered information about the following costs for 1988:

Direct materials used	$35,000
Indirect materials used	2,000
Direct labor	40,000
Indirect labor	15,000
Sales labor	25,000
Insurance on factory and machinery	4,000
Insurance on salespeople's cars	1,500
Depreciation on production machinery	5,000
Utilities of factory	6,200
Freight costs for units sold	2,400

Required   **1.** For this part, assume that the beginning and ending inventories for Cinderella had zero balances. Prepare a schedule of cost of goods sold for 1988.

2. Prepare the schedule of cost of goods sold a second time. This time assume the following inventories for 1988:

January 1, 1988:	
Work-in-process	$10,000
Finished goods	20,000
December 31, 1988:	
Work-in-process	12,000
Finished goods	16,000

(Check figure: Cost of goods sold = $109,200)

Problem B19-3

Calculating the year-end inventories for a manufacturer

At the end of 1986, the McLeod Company accumulated the following information:

Purchase of raw materials	$240,000
Materials used:	
Direct	200,000
Indirect	20,000
Direct labor accrued	240,000
Other factory overhead:	
Indirect labor	100,000
Utilities accrued.	7,000
Property taxes accrued	12,000
Payroll taxes	8,000
Cost of units completed in 1986.	280,000
Cost of units sold in 1986	330,000

Assume that the January 1, 1986, inventories were as follows:

Raw materials	$ 40,000
Work-in-process	100,000
Finished goods	160,000

Required   Determine the December 31, 1986, balances in each inventory account.

(Check figure: Finished goods, December 31, 1986 = $110,000)

Problem B19-4
Determining income with different assumptions about product and period costs

The Sutton Company manufactured 40,000 units during 1987 and sold 10,000 units at $40 per unit. The prime costs incurred during the year were $100,000 for direct materials and $120,000 for direct labor. The remaining costs incurred by Sutton during 1987 were $400,000, which had not been separated into manufacturing costs versus selling and administrative costs by year-end. The vice president of manufacturing believes that only $100,000 of the $400,000 is related to manufacturing, while the sales vice president argues that $320,000 of the $400,000 is manufacturing costs. The president has no idea how much of the $400,000 is associated with manufacturing, but she doesn't think it makes any difference. She contends that the income statement for the firm will be the same regardless of which department gets assigned the most costs.

Required
1. Do you agree with the president's opinion? Explain why or why not.
2. Prepare an income statement for 1987 based on the contention of the vice president of manufacturing.
3. Prepare an income statement for 1987 based on the contention of the vice president of sales.

(Check figure: Net income = $185,000)

4. Explain the difference in your answers to parts (2) and (3).

Problem B19-5
Preparing a detailed income statement for a manufacturer

The Elia Pizzeria, which produces 10-ounce pizzas, just completed operations for 1986. Mr. Michael, an accountant, has gathered the following data related to the year:

Labor:	
Direct laborers.	$160,000
Supervisors of production	60,000
Production janitors.	32,000
Administrative employees	40,000
Sales representatives	80,000
Raw materials used*	240,000
Depreciation:	
Building†	16,000
Machinery and equipment.	4,000
President's Orange computer	2,000
Utilities‡.	14,400
Property taxes†.	12,000
Shipping costs of units sold	10,000
Sales discounts	10,800
Sales.	800,000
Interest on long-term borrowing.	3,000

* $40,000 of which are for indirect materials.
† One-half relates to factory facilities; the remainder relates to selling and administrative facilities.
‡ Allocated on the basis of kilowatthours used in each department.

The kilowatthours used were as follows:

Production departments 10,000
Selling and administrative departments 2,000

Required

1. Prepare a schedule of cost of goods sold expense. There were no beginning or ending inventories.
2. Prepare the 1986 income statement for Elia Pizzeria.

(Check figure: Net income = $115,800)

Problem B19-6
Preparing a detailed income statement for a manufacturer

The Deferral Company has gathered the following information concerning the operations during 1988, and would like you to prepare a detailed income statement for the year:

Revenues

Sales for 1988 (of which $90,000 was returned) were $4,000,000. The costs of shipping the product were $60,000.

Materials and Supplies

Purchases of materials and supplies for the year were $1,000,000, which were added to a beginning inventory of $150,000. At year-end there was a $100,000 balance remaining in inventory. Of the materials and supplies used, three-fourths were used in production ($650,000 of which was direct materials) and the remaining one-fourth were used in the selling and administrative departments.

Salaries and Wages

The payroll for the year was $2,000,000, broken down as follows:

Direct laborers $1,300,000
Indirect laborers   400,000
Selling and administrative personnel   300,000

Insurance

A 3-year policy was purchased on January 1, 1988, for $30,000. The insurance was related to departments in the following manner:

Production. . . . . three-fifths
Selling and administrative . . . . two-fifths

Depreciation

The cost of the depreciable assets used by the company was $2,300,000, and the balances in Accumulated Depreciation on 1/1 and 12/31 were $950,000 and $1,200,000, respectively. All but 20% of the depreciable assets are used in production.

Inventories

The balances in Work-in-Process and Finished Goods were:

	January 1	December 31
Work-in-process	$180,000	$160,000
Finished goods	$220,000	$195,000

Other Items

Interest expense for 1988 was $27,000, and income taxes were 40% of income before tax.

Required

Prepare, in good form, a detailed income statement for Deferral Company.

(Check figure: Net income = $216,800)

Chapter 20

Product Costing Methods
Part 1: Job Order Costing

When you have finished studying this chapter, you should be able to:

- Explain the differences between job order costing and process costing
- Determine the flow of costs through the production accounts and integrate this flow into the accounting records with journal entries and general ledger accounts
- Understand the purpose of subsidiary ledgers and the types of subsidiary ledgers needed for job order costing
- Relate the different types of source documents to the events or transactions they represent
- Discuss the interrelationships of the journal entry, the general ledger accounts, the subsidiary ledger accounts, and the source documents
- Understand why the overhead that becomes part of the cost of the product is not the actual factory overhead incurred but rather the factory overhead applied
- Calculate the factory overhead rate and the factory overhead applied
- Explain the meaning of over- or underapplied overhead, why each comes about, and how each is accounted for at year-end

Product costing

In Chapter 19 we explained what we mean by the term ***product costing*** — the accumulation of costs associated with inventory and the assignment of these costs to the units in inventory. We stressed how important it is to properly determine the product costs for an organization in order to have correct amounts in cost of goods sold expense (on the income statement) and in inventory at year-end (on the balance sheet). We also defined the three types of product costs for a manufacturer (direct materials, direct labor, and factory overhead) and described the flow of product costs through the production accounts (from Raw Materials Inventory to Work-in-Process Inventory to Finished Goods Inventory, to Cost of Goods Sold Expense). What we did not do is explain exactly how the product costs are assigned to individual units, i.e., how do we determine the cost of each and every unit that is produced?

How to get a cost per unit

Do we spread the total production costs evenly over the many units being worked on — ending up with one unit costing exactly the same as any other — even when there may be obvious differences in the physical appearance, materials used, and attention given to different units? Or do we painstakingly keep track of the exact amount of materials, labor, and overhead used for each unit? Will each unit have a different cost — even when all units appear to be identical?

To answer these questions, we first need to know which cost accounting method — job order costing or process costing — is the more appropriate way to account for the product costs.

JOB ORDER COSTING AND PROCESS COSTING: AN INTRODUCTION

To begin to get an idea of what we mean by job order costing and process costing, consider the case of Bill Wiley.

Bill has recently inherited a great deal of money and has acquired a controlling interest in two quite different companies — the Bubbly Champagne Company and Heritage Construction Company. Bill has spent the entire afternoon completing a contract to build a custom home for a new client. All the details have been clearly laid out in the contract that was signed by both parties. On his way home, Bill stops off at the Bubbly warehouse to pick up a bottle of champagne, to celebrate the deal with his wife (after all, this will be the first house that Bill has ever undertaken to build for someone).

Cost accountants tend to think of the house as being produced according to a specific job order — one unit, different from any other unit — produced over an extended period of time. The champagne company would be producing bottles of champagne according to what cost accountants tend to regard as a process — thousands of units, each unit identical to the next. In both cases, the product will have to be "costed." But in each case, the product costing method will be quite different. For the house, accountants use a ***job order costing method.*** For the champagne, accountants use a ***process costing method.***

The difference has to do with how to calculate the cost of each unit

The basic difference between job order costing and process costing is in the method of keeping track of the costs of each unit or batch of units being produced. As you might well imagine, and as we'll show in this and the next chapter, the cost accountant for Heritage Construction accounts for the costs of the house in a very different way than the cost accountant for Bubbly Champagne accounts for the cost of each bottle of champagne.

In the next section we'll begin the explanation of the job order costing method of accounting. We'll explain all about the process costing method in Chapter 21.

JOB ORDER COSTING

In manufacturing situations that can be described by the following characteristics, job order costing is used to account for the cost of a finished product:

Characteristics of job order costing

1. Only a small number of units or a few batches of units are produced.

2. Each unit or batch is clearly identifiable and distinguishable from others produced within the same production environment.

3. There is a very discernible beginning and end to the production of each unit or batch.

4. Each unit or batch is produced according to customer specifications.

5. Considerable costs are represented in each unit produced.

The name of this method describes what it is all about: The manufacturer produces a specific product according to a customer's *order;* the manufacturer refers to the product while in production as a *job* and assigns it a job number as a way of keeping track of it and its *costs,* as it progresses toward completion. Industries that typically employ job order costing include furniture, heavy machinery, construction, printing, and shipbuilding—and any other industry, such as public accounting, advertising or auto repairs, in which it is necessary and possible to distinguish among costs of different items being produced.

Who uses job order costing?

The key to accumulating product costs in a job order costing situation is to make sure that the costs of a specific job are carefully separated from the costs of any other job. The accountant cannot allow the costs of different jobs to be commingled. For example, assume that Bill Wiley has just signed a contract with a second customer to build another house. When you look at the situation from the standpoint of either Bill Wiley or his customers, you should understand why it is so important to keep track of the costs of one job separate from the other. Naturally, neither customer wants to pay Bill for costs that may relate to the construction of the other's house. And, from Bill's viewpoint, when his accountant reports the revenues from the construction of one house on the income statement, Bill naturally assumes that the accountant matches the appropriate costs with those revenues. For these reasons the customers and Bill Wiley all agree that a method of accounting is needed that clearly separates the costs of the different projects—this method is job order costing.

You should understand that job order costing is used not only by manufacturers; it can be adapted to other types of organizations as well. For example, each of the clients audited by the CPA firm of Deloitte Haskins & Sells represents a different job, having distinctly different costs. Each car repair by a Toyota Service Center and each client's advertising campaign for the J. Walter Thompson Agency are also types of jobs.

Although we give all of our attention to job order costing for a manufacturer, many of the concepts we will introduce do apply to any type of organization that finds it necessary to distinguish among the costs of different projects that are being worked on.

Accounting Records in Job Order Costing

In the previous chapter we used **T-accounts** to show you how the product costs for a manufacturer flowed from one inventory account to another, finally ending up in cost of goods sold. This basic progression was from raw materials to work-in-process to finished goods to cost of goods sold expense. (See illustration at top of facing page.)

In this chapter we will look not only at the T-accounts for a manufacturer (which represent in a simple form the **general ledger accounts** for an organization), but we will also be concerned with the formal **journal entries** that record the flow of costs from one T-account to the next. And after you have studied this chapter and the one on process costing, you'll realize that the T-accounts and the journal entries are exactly the same for these two extreme methods.

General ledger and journal entries are the same for job order and process costing

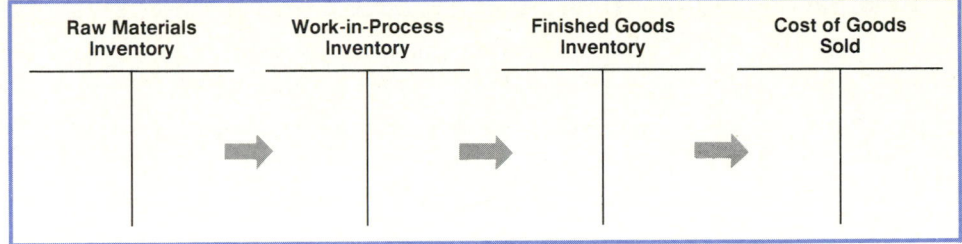

Subsidiary Ledgers

The job order costing method requires that a great deal of detail be maintained concerning the cost of its inventories. It is not enough merely to have general ledger accounts for raw materials, work-in-process, and finished goods; we also need a subsidiary ledger for each of these general ledger accounts.

Subsidiary ledgers provide a detailed breakdown of a general ledger account. In Chapters 6 and 7 we discussed the accounts receivable subsidiary ledger—a ledger that includes a different account for each different customer, detailing the transactions with that customer and the organization. The sum of the individual account balances in the subsidiary ledger for Accounts Receivable equals the balance in the general ledger account.

Manufacturers also maintain subsidiary ledgers for their inventories. The subsidiary ledger for work-in-process contains the basic document used in job order costing—the *job cost sheet.* For each job order there is a job cost sheet, on which are recorded the product costs (direct materials, direct labor, and factory overhead) associated with that job order.

When the job cost sheets for all unfinished jobs are combined, this makes up the subsidiary ledger for work-in-process. At the end of each reporting period the balance in the subsidiary ledger for work-in-process—which is the sum of the balances in the individual job cost sheets—should be equal to the balance in the general ledger account.

As soon as a job is completed, the job cost sheet is removed from the subsidiary ledger for work-in-process and becomes part of the subsidiary ledger for finished goods inventory. There are several additional subsidiary ledgers which will also be discussed in the example that begins on page 787 for Historical Replicas Company.

Source Documents

Where does the information come from?

The information concerning each event or transaction in the production operation that is recorded in subsidiary ledgers and general ledger accounts must come from some source that provides evidence of the event and its cost. This evidence is the *source document.* Examples of source documents are: (1) a purchase invoice, which indicates that a purchase took place, the quantity purchased, and from whom the purchase was made; and (2) a work ticket, which indicates the hours worked by an employee on each different job during a pay period. These and other source documents (stores requisition, clock card, utility bill, depreciation schedule, etc.) will be discussed as the chapter progresses.

Job Order Costing: A More Complete View

Now we want to show you, with Figure 20-1 (shown on page 786), a more complete view of a job order costing system—one that combines the three basic elements we have just discussed:

1. The flow of costs through the three general ledger inventory accounts

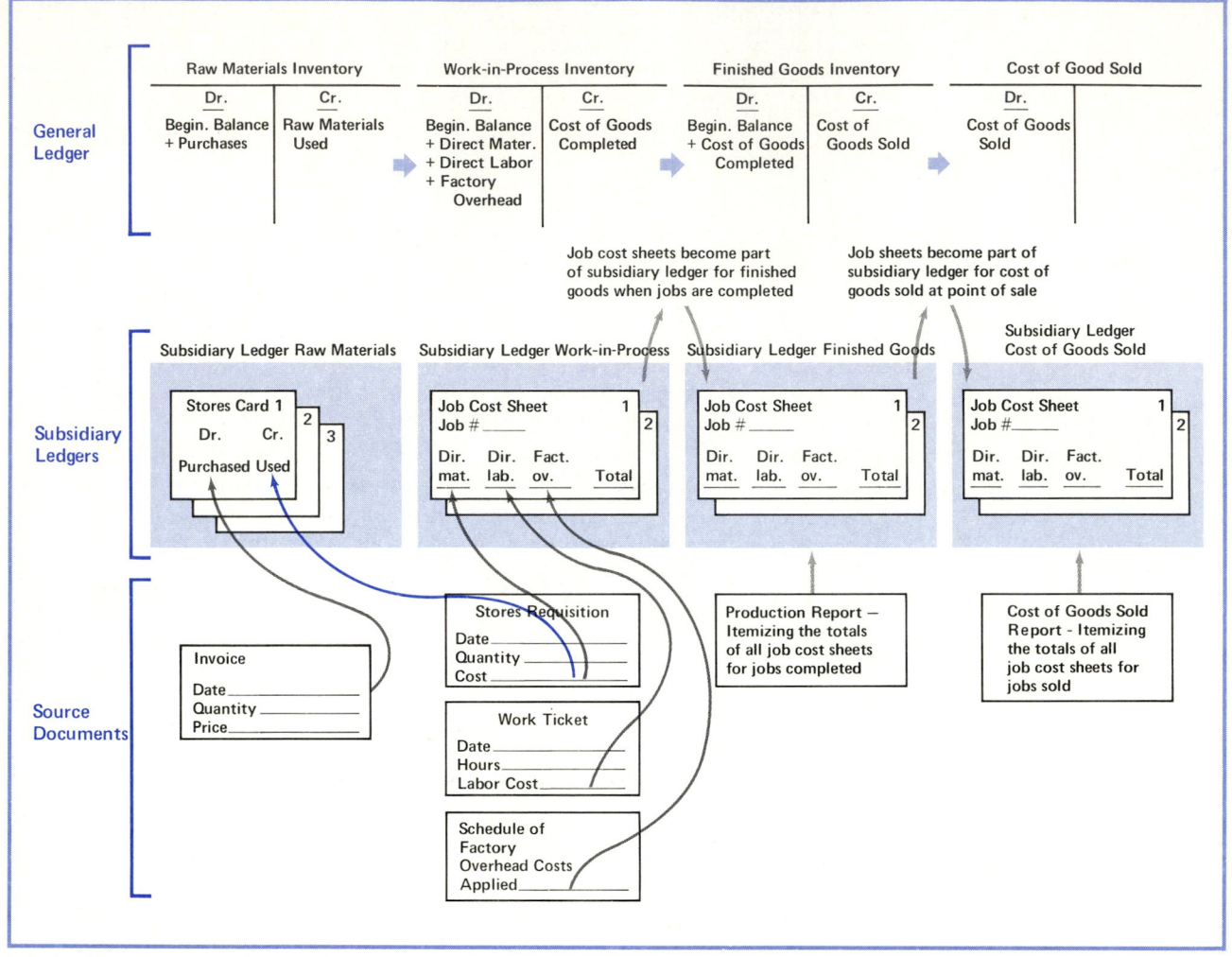

FIGURE 20-1   Job Order Costing System.
The complete view of job order costing shows: (1) the T-accounts from left to right across the top; (2) the subsidiary ledger below each T-account; and (3) the source documents.

2. The subsidiary ledgers for each general ledger inventory account

3. Selected source documents providing evidence concerning the flow of costs

The explanation of Figure 20-1   Across the top of Figure 20-1, running from left to right, you can see the T-accounts that record the progression of production costs through the general ledger of a manufacturer. Immediately below each general ledger account is the subsidiary ledger for that account. The subsidiary ledger for raw materials includes a different *stores card* for each different type of raw material; the subsidiary ledger for work-in-process keeps on file a different *job cost sheet* for each job. Notice that the job cost sheets make up the subsidiary ledgers for finished goods and cost of goods sold expense, as well as for work-in-process. As units are being produced the job cost sheets accumulate the costs that are assigned to work-in-process. When the units are completed, the job cost sheets become the subsidiary ledger for finished goods — now showing the detail of different jobs awaiting sale. Once the jobs are sold, the job cost sheets provide the detail for cost of goods sold expense.

Below the subsidiary ledgers in Figure 20-1 are source documents. For instance, the invoice provides evidence of the purchase of raw materials; the stores requisition tells us about the raw materials transferred to work-in-process; and the work ticket indicates the amount of labor employed on each job.

Now we should be ready to go on to the detailed illustration for job order costing, which begins with the example below.

THE HISTORICAL REPLICAS COMPANY

The Historical Replicas Company produces, to customer specifications, metal art of historical significance — such as Custer's Last Stand and *Star Trek's* Starship Enterprise. The company uses a single direct material, bulk metal, which is melted, cast, sculpted, and polished, all within one operating department.

At the end of January 1988, Historical Replicas was working on two unfinished jobs, no. 788 and no. 789; and had a finished job, no. 787, awaiting delivery. The general ledger accounts for each inventory show the following balances on January 31, 1988:

Raw Materials Inventory		Work-in-Process Inventory		Finished Goods Inventory	
Bal. 1/31 8,000		Bal. 1/31 37,000 (jobs 788 and 789)		Bal. 1/31 24,000 (job 787)	

Subsidiary Ledger Details

The balances shown in the general ledger inventory accounts for Historical Replicas are supported by the subsidiary ledger accounts on pages 788–790, in Exhibits 20-1, 20-2, and 20-3. Two stores cards are presented first in Exhibit 20-1, one card for bulk metal, the direct material, and the other card for metal polish, an indirect material. The balance in the stores card for bulk metal on January 31 is $7,800 (shown in the gray shaded area). When this amount is added to the $200 balance (shown in the gray shaded area) for the metal polish, the sum is $8,000, which is the balance in the general ledger for raw materials inventory.

Also notice in Exhibit 20-1 that the perpetual inventory system is being utilized. As you may recall from Chapter 5, when a *perpetual inventory system* is being maintained, the inventory accounts are continually updated as transactions take place. Each increase or decrease is recorded in the account as soon as it occurs and a new balance is determined. For simplicity, in Exhibit 20-1 we have shown all of the issues of bulk metal for January recorded as a single amount—$12,000 (see column 8 of first stores card), and for metal polish—$160 (see column 8 of second stores card). In actuality, each issue would be listed separately, with a new balance determined after each issue.

The perpetual inventory method is also employed for work-in-process and finished goods, as you can see in the *job cost sheets* in Exhibits 20-2 and 20-3.

The January 31 balance in the general ledger account for work-in-process, $37,000, represents the combined costs for the two unfinished jobs, 788 and 789. The subsidiary ledger accounts for these two jobs (the job cost sheets) are shown in Exhibit 20-2; the sum of the ending balances of $19,000 and $18,000 (shown in the gray

EXHIBIT 20-1   Subsidiary Ledger for Raw Materials: The Stores Cards.

The balances on January 31 are shown in the gray shaded area; and the balances on February 28 are shown in the blue shaded area.

STORES CARD

Stock No. ____1____

Item ____Bulk metal____

Date	Received			Issued				Balance		
	Pounds	Unit Cost	Total Cost	Requisi-tion No.	Pounds	Unit Cost	Total Cost	Pounds	Unit Cost	Total Cost
Bal. 1/1								0		0
1/10	19,800	$1.00	$19,800					19,800	$1.00	$19,800
1/14–1/31				1110–1121	12,000	$1.00	$12,000	7,800	$1.00	$ 7,800
2/3	30,200	$1.00	$30,200					38,000	$1.00	$38,000
2/4				1123	5,000	$1.00	$ 5,000	33,000	1.00	33,000
2/7				1124	7,000	1.00	7,000	26,000	1.00	26,000
2/22				1125	21,000	1.00	21,000	5,000	1.00	5,000

STORES CARD

Stock No. ____2____

Item ____Metal polish____

Date	Received			Issued				Balance		
	Cans	Unit Cost	Total Cost	Requisi-tion No.	Cans	Unit Cost	Total Cost	Cans	Unit Cost	Total Cost
Bal. 1/1								9	$40	$360
1/20–1/31				1109	4	$40	$160	5	$40	$200
2/1–2/28				1122	5	$40	$200	0	40	–0–

shaded areas) equals the $37,000 balance in work-in-process. You probably also observed that there was a job cost sheet in Exhibit 20-2 for job 790. This job was started in February, so naturally it didn't have a balance on January 31.

Finally, the balance of $24,000 in the finished goods general ledger account is represented by job 787, shown in Exhibit 20-3.

As you were examining the job cost sheets in Exhibits 20-2 and 20-3, you may have wondered what the factory overhead rate of $2 was (how it was determined and why we need to use it). This is an element of factory overhead that we will explain later in the chapter. So for now, do not be concerned with it.

Don't be concerned for now with the factory overhead rate of $2 per hour

EXHIBIT 20-2   Job Cost Sheets for Jobs 788, 789, and 790.
The job cost sheets show the 1/31 balances (in the gray shaded areas), the transactions for February, and the 2/28 balances (in the blue shaded areas).

JOB COST SHEET

Job No. ___788___

Customer ___L. Hooper___   Date Completed ___2/17___

Date Started ___1/28___   Date Delivered ___2/21___

	Direct Materials		Direct Labor			Factory Overhead		
Date	Requisition No.	Amount	Work Ticket No.	Hours	Amount	Rate	Amount	Total
1/28	1120	$7,000						
1/28–31			22111–22114	2,000	$8,000			
1/31						$2 per direct labor hour	$4,000	
Bal. 1/31		$7,000			$8,000		$4,000	$19,000
2/4	1123	$5,000						
2/1–2/17			22121–22130	1,500	$6,000			
2/17						$2 per direct labor hour	$3,000	
Completed costs		$12,000			$14,000		$7,000	$33,000

JOB COST SHEET

Job No. ___789___

Customer ___T. Pennachio___   Date Completed ___2/21___

Date Started ___1/29___   Date Delivered _____

	Direct Materials		Direct Labor			Factory Overhead		
Date	Requisition No.	Amount	Work Ticket No.	Hours	Amount	Rate	Amount	Total
1/29	1121	$3,000						
1/29–31			22115–22120	2,500	$10,000			
1/31						$2 per direct labor hour	$5,000	
Bal. 1/31		$3,000			$10,000		$5,000	$18,000
2/7	1124	$7,000						
2/1–2/21			22131–22134	5,000	$20,000			
2/21						$2 per direct labor hour	$10,000	
Completed costs		$10,000			$30,000		$15,000	$55,000

(Continued)

EXHIBIT 20-2   *(Continued)*

JOB COST SHEET

Job No. _____790_____

Customer _____A. Robertson_____   Date Completed _____

Date Started _____2/22_____   Date Delivered _____

Date	Direct Materials Requisition No.	Amount	Direct Labor Work Ticket No.	Hours	Amount	Factory Overhead Rate	Amount	Total
2/22	1125	$21,000						
2/22–2/28			22135–22140	2,500	$10,000			
2/28						$2 per direct labor hour	$5,000	
Bal. 2/28		$21,000			$10,000		$5,000	$36,000

EXHIBIT 20-3   Subsidiary Ledger for Finished Goods.
This job cost sheet represents the 1/31 balance in finished goods inventory.

JOB COST SHEET

Job No. _____787_____

Customer _____G. Nichols_____   Date Completed _____1/25_____

Date Started _____1/11_____   Date Delivered _____2/3_____

Date	Direct Materials Requisition No.	Amount	Direct Labor Work Ticket No.	Hours	Amount	Factory Overhead Rate	Amount	Total
1/11	1119	$6,000						
1/11–1/25			22100–22110	3,000	$12,000			
1/25						$2 per direct labor hour	$6,000	
Bal. 1/31		$6,000			$12,000		$6,000	$24,000

The Transactions for February

We'll discuss four things about each transaction

Each of the transactions related to production during February are now given, and as the transactions occur, they are numbered 1 through 9. For each transaction:

1. The source document providing the evidence of that transaction will be displayed.

2. The details of that transaction will be posted to subsidiary ledger accounts as soon as the transaction takes place.

EXHIBIT 20-4   The Invoice.
The invoice is the source document that gives evidence of a purchase of raw materials.

INVOICE

The Salvage 1 Junk Metal, Inc.   No. _____ 12114 _____
1969 Moon Drive
Canaveral, FL 32920   Date _____ 2/1/88 _____

Sold to: Historical Replicas Company
            527 Southshore Boulevard
            Land O'Ponds, FL 33539

Terms	FOB	Date Shipped
2/10, net 30	Shipping point	2/1/88

Description	Quantity	Unit Price	Amount
Bulk metal	30,200 lb	$1.00/lb	$30,200

---

3. The monthly summary general journal entry will be illustrated.

4. The journal entry will be posted to the general ledger accounts at month-end.

The Purchase of Raw Materials

The purchase of raw materials

On February 3, bulk metal in the amount of $30,200, purchased by the purchasing agent, was received and placed in the storeroom under the control of the storekeeper. As evidence of the purchase, Historical Replicas receives an *invoice* from its supplier, which is the *source document* for the purchase transaction. The invoice for the purchase of 30,200 pounds of bulk metal is shown in Exhibit 20-4. It indicates (1) the date, (2) the name of the supplier, (3) the terms of the purchase, (4) the quantity purchased, and (5) the total cost of the purchase.

As soon as the purchase of bulk metal is received, the subsidiary ledger for raw materials needs to be updated. You can see how this is done back in Exhibit 20-1, for the stores card for bulk metal.

At the end of the month, a single journal entry is made that summarizes all the purchases made during the month. Although there could have been numerous purchases from different suppliers, we are assuming that the entire month's purchases were made on February 3 from Salvage 1 Junk Metal, Inc. The following journal entry records this February purchase:

The journal entry to record a purchase of raw materials

1. Feb. 28   Raw Materials Inventory. 30,200
                        Accounts Payable (or Cash)   30,200
               Purchased raw materials on account (or for cash).

At the end of each month the debits and credits for each journal entry are posted to the general ledger. Exhibit 20-5 shows T-accounts for most of the general ledger accounts affected by entries 1–9 for Historical Replicas. Entry no. 1 for the purchase results in a debit to the T-account for Raw Materials Inventory and a credit to the T-account for Accounts Payable. The numbers in the T-accounts relate to the number of the entry being posted.

Each of the entries that follows will also be posted to T-accounts in Exhibit 20-5 (see pages 792–793). Therefore, you will need to refer back to this exhibit quite a few times before you are finished.

EXHIBIT 20-5   General Ledger Accounts for Historical Replicas Company.

The journal entries (1–9) from our illustration are posted to these accounts.

Raw Materials Inventory

Beg. Bal.	8,000	Transfer of direct and indirect materials	33,000 (2)
			200 (4)
Purchases	(1) 30,200		
End. Bal.	5,000		

Accounts Payable

Payments	30,000	Beg. Bal.	1,000
		Purchases	30,200 (1)
		End. Bal.	1,200

Salaries Payable

		Beg. Bal.	0
		Salaries earned in February:	
		Direct	36,000 (3)
Salaries paid in February	(6) 46,000	Indirect	10,000 (4)
		End. Bal.	0

Work-in-Process Inventory

Beg. Bal.	37,000		
Direct materials	(2) 33,000		
Direct labor	(3) 36,000	Completed jobs transferred to finished goods	88,000 (7)
Overhead applied	(5) 18,000		
End. Bal.	36,000		

Factory Overhead Incurred and Applied

Incurred in February:			*Applied in February:*
Ind. mat.	(4) 200		
Ind. labor	(4) 10,000		
Utilities	(4) 1,000		
Deprec.	(4) 2,800		18,000 (5)
	14,000		18,000

Use of Direct Materials

Direct materials are needed in production

During February, $33,000 of *direct* materials were transferred from raw materials to work-in-process. These materials were needed to (1) continue the work on jobs 788 and 789, that were begun in January, and (2) start work on job 790. The $33,000 was distributed to the three jobs in the following manner:

Date	Job	Amount
Feb. 4	788	$ 5,000
7	789	7,000
22	790	21,000
Total direct materials used		$33,000

Finished Goods Inventory

Beg. Bal.	24,000		
Jobs completed in February	(7) 88,000	Cost of jobs sold	57,000 (9)
End. Bal.	55,000		

Cost of Goods Sold Expense

Cost of jobs sold	(9) 57,000		

Sales Revenue

		Revenue from job nos. 787 and 788	85,500 (8)

Subsidiary ledgers affected by requisition: stores card and job cost sheets

To obtain the materials, a ***stores requisition,*** which is a source document representing a request for materials, is filled out by a supervisor or a designated individual in production and given to the storekeeper in exchange for the required materials. For example, the stores requisition for materials needed on February 4 for job 788 is illustrated in Exhibit 20-6 (page 794).

As you can see, stores requisition no. 1123 indicates that 5,000 pounds of bulk metal, having a cost of $5,000, is needed on February 4 by M. Angelo for job 788. Two subsidiary ledgers are affected by this transaction — the requisition of direct materials. First, the stores card is reduced by the $5,000 of direct materials issued to production. This is shown in Exhibit 20-1 as the first issue of raw materials in February; the second and third issues for February are for jobs 789 and 790.

The second subsidiary ledger affected by the use of direct materials is for work-in-process — the job cost sheets for jobs 788, 789, and 790. In Exhibit 20-2, $5,000 is entered in the direct materials column of the job cost sheet for job 788; $7,000 is

EXHIBIT 20-6
Stores Requisition.

A source document representing a request for materials needed in production.

STORES REQUISITION				

No. 1123

Date _____2/4_____

Job No. _____788_____

Requested by _____M. Angelo_____

Stock No.	Item	Quantity	Unit Cost	Amount
1	Bulk metal	5,000 lb	$1.00/lb	$5,000

assigned to the job cost sheet for job 789; and $21,000 is shown on the job cost sheet for job 790.

At the end of February, a summarized journal entry is made for the total direct materials used during the month. The appropriate entry is:

The journal entry and postings for direct materials

2. Feb. 28   Work-in-Process Inventory 33,000
                     Raw Materials Inventory.....................   33,000
                 Direct materials used during February, distributed to jobs as
                 follows:

                 Job no. 788 $ 5,000
                 Job no. 789   7,000
                 Job no. 790   21,000
                                $33,000

Following this journal entry, the debits and credits are posted to the general ledger accounts for raw materials and work-in-process. This posting is done in Exhibit 20-5, using the number 2 in the T-accounts to indicate the second entry.

Direct Labor

Direct labor: Labor costs easily traceable to a specific job

The labor that is easily traceable to the manufacture of a specific product is called direct labor. To determine the exact amount of direct labor cost incurred for a particular job, it is necessary for each employee to fill out a source document called a *work ticket* for each job worked on. A work ticket for a single laborer who is working on job 788 on February 6 might appear as shown in Exhibit 20-7; it shows the time involved on job 788, the hourly wage rate, and the total direct labor cost for the work performed.

EXHIBIT 20-7
Work Ticket.

The source document that identifies labor costs with a department and a specific job.

WORK TICKET	

22124

Employee _____O. B. Harris_____

Department _____Casting & Sculpting_____   Hours Worked _____8_____

Job. No. _____788_____   Rate _____$4.00_____

Date _____2/6_____   Total _____$32.00_____

We will now assume that a summary of all work tickets used during February indicates that $36,000 was spent for labor, distributed as follows to the three jobs:

Job	Hours	Rate	Amount
788	1,500	$4.00/hr	$ 6,000
789	5,000	4.00/hr	20,000
790	2,500	4.00/hr	10,000
Total direct labor	9,000		$36,000

Check the postings in the job cost sheets

In actual practice we would post the direct labor costs to the job cost sheets on a daily basis. Since the work occurred over quite a few days of the month, the job cost sheets that we are using would be quite lengthy and detailed if we did post all of the daily entries separately. Therefore, for the purpose of *simplicity only,* we will make one posting of direct labor to each job cost sheet to represent the many postings that would actually take place.

So now if you look back to Exhibit 20-2 you will see that $6,000 of direct labor costs have been posted during February to job 788, $20,000 to job 789, and $10,000 to job 790.

The summarized journal entry made on February 28 records a debit to Work-in-Process Inventory and a credit to Salaries Payable:

The month-end entry and posting for direct labor

3. Feb. 28   Work-in-Process Inventory 36,000
                   Salaries Payable............................   36,000
                   Direct labor earned by laborers during February, distributed
                   as follows:

                   Job no. 788 $ 6,000
                   Job no. 789   20,000
                   Job no. 790   10,000
                                 $36,000

The debits and credits in entry 3 are now posted, in total, to the general ledger accounts. Notice that the postings have been made by referring back to Exhibit 20-5 and finding entry 3 in the Work-in-Process and Salaries Payable T-accounts.

Due to the fact that we will have an additional accrual of wages—for indirect labor—in the section on factory overhead that comes next, we will postpone the required entry for the payment of salaries until after we have finished the section on factory overhead.

Factory Overhead Incurred

Factory overhead costs are the indirect costs of production

All factory costs other than direct materials and direct labor are classified as factory overhead. During February the factory overhead incurred was as follows:

Indirect materials	$ 200
Indirect labor..	10,000
Utilities	1,000
Depreciation	2,800
Total factory overhead incurred.........................	$14,000

The indirect materials are the raw materials that either (1) do not become an integral part of the finished good, or (2) do become a physical part of the finished good but are immaterial in amount. For example, indirect materials might include: glue, screws, polish, nails, varnish, maintenance supplies, and janitorial supplies. For Historical Replicas the indirect materials are the cans of metal polish.

The indirect labor relates to the production laborers who do not actually work on the jobs being produced. These laborers might be supervisors, maintenance people, material handlers, and janitors.

There are a variety of source documents related to these miscellaneous overhead items. A stores requisition would once again be needed to obtain the indirect raw materials from the storeroom; and work tickets would be filled out by employees to indicate the amount of labor time indirectly related to production. As we will discuss shortly, there is no attempt to pinpoint the exact amount of indirect materials or indirect labor associated with specific jobs. The stores requisition and the work ticket will only designate the department in which the indirect materials and indirect labor are used — not a specific job. The bill from the power company is the source document for the utility charges, and a depreciation schedule is a source document that indicates the amount of depreciation associated with February's production.

> *Source documents cannot identify specific jobs*

When we use indirect materials (the metal polish) we must update the appropriate stores card — the subsidiary ledger account for raw materials. If you look back to Exhibit 20-1 at the stores card for metal polish you will see a balance of $200 on January 31 (in the gray shaded area). If $200 of polish is used during February, the balance at the end of February would be reduced to zero (in the blue shaded area).

> *Update the stores card for metal polish. It's now zero*

All of the factory overhead costs incurred — the actual factory overhead — are accumulated during the period on *factory overhead cost sheets* — a subsidiary ledger that is similar to a job cost sheet. The difference is that the factory overhead cost sheets trace costs only to the department where the costs are incurred — but not to any of the jobs being produced in the department. In our example, Historical Replicas has only one production department, so it will have only one factory overhead cost sheet. Firms with many production departments will have a different overhead cost sheet for each department.

> *Factory overhead incurred goes to factory overhead cost sheets — not job cost sheets*

Each factory overhead cost sheet will have enough columns to accommodate the different types of factory overhead costs incurred throughout the month. Exhibit 20-8 shows a factory overhead cost sheet for the casting and sculpting department for the month of February, listing the four individual overhead items from above as well as the total for the month of $14,000. There will be a similar posting in each month of the year, the totals accumulating as the year progresses.

4. Feb. 28   Factory Overhead Incurred and Applied 14,000
            Raw Materials Inventory   200
            Salaries Payable   10,000
            Accounts (or Utilities) Payable   1,000
            Accumulated Depreciation   2,800
        To record overhead incurred in February.

Notice in entry 4 above, for the factory overhead costs incurred, that the debit was not to the same account that we used in Chapter 19 — Factory Overhead Incurred — but to a similarly named account instead — *Factory Overhead Incurred and Applied.* Whereas the two account titles may sound the same, the presence of the new word — *applied* — in the title represents a major change in how we account for factory overhead as a product cost.

EXHIBIT 20-8
Factory Overhead Cost Sheets.
The overhead cost sheet has a different column for each type of overhead incurred for a period. There is a different overhead cost sheet for each department.

FACTORY OVERHEAD COST SHEET					
Department		Casting, Sculpting			
Date	Indirect Materials	Indirect Labor	Utilities	Depreciation	Total
Jan.	. . .	. . .	. . .	. . .	. . .
Feb.	$200	$10,000	$1,000	$2,800	$14,000
Mar.	. . .	. . .	. . .	. . .	. . .
Apr.	. . .	. . .	. . .	. . .	. . .

In Chapter 19 we first debited Factory Overhead Incurred. And then at the end of each period, after all the factory overhead costs had been accounted for, we closed the account with a credit, and transferred the total to Work-in-Process with a debit. In this way, the actual overhead costs incurred ended up as product costs in work-in-process. In this chapter, however, you'll find out that there are certain problems associated with the actual factory overhead costs being product costs, and that factory overhead *applied* will be the product costs instead. In order to keep track of two different types of factory overhead — the actual costs incurred and the costs applied — we need to use an account with an expanded title. The account is Factory Overhead Incurred and Applied.

Assigning Factory Overhead Costs to Jobs   At this point you're probably thinking, "This certainly sounds confusing. Why don't we just continue using the same system that was introduced in Chapter 19 — first debiting Factory Overhead Incurred for the $14,000 and later transferring this total to Work-in-Process. Didn't we learn in Chapter 19 that factory overhead is a product cost just like direct materials and direct labor? And didn't we just assign the actual costs of direct materials and direct labor to work-in-process, in entries 2 and 3? So why don't we do the same thing for factory overhead; why don't we merely transfer the actual costs of $14,000 to Work-in-Process, just as we did in Chapter 19? Why aren't the actual factory overhead costs still the product costs?"

These are indeed extremely good questions. And the answers to these questions are vital if you are to understand the steps we are about to take for factory overhead.

Yes, factory overhead is definitely a product cost, just like direct materials and direct labor; and yes, factory overhead does need to be debited to Work-in-Process. However, for two very practical and important reasons, we are no longer going to use the actual factory overhead costs for product costing.

Reason No. 1: The Indirect Relationship   The first reason we don't debit Work-in-Process for the actual factory overhead incurred for a period is because of the relationship of overhead costs to the jobs in production. Direct materials and direct labor are costs that can be easily traced and assigned to the individual jobs to which they apply. This is why we refer to these costs as being "direct." When these costs are debited to Work-in-Process, it is an easy task to distribute the total to the various job cost sheets, just as we did in Exhibit 20-2.

Although factory overhead is also a product cost, it is indirectly rather than directly related to the jobs in production. Factory overhead is considered to be indirectly related to production because it is extremely difficult, if not impossible, to determine

Factory overhead can't be associated with specific jobs

the exact amount of actual overhead to associate with each different job. For example, the salary paid to a foreman is part of factory overhead. The foreman may be supervising numerous workers, each of whom may be working on several different jobs. Not only is it very difficult to determine the exact amount of time spent by the foreman supervising each worker, but it is even more difficult to determine the amount of time associated with each particular job. If the actual overhead incurred is assigned to Work-in-Process, then we also have to distribute the amount incurred to the job cost sheets. Because of the indirect relationship between factory overhead and the jobs worked on, there is no way to know how much overhead cost we should assign to each job cost sheet. As a result it normally isn't a good idea to debit Work-in-Process Inventory for the actual overhead incurred.

Reason No. 2: Fluctuating Activity   After you have read the first reason, you may say to yourself, "But it doesn't seem necessary to find out the exact amount of overhead associated with each job. All we have to do is spread the overhead incurred each month evenly among each job. Or better yet, we can spread the overhead evenly among the labor hours worked, and then assign the actual overhead to each job based on the number of hours used on each job that month."

The problem with this line of reasoning relates to the effect that fluctuating production activity from month to month can have on the cost per finished unit and the resulting monthly income statements. This is especially true when a substantial

Variable and fixed costs

portion of the overhead costs is fixed. The topic of fixed costs, along with variable costs, will be discussed in more detail in Chapter 22. We do feel that it is necessary however to provide a basic explanation of variable and fixed costs at this time — before we go on to explain the problem of fluctuating production activity.

Variable costs are costs that fluctuate, in total, in proportion to changes in activity — the more units you produce the more variable costs you have. Fixed costs are those costs that, in total, are not expected to change as activity changes — no matter how many units you produce, the total fixed costs remain the same.

The cost per unit can fluctuate dramatically when production fluctuates from period to period

Since fixed costs in total will be the same no matter how many units are produced, the fixed costs per unit can be very large or very small depending on the number of units produced.

Suppose, for example, that an organization expects its factory overhead to be completely fixed, amounting to $200,000 for an entire year, and that the amount incurred each month is the same amount — $16,667 ($200,000 ÷ 12 = $16,667). Suppose also that activity throughout the year is expected to fluctuate dramatically. Exhibit 20-9 shows that the overhead cost and also the total cost per unit or per job can be quite a bit different from month to month due to these fluctuations in activity.

Because of fluctuations in production throughout the year, the monthly overhead cost per unit is expected to be as high as $8,334 in January and as low as $1,389 in July. Combining these amounts with the $10,000 per unit for the direct materials and direct labor (assumed for simplicity — however unrealistic — to be the same amount per unit worked on), we get a total cost per unit of $18,334 in January and $11,389 in July. Looking at overhead costs and total units produced on an annual basis (the bottom line of Exhibit 20-9), we get an overhead cost per unit of $2,500 ($200,000 ÷ 80 = $2,500), and a total cost per unit of $12,500 ($10,000 + $2,500 = $12,500).

Now let's assume that the selling price is $17,500 per unit — which will generate a gross profit of $5,000 per unit ($17,500 − $12,500 = $5,000) if we use the total cost per unit on an annual basis. Many organizations, however, want to prepare income statements for their own use more frequently than once a year. If monthly income

EXHIBIT 20-9   Fluctuating Cost per Unit.
Notice how the average cost per unit is very high in January when few units are produced, and very low in July when many units are produced.

Month	Actual Overhead Costs	÷	Expected Units (or Jobs) to Be Produced	=	Overhead Cost per Unit	+	Direct Materials Plus Direct Labor per Unit	=	Total Cost per Unit
Jan.	$ 16,667		2		$8,334		$10,000		$18,334
Feb.	16,667		3		5,555		10,000		15,555
Mar.	16,667		4		4,167		10,000		14,167
July	16,667		12		1,389		10,000		11,389
Aug.	16,667		11		1,515		10,000		11,515
Nov.	16,667		3		5,555		10,000		15,555
Dec.	16,667		2		8,334		10,000		18,334
Year	$200,000		80		$2,500		$10,000		$12,500

statements are prepared using the monthly total cost per unit, the gross profit per unit would vary from month to month, shown as follows for three of the months:

Month	Sales Price	Total Cost/Unit	Gross Profit/Unit
Jan.	$17,500	$18,334	$ (834)
July	17,500	11,389	6,111
Nov.	17,500	15,555	1,945

The monthly gross profit is far below the $5,000 average of the year in January and November, but is above the average in July. This might create the impression that the production department was run poorly in January and November but that it was run efficiently in July. The fact is, however, that the only reason the monthly results appear to be so dramatically different is that the number of units to which the $16,667 monthly overhead was assigned fluctuated quite a bit. As you can see, the assignment of monthly actual overhead to units produced each month can cause meaningless interim income statements.

Assigning actual overhead costs to jobs can result in meaningless interim income statements

To conclude, there are two reasons that it is better *not* to debit Work-in-Process for the actual overhead incurred.

1. Because of the indirect relationship between overhead costs and units produced, there is no practical way to determine the amount of actual overhead that is incurred for each individual job produced.

2. When an organization experiences fluctuating production activity, the average cost per finished unit can be very large or very small, often causing meaningless interim income statements.

Factory Overhead Applied

What is factory overhead applied?

The factory overhead that we will now assign to different jobs and debit to Work-in-Process is called *factory overhead applied.* To determine the factory overhead applied, we use a *predetermined overhead rate.* What that means is this: At the beginning of the year each production department makes an estimate of the total overhead costs and expected activity for the year. When the estimated overhead costs are divided by the estimated activity, we get the predetermined overhead rate. During each month, the actual activity for that month is multiplied by the predetermined overhead rate, resulting in an overhead cost we call factory overhead applied.

The controller looks for a good way to measure activity

Now let's get back to Historical Replicas Company. Assume that the company controller, Steve Cobb, on January 1, 1988, wanted to calculate the company's predetermined overhead rate for 1988, and estimated the factory overhead for the year to be $200,000. He initially thought he would: (1) estimate the number of jobs (or units) to be worked on in 1988, (2) determine an average cost per job; and then (3) assign this average cost to each job produced as the year progressed. As a result, each job—no matter how long it took to produce—would have the same amount of factory overhead assigned to it.

Steve figured that the company would work on only five jobs during 1988, four of them during the first 2 months (jobs 787–790), and only one during the remaining 10 months of the year. Steve realized that by spreading the $200,000 evenly among the five jobs, this would result in a cost per job of $40,000. The more Steve thought about this approach, however, the less sense it made. A job that takes 10 months to complete should be assigned a much bigger portion of the total overhead for the year than a job that takes only 1 or 2 months to complete. Steve knew he needed to find a better way to measure activity for the year than the number of jobs to be worked on.

The thought then came to Steve that direct labor hours might be a more meaningful way to measure activity, since overhead costs for the year are probably more influenced by the number of hours worked than by the number of jobs completed.

By using direct labor hours, the overhead costs assigned to each job would better reflect the relative time, effort, and attention exerted on that job. A job taking 1,500 direct labor hours does not require as much attention as one taking 5,000 hours or 50,000 hours. Therefore, by assigning overhead costs to jobs based on the number of direct labor hours needed for each job, far less overhead would be assigned to the 1,500-hour job than to the 50,000-hour job—a more equitable manner of distribution.

On January 1, 1988, Steve estimated that the total direct labor hours for all jobs in 1988 would be 100,000 hours. He then determined an average overhead rate for 1988 using the following general formula:

Getting a predetermined overhead rate for Historical Replicas

$$\text{Predetermined factory overhead rate} = \frac{\text{estimated factory overhead costs for the year}}{\text{estimated activity for the year}}$$

Using the specific data for Historical Replicas, the rate is determined in the following manner:

$$\text{Predetermined factory overhead per direct labor hour} = \frac{\text{estimated factory overhead costs for the year}}{\text{estimated direct labor hours for the year}}$$

$$= \frac{\$200,000}{100,000 \text{ hours}}$$

$$= \$2.00 \text{ per direct labor hour}$$

For each direct labor hour worked during a month, whether it be in February, July, or November, $2.00 of factory overhead is assigned (or applied) to work-in-process.

The amount of overhead cost to be assigned to each specific job depends on the number of direct labor hours used on each job.

If you'll now look back to the discussion preceding entry 3 for direct labor, you can see that the total hours of direct labor used in February were 9,000, broken down by job as follows:

Job	Direct Labor Hours
788	1,500
789	5,000
790	2,500
Total	9,000

Using the predetermined overhead rate of $2.00 per direct labor hour, the total overhead assigned to production in February is:

Job	Activity for Month (direct labor hours)	×	Overhead Rate per Hour	=	Overhead Cost Assigned to Production
788	1,500	×	$2.00	=	$ 3,000
789	5,000	×	2.00	=	10,000
790	2,500	×	2.00	=	5,000
					$18,000

The overhead applied in February is $18,000. How much goes to each job?

The $18,000 of overhead costs assigned to production must be posted to the appropriate job cost sheets. Exhibit 20-2 (on pages 789–790) shows that the amount posted to the job cost sheet for job 788 is $3,000; for job 789 it is $10,000; and for job 790 it is $5,000.

The journal entry needed on February 28 to record the overhead costs applied is:

5. Feb. 28   Work-in-Process Inventory 18,000
                          Factory Overhead Incurred and Applied   18,000
                     Factory overhead applied to production, based on a $2 per
                     hour predetermined rate for 9,000 hours of direct labor dur-
                     ing February.

Now you can debit Work-in-Process for overhead — the overhead applied

Be sure to notice in entry 5 the account that is being credited — Factory Overhead Incurred and Applied. This is the account that we debited for the factory overhead *incurred* in entry 4. Now we are crediting it for the overhead *applied*.

The amounts shown in entry 5 are now posted to general ledger accounts. If you look back to Exhibit 20-5, notice that the Work-in-Process T-account has been debited for $18,000 and the Factory Overhead Incurred and Applied T-account has been credited for $18,000.

Can we measure activity in any other way? Dollars? Machine hours?

Alternative Measures of Activity   In the illustration for Historical Replicas, the controller decided to measure activity for the year in terms of *direct labor hours*. An alternative way to measure activity, which closely approximates the results of using direct labor hours, is *direct labor dollars*. Instead of the resulting rate being a cost per hour, it is a percentage of labor dollars. For those production situations that involve a great deal of machine work, the number of *machine hours* expected for the year could be a third possible way to measure activity, and the overhead rate would be a cost per machine hour.

The overhead incurred and applied for February aren't the same amount

Overapplied and Underapplied Overhead   Before we go on, let's look for a moment at what has been recorded during February for factory overhead. In entry 4 we debited the account, Factory Overhead Incurred and Applied, for $14,000 — the actual overhead incurred for the month. Now in entry 5, using an estimated average cost per direct labor hour of $2, we credited the same account, Factory Overhead Incurred and Applied, for $18,000 — the overhead applied to production in February. The details of these entries are shown below in the T-account for Factory Overhead Incurred and Applied:

Factory Overhead Incurred and Applied

	Incurred		Applied
(4)	200		
(4)	10,000		
(4)	1,000		
(4)	2,800	(5)	18,000
	14,000		18,000

As you can see, the credits exceed the debits by $4,000 — the excess of what was applied during February over what was actually incurred. Factory overhead for February is said to be $4,000 *"overapplied."*

The difference is either overapplied or underapplied

The difference for each month between the debits and credits in the Factory Overhead Incurred and Applied account is called the overapplied or underapplied overhead. If the credits exceed the debits, as they do above, the overhead is ***overapplied.*** If the debits exceed the credits, the overhead is ***underapplied.*** Do not be surprised when the debits and credits are not equal — we do not expect the amount incurred in a month to equal the amount applied. In fact, for a firm with fluctuating activity, we fully expect to have overapplied overhead in some months and underapplied overhead in the other months. By year-end we hope that the debits will be fairly close to the credits, that is, that the incurred will equal the applied. If there is not an equality by the end of the year, a special kind of entry will be made — one that is made only at the end of the year, not at the end of each month. We will discuss this problem later. For now, let's continue with the events of February for Historical Replicas.

Payment of Salaries

The labor costs accrued for the month of February were recorded in entry 3 (direct labor) and entry 4 (indirect labor — factory overhead). They totaled $46,000:

The payment of direct and indirect laborers

Direct labor.	$36,000
Indirect labor.	10,000
Total labor accrued.	$46,000

If you look at the Salaries Payable T-account in Exhibit 20-5, you will see credits totaling to this amount.

EXHIBIT 20-10
Clock Card.
A source document that
accumulates the total hours
worked by an employee during a
pay period. It is not the same as
a work ticket.

CLOCK CARD

Name ___Jerome Brown___

Pay Period ___February 1988___

Date	Time In	Time Out	Hours Regular	Overtime
2/1	8:00	12:00	4	
	1:00	5:00	4	
2/2	8:01	11:55	4	
	1:00	5:02	4	
2/25	8:03	12:00	4	
	1:00	4:55	4	

At the time of these accruals, we pointed out that each laborer would have to fill out a work ticket to indicate which department he was working in (for both direct laborers and indirect laborers) and which job he was working on (for direct laborers only). In addition, each laborer needs to keep track of the total hours that he has worked during the pay period—using a *clock card.* The clock card is a source document that informs the accounting department of the number of hours for which each laborer should be paid. The clock card does not specify which jobs the laborer has worked on; that is the purpose of the work ticket. A typical clock card for a single worker during February might appear as shown in Exhibit 20-10.

If we assume that the salaries are paid on the last day of each month and that the combined labor costs from clock cards for all employees is $46,000, then the appropriate entry to record the payment of salaries to laborers is shown below as entry 6:

6. Feb. 28   Salaries Payable 46,000
               Cash   46,000
               $36,000 was paid to direct laborers and $10,000 was paid to
               indirect laborers.

Entry 6 is posted to the appropriate general ledger accounts on February 28, which we show in Exhibit 20-5.

Completion of Jobs

Jobs are completed and transferred to finished goods

During February two jobs were completed, jobs 788 and 789. As the job cost sheets in Exhibit 20-2 indicate, the total costs of producing these jobs were $33,000 and $55,000, respectively. The total of these two, $88,000, is transferred from Work-in-Process to Finished Goods as shown by the following entry:

7. Feb. 28   Finished Goods Inventory 88,000
               Work-in-Process Inventory   88,000
               Completion in February of jobs 788 and 789, and transfer of
               costs ($33,000 and $55,000, respectively) to finished goods.

The debits and credits in entry 7 are posted to the appropriate general ledger accounts, shown in Exhibit 20-5. When the jobs are completed during the month, the job cost sheets for the completed jobs are removed from the work-in-process inventory subsidiary ledger and become part of the subsidiary ledger for finished goods inventory.

Historical Replicas might prepare a cost of production report as a source document for entry 7, listing the costs of the jobs completed during the period and transferred to finished goods. The information presented on the report would be taken from the job cost sheets that are transferred from the subsidiary ledger for work-in-process to the one for finished goods.

Sale of Completed Jobs

Jobs 787 (the beginning inventory of finished goods) and 788 (completed during February) were the only jobs sold during February. Their respective costs (shown in Exhibits 20-3 and 20-2) were:

Job 787	$24,000
Job 788	33,000
	$57,000

If each job is sold at a markup of 50% over cost, the sales price for each job would have been:

Jobs 787 and 788 are sold at a markup of 50% over cost

Job No.	Cost	50% Markup	Sales Price
787	$24,000	$12,000	$36,000
788	33,000	16,500	49,500
	$57,000	$28,500	$85,500

The entries to record the sales and cost of goods sold are shown in entries 8 and 9, respectively. First, we record the revenue:

You need two entries to record a sale: the revenue and the cost of goods sold

8. Feb. 28   Accounts Receivable (or Cash) 85,500
             Sales Revenue   85,500
             To record the sale of jobs 787 and 788 at prices of $36,000 and
             $49,500, respectively.

Next, we record the cost of goods sold:

9. Feb. 28   Cost of Goods Sold Expense. 57,000
             Finished Goods Inventory   57,000
             To record the cost of goods sold for jobs 787 and 788. The
             costs were $24,000 and $33,000, respectively.

Entries 8 and 9 are posted to the general ledger accounts in Exhibit 20-5. At the time of sale the job cost sheets for jobs 787 and 788 would be removed from the subsidiary ledger for finished goods and placed in the subsidiary ledger for cost of goods sold. The source documents for entry 8 are copies of the sales invoices, and the source document for entry 9 is a cost of goods sold report. The cost of goods sold report itemizes the costs, from the job cost sheets of jobs 787 and 788, that are transferred to the subsidiary ledger for cost of goods sold.

An important reminder: the journal entries shown in entries 1–9 and the posting to the general ledger T-accounts displayed in Exhibit 20-5 are made in summarized form at month-end. The detailed records maintained in the subsidiary ledger accounts for each job would in most cases be maintained daily.

The Interim Statement

What you need for financial statements in February

Assume that monthly financial statements are prepared on Februay 28. The income statement includes the sales of $85,500 and the cost of goods sold expense of $57,000 relating to the sales of jobs 787 and 788. In an actual situation there would also be operating expenses (selling and administrative), which were not included in this illustration. The balance sheet includes the following inventory balances taken from the T-accounts in Exhibit 20-5:

Raw Materials Inventory	$ 5,000
Work-in-Process Inventory	36,000
Finished Goods Inventory	55,000

The Raw Materials balance, $5,000, is supported by the stores card for bulk metal shown in Exhibit 20-1. The Work-in-Process balance, $36,000, represents the total from the job cost sheet for job 790 shown in Exhibit 20-2. Job 790 is still being worked on the last day of February. The balance in Finished Goods, $55,000, comes from the job cost sheet for job 789, which is also shown in Exhibit 20-2. Job 789 was finished in February and will probably be sold in March.

Year-End Handling of Over- or Underapplied Overhead

For the month of February, the actual overhead incurred was $14,000 and the amount applied was $18,000. These represent the debits and credits to the Factory Overhead Incurred and Applied T-account shown in Exhibit 20-5. There were also debits and credits to this account for January (which we did not show), and there will be additional debits and credits for the next 10 months of 1988. At the end of the year, on the debit side of Factory Overhead Incurred and Applied there will be accumulated overhead incurred for the full 12 months of 1988. On the credit side will.be accumulated 12 months of applied overhead. A question: By the end of the year, will the debits in this account equal the credits? Probably not.

In the ideal situation the applied overhead would exactly equal the overhead costs incurred; and to make matters even nicer, they would both equal the amount of overhead costs predicted for the year—the $200,000—which was used in the calculation of the factory overhead rate (look back at this calculation on page 800). In the more realistic situation, however, the applied overhead will not equal the actual overhead for the year, and neither one will be exactly $200,000.

To see how we handle this, let's assume this set of facts for Historical Replicas at year-end:

What if the incurred doesn't equal the applied?

■ At the end of the year, all the bills for overhead add up to a total of $204,000 in factory overhead costs actually incurred.

■ The sum of the work tickets for the year shows that 98,000 labor hours were worked in the manufacturing department. At the predetermined rate of $2.00 per direct labor hour, this means that during the year, $196,000 in overhead costs were applied to all units produced.

The T-account for Factory Overhead Incurred and Applied might look like this for 1988:

Factory Overhead Incurred and Applied

	Incurred	Applied
Jan.	20,000	12,000
Feb.	14,000	18,000
.	.	.
.	.	.
.	.	.
Dec.	16,000	18,000
Totals for 1988	204,000	196,000

In this more realistic case, the debits do not equal the credits—the actual overhead incurred does not equal the applied. The difference in the actual costs, of $204,000, and the applied costs, of $196,000, indicates that the overhead costs were underapplied by $8,000. In this case, the sum of the overhead costs applied to each unit produced does not add up to the total of overhead costs incurred. We don't find out until the end of the year that we didn't assign sufficient overhead costs to units produced to cover the actual overhead costs incurred. In this case, we should have assigned $8,000 more in overhead costs than was assigned.

How do we account for this $8,000 in underapplied overhead costs at the end of the year? Let's see.

The Factory Overhead Incurred and Applied account is a temporary, or nominal, account, which means that the balance must be closed—reduced to zero—at the end of the year. There are two ways to close this account. The first way is to close the Factory Overhead Incurred and Applied balance entirely to Cost of Goods Sold Expense:

Dec. 31   Cost of Goods Sold Expense 8,000
                  Factory Overhead Incurred and Applied   8,000
                  To close out the overhead account for the $8,000 of underapplied
                  overhead.

The second way to close the Factory Overhead Incurred and Applied account allocates the over- or underapplied overhead among the Work-in-Process, Finished Goods, and Cost of Goods Sold accounts, based on the ending balances in these accounts prior to the closing entry.

For example, assume that the *year-end* balances for these accounts are as follows (Caution: The balances shown in Exhibit 20-5 are only for the end of February, not for the end of the year):

Work-in-Process Inventory . . . . $ 40,000
Finished Goods Inventory. 60,000
Cost of Goods Sold Expense 700,000

AN IRS RULING
LIFO cannot be applied to certain jobs

The job order costing method is appropriate for manufacturing situations where a small number of units (or batches of units) are being produced, probably to customer specifications. In addition, each unit or batch is distinguishable from any other one, and each unit usually takes considerable time, attention, and costs to complete.

Although there are numerous examples of situations where job order costing is appropriate, accounting for construction projects should be one of the most obvious. Such was the case for Spang Industries, Inc., which was engaged in the fabrication of structural steel parts for bridges. Usually the production was done based upon customer specifications and took a minimum of a year to complete.

"To track the costs incurred and the revenues received under its long-term contracts, Spang relied upon the so-called job order system, which consisted of a series of primary accounts in which the flow of costs and revenues were traced. This system gathered costs as they were incurred and recorded income only upon shipment."

Spang reported its income for tax purposes to the IRS only when the project was completed; thus, it was using the income reporting method called completed contract. This reporting method includes income on the tax return at a later date than the alternative method of reporting income —percentage of completion. "Through the year prior to the fiscal year ended Jan. 1, 1970, reporting under the completed contract method was carried out by subtracting from the revenues earned on each contract completed during a taxable year all the costs incurred in the performance of the contract as reflected in the job cost summaries that were maintained over the life of the contract."

This manner of reporting is perfectly acceptable to the IRS. Unfortunately Spang went a little bit too far in its effort to reduce its tax bill in 1970. In that year, Spang attempted to apply the LIFO method to the ending inventories of work-in-process, an adjustment that had the effect of increasing the cost of goods sold and reducing the resulting income and income taxes. Not only did this change relate to 1970, but it was subsequently applied to the next three years, at which time Spang's tax returns were audited and the deductions related to the application of LIFO were disallowed and were returned to income.

Spang subsequently went to court seeking a refund of the additional taxes they were assessed. Nearly a decade later the U.S. Claims Court ruled that the completed contract method is not compatible with the LIFO method of inventory valuation in accounting for long-term contracts, and that Spang was not entitled to the refund that it was seeking.

"LIFO Incompatible with Completed Contract Method," *1984 The Bureau of National Affairs, Inc.; Daily Reporting for Executives,* Taxation and Accounting Section, August 23, 1984.

The $8,000 underapplied overhead is allocated to each account as follows:

	Ending Balance	Fraction of Total	×	Total Under-applied	=	Underapplied Overhead Allocated
Work-in-Process Inventory	$ 40,000	$\frac{40}{800}$	×	$8,000	=	$ 400
Finished Goods Inventory	60,000	$\frac{60}{800}$	×	8,000	=	600
Cost of Goods Sold Expense	700,000	$\frac{700}{800}$	×	8,000	=	7,000
	$800,000					$8,000

The closing entry using the second way would be the following:

The second way to close: It's tougher but it is GAAP

Dec. 31	Work-in-Process Inventory	400	
	Finished Goods Inventory	600	
	Cost of Goods Sold Expense	7,000	
	Factory Overhead Incurred and Applied		8,000

To close out the overhead account for the $8,000 of underapplied overhead.

EXHIBIT 20-11   Matrix Overview of Job Order Costing.
For each transaction, Exhibit 20-11 lists the entry, the subsidiary ledger, and the source document.

No.	Transaction	Journal Entry	Subsidiary Ledgers	Source Documents
1.	Purchase of raw materials	Raw Materials Inventory Accounts Payable	Stores cards	Invoice

2.	Use of direct materials	Work-in-Process Inventory
		   Raw Materials
		     Inventory
			Job cost sheets
			
			Stores cards
				Stores requisition

3.	Accrual of direct labor	Work-in-Process Inventory Salaries Payable	Job cost sheets	Work tickets

4.	Actual factory overhead incurred	Factory Overhead Incurred
		   and Applied
		     Miscellaneous credits
			Factory overhead cost
			   sheets
			Stores cards
				Stores requisition, work tickets, utility bills, depreciation schedules

5.	Factory overhead applied	Work-in-Process Inventory
		   Factory Overhead
		     Incurred and Applied
			Job cost sheets	Schedule showing the determination of the predetermined factory overhead rate

6.	Payment of salaries	Salaries Payable Cash		Clock cards

7.	Completion of jobs	Finished Goods Inventory
		   Work-in-Process
		     Inventory
			Job cost sheets	Cost of goods produced schedule

8.	Sale of jobs: revenue	Accounts Receivable
		   Sales
			Accounts receivable
			   subsidiary ledger
				Invoice

9.	Sale of jobs: costs	Cost of Goods Sold Expense
		   Finished Goods
		     Inventory
			Job cost sheets	Cost of goods sold expense schedule

This second approach is usually required in order to be in accordance with generally accepted accounted principles (GAAP). However, if the over- or underapplied overhead is immaterial in amount, then it is acceptable to use either of the two approaches we have shown. When it is immaterial, it makes little difference whether we allocate or not, because the differences in the cost of goods sold and the resulting net income under the two approaches is also immaterial. However, if the over- or underapplied overhead is extremely large, then the amounts for cost of goods sold and net income could be quite a bit different under the two approaches, and the recommended approach is mandatory.

An Overview of Job Order Costing

Now that you have completed reading the chapter, you may feel that there were so many details over so many pages that you wish you could put them all into perspective on a single page. We did. We have condensed the chapter into the most basic elements in Exhibit 20-11. We offer you a summary of job order costing, in matrix form. For each transaction, by reading from left to right, you can see the journal entry, subsidiary ledgers, and source documents affected.

CHAPTER SUMMARY

Job order costing is used to account for the manufacture of identifiable units or batches, which are often produced to customer specifications. The costs of each unit or batch of units—the job—are carefully determined and kept separate from the costs of each other job.

The journal entries required in the job order costing method trace the flow of manufacturing costs from one production account to another:

Raw Materials Inventory	Work-in-Process Inventory	Finished Goods Inventory	Cost of Goods Sold Expense

The main subsidiary ledger account employed in job order costing is the *job cost sheet.* The job cost sheet accumulates the product costs associated with each job. The total of all job cost sheets should be equal to the debit balance in Work-in-Process Inventory.

The costs of direct materials and direct labor are obviously related and easily traced to the different physical units of production. Therefore, the assignment of these costs to different jobs presents no difficulties. Factory overhead, however, is not related directly to units being produced throughout the year, and the actual overhead costs cannot be obviously or easily traced to the individual jobs. For this reason the factory overhead debited to Work-in-Process Inventory and assigned to the individual job cost sheets is the amount of *factory overhead applied* rather than the **actual factory overhead incurred.**

The overhead applied is debited to Work-in-Process Inventory and it is credited to *Factory Overhead Incurred and Applied.* The actual factory overhead costs incurred (rent, insurance, salaries, utilities, supplies, depreciation, repairs, etc.) are debited to Factory Overhead Incurred and Applied and are credited to a wide variety of miscellaneous accounts—such as Raw Materials Inventory, Accounts Payable, Unexpired Insurance, and Salaries Payable. The difference between the applied overhead and the actual overhead is called overapplied or underapplied overhead. If the applied exceeds the actual, it is *overapplied;* if the applied is less than the actual, it is **underapplied.** Overapplied overhead is represented by a credit balance in the account, Factory Overhead Incurred and Applied; underapplied overhead is represented by a debit balance. The balance must be closed out at year-end, either entirely to Cost of Goods Sold Expense or allocated among Work-in-Process Inventory, Finished Goods Inventory, and Cost of Goods Sold Expense.

IMPORTANT TERMS USED IN THIS CHAPTER

Clock card A source document that indicates the number of hours worked and salary earned by each employee during a pay period. (page 803)

Factory overhead applied (or assigned) The overhead debited to Work-in-Process for product costing purposes. Applied overhead is determined by multiplying a predetermined factory overhead rate by the activity for the period. (page 799)

Factory overhead cost sheet   The subsidiary ledger for factory overhead incurred and applied. This sheet itemizes for each department the types of factory overhead costs incurred. (page 796)

Factory Overhead Incurred and Applied   The general ledger account debited for factory overhead incurred and credited for factory overhead applied. (page 796)

Invoice   The source document for a purchase or sale. It indicates the quantity and cost of what is bought or sold. (page 791)

Job cost sheet   In job order costing, the basic document that accumulates the product costs associated with each job being worked on. The combination of all job cost sheets is the subsidiary ledger for work-in-process inventory. When units are completed and later sold, job cost sheets also provide the subsidiary ledgers for finished goods and cost of goods sold. (page 785)

Job order costing method   The method of accounting for the production of identifiable products, often to customer specifications. The costs of each job are carefully accumulated and kept separate from the costs of any other job. (page 783)

Overapplied overhead   The difference between factory overhead applied and factory overhead incurred when factory overhead applied is the greater amount. (page 802)

Source document   A document giving evidence of a transaction, and the amount involved. (page 785)

Stores card   A card indicating the receipts, withdrawals, and balance for each different type of raw material. The combination of all stores cards is the subsidiary ledger for raw materials inventory. (page 786)

Stores requisition   A written request presented to the storekeeper by the operating department to acquire raw materials needed for production. (page 793)

Subsidiary ledger   A file of accounts that provides the details of a general ledger account. The job cost sheets make up the subsidiary ledger for work-in-process inventory and the stores cards comprise the subsidiary ledger for raw materials inventory. (page 785)

Underapplied overhead   The difference between factory overhead applied and factory overhead incurred, when factory overhead incurred is greater. (page 802)

Work ticket   A source document that indicates the time and salary a direct laborer spends on a specific job and the time and salary an indirect laborer spends in a particular department. (page 794)

QUESTIONS

1. Explain the differences between *job order costing* and *process costing.* Give several examples for each of industries in which each method would be used.

2. Name and describe the inventory subsidiary ledger accounts for a manufacturer.

3. Explain why actual factory overhead incurred is not debited to Work-in-Process as part of the product costing purpose.

4. What is *factory overhead applied?* How is it determined?

5. What is *overapplied overhead? Underapplied overhead?*

6. What is the required accounting treatment for over- or underapplied overhead at year-end?

7. What is the purpose of the *job cost sheet?* What types of costs are recorded in the job cost sheets?

8. Explain what we mean by the term *source document,* and describe at least three examples of source documents.

9. Job order costing is the method used by most manufacturers of custom-made products to help control operations. Discuss what is wrong with this statement.

10. If the Factory Overhead Incurred and Applied account has a debit balance at the end of a year, does this mean that the account received nothing but debits during the year? Is overhead overapplied or underapplied for the year? What adjustment do we make for the overapplied or underapplied balance at the end of each month? At the end of the year?

EXERCISES

Exercise 20-1
Different ways to calculate the predetermined overhead rate

On January 1, 1989, the Walker Company estimates that the factory overhead for 1989 will be $500,000. It also estimates its direct labor hours and direct labor costs for the year to be 100,000 hours and $250,000, respectively. During January 1989, Walker worked on two jobs, neither of which was completed on January 31. The direct labor hours worked in January were 7,000. The costs incurred in January were as follows:

Direct labor:		
Job 1 (5,000 hours)	$ 12,500	
Job 2 (2,000 hours)	5,200	$ 17,700
Factory overhead.		50,000
Direct materials:		
Job 1	$ 80,000	
Job 2	100,000	180,000

a. Determine the factory overhead assigned to each job, if the actual overhead is split evenly between the jobs worked on.

b. Determine the factory overhead assigned to each job, if the actual overhead is allocated to the jobs based on the direct labor hours used in January on each job.

(Check figure: Job 1 = $35,714)

c. Determine the factory overhead assigned to each job if overhead is applied using a predetermined overhead rate, with the activity measured in terms of direct labor hours.

(Check figure: Job 1 = $25,000)

d. Answer part (c), but assume that activity was measured in terms of direct labor dollars.

e. Which approaches (a through d) would be recommended?

f. Was the factory overhead overapplied or underapplied in parts (c) and (d)? By what amounts?

Exercise 20-2
Determining product costs for a job

The O'Drobinak Manufacturing Company uses the job order costing method. On April 1, there were no incomplete jobs on hand. During April, the following facts related to production:

Direct materials.	$50,000
Direct labor (1,000 hours)	20,000
Factory overhead incurred.	7,000

Factory overhead is applied using a predetermined rate of 40% of direct labor cost. None of the jobs worked on during April was finished at month-end.

a. Determine the April 30 balance in Work-in-Process Inventory.

(Check figure: $78,000)

b. Determine the over- or underapplied overhead.

Exercise 20-3

Computing the over- or underapplied overhead

During April 1988, Woody's Puppy Chow Company incurred the following manufacturing costs:

Direct materials. $100,000
Direct labor (200,000 hours).   500,000
Factory overhead   275,000

Woody applies overhead to jobs at $1.50 per direct labor hour. Determine the amount of over- or underapplied overhead for April.

(Check figure: $25,000)

Exercise 20-4

Comparing results with and without predetermined factory overhead rates

On January 1, 1988, Moonie Manufacturing accountant Jimmy James makes the following estimates for the year:

	Estimated Factory Overhead	Estimated Direct Labor Hours
Jan.	$ 15,000	1,000
Feb.	20,000	2,000
Mar.	30,000	4,000
.	.	.
.	.	.
.	.	.
July	85,000	15,000
.	.	.
.	.	.
.	.	.
Dec.	25,000	3,000
For the year	$375,000	50,000

During the months of February and July, Moonie experiences the following:

	February	July
Actual factory overhead	$21,000	$81,000
Jobs worked on	2	4
Direct labor hours		
Job: .	.	.
.	.	.
.	.	.
6	1,200	—
7	600	—
.	.	.
.	.	.
.	.	.
21	—	6,000
22	—	4,000
23	—	5,000
24	—	1,000

Jobs 6–7 and 21–24 were the only jobs worked on during February and July, respectively.
a. Determine the overhead that would probably be assigned to job 6 in February and job 21 in July if Moonie was *not* using a predetermined factory overhead rate.
b. Answer part (a) again, this time assuming that Moonie *does* employ a predetermined factory overhead rate.
c. Determine the overapplied or underapplied factory overhead in February and in July.

(Check figure: July = $39,000)

Exercise 20-5
Working backward to original estimate

The Wilkie Company employs a job order costing system and uses a predetermined factory overhead rate of 125% of direct labor dollars. At the end of 1988, Wilkie's actual overhead incurred was $495,000, which resulted in $30,000 overapplied.
a. How much was spent by Wilkie in 1988 for direct labor?

(Check figure: $420,000)

b. If the estimated labor for the year had been $400,000, what would have been the estimated factory overhead costs for 1988, which was used to get the predetermined factory overhead rate on January 1, 1988?

Exercise 20-6
Allocating product costs among jobs

The Margie Wynn Advertising Agency uses a job order costing system for its different customer accounts. During January, the first month of operation, the agency accepted assignments from two customers, C. Huck and Melody Tune. The following costs were incurred:

Materials	$ 6,000
Labor	8,000
Overhead.	13,000

Wynn decided to employ a predetermined overhead rate of 200% of labor cost. The materials used were split evenly between the two jobs, but the labor was distributed two-thirds to the C. Huck job and one-third to the Melody Tune job.
    Determine the costs assigned to each job for January.

(Check figure: Huck = $19,000)

Exercise 20-7
Analyzing factory overhead incurred and applied

The Talavera Company uses a predetermined overhead rate for product costing purposes of $2.50 per machine hour. The following facts relate to 1988:

Direct labor hours	20,000
Machine hours	18,000
Factory overhead incurred.	$42,000

At year-end, Talavera had the following balances in the production accounts:

Raw Materials, Inventory	$20,000
Work-in-Process Inventory	30,000
Finished Goods Inventory	50,000
Cost of Goods Sold Expense	70,000

a. Determine the over- or underapplied overhead for 1988.

(Check figure: $3,000)

b. Show the general ledger account for Factory Overhead Incurred and Applied.
c. Prepare the closing entry required if the over- or underapplied overhead is closed entirely to Cost of Goods Sold Expense.
d. Prepare the closing entry if the over- or underapplied overhead is allocated to the appropriate production accounts.

PROBLEMS
Set A

Problem A20-1
Journal entries for job order costing

The Stones Corporation is a manufacturer that uses the job order costing method of product costing. At the beginning of 1988, it had the following general ledger balances related to production:

Raw Materials Inventory			Work-in-Process Inventory		
1988			1988		
1/1	200,000		1/1	500,000	

Finished Goods Inventory		
1988		
1/1	350,000	

The transactions for January 1988 are given below:
a. Raw materials purchased, $800,000.
b. Indirect materials used in production, $25,000.
c. Direct materials used in production, $750,000.
d. Direct labor employed, $1,000,000 (200,000 hours).
e. Additional factory overhead incurred:

Indirect labor	$150,000
Utilities	20,000
Property taxes	10,000
Prepaid insurance expired	5,000

f. Factory overhead applied, $1.25 per direct labor hour.
g. Cost of jobs completed, $2,100,000.
h. Cost of jobs sold, $1,900,000.
i. Sales revenue from jobs sold during January, $3,000,000.

Required
1. Prepare the proper journal entry for each transaction given above.
2. Determine the January 31 balance in each of the three inventory accounts.

(Check figure: Work-in-process = $400,000)

Problem A20-2
Completing the T-accounts for job order costing

The Banks Publishing Co. publishes yearbooks for high schools and universities, and uses a job order costing system to keep track of the orders from different schools. It keeps its records in T-accounts, which are shown in incomplete form below for 1989:

Raw Materials Inventory

1989		Direct	
1/1	20,000	Materials	130,000
Purchases	_____	Indirect	
		Materials	10,000
12/31	60,000		

Factory Overhead Incurred and Applied

1989			
Indirect			
Materials	_____		
Indirect		Factory	
Labor	100,000	Overhead	
Insurance	_____	Applied	_____
Depreciation	_____		
Other	30,000		
	_____		_____

Work-in-Process Inventory

1989			
1/1	150,000		
Direct			
Materials	_____		
Direct			
Labor	_____		
Factory			
Overhead			
Applied	_____		_____
12/31	120,000		

Salaries Payable

		1989	
Salaries		1/1	16,000
Paid	280,000	Direct	
		Labor	200,000
		Indirect	
		Labor	_____
		12/31	_____

Finished Goods Inventory

1989		Cost of	
1/1	120,000	Goods Sold	360,000
Cost of			
Goods			
Completed	_____		
12/31	_____		

Prepaid Insurance

1989		Insurance	
1/1	6,000	Used	2,000
12/31	4,000		

Cost of Goods Sold Expense

_____			

Accumulated Depreciation

		1989	
		1/1	30,000
		Depreciation	_____
		12/31	34,000

Additional Information

a. All purchases are for cash.

b. Factory overhead is applied at a rate of 70% of direct labor cost.

c. No fixed assets are retired during 1989.

Required   Complete the T-accounts above by filling in the missing blanks.

(Check figure: Cost of goods completed = $500,000)

Problem A20-3

Making journal entries and posting to subsidiary ledger

At the end of 1987 the Wetden Publishing Company was working with potential authors on a single new project, which is expected to be completed in 1988. Wetden makes use of the job costing method of accounting for its projects. The job cost sheet for the current project appears as follows on December 31, 1987:

Job No. _____ 121 _____

Authors _____ Icerman _____

Date Started _____ 1987 _____   Date Completed _____

Date	Direct Materials	Direct Labor		Overhead		Total
		Hours	Cost	Rate	Amount	
1987	$5,000	100	$1,000	$2 per direct labor hour	$200	$6,200

During 1988: (a) two additional projects were begun (jobs 122 and 123) for authors Black and Heck, respectively; (b) jobs 121 and 122 were finished; and (c) job 121 was sold. The following transactions took place during 1988;

Purchase of raw materials			$60,000
Usage of direct materials:			
Job 121		$25,000	
Job 122		20,000	
Job 123		6,000	51,000
Direct labor:			
Job 121 (1,500 hours)		$15,000	
Job 122 (1,450 hours)		15,000	
Job 123 (220 hours)		2,000	32,000
Factory overhead incurred:			
Indirect labor		$ 3,000	
Supplies		1,500	
Rent		1,000	5,500

Additional Information

a. Projects are priced to sell at 40% above their cost.

b. Overhead is assigned to jobs using a predetermined overhead rate, based on the number of direct labor hours worked.

Required

1. Prepare the journal entries to record the transactions for 1988.

2. Prepare job cost sheets for the three jobs.

(Check figure: Job 123 = $8,440)

3. Determine the over- or underapplied overhead for 1988.

(Check figure: $840)

Problem A20-4
Determining ending balances in inventory

The Zvirblis Company produces customized farm equipment, and uses the job order costing method to keep track of its different orders. Zvirblis applies factory overhead to each job (using direct labor hours) based on an overhead rate determined at the beginning of the year. At the end of January 1988, Zvirblis is working on two jobs. The cost information related to these two jobs is as follows:

	Job 105	Job 106
Direct materials	$ 4,000	$5,000
Direct labor (at $5 per hour)	10,000	9,500
Factory overhead applied	7,000	6,650

During February, the following direct costs were incurred to continue work on jobs 105 and 106 and to start 107:

	Job 105	Job 106	Job 107
Direct materials	$3,000	$4,000	$3,000
Direct labor (at $5 per hour)	2,625	4,200	6,300

The factory overhead incurred in February was $10,000.
Jobs 105 and 106 were finished during February, and job 105 was sold for $35,000.
There were no completed jobs in finished goods on February 1.

Required

1. Determine the February 28 balances in (a) Work-in-Process, and (b) Finished Goods; and Cost of Goods Sold for February.
2. Calculate the over- (or under) applied overhead for February.

(Check figure: $812)

Problem A20-5
A variety of miscellaneous questions

The Ware Company uses a job order costing system and had one incomplete job (job 21) on January 1, 1987.

	Job 21
Direct materials	$20,000
Direct labor	16,000
Factory overhead	8,000
	$44,000

The January 1, 1987, balances in Raw Materials and Supplies and in Finished Goods were $8,000 and $37,000, respectively.
On January 1, Ware estimated direct labor and factory overhead for three possible levels of activity for 1987:

	Pessimistic	Most Likely	Optimistic
Expected labor—Hours	60,000	70,000	80,000
—Dollars	$1,020,000	$1,190,000	$1,360,000
Estimated overhead	$ 560,000	$ 630,000	$ 700,000

Overhead is applied based on direct labor hours.

During January, the following costs were incurred:

Purchases:	
Raw materials.	$28,000
Supplies.	5,000
	$33,000
Requisitions:	
Raw materials	
Job 21	$ 3,000
Job 22	16,000
Supplies.	7,000
	$26,000
Production labor:	
Used on job 21 (200 hours)	$ 3,500
Used on job 22 (800 hours)	13,000
Foremen's salaries (120 hours)	1,440
Maintenance (200 hours).	1,500
Security (80 hours).	800
	$20,240
Other factory costs:	
Insurance.	$ 800
Property taxes.	900
Utilities.	450
	$ 2,150

Job 21 was finished in January and sold for $75,000. Job 22 was unfinished on January 31, 1987.

Required   **1.** What was the January 31 balance in Raw Materials and Supplies?
2. If the January 31 balance in Finished Goods was zero, what was the cost of goods sold for January?

(Check figure: $89,300)

3. How much was debited to Work-in-Process during January?
4. What was the under- or overapplied overhead for January 1987?

Set B

Problem B20-1
Preparing journal entries for job order costing

The Custom Couch Company produces luxury couches based on customer specifications. On January 1, 1988, the accountant, Jamie Lou, determines the following balances in the company's inventories:

Raw materials inventory	$425,000
Work-in-process inventory.	820,000
Finished goods inventory.	300,000

Required | For each transaction below:
1. Make the required journal entry.
2. Indicate the subsidiary ledger(s) and source document(s) that would be affected by the transaction.
3. Determine the new inventory balances on January 31.

Transactions

a. Purchased materials in the amount of $1,000,000.
b. Materials used in production were direct materials, $700,000; and indirect materials, $100,000.
c. Labor used in production amounted to $300,000 for direct labor, and $175,000 for indirect labor.
d. Miscellaneous items included:

Utilities	$18,000
Insurance.	7,000
Depreciation.	6,500

e. Factory overhead is applied at a rate of 80% of direct labor cost.
f. The jobs completed totaled $1,650,000.
g. The sales revenue for January was $3,000,000, and the cost of jobs sold was $1,700,000.

Problem B20-2
Completing T-accounts

The Bailey Company, which employs the job order costing method of accounting for its inventories, had the following incomplete general ledger accounts at the end of 1989:

Raw Materials Inventory

1989		Materials	
1/1	60,000	Materials	
Purchases	210,000	Used	201,000
12/31	———		

Work-in-Process Inventory

1989		Completed and	
1/1	96,000	Transferred	———
Direct Mat.	———		
Direct Labor	264,000		
Fac. Over.			
Applied	———		
12/31	———		

Finished Goods Inventory

1989		Sold	
1/1	———	Sold	———
Completed	600,000		
12/31	75,000		

Cost of Goods Sold Expense

Sold	645,000	

Accounts Payable

Paid	216,000	1989	
		1/1	6,000
		Purchases	210,000
		12/31	———

Factory Overhead Incurred and Applied

Ind. Labor	———	Applied	———
Insur.	90,000		
Deprec.	51,000		
Misc.	48,000		
	———		
	294,000		———

(Continued)

Salaries Payable

Paid	363,000	1989	
		1/1	3,000
		Dir. Labor	
		Accrued	_____
		Ind. Labor	
		Accrued	105,000
		12/31	_____

Additional Information

a. All purchases are made on account, and no returns were made to the supplier.

b. All raw materials are used directly in production.

c. Factory overhead was predicted to be $300,000 for 1989. The predetermined overhead rate was computed using direct labor hours for activity. The direct labor hours were estimated as 60,000 for the year. The actual direct labor hours for 1989 were 66,000.

Complete the T-accounts above by filling in the missing blanks.

Required

(Check figure: Factory overhead applied = $330,000)

Problem B20-3

Preparing journal entries and posting to subsidiary ledger

The LeRoy Roswell Company accepts special orders from customers to acquire and renovate classic cars. January 1988 was the first month of operation, and at month-end, one job (no. 1) was in work-in-process inventory. Its job cost sheet appeared as follows:

Job No. _____1_____

Customer _____Keith Watson_____

Date Started _____1/13/88_____   Date Completed _____

			Overhead		
Date	Direct Materials	Direct Labor	Rate	Amount	Total
Jan.	$3,200	$2,100	60% of direct labor	$1,260	$6,560

During February, $60,000 of materials were bought on account, and on February 7 two additional orders were accepted (Job nos. 2 and 3) from Mr. Watson. The following costs were incurred on the three jobs:

Direct materials:
Job 1 . . . . $10,000
Job 2   18,000
Job 3 . . . .   3,000 $31,000

Direct labor:
Job 1	$12,000	
Job 2	30,000	
Job 3	4,500	$46,500
Actual factory overhead:		
Indirect labor	$ 8,000	
Supplies	3,000	
Utilities	3,000	
Insurance	2,000	
Rent	6,000	22,000

Job no. 1 was completed and sold on February 14. Job no. 2 was completed on February 18. Sales are made at a markup of 80% above cost.

Overhead is assigned to jobs with a predetermined overhead rate, using direct labor costs as the measure of activity.

Required

1. Prepare the journal entries to record the transactions for February.
2. Prepare job cost sheets for the three jobs.

(Check figure: Job no. 3 = $10,200)

3. Prepare a factory overhead cost sheet for the renovation department.
4. Determine the over- or underapplied overhead for February.

(Check figure: $5,900)

Problem B20-4

Determining ending balances in inventory

Clyde Smith is in the home construction business and is usually working on several custom homes at one time. On July 1, 1989, Clyde was working on homes for Ray Moody and Ralph Trottier. The costs assigned to these homes on July 1 were as follows:

	Client	
	Moody	**Trottier**
Direct materials	$52,000	$61,000
Direct labor — Hours	2,000	4,200
— Dollars	$16,000	$34,650
Factory overhead applied as a percentage of direct labor costs.	$ 3,360	$ 7,277

During July, Clyde completed the Moody home, and started work on a new home for Mark Pace. The costs incurred during July were:

	Client		
	Moody	**Trottier**	**Pace**
Direct materials.	$10,000	$25,000	$20,000
Direct labor — Hours	200	1,000	800
— Dollars	$15,700	$ 8,200	$ 8,000

The factory overhead incurred during the month was $2,800.

Required

1. Determine the cost of goods sold expense for July (assume that Clyde is recognizing all revenues and expenses at completion).

(Check figure: $100,497)

2. Determine the balances in Work-in-Process and in Finished Goods on July 31.
3. Calculate the over- or underapplied overhead for July.

Problem B20-5

A variety of miscellaneous questions

Tammy Haskins runs a small CPA firm and has several clients at any one time. She determines her fee for each client by taking a 25% markup, on top of the costs of materials, direct labor, and office overhead applied. Tammy applies overhead to jobs based on direct labor hours.

On January 1, 1988, Tammy predicted that the office overhead would be $22,750 for the year. She also figured that the direct labor hours would be 2,600 ($31,200).

On December 1, 1988, Tammy's firm had only one client, and the costs associated with that client were as follows:

	T. Towne
Materials	$ 250
Direct labor	1,900
Office overhead applied	1,400
	$3,550

During December, two new clients were found, and the following costs were incurred:

Materials purchased	$ 500
Materials used:	
On Towne job	$ 50
On Fonte job	150
On Christe job	95
	$ 295
Labor:	
Secretary (160 hours)	$ 400
Accountants	
Used on Towne job (20 hours)	250
Used on Fonte job (120 hours)	1,450
Used on Christe job (85 hours)	1,000
Clean-up crew (40 hours)	100
	$3,200
Other costs:	
Rent	$ 500
Insurance	100
Utilities	150
	$ 750

The Towne job was completed and billed. The Fonte and Christe jobs were incomplete on December 31. The direct labor and office overhead for the first 11 months of 1988 were $28,000 (2,300 hours) and $20,000, respectively.

Required

1. Determine how much was debited to Work (or Jobs)-in-Process during December.
2. What was the balance in Work-in-Process on December 31?
3. What was the over- or underapplied overhead for December? For the entire year?

(Check figure: $4,489)

4. What was the sales revenue for Tammy Haskins for December?

Chapter 21

Product Costing Methods
Part 2: Process Costing

After you have completed studying this chapter, you should be able to:

- Understand job order costing and process costing, and what makes them different

- Explain what is meant by an "equivalent whole unit" and apply this concept to the different types of product costs

- Organize a process costing problem into its three basic steps and understand the relationship of each step to the other

- Explain the difference between the FIFO and weighted average methods of product costing

- Prepare a production report and a summary of costs report using the FIFO method of product costing

- Prepare a production report and a summary of costs report with the weighted average method of product costing

We just covered in detail *job order costing,* which is used to account for the costs of a manufactured product whenever:

1. There are only a small number of units or batches of units being produced.

2. Each unit or batch is probably being produced according to customer specifications.

3. Each unit or batch is easily distinguishable from any other unit or batch.

It was necessary for us to accumulate costs by job and to keep the costs of one job separate from the costs of each other job.

In this chapter we will look in detail at *process costing,* which you'll quickly realize is quite different from job order costing. In process costing it is not necessary for us to identify individual source documents (such as work tickets and materials requisitions) with specific jobs; nor will we need to maintain job cost sheets. In essence, it is not necessary to calculate exactly the cost of each unit individually—because all the units we're working on will be basically the same, and the cost of one unit will be identical to the cost of every other unit produced.

THE PROCESS COSTING METHOD

Process costing is used to determine the cost of units that:

1. Are produced continuously in large batches; and

2. Are indistinguishable from one another.

Industries using process costing

The "process" of manufacturing units like these comprises a sequence of several manufacturing steps, each step discernible from the others. For instance, juice in a citrus processing plant first passes through a process in which the fruit is squeezed, the juice is strained for seeds and pulp, and the juice is chilled. In the next process the juice is bottled in presterilized containers, which are sealed or capped. Finally, the bottles are packaged in boxes or cartons, and are sent to finished goods to await sale. Process costing is also used to account for "processed" products such as cement, paint, oil products, chemicals, flour, and pharmaceuticals.

Through process costing, not only can we determine the costs to be assigned to finished units, we can also determine the costs to be assigned at each manufacturing step for partially completed units. But, as you may well imagine, we don't use job order costing to determine the cost to be assigned to 1 gallon of orange juice or to 1 bottle of champagne. We don't try to determine the exact cost of any one unit produced in a process. Because all units are identical in a process manufacturing situation, it would be pointless to even try to distinguish the cost of one unit from any other unit.

What quantity should we use to get the cost per unit?

Instead, what we do in process costing is to: (1) determine the total production costs for an entire period; (2) determine the number of units produced during that period; and (3) divide the total costs by the units in production to get a cost per unit—which will be the same cost for each unit produced during that period. The key to understanding and using process costing is to realize exactly what we mean by the number of units produced.

Let's look first at an unrealistic but simple example of process costing. Then we will introduce some considerations that will make it more realistic, but less simple.

EXAMPLE 21-1

A very simple example

TRUVILLION COMPANY

The Truvillion Company produces an item that is processed through only one manufacturing stage. At the end of that one process the units are complete and are transferred to finished goods. During August, 80,000 units were started and completed, and $80,000 of production costs were incurred. There were no beginning or ending inventories of work-in-process for the month. The cost per unit for Truvillion in August is simply:

$$\text{Cost per unit} = \$80,000 \div 80,000 \text{ units} = \$1.00$$

What made Example 21-1 so simple is that there were no beginning and no ending inventories of work-in-process. In other words, all the units that were started during the period were also completed by the end of the period. Now, let's assume that not all the units are completed by the end of the period. That means there will be an ending inventory of work-in-process.

EXAMPLE 21-2

A little tougher example

TRUVILLION COMPANY

Assume for the Truvillion Company that: (1) there was no beginning inventory of work-in-process; (2) 80,000 units were started during August; (3) 76,000 units were completed by the end of the month; (4) the 4,000 incomplete units were left one-half completed; and (5) the production costs during the month were $78,000, and they were incurred evenly throughout the manufacturing process.

We don't use units started

Now, how do we calculate the cost per unit?

Do we divide the production costs of $78,000 by the 80,000 units started? No, because this would assign the same amount of cost to each of the units that are completed as would be assigned to each of the units that are only one-half completed.

We don't use units completed

Do we divide the $78,000 by the 76,000 units that were completed? No, because the $78,000 of production costs also helped to process the 4,000 units. Therefore, some of the costs should be assigned to the 4,000 units and not just to the 76,000 units.

We do use equivalent whole units

Here is the key—we have to give some consideration to the partially finished units—but not as much as to the completely finished units. We have to divide the $78,000 by the finished units plus some portion of the unfinished units. If the 4,000 units were exactly half-finished at the end of the period, then the work—and the costs—that went into them is equivalent to the work and costs that go into 2,000 finished units.

Thus, if we add together the finished units and the equivalent number of finished units that are still in process, we can spread the total costs over the "appropriate quantity" of units produced—the equivalent whole units. Here's how:

$$\begin{array}{c}\text{76,000 completed}\\\text{units}\end{array} + \left(\begin{array}{c}\text{4,000 in}\\\text{process}\end{array} \times \tfrac{1}{2} \text{ complete}\right) = \begin{array}{c}\text{78,000 equivalent}\\\text{whole units}\end{array}$$

$$\begin{array}{c}\text{Cost per}\\\text{unit}\end{array} = \$78,000 \div \begin{array}{c}\text{78,000 equivalent}\\\text{whole units}\end{array} = \begin{array}{c}\$1.00 \text{ per equivalent}\\\text{whole unit}\end{array}$$

Equivalent whole units is a new concept, which we must understand in order to learn the process costing method.

Equivalent Whole Units

The 80,000 units can be represented graphically, as shown:

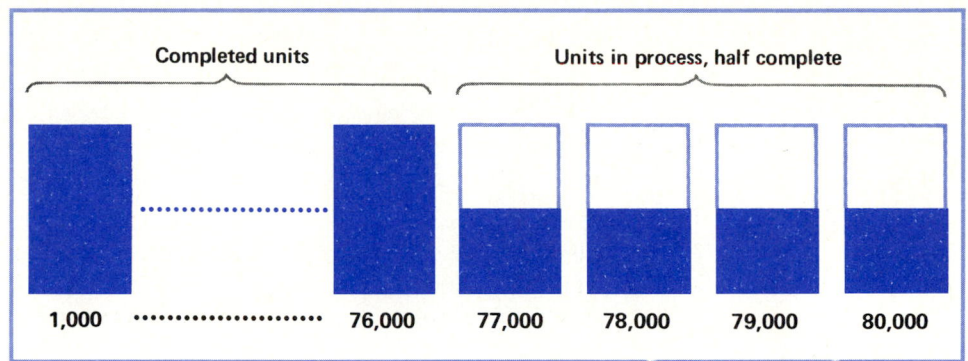

The first 76,000 units are completed and are represented as fully shaded boxes. The 4,000 half-complete units are represented by boxes that are half-shaded.

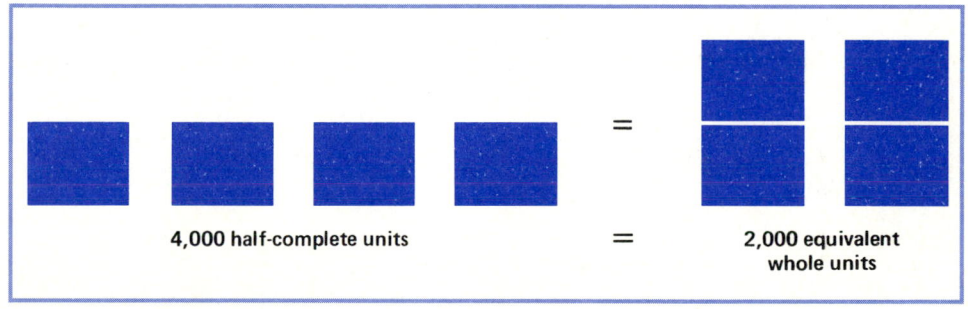

The 4,000 half-shaded boxes are the equivalent of 2,000 fully shaded boxes. There is a total of 78,000 shaded boxes—76,000 fully shaded and 4,000 half-shaded. The 78,000 boxes represent 78,000 equivalent whole units.

A Full Dosage of Costs

Equivalent units: A full dosage of costs

A good way to think of an equivalent whole unit is in terms of a "full dosage of costs." A completed unit requires 100% of all the costs needed to make it — saying it another way, a full dosage of cost must be added or incurred to make a whole unit. In the preceding example full dosages have been added to each of the 76,000 units to complete them. The 4,000 half-completed units each has only one-half of a full dosage of cost. If these 4,000 half-dosages of costs had been incurred instead to make only completed units, then the 4,000 half-dosages of costs would be equivalent to 2,000 full dosages of costs. The combination of 76,000 full dosages and 4,000 half-dosages produces 78,000 equivalent full dosages — or 78,000 equivalent whole units.

In Example 21-2, we assumed for simplicity that all production costs (direct materials, direct labor, and factory overhead) were incurred evenly throughout the production process. In the next example and in most problems, this will be assumed for direct labor and factory overhead (conversion costs) but not for direct materials. Direct materials are usually assumed to be added in a lump sum rather than in a continuous manner throughout production.

Basic Steps in the Process Costing Method

From these simple examples we have presented some basic ideas about how to determine the cost of units produced in a process. Now we will look in much greater detail at the accounting procedures involved in process costing. The basic steps are:

Three basic steps to process costing

1. *Tracing the physical flow* In this step we determine two things: the number of units completed during the period and the number of incomplete units still in production at the end of the period (the ending inventory).

2. *Preparing the production report* Based on the completed units and the ending inventory of work-in-process, which we determined in Step 1, we next calculate three things within the production report: the equivalent whole units, the total costs to account for, and the cost per equivalent whole unit.

3. *Preparing the summary of costs report* After the production report has been completed, we need to distribute the total costs to account for between these two groups of units: (1) the completed units; and (2) the units in ending inventory of work-in-process. We show this distribution in the *summary of costs report.*

The Comprehensive Illustration

The following example will demonstrate the three steps we have just discussed.

EXAMPLE 21-3

SPURRIER BALL COMPANY

The Spurrier Ball Company produces footballs that pass through two processing departments before they are completed. In the first department cowhide is cut and sewn into a football. In the second department, the balls are pumped with air and boxed. The steps in this production process are represented by the following diagram:

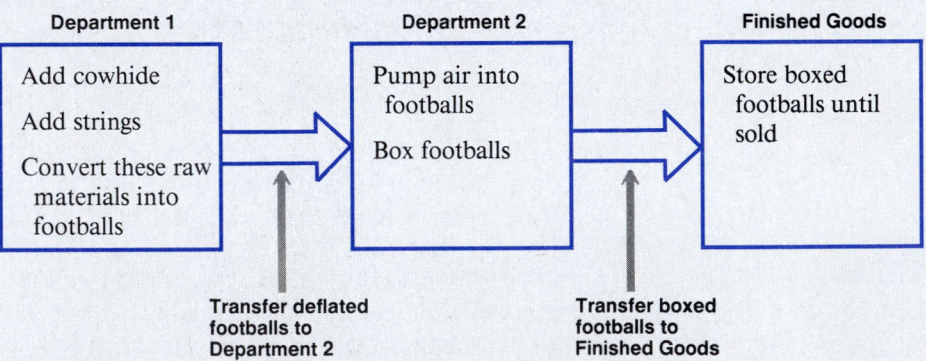

The flow of costs associated with these footballs is represented by the progression of T-accounts at the top of page 829.

Information concerning Department 1 is presented at this point. Additional information concerning Department 2 will be provided after the discussion of Department 1 is completed.

There are no beginning inventories in this Example

Two different raw materials are needed in Department 1. Cowhide is added at the beginning, and the strings are added when the work required on the footballs is one-half complete. Conversion costs (direct labor plus factory overhead) are incurred evenly throughout production.

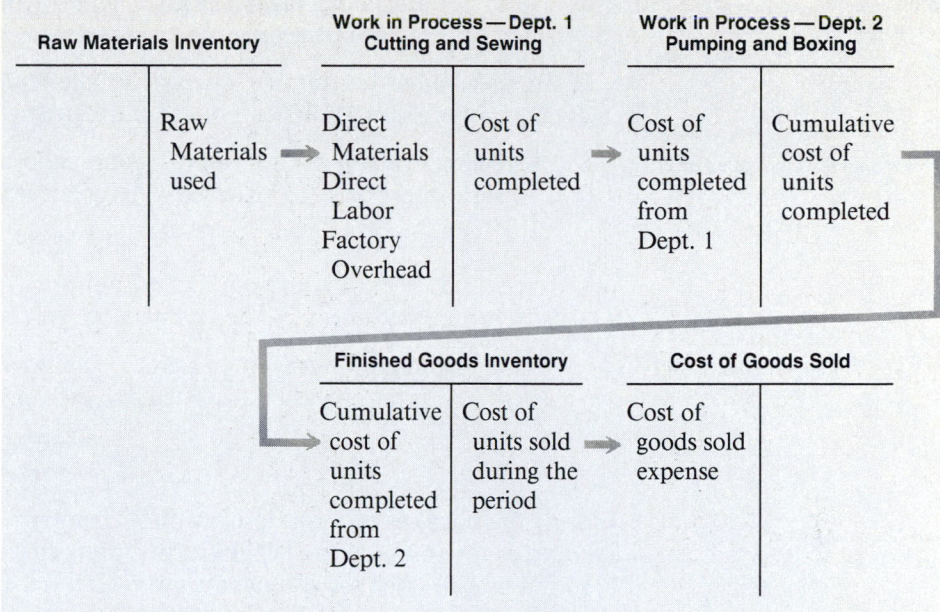

On August 1 there were no unfinished footballs in work-in-process. During August, 40,000 footballs were started. On August 31, there was an ending inventory of 20,000 footballs, each one exactly three-quarters complete.

The costs incurred during the month of August are as follows:

Costs incurred during August:
Cowhide	$120,000
Strings	20,000
Conversion costs.	148,750
Total costs to account for	$288,750

As Example 21-3 indicates, there are no incomplete footballs in process in Department 1 on August 1. For simplicity we are making this assumption for our initial set of exhibits. At a later point we will introduce a beginning inventory and point out just how it complicates matters.

Basic Steps for Department 1 — Assuming No Beginning Inventory

We will now go through the three basic steps for Spurrier Ball Company. The first step is to trace the physical flow.

STEP 1: Tracing the Physical Flow

We need the completed units and the ending inventory for the production report

At this step, remember, we determine two things: (1) the number of units completed during the period, and (2) at the end of the period, the number of units remaining in the ending work-in-process inventory. This information is necessary for the production report. In many process costing problems only one of these two quantities is known while the other must be determined. In most situations, we know the beginning inventory and we know the number of units that were started. The addition of these two represents the "total units to account for" in production.

$$\underset{\text{work-in-process}}{\text{Beginning inventory in}} + \underset{\text{started}}{\text{units}} = \underset{\text{account for}}{\text{total units to}}$$

If we also know the number of units in the ending work-in-process, we can calculate the number of units completed during the period, as follows:

Finding the completed units

$$\underset{\text{work-in-process}}{\text{Beginning inventory in}} + \underset{\text{started}}{\text{units}} = \underset{\text{account for}}{\text{total units to}} - \underset{\text{in work-in-process}}{\text{ending inventory}}$$

$$= \textbf{units completed}$$

Conversely, if we know the number of units completed we can determine the number of unfinished units, in the ending work-in-process:

Finding the number of incomplete units

$$\underset{\text{work-in-process}}{\text{Beginning inventory in}} + \underset{\text{started}}{\text{units}} = \underset{\text{account for}}{\text{total units to}} - \underset{\text{completed}}{\text{units}}$$

$$= \underset{\text{work-in-process}}{\text{ending inventory in}}$$

Tracing the physical flow for Spurrier Ball Company will be easy because we have assumed — for now — a zero beginning inventory in work-in-process in Department 1. We have been given the ending inventory for work-in-process, so what we need to calculate is the number of units that were completed during August. They are calculated as follows:

The completed footballs are 20,000

Beginning inventory, work-in-process (Department 1)	0 footballs
Add: Units started	40,000 footballs
Total to account for	40,000 footballs
Less: Ending inventory, work-in-process (Department 1)	20,000 footballs
Units completed and transferred to Department 2.	20,000 footballs

The 20,000 footballs that are finished in Department 1 and the ending inventory of 20,000 unfinished footballs now become the basis for calculations in the production report, enabling us to determine the number of equivalent whole units and the cost per equivalent whole unit.

STEP 2: Preparing the Production Report

The production report — part 1

Once the completed units and the units in the ending inventory of work-in-process have been determined, then we prepare the ***production report.*** The purpose of the production report is for us to calculate a cost per equivalent whole unit for each different product cost — direct materials, direct labor, and factory overhead. In the first part of the production report we will calculate the equivalent whole units (also called equivalent units).

Part 2

In the second part of the production report, we have to accumulate all the costs that are associated with the production of the period; this accumulation is referred to as the "total costs to account for." In most situations the ***total costs to account for*** will be found by adding together the costs of beginning inventory and the costs incurred during the period.

Part 3

In the third part of the production report, we will divide the total costs to account for by the equivalent whole units; the result is the ***cost per equivalent whole unit (CPEWU).***

EXHIBIT 21-1   Production Report for Department 1: No Beginning Inventories.
Department 1's production report calculates the CPEWU for each product cost. The total CPEWU—when there are no beginning inventories—is $7.75.

Product Cost	(1) Units Started and Completed	(2) Ending Inventory WIP	(3) Fraction Completed	(4) Equivalent Whole Units	(5) Total Costs to Account for	(6) Cost per Equivalent Whole Unit
Cowhide	20,000	20,000	1	40,000	$120,000	$3.00
Strings	20,000	20,000	1	40,000	20,000	.50
Conversion costs	20,000	20,000	$\frac{3}{4}$	35,000	148,750	4.25
					$288,750	$7.75

All the units started were also completed

The production report for Department 1 is provided in Exhibit 21-1. The first column indicates the number of units that were completed during August (20,000). But a close look at column 1 shows that it is labeled "Units Started and Completed," and not merely "Completed." Since there were no incomplete footballs in inventory on August 1, all the units that were completed had to have been started during August. The reason we use the more specific term "Units Started and Completed" will become clear when we discuss the FIFO and weighted average methods. For now don't be overly concerned.

In the second column of Exhibit 21-1, we've placed the number of footballs that are still in process on August 31 (20,000). Column 3 is the fraction of a full dosage of cost that has been added to the 20,000 footballs by August 31. To get column 4 we multiply column 2 by column 3 and add that result to column 1.

Remember, 40,000 units were started; and column 1 represents the 20,000 units from this batch that were completed during August. We can see and count every one of the footballs (and even throw a few passes if they weren't still deflated). Column 2 represents the footballs we cannot yet throw or kick because they haven't been completely sewn together. Nevertheless, between columns 1 and 2 we're talking about 40,000 footballs, although some of them (one-half in this example) are unfinished.

Let's now discuss columns 3 and 4 in more detail.

Column 3   The ending inventory of work-in-process is the key to determining equivalent whole units. The fraction of work completed for each cost, shown in column 3, represents the percentage of a full dosage of cost that has been added to the unfinished units (20,000) by the end of a period. To calculate the fraction of completion for the unfinished units, it is necessary to know and compare the following items:

1. How far the unfinished units have progressed in the production process by period-end

2. How and when the product costs are added to the units as they are manufactured (lump sum? sporadically? uniformly?)

The balls are three-quarters complete

For item 1, the ending inventory for Spurrier Ball Company of 20,000 footballs was said to be three-quarters complete—meaning that three-quarters of the total time and attention to be spent on each football has already occurred.

For item 2, we were told that:

1. Cowhide is added in a lump sum (all at one time) at the very beginning of production.

2. Strings (or laces) are added to the footballs in a lump sum, after the footballs have proceeded one-half of the way through the process.

3. Conversion costs are incurred uniformly (evenly) throughout the production process.

Let's take these in reverse order by looking first at the conversion costs — what should be its fraction in column 3?

(a) Conversion Costs   The ending inventory of 20,000 footballs is three-quarters complete. If it takes 4 hours to complete a football in Department 1, then at the end of the day on August 31, 3 of the required 4 hours of work has already taken place on each of the 20,000 footballs — thus the footballs are three-quarters complete. Conversion costs are assumed to occur evenly over the 4 hours of production. Therefore, if the footballs are three-quarters complete, then three-quarters of a full dosage of conversion costs has been incurred.

Since three-quarters of a full dosage of conversion costs has been added, the fraction in column 3 in the production report is $\frac{3}{4}$.

We now have the rule for determining the fraction applicable to ending inventory for conversion costs — it is:

■ *The fraction completed in the production report for conversion costs is always the same as the point in production reached by the units in the ending work-in-process.*

(b) Materials   Most of the time direct materials are not added to the process in a uniform manner, as in the case of the conversion costs. Therefore, the rule for determining the fraction in column 3 has to be different for materials than it is for conversion costs.

Most of the time we will assume that materials are added in a lump sum at a specific point in production. The fraction for column 3 depends on where the materials are added during the production process and how far along in this process the unfinished units are at month-end.

To get an idea of what we mean here, let's look at a time line diagram — which represents the production process going from beginning to end on a horizontal scale.

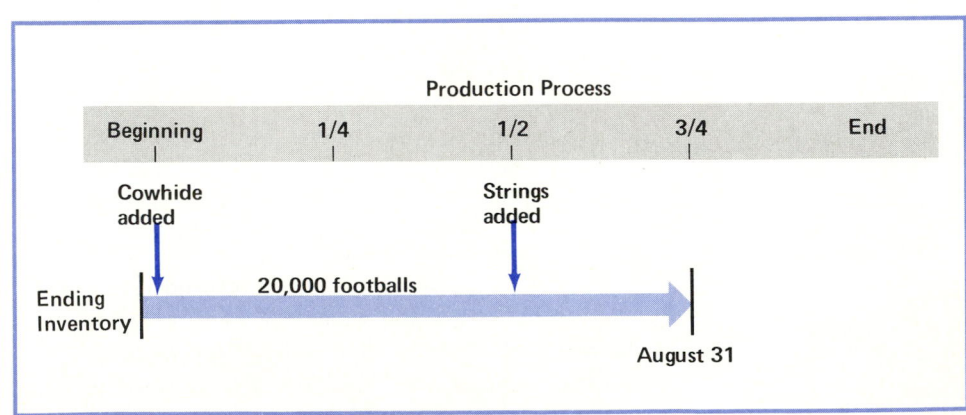

Cowhide gets a full dosage

The cowhide is introduced in the process at the very beginning of production. Since the footballs have progressed to the three-quarter point in production, the cowhide had to have already been added. And the fraction must be 1—a full dosage.

So do the strings

The strings are also added in a lump sum, but at the one-half point in production. The 20,000 footballs have already passed the one-half point, and there is no way to pass by without being strung. Each football, at the three-quarter point, has a full dosage of strings—the fraction is also 1.

Notice in the diagram that the downward arrows for cowhide and strings both intersect with the line representing the 20,000 footballs—where the lines intersect graphically represents that the materials have been added.

From this discussion, we can now generalize about the rules for determining the fraction applicable to the ending inventory for direct materials.

The rule for materials

- *For any materials that are added in a lump sum at a point in production earlier than the point reached by the units in the ending inventory, the fraction is 1.*

- *For any materials that are added in a lump sum after the point in production reached by the units in ending inventory, the fraction is 0.*

Column 1 plus column 2 times column 3

Column 4   Column 4 in Exhibit 21-1—the equivalent whole units—is found by multiplying column 3 by column 2 and adding the result to column 1. (It may be a little more elaborate when there is a beginning inventory involved.) The equivalent whole units for cowhide, strings, and conversion costs were determined as follows:

			Column from Exhibit 21-1		
	(1)	**+**	**[(2) × (3)]**	**=**	**(4)**
Cowhide	20,000	+	(20,000 × 1)	=	40,000 equivalent whole units
Strings	20,000	+	(20,000 × 1)	=	40,000 equivalent whole units
Conversion costs	20,000	+	(20,000 × $\frac{3}{4}$)	=	35,000 equivalent whole units

Total costs to account for: beginning inventory plus incurred

Columns 5 and 6   Column 5 is called the total costs to account for. That means, for each production cost, we add together the costs of the beginning work-in-process and the costs incurred during the entire month. For cowhide the cost of the beginning inventory given in Example 21-3 was zero (because there were no units in beginning inventory) and the costs incurred during August were $120,000. The total, $120,000 in cowhide costs, when divided by the equivalent whole units of 40,000 (column 4), results in a cost per equivalent whole unit of $3.00 (column 6). For the strings, the total costs to account for are incurred entirely in August, $20,000. The resulting *cost per equivalent whole unit* for the strings is $.50 ($20,000 ÷ 40,000).

CPEWU

Finally, the total conversion costs to account for are $148,750. Dividing that cost by the 35,000 equivalent whole units results in a conversion cost per equivalent whole unit of $4.25.

The total of all the total costs to account for in column 5 is the total of all the production costs represented in all the equivalent whole units worked on during the month. Thus, the total of all production costs to account for is $288,750 in our example. The total cost per equivalent whole unit in column 6 is $7.75.

Next, the total costs to account for, $288,750, is to be allocated between the 20,000 units completed and the 20,000 units remaining in work-in-process. We shall show you how to do that in the summary of costs report in Step 3.

EXHIBIT 21-2
Summary of Costs Report for Department 1: No Beginning Inventories.

Of the total costs to account for, $155,000 are transferred to Department 2 and the balance of $133,750 remains in work-in-process—Department 1.

Units completed and transferred to Department 2:		
20,000 × $7.75		$155,000*
Ending inventory—work-in-process:		
Cowhide 20,000 × 1 × $3.00	$60,000†	
Strings 20,000 × 1 × $ .50	10,000†	
Con. costs 20,000 × ¾ × $4.25	63,750†	133,750
		$288,750‡

* From Exhibit 21-1, column 1 × the sum of column 6.
† From Exhibit 21-1, column 2 × column 3 × column 6.
‡ This total agrees with the total in column 5 of Exhibit 21-1.

STEP 3: Summary of Costs Report

The purpose of the ***summary of costs report*** is to determine what part of the total costs to account for are assigned to the units completed and transferred to Department 2 and what part of these costs remain in Department 1, with the ending work-in-process. The number of completed units is multiplied by the combined costs per equivalent whole unit (this is simplified when there is no beginning inventory) for direct materials, direct labor, and factory overhead. We transfer this amount, with the units completed, to the next production department if there are several stages in production, or to finished goods inventory if the units have no additional processing to be performed. The cost of the ending inventory of work-in-process is calculated by multiplying the equivalent whole units that are still in process by the appropriate cost per equivalent unit.

This report (Exhibit 21-2) indicates that $155,000 is assigned to the completed units, which, upon transfer to Department 2, requires the following journal entry:

The transfer to Department 2

Work-in-Process Inventory—Department 2 155,000
    Work-in-Process Inventory—Department 1   155,000
Cost of completed units transferred from Department 1 to Department 2.

If Department 1 had been the only production department, then the 20,000 units would be transferred to finished goods and the debit in the entry above would be to Finished Goods Inventory rather than to Work-in-Process—Department 2.

Exhibit 21-2 also shows that the cost of the 20,000 unfinished footballs in Department 1 is $133,750 at the end of August. The $155,000 plus the $133,750 equal $288,750—which agrees with the total costs to account for at the bottom of column 5 in the production report.

The Illustration Complicated—A Beginning Inventory for Department 1

EXAMPLE 21-4

Up to here we have simplified the analysis by assuming that there was no beginning inventory in work-in-process. Now we will introduce a beginning inventory and see how the analysis is affected. The new facts are given in Example 21-4.

SPURRIER BALL COMPANY—DEPARTMENT 1: WITH A BEGINNING INVENTORY

Add to the basic facts given in Example 21-3 that Spurrier Ball Company now has a beginning inventory of 10,000 footballs, one-fifth complete. The cost of this inventory on August 1 is as follows:

Here's the beginning inventory

> Cost of 10,000 footballs
> ($\frac{1}{3}$ complete), Aug. 1:
>> Cowhide $30,000
>> Strings.   0
>> Conversion costs   7,570
>> $37,570

One other way in which the facts in Example 21-4 are different from Example 21-3 is that the costs incurred during August for Department 1 are now assumed to be:

The costs incurred are a little different from Example 21-3

> Costs incurred during Aug.:
>> Cowhide $120,000
>> Strings   25,000
>> Conversion costs   172,430
>> $317,430

The number of footballs started during August is still 40,000, and the inventory of work-in-process on August 31 is still 20,000 footballs, three-fourths complete.

Once again we will go through the three basic steps for Department 1 for Spurrier Ball Company. This time, however, some of the mechanics will be a little more complicated, due to the 10,000 footballs in beginning inventory.

STEP 1: Tracing the Physical Flow

In this example, there are now 10,000 footballs in beginning inventory, in addition to the 40,000 footballs that were started. Because of these 10,000 additional footballs, the number completed is now 30,000, instead of the 20,000 calculated in the previous example.

> Beginning inventory, Department 1. . . . . 10,000 footballs — 10,000 additional footballs
> Add: Units started . . . . 40,000 footballs
> Total to account for . . . . 50,000 footballs — includes 10,000 additional footballs
> Less: Ending inventory, Department 1 . . . . 20,000 footballs
> Units completed and transferred to Department 2 . . . . 30,000 footballs — includes 10,000 additional footballs

We logically assume that the beginning inventory is completed first

An important assumption that we make concerning the 10,000 footballs not yet finished in Department 1 on August 1 is that these footballs are the first 10,000 (of the total of 30,000) to be completed in August. Only after we complete the beginning inventory do we complete those units that we start from scratch during August. The schedule above indicates that 30,000 footballs are completed in August. If 10,000 of this total came from the beginning inventory, where must the remaining 20,000 have come from? There can be only one possibility: They were part of the 40,000 units that were started during the month. Therefore, of the 40,000 units that were started, 20,000 were completed and the remaining 20,000 were incomplete at the end of the month. The diagram on page 836 should help to clarify these relationships:

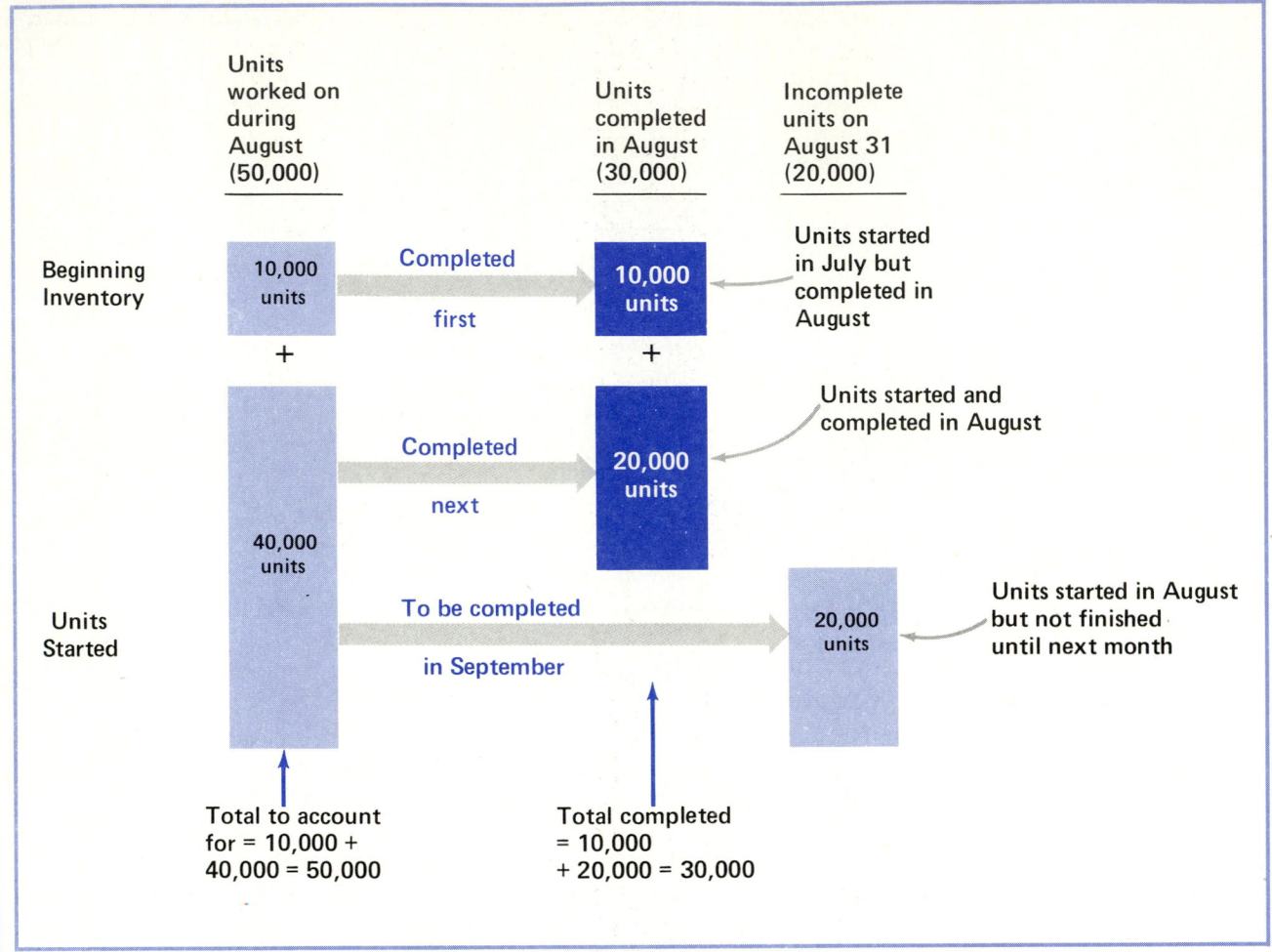

Whenever there is a beginning inventory in work-in-process that is completed in the current period, this means that some of the total work needed to produce these units has already occurred—last period—and the remainder will occur in the current period. In our example, part of the work (and costs related to this work) needed to produce the 10,000 units in the August 1 inventory took place in July, and the remaining work (and related costs) to complete these units took place in August. In other words, some of the 10,000 equivalent units relate to July and some relate to August. The critical questions are:

The problem is how to account for the beginning inventory

How do we account for that part of the 10,000 equivalent units that were produced during July—in the August production report?

What do we do in this month's production report with the costs incurred last period to work on the beginning inventory?

Do we include or exclude the equivalent units and related costs of the beginning inventory in this month's production report?

FIFO and weighted average   ***FIFO versus Weighted Average***   Whether we include or exclude the equivalent units and related costs of the beginning inventory in the August production report depends on the process costing method we use to determine equivalent units. With the FIFO method, we *exclude* them. But with the weighted average method, we *include* them. Let's now see what the basic differences are in these two methods. Later we will look at each method in much greater detail.

First, FIFO

With the ***FIFO method*** we keep separate track of the work that was performed last period on the beginning inventory and the work performed during the current period. The equivalent units of the current period *includes* the work performed to complete the beginning inventory plus any work that was performed on the units that were started this period, and *excludes* the equivalent units that were in the beginning inventory. When the total number of equivalent units are divided into the total costs (which exclude the costs of the beginning inventory), the resulting cost per equivalent whole unit (CPEWU) relates only to the work performed in the current period. As suggested by the name of the method—FIFO—the first units assumed to be completed are the ones in beginning inventory. Their costs are composed of two parts: the cost of the beginning inventory (incurred last period), and the costs incurred this period to complete the beginning inventory. The next group of units to be completed are assumed to come from the units that were started in the current period; their cost is based entirely on the current CPEWU.

Now, weighted average

With the ***weighted average method,*** we combine the units from the beginning inventory with the units that were worked on in the current period, and treat the combination as if all the units were worked on entirely in the current period. We then combine the costs of the beginning inventory with the costs incurred currently and treat them as if they were all incurred in the current period. Therefore, when we calculate the equivalent units, they *include* the equivalent units from the beginning inventory. When this total number of units is divided into the total costs to account for—which *includes* the costs of the beginning inventory—we come up with a weighted average cost per equivalent unit—which is the same for all units, whether they came from beginning inventory or from current production. The resulting cost of completed units that is transferred to the next department is found simply by multiplying the average cost per equivalent unit by all the units that were completed.

This is a different set of facts from Example 21-4; it is for purposes of comparing the two methods only

A graphic comparison of FIFO and weighted average is provided in Figure 21-1. We are assuming that there are 10,000 units, one-half complete in the beginning inventory, representing 5,000 equivalent whole units. In addition, we are assuming that the equivalent units of work performed in the current period were 31,000; that 30,000 equivalent units are completed during the period; and that there are 12,000 units, one-half complete at the end of the period—representing 6,000 equivalent whole units. All of the related costs are shown in the blocks at the bottom of each diagram. Do not worry about how we got the 31,000 equivalent whole units that were worked on—your only concern for now should be how the units and costs are distributed differently under FIFO and weighted average.

Go back now three paragraphs, and reread the discussion concerning each method as you study the diagrams in Figure 21-1 (pages 838–839). The purpose of these diagrams is to give you a general understanding of the differences in the two methods before you study either of them in detail. Certain things have been simplified to facilitate the analysis; so if you later compare the diagrams to the production report or summary of costs report for either method, you may find some minor inconsistencies.

Selection of a Method   You now may be asking yourself: Which method is the better of the two? Which method am I going to have to learn? The answer to the first

FLOW OF EWUs AND COSTS FOR FIFO

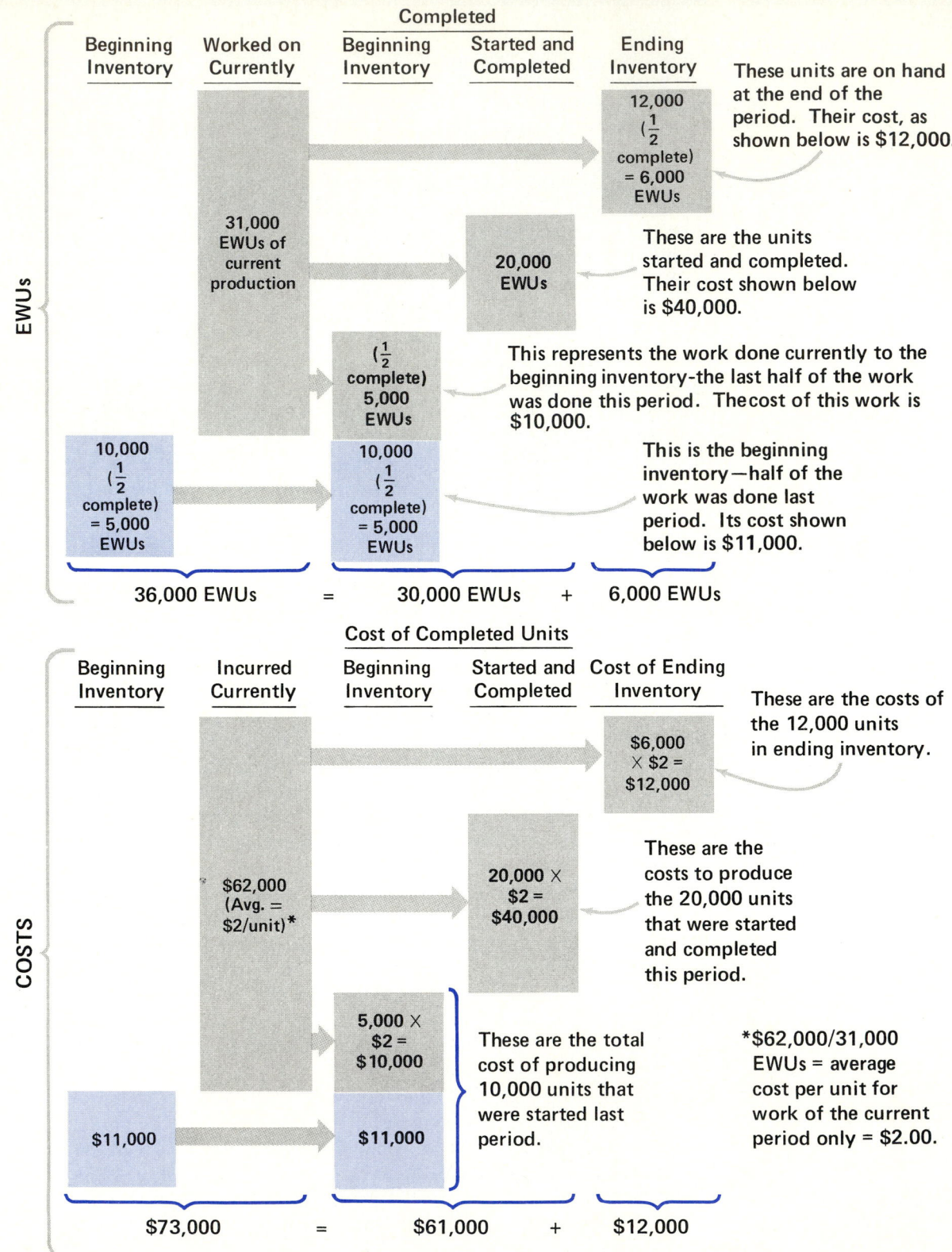

FIGURE 21-1   **A Comparison of FIFO and Weighted Average.**
The top part of each diagram for each method shows the equivalent units that were worked on during each period. Some of what was

FLOW OF EWUs AND COSTS FOR WEIGHTED AVERAGE

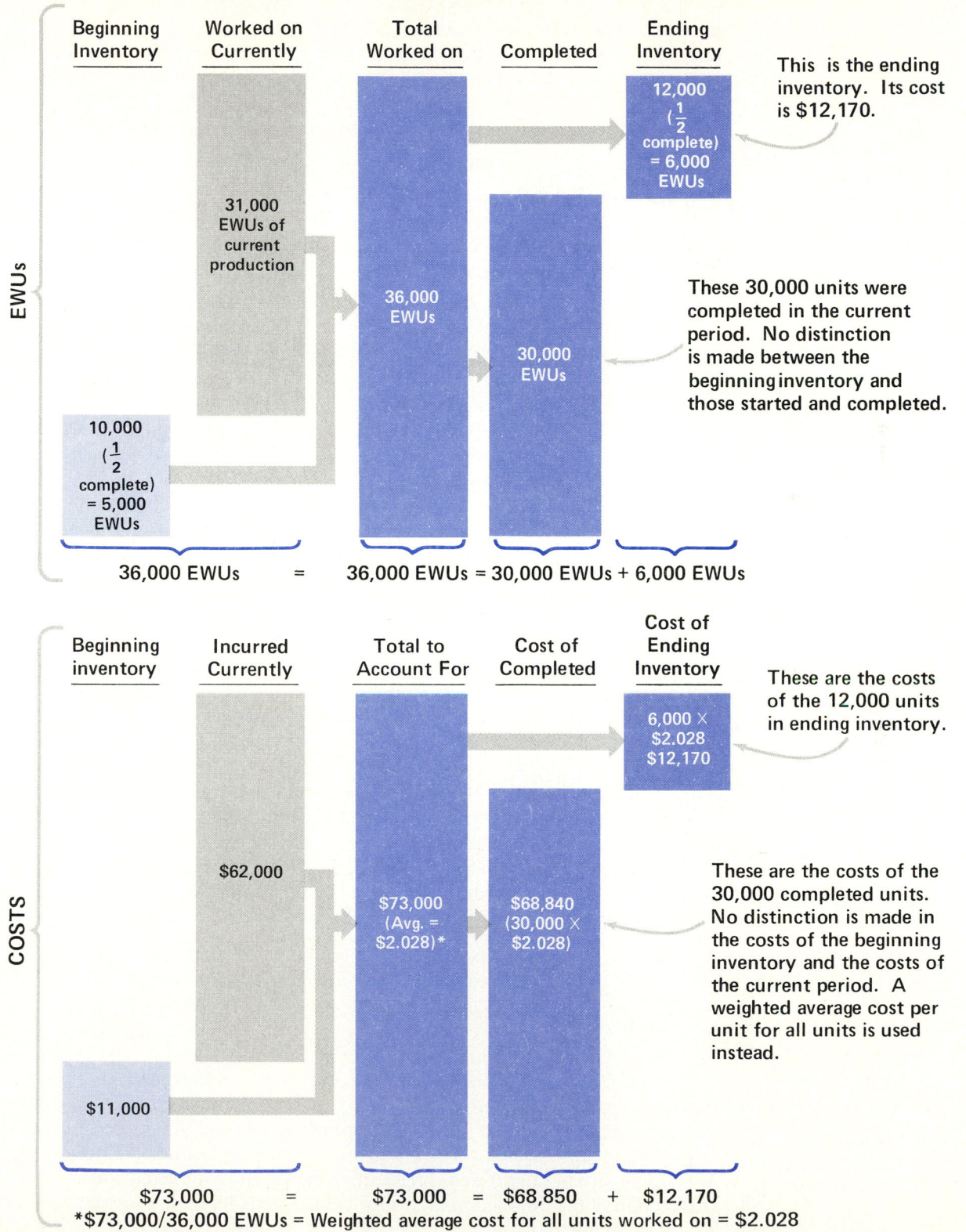

Beginning Inventory	Worked on Currently	Total Worked on	Completed	Ending Inventory

31,000 EWUs of current production

12,000 ($\frac{1}{2}$ complete) = 6,000 EWUs

This is the ending inventory. Its cost is $12,170.

36,000 EWUs

30,000 EWUs

These 30,000 units were completed in the current period. No distinction is made between the beginning inventory and those started and completed.

10,000 ($\frac{1}{2}$ complete) = 5,000 EWUs

36,000 EWUs = 36,000 EWUs = 30,000 EWUs + 6,000 EWUs

EWUs

Beginning inventory	Incurred Currently	Total to Account For	Cost of Completed	Cost of Ending Inventory

$62,000

6,000 × $2.028 $12,170

These are the costs of the 12,000 units in ending inventory.

$73,000 (Avg. = $2.028)*

$68,840 (30,000 × $2.028)

These are the costs of the 30,000 completed units. No distinction is made in the costs of the beginning inventory and the costs of the current period. A weighted average cost per unit for all units is used instead.

$11,000

COSTS

$73,000   = $73,000 = $68,850 + $12,170

*$73,000/36,000 EWUs = Weighted average cost for all units worked on = $2.028

worked on had already been started last period. The bottom part of each diagram shows the total costs to account for (beginning inventory costs plus costs incurred in the current period), and how they are assigned to the completed units and ending inventory.

839

question depends on who you ask; and the answer to the second depends on your teacher. Let's look first at some possible answers to the first question.

Arguments for using FIFO

Proponents of FIFO argue that it is preferable because:

1. It provides for a theoretically preferable matching of costs and revenues.

2. It is a better approximation of the physical flow of goods.

3. It often is the required method on the CPA exam.

On the other hand, proponents of the weighted average method counter with the following reasons for using weighted average:

Arguments for using weighted average

1. It is far easier to learn and to apply in practice.

2. Many more companies use weighted average than use FIFO in the real world.

As we said above, the method that you now learn will probably depend on the method your teacher prefers. *For this reason we are assuming that you will be using one method or the other, but not both.* Based on this assumption, *we will cover each method in detail as if it is the only one you will learn.* This means that if you do cover both methods there will be some redundancy within the two discussions. If you are only covering the FIFO method you will need to read pages 840–850; but if you are only covering weighted average, skip now to page 850 and read through to the end of the chapter.

THE FIFO METHOD OF PROCESS COSTING

Step 1 in the preparation of a process costing solution — tracing the physical flow — was done in the previous section. Remember, there were 30,000 units completed, and 20,000 units were in the ending inventory, three-quarters complete. The remaining facts were given in Example 21-4. We can now go to Step 2.

STEP 2: Preparing the Production Report

The first thing we need to do under the ***FIFO method*** is to distinguish between the units completed from the beginning inventory (they were started in July and finished in August) and the units that were started and completed in August. In most problems like the one we're doing for Spurrier Ball Company, the beginning inventory is given, but the units started and completed must be determined. We can calculate the units started and completed in the following manner:

Separation of completed units into two parts

$$\text{Units started and completed} = \text{total units completed} - \text{beginning inventory}$$

$$= \quad 30{,}000 \quad - \quad 10{,}000$$

$$= \quad 20{,}000$$

Next we must show, in the first column of the production report (units completed), which units were completed from the beginning inventory and which units were started and completed. To make that distinction, we need three columns — (1a) the beginning inventory, (1b) a fraction to apply to the beginning inventory (which we will explain in a moment), and (1c) the units started and completed. For this example, this section of the production report for Department 1 will now appear as shown at top of the facing page.

Column 1b represents the fraction of a full dosage of costs incurred in the current period (in this case during August) to complete the units that were started last period.

Notice that the sum of columns 1a and 1c always equals the total number of completed units

Product Cost	Completed		
	(1a) Beginning Inventory	(1b) Fraction	(1c) Started and Completed
Cowhide	10,000	0	20,000
Strings	10,000	1	20,000
Conversion costs	10,000	$\frac{4}{5}$	20,000
		30,000	

[The fraction can also be expressed in decimal form or as a percentage (e.g., $\frac{4}{5} = 0.80 = 80\%$).] To determine this fraction we need to know the following two bits of information:

Determining the fraction to place in column 1b

1. How far the beginning inventory progressed in the production process by the end of last period.

2. How and when the product costs are added to the units as they are manufactured (lump sum, sporadically, uniformly).

We know from the information given in Example 21-4 that the 10,000 footballs were only one-fifth complete on August 1, so very little work had been done in July. We are also reminded that cowhide is added at the beginning of production; strings are added at the one-half point in production; and conversion costs are incurred evenly throughout production.

Four-fifths of the conversion process is left to complete the beginning inventory

Conversion Costs   During July, one-fifth of the work had already been done to complete the 10,000 footballs. Since conversion costs are incurred evenly throughout production, one-fifth of a full dosage of costs must already have been added to these footballs by the end of July. Therefore, to complete the 10,000 footballs in August, the remaining four-fifths of a full dosage is needed—the fraction in column 1b.

Cowhide was added last period

Cowhide   Since cowhide is added in a lump sum at the beginning of production, and since the 10,000 footballs were one-fifth complete in July, all of the cowhide must have been added to these footballs when they were begun in July. This also means that none of the cowhide needs to be added to the 10,000 footballs in August to complete them. Therefore none of the full dosage was added in August; thus the fraction in column 1b is zero.

The strings were added this period

Strings   If the strings are added only after the footballs get halfway through production, there is no way that the strings could have already been added to the 10,000 footballs in July. The process had not progressed far enough in July for the strings to have been added—the footballs got only one-fifth of the way through the process. Therefore, the full dosage of the cost of strings must have been added in August to complete the footballs; thus the fraction for strings in column 1b is 1.

The Completed Production Report   The completed production report for Department 1 is shown in Exhibit 21-3.

EXHIBIT 21-3   Production Report for Department 1: FIFO.

Now that we have a beginning inventory, we have to use either FIFO or weighted average. The production report in this exhibit uses the FIFO method.

	Units Completed							
Product Cost	(1a) Beginning Inventory WIP	(1b) Fraction Completed	(1c) Started and Completed	(2) Ending Inventory WIP	(3) Fraction Completed	(4) Equivalent Whole Units	(5) Total Costs to Account for	(6) Cost per Equivalent Whole Unit
Cowhide	10,000	0	20,000	20,000	1	40,000	$120,000	$3.00
Strings	10,000	1	20,000	20,000	1	50,000	25,000	.50
Conversion costs	10,000	$\frac{4}{5}$	20,000	20,000	$\frac{3}{4}$	43,000	172,430	4.01
							$317,430	$7.51

Under (1a), (1b), (1c): 30,000

Costs of Beg. Inv. → { 30,000 / 7,570 } Costs incurred during August

$355,000

As you can see, columns 2 and 3 are exactly the same as they were in Exhibit 21-1; and since we discussed these columns in detail in an earlier section, we will not discuss them any further here. Column 4, however, deserves special attention because the calculation of the equivalent units shown in it is affected by the beginning inventory.

We calculate the equivalent units using FIFO in the following manner (using columns 1a–4 of Exhibit 21-3):

There are several parts to Equivalent Whole Units for FIFO.

Product	(1a) Beginning (Inventory	×	Fraction)	+	(1c) Started and Completed	+	(2) Ending (Inventory	×	(3) Fraction)	=	(4) Equivalent Whole Units
Cowhide	(10,000	×	0)	+	20,000	+	(20,000	×	1)	=	40,000
Strings	(10,000	×	1)	+	20,000	+	(20,000	×	1)	=	50,000
Conversion costs	(10,000	×	$\frac{4}{5}$)	+	20,000	+	(20,000	×	$\frac{3}{4}$)	=	43,000

Look now at column 5 in Exhibit 21-3 — the total costs to account for. Remember, we mentioned earlier that these costs are represented by the addition of beginning inventory costs plus costs incurred during the current period. In Exhibit 21-1 there were no beginning inventory costs — because there were no units in beginning inventory. Now, however, we do have a beginning inventory, and its cost is $37,570 ($30,000 for cowhide plus $7,570 for conversion costs). This amount — shown in the lower portion of column 5 — is added to the $317,430 ($120,000 + $25,000 + $172,430) that was incurred during August. The total for column 5 is $355,000.

How to handle costs of beginning inventory

You may be wondering if it makes any difference just how we combine the costs of beginning inventory plus the costs incurred in the current period. In Exhibit 21-3 we added the beginning inventory costs, $37,570, to the sum of the three costs incurred during August, $317,430. Would it have been okay to individually add the corresponding components of the beginning inventory costs and the costs incurred currently? For example, couldn't we have added together the $30,000 and $120,000 for cowhide and merely place the total of $150,000 on the first line under column 5, and then done the same thing for strings and conversion costs? Wouldn't the total for column 5 still be $355,000?

Although the total may still be $355,000, this alternative is not acceptable. Here's why:

The equivalent whole units in column 4 represent equivalent whole units of work performed *in the current period only.* These equivalent whole units exclude the work performed on the 10,000 units in the previous period. Remember, when we determined each fraction (column 1b) to multiply by the beginning inventory of 10,000 footballs, we said that it represented the fraction of a full dosage of work that was incurred *in the current period.* That fraction of a full dosage representing work of *the previous period* was included in that period and therefore is not included in the current month's production report.

Because: (1) the equivalent whole units represent the denominator of the cost per equivalent whole unit calculation (CPEWU), and (2) the equivalent whole units include only the work of the current period, for the sake of consistency the number of equivalent whole units must be divided into a numerator that represents costs incurred *in the current period only.* For FIFO we calculate the CPEWU using the following numerator and denominator:

CPEWU for FIFO

$$\text{CPEWU} = \frac{\text{costs incurred in current period}}{\text{equivalent units of work performed in current period}}$$

As you can tell from Exhibit 21-3, for cowhide the CPEWU is $3.00, which represents the costs incurred of $120,000, divided by the equivalent whole units, 40,000. In a like manner the respective CPEWUs for strings and conversion costs are $.50 ($25,000 ÷ 50,000) and $4.01 ($172,430 ÷ 43,000).

STEP 3: Preparing the Summary of Costs Report

The last step we need to take is to allocate the total costs to account for — the $355,000 — between the 30,000 completed units and the 20,000 units that are still in process on August 31. We do this in the *summary of costs report.*

The costs that we assign to the 30,000 completed units — when we are using FIFO — are made up of three parts. They are:

Three parts to the cost of completed units

1. The costs assigned to the 20,000 units started and completed in August

2. The costs of the 10,000 units in beginning inventory (these costs were incurred last period)

3. The costs to complete the 10,000 units in beginning inventory (these costs are incurred in the current period)

The summary of costs report for Department 1 of Spurrier Ball Company is shown in Exhibit 21-4. The cost of the units started and completed is $150,200 (20,000 × $7.51); the cost of the beginning inventory is $37,570 ($30,000 + $7,570); and the cost of completing the beginning inventory is $37,080 ($0 + $5,000 + $32,080). The total of these three parts is $224,850, which is the amount that is transferred with the 30,000 footballs to the second processing department, Department 2, where they are pumped with air and boxed.

The cost assigned to the ending inventory is $130,150 ($60,000 + $10,000 + $60,150), and when this amount is added to the $224,850, the total is $355,000, which agrees with the total in column 5 of the production report in Exhibit 21-3.

Perhaps now would be a good time to stop and look at what we've been doing in

EXHIBIT 21-4   Summary of Costs Report for Department 1: FIFO.
Because of the beginning inventory there are three parts to the calculation of the cost of the completed units—for FIFO.

Units completed and transferred to Department 2:
   Started and completed 20,000 × $7.51 . . . . $150,200
   Beginning inventory
      Cost of beg. inv. $37,570
      Costs to complete
         Cowhide 10,000 × 0 × $3.00. . . . . . $ 0
         Strings 10,000 × 1 × $.50.   5,000
         Con. costs 10,000 × $\frac{4}{5}$ × $4.01   32,080   37,080
      Total costs of producing beginning inventory   74,650
   Total costs of 30,000 completed units $224,850
Ending inventory—work-in-process
   Cowhide 20,000 × 1 × $3.00 . . . . $ 60,000
   Strings 20,000 × 1 × $.50   10,000
   Con. costs 20,000 × $\frac{3}{4}$ × $4.01.   60,150
   Total costs of ending inventory.   130,150
                           $355,000

Total costs of beginning inventory = $37,570 + $37,080 = $74,650

Total costs of units completed and transferred = $150,200 + $74,650 = $224,850

Total cost of ending inventory = $60,000 + $10,000 + $60,150 = $130,150

Total costs to account for = $224,850 + $130,150 = $355,000

EXHIBIT 21-5   T-Account Approach for Department 1: FIFO.

Work-in-Process — Department 1	
Beginning inv.—10,000 units ($30,000 + $7,570) $ 37,570	
PLUS	
Costs incurred in August to complete beg. inv. and start 40,000 more ($120,000 + $25,000 + $172,430) 317,430	
EQUALS	
Total costs to account for, associated with all 50,000 units $355,000	**LESS** Cost of 30,000 units that were completed in Department 1 ($37,570 + $37,080 + $150,200) $224,850
EQUALS	
Ending inv.—20,000 units ($60,000 + $10,000 + $60,150) $130,150	

The combination of these three costs —$224,850—is assigned to the 30,000 units that are transferred to Department 2 in August. Department 2 will call these costs "transferred-in costs."

To Work-in-Process —Dept. 2

Department 1 from a T-account approach. Exhibit 21-5 shows how the units and dollars flow through Department 1 on their way to Department 2. It shows that the $355,000 of total costs to account for—which we determined in the Exhibit 21-3 production report—are allocated between the completed units ($224,850) and the incomplete units ($130,150)—which we calculated in the Exhibit 21-4 summary of costs report. You can see the $224,850 going from Department 1 to 2 on the credit side of the Work-in-Process T-account, and the $130,150 remaining as the debit balance at the bottom of the Work-in-Process T-account.

The Illustration Continued

The 30,000 completed footballs are transferred from Department 1 to Department 2, where they are pumped with air and boxed. The costs of the 30,000 footballs transferred, $224,850, becomes a cost of Department 2. The costs transferred into Department 2 are referred to as "transferred-in costs" and will be treated like the costs of any other direct material. Example 21-5 provides the information we need to know about Department 2.

EXAMPLE 21-5

Department 2 of Spurrier Ball Company

SPURRIER BALL COMPANY—DEPARTMENT 2: FIFO

In Department 2 of Spurrier Ball Company, footballs that are transferred in from Department 1 are pumped with air and boxed for shipment. On August 1, there were 5,000 footballs (one-half complete) being processed in Department 2, and during August, the 30,000 footballs completed in Department 1 were introduced into Department 2. Of the 35,000 footballs (5,000 + 30,000) worked on during August, 29,000 were finished by August 31, and the footballs in ending work-in-process are two-thirds complete.

The costs of the August 1 beginning inventory of 5,000 unfinished balls and the costs incurred during August are as follows:

Cost of 5,000 footballs, Aug. 1:		
Transferred-in costs (costs transferred from Department 1 to 2 during July)	$ 34,000	
Conversion costs.	2,400	$ 36,400
Costs incurred during August:		
Transferred-in costs (costs transferred from Department 1 to 2 in current period)	$224,850	
Conversion costs.	30,600	
Boxes.	7,250	262,700
Total costs to account for		$299,100

Basic Steps for Department 2

The cost per equivalent whole unit in Department 2 is found in the same way as it was in Department 1.

The footballs that are finally finished and boxed in Department 2 will be transferred directly to finished goods inventory to await sale to customers. Let's now do the three basic steps for Department 2.

STEP 1: Tracing the Physical Flow

We know that during the month of August, 29,000 footballs were finished in Depart-

EXHIBIT 21-6   Production Report for Department 2: FIFO.
The second processing department will always have transferred-in costs—the costs that are transferred from one processing department to another.

	Units Completed							
Product Cost	(1a) Beginning Inventory WIP	(1b) Fraction Completed	(1c) Started and Completed	(2) Ending Inventory WIP	(3) Fraction Completed	(4) Equivalent Whole Units	(5) Total Costs to Account for	(6) Cost per Equivalent Whole Unit
Transferred-in costs	5,000	0	24,000	6,000	1	30,000	$224,850	$7.495
Boxes	5,000	1	24,000	6,000	0	29,000	7,250	.250
Conversion costs	5,000	½	24,000	6,000	⅔	30,500	30,600	1.003
							$262,700	$8.748

29,000

Cost of Beg. Inv. → 34,000
2,400   *Costs incurred during August*
$299,100

STEP 2: Preparing the Production Report

ment 2. The footballs that were not finished in Department 2 at the end of August are determined as follows:

Beginning inventory, work-in-process (Department 2)	5,000 footballs
Add: Units started (transferred-in from Department 1 during August)	30,000 footballs
Total to account for	35,000 footballs
Less: Units completed and transferred to finished goods	29,000 footballs
Ending inventory, work-in-process (Department 2)	6,000 footballs

The production report for Department 2 (Exhibit 21-6) shows that three costs go into the final boxed product—the costs of making the football in the previous department (the transferred-in costs), the box in which the football is packaged, and the conversion costs of pumping air into the balls and packaging the balls.

Completed Units Columns 1a and 1c indicate that a total of 29,000 footballs were completed in Department 2 during August. Of this total, 5,000 (column 1a) were in process on August 1; the remaining 24,000 (column 1c) were started and completed during August. Column 1b—fraction completed—indicates the fraction (or percentage) of a full dosage of costs incurred during August to complete the beginning inventory.

The 5,000 footballs had progressed halfway through the production process in July—therefore one-half of the time and attention that these units will get was received during July, and the remaining one-half of the total time and attention takes place during August. Since the conversion costs are spread evenly over the production process, one-half of the full dosage of conversion costs takes place in August to do the last one-half of the work on the incomplete units. The fraction for conversion costs in column 1b, therefore, is ½.

The box is added at the end of processing—only a fully pumped football will be packaged in a box. Since the 5,000 footballs were only one-half complete in July,

The ending inventory is 6,000 footballs

The beginning inventory had been worked on in July

Conversion costs are ½

The box is added this period

These transferred-in costs came to Dept. 2 last month

The full dosage was added in July

Now we get the fractions for ending inventory

Conversion costs = $\frac{2}{3}$

The box will be added next period

Transferred-in costs are 1

there was no way that a box could already have been added to them. The box had to have been added during August—when the 5,000 footballs were completed. The fraction in column 1b is 1.

Now we come to the transferred-in costs. Remember, these represent the costs assigned to units that are transferred from Department 1 to Department 2. Normally we treat transferred-in costs just like the costs for a material that is added at the beginning of production. This is because the processing of units transferred into a new department usually begins as soon as the units are received, so the costs transferred with these units—the transferred-in costs—become the responsibility of the receiving department as soon as the work begins in the receiving department. This is just like the costs of raw materials that are transferred from a storeroom directly to the production department at the start of production. The only difference is in the name; instead of being called direct materials (such as cowhide, strings, or package), they are called transferred-in costs.

If the transferred-in costs are treated the same as any raw material added at the beginning of production, then the fraction is just as easy to determine as it is for a direct material. Remember that the 5,000 units (as well as the transferred-in costs assigned to these units) in the beginning inventory on August 1 would have been transferred from Department 1 to Department 2 during July. Therefore the work (pumping and packaging) began on the 5,000 footballs in Department 2 sometime last month. Any costs—such as direct materials or in this case the transferred-in costs—that are added at the beginning of production would had to have been completely added to the 5,000 footballs last month, because that is when they were begun. Therefore, none of the full dosage of costs remains to be added in August, and the fraction must be 0.

Ending Inventory   In column 2 we see the 6,000 footballs (two-thirds complete) that were still in process at the end of August, and column 3 indicates the fraction of a full dosage of each cost that was added during August to these footballs. Since conversion costs are incurred evenly throughout production, and since two-thirds of the total time and attention have taken place during August in order to get the footballs to the two-thirds stage in production, two-thirds of a full dosage of conversion costs took place in August. The fraction in column 3 is $\frac{2}{3}$.

Since the box is added at the end of production, and since the footballs are only two-thirds complete, there is no way that the box has yet been added to the ending inventory; therefore its fraction in column 3 is 0.

And now for the transferred-in costs. Since the 6,000 footballs in ending inventory are from the batch of 30,000 that were transferred from Department 1 to Department 2 in August, this means that the 6,000 footballs were all begun in August. Remember, we treat transferred-in costs just like a direct material added at the beginning of production. Since production on the 6,000 footballs has already begun—in fact, they are all two-thirds complete—the fraction for the transferred-in costs is 1, just as it would be for a direct material added at the beginning of production.

Costs per Equivalent Whole Unit (CPEWU)   Once again we can calculate the equivalent units in column 4 rather simply. We merely add together the equivalent units from three sources: (1) beginning inventory, (2) units started and completed, and (3) units in ending inventory. (See illustration at top of page 848.)

Remember that the total costs to account for is the sum of two groups of costs: the costs of beginning inventory plus the costs incurred during the current period. When we are using FIFO, however, we need to remember to place these two groups in two

Calculating EWUs for Department 2: FIFO.

	(1a) Beginning (Inventory	×	(1b) Fraction)	+	(1c) Started and Completed	+	(2) Ending (Inventory	×	(3) Fraction)	=	(4) Equivalent Whole Units
Transferred-in costs	(5,000	×	0)	+	24,000	+	(6,000	×	1)	=	30,000
Package	(5,000	×	1)	+	24,000	+	(6,000	×	0)	=	29,000
Conversion costs	(5,000	×	$\frac{1}{2}$)	+	24,000	+	(6,000	×	$\frac{2}{3}$)	=	30,500

Remember: Incurred at the top, beginning inventory at the bottom

CPEWU

different sections of column 5 in Exhibit 21-6. The costs incurred ($224,850, $7,250, and $30,600) go at the top; these are the ones we divide by the equivalent units to get the CPEWU. The costs of the beginning inventory ($2,400 and $34,000) go at the bottom; these do not enter into the calculation of CPEWU.

For the transferred-in costs, the costs of the current period (these were assigned to the 30,000 units transferred from Department 1 to Department 2 during August) were $224,850; and when these were divided by the equivalent units of 30,000, we got the CPEWU of $7.495—which you can see in column 6. The beginning inventory costs of $34,000 (these are costs that were assigned to the 5,000 units transferred from Department 1 to Department 2 last period but were incomplete in Department 2 at the end of last period) are shown in the bottom portion of column 5.

The costs incurred during the current period for the boxes were $7,250; and when we divide them by the equivalent units of 29,000, we get the CPEWU of $.25. There were no beginning inventory costs for the boxes in column 5 because the box had not yet been added to the units as of the beginning of August.

Finally we come to the conversion costs. When the costs incurred during August—$30,600—are divided by the equivalent units of 30,500, we get a CPEWU of $1.003.

EXHIBIT 21-7   Summary of Costs Report for Department 2: FIFO.
The total cost of the 29,000 completed units transferred to finished goods inventory is $250,109.

Units completed and transferred to finished goods:
Started and completed 24,000 × $8.748 . . . . $209,952
Beginning inventory
  Cost of beg. inv.. . . . . $36,400   *Total costs of beginning inventory = $34,000 + $2,400 = $36,400*
  Costs to complete
    Trans.-in 5,000 × 0 × $7.495 . . . . . $ 0
    Box 5,000 × 1 × $.25 1,250
    Con. costs 5,000 × $\frac{1}{2}$ × $1.003 2,507   3,757
  Total costs of producing beginning inventory. 40,157
Total costs of 29,000 completed units. . . . . $250,109   *Total costs of units completed and transferred = $209,952 + $40,157 = $250,109*
Ending inventory—work-in-process
  Transferred-in costs 6,000 × 1 × $7.495 . . . . $ 44,970
  Box 6,000 × 0 × $.25 0
  Conversion costs 6,000 × $\frac{2}{3}$ × $1.003 4,012   *Total cost of ending inventory = $44,970 + $4,012 = $48,982*
  Total costs of ending inventory. 48,982
                           $299,091*   *Total costs to account for = $250,109 + $48,982 = $299,091**

* $9 error due to rounding of $1.003 in production report.

EXHIBIT 21-8   T-Account Approach for Department 2: FIFO.

Work-in-Process — Department 2

Beginning inv. — 5,000 units
($34,000 + $2,400) $ 36,400

PLUS

Costs incurred in August to
complete beg. inv. and start
30,000 more ($224,850 +
$7,250 + $30,600)   262,700

EQUALS

The combination of these three costs — $250,109 — is assigned to the 29,000 units that are transferred to finished goods in August.

Total costs to account for,
associated with all
35,000 units $299,100

LESS

Cost of 29,000 units that were
completed in Department 2
($36,400 + $3,757 +
$209,952) $250,109   *To Finished Goods Inventory*

EQUALS

Ending inv. — 6,000 units
($44,970 + $4,012) $ 48,982

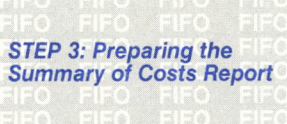

STEP 3: Preparing the Summary of Costs Report

The costs of the boxed footballs are made up of three parts

The costs of beginning inventory, $2,400, are shown separately at the bottom of column 5.

The final step is to allocate the total costs to account for in column 5 between the completed units and the ending inventory. We do this once again in the summary of costs report, shown in Exhibit 21-7.

The costs assigned to the 29,000 footballs that were completed during August are composed of three parts:

1. The cost assigned to the units started and completed in August = 24,000 × the total CPEWU of $8.748.

2. The cost of the 5,000 footballs in beginning inventory = $36,400 ($34,000 + $2,400).

3. The costs incurred during August to complete the 5,000 footballs = $3,757 ($1,250 + $2,507). The $250,109 total is the amount that we transferred with the 29,000 footballs to finished goods inventory.

The ending inventory $48,982 ($44,970 + $4,012), represents the balance in work-in-process — Department 2 on August 31. When we add this amount to the cost of completed units, $250,109, we get a total of $299,091, which agrees (except for a $9 rounding error) with the total for column 5 in the production report.

The journal entry required to transfer the costs from Work-in-Process—Department 2 to Finished Goods is as follows:

The final transfer

Finished Goods Inventory. 250,109
    Work-in-Process—Department 2.   250,109
Cost of completed units transferred from Department 2 to Finished Goods.

Let's look now at the Work-in-Process T-account for Department 2. As you can see in Exhibit 21-8, the total costs to account for of $299,100—which we determined in the Exhibit 21-6 production report—are allocated between the 29,000 completed units and the 6,000 incomplete units—which we did in the Exhibit 21-7 summary of costs report. The costs that are transferred to finished goods with the 29,000 units—the $250,109—are shown as a credit in the Work-in-Process T-account, and the cost of the 6,000 unit ending inventory is shown as the debit balance at the bottom of the Work-in-Process T-account.

THE WEIGHTED AVERAGE METHOD OF PROCESS COSTING

Be sure you are familiar with Example 21-4

In Example 21-4 you were given an expanded set of facts for the Spurrier Ball Company. There were 10,000 units, one-fifth complete, in beginning inventory. The number of units that were started and the number that were in the ending work-in-process for Department 1 for August were still 40,000 and 20,000 footballs, respectively. By doing Step 1—tracing the physical flow—we learned that there were 30,000 footballs completed during August, rather than the 20,000 that were completed in the original example (Example 21-3) for Spurrier. We are now ready to go to Step 2.

STEP 2: Preparing the Production Report

You've already learned the basic format back in Exhibit 21-1

The production report that we use with the weighted average method has exactly the same format as the one used in Exhibit 21-1. As a matter of fact, all of the procedures will be exactly the same—only the numbers will be different. The numbers are different because there are now 10,000 units (and related costs) in beginning inventory, which were assumed to be zero in the original example. This means that you have already basically learned the weighted average method, and now only need to see how to include the beginning inventory in the production report. Remember, as we pointed out in the section comparing FIFO to weighted average, for weighted average we merge the beginning inventory (and costs) with the current production (and costs) and treat the combined totals as if there was one homogeneous group of units and one homogeneous group of costs. The resulting CPEWU is a weighted average—just as the name implies—found by dividing the combined units of last period and this period into the combined costs of last period and this period.

The reason for the name

The completed production report (which is combined with the summary of costs report) is shown in Exhibit 21-9. As you look it over, notice the following similarities and differences in Exhibit 21-9 and Exhibit 21-1.

The completed units are now 10,000 higher

Column 1   Column 1 in Exhibit 21-9 shows the number of units that were completed in August, 30,000. This is 10,000 higher than the number shown in column 1 of Exhibit 21-1 because of the additional 10,000 units in the beginning inventory. Also, column 1 is labeled "completed" in Exhibit 21-9, whereas it was called "started and completed" in Exhibit 21-1. This is because in Exhibit 21-1 we were assuming no

EXHIBIT 21-9   Combined Production Report and Summary of Costs Report for Department 1: Weighted Average.
Weighted average is simpler because we do not keep the units in beginning inventory separate from those that were started and completed.

Production Report

Product Cost	(1) Units Completed	(2) Ending Inventory, Work-in-Process	(3) Fraction Completed	(4) Equivalent Whole Units	(5) Total Costs to Account for		(6) [(5) ÷ (4)] Cost per Equivalent Whole Unit
Cowhide	30,000	20,000	1	50,000	$ 30,000		
					120,000	$150,000	$3.00
Strings	30,000	20,000	1	50,000	0		
					$ 25,000	25,000	.50
Conversion costs	30,000	20,000	$\frac{3}{4}$	45,000	$ 7,570		
					172,430	180,000	4.00
						$355,000	$7.50

Summary of Costs Report:

Units completed and transferred to Department 2:

30,000 × $7.50 . . . . $225,000

Ending inventory—work-in-process:

Cowhide	20,000 × 1 × $3.00	$60,000
Strings	20,000 × 1 × $ .50	10,000
Conversion costs	20,000 × $\frac{3}{4}$ × $4.00	60,000	130,000
Total costs to account for		$355,000

Look back at pages 831–833 for explanation

beginning inventory, therefore all the units that were completed in August came from the units that were started during August.

Columns 2 and 3   The headings, numbers, and explanations of the numbers in columns 2 and 3 in Exhibit 21-9 are exactly what they were in the comparable columns of Exhibit 21-1. Since we discussed these columns in detail when we discussed Exhibit 21-1, we will not discuss them any further here.

Column 4   The equivalent whole units in column 4 of Exhibit 21-9 are calculated in exactly the same manner as they were in Exhibit 21-1. The results in Exhibit 21-9 for each product cost are 10,000 units higher than they were in Exhibit 21-1, since the completed units are now 10,000 higher. The calculation of equivalent whole units in Exhibit 21-9 is done as follows:

EWUs for weighted average—Department 1.

	Column in Exhibit 21-9					
	1	+	(2	×	3)	=	4
Cowhide	30,000	+	(20,000	×	1)	=	50,000 equivalent whole units
Strings	30,000	+	(20,000	×	1)	=	50,000 equivalent whole units
Conversion costs	30,000	+	(20,000	×	$\frac{3}{4}$)	=	45,000 equivalent whole units

CPEWU for cowhide

Total costs to account for = beg. inv. plus incurred

CPEWU for strings

CPEWU for conversion costs

STEP 3: Preparing the Summary of Costs Report

We're combining two reports into one

Cost of completed units

Department 2 will refer to the $225,000 as transferred-in costs

Columns 5 and 6 The costs that are included in column 5 of Exhibit 21-9 are higher than they were in Exhibit 21-1. Once again the reason is the beginning inventory. Since there are now 10,000 footballs in the beginning inventory, there will also be costs associated with those footballs. For cowhide, the beginning inventory costs were $30,000, which when added to the $120,000 incurred gives us a total to account for of $150,000. When this combination is divided by the equivalent whole units for cowhide of 50,000, we get a CPEWU of $3.00:

$$\text{CPEWU} = \frac{\text{total costs to account for}}{\text{equivalent whole units}} = \frac{\$150,000}{50,000} = \$3.00$$

For the strings, there were no beginning inventory costs, because the strings had not been added last period to the 10,000 footballs in beginning inventory. Remember, strings are added when the footballs are one-half complete. Since the footballs were only one-fourth complete at the beginning of August, there is no way they could have progressed far enough during July to have been strung. Therefore the total costs to account for are represented entirely by the costs incurred during August, $25,000; and the resulting CPEWU is $.50 ($25,000 ÷ $50,000).

Finally, the total conversion costs to account for are $180,000 ($7,570 in beginning inventory plus $172,430 incurred in August). Dividing that cost by the 45,000 equivalent whole units results in a conversion cost per equivalent whole unit of $4.00.

The total of all the total costs to account for in column 5 of Exhibit 21-9 is the total of all the production costs represented in all the equivalent whole units worked on during the month. Thus, the total of all the production costs to account for is $355,000 in our example. The total cost per equivalent whole unit in column 6 is $7.50.

Next, the total costs to account for will be allocated between the 30,000 completed and the 20,000 units remaining in work-in-process. We will do this in Step 3.

As we mentioned before, the purpose of the summary of costs report is to determine what portion of the total costs to account for are to be assigned to the completed units and transferred with those units to the next department, and what part of these costs will remain in Department 1, assigned to the units in the ending inventory.

The summary of costs report for Department 1 is combined with the production report in Exhibit 21-9. We have combined these two reports in order to show you, with the use of arrows: (1) exactly where each number in the summary of costs report comes from; and (2) how closely related the summary of costs report is to the production report.

Notice also that the summary of costs report in Exhibit 21-9 uses exactly the same format as we used in Exhibit 21-2, where there was no beginning inventory. The numbers will be different in the two reports, however, because of the additional 10,000 units in Exhibit 21-9.

Exhibit 21-9 indicates that $225,000 is assigned to the completed units (30,000 × $7.50), which, upon transfer to Department 2, requires the following journal entry:

```
Work-in-Process—Department 2...........................  225,000
    Work-in-Process—Department 1......................              225,000
Cost of completed units transferred from Department 1 to Depart-
ment 2.
```

EXHIBIT 21-10   T-Account Approach for Department 1: Weighted Average

Work-in-Process — Department 1	
Beginning inv.— 10,000 units ($30,000 + $7,570) $ 37,570	
PLUS	
Costs incurred in August to complete beg. inv. and start 40,000 more ($120,000 + $25,000 + $172,430) 317,430	
EQUALS	
Total costs to account for, associated with all 50,000 units $355,000	*$225,000 is assigned to the 30,000 units that are transferred to Department 2 in August. Department 2 will call these costs "transferred-in costs."*
	LESS
	Cost of 30,000 units that were completed in Department 1 ($30,000 × $7.50) $225,000 *To Work-in-Process — Dept. 2*
EQUALS	
Ending inv.— 20,000 units ($60,000 + $10,000 + $60,000) $130,000	

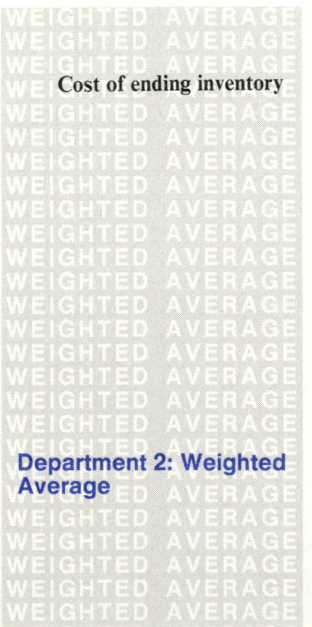

Cost of ending inventory

Exhibit 21-9 also indicates that the cost of the 20,000 footballs on August 31 in Department 1 is $130,000 — representing $60,000 for cowhide, $10,000 for strings, and $60,000 for conversion costs. When the $130,000 is added to the costs assigned to completed units, $225,000, the total is $355,000, which agrees with the total at the bottom of the total costs to account for column (column 5) of the production report.

Let's now look at what we've been doing in Department 1 from a T-account approach. Exhibit 21-10 shows how the units and dollars flow through Department 1 on their way to Department 2. It shows that the $355,000 of total costs to account for (which we determined in the Exhibit 21-9 production report) are allocated between the completed units, $225,000, and the incomplete units, $130,000 (which we calculated in the Exhibit 21-9 summary of costs report). You can see the $225,000 going from Department 1 to 2 on the credit side of the T-account, and the $130,000 remaining as the debit balance at the bottom of the Work-in-Process T-account.

Department 2: Weighted Average

The 30,000 completed footballs are transferred from Department 1 to Department 2, where they will be pumped with air and boxed. The costs assigned to these 30,000 footballs are $225,000, and they are transferred with the footballs to Department 2. When Department 2 receives these costs, it refers to them as "transferred-in costs" and treats them like the costs of any other direct material.

The facts related to Department 2 are provided in Example 21-6, on page 854.

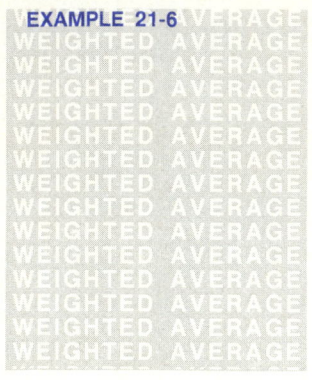

EXAMPLE 21-6

SPURRIER BALL COMPANY—DEPARTMENT 2: WEIGHTED AVERAGE

In Department 2 of Spurrier Ball Company, footballs that are transferred in from Department 1 are pumped with air and boxed for shipment. At the beginning of August, there were 5,000 footballs (one-half complete) being processed in Department 2. During August, the 30,000 footballs completed in Department 1 were introduced into Department 2. Of the 35,000 footballs (5,000 + 30,000) worked on during August, 29,000 were finished by August 31, and the footballs in the ending work-in-process are two-thirds complete.

The costs of the August 1 beginning inventory of 5,000 unfinished footballs and the costs incurred during August are as follows:

This is the same as Example 21-5 under FIFO except for the transferred-in costs of $225,000

Cost of 5,000 footballs, Aug. 1:		
Transferred-in costs (costs transferred from Dept. 1 to Dept. 2 during July)	$ 34,000	
Conversion costs	2,400	$ 36,400
Costs incurred during Aug.:		
Transferred-in costs (costs transferred from Dept. 1 to Dept. 2 in current period)	$225,000	
Conversion costs	30,600	
Boxes	7,250	262,850
Total costs to account for		$299,250

Basic Steps for Department 2

The cost per equivalent whole unit in Department 2 is found in the same way as it was in Department 1.

The footballs that are finally finished and boxed in Department 2 will be transferred directly to finished goods inventory to await sale to customers. Let's now do the three basic steps for Department 2.

STEP 1: Tracing the Physical Flow

We know that during the month of August 29,000 footballs were finished in Department 2. The footballs that were not finished in Department 2 at the end of August are determined as follows:

The ending inventory is 6,000 footballs.

Beginning inventory, work-in-process (Department 2)	5,000 footballs
Add: Units started (transferred-in from Department 1 during August)	30,000 footballs
Total to account for	35,000 footballs
Less: Units completed and transferred to finished goods	29,000 footballs
Ending inventory, work-in-process (Department 2)	6,000 footballs

STEP 2: Preparing the Production Report

The production report for Department 2 (Exhibit 21-11) shows that three costs go into the final boxed product—the costs of making the football in the previous department (the transferred-in costs), the box in which the football is packaged, and the conversion costs of pumping air into the balls and packaging the balls.

EXHIBIT 21-11   Combined Production Report and Summary of Costs Report for Department 2: Weighted Average.
Under weighted average the cost assigned to the 29,000 completed units is calculated in a single step in the summary of costs report.

Production Report

Product Cost	(1) Units Completed	(2) Ending Inventory, Work-in-Process	(3) Fraction Completed	(4) Equivalent Whole Units	(5) Total Costs to Account for		(6) Cost per Equivalent Whole Unit
Transferred-in costs	29,000	6,000	1	35,000	$ 34,000		$7.40
					225,000	$259,000	
Boxes	29,000	6,000	0	29,000	0		.25
					$ 7,250	7,250	
Conversion costs	29,000	6,000	$\frac{2}{3}$	33,000	$ 2,400		1.00
					30,600	33,000	
						$299,250	$8.65

Summary of Costs Report:

Footballs completed and transferred to finished goods

29,000 × $8.65 . . . . $250,850

Ending inventory—work-in-process (Department 2):

Transferred-in costs	6,000 × 1 × $7.40	$44,400	
Boxes	6,000 × 0 × $ .25	0	
Conversion costs	6,000 × $\frac{2}{3}$ × $1.00	4,000	48,400
Total costs to account for	. . . .		$299,250

Columns 1 and 2 indicate the number of complete and the number of incomplete footballs. The fraction of a full dosage of each production cost added to each of the 6,000 incomplete footballs is shown in column 3.

The fraction for conversion costs is $\frac{2}{3}$

The 6,000 footballs have progressed two-thirds of the way through the production process—therefore two-thirds of the time and attention that these units will get has already been received during August. Since the conversion costs are spread evenly over the production process, two-thirds of a full dosage of conversion costs has been incurred to do two-thirds of the work on the incomplete units. The fraction for conversion costs in column 3, therefore, is $\frac{2}{3}$.

The box is a 0

The box is added at the end of processing—only a fully pumped football will be packaged. Since the 6,000 units are only two-thirds complete, there is no way that a box has been added to any of the 6,000 incomplete units. The fraction is a 0.

Finally, we come to the transferred-in costs (which are the dollars assigned to units transferred from Department 1 to Department 2). During August, 30,000 units were completed in Department 1 at a cost of $225,000, and transferred to Department 2. Normally the processing of units transferred into a new department begins as soon as the units are received, so transferred-in costs are just like the costs of a direct material added at the beginning of production. The only difference is in the name; instead of being called direct materials (such as cowhide, strings, or package), it is called transferred-in costs.

If the transferred-in costs are the same as any other direct material that is added in a lump sum at the beginning of production, then the fraction is just as easy to deter-

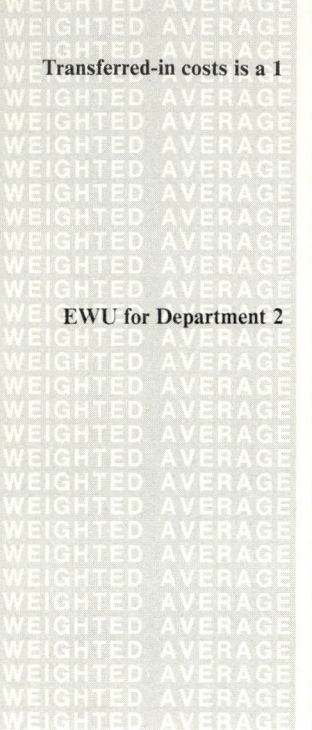

Transferred-in costs is a 1

EWU for Department 2

mine as it is for a direct material. Since the costs are added at the beginning, they had to have been added to the 6,000 units that are two-thirds complete—the fraction is a 1.

The equivalent whole units (column 4) for each production cost are calculated as before, as follows:

	Column from Exhibit 21-8			
	(1)	**+**	**[(2) × (3)] =**	**(4)**
Transferred-in costs	29,000	+	(6,000 × 1) = 35,000 equivalent whole units	
Package	29,000	+	(6,000 × 0) = 29,000 equivalent whole units	
Conversion costs	29,000	+	(6,000 × $\frac{2}{3}$) = 33,000 equivalent whole units	

The data in columns 5 and 6 for Department 2 are determined in the same manner as they were for Department 1.

The total costs to account for (column 5) are determined by adding together the costs of beginning inventory and the costs incurred during the period. And the costs per equivalent whole unit (column 6) are still determined by dividing the total costs to account for (column 5) by the equivalent whole units (column 4).

The total cost of producing an equivalent whole unit is $8.65 per unit, shown in column 6. The total costs to account for, for Department 2, are $299,250, shown at the bottom of column 5. This total of $299,250 will be allocated between the com-

EXHIBIT 21-12   T-Account Approach for Department 2: Weighted Average

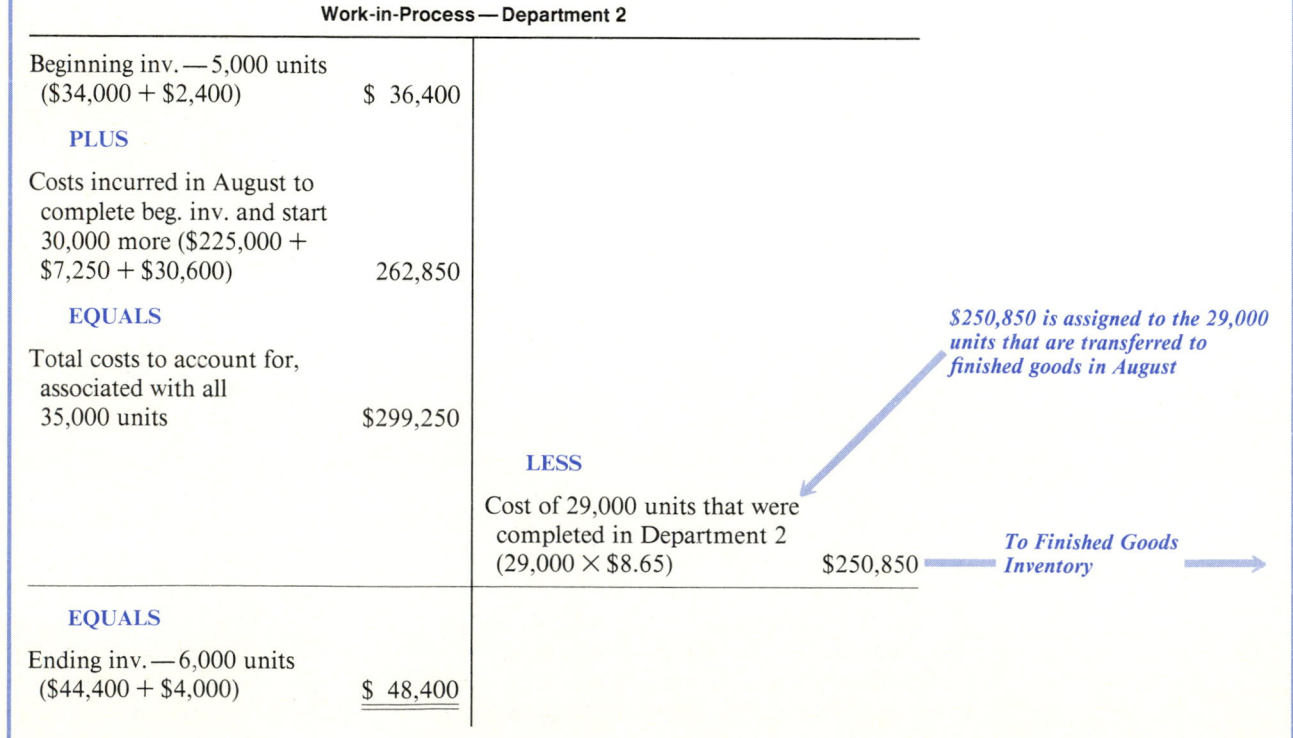

Work-in-Process — Department 2	
Beginning inv. — 5,000 units ($34,000 + $2,400) $ 36,400	
PLUS	
Costs incurred in August to complete beg. inv. and start 30,000 more ($225,000 + $7,250 + $30,600) 262,850	
EQUALS	*$250,850 is assigned to the 29,000 units that are transferred to finished goods in August*
Total costs to account for, associated with all 35,000 units $299,250	
	LESS
	Cost of 29,000 units that were completed in Department 2 (29,000 × $8.65) $250,850 ➝ *To Finished Goods Inventory*
EQUALS	
Ending inv. — 6,000 units ($44,400 + $4,000) $ 48,400	

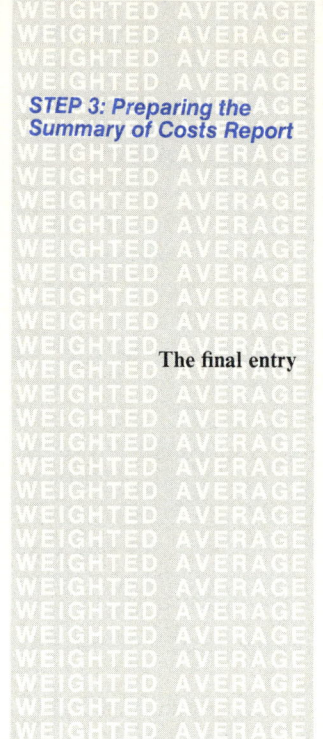

STEP 3: Preparing the Summary of Costs Report

The final entry

pleted units (29,000) and the incomplete units (6,000) in the final step—the summary of costs report.

The summary of costs report for Department 2 is shown below the production report in Exhibit 21-11. It shows that the cost of 29,000 footballs transferred to finished goods is $250,850 and the costs assigned to the 6,000 unfinished footballs in Department 2 is $48,400. The total of these two ($250,850 + $48,400) equals $299,250, which corresponds with the total for column 5 in the production report.

The journal entry required to transfer the costs from Work-in-Process—Department 2 to Finished Goods Inventory is as follows:

Finished Goods Inventory. 250,850
    Work-in-Process Inventory—Department 2   250,850
Cost of completed units transferred from Department 2 to Finished Goods.

The T-account for Department 2 is shown in Exhibit 21-12. The total costs to account for of $299,250 (which we determined in the production report part of Exhibit 21-11) are allocated between the 29,000 completed units and the 6,000 incomplete units (which we calculated in the summary of costs report part of Exhibit 21-11). The costs that are transferred to finished goods with the 29,000 units, the $250,850, are shown as a credit in the Work-in-Process T-account, and the cost of the 6,000 unit ending inventory, $48,400, is shown as the debit balance at the bottom of the Work-in-Process T-account.

CHAPTER SUMMARY

The ***process costing method*** is used by companies that produce a large quantity of physically indistinguishable units in a continuous process. Since all units are identical, it is impractical and probably impossible to distinguish the exact cost of one unit from another. The cost per unit is determined by dividing the equivalent whole units produced during the period into the total costs to account for of that period.

In process costing the output is measured in ***equivalent whole units.*** This represents all fully completed units and the number of units that could be obtained if partially completed units could be somehow magically glued together to make whole ones. More realistically, equivalent whole units might be viewed as the number of units to which a full dosage of costs has been applied.

There are three basic steps in all process costing situations:

1. Tracing the physical flow
2. Preparing the production report
3. Preparing a summary of costs report

The first step determines the units completed and the units in the ending work-in-process. Based on what was determined in the first step, the next step (1) determines the equivalent whole units for each product cost, (2) accumulates the total costs to account for, and (3) computes the costs per equivalent unit.

The third step allocates the total costs to account for between the units completed and the units in the ending work-in-process.

There are two different methods of process costing: ***FIFO*** and ***weighted average.*** These methods differ in the way they handle the partially completed units in the beginning inventory, in both the production report and the summary of costs report.

With FIFO the completed units are first separated into two parts in the *production report*—the partially completed units in the beginning inventory and the units started and completed during the period. FIFO then assigns to the beginning inventory a fraction representing the fraction of a full dosage of costs added in the current period to complete these units. The number of equivalent whole units (EWU) in the production report for each different product cost is determined as follows:

$$EWU = \begin{bmatrix} \text{begin.} & \text{fraction com-} \\ \text{inv. of} \times & \text{pleted (in} \\ \text{WIP} & \text{current period)} \end{bmatrix} + \begin{matrix} \text{started} \\ \text{and} \\ \text{completed} \end{matrix} + \begin{bmatrix} \text{ending} & \text{fraction com-} \\ \text{inv. of} \times & \text{pleted (in} \\ \text{WIP} & \text{current period)} \end{bmatrix}$$

The equivalent whole units in the production report represent work done in the current period only—the equivalent units of work done last period to the beginning inventory are excluded. In the total costs to account for column of the production report, FIFO separates the total costs into two groups: the costs incurred in the current period (these are the ones divided by the equivalent units to get the CPEWU) and the beginning inventory costs (these costs do not enter into the CPEWU calculation). Within the *summary of costs report,* the costs assigned to the completed units are made up of three parts: (1) the costs to produce the units started and completed; (2) the costs of the partially completed units in the beginning inventory (incurred in the previous period); and (3) the costs to complete the beginning inventory (incurred in the current period).

When the weighted average method is used, no distinction is made within the production report between the units that were in beginning inventory and the units that were worked on in the current period. The equivalent whole units (EWU) for the current period include all of the beginning inventory even though some of the work may have been done in the previous period. The calculation is:

$$EWU = \begin{matrix} \text{all} \\ \text{completed} \\ \text{units} \end{matrix} + \begin{bmatrix} \text{ending} & \text{fraction com-} \\ \text{inv. of} \times & \text{pleted (in} \\ \text{WIP} & \text{current period)} \end{bmatrix}$$

In the total costs to account for column, no distinction is made between the costs of the beginning inventory and the costs incurred in the current period. They are simply added together and treated as if they all occurred in the current period. These combined costs are then divided by equivalent whole units to get a weighted average CPEWU. This CPEWU is the same for all units, whether they were worked on entirely in the current period or were worked on partially during the previous period and partially during the current period. Under weighted average, in the summary of costs report the cost of completed units is calculated in one simple step—as the number of units completed multiplied by the total CPEWU.

Cost per equivalent whole unit   Total costs to account for divided by the equivalent whole units. It represents the full dosage of each production cost assigned to each equivalent whole unit. (page 830)

Equivalent whole units   A measure of productive output in process costing manufacturing—measuring whole completed units as well as units not yet completed. It represents the number of units to which a full dosage of costs is applied. It is computed by adding (1) the completed units and (2) the units in the ending inventory of work-in-process multiplied by the fraction completed. Also called just equivalent units. (page 827)

FIFO method   The process costing method that distinguishes the work of the current period from that of the previous period. This method separates the units in beginning inventory from those that were started and completed; the CPEWU is calculated by dividing the costs of the current period by the equivalent units of work for the current period. (page 837)

Job order costing method   The method of accounting for the production of identifiable products, often to customer specifications. The costs of each job are carefully accumulated and kept separate from the costs of any other job. (page 825)

Process costing method   The method of accounting for the production of a large volume of indistinguishable units in a continuous process. An average cost is determined by dividing the production costs by the equivalent whole units of production. (page 825)

Production report   A basic step in the process costing method — a format for calculating the cost per equivalent whole unit. (page 830)

Summary of costs report   The final step in the process costing method in which the total costs to account for are allocated between the completed units and the ending inventory of work-in-process. (page 828)

Total costs to account for   The total of the costs of the beginning inventory of work-in-process and all the product costs incurred during the current period. (page 830)

Weighted average method   The process costing method that makes no distinction between the units that were completed from the beginning inventory and those that were started and completed in the current period. The CPEWU is calculated by dividing the combination of beginning inventory costs plus costs incurred currently, by the equivalent units for the period. The equivalent units include some work of the previous period. (page 837)

QUESTIONS

1. Explain the differences between *job order costing* and *process costing.* Give several examples for each of industries in which each method would be used.

2. The difference between job order costing and process costing is described by some as the breadth of the denominator. Explain what might be meant by this statement.

3. Job order costing and process costing are extremes of product costing. Describe a situation in which a combination of the two methods might be employed.

4. Explain the meaning of the term *equivalent whole units.* How is it determined?

5. The cost per equivalent whole unit is computed by dividing the costs incurred for the period by the number of units completed. Do you agree? Why?

6. Explain how the fraction completed column in the production report is determined for materials added in a lump sum.

7. Will equivalent whole units be less than, equal to, or greater than the number of units completed? Explain.

8. In process costing, what is the purpose of: **(a)** the production report, and **(b)** the summary of costs report?

9. Explain the differences between the FIFO and weighted average methods of process costing.

10. What are the three basic steps in the solution to any process costing problem?

11. Why is it so much easier to solve a process costing problem with FIFO when there is no beginning inventory in work-in-process?

12. We ignore the beginning inventory in work-in-process whenever we use the FIFO method of process costing. Comment.

13. As long as the totals in the summary of costs report agree with the total costs to account for column in the production report, we are assured of having done a process costing problem correctly. Do you agree? Why?

14. When there is no beginning inventory in work-in-process, the equivalent whole units under FIFO and weighted average will always be identical. Discuss why you believe this statement to be true or false.

15. Explain what is meant by the term ***transferred-in costs.***

EXERCISES

Exercise 21-1
Filling in the blanks for the percentage complete — ending WIP

During December 1988 the NA Beer (NA meaning no alcohol) Company completed 75,000 units and had 15,000 units still in process on December 31. NA uses four ingredients in its production process:

    Material A: added at the beginning of production
    Material B: added when production is one-half complete
    Material C: added at the end of production
    Material D: incurred evenly throughout production
    Conversion costs: incurred evenly throughout production

There are three different situations listed below. Each one represents a possible point in production that the 15,000 units in inventory have reached by month-end. For each situation, fill in the blanks for each product cost that indicates the fraction completed in determining equivalent whole units.

	Ending Inventory		
Product Cost	$\frac{2}{5}$ **Complete**	$\frac{3}{5}$ **Complete**	$\frac{3}{4}$ **Complete**
Material A	_____	_____	_____
Material B	_____	_____	_____
Material C	_____	_____	_____
Material D	_____	_____	_____
Conversion costs	_____	_____	_____

Exercise 21-2
Percentage complete — beginning WIP (FIFO)

Refer again to the facts in Exercise 21-1. Now assume that there is a beginning inventory on December 1 of 10,000 units, and you are using the FIFO method. Once again there are three situations below, but this time they represent the beginning inventory rather than the ending inventory. This time you are to fill in the blanks with a fraction that represents the fraction (or percentage) of a full dosage needed to complete the beginning inventory during December.

Product Cost	Situations — Beginning Inventory		
	$\frac{2}{5}$ Complete	$\frac{3}{5}$ Complete	$\frac{3}{4}$ Complete
Material A	_____	_____	_____
Material B	_____	_____	_____
Material C	_____	_____	_____
Material D	_____	_____	_____
Conversion costs	_____	_____	_____

Exercise 21-3

Tracing the physical flow

The first step in the process costing method is to trace the physical flow. The items listed below are needed to make this computation. Fill in the blanks for the unknown quantities.

	Situations		
	1	2	3
Beginning inventory, work-in-process	20,000		44,000
Units started	60,000	120,000	
Total to account for		190,000	200,000
Ending inventory, work-in-process	20,000	55,000	
Units sold			180,000

Exercise 21-4

Preparing a summary of costs report — weighted average

The production report for the Montana Manufacturing Company is shown below. Based on the information in it, prepare the summary of costs report. Assume that there was a 40,000-unit beginning inventory in work-in-process, one-fourth complete. Montana Company uses the weighted average method.

Product Cost	Units Completed	Ending Inventory, Work-in-Process	Fraction Complete	Equivalent Whole Units	Total Costs to Account for		Costs per Equivalent Whole Unit
Material A	240,000	50,000	1	290,000	$ 74,200 500,000 0	$574,200	$1.98
Package	240,000	50,000	0	240,000	$ 96,000	96,000	.40
Conversion costs	240,000	50,000	$\frac{2}{5}$	270,000	$ 10,000 260,000	270,000 $940,200	1.00 $3.38

(Check figure: Cost of ending work-in-process = $129,000)

Exercise 21-5

Preparing a summary of costs report — FIFO.

Assume the same facts as in Exercise 21-4, except that Montana Company uses the FIFO method, and the production report is as given on page 862:

| | Units Completed | | | | | | | |
Product Cost	Beginning Inventory, Work-in-Process	Fraction Completed	Units Started and Completed	Ending Inventory, Work-in-Process	Fraction Complete	Equivalent Whole Units	Total Costs to Account for	Costs per Equivalent Whole Unit
Material A	40,000	0	200,000	50,000	1	250,000	$500,000	$2.00
Package	40,000	1	200,000	50,000	0	240,000	96,000	.40
Conversion costs	40,000	$\frac{3}{4}$	200,000	50,000	$\frac{3}{5}$	260,000	260,000	1.00
							$856,000	$3.40
							74,200	
							0	
							10,000	
							$940,200	

(Check figure: Cost of completed goods = $810,200)

Exercise 21-6
Completing a production report — FIFO

Below is a partial report for the Justin Tyme Stopwatch Company. Fill in the blanks that will complete the report. Justin uses the FIFO method.

| | Units Completed | | | | | | | |
Product Cost	Beginning Inventory, Work-in-Process	Fraction Completed	Units Started and Completed	Ending Inventory, Work-in-Process	Fraction Complete	Equivalent Whole Units	Total Costs to Account for	Costs per Equivalent Whole Unit
Material A	2,000	0	6,000	1,000	1	_____	$ _____	$2.50
Material B	2,000	1	6,000	1,000	_____	8,000	16,000	_____
Conversion costs	2,000	$\frac{1}{5}$	6,000	1,000	_____	_____	28,600	4.00
							$ _____	$ _____
							$ 4,800	
							0	
							6,240	
							$ _____	

Exercise 21-7
Completing a production report — weighted average

The incomplete production report for Tums Petroleum is shown below. Fill in the missing blanks, assuming that Tums uses the weighted average method.

Product Cost	Completed	Ending Inventory	Fraction Complete	Equivalent Whole Units	Total Costs to Account for	Cost per Equivalent Whole Unit
Material A	50,000	10,000	_____	60,000	$270,000	$ _____
Material B	50,000	10,000	0	_____	_____	5.00
Conversion costs	_____	10,000	_____	57,500		
					$ _____	$11.00

Exercise 21-8
Preparing a production report and summary of costs report for the second of two departments — FIFO

The Connors Company produces a product that goes through an assembly and finishing department prior to completion. During October, 10,000 units were completed in the assembly department at $5 per unit and transferred to the finishing department. On October 1, there was a 4,000-unit beginning inventory in the finishing department, one-fourth complete, and on October 31 there was an inventory of 2,000 units, one-half complete. The conversion costs incurred in October for the finishing department were $27,000.

The costs of the beginning inventory were:

Conversion costs.	$ 2,500
Transferred-in costs.	19,800
	$22,300

Prepare a production report and summary of costs report for the finishing department using the FIFO method.

(Check figure: Cost per equivalent whole unit for transferred-in costs = $5.00)

Exercise 21-9
Preparing a production report and summary of costs report for the second of two departments — weighted average

Solve Exercise 21-8 using weighted average instead of FIFO.

(Check figure: Cost of completed units = $87,060)

Exercise 21-10
Tracing the physical flow through two departments

The Arias Company produces a product that goes through two processing departments before it is completed and transferred to finished goods. Fill in the blanks for the two departments for the two independent situations A and B:

	Situation A		Situation B	
	Dept. 1	**Dept. 2**	**Dept. 1**	**Dept. 2**
Beginning inventory	3,000	4,500	11,000	14,000
Units started (or transferred-in)	20,000			66,000
Total to account for				80,000
Ending inventory		1,500	2,400	
Units completed	15,000			70,000

PROBLEMS
Set A

Problem A21-1
Preparing a production report and summary of costs report — FIFO

The Wilson Manufacturing Company produces soccer balls for the Tampa Bay Rowdies in a continuous process. During the month of July, 40,000 balls were started; at the end of the month, 2,000 were still in process, one-tenth complete. There were no balls in process on July 1.

The only two product costs are for direct materials (which are added in their entirety at the beginning of production) and conversion costs (which are incurred uniformly throughout production). The costs incurred during July were $160,000 for the direct materials and $114,600 for conversion costs.

Required

Prepare a production report and a summary of costs report using the FIFO method.

(Check figure: Cost of balls completed = $266,000)

Problem A21-2
Preparing a production report and summary of costs report — FIFO

The Rodney Corporation makes a citrus-flavored drink, called Pick Me Up, which is being used at more and more universities. It not only replaces the liquids lost through perspiration, it also provides daily requirements of all important nutrients needed by the human body. This allows coaches to practice straight through dinner, thereby saving the university the costs of one meal per day for the entire team.

During September 1988, the Rodney Corporation started 50,000 gallons of Pick Me Up and completed 45,000. The inventory on September 30 was 7,500 gallons, one-half complete. The production costs incurred during September were as follows:

Direct materials. $50,000
Conversion costs   95,625

The inventory on September 1 was three-fourths complete. The costs of this inventory were $2,500 for direct materials and $3,750 for conversion costs. Direct materials are added at the beginning of production.

Required

1. Prepare a production report using the FIFO method.
2. Prepare a summary of costs report.

(Check figure: Cost of units completed and transferred to finished goods = $136,725)

3. Prepare the journal entry to record the transfer of completed units to Finished Goods Inventory.

Problem A21-3
Preparing a production report and summary of costs report— weighted average

Required

Using the information given in Problem A21-2, do the same three requirements assuming that Rodney Corporation uses the weighted average method.

[Check figure for part (2): Cost of goods completed = $136,733]

Problem A21-4
Using weighted average with several materials

On December 1, 1988, the SKW Company had 8,000 units in work-in-process, one-fourth complete. The costs of this inventory were:

Material S $14,000
Material K   8,000
Conversion costs 12,250

During December, 32,000 units were started, of which 25,000 were completed by month-end. The costs incurred during December were:

Material S $66,000
Material K 57,000
Material W 12,500
Conversion costs 74,000

Material S is added at the beginning of production. Material K is added evenly during the process until the units are one-half complete. Material W is added entirely at the end of production. The ending work-in-process is 25% complete, and SKW uses the weighted average method of process costing.

Required

1. Determine the cost assigned to completed units transferred to finished goods in December.

(Check figure: $187,500)

2. Determine the cost of the December 31 balance in Work-in-Process.

Problem A21-5
Using FIFO with several materials

Assume that the SKW Company uses the FIFO method instead of weighted average.

Required

1. Determine the cost assigned to completed units transferred to finished goods in December.

(Check figure: $187,439)

2. Determine the cost of the December 31 balance in Work-in-Process.

Problem A21-6

FIFO process costing—several materials and transferred-in costs

The Jetson Company produces a packaged fruit drink called Persimmon Punch. The persimmons are ground and blended in Process 1; pink artificial coloring is added in Process 2; and the concoction is chilled and packaged (at the end of processing) in Process 3.

On January 1, 1987, there were 30,000 pints of flavored punch in Process 3, one-third complete. During January, 100,000 pints were transferred from Process 2 to Process 3, and at the end of January there were 25,000 pints of punch awaiting packaging, four-fifths complete.

The January 1 costs of inventory were:

Conversion costs.	$ 500
Transferred-in costs	6,000

During December, the average cost of producing a pint in Process 2 was $.20 per pint. In addition, the costs incurred for Process 3 during January were:

Conversion costs.	$5,750
Cartons.	4,200

The Jetson Company uses the FIFO method for all three processes.

Required   Prepare a production report and a summary of costs report for Process 3 for January.

(Check figure: Cost of completed units = $30,450)

Problem A21-7

Weighted average process costing—several materials and transferred-in costs

Required

Assume the same facts as in Problem A21-6. This time prepare a production report and summary of costs report using the weighted average method.

(Check figure: Cost of ending inventory = $6,000)

Problem A21-8

Production report and summary of costs report—two departments—FIFO

The Silver Trinkets Company makes sterling silver pacifiers in two production processes. In the first the metal is finely molded. In the second process the pacifiers are polished and boxed (100 pacifiers to a box). The silver metal is added entirely at the beginning of Process 1, and the pacifiers are boxed at the end of Process 2.

	Molding	Polishing
Beginning balance (November 1), pacifiers.	10,000	3,000
Pacifiers started or transferred-in	50,000	?
Completed units:		
Pacifiers.	55,000	n/a
Boxes	n/a	450
Completion percentage:		
Beginning inventory.	75%	50%
Ending inventory.	25%	75%
Costs of beginning inventory:		
Metal	$1,000,000	$ n/a
Boxes	n/a	0
Conversion costs	200,625	12,000
Transferred-in costs	n/a	375,000
Costs incurred in November:		
Metal	5,000,000	n/a
Conversion costs	1,486,875	426,000
Boxes	n/a	90,000

Required

1. Using the FIFO method, prepare the production report and summary of costs report for the molding department for November.

(Check figure: Cost of pacifiers transferred to polishing = $7,149,375)

2. Using the FIFO method, prepare the production report and the summary of costs report for the polishing department for November.

(Check figure: Cost of ending inventory = $1,767,870)

Problem A21-9

Production report and summary of costs report for two departments—weighted average.

Required

Using the weighted average method, repeat the requirements of Problem A21-8.

(Check figures: Cost of pacifiers transferred to Department 2 = $7,150,000, and cost of boxes transferred to finished goods = $6,288,300)

Problem A21-10

Preparing all process costing reports for two departments for two months—weighted average

On January 1, the Warhawk Weapons Company begins production of a new handgun called Saturday Night Extra-Special. All the materials are added at the beginning of the Assembly Department, and completed guns are transferred to a second department, which inspects each gun before it is transferred to finished goods. The following facts are given for each department, one month at a time:

January

During the first month of operation, production was started on 1,000 guns in the Assembly Department, of which 800 were completed. The costs incurred in January were $5,000 for direct materials and $2,125 for conversion costs. The ending inventory was one-fourth complete at the end of the month.

In the Inspection Department, 700 guns were completely inspected and given the green light to be sold. They were transferred to finished goods. The remaining guns were one-half inspected on January 31. The conversion costs incurred during January were $750.

February

During February, 1,400 guns were started, of which 400 (three-fourths complete) were unfinished on February 28. The Assembly Department incurred $7,350 of costs for direct materials and $3,770 for conversion costs.

The costs incurred in the Inspection Department during February were $1,155 for conversion costs. There were 300 guns still on hand at the end of February, which had been only one-third inspected.

Required

1. Prepare the production report and summary of costs report for the Assembly Department for January. Also make the appropriate journal entry for the transfer to the Inspection Department.
2. Prepare the production report and summary of costs report for the Inspection Department for January. Also make the journal entry to record the transfer to finished goods.

(Check figure: Cost of guns completed = $5,953)

3. Prepare the production report and the summary of costs report for the Assembly Department for February. Once again, make the correct entry to record the transfer.

(Check figure: Cost of guns completed = $9,378)

4. Prepare the production report and the summary of costs report for the Inspection Department for February. One last time, make the correct entry to record the transfer.

Problem A21-11

Preparing all process costing reports for two departments for two months—FIFO

The Warhawk Weapons Company discussed in Problem A21-10 is interested in using the FIFO method, rather than the weighted average method, to account for its two departments.

Required

1. Prepare the production report and summary of costs report for the Assembly Department for January. Also make the appropriate journal entry for the transfer to the Inspection Department.

2. Prepare the production report and summary of costs report for the Inspection Department for January. Also make the journal entry to record the transfer to finished goods.

(Check figure: Cost of guns completed = $5,950)

3. Prepare the production report and the summary of costs report for the Assembly Department for February. Once again, make the correct entry to record the transfer.

(Check figure: Cost of guns completed = $9,365)

4. Prepare the production report and the summary of costs report for the Inspection Department for February. One last time, make the correct entry to record the transfer.

Set B

Problem B21-1
Preparing production report and summary of costs report—FIFO

The Sweet-Tooth Candy Company produces a snackbar called Baby Brett in a single process. All ingredients (sugar, syrup, nuts, flour, etc.) are added at the beginning of production, and a package is added at the very end. At the beginning of 1987 there were no snackbars in process (the ones that would have been on hand were spoiled when the power went off the previous night). During January, 1,000,000 snackbars were begun, of which 300,000 were still in process (one-third complete) on January 31.

The costs incurred during January were as follows:

Ingredients	$150,000
Conversion costs	80,000
Package	7,000

Sweet-Tooth Company uses the FIFO method of cost accounting.

Required

1. Prepare a production report for January.

(Check figure: Total CPEWU = $.26)

2. Prepare the summary of costs report for January.
3. Make the journal entry that would be needed to record the transfer of completed snackbars.

Problem B21-2
Preparing a production report and summary of costs report—weighted average

On March 1, 1989, the Henry Erin Bat Company, which produces metal baseball bats for Little League baseball teams, had 7,000 unfinished bats in process. Each one was about 25% complete. Its costs were:

Direct materials.	$10,400
Direct labor	5,000
Factory overhead.	1,600

During March, 23,000 bats were started; at the end of March, there were 5,000 bats remaining in work-in-process, three-fifths complete. The costs incurred in March were $34,600 for direct materials, $80,000 for direct labor, and $26,400 for factory overhead. The direct materials are added at the beginning of the production process, and all conversion costs are incurred smoothly over the entire production process. The FIFO method is used by the company to account for the production process.

Required

Prepare each of the following:
1. The production report
2. The summary of costs report

(Check figure: Cost of ending work-in-process = $19,682)

Problem B21-3
Preparing a production report and summary of costs report—weighted average

Assume that the Henry Erin Bat Company in Problem B21-2 would rather use the weighted average method than FIFO.

Required

Prepare each of the following:
1. The production report
2. The summary of costs report

(Check figure: Cost of ending work-in-process = $19,607)

Problem B21-4
Using weighted average with several materials

The George Orwell Manufacturer started 81,000 units during August 1989, and completed 66,000 during the month. Orwell uses three materials in production. Material A is added at the beginning of the process; material B is added evenly throughout production, and material C is added after production is 80% complete.

On August 1, Orwell had a 9,000-unit beginning inventory, 30% complete. Its costs were:

Material A	$8,400
Material B	4,020
Conversion costs	4,800

The costs incurred during August were:

Material A	$ 81,600
Material B	103,980
Material C	33,000
Conversion costs	120,300

The August 31 inventory was 25% complete.

Required

Using the weighted average method, determine each of the following:
1. The costs assigned to Finished Goods Inventory in August.

(Check figure: $312,708)

2. The cost of the August 31 balance in Work-in-Process.

Problem B21-5
Using FIFO with several materials

Read the facts above for George Orwell Manufacturer, but assume that the FIFO method is being used.

Required

Using the FIFO method, determine each of the following:
1. The costs assigned to Finished Goods Inventory in August.

(Check figure: $312,458)

2. The cost of the August 31 balance in Work-in-Process.

Problem B21-6
Using FIFO costing with several materials and transferred-in costs

The Dr. Pibber Bottling Company produces a soft drink called Pepper Power. The ingredients for Pepper Power are mixed in Department 1, bottled in Department 2, and capped and packaged (six to a carton) in Department 3. During December, 200,000 bottles (at $.08 per bottle) are transferred from Bottling to Capping. On December 1 there were 10,000 uncapped bottles in the Capping Department, one-fourth complete; and during December, 32,500 cartons were transferred to finished goods. The ending inventory of capped bottles were one-half complete.

The December 1 inventory had the following costs:

Transferred-in costs	$1,000
Conversion costs	175

The costs incurred during December in the Capping Department were as follows:

Conversion costs	$5,900
Caps (added at the one-third point in production) . .	2,100
Cartons (added at the end of production)	3,900

Required | Prepare a production report and summary of costs report for Dr. Pibber. Use the FIFO method of costing the product. Calculate the equivalent units and the CPEWU in terms of the number of bottles.

(Check figure: Total CPEWU = $.1395/bottle)

Problem B21-7

Using weighted average costing with several materials and transferred-in costs

Required

Prepare the production report and summary of costs report for the Dr. Pibber Company in Problem B21-6. Use the weighted average method to cost the product, and make all calculations in terms of the number of bottles produced.

(Check figure: Total CPEWU = $.141/bottle)

Problem B21-8

Production report and summary of costs report for two departments—FIFO

The Swinging Door Company produces high-quality leaded glass doors that pass through an assembly department and a finishing department prior to completion. The wood is added at the beginning of assembly; the leaded glass is added at the 50% point in finishing; and a package is added at the very end of finishing. These additional facts relate to production for Swinging Door during November:

	Assembly	Finishing
Beginning inventory, doors	2,500 ($\frac{1}{2}$ complete)	4,500 ($\frac{2}{3}$ complete)
Doors started, or transferred-in.	12,500	?
Completed doors.	8,000	10,500
Ending inventory, doors	7,000 ($\frac{6}{7}$ complete)	2,000 ($\frac{1}{4}$ complete)
Cost of beginning inventory:		
Wood . . . . $	190,000	n/a
Transferred-in costs	n/a	$434,000
Leaded glass	n/a	214,500
Package	n/a	0
Conversion costs	11,750	12,950
Costs incurred in November:		
Wood	1,025,000	n/a
Leaded glass	n/a	300,000
Package	n/a	21,000
Conversion costs	191,250	36,000
Method to be used.	FIFO	FIFO

Required | 1. Prepare a production report and summary of costs report for the assembly department.

(Check figure: Costs transferred to finishing = $754,000)

2. Prepare a production report and summary of costs report for the finishing department.

(Check figure: Costs transferred to finished goods = $1,581,200)

Problem B21-9

Production report and summary of costs report for two departments—weighted average

Required

Using the weighted average method, repeat the requirements of Problem B21-8.

(Check figure: Cost of doors transferred to finishing department = $764,000)

Problem B21-10
Preparing all process costing reports for two departments for two months — weighted average

The Irving Eastern Book Company produces sleazy romance novels in two departments, Binding and Proofing. All materials are added at the beginning of production in the Binding Department. Bound books are transferred to Proofing, where they are inspected to be sure that all the pages are included, the binding is secure, and the printing is legible.

The following facts relate to Irving's production during January 1988:

Binding Department: On January 1, there were 10,000 books in process (one-fifth complete). Costs were $1,000 for direct materials and $2,500 for conversion costs. During the month, 90,000 books were started and 80,000 were completed. The remaining books were three-fourths complete on January 31. The costs incurred in January were $9,000 for direct materials and $83,700 for conversion costs.

Proofing Department: The beginning inventory was 2,000 books (one-fifth complete). The costs assigned to these books were $2,000 for transferred-in costs and $200 for conversion costs. The January 31 balance in inventory was 4,000 books (one-half complete). The conversion costs for January in the Proofing Department were $39,800.

The facts given below relate to production for February:

Binding Department: 60,000 books were begun in February, and there were 30,000 in process at the end of February, two-thirds complete. The direct materials costs for February were $7,500, and the conversion costs were $57,750.

Proofing Department: The number of books that were transferred to finished goods during February were 45,000. The books that were still in process at the end of the month were one-third complete. The conversion costs for the month were $25,300.

The Irving Eastern Company uses the weighted average method to account for its production costs in both the Binding and the Proofing Departments.

Required

Prepare the production report and summary of cost report for:
1. The Binding Department for January

(Check figure: Cost of books transferred = $80,560)

2. The Proofing Department for January
3. The Binding Department for February

(Check figure: Cost of books transferred = $56,910)

4. The Proofing Department for February

Problem B21-11
Preparing all process costing reports for two departments for two months — using FIFO

Assume that Irving Eastern Book Company, discussed in Problem B21-10, is using the FIFO method rather than weighted average to account for its Binding and Proofing Departments.

Required

Prepare the production report and summary of cost report for:
1. The Binding Department for January

(Check figure: Cost of books transferred = $80,700)

2. The Proofing Department for January
3. The Binding Department for February

(Check figure: Cost of books transferred = $56,000)

4. The Proofing Department for February

Chapter 22

The Contribution Approach to Cost-Volume-Profit Analysis

In this chapter you will learn the following:

- The terms *variable costs* and *fixed costs*
- How to show variable costs and fixed costs graphically
- What the *relevant range of activity* means
- What the *contribution margin income statement* is and how it is different from the *traditional income statement*
- What a *breakeven point* is and how to calculate it
- How to show graphically the many variables involved in cost-volume-profit analysis
- What the simplifying assumptions are for cost-volume-profit analysis
- How to use cost-volume-profit analysis for a multi-product firm
- The difference between the direct costing and absorption costing methods

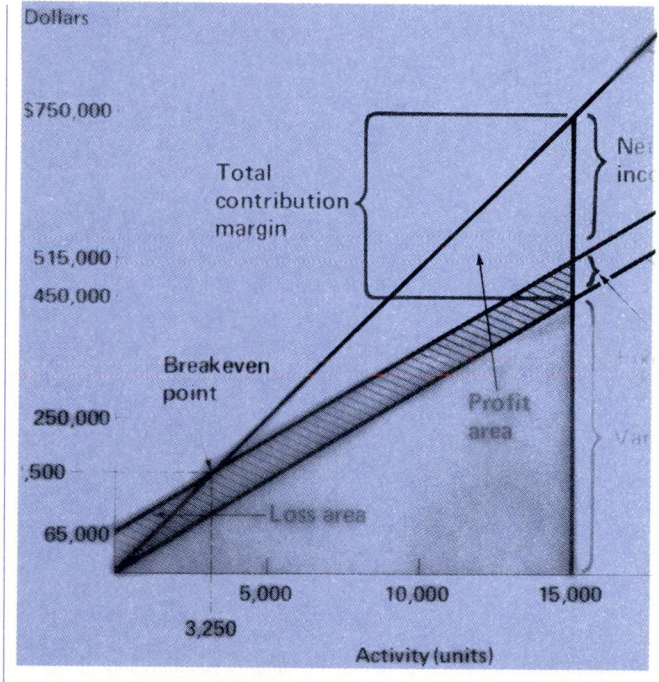

In Chapter 19 we looked closely at product costs—those costs assigned to inventory when incurred, and expensed when the units are sold—as well as period costs—those costs that are expenses when incurred. We also discussed how product costs and period costs could be total costs—the sum of all costs for a center of activity—or average costs—the total costs divided by the activity of the center to which they relate.

Now we will look at the *behavior* of product costs and period costs. That is, we will look at how those costs, whether in total or on the average, respond to changes in activity. We will be concerned with classifying costs as variable, fixed, or mixed.

Then we will explain in detail a tool used by accountants to help managers plan for the short run—a tool that can be used only if the accountant knows which costs are variable and which costs are fixed. We refer to this tool as cost-volume-profit analysis.

THE THREE TYPES OF COSTS: VARIABLE, FIXED, AND MIXED

Variable and fixed costs: Defined in terms of how the total cost responds to changes in activity

There are three types of costs: variable, fixed, and mixed. The type of cost that a particular cost is depends on how *its total behaves or responds to changes in activity.*

A *variable cost,* in total, changes in the same direction and in direct proportion to changes in activity. The costs of direct materials, direct labor, supplies, and sales commissions are a few examples of variable costs.

A *fixed cost,* in total, does not change in response to changes in activity. That's the simplest definition. A more complete definition is as follows: For a given period of time and within a relevant range of activity, a total fixed cost does not change in response to changes in activity. Rent, depreciation, property taxes, and certain salaries are examples of fixed costs. We will explain a little later what we mean by *for a given period of time* and *within a relevant range of activity.*

Mixed costs: a combination of variable and fixed costs

Mixed costs are a combination of variable costs and fixed costs. Part of a mixed cost is not expected to respond to changes in activity—the fixed cost component—and part is expected to respond to changes in activity—the variable cost component. An example of a mixed cost is a utility bill. Part of it is fixed—you will be charged this amount even if you don't turn on the electricity; and part of it is variable—the more kilowatthours you use, the higher your cost.

VARIABLE AND FIXED COSTS AND CHANGES IN ACTIVITY

AVC is constant but AFC varies inversely with activity

The next step to understanding the behavior of costs is to see how average variable costs respond to changes in activity, and how average fixed costs respond to changes in activity. Let's first take a look at the relationship of total and average costs to activity, and see how it differs for variable costs and fixed costs. For variable costs, in order for the total to change in direct proportion to changes in activity, the average variable cost (such as a variable cost per hour or per unit) will have to remain the same, regardless of the level of activity. For example, if the variable cost per unit is $4 when 10 units are produced, it is also $4 per unit when 100 or 1,000 units are produced. Only if the *average* variable cost remains unchanged will the *total* variable costs change in direct proportion—represented by a straight line on a graph—to changes in activity. On the other hand, for *total* fixed costs to remain unchanged in response to changes in activity, the *average* fixed costs must be inversely related to activity. That is, the greater the amount of activity, the lower the average fixed cost; and the lower the amount of activity, the higher the average fixed cost.

In Example 22-1 we'll show you what we mean. Look carefully at the total and average variable and fixed costs and notice how they respond to changes in activity.

In this example we are measuring activity by the number of units produced, and the average costs are costs per unit. You may remember that in Chapter 19 we mentioned that activity can be measured in many ways—units produced, hours, requisitions, or square feet, to name a few—and that an average can be a cost per unit, as shown in Example 22-1, a cost per hour, a cost per requisition, or a cost per square foot.

EXAMPLE 22-1

THE HARRIS COMPANY

During 1988, the Harris Company expects its variable costs to be $4 per unit and its total fixed costs to be $10,000. The company predicts its variable and fixed costs at several possible levels of activity for the year. First the total costs:

Activity (in units)		Variable Cost per Unit		Total Variable Costs	Total Fixed Costs
100	×	$4	=	$ 400	$10,000
150	×	$4	=	$ 600	$10,000
500	×	$4	=	$2,000	$10,000
1,000	×	$4	=	$4,000	$10,000
1,200	×	$4	=	$4,800	$10,000
1,500	×	$4	=	$6,000	$10,000

Now the average costs are calculated for these same levels of activity:

Activity (in units)	Variable Costs per Unit	Fixed Costs per unit (rounded)
100	$4 ($400 ÷ 100)	$100 ($10,000 ÷ 100)
150	$4 ($600 ÷ 150)	$ 67 ($10,000 ÷ 150)
500	$4 ($2,000 ÷ 500)	$ 20 ($10,000 ÷ 500)
1,000	$4 ($4,000 ÷ 1,000)	$ 10 ($10,000 ÷ 1,000)
1,200	$4 ($4,800 ÷ 1,200)	$ 8 ($10,000 ÷ 1,200)
1,500	$4 ($6,000 ÷ 1,500)	$ 7 ($10,000 ÷ 1,500)

If we add together the totals for each activity level for variable and fixed costs, we get mixed costs. For the activity levels of 100 units and 150 units, the mixed costs are $10,400 ($400 + $10,000) and $10,600 ($600 + $10,000), respectively.

These total and average variable and fixed costs are represented in graphical form in Figure 22-1. The relationship between activity and total variable costs is shown in graph 1; between activity and total fixed costs, in graph 2. Graphs 3 and 4 depict the relationships between activity and the average costs. For all graphs in this section of the book, the horizontal axis represents activity (units in this example) and the vertical axis represents dollars of cost (or revenue).

AVC and TFC are constant   As you look over the four graphs, remember what we mentioned earlier. For the variable costs, the average is unchanging, so the total will be in the form of a straight line coming out of the origin. For the fixed costs, the total is not expected to change, so the average will decrease as activity increases.

A Given Period of Time   According to the way we define a fixed cost, its total is not expected to respond to changes in activity. Now, this does not mean that a fixed cost will remain the same indefinitely, nor that a fixed cost will remain the same regardless of how high or low

FIGURE 22-1
Graphs for Variable and Fixed Costs.
The TVC changes in direct proportion to changes in activity with a constant AVC of $4.00. For fixed costs the TFC remains at $10,000 but the AFC decreases with greater activity.

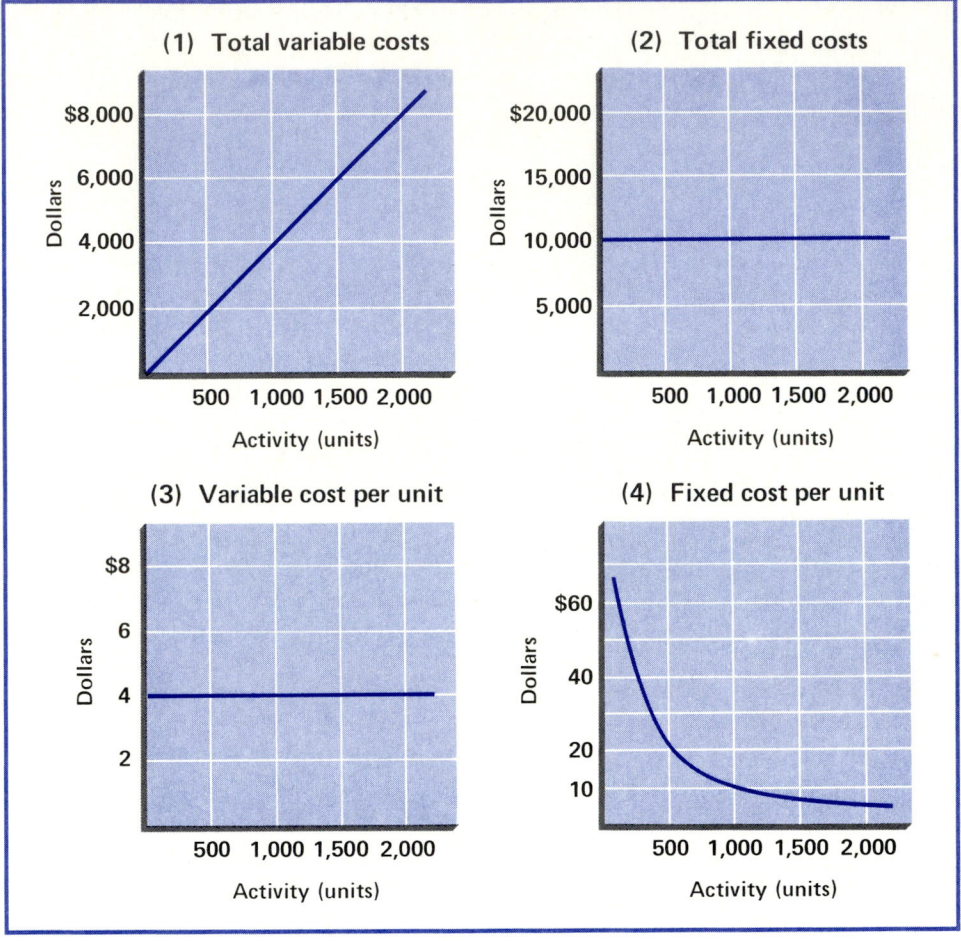

activity is expected to be. The more complete definition we gave for a fixed cost was that it is not expected to change in total, in response to changes in activity:

1. For a given period of time

2. Within a "relevant range" of activity

Let's first see what we mean by *for a given period of time.* Then we will explain what we mean by *within a relevant range of activity.*

Assume that you are trying to predict how much three costs (making up part of the $10,000 total in Example 22-1), will be in 1988. During 1987 these costs were:

Property taxes $1,500
Insurance   500
Rent. 4,000

You know that your property has recently been appraised at a greater value than it was a year ago, so you expect your property taxes and insurance to increase by 20% in

1988. According to your lease, the rent will automatically drop to $3,500 if you renew for an additional 5 years—and you do plan to renew.

The following are your predictions for 1988:

Property taxes	$1,800
Insurance	600
Rent.	3,500

Fixed costs can change, and still be fixed

These costs are all fixed—they just happen to be different in 1988 than they were in 1987. Many fixed costs are fixed only for a single period of time; the fact that they change from one period to another in no way affects their classification as fixed.

Not only can fixed costs change from one period to the next, they can also be a different amount than you predicted them to be. For instance, if in 1988 your county government started assessing property taxes at 100% of fair market value instead of 80%, you might get a property tax bill for 1988 of $2,250. These property taxes are still considered to be fixed costs even though they are different from the amount that you expected, $1,800.

A Relevant Range of Activity

Fixed costs aren't the same at *all* levels of activity

As you may have already guessed, the ***relevant range of activity*** is a range of activity in which the fixed costs do not respond to changes in activity. Stated in more general terms, it is only within the relevant range of activity that *all* assumptions concerning the behavior of costs are expected to be valid.

Assume that the Harris Company in Example 22-1 is operating at a full capacity of 1,500 units and wants to increase its production to 3,000 units. Is it reasonable to expect the fixed costs to remain at $10,000 if Harris increases its capacity to accommodate production of 3,000 units? Of course not. Additional machinery must be acquired, resulting in more depreciation, more salaried supervisors for additional workers, more insurance, and additional property taxes. All of these costs combine into a higher fixed cost, corresponding to the higher level of activity.

A higher range means more fixed costs

Assume that the additional fixed costs needed by Harris to increase the capacity would be $5,000, increasing the total fixed costs from $10,000 to $15,000. Assume also that the new capacity can now produce as many as 3,000 units. If Harris expects to produce from zero to 1,500 units each year, that represents one relevant range of activity for which the fixed costs would be only $10,000. But if Harris wants to expand the maximum capacity from 1,500 to 3,000 units, that higher range—from 1,501 to 3,000 units—would represent a higher relevant range of activity, and the fixed costs for this higher range would be $15,000.

The graph depicting these two relevant ranges for Harris Company is shown in Figure 22-2. Other relevant ranges of activity are possible. For example, if Harris Company increased its maximum productive capacity from 3,000 to 5,000 units, then that range—between 3,000 and 5,000 units—would represent a higher range requiring higher amounts of fixed costs.

Relevant Range and Variable Costs

The variable cost rate can change when you go to a new relevant range

In the previous section we defined the relevant range as a range of activity in which total fixed costs are not expected to change. The concept of a relevant range doesn't apply only to fixed costs, however. That is why we added to the definition that *all* cost behavior assumptions are valid only within the relevant range—this includes the assumptions for variable costs as well as for fixed costs.

We say that variable costs, in total, change in direct proportion to changes in

FIGURE 22-2
Fixed Costs and Relevant Ranges.
The fixed costs are $10,000 for 0–1,500 units (relevant range no. 1) but will be $15,000 for 1,501–3,000 units (relevant range no. 2).

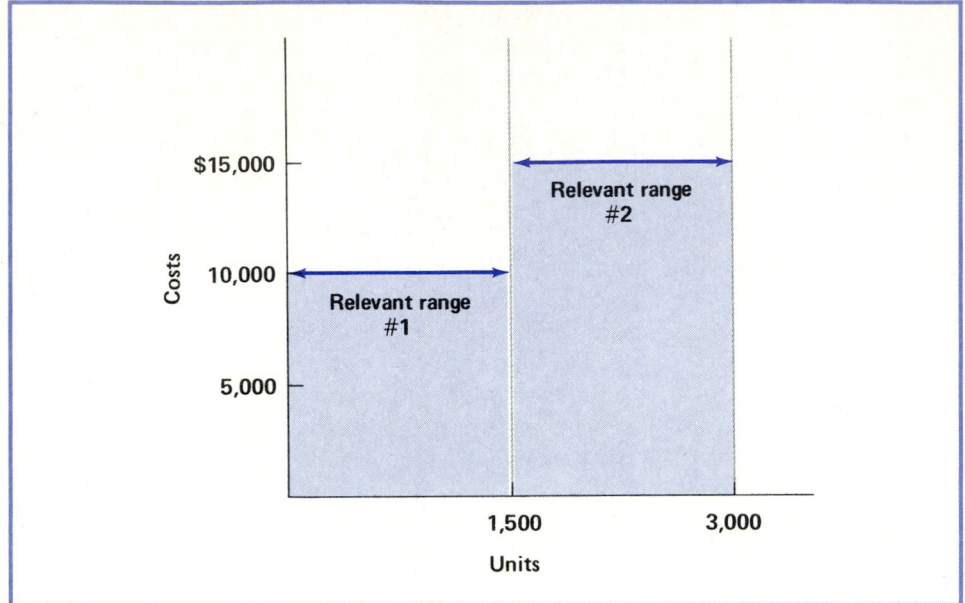

activity, and that average variable costs are constant. Are these statements true no matter how few or how many units we make?

In reality, it is quite possible that the average cost is different for different relevant ranges of activity, just as the total fixed costs are different. Do not worry about the average variable cost changing, however, because we will assume that all activity takes place in a single relevant range. At this point you need only remember that variable costs do behave in the manner we described within a single relevant range of activity.

COST-VOLUME-PROFIT ANALYSIS

C-V-P: analysis of interacting variables

Now that we know what variable and fixed costs are, we are ready to study an extremely useful accounting tool called cost-volume-profit analysis. In cost-volume-profit analysis accountants recognize that there are many interacting variables that affect an organization's profits—such things as the sales price of a product, the variable costs per unit, the fixed costs, and the volume of production and sales. *Cost-volume-profit (C-V-P) analysis* evaluates the relationships among these interacting variables and the effect that changes in these variables have on an organization's profits.

A simple example

For example, assume that a new publisher, Prentiss Hill, has just signed its first author to write a Fundamentals of Accounting textbook. They have determined that their variable costs will average $30 per book and their fixed costs will total $65,000. Since they expect the book to be far superior to any of its competition, they plan to sell it for a whopping price of $50 per book. The president is naturally concerned with making a profit in the first year, and asks the controller, Cindy Kinsey, to figure out how many books they will have to sell to break even.

An hour later Cindy reports back to the president with what she has learned:

1. If the company can sell at least 3,250 books, they will do no worse than break even.

2. Based on the sales manager's projections for the first year of sales of 8,000 books, the company can expect to show a profit of $95,000.

Breakeven means zero profit

Just how Cindy was able to make these calculations — and much more — will be explained in the remainder of this chapter. First, however, let's explain what a breakeven point is and how she calculated it.

The ***breakeven point*** is the number of units sold (or dollars of sales) that will guarantee a zero profit for the firm. Cindy found this point — in units — by starting with the following general equation:

$$\text{Total sales} - \text{total costs} = \text{net income}$$

Keeping in mind that total costs will be made up of variable costs and fixed costs, the equation becomes:

$$\frac{\text{Total}}{\text{sales}} - \frac{\text{variable}}{\text{costs}} - \frac{\text{fixed}}{\text{costs}} = \text{net income}$$

And now, taking it a little bit further, we get:

The unknown in this equation is the number of units sold

$$\left(\frac{\text{Sales}}{\text{price}} \times \frac{\text{units}}{\text{sold}}\right) - \left(\frac{\text{variable}}{\text{cost per}} \times \frac{\text{units}}{\text{sold}}\right) - \frac{\text{fixed}}{\text{costs}} = \frac{\text{net}}{\text{income}}$$

Since Cindy did not know how many units would have to be sold in order to break even, she substituted the letter X in the equation for units sold, let net income = 0, or breakeven, and solved the equation in the following manner:

When $X = 3,250$ units, income = $0.

$$\$50X - \$30X - \$65,000 = \$0$$
$$\$20X = \$65,000$$
$$X = \$65,000 \div 20 = 3,250 \text{ units}$$

THE CONTRIBUTION MARGIN FORMAT TO THE INCOME STATEMENT

The next thing we want to do is to prove that 3,250 units is indeed the breakeven point. In order to do this we need to prepare an income statement that uses a format that emphasizes the behavior of costs. The income statement typically used with cost-volume-profit analysis is called the ***contribution margin format income statement*** (also called the ***behaviorial format income statement***). It looks like this:

The contribution margin format takes a behavioral approach to cost classifications

Sales

Less: Variable Costs

Equals: Total Contribution Margin

Less: Fixed Costs

Equals: Net Income

For this format, we add up all the variable costs (production, selling, and administration) and subtract this total from sales. We call the difference the ***total contribution margin,*** which is why this format is referred to as the ***contribution margin format income statement.*** We then add together all fixed costs (production, selling, and administration) and subtract them from the contribution margin to get net income.

Now let's look back at Prentiss Hill Company, but in somewhat more detail. We will use the expanded set of facts in Example 22-2 to explain the contribution margin format income statement.

EXAMPLE 22-2

The simple example expanded

THE PRENTISS HILL COMPANY

The Prentiss Hill Company sells a new book for $50 per book. Variable and fixed costs are expected to be:

Variable costs:	
Direct materials	$10/unit
Direct labor	15/unit
Variable overhead	3/unit
Variable selling	2/unit
Total	$30/unit
Fixed costs:	
Factory overhead	$40,000
Selling	25,000
Total	$65,000

There were no beginning or ending balances in work-in-process or finished goods.

The contribution margin income statement for Prentiss Hill Company at the break-even point of 3,250 units is shown in Exhibit 22-1.

$$TCM = total\ sales - TVC$$

The key item in the contribution margin statement is the **total contribution margin,** which is the dollar amount of sales remaining after the variable costs have been subtracted. In Exhibit 22-1 the total contribution margin is $65,000 ($162,500 − $97,500). If the total contribution margin is greater than the fixed costs, there is a profit; if it is less than the fixed costs, there is a loss; and if it is equal to the fixed costs, the firm is breaking even. Notice in Exhibit 22-1 that the total contribution margin is exactly equal to the fixed costs—therefore 3,250 units must be the breakeven point.

If you recall, when Cindy Kinsey calculated the breakeven point, she also found out that the sales personnel were predicting sales for the year of 8,000 units—well in

EXHIBIT 22-1
Contribution Margin Format Income Statement—At Breakeven.

Total contribution margin is total sales less total variable costs, or $65,000. This is the amount contributed to the coverage of fixed costs. In this situation the TCM is exactly equal to the fixed, so there is no profit.

PRENTISS HILL COMPANY
Income Statement
Year Ended December 31, 1989

Sales Revenue (3,250 books × $50)			$162,500
Total Variable Costs:			
Direct Materials (3,250 books × $10)	$32,500		
Direct Labor (3,250 books × $15)	48,750		
Variable Overhead (3,250 × $3)	9,750	$91,000	
Variable Selling (3,250 books × $2)		6,500	97,500
Total Contribution Margin			$ 65,000
Fixed Costs:			
Fixed Factory Overhead		$40,000	
Fixed Selling		25,000	65,000
Net Income			$ 0

EXHIBIT 22-2
Contribution Margin Format Income Statement—At a Profitable Level of Sales.
Total contribution margin is now $160,000—$95,000 in excess of the fixed costs of $65,000.

PRENTISS HILL COMPANY
Income Statement
Year Ended December 31, 1989

Sales Revenue (8,000 books × $50)			$400,000
Total Variable Costs:			
Direct Materials (8,000 books × $10)	$ 80,000		
Direct Labor (8,000 books × $15)	120,000		
Variable Overhead (8,000 books × $3)	24,000	$224,000	
Variable Selling (8,000 books × $2)		16,000	
Total Variable Costs			240,000
Total Contribution Margin			$160,000
Fixed Costs:			
Fixed Factory Overhead		$ 40,000	
Fixed Selling		25,000	65,000
Net Income			$ 95,000

---

excess of the breakeven point of 3,250 units. Let's see now, in Exhibit 22-2, what the income statement looks like if the sales personnel are correct.

TCM exceeds TFC by $95,000—the net income

As you can see, when the sales are 8,000 units, the total contribution margin is $160,000, which is far in excess of the fixed costs of $65,000. The excess of $95,000 is, of course, the net income. So you can see that the key to generating a profit is to sell enough units so that the resulting total contribution margin is greater than the fixed costs.

In Chapter 19 we prepared income statements that used the following format:

The traditional format income statement

Sales

Less: Cost of Goods Sold

Equals: Gross Margin

Less: Selling and Administrative Expenses

Equals: Net Income

Traditionally the income statement follows this format and that is why we call this statement the ***traditional format income statement.*** When we use this format we group costs within the income statement according to the *function* of each cost—i.e., production, selling, and administration. That is why it is also referred to as the ***functional format income statement.***

Superiority of the Contribution Margin Format

The contribution margin format is better suited for evaluating the effect on profits of a change in a variable

It is possible to calculate income using either the traditional or contribution margin format. We will employ primarily the contribution margin format, however, because it seems to be more naturally suited for analyzing the interacting variables that make up net income.

Whichever method we use, we still need to know which costs are variable and which costs are fixed. Since the contribution margin format uses a behavioral approach to grouping costs on the income statement, it is extremely easy to keep track of how each group of costs responds to a change in activity. Because the traditional format groups costs according to their function, each group is a combination of variable and fixed costs. As a result it is more difficult, and sometimes impossible, to predict accurately how each group will respond to a change in activity.

Therefore, whenever you are required to prepare an income statement, we recommend that you use the contribution margin format unless you are told specifically to do otherwise.

Our recommendation of the contribution margin format has to do with helping managers make decisions—not with publishing financial statements for external parties. For financial reporting purposes you must use the traditional format in order to comply with generally accepted accounting principles (GAAP).

We will discuss both formats again in a later section of this chapter, when we compare the direct costing and absorption costing methods of product costing.

ADDITIONAL TERMS USED IN COST-VOLUME-PROFIT ANALYSIS

We know from Exhibit 22-2 that the total variable costs for Prentiss Hill were $240,000, and that the total contribution margin was $160,000. Before we go any further into cost-volume-profit analysis, we also need to know what the variable costs and contribution margin are:

1. On a per-unit basis, and

2. As a percentage of sales dollars.

We will look first at the per-unit figures and then at the percentage figures for the variable costs.

Variable Cost per Unit (VCU)

$$VCU = \frac{TVC}{units}$$

Although we were actually given the variable cost per unit in Example 22-1, if it had not been given we still could have calculated it based only on the totals from Exhibit 22-1 or 22-2. Using Exhibit 22-2, we could have used the following reasoning: Since Prentiss Hill incurs $240,000 of variable costs to produce and sell 8,000 units, the average variable cost per unit (VCU) must be:

$$\text{Variable cost per unit (VCU)} = \frac{\text{total variable costs}}{\text{units sold}}$$

$$= \frac{\$240,000}{8,000 \text{ units}}$$

$$= \$30$$

For each additional unit produced and sold, Prentiss Hill's total costs increase by $30.

Look now at Exhibit 22-3. You can see that it is the same as Exhibit 22-2 except that we've added columns for units, per unit, and percentages, in addition to the columns for the total dollars. The $30 per unit cost (VCU) is simply the $240,000 divided by the 8,000 units.

Variable Cost Percentage (VC%)

$$VC\% = \frac{TVC}{\text{sales dollars}}$$

The *variable cost percentage* (or *variable cost ratio*) represents the portion of total sales that is needed to cover the variable costs; it is the percentage that variable costs are to sales dollars. The variable cost percentage (VC%) for Prentiss Hill is 60%, which can be determined several different ways. The first way uses total dollars:

$$\text{Variable cost percentage (VC\%)} = \frac{\text{total variable costs}}{\text{total sales dollars}} \times 100\%$$

$$= \frac{\$240,000}{\$400,000} \times 100\%$$

$$= 60\%$$

EXHIBIT 22-3
Contribution Margin Format Income Statement—Showing Totals, Per Units, and Percentages.

PRENTISS HILL
Income Statement
Year Ended December 31, 1989

	Total Dollars	Units	Per Unit	%
Sales Revenue	$400,000	8,000	$50	100%
Variable Costs:				
Direct Materials	$ 80,000			
Direct Labor	120,000			
Variable Overhead	24,000			
Variable Selling	16,000			
Total Variable Costs	240,000	8,000	30	60%
Total Contribution Margin	$160,000	8,000	$20	40%
Fixed Costs:				
Fixed Factory Overhead	$ 40,000			
Fixed Selling	25,000	65,000		
Net Income	$ 95,000			

SP   *VCU*   *VC%*   *CMU*   *CM%*

The $240,000 of variable costs average $30 per unit and 60% of sales. The $160,000 of contribution margin is $20 per unit and 40% of sales.

If you look at Exhibit 22-3, you can see the 60% under the percentage column in the income statement. This means that the variable costs average 60% of sales dollars; or that 60% of the sales dollars are needed to cover the variable costs.

Although we just calculated variable costs as a percentage of sales, we could just as well calculate this relationship in decimal ratio form. For example, 60% is the same as .60 (the variable cost ratio), since $.60 \times 100\% = 60\%$. For simplicity we will use one notation—VC%—to represent the variable cost percentage (60%) or the variable cost ratio (.60).

The second way to calculate the VC% uses the variable cost per unit and the sales price, as follows:

$$VC\% = \frac{VCU}{SP}$$

$$VC\% = \frac{\textbf{variable cost per unit}}{\textbf{sales price per unit}}$$

$$= \frac{\$30}{\$50}$$

$$= .60 \text{ (or 60\%)}$$

There is a third way to calculate the VC%; it relates to an understanding of the contribution margin percentage (CM%), which we discuss in a later section.

Contribution Margin per Unit (CMU)

In Exhibit 22-2, Prentiss Hill had a total contribution margin of $160,000. We can determine the amount that each unit contributes—the *contribution margin per unit (CMU)*—in two different ways. In the first way we merely subtract the variable cost per unit from the sales price per unit:

$$CMU = SP - VCU$$

Contribution margin per unit (CMU) = sales price per unit − variable costs per unit

$$= \$50 - \$30 = \$20$$

This means that each time a unit is sold, it provides, or *contributes,* the difference between the sales price and the unit variable costs toward covering the fixed costs needed to produce and sell all the units. In this case, each unit sold contributes $20 toward paying for the fixed costs. Furthermore, once the total fixed costs are covered, then the $20 represents the amount that each unit sold contributes to net income — that is, every time a unit is sold, the profits increase by $20.

Notice now where the $20 per unit is in Exhibit 22-3. It is right below the $30 in the per-unit column of the income statement ($50 − $30 = $20).

The second way to calculate the CMU is to divide the total contribution margin by the number of units sold:

$$CMU = \frac{TCM}{units}$$

$$CMU = \frac{\text{total contribution margin}}{\text{units sold}}$$

$$= \frac{\$160,000}{8,000 \text{ units}}$$

$$= \$20 \text{ per unit}$$

If 8,000 units contribute $160,000, then each unit must contribute $20.

Contribution Margin Percentage (CM%)

The *contribution margin percentage* (or *contribution margin ratio*) represents the portion of total sales that remains after the variable costs have been subtracted. It can be determined in three ways.

The first way is to divide the total contribution margin by total sales dollars. For Prentiss Hill, it would be as follows:

$$CM\% = \frac{TCM}{dollar\ sales}$$

$$\text{Contribution margin percentage (CM\%)} = \frac{\text{total contribution margin}}{\text{total sales dollars}} \times 100\%$$

$$= \frac{\$160,000}{\$400,000} \times 100\%$$

$$= 40\%$$

Now look one last time at Exhibit 22-3, and notice where the contribution margin percentage of 40% is. You'll find it directly below the 60% in the % column of the income statement.

Forty percent of the sales dollars remain after the variable costs have been subtracted; this means that 40% of the sales are contributed to the coverage of fixed costs.

In ratio form, 40% is the same as .40 (the contribution margin ratio), since .40 × 100% = 40%. For simplicity we will use the notation CM% to represent both the contribution margin percentage (40%) and the contribution margin ratio (.40).

A second way to calculate the CM% involves the contribution margin per unit and the sales price per unit:

$$CM\% = \frac{CMU}{SP}$$

$$CM\% = \frac{CMU}{\text{sales price per unit}} \times 100\%$$

$$= \frac{\$20}{\$50} \times 100\%$$

$$= 40\% \text{ (or .40)}$$

Finally, we can calculate the CM% by subtracting the variable cost percentage from 100%, or the variable cost ratio from 1:

CM% = 100% (or 1) minus VC%

$$\textbf{CM\% = 100\% - VC\%} \quad \text{or} \quad \textbf{CM\% = 1 - VC\%}$$
$$= 100\% - 60\% \qquad\qquad = 1 - .60$$
$$= 40\% \qquad\qquad\qquad = .40$$

If the CM% = 1 − VC%, then conversely the VC% = 1 − CM%. For Prentiss Hill, its VC% can be calculated this third way:

VC% = 100% (or 1) minus CM%

$$\textbf{VC\% = 100\% - CM\%} \quad \text{or} \quad \textbf{VC\% = 1 - CM\%}$$
$$= 100\% - 40\% = 60\% \qquad = 1 - .40 = .60$$

We have shown you several ways to calculate the variable cost percentage, the contribution margin per unit, and the contribution margin percentage. Although it will not be necessary for you to use all of these approaches in any one situation, it is likewise improbable that you can use a single approach in all situations. The easiest (and sometimes the only) way to determine the variable cost percentage, the contribution margin per unit, or the contribution margin percentage may depend on the exact information you are given. Therefore, it is probably a good idea for you to try to understand each of the approaches we discussed, rather than just the one that seems to be the easiest to calculate for Example 22-2. The easiest way for Example 22-2 may not be the easiest way in another situation.

TECHNIQUES OF COST-VOLUME-PROFIT ANALYSIS

In the previous section we calculated the breakeven point for Prentiss Hill. At that time, however, you were not familiar with many of the relevant terms used in C-V-P analysis, so we did not point out to you several things:

1. There are two different techniques for doing C-V-P analysis; we presented only one of them.

2. The techniques can be used to determine the level of sales needed to generate any desired amount of profit, and not just the breakeven point.

3. The techniques can be used to calculate the answer in either unit sales or dollar sales; we only showed you how to calculate the answer in unit sales.

We will now show you *both* methods of calculating (in *both* unit and dollar sales) the level of sales needed to generate *any* desired income.

Income Equation Technique

Sales − TVC − TFC = net income

The first technique is referred to as the ***income equation technique.*** This approach is the one you learned in the earlier section. It derives its name from the format for the contribution margin income statement. It is:

$$\begin{matrix} \textbf{Sales price} & \textbf{VCU times} & \textbf{total} & \\ \textbf{times units} - & \textbf{units} & -\textbf{fixed} = & \dfrac{\textbf{net}}{\textbf{income}} \\ \textbf{sold} & \textbf{sold} & \textbf{costs} & \end{matrix}$$

Let *X* be the number of units to be sold

Since we are looking for the number of units to be sold, we designate that unknown quantity as *X*. Substituting *X* into the income equation for the units sold and substituting zero for net income, we have a breakeven point of 3,250 units, just as we did before:

$$\$50X - \$30X - \$65,000 = \$0$$

$$X = \frac{\$65,000}{\$20}$$

$$= \underline{3,250 \text{ units}}$$

Just substitute net income for zero in the income equation

Let's assume for a moment that Prentiss Hill has greater aspirations than merely breaking even, and wants to know how many units need to be sold to show a profit of $95,000. The only difference now is that we substitute $95,000 (instead of zero) for net income in the equation. We now get an answer of 8,000 units:

$$\$50X - \$30X - \$65,000 = \$95,000$$

$$\$20X = \$160,000$$

$$X = \frac{\$160,000}{\$20}$$

$$= \underline{\underline{8,000 \text{ units}}}$$

We can get dollars by multiplying X times SP

Once we know how many *units* we have to sell, we can get the total sales revenue by multiplying the units times the sales price. At breakeven the sales dollars are:

$$3,250 \text{ units} \times \$50 = \underline{\underline{\$162,500}}$$

And for a profit of $95,000, the sales dollars are:

$$8,000 \text{ units} \times \$50 = \underline{\underline{\$400,000}}$$

Or we can let X = sales dollars in the equation

Or, we can solve for the total sales dollars directly, without first calculating the answer in units. We do this with the following equation:

Sales dollars − (VC% times sales dollars) − fixed costs = net income

In this equation, sales dollars is the unknown and is designated as X. Solving for the equation, we first get the breakeven point:

$$X - \text{VC\%}(X) - \textbf{fixed costs} = \textbf{net income}$$

$$X - .60X - \$65,000 = \$0$$

$$.40X = \$65,000$$

$$X = \frac{\$65,000}{.40}$$

$$= \underline{\underline{\$162,500}}$$

If Prentiss Hill desires a profit of $95,000, then sales have to be $400,000, determined as follows:

$$X - .60X - \$65,000 = \$95,000$$

$$.40X = \$160,000$$

$$X = \frac{\$160,000}{.40}$$

$$= \underline{\underline{\$400,000}}$$

Contribution Margin Technique

The second approach that we can use for cost-volume-profit analysis is called the *contribution margin technique.* If we designate X to represent unit sales, then our solution will be in units, using the following equation:

In the numerator, TFC + NI = the TCM at the unknown level of sales, X

$$X = \frac{\textbf{total fixed costs} + \textbf{net income}}{\textbf{CMU}}$$

By substituting zero for net income, once again we get a breakeven point of 3,250 units:

$$X = \frac{\$65,000 + \$0}{\$20} = \underline{\underline{3,250 \text{ units}}}$$

If we desire a $95,000 profit, we get an answer of 8,000 units:

$$X = \frac{\$65,000 + \$95,000}{\$20}$$

$$= \frac{\$160,000}{\$20} = \underline{\underline{8,000 \text{ units}}}$$

The contribution margin technique is actually the last step in the income equation technique

Notice that the last step in the income equation technique is identical to the only step in the contribution margin technique. This is because the contribution margin technique is a variation of the income equation technique. There are two advantages of using the contribution margin technique: (1) It involves fewer steps, and (2) it can be employed when the CMU is given but the sales price and VCU are not individually known.

If you want your solution to be in dollar sales rather than unit sales, let X represent the dollar sales and use the following formula:

$$X = \frac{\text{total fixed costs} + \text{net income}}{\text{CM\%}}$$

In order to break even, Prentiss Hill's dollar sales must be $162,500:

$$X = \frac{\$65,000 + \$0}{.40} = \underline{\underline{\$162,500}}$$

And in order to show a profit of $95,000, dollar sales will have to be $400,000, determined as follows:

$$X = \frac{\$65,000 + \$95,000}{.40} = \underline{\underline{\$400,000}}$$

In each of the calculations above we added together the fixed costs plus net income in the numerator of the formula. But do you know what the numerator of this formula represents? Look back at Exhibit 22-2 to the bottom of the income statement. Going from the bottom up, add the net income and fixed costs together—what do you get? The $95,000 plus $65,000 totals to $160,000, which is the total contribution margin. That means that the numerator represents the amount of total contribution margin that must be generated by some level of sales that will be just enough to cover the fixed costs and leave the desired profit remaining.

Margin of Safety

A firm is said to have a ***margin of safety*** when its sales are in excess of breakeven. We calculate a margin of safety by subtracting the breakeven sales from the actual or budgeted sales for the period. Prentiss Hill expected its sales to be 8,000 units ($400,000) during its first year of operation, and determined its breakeven point to be 3,250 units ($162,500). For these data the margin of safety (in units) is:

MS = actual sales − BE sales

$$\begin{matrix} \textbf{Margin} \\ \textbf{of} \\ \textbf{safety} \end{matrix} = \begin{matrix} \textbf{actual or} \\ \textbf{budgeted} \\ \textbf{sales} \end{matrix} - \begin{matrix} \textbf{breakeven} \\ \textbf{sales} \end{matrix}$$

$$= \textbf{8,000} - \textbf{3,250} = \textbf{4,750 units}$$

We can also measure margin of safety in terms of sales dollars:

$$\text{Margin of safety} = \$400,000 - \$162,500 = \$237,500$$

The margin of safety expresses the amount that a firm's sales can decrease without experiencing a loss. For Prentiss Hill, its sales can drop by as much as 4,750 units (or $237,500) before it has to worry about a loss for the year.

Effect of Income Taxes

Thus far we have ignored a very significant expense that appears on the income statement of many organizations: income taxes. Let's now look briefly at that expense and see how it affects the cost-volume-profit analysis.

Taxes = tax % times income before tax

If we add the complication of income taxes (at 40% of income before tax) to the income statement of Prentiss Hill, the expanded income statement (for 8,000 units) appears as shown in Exhibit 22-4:

EXHIBIT 22-4
Income Statement—Income Tax Effects Considered.
What we called net income in Exhibit 22-2—$95,000—is actually income before tax, when we have income tax to consider.

	8,000 Units
Sales Revenue	$400,000
Total Variable Costs	240,000
Total Contribution Margin	$160,000
Fixed Costs	65,000
Income before Tax	$ 95,000
Income Tax @ 40%	38,000
Net Income	$ 57,000

Notice in Exhibit 22-4 that what we've been calling "net income"—the $95,000—is actually "income before tax," for an organization that has to pay taxes. And what we will now properly refer to as "net income"—the $57,000—is "income after tax."

Now let's suppose further that you were asked: "How many units must Prentiss Hill sell in order to have a net income of $57,000?" Naturally your answer would be 8,000 units. But in order to get that answer, which amount of income would you place in the numerator of the C-V-P formula—net income or income before tax? As we showed previously, it has to be $95,000, and that amount is the income before tax. Therefore, whenever we deal with a company that pays taxes, the C-V-P formula is:

Income in the numerator is income before tax

$$X = \frac{\text{income before tax} + \text{fixed costs}}{\text{CMU}}$$

where X represents unit sales.

What do you do if you don't know the amount of income before tax—what if you have only net income? In that case you need to convert the net income to income before tax. You make this conversion with the following formula:

$$\text{Income before tax} = \frac{\text{net income}}{1 - \text{tax rate}}$$

If the net income is $57,000 and the tax rate is 40%, then the income before tax is determined like this:

Converting net income to income before tax

$$\text{Income before tax} = \frac{\$57,000}{1 - .40}$$

$$= \frac{\$57,000}{.60} = \underline{\underline{\$95,000}}$$

Finally, all of this discussion might naturally prompt you to ask: "When I see the term 'net income,' how will I know if it means income before tax or income after tax?" That's a good question.

If you first accept the fact that the last item on an income statement is the only item that should ever be called "net income," then we can answer your question with the following rule:

When there are no taxes

If there is no mention of income taxes in the problem, then net income means income before tax—because the income before tax is the last item on the income statement.

But:

When there are taxes

If income taxes are being considered in the problem, then net income means income after tax.

In most of the problems at the end of the chapter, there is no mention of income taxes, so the term *net income* will usually mean income before tax.

GRAPHICAL APPROACH TO COST-VOLUME-PROFIT ANALYSIS

Up to this point we have used income statements and equations to analyze the relationships among revenue, costs, volume, and profit. Now we will use a graphical approach to analyze these interacting variables.

Figures 22-3 on page 888 and 22-4 on page 889 present two similar, yet different approaches to a cost-volume-profit graph for Prentiss Hill. In both graphs the horizontal axis represents activity (unit sales) and the vertical axis measures dollars of revenues, costs, and profits.

Traditionally the sales line is drawn having a 45° angle extending from the origin upward and to the right. The total costs line begins at $65,000 (the fixed costs) on the vertical axis and also extends upward and to the right—but with a smaller slope than that of the sales line. The intersection of the sales line and the total costs line is the breakeven point (3,250, $162,500).

At levels of activity above the breakeven point of 3,250 units, the firm will have a profit, as shown by the gray-shaded ***profit area*** in both graphs. But for levels of activity below 3,250 units, the firm will experience a loss, as shown by the light blue-shaded ***loss area.***

The graphs differ in how the total costs line is derived

The main difference between Figures 22-3 and 22-4 is the manner in which the cost lines are drawn. In Figure 22-3, the fixed costs line ($65,000) is drawn first. The variable costs line is not shown, but the total costs line represents the addition of the variable costs to the fixed costs. Thus the variable costs are said to be graphed above the fixed costs. In Figure 22-4, the variable costs line is drawn first, to which is added the fixed costs, resulting in the total costs line. In Figure 22-4 the fixed costs are graphed above the variable costs.

Does it make any difference which graph we use? Do both graphs show the same relevant information—but in different ways?

Look carefully at the graph in Figure 22-4 and see if you can find anything important that is missing from Figure 22-3—something that we have been emphasizing throughout this chapter.

The horizontal axis is unit sales
and the vertical axis is dollars.
The total costs line is derived by
adding the variable costs to the
fixed costs line. The breakeven
point is 3,250 units ($162,500).

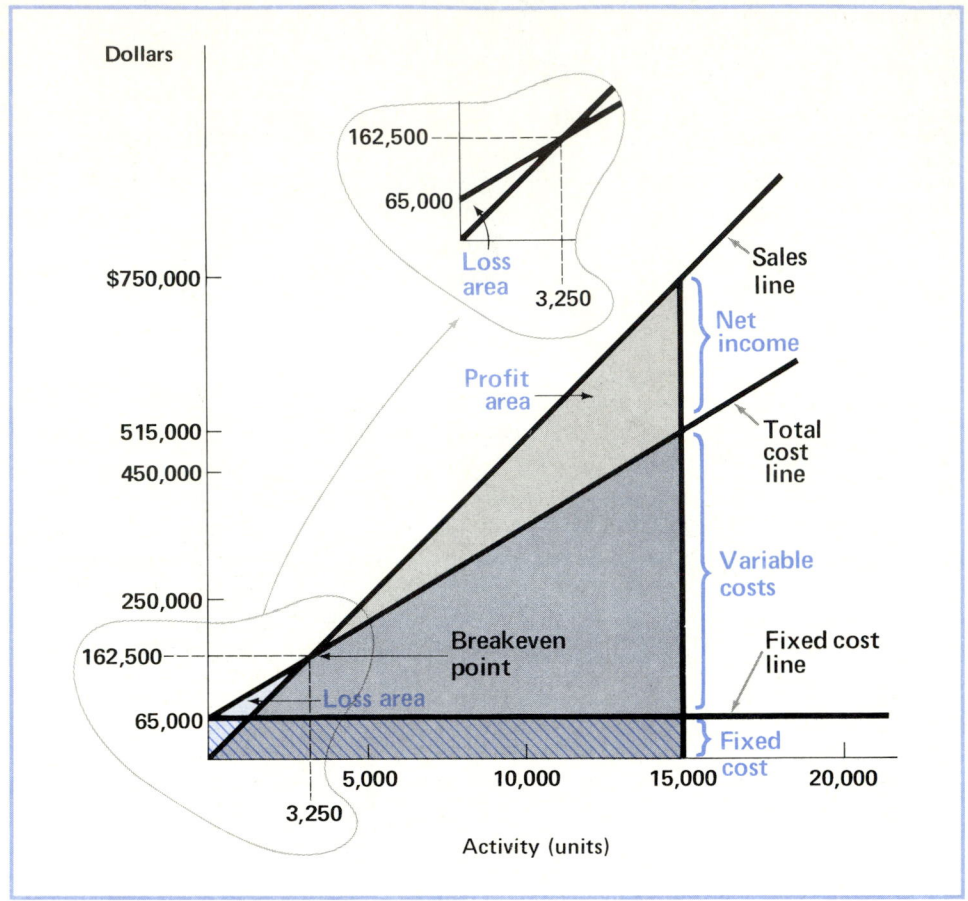

How about the total contribution margin?

It's easy to see TCM in Figure 22-4

Remember, total contribution margin is the difference between total sales and total variable costs. Since the variable costs line is drawn in Figure 22-4, it is easy to see the total contribution margin — it is the vertical distance from the sales line to the variable costs line. By reading the dollars from the vertical axis you can see in Figure 22-4 that the total contribution margin for 15,000 units is as follows:

Total Sales.	$750,000
Total Variable Costs	450,000
Total Contribution Margin	$300,000

You can also easily see in Figure 22-4 what the total contribution margin would be for any level of activity from zero to 15,000 units — it is represented by the dashed area between the sales line and the variable costs line.

FIGURE 22-4
Cost-Volume-Profit Graph:
Fixed Costs on Top of
Variable Costs.

The total costs line is derived by adding the fixed costs to the variable costs line. Total contribution margin is the distance from the sales line to the variable costs line.

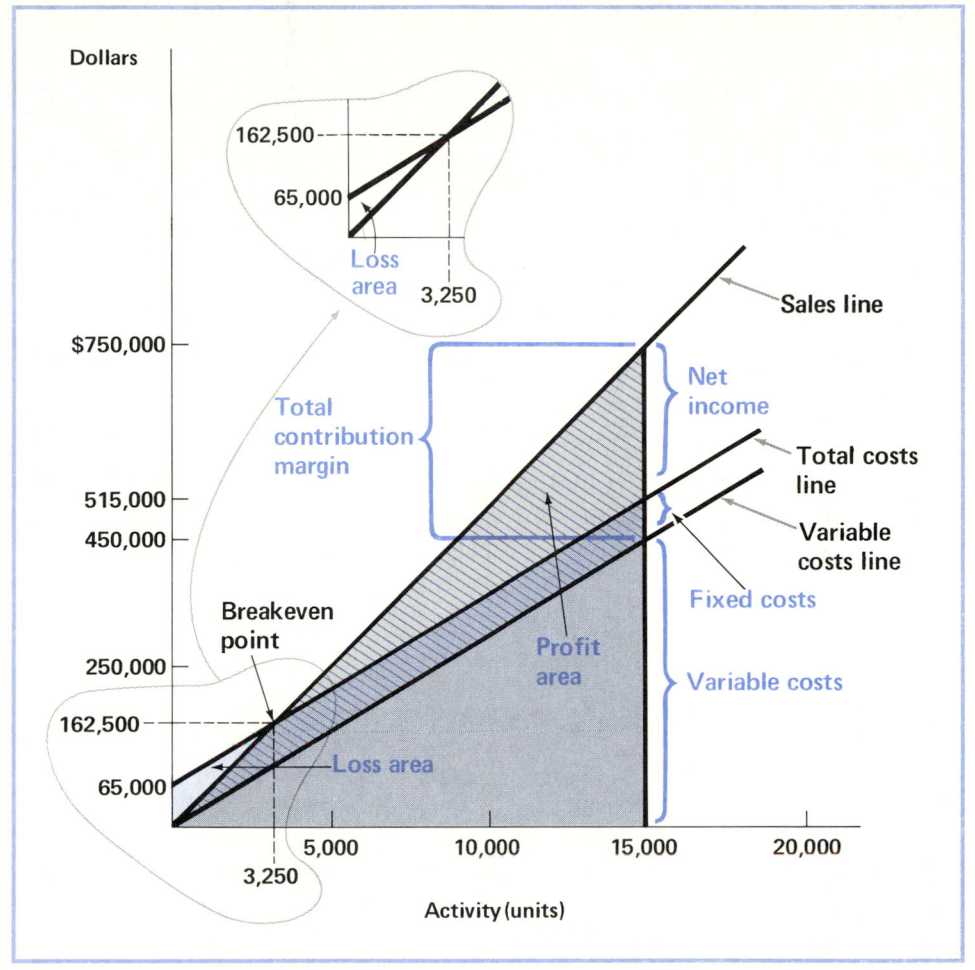

Because it is so easy to visually determine the total contribution margin in Figure 22-4, we often refer to that graph as the ***contribution margin cost-volume-profit graph.***

You can't see TCM in Figure 22-3

It is much more difficult to find the total contribution margin in Figure 22-3. At 15,000 units there is no vertical distance from one line to another representing total contribution margin, and there is no way to show a dashed area for total contribution margin in the range of activity from zero to 15,000 units.

Therefore we feel that the graph in Figure 22-4 is the better of the two graphs, because of the emphasis given to contribution margin. We recommend that you use the contribution margin approach whenever you are preparing a cost-volume-profit graph, unless you are specifically told to do otherwise.

ASSUMPTIONS
UNDERLYING COST-
VOLUME-PROFIT
ANALYSIS

When we use the cost-volume-profit model, our projections for an organization are reliable only if the assumptions we make about the model are valid. The assumptions we make relate to the interacting variables in the model—each of which is assumed to remain unchanged during the period that the model is used. We make six assumptions about the cost-volume-profit model. They are as follows:

The six assumptions of C-V-P analysis

1. Volume or activity (usually measured in units produced and sold) is the only variable affecting the behavior of costs.

2. Fixed and variable costs can be separated and accurately classified.

3. The variable cost per unit and the total fixed costs are expected to remain the same within the relevant range of cost-volume-profit analysis.

4. The sales price remains the same within the relevant range of cost-volume-profit analysis.

5. The analysis either involves a single product, or for a multi-product firm the sales mix remains the same.

6. There is no significant difference in beginning and ending inventories of finished goods (that is—units produced equal units sold).

When we originally used the cost-volume-profit model, we assumed that Prentiss Hill sold a single product for $50 per unit and that the variable and fixed costs were $30 per unit and $65,000 per year, respectively. We then calculated the breakeven point for Prentiss Hill:

$$X = \frac{\$65,000 + \$0}{\$50 - \$30} = \frac{\$65,000}{\$20} = \underline{\underline{3,250 \text{ units}}}$$

If any variable changes in the C-V-P analysis, so do our results

The only way that Prentiss Hill will actually break even when 3,250 units are sold is if the variables used in the model—the sales price, the variable costs per unit, and the total fixed costs—remain the same as they were predicted to be. If any one of these variables changes, then our projection for breakeven will be incorrect.

Just because our projection is incorrect does not mean, however, that there is anything wrong with the cost-volume-profit model. It merely signals the need to revise the model in order to accommodate the changes. For example, if:

1. The sales price is $55 instead of $50;

2. The variable costs per unit go from $30 to $32; and

3. The fixed costs decrease by $1,000 to $64,000,

then the model is revised to include these changes and the projected breakeven point is now 2,783 units:

$$X = \frac{\$64,000 + \$0}{\$55 - \$32} = \frac{\$64,000}{\$23} = \underline{\underline{2,783 \text{ units}}}$$

Based on our discussion in this chapter, you should have no trouble understanding what the first four assumptions mean. On the other hand, we have not yet given you enough of a foundation to understand the significance of assumptions 5 and 6. So the remainder of this chapter is devoted entirely to the last two assumptions—what they mean and how they affect the cost-volume-profit analysis.

COST-VOLUME-PROFIT ANALYSIS FOR THE MULTI-PRODUCT FIRM

Assumption 5—an unchanging sales mix

Up until this point we have assumed that Prentiss Hill planned to sell just one product—the fundamentals of accounting textbook. However, most firms in the real world sell many products—thus explaining why we will refer to them as multi-product firms. The C-V-P analysis for the multi-product firm is nearly the same as that for the single-product firm, but the differences that do exist are significant enough to warrant our attention.

We will now assume that Prentiss Hill decides to publish an intermediate accounting text as well as the fundamentals text, which makes Prentiss Hill a multi-product firm. The facts concerning the two products are shown in Example 22-3.

EXAMPLE 22-3

THE MULTIPLE PRODUCTS OF PRENTISS HILL

Assume now that Prentiss Hill plans to produce and sell two accounting textbooks in their second year of operation. Their marketing managers assure the president that they will continue to sell 8,000 copies of the fundamentals text, but will in addition sell 2,000 copies of the new intermediate text.

Relevant data pertaining to the two texts are as follows:

	Fundamentals Text	Intermediate Text
Sales price.	$50	$55
Variable cost per unit	30	40
Contribution margin per unit	$20	$15

The two products will be produced within the same production facility, so the fixed costs will continue to be $65,000 no matter how many units of each text are produced. For simplicity, these fixed costs are split evenly between the two products in determining product-line income statements.

Based on the facts in Example 22-3, three income statements are shown in Exhibit 22-5 — two for the individual product lines (fundamentals and intermediate) and one for the organization as a whole.

Looking at the combined income statements in Exhibit 22-5, you can see that Prentiss Hill should be able to earn a total of $125,000 during their second year if they can sell 10,000 textbooks. But how many must they sell in order to break even; or to have a profit of $95,000, or any other desired amount? The answer to these questions can be supplied by the same C-V-P formulas that we've been using all along — with just a few modifications.

Sales Mix

Sales mix is a relative concept

The first thing we need to do is to introduce a new term — sales mix — a term that has meaning only for a multi-product firm. The *sales mix* for a multi-product firm represents the percentage of total sales that is distributed to each product line. We

EXHIBIT 22-5
Product-Line Income Statements.

The sales for Prentice Hill are now 10,000 units. There are two products—Fundamentals and Intermediate.

	Funda-mentals, 8,000 u	Inter-mediate, 2,000 u	Total 10,000 u
Sales Revenue.	$400,000	$110,000	$510,000
Total Variable Costs.	240,000	80,000	320,000
Total Contribution Margin	$160,000	$ 30,000	$190,000
Fixed Costs (allocated one-half to each)	32,500	32,500	65,000
Net Income	$127,500	$ (2,500)	$125,000

might also think of the sales mix as the percentages that the sales of each product line are to the combined sales for all product lines of the firm. The sales mix percentage for each product line for Prentiss Hill is:

$$\text{Sales mix \%} = \frac{\text{sales of individual product line}}{\text{sales of all product lines combined}}$$

The sales mix for a firm can be measured in terms of unit sales or dollar sales. For Prentiss Hill, the sales mix, in unit sales, is calculated as follows:

Sales mix based on unit sales — 80% : 20%

Product	Unit Sales	Sales Mix
Fundamentals	8,000 u	80% (8,000 ÷ 10,000)
Intermediate	2,000 u	20% (2,000 ÷ 10,000)
	10,000 u	100%

The fundamentals text represents 80% of total unit sales and the intermediate text represents 20% of total unit sales.

     The sales mix, in dollar sales, for Prentiss Hill would be calculated in the following manner:

Sales mix based on dollar sales — 78% : 22%

Product	Dollar Sales	Sales Mix
Fundamentals	$400,000	78.4% ($400,000 ÷ $510,000)
Intermediate	110,000	21.6% ($110,000 ÷ $510,000)
	$510,000	100.0%

Everything changes when the sales mix changes

     As we shall see in a moment, the sales mix for an organization has an effect on the contribution margin per unit (CMU), or contribution margin percentage (CM%), that we use in the C-V-P formulas. When the sales mix changes we get a new CMU (or CM%), and a new CMU (or CM%) requires that we revise the C-V-P model. In the example that follows, we will only use the sales mix that is measured in terms of units, and show how it affects the C-V-P analysis that uses CMU.

Sales Mix and C-V-P Analysis

Four steps to C-V-P analysis for a multi-product firm

There are four steps in doing C-V-P analysis for a multi-product firm:

1. The first step is to determine the sales mix. This we have already done.

2. The second step is to calculate the weighted average contribution margin per unit. This we can do in one of two ways. The first way is to divide the total contribution margin for all products combined by the total unit sales. For Prentiss Hill it is:

$$\frac{\text{Weighted}}{\text{average CMU}} = \frac{\text{total CM}}{\text{(all products)}} \div \frac{\text{total units}}{\text{(all products)}}$$

$$= \$190,000 \div 10,000 = \$19 \text{ per unit}$$

A second way to calculate the average CMU is to multiply each individual CMU by its respective sales mix percentage, and then add together the individual multiplications. We can do this for Prentiss Hill as follows:

Weighted average CMU

Product	Individual CMU		Sales Mix %		Average CMU
Fundamentals.	$20	×	80%	=	$16
Intermediate.	$15	×	20%	=	3
					$19 per unit

Either way we do it we get an average CMU of $19 per unit.

3. The third step is to use the traditional C-V-P formula—placing total fixed costs and desired income for all products combined in the numerator, and the average CMU in the denominator. For Prentiss Hill, the breakeven point (in units) for both products combined is:

This is for both products combined

$$X = \frac{\$65,000 + \$0}{\$19 \text{ per unit}} = 3,421 \text{ units}$$

And the level of sales needed to generate a profit of $95,000 is:

$$X = \frac{\$65,000 + \$95,000}{\$19 \text{ per unit}} = 8,421 \text{ units}$$

4. The fourth step is to allocate the answer from Step 3 between the different product lines, by multiplying each product's sales mix percentage times the total unit sales. For Prentiss Hill the allocation of the breakeven units of 3,421 is:

This is by product line

Product	Total Sales		Sales Mix %		Allocation to Products
Fundamentals	3,421	×	80%	=	2,737
Intermediate	3,421	×	20%	=	684
					3,421

We allocate the 8,421 units in exactly the same manner to determine the sales units of the two products that provides a profit of $95,000 for the firm.

Before we stop, it is also important for you to know what assumption the accountant makes concerning the sales mix when doing C-V-P analysis. The accountant assumes—unless told specifically otherwise—that *the sales mix remains the same,* which is assumption 5 on page 890. For Prentiss Hill this means that we are assuming that the fundamental text sales will be 80% and the intermediate text sales will be 20% of total sales—regardless of how many texts are sold in all. The breakeven point of 3,421 units is correct only with the 80% : 20% sales mix. It would not be the breakeven point for any other sales mix.

Assumption 5

The unit sales needed to generate a $95,000 profit is 8,421 units only with the 80% : 20% sales mix, and will not be correct for any other sales mix.

In addition, we showed a profit in Exhibit 22-5 of $125,000, for combined sales of 10,000 units. That is the amount of profit for that level of sales only if the sales mix is 80% : 20%. For any other sales mix, the profit for combined sales of 10,000 units will be a different amount.

You see, when the sales mix changes, so does the average CMU. And when the average CMU changes, so too does every answer in the C-V-P analysis.

Direct versus Absorption Costing

Assumption 6 — unchanging inventories, or production (Qp) equals sales (Qs)

The sixth assumption underlying cost-volume-profit analysis is that there are no significant differences in the beginning and ending inventories of finished goods. Stated another way, the assumption is that the number of units produced during the period equals the number of units sold. Obviously, since only manufacturers produce the units they sell, this assumption does not concern nonmanufacturing organizations.

In order to understand the meaning of this assumption, let's first remind ourselves of the two formats of income statements that we have used in this course. The one on the left below is the one we've used primarily within this chapter. It is the ***contribution margin format*** (or ***behavioral format***). The one on the right was used in Chapter 19 and is the one most often used in financial statements issued to the public. It is called the ***traditional format*** (or ***functional format***).

Different formats for different product costing methods

Contribution Margin Format	Traditional Format
Sales	Sales
Less: Total Variable Costs	Less: Costs of Goods Sold
Equals: Total Contribution Margin	Equals: Gross Margin
Less: Total fixed costs	Less: Selling and Administrative
Equal: Net Income	Equals: Net Income

The contribution margin format to an income statement is used whenever a firm is employing the ***direct costing method*** of product costing; and the traditional method is used whenever a firm is employing the ***absorption costing method*** of product costing.

Definitions of Direct and Absorption Costing

Absorption costing (AC) — fixed factory overhead (FFO) is a product cost

The difference between absorption costing and direct costing is that fixed factory overhead is a product cost under absorption costing but a period cost under direct costing.

Under ***absorption costing*** the product costs are direct materials, direct labor, variable factory overhead, and fixed factory overhead. Remember that as product costs, all of these costs are assigned to inventory when units are produced, and become expenses (as part of cost of goods sold expense) only when the units to which they are assigned are sold. All costs that are assigned to the unsold units remain as an asset on the balance sheet. All selling and administrative costs are period costs and are expensed when incurred.

Direct costing (DC) — FFO is a period cost

For ***direct costing*** the product costs include direct materials, direct labor, and variable factory overhead. We only assign the variable manufacturing costs to the units produced; only variable manufacturing costs are expensed (as part of variable cost of goods sold expense) when the units are sold. And nothing but the variable manufacturing costs are assigned to the unsold units that remain on the balance sheet as an asset. Fixed factory overhead is not a product cost; it is a period cost, which, like the selling and administrative costs, is expensed when incurred.

EXHIBIT 22-6   Income Statements—Using the Contribution Margin Format and the Traditional Format.
As long as assumption 6 is valid—that the quantities produced and sold are the same—the incomes for direct costing and absorption costing are equal.

Contribution Margin Format		Traditional Format	
Sales	$400,000	Sales	$400,000
Variable Costs—Cost of Goods Sold:		Cost of Goods Sold:	
Direct Materials. . . . . $ 80,000		Direct Materials. . . . . $ 80,000	
Direct Labor. 120,000		Direct Labor. 120,000	
Variable Overhead 24,000		Variable Overhead 24,000	
Variable Costs of Goods Sold. . . $224,000		Fixed Overhead. 40,000	
Variable Selling. 16,000		Cost of Goods Sold	264,000
Total Variable Costs	240,000	Gross Margin.	$136,000
Total Contribution Margin	$160,000		
		Selling Costs:	
Fixed Costs:		Variable. . . . . $ 16,000	
Factory Overhead $40,000		Fixed. 25,000	
Selling. 25,000		Total Selling Costs.	41,000
Total Fixed Costs	65,000	Net Income.	$ 95,000
Net Income	$ 95,000		

Using the same facts that were given in Example 22-2 for Prentiss Hill, the income statements for both methods are shown in Exhibit 22-6, based on the 8,000 units that were produced and sold. The key facts from Example 22-2 were as follows:

Sales price	$50 per unit
Variable costs:	
Direct materials . . . . $10 per unit	
Direct labor . . . . 15 per unit	
Variable overhead . . . . 3 per unit	
Variable selling. . . . . 2 per unit	
Total variable costs	$30 per unit
Fixed costs:	
Factory overhead $40,000	
Selling 25,000	
Total fixed costs	$65,000

The most important thing to notice in Exhibit 22-6 is the bottom line of the statement for each method—the net income. The fact that the net incomes for direct costing and absorption costing are both $95,000 helps explain the significance of assumption 6 on page 890.

The significance of the sixth assumption, that the number of units produced equals the number of units sold, is as follows:

If $Q_p = Q_s$, net incomes are equal

1. If the assumption is valid, then the net income (and the breakeven point) under direct costing (which uses the contribution margin format) will be exactly the same as the net income (and the breakeven point) for absorption costing (which uses the traditional format). This is because the amount of fixed factory overhead expensed

as part of cost of goods sold, for absorption costing, is exactly the same as the amount of fixed factory overhead expensed as a period cost, for direct costing. Notice in Exhibit 22-6 that the amount of fixed factory overhead that was expensed was $40,000 under both methods.

If $Qp \neq Qs$, net incomes are not the same

2. But if the assumption is not valid — that is, if the number of units produced is not equal to the number of units sold — then the net income (and the breakeven point) for direct costing will be different from the net income (and breakeven point) for absorption costing. This is because the fixed factory overhead expensed under absorption costing, in cost of goods sold, will no longer equal the amount of fixed factory overhead expensed as a period cost, under direct costing. An example of this situation occurs when the number of units produced exceeds the number sold. In this situation, some of the $40,000 of fixed factory overhead that is assigned to the units produced under absorption costing will still be in finished goods inventory at the end of the period, because some of the units produced were not sold. Therefore, some of the $40,000 is not expensed in the current period. Under direct costing, however, all of the $40,000 of fixed factory overhead is expensed, because as a period cost fixed factory overhead is expensed when incurred.

Since more fixed overhead is expensed under direct costing than absorption costing, the net income for direct costing will be less than the net income for absorption costing.

In the situation where the number of units sold exceeds the number of units produced, the results for direct and absorption costing will be just the reverse; that is, the income for direct costing will be higher than the income for absorption costing.

CHAPTER SUMMARY

Costs are either variable, fixed, or mixed. *Variable costs* in total change in the same direction and in direct proportion to changes in activity. In order for the total variable cost to change in direct proportion, the average variable cost must remain unchanged. That is, no matter how low or high the activity is, the average variable cost does not change.

Fixed costs, in total, are not expected to change in response to changes in activity (1) for a given period of time, and (2) within a relevant range of activity. Average fixed costs vary inversely with activity — the lower the activity, the higher the average fixed cost, and vice versa.

A *mixed cost* contains both variable and fixed cost components.

The *relevant range* is the range of productive activity within which the assumptions of cost behavior are expected to be valid, that is, within which the total fixed costs and average variable costs will remain unchanged. The total fixed costs and the variable cost rate may change as you go from one relevant range to another.

Cost-volume-profit analysis is used by accountants to analyze and evaluate the relationships among interacting variables — prices, costs, and activity — and the effect that a change in these variables has on profits. Our approach to cost-volume-profit analysis emphasizes the separation of costs based on their behavior. The income statement that separates the variable and fixed costs is called the *contribution margin format income statement.* Within this statement, all variable costs are grouped together and subtracted from sales; the difference is called the *total contribution margin.* Then the fixed costs are combined and subtracted from the total contribution margin, leaving net income. Although the *traditional* (or *functional*) *format* is usually employed in financial statements issued to external users, the contribution margin approach is considered superior for internal decision making.

One way that we can use cost-volume-profit analysis involves the determination of a level of sales that will generate a desired amount of profit. One such level of sales is the ***breakeven point,*** where the income is zero, because the sales and total costs are equal. We use two techniques in cost-volume-profit analysis: the ***contribution margin technique*** and the ***income equation technique.***

The ***sales mix*** for a multi-product firm represents the percentage of total sales distributed to each product line. Different products usually have different contribution margins per unit. Therefore, the weighted average contribution margin per unit (for all products) depends on the proportion that each product's sales are to total sales. And, since the cost-volume-profit formulas use a weighted average ***contribution margin per unit,*** the results of the analysis depend on the sales mix assumed. In order for cost-volume-profit predictions to be correct, the sales mix that actually comes about must be the same as the sales mix originally assumed in the C-V-P model.

An important assumption underlying cost-volume-profit analysis is that there are no significant differences in beginning and ending inventories of finished goods; or, stated another way, that the units produced are equal to the units sold. Only when this assumption is true will the net income for direct costing be equal to the net income for absorption costing. ***Direct costing*** defines product costs as variable manufacturing costs. Fixed factory overhead is a period cost, and is thus expensed when incurred. ***Absorption costing*** defines product costs as both variable and fixed manufacturing costs. The fixed factory overhead is expensed when the units are sold, rather than when the costs are incurred. The income under absorption costing is higher than for direct costing whenever production exceeds sales. When sales exceed production, income under direct costing is higher than income for absorption costing.

IMPORTANT TERMS USED IN THIS CHAPTER

Absorption costing method   A product costing method that assigns variable and fixed manufacturing costs to units being produced. The product costs include direct materials, direct labor, variable overhead, and fixed factory overhead. These costs are expensed only when the units to which they are assigned are sold. (page 894)

Breakeven point   The level of sales (measured in units or dollars) for an organization at which net income is zero. At breakeven, total costs equal total sales dollars. (page 877)

Contribution margin format income statement   An income statement in which variable costs are separated from fixed costs. The variable costs are subtracted from sales to get total contribution margin. Fixed costs are subtracted next, resulting in net income. Also known as the ***behavioral format income statement.*** (page 877)

Contribution margin percentage (CM%)   The percentage of total sales that remains after the variable costs are subtracted. (page 882)

Contribution margin per unit (CMU)   The sales price less the variable costs per unit. The CMU is the amount that each unit sold contributes to the coverage of fixed costs and to the accumulation of profits. It is the amount that is added to net income every time an additional unit is sold. (page 881)

Contribution margin technique   A method used in cost-volume-profit analysis. The level of sales that will generate a desired profit is determined by dividing the fixed costs plus net income by the contribution margin per unit (or contribution margin percentage). (page 884)

Cost-volume-profit (C-V-P) analysis   A tool used by accountants to assist managers in the analysis and evaluation of the relationships among prices, costs, and activity; and the effect that changes in these variables have on profits. (page 876)

Direct costing method   A product costing method that treats only the variable manufacturing costs as product costs. These costs include direct materials, direct labor, and variable factory overhead. Fixed factory overhead is a period cost rather than a product cost and is expensed when incurred. (page 894)

Fixed costs   Costs that in total are expected to remain unchanged in response to changes in activity during a period of time and within a relevant range of activity. (page 872)

Income equation technique   A method used in cost-volume-profit analysis. The level of sales needed to generate a desired profit is determined by substituting X (for unit sales or dollar sales) into the equation for net income: sales − variable costs − fixed costs = net income. (page 883)

Mixed cost   A cost that contains both variable and fixed costs. (page 872)

Relevant range of activity   The range of activity within which a firm expects to operate and for which the assumptions concerning the behavior of costs are assumed to be valid. (page 875)

Sales mix   For a multi-product firm, the percentage of total sales that is distributed to each product line. (page 891)

Total contribution margin   Total sales revenue less total variable costs. It is the amount contributed by sales to the coverage of fixed costs. If the total contribution margin is greater than the fixed costs, there is a profit; if the reverse is true, there is a loss. (page 878)

Traditional format income statement   An income statement format that separates costs on the income statement according to their functions—production, selling, and administration. The cost of goods sold is subtracted from sales to get gross profit; and net income remains after the selling and administrative expenses are subtracted from gross profit. Also called the *functional format income statement.* (page 879)

Variable cost percentage (VC%)   The percentage of total sales needed to cover the variable costs; the percentage that total variable costs are to sales revenue. (page 880)

Variable cost per unit (VCU)   The amount by which total costs increase for each additional unit produced and sold. (page 880)

Variable costs   Costs that in total change in the same direction and in direct proportion to changes in activity. (page 872)

QUESTIONS

1. List and define the three types of costs classified by behavior.

2. "A variable cost can be defined as one that changes." Comment.

3. "If a certain cost changes, it cannot be a fixed cost." Do you agree? Explain.

4. Discuss the importance of activity to the definitions of *variable* and *fixed* costs.

5. "The more activity increases, the lower the fixed cost per unit will be. Therefore, fixed costs can really be classified as variable costs." Explain why you agree or disagree with these statements.

6. Which of the product costs of a manufacturer would be classified as variable and which would be classified as fixed?

7. Discuss the concept of *relevant range* and how it affects the definitions of variable and fixed costs.

8. Explain the differences between the *contribution margin format* and the *traditional format* to an income statement.

9. "The terms *total contribution margin* and *total gross margin* are synonymous." True or false? Explain.

10. The increase in net income generated by an increase in activity is identical to the increase in total contribution margin, as long as which assumption underlying cost-volume-profit analysis is valid?

11. Define the term *breakeven point.* Is the term *breakeven analysis* identical to the term *cost-volume-profit analysis?* Explain.

12. If a firm's sales are expected to increase by 50% in an upcoming period, what will happen to the breakeven point? Explain.

13. Given the formula for the cost-volume-profit relationship:

$$X = \frac{\text{fixed costs} + \text{income}}{\text{CMU}}$$

Is the income before or after taxes?

14. A firm sells two products, A and B, both of which are expected to represent 50% of total sales during the first year of operation. Following the first year, it was determined that the sales mix for A and B was 75% : 25% respectively. Discuss the consequence of this change in sales mix for the cost-volume-profit analysis of the firm.

15. Explain what is meant by the term *sales mix.*

16. "The income taxes for a firm operating at its breakeven point of 2,000 units are twice those for a firm operating at its breakeven of 1,000 units." Do you agree? Explain.

17. Define the terms *direct costing* and *absorption costing.*

18. Explain why the net income for absorption costing is higher than for direct costing, when the finished goods inventory increases.

19. Discuss the significance of the cost-volume-profit assumption, "There are no significant changes in the beginning and ending inventories."

EXERCISES

Exercise 22-1
Filling in the missing blanks of a contribution margin income statement

Fill in the blanks for each of the income statements below. The sales price in each situation is $10.

	A	B	C
Sales Revenue	$200,000	$?	$?
Variable Costs	$100,000	$?	$?
Total Contribution Margin	$?	$100,000	$120,000
Fixed Costs	$ 30,000	$ 50,000	$?
Net Income	$?	$?	$?
Units Sold	?	40,000	30,000
Breakeven (in units)	?	?	10,000

[Check figure: New Income (C) = $80,000]

Exercise 22-2

Finding the unknown variables

For each independent situation below, fill in the missing spaces for the unknown items:

[Check figure: Sales price (III) = $150]

	I	II	III
Sales price.	$150	$?	$?
Variable cost per unit	$120	$24	$?
Contribution margin per unit	$?	$?	$60
Variable cost percentage	?	20%	?
Contribution margin percentage	?	?	40%

Exercise 22-3

C-V-P analysis for a single product

The Macho-Man Exercise Studio sells packages of exercise classes for $250 per package. Its variable costs average $100 per package, and the fixed costs are $4,000 per month.

a. How many packages would have to be sold for Macho-Man to break even each month?

(Check figure: 27 packages)

b. How many packages would have to be sold each month if a $36,000 profit is desired?

c. What would be the margin of safety (in units) for Macho-Man if 40 packages are sold each month?

d. Using a contribution margin format, prepare an income statement for a month in which 40 exercise classes are sold.

Exercise 22-4

Doing C-V-P analysis with and without tax effects

The Tobacco-Free Institute produces and sells a single sized carton of smokeless cigarettes for $20 per carton. Its expected costs are as follows:

Variable manufacturing costs. . $8.00/carton   Fixed selling costs $20,000
Variable selling costs . . . . . . $4.00/carton   Tax rate. 40%
Fixed manufacturing costs. . . . $60,000

a. Using a contribution margin format, prepare an income statement (after tax) for the company if 200,000 cartons are sold in 1988.

(Check figure: Net Income = $912,000)

b. Compute the breakeven point (in dollars).

c. If 200,000 cartons are sold, determine the margin of safety, in units and in dollars.

d. Determine the number of cartons that must be sold in order to generate an aftertax net income of $800,000.

(Check figure: 176,667 cartons)

Exercise 22-5

C-V-P analysis for two products

The McEnconnors Company sells two tennis racket models—the Prince and the Pauper. The contribution margins per unit, respectively, are $40 and $20. The fixed costs for the company are $35,000. Sales are expected to be distributed to Prince and Pauper in a 40%:60% ratio.

a. Determine the number of units of each product that must be sold in order for McEnconnors to show a $50,000 profit, assuming that the sales mix is exactly as expected.

b. If the sales mix changes from 40%:60% to 50%:50%, the number of units of each product that would be required to have a profit of $50,000 would now be what?

(Check figure: Prince = 1,416.50 units)

Exercise 22-6

Breakeven for different machines

The Disco Beat Company used to sell records, but was unable to make any money, so now it sells computer diskettes for $25 per package of 10 diskettes. Disco Beat is trying to decide whether to purchase an automatic or a semiautomatic machine. If the automatic is purchased, the company's variable and fixed costs will be $15 and $20,000, respectively. However, if the semiautomatic machine is acquired, these costs will be $18 and $16,000.

a. Determine the firm's breakeven point (in units) for each different situation described above.

b. Determine the net income for each situation if 1,300 packages are sold; if 3,500 packages are sold.

c. Determine the level of sales (in packages) for which the net income for the two situations would be the same.

(Check figure: 1,333⅓ units)

d. Discuss whether the automatic or the semiautomatic machinery should be bought.

e. Answer requirement (c), assuming that the variable cost per unit for the automatic machine is $19 rather than $15.

Exercise 22-7

Determining margin of safety

The Diana Leonard Skin Cream Company sells a 10-oz bottle of skin cream called Soft-as-a-Baby for $50 a bottle. The variable and fixed costs of producing and selling each bottle are $8 and $65,000, respectively. If Diana sells 2,200 bottles of Soft-as-a-Baby in 1989, what will be her margin of safety, in both units and dollars?

(Check figure: 652 bottles)

Exercise 22-8

Identifying line segments on C-V-P graphs

Presented below are two graphs depicting different views toward cost-volume-profit analysis.

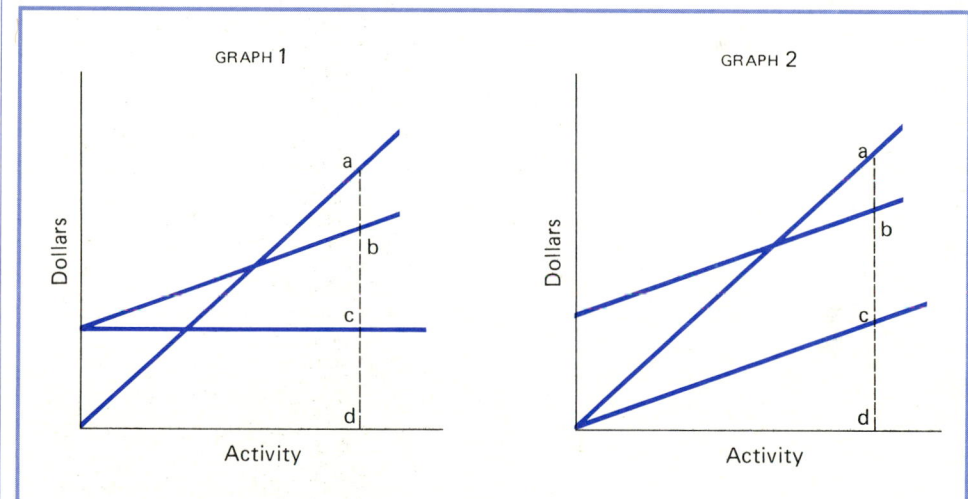

For each graph, identify the items described by placing the appropriate letters for the line segments in the spaces provided.

	Graph 1	Graph 2
Example: Sales revenue	ad	ad
a. Total variable costs.	———	———
b. Total fixed costs.	———	———
c. Total contribution margin	———	———
d. Net income.	———	———

Exercise 22-9

Drawing a C-V-P graph — including taxes and dividends

Draw a cost-volume-profit graph in which the variable costs are drawn first and the fixed costs are then added to the variable. Include within the graph a line that represents the effect of taxes on income, assuming that there is no tax impact when losses occur. Also include a line to represent dividends, when paid as a constant percentage of net income (after tax).

Exercise 22-10
Doing C-V-P analysis: before and after taxes

The Jimmy Moon Company had the following income statement for 1988:

Sales Revenue	$320,000
Variable Costs	240,000
Total Contribution Margin	$ 80,000
Fixed Costs	54,000
Income before Tax	$ 26,000
Income Tax	10,400
Net Income	$ 15,600

a. If Jimmy expects to have an income before tax of $56,000 in 1988, how great must its sales revenue be?

b. If Jimmy desires an aftertax net income of $40,000 in 1988, how many dollars of sales must be generated?

(Check figure: $482,668)

Exercise 22-11
Analyzing the effect of a change on a key variable

For each situation in the table below, determine the effect on the total contribution margin, the breakeven point, and the net income for the firm. Choose one of the five following effects for each answer:

a. Doubles
b. Increases more than double
c. Increases less than double
d. No change
e. Decreases

Place the correct letter in the spaces provided.

	Effect on:		
	Total Contribution Margin	Breakeven Point	Net Income*
1. Units sold double.	—	—	—
2. The sales price doubles.	—	—	—
3. The variable cost per unit increases by 10%.	—	—	—
4. The sales price and the variable cost per unit both double.	—	—	—
5. Fixed costs double.	—	—	—
6. Fixed costs are cut in half.	—	—	—
7. The sales mix changes from 40%:60% to 70%:30% for products having contribution margins per unit of $20 and $30, respectively.	—	—	—

* Before taxes.

Exercise 22-12
C-V-P analysis: changing variables

The Pace Company sells a single product called New Spice Deodorant. The Pace Company's 1989 income statement is shown below:

Sales (10,000 jars @ $3 per jar)	$ 30,000
Variable Costs	(13,500)
Fixed Costs (advertising)	(12,000)
Net Income	$ 4,500

a. Determine the breakeven point (in dollars)
b. How many units need to be sold in order to show a profit of $20,000?
c. A 25% increase in advertising, accompanied by a 6% reduction in the sales price, is expected to increase unit sales by 30%. What will be the new net income?

(Check figure: $4,110)

Exercise 22-13
C-V-P analysis: desired income stated as a % of sales

The Sibbald Nursery sells all its plants for $5 a plant. Its variable costs average $1.50 per plant and its fixed costs are $10,000. In 1988, Sibbald sold 9,000 plants.
a. How many plants have to be sold so that Sibbald will have a net income of 20% of sales dollars?
b. Sibbald is going to reduce its price from $5 to $4.80, because the variable costs are expected to drop by $.40 per plant. How many plants will have to be sold in 1989 in order to yield the same net income as in 1988?

(Check figure: 8,514 plants)

Exercise 22-14
Determining the product costs per unit for direct and absorption costing

The Mitchell Company plans to produce and sell 10,000 units in 1986, and expects the following costs for the year:

Direct materials	$10/unit
Direct labor	15/unit
Variable overhead	3/unit
Variable selling	2/unit
Variable administrative	1/unit
Fixed overhead	100,000
Fixed selling	60,000
Fixed administrative	30,000

The sales price is $50 per unit.
a. Compute the product cost per unit for the absorption costing method.

(Check figure: $38)

b. Compute the product cost per unit for the direct costing method.
c. Prepare an income statement for Mitchell Company:
    (1) Using the absorption costing method
    (2) Using the direct costing method

PROBLEMS
Set A

Problem A22-1
Integrating taxes and dividends into C-V-P analysis

During 1988 the Pinella Company produced and sold 10,000 baseball batting gloves. Based on this level of activity, the following cost per unit statement was prepared:

Sales Price		$150/glove
Variable Manufacturing Cost	$40	
Fixed Manufacturing Cost	10	50/glove
		$100/glove
Variable Selling Costs	$20	
Fixed Selling Costs	4	24/glove
Income before Taxes		$ 76/glove
Income Tax		38/glove
Net Income		$ 38/glove

In addition, 40% of the net income was paid out to stockholders as dividends.

Required

1. If 15,000 gloves are produced and sold during 1989, prepare an income statement using the contribution margin format.
2. If the company desires an income before tax of $600,000 in 1989, how many gloves must be sold?
3. If the company wants to increase its retained earnings (after dividends are paid at 40%) during 1989 by $660,000, how many gloves must be sold?

(Check figure: 26,000 gloves)

Problem A22-2
Preparing income statements for different assumptions

During the year 1987, the Billy Martin Company produced and sold 15,000 boxing punching bags and prepared the following income statement:

Sales Revenue.		$600,000
Cost of Goods Sold:		
Direct Materials	$ 80,000	
Direct Labor	100,000	
Variable Overhead	40,000	
Fixed Overhead	60,000	280,000
Gross Profit		$320,000
Selling and Administrative:		
Variable	$130,000	
Fixed	70,000	200,000
Net Income		$120,000

There were no beginning or ending inventories of finished goods.

Required

1. Reconstruct the income statement using the contribution margin format.
2. If the number of units increases by 20% because of a 5% decrease in the sales price, and the fixed overhead increases by $5,000, prepare a new income statement.
3. Calculate the breakeven point for the facts described in part (2), and prepare another income statement for that level of activity.

(Check figure: Breakeven = 7,800)

Problem A22-3
C-V-P analysis with changing assumptions

Ronald Reagen starts a small manufacturing company that will produce and sell gourmet jelly beans for $5 a jar. The company controller, David Stocker, estimates the following data concerning activity for its first year of operation, 1989:

Expected sales	150,000
Direct materials	$1.00/jar
Direct labor	$ .75/jar
Variable overhead	$ .25/jar
Fixed overhead	$ 80,000
Variable selling	$ .20/jar
Fixed selling	$ 60,000

There are no beginning or ending inventories of finished goods.

Required

1. How many jars will have to be sold in 1989 in order to show a profit of $200,000?
2. If the company is to generate a profit of 25% of sales, what must its dollar sales be?
3. Looking ahead to 1990, Mr. Reagen plans to increase the sales price by $1. In addition, he expects the fixed manufacturing costs to increase by 10%. How many jars will he have to sell in 1990 to have the same income he expects for 1989?

(Check figure: 112,632 jars)

Problem A22-4

Doing C-V-P analysis with
different relevant ranges

The Leaded Bottoms Company manufactures kewpie dolls for carnivals and sells them for $2 per kewpie. The variable costs of manufacturing and selling are $1 and $.25 per kewpie, respectively. The fixed costs are based on the following ranges of activity:

Range of Activity	Fixed Costs
0–40,000 kewpies	$35,000
40,001–75,000 kewpies	50,000
75,001–125,000 kewpies (maximum capacity)	70,000

During 1988, Leaded Bottoms produced and sold 45,000 kewpies.

Required

1. Determine the net income for Leaded Bottoms for 1988.
2. How many additional kewpies (above the 45,000) would Leaded Bottoms need to sell in order to break even, if the additional kewpies will be sold for only $1.90?
3. Answer requirement (2) except assume that the company wishes to generate a profit of $6,000.

(Check figure: 65,000 units)

4. What is the maximum profit that could be earned by Leaded Bottoms (disregard requirements 2 and 3)?
5. Leaded Bottoms wants to produce and sell 85,000 units but does not want to incur any additional fixed costs. The company production supervisor decides to pay double time for labor in order to produce the 10,000 kewpies above the second range of activity. If the labor costs are three-fourths of the variable manufacturing costs, determine the profit the company should earn.

(Check figure: $6,250)

Problem A22-5

C-V-P analysis for a multi-
product firm

The Jackson's T-Shirt Emporium sells two types of t-shirts: the Michael and the Group. A condensed income statement is shown below for the company's first year of operation:

	Michael	Group	Total
Total Contribution Margin	$1,000,000	$600,000	$1,600,000
Fixed Costs.	400,000	250,000	650,000
Net Income	$ 600,000	$350,000	$ 950,000
Shirts Sold	100,000	150,000	250,000

Required

1. Determine the sales mix for the two products.
2. Determine the weighted average contribution margin per unit.
3. Determine the breakeven point for the firm as a whole. How many shirts of each type would be sold?

(Check figure: 40,625 Michael shirts)

4. Prepare income statements for the firm as a whole and for each product line, based on your answer in requirement (3).

Problem A22-6

Analyzing the effect of changing
variables

During 1988, The Gustavo Company produced and sold 10,000 units of its product line, which resulted in a profit of $100,000. Its fixed costs were $200,000, which were $25,000 less than they were expected to be in 1989. Gustavo plans to revise his sales price in such a way as to increase the contribution margin per unit by $2 during 1989.

Required

1. Gustavo would like to double the 1988 profit in 1989; how many units will he have to sell in 1989 in order to accomplish this goal?
2. Assume instead that the fixed costs are going to remain the same in 1989 as they were in 1988, but that the contribution margin is still going to increase by $2 per unit. How many units will Gustavo have to sell in 1989 in order to earn as much income in 1989 as he did in 1988?
3. Assume now that the fixed costs are going to increase by $50,000, and that the contribution margin per unit is going to change, but we're not sure what it is going to be. Finally, assume that the 1989 sales are expected to be 15,000 units. What will the contribution margin per unit have to be in 1989 in order to earn a profit of $150,000?

(Check figure: $26.67)

Set B

Problem B22-1
Integrating taxes and dividends into C-V-P analysis

During 1988 The Delorean Miniatures produced and sold 20,000 miniature car kits at $50 per kit. Based on this level of activity, the average costs were as follows:

Variable manufacturing costs	$15.00/kit
Variable selling	5.00/kit
Fixed manufacturing	10.00/kit
Fixed selling	2.50/kit
Income taxes (at 40% of income before tax)	7.00/kit

In addition, 30% of income is paid out as dividends each year.

Required

1. If 30,000 kits are produced and sold in 1988, prepare a contribution margin format income statement.
2. If the company desires a profit of $220,000 in 1988 (before tax), how many units need to be sold?
3. If the company wants $150,000 of profits to remain after the payment of dividends, how great must the dollar sales be in 1988?

(Check figure: $1,011,900)

Problem B22-2
Preparing different income statements for changing assumptions

The Charlie Moore Farms hatched and sold 400,000 packages of chicken eggs during 1987, incurring the following revenues, expenses, and income:

Sales		$200,000
Cost of Goods Sold:		
Direct Materials	$50,000	
Direct Labor	25,000	
Variable Overhead	12,500	
Fixed Overhead	37,500	125,000
Gross Profit		$ 75,000
Selling and Administrative Expenses*		30,000
Net Income		$ 45,000

* $15,000 of this total is fixed.

Required

1. Prepare the income statement using the contribution margin format.
2. Due to a 20% drop in the variable manufacturing costs per unit, Charlie plans to lower the price per package by $.05 in 1988. He expects that this change will stimulate an increase in sales of 25,000 packages. Prepare an income statement calculating the expected income for 1988.

(Check figure: net income = $48,437)

3. Determine the breakeven point (in dollar sales) for 1988.

Problem B22-3
C-V-P analysis—desired income stated in % and per unit

The Galaxy Video Arcade estimates that each of its customers spends an average of $10 per visit. Based on past experience, the owner, Pac Boy, estimates his costs as follows:

Variable operating $6.50/customer
Salaries $30,000/year
Rent and machine leasing 20,000/year
Advertising. 10,000/year

Required

1. How many customers will Galaxy have to have in order to have a profit of $25,000?
2. What will the total revenues have to be in order to show a profit of 30% of sales?
3. If Galaxy wants to generate a profit of $1 per customer, how many customers must they have during the year?

(Check figure: 24,000)

Problem B22-4
Doing C-V-P analysis with several relevant ranges of activity

The Hubbard and Annaheim CPA Firm bills its services to customers at $50 per billable hour, and estimates that the variable costs of running their office average $30 per billable hour. The level of fixed costs depends on the number of employees working for the firm. All fixed costs, other than salaries, will be the same no matter how much business the firm can attract. The total fixed costs will be as follows:

Number of Employees	Fixed Costs
One (for 0–2,000 billable hours)	$60,000*
Two (for 2,001–3,600 hours)	75,000
Three (for 3,601–6,000 hours)	95,000

* Includes costs of insurance, advertising, rent, etc., in addition to salaries.

During the past year, Hubbard and Annaheim employed two staff employees and were able to charge customers for 3,500 billable hours.

Required

1. Determine the income for last year.
2. How many billable hours must Hubbard and Annaheim have in order to break even?
3. What is the maximum profit possible for the firm of Hubbard and Annaheim?

(Check figure: $25,000)

Problem B22-5
C-V-P analysis for a multi-product firm

The Napa Valley Wine Stand sells bottles of wine at the side of the road. Its motto is "We sell our wine just in time." Napa sells two types of wine—Chipper Chablis and Rose' Red—both of which are bought at the back door of local wineries. During 1987 Napa sold 2,000 bottles of Chipper Chablis and 3,000 bottles of Rose' Red. The income statement for Napa for 1987 is given below:

	Chipper Chablis	Rose' Red	Total
Sales	$4,000	$9,000	$13,000
Variable Costs	1,000	3,000	4,000
Total Contribution Margin	$3,000	$6,000	$ 9,000
Fixed Costs.	750	750	1,500
Net Income	$2,250	$5,250	$ 7,500

Required

1. Determine the sales mix for Chipper Chablis and Rose' Red.
2. Compute the weighted average contribution margin per bottle.

3. Using your answer to requirement (2), determine the breakeven point for the entire firm. How much of each product must be sold in order to break even?

(Check figure: Chipper Chablis = 333 bottles)

4. Prepare the income statement for each product line and for the firm as a whole, based on the answers to requirement (3).

Problem B22-6
Evaluating effect of changing assumptions for key variables

The Merrick Merry Minstrels specializes in "Surprises" for unsuspecting people on such momentous occasions as birthdays, anniversaries, and any good time. They charge the same price no matter what the occasion is or who the unsuspecting person is. The net income earned by the Merrick Merry Minstrels in 1988 was $25,000, based on 250 surprises during the year. The fixed costs of running Merrick Merry Minstrels are $5,000 per year.

Required

1. How many surprises does Merrick have to perform each year in order to break even?
2. Merrick plans to increase its fee next year by $25 per surprise. How many surprises will it have to perform in order to earn a profit in 1989 equal to that in 1988?
3. Disregard the change in requirement (2). Instead, assume that the fixed costs are going to increase by 20% in 1989 but that Merrick still expects the income for the year to double. What will be Merrick's margin of safety in 1989?

(Check figure: 417)

Chapter 23

The Master Budget

When you have finished studying this chapter you should have learned:

- What a master budget is and how it is used to assist management in the planning function
- Who the participants are in the budgetary process
- How important the sales forecast is in preparing the master budget
- What the different types of operating budgets and financial budgets are
- How the historical cost balance sheet relates to the master budget
- How to prepare a master budget

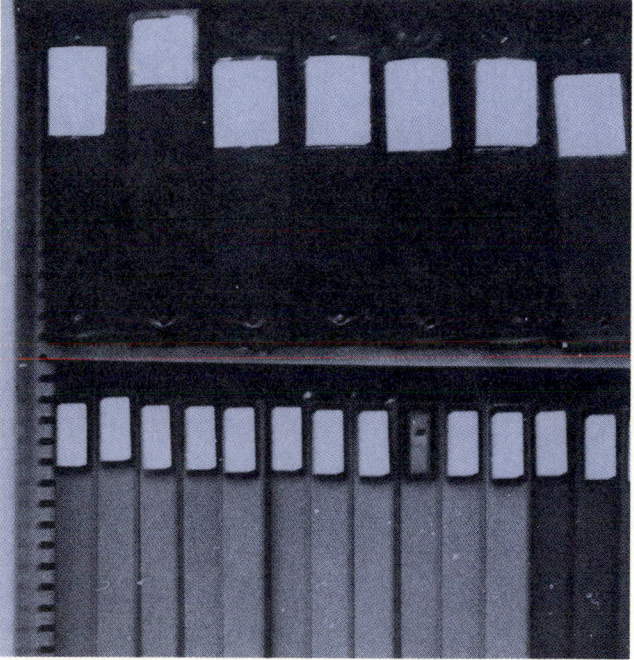

In almost every business organization there are a number of different activities going on at the same time, such as selling, producing, purchasing, distributing, and financing. All of these activities are interrelated in such a way that together they affect the attainment of the organization's objectives. Thus, planning for an entire organization means planning for each of the specific activities within it. Further, it means planning the individual activities to achieve goals that lead smoothly to the attainment of overall organization goals as well.

The master budget is a comprehensive budget for the entire firm

The ***master budget*** is a comprehensive budget that expresses the overall business plan for the whole organization for a period covering 1 year or less. The master budget:

1. Recognizes the relationships among the interacting activities of the departments within the organization

2. Summarizes the individual budgets of these departments

3. Combines the individual budgets into a harmonious composite for the firm as a whole

The master budget actually consists of two types of budgets: (1) operating budgets, and (2) financial budgets.

Operating budgets

Operating budgets express the expected results of the firm's operations during the budget period. Operating budgets contain expectations of "when" and "how much" with respect to such things as revenues, expenses, and net income. The typical schedules and statements included in the operating budget are the:

- Sales forecast
- Production budget (only for a manufacturer)
- Selling and administrative expenses budget
- Budgeted income statement
- Budgeted retained earnings statement

Financial budgets

Financial budgets include statements that report on the projected sources of cash and other resources used in operations, as well as the uses of that cash and other resources; and, of course, the ending balances in cash and other resources. This category is composed of the:

- Budgeted statement of cash receipts and disbursements
- Budgeted balance sheet

Before we discuss how to prepare the master budget, let's first consider the reasons for budgets and who the main participants are in preparing the budget and responding to it.

REASONS TO USE BUDGETS

There are more reasons to use budgets than not to use budgets

People who don't understand the purposes of budgets and how to use them, often characterize them with these objections:

"Budgets are too costly."

"My firm is small and uncomplicated. I can do all my planning in my head."

"The employees don't respond well to the pressure imposed on them by budgets."

Although there may be some basis for these objections, budgets do offer advantages and benefits that should far outweigh any costs or disadvantages, regardless of the type and size of firm.

Three ways in which budgets can benefit all firms include: (1) better planning, (2) control of performance, and (3) communication and coordination.

Better Planning

Budgets help managers plan

Budgets indicate to management: (1) how profitable the firm is expected to be, and (2) the resources that are expected to be generated or used during the forthcoming budget periods. When changes from normal operating activities are being considered, a budget can also inform the manager of the consequences of alternative courses of action, providing a basis for deciding which will be the best alternative. Without a budget, a manager can only hope that he or she is going in the best direction and has little idea of the ultimate results to expect.

Managers who prepare budgets for the first time usually are surprised by what they learn about the group they manage and its activities. For example, the sales manager may learn that the average collection period for sales to customers is 120 days for items sold with credit terms of 2/10, net 30. A production manager may find out that the new machine that is so badly needed may not generate enough cash flows over the useful life to pay for itself. Both of these managers may realize that they couldn't plan as well in their heads as they can with a budget.

Control of Performance

Budgets help managers control

In many organizations, control systems are developed to evaluate the actual performance of employees based on some predetermined measure of what their performance is expected to accomplish. The budget is an integral part of such a system since it represents the standard against which actual performance is compared. The performance report, prepared by the accountant, shows the actual results, the budgeted results, and any differences between actual and budget, referred to as variances. Any significant variances are noted and analyzed in an attempt to identify what caused them. Once the cause is identified, the appropriate remedy can be determined and set into action in an attempt to shrink these differences between actual and budget during the next performance report period.

If the expectations in the budget are communicated to all concerned at the beginning of a period, the employees will have been informed of exactly what is expected of them and the basis for their evaluation at the end of the period.

The type of budget used in a performance report for *controlling operations* is called a flexible budget, which we will cover in detail in the next chapter. For now, we will continue to be concerned with the master budget, a tool used by accountants to assist in the *planning of operations.*

Communication and Coordination

Budgets provide communication and coordination

The overall goals of the organization must be communicated to the managers of each of the departments within the organization. The overall goals must be understood by the middle- and lower-level managers and accepted by them as consistent with their own goals.

If the managers of different departments believe that by helping to attain the company's goals they also accomplish their own goals, the chances are good that the efforts, activities, and goals of all managers will be coordinated toward achieving the goals of the organization. If each department is interested only in its own performance, all the departments may become competitive rather than cooperative, and the organization as a whole may suffer.

Once the organization's overall goals have been communicated to each department, the manager of that department is responsible for the budget for his depart-

CAN BUDGETS SERVE ALL MASTERS?

A senior design engineer for a large automobile manufacturer recently complained to one of his employees:

"Those marketing guys want everything. They've decided that what they need in the next design series is The All-American Car. They say it's got to be large enough for a family of five (plus dog), small enough to drive in city traffic, powerful enough to pull a camp trailer, sporty enough so that the man of the house feels that what he's driving is only a few steps removed from a Formula One, luxurious enough to be seen at the country club, safe enough to meet all the federal standards, and it must get 35 miles per gallon and list for under $3,499. What the hell do they expect? One car can't do everything."

The frustrations of the automobile design engineer are not entirely different from those of the company controller who was recently asked why he couldn't design a budgeting system to meet all the requirements that managers throughout the company were placing upon it. The treasurer said he wanted a budget that was realistic enough for cash planning purposes. The marketing vice-president said he needed a budget that would motivate the sales force. The production chief told the controller he needed it to evaluate operating efficiency. The president asked that it be used as the primary coordination device to harmonize all the company's activities. Finally, a consultant came in and told the controller that he ought to be using the budget as a tool for management development. Like the design engineer, the controller rightly asked, "How can one budget be asked to do everything?"

The problems the design engineer and the company controller face in these hypothetical examples arise from the fact that both automobiles and budgeting systems serve multiple roles—at the same time they may be many things to many people. And the problem would be greatly simplified if none of multiple roles conflicted with any of the others. Unfortunately, this is not the case. A car cannot be luxurious and powerful if at the same time it must be inexpensive and economical. Similarly, a budget cannot fill equally well all the tasks that managers within an organization may wish to assign to it.

ment and for coordinating his budget with the budgets of the other departments. Each budget becomes an integral part of the master budget.

If the organization does not prepare a master budget, the managers of each department might not consider the effects of implementing the plans for their goals on the attainment of goals of other departments and the goals of the organization as a whole.

PARTICIPANTS IN THE BUDGETARY PROCESS

All areas of an organization participate in the budget preparation

Managers at all levels in an organization must actively participate in preparing the master budget if it is to be a truly useful tool. The major source of information in the budget is supplied by the departments to which the budgets apply. Thus, sales managers, production supervisors, and purchasing agents are as involved in the budgetary process as the accounting department personnel and top-level company executives.

Most larger organizations have a ***budget committee,*** composed of top executives of the different divisions or departments of the company. A budget director and the budget committee provide guidance and coordination as the budget is prepared. Also, the budget committee makes sure:

1. There are guidelines for preparing the budget.

2. These guidelines are communicated to and followed by the people who prepare the budget.

3. Any conflicts among departments regarding their own goals or the organization's are resolved.

4. The budget package is completed and promptly submitted to the president.

The accountant's role in the budget process

The ***budget director*** is the member of the budget committee responsible for much of the mechanical compilation of the budget; that is, he develops the many schedules and statements that make up the master budget. The budget director — who is probably an accountant serving on the controller's staff — deals directly with the managers of different departments by:

1. Providing them with useful historical data to assist in their estimates for the coming period

2. Making computations based on their estimates

3. Combining the budgets of the individual subunits into a complete and integrated package — the budget package[1]

PREPARING THE MASTER BUDGET

Preparing a master budget is a sequence of many steps, each subsequent step built on the preceding steps. We will take you through a detailed illustration for a typical company, step by step, from beginning to end, explaining the process as we move along and pointing out the specific things for you to learn about preparing any master budget.

The illustration for Underhill Company (see Example 23-1) begins with:

1. The company's balance sheet, which is for the day before the master budget period begins

2. Predictions of activity for the forthcoming budget period

3. Other relevant information describing the company's policies and expectations — such as sales terms, collection experience, desired ending inventories, and minimum cash balances

The illustration then continues, preparing the following supporting schedules in the sequence listed:

1. The sales forecast
2. The production budget
3. Costs of production
4. Purchases
5. Cost of goods sold expense
6. Selling and administrative expenses

Finally, based on the information in these schedules, the illustration concludes with the budgets for:

- The statement of cash receipts and disbursements
- The income statement and retained earnings statement
- The balance sheet

The illustration we will discuss is for a manufacturing firm rather than a service firm or a merchandising firm. Once you know how to develop the budgetary process for a manufacturer, it is not difficult to adapt what you have learned to other types of organizations. As we proceed through the example, we will specify and explain the steps that are different for an organization that doesn't produce the product it sells. At the end of the chapter we have a self-study problem for a retailer that you will want to work through.

---

[1] Robert N. Anthony and Glenn A. Welsch, *Fundamentals of Management Accounting* (Homewood, Ill.: Richard D. Irwin, Inc., 1977), p. 491.

The underlying principles of financial accounting that you learned in Chapters 1 through 18 of this text apply just as well to the preparation of budgeted financial statements as they do to the preparation of historical financial statements. The only difference is that budgeted statements portray what we expect in the future, whereas historical statements show what actually happened in the past. Budgeted statements involve a great deal of subjectivity and uncertainty; historical statements deal with more factual and objective evidence.

The Underhill Company

The Underhill Company: Read the facts carefully before you look at the schedules that follow

The remainder of this chapter involves the preparation of a master budget for Underhill Company. Read carefully the facts about Underhill Company that we give you in Example 23-1. Then proceed carefully through each of the schedules and statements that follow. It is important for you to understand each step before you proceed to the next.

EXAMPLE 23-1

UNDERHILL COMPANY

The Underhill Company produces a good luck charm requiring a single raw material. Its controller, Kelly Hernandez, has decided to prepare a master budget for the first quarter of 1988. She starts with the balance sheet for December 31, 1987, shown in Exhibit 23-1.

EXHIBIT 23-1

This is the balance sheet on 12/31/87—at the end of the year preceding the master budget period. The last step in the master budget will be another balance sheet—the budgeted balance sheet for 3/31/88

UNDERHILL COMPANY
Balance Sheet
December 31, 1987

Assets		Liabilities	
Cash	$ 102,250	Accounts Payable	$ 46,000
Accounts Receivable	75,000	Dividends Payable	80,000
Inventories:		Total Liabilities	$126,000
Raw Materials	8,000		
Finished Goods	75,000*	**Stockholders' Equity**	
Machinery	420,000	Capital Stock	$200,000
Accumulated Depreciation . .	(126,000)	Retained Earnings	228,250
			$428,250
		Total Liabilities and	
Total Assets	$ 554,250	Stockholders' Equity.	$ 554,250

* 5,000 units at $15 per unit.

Next, the vice president of sales provides Kelly with his best prediction of sales for the first 4 months of 1988 as shown below.

	Unit Sales	Dollar Sales
January	10,000	$250,000
February	20,000	500,000
March	24,000	600,000
April	18,000	450,000

Sales predictions and collection experience

Sales for December 1987 were 8,000 units, totaling $200,000. During the past year cash sales averaged 25% of total sales. In addition, one-half of the credit sales were

Minimum inventories

typically collected in the month of sale, and the remaining one-half in the month following the sale. These past averages are expected to pertain to Quarter I, 1988, as well. No discounts are offered by the company, and bad debts are not expected to occur.

Kelly feels it is necessary to maintain ending inventories of both finished goods and raw materials as a safety measure against a sudden surge in demand for the charms. The desired month-end inventory of finished goods will be equal to 50% of the following month's unit sales. Starting in January the desired ending inventory for raw materials will be $10,000 each month.

Kelly estimates the costs of production to be:

Costs of production

Direct materials . . . . $5 per unit
Direct labor . . . . $6 per unit
Variable overhead . . . . $3 per unit
Fixed overhead . . . . $15,000 per month

All units started in production each month will be completed during that period, and the beginning and ending balances in work-in-process inventory are assumed to be zero. All labor and overhead costs for the production department (other than depreciation on production machinery—totaling $2,000 per month) will be paid when incurred.

All purchases are on account

All purchases will be made on account and will be paid in full in the month following purchase.

S & A

The selling and administrative expenses are expected to be $2 per unit variable and $8,000 per month fixed. These expenses (other than the depreciation of office equipment in the selling and administrative departments—totaling $1,500 per month) will be paid in the month incurred.

Dividends

Dividends of $80,000 are paid during the first month of each quarter, after being declared in the previous month.

Machine purchase

In January the company plans to purchase a new machine costing $30,000. The $2,000 of depreciation given previously for the production overhead includes expected depreciation on this machine.

Cash balance and loans

The treasurer, Gus LaBretta, recommends that a minimum cash balance of $50,000 be maintained during each month. Whenever the company anticipates falling below that amount, a short-term loan will be taken out at the beginning of that month. The loan will be repaid when cash becomes available. Interest will accrue at 14% of the unpaid balance and will be paid when the principal is repaid (based on the amount of principal repaid). All repayments take place at the end of the month.

Relationship of the December 31, 1987, Balance Sheet to the 1988 Budgets

Every item in the 12/31/87 balance sheet is needed in preparing the master budget

The balance sheet (Exhibit 23-1) on December 31, 1987, serves as the starting point for the anticipated activities of 1988. Each account balance given in the December 31, 1987, balance sheet is in some way employed in the budgeted schedules and statements for 1988.

For example, the cash balance of $102,250 on December 31, 1987, becomes the January 1, 1988, cash balance to start off the cash receipts and disbursements budget for the forthcoming quarter. (Take a peek at Exhibit 23-12, beginning cash balance for January—line 9.) Similarly, the $8,000 balance on December 31, 1987, for raw materials inventory becomes the starting point, or the beginning inventory in the schedule of purchases budgeted for January 1988 (see Exhibit 23-8 on page 923—line 4). All the balances in the accounts on the December 31, 1987, balance sheet are used in a similar way in preparing the schedules and statements that eventually form the master budget.

With this brief introduction, we will now help you to become more familiar with each of the schedules and statements that make up the master budget.

The Operating Budgets

The Sales Forecast

The cornerstone of all budgeting: the sales forecast

The first step in the budget process is the ***sales forecast***—a prediction of expected sales throughout the budget period. The responsibility for developing the sales forecast is assigned to a top-level marketing officer. The sales forecast is considered the starting point for all budgeting (whether it be for a manufacturer or a nonmanufacturer) because all the other budgets—that is, all the elements of the master budget—depend on it.

Figure 23-1 shows the relationships among the schedules and statements comprising the master budget and the sequence in which each is developed. Notice that none of the steps in the figure can be determined until after the sales forecast (Step 1) is developed.

For example, not until the sales are forecast is it possible to determine the number of units that have to be produced (Step 3). Then, only after the production budget is prepared, can we estimate the materials needed (Step 5), the required purchases (Step 6), and conversion costs (Step 7) needed for production.

The schedule of collections (Step 2) depends on the sales forecast and so does the selling expense budget (Step 4).

The four budgeted financial statements (Steps 8 through 11) depend on the estimates in all the preceding budgeted schedules (Steps 2 through 7) which, of course, depend on the sales forecast. So, everything in a master budget depends on the sales forecast. That's the main thing you should understand from this figure. As we proceed we will show you in detail exactly how each of the budgeted schedules and statements develops from the budgets that precede it.

Sales Forecast and Reliability   The accuracy of the sales forecast will determine the reliability of all the other budgeted schedules and statements. As a result, the sales forecast is the most important as well as the most difficult step. It is difficult because future sales are influenced by such diverse factors as:[2]

Factors to consider in the sales forecast

- Past sales (last year's, last month's, the same month last year)
- Industry conditions
- Advertising
- GNP and disposable income
- Population
- Quality of sales personnel
- Production capacity
- Prediction of salesforce

Not only are these factors often uncontrollable, but it is also difficult to determine which factors will have an influence on sales and to what extent. The sales executive, with the help of others, is expected to consider all these factors and derive, either subjectively or statistically, an accurate prediction of (or one that closely approximates) sales for each period. This is not an easy task.

[2] Charles T. Horngren, *Cost Accounting: A Managerial Emphasis,* 5th ed. (Englewood Cliffs, N.J.: Prentice-Hall, Inc., 1982), p. 141.

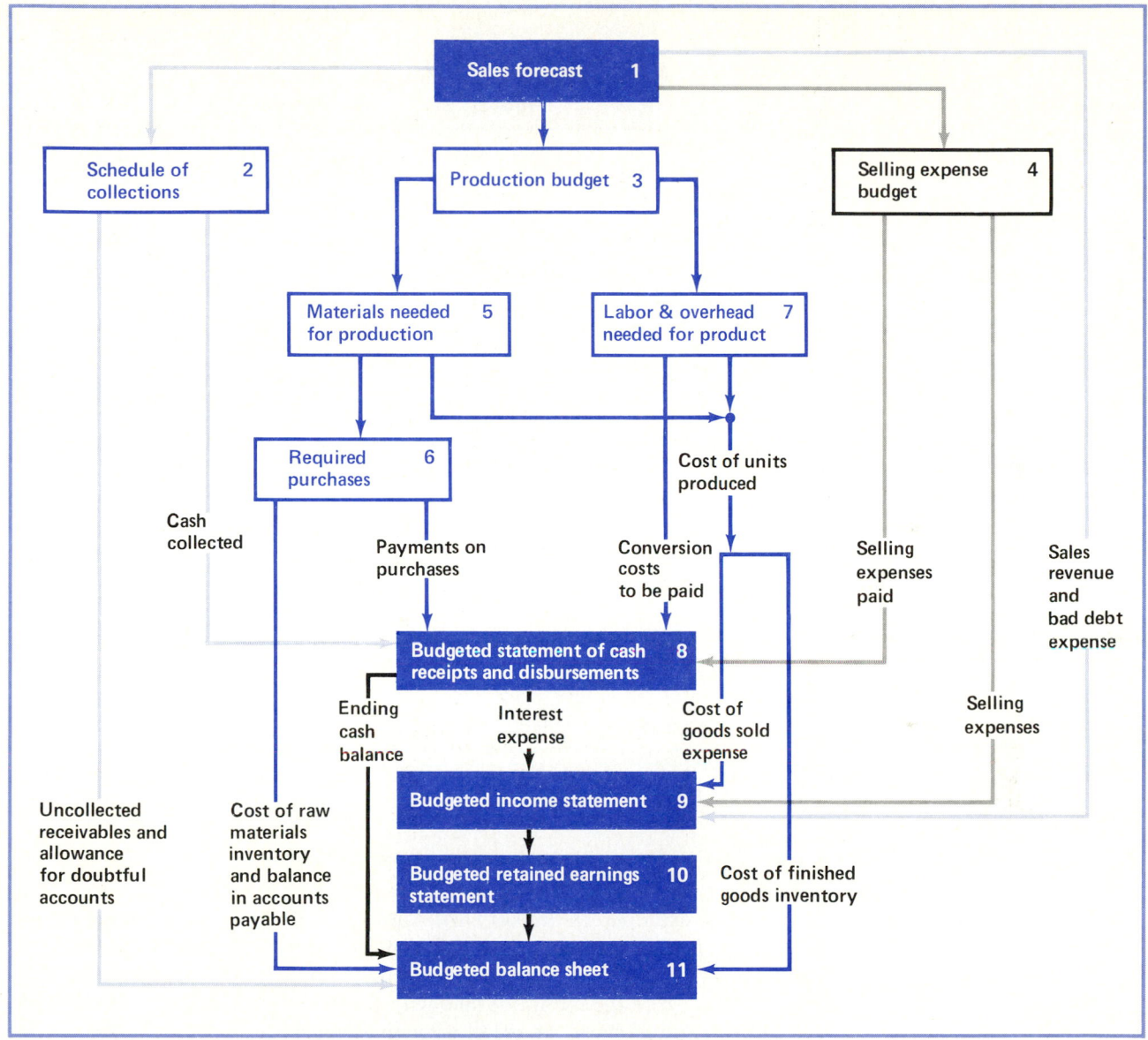

FIGURE 23-1   The Master Budget: The Relationship of the Parts That Make Up the Whole.
Every step we take in preparing the master budget depends on the sales forecast (Step 1). Each step we take leads toward the final product—the budgeted financial statements (Steps 8–11).

Sales are the basis for cash collections

The sales forecast for Quarter I, 1988, for Underhill Company is shown in Exhibit 23-2 (page 918). The total sales are broken down into cash sales (25%) and credit sales (75%). In addition, Exhibit 23-2 includes the sales for the month of December —because only one-half of the credit sales of that month were collected in 1987, the other one-half will be collected in January of 1988. We need to show where the cash collections (shown in Exhibit 23-3) in January come from—some will come from January's sales and some will come from December's sales.

The arrows from the sales forecast (Exhibit 23-2) to the ***cash collections budget*** (Exhibit 23-3) point out the month in which each month's sales are expected to be

EXHIBIT 23-2   Past and Future Sales.
The sales are 25% cash and 75% credit. Total forecasted sales for Quarter I are $1,350,000.

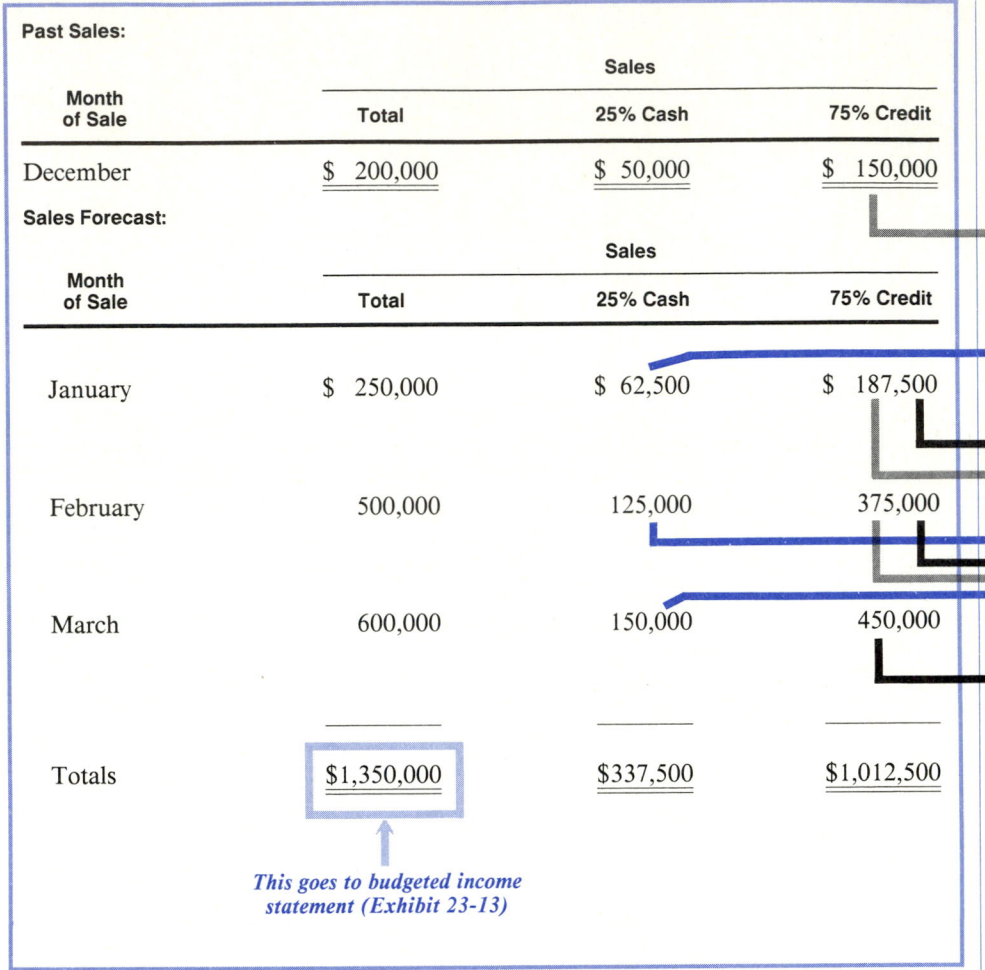

Past Sales:

Month of Sale	Total	Sales 25% Cash	75% Credit
December	$ 200,000	$ 50,000	$ 150,000

Sales Forecast:

Month of Sale	Total	Sales 25% Cash	75% Credit
January	$ 250,000	$ 62,500	$ 187,500
February	500,000	125,000	375,000
March	600,000	150,000	450,000
Totals	$1,350,000	$337,500	$1,012,500

This goes to budgeted income statement (Exhibit 23-13)

collected. For example, in January the sales of $250,000 are $62,500 cash and $187,500 credit. The cash sales are obviously collected in the month of sale (shown by the dark blue arrow). Based on the facts given in Example 23-1, 50% of the credit sales are to be collected in the month of sale, with the balance collected in the following month. Therefore, 50% of the credit sales in January, or $93,750, is collected in January (the black arrow). The remaining $93,750 is collected in February (the light gray arrow).

The cash collections for each month are composed of three parts. For January, they are:

1. The cash sales of the month, $62,500

2. The collection of 50% of December's credit sales, $75,000

3. The collection of 50% of January's credit sales, $93,750

The total of these three specific cash collections is $231,250 for January. The total of these categories of collections is $406,250 for February and $562,500 for March. These totals, representing expected cash receipts each month during the first quarter, are transferred to the first line of the ***budgeted statement of cash receipts and disburse-***

EXHIBIT 23-3   Budgeted Schedule of Cash Collections: Quarter I, 1988.

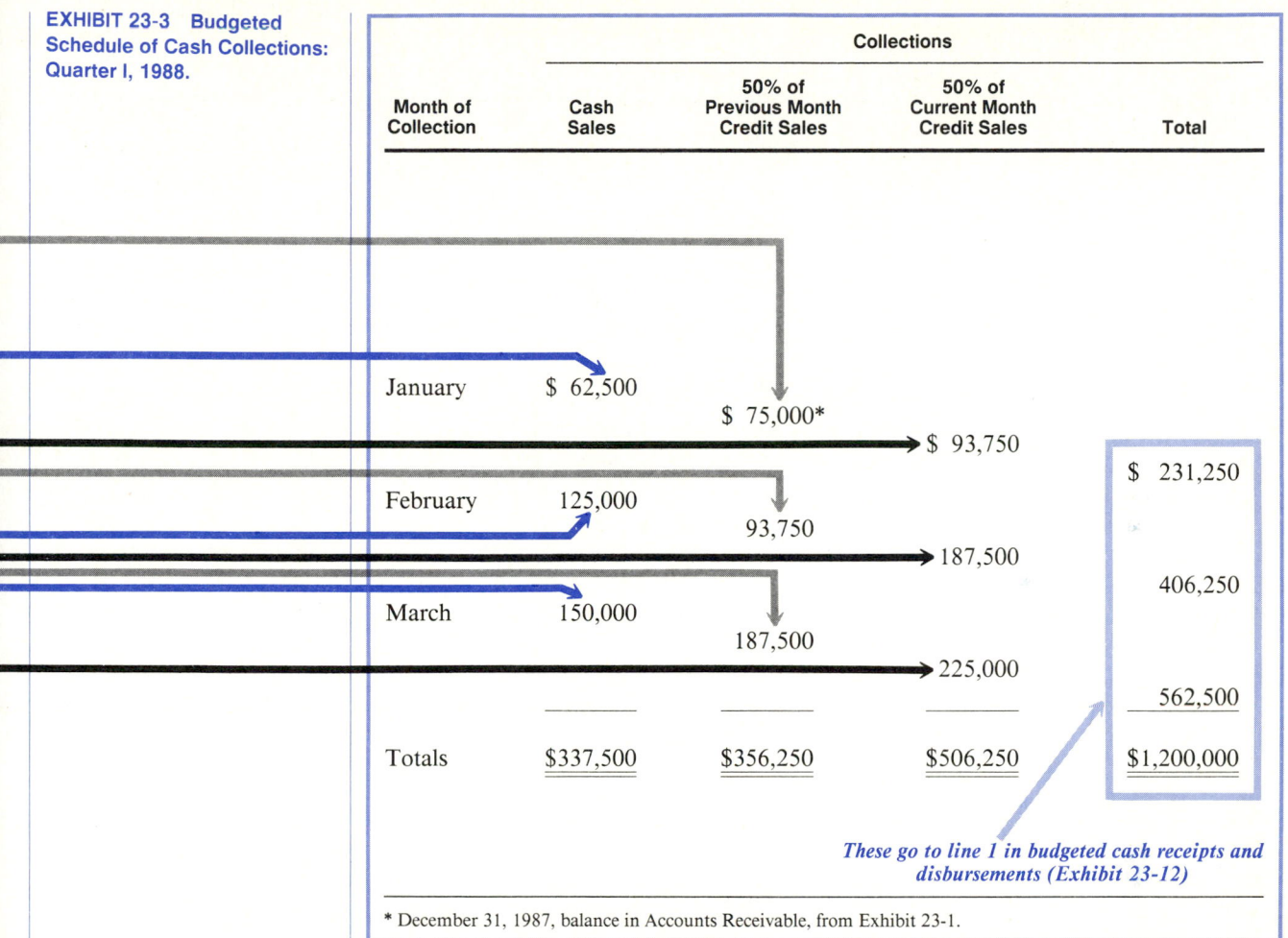

Month of Collection	Cash Sales	Collections 50% of Previous Month Credit Sales	50% of Current Month Credit Sales	Total
January	$ 62,500	$ 75,000*	$ 93,750	$ 231,250
February	125,000	93,750	187,500	406,250
March	150,000	187,500	225,000	562,500
Totals	$337,500	$356,250	$506,250	$1,200,000

These go to line 1 in budgeted cash receipts and disbursements (Exhibit 23-12)

* December 31, 1987, balance in Accounts Receivable, from Exhibit 23-1.

ments (Exhibit 23-12). This budget lists the different types of budgeted receipts and disbursements for each month of the quarter. It also indicates if any financing is needed during the quarter. We will look at this budget in detail after we have completed all of our supporting schedules.

Although budgeted income statements and budgeted balance sheets can be prepared monthly, *for simplicity these statements are being prepared only on a quarterly basis* in this illustration.

The total forecasted sales for the quarter, $1,350,000, is transferred to the first line in the budgeted income statement (Exhibit 23-13).

The balance in Accounts Receivable represents the uncollected credit sales on March 31, 1988. For Underhill Company this is simply the 50% of March's credit sales that are expected to be collected in April. A useful general format for obtaining a balance in Accounts Receivable is shown in Exhibit 23-4.

The uncollected receivables go on the balance sheet

One-half of the budgeted credit sales of March, $225,000 — the uncollected portion — is the budgeted balance in Accounts Receivable on March 31. This amount is transferred to the budgeted balance sheet (line 2 in Exhibit 23-15).

In this example we have assumed that all credit sales would eventually be collected — no bad debts expense was expected. More realistically, we probably should have assumed that some of the accounts are going to go bad. If Underhill had

EXHIBIT 23-4
Expected Balance in Accounts Receivable:
March 31, 1988.

The Accounts Receivable balance on 3/31/88 goes to the budgeted balance sheet (Exhibit 23-15).

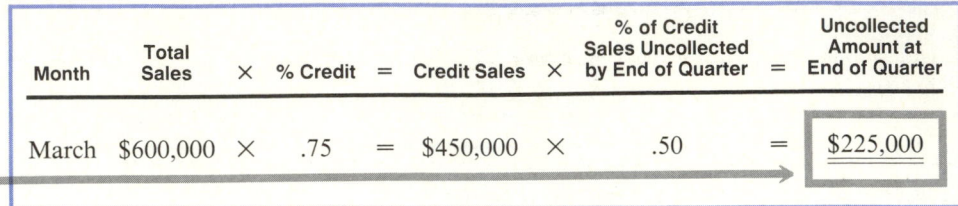

Month	Total Sales	×	% Credit	=	Credit Sales	×	% of Credit Sales Uncollected by End of Quarter	=	Uncollected Amount at End of Quarter
March	$600,000	×	.75	=	$450,000	×	.50	=	$225,000

expected some bad debts and had been using an estimation method for bad debts—such as percentage of sales—a few things would be different. First, there would have been an Allowance for Uncollectibles account on the December 31, 1987, balance sheet. Next, we would have some bad debts expense in the budgeted income statement—Exhibit 23-13. Finally, the Allowance for Uncollectibles account would have to be adjusted for the additional estimated bad debts in Quarter I. When you go through the self-study problem at the end of the chapter, you'll get a chance to see just how the schedules and statements would be affected by the complication of having bad debts.

The sales forecast, the cash collections budget, and the schedule for calculating the expected balance in Accounts Receivable are represented by Steps 1 and 2 in the flow chart in Figure 23-1. And as you just saw, these budgets are eventually reflected (with light blue lines in Figure 23-1) in the budgeted statement of cash receipts and disbursements (for the cash collections), the budgeted income statement (for the sales revenue), and the budgeted balance sheet (for the ending balance in Accounts Receivable).

The Production Budget

If we were preparing a master budget for a retailer or a wholesaler instead of a manufacturer, we would skip the next few sections and go right to the calculation of purchases on page 923. If the organization were a service type of company, we would jump directly to the discussion of selling and administrative expenses on page 926. But our example is for a manufacturer, so we will now continue on with the next logical step for the manufacturer—the production budget.

The *production budget* indicates the units that need to be produced in each future period to meet the expected sales. In this budget the production department must decide the amount of finished goods inventory that must be on hand at the end of each month during the budget period. Every manufacturer should maintain some minimum level of finished goods inventory to help stabilize production from month to month, and to avoid the possibility of losing sales when demand exceeds the balance in finished goods. Once the required—the **desired** minimum—ending inventory in finished goods has been determined, the production required during each month of the budget period can be calculated with the following schedule:

Determining the units to be produced

> Desired minimum ending inventory of finished goods
> plus
> Unit sales expected for the forthcoming period
> equals
> Total inventory needs for the forthcoming period
> less
> Beginning inventory of finished goods
> equals
> Units to be produced

**EXHIBIT 23-5   Budgeted Unit Production Report:
Quarter I, 1988.**
Based on the forecasted sales and desired minimum ending inventories of finished goods, the units to be produced are determined for each month of Quarter I.

	January	February	March
Desired minimum ending inventory, finished goods*.	10,000	12,000	9,000
Sales for month.	10,000	20,000	24,000
Total needs for month	20,000	32,000	33,000
Beginning inventory, finished goods.	5,000†	10,000‡	12,000‡
Units to be produced	15,000	22,000	21,000

These units are needed in Exhibit 23-6

* 50% of sales (in units) for February, March, and April, respectively.
† Given in the footnote to the 12/31/87 balance sheet (Exhibit 23-1).
‡ The desired ending inventory of each previous month.

The minimum ending inventory balance determined to be needed each period may be expressed:

1. In absolute terms, which would be the same amount, regardless of the level of future inventory needs. For example, Underhill may desire an ending inventory of 10,000 units, whether the following month's sales are expected to be 50,000 units or 1,000 units.

2. In relative terms, which would probably be determined as a percentage of sales expected in future months. For example, Underhill may prefer its ending inventory of finished goods always to be at least 50% of the next month's expected unit sales.

Assuming that Underhill decides to use the second policy mentioned above, then on January 31, the company will want its inventory to be at least 50% of unit sales for February. Since the sales for February are expected to be 20,000 units, the inventory of finished goods on January 31 should be at least 10,000 units. The required ending inventories for February and March are determined in a similar manner.

Starting with the figures for required ending inventory of finished goods each month, the number of units to be produced are determined in Exhibit 23-5 — 15,000 units in January, 22,000 units in February, and 21,000 units in March.

Budgeted Costs of Production Report

Based on the units to be produced each month, as shown in the production report, the budgeted costs of producing the units are determined as shown in Exhibit 23-6.

The variable production costs are based on the following rates per unit:

Direct materials . . . . $5 per unit
Direct labor . . . . 6 per unit
Variable overhead . . . . 3 per unit

These per-unit rates are assigned to the budgeted units of production, 15,000, 22,000, and 21,000 for the 3 months of the quarter. The fixed factory overhead assigned to production is expected to be $15,000 per month regardless of activity. For the 3

EXHIBIT 23-6   Budgeted Costs of Production Report: Quarter I, 1988.

Starting with the units to be produced (Exhibit 23-5), the budgeted costs of production are calculated for each month. The average cost per unit for the quarter is $14.78.

	January	February	March	Total for the Quarter
Units to be produced	15,000	22,000	21,000	58,000
Direct materials ($5 per unit)	$ 75,000	$110,000	$105,000	$290,000
Direct labor ($6 per unit)	90,000	132,000	126,000	348,000
Variable overhead ($3 per unit)	45,000	66,000	63,000	174,000
Fixed overhead*	15,000	15,000	15,000	45,000
Total production costs	$225,000	$323,000	$309,000	$857,000
				÷ 58,000 units
				=$ 14.78 per unit

* The $15,000 includes $2,000 of depreciation on production machinery.

months combined, the total production costs ($857,000) divided by the total budgeted units of production (58,000) results in an expected average cost per unit produced of $14.78. (In the next section this cost per unit will be assigned to the ending inventory of finished goods to determine the budgeted cost of goods sold expense.)

Budgeted Schedule of Cost of Goods Sold Expense

The cost of goods sold expense predicted for Quarter I is calculated in Exhibit 23-7. The beginning inventory of finished goods, $75,000, was given in the December 31, 1987, balance sheet (Exhibit 23-1). The total costs of production for the quarter come from Exhibit 23-6, and the ending inventory, $133,020, is calculated by applying the FIFO method to the desired ending inventory of 9,000 units from Exhibit 23-5 at the end of March. Under the FIFO method, the ending inventory comes from current production, which should have an average cost of $14.78 per unit (Exhibit 23-6). For simplicity a single average for the quarter was determined rather than a different one for each month's production. The cost of the ending inventory is:

$$9{,}000 \text{ units} \times \$14.78 \text{ per unit} = \$133{,}020$$

Subtracting the cost of the ending inventory from the total available for sale leaves $798,980, which is the cost of goods sold expense.

EXHIBIT 23-7
Budgeted Schedule of Cost of Goods Sold Expense: Quarter I, 1988.

January 1, finished goods inventory	$ 75,000
Cost of production: Quarter I (Exhibit 23-6)	857,000
Total available for sale	$932,000
March 31, finished goods inventory	133,020
Cost of goods sold expense	$798,980

This goes on the budgeted balance sheet (Exhibit 23-15)

This goes on line 2 of the budgeted income statement (Exhibit 23-13)

The budgeted cost of goods sold goes on the budgeted income statement

The cost of goods sold expense is subtracted from the sales revenue in the budgeted income statement (Exhibit 23-13), yielding a budgeted gross profit of $551,020. And the ending inventory for finished goods of $133,020 is an asset in the March 31, 1988, budgeted balance sheet (Exhibit 23-15).

Purchases and Payments

What raw materials we purchase depends on what we need in production

A major item included in the budgeted costs of production report (Exhibit 23-6) is the budgeted amount of direct materials needed for each month's production. These estimates enable us to calculate the raw materials that have to be purchased in each period as well as the cash needed to pay for them.

Just as a firm sets a policy regarding the minimum quantity of finished goods inventory it likes to have at the end of each accounting period, so also may that firm decide on a policy about the minimum quantity of raw materials inventory at the end of a period. Knowing what the required—or desired—minimum raw materials balance must be makes it possible to calculate the purchases of raw materials needed to fulfill that balance. Some minimum quantity of raw materials must be kept on hand at all times so that production is not disrupted when the demand to produce finished goods is greater than anticipated.

Once the required ending inventory for raw materials has been determined, the amount of raw materials to be purchased each period is calculated according to the following schedule:

Determining purchases for a manufacturer

> Desired ending inventory of raw materials
> plus
> Raw materials needed for production
> equals
> Total needs for the period
> less
> Beginning inventory of raw materials
> equals
> Required purchases of raw materials

The **budgeted schedule of purchases** for the Underhill Company is provided in Exhibit 23-8. The minimum required ending inventory of raw materials of $10,000

EXHIBIT 23-8   Budgeted Schedule of Purchases: Quarter I, 1988.

Notice that the desired ending inventory of one month becomes the beginning inventory of the next month. Also, the desired ending inventory of March goes on the budgeted balance sheet.

	January	February	March
Desired ending inventory, raw materials (given in Example 23-1)	$10,000	$ 10,000	$ 10,000
Materials needed for production of month (Exhibit 23-6)	75,000	110,000	105,000
Total needs	$85,000	$120,000	$115,000
Beginning inventory, raw materials	8,000	10,000	10,000
Purchases for month	$77,000	$110,000	$105,000

March's ending inventory goes on the budgeted balance sheet (Exhibit 23-15)

The purchases are needed to get cash payments (Exhibit 23-9)

EXHIBIT 23-9   Schedule of Purchase Payments: Quarter I, 1988.

The purchases are paid for in the following month. The March purchase will be paid in April—it is an account payable on March 31.

	December	Quarter I			April
		January	February	March	
Purchases	$46,000	$77,000	$110,000	$105,000*	
Payments—in month following purchase .		$46,000	$ 77,000	$110,000	$105,000

* On March 31, the unpaid purchases represent the balance in Accounts Payable.

Trace these to line 2 of the budgeted cash receipts and disbursements (Exhibit 23-12)

each month was given in Example 23-1. The beginning inventory for January was taken from the December 31, 1987, balance sheet (Exhibit 23-1). Finally, the beginning raw materials inventory for February is the ending inventory for January; and the beginning inventory for March is the ending inventory for February. The expected ending inventory for March of $10,000 is classified as an asset in the budgeted balance sheet on March 31, 1988 (Exhibit 23-15).

The purchases shown in the budgeted schedule of purchases (Exhibit 23-8) are not paid for in the month of purchase. Instead, Underhill Company typically pays for its purchases in the month following the purchase. The schedule of purchase payments (Exhibit 23-9) indicates what the cash payments will be in each month.

The payments in January, $46,000, are for the purchases of December. Since these purchases were not paid for before December 31, 1987, they appeared as the balance in Accounts Payable on the December 31, 1987, balance sheet (Exhibit 23-1). The cash payments in February and March are for the purchases of January and February. The purchases of March ($105,000) will not be paid for until April, so this $105,000 of unpaid bills represents the balance in Accounts Payable in the March 31, 1988, budgeted balance sheet (Exhibit 23-15).

The cash payments from Exhibit 23-9 are listed on the first line under disbursements in the budgeted statement of cash receipts and disbursements (Exhibit 23-12).

If the Underhill Company were a retailer or wholesaler instead of a manufacturer, the purchases would be for merchandise inventory rather than raw materials inventory. The schedule of purchases for a retailer and a wholesaler is slightly different than for a manufacturer, as shown below:

Determining purchases for a nonmanufacturer

Desired ending inventory of merchandise
plus
Merchandise needed for current sales
equals
Total needs for the period
less
Beginning inventory of merchandise
equals
Required purchases

If the company were a service firm, there would be no purchases because service firms don't have inventories.

In the situation we've been examining for Underhill Company in Example 23-1, we found that the purchases were dependent on the company policy concerning a desired ending inventory for raw materials. Sometimes the company policy concerning purchases is stated more directly. Instead of specifying a desired ending inventory and calculating purchases as we did in Exhibit 23-8, the company may come up with a policy that specifies that purchases will be based entirely on future sales. For example, the policy may be to purchase each month enough to cover the sales of the following month. This situation would actually be a lot easier than what we've been doing; all you'd have to do is figure out what the sales are for the period covered by the policy, and then buy that amount one month earlier. If you want to see how this works, take a look at the self-study problem for a retailer at the end of this chapter.

Cash Disbursements for Conversion Costs

Depreciation is a noncash item

The conversion costs (direct labor plus fixed and variable factory overhead) listed in the budgeted costs of production report (Exhibit 23-6), with the exception of depreciation, are to be paid for when incurred. Exhibit 23-6 shows $15,000 of fixed factory overhead. This amount includes $2,000 in depreciation costs. But depreciation does not involve a cash outlay. Therefore, the actual cash outlay for fixed factory overhead each month is $13,000, or $2,000 less than the $15,000 shown in the budgeted costs of production report. Exhibit 23-10 lists the monthly budgeted cash payments for conversion costs, which are also listed in the second line under disbursements in the budgeted statement of cash receipts and disbursements (Exhibit 23-12).

The budgeted production reports (Exhibits 23-5 and 23-6), the budgeted cost of goods sold expense (Exhibit 23-7), the budgeted schedules of purchases and payments of purchases (Exhibits 23-8 and 23-9), and the budgeted schedule of disbursements for conversion costs (Exhibit 23-10) are represented by Steps 1, 3, 5, 6, and 7 in the flow chart for the master budget (Figure 23-1).

As you saw, the budgets in Exhibits 23-5 through 23-10 are also reflected in the budgeted financial statements (shown in Figure 23-1 with dark blue lines). For the budgeted income statement (Exhibit 23-13) we got the budgeted cost of goods sold expense from Exhibit 23-7. For the budgeted statement of cash receipts and disbursements (Exhibit 23-12) we got the budgeted purchase payments from Exhibit 23-9 and the budgeted disbursements for conversion costs from Exhibit 23-10. Finally, for the budgeted balance sheet (Exhibit 23-15) we got the finished goods inventory balance

EXHIBIT 23-10
Budgeted Schedule of Disbursements for Conversion Costs:
Quarter I, 1988.

	January	February	March
Direct labor.	$ 90,000	$132,000	$126,000
Variable overhead.	45,000	66,000	63,000
Fixed overhead.	13,000	13,000	13,000
Total disbursements	$148,000	$211,000	$202,000

Trace these to line 3 in the budgeted cash receipts and disbursements (Exhibit 23-12)

EXHIBIT 23-11   Budgeted Schedule of Selling and Administrative Items—Expenses and Disbursements: Quarter I, 1988

Total expenses less $1,500 of depreciation equals total disbursements. Remember, depreciation is a noncash expense.

	January	February	March	Total	
Variable*	$20,000	$40,000	$48,000	$108,000	*The total expenses go to the budgeted income statement (Exhibit 23-13)*
Fixed	8,000	8,000	8,000	24,000	
Total expenses	$28,000	$48,000	$56,000	$132,000	
Total disbursements†	$26,500	$46,500	$54,500	$127,500	*The disbursements are found in line 4 of budgeted cash receipts and disbursements (Exhibit 23-12)*

* $2 per unit sold × the number of units sold in each month.
† Total expenses less the $1,500 per month for depreciation of office equipment—a noncash expense.

from Exhibit 23-7, the raw materials inventory balance from Exhibit 23-8, and the accounts payable balance from Exhibit 23-9.

Selling and Administrative Expenses

Both manufacturers and nonmanufacturers have S & A costs

Selling expenses are the costs of promoting, selling, and shipping the product to customers. These costs include a variety of items that can be divided into variable and fixed costs.

Variable selling costs, such as commissions and shipping costs, can be estimated by taking a percentage of the estimated total sales dollars or by multiplying a cost per unit by the number of units sold.

Fixed selling costs include salaries, advertising, rent, and depreciation. They are budgeted at an unchanging amount per month.

Administrative costs are associated with such activities as giving overall direction to the company and providing services for personnel. Although most administrative costs are fixed, some items such as supplies and telephone costs are variable costs.

The selling and administrative expenses for Underhill Company are estimated to be $2 per unit variable and $8,000 per month fixed. Based on the budgeted sales of 10,000, 20,000, and 24,000 units for the first 3 months of 1988, a budget is prepared for the selling and administrative expenses.

As shown in Exhibit 23-11, the total budgeted expenses for the quarter, $132,000, is transferred to the budgeted income statement (Exhibit 23-13).

Cash disbursements for selling and administrative items, with the exception of depreciation, are made when the expense is incurred. Thus the total expenses for each month, less the $1,500 of depreciation, represents the selling and administrative cash disbursements for each month. These monthly disbursements are also listed as the third line of disbursements in the budgeted statement of cash receipts and disbursements (Exhibit 23-12).

The schedule for selling and administrative items (Exhibit 23-11) is represented by Step 4 in the master budget flow chart (Figure 23-1). The gray arrows from Step 4 lead to: (1) Step 9 for the selling and administrative *expenses* that go on the budgeted income statement (Exhibit 23-13), and (2) Step 8 for the selling and administrative *disbursements* going on the budgeted statement of cash receipts and disbursements (Exhibit 23-12).

A Financial Budget: The Statement of Cash Receipts and Disbursements

We have not yet completed all of the operating budgets—the budgeted income statement lacks one step and the budgeted retained earnings statement hasn't been started. We cannot complete these operating budgets until we have finished the budgeted cash receipts and disbursements statement—the first of two financial budgets.

The only item missing from the budgeted income statement is interest expense. And we cannot calculate interest expense until we know if any financing is needed during the forthcoming quarter. We find out what financing is necessary in the budgeted statement of cash receipts and disbursements—and only then can we determine interest expense.

The purpose of the ***budgeted statement of cash receipts and disbursements*** is to show the amount and source of cash inflows and cash outflows expected throughout the budget period, and the resulting anticipated cash balances at key times during the budget period. This budget indicates to management when cash receipts will be far in excess of cash disbursements, resulting in large cash balances. In this situation, management knows how long the excess cash will be available and must decide how it should be invested to earn maximum returns. The budgeted statement also points out when cash outflows are expected to be much larger than cash receipts, which should lead to seriously low cash balances. This information allows management enough time to arrange financing so that when the day comes to meet payrolls, distribute dividends, and pay creditors, the cash will be available.

The many items to be included in the budgeted statement of cash receipts and disbursements can be arranged in a variety of ways. The general format given below will be employed in this text:

Form for budgeted statement of cash receipts and disbursements

> Cash receipts
> less
> Cash disbursements
> equals
> Difference in cash receipts and cash disbursements
> plus
> Beginning cash balance
> equals
> Ending cash balance (assuming no financing, repayments, or investments)
> plus
> Financing arranged to attain a minimum cash balance
> less
> Repayments of financing
> less
> Investment of excess cash
> equals
> Ending cash balance

You might want to envision this statement in terms of Figure 23-2. Try to imagine the beginning cash balance as a water level within a bucket. During the budget period this level is increased by cash receipts and decreased by cash disbursements. If the cash receipts during the budget period are greater than the cash disbursements, the water (or cash) level will go up. But if the cash receipts are less than the cash disbursements, the water (or cash) level will go down. When there is a decrease, the level of

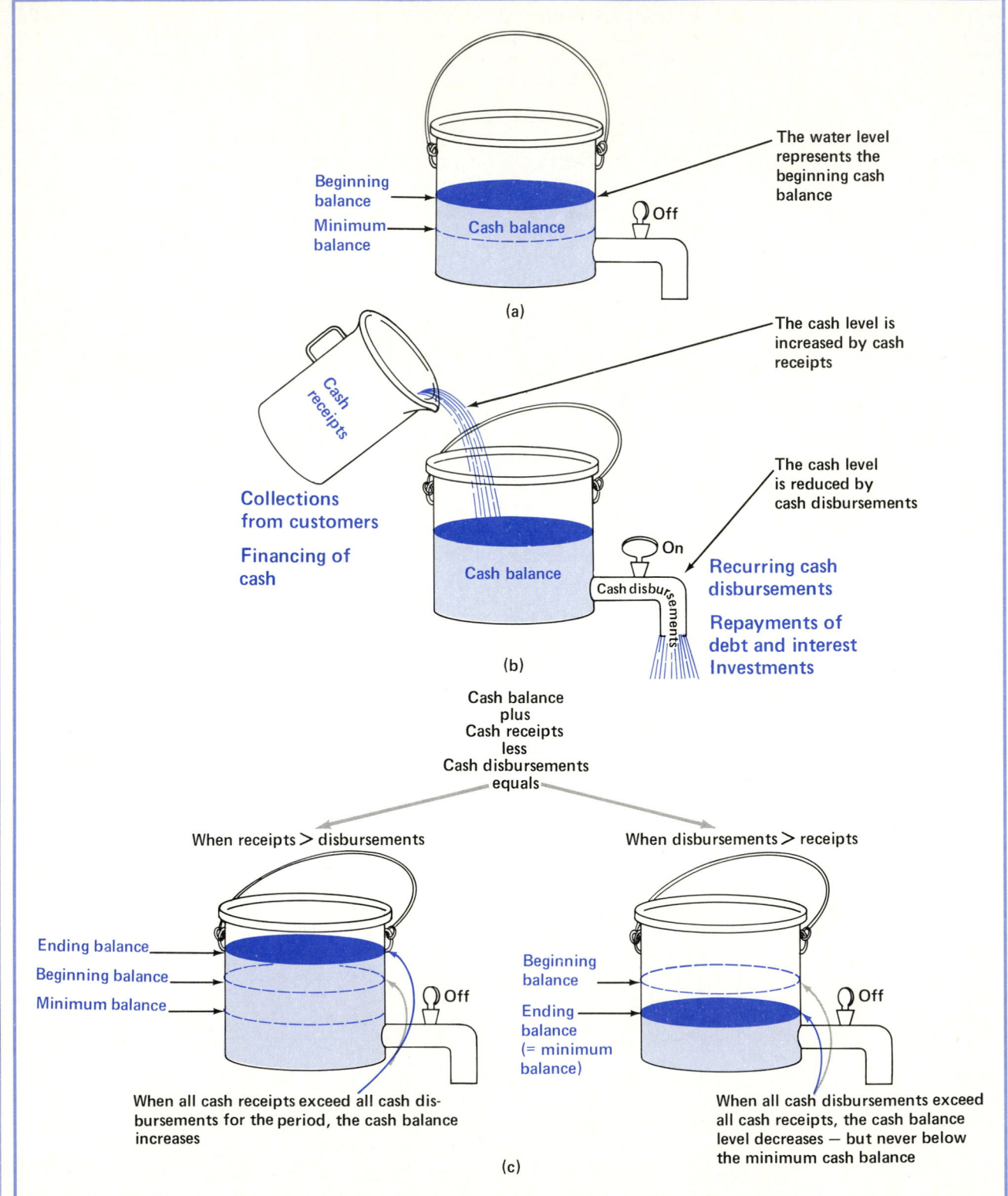

The water level represents the beginning cash balance

Beginning balance

Minimum balance

Cash balance

Off

(a)

The cash level is increased by cash receipts

Cash receipts

Collections from customers

Financing of cash

Cash balance

On

Cash disbursements

The cash level is reduced by cash disbursements

Recurring cash disbursements

Repayments of debt and interest Investments

(b)

Cash balance
plus
Cash receipts
less
Cash disbursements
equals

When receipts > disbursements

When disbursements > receipts

Ending balance
Beginning balance
Minimum balance

Off

When all cash receipts exceed all cash disbursements for the period, the cash balance increases

Beginning balance

Ending balance (= minimum balance)

Off

When all cash disbursements exceed all cash receipts, the cash balance level decreases — but never below the minimum cash balance

(c)

FIGURE 23-2   The Budgeted Statement of Cash Receipts and Disbursements, Viewed as a Changing Water Level in a Bucket of Cash.

**EXHIBIT 23-12   Budgeted Statement of Cash Receipts and Disbursements:
Quarter I, 1988.**
There is excess cash in February and March but a deficiency in January. Therefore financing is required in January which should be repaid in February. The interest expense of $1,097 goes on the budgeted income statement, and the March 31 cash balance, $269,653, goes on the budgeted balance sheet.

	January	February	March
Cash receipts (Exhibit 23-3)	$231,250	$406,250	$562,500
Cash disbursements:			
Purchase payments (Exhibit 23-9).	$ 46,000	$ 77,000	$110,000
Conversion costs (Exhibit 23-10)	148,000	211,000	202,000
Selling and Adm. (Exhibit 23-11)	26,500	46,500	54,500
Dividends paid	80,000	–0–	–0–
Purchase of machinery	30,000	–0–	–0–
Total cash disbursements	$330,500	$334,500	$366,500
Receipts less disbursements	$ (99,250)	$ 71,750	$196,000
Beginning cash balance (Exhibit 23-1 for Jan.).	102,250	50,000	73,653
Ending cash balance if no financing or repayments	$ 3,000	$121,750	$269,653
Financing required to attain minimum $50,000 balance	47,000	–0–	–0–
Repayments: Principal	–0–	(47,000)	–0–
Interest.	–0–	(1,097)*	–0–
Ending cash balance	$ 50,000	$ 73,653	$269,653

Goes to budgeted income statement (Exhibit 23-13)

Goes to budgeted balance sheet (Exhibit 23-15)

* $47,000 × .14 = $6,580 per year × $\frac{2}{12}$ = $1,097 for 2 months.

cash will be somewhere below the beginning level but never below the minimum level.

The budgeted statement of cash receipts and disbursements for the Underhill Company is presented in Exhibit 23-12.

The cash receipts and the first three types of cash disbursements for purchases, conversion costs, and selling and administrative costs have already been discussed. The cash disbursement for the dividends paid in January follows from the December 1987, declaration. If you refer back to the balance sheet on December 31, 1987, in Exhibit 23-1, you'll see the $80,000 liability for dividends payable.

The $80,000 of dividends declared in March will be paid in April and therefore do not affect the budgeted statement of cash receipts and disbursements during Quarter I. However, the dividends declared in March do reduce retained earnings (Exhibit 23-14) at that time, and the related liability for the April payment must be included in the March 31, 1988, budgeted balance sheet (Exhibit 23-15).

The cash disbursement of $30,000 is for the January cash purchase of machinery. The depreciation of machinery is not included in this budgeted statement because it is a noncash item. It is included in the budgeted income statement, however, as a part of the cost of goods sold expense and as a part of selling and administrative expenses.

Notice in Exhibit 23-12 that in January the cash disbursements are expected to exceed the cash receipts by $99,250, which reduces the beginning cash balance of $102,250 to only $3,000. The $3,000 represents what the Underhill Company's January 31 cash balance will be if no financing is arranged for that month. Had the receipts less disbursements been exactly −$102,250, the January 31 balance would be zero, a situation that the company would not want to have.

Minimum cash balance

To avoid the possible consequences of being out of cash, it is common to set a minimum cash balance to be maintained throughout each month. If at any time during the month the company expects its cash balance to fall below the minimum, financing should be arranged before the deficiency arises.

The Underhill Company sets a minimum cash balance of $50,000. To attain this level, it is necessary to borrow $47,000 at the beginning of January. This borrowing, when integrated into Exhibit 23-12, causes the expected January 31 balance to be the required minimum, $50,000. This ending balance for January then becomes the beginning cash balance for February.

During February, cash receipts should exceed cash disbursements by $71,750, which when added to the $50,000 beginning cash balance provides a $121,750 balance, far in excess of the required minimum. This $121,750 is not really the February 28 cash balance, however. It isn't, because the loan made during January must first be repaid, as soon as excess cash—above the $50,000 minimum—is available. Therefore, the entire $47,000 loan will be repaid plus interest of $1,097. The interest is for 2 months, since the principal was borrowed at the beginning of January and will not be repaid until the end of February. The February 28 cash balance is $73,653 and the March 31 balance is $269,653. Both these balances are far in excess of the required minimum balance desired.

It would be prudent to invest the excess in March, $219,653 ($269,653 − $50,000), in short-term securities if the firm wants to use all of its resources in the most profitable manner.

The March 31 cash balance of $269,653 is transferred to the asset section of the March 31 budgeted balance sheet (Exhibit 23-15). In Figure 23-1 this transfer is shown by the black line going from Step 8 to Step 11.

The Budgeted Statements of Income and Retained Earnings

Only now can we complete the *budgeted income statement.* We see from Exhibit 23-12 that the interest expense is $1,097. (In Figure 23-1 this is represented by the black line going from Step 8 to Step 9.) When we subtract this amount from the operating income in Exhibit 23-13, we get the net income—$417,923.

What if we have an unpaid note on 3/31?

For a moment let's assume instead that on March 1, 1988, we need to borrow an additional $20,000, which we will not repay until Quarter II. In this situation, is there

EXHIBIT 23-13
Budgeted Income Statement: Quarter I, 1988.
The budgeted net income will be transferred to the budgeted statement of retained earnings.

Sales (Exhibit 23-2).	$1,350,000
Cost of Goods Sold Expense (Exhibit 23-7)	798,980
Gross Profit.	$ 551,020
Selling and Administrative Expenses (Exhibit 23-11)	132,000
Operating Income.	$ 419,020
Interest Expense (Exhibit 23-12)	1,097
Net Income.	$ 417,923

any additional interest in either the budgeted statement of cash receipts and disbursements, or in the budgeted income statement?

Since we will not pay the interest on the $20,000 loan until we repay the loan, there won't be any additional interest in the budgeted statement of cash receipts and disbursements. However, since the $20,000 loan will be outstanding for the month of March, there will be 1 month of interest expense. It will be:

$$\$20,000 \times .14 \times \tfrac{1}{12} = \$233$$

which we would add to the $1,097 of interest expense already shown on the budgeted income statement. In addition, the March 31 budgeted balance sheet would include a current liability for Notes Payable—$20,000, and a current liability for Interest Payable—$233.

In the December 31, 1987, balance sheet from Exhibit 23-1, you can see that the January 1, 1988, balance in Retained Earnings is $228,250. We can now add the budgeted net income for Quarter I, $417,923, to this beginning balance—the total being $646,173 as shown in Exhibit 23-14. From this amount, the dividends of $80,000—declared in March—are subtracted. The remainder of $566,173—the March 31 *budgeted balance in retained earnings*—is transferred to the budgeted balance sheet (Exhibit 23-15).

Underhill expects stockholders' equity to increase by $337,923 ($417,923 − $80,000) in Quarter I

EXHIBIT 23-14
Budgeted Retained Earnings Statement:
Quarter I, 1988.

The budgeted balance in Retained Earnings, $566,173, now goes on the budgeted balance sheet.

Retained Earnings, Jan. 1, 1988 (Exhibit 23-1)	$228,250
Net Income (Exhibit 23-13).	417,923
	$646,173
Dividends Declared.	80,000
Retained Earnings, Mar. 31, 1988.	$566,173

The Budgeted Balance Sheet

The *budgeted balance sheet* is now shown in Exhibit 23-15. It represents the culmination of the budgeted schedules and statements that we discussed in previous sections. It is the final step (Step 11) in the master budget flow chart of Figure 23-1. We have already discussed all of the items in the balance sheet with the exception of Capital Stock, Machinery, and Accumulated Depreciation.

Since there are no capital stock transactions expected during Quarter I, the bud-

EXHIBIT 23-15
Budgeted Balance Sheet:
March 31, 1988.

This is what Underhill expects its assets, liabilities, and stockholders' equity accounts to look like on March 31, 1988

Assets		Liabilities	
Cash (Exhibit 23-12)	$ 269,653	Accounts Payable	
Accounts Receivable		(Exhibit 23-9).	$105,000
(Exhibit 23-4).	225,000	Dividends Payable	80,000
Inventories:		Total Liabilities	$185,000
Raw Materials			
(Exhibit 23-8)	10,000	**Stockholders' Equity**	
Finished Goods		Capital Stock.	$200,000
(Exhibit 23-7)	133,020	Retained Earnings	
Machinery	450,000	(Exhibit 23-14).	566,173
Accumulated Depreciation . . .	(136,500)	Total Stockholders' Equity . . .	$766,173
		Total Liabilities and	
Total Assets.	$ 951,173	Stockholders' Equity	$951,173

geted balance of $200,000 in Capital Stock shown in Exhibit 23-15 is exactly what it is on December 31, 1987 (Exhibit 23-1).

The December 31, 1987, balance in the Machinery account (Exhibit 23-1) is $420,000. With the $30,000 purchase of machinery during January, the balance on March 31 should be $450,000. The balance in Accumulated Depreciation is $126,000 in the December 31, 1987, balance sheet, and during Quarter I, the depreciation was:

Production machinery (3 × $2,000 per month)...................	$ 6,000
Selling and administrative machinery (3 × $1,500 per month)...........	4,500
	$10,500

When we add the $10,500 of depreciation to the December 31, 1987, balance in Accumulated Depreciation, we get $136,500—the amount shown in the budgeted balance sheet of Exhibit 23-15.

Notice in Exhibit 23-15 that the totals for assets, liabilities, and stockholders' equity result in the proper balance of the accounting equation:

$$\text{Assets} = \text{Liabilities} + \text{Stockholders' Equity}$$

$$\$951,173 = \$185,000 + \$766,173$$

$$\$951,173 = \$951,173$$

The process of preparing the master budget started with the balance sheet on December 31, 1987; continued on with numerous budgeted schedules and statements; and finally, now, ends with the preparation of the budgeted balance sheet for March 31, 1988.

The Budget's Use — After the Fact

The budget has been employed thus far to predict the consequences of future expectations. After the budget period has passed, the actual results are collected and compared to the estimates in a budget to decide if the firm operated according to plan. This comparison is made in the performance report. What type of budget to include in the performance report—the master budget or a flexible budget—is discussed in the next chapter.

PROBLEM FOR SELF-STUDY

Throughout this chapter we have discussed the steps in the preparation of a master budget for a manufacturer. Although we did discuss a few differences that you would experience if you were doing the work for a retailer or a wholesaler instead, we thought it might be a good idea for you to have a separate problem for a retailer. This is what you'll now find in the problem for self-study. The fact that the problem is for a different type of organization is not the only difference from Example 23-1 for Underhill Company. We'll also find a few other differences in Example 23-2 for Elia Sangria Company. So as you go through this problem you might want to give special attention to the following items:

1. Purchases are calculated differently. Instead of having a policy of maintaining some desired ending inventory, the inventory policy now will simply be to purchase enough inventory each month to cover the following month's sales.

2. In order to simplify the mechanics, we are going to prepare the master budget for only 2 months instead of for an entire quarter.

3. The company in our example expects to have some bad accounts. Therefore you'll

see "Bad Debts Expense" on the income statement and "Allowance for Uncollectibles" on the balance sheet.

4. The amount that we have to borrow in the budgeted statement of cash receipts and disbursements is not fully repaid by the end of the budget period. As a result, you'll see notes payable and interest payable on the budgeted balance sheet; and more interest expense on the income statement than you'll have in the budgeted statement of cash receipts and disbursements.

Let's look now at the master budget for Elia Sangria Company.

EXAMPLE 23-2

MASTER BUDGET FOR A RETAILER

The Elia Sangria Company began operation in December of last year, and expected to have the following balance sheet at year-end:

ELIA SANGRIA COMPANY
Balance Sheet
December 31, 1987

Assets			Liabilities		
Cash.		$ 50,000	Accounts Payable		$160,000
Accounts					
Receivable	$80,000				
Less: Allowance for			**Stockholders' Equity**		
Bad Debts	(8,000)	72,000	Capital Stock	$50,000	
Merchandise					
Inventory.		100,000	Retained		
			Earnings.	12,000	62,000
Total Assets.		$222,000	Total Liabilities and		
			Stockholders' Equity		$222,000

Elia had sales in December of $100,000, and expects the sales of the first quarter of 1988 to be:

January	$150,000
February	200,000
March	225,000

Elia expects that 20% of all sales will be cash sales; and of the credit sales, 90% will be collected in the month following sale, and the remaining 10% will go uncollected. No bad accounts have been *written off* in December, nor are any expected to be during the first few months of 1988.

The cost of merchandise averages about 60% of retail prices. The company's policy, starting in January, concerning merchandise purchases is to buy enough each month to cover the following month's sales — at cost. December's purchases — since it was the first month in its life — were substantially higher than what the new policy will require. All purchases are on credit, and will be paid for 1 month after purchase.

The variable operating costs should average 10% of sales, and the fixed operating costs will be $10,000 in January and $6,000 in February. Disbursements for these expenses will be made in the month incurred.

Elia hopes to maintain a minimum cash balance of $20,000. If the cash balance falls below this amount, Elia plans to borrow money to meet its needs, at a rate of 15% per annum. All borrowings and repayments will be made at the beginning and end of the month, respectively. Interest will be paid based on the amount of principal repaid. All borrowings and repayments will be made in multiples of $1,000.

The controller for Elia now prepares the following master budget for the first 2 months of 1988:

STEP 1　Past and Future Sales — The Sales Forecast　　　　**STEP 2　Cash Collections**

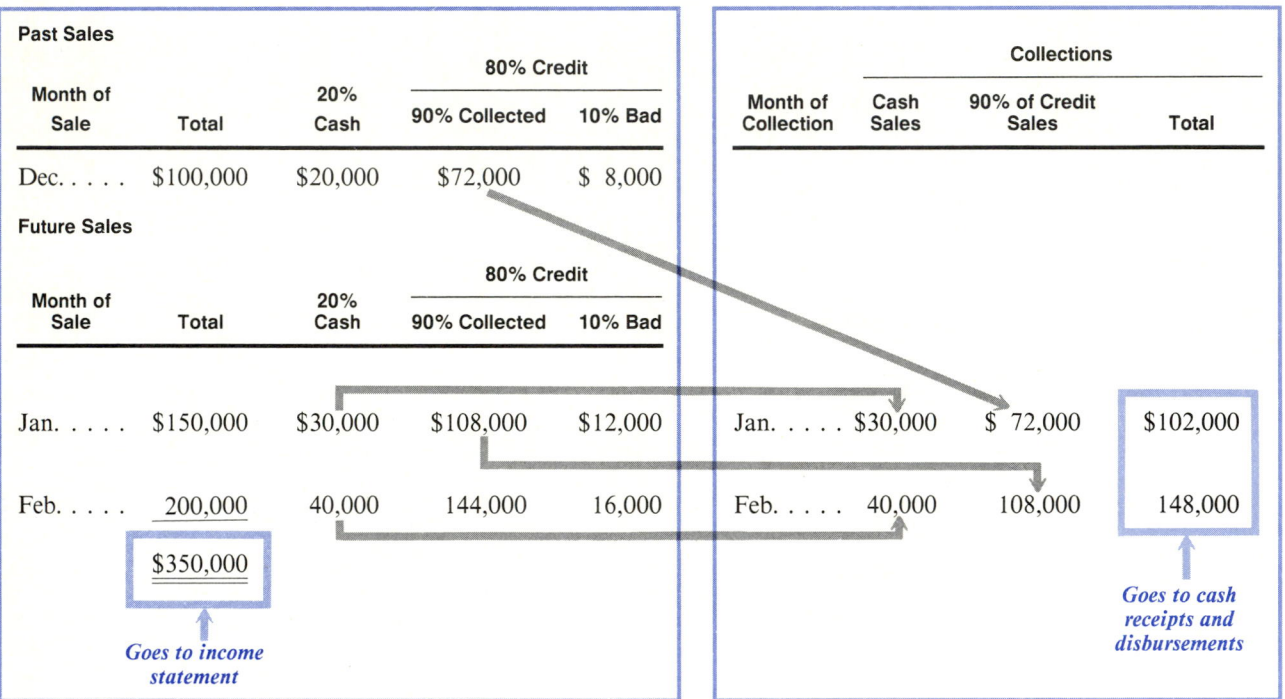

STEP 3　Uncollected Balance in Accounts Receivable, Bad Debts Expense, and Allowance for Uncollectibles

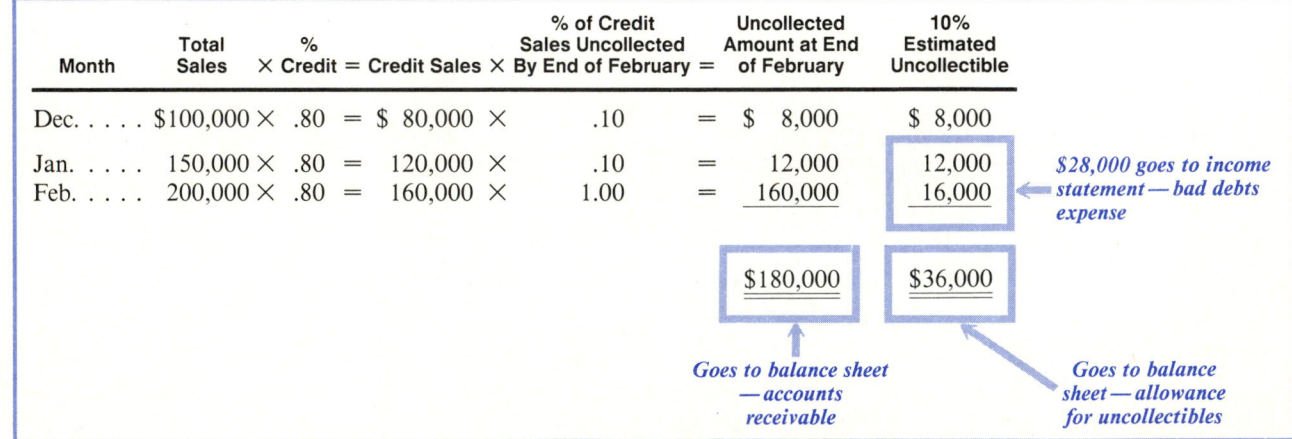

STEP 4   Schedule of Purchases and Payments, and Ending Balance in Inventory

	Month of Sale		
	January	February	March
Sales.	$150,000	$200,000	$225,000
Cost of sales %	×.60	×.60	×.60
Cost of goods sold	$ 90,000	$120,000	$135,000

	December	January	February	March
Purchases.	$160,000*	$120,000	$135,000 ← *Accounts payable, 2/28/88*	
Payment.		$160,000	$120,000	$135,000

* Shown as 12/31/88 balance in Accounts Payable.

February 28 Balance in Merchandise Inventory

Balance, January 1		$100,000
Purchases:		
January	$120,000	
February.	135,000	255,000
Total available		$355,000
Less: Cost of sales:		
January	$ 90,000	
February.	120,000	210,000
Ending inventory		$145,000

Goes to balance sheet

**STEP 5
Schedule of Variable
Operating Costs — Expenses
and Disbursements**

	Month of Sale		
	January	February	Total
Sales	$150,000	$200,000	$350,000
Variable costs %	×.10	×.10	×.10
Variable operating costs	$ 15,000	$ 20,000	$ 35,000

*Goes to cash
receipts and
disbursements*

*Goes to
income
statement*

STEP 6   Budgeted Statement of Cash Receipts and Disbursements

	January	February
Cash receipts.	$102,000	$148,000
Cash disbursements:		
Purchase payments	$160,000	$120,000
Variable operating costs	15,000	20,000
Fixed operating costs	10,000	6,000
Total cash disbursements	$185,000	$146,000
Receipts less disbursements	$ (83,000)	$ 2,000
Beginning cash balance	50,000	20,000
Ending cash balance if no financing or repayments	$ (33,000)	$ 22,000
Financing required to maintain minimum cash balance of $20,000	$ 53,000	$ -0-
Repayments—Principal	-0-	(1,000)
—Interest	-0-	(25)
Ending cash balance	$ 20,000	$ 20,975

Net of these two—$52,000—is in Notes Payable

Part of interest expense (additional interest associated with $52,000 note payable)

Goes to balance sheet

STEP 7
Income Statement

Sales		$350,000
Cost of Goods Sold.		210,000
Gross Profit		$140,000
Operating Costs:		
Variable	$35,000	
Fixed	16,000	
Bad Debts	28,000	79,000
Operating Income		$ 61,000
Interest Expense.		1,325*
Net Income.		$ 59,675

This amount is added to the beginning balance in Retained Earnings to get the 2/28/88 balance on the balance sheet

* See the footnote to the balance sheet.

STEP 8   Balance Sheet

Assets			Liabilities and Owners' Equity		
Cash.		$ 20,975	Accounts Payable	$135,000	
Accounts Receivable	$180,000		Notes Payable	52,000	
Less: Allowance for Bad Debts	(36,000)	144,000	Interest Payable.	1,300*	$188,300
Merchandise Inventory.		145,000	Capital Stock	$ 50,000	
			Retained Earnings	71,675	121,675
Total Assets		$309,975	Total Liabilities and Owners' Equity		$309,975

* The $1,300 is interest that has accrued on the $52,000 note, at 15%, for 2 months. When added to the amount of interest paid on the payment of $1,000 in principal—$25—we get total interest of $1,325, which we find on the income statement.

CHAPTER SUMMARY

The *master budget* provides an overall view of the short-term effects that a forecasted level of sales should have on operating results and financial position. The master budget is made up of *operating budgets* and *financial budgets.*

Operating budgets include schedules and statements associated with the estimated revenues, expenses, and resulting income.

Financial budgets report on the sources, uses, and ending balances of cash and other resources used in operations.

Three ways in which budgets can benefit all firms include: (1) better planning, (2) control of performance, and (3) communication and coordination.

All departments in an organization should actively participate in preparing the master budget. Most large companies have a *budget committee* which provides guidance and coordination in preparing the budget.

The starting point in the budgetary process is the preparation of the *sales forecast.* All other elements of the budget depend on the sales forecast.

For a manufacturer, the next most important forecast is determined in the *production budget,* which calculates the units that need to be produced in each future period based on the sales forecast. Once the production budget is completed, it is then possible to determine the costs of production, estimated costs of goods sold, and the required purchases of raw materials.

Once the following four budgeted financial statements are prepared, the master budget is completed:

1. The budgeted income statement
2. The budgeted retained earnings statement
3. The budgeted statement of cash receipts and disbursements
4. The budgeted balance sheet

IMPORTANT TERMS USED IN THIS CHAPTER

Budget committee A committee composed of top-level executives from departments within the organization and a budget director. The budget committee provides guidance and coordination in the preparation of the budget. (page 912)

Budget director The member of the budget committee responsible for putting together the many schedules and statements that make up the master budget. (page 912)

Budgeted balance sheet A statement depicting the estimated assets, liabilities, and stockholders' equity at the end of a budget period. (page 931)

Budgeted income statement A statement listing the predicted revenues, expenses, and resulting income for a budget period. (page 930)

Budgeted retained earnings statement A statement showing the estimated change in the retained earnings balance during a budget period. (page 931)

Budgeted schedule of cash collections A monthly schedule listing the estimated collection from cash and credit sales. (page 917)

Budgeted schedule of purchases A schedule determining the raw materials that must be purchased for production needs (for a manufacturer); or the merchandise that must be purchased to meet sales demand (for a retailer or wholesaler). (page 923)

Budgeted statement of cash receipts and disbursements A statement listing the different types of anticipated cash receipts and disbursements for a budget period, as well as the estimated ending cash balance. It helps management to be aware when extra cash may be available for investment, or when potential cash shortages may require additional short-term financing. (page 918)

Financial budgets A category of the master budget that includes statements reporting on the projected sources, uses, and ending balances for cash and other resources used in company operations. (page 910)

Master budget A comprehensive budget that expresses the overall business plan for the organization for a period covering 1 year or less. (page 910)

Operating budgets A category of the master budget that includes schedules and statements related to budgeted revenues, expenses, and income. (page 910)

Production budget A schedule indicating the units that have to be produced during a budget period. (page 920)

Sales forecast The starting point for all budgeting—the projection of sales for the budget period. (page 916)

QUESTIONS

1. Why is the sales forecast often referred to as the starting point in all budgeting?

2. Discuss three purposes or benefits from budgeting.

3. The master budget includes all budgets prepared by accountants to assist in both long-range and short-range planning. Do you agree? Explain.

4. List several factors that affect the sales forecast.

5. The accountant bears sole responsibility for the preparation of all aspects of the master budget. Comment.

6. If the sales forecast is considered the starting point for all budgeting, why is it that the forecast cannot be made until the selling expense budget has been at least partially completed?

7. Explain the differences between historical financial statements and budgeted financial statements.

8. Why should human problems be considered in the preparation of a master budget?

9. For control purposes, actual results for the current period should be compared to the actual results for the previous period. Do you agree? Explain.

10. Why does a firm maintain minimum balances in finished goods inventory?

11. In order to avoid the consequences of running out of cash, a firm should maintain as much cash on hand as possible. Comment.

12. Discuss the purposes of preparing a budgeted statement of cash receipts and disbursements.

13. Why isn't depreciation expense included in the budgeted statement of cash receipts and disbursements?

14. When a firm expects high sales volume and significant profits for a period, this should guarantee the existence of an adequate inflow of cash. Comment.

15. The budgeted cost of goods sold equals the combined costs of materials, labor, and overhead assigned to production during a period. Do you agree? Explain.

16. Explain why dividends to be declared during a budget period might not be included in the budgeted statement of cash receipts and disbursements.

EXERCISES

Exercise 23-1
Tracing the balance sheet items to the budgeted schedules and statements

On March 31, 1988, the Navritalova Company prepared the following balance sheet at the end of Quarter I, prior to preparing a master budget for Quarter II:

NAVRITALOVA COMPANY
Balance Sheet
March 31, 1988

Assets		Liabilities	
Cash	$ 4,000	Accounts Payable	$ 32,000
Accounts Receivable	40,000	Notes Payable, due 6/1/88	30,000
Allowance for Uncollectibles	(2,000)	Interest Payable on Note	1,000
Merchandise Inventory	70,000	Total Liabilities	$ 63,000
Prepaid Insurance	1,600	**Stockholders' Equity**	
Equipment	20,000	Capital Stock	$ 40,000
Accumulated Depreciation	(4,000)	Retained Earnings	37,000
Patent	2,400	Total Stockholders' Equity	$ 77,000
Total Assets	$140,000	Total Liabilities and Stockholders' Equity	$140,000

Indicate how each account on the March 31, 1988, balance sheet will affect the Quarter II master budget. For example, the cash balance of $4,000 is added to the difference in cash receipts and disbursements in the statement of cash receipts and disbursements.

Exercise 23-2
Distinguishing income statement items from cash receipts and disbursements

There are several items described below affecting the budgeted income statement and budgeted statement of cash receipts and disbursements for July 1987. For each item, determine: (1) the amount of revenue (or expense) to be shown in the budgeted income statement; and (2) the amount of cash receipts (or disbursements) included in the budgeted statement of cash receipts and disbursements.

a. Uncollected sales from June are $48,000. Sales for July should be $300,000, 30% of which are for cash. Credit sales are collected 60% in the month of sale and 40% in the following month. No bad debts are expected.

b. Cost of goods sold averages 65% of sales. The beginning and desired ending inventories for July are $24,000 and $36,000, respectively. All purchases are paid for in the month of purchase.

c. A 3-year insurance policy, costing $1,350, was purchased in the middle of the month.

d. Machinery costing $45,000 was purchased in June. The estimated useful life is 10 years.

e. Dividends of $300,000 were declared in July to be paid in August.

f. Wages earned during the first 2 weeks of each month are paid 3 days into the third week. Wages earned during the last 2 weeks of each month are paid on the third day of the next month. Wages are earned by workers as follows:

	Wages
June:	
First 2 weeks	$13,200
Last 2 weeks	14,100
July:	
First 2 weeks	$14,400
Last 2 weeks	15,300

Exercise 23-3
Calculating purchases, after the desired ending inventory is determined

The Solid Binding Textbook Company sells its only book, *Principles of Macrame,* in many university bookstores throughout the country. One of these bookstores—at the University of Cripp—buys the books from Solid Binding for $12 per text and marks them to sell at 50% over cost. On September 1, 1987, the bookstore has 1,500 texts on hand. They expect student enrollment in the initial macrame courses to be 1,200, 1,000, 900, and 300 in Quarters I through IV, respectively, of the 1987–1988 academic year. In addition, sales are expected to be 1,300 texts in Quarter I of the 1988–1989 school year. The bookstore plans to maintain at the end of each upcoming quarter enough texts to cover 150% of the following quarter's forecasted sales.

Purchases will be made at the end of each quarter and paid for within 30 days of purchase. Accounts Payable on August 31, 1987, has a balance of $17,400.

Determine the unit purchases and cash payments for each quarter of the 1987–1988 academic year.

(Check figure: Purchases for Quarter I = 1,200 books)

Exercise 23-4
Determining purchases— desired ending inventory is given

The Carny Medication Company produces a product called Snake-Eye Elixir, which is sold at circus and carnival side shows. Each 12-ounce bottle, which contains 3 ounces of alcohol, is to be used for medicinal purposes only.

During September and October of 1987, Carny expects to produce 30,000 and 40,000 bottles of elixir. Also, Carny hopes to maintain on hand at least 5,000 ounces of alcohol at all times—beginning in September.

On September 1, 1987, Carny has 4,800 ounces of alcohol in the raw materials inventory. The cost per ounce of alcohol is $.12.

Determine the cost of purchases for September and October.

(Check figure: October purchases = $14,400)

Exercise 23-5
Preparing a budgeted statement of cash receipts and disbursements

During the last 2 months of 1988, the Muncies Candy Bar Company expects the following items concerning its cash flow:

	November	December
Cash receipts	$100,000	$130,000
Cash disbursements	112,000	125,000

The November 1 cash balance was $18,000, and the company requires a minimum cash balance each month of $12,000.

If a cash deficiency is expected during a month, a loan is arranged at the beginning of that month, at 12% interest. Any repayments of principal plus interest based on the principal repaid are made at the end of the month, when cash becomes available. All borrowing and repayments of principal are made in multiples of $1,000.

Prepare a statement of cash receipts and disbursements for November and December.

(Check figure: Ending cash balance for December = $12,920)

Exercise 23-6
Preparing a budgeted statement of cash receipts and disbursements

Due to financial setbacks during 1988, the Lutz Butler Corporation was severely short of cash at the end of the year. The company treasurer found it necessary to take out an $80,000 loan on December 31, at 16%, to be repaid in the next month or two from cash generated from operations. During January the cash receipts and disbursements from operations are expected to be $400,000 and $240,000, respectively.

Lutz Butler plans to maintain a minimum cash balance of $10,000, which is the actual balance on January 1.

Any cash (in $1,000 multiples) in excess of the minimum will be invested at the end of the month to earn 10% interest.

Dividends of $50,000 will be paid in January, and a 2-year insurance policy costing $4,000 will be taken out in the same month.

Prepare a statement of cash receipts and disbursements for January 1988.

(Check figure: Ending cash balance = $10,933)

PROBLEMS
Set A

Problem A23-1
Preparing a sales forecast and schedule of cash collections

John Stanton, the budget director for Crete Corporation, is in the midst of preparing the master budget for the third quarter of 1987. The sales vice president has supplied John with the following sales projections for July through September:

	Sales
July	$150,000
August	180,000
September.	240,000

Cash sales are expected to be 30% of total sales and credit sales are expected to be collected in the following manner:

- 40% in the month of sale
- 50% in the month following sale
- 10% uncollectible

On July 1, 1987, the Accounts Receivable balance is $60,000, of which $18,000 is expected to be uncollectible.

Required

1. Prepare a sales forecast for the 3 months of Quarter III, 1987.
2. Prepare a schedule of collections for the 3 months of Quarter III, 1987.

[Check figure: Total cash collections (July) = $129,000]

3. Determine what the September 30, 1987, balance in Accounts Receivable is expected to be assuming that uncollectible accounts have still not been written off by that time.

(Check figure: $141,900)

Problem A23-2
Calculating monthly cash collections

In the months of November and December 1988, the Davidson Company had sales revenues of $33,000 and $40,000, respectively. The sales predictions for the first quarter of 1988 are as follows:

	Sales
January	$25,000
February.	35,000
March	20,000

Cash sales are 60% of total sales and no credit sales are expected to be uncollectible. Davidson offers a 5% cash discount on credit sales paid off in the month of sale.

Collection experience for the company is expected to be:

- 70% collected in the month of sale (with discount)
- 30% collected in the month following sale (without discount)

The Accounts Receivable balance (recorded at the gross amount of sales) on December 31, 1987, was $4,800.

Required

Prepare a schedule of cash collections for the months of January, February, and March 1988.

[Check figure: Cash collections (February) = $33,310]

Problem A23-3
Determining the month ending cash balance

Mina Pawpaw is about to prepare a cash budget for the first time for her shop, Mina's Wickery. On July 1, 1988, the shop's balance in Accounts Receivable was $4,932. From this balance only $1,868 is expected to be collectible, and this amount should all be collected in July.

Mina projects the sales for July and August to be $32,000 and $30,000, respectively. Typically, 80% of sales are cash sales. Of the credit sales, one-third is expected to be collected in July and the same amount in August. The remaining one-third will probably go uncollected.

Mina purchases wicker materials 1 month in advance of their expected sales. The cost of the wicker materials averages 60% of their retail value. All purchases are paid for in the month of purchase.

The following operating expenses are expected for the month of July:

	Expenses
Utilities.	$1,000
Salaries.	4,800
Property taxes	200
Advertising	3,000
	$9,000

Utility bills are received at the end of each month and paid for at the beginning of the following month (the June utility bill was $900). Salaries are paid at the end of the month. Property taxes for the year of $2,400 ($200 × 12 months) are paid to the county on July 1. A $3,000 payment to WYRN-TV for four commercials to be aired in July was made on June 30.

Required

Prepare a budgeted statement of cash receipts and disbursements for July. Assume a July 1 cash balance of $4,000 and that no minimum cash balance is desired.

(Check figure: Ending cash balance = $7,501)

Problem A23-4
Determining net income and cash receipts and disbursements

Sandy Grinnell has been working for a large national CPA firm for about 1 year. However, in August 1988, when she learned that she had passed the CPA exam, she decided to open her own practice. After 2 months of preparation, she finally opened her doors on October 15. One of the first things she decided to do was to prepare a cash budget for November.

Her client fees in October were $1,000, none of which were collected in that month. Grinnell expects to collect $800 of this amount in November. The remaining amount relates to a client who skipped town after Grinnell prepared a tax return that indicated a massive liability to the IRS. The fees for November are expected to be $2,000, and Grinnell anticipates collecting nearly the entire amount in that month, since she will not turn over her finished reports to her clients until the cash is received. Only 10% will remain to be collected in December.

Grinnell expects the following cash disbursements in November:

Salaries of $400 for a part-time college student and a full-time secretary.
Payment of $120 for her professional licenses for the year: November 1988 – October 1989.
Purchase of office furniture for $3,600. The useful life of the furniture is 6 years.
Utilities for October of $150. The November bill, to be paid in December, is estimated to be $175.

In addition, on October 15, 1988, Grinnell signed a 3-month lease and made a prepayment of $1,200 at that time.

Required   1. Prepare a budgeted income statement for the month of November.

(Check figure: net income = $965)

2. Assume that Grinnell had a November 1, 1988, cash balance of $4,000. Prepare a budgeted statement of cash receipts and disbursements for November.

(Check figure: Ending cash balance = $2,330)

Problem A23-5
Preparing a statement of cash receipts and disbursements

Gales Metalworks, which manufactures steel lawn furniture, had sales in December 1988 of $3,750,000. Each piece of furniture was priced to sell at $150 and is expected to remain at the same price for the next 4 to 6 months.

Sales for the first 4 months of 1989 were projected to be the following:

	Sales
January	20,000 units
February	40,000 units
March	35,000 units
April	30,000 units

Cash sales average 25% of total sales, and credit sales are typically collected in full in the month following sale.

Starting in January, the company wants to maintain the following ending inventories to assure never being out of stock:

	Ending Inventory
Raw materials	180,000 pounds
Finished goods	75,000 units

The January 1 balances in raw materials and finished goods were 210,000 pounds and 60,000 units, respectively. The January 1 and January 31 balances in work-in-process are and will be zero.

Six pounds of raw materials (at $2.50 per pound) are required for each finished unit.
Purchases of raw materials are all for cash.
Additional costs for Gales Metalworks during January are:

	Costs
Direct labor	$1,800,000
Factory overhead (including $100,000 of depreciation)	1,000,000
Selling department costs	400,000

All payments are made when the costs are incurred.

The January 1 cash balance for Gales is $75,000, but it hopes to maintain at least a $100,000 ending cash balance beginning in January. All financing, if necessary, is made at the beginning of the month. Repayments will include interest at 12% of the principal repaid.

Required   Prepare a budgeted statement of cash receipts and disbursements for January.

(Check figure: Payments for purchases = $450,000)

Problem A23-6

Preparing a complete master budget

The Pinacina Company, which sells a hair dye called Natural, has just completed operations for 1988 and has prepared the balance sheet shown in the middle of this page.

All sales are credit sales. Collections are expected to be made in the following manner:

- 50% collected in the month of sale
- 30% collected in the first month after sale
- 20% collected in the second month after sale

The actual sales for November and December 1988 were $120,000 and $140,000, respectively. The projected sales for upcoming months are as follows:

	Projected Sales
January 1989	$160,000
February 1989	160,000
March 1989	130,000
April 1989	100,000

PINACINA COMPANY
Balance Sheet
December 31, 1988

Assets		Liabilities	
Cash	$ 11,000	Accounts Payable.	$ 48,000
Accounts Receivable.	94,000	Notes Payable	40,000
Merchandise Inventory	80,000	Interest Payable	666
Building.	50,000	Total Liabilities	$ 88,666
Accumulated Depreciation.	(2,400)		
Prepaid Insurance	9,000	**Stockholders' Equity**	
		Capital Stock	$ 80,000
		Retained Earnings	72,934
		Total Stockholders' Equity.	$152,934
Total Assets	$241,600	Total Liabilities and Stockholders' Equity	$241,600

The sale price for all months is $10 per bottle.

Sixty percent of the purchases are made on account, and all credit purchases are to be paid in the month following purchase. Pinacina Company desires to maintain the following ending inventories each month of Natural (at $5 per bottle):

	Ending Inventories
November 1988	14,000 bottles
December 1988	16,000 bottles
January 1989.	16,000 bottles
February 1989	12,000 bottles
March 1989.	8,800 bottles

The only transactions recorded in Accounts Payable are for purchases of merchandise. The prepayment of insurance was made on October 1, 1988, for a 1-year policy. The monthly cash operating expenses of $20,000 are paid when incurred. Depreciation expense is $200 per month.

Pinacina plans to declare and pay dividends during March 1989 amounting to $50,000. In addition, a new building, costing $150,000, will be purchased at the end of March 1989, for cash.

The note payable shown in the December 31, 1988, balance sheet was signed on November 1, 1988, and is due to be repaid plus 10% interest on January 31, 1989. If any future monthly cash balance is expected to fall below a minimum of $10,000, additional financing will have to be arranged at 12% interest, at the beginning of that month.

Required

Prepare the following for Quarter I, 1989:

1. Budgeted income statement

(Check figure: Net income = $160,460)

2. Budgeted retained earnings statement

3. Budgeted statement of cash receipts and disbursements

[Check figure: Cash balance (January 31) = $16,000]

4. Budgeted balance sheet

(Check figure: Total assets = $354,000 and total liabilities = $90,606)

Be sure to include all supporting schedules.

Set B

Problem B23-1
Preparing sales forecast and schedule of cash receipts

Bob Cox, the sales vice president of Video View, has just given the budget director the sales forecast for the first quarter of 1988. Sales are projected to be 22,500 units in January; 12,000 units in February; and 13,500 units in March.

Video View sells its cassette tapes for $8 each, and expects to collect its sales in the following manner:

Cash sales.	15%
Credit sales.	85%
Collected in month of sale 30%	
Collected in month following sale 60%	
Uncollectible. 10%	

On January 1, 1988, Video View had a balance in Accounts Receivable of $97,500. Of this amount, $11,820 is expected to be uncollectible.

Required

1. Prepare a sales forecast for the first 3 months of 1988.

2. Prepare a schedule of cash collections for the same months.

[Check figure: Total cash collections (January) = $158,580]

3. Determine the predicted March 31, 1988, balances in Accounts Receivable and Allowance for Doubtful Accounts (assume that no accounts were written off during the quarter).

(Check figure: Accounts Receivable = $99,540)

Problem B23-2
Determining the cash collections from sales—discounts offered

During May and June 1989, Center's Wholesale had sales of $400,000 and $600,000, respectively. During the next 3 months, sales are forecasted to be:

	Sales
July.	$ 500,000
August	1,000,000
September.	750,000

In the past, credit sales were 80% of total sales, and this experience is expected in the future months as well. All credit sales are considered collectible. The firm offers a 3% cash discount on credit sales, and it is expected that many customers will take advantage of the discounts within the allowed payment period.

The collection of credit sales typically occurs in the following manner:

- 40% in the month of sale (with discounts)
- 40% in the first month following sale (without discounts)
- 20% in the second month following sale (without discounts)

The June 30 balance in Accounts Receivable (recorded at gross amount of sales) is $330,000.

Required Prepare a schedule of cash collections for July, August, and September.

[Check figure: Total cash collections (September) = $782,800]

Problem B23-3
Determining the month's ending cash balance

Gary Smiley runs a chain of florist shops called Gary's Garden, and is about to prepare his first cash budget. On August 1, customers owe the shops $350 for sales made in June and $3,150 for sales made in July. Gary expects all of the June receivables and $1,050 of the July receivables to go uncollected. He predicts sales for August and September to be $35,000 and $28,000, respectively. Typically 70% of the sales are for cash. The credit sales should be collected as follows:

- 70% in the first month
- 20% in the second month
- 10% uncollectible

Gary has decided to purchase enough flowers each month to cover that month's sales. Flowers are purchased to sell at a markup of 100% of cost, and are paid for within 10 days of purchase. This means that approximately one-third of each month's purchases are paid for in the subsequent month. The purchases for July were $13,125.

The following expenses will be incurred in August:

	Expenses
Salaries	$ 2,800
Utilities	875
Rent	5,250
Gasoline	350
Advertising	875
Total	$10,150

Salaries and gasoline are paid for when incurred. Utilities are paid for in the following month (the July utility bill was $787). Three months of prepaid rent were paid on July 1. On August 1 an advance of $1,750 was given to an advertising agency for 2 months of promotion.

The cash balance for Gary's Garden on August 1 was $2,625. No minimum balance has been set for the month-end.

Required Prepare a budgeted statement of cash receipts and disbursements for August.

(Check figure: Ending cash balance = $14,846)

Problem B23-4
Preparing statements of income and cash receipts and disbursements

Robert Knealson recently passed his bar examination and has opened a law office. September was his first month of business, and Knealson has decided to prepare budgets starting in October. All client fees in September were billed on account. At the end of September, $2,000 of the fees were uncollected. Half of that amount is expected to be collected in October. The remaining one-half is not expected to be collected, since the client, destitute at the time, died upon hearing the guilty verdict. In addition, Robert has a 30-day note receivable, dated September 15, from Ann Kirstin, for $3,000, expected to be collected on October 15 (plus 10% annual interest), when the life insurance of Ann's late husband is paid.

During October, Robert expects the law fees to be $8,000, 20% of which will be cash fees for wills and quickie divorces. The credit fees are expected to be collected one-half in each of the following 2 months.

Robert expects the following cash disbursements during October:

A $3,000 purchase of law books on October 1, which are expected to have a 10-year useful life.
Prepayment of $1,000 for 2 months rent on October 1.
Salary of $200 for a full-time law student.
Birthday presents for the children of three judges, costing $1,600.
Advertising in the *Florida Enquirer* newspaper, $2,000.

On October 1, Robert had a cash balance of $75.

Required

1. Prepare a budgeted income statement for October.

(Check figure: Net income = $3,687.50)

2. Determine how much cash Knealson would have to borrow during October (if any) in order to attain an October 31 ending cash balance of $200.

(Check figure: $2,300)

Problem B23-5
Preparing a statement of cash receipts and disbursements

Rube's Tubes is a manufacturer that produces a product taking a single raw material. The controller, Dave Knight, prepares a master budget each month and is currently in the process of preparing the November budget. The actual sales for October (at a $150 sales price) and the forecasted sales for the next 4 months are provided below by the sales vice president, Tom Kinsey:

	Sales
October	25,000 units
November.	20,000 units
December	40,000 units
January	35,000 units
February.	30,000 units

The sales are broken down as follows:

- 20% for cash
- 80% for credit, to be collected in the first month after the sale

The desired ending inventories are determined to be:

- Finished goods—the next 2 months' sales (in units)
- Raw materials—the next month's production requirements

The beginning and ending inventories of work-in-process are immaterial in amount. The November 1 inventories for finished goods and raw materials are 60,000 units and 105,000 pounds, respectively. It takes 3 pounds of raw materials for each finished unit, each pound costing $5. All purchases are for cash.

Other costs for Rube's Tubes during November are predicted to be as follows:

Direct labor	$1,800,000
Factory overhead.	1,000,000
Selling and administration.	400,000

Included in the factory overhead is $100,000 of depreciation. All cash payments are made for the items above when the cost is incurred.

The cash balance on November 1 is $75,000, and the company hopes to maintain, starting in November, a minimum cash balance each month of $150,000. If financing is required, loans will be taken out at the beginning of the month at 10% interest.

Required   Prepare a budgeted statement of cash receipts and disbursements for November.

(Check figure: Payments for purchases = $450,000)

Problem B23-6
Preparing a complete master budget

The Quickie Wipes Company sells disposable moist wipes for babies at $2.50 per package (500 wipes per package). Although the company will begin its fourth month of operation on January 1, 1988, the controller is about to prepare the company's first master budget for the first quarter of 1988. The balance sheet for Quickie on 12/31/87 is given below:

QUICKIE WIPES
Balance Sheet
December 31, 1987

Assets		Liabilities	
Cash	$ 11,000	Accounts Payable.	$ 48,000
Accounts Receivable.	99,000	Notes Payable	40,000
Allowance for Doubtful Accounts	(18,000)	Interest Payable	666
Merchandise Inventory	80,000	Total Liabilities	$ 88,666
Prepaid Rent.	9,000		
		Stockholders' Equity	
		Capital Stock	$ 80,000
		Retained Earnings	12,334
		Total Stockholders' Equity.	$ 92,334
Total Assets	$181,000	Total Liabilities and Stockholders' Equity	$181,000

The note was signed on November 1, 1987, and is due to be repaid on January 31, 1988, at 10% annual interest. If any future monthly cash balance is expected to fall below a minimum of $8,000, additional financing will have to be arranged at the beginning of that month.

Sales are all on credit. Collections are expected to be 50% in the month of sale; 30% in the first month after sale; 15% in the second month after sale, and 5% will be uncollectible (estimated and recorded at the end of each quarter). No accounts considered as bad have been written off the books.

The actual sales for the last quarter and the predicted sales for the next 4 months (assuming a $2.50 sales price) are:

	Sales
October 1987	$100,000
November 1987	120,000
December 1987	140,000
January 1988	160,000
February 1988	160,000
March 1988	130,000
April 1988	100,000

Purchases for cash are 40% of all purchases, and all of the credit purchases will be paid in the month after purchase. Quickie desires the following monthly ending inventories for its wipes:

	Ending Inventory
November 1987.	56,000 packages
December 1987.	64,000 packages
January 1988	64,000 packages
February 1988.	48,000 packages
March 1988	35,200 packages

The cost of the inventory is $1.25 per package. The only transactions recorded in Accounts Payable are for purchases of merchandise. The prepayment for rent was made on October 1 for a 1-year lease. A $200,000 cash purchase of land is planned for March. The operating expenses are paid when incurred. They amount to $20,000 per month.

Required   Prepare the following statements for Quarter I, 1988:
1. Budgeted income statement

(Check figure: net income = $138,504)

2. Budgeted statement of retained earnings
3. Budgeted statement of cash receipts and disbursements (month by month)

(Check figure: Cash balance, February 28 = $67,000)

4. Budgeted balance sheet

(Check figure: Total assets = $340,500 and total liabilities = $109,622)

Be sure to include all necessary supporting schedules.

Chapter 24

The Flexible Budget, Standard Costs, and Variance Analysis

After you finish reading this chapter, you will have learned:

- What a performance report is used for
- What a responsibility center is and how it relates to responsibility accounting
- The distinction between static budgets and flexible budgets, and why flexible budgets should be used in performance reports
- What standard costs are and the different ways they are used
- How the standard costs for direct materials, direct labor, and factory overhead are determined
- How to prepare a performance report and calculate the price variance, quantity variance, and flexible budget variance for each product cost
- Why and how we calculate a predetermined rate for fixed factory overhead; what fixed factory overhead applied is; and how to calculate a volume variance for fixed factory overhead
- How to determine which variances need to be investigated

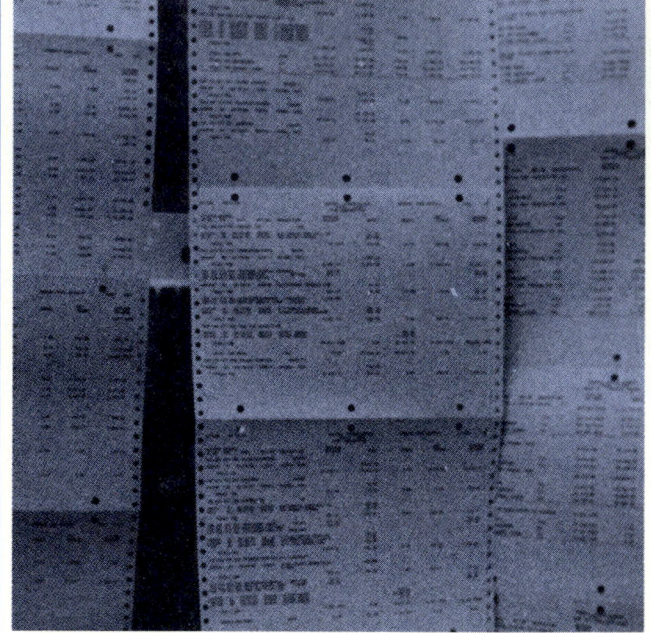

In the previous chapter you learned that the master budget is a tool that looks into the future, characterizing in a quantitative way the things that should happen during the budget period if sales occur as forecasted. Here, we are going to look back over the budget period, after it is completed, to compare what should have happened with what did indeed happen. We will calculate the differences between "budgeted" and "actual" results in order to help managers control their current operations.

When we look back on what we have done, the budget we must compare to the actual results is the flexible budget, not the master budget. The master budget tells us what we expect — before a period begins — for the level of activity expected in the forthcoming period. *The flexible budget tells us — after the fact — what we expect to have happened for the level of activity that has actually taken place.*

In this chapter we will explain exactly what a flexible budget is, and why we use it instead of the master budget in the performance report. In addition, we will show you how to prepare a performance report, and explain how it is used by accountants to help management control current operations. We will also explain what standard costs are, and the role they play in flexible budgets and performance reports. And we will discuss the different types of **variances,** which are the *differences* between the actual results and the flexible budget.

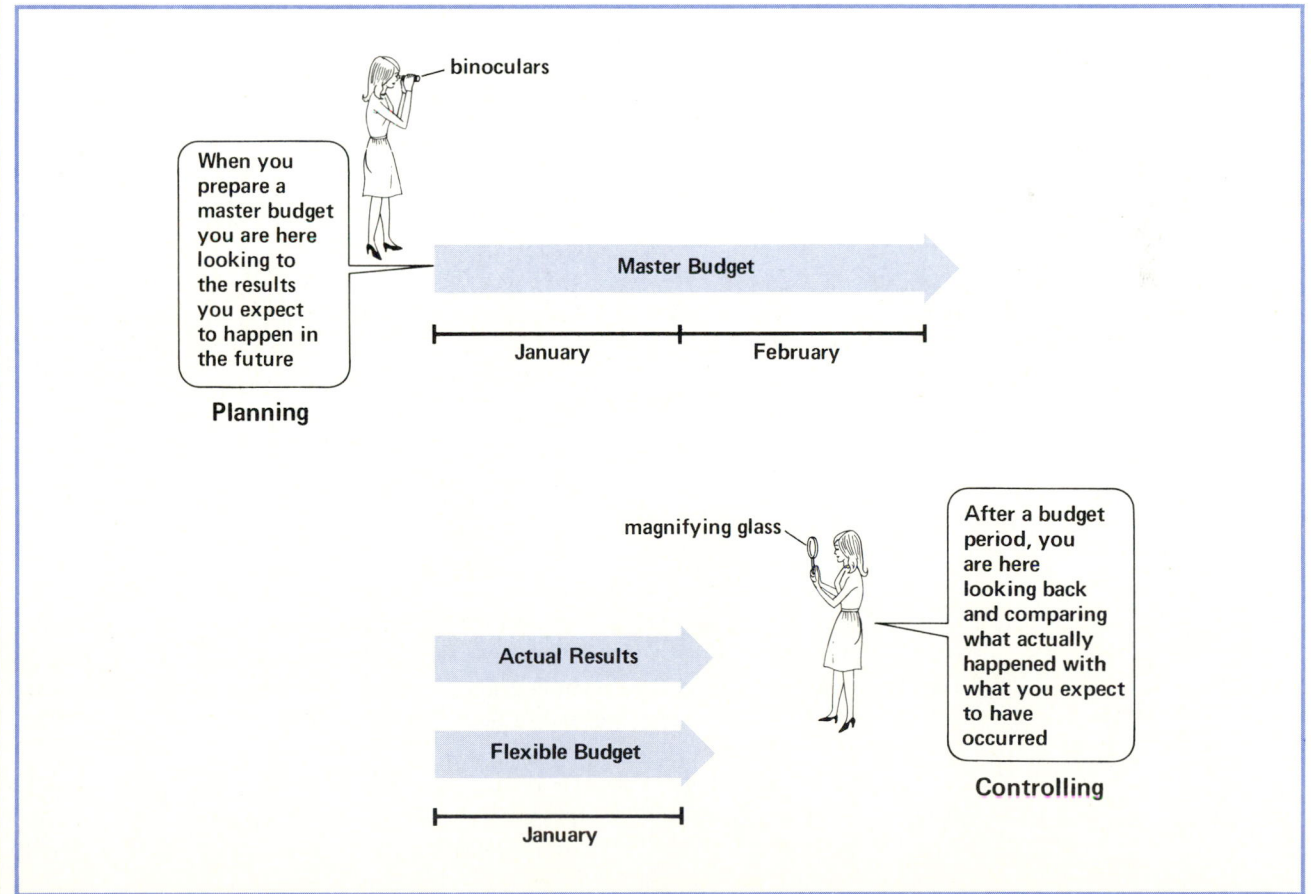

Comparing Master Budgets to Flexible Budgets: A Matter of Viewpoints.

**THE PERFORMANCE
REPORT**

From Example 23-1, recall that Underhill Company budgeted 15,000 units to be produced in January (see page 921) and that production costs were budgeted for that month based on the following estimates:

Direct materials	$5/unit
Direct labor.	$6/unit
Variable overhead.	$3/unit
Fixed overhead.	$15,000/month

The total budgeted production costs for January were given in Exhibit 23-6. They were:

	Budgeted Costs of Production (for 15,000 units) in January
Direct materials (15,000 × $5/unit)	$ 75,000
Direct labor (15,000 × $6/unit).	90,000
Variable overhead (15,000 × $3/unit).	45,000
Fixed overhead	15,000
	$225,000

Let us assume for now that on January 31 we learn that 15,000 units were actually produced—exactly the number Underhill predicted on January 1—and that the actual costs of producing these units were as follows:

	Actual Costs of Producing 15,000 Units in January
Direct materials.	$ 76,000
Direct labor	93,000
Variable overhead	44,000
Fixed overhead	14,900
	$227,900

We can now compare the budgeted results to the actual results for January in a performance report, shown in Exhibit 24-1. *Remember, we have assumed that 15,000 units were budgeted to be produced, and that exactly 15,000 units were actually produced.* (When the units budgeted are equal to what is actually produced, the master budget and the flexible budget are exactly the same, so there is no reason to be concerned with which budget we should use. We will discuss this issue in more detail later.)

To begin to control operations for the period, management, with the accountant's help, looks at the performance report, examines the information in the differences column, and asks several questions that require immediate answers. Management asks questions such as:

**Important questions to ask
about the performance report**

1. Who is responsible for the differences—the variances—that appear in the performance report?

EXHIBIT 24-1
Performance Report
—Underhill Company.
(In This Case, Units Produced Equal Units Budgeted.)
A comparison of actual and budgeted results when units produced equal units budgeted.

	Actual Costs of Producing 15,000 Units	Budgeted Costs of Producing 15,000 Units	Total Differences*
Direct materials.	$ 76,000	$ 75,000	$1,000 U
Direct labor	93,000	90,000	3,000 U
Variable overhead	44,000	45,000	1,000 F
Fixed overhead	14,900	15,000	100 F
	$227,900	$225,000	$2,900 U

* Differences shown with the letter U are unfavorable, meaning that the actual costs are over budget, and those shown with the letter F are favorable, indicating that the actual costs are under budget.

2. Which differences should be investigated?

3. What is the cause of each difference that is to be investigated?

4. What (if any) corrective actions need to be taken?

As we progress through this chapter, you should begin to understand why these questions are so important, and how the accountant can help management answer each of them to management's satisfaction.

RESPONSIBILITY ACCOUNTING

Responsibility center: Unit of activity, authority, and responsibility

Before you can answer the first question, it is necessary to understand what we mean by two very important terms: responsibility centers and responsibility accounting.

A *responsibility center* is an area of activity within an organization over which an individual has been delegated authority, and assigned the responsibility for the activities of that area for a period of time. Within the Underhill Company there are responsibility centers for at least each of the production, selling, and administrative departments. In Exhibit 24-1 the activities of the production department were reported in the performance report; therefore, the responsibility center in that report is the production department. Within each department there can be numerous smaller responsibility centers as well. For example, the production department could have responsibility centers for individual workers, for a foreman supervising a group of workers, or for a superintendent over several foremen (each of whom supervises a group of workers). A responsibility center can be very small or quite large.

Responsibility accounting is based on responsibility centers

Responsibility accounting is the process of:

1. Designating the responsibility centers

2. Delegating authority to individuals within the responsibility centers

3. Preparing budgets, accumulating actual results, and preparing performance reports for the responsibility centers

4. Holding the individuals with authority responsible or accountable for their actions

So you see, responsibility centers are the heart of a responsibility accounting system. For once we know what the responsibility centers are, and who is in charge, then budgets can be formulated and put into action; actual costs can be accumulated after the fact; and performance reports can be prepared and evaluated. Then the process starts all over again — for each responsibility center.

Responsibility accounting is the backbone of all planning and control systems.

Controllable and Uncontrollable Costs

Controllable costs: Significant influence during a period of time

Within each responsibility center the costs that a manager is held responsible for are those that are controllable by him or her. **Controllable costs** are costs within a responsibility center that can be significantly influenced by the manager of that center during a given period of time. If a manager has no influence over a cost during a given period of time, then the cost is an **uncontrollable cost** (a noncontrollable cost). If costs are uncontrollable, it doesn't make sense to hold a manager accountable when the actual costs are not what they should be.

To determine if a cost is controllable or uncontrollable, you must consider two things: (1) the responsibility center and manager to which the cost relates, and (2) the period of time covered by the performance report.

First, you do not classify a cost as controllable just because there is someone, somewhere, who exerts influence over the cost. Instead, you specify that a cost is controllable or uncontrollable because there is or is not influence by a manager at a specific level of responsibility within the organization. For example, when classifying the cost of direct materials in the assembly department as controllable or uncontrollable, you first need to know: "For whom am I considering it controllable or uncontrollable?" If the answer is the production foreman in assembly, then the cost is probably controllable. If the answer is the vice president of sales, then the cost is definitely uncontrollable.

Second, whether or not a cost is controllable depends on the period of time covered by the performance report. In the extreme long run, such as 50 years, every cost within an organization is controllable by someone. On the other hand, in the extreme short run, such as 1 second, there are probably no costs that are controllable by anyone. Which period of time we are using to classify costs as controllable or uncontrollable can make a big difference.

The performance of a responsibility center and the manager of that center might be evaluated as frequently as daily, weekly, or monthly. Or performance might be evaluated for longer periods of time — such as quarterly or annually. If a manager's performance is evaluated only once a year, then controllable costs are any costs that he or she can influence during a full 365-day period. On the other hand, if performance is evaluated each and every day, then a controllable cost is one that can be influenced on a day-to-day basis.

For our purposes we will classify any cost as controllable if a manager has a significant amount of influence over it, during a period of 1 year or less.

The concept of controllability is simple to define and easy to understand, but may be quite difficult to apply in a real-world situation. This is because some costs are influenced by many people, with no single individual exerting an obviously significant amount of influence.

For example, assume that a maintenance department takes far more time to repair a machine than it should have taken. Who has the most influence on the cost of this repair? Is it the maintenance foreman who didn't keep track of the work being performed by the repairman? Or could it be the production foreman who postponed normal maintenance during the busy periods and allowed his workers to misuse the machinery?

There is no simple answer, but a useful guideline might be that the individual to be assigned responsibility for controlling a cost is the one having the greatest day-to-day continuing influence over that cost.

Once a cost has been determined as controllable at one level of responsibility, it is also considered controllable at all higher levels of responsibility in the chain of command. To understand this, refer back to page 734, which shows a simple organization chart for a typical manufacturer. If a cost is classified as controllable by a foreman in production department no. 1, it would also be considered controllable by the production superintendent, the vice president of manufacturing, and the president. If a cost is controllable by sales manager no. 1, it is also controllable by the vice president of sales and the president.

Behavior of Costs versus Controllability

Are all controllable costs variable?

A common misconception is that variable costs are synonymous with controllable costs, and fixed costs are synonymous with uncontrollable costs.

All variable costs, however, are not necessarily controllable; and all fixed costs are not categorically uncontrollable. Remember, controllability deals with a manager's ability to influence the amount of a cost during a period. Behavior of costs refers to the relationship between total costs and activity.

There are variable and fixed costs that are clearly controllable, and variable and fixed costs that are clearly uncontrollable. For example, the direct material costs (variable) and salaries of production foremen (fixed) are controllable by the vice president of manufacturing, but the sales commissions (variable) and the president's salary (fixed) are uncontrollable by the vice president of manufacturing.

Distinguishing Responsibility from Blame

Responsibility isn't the same as blame

Another common misunderstanding concerns the difference between "responsibility" and "blame." They are not synonymous. Assigning someone the responsibility is not the same as placing the blame.

For example, referring back to the performance report in Exhibit 24-1, you can see that the direct labor costs were $3,000 higher than they were expected to be. The fact that production foremen are assigned responsibility to control the performance of workers does not, however, automatically mean that they are blamed for the $3,000 difference. First of all, it is possible that the unfavorable difference was beyond anyone's control. A plausible explanation could be that a damaging storm caused a shutdown for several days during which time the laborers were still paid. Or the unfavorable difference might have been due to lack of foresight in the budget, which did not anticipate the higher wage rates that went into effect during the period. Still another likely cause for the difference might be the actions of another department. The sales manager may have accepted a large unexpected rush order that forced costly overtime work; or the purchasing agent may not have acquired the materials in time for production, causing lengthy idle time.

In each situation, the production foreman assumes initial responsibility for the unfavorable difference, but the blame was placed on someone else, or on no one at all. This is not to say that the foreman could not have been blamed, for indeed the differences could have been due to the workers' inadequate supervision. *The point is simply that responsibility and blame are not synonymous.*

A way to distinguish the two terms might be as follows: Responsibility is assigned before a cause is determined. Blame is assigned only after a cause has been determined. Setting responsibilities assures that someone can be asked, "What went wrong?" Only after this question is answered can the second question be asked: "Who's to blame?"

USE OF A STATIC BUDGET

The performance report in Exhibit 24-1 compared the actual results to a budget based on 15,000 units. We assumed that the number of units actually produced was the same as the number of units budgeted for production.

Let us now assume that only 12,500 units were actually produced, whereas 15,000 units had been budgeted for production. The performance report comparing the actual costs to make 12,500 units to the master budget for the 15,000 budgeted units is shown in Exhibit 24-2. The actual costs are much less than they were in Exhibit 24-1 (when we assumed that 15,000 units were actually produced), which is to be expected since we have now produced 2,500 fewer units. The master budget, how-

	Actual Costs (12,500 units)	Master Budget (15,000 units)	Difference
Direct materials	$ 65,000	$ 75,000	$10,000 F
Direct labor.	78,000	90,000	12,000 F
Variable overhead.	39,000	45,000	6,000 F
Fixed overhead.	14,900	15,000	100 F
	$196,900	$225,000	$28,100 F

ever, is the same as it was in Exhibit 24-1 because the master budget is based on the prediction that we made at the beginning of the month. Since the master budget remains the same regardless of the number of units actually produced, it is often referred to as a *static (or unchanging) budget.*

Each actual cost in Exhibit 24-2 is less than the budgeted cost — designated as favorable by the letter F beside each difference. The total of the individual differences, $28,100 F, is significant and might result in the responsible parties being praised for their efficient performance during January.

It would be a mistake, however, to conclude from this favorable difference that production was conducted in an efficient manner. Efficiency had nothing to do with it. Remember, the actual costs of production were based on 2,500 fewer units than were the budgeted costs. Even if the workers were grossly inefficient, doesn't it seem reasonable to expect them to incur less actual variable costs in the production of only 12,500 units than they were expected to incur for the production of 15,000 units? The only thing we know for sure from Exhibit 24-2 is that the production department was unable to reach the 15,000-unit production goal set by management, and as a result, the actual costs were less than predicted. Whether or not the 12,500 units were produced for more or less costs than they should have been has yet to be determined.

Just in case you're not yet convinced of the irrelevance of the differences in the performance report when the master budget is compared to the actual results, we will now take the situation to an extreme. We will now assume that there was zero actual production for the month even though we had expected 15,000 units to be produced. The actual variable costs would, of course, be zero, as you can see in the performance report of Exhibit 24-3. The comparison of these zero actual costs to the unchanging master budget amounts now results in fantastically favorable variances. Do the $210,100 of favorable variances in Exhibit 24-3 have any meaning or relevance? Of course not!

Rule: Don't use the master budget in the performance report

Although Exhibit 24-3 represents an extreme and silly situation, it should help to plant an important generalization in your minds: *When the master budget is included in the performance report, it results in irrelevant and meaningless variances.* This is

	Actual Costs (zero units)	Master Budget (15,000 units)	Difference
Direct materials	$ –0–	$ 75,000	$ 75,000 F
Direct labor.	–0–	90,000	90,000 F
Variable overhead.	–0–	45,000	45,000 F
Fixed overhead.	14,900	15,000	100 F
	$14,900	$225,000	$210,100 F

because the master budget is a static, unchanging prediction of what the costs might be in the upcoming period, rather than an indication of what the costs are expected to be to produce the actual units worked on. When the master budget is used in the performance report, as it was in Exhibits 24-2 and 24-3, it is not possible to determine if the organization was operated effectively or efficiently.

Effectiveness and Efficiency

Effectiveness refers to the attainment of objectives. It is measured by comparing the actual output (the finished units produced by the organization) to the original goals. *Efficiency* refers to the relationship of inputs to outputs, that is, how well the company controls the use of its inputs (materials, labor, and overhead) in generating the outputs (the finished units).[1]

You can be effective but not efficient, and vice versa

For example, let's assume that you have a mouse in your kitchen, and you want to kill it. If you decide to solve your problem by having an exterminator's tent put on your house (at a cost of $300), your approach would be quite effective — a dead mouse. However, it wouldn't be very efficient — $300 for one little mouse? Assume instead that you borrow the ferocious cat from next door and she kills your mouse in exchange for a box of catnip treats (costing $.49). Now you have been both effective — a dead mouse — and efficient — a cost of only $.49.

Let's now look back at the performance report in Exhibit 24-2 for Underhill Company. Unfortunately, the differences that are shown give us no indication whether the production department was run effectively, efficiently, or both. Each difference is actually a combination of effectiveness and efficiency. Part of each difference exists because the department produced 2,500 fewer units than were hoped for — this means that we were not effective. The other part of each difference exists because the 12,500 units were produced for either more or less than they might have been — this is where efficiency comes in.

From now on our main concern is with efficiency

Although management naturally has to be concerned with both the effectiveness and efficiency of its operation, within this chapter we are concerned primarily with management's interest in efficiency. Performance reports must provide variances that isolate efficiency rather than a confusing combination of efficiency and effectiveness. The only way to do this is to compare the actual costs to a budget that indicates what the costs are expected to be for the units actually produced. Such a budget is a flexible budget.

THE FLEXIBLE BUDGET

Flexible budgets are predictions of costs at different levels of activity

The master budget is based on the single most likely level of activity to take place, and it is prepared before any activity at all occurs. A *flexible budget* is a prediction of costs at various levels of activity, based on a knowledge of how costs are expected to behave in response to activity. A flexible budget can be prepared before a period begins, indicating what the predicted costs might be for many possible levels of future activity — one of which will probably be the master budget level. Or a flexible budget can be prepared after the period is completed and the actual activity is known; in this case a flexible budget indicates the costs that you would expect for the actual production that has just taken place.

For example, the best estimate of production activity for the Underhill Company during January 1988 (Exhibit 23-5 from the previous chapter) was 15,000 units. However, budgets for activity above and below that level of production might have also been useful.

The Underhill Company may have wanted to know the possible effect on the

---

[1] Robert N. Anthony, *Planning and Control Systems: A Framework for Analysis* (Boston: Harvard Business School, 1965), pp. 27–28.

EXHIBIT 24-4   Flexible Budgets for January.
Here flexible budgets are prepared for three levels of possible future activity. One of these is the master budget level.

	Budgeted Cost per Unit	Flexible Budgets		
		14,000 Units	Master Budget, 15,000 Units	16,000 Units
Direct materials.	$5	$ 70,000	$ 75,000	$ 80,000
Direct labor	6	84,000	90,000	96,000
Variable overhead	3	42,000	45,000	48,000
Fixed overhead	n/a	15,000	15,000	15,000
Total production costs		$211,000	$225,000	$239,000

company's financial statements if the results were different from its best estimate. Flexible budgets help to provide this kind of information. Exhibit 24-4 portrays flexible budgets for the production department for January at several possible levels of production—the master budget level, as well as above and below that level. If production is anywhere between 14,000 and 16,000 units, the company will have a good idea of what the costs will be for the month.

Flexible budgets, such as the one in Exhibit 24-4, are prepared before the period begins, to assist management in planning for that period. When January's production of 12,500 units is completed and the actual costs of producing that quantity are determined, another flexible budget must be prepared, this one to be used in the performance report for control purposes. This flexible budget is based on the actual units—12,500—produced during January.

The performance report based on the flexible budget for 12,500 units is provided in Exhibit 24-5. The budgeted variable costs are based on the budgeted per-unit costs (column 1 in Exhibit 24-4) multiplied by 12,500 units; the budgeted fixed costs are the same amount, $15,000.

The difference between actual costs and the flexible budget based on the units produced is referred to as the ***flexible budget variance*** (which some people call the controllable variance). Notice that we are now using the term *variance* rather than *difference* in column 3. A difference is a general term meaning that two numbers are not the same amount; when this difference occurs in a performance report, it is referred to as a variance, a more specific term.

From the flexible budget variances we can determine whether or not the units were produced efficiently. In Exhibit 24-5 you can see that each of the actual variable costs is higher than the corresponding costs in the flexible budget, resulting in unfavorable

EXHIBIT 24-5
Performance Report: Flexible Budget Based on Units Produced.
Now a flexible budget is prepared based on the units that were actually produced. When subtracted from the actual results we have the flexible budget variance.

	Actual Costs (12,500 units)	Flexible Budget, Based on Units Produced (12,500 units)	Total Flexible Budget Variance
Direct materials	$ 65,000	$ 62,500	$2,500 U
Direct labor	78,000	75,000	3,000 U
Variable overhead	39,000	37,500	1,500 U
Fixed overhead	14,900	15,000	100 F
Total production costs	$196,900	$190,000	$6,900 U

flexible budget variances. Based on these unfavorable variances we can now say that the 12,500 units were not made very efficiently—we spent more to make the 12,500 units than we expected to spend.

We can determine if Underhill Company is *effective* or not by comparing the actual units produced to the number of units originally estimated in the master budget. Since 2,500 fewer units were produced than anticipated, the company was not as effective as it could have been. Producing and selling 2,500 fewer units than expected reduces net income because we will have a lower contribution margin as a result of not having sold these 2,500 units.

We can determine the dollar measure of effectiveness by:

The master budget can be used to measure effectiveness

1. Preparing a budgeted income statement for Underhill based on production and sales of 12,500 units.

2. Comparing this statement to the budgeted income statement based on the master budget level of activity, 15,000 units.

3. The difference in the budgeted net incomes on the two statements is the dollar measure of effectiveness.

If the budgeted net income is higher at the master budget level of activity, this means that we will have less income than originally expected because of producing and selling fewer units. This is the situation for Underhill who produced and sold 2,500 fewer units than originally estimated.

If the budgeted net income is lower for the master budget level of activity, this means that our net income will be higher than expected because we produced and sold more units than we originally estimated.

We can determine the dollar measure of effectiveness in an easier manner—it will not be necessary to prepare complete comparative statements of budgeted net income. We can do this with the following formula:

Effectiveness is measured in terms of lost profits by not reaching our original goal

$$\begin{array}{c}\textbf{Measure of} \\ \textbf{effectiveness}\end{array} = \begin{array}{c}\textbf{difference} \\ \textbf{in profits}\end{array} = \begin{array}{c}\textbf{difference in units} \\ \textbf{budgeted and units} \\ \textbf{actually produced}\end{array} \times \begin{array}{c}\textbf{contribution} \\ \textbf{margin per} \\ \textbf{unit}\end{array}$$

For the Underhill Company, the contribution margin per unit was $9.

Sales price.		$25
Variable costs per unit:		
Direct materials	$5	
Direct labor	6	
Variable overhead	3	
Variable selling.	2	16
Contribution margin per unit		$ 9

Based on the difference between the units actually produced, 12,500, and the units originally budgeted, 15,000, the amount of profit lost by Underhill due to ineffectiveness was:

$$\text{Difference in profits} = (15,000 \text{ units} - 12,500 \text{ units}) \times \$9/\text{unit}$$
$$= 2,500 \text{ units} \times \$9/\text{unit}$$
$$= \underline{\$22,500}$$

Since Underhill produced and sold 2,500 fewer units than it planned to , its net income will be $22,500 less than it was originally estimated to be.

Thus far, we have been concerned with predictions of what actual costs "will be" or "would have been" rather than what the costs "should be" or "should have been." For example, suppose that we know that a worker can make a unit for $10, as long as he shows a reasonable amount of care and concentration. We expect to produce 1,000 units next month and are preparing the master budget. We learn from the worker's supervisor that the worker has not been performing as well as he can because of personal problems. So, instead of budgeting $10,000 (1,000 units × $10), we budget the costs to be 10% higher — $11,000 (1,000 × $11). The $11,000 is a prediction of what the actual costs "will be"; it does not indicate what the costs "should be" — 1,000 units × $10 = $10,000.

Now let's assume that the month is over; that 1,200 units have actually been produced; and we are now preparing the flexible budget for the performance report. Remembering what the supervisor told us about the worker's personal problems, we budget the costs at $13,200 (1,200 × $11). This amount is an estimate of what we think the actual costs "would have been," to make 1,200 units; it does not indicate what the costs "should have been" to make the 1,200 units − 1,200 × $10 = $12,000.

When we estimate what costs "should be" instead of "will be" (when we look into the future), and what costs "should have been" instead of "would have been" (when we look back at the past), we are dealing with a type of costs we call "standard costs." **Standard costs,** which are carefully predetermined estimates of what costs "should be" or "should have been," are target costs to aim for rather than merely anticipated actual results. Standard costs are determined in an extremely careful manner rather than merely being roughly estimated. They may be used for several purposes, including:

1. Building master budgets
2. Evaluating performance with flexible budgets
3. Product costing

We can use standard costs in the preparation of the master budget, in which case the budget represents *what we think the costs should be in the forthcoming period, instead of what we think the actual costs will be.* For our worker mentioned above, who had personal problems, we would budget $10,000 for the period instead of $11,000. Now during the period control will be exerted to reach the $10,000 goal. If we set out to attain a $10,000 goal we have a better chance of reaching it than if we set our goal at $11,000 and hope to spend only $10,000. If we aim at $11,000, we will probably have a self-fulfilling prophecy.

The flexible budget shown in Exhibit 24-5 provided a rough estimate of what the "actual costs were expected to be" in producing 12,500 units. If the company were using a standard cost system, and if the per-unit costs were standard costs per unit, the *same flexible budget would represent what the costs "should have been" in producing 12,500 units.*

If managers are to determine the causes of variances and take the necessary corrective action to reduce variances to an acceptable amount in the next period, it is better that the variances represent the deviations of costs from what they "should have been" than from what they "were expected to be." If costs are exactly as we expect them to be, we might not realize that what we expect is based on an inefficiently run operation, and that a zero difference between actual and expected does not necessarily mean that adequate control is being exerted. The use of standards gives better assurance to managers that: (1) the operation is being properly controlled when variances are zero or insignificant, and (2) a significant variance means that the operation is out of control, warranting the time and costs of an investigation.

Before we go on to the third purpose for using standard costs, remember one important point: The master budget and the flexible budget are merely mechanical tools used by accountants to predict costs at different levels of activity and at different points in time; *standard costs represent the type of costs* being predicted in the master budget and the flexible budget.

Product Costing

Standard costs make good inventory costs

Product costs are those that are associated with and assigned to units in inventory. The costs are classified as assets until the units are sold, at which time they become an expense — cost of goods sold. The costs assigned to units in inventory can be actual costs or standard costs.

Proponents of standard costing contend that for units in inventory, the definition of an asset — a resource having a future economic benefit — is better met by assigning standard costs rather than actual costs to inventory. They argue that standard costs, not actual costs, provide future economic benefits in terms of revenues generated from the sale of units. What they mean is this.

Let's suppose that after all the production is said and done, and all the units are on the shelves in inventory waiting for sale, and all the costs are determined, it turns out that the actual costs are higher than the standard costs. The difference — the excess costs — at this point cannot be passed on to buyers in terms of higher prices. (Remember, the selling price was set much earlier when the costs were budgeted. And more than likely, that price has been advertised or committed to in some way to customers.) Therefore, that part of the actual costs above the standard costs, which we tend to think of as "the excess costs" and which we refer to as "unfavorable variances," provides no future benefits and, as a result, should not be considered a cost of this particular asset, the units in inventory.

How, then, do we account for the part of the actual costs in excess of standard costs, that is, the unfavorable variances? These costs are considered by proponents of standard costing to be losses for the period, which should be deducted on the income statement when they occur.

Types of Standards — A Matter of Tightness

A standard cost represents the amount it should cost to produce a unit of output. But is the amount it should cost based on extremely tight or lax conditions? Is a standard cost the least amount it can ever cost to make a unit, or is it the cost to make a unit when workers are merely doing a pretty good job? Is a standard virtually impossible, or relatively easy to attain? The answers to these questions depend on the types of standard that we use — ideal standards or currently attainable standards.

Ideal Standards

Ideal standards are usually impossible to attain for a sustained period of time

Ideal standards represent what it should cost to produce a unit if production conditions are perfect. This assumes that workers can perform at peak efficiency 100% of the time, that all units are 100% perfect, that there are no spoiled or defective units, that machines never break down, and overtime is never necessary. Of course, all of these things do occur; they are expected and are even accepted, within reasonable limits, as part of the process of production. Thus we realize that it is impossible for workers and machinery to attain these standards of perfection, resulting in variances that are always unfavorable.

One possible consequence of using ideal standards is that there may be a negative response on the part of employees to improve. If they can never attain the goal, they might develop an attitude of "why try?" Instead of standards helping to find and eliminate inefficiencies, they might cause greater inefficiencies.

Currently attainable standards provide allowances for normal and acceptable imperfections in the production process. Currently attainable standards are realistic expectations of what should be accomplished under continuing efficient operating conditions.

They are not easy to attain, but they are possible to attain.

Currently attainable standards are recommended over ideal standards for several reasons:

1. The master budget will be a more useful planning device if it offers a realistic approximation of future expectations.

2. Since currently attainable standards give a realistic indication of what workers should have accomplished, any variances that result will provide a better clue to areas that need to be investigated.

3. Currently attainable standards are more likely to be recognized by workers as reasonable expectations of management, and are thereby more likely to motivate workers in a positive manner.

Standard costs are set for each type of production cost—direct materials, direct labor, and factory overhead. Each of these standards has two components: (1) a price standard and (2) a quantity standard. A *price standard* measures the dollar cost that should be paid for each of the inputs needed for production. For direct materials the inputs can be measured in gallons, pounds, bottles, packages, etc. For direct labor and variable overhead, inputs are usually measured in hours.

A *quantity standard* represents the quantity of each input that should be used for each unit completed.

Variances occur whenever actual results are different from the standard. Because there are two components of a standard cost, there are also two corresponding variances—the *price variance* and the *quantity variance.* The addition of the price variance and quantity variance is the *total flexible budget variance* (or just flexible budget variance). There is a price variance, a quantity variance, and a flexible budget variance for each variable production cost (direct materials, direct labor, and variable overhead). For fixed overhead there is a price variance, but there is no quantity variance.

In addition, there is a different type of variance just for fixed factory overhead—the volume variance. We will postpone discussion of this variance until the end of the chapter.

The terms standard cost and flexible budget are often used interchangeably, which is acceptable, even though they do mean different things. As we mentioned earlier, the flexible budget is the tool for predicting costs, and standard costs are the type of costs being predicted. Since the only costs that we will now be predicting in the flexible budgets are standard costs, we will refer to the flexible budgets and to the standard

Currently Attainable Standards

Currently attainable standards are realistic expectations

Categories of Standards and Variances

Price variance plus quantity variance equals the total flexible budget variance

Standard Costs and Flexible Budgets

The flexible budget is a tool for predicting costs. Standard costs are the type of cost being predicted

costs within the flexible budgets as if they were the same. A second way that these two terms differ relates to whether we are referring to total dollars or per-unit dollars. The term standard cost technically refers to a cost per unit, or per pound, or per hour, rather than to the total costs for some level of activity. Conversely, the term "flexible budget" technically is a measure of total dollars, rather than dollars per unit or per hour. For example, if a standard cost is $5 per unit, then the flexible budget for 1,000 units is $5,000. Once again there is a conceptual difference in the two terms, but the difference has tended to blur through indiscriminate usage. So the $5 per unit standard cost might be referred to as the flexible budget per unit and the $5,000 flexible budget might be called the total standard costs. This will be perfectly acceptable.

AN ILLUSTRATION OF STANDARD COSTING

For the purpose of this illustration, additional details concerning the production costs of the Underhill Company are provided in Example 24-1.

EXAMPLE 24-1

THE UNDERHILL COMPANY

The Underhill Company has recently developed a standard cost system for the control of its production operations. According to the controller, Kelly Hernandez, the following standards for variable costs have been set for the production of each unit (a good luck charm):

Direct materials . . . . $\frac{1}{2}$ lb/unit @ $10.00/lb = $5.00/unit
Direct labor . . . . 2 hr/unit @ $3.00/hr = $6.00/unit
Variable overhead . . . . 2 hr/unit @ $1.50/hr = $3.00/unit

Fixed overhead is budgeted at $15,000 per month.
   At the beginning of January 1988, 15,000 units were budgeted for production. There were only 12,500 units actually produced during the month. The actual results for the month's production were as follows:

6,404 pounds purchased and used, at a cost of $10.15 per pound

26,621 hours worked

$78,000 of direct labor costs ($2.93 per hour)

$39,000 of variable overhead costs ($1.465 per hour)

$14,900 of fixed overhead

We will use these details to calculate the standard costs and the variances. The standard costs per unit are the same as the budgeted costs per unit shown in Exhibit 24-4.
   In Exhibit 24-4 we assumed that the per-unit amounts represented what we *expected the actual costs to be* during production. Now we are assuming—by using standards—that the per-unit amounts are what *"it should" cost* to produce each unit. In addition, each per-unit standard cost is broken down into a price standard and a quantity standard, which will allow us to determine individually the price and quantity variances as well as the total flexible budget variance. In Exhibit 24-5 we were only able to calculate the flexible budget variance.

Direct Materials

The purchasing agent is responsible for direct material price variances

The purchasing agent is usually the person responsible for determining the standard price for materials. He or she is also responsible for acquiring the proper quantity and quality of materials required for production at the standard price. Determining the standard price can be a difficult task because it often is no more than a guess of what price the suppliers will be charging in the future rather than a carefully determined calculation of the price the company "ought" to be charged.

The purchasing agent shops around to find the best price, being sure to take into consideration cash and quantity discounts and different means and costs of transportation. Having set the standard price, purchases in the future at any other price result in a price variance.

Quantity standards are set by the engineering department in companies that have one. Otherwise, the quantity standard will probably be determined by production superintendents and foremen based on their working knowledge of the materials needed for each unit, as well as the ability of laborers and the quality of machinery to be used.

The quantity standard is converted into dollars by the accounting department. For example, Underhill Company has a standard quantity for direct materials of $\frac{1}{2}$ pound per unit. In dollars this standard converts to $5.00 per unit ($\frac{1}{2}$ pound per unit $\times$ $10 per pound). And the flexible budget for the 12,500 units produced is $62,500 (12,500 units $\times$ $5 per unit).

Production foremen are responsible for seeing that workers in their departments use the correct amount of materials. If the actual usage is different from the standard allowed for the units produced there will be a quantity variance.

Calculating the Variances

The purchasing agent has a responsibility to pay the established standard price (the "price" charged by the supplier becomes the "cost" for the buyer) for whatever he or she purchases. If a purchase is made at a different price than the standard price, then the resulting price variance should be based on the quantity purchased even if some of the purchase is not used in production until a later period. The price variance is not based on the quantity used (unless the quantity used happens to be the same as the quantity purchased) because the event causing the variance is the purchase of materials at a price different from standard—not the usage of materials. Furthermore, a price variance must be recognized at the time of purchase, not later when the material is used. If recognition is postponed to a time later than the event that caused the price variance, the explanation for paying the excessive price would no longer be very useful information.

The ***materials price variance*** (direct materials) can be computed using the following formula:

The materials price variance is based on the quantity purchased

$$\text{Materials price variance} = \text{actual quantity purchased} \times \text{*difference* between the *actual* and *standard* cost per unit of input purchased}$$

Based upon the information in Example 24-1, the price variance for Underhill Company, where the materials price standard is $10.00 per pound, is:

$$\text{Materials price variance} = 6{,}404 \text{ lb} \times (\$10.15 - \$10.00)$$

$$= 6{,}404 \text{ lb} \times \$.15/\text{lb} = \$960 \text{ U}$$

The $960 materials price variance is considered to be unfavorable because the actual price paid for each pound purchased ($10.15) was higher than it should have been ($10.00).

The *materials quantity variance* (direct materials) is based on the difference between the actual quantity used and the standard quantity allowed. The *standard quantity allowed* represents the quantity of direct materials that should have been used to make the units produced during the period. If this quantity is different from the actual quantity used, there is a quantity variance.

The dollar amount of the materials quantity variance can be calculated with the following formula:

You use the standard price to get the quantity variance

$$\text{Materials quantity variance} = \begin{array}{c} \textit{difference} \text{ between} \\ \textit{actual} \text{ quantity used} \\ \text{and } \textit{standard} \text{ quantity} \\ \text{allowed} \end{array} \times \begin{array}{c} \textit{standard} \text{ cost per} \\ \text{unit of input} \end{array}$$

The materials quantity variance for the Underhill Company, where the materials quantity standard is $\frac{1}{2}$ pound per unit, is:

$$\begin{aligned} \text{Materials quantity variance} &= [6{,}404 \text{ lb} - (\tfrac{1}{2} \text{ lb})(12{,}500 \text{ units})] \times \$10.00/\text{lb} \\ &= (6{,}404 \text{ lb} - 6{,}250 \text{ lb}) \times \$10.00/\text{lb} \\ &= 154 \text{ lb} \times \$10.00/\text{lb} = \$1{,}540 \text{ U} \end{aligned}$$

The materials quantity variance (also known as the *materials usage variance*) of $1,540 is unfavorable: Instead of using 6,250 pounds to produce 12,500 units, 6,404 pounds were used, or 154 pounds too many.

The total flexible budget variance for direct materials is then:

FBV = PV + QV

Total flexible budget variance = price variance + quantity variance

Total flexible budget variance = $960 U + $1,540 U = $2,500 U

Another approach to calculating variances makes use of an analysis that is quite similar in appearance to a performance report. This approach, called a three-column analysis, is presented in Exhibit 24-6. Notice that in columns 2 and 3 of Exhibit 24-6 we are once again using the term "flexible budget." We started with a standard cost per unit or per pound, and now we are converting these unit standards into total dollars with the flexible budget. Remember that when we have a standard cost system, the flexible budget indicates what the costs "should have been" for a specified level of activity. Column 2 (the flexible budget based on the actual quantity) indicates that we should have spent $10 per pound for each of the 6,404 pounds that were purchased—we should have spent $64,040 to acquire the direct materials. Column 3 (the flexible budget based on the standard quantity allowed) indicates that we should have used 6,250 pounds at a price of $10 per pound to make 12,500 units—we should have spent $62,500 to make 12,500 units.

Refer back to Exhibit 24-5 (on page 958), and compare the first line across, direct materials, to this expanded three-column analysis in Exhibit 24-6. In both figures, the actual costs are $65,000; the flexible budget costs (column 3 in Exhibit 24-6) are $62,500; and the total flexible budget variance is $2,500. Exhibit 24-6 shows that, with the addition of the flexible budget based on actual quantity (column 2 in Exhibit 24-6), the $2,500 can be broken down into price and quantity variances. The flexible budget in column 3 is based on the standard quantity allowed to produce 12,500 units (6,250 pounds); the flexible budget in column 2 is based on the actual quantity used to produce 12,500 units (6,404 pounds). Column 2, the flexible budget based on the

EXHIBIT 24-6
Three-Column Analysis for
Direct Materials.
(Quantity Used = Quantity
Purchased)
We have a price variance
because we paid too much for
what we bought. We have a
quantity variance because we
used too many pounds.

Remember, we are now
assuming that we purchase and
use the same number of
pounds—6,404

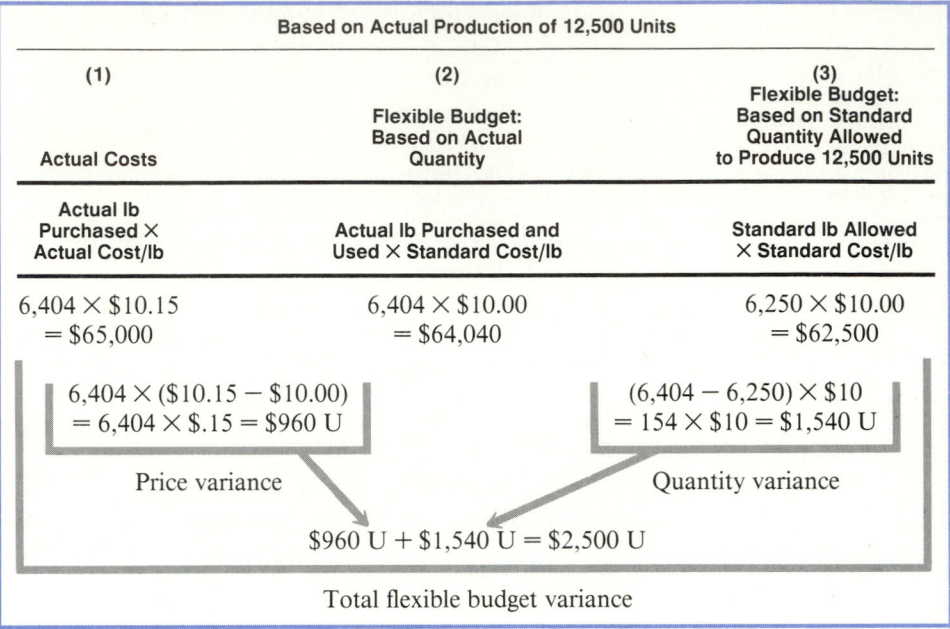

quantity purchased and used (6,404 pounds $\times$ \$10 = \$64,040), is compared to the actual costs for what was purchased to get the price variance, and it is compared to the flexible budget in column 3 to get the quantity variance.

In Exhibit 24-6 we found the flexible budget variance (\$2,500 U) by adding together the price variance (\$960 U) and the quantity variance (\$1,540 U). We could also have calculated the flexible budget variance by subtracting column 3 (\$62,500) from column 1 (\$65,000). *A warning, though, if you use this second approach: It doesn't work for direct materials if the quantities purchased and used are different amounts (see Exhibit 24-7).*

Example 24-1 specified that 6,404 pounds were purchased and all of it was used. If the quantity used were different from the quantity purchased, the formula for calculating the price variance would be the same. However, the three-column analysis for direct materials would need some minor adjustments. Assume that 6,404 pounds were used in production, but that 6,500 pounds were purchased. The three-column analysis would be as shown in Exhibit 24-7.

The price variance is \$975 unfavorable because 6,500 pounds were purchased. When we assumed that 6,404 were purchased, the price variance was \$960 unfavorable. *The fact that 6,404 pounds were actually used in production has no bearing on the price variance and how we calculate it. The actual quantity used only enters into the quantity variance calculation.*

The flexible budget variance is now \$2,515 U, found by adding together the price variance (\$975 U) and the quantity variance (\$1,540 U). Notice now, however, that the alternative way of determining the flexible budget variance no longer works for direct materials. When we subtract column 3 (\$62,500) from column 1 (\$65,975), we get \$3,475 U—which is not the same as \$2,515 U.

The Cause of Each Variance
Now find out what went wrong.

Once the variances are calculated, the next step for a manager is to find out what caused them.

EXHIBIT 24-7
Three-Column Analysis for Direct Materials.
(Quantity Purchased Different from Quantity Used.)
When the quantity purchased and used aren't the same, the middle column is split into two parts: the actual quantity purchased and the actual quantity used.

	Based on Actual Production of 12,500 Units		
(1)	**(2)**		**(3)**
	Flexible Budget: Based on Actual Quantity		**Flexible Budget: Based on Standard Quantity Allowed to Produce 12,500 Units**
Actual Costs			
Actual lb × Actual Cost/lb	**Actual lb × Standard Cost/lb**		**Standard lb Allowed × Standard Cost/lb**
	Quantity Purchased	**Quantity Used**	
6,500 × $10.15 = $65,975	6,500 × $10 = $65,000	6,404 × $10 = $64,040	6,250 × $10 = $62,500

$$6,500 \times (\$10.15 - \$10.00)$$
$$= 6,500 \times \$.15 = \$975 \text{ U}$$

Price variance

$$(6,404 - 6,250) \times \$10$$
$$= 154 \times \$10 = \$1,540 \text{ U}$$

Quantity variance

$$\$975 \text{ U} + \$1,540 \text{ U} = \$2,515 \text{ U}$$

Total flexible budget variance

Was the price variance due to a change in the price? Buying in too small a quantity? Buying better quality materials than are required?

Was the quantity variance due to improper standards? Machine breakdowns? Poor workmanship? Poor-quality materials?

Only after the causes have been determined can corrective action be taken. The standard may need to be revised; the laborers may need additional training; the purchasing agent may need to shop around for better deals. If the information revealed by the variances is not put to good use in making these kinds of corrections, then the costs of devising, implementing, and applying a standard cost system will be wasted.

Standard Costs and Product Costing

The product costs were the standard costs in column 3

Thus far, all of our attention in this section has been directed to using standards and flexible budgets to control operations. Remember that standard costs can also be used for product costing. If we do decide to assign standard costs instead of actual costs to the units produced, what amount of standard costs do we assign to the 12,500 units? If you look back to Exhibit 24-7, you'll see the answer. Column 3 is standard pounds multiplied by the standard cost per pound:

$$6,250 \text{ lb} \times \$10/\text{lb} = \underline{\$62,500}$$

The flexible budget of $62,500 represents how much we "should have spent" to make 12,500 units. This is the amount to assign to the units produced.

The flexible budget in column 2 does not represent the standard costs of producing 12,500 units because it is based on the actual pounds used (6,404), not the standard pounds allowed (6,250).

Direct Labor

Price standard

The labor price (or rate) standard is not usually set by management and imposed upon workers. Instead, labor rates are typically determined by either labor contracts negotiated between management and labor, or by local conditions of supply and demand for labor. The exact rates may also depend on conditions within the company, since different rates apply based on a worker's position, seniority, and the difficulty or skill of tasks performed. All of the factors affect the direct labor price standard.

Quantity standard

Labor quantity standards (also called labor efficiency standards) are often difficult to establish. Given a variety of workers, each with different skills and abilities, the idea behind a labor quantity standard is to determine what an average worker under continuing normal conditions can accomplish. The method of making such a determination is called a *time and motion study* and is conducted by the engineering department. A time and motion study is a scientific analysis of an entire labor operation and its component parts, determining how to best make and what amount of time it should take to do each part, so that the entire operation can be performed most efficiently.

Another way to set labor quantity standards is with test runs. Test runs of the labor operation are conducted under controlled conditions for a short period of time; the results are observed, documented, and analyzed. Based on these results, labor quantity standards are set.

Foremen are usually held responsible for both the labor price (or rate) variance and the labor quantity (or efficiency) variance. Labor price variances should be quite small, since the rates are not usually subject to sudden change. However, they will probably not be zero, because there will be cases where a worker earning one rate is substituted for another earning a different rate, and also because of overtime premiums.

Calculating the Variances

Direct materials variances are calculated for two distinct events—the purchase of materials and the subsequent use of those materials.

For direct labor, these two events occur simultaneously—the labor hours are purchased and used at exactly the same time. Therefore, the labor price variance and labor quantity variance are both calculated, based on the actual hours that are used (or worked).

The labor price variance is based on the actual hours worked

The actual hours are purchased and used

The *labor price variance* is calculated using the following formula:

$$\text{Labor price variance} = \text{actual hours worked} \times \begin{array}{l}\textit{difference} \text{ between the} \\ \textit{actual} \text{ wage rate and} \\ \textit{standard} \text{ wage rate}\end{array}$$

Notice the similarity of variances

Compare this formula with the one for the materials price variance; note the similarities. Although labor deals with hours worked rather than quantity purchased, and the price for labor is a wage rate rather than a cost per pound, the formula for the price variance for materials and the one for labor have exactly the same form. Notice the colored words in the formula for the labor price variance and compare these words to the colored words in the formula for the materials price variance; and then compare them to the formula for the variable overhead price variance that comes later. All three price variances involve an actual quantity multiplied by the difference between actual and standard prices.

For Underhill Company, where the labor price standard is $3.00 per hour, the labor price variance is:

$$\text{Labor price variance} = 26{,}621 \text{ hr} \times (\$2.93 - \$3.00)$$
$$= 26{,}621 \text{ hr} \times \$.07/\text{hr} = \$1{,}863 \text{ F}$$

The labor price variance of $1,863 is favorable because the actual wage rate paid to workers ($2.93) was less than the standard rate ($3.00) set for the operation.

The *labor quantity variance* uses the following formula:

Use the standard rate per hour for the quantity variance

$$\text{Labor quantity variance} = \begin{array}{c} \textit{difference} \textbf{ between} \\ \textit{actual} \textbf{ hours worked} \\ \textbf{and } \textit{standard} \textbf{ hours} \\ \textbf{allowed} \end{array} \times \begin{array}{c} \textit{standard} \\ \textbf{rate per hour} \end{array}$$

The term **standard hours allowed** represents the direct labor hours that should have been worked to produce the units completed during the period.

The formula for a direct labor quantity variance can be shown as having the same form as the formulas for the direct materials quantity variance and variable overhead quantity variance. Each quantity variance involves a difference between actual quantity used and standard quantity allowed, the difference multiplied by a standard price. Recognizing the similarities in variances for materials, labor, and variable overhead can be helpful in learning, understanding, and remembering them. It is easier to learn two basic variances—price variance and quantity variance—and to adapt them to the three production costs, than it is to learn six variances as if they were completely dissimilar.

The labor quantity variance for Underhill Company, where the labor quantity standard is 2 hours per unit, is:

$$\begin{aligned} \text{Labor quantity variance} &= [26,621 \text{ hr} - (2 \text{ hr} \times 12,500 \text{ units})] \times \$3.00/\text{hr} \\ &= (26,621 \text{ hr} - 25,000 \text{ hr}) \times \$3.00/\text{hr} \\ &= 1,621 \text{ hr} \times \$3.00/\text{hr} = \$4,863 \text{ U} \end{aligned}$$

The labor quantity variance is unfavorable, since 1,621 actual hours were used in excess of the standard allowed ($26,261 - 25,000 = 1,621$ hours).

The total flexible budget variance for direct labor is the sum of the labor price variance and the labor quantity variance.

FBV = PV + QV

Total flexible budget variance = $1,863 F + $4,863 U = $3,000 U

The three-column approach to calculating the direct labor variances is shown in Exhibit 24-8 at the top of page 970.

Notice in Exhibit 24-8 that the total flexible budget variance can be found in two ways. In addition to the way shown in the exhibit ($1,863 F + $4,863 U = $3,000 U), you can also find it by subtracting column 3 from column 1 ($78,000 − $75,000 = $3,000 U).

The Cause of Each Variance

What is the cause of each variance?

Once we have calculated the variances, it is then necessary to determine their causes and to take corrective action when warranted. A price variance can occur when different workers are used on a job rather than the ones that we expected. For example, we may use a worker with less seniority, and therefore pay a lower wage rate than we had planned on.

Labor quantity variances can occur for a variety of reasons. It could be that the worker mentioned above is paid a lower wage rate because of his inexperience, which could result in his taking longer to finish the job than the worker we planned on using would have taken. Other causes include machine breakdowns, defective materials, poor workmanship, and inadequate supervision.

EXHIBIT 24-8
Three-Column Analysis for Direct Labor.
For direct labor the hours purchased and used are always the same. So column 2 never has to be split into two parts as we do for direct materials.

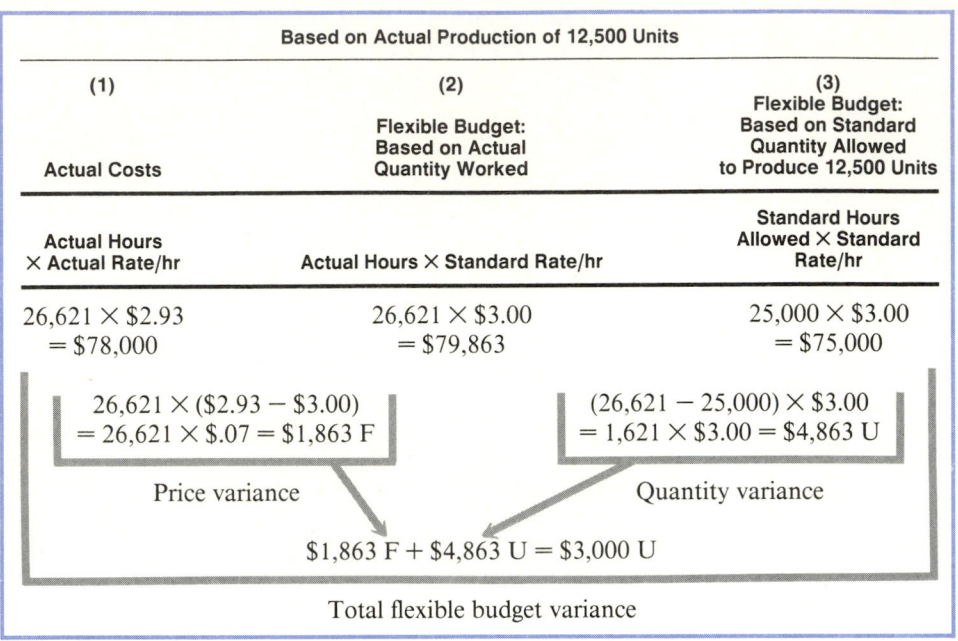

Based on Actual Production of 12,500 Units

(1) Actual Costs	(2) Flexible Budget: Based on Actual Quantity Worked	(3) Flexible Budget: Based on Standard Quantity Allowed to Produce 12,500 Units
Actual Hours × Actual Rate/hr	Actual Hours × Standard Rate/hr	Standard Hours Allowed × Standard Rate/hr
26,621 × $2.93 = $78,000	26,621 × $3.00 = $79,863	25,000 × $3.00 = $75,000

26,621 × ($2.93 − $3.00)
= 26,621 × $.07 = $1,863 F

Price variance

(26,621 − 25,000) × $3.00
= 1,621 × $3.00 = $4,863 U

Quantity variance

$1,863 F + $4,863 U = $3,000 U

Total flexible budget variance

Standard Costs and Product Costing

The product costs are the standard costs

If we are using standard costs for product costing as well as for control—that is, we are assigning standard costs to the units produced instead of assigning actual costs—then the amount we would assign is $75,000. This is the standard hours allowed multiplied by the standard rate per hour (25,000 hours × $3.00 per hour) that we find in column 3 of Exhibit 24-8. The $75,000 represents how much Underhill Company should have spent to produce 12,500 units.

Therefore, just as we saw for direct materials, column 3 serves two purposes:

Column 3 is used for both control and product costing

1. It is the flexible budget based on standard hours allowed, which we use to calculate the quantity variance and the flexible budget variance. We use it in this manner to help managers *control.*

2. It is also the dollar amount that we assign to the units produced when we are using a standard cost system for *product costing.*

Variable Factory Overhead

Direct materials and direct labor are direct costs because they are either physically related to or become an integral part of the units produced. It is possible to determine the exact amount of direct materials and direct labor going into each unit. To set standards for direct materials and direct labor, engineers figure the exact quantity of materials and hours of direct labor that should go into each unit. From these quantities the standard costs per unit are calculated, representing the costs that should be incurred to produce each and every unit.

Variable overhead is indirectly related to production

Variable overhead costs are indirectly related to production. This means that although the costs are necessary, they cannot be closely, or directly, associated with specific units of production. For this reason setting standards for variable overhead costs is somewhat different from setting standards for direct materials and direct labor. Rather than determining an exact amount of variable overhead that should be incurred every time a unit is completed, an average is determined instead. The average represents how much overhead should be incurred per unit in a batch of units produced over an extended period of time.

For example, assume that the standard costs per unit for the production of For-mica top tables includes $2.00 for Formica (a direct material) and $.50 for utilities (an indirect item of variable overhead).

Each table would require one Formica table top and thus $2.00 of materials cost, whether it was the first, tenth, or one-thousandth table produced.

The $.50 per table for utilities has a different explanation. It would not be reason-able to expect the utility bill to increase by exactly $.50 every time a table was finished. However, over a longer period of time, say a month, we might expect the total utility bill to average $.50 per table.

In order to develop standards for variable overhead, it is necessary to deal with averages rather than exact costs per unit. We can determine these averages with the aid of statistical tools for evaluating the behavior of costs. These tools are beyond the scope of this text, however, and will be covered in your upper-level statistics and cost accounting courses. For our purposes, we'll merely accept the fact that Underhill Company has evaluated the behavior of its total overhead costs and has determined that the variable overhead costs should average $1.50 per hour. And since we already know (from the discussion of direct labor) that the standard hours allowed per unit are 2, the standard variable overhead rate per unit is $3.00, determined as follows:

$$\text{Variable overhead cost per unit} = \text{standard hours/unit} \times \frac{\textbf{variable overhead cost}}{\textbf{per hour}}$$

Variable overhead cost per unit = 2 hr/unit × 1.50/hr = $3.00/unit

Calculating the Variances

The calculation of price and quantity variances for variable overhead are nearly the same as those for direct labor. The ***variable overhead price (or spending) variance*** is:

The price variance is just like direct labor's

$$\frac{\textbf{Variable overhead}}{\textbf{price variance}} = \frac{\textit{actual}}{\textbf{hours worked}} \times \frac{\textit{difference} \textbf{ between } \textit{actual}}{\substack{\textbf{cost/hour and } \textit{standard} \\ \textbf{cost/hour}}}$$

For Underhill Company, it would be:

Variable overhead price variance = 26,621 hr × ($1.465 − $1.50)

= 26,621 hr × $.035/hr = $932 F

The price variance is favorable because the average variable overhead cost in-curred per hour ($1.465) was $.035 less than it was expected to be ($1.50), for the 26,621 actual hours employed in production.

The formula for the ***variable overhead quantity variance*** is:

So is the quantity variance

$$\frac{\textbf{Variable overhead}}{\textbf{quantity variance}} = \frac{\textit{difference} \textbf{ between } \textit{actual}}{\substack{\textbf{hours worked and } \textit{standard} \\ \textbf{hours allowed}}} \times \frac{\textit{standard} \textbf{ cost}}{\textbf{per hour}}$$

The quantity variance for Underhill is:

$$\frac{\text{Variable overhead}}{\text{quantity variance}} = (26,621 \text{ hr} - 25,000 \text{ hr}) \times \$1.50/\text{hr}$$

= 1,621 hr × $1.50/hr = $2,432 U

The quantity variance for variable overhead is based on the difference in actual hours (26,621 hours) and standard hours (25,000 hours) of direct labor. Once these

EXHIBIT 24-9
Three-Column Analysis for Variable Overhead.
The total flexible budget variance for variable overhead is the amount over- or underapplied.

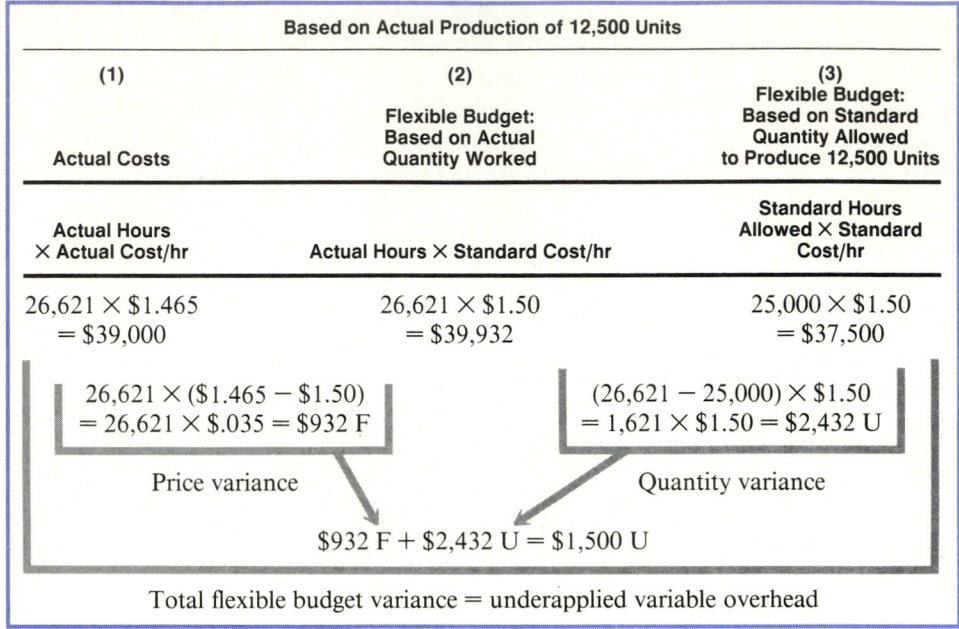

	Based on Actual Production of 12,500 Units	
(1)	**(2)** Flexible Budget: Based on Actual Quantity Worked	**(3)** Flexible Budget: Based on Standard Quantity Allowed to Produce 12,500 Units
Actual Costs		
Actual Hours × Actual Cost/hr	Actual Hours × Standard Cost/hr	Standard Hours Allowed × Standard Cost/hr
26,621 × $1.465 = $39,000	26,621 × $1.50 = $39,932	25,000 × $1.50 = $37,500

26,621 × ($1.465 − $1.50)
= 26,621 × $.035 = $932 F

(26,621 − 25,000) × $1.50
= 1,621 × $1.50 = $2,432 U

Price variance   Quantity variance

$932 F + $2,432 U = $1,500 U

Total flexible budget variance = underapplied variable overhead

two quantities are determined, the dollar amount of quantity variance is derived by multiplying the quantity difference by the standard cost per hour.

The total flexible budget variance for variable overhead is the sum of the price variance and the quantity variance:

$FBV = PV + QV$

$$\begin{array}{l}\text{Total flexible}\\\text{budget variance}\\\text{for variable}\\\text{overhead}\end{array} = \$932\text{ F} + \$2,432\text{ U} = \$1,500\text{ U}$$

The three-column approach for determining the variable overhead variances is shown in Exhibit 24-9.

The flexible budget variance of $1,500 U in Exhibit 24-9 can also be found by subtracting column 3 from column 1 ($39,000 − $37,500 = $1,500 U).

The Cause of Each Variance

The VO quantity variance is closely related to direct labor

Since variable factory overhead is closely related to the number of direct labor hours used in production, anything that causes a quantity variance for direct labor also results in a quantity variance for variable overhead. So once we have determined the hours of variance for direct labor, and the causes of the variance, then we have also determined the hourly variance and causes for variable overhead. The only difference between the quantity variances for direct labor and variable overhead is the standard rate that is multiplied by the difference in actual and standard hours.

The VO price variance is a residual

The variable overhead price (or spending) variance represents the remainder of the flexible budget variance — the portion that is not explained by the quantity variance. It may arise for a variety of reasons, the exact cause depending on the specific overhead cost being evaluated. It could be that the best measure of activity for some of the overhead costs may not be hours of labor, but that for convenience the same measure of activity is being used for all overhead costs. As a result, the standard rate per hour may not result in as precise an estimate of costs in the flexible budget as we would like — resulting in a price variance. On the other hand, a price variance could be explained by paying a higher average hourly rate than we should have for the indirect laborers. Or it could even be due to the inefficient use of supplies that wasn't already explained by the quantity variance (i.e., wasn't due to the use of too many direct labor hours).

Standard Costs and Product Costing

The product costs come from column 3—standard times standard

We have used column 3 in Exhibit 24-9 as the flexible budget based on standard hours allowed to get the quantity variance and the flexible budget variance. We're sure you remember that column 3 can also be used for a second purpose—for product costing. If we are using the standard cost system for product costing, then the dollar amount we assign to the 12,500 units produced is $37,500—the standard hours allowed multiplied by the standard rate per hour. The $37,500 is the amount of variable overhead costs that "should have been" incurred to produce 12,500 units.

For variable overhead the flexible budget variance is also called the over- or underapplied overhead. If you think back to Chapter 20, you may remember that we called the factory overhead assigned to production, for product costing, the "overhead applied." Well, we still do—so the $37,500 in column 3 can also be called the "variable overhead applied." The difference in actual overhead costs and overhead applied was called the over- or underapplied overhead in Chapter 20—and it still is. Therefore, the difference of $1,500 can either be called the total flexible budget variance or the underapplied overhead.

More Detail for Variable Overhead

Variable overhead should actually be evaluated on an item-by-item basis

Actually, the variable overhead costs and variances shown in Exhibit 24-9 would probably be broken down into many specific variable overhead costs. An analysis of the variances would be performed for each cost item so that management would have the information needed to take corrective actions. For example, the $932 F price variance and the $2,432 U quantity variance from Exhibit 24-9 might comprise the following items:

	Price Variance	Quantity Variance
Supplies.................................	$1,800 U	$ 811 U
Utilities	600 U	405 U
Indirect labor	3,332 F	1,216 U
	$ 932 F	$2,432 U

Each variance might have its own cause, its own person bearing responsibility for that item, and its own necessary corrective action.

If each of the variable overhead cost items have to be treated individually rather than collectively, this means that separate variance calculations must be made for each item. But this should present no problem, because the variance formulas that you will use are the same, it's just that now they'll be used with specific items instead of for all variable overhead items combined. Take supplies, for example. If the individual standard cost per hour is $.50, and the actual rate averaged $.5676 per hour, the price variance is simply:

$$\text{Variable overhead price variance} = \text{actual hours worked} \times \text{difference between actual cost per hour and standard cost per hour}$$

$$\text{Variable overhead price variance} = 26,621 \times (\$.5676 - \$.50) = 26,621 \times \$.0676 = \$1,800 \text{ U}$$

And the variable overhead quantity variance for supplies would be:

The 1,621 excess hours are the same as for direct labor

$$\frac{\text{Variable overhead}}{\text{quantity variance}} = \frac{\text{difference between actual hours and}}{\text{standard hours allowed}} \times \frac{\text{standard cost}}{\text{per hour}}$$

$$\frac{\text{Variable overhead}}{\text{quantity variance}} = (26{,}621 - 25{,}000) \times \$.50 = 1{,}621 \times \$.50 = \$811 \text{ U}$$

Naturally, we would then calculate the variances for utilities and indirect labor in a similar manner.

A Choice in Terminology

Throughout our discussion of the variable production costs (direct materials, direct labor, and variable overhead), we have referred to price and quantity standards, and price and quantity variances. Because other texts use different terms, we usually gave you an alternative name that you could use. For example, the term usage variance is an acceptable alternative to quantity variance for direct materials.

We use only one set of terms in this text—price and quantity—to emphasize the similarity in form of each type of variance whether we calculate it for direct materials, direct labor, or variable overhead. We feel that you should have no trouble learning two types of variances—and then applying each type to a different variable production cost.

If you'd prefer a choice instead, take a look at Exhibit 24-10. It gives a list of commonly used terms for our price and quantity variances, and it also gives a summary of the formulas for calculating each variance.

EXHIBIT 24-10
Summary of Variances for Variable Production Costs.
This exhibit gives commonly used alternative terms for our price and quantity variances. It also shows how to calculate each price and quantity variance.

Variances: Terminology Employed in Text	Commonly Used Alternatives	Formula
Direct materials:		
Price variance	None	Difference in actual and standard price × actual quantity purchased
Quantity variance	Usage variance	Difference in actual quantity used and standard quantity allowed × standard price
Direct labor:		
Price variance	Rate variance	Difference in actual and standard rate per hour × actual hours worked
Quantity variance	Efficiency, time, or usage variance	Difference in actual hours worked and standard hours allowed × standard rate per hour
Variable overhead:		
Price variance	Spending variance	Difference in actual and standard cost per hour × actual hours worked
Quantity variance	Efficiency variance	Difference in actual hours worked and standard hours allowed × standard cost per hour

Fixed Factory Overhead

Our analysis of fixed factory overhead is somewhat different than it is for direct materials, direct labor, and variable overhead. Although we can use a similar multi-column format as we used for the variable cost items, there will be several differences:

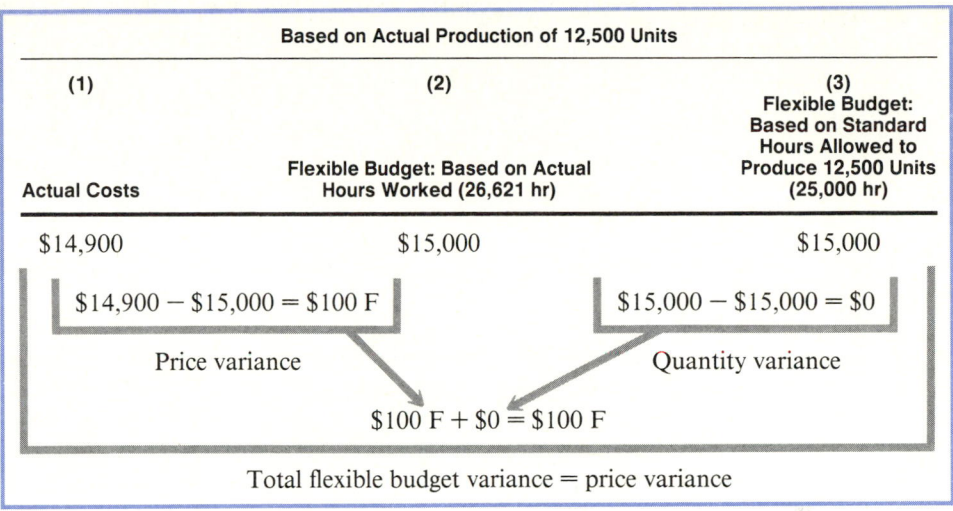

1. We do not have a quantity variance for fixed factory overhead.

2. Although there is a price variance for fixed factory overhead, we do not calculate it in the same manner.

3. We will have to expand the three-column format to four columns, when we introduce a new variance — the volume variance.

The analysis of fixed overhead differs from the analysis of the variable costs

The fixed factory overhead for Underhill Company is expected to be $15,000 per month. Since total fixed costs are not expected to change in response to changes in activity, this $15,000 is the amount we budget, regardless of activity. Therefore, the flexible budget based on actual hours of 26,621 and the flexible budget based on the standard hours allowed of 25,000, are both the same amount — $15,000. You can see this when you look at columns 2 and 3 in Exhibit 24-11.

Graphically, the flexible budget for fixed factory overhead looks like this:

Budgeted fixed factory overhead is the same at all levels of activity

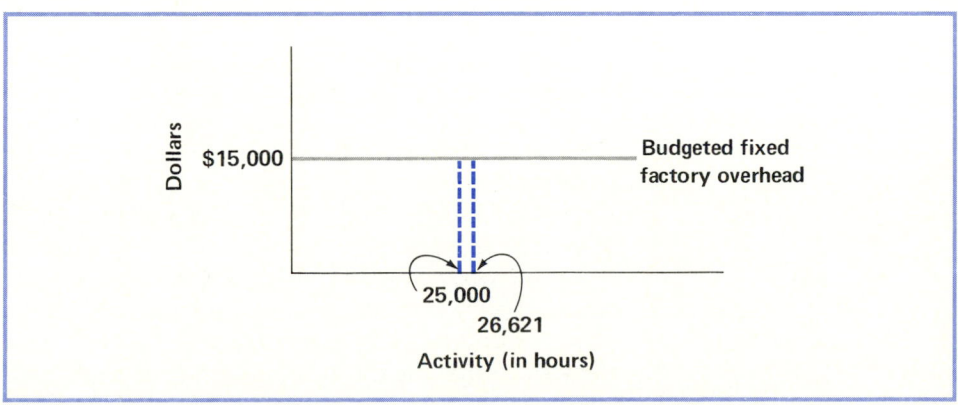

If the hours in our performance report were 15,000 or 21,000 or 28,000 instead, the flexible budget for fixed factory overhead would still be $15,000.

Calculating the Price Variance

When we subtract the budgeted fixed factory overhead (column 2) in Exhibit 24-11 from the actual costs incurred (column 1), we get a favorable *fixed overhead price (or spending) variance* of $100:

Price variance for fixed equals actual less budgeted

$$\text{Fixed factory overhead price variance} = \text{actual costs} - \text{flexible budget for fixed factory overhead}$$

$$\text{Fixed factory overhead price variance} = \$14{,}900 - \$15{,}000 = \$100 \text{ F}$$

Notice that we did not calculate the fixed overhead price variance in the same way as we did for the variable overhead price variance (difference in the actual and the standard rate per hour × actual hours). Not only didn't we do it that way in Exhibit 24-11, we will *never* do it that way—because the price variance for fixed factory overhead is not affected by the number of actual hours that we use.

The quantity variance is always zero

Now look at columns 2 and 3 in Exhibit 24-11. Since the amount of fixed factory overhead that we budget for the actual hours and for the standard hours are the same (and will *always* be the same) there is *never* a quantity variance for fixed factory overhead. And since the quantity variance is zero, the total flexible budget variance for fixed factory overhead will always equal its price variance.

The price variance always equals the total flexible budget variance for the total fixed overhead

$$\text{Total flexible budget variance for fixed factory overhead} = \text{price variance} + \text{quantity variance}$$

$$\text{Total flexible budget variance for fixed factory overhead} = \text{price variance} + \$0$$

$$= \text{price variance}$$

Most likely, the total fixed costs shown in Exhibit 24-11 are not represented by merely one item. Instead there are probably numerous fixed costs (depreciation, part of the utilities, salaries, property taxes, etc.) making up the total. For control purposes, it would be necessary to calculate price variances for each of the different fixed costs, prior to determining their causes.

The reasons for the fixed overhead price variance

The reason we have price variances is simply that we spent more or less than we expected to. It could be that top management decides to reward a department manager with a bonus in addition to his fixed salary, for outstanding performance during the current period. It could be that depreciation was different than predicted due to an unexpected sale of depreciable assets or because of a change in the method of depreciation. Or it might be that the county decreases property tax rates or begins to assess property taxes on an amount closer to market value.

The product costs for fixed overhead do not come from column three

In our discussion of direct materials, direct labor, and variable overhead, we pointed out that the third column in the performance report served two purposes:

1. For control purposes, it is the flexible budget, based on the standard hours allowed, that we use to determine the quantity variance and the flexible budget variance.

2. For product costing purposes, it is the amount of standard costs assigned to units produced.

Does column 3 also serve these same two purposes for fixed factory overhead? No, it does not—although we do use it to help control operations by getting a flexible budget variance, we do not use it for product costing.

Fixed Factory Overhead and Product Costing

If budgeted costs were product costs then the per unit cost would fluctuate dramatically

Let's assume for a moment that we do use column 3 in Exhibit 24-11—the budgeted fixed factory overhead—for product costing. This means that we will assign (or apply) the $15,000 to the 12,500 units produced, resulting in a cost per unit of $1.20:

$$\$15,000 \div 12,500 \text{ units} = \underline{\$1.20}/\text{unit}$$

Now let's see what the cost per unit would be if only 8,000 units were produced, or, if as many as 20,000 units were produced:

$$\$15,000 \div 8,000 = \$1.875/\text{unit for 8,000 units}$$

$$\$15,000 \div 20,000 = \$.750/\text{unit for 20,000 units}$$

Depending on the number of units produced, the fixed overhead per unit can fluctuate quite a bit. And, if you remember from our discussion of factory overhead on pages 797–801 of Chapter 20 on job order costing, when the overhead costs per unit fluctuate dramatically we may, as a consequence, have meaningless monthly income statements.

For product costing we calculate a predetermined fixed overhead rate

We discussed overhead rates first in Chapter 20

A Predetermined Rate for Fixed Factory Overhead   So, what do we do? How do we assign fixed factory overhead to production? We can find the answers to these questions by once again referring back to Chapter 20, where we are reminded that we need to get a predetermined overhead rate for fixed factory overhead, and assign that unchanging rate to the units produced (or hours used in production) in each month. We will calculate this rate at the beginning of the year, and we will use it only for product costing—we will not use it to calculate a price or a quantity variance.

If you look back at page 800 in Chapter 20, you'll see that we got a predetermined overhead rate in the following manner:

$$\frac{\text{Predetermined factory}}{\text{overhead rate}} = \frac{\text{estimated overhead for the year}}{\text{estimated activity for the year}}$$

Although we will use basically the same formula in this chapter, we will make the following changes:

1. We will use the formula only to calculate a rate for fixed factory overhead, since we have already discussed how we get a rate for variable overhead.

2. The numerator of the overhead rate in Chapter 20 related to what the actual overhead costs were expected or estimated to be; we will now be interested in what the overhead costs "should be." Therefore, instead of calling the numerator *estimated overhead for the year,* we will use the term *budgeted fixed overhead for the year.*

Normal activity is the denominator of the fixed overhead rate calculation

3. We will now refer to the denominator of the formula for calculating a fixed overhead rate as **normal activity.** Normal activity may be a prediction of activity for a single year, or it may be a prediction of average activity over a period of 4 or 5 years.

With these changes, our formula for the predetermined rate for fixed factory overhead is:

$$\text{Predetermined fixed}\atop\text{factory overhead rate} = \frac{\text{budgeted fixed factory overhead for the year}}{\text{normal activity}}$$

Assume that the budgeted fixed overhead for the year for Underhill Company is $180,000 ($15,000 per month for 12 months); the normal activity in units is 180,000; and the standard hours allowed is 2 hours per unit.

In most standard cost systems, normal activity is measured in terms of "standard hours." Therefore, the first thing we need to do is to convert normal activity measured in units to normal activity measured in standard hours:

$$180,000 \text{ units} \times 2 \text{ hr/unit} = 360,000 \text{ standard hours of normal activity}$$

Next, we calculate the fixed overhead rate per standard hour:

The rate: using annual costs and activity

$$\text{Predetermined fixed overhead}\atop\text{rate per standard hour} = \frac{\$180,000}{360,000 \text{ standard hours of normal activity}}$$

Fixed Factory Overhead Applied   Now that we have a fixed overhead rate per standard hour of $.50, we can assign fixed factory overhead to the 12,500 units produced in January. We do this by multiplying $.50 per standard hour times the standard hours allowed to produce these units. For 12,500 units, the standard hours allowed are 25,000 (12,500 × 2 hours per unit)—just like they were for direct labor and variable overhead—and the fixed overhead assigned to production (called "fixed overhead applied") is:

The applied is standard hours × standard rate

$$\text{25,000 standard}\atop\text{hours allowed} \times \text{\$.50 per}\atop\text{standard hour} = \$12,500 \text{ fixed overhead applied}$$

In order to integrate the fixed overhead applied into the multi-column analysis, we

EXHIBIT 24-12
Four-Column Analysis for Fixed Factory Overhead.
Column 4 is the fixed overhead applied, which we need only for product costing. We still use the first three columns to aid in control. The difference in the budget and the applied is the volume variance.

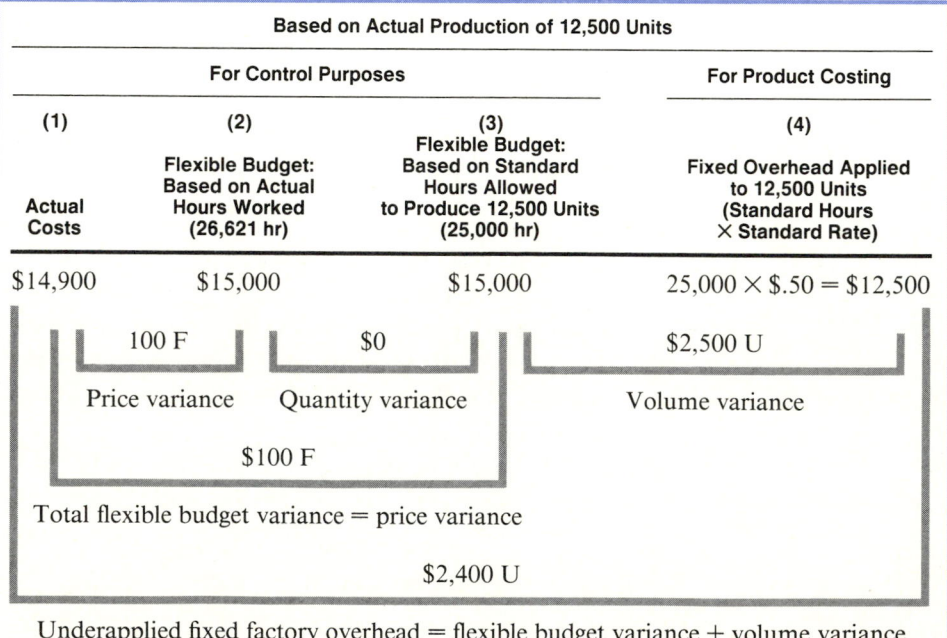

Based on Actual Production of 12,500 Units			
For Control Purposes			For Product Costing
(1)	(2)	(3)	(4)
Actual Costs	Flexible Budget: Based on Actual Hours Worked (26,621 hr)	Flexible Budget: Based on Standard Hours Allowed to Produce 12,500 Units (25,000 hr)	Fixed Overhead Applied to 12,500 Units (Standard Hours × Standard Rate)
$14,900	$15,000	$15,000	25,000 × $.50 = $12,500
	100 F	$0	$2,500 U
	Price variance	Quantity variance	Volume variance
	$100 F		
Total flexible budget variance = price variance			
$2,400 U			
Underapplied fixed factory overhead = flexible budget variance + volume variance			

need to use four columns instead of the three that we have been using. Look now at Exhibit 24-12, which has four columns, and notice how it is exactly the same as Exhibit 24-11, except that column 4 — the fixed overhead applied — has been added.

We are introducing a new variance in Exhibit 24-12 — the *fixed overhead volume variance.* It is the difference between:

1. The fixed overhead budgeted of $15,000 in column 3 — which is the amount that *should* be incurred during January's production; and

2. The fixed overhead applied of $12,500, in column 4 — which is the amount we assign (apply) to the units produced, based on a predetermined fixed overhead rate.

The volume variance (also called the idle capacity variance) of $2,500 means that we have *applied* fewer dollars to the units that were produced, than we *budgeted* to spend during the month.[2]

Since the fixed overhead applied of $12,500 is less than the actual costs of $14,900, the difference of $2,400 in Exhibit 24-12 is the amount of underapplied fixed factory overhead. This is made up of two parts: the $100 F flexible budget variance and the $2,500 U volume variance.

Frequency of Variance Investigation

The formal performance reports and spotlighting of variances displayed in this chapter are prepared each month in summary form. For these reports to be meaningful and helpful, significant variances must be investigated promptly and corrective actions put into effect as soon as possible. For direct materials and direct labor, this means tracing variances to responsibility centers as they occur on an hourly or daily basis. For factory overhead, it would be both impractical and impossible to attempt to exert control so frequently. First of all, the individual overhead cost items are not significant enough in amount to justify the costs of such a control system. Second, as we discussed in an earlier section, the expected relationships between overhead costs and production activity may be valid over long periods of time but not for periods as short as a day — much less an hour. Therefore, control of overhead will likely be performed over no shorter period of time than a month.

Materiality and Variance Investigation

Although we discussed the concept of *management by exception* in the Overview chapter, we need to mention it again at this time. The term means that all material ("material" in the sense of "significant" or "meaningful") variances are to be spotlighted on the performance report, so only those variances warranting evaluation will be investigated. The emphasis is placed on the word "material," for if the variances are insignificant in amount, not only might the causes never be determined but the benefits to the firm of eliminating the variances could not outweigh the costs of investigation and corrective action.

Volume Variances
The volume variance is the difference in columns 3 and 4

Why do we have a volume variance?

Over- or underapplied fixed overhead = total flexible budget variance + volume variance

The more timely the better

It only makes sense to evaluate significant variances

---

[2] Another way to calculate the volume variance is with the following formula:

$$\text{Fixed overhead volume variance} = \left(\text{standard hours allowed} - \text{normal activity in hours}\right) \times \text{fixed overhead rate per hour}$$

$$= (25{,}000 \text{ hr} - 30{,}000 \text{ hr}) \times \$.50 \text{ per hour} = \$2{,}500 \text{ U}$$

Because we operated at 5,000 hours below normal capacity, and for each of these 5,000 hours we failed to apply the $.50 rate, as a result we applied $2,500 less to production than we budgeted for the period.

Just how do we determine if a variance is material? There is no perfect answer, but there are several approaches that we might be able to take:

1. Hunch — managers may feel that they can intuitively detect when a process is out of control and requires investigation. This approach is not considered theoretically valid.

2. Absolute amounts — a fixed dollar amount is set. If the variance exceeds that amount it is investigated.

3. Percentage of standard — a percentage, such as 10%, is decided upon. If the variance is greater than this percentage of the standard, it is investigated.

4. Statistical control limits — boundaries can be set above and below the standard representing an allowable number of standard deviations away from the standard. This approach is based on a belief that results that fall within the control limits are caused by random influences for which no cause can be determined. Results falling outside the limits are considered to be due to systematic and determinable causes and should be investigated.

DO STANDARD COSTS FUEL INFLATION?

The "ratchett effect" is a term economists use to describe the tendency of prices to climb higher and higher, resisting the downward pressures of the market place (even in times of low demand) and refusing to return to former levels even if the cost elements that apparently caused the rise . . . have done so.

What causes the ratchett effect? The budgetary process and the financial control systems of American business must take a share of the blame. . . .

How can a financial control system encourage higher costs? It does so by allowing cost increases to generate favorable variances. Here is how this comes about.

In their planning, companies project expected rates of increases in costs. Then they budget the expected increases.

In 1974, as a plant manager for Rockwell International, I was told by my division headquarters to budget an 8% increase in materials prices for 1975. I did so and the new budget, once approved, was used to establish our plant's standard costs for 1975.

As a result I got gold stars all year for a favorable purchase price variance because I was able to buy raw materials at only 6% above the previous year's costs. I was motivated by the variance reports not so much to force suppliers to hold their price level as to prevent them from increasing them beyond 8%.

We got increases, perhaps because we planned them. At any rate, we no doubt resisted them less because our variance reports showed as favorable any cost increases less than those planned. Spread this experience to the entire private sector and the result is an appalling effect on inflation. Bigger budgeted increases lead to higher toleration of cost increases which lead to more inflation and still larger budgeted cost increases. . . .

Nowadays, when the standard cost line takes a quantum leap ahead every year, many managers are "achieving" favorable cost variances every year. Are they better managers than those of the 1960s? No, their grading scale is inflating faster than their costs.

The cure for this industrial gradeflation is fairly simple: let standard costs stand for at least three years. I will argue with those that insist that this cure will lead to unrealistic standards. Standard costs are what management feels costs should be, not what management fears they may become.

CHAPTER SUMMARY

Accountants prepare performance reports to help managers control their operations. Within a *performance report,* actual results are compared to budgeted results and the differences are spotlighted for investigation. A performance report should use a *flexible budget* rather than the master budget.

The master budget is a *static budget;* that is, it is an "inflexible budget" prepared before a period begins for a single unchanging level of expected activity. The flexible budget can be prepared for various levels of activity, one of which is the activity that actually takes place during a period. Comparing actual results to a static budget does not help a manager tell if production was operated efficiently or not. Since a flexible budget is prepared for the level of activity that has just taken place, it provides more meaningful information in the performance report; that is, the manager can tell if the activities were or were not performed efficiently.

In the performance report a flexible budget can either be an estimate of what the actual costs were expected to be or an estimate of what the costs should have been. *Standard costs* are carefully predetermined estimates of what costs should be or should have been. When standard costs are used with flexible budgets, the performance report provides an even better measure of comparison. Rather than merely comparing actual costs to what costs were expected to be, standards provide a comparison to what the costs should have been. Standard costs are used not only for controlling performance; they can also be used for (1) building better master budgets and (2) product costing.

For each variable production cost, there is a *price standard* and *quantity standard.* If actual costs differ from standard costs, there will be a *price variance* and a *quantity variance.* The sum of the price variance and the quantity variance is the *total flexible budget variance.* The price variance is calculated for direct materials, direct labor, and variable overhead in the following manner:

$$\text{Price variance} = \text{actual quantity} \times \begin{array}{c} \text{difference between} \\ \text{actual and standard} \\ \text{costs per unit of} \\ \text{input} \end{array}$$

And the quantity variance is calculated as follows:

$$\text{Quantity variance} = \begin{array}{c} \text{difference between} \\ \text{actual quantity used} \\ \text{and standard} \\ \text{quantity allowed} \end{array} \times \begin{array}{c} \text{standard} \\ \text{cost per} \\ \text{unit of} \\ \text{input} \end{array}$$

The price variance for fixed overhead is simply the difference between the actual costs and the budgeted costs. There will never be a quantity variance for fixed overhead.

There will be a variance for fixed factory overhead that we do not have for any other cost; this is the *fixed overhead volume variance.* The volume variance is the difference between the budgeted fixed overhead and the fixed overhead applied. The fixed overhead applied is found by multiplying the predetermined fixed overhead rate (budgeted fixed overhead ÷ normal activity) times the standard hours allowed.

Management by exception means that we should only investigate significant variances. We can use several approaches to determine if a variance is significant. These approaches include: (1) hunch, (2) an absolute amount, (3) a percentage of standard, and (4) statistical control limits.

IMPORTANT TERMS USED IN THIS CHAPTER

Controllable cost A cost that can be significantly influenced by a manager of a responsibility center during a given period of time. (page 954)

Currently attainable standards Standards that allow for realistic amounts of normal inefficiencies. (page 962)

Effectiveness A measure of whether or not objectives were attained; determined by comparing actual output to the original goals. (page 957)

Efficiency A measure of the relationship of inputs to outputs; a determination of how well a company controls its inputs to generate outputs. We compare the actual inputs (direct materials, direct labor, and factory overhead) to what we expected them to be based on the actual output (the finished unit). (page 957)

Fixed overhead price variance The difference between the actual fixed overhead cost and the budgeted fixed overhead cost. Also called the controllable variance or the spending variance. (page 976)

Fixed overhead volume variance The difference between the budgeted fixed overhead and the applied fixed overhead (where the applied is the standard hours allowed × standard fixed overhead rate per hour). (page 979)

Flexible budget A prediction of costs at various levels of activity, based on a knowledge of how costs relate to changes in activity. Once we know what activity might be in the future or was in the past, we can estimate the costs at that level of activity. (page 957)

Ideal standards Standards representing what it should cost to produce a unit under perfect conditions. (page 961)

Labor price variance The actual hours worked multiplied by the difference between the actual wage rate paid and the standard wage rate. Also known as a labor rate variance. (page 968)

Labor quantity variance The difference between the actual hours worked and the standard hours allowed, multiplied by the standard wage rate. Also called the labor efficiency variance. (page 969)

Materials price variance For a particular direct material, the actual quantity purchased multiplied by the difference between the actual cost per unit of input and the standard cost per unit of input. (page 964)

Materials quantity variance For a particular direct material, the difference in the actual quantity used and standard quantity allowed, multiplied by the standard cost per input used. Sometimes called the materials usage variance. (page 965)

Normal activity The level of activity used in the denominator of the calculation for the predetermined fixed overhead rate. (page 977)

Price standard The dollar amount that should be paid for each of the inputs needed for production (e.g., a cost per pound or a rate per hour). (page 962)

Price variance A variance that results whenever the actual price paid and the standard price allowed for a unit of input differ. (page 962)

Quantity standard The amount of each input that should be used to produce a unit (such as the required number of pounds per unit or hours per unit). (page 962)

Quantity variance A variance that results when the actual quantity of inputs used differs from the standard quantity allowed for the units actually produced. (page 962)

Responsibility accounting The process within an organization of: (1) designating the responsibility centers; (2) delegating authority to individuals within each responsibility center; (3) preparing budgets, accumulating actual results and preparing performance reports for responsibility centers; and (4) holding the individuals with authority responsible for their actions. (page 953)

Responsibility center An area of activity over which an individual has been delegated the authority to plan and control the activities and has been assigned responsibility for the activities. (page 953)

Standard costs Carefully predetermined estimates of what costs should be or should have been. (page 960)

Standard hours allowed The labor hours that should have been worked to make the units that were produced during the period. (page 969)

Standard quantity allowed The quantity of direct materials that should have been used to make the units produced during the period. (page 965)

Static budget A budget that is based on a single and unchanging level of predicted activity. Master budgets are static budgets. (page 956)

Time and motion studies A method used by engineers to determine labor quantity standards. (page 968)

Total flexible budget variance The sum of the price variance and the quantity variance for any predicted cost item. (page 962)

Variable overhead price variance The actual hours worked multiplied by the difference between the actual and standard costs per hour. Sometimes referred to as the variable overhead spending variance. (page 971)

Variable overhead quantity variance The difference between the actual hours worked and the standard hours allowed, multiplied by the standard variable overhead cost per hour. Also known as the variable overhead efficiency variance. (page 971)

QUESTIONS

1. What is the difference between a *static budget* and a *flexible budget?*

2. Distinguish *flexible budgets* from *standard costs.*

3. Why shouldn't the master budget be compared to actual results in the performance report when the efficiency of a responsibility center is being evaluated?

4. Define *responsibility accounting.*

5. Distinguish *responsibility* from *blame.*

6. Discuss how to determine if costs are controllable or noncontrollable.

7. All variable costs are controllable and all fixed costs are noncontrollable. Do you agree? Explain.

8. Discuss why it would be preferable to compare the actual results for the current period to standard costs rather than to the actual costs of the previous period.

9. Define the term *standard cost,* and list three uses for standard costs.

10. How can a manager determine if a variance is material enough to warrant investigation?

11. What is the difference in the concepts of effectiveness and efficiency?

12. Is it possible for a responsibility center to be effective but not efficient? Explain.

13. Which type of standards do you feel will better motivate employees toward company goals? Ideal or currently attainable? Explain.

14. Define *ideal* and *currently attainable standards.*

15. Define what is meant by a *price variance*. A *quantity variance*.

16. The purchasing agent should be blamed for all price variances. Do you agree? Explain.

17. Who should be held responsible for the extra production costs caused by a rush sales order? Explain.

18. Why is there no quantity variance for fixed overhead?

19. The accountant is solely responsible for the development of standards used in a standard cost system. Discuss why you feel this statement is correct or incorrect.

20. Fixed overhead applied represents the amount of fixed overhead that should have been incurred during a period of time. Comment.

21. Explain why a department might have a fixed overhead volume variance.

EXERCISES

Exercise 24-1
Analysis of variance for direct materials

On January 1, 2,000 units were budgeted for production. During the month, 3,800 gallons of direct materials were purchased for $6.25 per gallon and 3,500 gallons were used in the production of 2,400 units. The standards for direct materials were $1\frac{1}{2}$ gallons per unit at $6.00 per gallon.

Compute the price, quantity, and total flexible budget variances for direct materials. Indicate with a U or an F if the variance is unfavorable or favorable.

(Check figure: Price variance = $950 U)

Exercise 24-2
Analysis of variance for direct labor and variable overhead

The Howsman Hose Company makes a product expected to require 6 hours to produce. The standard direct labor and variable overhead rates per hour are $2.50 and $1.25, respectively. During January, 600 units were produced although 500 units had been budgeted. The actual conversion costs were:

Direct labor . . . . $7,840 (3,200 hours)
Variable overhead $4,160

Determine the price, quantity, and total flexible budget variances for each of the conversion costs. Indicate with a U or an F if the variances are unfavorable or favorable.

(Check figure: Labor quantity variance = $1,000 F)

Exercise 24-3
Calculating variances for direct materials and direct labor

Spartacus Company produces vitamins and uses standards to help control its operations. During January, the 10,000 cases budgeted for production were actually produced. Purchases and usage of direct materials were 3,200,000 ounces at a cost of $.14 per ounce. The direct labor incurred for January was 4,850 hours at $10.25 per hour.

The standards per case are as follows (for direct materials and direct labor):

Direct materials: 300 ounces at $.15 per ounce = $45.00 per case
Direct labor: $\frac{1}{2}$ hour at $10.00 per hour = $5.00 per case

Determine the price, quantity, and total flexible budget variances for direct materials and direct labor. Indicate whether each variance is favorable (F) or unfavorable (U).

(Check figure: Direct materials flexible budget variance = $2,000 F)

Exercise 24-4
Determining unknowns from a performance report

During August 1988, the Skibinski Corporation produced 10,500 units, exactly the same as what had been budgeted for the month. The standards that Skibinski uses to help control production are as follows:

Direct materials: 2 pounds per unit at $1.75 per pound
Direct labor: $4\frac{1}{2}$ hours per unit at $4.50 per hour

During August, Skibinski purchased and used the same quantity of raw materials. The performance report for August spotlighted the following variances:

Direct materials:	
Price variance	$ 5,000 F
Quantity variance.	1,750 F
Direct labor:	
Price variance	$25,000 U
Quantity variance.	12,375 U

Determine the following:

a. The actual pounds purchased and used

(Check figure: 20,000)

b. The actual price paid per pound
c. The actual hours worked
d. The actual rate paid per hour

(Check figure: $5.00)

e. The total flexible budget variances for direct materials and direct labor

Exercise 24-5

Distinguishing effectiveness from efficiency

The Watson Company produces a hair product called Greasy Adult Stuff and uses a standard cost system. The predetermined standards per case for direct labor are $\frac{1}{2}$ hour at $7.00 per hour. The cases produced during January were 100, which was 20 less than the cases budgeted. The actual costs for January were $420 (56 hours). The product is sold at a price to contribute $5 per case.

Determine dollar measures of the company's: **(a)** effectiveness, and **(b)** efficiency for January.

Exercise 24-6

Determining the budgeted units for an ineffective month

The Waikiki Hula Skirt Company produced 5,000 boxes during the month, spending $151,000 of variable production costs. The sales price and standard variable costs per box were:

Sales price	$60
Direct materials	$10
Direct labor	12
Variable overhead	8
Variable selling	4

Waikiki earned $5,200 less profit than originally predicted, due to producing and selling fewer units than budgeted.

How many units were budgeted for the month?

(Check figure: 5,200 units)

Exercise 24-7

Determining the variances for fixed overhead

Schleman Faucets, which produces washerless faucets, determined that the standard time to produce a faucet is 30 minutes.

During March, Schleman produced 80,000 faucets, which was 40,000 faucets below the average monthly normal activity.

Schleman budgeted its fixed costs to be $60,000 per month, but actually incurred $56,000 during March.

Determine the price variance, quantity variance, and volume variance for fixed overhead.

(Check figure: Volume variance = $20,000 U)

Exercise 24-8

Analyzing fixed overhead

At the beginning of the year, Harvey Electrical Products budgeted its annual fixed costs to be $360,000 ($30,000 per month). During the first month of the year, the actual fixed costs were $33,000.

In addition, Harvey's standard cost system specified that 2 hours be used per unit. During January, 6,600 hours were employed to produce 3,000 units.

The normal activity for Harvey is 30,000 units per year.

Calculate the following variances for Harvey Electrical:

a. Fixed overhead price variance
b. Fixed overhead quantity variance
c. Fixed overhead flexible budget variance
d. Fixed overhead volume variance
e. Fixed overhead over- (or under)applied

For each variance, specify whether it is unfavorable (U) or favorable (F).

Exercise 24-9
Working backward to get unknowns

The Willjack Company produces pennants for all the teams in the SASL (South American Soccer League). Willjack budgeted $400,000 of fixed overhead for 1988, but had the following actual results for the year:

Fixed overhead incurred $425,000
Standard fixed overhead applied (based on 105,000 standard hours allowed). .   420,000

The standard time allowed per case of pennants was 4 hours; and the actual hours incurred in 1988 were 111,000.

Determine each of the following based on the facts given above.

a. What was the standard fixed overhead rate for Willjack?
b. How many units were produced during 1988?
c. What is Willjack's normal activity (in hours)?

Exercise 24-10
Evaluating variable and fixed factory overhead

Lindsay Company uses standard costs and flexible budgets for control and product costing. Its standards for conversion costs are as follows:

Direct labor. . . . . 3 hours per unit at $4 per hour
Variable overhead . . . . 3 hours per unit at $2 per hour

Fixed overhead:
  Budgeted $150,000
  Applied . . . . 3 hours per unit at $1 per hour

During December, 40,000 units were produced and the actual results were:

Actual hours worked . . . . 125,000 hours

Actual overhead costs:
  Variable. $255,000
  Fixed.   156,000

Calculate the price variance, quantity variance, and flexible budget variance for variable overhead. In addition, calculate the price variance, flexible budget variance, and volume variance for fixed overhead.

(Check figure: Volume variance = $30,000 U)

PROBLEMS
Set A

Problem A24-1
Preparing flexible budgets prior to and after production is completed

Talavera Company manufactures track shoes and utilizes flexible budgets and standard costs to control its operations. The master budget for October's expected production of 60,000 units is shown at the top of page 987. All the costs are variable.

	Master Budget
Direct labor.	$120,000
Supplies	6,000
Utilities	3,000
	$129,000

Required

1. Prepare flexible budgets for 45,000, 54,000, and 66,000 units of production.

(Check figure: Total costs for 45,000 units = $96,750)

2. The actual units produced were 75,000. Prepare a performance report if the actual costs were:

	Actual Costs
Direct labor	$147,000
Supplies.	9,000
Utilities	3,900
	$159,900

The report should include three columns for each cost: (1) actual costs, (2) flexible budget, and (3) total flexible budget variance.

Problem A24-2
Preparing flexible budgets

Referring to Problem A24-1, assume that the standard hours allowed per unit are 2.

Required

1. List the standard costs per unit from the previous problem.
2. List the standard costs per hour.

(Check figure: Direct labor = $1.00)

3. Prepare flexible budgets for 105,000, 120,000, and 135,000 hours.

(Check figure: Total costs at 105,000 hours = $112,875)

4. If the standard and actual hours for the month were 150,000 and 156,000 hours, respectively, prepare a performance report with six columns for each cost: (1) actual costs, (2 and 3) two flexible budgets, (4) price variance, (5) quantity variance, and (6) total flexible budget variance.
5. Compare the results from part (4) in this problem to those from part (2) of the previous problem.

Problem A24-3
Determining variances for all production costs

Standard costs for Flying High Flagpole Company have recently been developed by the company controller with the help of a management consulting firm. They are the following:

Direct materials: 100 pounds per flagpole at $.05 per pound = $5.00 per flagpole
Direct labor: 1 hour per flagpole at $2.00 per hour = $2.00 per flagpole
Variable overhead: 1 hour per flagpole at $1.00 per hour = $1.00 per flagpole
Fixed overhead: $12,000 per month

During December, 1,200 flagpoles were budgeted for production (which was also the normal activity for the month), but only 1,000 were produced. The actual results related to this production were as follows:

Direct materials: 104,000 pounds purchased at $.045 per pound; 110,000 pounds used
Direct labor: 1,120 hours at $2.075 per hour
Variable overhead: $1,140
Fixed overhead: $12,850

Required   Compute the individual and total flexible budget variances for each production cost. Indicate if each variance is favorable or unfavorable. Also determine the volume variance for fixed factory overhead.

(Check figure: Materials price variance = $520 F)

Problem A24-4
Calculating variances for the prime costs: two materials and two labor operations

The Barge Corporation brews a beer from nuclear power plant river water that glows in the dark. Production requires the use of two materials and two labor operations. The standards for these prime costs are as follows:

	Quantity	Price
Material A	3 lb/barrel	$2/lb
Material B	10 gal/barrel	$3/gal

	Operation	
	1	2
Direct labor:		
Hours per barrel	2	1
Rate per hour	$4.00	$6.00

During the period, 25,000 barrels were finished. Purchases totaled 100,000 pounds ($2.15 per pound) for material A and 200,000 gallons ($2.95 per gallon) for material B. The pounds and gallons used in production were 78,000 and 240,000, respectively.

The direct labor costs for the period were:

	Operation	
	1	2
Total hours	51,000	26,500
Rate per hour	$3.75	$6.10

Required   Compute all individual and total variances for: **(1)** each direct material, and **(2)** each direct labor operation.

(Check figure: Direct labor price variance for operation 1 = $12,750 F
and for operation 2 = $2,650 U)

Problem A24-5
Figuring out the unknowns based on a partial performance report

Frazier Pool Supplies produces pumps for pool filtering systems, and uses standard costs and flexible budgets to help control its operations. At the end of August, the chief cost accountant, Clara Williams, prepared the production report shown at the top of page 989. Read it carefully and then answer the four questions below.

Required   1. Determine the price variance, quantity variance, and total flexible budget variance for each of the four production costs included in the performance report.
2. If the standard costs for direct labor are: 8 hours per unit at $5 per hour = $40 per unit, how many units were produced? What were the actual hours used and actual rate paid?

(Check figure: Actual rate paid = $4.737)

3. If the direct materials required are 4 pounds per unit, what were the standard pounds allowed for production and the actual pounds used? What is the standard price per pound and the actual price paid?

(Check figure: Actual pounds used = 16,800)

		Flexible Budgets	
	Actual Costs	Based on Actual Quantity	Based on Standard Quantity
Direct materials	$ 28,000	$ 28,800*	
		25,200†	$ 24,000
Direct labor.	144,000	152,000	160,000
Variable overhead.	30,800	30,400	32,000
Fixed overhead.	32,000	30,000	30,000

* Based on the amount purchased.
† Based on the amount used in production.

4. What was the standard rate per hour for variable overhead? What was the average actual rate per hour paid for variable overhead?

(Check figure: Actual rate = $1.013)

Problem A24-6

Evaluating variances for all production reports

The Nettles Corporation manufactures the bases used by the Greengrass Valley Baseball League, and controller Luci Van Pelt prepared the following master budget for 1988:

	Master Budget* (2,000 bases)
Direct materials	$ 8,000
Direct labor.	16,000
Variable overhead.	6,000
Fixed overhead.	12,000
	$42,000

* The normal activity per month is also 2,000 bases.

Quantity standards for these production costs were 4 pounds and 2 hours per unit.

During May, 9,800 pounds of direct materials were purchased and 10,400 pounds were used in the production of 2,500 units. The price paid per pound was $.95. In addition, 5,500 hours were worked and actual conversion costs were:

Direct labor.	$19,000
Variable overhead.	7,800
Fixed overhead.	11,800
	$38,600

Required   Determine the price, quantity, and total flexible budget variances for each of the production costs. Also compute the volume variance for fixed overhead. Indicate whether each variance is favorable (F) or unfavorable (U).

(Check figure: Materials quantity variance = $400 U)

Problem A24-7

Preparing income statements at the actual and budgeted levels of activity

The Melva Parachute Company budgeted 5,000 parachutes for production for August 1987. Each parachute is expected to be sold for $150. The controller expects the following costs for the month:

Variable production costs . . . . $60 per parachute
Variable selling costs . . . . $40 per parachute

Fixed production costs . . . . $200,000 per month
Fixed selling costs . . . . $40,000 per month

The company managed to produce and sell only 4,000 parachutes in August. Each one was sold for $148. The actual costs for the month were as follows:

Variable production costs $275,000
Variable selling costs.   190,000
Fixed production costs   210,000
Fixed selling costs   39,000

Required   **1.** Prepare income statements using the contribution margin format with the following five column headings:

(1)	(2)	(3)	(4)	(5)
Actual Results	**Difference**	**Flexible Budget for Units Produced**	**Difference**	**Master Budget**

[Check figure: Net income for flexible budget = ($40,000)]

2. Analyze what the difference columns (2 and 4) represent.

Set B

Problem B24-1
Preparing flexible budgets before production and after production is finished

The Duda Company manufactures tape measures and uses flexible budgets and standard costs to control its operations. Given below is the master budget for December's expected production:

	Master Budget (20,000 units)
Direct labor	$60,000
Supplies	4,000
Utilities.	2,000
Rent.	1,200
	$67,200

Required   **1.** Prepare flexible budgets for 17,000, 21,000, and 25,000 units of production. (All costs except rent are variable.)

(Check figure: Total costs for 17,000 units = $57,300)

2. The actual units produced during December were 19,000, and the actual costs incurred were:

Direct labor.	$55,100
Supplies	3,840
Utilities	1,920
Rent	1,400
	$62,260

Prepare a performance report. The report should include three columns for each cost: (1) actual costs, (2) flexible budget, and (3) flexible budget variance.

Problem B24-2

Preparing flexible budgets for the actual hours and for the standard hours allowed

Referring to the previous problem, assume that the standard hours allowed per unit are 6.

Required

1. List the standard costs per unit from the previous problem.
2. Compute and list the standard costs per hour.

(Check figure: Direct labor = $.50 per hour)

3. Prepare flexible budgets for 100,000, 120,000, and 130,000 hours.

(Check figure: total for 100,000 hours = $56,200)

4. If the standard and actual hours for the month were 114,000 and 117,000 hours, respectively, prepare a performance report having six columns for each cost: (1) actual costs, (2 and 3) two flexible budgets, (4) the price variance, (5) the quantity variance, and (6) the flexible budget variance.

Problem B24-3

Determining variances for all production costs

Sirrock Company manufactures leather belts, and uses standard costs to assist in the control and product costing of its operations. The standard costs of producing a leather belt are:

Direct materials: 3 pounds per belt at $2.00 per pound = $6.00 per belt
Direct labor: 2 hours per belt at $5.00 per hour = $10.00 per belt
Variable overhead: 2 hours per belt at $.50 per hour = $1.00 per belt
Fixed overhead: $5,000 per month

During February, 1,250 belts were budgeted for production (which was also the average monthly normal activity), but 1,000 belts were actually produced. The actual results for February were as follows:

Direct materials:	
3,500 lb were purchased (3,300 lb were used)	$7,350
Direct labor:	
1,900 hr were worked.	9,405
Variable overhead	1,140
Fixed overhead	5,200

Required Compute the individual and total variances for each production cost. Indicate if each variance is favorable or unfavorable.

(Check figure: Direct labor quantity variance = $500 F and fixed overhead volume variance = $1,000)

Problem B24-4

Analyzing two direct materials and two labor operations

The Carter Bottling Company produces a product that tastes exactly like beer, but has no alcohol or caffeine and very few calories. The key difference in its beer is the substitution of soybeans for barley. Information concerning its raw materials during May 1989 is as follows:

	Hopz	Soybeans
Standards	2 lb/case @ $.50/lb	1 lb/case @ $3/lb
Actual results:		
Purchased	18,000 lb @ $.60/lb	10,500 lb @ $2.70/lb
Used	19,500 lb	10,333 lb

Information concerning the labor operations is given on page 992.

	Operation 1	Operation 2
Standards....................	$\frac{1}{2}$ hr/case @ $7.00/hr	1 hr/case @ $4.00/hr
Actual results	4,950 hr @ $7.50/hr	10,500 hr @ $3.90/hr

The cases produced during February numbered 10,000.

Required   Determine all individual and total variances for **(1)** each raw material and **(2)** each labor operation.

(Check figure: Direct materials price variances: Hopz = $1,800 U and soybeans = $3,150 U)

Problem B24-5
Calculating the unknown from a partial performance report

An incomplete performance report is given below for the Reflecto Wall Mirror Company:

	Actual Costs	Flexible budget	
		Based on Actual Quantity	Based on Standard Quantity
Direct materials	$25,000	$30,000*	
		27,600†	$27,000
Direct labor......................	40,375	38,000	36,000
Variable overhead...............	7,125	7,600	7,200
Fixed overhead	2,000	2,300	2,300

* Based on the quantity purchased.
† Based on the quantity used.

Required   1. Determine the price variance, the quantity variance, and the total flexible budget variance for each of the four production costs shown above.
2. If the standard costs for direct labor are 3 hours per mirror at $8.00 per hour = $24 per mirror, how many mirrors were produced? What were the actual hours used and the actual labor rate paid per hour?

(Check figure: Mirrors produced = 1,500)

3. If the direct materials required are 30 pounds per mirror, what were the standard pounds allowed for production and the actual pounds used? What is the standard price per pound and the actual price paid?

(Check figure: Pounds purchased = 50,000)

4. What was the standard rate per hour for variable overhead? What was the average actual rate per hour paid for variable overhead?

(Check figure: Standard rate = $1.60 per hour)

Problem B24-6
Evaluating variances for all production costs

The Xenon Corporation manufactures the kicking tees used by the American Football League. Its controller, Danny Trivillon, prepared the following master budget for August 1988 based on anticipated production of 2,000 kicking tees (which was also the normal level of activity):

	Master Budget
Direct materials	$4,000
Direct labor	3,000
Variable overhead	1,000
Fixed overhead	500
	$8,500

Quantity standards are 2 gallons and $\frac{1}{2}$ hour per unit.

During August, 2,400 kicking tees were produced and the actual costs incurred were:

Direct materials	$6,450*
Direct labor	4,500
Variable overhead	1,200
Fixed overhead	525

* Based on the gallons purchased.

In addition, 6,000 gallons were purchased during August and 5,200 gallons were used. The actual hours needed for production were 1,400.

Required   Determine the price, quantity, and total flexible budget variances for each of the production costs. In addition, calculate the fixed overhead volume variance. Indicate whether each variance is favorable (F) or unfavorable (U).

(Check figure: Materials quantity variance = $400 U)

Problem B24-7
Preparing income statements at the actual and budgeted levels of activity

The Repass Company sells lightning surge protectors for television sets, at $18 per unit. Repass expected to produce and sell only 3,000 units during August, but was able to produce and sell 4,000 units due to a substantial increase in lightning storms in several areas of the country. The standard and actual results for the month are as follows:

	Standard	Actual
Variable manufacturing costs	$6/unit	$6.50/unit
Variable selling costs	$3/unit	$2.80/unit
Fixed manufacturing costs	$20,000/month	$20,600
Fixed selling costs	$3,000/month	$3,500

Repass' actual revenues for August were $75,000.

Required   1. Prepare income statements using the contribution margin format with the following five column headings:

Actual Results	Difference	Flexible Budget for Units Produced	Difference	Master Budget

(Check figure: Net income for middle column = $13,000)

2. Analyze the results for each of the difference columns.

Chapter 25

Relevant Information for Special Decisions

After you have finished studying this chapter, you will understand:

- What we mean by the term *relevant information*
- When it is appropriate to accept a special order
- When to drop an unprofitable product line
- How to maximize the profits in a multi-product firm
- When an organization should produce its raw materials internally rather than buy them from an outside supplier
- What we mean by a *joint product;* and what happens to the joint product at the stage in production called the *split-off point*
- How to decide if a joint product should be sold at the split-off point or processed further
- Whether to scrap or rework defective units

The profits that a firm reports in a particular year are a reflection of the decisions that its managers made in that year and in preceding years. And the decisions that managers make today will have an impact on next year's profits, and maybe on the profits for many years after that. Decisions such as the price at which to sell a product, whether to accept a special order at a price that is lower than the regular price, and whether to drop an apparently unprofitable product line, all put managers in a position of choosing between at least two, and perhaps more, alternatives. In each case the manager is expected to select the alternative that is the most profitable for the firm as a whole.

This is where the accountant comes in. The manager depends on the accountant to provide complete and pertinent information concerning each alternative. Only with all the facts can the manager make the correct choice. The information that accountants provide managers to help them make these decisions must have a special quality: The information must be *relevant.* In this chapter we will be concerned with those decisions that primarily affect the organization's short-run profit picture, and with the information that is relevant to the short-run decision alternatives. In Chapter 26, we will direct our attention to those decisions that have an impact on long-run profits.

THE CONCEPT OF RELEVANCE

Two criteria for relevance

In order for information (costs or revenue) to be ***relevant*** to a decision, the information must meet two criteria. It must (1) relate to the future, and (2) be different for each alternative being considered. Information that fails to meet either one of these two criteria is considered to be ***irrelevant.***

First, the information must relate to the future — because all decisions relate to the future. Managers are concerned with what they are going to do today and tomorrow; it is too late for them to dwell on what they could have done yesterday or last year. Since the alternatives under consideration involve possible future courses of action, the information that accountants gather should also be about the future. *The past is irrelevant.*

In order for information to be relevant, it must also be different for the alternatives being considered. Otherwise there is no quantitative basis for a decision. If the facts are the same concerning different courses of action, how can we decide if one course of action is better than any other?

Assume for a moment that you are trying to decide where you want to go to dinner, and are considering only two possibilities — McDonald's and Burger King — both of which are on University Avenue. The last time you went to McDonald's, a hamburger, fries, and a cola cost you $1.59; the same dinner cost you only $1.49 at Burger King. You've heard, however, that a hamburger, cola, and fries now costs $1.79 at McDonald's and $1.85 at Burger King. You figure that it will cost $.50 for gas no matter which place you go. Assuming that you like the meals as much at McDonald's as you do those at Burger King, where would you go for dinner in order to keep your costs as low as possible?

The key to any decision — whether it is as simple as where to go to dinner or extremely complex — is to first decide what information is relevant to the decision and what information is irrelevant. For the situation above, the only information that is relevant is the cost that you will pay today for dinner — $1.79 at McDonald's and $1.85 at Burger King. These are the only costs that both (1) relate to the future and (2) are different for the two alternatives. The amounts you paid the last time you went to dinner are irrelevant, because they relate to the past. The cost of gasoline is irrelevant, because it is the same amount whether you go to McDonald's or Burger King. Therefore, if you want to minimize the cost of dinner, go to McDonald's and save $.06 ($1.85 − $1.79).

As you might expect, the decision situations that we are going to discuss later in this chapter are a bit more complicated than the one above. However, the concept of relevance never changes — if you know the two criteria for relevance, you should be able to apply the concept to any situation. Unfortunately, some students have trouble with the concept of relevance because they confuse it with other concepts discussed earlier in the text.

Just in case you might be one of these students, let's see how you answer the following questions. Are relevant costs the same as variable costs? Must information be accurate to be relevant? Is information that relates to the past *ever* relevant? Is information that relates to the past *always* useless? The correct answer to each of these questions is definitely *no.* Therefore, if you answered *yes* to any of them, be sure to read the next three sections very carefully — because there is probably still something missing in your understanding of this important concept.

Relevance vs. Variable and Fixed Costs
Is relevant the same as variable?

A common mistake is to conclude that relevant costs and variable costs mean the same thing, or that irrelevant costs and fixed costs mean the same thing. Variable and fixed costs are defined in terms of how total costs respond to changes in activity, not in terms of whether or not the totals are different for alternative courses of action.

Variable costs can be relevant or irrelevant; fixed costs can be relevant or irrelevant. Whether or not each cost is relevant depends on the alternatives being considered. For example, assume that a firm is considering the purchase of two new machines, each having a 4-year life. Each machine produces the same product and each product requires the same amount of direct materials — $36,000 per year. Machine 1 costs $100,000 and machine 2 costs $200,000. The direct labor costs on machine 1 are much higher than those for machine 2 — $50,000 vs. $32,000 per year. The supervisor who is currently employed by the firm is capable of overseeing the operations of either machine. His annual salary is $25,000.

In this example there are both (1) relevant and irrelevant variable costs; and (2) relevant and irrelevant fixed costs, as shown below:

	Relevant Cost	Irrelevant Cost
Variable cost	Direct labor of $50,000 vs. $32,000 per year	Direct materials of $36,000 per year
Fixed cost	Depreciation of $25,000 per year ($100,000 ÷ 4 years) vs. $50,000 per year ($200,000 ÷ 4 years)	Supervisor's salary of $25,000 per year

Although the direct materials and supervisor's salary do relate to the future, they are irrelevant because they will be the same amount regardless of which machine is purchased. Both direct labor and depreciation relate to the future and are different for the alternatives being considered — therefore, they are both relevant.

Relevance vs. Usefulness
Is the past always irrelevant?

The first of two criteria for relevance is that the information must relate to the future. Since information about the past does not meet this requirement, all past information is irrelevant. Past (or historical) information relates to events that have already occurred — there is nothing that can be done to change that fact, regardless of the alternatives being considered.

Does the fact that past information is always irrelevant also mean that past information is always useless? Definitely not! Being irrelevant does not necessarily mean being useless.

Information about the past can help us to predict the future. In this way the past is useful even though it isn't relevant. Assume that we are trying to predict the labor costs for one of two new projects. Last year the labor costs were $40,000 (8,000 hours at $5 per hour) for an old project. We know that the labor rates are going to increase by 20% and that the labor hours will be 10% less than they were in the past. The prediction of future labor costs of $43,200 (7,200 hours at $6 per hour) is relevant, as long as it is also different from the labor costs of the other project under consideration. The past labor costs (8,000 hours and a $5 rate) helped us to predict the relevant costs — they were useful, but they were not relevant.

Relevance vs. Accuracy

Relevant is not the same as accurate

Another common mistake is to confuse being accurate with being relevant. These concepts, however, are not the same. Accurate information is information that is precise or exact; relevant information is information that relates to the future and is different for the alternatives being considered.

Accuracy is indeed a desirable characteristic — we would like the information that we as accountants provide managers to be accurate. Unfortunately, that is not always possible. Since relevant information must relate to the future, it involves predictions. Predictions are estimates — and estimates are, more often than not, inexact.

If it was necessary for information to be accurate in order to be relevant, there would be very little information that accountants could give managers to help them make decisions about the future.

QUANTITATIVE VS. QUALITATIVE FACTORS

Qualitative factors are important too

When a manager makes a decision he or she needs to consider both the quantitative and the qualitative factors involved in the decision. Quantitative factors are those that can be measured with some reasonable degree of precision in dollars and cents. The fact that dropping a product line will eliminate a supervisor's salary of $20,000 is a quantitative factor.

Qualitative factors are those that cannot be expressed with a reasonable degree of precision in dollars and cents, yet may still have a significant influence on a manager's decision. For example, if a firm is considering moving its manufacturing facilities from Delaware to Mexico, a qualitative factor may be the effect on morale of the employees who are forced to move. If a firm is considering the installation of safety equipment in its mines, a qualitative factor would be the health and protection of its employees.

It's not that qualitative factors have no financial effect on a decision; it's just that the financial effect cannot be measured. Obviously, if a move to Mexico causes the employees to become disgruntled, then operating profits will be lower than they would be otherwise. However, if no one knows for sure if the move will affect morale — nor how much low morale could hurt the profits — then there is no objective way in which a manager can integrate these factors — in dollars and cents — into the analysis.

It will be up to the individual manager to assess subjectively the importance of a qualitative factor in a decision situation. Qualitative factors may be given very little weight in some situations but may be the determining factor in others.

THE RELEVANCE OF RELEVANCE TO THE BANKING INDUSTRY

"In the midst of scurrying for profits, is it possible that banks are putting the cart before the horse? Is sufficient reliable information available to support rationally current decisions and to evaluate the options facing banks? How can bankers obtain the kind of timely, relevant information needed to shift course quickly when required by economic and environmental changes? More specifically, how can bankers determine future approaches to marketing strategies, pricing policies, product mix, productivity levels and systems development?

To answer these challenges, banks must produce service/product line cost and profitability information." Unfortunately until recently banks were in the relative dark ages when it came to reliable and useful cost systems. For a variety of reasons banks found that gathering relevant cost information to assist managers in the decision process, was usually too time consuming, too difficult, and too expensive to obtain. Today however with new, improved and more efficient data processing systems,

many banks are finding it possible to significantly improve the cost accounting systems within their banks. An example is Central Bank of San Francisco.

"In 1980, the bank's senior management team obtained current information regarding the cost of transactions and the profitability of products and services. The bank had decided that it would price its products to produce a profit or, where competition prohibited flexible pricing, it would attempt to reduce expenses and increase productivity to improve profitability. Up to this point, the bank relied on general industry trends, peer group data, or the competition to set prices and measure costs. What senior management now wanted was specific relevant data about Central Bank, produced at a reasonable cost and on a timely basis."

What it got was a system that "identifies the components of costs and permits Central Bank to uncover inefficiencies and fine tune products. It also allows the bank to review transaction, product line, account

and branch productivity levels from one period to the next. Thus the impact of changes in workload, procedures, systems and training can be monitored. Central uses this information to improve its pricing, or to assist in determining how to make a product profitable. . . .

The cost system caused Central Bank to reexamine a number of its services. For example, the bank noticed that the high costs associated with its traveler's check service were higher than those of other banks utilizing the cost system. When staff analyzed the cost system's underlying documentation for traveler's checks, they found redundant controls, unnecessary dual custody and excessive transaction time. The bank reacted by reaching an agreement with its check vendor requiring changes to its procedures."

"Cost Analysis: Necessary Evil or Management Tool of the 80s?", *The Magazine of Bank Administration,* published by Bank Administration Institute, October, 1983, p. 60.

Since the accountant is involved primarily with the quantitative factors in a decision situation, the quantitative factors are the ones that we emphasize in this chapter. However, if the accountant is to be of real assistance to managers, he or she should attempt to quantify as many qualitative factors as possible, thereby reducing the amount of subjectivity in a manager's decision.

TYPES OF DECISION SITUATIONS

We will discuss six different types of decision situations. Each situation requires that a manager decide the course of action that will maximize his or her firm's short-run profits.

Managers face many more decisions in their day-to-day operations than the ones we will present; our six are merely a representative sample. However, by the time you have finished studying this chapter, you should be able to adapt what you have learned to many other decision situations as well.

The six decision situations we will discuss are:

1. The special order

2. Dropping a product line

3. Maximizing profits in a multi-product firm

4. Make or buy

5. Joint products — sell or process further

6. Scrap or rework defective units

The Special Order

The special order situation

Imagine that you are a manufacturer of volleyballs and are currently producing at 80% of full capacity. Your customers have always been exclusively American companies, but last week you were approached by a representative of the Chinese government. The Chinese are some of the finest volleyball players in the world, but they have temporarily run out of quality balls in their preparation for the 1988 Summer Olympics. They hope that you will use your idle capacity to produce a special order of volleyballs. The catch is that the price they are offering is below your regular price. You'd certainly like the business, but you'd really hate to reduce your price. What should you do?

The first thing you *shouldn't* do is to reject the offer simply because the price is lower than you would normally like it to be. You need to evaluate the offer in a great deal more depth. Manufacturers are often receptive to accepting a special order at a reduced price — but only if the conditions are right. The necessary conditions are as follows:

1. There must be excess productive capacity.

2. The order must be from a customer in a market different from the one in which the manufacturer normally sells — an unrelated market.

Idle capacity is necessary for a special order

It is important that there is excess capacity available; otherwise you would have to reduce production and sales to regular customers to make sales to one-time customers. Not only would you have to sell the same units at a lower price, but your regular customers would be forced to find other suppliers and their business might be permanently lost to the firm. It's one thing to reduce the price in order to sell units that you wouldn't otherwise sell and quite another to reject the business of a regular customer in order to accept one-time business at a lower price.

Special orders should come from a special market

Also, it is usually important that special orders be accepted only when they come from an unrelated market. You might accept the special order from the Chinese government, of whom your regular customers are probably unaware. On the other hand, you might reject the same offer from an American buyer, since your regular customers could easily learn about the reduced price you were offering a competing company and demand that similar concessions be granted to them. This could result in either reduced prices to all customers or a loss of regular customers. Either way, if you accept a special order in a related market as a temporary use of excess capacity to boost short-run profits, you may seriously affect your long-run pricing structure and long-run net income.

For this reason it is always necessary for the accountant and the manager to consider the impact that a special order might have on long-run profits, as well as the profits in the short run. As a matter of fact, this is an important consideration in all the short-run decision situations we will discuss in this chapter. To simplify matters however, we will always assume — unless we state specifically otherwise — that the long-run profit picture will not be affected by the decision to maximize short-run profits.

We will now look in depth at the special order for volleyballs for the Set and Spike Athletic Equipment Company. The facts are provided in Example 25-1.

EXAMPLE 25-1
   An example of a special order

THE SET AND SPIKE ATHLETIC EQUIPMENT COMPANY

The Set and Spike Athletic Equipment Company produces a wide range of athletic equipment, but it specializes in nets, balls, and shinguards for volleyball teams. Set and Spike normally sells its top-grade volleyball—called Olympic Gold—for $100 a box (which contains four balls). Set and Spike is currently considering a special order from the Chinese government for 1,000 boxes at $78 per box. Since the deal is quite hush-hush—only Set and Spike, the Chinese government, and the CIA are aware of it—production and sales of volleyballs to Set and Spike's regular customers will not be affected in any way. The income statement for Set and Spike, without the special order, was budgeted for 1988 as follows:

Sales (5,000 boxes)	$500,000
Cost of goods sold.	400,000
Gross margin.	$100,000
Operating expenses	110,000
Net income	($ 10,000)

The cost of goods sold includes both variable costs ($40 per box) and fixed costs ($200,000 per period). This is also true for the operating costs ($10 per box sales commission and $60,000 fixed). If the special order is accepted, Set and Spike will not pay a sales commission to its own sales representatives, but a CIA agent will receive $5,000 for arranging the deal. Should Set and Spike accept the order?

At first glance, you might be tempted to reason that the order should be rejected because the $78 price is less than the cost of producing each box:

$$\frac{\text{Cost of goods}}{\text{sold per box}} = \frac{\$400,000}{5,000 \text{ boxes}} = \$80 \text{ per box}$$

The gross margin is a negative $2 per box ($78 − $80). If a 1,000-box order is accepted, then won't the gross margin be a negative $2,000? And since the gross margin is negative, won't net income also be negative?

   We hope you do not agree with this line of reasoning, because it can lead to serious mistakes in the decisions you may make in this chapter. The fact of the matter is that the order should be accepted, because the profits for the firm can be substantially improved. You may wonder how this can be true, since the cost of goods sold per unit is greater than the sales price. The problem is that the income statement in Example 25-1 has been prepared using the traditional format—that is, sales − cost of goods sold = gross profit − operating expenses = net income.

   Included within the cost of goods sold for Set and Spike is $200,000 of fixed factory overhead. When we calculated the cost per box of $80, we concluded that each additional box would cost an additional $80 to produce. This is not true, however, because the total fixed overhead is not expected to increase with additional production—it is assumed to remain the same. Therefore the cost of goods sold will not increase by $80,000 (1,000 boxes × $80), but will instead increase by only $40,000—which is just the variable portion of cost of goods sold:

Additional variable manufacturing costs (1,000 boxes × $40).	$40,000
Additional fixed manufacturing costs	0
Additional cost of goods sold.	$40,000

So you see, the additional sales of $78,000 will be greater—not less—than the additional cost of goods sold of $40,000, by $38,000, or $38 per unit ($78 − $40).

This type of reasoning error can be a problem any time the traditional format is used. Since cost of goods sold is often mentioned on a per-unit basis, it is a simple mistake to forget that some fixed costs have gone into that per-unit calculation. It is also easy to forget that the cost of goods sold cannot be calculated by simply multiplying the average cost per unit by the number of units sold—the variable and fixed costs must be calculated separately.

Unit costs can lead you astray

Warning: Beware of unit costs—when they include a fixed portion.

The easiest way to avoid this problem is to use the ***contribution margin format*** for an income statement, which requires that variable costs and fixed costs be evaluated separately. The contribution margin format, in case you've forgotten, is as follows:

Sales
Less: Total variable costs
Equals: Total contribution margin
Less: Fixed costs
Equals: Net income

A Better Approach

We will now analyze the situation correctly, this time using the contribution margin format for the income statement. First of all we will revise the original budgeted income statement for Set and Spike given in Example 25-1:

Sales (5,000 boxes at $100 per box)		$500,000
Variable costs:		
Manufacturing (5,000 boxes at $40 per box).	$200,000	
Operating (5,000 boxes at $10 per box)	50,000	250,000
Total contribution margin (5,000 boxes at $50 per box).		$250,000
Total fixed costs:		
Manufacturing	$200,000	
Operating	60,000	260,000
Net income		($ 10,000)

Next, we will present the facts about the special order decision in a three-column decision format. As you can see in Exhibit 25-1, the first column shows Set and Spike's loss ($10,000) if we reject the order—the status quo. The second column shows Set and Spike's expected income if we accept the special order. And the third column reports the differences in columns 1 and 2—only relevant items appear in the difference column.

EXHIBIT 25-1
Contribution Margin Format to Solution.
The additional contribution margin by accepting the order ($38,000) exceeds the fixed costs ($5,000). Accept the order!

| | Alternatives | | |
	1 Reject Order	2 Accept Order	3 Difference
Sales	$500,000	$578,000	$78,000
Variable costs:			
Manufacturing	$200,000	$240,000	($40,000)
Operating—sales commissions.	50,000	50,000	—
Total variable costs	$250,000	$290,000	($40,000)
Total contribution margin	$250,000	$288,000	$38,000
Fixed costs:			
Manufacturing	$200,000	$200,000	—
Operating.	60,000	65,000	(5,000)
Total fixed costs	$260,000	$265,000	($ 5,000)
Net income	($ 10,000)	$ 23,000	$33,000

The sales are expected to increase by $78,000 (1,000 additional boxes × $78 per box), more than enough to offset the additional variable costs of $40,000 (1,000 additional boxes × $40 per box). There are no additional variable operating costs because sales commissions are not to be paid on the special order—the variable operating costs are irrelevant. The additional contribution margin of $38,000 ($78,000 − $40,000) exceeds the additional fixed operating costs (the CIA agent's fee) of $5,000, by $33,000—which is the increase in net income from accepting the special order. The fixed manufacturing costs are irrelevant because they are expected to be $200,000 with or without the special order.

As you can see, the special order should be accepted — because profits are expected to increase by $33,000.

Although we strongly recommend that you use the contribution margin format in order to minimize the likelihood of errors, this doesn't mean that we are saying that it is impossible to get the correct answer with the traditional format. As long as you properly separate the variable and fixed costs within each functional cost grouping of the traditional format, you can get the same answer as we showed in Exhibit 25-1 for the contribution margin approach.

Although the same solutions can be obtained with the traditional approach, we will use the contribution approach exclusively throughout this chapter. The contribution approach is more easily adapted to any type of analysis, and it is less likely to lead to improper conclusions such as those we made with the traditional approach.

Dropping a Product Line

Changing a firm's sales mix

Firms are referred to as ***multi-product*** firms when they sell more than a single line of products. We first introduced the idea of a multi-product firm in Chapter 22—in cost-volume-profit analysis. At that time, we defined ***sales mix*** as the proportion of total sales that is distributed to each product line. We showed how to calculate the breakeven point for a multi-product firm, and discussed the significance of a change in the sales mix on a firm's profits. In this section, we are going to talk about dropping entire product lines—decisions that can result in rather abrupt changes in the sales mix. You need to be able to determine when a product line is no longer profitable and should be eliminated.

Let's look at the situation for Gas Glow Grill Company in Example 25-2 and see if any changes are advisable for its product lines.

EXAMPLE 25-2

THE GAS GLOW GRILL COMPANY

The Gas Glow Grill Company sells three models of barbeque grills: Super Deluxe, Deluxe, and Matchless. Its income statement for 1988 showed a profit for the firm as a whole. However, one of the three product lines reported a loss as shown below:

	Super Deluxe	Deluxe	Matchless	Total
		Model		
Sales	$200,000	$240,000	$200,000	$640,000
Variable expenses (and % of total sales)	120,000 (.60)	180,000 (.75)	160,000 (.80)	460,000 (.72)
Total contribution margin (and % of total sales) . .	$ 80,000 (.40)	$ 60,000 (.25)	$ 40,000 (.20)	$180,000 (.28)
Fixed expenses .	60,000	50,000	50,000	160,000
Net income. . . .	$ 20,000	$ 10,000	($ 10,000)	$ 20,000

The controller, Neon Propane, thinks that Matchless should be dropped. Not only does it have the smallest contribution margin ratio of the three products ($40,000 ÷ $200,000 = 20%), but it is the only product line showing a loss. Neon says, "If we drop Matchless, we can improve our profits by the $10,000 loss that we eliminate."

Neon was partially right about Matchless—that is, it does have the smallest contribution margin ratio of the three product lines, and it is the only product line with a loss. Neon was wrong, however, in his conclusion—that Matchless should be dropped.

Before we explain why Neon was wrong, we want to first point out two important assumptions that we are making—assumptions that you must also make until we tell you differently. They are as follows:

Fixed costs don't change and excess capacity is needed

1. The total fixed costs are not affected by the decision and will remain the same.

2. The excess capacity will not be used in any other productive manner, such as producing more of another product line or renting it to an outsider.

The solution is really quite simple, because the only thing that changes for Gas Glow Grill if Matchless is dropped is its total contribution margin. Since Matchless has a contribution margin of $40,000, if it is dropped, the contribution margin for the entire firm will fall by $40,000. And when the contribution margin falls by $40,000 —with no change in the fixed costs—the profits will also fall by $40,000. The profits will not improve by $10,000, as Neon believed they would.

EXHIBIT 25-2
Comparative Analysis — Drop Matchless.

	Totals		
	1 Keep Matchless	2 Drop Matchless	3 Difference
Sales	$640,000	$440,000	($200,000)
Variable expenses	460,000	300,000	160,000
Total contribution margin	$180,000	$140,000	($ 40,000)
Fixed expenses	160,000	160,000	—
Net income	$ 20,000	($ 20,000)	($ 40,000)

Don't drop Matchless, because it does make a contribution to fixed costs

Is this the same conclusion that you reached when you first read the example, or did you agree with Neon Propane's reasoning for dropping the product line? Neon thought that the entire loss of $10,000 would be eliminated if Matchless were dropped by Gas Glow. For this to be true, not only would the contribution margin of $40,000 have to be eliminated, but the fixed costs of $50,000 would have to be eliminated as well. Remember, however, that we assumed that the total fixed costs aren't affected by the decision. So if Matchless is dropped, the $50,000 of fixed costs are not eliminated, but are instead distributed to Deluxe and Super Deluxe.

If you look now at the three-column format in Exhibit 25-2, you can see that the fixed costs are $160,000 whether or not Gas Glow drops Matchless. Also, notice that the profits will continue to be $20,000 if Gas Glow leaves well enough alone (column 1), but will fall to a negative $20,000 if it drops the line (column 2) — resulting in a reduction in net income of $40,000 (column 3).

Utilizing Excess Capacity

Now let's use excess capacity productively

Let's now assume a slightly more complicated situation for Gas Glow Grill Company. First, we'll assume that $20,000 of the $50,000 of fixed costs for Matchless are for a supervisor's salary that can be eliminated if the line is dropped. Second, the productive capacity that had been used for Matchless will now be used to produce additional Deluxe models, increasing the sales of Deluxe from $240,000 to $340,000. The solution to the revised example for Gas Glow is shown in Exhibit 25-3. We now see that Matchless should be dropped.

The total sales will be $540,000 if Matchless is dropped and Deluxe is expanded. This is a reduction in the total sales of $100,000. The variable expenses will also be lower — by $85,000, resulting in a reduced contribution margin for Gas Glow of $15,000. Since a product-line supervisor will be terminated, the $20,000 savings in

EXHIBIT 25-3
Comparative Totals — Drop Matchless, Produce Additional Deluxe.
By dropping Matchless and increasing Deluxe, the net effect on contribution margin is to reduce it by $15,000. The reduction in fixed costs of $20,000, however, offsets the negative contribution margin by $5,000.

	Totals		
	1 Keep Matchless	2 Drop Matchless	3 Difference
Sales	$640,000	$540,000*	($100,000)
Variable expenses	460,000	375,000†	85,000
Total contribution margin	$180,000	$165,000	($ 15,000)
Fixed expenses	160,000	140,000	20,000
Net income	$ 20,000	$ 25,000	$ 5,000

* Super Deluxe + Deluxe = $200,000 + $340,000 = $540,000.
† Super Deluxe + Deluxe = $200,000 (.60) + $340,000 (.75) = $120,000 + $255,000 = $375,000.

fixed costs is great enough to offset the reduced contribution margin. The net effect is to increase net income by $5,000.

Adding a Product Line

Another possibility that might be considered by Gas Glow Grill Company if Matchless is dropped is to add a new product line rather than expanding the production of Deluxe. However, since the analysis of this alternative is very similar to that of expanding the production of Deluxe, it is not necessary to discuss it separately.

Maximizing Profits in a Multi-Product Firm

In the previous section we discussed how the Gas Glow Grill Company tried to improve its profits by dropping and/or expanding product lines. Of the three possibilities that Gas Glow considered—(1) continue to produce and sell all three lines, (2) drop Matchless, and (3) drop Matchless and increase the sales of Deluxe—the most profitable alternative was number 3. If Matchless is dropped and the sales of Deluxe are increased, the net income should increase from $20,000 to $25,000.

Is there a maximum profit? Is there a best sales mix?

Even though $25,000 is the maximum net income for the three alternatives that were mentioned, is it also the maximum net income that Gas Glow could possibly earn? Might there be any other combination of product lines that could increase the net income above $25,000? For example, since Super Deluxe has the highest contribution margin percentage—40% (see Example 25-2)—maybe the excess capacity from dropping Matchless should be used to increase production of Super Deluxe; or maybe both Matchless and Deluxe should be dropped and the entire capacity for Gas Glow Grill should be used to produce and sell nothing but Super Deluxe.

Already we have mentioned a half-dozen possibilities, and we could probably come up with a half-dozen more. Even then, however, we might not have stumbled upon the optimum combination of product lines—the optimum *sales mix*—that would maximize the profits of Gas Glow.

Is it even possible to determine an optimum sales mix for a multi-product firm without doing exactly what we are doing now—that is, trying as many possible combinations as we can think of? Yes, it is possible, but it is necessary first to answer three important questions:

Key variables for finding best sales mix

1. What is the contribution margin per unit (or contribution margin percentage) for each product line?

2. What resources (capacity, labor, materials, customers) does the firm possess for the production and sale of its product lines?

3. What restrictions (constraints) are placed upon the use of the firm's resources in the production and sale of each product line?

Unless we find the answers to these questions, there is no way to determine an optimum sales mix for Gas Glow. At first, it might seem reasonable to conclude that all of the firm's resources would be best utilized by producing nothing but Super Deluxe—after all, it does have the highest contribution margin ratio.

Suppose, however, that when we answer questions 2 and 3 above, we find out the following facts about Super Deluxe:

The product with the best contribution margin per unit or ratio may not be the best product

1. The demand from customers for Super Deluxe is currently at a maximum.

2. It takes longer to produce Super Deluxe than either of the other models, and the total hours of machine time are limited.

3. More highly qualified laborers are required to work on Super Deluxe than the other models, and qualified laborers are scarce.

4. Super Deluxe requires a raw material that is nearly impossible to acquire in greater amounts.

Constraints are restrictions on production and sales

Each of these facts represents a restriction, or **constraint,** on Gas Glow's ability to produce and sell what at first glance appears to be its most profitable product line. Should Gas Glow shift all of its productive capacity to Super Deluxe in light of this information? Because of these constraints, it would be foolish for Gas Glow to produce and sell nothing but Super Deluxe. In fact, the constraints could be so restrictive that it might be better if Super Deluxe were not produced at all.

Maximum Profits for Gas Glow

More details for Gas Glow

Based on the original facts for Gas Glow in Example 25-2, let's assume that you are now given a more detailed set of facts related to the income statement of Gas Glow for 1988:

	Super Deluxe	Deluxe	Matchless
Sales price	$ 400	$ 240	$ 100
Variable cost per unit.	240	180	80
Contribution margin per unit.	$ 160	$ 60	$ 20
Unit sales	500	1,000	2,000
Total contribution margin.	$80,000	$60,000	$40,000
Fixed expenses	60,000	50,000	50,000
Net income	$20,000	$10,000	($10,000)

We also find out that it takes 10 hours to make one Super Deluxe; 4.8 hours for one Deluxe; and 1 hour for each Matchless. The total available production hours are 11,800.

Production constraint: hours per unit and limited total hours

For now, we are going to consider only one constraint for Gas Glow — the number of hours that it takes to produce each grill. When there is only one constraint, the solution can be derived quite simply — the solution will always be to produce and sell a single product. Do you have any idea which product it will be?

What we need to do is to convert the contribution margin per unit to a contribution margin per hour — the product with the highest contribution margin per hour will be the best.

Contribution margin per unit of the constraining factor: contribution margin per hour

$$\text{Contribution margin per hour} = \frac{\text{contribution margin per unit}}{\text{number of hours per unit}}$$

$$\text{CM per hour (Super Deluxe)} = \frac{\$160}{10 \text{ hours}} = \$16 \text{ per hour}$$

$$\text{CM per hour (Deluxe)} = \frac{\$60}{4.8 \text{ hours}} = \$12.50 \text{ per hour}$$

$$\text{CM per hour (Matchless)} = \frac{\$20}{1 \text{ hour}} = \$20 \text{ per hour}$$

Lo and behold, Matchless has the highest contribution margin per hour — and this is the product we kept wanting to dump! For every one of the 11,800 hours, Matchless contributes $20 toward the coverage of fixed costs, while Super Deluxe contributes $16 and Deluxe contributes $12.50. If the full 11,800 hours of production are used to produce only one product line, the income statements for each line would be as follows:

Maximize profits with Matchless

	Super Deluxe	Deluxe	Matchless
Contribution margin per hour	$ 16.00	$ 12.50	$ 20.00
Total hours of capacity.	11,800	11,800	11,800
Total contribution margin.	$188,800	$147,500	$236,000
Fixed costs.	160,000	160,000	160,000
Net income	$ 28,800	($ 12,500)	$ 76,000

The most profit that is possible for Gas Glow to earn is $76,000 — when Matchless is the only product that is produced and sold.

You may say, "How can this be true? Matchless looks like such a loser. Super Deluxe contributes eight times as much per unit as Matchless does — $160 vs. $20."

The key point is that Matchless is not a loser once you consider how many hours it takes to make a unit of each product line. Although Matchless has a much lower contribution margin per unit than either of the other two products, the fact that it takes so little time to produce — 1 hour — makes up for its deficiency.

Notice below how many more units of Matchless can be produced each year than can be produced for Super Deluxe or Deluxe:

Less hours per unit means that more units can be produced

	Super Deluxe	Deluxe	Matchless
Total hours of capacity	11,800	11,800	11,800
Hours per unit	÷ 10	÷ 4.8	÷ 1
Maximum units that can be produced.	1,180	2,458*	11,800
Contribution margin per unit	$ 160	$ 60	$ 20
Maximum contribution margin	$188,800	$147,500	$236,000
Fixed costs	160,000	160,000	160,000
Maximum net income	$ 28,800	($ 12,500)	$ 76,000

* Rounded.

Gas Glow can produce 11,800 units of Matchless but only 2,458 units of Deluxe and 1,180 units of Super Deluxe. Matchless may have a much smaller contribution margin per unit than either of the other two products — but because of its significant advantage in the number of units that can be produced, the total contribution margin and net income for Gas Glow is highest when Matchless is produced.

More than One Constraint   In a more realistic setting, a company such as Gas Glow Grill would probably have more than one — and possibly numerous — constraints to worry about. For example, there might be more than one production constraint, especially if the products were produced in two or more departments. In addition, there could be a limit on the maximum sales potential for each product. As the number of constraints grows, the level of difficulty seems to expand at an even greater rate—so much so that it would become almost impossible to solve certain problems without the aid of a sophisticated quantitative tool called **linear programming.** The discussion of multiple constraints and the use of this tool is deferred to an upper-level quantitative methods course.[1]

Make or Buy

Reasons to make: cost, quality, and availability

Reasons to buy: lower cost and better use of productive capacity

A manufacturer is often faced with an interesting option: It can buy the raw material that goes into its finished product, or it can produce its own raw material. Sometimes it is more economical to produce the raw material internally. Also, the manufacturer is able to maintain better control over the quality and availability of a raw material if it is made internally. On the other hand, the main problem with producing one's own raw materials is that this may require some of the firm's productive capacity to be taken away from the production of the finished product. What good does it do to produce one's own raw materials if there is little remaining capacity for producing the main product? The main product might cost less, but the firm may not be able to make and sell enough of its main product line to be profitable.

To be complete, any analysis of making vs. buying raw materials must be concerned with utilizing all of the productive capacity in the most effective manner. In order for a manufacturer even to consider making its own raw materials, there must be productive capacity that is idle—and therefore available for an alternative use.

The Analysis

The analysis of a make-or-buy decision simply determines the relevant costs of making the material and compares that amount to the relevant costs of buying it from an outsider. A typical make-or-buy situation is presented in Example 25-3 for Frankensense Company.

EXAMPLE 25-3

To make or buy Roo Myrr

FRANKENSENSE COMPANY

The Frankensense Company produces a perfume called Breathless. One hundred thousand ounces of one of the ingredients, Roo Myrr, is currently being produced by Frankensense for the following costs:

Direct materials	$600,000	$6.00/oz
Direct labor	100,000	1.00/oz
Variable overhead	50,000	.50/oz
Fixed overhead	50,000	.50/oz
	$800,000	$8.00/oz

Frankensense is considering purchasing the 100,000 ounces from CinDi Lauder Company for $7.25 per ounce plus shipping costs of $.40 per ounce. The productive capacity that is currently being used to manufacture Roo Myrr will be used to produce additional units of another product line—After Dark. The additional contribution margin that can be generated from After Dark is $20,000.

The solution for Example 25-3 is given in Exhibit 25-4. The first column shows the total costs to make Roo Myrr; the second column shows the total costs of purchasing

[1] A simple example of a company with two constraints is given in Problems A25-3 and B25-3.

EXHIBIT 25-4
A Comparison of Make or Buy Roo Myrr.

Frankensense is $5,000 better off by buying Roo Myrr. The additional contribution margin of $20,000 from After Dark is an opportunity cost.

| | Alternatives | | |
	1 Make Roo Myrr	2 Buy Roo Myrr	3 Difference
Variable costs:			
Direct materials	$600,000	$ —	$600,000
Direct labor	100,000	—	100,000
Variable overhead	50,000	—	50,000
Shipping costs	—	40,000	(40,000)
Purchase of 100,000 oz	—	725,000	(725,000)
	$750,000	$765,000	($ 15,000)
Fixed overhead	50,000	50,000	—
Total actual costs	$800,000	$815,000	($ 15,000)
Additional contribution margin for After Dark	—	(20,000)	20,000
Net costs	$800,000	$795,000	$ 5,000

Roo Myrr; and the third column shows the difference between the costs of making and buying Roo Myrr.

For the variable items, the costs of buying are $15,000 higher than the costs of making ($765,000 − $750,000). And the fixed overhead is $50,000 regardless of Frankensense's decision. Remember: For all the decision situations that we evaluate in this chapter, the total fixed costs are assumed to remain the same regardless of activity, unless we give you specific information to the contrary. It is possible, for example, that in a situation such as this one, the fixed costs could change, possibly due to a reduction in the number of supervisors needed. However, we are not assuming a change of that sort for Frankensense.

Total fixed costs are assumed to remain the same

The final item in Exhibit 25-4 concerns the additional contribution margin that Frankensense can generate from After Dark if Roo Myrr is purchased. If this item were left out of the analysis, Frankensense would probably decide to continue making Roo Myrr—because the costs of buying it are $15,000 higher than the costs of making it. However, since Frankensense can increase its contribution margin by $20,000 on After Dark only if it buys Roo Myrr, the additional contribution is relevant to the decision. And the net effect is to increase its profits by $5,000 ($20,000 − $15,000)—by purchasing Roo Myrr from an outside supplier.

Opportunity Costs

The additional contribution margin of $20,000 that is listed at the bottom of Exhibit 25-4 is called an opportunity cost.

Opportunity costs are foregone profits

An *opportunity cost* is the profit foregone or lost by a firm in taking one course of action rather than another. It relates to an opportunity that is given up, or sacrificed. It is not an actual cash outlay as other costs usually are. Instead, it is a cash inflow that the firm sacrifices by accepting one alternative over another. If Frankensense decides to continue making Roo Myrr, it is giving up $20,000 of additional profit from After Dark.

In Exhibit 25-4, we've shown the opportunity cost as additional income in the buy column; this reduces the total costs of the purchase alternative from $815,000 to $795,000. The $5,000 balance at the bottom of the difference column indicates that the buy alternative is preferable.

Another good example of an opportunity cost that could relate to Frankensense's company is rent income. Ceasing production of Roo Myrr might release floor space that could be rented to outsiders. The rent foregone by making Roo Myrr would be an opportunity cost, and it, too, would be relevant to the decision.

Joint Products

There are many production processes that begin with a single raw material and end up with two or more final products. A prime example involves the many final products that come from a single steer—hides, hamburger, steaks, pet food, etc. Another is a barrel of crude oil that ends up being kerosene, regular and unleaded gasoline, and other petroleum products. Other examples can be found in the lumber and chemicals industries.

Joint products: A single product splits into two or more products

The raw material is treated as a single product up until a point in production called the ***split-off point.*** At this point the single product divides into two or more products called ***joint products.*** The joint products are not individually identifiable until the split-off point.

The costs of producing the single product up to the split-off point are the ***joint product costs.*** These costs are common to all the units produced and cannot be associated directly with the units once they split into the individual products. Take, for example, the costs of raising a herd of cattle. The costs of buying, feeding, caring for, and transporting each cow to market are the joint product costs. When the cows are slaughtered—the split-off point—there really is no way to tell how much of the joint costs were costs of the hide, the hamburger, or the steaks.

This processing of cattle is depicted in the following simplified diagram:

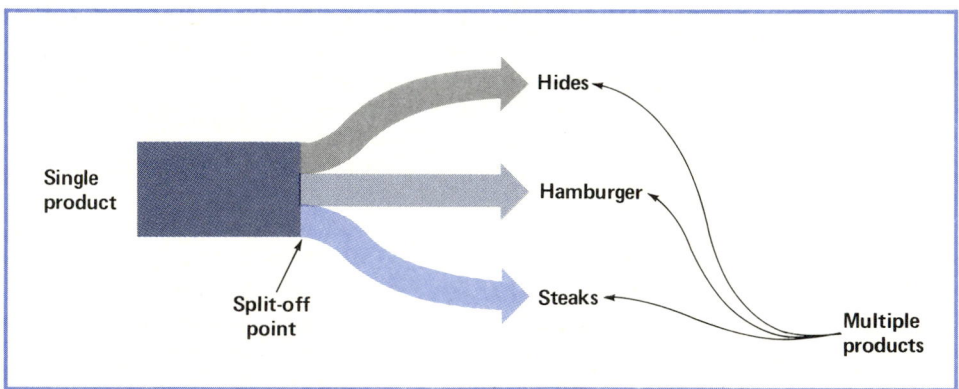

Choices at split-off

Sometimes we can sell a joint product immediately after the split-off point. In other situations we may have to process the joint product beyond the split-off before it can be sold. We may even have the option of selling at split-off or processing further.

A Useful Diagram

A more elaborate diagram for joint products is shown at the top of the facing page. It shows both the sales at split-off and any additional processing that may be needed for two joint products, product A and product B.

This type of diagram can be very useful when you do your homework. If you place the key facts from a problem into the appropriate positions in the diagram, you can get a complete overview of what you are about to evaluate. We'll do this for you in a moment in our example on joint products.

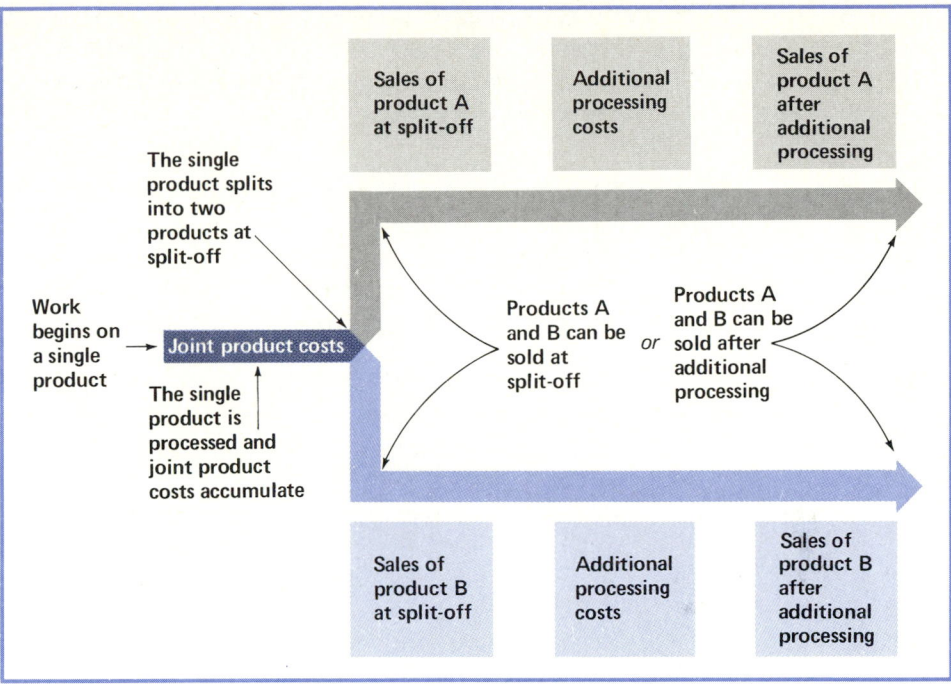

Sell at Split-Off or Process Further

When a firm has the option of selling a joint product at the split-off point or processing it further, it will naturally select that option with the more favorable effect on profits. The key to making the correct decision is knowing which information is relevant and which information is irrelevant.

Let's look at such a situation for Jimmy Joe in Example 25-4. Although Jimmy Joe is a farmer rather than a manufacturer, the concepts still apply.

EXAMPLE 25-4

JIMMY JOE'S PEANUT FARM

Jimmy Joe James has recently purchased substantial farmland in Georgia and is currently growing peanuts. At harvest time the crop is divided into nuts and shells. The nuts can be sold immediately to a grocery store chain or processed into vegetable oil. The shells can be burned or ground into a powder. The powder can be sold to a drug company, which uses it in a new medicine for acne.

The costs of growing the crop, harvesting it, and separating it into the two products are $400,000. At harvest, the following information pertains to the choices for Jimmy Joe:

	Sales at Harvest Time (split-off)	Additional Processing Costs	Sales after Additional Processing
Nuts.	$750,000	$500,000	$1,200,000
Shells	0	50,000	100,000

What actions should Jimmy Joe take to maximize profits?

The first step we need to take to solve Example 25-4 is to get an overview of the situation. This overview is provided in the diagram below, in which we have substituted all the numbers given in Example 25-4 into the general format that we discussed on the previous page.

All the facts for Jimmy Joe are in this diagram

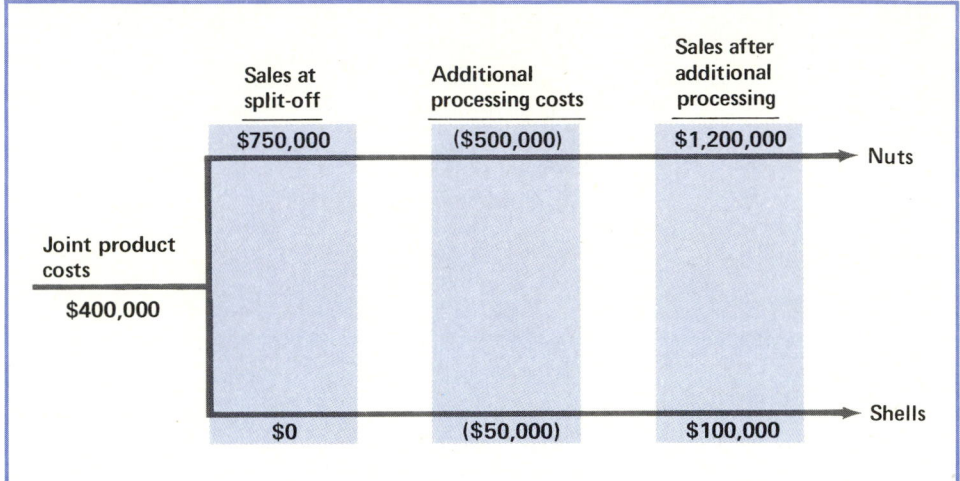

Notice in this diagram that the only way you can produce nuts and shells is to spend $400,000 developing the crop up to the split-off point. No matter what you decide to do with the nuts and shells — that is, sell at split-off or process further — you have to first spend the $400,000. Since the joint product costs are not affected by the decision you make, they must be irrelevant to the decision.

The items that are relevant to the decision of selling at split-off or processing further are those that come after the single product splits into two or more joint products. Let's look now at the relevant items, first for the nuts and then for the shells.

For nuts, it's better to sell at split-off

For the nut crop, you can see in the diagram that there are two choices. You can sell it at split-off for $750,000 or you can process it further. If you spend $500,000 to process the nut crop further, you can then sell it for $1,200,000, a net of $700,000 ($1,200,000 − $500,000). If you were Jimmy Joe, would you rather have the $750,000 or the $700,000? Assuming that you'd like to make as big a profit as possible, we feel sure that you would rather have the $750,000 — you would sell the nuts at the split-off point.

For shells: Sell after processing

Although technically you have two choices for the shells, disposing of them at the split-off would probably be your last resort. By processing them further, Jimmy can increase his profits by $50,000 ($100,000 − $50,000). Since this is obviously preferable to receiving zero at the split-off, the shells should be processed further.

The format that accommodates this evaluation of nuts and shells is presented in Exhibit 25-5. It shows that the maximum profit before subtracting the joint costs is $800,000 — if the nuts are sold at split-off and the shells are processed further. After the joint costs are deducted, the maximum profit for Jimmy Joe's farm is $400,000.

Product Costing vs. Special Decisions

The main issue concerning joint products is what to do with them — sell them at split-off or process them further. A second issue concerns the distribution of joint product costs to the joint products. The joint product costs are *product costs* — costs that are assigned to inventory when incurred and that are expensed (to cost of goods

EXHIBIT 25-5
Sell at Split-Off or Process Further — An Incremental Approach.
What to do depends on this: Is incremental profit from processing further less than or greater than sales at split-off?

	Sell at Split-Off Point	Sell after Processing	− Additional Processing Costs	= Net	Best Decision
			Process Further		
Nuts	$750,000	$1,200,000	− $500,000	= $700,000	$750,000 Sell at split-off point
Shells	0	100,000	− 50,000	= 50,000	50,000 Sell after processing

Maximum profits before joint product costs $800,000
Joint product costs   400,000

Maximum profits $400,000

Income statement for joint products

sold) when the units to which they are assigned are sold. The joint product costs of $400,000 for Jimmy Joe were incurred to produce both nuts and shells. In order to make income statements for the nuts and the shells, we need to know the amount of the joint product costs that is assigned to each.

The problem is, how do we tell exactly how much of the joint product costs was incurred because of the shells and how much was incurred because of the nuts, so that we can assign to each joint product the amount of joint cost that is related to it? The answer is that there is no way to tell exactly how much cost relates to each joint product. So what do we do? We use one of two methods to rather arbitrarily allocate the joint costs to the joint products.

One method allocates the joint product costs based on the quantity of each joint product — the *physical volume method.* For instance, assume that we determine the number of pounds of nuts and shells at the split-off point. If the nuts represent three-fourths of the total weight, then we allocate three-fourths of the joint costs ($\frac{3}{4} \times$ $400,000 = $300,000) to nuts and the remaining one-fourth ($\frac{1}{4} \times$ $400,000 = $100,000) to shells. The net income for nuts would be $450,000 ($750,000 − $300,000) and for shells would be a loss of $50,000 ($100,000 − $50,000 − $100,000), combining to a total of $400,000 — which is the maximum profit possible for Jimmy Joe — just as we proved in Exhibit 25-5.

At this point you may be tempted to suggest that we not sell shells at all because of the $50,000 loss. However, remember that the joint costs of $400,000 are irrelevant to any decision concerning what we should do with each product. Therefore, the amount of joint costs we allocate to each product — and the resulting income for that product — is also irrelevant to this decision. We concluded from Exhibit 25-5 that the very best we can do is a $400,000 profit, and that's exactly what we have: $450,000 + $(50,000) = $400,000. If we did stop selling shells altogether, the full $400,000 would still be incurred, and would be assigned completely to the nuts. Consequently, it's net income, and the income for the firm as a whole would drop to $350,000 ($750,000 − $400,000).

The other method allocates the joint product costs to the joint products based on the relative sales value of each product at the split-off point. This method is called the *relative sales value method,* which we also discussed in Chapter 10. If a product has no sales value at the split-off point, but can be sold after further processing (which is the situation we have for the shells), the net of the sales after further processing, less the additional processing costs, is substituted for the sales at split-off. For example, we allocate the $400,000 of joint costs for Jimmy Joe between nuts and shells in the following manner:

Product	Sales Value	Fraction		Joint Cost		Allocation of Joint Cost
Nuts	$750,000	750/800	×	$400,000	=	$375,000
Shells	50,000*	50/800	×	$400,000	=	25,000
	$800,000					$400,000

* Since there is no sales value at split-off for the shells, the net of $100,000 − $50,000 = $50,000 is substituted.

When we prepare individual income statements for the nuts and shells, we assign $375,000 of the joint costs to nuts and the remaining $25,000 to shells, leaving us with an income for nuts of $375,000 ($750,000 − $375,000) and for shells of $25,000 ($100,000 − $50,000 − $25,000). The combined income once again is $400,000, the maximum profit possible for Jimmy Joe.

Defective Units

Defective units do not meet production standards

When a manufacturer produces finished goods for sale, it is important that the product meet all quality and dimensional (size and shape) standards. When an unsatisfactory unit—a **defective unit**—is sold, there is a good chance that the customer will either return it for a good one, ask for a refund, or stop purchasing from the company altogether. When a bad unit is returned by a customer or is detected as bad before it is sold, the manufacturer can dispose of it for a minimal value or rework it so that it can be sold at close to the regular price. As you might expect, the existence of defective units can seriously erode a manufacturer's profit margin.

Can Defective Units Be Avoided?

Don't try to eliminate all defective units

What would you do if you had defective units? Would you make every effort to produce 100% of your output without a single bad unit? Or would you simply not worry about the problem because there is nothing that you could do about it? Your answer is, hopefully, somewhere in between these two extremes.

Most companies are aware that some units will be defective and even expect a certain amount of bad units to accompany the good units. A reasonable number of defective units is considered a normal or acceptable part of continuing efficient operations, given the current quality of materials, laborers, machinery, and supervision. If you attempted to eliminate all defective units you would have to incur substantial additional costs to improve the overall quality of the production process. The additional costs are often greater than the benefits of eliminating a small amount of defective units. As a result, most organizations look upon this small quantity of defective units as a necessary evil.

Whenever the number of defective units exceeds an acceptable level (probably set as a percentage of total production), every effort must be made to find the cause and eliminate the problem. Defective units in excess of an acceptable level are not a part of continuing efficient operations. Based on the current quality of materials, laborers, machinery, and supervision, there is no reason to have excess defective units—they are not a necessary evil. The system of controls will have to be tightened.

Scrap or Rework

Accepting the fact that some defective units will probably occur, what should a firm

As long as we're going to have defective units, let's make the best of the situation

do with them—sell them as is, when they are detected, or correct their deficiencies and then sell them at a price much closer to the regular price? Let's look to Example 25-5 and its solution in Exhibit 25-6.

EXAMPLE 25-5

CASAROJO CEILING FAN

At the beginning of 1988, the Casarojo Ceiling Fan Company budgets production of 100,000 fan blades, of which it expects 10% to be defective. At the point of inspection, defective units can be sold for $3 per blade as irregulars or reworked so that they can be sold for the normal price of $10. The costs assigned to each blade up until the inspection point are as follows:

Direct materials	$1.50
Direct labor.	1.20
Variable overhead	1.00
Fixed overhead ($30,000 ÷ 100,000 blades)	.30
	$4.00

The additional costs of reworking each blade so that it can be sold as a regular are as follows:

Direct materials	$.90
Direct labor	.60
Variable overhead	.50

The selling costs average $1 per blade, whether the units are sold as regulars or irregulars. Should the defective units be sold at $3 per blade or reworked to sell at $10 per blade?

Let's first see which items are irrelevant to the decision.

Casarojo expects to produce 100,000 blades in 1988—10,000 of which are expected to be defective. Since Casarojo doesn't know which blades are defective until the inspection point, it must produce all 100,000 units at least until they are inspected. At that point, the 10,000 defective blades are withdrawn from production and the 90,000 good ones continue on.

The cost of making 100,000 blades up to the point of inspection is $4.00 per unit—a total of $400,000. Look what happens to the $400,000 in the diagram at the top of the next page.

The $40,000 assigned to the defective blades could not be avoided—the costs had to be incurred in order to get the blades to the inspection point. They are the same amount whether the defective blades are scrapped or reworked. Since these costs are not different for the alternatives being considered—scrap or rework—they are irrelevant to the decision. The only production costs that are relevant are the additional costs to rework the defective blades.

The other item that is irrelevant to the decision is the $1 per blade selling cost. It costs the same amount to scrap a blade as it does to sell a reworked one.

The solution to Example 25-5 is shown in Exhibit 25-6. In column 1 you can see

The production costs up to inspection occur no matter what you do later: They're irrelevant

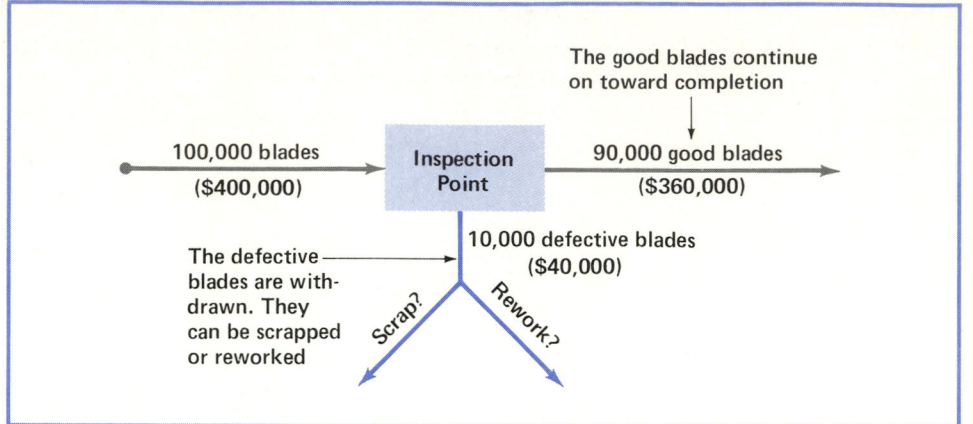

the sales and the costs if we sell the 10,000 defective blades at the inspection point. The sales are 10,000 blades at $3 per blade, and the costs are the 10,000 blades multiplied by the original per-unit costs given in Example 25-5. In column 2 we show the consequences of reworking the 10,000 defective units and selling them for $10 per blade. The production costs shown in column 2 are a combination of the costs of producing the blades up to the inspection point at one cost per unit, plus the costs to rework the blades at different costs per unit. For example the direct materials in column 2 are:

Costs to produce up to inspection point (10,000 blades × $1.50)........	$15,000
Costs to rework (10,000 blades × $.90).........................	9,000
	$24,000

Notice also that the items we pointed out as being irrelevant to the decision—the variable selling and the fixed costs—are the same amounts in column 1 as they are in column 2. As a result, there are nothing but zeroes for these two in the difference column.

EXHIBIT 25-6
Defective Units—Scrap or Rework—Irrelevant Production Costs Included.

	(1) Sell at Inspection Point	(2) Rework	(3) Difference
Sales	$30,000	$100,000	$70,000
Variable costs:			
Direct materials	$15,000	$ 24,000	($ 9,000)
Direct labor	12,000	18,000	(6,000)
Variable overhead.....................	10,000	15,000	(5,000)
Variable selling.......................	10,000	10,000	—
	$47,000	$ 67,000	($20,000)
Contribution margin......................	($17,000)	$ 33,000	$50,000
Fixed costs	30,000	30,000	—
Income from defective units.................	($47,000)	$ 3,000	$50,000

Column 3 is the difference column. In it we see that the revenues are $70,000 higher if we rework the blades, and the costs are $20,000 higher for reworking. The net, $50,000, means that we will have an additional $50,000 of income if we rework the defective blades rather than selling them at the inspection point.

CHAPTER SUMMARY

Managers face a variety of decisions that affect both long-run and short-run profits. Accountants have the responsibility to assist management in the decision-making process by providing them with information that is relevant to the decision at hand. In order for information to be *relevant,* it must meet two criteria: First, it must relate to the future. Second, it must be different for the alternatives being considered. Past information cannot be relevant, but it may be useful in projecting relevant information. Although we prefer relevant information to be as *accurate* as possible, information does not have to be accurate to be relevant.

Managers need to consider both quantitative and qualitative factors when making a decision. *Quantitative* factors are those that can be measured in dollars and cents. *Qualitative* factors cannot be measured in dollars and cents but may still have a significant effect on a decision.

An organization is often receptive to accepting a *special order* at a reduced price from a customer in an unrelated market. Two important considerations in a special order are: (1) that excess capacity is available, and (2) that the reduced price for a special order will not hurt the firm's pricing structure with regular customers.

Multi-product firms attempt to maximize profits by determining an optimum *sales mix* for their many products. This may involve dropping an entire line or merely revising slightly the percentage of total sales distributed to different products. In order to determine the optimum mix, consideration must be given to each product's contribution margin per unit, the resources of the firm, and the constraints imposed on those resources by each product.

Many organizations produce the raw materials needed for a finished good as well as the finished good itself. They may find it more economical to purchase the raw materials from an outsider, and they may wish to free productive capacity for more profitable uses. In this case, consideration needs to be given to the most effective use of idle capacity.

Joint products come about when a single product divides into two or more products at a *split-off point.* An important decision for a firm with joint products is whether to sell them at split-off or process them further. The joint product should be processed further if the incremental revenue (sales after processing less additional processing costs) exceeds the sales at split-off. *Joint product costs* are always irrelevant to the decision.

Defective units are items that fail to meet quality or dimensional standards of production. They can be scrapped when detected as defective, or reworked and sold at a price close to the regular price. Defective units should be reworked whenever the incremental profit (sales after reworking less additional costs of reworking) from reworking is greater than the scrap value (sales at the inspection point).

IMPORTANT TERMS USED IN THIS CHAPTER

Accuracy   A quality of information; exactness, or preciseness. (page 997)

Constraints   Restrictions on a firm's ability to produce and sell an unlimited amount of different product lines. (page 1006)

Contribution margin format   An income statement format in which variable costs are subtracted from sales, and fixed costs are subtracted from the difference (the total contribution margin). (page 1001)

Defective units   Units that do not meet dimensional or quality-of-production standards and that can be either scrapped when detected as defective or reworked and sold at a price closer to the regular price. (page 1014)

Joint product costs   The costs associated with a single product up until the split-off point in a joint product situation. (page 1010)

Joint products   Multiple products that result from the division of a single product at a split-off point in production. (page 1010)

Opportunity cost   The measurable sacrifice (or lost profits) of rejecting one alternative in order to accept another. (page 1009)

Relevant information   Information that: (1) relates to the future, and (2) is different for the alternatives being considered. (page 995)

Sales mix   For a multi-product firm, the percentage of total sales distributed to each product line. (page 1002)

Split-off point   A point in production at which a single product divides into two or more joint products. (page 1010)

Traditional format   An income statement format in which cost of goods sold is subtracted from sales, leaving the gross margin; operating costs are then subtracted from the gross margin. (page 1002)

QUESTIONS

1. Explain what is meant by the term *relevant information.*

2. "Information must be accurate in order to be relevant." Comment.

3. All differential costs relate to relevant items. Why?

4. What is an *opportunity cost?*

5. "Opportunity costs are always relevant." Do you agree? Explain.

6. Since past costs are irrelevant, is it possible for them to be useful? Explain.

7. "A special order should be accepted only if the gross profit for the special order is positive." Comment.

8. "In a multi-product firm, the firm can maximize profits by producing and selling only that product with the highest contribution margin per unit." Comment.

9. Explain several reasons why a firm would make a raw material needed in production rather than buy it from an outside supplier.

10. Why are joint product costs irrelevant to the decision of selling at split-off or processing further?

11. What is a *defective unit?* Why would a firm be willing to accept the occurrence of defective units rather than trying to eliminate them completely?

12. Give some examples of both quantitative factors and qualitative factors in a make-or-buy decision, and in a decision to accept or reject a special order.

13. Discuss completely whether the following statements are true or false:

    a. A product should always be dropped by a firm when its product line income is negative.
    b. As long as a product line is showing a profit, it should never be dropped.
    c. It's not that important whether a product line has a positive or negative contribution margin. What's important is whether or not it has a favorable amount of net income.

EXERCISES

Exercise 25-1
Deciding whether to accept or reject a special order

The General Electronics Corporation sells cordless phones that double as Walkman radios for $100 apiece. The per-unit costs for the phones are shown below (based on normal sales of 20,000 phones per year):

Cost of goods sold (including $20 for fixed factory overhead) $60
Selling costs (including $10 of fixed selling costs: the remaining costs are shipping costs). 30

The sales vice president is offered a unit price of $56 for a special order of 3,000 phones by an Eskimo village. The village representative will pick up the order at the door, since shipments to his remote village take 6 months for delivery. The vice president suggests that the order be rejected when he learns that it costs $60 to produce each phone.

What would you suggest? How much more (or less) income will General Electronics have by accepting the order?

(Check figure: $48,000)

Exercise 25-2
Determining if an unprofitable product should be dropped

The Upbeat Company sells three products, but is considering dropping at least one of them because it looks like a couple are losing money for the firm.

	Product		
	A	B	C
Sales	$100,000	$60,000	$55,000
Variable costs	55,000	50,000	60,000
	$ 45,000	$10,000	($ 5,000)
Fixed costs	15,000	15,000	15,000
Net income.	$ 30,000	($ 5,000)	($20,000)

a. Should any product line be dropped? Why? Show calculations to support your conclusion.
b. Prepare income statements for each product if the $45,000 of fixed costs is distributed to A, B, and C in a 60%:20%:20% ratio. Compare the total income to what it is in the original situation. Should any product be dropped now?

(Check figure: $5,000)

Exercise 25-3
Determining whether a new product line will improve profits

Currently the Bruno Company has only one product line, but is considering the addition of a second line in 1988. Information related to the new product line is as follows:

Sales price . . . . $ 25
Variable costs per unit . . . . $ 20
Unit sales.   8,000
Fixed costs allocated to new product line $40,000

The projected income statement for Bruno if the new line is not added is shown below:

Sales (8,000 units).	$525,000
Variable costs.	260,000
	$265,000
Fixed costs.	80,000
Net income	$185,000

Should Bruno add the new line? Why or why not?

(Check figure: Net income if added = $225,000)

Exercise 25-4

Multiple products: maximize profits—one constraint

The O'Donohue Company sells two products, A and B, that have contribution margins per unit of $6 and $4, respectively. A takes 3 hours to produce and B requires 1 hour.

The company can sell all it produces; and the fixed costs are $17,000.

Which product should be produced? Why?

Exercise 25-5

Deciding to make or buy a part that goes into the finished product

The Reeves Corporation is currently producing 10,000 parts that go into the production of its main product line. The costs of producing this part are:

Direct materials	$1.50
Direct labor.	.75
Total overhead.	1.25*
	$3.50

* 60% is for variable overhead.

The vice president of production is considering buying the part from a supplier for $3.15 each, and discontinuing its production. He determines that four-fifths of the fixed overhead will exist regardless of the decision. The remainder will occur only if the part is produced.

Determine if the part should be purchased or produced internally. Provide supporting computations for your answer.

(Check figure: Produce is preferable by $500)

Exercise 25-6

Deciding if it's better to sell a joint product at split-off or to process further

The Banana Split Fruit Company makes a product that breaks into three products at a split-off point. Information concerning the three products is as follows:
1. Product X can be sold at the split-off point for $90,000, or processed further (additional processing costs are $35,000) to sell for $115,000.
2. Product Y can be sold only after additional processing (additional processing costs are $40,000) for $70,000.
3. Product Z can be sold only at the split-off point, for $60,000.
The joint product costs are $135,000.

Determine whether each product should be sold at the split-off point or after additional processing. What is the maximum profit possible for Banana Split?

(Check figure: Maximum profits = $45,000)

Exercise 25-7

Maximizing profits in a joint product situation

The Energetics Company in 1989 produced two chemicals, Oxydol and Pectic, from a single compound. The following income statement relates to that year:

	Oxydol	Pectic	Total
Sales	$150,000	$220,000	$370,000
Additional processing costs	$ 60,000	$180,000	$240,000
Allocated joint product costs	45,000	50,000	95,000
	$105,000	$230,000	$335,000
Net income	$ 45,000	($ 10,000)	$ 35,000

a. Energetics is considering dropping Pectic (due to its reported loss and the fact that it cannot be sold at split-off). Prepare a new income statement if this action is taken. Is it a good idea to drop the product?
b. Assume instead that Energetics can sell Oxydol and Pectic at the split-off point for $100,000 and $35,000, respectively. Where should each product now be sold in order to maximize profits? What are the maximum profits possible?

(Check figure: Maximum profits = $45,000)

Exercise 25-8

Deciding to scrap or rework defective units

The Huff Corporation expects 2,000 units to be defective during the next month out of a total production of 30,000 units. The cost of producing each unit is $15 (including $2 of fixed overhead). The defective units can be scrapped for $4 per unit or reworked so that they can be sold for $16 each. The regular sales price is $24, and the variable costs of reworking the defective units are $13 per unit. Should the defective units be scrapped or reworked?

(Check figure: Difference in alternatives = $2,000)

PROBLEMS
Set A

Problem A25-1

Should a product line be dropped?

The Patriotic T-Shirt Company, an official sponsor of the 1984 Olympics, is still selling 1984 Olympic T-shirts in 1987. The president feels that the "USA-'84" shirt is the only profitable line—after looking at the 1986 income statement below. He insists that the "Gold Rush-'84" and "LA-'84" be dropped.

	Product			
	USA-'84	Gold Rush-'84	LA'-84	Total
Sales	$450,000	$300,000	$500,000	$1,250,000
Cost of goods sold:				
Variable	$200,000	$180,000	$300,000	$ 680,000
Fixed	45,000	40,000	50,000	135,000
	$245,000	$220,000	$350,000	$ 815,000
Gross profit	$205,000	$ 80,000	$150,000	$ 435,000
Selling and administrative:				
Variable	$ 50,000	$ 60,000	$210,000	$ 320,000
Fixed	30,000	30,000	40,000	100,000
	$ 80,000	$ 90,000	$250,000	$ 420,000
Net income	$125,000	($ 10,000)	($100,000)	$ 15,000

Required

1. Assuming that the total fixed costs will not be affected by the decision, should any product line be dropped? Why? By what amount will income change?
2. Assume for this part only that Gold Rush-'84 and LA-'84 are being dropped, and that the fixed overhead costs that are reduced by dropping each line are $30,000 and $25,000, respectively. By how much will the deletion of these products increase or decrease the net income for the firm?

(Check figure: $5,000)

Problem A25-2

Preparing income statements and maximizing profits for joint products

The Generic Component Company produces a liquid in a heating process, which at 525° splits into two products that can be sold to drug manufacturing companies.

The first product, TR3, can be sold at the split-off point for $2,400,000, or processed further. The product's additional processing will cost $450,000, but will increase the sales to $3,600,000.

The second product, SX100, can also be sold at split-off or processed further. Sales at split-off would be $1,800,000, and after additional processing, $2,250,000. The additional processing costs will be $600,000. The joint product costs are $3,000,000.

Required

1. Draw a diagram depicting the situation above.
2. Assume that the joint costs are allocated $1,050,000 to TR3 and $1,950,000 to SX100. If all the products are sold at split-off, what would be the income for the firm as a whole as well as for each product?
3. Answer requirement (2) but assume that both products are sold after additional processing.

4. In order to maximize profits for the firm, should each product be sold at split-off or processed further?
5. Using the answer to requirement (4), and assuming the same cost allocation as in requirement (2), determine the income for the firm as a whole as well as for each product line.

(Check figure: Net income = $1,950,000)

Problem A25-3

Two products with constraints

The Toysuki Company produces two models of television sets. The following information relates to the production and sale of each model:

	Portable	Console
Sales price	$ 400	$ 500
Variable cost per unit.	$ 320	$ 300
Allocated fixed costs	$1,620,000	$3,580,000
Hours needed to produce	2	10
Maximum unit sales	100,000	20,000

The total hours of productive capacity are 250,000.

The controller is trying to decide how to distribute the productive capacity to the two products in order to maximize profits, and asks for your advice.

Required   Determine the number of units of each product to be produced and sold in order to maximize profits. What are the maximum possible profits for Toysuki?

(Check figure: Maximum profits = $3,800,000)

Problem A25-4

The special order: deciding to accept or reject

The Stickney Stuffing Company produces and sells cases of bread crumb stuffing. During 1988 Stickney had the following operating results:

Sales ($25 per case)		$75,000
Cost of goods sold:		
Variable	$25,000	
Fixed	5,000	30,000
Gross profit		$45,000
Selling and administrative:		
Variable	$15,000*	
Fixed	3,000	18,000
Net income		$27,000

* 40% for sales commissions and the remainder for shipping.

Stickney is considering a special order from Golden Fresh Poultry, during a slow month, to sell 1,000 cases at $15 per case. If the order is accepted, there will be no sales commissions on the transaction. Since it is a one-time deal, Stickney figures it can cut variable production costs by 20% per unit (by using cheaper materials).

Required | Determine whether or not the special order should be accepted. What will be the effect on profits of the firm if the order is accepted?

(Check figure: Change in profits = $5,333)

Problem A25-5
Determining whether profits will improve by making instead of buying a raw material

The Impredrin Corporation produces and sells an aspirin called Tylenun. In the past, one of the raw materials, Buffer, was purchased from a supplier, but Impredrin is now considering producing it internally.

During 1987, 10,000 pounds of Buffer will be required for production, which if purchased externally will cost $5.25 per pound. The costs of receiving and handling these purchases of Buffer average $.60 per pound.

The costs of producing Buffer internally are given below:

Direct materials.	$1.00/lb
Direct labor	4.00/lb
Variable overhead	.50/lb
Fixed overhead	.75/lb
	$6.25/lb

The fixed overhead for the company in total will not change. Some of the total is assigned to the production of Buffer, since it does utilize some of the productive capacity.

Required | Determine if Buffer should be produced internally or purchased from an outside supplier.

(Check figure: Difference in profits = $3,500)

Problem A25-6
Determining whether improvements should be made that can eliminate defective units

Each year Moody Blues Company produces 25,000 record players, of which 2,000 are found to be defective prior to sale. A record player regularly sells for $75, but a defective unit can only be scrapped for $25. The chief engineer, Ray Virginian, feels that the process can be improved enough to eliminate all defective units, but the controller, Regina Christy, is doubtful that the changes would be cost-beneficial. Regina determines the following cost relationships expected for the coming year, with and without the proposed changes:

	Without Improvements	With Improvements
Direct materials	$20.00/unit	$22.50/unit
Direct labor	10.00/unit	11.00/unit
Variable overhead	5.00/unit	5.00/unit
Fixed overhead	4.00/unit	4.00/unit
Fixed selling	3.00/unit	3.20/unit

Required | Should Ray Virginian be allowed to implement his proposed improvements? Support your answer with computations in good form.

(Check figure: Difference in profits = $7,500)

Problem A25-7

Multiple products—
miscellaneous questions

The controller of Sonymax Electronics has prepared the following product-line income statements for 1988, and the president is extremely dissatisfied with the profits from his SR25 and SR100 lines:

	SR25	SR50	SR100
Sales	$500,000	$300,000	$250,000
Variable costs:			
Production.	$300,000	$105,000	$110,000
Selling.	100,000	45,000	40,000
	$400,000	$150,000	$150,000
Fixed costs (allocated by set ratio):			
Production.	$ 75,000	$ 60,000	$ 70,000
Selling.	50,000	40,000	50,000
	$125,000	$100,000	$120,000
Income.	($ 25,000)	$ 50,000	($ 20,000)
Units produced and sold	12,500	15,000	8,000

Required

Answer each *independent* question below:
1. What will be Sonymax's profits if SR25 or SR100 is dropped? Would you recommend that either one be dropped?
2. Assume, in this part only, the following facts: Sonymax is considering a special order of 2,000 units for SR50 at $14 a unit. It will not be necessary to incur any additional shipping costs (and shipping costs are two-thirds of the variable selling costs). If Sonymax accepts the special order, the variable production costs will be $3 higher per unit due to paying higher labor rates for overtime work. Should the order be accepted? Show all work.
3. Sonymax is hoping to shift some of the production and sales from SR25 to SR100. It wants to have a sales mix of 20:40:40 for SR25, SR50, and SR100, respectively. How many units would the firm have to sell to generate a profit of $75,000 if the desired sales mix can be attained? (See Chapter 22, the sales mix section.)
4. Assume in this part only that it takes 1 hour to produce SR25, 2 hours for SR50, and 4 hours for SR100; and that the total hours of machine time available are 74,500 per year. In addition, the maximum demand for each product is estimated to be:

	Maximum Sales
SR25.	25,000
SR50.	30,000
SR100.	19,000

How many units of each product line should be sold in order to maximize profits? What is the amount of maximum profits possible for Sonymax?

Set B

Problem B25-1
Increasing profits by dropping or adding product lines

The Jordan Company sells three products, and has prepared the following income statements for 1987:

			Product	
	S	F	U	Total
Sales.	$100,000	$80,000	$150,000	$330,000
Cost of goods sold	65,000	75,000	70,000	210,000
Gross margin	$ 35,000	$ 5,000	$ 80,000	$120,000
Operating expenses	40,000	35,000	35,000	110,000
Net income	($ 5,000)	($30,000)	$ 45,000	$ 10,000

The fixed costs included in cost of goods sold and operating expenses are as follows:

Fixed Costs Included in:	Cost of Goods Sold	Operating Expenses
Product S.	$25,000	$20,000
Product F.	15,000	10,000
Product U	20,000	25,000
	$60,000	$55,000

Required
1. Reconstruct the income statement in the contribution margin format.
2. Should any of the product lines be dropped? Why?
3. Assume in this part only that products S and F are dropped, and that the fixed overhead costs that could be reduced by dropping each line are $10,000 and $8,000, respectively. By how much would the profits for the firm be reduced or increased?

(Check figure: $17,000)

4. Disregarding requirement (3), assume that product N is added, having sales of $90,000 and a variable cost ratio of 35%. Assume also that the total fixed overhead and fixed operating costs will not change, but that $25,000 ($15,000 factory overhead and $10,000 operating expenses) of the total will be allocated to this new line. By how much will net income change by the addition of product N?

(Check figure: $58,500)

Problem B25-2
Preparing income statements for joint products, and maximizing profits

The Stockstill Lumber Company incurs costs of $200,000 in cutting and transporting trees to the sawmills, at which time they split into three products: wood, pulp, and sawdust.
Wood can be sold immediately for $170,000 or processed further in order to be sold for $185,000. Pulp can be sold at split-off for $120,000 or after processing for $130,000. Sawdust can be sold only at split-off for $40,000. The additional processing costs are $10,000 for wood and $20,000 for pulp.

Required
1. Draw a diagram depicting the situation described above.
2. Assume that the joint costs are allocated as follows: $80,000 to wood, $70,000 to pulp, and $50,000 to sawdust. If all products are sold at split-off, what would be the income for each product and the firm as a whole?

3. Answer requirement (2), but assume that wood and pulp are sold after additional processing.
4. Should each product be sold at split-off or processed further? Determine the maximum profits for the firm.

(Check figure: $135,000)

Problem B25-3

Multiple products — maximizing profits

The Cuomo Corporation is about to introduce two new product lines that will share the facilities of a single plant. Estimates concerning the potential per-unit revenues and costs are given below:

	Product X	Product Y
Sales price	$100	$200
Cost of goods sold:		
Variable	$ 20	$ 80
Fixed	10	15
	$ 30	$ 95
Gross profit	$ 70	$105
Operating (all variable)	$ 10	$ 20
Income	$ 60	$ 85

In addition, it will take 2 hours to make one unit of product X and 4 hours to make one unit of product Y. The total productive capacity is 100,000 hours, and Cuomo can sell all the units it produces.

Required

1. How many units of each product need to be produced and sold in order to maximize profits for Cuomo?
2. Assume now that the maximum demand for X and Y is 15,000 and 20,000 units, respectively. How many units of each product should be produced and sold in order to maximize profits? What is the maximum total contribution margin for Cuomo?

(Check figure: Product Y = 17,500 units)

Problem B25-4

The special order: deciding to accept or reject

The Winfield Corporation produces baseball batting helmets priced to sell for $16 per helmet but is considering a special order for 5,000 helmets at only $14 per helmet. In 1986, 25,000 helmets were produced and sold, 6,000 below full capacity. The income statement for 1986 is shown below:

Sales		$400,000
Cost of Goods Sold:		
Direct Materials	$40,000	
Direct Labor	30,000	
Variable Overhead	25,000	
Fixed Overhead	12,500	107,500
Gross Profit		$292,500
Operating Expenses:		
Variable Selling	$50,000	
Fixed Selling	20,000	70,000
Net Income		$222,500

The additional information relates to the special order. The materials used will be of an inferior quality, costing $.20 less per helmet. Direct labor will require 10% fewer hours, and variable overhead fluctuates with direct labor hours. Shipping costs of $.25 per helmet will not have to be paid by Winfield, since the helmets will be picked up by the customer at the factory door. Finally, if the deal goes through, the sales representative will receive a bonus of $1,000.

Required   Should the special order be accepted or rejected? Show details to support your answer.

(Check figure: Difference = $43,350)

Problem B25-5

Determining whether profits will be better by making or buying a part

The Amplex Radio Company makes its own circuit boards, which are used in the production of its radio lines. One circuit board, FX12, was used in 10,000 radios last year. The costs of producing FX12 were:

Direct materials	$ 8,000
Direct labor.	12,000
Variable overhead.	4,000
Fixed overhead.	16,000
	$40,000

Amplex is considering purchasing the 10,000 circuit boards from Beta Electronics for $2.70 per board (plus shipping costs of $.10 per board).

The fixed overhead above represents the salary of a supervisor who will be used to supervise additional production of the major product line if the part is purchased.

If the boards are purchased, the released capacity can be used to produce 500 additional radios, bringing the total to 10,500 radios. The contribution margin per radio is expected to be $10 and the fixed costs of producing the 10,000 radios is $60,000.

Required   Determine whether the circuit boards should be purchased or produced internally.

(Check figure: Difference = $1,000)

Problem B25-6

Deciding whether defective units should be completely eliminated

The Murray Corporation is operating at full capacity of 20,000 units per year. The costs of production for 1988 were the following:

Direct materials ($10/u)	$200,000
Direct labor ($9/u)	180,000
Variable overhead ($4/u)	80,000
Fixed overhead.	200,000
	$660,000

Murray's selling costs were $100,000, all of which were fixed. Each year 10% of production is found to be defective, leaving only 18,000 units to be sold at the regular price of $50 per unit. The defective units are scrapped for only $12 per unit.

Murray is considering making improvements in the production department in order to eliminate the occurrence of defective units. This will entail the following: (1) paying an extra $1 per unit for better-quality materials; (2) spending additional labor time on each unit, increasing the cost per unit by 15%; (3) hiring an additional supervisor for $20,000 per year; and (4) providing additional maintenance on machinery, costing $4,000 per year.

Required   Determine if the improvements should be made by Murray Company in order to eliminate the occurrence of defective units.

Problem B25-7
Miscellaneous questions
concerning multiple products

The Longex Watch Company produced and sold a total of 72,000 digital watches in 1988. This total is broken down by product line in the 1988 income statement:

	Product Line		
	Luxury	Diver	Sports
Unit Sales	20,000	2,000	50,000
Sales Revenue	$5,000,000	$2,000,000	$8,000,000
Cost of Goods Sold:			
Variable	$4,000,000	$1,500,000	$3,500,000
Fixed	800,000	600,000	1,000,000
	$4,800,000	$2,100,000	$4,500,000
Gross Profit	$ 200,000	($ 100,000)	$3,500,000
Operating Expenses:			
Variable	$1,100,000	$ 300,000	$ 500,000
Fixed	500,000	100,000	500,000
	$1,600,000	$ 400,000	$1,000,000
Net income	($1,400,000)	($ 500,000)	$2,500,000

Required

Answer each question below. Each question is completely independent of any other question.

1. Which product(s), if any, should be dropped? Support your answer with organized calculations.

2. Assume now that Longex is considering a special order with the Russian sports federation for 5,000 sports watches, at a price of $90 per watch. Longex salespeople usually work on a fixed salary, but if this order is accepted, the salesperson who arranged the deal will receive a $2,000 bonus. Since production of Diver watches is rather slow, one of the foremen for this product line (who is paid $25,000 per year) will supervise production of the special order. Longex figures that it can reduce the variable production costs by 20% per unit, by substituting questionable materials for what is usually used. By what amount will Longex's income change if the special order is accepted?

3. Assume now that Longex is going to drop Luxury, and will attempt to sell Diver and Sports in a 50:50 ratio. If this sales mix can indeed be achieved, how many watches (in total) must Longex sell in order to show a combined profit of $1,000,000?

4. Assume finally that there are two constraints on Longex's production and sale of watches. The constraints are shown below:

	Hours to Produce per Unit	Maximum Sales Demand
Luxury	4	25,000
Diver	2	20,000
Sports	1	100,000

In addition, the total hours of machine capacity are 134,000. How many units of each product line should be sold in order to maximize profits? What are the maximum profits possible for Longex?

Chapter 26

Capital Budgeting

After you have completed studying this chapter, you should understand the following things:

- What is meant by the term capital budgeting
- The steps to be taken by an organization in the capital budgeting process
- The difference between discounted cash flow methods and nondiscounted cash flow methods; and which specific methods belong to each group
- How to compute the net present value and internal rate of return for a project; and the criteria for accepting or rejecting a project when these methods are used
- How to compute the nondiscounted cash flow methods—payback and accountant's rate of return; and how to evaluate the results of each of these methods
- The weaknesses of the nondiscounted cash flow methods; and why the methods are popular in spite of these weaknesses.

In Chapter 25 we discussed many types of decisions that managers must make in running their day-to-day operations. A common element of each was that it involved the use of current productive capacity; that is, it was not necessary to purchase or build additional fixed assets in order to implement the decision. In our role as accountants we tried to help the managers determine the most profitable way for them to use that productive capacity. The effect of each decision was primarily on our short-run profits — 1 year or less.

Changes in productive capacity have long-run consequences

Once we decide to change our productive capacity, the impact on our profits will be felt for many years into the future. For instance, we might consider increasing the size of our factory; replacing old productive assets with new ones; or substituting machinery for labor.

For every decision that you as a manager make, whether the decision affects the short run or the long run, it is naturally very important to give careful consideration to all the relevant factors that are involved. Few decisions, however, require the same amount of time-consuming and diligent attention as do those that involve changes in an organization's productive capacity. This is true because:

1. The decision usually involves a significant outlay of resources, which commits the organization to a project for an extended period of time.

2. The success or failure of the project depends on a future that is unknown, or uncertain at best.

3. The possible losses that can result from a poor decision concerning a single project might be so great as to threaten the continued existence of the organization.

4. If the future proves that a poor decision has been made, it may be too late to avoid much of the impact of that decision.

Since changes in productive capacity can have such a significant effect on the long-run profits of an organization, accountants have to be able to help managers make the right decision. Therefore, accountants need to have reliable evaluation methods at their disposal. There are, in fact, quite a few evaluation methods that are available to accountants — they are called capital budgeting methods — and some are more reliable than others.

THE CAPITAL BUDGETING PROCESS

Capital budgeting:
— planning
— acquisition and financing
— long-term investments

Steps in the capital budgeting process

Capital budgeting is a process that helps managers plan for the acquisition and financing of long-term investments — primarily in fixed assets.[1] The capital budgeting process involves eight steps, which must be taken one step at a time.

The eight steps in the capital budgeting process are:

1. Determine the investment needs of the organization.

2. Determine the investment opportunities that meet the needs of the organization.

3. Gather the relevant information concerning the investment opportunities to be evaluated.

4. Determine the method(s) to be employed in evaluating the investment proposals.

5. Calculate the results for the method(s) using the relevant information.

---

[1] Although our emphasis is placed primarily on investments in fixed assets, the concepts and tools involved in capital budgeting apply equally well to investments that do not involve changes in an organization's productive capacity. We discuss these other applications on page 1049 at the end of this chapter.

6. Determine the criteria to be used for deciding whether an investment proposal is to be accepted or rejected.

7. Determine which investments meet the criteria for acceptance.

8. Determine a means of financing these investments.

Steps 1 and 2 — Determine investment needs and alternative opportunities

In the first two steps management needs to take a good hard look at the organization, and decide what it has to do now, in order to reach its objectives for 5, 10, and 15 years down the road. What changes are needed in the current and future productive capacity in order to be on the right track? Once the needs of the organization have been determined, then all alternative ways of satisfying these needs must be specified.

For example, assume that the management of Home Video, Inc., which currently has a 2% share of the home video market, predicts that the firm will maintain that share over the next 10 years, but that the total market will quadruple. In order to meet this explosive demand, Home Video's capacity will have to be doubled within the next 2 years. Should the present capacity be maintained, and double and triple work shifts be started; should additional space be rented when needed and more machinery purchased; or should a second factory building be constructed? If Home Video is sure that there are no other practical ways to meet its needs, then it could go on to Step 3 in the capital budgeting process — the gathering of relevant information concerning the alternatives to be evaluated.

Remember that in Chapter 25 we learned that *relevant information* represents that information which (1) relates to the future, and (2) is different for the alternatives that are being considered in the decision. Within this chapter all relevant information can be placed in one of two categories. And these two categories — the key factors of Step 3 — are common to all capital budgeting situations. The two key factors are:

Step 3 — Relevant information: net incremental investment and incremental cash flows

1. The net incremental investment
2. The incremental cash flows

The *net incremental investment* represents the outlay of resources made at the very beginning of a new project. The *incremental cash flows* represent the additional cash generated by the firm during the life of a project due to the net incremental investment that was made at the beginning of the project.

Step 4 — Select a capital budgeting method

The fourth step in the capital budgeting process is the selection of a capital budgeting method that we can use to evaluate the relevant information about a capital budgeting proposal.

We are going to look at four different capital budgeting methods. The four methods are classified as either discounted cash flow methods or nondiscounted cash flow methods. They are:

1. Discounted cash flow methods
   a. Net present value   b. Internal rate of return
2. Nondiscounted cash flow methods
   a. Payback period   b. Accountant's rate of return

Step 5 — Calculate results for capital budgeting method

Once we decide which method (or methods) to use to evaluate the investment proposals, we then do Step 5 — we calculate the results for each method, using the procedures that are discussed in the remaining pages of this chapter.

CAPITAL BUDGETING: TO SOME AN UNREWARDING EXPERIENCE

At a recent management conference, an upper level executive of a prosperous high-technology company was asked to name his most difficult problem. Instead of citing Japanese competition or the constant need in that business to come up with innovative technology, the executive stated simply "trying to convince my CEO and board to approve an idea for a new investment project."

Many managers will agree that getting a project through a corporate capital appropriations committee can be one of the most frustrating and unrewarding experiences of corporate life. Battles wage against a background of high interest rates, tight budgets, and increasing sensitivity to investment risk. Typically, two sides develop; strategists, who look at a project for what it might accomplish, are pitted against quantitative an-

alysts, who look at it for what it will cost. Often, the only result is a stalemate.

Steps 6 and 7—Determine and use criteria for acceptability

As you can tell from the list of steps, Step 5 is not the last step. The net present value for a project does not automatically tell us if it is good enough to warrant our purchase. That's where the criteria—Steps 6 and 7—come in. The criteria are simply guidelines that tell us what is an acceptable answer and what is not. If the results for a project do not meet certain minimum standards, then that project is dropped from further consideration. For example, when we use the net present value method, the guideline says that the net present value must be greater than or equal to zero, or the project is unacceptable.

Step 8—Determine means of financing

Once we decide which project or projects to invest in, the last step in the capital budgeting process is deciding how to finance the investment. Should we finance with debt, or stock, or internally generated funds? The answer to this question is beyond the scope of this text, but will likely be discussed in detail in your finance courses.

DISCOUNTED CASH FLOW METHODS

For discounted cash flow methods we need to understand present value concepts

The main characteristic of the ***discounted cash flow methods*** is that they consider the time value of money through the application of present value analysis. We introduced the concept of present value in Chapter 15 and showed you how to apply the concept to long-term liabilities. In this chapter we will take the same concept but apply it to capital budgeting. First though, let's review some of what you learned back in Chapter 15.

The Concept of Present Value

A review of present value

Present value analysis recognizes the time value of money, that is, that cash invested today will accumulate to greater amounts in future periods, due to the compounding of interest. For example, if $1 is invested today (referred to as time period zero), at 10%, the $1 will accumulate in the following manner:

Investment today	$1.000
Interest in year 1 @ 10%	.100 ($1.000 × .10)
Investment at end of year 1	$1.100
Interest in year 2	.110 ($1.100 × .10)
Investment at end of year 2	$1.210
Interest in year 3	.121 ($1.210 × .10)
Investment at end of year 3	$1.331

By the end of 3 years, interest of $.331 ($.100 + $.110 + $.121) will have been added to the $1 investment, totaling $1.331.

This accumulation of cash can also be shown by the following diagram:

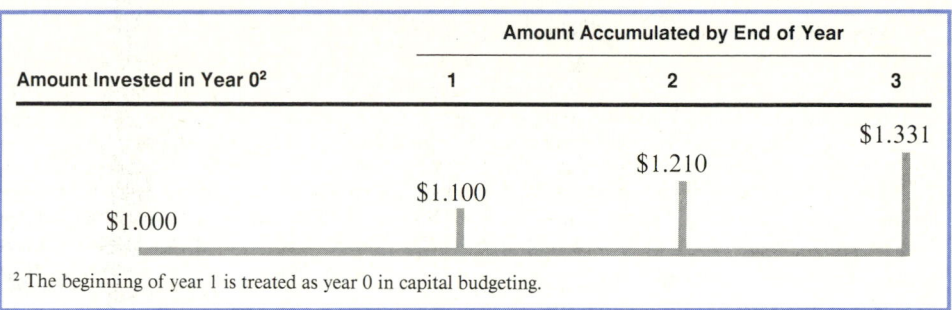

	Amount Accumulated by End of Year		
Amount Invested in Year 0[2]	1	2	3
			$1.331
		$1.210	
	$1.100		
$1.000			

[2] The beginning of year 1 is treated as year 0 in capital budgeting.

A lump sum accumulates into the future

Let's assume now that instead of investing $1, you want to invest $10,000. What amount would $10,000 accumulate to in 3 years? One way to find out is to multiply the amount that $1.00 accumulates to in 3 years, $1.331, by the $10,000 investment:

$$\$1.331 \times \$10,000 = \underline{\$13,310}$$

Another way is with the diagram:

	Amount Accumulated by End of Year		
Amount Invested in Year 0[2]	1	2	3
			$13,310
		$12,100	
	$11,000		
$10,000			

[2] The beginning of year 1 is treated as year 0 in capital budgeting.

You would have $13,310 in your account in 3 years.

The value today of a future lump sum

Now let's turn things around just a bit. Assume instead, that you know that you want to have $13,310 in your bank account in 3 years but are wondering how much you have to invest today at 10% to accumulate to $13,310. Naturally we know from above that the amount is $10,000. But, assuming for a moment that we do not know, we could determine it by doing the reverse of the computation above. That is:

$$\$13,310 \div 1.331 = \underline{\$10,000}$$

An alternative way to show this computation is:

$$\$13,310 \times \frac{1}{1.331} = \underline{\$10,000}$$

And, one final way is as follows:

$$\$13,310 \times .7513 = \underline{\$10,000}$$

The number .7513 is merely the decimal form for the fraction 1/1.331. This number .7513 is called the present value of $1 in 3 years at 10%. What it means is that $.7513 invested today at 10% will accumulate to $1 in 3 years:

Invest	$.7513
Interest in year 1	.0751
	$.8264
Interest in year 2	.0826
	$.9090
Interest in year 3	.0909
Accumulation at the end of 3 years	$.9999 = $1.0000 (rounded)

When we multiply .7513 by $13,310, the $10,000 result represents the present value of $13,310 in 3 years, at 10%—meaning that $10,000 invested today at 10% will accumulate to $13,310 in 3 years.

PV of $1 table: little *p – n – slash – i*: $p_{\overline{n}|\,i}$

The number .7513 is found in the present value of $1 table in Chapter 15 (Table 15-1) at the intersection of the 10% column and the 3-year row. The present value of $1 for other combinations of years and interest rates can also be found in Table 15-1. Therefore, any time you need to determine the present value of some lump-sum amount of cash in the future, you merely find the appropriate number (called a present value factor) in Table 15-1 and multiply it by the future lump sum. You will be making quite a few of these present value calculations in this chapter, so you had better know how to do them.

Another example: should land be purchased?

Let's change our example now to one that obviously involves a capital budgeting situation. Mr. Cincy is looking for a good real estate investment, and goes to see Mr. Driessen, a real estate agent. Mr. Driessen shows Mr. Cincy a piece of land costing $20,000 and assures Mr. Cincy that if the land is held for 2 years, it will have a resale value of $24,000—an appreciation of $4,000. Should Mr. Cincy buy the land?

Estimating that he can earn 12% interest in a CD, Cincy computes first:

Investment	$20,000
Interest in year 1 (.12 × $20,000)	2,400
	$22,400
Interest in year 2 (.12 × $22,400)	2,688
Investment at end of year 2	$25,088

If $20,000 is invested in a CD, Mr. Cincy sees that he can have $25,088 in 2 years, $1,088 more than he will have if he buys and then resells the land.

Mr. Cincy also evaluates the situation a second way—this way being very similar to one of the discounted cash flow methods we will discuss in a moment. He finds the present value of receiving $24,000 in 2 years:

$$.7972 \times \$24,000 = \underline{\$19,133}$$

The $19,133 is the amount that could be invested today, at 12%, in order to have $24,000 in 2 years. Given the choice of investing $19,133 in a CD or $20,000 in land, but receiving the same $24,000 in 2 years under both alternatives, Mr. Cincy makes the logical choice—turn down Mr. Driessen's deal—or get a lower price from him.

Now we are about ready to discuss the two discounted cash flow methods—net present value and internal rate of return. The facts we will present in Example 26-1 provide the input for these two methods, as well as for the two nondiscounted cash flow methods that follow.

The Illustration

Everything is the same for two projects except the timing of cash flows

The illustration we will show you in Example 26-1 involves two machines that cost the same amount of money, have the same life, and generate the same amount of incremental cash flows over their lives. The only difference in the two machines is the timing of the incremental cash flows. One of the machines is expected to generate the same amount of cash flow in each year (an annuity), while the other machine is expected to experience greater cash flows in the early years than in the later years of life.

For each capital budgeting method that we discuss in this chapter, the calculations of the method, and in some cases the usefulness of that method, depend on the timing of the cash flows. In all but one of the methods, the solution is different when the cash flows are the same each year from the solution when the cash flows are not the same each year. When we get different solutions we know that they are due entirely to the different timing of cash flows—since all other facts about the two machines are identical.

EXAMPLE 26-1

HUBBARD CONTRACTING

Craig Hubbard, the owner of a local road building company, is considering an investment in one of two projects, A or B. Each project requires a $10,000 incremental outlay for a different earth-moving machine—which we will call machines A and B. Both machines have an expected 8-year life. The total incremental cash flows over the 8-year life is $16,000 for both machines, but the distribution of this total to individual years is quite a bit different.

Cash flows are even for project A and uneven for project B

Year of Life	Incremental Cash Inflows	
	Project A	Project B
1	$ 2,000	$ 4,000
2	2,000	3,000
3	2,000	3,000
4	2,000	2,000
5	2,000	1,000
6	2,000	1,000
7	2,000	1,000
8	2,000	1,000
Total	$16,000	$16,000

When discounted cash flow methods are employed, Craig will use an interest rate of 10%. This rate, referred to in capital budgeting as the cost of capital or minimum desired rate of return, will be represented by the letter "r." This is the cost of raising funds to finance the project.

Net Present Value Method

The first discounted cash flow method that we discuss is the ***net present value method.*** The steps we take in the net present value method are very similar to what we did for Mr. Cincy when we decided not to purchase the land from Mr. Driessen for $20,000.

In the net present value method, we first calculate the present value of all future cash flows and then compare this amount to the amount of required initial cash outlay (the net incremental investment). If the present value of the net cash receipts exceeds the outlay, the project is acceptable. If the present value is less than the outlay, the project must be rejected. We only accept projects with positive NPVs because a positive NPV means that the value of what we get back from the investment—measured by the present value of future cash flows—is greater than what it costs us to invest in the project. And only when we invest in a project with a positive NPV will the value of the firm as a whole be increased.

The steps we take in this process are the same, whether the cash flows are the same amount each year (an annuity) or a different amount each year. They are:

STEP 1: Determine the total present value (TPV) of the future cash flows using the appropriate interest rate, r (referred to as the ***cost of capital*** or the minimum desired rate of return).

STEP 2: Subtract the cash outlay for the net incremental investment from TPV. This difference is called the ***net present value*** (NPV).

NPV = TPV less investment

STEP 3: If the NPV is positive, the project is acceptable. If the NPV is negative, it is rejected. If it is zero, the decision maker is indifferent to accepting or rejecting.

Using these steps, we will now compute the NPV for project A and then decide if it is acceptable or not.

Project A

When the cash flows in each year are the same amount, we can determine their total present value in one of two ways. We can individually find the present value of each $2,000 receipt for years 1 through 8 using only the present value of $1 table (Table 15-1). Or we can use a simpler approach in which we use the present value of an ordinary annuity of $1 table (Table 15-2), and make one calculation instead of eight.

You see, the present value of an ordinary annuity table is closely related to the present value of $1 table. Specifically, any number—a factor—in the present value of an annuity table is simply the summation of the numbers—the factors—from the present value of $1 table. For example, at 10% the first eight factors from the present value of $1 table are as follows:

PV of $1 @ 10% in 1 year $(p_{\overline{1}\|10\%})=$	.909
PV of $1 @ 10% in 2 years $(p_{\overline{2}\|10\%})=$	.826
PV of $1 @ 10% in 3 years $(p_{\overline{3}\|10\%})=$	.751
PV of $1 @ 10% in 4 years $(p_{\overline{4}\|10\%})=$	.683
PV of $1 @ 10% in 5 years $(p_{\overline{5}\|10\%})=$	.620
PV of $1 @ 10% in 6 years $(p_{\overline{6}\|10\%})=$	.564
PV of $1 @ 10% in 7 years $(p_{\overline{7}\|10\%})=$	.513
PV of $1 @ 10% in 8 years $(p_{\overline{8}\|10\%})=$	.466

Summation of PV of $1 factors, at
10%, for years 1–8   = 5.332

PV of annuity table:
Big P – little n – slash – i: $P_{\overline{n}\|i}$

The summation of present value factors for 8 years at 10% equals 5.332. If you now look at the present value of an ordinary annuity table (Table 15-2) for 8 years at 10%, you will see the same number: 5.334. (The difference between the 5.332 above and 5.334 is due to rounding in the calculations of present value factors.)

Using this annuity factor of 5.334 ($P_{\overline{8}|10\%}$), the steps in computing net present value are:

STEP 1: TPV = PV of \$2,000 @ 10% for 8 years:
$$= P_{\overline{8}|10\%} \times \$2,000$$
$$= 5.334 \times \$2,000 = \underline{\$10,668}$$

NPV for project A is positive: It's acceptable

STEP 2: NPV = TPV − net incremental investment
$$= \$10,668 - \$10,000 = \underline{\$668}$$

STEP 3: Since NPV of \$668 is > \$0, or positive, the project is acceptable.

Notice that in Step 3 we used the term "acceptable" rather than "accepted." Since only one of the two projects, A or B, will be purchased, the two are referred to as being ***mutually exclusive*** — the acceptance of one project automatically results in the rejection of the other. Even though the NPV of \$668 for project A is acceptable, we will accept project A over project B only if the NPV of project B is not higher than \$668.

If we were not comparing projects A and B for the same purpose, then they would not be mutually exclusive, and the acceptance of one would not automatically preclude the acceptance of the other. If this were the case, then whether or not we do accept all acceptable projects (NPV > 0) depends on the availability of funds. It might be that we accept all projects with a positive NPV. However, if the funds budgeted for capital projects are limited, then we would have to rank the projects according to the NPVs, and we would accept the projects with the highest NPVs until the available funds for investment purposes are exhausted.

Project B

The cash inflows expected for project B are not the same amount each year — they do not represent an annuity — thus we cannot determine TPV with the PV of an ordinary annuity of \$1 table (Table 15-2). Instead, we need to use the PV of \$1 table (Table 15-1) and separately compute the present value of each cash inflow. The steps are:

STEP 1: TPV

PV of \$4,000 @ 10% in year 1 = \$4,000 × .909 =	\$ 3,636
PV of \$3,000 @ 10% in year 2 = \$3,000 × .826 =	2,478
PV of \$3,000 @ 10% in year 3 = \$3,000 × .751 =	2,253
PV of \$2,000 @ 10% in year 4 = \$2,000 × .683 =	1,366
PV of \$1,000 @ 10% in year 5 = \$1,000 × .620 =	620
PV of \$1,000 @ 10% in year 6 = \$1,000 × .564 =	564
PV of \$1,000 @ 10% in year 7 = \$1,000 × .513 =	513
PV of \$1,000 @ 10% in year 8 = \$1,000 × .466 =	466
	TPV = \$11,896

NPV for project B is positive: It's acceptable, and higher than NPV for project A

STEP 2: NPV = TPV − net incremental investment
$$= \$11,896 - \$10,000$$
$$= \underline{\$1,896}$$

STEP 3: The NPV of \$1,896 is greater than zero, so it is acceptable.

Not only is project B acceptable, but since its NPV is also greater than the NPV for project A, it is probably the one we would choose—if only the two projects are being compared.

Intuitively, you might have expected the NPV for project B to be greater than the NPV for project A without making any computations. Both projects A and B are expected to generate the same total amount of cash inflows, $16,000, during the same 8 years of useful life, for the same amount of investment, $10,000. Since the total cash inflows are the same, $16,000, the timing of the cash inflows is the clue to which project is the better of the two. Project B promises greater cash inflows than project A in years 1 to 3 but less cash inflows than project A in years 5 to 8. By looking at the factors in the present value of $1 table for years 1 through 8, you can see that the present value of early year cash flows is more valuable than the present value of later year cash flows. Therefore, the present value of the $16,000 distributed to the 8 years of project B has to be greater than the same $16,000 distributed to the 8 years of project A.

An Adaptable Format for NPV

An easy-to-use format for NPV—especially for harder problems

The calculations for project B were a little more cumbersome than they were for project A because of the uneven stream of cash inflows for project B. Even so, they were still rather simple and straightforward, when compared to what they can be in some capital budgeting problems. So let's now make project B somewhat more complicated so we can show you a useful format for calculating NPV that is really needed only when the problems get a little more difficult.

EXAMPLE 26-2

> Assume in Example 26-1 that the machine acquired for project B is expected to require a $500 major overhaul at the end of year 5. In addition, the acceptance of project B will require the use of building space that is currently being leased to Apex Company for $200 per year. Finally, the machine can be sold for $2,500 at the end of the project's useful life.

In addition to the cash receipts from operations, there now is also a major overhaul, a disposal, and some lost rentals.

The new solution for project B is presented in Exhibit 26-1. What we want to emphasize in this solution is the format that we are using to compute NPV—a format that can be easily adapted to any NPV situation—no matter how simple or detailed the situation may be.

The key to the format is in the headings that run from left to right across the top of the page:

Description	PV Factor	PV of Cash Flows	Yearly Sketch of Cash Flows								
			0	1	2	3	4	5	6	7	8

The format organizes your work under easy-to-use headings

The first two items in Exhibit 26-1 come from the original facts in Example 26-1. The initial outlay of $10,000 goes in year 0 (the beginning of year 1), and its present value is $(10,000)—shown in parentheses to represent an outflow. The cash receipts from

EXHIBIT 26-1 Solution to Example 26-2.
For each item described: (1) Put the cash in the sketch of cash flows, (2) find the correct PV factor, and (3) multiply to get PV.

Description	10% Present Value Factor	10% Present Value	Yearly Sketch of Cash Flows								
			0	1	2	3	4	5	6	7	8
Net incremental investment	1.000	$(10,000)	$(10,000)								
Cash receipts from operations: Year											
1	.909	3,636		$4,000							
2	.826	2,478			$3,000						
3	.751	2,253				$3,000					
4	.683	1,366					$2,000				
5	.620	620						$1,000			
6	.564	564							$1,000		
7	.513	513								$1,000	
8	.466	466									$1,000
Major overhaul	.621	(311)						(500)			
Opportunity cost: lost rentals	5.334	(1,067)		(200)	(200)	(200)	(200)	(200)	(200)	(200)	(200)
Disposal of machine	.466	1,165									2,500
Net present value		$ 1,683									

operations are shown in the sketch of cash flows for years 1 through 8, and eight different present value computations are made.

The last three items come from the additional complications introduced in Example 26-2. The major overhaul is placed in the year 5 column of the sketch of cash flows, and its present value at 10% is determined to be $(311). The $200 per year of lost rentals represents an opportunity cost to the firm. Even though they will not actually be cash outflows, they will still have a negative effect on the firm's cash position. If the space were rented, the cash receipts would be $200 per year. But if the space is not leased, the cash receipts will be reduced by the $200—the opportunity foregone. The present value of the annuity of reduced rentals is $(1,067). Finally, the firm expects to sell the machine at the end of its useful life for $2,500. This amount goes in the year 8 column and its present value is $1,165. The NPV of project B is now $1,683, which is still positive and therefore acceptable.

As long as the facts within a problem are no more complicated than they were originally in Example 26-1, there really is no reason for you to use the format we've just shown you. However, for the more complicated situations, we recommend that you use the format shown in Exhibit 26-1, because all the facts in the solution can be easily seen and followed by you or anyone reviewing your work.

Internal Rate of Return

Changing rates mean different NPVs

When we determined the NPV for project A from Example 26-1, using a 10% cost of capital, we got an NPV of $668. If we had used any rate other than 10%, the NPV would naturally have been different. Let's see what the NPV would have been if we had used 8% or 12%, rather than 10%.

8%	12%
TPV $= P_{\overline{8}|8\%} \times \$2,000$ per year	TPV $= P_{\overline{8}|12\%} \times \$2,000$ per year
$= 5.746 \times \$2,000$	$= 4.967 \times \$2,000$
$= \$11,492$	$= \$9,934$
NPV $= \$11,492 - \$10,000 = \underline{\$1,492}$	NPV $= \$9,934 - \$10,000 = \underline{\$(66)}$

After we compare the results for NPV at 8%, 10%, and 12%, we can make the following conclusions:

1. The higher the cost of capital, the smaller the NPV; and the smaller the cost of capital, the higher the NPV.

2. NPV can either be positive or negative, depending on the cost of capital.

When NPV = zero, this rate is the IRR

If the second conclusion is true, then it must also be correct to conclude that there is an interest rate for which the TPV exactly equals the incremental investment — resulting in an NPV of zero. Since NPV is positive at 8% and 10% and negative at 12%, it must be zero for some rate in between 10% and 12%. When we have found that rate, at which the NPV of the project is zero, we will have found the ***internal rate of return*** for the project.

The IRR is the effective rate earned on a project

The internal rate of return (IRR) is the actual, effective, or true rate of return that we are earning on a project. So once we have determined the IRR, we then compare this rate to the cost of capital, r, in order to decide whether or not the project is acceptable. If the project is earning a rate of return that is greater than it costs to finance the project (IRR $> r$), the project is acceptable; if the reverse is true

Criteria for acceptance with IRR

(IRR $< r$), then the project is rejected; and if the internal rate of return equals the cost of capital (IRR $= r$), then we are indifferent to accepting or rejecting.

Project A

We can always determine the IRR by doing what we did in the discussion above. When we calculated the NPV at different costs of capital, we found that the NPV was positive at one rate but negative at the next. We then knew that the IRR must be in between the two rates. Although this approach is necessary for projects with uneven cash flows, there is a much easier way to calculate IRR for projects that have an even stream of cash receipts.

To find IRR — search for the factor

Since the cash receipts for project A are the same amount each year — an annuity — why don't you first turn back to Table 15-2, which is the present value of an ordinary annuity table. We will be looking for a specific number in that table — a present value of an annuity factor. We want to find that factor which we can multiply by the $2,000 cash receipts per year to give us a TPV of $10,000 and an NPV of zero. The only factor that can do this, of course, is 5.000. Now try to find this factor in the row for 8 years. If you find it, then the interest rate at the top of the column having the factor will be the IRR.

Although you will not find the exact factor that you want, you can get awfully close. As you can see, the factor 5.000 falls in between the factors of 5.334, for 10%, and 4.967, for 12%. Therefore, just as we concluded in the previous section, the IRR must be between 10% and 12%. Now that we know approximately where it is, we need to use interpolation to calculate the exact rate. *Interpolation* is a procedure used to find an exact answer when you know it lies between two other numbers.

The discussion above for determining the IRR *for projects having even cash flows* can be converted into the following list of mechanical steps:

STEP 1: Divide the net incremental investment by the cash flow expected per year. This results in a PV of an annuity factor ($P_{\overline{n}|i}$):

$$\text{Factor} = \frac{\textbf{net incremental investment}}{\textbf{cash flow per year}}$$

$$= \frac{\$10,000}{\$2,000} = 5.000$$

The PV of annuity table is used only when we have an annuity

STEP 2: Go to the PV of an annuity of $1 table (Table 15-2) and find the row representing the life of the project. Scan across this row looking for the factor determined in Step 1. It will probably be between the factors for two other interest rates.

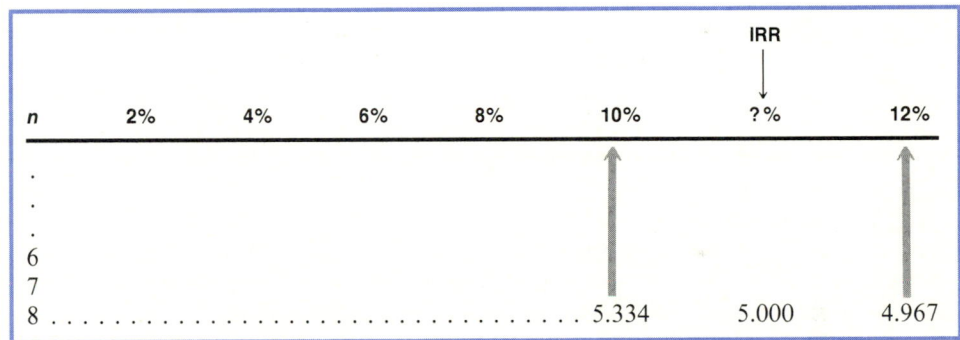

n	2%	4%	6%	8%	10%	?%	12%
.							
.							
.							
6							
7							
8						5.334	5.000	4.967

Interpolation — finding an exact IRR

STEP 3: Find the exact IRR by the process of interpolation. This involves first of all finding out the ratio of: the distance from 5.334 to 5.000, to the distance from 5.334 to 4.967. The distance from 5.334 to 4.967 is .367, which is the subtraction of factors immediately above and below 5.000.

10%	5.334
12%	4.967
	.367

The distance from the factor for 10% (5.334) to the factor for the exact IRR (5.000) is .334.

10%	5.334	5.334
?	5.000	
12%		4.967
	.334	.367

The factor 5.000 is 91% of the way from 5.334 to 4.967.

$$\frac{.334}{.367} = 91\%$$

The exact IRR is 91% of the way from 10% to 12% (the interest rates for 5.334 and 4.967). So the exact IRR is 1.82% above 10%.

$$.91 \times (12\% - 10\%) = 1.82\%$$

When added to 10%, IRR becomes 11.82%:

$$\text{IRR} = 10\% + 1.82\% = \underline{11.82\%}$$

STEP 4: Compare the IRR to r, the cost of capital—which, remember, is the cost of the money used to finance the project. If IRR $> r$, the project is acceptable. If IRR $< r$, the project is rejected. If IRR $= r$, the decision maker is indifferent to accepting or rejecting. Since the IRR of 11.82% $>$ 10%, the project is acceptable.

The reason we consider a project to be acceptable when its IRR exceeds r is that it means that the actual return being earned on the project is greater than the cost of funds that will be used to finance the project. And since we can earn more with those funds than it costs to raise the funds, the value of the firm will increase by investing in the project.

Project B

For uneven cash flows use trial and error for IRR

We will not be able to calculate the IRR for project B in the same way that we did for project A. The only reason that we were able to use the present value of an annuity table for project A is that the cash receipts for project A were an annuity. *Since the cash receipts for B are not an annuity, we cannot use the annuity table to calculate IRR*—we need to find another approach. The other approach is called *trial and error.* First however, let's remind ourselves what the IRR represents: The IRR is an interest rate—representing what the project is actually earning for the firm—and when we calculate the TPV of a project at that rate, the TPV equals the incremental investment (the NPV is zero).

For project B we are trying to find that rate of interest which will give us a TPV for

Year		
1	$4,000 \times p_{\overline{1}|14\%} = \$4,000 \times .877 =$	$ 3,508
2	$3,000 \times p_{\overline{2}|14\%} = 3,000 \times .769 =$	2,307
3	$3,000 \times p_{\overline{3}|14\%} = 3,000 \times .675 =$	2,025
4	$2,000 \times p_{\overline{4}|14\%} = 2,000 \times .592 =$	1,184
5	$1,000 \times p_{\overline{5}|14\%} = 1,000 \times .519 =$	519
6	$1,000 \times p_{\overline{6}|14\%} = 1,000 \times .456 =$	456
7	$1,000 \times p_{\overline{7}|14\%} = 1,000 \times .400 =$	400
8	$1,000 \times p_{\overline{8}|14\%} = 1,000 \times .351 =$	351
	TPV	$10,750
	Less: Incremental investment	10,000
	NPV	$ 750

IRR isn't 10%, since NPV > 0.
Go higher

the future cash flows of $10,000—exactly equal to the incremental investment. If you look back to the original calculation of NPV for B, using the 10% cost of capital, you'll see that the TPV was $11,896 and the NPV was $1,896. The interest rate of 10% cannot be the IRR, because the NPV at this rate is not zero.

If we're going to determine what the IRR is, we need to calculate the NPV at another rate and see if it will be zero. Remember one of our conclusions earlier: A higher interest rate results in a lower NPV. So if we calculate the NPV for project B at a rate higher than 10%, we know that the NPV will drop below $1,896, and possibly as far as zero. Using an interest rate of 14%, we see (in the illustration at the bottom of page 1042) that the NPV drops to $750.

It's not 14% either. Go a little
higher

Since at 14% the NPV is not zero, then 14% cannot be the IRR. And, since the NPV is still positive, the IRR must be higher than 14%. By repeating the NPV calculation at 18%, we get a negative NPV:

Year		
1	$4,000 \times p_{\overline{1}|18\%} = \$4,000 \times .847 =$	$ 3,388
2	$3,000 \times p_{\overline{2}|18\%} = 3,000 \times .718 =$	2,154
3	$3,000 \times p_{\overline{3}|18\%} = 3,000 \times .609 =$	1,827
4	$2,000 \times p_{\overline{4}|18\%} = 2,000 \times .516 =$	1,032
5	$1,000 \times p_{\overline{5}|18\%} = 1,000 \times .437 =$	437
6	$1,000 \times p_{\overline{6}|18\%} = 1,000 \times .370 =$	370
7	$1,000 \times p_{\overline{7}|18\%} = 1,000 \times .314 =$	314
8	$1,000 \times p_{\overline{8}|18\%} = 1,000 \times .266 =$	266
	TPV	$ 9,788
	Less: Incremental investment	10,000
	NPV	$ (212)

Now NPV < 0, so IRR must be
between 14% and 18%

Once again the NPV is not zero. However, since the NPV is greater than zero at 14% and is less than zero at 18%, the interest rate for which NPV = 0 (the IRR) must be between 14% and 18%.

The steps for IRR, that we have just described, for any situation that involves *uneven cash flows,* are:

STEP 1: Select any interest rate and calculate the NPV of the cash flows, using the PV of $1 table.

STEP 2: If the NPV is not zero repeat Step 1. If the NPV in Step 1 is > 0, repeat using a higher interest rate. If the NPV is < 0, repeat using a lower interest rate.

STEP 3: Continue repeating Step 2 until you have an NPV > 0 and an NPV < 0.

Once we have an approximate IRR, we then complete the process with Steps 4 and 5:

STEP 4: Interpolate to determine the exact IRR.

STEP 5: Compare the IRR to *r* and decide if the project is acceptable or to be rejected.

Picking up with Step 3 for project B, we see that the TPV and NPV at 14% and 18% are as follows:

	14%	18%
TPV..	$10,750	$ 9,788
Incremental investment	10,000	10,000
NPV..	$ 750	$ (212)

Using interpolation, we find that the exact IRR is 17.12%.

The final step of trial and error is also interpolation

	TPV	TPV
14%	$10,750	$10,750
?	10,000	
18%		9,788
	$ 750	$ 962

$$\frac{\$750}{\$962} = 78\% \times (18\% - 14\%) = \quad 3.12\%$$

$$+ \underline{14.00\%}$$

$$IRR = \quad \underline{17.12\%}$$

Both projects A and B have IRRs that are higher than the cost of capital of 10%— they are both acceptable projects. Since they are mutually exclusive, we will choose project B over project A because of the higher IRR (17.12% > 11.82%).

Comparison of Results Using NPV and IRR

Whenever we are evaluating the acceptability of a project, it shouldn't make any difference whether we are using the NPV method or the IRR method—the answer will be the same. If the NPV method indicates acceptability, so will the IRR. If the NPV method dictates rejection, the same will be true for IRR. In order for you to keep track of the relationships between the NPV and the IRR, Exhibit 26-2 may be helpful.

**EXHIBIT 26-2
Relationships of NPV and IRR.**

The decisions for NPV and IRR should be the same.

When the NPV Is:	The IRR Will Be:	Decision
NPV > 0	IRR > r	Project is acceptable
NPV < 0	IRR < r	Reject project
NPV = 0	IRR = 0	Indifferent to accepting or rejecting

NONDISCOUNTED CASH FLOW METHODS

We don't use PV tables for these methods

As the name should imply the distinguishing characteristic of the **nondiscounted cash flow methods** is that they do not require the use of present value techniques. Accountants usually consider these methods to be inferior to the discounted cash flow methods, because they do not explicitly consider the time value of money. However, we should still be interested in learning about these methods for the following reasons:

1. Many organizations still use these methods, so it is important for us to understand all the methods that are being used.

2. Some of the methods may be very useful when employed in conjunction with one of the discounted cash flow methods.

3. In certain circumstances a nondiscounted cash flow method may be more appropriate than a discounted cash flow method.

Payback Period Method

Payback is the number of years to recoup investment

The *payback period* (PP) is the number of years needed for a project to accumulate enough cash to pay for the initial cost of the investment. The calculation of the payback period depends on the timing of the stream of cash flows. Are they even or uneven?

Project A

When the stream of cash flows is even, we determine the payback period by dividing the incremental investment by the cash inflows per year. For project A, we do the following:

$$\text{Payback period (PP)} = \frac{\text{incremental investment}}{\text{cash flow per year}}$$

$$PP = \frac{\$10,000}{\$2,000} = 5 \text{ years}$$

For project A it takes 5 years for the accumulation of cash flows at $2,000 per year to pay for the $10,000 investment.

For a project with even cash flows, the PP is the factor for IRR

If you look carefully at the payback calculation, it should look familiar—the payback for project A is calculated in the same manner as we calculated the factor in the IRR method. In fact, this factor will always be the same—but only for projects having an even stream of cash flows.

Project B

We cannot take the same approach for project B as we did for project A. The reason is due to the fact that project B's cash flows do not represent an annuity. Instead, we need to accumulate the cash flows, 1 year at a time, until the total amount accumulated is equal to the incremental investment. We can do this for project B in the following manner:

Accumulate cash flows until they equal the investment

Year	Cash Flow per Year	Cumulative Cash Flow
1	$4,000	$ 4,000
2	3,000	7,000
3	3,000	10,000

It should take exactly 3 years for the cash flows of project B to accumulate to the $10,000 incremental investment.

Let's assume for a moment that the incremental investment for B is $10,500 instead of $10,000. If this were the case, then the cumulative cash flows at the end of 3 years would not fully pay for the investment. Instead, the payback period would be somewhere into the fourth year, as you can see on the next page.

Year	Cash Flow per Year	Cumulative Cash Flow
1	$4,000	$ 4,000
2	3,000	7,000
3	3,000	10,000
Payback period		**10,500**
4	2,000	12,000

At some point during the fourth year, the investment of $10,500 will be fully paid for. If we assume that the cash flows are generated evenly throughout the year, the exact answer can be determined by interpolation.

		Cumulative Cash Flows
End of year 3	$10,000	$10,000
Needed to pay for investment........................	10,500	
End of year 4		12,000
Differences	$ 500	$ 2,000

$$\text{Fraction of year} = \frac{\textbf{cash flow needed during year to pay for investment}}{\textbf{cash flow for full year}}$$

$$= \frac{\$500}{\$2,000} = .25 \text{ year}$$

Payback period = 3 years + .25 year = 3.25 years

Now the payback period would be 3.25 years, which places it near the end of March in year 4.

Decision Criteria and Resulting Weaknesses of the Payback Period Method

Is there life after payback?

If we accept or reject projects based entirely on the project's payback period, we would naturally select those projects with the shorter payback periods. In the original set of facts in Example 26-1, we would select project B, because it has a shorter payback period (3.0 years) than did project A (5.0 years). The choice of project B over project A is consistent with the choice we made when we used the NPV and IRR methods. But is this just a coincidence, or will the payback period method *always* yield results that are consistent with the discounted cash flow methods?

The problem with the payback period method is that it oftens evaluates projects differently than do NPV and IRR—for two main reasons. First, as the name— nondiscounted cash flow methods—implies, the payback period method ignores the time value of money. And second, the payback period ignores the useful life of the project. For example, pretend for a moment that the life of project B is only 3.1 years—barely longer than the payback period—and project A still has a payback of 5 years and a useful life of 8 years. The payback period of 3 years for project B is still better than the 5 years for project A. But does this mean we should still choose B over A, simply because B has the shorter payback period? Of course not! For when we calculate the new IRR for project B, we find that it is now approximately 1% (please don't be concerned with how this was calculated), which is not only far below the 11.82% for A, but is now less than our *r* of 10%—it is no longer even acceptable.

Since the payback method does have some serious weaknesses, you might ask: "Do any firms use this method, and if so, why?" The answer is definitely yes, and for several reasons. These include:

In spite of its shortcomings, it can be useful

1. Payback is simple to calculate and understand. The discounted cash flow methods seem overly complicated to many potential users.

2. Payback can be used in conjunction with the discounted cash flow methods. If a project has an undesirable payback period, it might be a waste of time determining the IRR or the NPV.

3. A company in a poor liquidity position may be more interested in a project having a quick return of the cost and a short life, than with a project having a longer payback period but an extremely long life and high rate of return.

4. A company that is considering a high-risk project, which could cause the company to go out of business if the project fails, once again may prefer the project with the short payback period regardless of the potential long-run profits on alternative opportunities.

Accountant's Rate of Return

The ARR is the only method that uses averages

The final capital budgeting method we will look at is the ***accountant's rate of return*** (ARR), which is also known as the accounting rate of return, or the unadjusted rate of return. Rather than emphasizing cash flows as do all the other methods, this method seems to stress accrual-based accounting income. The ARR is the percentage that the expected average annual income will be of the investment required to generate this income. The ARR is determined with the following formula:

$$\text{ARR} = \frac{\textbf{average net income}}{\textbf{incremental investment}}$$

The ARR is an *average rate of return for the entire life of a project.* Since it is an average, it makes no difference if the cash flows are even or uneven. Whenever we calculate an average, we merely divide the total cash flows by the number of years — it makes no difference if the total cash all comes in at the beginning of a project; if it all comes in at the end of a project; or if it is distributed evenly over the life of a project. The fact that the timing of a project's cash flows has no effect on the results for ARR is a serious weakness of the ARR method.

Is net income the same as cash flows?

We have just been talking about cash flows for a project — the timing, the total, and the average. When you look at the formula for ARR, however, you see that there is no mention of cash flows. The numerator is average net income, not average cash flows.

Net income and cash flows aren't equal, but they are related

This may be true, but since net income and cash flows are closely related, we have no trouble converting the ARR formula into a form that will better accommodate the facts we have been given. The main difference between the cash flows from operations of an organization and the net income of an organization is depreciation. Therefore, the relationship of cash flows to net income is as follows:

$$\textbf{Cash flows} - \textbf{depreciation} = \textbf{net income}$$

Now we can substitute the term, ***average cash flows − depreciation,*** for average net income, in the numerator of ARR, and we get:

$$\text{ARR} = \frac{\textbf{average cash flows} - \textbf{depreciation}}{\textbf{incremental investment}}$$

or
$$ARR = \frac{ACF - D}{I}$$

If a project has a salvage value, don't forget to subtract it in computing depreciation

Depreciation (D) is determined by:

$$D = \frac{\text{incremental investment} - \text{salvage value}}{\text{useful life of investment}}$$

or
$$= \frac{I - S}{L}$$

which is the formula for straight-line depreciation. An important point: The cash flows in the numerator of ARR are cash flows from the operations of the project, they do not include nonoperating cash items such as the salvage value. The cash receipt for salvage is included only in the calculation of depreciation.

Now let's calculate the ARR for projects A and B.

Project A

Since the cash flows for project A are the same each year, $2,000, we do not have to calculate the average cash flows for the numerator of ARR—the annual amount is also the average. The average depreciation for project A is $1,250 per year:

$$D = \frac{\$10,000 - \$0}{8 \text{ years}} = \$1,250$$

And the ARR for project A is:

$$ARR = \frac{\$2,000 - \$1,250}{\$10,000} = \frac{\$750}{\$10,000} = 7.50\%$$

Net income should average 7.50% of investment for project A

And here's what an ARR of 7.50% means. For an investment of $10,000, the income earned from this investment, $750 per year, averages 7.50% of the initial cost of the investment over the 8-year useful life. As you might expect, the higher the ARR, the better the project, and in order for a project to be acceptable, the ARR must be higher than the cost of capital, r.

Both ARR and IRR are rates of return that we expect to be earned by a proposed capital project. The difference is that IRR considers the time value of money while ARR assumes that all cash flows received throughout the life of a project are of equal value. Even though we may find that in some situations ARR and IRR may have similar answers, you should use IRR whenever possible. In many situations the results of the two methods are quite a bit different, and the results of IRR are always conceptually superior.

Project B

Since this project has an uneven stream of cash flows, the first thing we need to do is compute the average cash flow (ACF). The average cash flows for project B, over its useful life of 8 years, is $2,000, the same as project A:

$$ACF = \frac{\text{total cash flows (from operations) for entire useful life}}{\text{useful life}}$$

$$= \frac{\$16,000}{8 \text{ years}} = \$2,000 \text{ per year}$$

The ARR for project B is now

$$ARR = \frac{\$2,000 - \$1,250}{\$10,000} = \frac{\$750}{\$10,000} = 7.50\%$$

which is identical to the answer for project A.

Similarity of Answers

ARR for projects A and B are equal because we use averages

The ARR for projects A and B are both 7.50%. The reason for this is that the calculations involve averages. Since the total cash flows and the useful lives are the same for the two projects, the average cash flows are equal. And since the net incremental investment of $10,000 is also the same for both alternatives, the resulting answers are identical.

It is no coincidence that these two answers are identical. We purposely constructed the example to make this happen, so that the weakness of the method would be obvious. If you were the decision maker, would you be indifferent to selecting project A or B? Hopefully not. Instead, wouldn't you select the project that returns the total of $16,000 on the $10,000 investment in the more timely manner? This is what project B does, because of its heavier emphasis on early-year cash flows. Remember: when different projects have different timings of cash flows, the ARR method is not capable of discriminating one project from the other. Only NPV and IRR can do that properly.

Even though the ARR is inferior to the discounted cash flow methods, unfortunately it is still a popular method for many decision makers. The reasons are simple:

1. ARR emphasizes net income rather than cash flows; this is more consistent with the accounting model employed in financial accounting.

2. ARR does not require using present value tables, which to many users are still confusing and overly complicated.

ALTERNATIVE USES OF CAPITAL BUDGETING

Capital budgeting isn't only for fixed assets

Early in this chapter we defined capital budgeting as planning for the acquisition and financing of long-term investments, primarily property, plant, and equipment. The four methods that we introduced all dealt with the question of whether or not to acquire a fixed asset, or which fixed asset it would be better to buy. Although the capital budgeting methods have obvious uses in fixed asset decisions, they are not limited to these applications. Quite the contrary, there are numerous other situations that provide opportunities for the use of these methods as well.

As a matter of fact, any situation faced by management that has the same characteristics as the purchase decision for a fixed asset may be ideal for capital budgeting. The key characteristics of a purchase decision that are also found in numerous other decision situations are the following:

1. A large initial outlay of resources at year 0

2. An expectation that the incremental benefits in future years will adequately compensate the organization for its outlay of resources.

Each of the decision situations described below has these characteristics — so each could have capital budgeting techniques employed as part of its analysis.

1. Should the plant rearrange its machinery in order to provide a more efficient flow of materials through the different stages of production?

THE ANALOGY OF CAPITAL BUDGETING TO CALL OPTIONS

Based on my research into the investment and capital budgeting decisions of companies . . . I've concluded that one answer is to think of investment opportunities as analogous to ordinary call options on securities. Most managers are familiar with call options since they trade actively on public exchanges and such options are often an important part of a compensation package.

Securities options give the owner the right (as distinct from an obligation) to buy a security at a fixed, predetermined price, (called the exercise price) on or before some fixed date (the maturity date). By way of analogy, a discretionary opportunity to invest capital in productive assets like plant, equipment, and brand names at some future point in time is like a call option on real assets, or a "growth option." The cost of the investment represents the option's ex-

ercise price. The value of the option (its underlying security) is the present value of expected cash flows plus the value of any new growth opportunities.

2. Would the advantages of reduced competition offset the cost of purchasing a patent to a new process?

3. Should we undertake a substantial advertising campaign that holds the promise of significantly increasing our sales for several years?

EXHIBIT 26-3   Comparative Overview of Capital Budgeting Methods.

This exhibit provides a brief definition of each capital budgeting method. It also indicates how to calculate the method and how to determine if a project is acceptable.

Method	Definition	Calculation	Criteria for Acceptance — Acceptable if:
NPV	The amount of present value of future cash inflows in excess of net incremental investment	NPV = PV of cash flows @ r, less net incremental investment (for both even and uneven streams of cash flows)	NPV > 0
IRR	Actual rate earned on a project; the rate for which NPV = 0	1. Even cash flows: $$\text{Factor} = \frac{\text{investment}}{\text{cash flows}}$$ Find the interest rate in PV of annuity of \$1 table that has this factor. 2. Uneven cash flows: trial and error—using the PV of \$1 table.	IRR > r
PP	Number of years needed to recoup the original investment	1. Even cash flows: $$\text{PP} = \frac{\text{investment}}{\text{cash flows}}$$ 2. Uneven cash flows: Accumulate cash flows until cumulative amount equals incremental investment.	Short number of years
ARR	Average net income per dollar of investment	$$\text{ARR} = \frac{\text{avg. cash flows} - \text{avg. deprec.}}{\text{investment}}$$ (for both even and uneven cash flows).	ARR > r

4. Should we develop an in-house training facility to minimize the amount of on-the-job training required for new employees?

These situations are not an all-inclusive list. We merely wanted to give you enough examples so that you won't associate capital budgeting only with fixed asset acquisitions.

FOR YOUR REVIEW

You may now find it helpful to refer to Exhibit 26-3, which summarizes the key items in each of the four capital budgeting methods we have discussed in Chapter 26. For each method, there is a brief (1) definition, (2) description of the required calculation, and (3) explanation of the criteria for accepting or rejecting projects.

CHAPTER SUMMARY

Capital budgeting is planning for the acquisition and financing of long-term investments—primarily in fixed assets. The capital budgeting methods used to evaluate investment proposals fall into two categories: *discounted cash flow methods* and *nondiscounted cash flow methods.* The former methods involve the use of present value analysis, while the latter methods do not.

The two discounted cash flow methods are *net present value* (NPV) and *internal rate of return* (IRR). The net present value method finds the present value of all future cash flows and from this amount subtracts the *net incremental investment* for the project. If the excess (the NPV) is positive the project is acceptable, and if it is negative it is rejected.

The internal rate of return is the exact rate of return to be earned on the project. It represents that rate of interest for which the total present value of future cash flows equals the incremental investment. Expressed a little differently, it is the rate for which the NPV is zero. If the IRR is greater that the *cost of capital,* the project is acceptable; but if it is less than the cost of capital, it is rejected.

The nondiscounted cash flow methods include: (1) the payback period method, and (2) the accountant's rate of return method. The *payback period* is the number of years needed for a project to accumulate enough cash flows to pay for the initial cost of the investment. The weaknesses in this method are that: (1) the time value of money is not considered, and (2) the life of the project beyond the payback period is disregarded.

The *accountant's rate of return* is the percentage that the average expected annual net income is to the investment required to generate this income. The accountant's rate of return is the only method in which averages are employed and allowed. In all other methods, the use of an average would distort the answer.

IMPORTANT TERMS USED IN THIS CHAPTER

Accountant's rate of return   The ratio of the average annual net income from a project, to the investment required to generate this income (average net income divided by investment). (page 1047)

Capital budgeting   The planning for the acquisition and financing of long-term investments. (page 1030)

Cost of capital   The interest rate for determining the total present value of cash flows in a capital budgeting problem. (See minimum desired rate of return.) (page 1036)

Discounted cash flow methods The category of capital budgeting methods that employs present value analysis. The two discounted cash flow methods are net present value and internal rate of return. (page 1032)

Incremental cash flows The cash generated by the incremental investment in capital budgeting. (page 1031)

Internal rate of return That interest rate for which the net present value of an investment is zero. It is the exact rate of return to be earned on a project. (page 1040)

Interpolation The process of finding an exact answer when it falls between two other numbers. (page 1041)

Minimum desired rate of return The interest rate used to determine the total present value of cash flows in a capital budgeting problem. (See cost of capital.) (page 1036)

Net incremental investment The required outlay of resources to obtain a fixed asset and prepare it for productive use. (page 1031)

Net present value The difference between the total present value of future cash flows and the incremental investment of a project. (page 1036)

Nondiscounted cash flow methods The category of capital budgeting methods that does not use present value analysis. The category includes: (1) payback period, and (2) accountant's rate of return. (page 1044)

Payback period The number of years needed for a project to accumulate enough cash flows to pay for the initial cost of the investment. (page 1045)

Trial and error The manner of determining the internal rate of return when the cash flows from a project are not the same each year. (page 1042)

QUESTIONS

1. Define *capital budgeting.*

2. Give several decision situations in which the capital budgeting planning models discussed in this chapter would be applicable.

3. What is the main difference between the capital budgeting methods that are classified as *discounted cash flow methods* and those that are called *nondiscounted cash flow methods?*

4. What are the two most important factors to be considered in the use of all capital budgeting methods? Name three other factors common to the use of most capital budgeting methods.

5. The cash flows from operations needed for all capital budgeting methods usually refer to cash generated from the continuing, repetitive use of a fixed asset. Name five types of cash flows that might appear in the capital budgeting problem that would probably be treated separately from the cash flows from operations.

6. Is it the amount or the timing of cash flows that affects the net present value of a project?

7. Explain why an understanding of the time value of money is important in capital budgeting analysis.

8. The higher the cost of capital, the lower the net present value. Do you agree? Explain.

9. The higher the cost of capital, the higher the internal rate of return. Do you agree? Explain.

10. The net present value can be positive or zero, but never negative. Do you agree? Explain.

11. As long as the net present value of a project is greater than zero, the project should always be purchased by the firm. Comment.

12. Define the *internal rate of return.*

13. The internal rate of return is another name for the cost of capital. Comment.

14. What are the criteria for acceptance or rejection of a project using the internal rate of return method?

15. Explain what is meant by the *trial-and-error method.*

16. If the nondiscounted cash flow methods are inferior to the discounted cash flow methods, why do you have to learn them?

17. When two projects are being compared, the one with the greater cash flows in the early years of life will always have the greater NPV. Discuss whether you agree or disagree with this remark.

18. Explain how a discounted cash flow method and a nondiscounted cash flow method might be used together to evaluate a capital project.

19. Financial accounting and capital budgeting relate to different time periods and different segments within the organization. Explain what we mean by this observation.

20. The selection of a depreciation method will not affect the accountant's rate of return. Why?

21. The accountant's rate of return will be higher if the cash flows from a project are heavier in the early years of life rather than in the later years. Do you agree? Explain.

EXERCISES

Exercise 26-1

Miscellaneous present value questions

Answer each of the miscellaneous present value questions, using Tables 15-1 and 15-2.
a. What is the factor for the present value of $1 at 6% for 8 years?
b. What is the factor for $P_{\overline{10}|8\%}$?
c. How much must be invested today to accumulate to $1 in 5 years, at 10%?
d. How much must be invested today at 4% in order to receive $1 per year for 4 years?
e. What is the maximum amount that you would invest today at 12% in exchange for 8 annual receipts of $10,000?
f. If you invest $321 today, which will accumulate to $1,000 in 10 years, at what interest rate is the money invested?
g. If an investment of $6,144 at 10% promises a return of $1,000 per year, for how many years would the $1,000 be expected?
h. What is the present value of $2,500 per year for 20 years if the interest rate is 8%?
i. If the payback period for a 5-year machine is 3.604 years, what is the internal rate of return?
j. If the internal rate of return for a 15-year project is 6%, what is its payback?
k. What is the present value of the following cash flows for an *r* of 4%?

Year	Cash flow
1	$ 8,000
2	6,000
3	7,000
4	4,000
5	3,000
	$28,000

l. If the NPV for a project is zero using a cost of capital of 11%, what is its internal rate of return?

Exercise 26-2
Determining the characteristics of different capital budgeting methods

For each description given below, place an X in the column(s) representing the method(s) to which the description applies:

	PP	ARR	NPV	IRR
a. **Example:** The answer is stated in number of years.	X	—	—	—
b. The answer is given in dollars.	—	—	—	—
c. The answer is stated as a percentage.	—	—	—	—
d. Acceptable whenever the answer is positive.	—	—	—	—
e. Disregards the concept of time value of money.	—	—	—	—
f. An averaging technique.	—	—	—	—
g. The answer is influenced by the life of the project.	—	—	—	—
h. Includes depreciation in the computation.	—	—	—	—
i. Is not affected by timing of cash flows.	—	—	—	—
j. Dependent on the value of r.	—	—	—	—

Exercise 26-3
Compute all the methods for even cash flows

The Bellafonte Company is considering the acquisition of a new machine that will cost $10,000 and have an expected 5-year useful life. The new machine should generate $2,800 per year in cash savings. The cost of capital is 12%.

Compute the following:
a. Payback period
b. Net present value
c. Internal rate of return

(Check figure: 12.393%)

d. Accountant's rate of return (assume, for this part, a $400 disposal value at the end of year 5)

Exercise 26-4
NPV for different costs of capital

One of the machines at the Burford License Plate Company has just broken down. Burford realizes that a new machine must be purchased immediately, since the production of 1989 plates is about to begin. The most efficient machine available would cost $36,040, but will generate additional cash flows per year of $10,000 over an estimated 5-year useful life. Burford has decided to employ the net present value method.
a. Would the machine be acceptable if the cost of capital for Burford was 10%?
b. Would the machine be acceptable if the cost of capital was 15%?

[Check figure: NPV = $(2,520)]

c. Is there any interest rate in the present value tables for which the NPV = 0? If so, what is it, and what is the name given for this rate?

Exercise 26-5
NPV and IRR for uneven cash flows

The Phelps Company is about to spend $29,200 for a new machine that promises the following annual cash inflows:

Year	Cash Inflow
1	$20,000
2	10,000
3	4,000
	$34,000

a. If the cost of capital is 10%, compute the net present value.
b. Is the answer to part **(a)** above the internal rate of return? Why?
c. Compute the net present value using a rate of: (1) 8%, and (2) 12%.

[Check figure: NPV = $(546) for 12%]

d. Where is the internal rate of return? Why?

Exercise 26-6
Comparing IRR to ARR

The R. J. West Secretarial Pool is considering the purchase of new Tangerine PC computers for the secretaries to use. The computers would replace several typewriters and one copying machine. The net incremental investment for the computer is $15,000 and for the word processing software, $1,000.

　R. J. expects to save $4,000 annually in operating costs (labor, typing, and copying) over the 5-year useful lives. At the end of 5 years, R. J. expects to sell the computers and software for $3,000. The firm's cost of capital is 10%.
a. Calculate the internal rate of return for this project.
b. Calculate the accountant's rate of return.

(Check figure: 8.75%)

c. Discuss whether or not the project should be accepted.

Exercise 26-7
Calculating *r* and IRR

Kim Knight of Florida Fried Chicken decided to invest in a new chicken fryer, costing $750, because the projected net present value was $237.40. The fryer had an estimated life of 6 years; a salvage value at the end of 6 years of $100; and was expected to save $200 per year in operating costs.
a. What was Kim's cost of capital?
b. What was the project's expected internal rate of return?

(Check figure: 17.46%)

Exercise 26-8
Weakness of payback

The Mangrove Gardens Ski Show is considering the purchase of two new boats. The first boat—the Streak—will cost $14,400 and generate new cash inflows of $2,400 per year. The second boat—the Typhoon—costs $15,000 and should generate net cash inflows of $3,000 per year.
a. Compute the payback period for each machine.
b. Based only on the answer to part **(a)**, which machine should be acquired?
c. If the useful lives of Streak and Typhoon are 15 years and 6 years, respectively, determine the internal rate of return for each.

(Check figure: Streak = 5.47%)

d. Using IRR, would the decision to invest be the same as in part **(b)**?

Exercise 26-9
Working backwards to get the payback period

The Fourth National Bank of Arcadia will probably invest $20,000 in several new sophisticated money-counting machines. The life of the machines is 10 years. What is the payback period if the accountant's rate of return is 15%?

(Check figure: 4.0 years)

Exercise 26-10
Capital budgeting methods

For each of the situations below, fill in the missing blanks concerning several capital budgeting methods:

	Situation		
	1	2	3
Initial investment	$60,000	$_____	$50,000
Cash flow per year	$10,000	$4,000	$10,000
Life	10 years	8 years	9 years
Discount rate	10%	10%	_____%
Salvage value	$0	$2,000	$0
Net present value	$_____	$2,268	$18,010
Internal rate of return	_____%	_____%	_____%
Payback period	_____	_____	5 years
Accountant's rate of return	_____%	_____%	_____%

[Check figures: IRR for (1) = 10.58%; investment for (2) = $20,000; IRR for (2) = 12.97%]

Exercises 26-11
Computing the life based on results of ARR

Radio Station WJCS has purchased a new turntable that promises to reduce operating costs by $300 per year. The turntable, which costs $1,500, is expected to have an accountant's rate of return of 10%. At the end of its useful life, the turntable should be sold for $300.
    Determine the expected useful life of the turntable.

(Check figure: Depreciation = $150)

PROBLEMS
Set A

Problem A26-1
For uneven stream, calculate PP, ARR, and IRR

The Brenda's Isometric Gym is considering the purchase of an exercise machine that is expected to reduce operating costs over the next 4 years. If purchased for $2,000, the operating costs should be reduced by the following amounts:

Year	Reduced Labor Costs
1	$700
2	800
3	900
4	300

The gym's cost of capital is 11%.

Required

1. Determine the payback period.
2. Compute the internal rate of return. Based on this answer, should the machine be purchased?
3. Determine the accountant's rate of return.

(Check figure: 8.75%)

Problem A26-2
Should we keep or replace an old machine?

The Chapman Contracting Company is considering the replacement of an old steam shovel with a new one. The old steam shovel was purchased 3 years earlier for $70,000. It presently can be sold for $54,000, but if kept until the end of its remaining 4-year useful life it can be sold for only $6,000.
    The new steam shovel will cost $216,000 and will have a 4-year useful life. At the end of that time it is expected that it can be sold for $36,000. The cash operating costs using the new steam

shovel should be $650,000 per year, $80,000 lower than the operating costs if the old steam shovel is kept.

If the old steam shovel is kept, it will need a $6,000 major overhaul immediately and another costing $6,400 in 2 years.

The company's cost of capital is 10%.

Required

Using the present value method, determine if the old steam shovel should be kept or replaced. Compute the present values for the keep and replace decisions separately.

[Check figure: Present value for replace = $(2,197,262)]

Problem A26-3
Finding the NPV for a new bus

An ex-football player, Bubba Karras, is now working for the county recreation department and is trying to convince the county commissioners to purchase a used bus to transport kids to the summer sports camps. Bubba feels that the bus could substantially increase enrollment. The bus costs $3,500 and should last for 5 years. At the end of its useful life, the bus is expected to have a disposal value of $1,000.

The additional enrollments are expected to increase cash receipts by $3,000 per year but will necessitate hiring another part-time coach for $1,500 per year.

At the end of 2 years it is expected that the bus will need to undergo $500 of repairs in order to last the 3 remaining years.

Required

Using the net present value method, determine if the equipment should or should not be purchased. Assume a 12% cost of capital.

(Check figure: NPV = $2,074)

Problem A26-4
To buy or not to buy a patent

The administrator of City Hospital is approached by an inventor, D. Jossi, who is trying to sell a newly patented invention. If purchased, the invention would enable City Hospital to convert its semiautomatic x-ray machinery to automatic. Such a change would enable City Hospital to reduce its variable costs of operation. The patent would cost $70,000, and it would be necessary to spend an additional $30,000 to make the machinery conversions. The variable cost per x-ray using the semiautomatic machinery is $9, and the expected cost of using the automatic machinery is $7 per x-ray.

Patients are billed for x-rays at $17 a piece. If the machinery is converted to automatic, 12,000 x-rays can be processed, 3,000 more than are possible with the semiautomatic machinery.

The machinery has a remaining 5-year life and will have a $2,000 higher salvage in 5 years if it is fully automated. The patent is expected to be sold for $5,000 in 5 years.

The cost of capital is 12%.

Required

Using the net present value method, decide if City Hospital should purchase the patent from D. Jossi.

(Check figure: NPV for semiautomatic = $259,488)

Problem A26-5
Calculating NPV for rearrangement of plant

The president of Instant Charge Battery Corporation has asked the management advisory department of its CPA firm to help it decide if production efficiency can be improved by rearranging the plant layout. The consultant's report recommended that rearrangements should be undertaken and that the costs of rearrangement would be $300,000. The consultant estimated that such a change would substantially reduce direct labor during the next 5 years. In the first year, direct labor should decrease by $1.50 per unit produced. For years 2 to 5 the reduction should increase to $3 per unit. In addition, one less foreman will be needed in each of the 5 years, a savings of $17,000 per year.

The units to be produced in each year are expected to be 20,000 in year 1; 22,000 in year 2; and 30,000 per year for years 3–5.

Required | Using the net present value method, determine whether or not the plant layout should be rearranged. The firm's cost of capital is 12%.

[Check figure: NPV = $(12,800)]

Problem A26-6
Comprehensive NPV—
Renovate a facility

Cheap Way is a discount store in Florida that has decided to upgrade the quality of its merchandise in order to appeal to a different group of customers. To do this, Cheap Way plans to completely renovate its facility—which had originally been an abandoned airplane hanger—by changing the store front; lowering the ceiling; replacing the flooring and store fixtures; and upgrading the cash registers as well as everything else inside and out. This will require a capital outlay of $1,000,000 on January 1, 1988. In addition, Cheap Way will change its name to Luxury for Less, and spend $50,000 in 1988 and 1989 promoting the changes to the public.

Cheap Way expects to be able to sell its old fixtures for $25,000 at the beginning of 1988, if the renovation take place.

Once the renovations have been made, Cheap Way anticipates a substantial increase in cash receipts—probably slow at first, but growing dramatically after the first or second year. Cheap Way's accountant, Robin West, has come up with the following projections over the 5-year useful life of the new project:

Additional Operating Receipts	
1988	$ 100,000
1989	150,000
1990	600,000
1991	600,000
1992	800,000
	$2,250,000

One significant increase in operating costs (not included in net operating receipts above) that Cheap Way expects is for salaries for sales personnel. Due to the change in emphasis from a discount store to a luxury outlet, many more employees will be needed. The additional salaries should be about $50,000 in 1988 and 1989 and $100,000 for the next 3 years.

Currently Cheap Way is leasing some space to the Injuries Can Be Profitable Law Firm, for $12,000 per year. Since Cheap Way plans to break the lease, it will no longer be receiving the annual rentals. In addition, it will be necessary for Cheap Way to compensate the law firm $7,500 on January 1, 1988, for breaking the lease.

Required | Calculate the net present value for the planned renovation for Cheap Way. Use a cost of capital of 15%.

[Check figure: $(23,024)]

Set B

Problem B26-1
Payback, IRR, ARR

The National Vertigo Society is a little-publicized charity that uses a great number of volunteers to label, lick, and stamp envelopes. If a new machine is purchased to lick envelopes, the society expects the labor costs to decrease substantially. The company's cost of capital is 14%. The machine will cost $2,100 and is expected to last 5 years. During that time, the reduced labor costs are predicted to be:

Year	Reduced Labor Costs
1	$300
2	450
3	750
4	750
5	900

Required

1. Determine the payback period.
2. Compute the internal rate of return. Based on this answer, should the new machine be purchased?

(Check figure: 12.78%)

3. Determine the accountant's rate of return.

Problem B26-2
Comparing keep to replace for an old machine

The Hogan Construction Company is considering the replacement of an old crane with a new one. The old crane was purchased 3 years earlier for $100,000 and has a remaining book value of $61,000. It can be sold for $48,000 if disposed of at the present time, or $9,000 if disposed of at the end of its 4-year remaining useful life.

The new crane will cost $125,000 and is expected to have a $12,000 disposal value in 4 years. The cash operating costs for the old and new crane, respectively, will be $250,000 and $200,000 per year. If the old crane is kept, it will require a major repair costing $10,000 at the end of 2 years.

The company's cost of capital is 8%.

Required

Using the present value method, determine if the old crane should be kept or replaced. Compute the present values for the keep and replace decisions separately.

(Check figure: Difference in present value = $99,375)

Problem B26-3
Calculating NPV for an equipment purchase

Billie Joe Everrett, a tennis star for 25 years, has just retired and opened a tennis complex. One thing that Billie Joe would like to purchase is a ball machine — which automatically tosses balls to players every few seconds, with a variety of speeds, spins, and trajectories. The ball machine costs $1,800 and is expected to last for 6 years. At the end of its useful life, it should have a disposal value of $300.

The machine is expected to generate additional cash receipts for the complex of $5,000 per year. It will require the addition of one part-time employee at an annual salary of $4,000. Finally, an overhaul will probably be required at the beginning of year 5, costing $400.

Required

Using the net present value method (assuming a 12% cost of capital), determine whether or not the ball machine should be purchased.

(Check figure: NPV = $2,209)

Problem B26-4
Computing the NPV of a patent

The president of Trim Lines Jeans Company is approached by an inventor, M. Carnac, concerning a new patent. The patent would enable Trim Lines to convert its manual machinery to semiautomatic, thereby reducing the labor costs of production. The patent would cost $900,000, and it would require an additional $300,000 to make the machinery conversions. The variable costs per unit using the manual and semiautomatic machinery will be $10 and $8, respectively.

If Trim Lines decides to acquire the patent, it will produce and sell 100,000 units per year for the next 5 years. If Trim Lines continues to use the manual equipment, the production and sales will be only 70,000 units per year. The sales price will be $16 per unit regardless of the decision made.

The patent will be worthless in 5 years, but the semiautomatic machinery will have a $15,000 higher disposal value than would the manual machinery.

The cost of capital for Trim Lines is 10%.

Required

Using the net present value method, decide if Trim Lines should purchase the patent from M. Carnac.

(Check figure: NPV for patent = $1,841,300)

Problem B26-5
Should a plant layout be rearranged?

A foreman on the assembly line at Mitsui Motorscooters took advantage of the company's suggestion box to recommend that the arrangement of machinery within the factory be changed. The foreman felt that the efficiency of the production operation could be vastly improved by arranging machinery in such a way that the flow of goods from one worker to another was more orderly and less time-consuming.

The president of Mitsui hired a team of consultants to determine if the foreman was correct. The final report of the consultants not only supported the foreman's claim but made suggestions on how it should be done. It was estimated by the consulting team that it would cost $375,000 to make the rearrangements but that there would be substantial reductions in the costs of production over the next 5 years. The direct labor costs would be reduced by $1 per unit in year 1. In years 2 through 5, after the laborers had become more familiar with the revised flow of production, the direct labor costs should be reduced by $2 per unit. In addition, one less foreman will be needed in years 2 through 5, a savings of $10,000 per year.

The units to be produced during the next 5 years are predicted to be:

Year	Product
1	50,000
2	60,000
3	75,000
4	75,000
5	75,000

The consultants charged the company $15,000 for the analysis and final report, and the foreman received $500 for his suggestion.

Required

Using the net present value method, determine whether or not the plant layout should be rearranged. The cost of capital is 15%.

(Check figure: NPV = $42,730)

Problem B26-6
Expansion of business — Comprehensive NPV

In 1985 — three years ago — Dr. Mel Practise opened a new chiropractic clinic in a building he built for $100,000. Mel uses one-half of the building for his practice and leases the remainder to a dentist for $5,000 per year (on a 5-year lease).

Mel is currently considering expanding his practice by adding an associate, whom Mel will pay a guaranteed annual salary. Mel anticipates a great boom in business, which will necessitate his canceling the dentist's lease in order to use the entire building. It will cost Mel $10,000 to break the lease on January 1, 1988.

If Mel does expand his practice, he will have to furnish the additional space with furniture, cabinets, desks, rugs, and equipment — which should cost $75,000. In 5 years Mel plans to sell the furnishings for $13,000 and move to a new location.

Mel expects the cash receipts from his practice to increase substantially over the next 5 years with the addition of a second doctor.

Additional Cash Receipts	
1988	$ 65,000
1989	85,000
1990	100,000
1991	175,000
1992	200,000
	$625,000

The main additional cash disbursement that Mel expects annually is the salary of the new doctor and one new nurse. These additional expenditures should be:

	Doctor	Nurse
1988	$ 30,000	$15,000
1989	30,000	15,000
1990	50,000	18,000
1991	50,000	18,000
1992	50,000	18,000
	$210,000	$84,000

In addition, Mel expects his malpractice insurance to increase by $5,000 per year because of the addition of the second doctor to his practice.

Because Mel is located in a bad part of town and gets little walk-in business, he feels that he'll need to advertise his expansion, in order to reach new potential customers. Mel plans to spend $15,000 on promotions during 1988.

Required   Determine the net present value for Mel Practise's expansion, using a cost of capital of 12%.

Chapter 27   Income Taxes

After studying this chapter, you should be able to:

- Distinguish between gross income, adjustments to income, itemized deductions, and exemptions.
- Explain the importance of adjusted gross income.
- Determine taxable income and calculate income taxes for individuals.
- Compute the net profit or (loss) from a business or profession operated as a proprietorship.
- Distinguish between income tax reported on the income statement and taxes paid to the government.

Did you know that about one-half of the income that large corporations earn is paid to the federal government in the form of income taxes? Not only does the federal government tax income, but so do most states, and so do many cities. These taxes provide a substantial source of revenue for the various governments. For the federal government, half of its revenues come from income taxes. It may surprise you to know that individuals contribute $4\frac{1}{2}$ times the amount of income taxes that corporations do. Income taxes are levied on individuals, corporations, estates, and trusts; but proprietorships and partnerships do not pay income taxes. The income from these businesses is reported by the owners on their individual tax returns.

The objectives of income taxation differ from those of financial accounting

The relationship between accounting and income taxes is very close. A large portion of the income tax provisions rests on accounting principles that we have learned or will learn in this text. But you must understand that the objectives of income taxation and financial reporting are not identical. We all know the major objective of income taxation. It is to generate revenues to pay for the governmental services we use. The tax laws are also used to stimulate or slow down the national economy, and to encourage full employment. By now we know that financial accounting's objective is to report fairly a business entity's financial position and results of operations. Owners of these business entities would, of course, hope to minimize their income taxes in accordance with the tax regulations. A business may select one accounting alternative, such as straight-line depreciation, to report fairly operating results. But when preparing the tax return, a vastly accelerated method is allowed and would be selected to minimize the tax liability. A knowledge of accounting is essential when complying with the provisions of the tax laws. A knowledge of income taxes is essential for efficiently managing a business.

Our discussion of income taxes in this text must, by necessity, be brief. We will consider only the very basic tax provisions. Those of you interested in additional information on federal income taxes are referred to the excellent *free* publications of the Internal Revenue Service, such as Publication 17, *Your Federal Income Tax,* and Publication 334, *Tax Guide for Small Business.*

We will begin our discussion with a consideration of individual income taxes, progress to include income from proprietorships and partnerships, and conclude with a brief discussion of corporate taxation.

FEDERAL INCOME TAX FOR INDIVIDUALS

The taxes we pay are based on taxable income, which is gross income minus adjustments to income minus itemized deductions minus exemptions

Our tax laws are codified in the U.S. Internal Revenue Code and enforced by the Internal Revenue Service (IRS).

Most of us must report our last year's income to the IRS by April 15 of this year. We do this on a U.S. Individual Tax Return, which is commonly referred to as a Form 1040. If our income consists of only salary, dividends, and interest, we can use the cash basis of accounting to prepare our tax return. The amount of tax we must pay is determined by applying the appropriate tax rate to our *taxable income.* Now, the way we arrive at taxable income is to start with *gross income* and to subtract three things—*adjustments to income, itemized deductions,* and *exemptions.* Our friends at the IRS have gone to great lengths to tell us what each of these terms means. And that's where we will start our discussion.

Gross Income

Wages and salaries are considered gross income. But so are a number of other things

Gross income means everything we receive for personal services as well as any income from other sources. This includes wages and salaries. And it also includes interest, dividend, rental, retirement, royalty, pension, annuity, farm, alimony, business, and partnership income.

There are certain gross income items the tax code exempts or excludes from taxation. Some examples are interest on certain notes and bonds of state and local governments; up to $100 of the total qualifying dividends [$200 for a married couple filing a return together (called a *joint return*)]; and undergraduate scholarships for which no services are required.

Adjustments to Income

Moving expenses may be considered as an adjustment to income

The first subtraction from gross income is *adjustments to income.* We can include in this item moving expenses in connection with a change of residence due to a job transfer or new employment; employee business expenses in excess of amounts reimbursed by the employer, and alimony paid. The difference between gross income and adjustments to income is called *adjusted gross income* (AGI). This is an important figure because AGI is used as a basis for computing several itemized deductions — medical expenses, drug expenses, and state sales taxes. If you make an error in AGI, some itemized deductions will also be wrong.

Adjusted gross income is the difference between gross income and adjustment to income

Let's look at an example to see how AGI is computed. Assume that during the current year Adam and Eve Taxpayer received $25,100 in salaries, $250 in interest, and $700 in dividends. Included in the interest is $50 from City of Bethlehem bonds. Adam and Eve incurred $2,500 of expenses in a job transfer from Tulsa, Oklahoma, to Bethlehem, Indiana, and $400 in employee business travel and entertainment expenses not reimbursed by the employer. The computation of adjusted gross income would look like this:

Calculation of adjusted gross income

Gross income:		
Wages, salaries, tips, etc.		$25,100
Interest income ($250 − $50 exempt)	$ 200	
Dividends ($700 − $200 exclusion)	500	700
Total income		$25,800
Adjustments to income:		
Moving expenses	$2,500	
Employee business expenses	400	
Total adjustments		(2,900)
Adjusted gross income.		$22,900

Itemized Deductions

Itemized deductions are personal expenses

Itemized deductions are personal expenses and they are broken down into six categories. These categories are medical and dental expenses, taxes, interest expense, contributions, casualty or theft losses, and miscellaneous deductions. The total of the itemized deductions is subtracted from AGI.

The zero-bracket amount is a standard deduction that everybody can use instead of itemizing deductions

You don't *have* to itemize your deductions because the tax code allows everybody a standard deduction called a *zero-bracket amount.* This is $3,400 for married taxpayers filing a joint return, $2,300 for single taxpayers, and $1,700 for married taxpayers filing separately. Of course, if your itemized deductions exceed the zero-bracket amount, you will want to itemize. But since this standard deduction is allowed for everybody, the appropriate zero-bracket amount must be subtracted from the sum of itemized deductions to arrive at the total deductions allowed.

Medical and dental expenses are payments we made for the diagnosis, cure, relief, treatment, or prevention of disease. These include doctors' and dentists' fees, hospital service costs, medical and hospital insurance premiums, and prescription medicines and drugs. The tax code limits the amount of medical and dental expenses we can

Only those medical and dental expenses that exceed 5% of AGI can be deducted

deduct. Only the amount of medical and dental expenses that exceed 5% of AGI may be deducted.

If we have received any reimbursement payments from insurance companies, we must subtract them from the total medical and dental expenses.

Here's how Adam and Eve Taxpayer would compute their medical and dental expense itemized deduction. Remember that Adam and Eve have an AGI of $22,900; they also have the following medical expenses: doctor and hospital bills, $2,829; medical insurance premiums, $700; medicines and drugs, $375. The medical insurance paid $1,450 for doctors and hospital bills and $125 for medicine and drugs. The medical expense deduction is determined as follows:

Calculation of the medical expense allowance

Prescription medicines and drugs ($375 − $125)	$ 250
Doctors, dentists, hospitals, insurance ($2,829 + $700 − $1,450).	2,079
Total	$2,329
Less 5% of adjusted gross income	(1,145)
Total medical and dental expenses	$1,184

We can deduct certain taxes

Taxes that we are allowed to deduct include state, local, or foreign income taxes; state, local, or foreign real property taxes; state or local personal property taxes; and state or local general sales taxes. Federal income taxes and social security taxes are not deductible.

The IRS provides us with an optional state sales tax table (see Exhibit 27-1, below) to use in lieu of providing detailed listings of the items on which sales tax was paid.

EXHIBIT 27-1   An Excerpt from the Optional State Sales Tax Tables.

Income	Idaho 1	2	3	4	5	Over 5	Illinois[4] 1&2	3&4	5	Over 5	Indiana 1&2	3&4	5	Over 5
$ 1–$ 8,000	97	118	127	137	150	169	121	143	153	162	117	139	148	157
$ 8,001–$10,000	114	135	148	160	174	195	143	169	180	191	137	163	173	183
$10,001–$12,000	130	151	167	181	196	218	163	193	206	217	156	186	197	207
$12,001–$14,000	144	165	185	200	216	240	182	216	230	242	173	207	219	230
$14,001–$16,000	158	178	202	219	236	260	200	238	253	266	189	227	240	252
$16,001–$18,000	171	191	218	236	254	280	217	259	275	288	205	246	260	272
$18,001–$20,000	184	203	234	253	271	298	233	279	296	309	220	264	279	291
$20,001–$22,000	196	214	249	269	288	315	249	299	316	330	234	282	298	310
$22,001–$24,000	208	225	263	284	304	332	264	318	336	350	248	299	316	328
$24,001–$26,000	219	235	277	299	319	348	279	336	355	369	261	316	333	346
$26,001–$28,000	230	245	290	314	334	364	294	354	373	388	274	332	350	363
$28,001–$30,000	241	255	303	328	349	379	308	372	391	407	287	347	366	379
$30,001–$32,000	251	264	316	342	363	394	322	389	409	425	299	362	382	395
$32,001–$34,000	261	273	328	355	377	408	335	406	426	442	311	377	397	411
$34,001–$36,000	271	282	340	368	390	422	348	422	443	459	323	392	412	426
$36,001–$38,000	281	290	352	381	403	436	361	438	460	476	334	406	427	441
$38,001–$40,000	291	298	363	393	416	449	374	454	476	493	345	420	442	456
$40,001–$100,000 . . . . (See Step 3B)	15	15	18	20	21	22	19	23	24	25	17	21	22	23

The tables are based on *adjusted gross income.* We can increase the amount of state sales tax obtained from the table for sales taxes paid on the following acquisitions: Automobiles, motorcycles, motor homes, trucks, boats, planes, or homes. The general sales tax for Adam and Eve Taxpayer (Indiana residents), whose family size is 4 and whose AGI is $22,900, is found in the Optional State Sales Tax Tables to be $299.

In addition to the general sales tax, Adam and Eve paid $509 in real estate taxes and $420 in state and local income taxes, for a total of $1,228.

Interest deductions are allowed for sums paid for the use of borrowed money, such as mortgage interest, finance charges separately stated, bank credit card plan interest, note discount interest, interest on personal loans, and installment plan interest. The most common type of personal interest is the interest on a home mortgage. Usually the company holding the mortgage will provide a statement at year-end itemizing the amount of interest paid. Interest paid by Adam and Eve Taxpayer is:

Calculation of interest deduction

Home mortgage interest.	$1,750
Credit and charge cards	125
Interest on auto installment notes	315
Total interest.	$2,190

Charitable contributions are deductible if we make them to qualified organizations. Churches, most educational organizations, nonprofit hospitals, community chest, and the United Fund are examples of qualified organizations. Nonqualified organizations are chambers of commerce, civic leagues, communist organizations, and social clubs. The amount of deductible contributions is generally limited to 50% of adjusted gross income. Contributions in excess of the limit can be carried over and deducted in each of the next 5 years until it is used up. Adam and Eve Taxpayer made the following qualified contributions:

The First United Church	$450
United Fund	100
South Bend High School	50
Total	$600

Casualty and theft losses are deductible if the occurrence and amount of the loss can be proven. Losses are deductible only to the extent that the loss for each personal casualty or theft is in excess of $100 and 10% of AGI. Adam and Eve Taxpayer had no casualty or theft losses for the current tax year.

Miscellaneous deductions are in addition to the itemized deductions we listed above. Miscellaneous deductions may be classified into three groups: employee expenses, expenses of producing income, and other expenses. In the first group the following items are deductible: certain employment agency fees, dues to professional societies, part of home used regularly and exclusively for work, union dues, subscriptions to professional journals, and small tools. Deductible expenses of producing income are certain legal and accounting fees, expenses of an income-producing hobby, gambling losses to the extent of winnings, safe deposit box rentals, and certain interest. Certain appraisal fees and tax counsel and assistance fall into the third group of miscellaneous deductions. Adam and Eve Taxpayer had the following miscellaneous deductions:

Union dues	$250
Small tools	55
Safe deposit box	15
Total	$320

It's now time to summarize the itemized deductions for Adam and Eve. Don't forget that if the total exceeds the zero-bracket amount ($3,400 for Adam and Eve), we must subtract the zero-bracket amount from the total. And if the total is less than the zero-bracket amount, we will claim no itemized deductions since the standard deduction will be used.

Here is a summary of Adam and Eve's itemized deductions:

Total medical and dental	$1,184
Total taxes	1,228
Total interest	2,190
Total charitable contributions	600
Total casualty or theft losses	0
Total miscellaneous	320
Total	$5,522
Less appropriate zero-bracket amount	(3,400)
Total itemized deductions	$2,122

Exemptions

We are allowed a $1,000 deduction for each personal exemption. Personal exemptions are allowed for ourselves, our spouses, and anyone who qualifies as a dependent. Additional exemptions are allowed for age and blindness. Adam and Eve Taxpayer have two dependent children, therefore their exemptions total four and a $4,000 deduction is allowed.

Taxable Income and the Tax Computation

We are just about ready to determine Adam and Eve's tax liability. We first need to compute taxable income, then apply the appropriate tax rate. Their taxable income is:

Gross income		$25,800
Adjustments to income		2,900
Adjusted gross income		$22,900
Less: Itemized deductions	$2,122	
Exemptions	4,000	6,122
Taxable income		$16,778

For Adam and Eve the appropriate tax rate is found in Schedule Y (see Exhibit 27-2). The reference to *line 37* in the schedule is to taxable income.

MAJOR CHANGES EXPECTED IN THE TAX LAWS

On May 28, 1985 President Reagan in an address to the nation presented his proposals for major tax reform. His plan is designed to raise the same amount of total revenue for the United States Treasury, but to radically change the system for the sake of fairness, simplicity, and growth. Throughout the 1985 year and into 1986 Congress is expected to consider the President's proposal. Eventually, Congress will act on the tax proposal and it will be signed into law. Substantial changes will be made in the President's proposals due to the pressures of various groups with vested interests. Thus it is impossible to tell what the final law will look like. Consequently, your text and the problem material will use the 1985 tax provisions. Several of the President's proposed changes are listed here.

Individual Tax Rates	Currently there are 14 rate brackets starting at 11% and going up to 50%. The proposal suggests only 3 rate brackets, 15%, 25%, and 35%.
Exemptions	The $1,000 exemption would be raised to $2,000.
Zero-Bracket Amount	The $3,400 zero-bracket amount would be increased to $4,000 for joint returns ($2,900 for a single return and $3,600 for Heads of Households).
State and Local Income and Property Taxes	These taxes would not be deductible. We can expect a major fight over this issue.
Corporate Tax Rates	Graduated up to 33%.
Depreciation	A Capital Cost Recovery System would replace the Accelerated Cost Recovery System for depreciable property placed in service on or after Jan. 1, 1986. In place of the 3-, 5-, 10-, and 15-year property classifications of ACRS there would be six classes for CCRS. The President's proposal would allow for assets to be depreciated at values adjusted each year for the effects of inflation. This would result in depreciating more than the cost of the assets.
Investment Tax Credit	The investment tax credit would be repealed.

**EXHIBIT 27-2
Schedule Y
Married Taxpayers and
Qualifying Widows and
Widowers.**
Married filing joint returns and qualifying widows and widowers.

Use This Schedule if You Checked Filing Status Box 2 or 5 on Form 1040—			
If the Amount on Form 1040, Line 37 is: Over—	But Not Over—	Enter on Form 1040, Line 38	Of the Amount Over—
$ 0	$ 3,400	—0—	
3,400	5,500	. . . . 11%	$ 3,400
5,500	7,600	$ 231 + 12%	5,500
7,600	11,900	483 + 14%	7,600
11,900	16,000	1,085 + 16%	11,900
16,000	20,200	1,741 + 18%	16,000
20,200	24,600	2,497 + 22%	20,200
24,600	29,900	3,465 + 25%	24,600
29,900	35,200	4,790 + 28%	29,900
35,200	45,800	6,274 + 33%	35,200
45,800	60,000	9,772 + 38%	45,800
60,000	85,600	15,168 + 42%	60,000
85,600	109,400	25,920 + 45%	85,600
109,400	162,400	36,630 + 49%	109,400
162,400	. . . . . .	62,600 + 50%	162,400

The tax for Adam and Eve amounts to $1,881, which we calculate like this:

		Tax
Taxable income.	$16,778	
Tax on $16,000	(16,000)	$1,741
Tax on excess at 18%.	$ 778	140
Total tax.		$1,881

Adam and Eve, having taxable income less than $50,000, could have used the Tax Table (Exhibit 27-3, page 1069) to compute their tax for the year. The amount of the

EXHIBIT 27-3 Excerpts from the Tax Table.

(Based on taxable income for persons with taxable incomes of less than $50,000.)

If Line 37 (Taxable Income) Is —		And You Are —				If Line 37 (Taxable Income) Is —		And You Are —			
At Least	But Less Than	Single	Married Filing Jointly *	Married Filing Separately	Head of a Household	At Least	But Less Than	Single	Married Filing Jointly *	Married Filing Separately	Head of a Household
		Your Tax Is —						Your Tax Is —			
14,400	14,450	1,886	1,489	2,264	1,791	20,000	20,050	3,212	2,466	3,937	2,972
14,450	14,500	1,896	1,497	2,276	1,800	20,050	20,100	3,225	2,475	3,954	2,984
14,500	14,550	1,906	1,505	2,289	1,809	20,100	20,150	3,238	2,484	3,970	2,996
14,550	14,600	1,916	1,513	2,301	1,818	20,150	20,200	3,251	2,493	3,987	3,008
14,600	14,650	1,926	1,521	2,314	1,827	20,200	20,250	3,264	2,503	4,003	3,020
14,650	14,700	1,936	1,529	2,326	1,836	20,250	20,300	3,277	2,514	4,020	3,032
14,700	14,750	1,946	1,537	2,339	1,845	20,300	20,350	3,290	2,525	4,036	3,044
14,750	14,800	1,956	1,545	2,351	1,854	20,350	20,400	3,303	2,536	4,053	3,056
14,800	14,850	1,966	1,553	2,364	1,863	20,400	20,450	3,316	2,547	4,069	3,068
14,850	14,900	1,976	1,561	2,376	1,872	20,450	20,500	3,329	2,558	4,086	3,080
14,900	14,950	1,986	1,569	2,389	1,881	20,500	20,550	3,342	2,569	4,102	3,092
14,950	15,000	1,996	1,577	2,402	1,890	20,550	20,600	3,355	2,580	4,119	3,104
16,600	16,650	2,375	1,854	2,864	2,219	22,000	22,050	3,732	2,899	4,597	3,452
16,650	16,700	2,386	1,863	2,878	2,229	22,050	22,100	3,745	2,910	4,614	3,464
16,700	16,750	2,398	1,872	2,892	2,239	22,100	22,150	3,758	2,921	4,630	3,476
16,750	16,800	2,409	1,881	2,906	2,249	22,150	22,200	3,771	2,932	4,647	3,488
16,800	16,850	2,421	1,890	2,920	2,259	22,200	22,250	3,784	2,943	4,663	3,500
16,850	16,900	2,432	1,899	2,934	2,269	22,250	22,300	3,797	2,954	4,680	3,512
16,900	16,950	2,444	1,908	2,948	2,279	22,300	22,350	3,810	2,965	4,696	3,524
16,950	17,000	2,455	1,917	2,962	2,289	22,350	22,400	3,823	2,976	4,713	3,536
18,600	18,650	2,848	2,214	3,475	2,636	25,000	25,050	4,573	3,571	5,694	4,233
18,650	18,700	2,861	2,223	3,492	2,648	25,050	25,100	4,588	3,584	5,713	4,247
18,700	18,750	2,874	2,232	3,508	2,660	25,100	25,150	4,603	3,596	5,732	4,261
18,750	18,800	2,887	2,241	3,525	2,672	25,150	25,200	4,618	3,609	5,751	4,275
18,800	18,850	2,900	2,250	3,541	2,684	25,200	25,250	4,633	3,621	5,770	4,289
18,850	18,900	2,913	2,259	3,558	2,696	25,250	25,300	4,648	3,634	5,789	4,303
18,900	18,950	2,926	2,268	3,574	2,708	25,300	25,350	4,663	3,646	5,808	4,317
18,950	19,000	2,939	2,277	3,591	2,720	25,350	25,400	4,678	3,659	5,827	4,331
						42,400	42,450	10,708	8,658	12,803	9,900
						42,450	42,500	10,729	8,675	12,824	9,917
						42,500	42,550	10,750	8,691	12,845	9,935
						42,550	42,600	10,771	8,708	12,866	9,952
						42,600	42,650	10,792	8,724	12,887	9,970
						42,650	42,700	10,813	8,741	12,908	9,987
						42,700	42,750	10,834	8,757	12,929	10,005
						42,750	42,800	10,855	8,774	12,950	10,022

tax from the table is found in the $16,750 to $16,800 bracket under "Married Filing Jointly" and is seen to be $1,881.

At this point Adam and Eve Taxpayer must compare the tax amount of $1,881 to the amount that has been withheld from their salaries by their employers in order to determine whether a refund is due or an additional amount must be mailed to the Internal Revenue Service by April 15. Assuming that the amount withheld is $2,387, Adam and Eve can expect a $506 refund upon filing their tax return.

PROPRIETORSHIPS

Income or loss from a proprietorship is part of an individual's gross income

Proprietorships are not taxable. However, the income or loss from a proprietorship is part of the owners' total gross income. Proprietorship income or loss must be reported on Schedule C (Form 1040), which is an income statement. The income or loss from the proprietorship is then transferred to Form 1040 to be included in gross income.

Schedule C, in general, is identical in form to the business entity's income statement. However, certain revenues and expenses may differ in amount from the income statement. That is because a different accounting method may be selected or required on the tax return. Where a selection can be made, we would select that alternative which would lower taxable income. For financial reporting, with the objective of fairly presenting operating results, a different accounting alternative may be selected.

Depreciation provides us with a good example. The tax law allows the accelerated cost recovery system (ACRS) to be used for most assets placed in service after December 31, 1980. For financial reporting, the straight-line method will most likely be selected.

Under ACRS assets are classified as 3-year property (autos, light trucks), 5-year property (equipment, furniture and fixtures, computers), or 15-year property (buildings). You must use these percentages to depreciate each class of property:

ACRS depreciation schedule

	3-Year	5-Year	15-Year
Year 1	25%	15%	12%
Year 2	38%	22%	10%
Year 3	37%	21%	9%
Year 4		21%	8%
Year 5		21%	7%
Year 6			7%
Years 7–15			6%

So for a $9,000 light truck purchased for business purposes, we could record depreciation over 3 years like this:

Year	ACRS Rate	Calculation	Depreciation
1	25%	.25 × $9,000	$2,250
2	38%	.38 × $9,000	3,420
3	37%	.37 × $9,000	3,330
Total			$9,000

Please note that even if the asset has a salvage value, it is *not* deducted from the $9,000.

Inventories provide another example. We could select the LIFO method of inventory cost identification. Before this selection is made, we should determine whether or not the LIFO selection will have a material effect on reducing taxable income. If a significant reduction is not evident, it may not be justifiable using LIFO since generally increased recordkeeping costs are incurred when LIFO is used. Further, if LIFO is selected, the tax code requires that it must also be used for financial statement purposes.

Our taxpayers, Adam and Eve, have some income that must be reported on Schedule C. Specifically, Adam operates a business as a proprietorship. Eve earns $10,000 in salary as a typist for a local CPA. Adam would determine his net profit from the business like this:

Schedule C profit or (loss) from business or profession

Part I: Income
Gross receipts or sales $380,000
Less: Returns and allowances   5,000
Balance $375,000
Less: Cost of goods sold   225,000
　　Gross profit $150,000

Part II: Deductions
Advertising . . . . $ 4,600
Bad debts from sales or service   450
Depreciation   10,000
Insurance   2,350
Interest on business indebtedness   750
Pension and profit-sharing plans   7,500
Rent on business property   4,800
Supplies   1,800
Telephone   650
Utilities   3,600
Wages   98,400   134,900
Net profit . . . . $ 15,100

The net profit of $15,100 would be added to other items of gross income to determine total income for Adam and Eve Taxpayer.

Calculation of gross income

Gross income:
Wages, salaries, tips, etc. $10,000
Interest income ($250 − $50 exempt)   200
Dividends ($700 − $200 exclusion)   500
Business income or (loss) (attach Schedule C)   15,100
　　Total income $25,800

Notice the total income is the same amount as previously reported. We adjusted the example by reducing the wages from $25,100 to $10,000 and adding the $15,100 business income. The rest of the Form 1040 tax return would then be identical to what we showed you before.

On the following five pages we have included an actual completed tax return for Adam and Eve Taxpayer. This should help you see how Schedule A—Itemized Deductions, Schedule B—Interest and Dividend Income, and Schedule C—Profit or (Loss) from a Business or Profession, tie in to the basic Form 1040.

EXHIBIT 27-4a   U.S. Individual Income Tax Return, Form 1040 (Side 1).

Form **1040**
Department of the Treasury—Internal Revenue Service

U.S. Individual Income Tax Return 1984 (O)

For the year January 1-December 31, 1984, or other tax year beginning _____ , 1984, ending _____ , 19___ | OMB No. 1545-0074

Use IRS label. Otherwise, please print or type.

Your first name and initial (if joint return, also give spouse's name and initial) | Last name

Adam and Eve Taxpayer

Your social security number: 126 : 72 : 3415

Present home address (Number and street, including apartment number, or rural route)

1425 Lehigh Drive

Spouse's social security number: 615 : 10 : 4201

City, town or post office, State, and ZIP code

Bethlehem, Indiana   33511

Your occupation **Boilermaker**

Spouse's occupation **Typist**

Presidential Election Campaign ▶ Do you want $1 to go to this fund? . . . . [x] Yes [ ] No

If joint return, does your spouse want $1 to go to this fund? . . [x] Yes [ ] No

Note: Checking "Yes" will not change your tax or reduce your refund.

For Privacy Act and Paperwork Reduction Act Notice, see Instructions.

Filing Status

Check only one box.

1 [ ] Single

2 [x] Married filing joint return (even if only one had income)

3 [ ] Married filing separate return. Enter spouse's social security no. above and full name here. _____

4 [ ] Head of household (with qualifying person). (See page 5 of Instructions.) If the qualifying person is your unmarried child but not your dependent, write child's name here. _____

5 [ ] Qualifying widow(er) with dependent child (Year spouse died ▶ 19___). (See page 6 of Instructions.)

Exemptions

Always check the box labeled Yourself. Check other boxes if they apply.

6a [x] Yourself   [ ] 65 or over   [ ] Blind

b [x] Spouse   [ ] 65 or over   [ ] Blind

} Enter number of boxes checked on 6a and b ▶ **2**

c First names of your dependent children who lived with you **Thomas**

Julia

Enter number of children listed on 6c ▶ **2**

d Other dependents:

(1) Name	(2) Relationship	(3) Number of months lived in your home	(4) Did dependent have income of $1,000 or more?	(5) Did you provide more than one-half of dependent's support?

Enter number of other dependents ▶ **4**

e Total number of exemptions claimed (also complete line 36). . . . .

Add numbers entered in boxes above ▶ [ ]

Income

Please attach Copy B of your Forms W-2, W-2G, and W-2P here.

If you do not have a W-2, see page 4 of Instructions.

7	Wages, salaries, tips, etc.	7	10,000
8	Interest income *(also attach Schedule B if over $400)* . . .	8	200
9a	Dividends *(also attach Schedule B if over $400)* 700 , 9b Exclusion 200		
c	Subtract line 9b from line 9a and enter the result	9c	500
10	Refunds of State and local income taxes, from the worksheet on page 9 of Instructions *(do not enter an amount unless you itemized deductions for those taxes in an earlier year—see page 9)*	10	
11	Alimony received	11	
12	Business income or (loss) *(attach Schedule C)*	12	15,100
13	Capital gain or (loss) *(attach Schedule D)*	13	
14	40% of capital gain distributions not reported on line 13 (see page 9 of Instructions) . . .	14	
15	Supplemental gains or (losses) *(attach Form 4797)*	15	
16	Fully taxable pensions, IRA distributions, and annuities not reported on line 17 . . .	16	
17a	Other pensions and annuities, including rollovers. Total received 17a		
b	Taxable amount, if any, from the worksheet on page 10 of Instructions	17b	
18	Rents, royalties, partnerships, estates, trusts, etc. *(attach Schedule E)* . . .	18	
19	Farm income or (loss) *(attach Schedule F)*	19	
20a	Unemployment compensation (insurance). Total received 20a		
b	Taxable amount, if any, from the worksheet on page 10 of Instructions	20b	
21a	Social security benefits. (see page 10 of Instructions) . . . 21a		
b	Taxable amount, if any, from the worksheet on page 11 of Instructions	21b	
22	Other income (state nature and source—see page 11 of Instructions) _____	22	
23	Add lines 7 through 22. This is your **total income** . . . . ▶	23	25,800

Please attach check or money order here.

Adjustments to Income

(See Instructions on page 11)

24	Moving expense *(attach Form 3903 or 3903F)*	24	2,500	
25	Employee business expenses *(attach Form 2106)*	25	400	
26a	IRA deduction, from the worksheet on page 12	26a		
b	Enter here IRA payments you made in 1985 that are included in line 26a above ▶			
27	Payments to a Keogh *(H.R. 10)* retirement plan	27		
28	Penalty on early withdrawal of savings	28		
29	Alimony paid	29		
30	Deduction for a married couple when both work *(attach Schedule W)*	30		
31	Add lines 24 through 30. These are your **total adjustments** . . . . ▶	31	2,900	

Adjusted Gross Income

32	Subtract line 31 from line 23. This is your **adjusted gross income**. If this line is less than $10,000, see "Earned Income Credit" (line 59) on page 16 of Instructions. If you want IRS to figure your tax, see page 12 of Instructions. . . . . . . ▶	32	22,900

EXHIBIT 27-4b (Side 2)

Form 1040 (1984)   Page **2**

Tax Compu- tation	**33**	Amount from line 32 (adjusted gross income)	**33**	22,900
	34a	If you itemize, attach Schedule A (Form 1040) and enter the amount from Schedule A, line 26	**34a**	2,122
(See Instruc- tions on page 13.)		**Caution:** If you have unearned income and can be claimed as a dependent on your parent's return, check here ▶ ☐ and see page 13 of the Instructions. Also see page 13 if: • You are married filing a separate return and your spouse itemizes deductions, OR • You file Form 4563, OR • You are a dual-status alien.		
	34b	If you do not itemize deductions, and you have charitable contributions, complete the worksheet on page 14. Then enter the allowable part of your contributions here	**34b**	
	35	Subtract line 34a or 34b, whichever applies, from line 33	**35**	20,778
	36	Multiply $1,000 by the total number of exemptions claimed on Form 1040, line 6e	**36**	4,000
	37	Taxable Income. Subtract line 36 from line 35	**37**	16,778
	38	Tax. Enter tax here and check if from ☐ Tax Table, ☐ Tax Rate Schedule X, Y, or Z, or ☐ Schedule G	**38**	1,881
	39	Additional Taxes. (See page 14 of Instructions.) Enter here and check if from ☐ Form 4970, ☐ Form 4972, or ☐ Form 5544	**39**	
	40	Add lines 38 and 39. Enter the total . . . . ▶	**40**	1,881

Credits (See Instruc- tions on page 14.)	**41**	Credit for child and dependent care expenses (attach Form 2441)	**41**	
	42	Credit for the elderly and the permanently and totally disabled (attach Schedule R)	**42**	
	43	Residential energy credit (attach Form 5695)	**43**	
	44	Partial credit for political contributions for which you have receipts	**44**	
	45	Add lines 41 through 44. These are your total personal credits . . .		**45**
	46	Subtract line 45 from 40. Enter the result (but not less than zero) . .		**46**
	47	Foreign tax credit (attach Form 1116)	**47**	
	48	General business credit. Check if from ☐ Form 3800, ☐ Form 3468, ☐ Form 5884, ☐ Form 6478	**48**	
	49	Add lines 47 and 48. These are your total business and other credits		**49**
	50	Subtract line 49 from 46. Enter the result (but not less than zero). . . . . . . ▶		**50**

Other Taxes (Including Advance EIC Payments)	**51**	Self-employment tax (attach Schedule SE)		**51**
	52	Alternative minimum tax (attach Form 6251)		**52**
	53	Tax from recapture of investment credit (attach Form 4255)		**53**
	54	Social security tax on tip income not reported to employer (attach Form 4137) . . .		**54**
	55	Tax on an IRA (attach Form 5329)		**55**
■	**56**	Add lines 50 through 55. This is your **total tax** . . . . ▶		**56**

Payments Attach Forms W-2, W-2G, and W-2P to front.	**57**	Federal income tax withheld	**57**	2,387
	58	1984 estimated tax payments and amount applied from 1983 return.	**58**	
	59	Earned income credit. If line 33 is under $10,000, see page 16 . .	**59**	
	60	Amount paid with Form 4868	**60**	
	61	Excess social security tax and RRTA tax withheld (two or more employers)	**61**	
	62	Credit for Federal tax on gasoline and special fuels (attach Form 4136) . . .	**62**	
	63	Regulated Investment Company credit (attach Form 2439) . . .	**63**	
	64	Add lines 57 through 63. These are your **total payments** . . . . . . ▶	**64**	2,387

Refund or Amount You Owe	**65**	If line 64 is larger than line 56, enter amount **OVERPAID** . . . . ▶	**65**	
	66	Amount of line 65 to be **REFUNDED TO YOU** . . . . ▶	**66**	506
	67	Amount of line 65 to be applied to your 1985 estimated tax . . . ▶ **67**	0	
	68	If line 56 is larger than line 64, enter **AMOUNT YOU OWE.** Attach check or money order for full amount payable to "Internal Revenue Service." Write your social security number and "1984 Form 1040" on it . . . ▶ (Check ▶ ☐ if Form 2210 (2210F) is attached. See page 17 of Instructions.) $	**68**	

Please Sign Here
Under penalties of perjury, I declare that I have examined this return and accompanying schedules and statements, and to the best of my knowledge and belief, they are true, correct, and complete. Declaration of preparer (other than taxpayer) is based on all information of which preparer has any knowledge.

▶ *Adam Taxpayer* ▶ |4-15-85| ▶ *Eve Taxpayer*
Your signature   Date   Spouse's signature (if filing jointly, BOTH must sign)

Paid Preparer's Use Only

Preparer's signature ▶		Date	Check if self-employed ☐	Preparer's social security no.
Firm's name (or yours, if self-employed) and address ▶			E.I. No.	
			ZIP code	

EXHIBIT 27-5a   Schedule A (Itemized Deductions).

SCHEDULES A&B (Form 1040) Department of the Treasury Internal Revenue Service (O)		**Schedule A—Itemized Deductions** (Schedule B is on back) ▶ Attach to Form 1040. ▶ See Instructions for Schedules A and B (Form 1040).			OMB No. 1545-0074 19**84** 07

Name(s) as shown on Form 1040   Adam and Eve Taxpayer   Your social security number   126 : 72 : 3415

Medical and Dental Expenses (Do not include expenses reimbursed or paid by others.) (See Instructions on page 19)	**1** Prescription medicines and drugs; and insulin (375–125)	**1**	250	
	2 a Doctors, dentists, nurses, hospitals, insurance premiums you paid for medical and dental care, etc. (2829+700 −1450)	**2a**	2079	
	b Transportation and lodging	**2b**		
	c Other (list—include hearing aids, dentures, eyeglasses, etc.) ▶.................	**2c**		
	3 Add lines 1 through 2c, and write the total here	**3**	2329	
	4 Multiply the amount on Form 1040, line 33, by 5% (.05)	**4**	1145	
	5 Subtract line 4 from line 3. If zero or less, write -0-. **Total** medical and dental . ▶	**5**		1,184
Taxes You Paid (See Instructions on page 20)	**6** State and local income taxes	**6**	420	
	7 Real estate taxes	**7**	509	
	8 a General sales tax (see sales tax tables in instruction booklet)	**8a**	299	
	b General sales tax on motor vehicles	**8b**		
	9 Other taxes (list—include personal property taxes) ▶........	**9**		
	10 Add the amounts on lines 6 through 9. Write the total here. **Total** taxes . ▶	**10**		1,228
Interest You Paid (See Instructions on page 20)	**11 a** Home mortgage interest you paid to financial institutions	**11a**	1,750	
	b Home mortgage interest you paid to individuals (show that person's name and address) ▶........................	**11b**		
	12 Total credit card and charge account interest you paid	**12**	125	
	13 Other interest you paid (list) ▶ Auto loan	**13**	315	
	14 Add the amounts on lines 11a through 13. Write the total here. **Total** interest . ▶	**14**		2,190
Contributions You Made (See Instructions on page 20)	**15 a** Cash contributions. (If you gave $3,000 or more to any one organization, report those contributions on line 15b.)	**15a**	600	
	b Cash contributions totaling $3,000 or more to any one organization. (Show to whom you gave and how much you gave.) ▶............................	**15b**		
	16 Other than cash (attach required statement)	**16**		
	17 Carryover from prior year	**17**		
	18 Add the amounts on lines 15a through 17. Write the total here. **Total** contributions . ▶	**18**		600
Casualty and Theft Losses	**19** Total casualty or theft loss(es). (You must attach Form 4684 or similar statement.) (see page 21 of Instructions) . ▶	**19**		
Miscellaneous Deductions (See Instructions on page 21)	**20** Union and professional dues	**20**	250	
	21 Tax return preparation fee	**21**		
	22 Other (list type and amount) ▶.................. ......Small tools ......Safe deposit box	**22**	55 15	
	23 Add the amounts on lines 20 through 22. Write the total here. **Total** miscellaneous . ▶	**23**		320
Summary of Itemized Deductions (See Instructions on page 22)	**24** Add the amounts on lines 5, 10, 14, 18, 19, and 23. Write your answer here.	**24**		5,522
	25 If you checked Form 1040 { Filing Status box 2 or 5, write $3,400 / Filing Status box 1 or 4, write $2,300 / Filing Status box 3, write $1,700 }	**25**		3,400
	26 Subtract line 25 from line 24. Write your answer here and on Form 1040, line 34a. (If line 25 is more than line 24, see the Instructions for line 26 on page 22.) . ▶	**26**		2,122

For Paperwork Reduction Act Notice, see Form 1040 Instructions.   Schedule A (Form 1040) 1984

EXHIBIT 27-5b   Schedule B (Interest and Dividend Income).

Schedules A&B (Form 1040) 1984   **Schedule B—Interest and Dividend Income**   08   OMB No. 1545-0074   Page **2**

Name(s) as shown on Form 1040 (Do not enter name and social security number if shown on other side.) | Your social security number

Part I Interest Income

(See Instructions on pages 8 and 22)

Also complete Part III.

If you received more than $400 in interest income, you must complete Part I and list ALL interest received. If you received interest as a nominee for another, or you received or paid accrued interest on securities transferred between interest payment dates, or you received any interest from an All-Savers Certificate, see page 22.

Interest income		Amount
1 Interest income from seller-financed mortgages. (See Instructions and show name of payer.) ▶	1	
2 Other interest income (list name of payer) ▶		
	2	
3 Add the amounts on lines 1 and 2. Write the total here and on Form 1040, line 8 ▶	3	

Part II Dividend Income

(See Instructions on pages 8 and 22)

Also complete Part III.

If you received more than $400 in gross dividends (including capital gain distributions) and other distributions on stock, or you are electing to exclude qualified reinvested dividends from a public utility, complete Part II. If you received dividends as a nominee for another, see page 22.

Name of payer		Amount
4 Bethlehem Steel Company		700
	4	
5 Add the amounts on line 4. Write the total here	5	700
6 Capital gain distributions. Enter here and on line 15, Schedule D.*	6	
7 Nontaxable distributions. (See Schedule D Instructions for adjustment to basis.)	7	
8 Exclusion of qualified reinvested dividends from a public utility. (See page 23 of Instructions.)	8	
9 Add the amounts on lines 6, 7, and 8. Write the total here	9	
10 Subtract line 9 from line 5. Write the result here and on Form 1040, line 9a ▶	10	700

If you received capital gain distributions for the year and you do not need Schedule D to report any other gains or losses, do not file that schedule. Instead, enter 40% of your capital gain distributions on Form 1040, line 14.

Part III Foreign Accounts and Foreign Trusts

(See Instructions on page 23)

If you received more than $400 of interest or dividends, OR if you had a foreign account or were a grantor of, or a transferor to, a foreign trust, you must answer both questions in Part III.

	Yes	No
11 At any time during the tax year, did you have an interest in or a signature or other authority over a bank account, securities account, or other financial account in a foreign country? (See page 23 of the Instructions for exceptions and filing requirements for Form TD F 90-22.1.)		X
If "Yes," write the name of the foreign country ▶		
12 Were you the grantor of, or transferor to, a foreign trust which existed during the current tax year, whether or not you have any beneficial interest in it? If "Yes," you may have to file Forms 3520, 3520-A, or 926.		X

For Paperwork Reduction Act Notice, see Form 1040 Instructions.   **Schedule B (Form 1040) 1984**

☆ U.S. GOVERNMENT PRINTING OFFICE: 1984—0-423-082 58-040-1110

EXHIBIT 27-6   Schedule C (Profit or Loss from Business or Profession).

SCHEDULE C
(Form 1040)

Department of the Treasury
Internal Revenue Service (0)

Profit or (Loss) From Business or Profession
(Sole Proprietorship)
Partnerships, Joint Ventures, etc., Must File Form 1065.

▶ Attach to Form 1040 or Form 1041.   ▶ See Instructions for Schedule C (Form 1040).

OMB No. 1545-0074

19 83
09

Name of proprietor	Social security number of proprietor
Adam Taxpayer	126 : 72 : 3415

A Main business activity (see Instructions) ▶ Retail Sales   ; product ▶ Plumbing supplies

B Business name and address ▶ 326 Front Street
Lutz, Indiana   33605

C Employer identification number

2 | 7 | 3 | 1 | 6 | 5 | 3 | 1 | 0

D Method(s) used to value closing inventory:
(1) ☐ Cost   **(2)** ☒ Lower of cost or market   **(3)** ☐ Other (attach explanation)

E Accounting method: **(1)** ☐ Cash   **(2)** ☒ Accrual   **(3)** ☐ Other (specify) ▶ . . . .

	Yes	No
F Was there any major change in determining quantities, costs, or valuations between opening and closing inventory? . . . . If "Yes," attach explanation.		X
G Did you deduct expenses for an office in your home?		X

PART I.—Income

1 a Gross receipts or sales	1a	380,000
b Less: Returns and allowances	1b	5,000
c Subtract line 1b from line 1a and enter the balance here	1c	375,000
2 Cost of goods sold and/or operations (Part III, line 8)	2	225,000
3 Subtract line 2 from line 1c and enter the **gross profit** here.	3	150,000
4 a Windfall Profit Tax Credit or Refund received in 1983 (see Instructions)	4a	
b Other income	4b	
5 Add lines 3, 4a, and 4b. This is the **gross income** . . . . ▶	5	150,000

PART II.—Deductions

6 Advertising	4,600	**23** Repairs		1,800
7 Bad debts from sales or services (Cash method taxpayers, see Instructions) .	450	**24** Supplies (not included in Part III) . .		
8 Bank service charges.		**25** Taxes (Do not include Windfall Profit Tax here. See line 29.)		
9 Car and truck expenses		**26** Travel and entertainment . . .		3,750
10 Commissions		**27** Utilities and telephone		
11 Depletion		**28 a** Wages 98,400		
12 Depreciation and Section 179 deduction from Form 4562 (not included in Part III) .	10,000	**b** Jobs credit		
		c Subtract line 28b from 28a . .		98,400
		29 Windfall Profit Tax withheld in 1983		
13 Dues and publications		**30** Other expenses (specify):		
14 Employee benefit programs		**a**		
15 Freight (not included in Part III) . . .	2,350	**b**		
16 Insurance	750	**c**		
17 Interest on business indebtedness . .		**d**		
18 Laundry and cleaning		**e**		
19 Legal and professional services . . .		**f**		
20 Office expense		**g**		
21 Pension and profit-sharing plans . . .	7,500	**h**		
22 Rent on business property	4,800	**i**		

31 Add amounts in columns for lines 6 through 30i. These are the **total deductions** . . . . ▶	31	134,400
32 Net profit or (loss). Subtract line 31 from line 5 and enter the result. If a profit, enter on Form 1040, line 12, and on Schedule SE, Part I, line 2 (or Form 1041, line 6). If a loss, go on to line 33	32	15,600

33 If you have a loss, you must answer this question: "Do you have amounts for which you are not at risk in this business (see Instructions)?" ☐ Yes ☐ No
If "Yes," you must attach Form 6198. If "No," enter the loss on Form 1040, line 12, and on Schedule SE, Part I, line 2 (or Form 1041, line 6).

PART III.—Cost of Goods Sold and/or Operations (See Schedule C Instructions for Part III)

1 Inventory at beginning of year (if different from last year's closing inventory, attach explanation)	1	12,360
2 Purchases less cost of items withdrawn for personal use	2	228,850
3 Cost of labor (do not include salary paid to yourself)	3	
4 Materials and supplies	4	
5 Other costs	5	
6 Add lines 1 through 5.	6	241,210
7 Less: Inventory at end of year	7	16,210
8 **Cost of goods sold and/or operations.** Subtract line 7 from line 6. Enter here and in Part I, line 2, above. . .	8	225,000

For Paperwork Reduction Act Notice, see Form 1040 Instructions.
⬦ U.S. GOVERNMENT PRINTING OFFICE 390-079-1983   13-134-8150

Schedule C (Form 1040) 1983

CONFUSING TERMS

We need to make a few final comments on income taxes for individuals. Many taxpayers confuse the tax meaning of the terms credits, deductions, exemptions, and exclusions. Each of these terms has a specific tax meaning. We haven't discussed credits in this brief presentation, but they are an important part of the tax code. Tax credits are allowed for such things as earned income (certain individuals can get a refundable tax credit of up to $550 if their earned income is less than $11,000); credit for the elderly (individuals age 65 or over can receive a 15% credit against their tax on all types of income up to a maximum of $2,500 for single persons and $3,750 for a couple filing a joint return); and qualified business property (a percentage of the qualified investment—called the Investment Tax Credit). The point we want to make is that credits are subtracted directly from the amount of the taxes due.

If the tax computed by an individual amounts to $15,000 and the investment tax credit is determined to be $900, then the credit is subtracted from the amount of taxes due and the amount paid to the Internal Revenue Service is $14,100 ($15,000 − $900).

Deductions are subtractions from gross income (moving expenses, for example), subtractions from adjusted gross income (medical expenses, for example), and expenses (a business-related deduction, such as depreciation). All of these items reduce the income subject to taxation.

Exemptions are fixed allowances in place of personal, living, or family expenses. They are allowed at the amount of $1,000 for each entitled exemption. The allowable exemptions are for dependents, old age, and blindness. Exemptions, like deductions, are subtractions from income.

Finally, *exclusions* are items that are not included in the determination of gross taxable income. Interest on state and municipal bonds are entirely excluded from gross income. So are the proceeds of life insurance policies paid by reason of death; and the $100 dividend exclusion ($200 on a joint return).

PARTNERSHIPS

Partnerships are not taxable, but they must prepare a return

Like proprietorships, partnerships are not taxable. But partnerships are required to prepare a return, U.S. Partnership Return of Income, Form 1065.

The partnership return must be accompanied by several important schedules. For each partner a Schedule K-1 Partner's Share of Income, Credits, Deductions, etc., must be prepared. A copy of Schedule K-1 is given to each partner so that the partner's share of the partnership income may be reported on the individual partner's personal Form 1040 tax return as part of gross income. A partnership balance sheet is required on Schedule L and a reconciliation of partners' capital accounts is required on Schedule M.

CORPORATIONS

Corporations are taxable and must file an income tax return using Form 1120, U.S. Corporation Income Tax Return. This form, which is supported by various schedules, is also similar to an income statement. The corporation is, for the most part, subject to the same rules of income and deduction determination as the proprietorship and partnership. Certain special deductions, however, are available to the corporation. Two such provisions are briefly mentioned below.

A corporation may deduct 85% of the dividends from taxable domestic corporations. Charitable contributions made by a corporation are deductible to a limit of 10% of taxable income. Excess contributions may be carried over to each of the following 5 years.

The corporation tax is based on its taxable income determined according to the following schedule:

If the Taxable Income Is: Over —	But Not Over —	The Tax Is	Of the Amount Over —
$ 0	$ 25,000	15%	$ 0
25,000	50,000	$ 3,750 + 18%	25,000
50,000	75,000	8,250 + 30%	50,000
75,000	100,000	15,750 + 40%	75,000
100,000	—	25,750 + 46%	100,000

If you are a shareholder of a corporation, you face a double taxation problem. First, the income earned by the corporation is taxed. Then, as the income is distributed to you in the form of dividends, it is taxed as part of your personal income.

Certain corporations, having no more than 35 shareholders, may elect not to be subject to income tax. They are treated as partnerships. These are referred to as Subchapter S corporations. Shareholders must report on their individual tax returns under gross income the dividends received from the corporations plus their pro rata shares of the corporation's undistributed taxable income. Salaries received from the corporation would, of course, also be included as gross income on the individual's return. Form 1120-S is used to report Subchapter S corporations. If a Subchapter S election is made, the dividend exclusion is not allowed on the individual shareholder's personal return.

Taxpayers would generally elect the Subchapter S option if the amount of total tax on the individual returns under Subchapter S is less than the tax on the individual returns plus the corporate return. For example, assume that a corporation owned equally by four shareholders has taxable income for the current year of $19,600. Further assume that each of the shareholders is married and files a joint return and has personal income of $17,000 before consideration of the income (or dividends) of the corporation. If the Subchapter S option is not elected, the corporation's aftertax income would be determined as follows:

Corporate income before taxes	$19,600
Less: Income taxes ($19,600 × 15%).	2,940
Corporate income after taxes.	$16,660

The corporation distributes the $16,660 income as dividends equally to the four shareholders, $4,165 to each. The amount of aftertax income for each of the four shareholders would be:

Taxable income before receiving dividends	$17,000
Dividend income ($4,165 − $200 exclusion)	3,965
Taxable income.	$20,965
Tax from Schedule Y [$2,497 + (.22)($20,965 − $20,200)].	2,665
Income after tax.	$18,300

DO SOMETHING EVEN IF IT'S WRONG

"Corporate executives view the nation's ever-changing tax code as an exotic form of governmental torture, a mine field through which they must annually pick their way, constantly alert for tax traps that could maim corporate earnings." So writes Gary Hector in the November 26, 1984, *Fortune* magazine. The point of this article is that executives must make decisions concerning long-range projects costing many millions of dollars that will affect their corporation's earnings for years to come, and the tax consequences of those decisions may not be known at the same time the decision needs to be made.

When Congress considers new tax legislation, corporate tax staffs work overtime analyzing the effect of congressional thinking on their corporate projects. Changes in congressional thinking naturally cause changes in analyzing projects. Even when tax legislation is passed by Congress, corporate executives are shooting in the dark because the Internal Revenue Service must interpret what Congress had in mind by is-

suing tax regulations. And that may be months (even years) after the legislation is passed.

Executives are paid handsomely for their decision making ability so there comes a time when a decision must be made. Considering that there are many options available for investment opportunities, rational executives would select those projects that provide an adequate return within an acceptable risk factor. And the uncertainty of the tax situation may move an acceptable project to an unacceptable status. Sometimes, however, decisions have to be made concerning existing projects when the tax status is uncertain.

Take for example the decision National Semiconductor Corporation had to make in 1985. During the first half of 1985 the company installed $50 million of equipment in its new research and development (R&D) facility. Now at that time Congress was considering whether or not to renew the 25% tax credit for research and development expenditures. If the tax credit was extended

National Semiconductor would be better off leasing the equipment. But if the tax credit was not extended the better decision would be to buy the equipment and take the investment tax credit.

Or consider Liggett & Myers, the leading U.S. manufacturer of generic cigarettes. In 1982 Congress increased the excise tax on cigarettes from 8 cents a pack to 16 cents a pack. This caused regular cigarette sales to drop and generic sales to increase. In 1985 Congress was considering whether or not to continue the excise tax or to allow it to revert back to 8 cents a pack. With the excise tax at 8 cents generic sales might evaporate. So if the law held at 16 cents it would be best to expand generic sales, but if the law went to 8 cents a better decision would be to switch back to brand names. And the decision had to be made before Congress acted.

Under Subchapter S the amount of income after tax for each shareholder would be:

Taxable income before including Subchapter S income.	$17,000
Subchapter S income ($19,600 ÷ 4).	4,900
Taxable income.	$21,900
Tax from Schedule Y [$2,497 + (.22)($21,900 − $20,200)].	2,871
Income after tax	$19,029

Each shareholder is better off by $729 ($19,029 − $18,300) by electing the Subchapter S option.

INCOME TAXES AND THE FINANCIAL STATEMENTS

We are now going to discuss a very difficult and controversial topic. It is called *income tax allocation,* and it arises because of the differences between financial accounting and tax accounting. Remember, we stated when we started this chapter that the objective of financial accounting is to report fairly a business entity's financial position (the balance sheet) and results of operations (the income statement). We do this by following generally accepted accounting principles. And we must also prepare tax returns fairly, in accordance with the tax code. For many transactions the amount we show on the financial statements and the amount we show on the tax return are identical. But certain transactions are treated differently on the tax return than on the financial statements. It is these transactions that cause the problem.

We need look at only one of these transactions to see the problem, but it will take us a few pages to explain why it is a problem. The transaction we will look at is depreciation. Let's work with several light trucks costing a total of $70,300. The trucks have a 5-year life and will be depreciated on the financial statements using the straight-line method. That works out to be $14,060 per year ($70,300 ÷ 5 years). But on the tax return we will use the ACRS for 3-year property (25%, 38%, and 37%). And that will be $17,575 the first year, $26,714 the second year, and $26,011 the third year. Now let's assume that we have income before depreciation and income taxes of $44,060 for each of the next 5 years, say, 1985 to 1989.

If the income tax rate is 40%, this is how the net income would be determined on the five income statements:

	1985	1986	1987	1988	1989	Total
Income before Depreciation and Income Taxes	$44,060	$44,060	$44,060	$44,060	$44,060	$220,300
Depreciation Expense	14,060	14,060	14,060	14,060	14,060	70,300
Income before Income Tax	$30,000	$30,000	$30,000	$30,000	$30,000	$150,000
Income Tax Expense	12,000	12,000	12,000	12,000	12,000	60,000
Net Income	$18,000	$18,000	$18,000	$18,000	$18,000	$ 90,000

The income statements reflect $18,000 net income each and every year and the income taxes are a constant $12,000. That's because we followed generally accepted accounting principles. The income tax expense is considered to be an expense of doing business, the company is considered to be a going concern, and the matching concept tells us to match the expenses incurred in the period against the revenues. The income tax expense is determined by taking the *accounting income* subject to income taxes and computing the income tax expense on that income. All well and good. But we do not pay $12,000 taxes each and every year. We will pay $60,000 over the 5 years, but not $12,000 each year. This is what we have to pay the government in each of the 5 years:

	1985	1986	1987	1988	1989	Total
Income before depreciation	$44,060	$44,060	$44,060	$44,060	$44,060	$220,000
Tax depreciation	17,575	26,714	26,011			70,300
Taxable income	$26,485	$17,346	$18,049	$44,060	$44,060	$150,000
Taxes payable	10,594	6,938	7,220	17,624	17,624	60,000

We use the tax depreciation to compute taxable income, and the income taxes we pay are computed to be 40% of taxable income. Now let's make the entry to record the tax expense for the year 1985:

Income Tax Expense ($30,000)(.4)	12,000	
Deferred Income Taxes		1,406
Income Taxes Payable ($26,485)(.4)		10,594

To record income tax expense and liability for income taxes for the year.

The debit of $12,000 to Income Tax Expense does not equal the credit of $10,594 to Income Tax Payable. The debits do not equal the credits. A credit balance of $1,406 is created, which we call ***Deferred Income Taxes.*** The view is that $1,406 of income taxes are deferred until later years when the income taxes payable will exceed the income tax expense. Remember that the total income tax expense is $60,000, as is the total income taxes payable. It is the timing of the two items (book depreciation and tax depreciation) that is causing the temporary imbalance. Look at the summary entries below for the 5-year period of time and you can see how the deferred income taxes are eventually paid:

	1985	1986	1987	1988	1989	Total
Income Tax Expense	$ 12,000	$12,000	$12,000	$ 12,000	$ 12,000	$60,000
Deferred Income Taxes	(1,406)	(5,062)	(4,780)	5,624	5,624	
Income Taxes Payable.	(10,594)	(6,938)	(7,220)	(17,624)	(17,624)	60,000

Note that the items in parentheses are credits.

In the first 3 years we have ***originating*** deferred income taxes and in the last 2 years we have ***reversing*** deferred income taxes.

The deferred income tax account would appear on the balance sheet as a liability. And here is where the controversy starts.

The deferred income tax is *not a liability.* We only owe the government $10,594 in 1985, we do not owe the government $12,000. But that is what we have recorded as the tax expense. The deferred income tax balanced the tax entries, and we can see that over the next 5 years the tax expense and the taxes payable will both equal $60,000. But the fact remains that as of the end of 1985, we owe the government $10,594, not $12,000. What we have done is to use accounting income subject to taxation to determine the income tax expense. Well, why not just subtract from the $30,000 accounting income before taxes the amount of the taxes payable? This is what would result:

	1985	1986	1987	1988	1989	Total
Income before Income Taxes	$30,000	$30,000	$30,000	$30,000	$30,000	$150,000
Income Taxes Payable . .	10,594	6,938	$ 7,220	17,624	17,624	60,000
Net Income	$19,406	$23,062	$22,780	$12,376	$12,376	$ 90,000

If we report these figures as net income, look how our net income bounces around. We had $30,000 income before taxes each year. Doesn't it seem to follow, then, that the net income should also be a constant percentage of the income before taxes, or $18,000 in this case? But that's what we did before, and we created that funny liability that isn't a liability — deferred income taxes. One more thought and we can leave this topic for the accountants to solve. We said that over the 5 years the originating deferred income taxes will reverse themselves. That's true of any individual item such as our $70,300 of light trucks, but suppose that we buy some more light trucks in 1990 and more every year thereafter. It's true that the first group of light trucks will be retired in 1989, but they will be replaced that year and some additional trucks will be acquired. The point is that the asset causing the depreciation book and tax differences will continue to grow, and as a result the deferred income tax account in the *aggregate* will also grow. It will not reverse (in the aggregate). The fact is that many corporations in the United States today have very substantial deferred tax accounts on their books. And the meaning of these accounts is in question.

CHAPTER SUMMARY

Income taxes are imposed on individuals and corporations, not proprietorships and partnerships. The amount of income taxes an individual must pay is determined by applying the appropriate tax rate to the individual's *taxable income.* And an individual's taxable income is determined by starting with *gross income* (salaries and wages, interest income, dividend income, business income, partnership income, rent income, royalty income, farm income, and other income) and subtracting *adjustments to income.* Adjustments to income include such items as moving expenses and employee business expenses. The difference between gross income and adjustments to income is called *adjusted gross income* (AGI), which is a very important figure because a number of calculations are based on this figure and several tax tables use this figure. From adjusted gross income we subtract the itemized deductions and exemptions to arrive at taxable income. *Itemized deductions* consist of such items as medical expenses in excess of 5% of AGI; taxes (state and local income taxes, real estate taxes, and general sales taxes); interest expense; contributions; casualty and theft losses; and miscellaneous deductions. The total of the itemized deductions must be reduced by the *zero-bracket amount,* which is an allowance for itemized deductions the tax code gives every taxpayer, $3,400 for a married individual filing a joint return, $2,300 for an individual filing a single return, and $1,700 for a married individual filing a separate return.

Exemptions are deductions the tax code allows for personal expenses at the rate of $1,000 for each exemption. We are allowed exemptions for ourselves, our spouses, and anyone who qualifies as a dependent. Additional exemptions are allowed for age and blindness.

The amount of the tax liability is determined by selecting the appropriate tax schedule, such as Schedule Y, and applying the proper tax rate to the taxable income to calculate the tax liability, or by using the tax table if the adjusted gross income is less than $50,000.

If a business is operated as a proprietorship a Schedule C, Profit or (Loss) from Business or Profession, must be included with the individual return and the income or loss picked up as part of the gross income figure. The Schedule C is very much like an income statement except that tax rules are used to determine the revenues and expenses rather than generally accepted accounting principles. In many cases we have a choice as to the method of reporting the expense or revenue; for example, we could use the installment sales method of reporting revenues and the Accelerated Cost Recovery System (ACRS) method of reporting depreciation.

Corporate income taxes are based on applying the proper corporate tax rate to the corporate taxable income. Corporations with no more than 35 shareholders can elect to have the corporate taxable income reflected on the individual shareholders' tax returns, and consequently these corporations, called Subchapter S corporations, do not pay income taxes. The individual shareholders pay income taxes on the corporate earnings as part of their individual taxable income.

Income tax allocation is a difficult and controversial topic in financial accounting. It arises because there are differences between the way we report certain transactions on the financial statements and the way the same transactions are reported on the tax return. The income tax expense on the income statement is measured by applying the appropriate tax rate to the accounting income subject to income taxes. But the tax liability is determined by applying the appropriate tax rate to taxable income. The difference is called *deferred income taxes* and is reported as a liability on the balance sheet.

IMPORTANT TERMS USED IN THIS CHAPTER

Adjusted gross income   The difference between gross income and adjustments to income. (page 1064)

Adjustments to income   Subtractions from gross income such as moving expenses or employee business expenses. (page 1064)

Exemptions   A $1,000 deduction allowed for each taxpayer, his or her spouse, for each person who qualifies as a dependent, and for age and blindness. (page 1067)

Gross income   The total of various revenues of corporations. For individuals it consists of everything received for personal services as well as income from other sources. (page 1063)

Income tax allocation   The process of measuring income tax expense according to generally accepted accounting principles and income taxes payable according to the tax code, resulting in a difference called deferred income taxes. (page 1079)

Itemized deductions   Six categories of personal expenses that qualify as subtractions from adjusted gross income. (page 1064)

Subchapter S corporation   A tax election to have a corporation taxed as a partnership. (page 1078)

Taxable income   The result of subtracting adjustments to income, deductions, and exemptions from gross income. It is the base on which the tax rates are applied. (page 1067)

Zero-bracket amount   A standard deduction in lieu of the itemized deductions. (page 1064)

QUESTIONS

1. A business operated as a proprietorship or partnership does not pay any income taxes. Explain.

2. The only purpose of the tax laws is to generate revenues to finance government services. Comment.

3. How does an individual determine the amount of income that is subject to federal taxes?

4. The following terms are commonly used when preparing individual tax returns. Explain each term: *gross income, adjustments to income, itemized deductions,* and *exemptions.*

5. What is the difference between *adjustments to income* and *adjusted gross income?*

6. How is the medical expense deduction determined on an individual tax return?

7. Why is the figure *adjusted gross income* so important?

8. How is the deduction for sales taxes determined on an individual tax return?

9. The total amount of the itemized deductions for an individual is not the amount that the tax law allows an individual to claim on the tax return. Why not?

10. How does an individual determine the amount of taxes that he or she must pay to the Internal Revenue Service after the amount of taxable income has been determined?

11. How does the Schedule C Profit or (Loss) from Business or Profession differ from an income statement?

12. Explain the difference between the terms *credits, deductions, exceptions,* and *exclusions.*

13. What is a *Subchapter S* corporation?

14. A corporation consisting of 15 stockholders should always select the Subchapter S option. Comment.

15. A corporation will pay taxes on the amount of net income it reports on its income statement. Comment.

16. What does the term *income tax allocation* mean?

EXERCISES

Exercise 27-1
Determining the amount of the medical deduction

Philip Pirrip and his wife have an adjusted gross income of $40,000 for the 1985 tax year. They have incurred the following medical and dental expenses: medical insurance premiums, $850; hospital bills totaling $4,500; drugs $700; dental bills totaling $1,250; other medical bills totaling $900. They have been reimbursed by their insurance company $2,300 on the hospital bill, $150 on the drugs, and $300 on the other medical bills. How much will Mr. and Mrs. Pirrip be allowed for the medical and dental deduction?

(Check figure: $3,450)

Exercise 27-2
Calculating the tax liability

Mr. and Mrs. Joe Gargery's gross income for 1985 amounts to $60,000. They are entitled to $6,300 of adjustments to income, a total of $8,500 itemized deductions before considering the zero-bracket amount, and six exemptions. A joint return is to be filed. Compute their tax liability for the year using both the tax table and Schedule Y.

(Check figures: $8,724; $8,716)

Exercise 27-3
Determining the amount of sales tax

Complete the table below using the proper optional sales tax table for the facts as presented:

State	Adjusted Gross Income	Exemptions	Optional Sales Tax
Indiana	$15,000	5	
Illinois	27,500	2	
Idaho	38,700	4	

Exercise 27-4
Calculating the corporate tax liability

Determine the amount of the corporate tax liability for a corporation having taxable income of:
a. $19,600   b. $40,700   c. $63,200   d. $6,500,000

[Check figure item (b): $6,576]

Exercise 27-5
Income tax expense journal entry

The Jolly Bargeman, a corporation, reports income before taxes on its income statement of $50,000 and has taxable income of $40,000 for the year 1985.

Prepare the general journal entry to record the tax expense and the taxes payable for the year assuming a 40% corporate tax rate.

Exercise 27-6
Preparing a table calculating deferred taxes

Barnard's Inn, Inc., acquired a new asset on January 1, 1985, costing $693,000. The asset is to be depreciated over 10 years using the straight-line method on the income statement, but it qualifies as a 5-year-life asset under the ACRS rules for the tax return. If the tax rate is 45%, what will be the balance in the deferred tax account at the end of year 6?

(Check figure: $124,740)

PROBLEMS
Set A

Problem A27-1
Preparing a comprehensive tax return

Mr. and Mrs. Herbert Pocket need help in preparing their tax return for the current year, and they have asked that you assist them. Mr. Pocket is employed by the Havisham Brewery as a brewmaster at a salary of $32,500. Mrs. Pocket earned $2,700 income as an Avon salesperson. In addition, the Pockets received dividends amounting to $2,500 and interest of $2,000. Included in the interest is income of $400 from the City of Indianapolis, Indiana, municipal bonds.

Mr. Pocket attended the Annual Brewmaster's convention in St. Louis in April of this year. He spent $375 for air fare, $425 for the motel (including meals), and $500 for registration fees. Upon his return he was reimbursed $750 by the Havisham Brewery.

The Pockets have a medical insurance policy with Blue Cross for which they paid $650 in premiums. They filed and received payment on claims for drugs, $175; hospital bills, $1,525; and doctors' bills, $1,250. The couple spent $650 on drugs, $2,514 for surgery on Mr. Pocket's kidney stone at Indianapolis General Hospital, and $1,800 to various doctors and dentists.

Mr. and Mrs. Pocket paid $1,050 in state income taxes, $1,790 in real estate taxes, and will use the optional sales tax table for the State of Indiana to determine the general sales taxes.

Interest on their home mortgage for the year amounted to $3,750, and the couple paid the following additional interest charges: credit cards, $150; auto loans, $1,760; and department store revolving charge accounts, $35.

Contributions paid by the Pockets were: First Church, $1,000; United Fund, $450; Girl Scouts, $100. The couple had no casualty losses during the year. On April 15 they paid an accountant $375 to help them with last year's tax return. Mr. Pocket belongs to the American Brewmaster's Association, which costs him $250 in annual membership fees.

Required

Prepare the tax return for the Pockets assuming that they are entitled to five exemptions and that they have $3,275 withheld by the Havisham Brewery for income taxes.

(Check figure: Tax due $309)

Problem A27-2
Determining the correct amount of tax liability

A recent article in the *Canterbury Clarion* revealed that Mr. Uriah Heep, Attorney at Law, was accused of misappropriating substantial sums entrusted to him by his partner, Mr. Wickfield, and a client, Miss Betsie Trotwood. Representing Mr. Wickfield and Miss Trotwood were two local attorneys, Mr. David (Trotwood) Copperfield—Miss Trotwood's nephew—and Mr. Tommy Traddles. As the local internal revenue agent you are interested in the case and become concerned that perhaps Mr. Heep has failed to file his most recent tax return properly. You request the Internal Revenue Center in Ogden, Utah, to send to your office in Pocatello, Idaho, a copy of Mr. Heep's return. The information contained on the return is summarized on page 1086.

From Schedule C			From Form 1040	
Receipts from law practice...............		$225,000	Business income	$44,000
Deductions:			Medical expenses................	(4,000)
Depreciation on			Taxes	(5,000)
Canterbury office	$25,000		Interest	(7,700)
Insurance	10,000		Contributions..................	(4,000)
Rent on office building	18,000		Casualty losses	(2,000)
Supplies	36,000		Miscellaneous.................	(4,500)
Telephone..................	12,000		Exemptions	(8,000)
Utilities	5,000		Taxable income................	$ 8,800
Wages	75,000		Taxes paid	$ 688
Total		181,000		
Net profit.........................		$ 44,000		

You exercise your legal right to obtain access to Mr. Heep's bank accounts with the Fifth National Bank of Canterbury, Idaho, and find the following information:

Cash Deposits

From law practice	$495,000
Cash dividends	25,000
Receipts from Blue Cross................	1,600

Cash Payments

State Farm Insurance	$ 1,000	Boise City Hospital..................	$1,950
Canterbury Office Rentals	6,000	Dr. Strong.	500
Ada County Office Supply	3,600	Idaho Drug Store	250
Boise Telephone Company..............	1,200	Property Taxes......................	870
Moscow Electric Company..............	500	Interest on Mortgage.................	971
Mrs. Peggotty	14,500	United Fund	10
Mr. Micawber	12,500	Blue Cross Premiums	380

Based on the above, you request a meeting with Mr. Heep to explain where he arrived at the figures on his tax return. At the meeting Mr. Heep, who states that he is indeed a most humble man, informs you that Mrs. Peggotty and Mr. Micawber are law clerks in his office and that Dr. Strong is the principal of the local school. Mr. Heep states that his business is mostly in cash and that he did not keep accounting records. The figures on the return represent his best judgment as to what he received and what he spent. The $1,600 from Blue Cross is for Mrs. Heep's illness, for which she was confined to the hospital.

You determine that Mr. Heep is married and is entitled to three exemptions. He claimed eight exemptions because he and his wife often feel like they are over 65 and sometimes have difficulty seeing at night. In addition, his dog Jip lives with them and they love him like a child. You determine that Mr. Heep is entitled to $579 in state sales taxes.

Required   Determine the correct amount of taxes that Mr. Heep should have paid.

(Check figure: Tax liability = $220,150)

Problem A27-3

Determining the corporate tax liability

Pumblechock Products, Inc., has just completed its first year of operations. Presented below is its income statement for the year ended December 31, 1985:

PUMBLECHOCK PRODUCTS, INC.
Income Statement
Year Ended December 31, 1985

Sales.		$1,950,000
Cost of Goods Sold		810,000
Gross Profit		$1,140,000
Operating Expenses:		
Salaries Expense.	$285,000	
Depreciation Expense	61,250	
Bad Debts Expense	12,500	
Interest Expense.	175,000	
Repairs Expense.	8,750	
Travel and Entertainment Expense	16,500	
Pollution-Control Amortization.	4,000	
Total Operating Expenses		563,000
Net Income		$ 577,000

Mr. Pumblechock is aware that he must prepare a federal tax return, and he asks your help with that task. He provides you with the following information:

a. Included in the sales figure are $150,000 of sales that were made in late November and in the month of December. Collections on these sales have not yet been received. The cash basis of accounting will be used on the tax return except for inventories.

b. The cost of goods sold was determined by using the FIFO method. If the LIFO method had been used, the cost of goods sold would have been $1,050,000. You advise Mr. Pumblechock that he should use the LIFO method because it will result in lower taxes, *but* that he must also use the LIFO method on the income statement. Mr. Pumblechock agrees to this.

c. From the balance sheet you observe the following accruals:

Salaries	$10,800
Interest.	12,500
Repairs	750
Travel and Entertainment	1,500

d. The amount of bad debts write-offs for the year were $7,250.

e. On January 1, 1985, the company acquired $90,000 of panel trucks, $180,000 of equipment, and a building costing $1,250,000 by borrowing $1,520,000 at 14% interest. For the income statement these assets were depreciated on the straight-line basis over 5, 15, and 40 years, respectively. The Accelerated Cost Recovery System must be used on the tax return.

f. The pollution-control facility was acquired on January 1 at a cost of $60,000 and is being amortized over 15 years. The tax law allows a 60-month amortization period.

Required

Revise the income statement to confirm to information that will be reported on the tax return (this would be Form 1120) to determine the taxable income and compute the amount of the tax liability.

(Check figure: Tax liability = $14,715)

Problem A27-4
Calculating the aftertax income using the Subchapter S election

Mr. and Mrs. James Steerforth own 30% of the Blunderstone Building Corporation, which qualifies as a Subchapter S corporation. In 1985 the corporation distributed all its profits as cash dividends to its shareholders. Presented below is a table listing different levels of pretax corporate income and the Steerforth's taxable income before receiving dividends from the Blunderstone Building Corporation:

Pretax Corporate Income	Individual Taxable Income before Receipt of Dividends
$ 300,000	$25,000
2,500,000	40,000

Required

For each level of pretax corporate income and the corresponding individual taxable income, compute the amount of aftertax income the Steerforths would have, assuming first that the Subchapter S election is not made, and then that the election is made. Use Schedule Y to compute the individual tax.

(Check figure: Aftertax income, Subchapter S elected at the $300,000 level = $75,626)

Problem A27-5
Determining the amount of deferred income taxes

Yarmouth Shipbuilding Company has reported income before taxes and depreciation of $100,000 for each of the 5 years between 1985 and 1989. The company's only depreciable asset consists of a company car acquired at a cost of $15,000 on January 1, 1985. The car is being depreciated over 5 years on the financial statements, but the Accelerated Cost Recovery System is being used on the tax return.

Required

1. Prepare a schedule that will compute net income for each of the 5 years assuming a 45% tax rate and that income tax allocation procedures are being followed.
2. Prepare a schedule that will compute income taxes payable for each of the 5 years.

(Check figure: Taxes payable, 1987 = $42,502)

3. Prepare general journal entries that will show the amount of the deferred income taxes at the end of each of the 5 years.

Problem A27-6
Determining the balance in the deferred tax account

Murdstone and Grinby's started business on January 1, 1982. On that date they acquired $75,000 of depreciable assets having a 5-year life for the financial statements but qualifying for the 3-year classification under the Accelerated Cost Recovery System for tax purposes. Each year thereafter the company acquired $75,000 of depreciable assets to handle their expanding business.

Required

Prepare a schedule computing the balance in the Deferred Income Tax account as of December 31, 1986, assuming a 45% tax rate.

(Check figure: Deferred income taxes, 1986 = $29,700)

Set B

Problem B27-1
Preparing a comprehensive tax return

Mr. and Mrs. Oliver Twist and their three children live in London, Illinois. The Twists' former accountant has retired and the couple is aware that you are studying business administration at the University of Northern Illinois and consequently ask if you will help with their tax return. Mr. Twist is engaged by Fagin Enterprises, where he earned $25,750. In addition, he earned $3,900 as a part-time employee at Sowerberry's Funeral Home and $1,750 dividends from the London Corporation. He also received $1,100 interest income including $175 from the city of London bonds.

In June of the 1985 tax year Mr. Twist attended the 14th Annual Pickpocketeers Convention, held at the Old Bailey Convention Center in downtown Burbank, California. His employer gave Mr. Twist $600 to attend the convention, but Mr. Twist spent $250 for the registration fee, $315 for airline tickets, and $425 for the hotel room and meals.

The Twists' son suffered a series of illnesses during the year that required hospitalization. The hospital bill was $3,353, of which the insurance policy covered only $2,475. Doctors' and dentists' bills for the son and the rest of the family amounted to $1,450 ($925 covered by insurance), and medicines and drugs amounted to $926 ($250 covered by insurance). The insurance policy was paid for by a $40 monthly payroll deduction.

In addition to the medical deductions, the Twists had the following deductible items:

Accounting services (for last year's return paid this year)...	$ 450	Illinois state income taxes	$ 650
		Red Cross...............	450
Auto loans (interest)........	1,150	Real estate taxes...........	1,435
Credit cards (interest)	370	Union dues.............	300
General sales taxes	?	United Church of London	1,000
Home mortgage interest......	1,950	United Fund............	600

Required

Using the information provided, prepare the tax return for the Twists assuming that federal income taxes have been withheld at a rate of $200 per month by Fagin Enterprises and that no taxes have been withheld by Sowerberry's.

(Check figure: Tax due = $136)

Problem B27-2
Determining the correct amount of tax liability

Presented below is information extracted from the 1985 tax return submitted by Mr. and Mrs. Bill Sikes:

From Schedule C		From Form 1040	
Receipts from professional activities	$125,000	Business income	$66,380
		Medical expenses.........	17,500
Insurance..............	600	Taxes	6,945
Rent.................	3,600	Interest	15,100
Supplies	450	Contributions...........	22,500
Telephone	270	Exemptions	6,000
Utilities..............	700	Taxable income	(1,665)

The Internal Revenue Service has determined, from a review of the Sikes' bank accounts, business records, and information obtained from customers and suppliers, the following information:

Receipts from customers amounted to $297,400.
Insurance expense was $150 per month.
Supplies were $900.
Telephone bills amounted to $2,700.
Wages paid to employees amounted to $73,000.
The rent and utilities were correct.

A review of the personal affairs of the couple revealed the following:

Dividends of $4,500 were received and the couple had $7,500 of unreimbursed moving expenses.

Bills for drugs were $3,200 and for other medical $12,185, a total of $15,385. However, the couple was reimbursed by insurance policies $800 on drugs and $2,500 on other medical expenses.

Property taxes and state income taxes were $870 and $2,300, respectively. General sales taxes were $775.

Interest was paid on the home mortgage, $3,300; and on auto loans, $1,800.

Contributions were made to the church, $1,950; and the Boy Scouts, $300.

The couple have two children, ages 6 and 4.

Since the reported taxable income was a negative $1,665, the couple did not pay any income taxes.

Required   Prepare a corrected tax return for Mr. and Mrs. Sikes.

(Check figure: Tax = $80,448)

Problem B27-3

Determining the corporate tax liability

Limbkins, Inc., operates an import-export business in Somewhere, New York. The business commenced operations on January 1, 1985, and was very successful. Presented below are the ledger accounts reflecting the accrual basis of accounting for the first year of operations:

Sales	$790,000	Bad Debts Expense	$5,400
Cost of Sales	559,000	Rent Expense	3,600
Salaries Expense	115,000	Repair Expense	2,100
Depreciation Expense	15,000	Organizational Costs	500
Interest Expense	13,500		

The federal tax return is due within a few days and the president of the company, Mr. Limbkins, asks you to prepare the return. You are able to obtain the following information:

a. The company acquired $50,000 of light trucks and autos, which it is depreciating over 5 years on the income statement. In addition, it acquired equipment costing $75,000, depreciating this amount over 15 years. The Accelerated Cost Recovery System will be used on the tax return.

b. The organization cost is being written off over 10 years on the income statement, but the tax law allows a write-off over 5 years.

c. If the LIFO method of inventory valuation is used on the tax return, it must also be used on the income statement. The FIFO method was used. LIFO would have increased the cost of goods sold by $12,300. Mr. Limbkins agrees to use LIFO and revise the income statement.

d. Sales in the amount of $4,500 have not yet been collected. Only the cash sales need be reported on the tax return.

e. The following accruals appear on the balance sheet:

Interest Payable	$2,500	Repairs Payable	$350
Salaries Payable	1,950		

f. Prepaid rent on the balance sheet totals $1,800.

g. Bad debts written off during the year amounted to $3,250.

Required   Using the information provided, prepare the 1985 corporate tax return.

(Check figure: Tax liability = $9,750)

Problem B27-4

Calculating the aftertax income using the Subchapter S election

Mr. and Mrs. Bumble have an ownership interest in a corporation that qualifies for the Subchapter S treatment. All the profits have been distributed by the corporation to the stockholders. Presented on page 1091 are two different levels of ownership, corporate income, and individual taxable income.

Ownership Interest	Pretax Corporate Income	Individual Taxable Income before Dividends
20%	$450,000	$30,000
40%	140,000	15,000

Required   Compute the amount of aftertax income for each case, assuming first that the Subchapter S election is not taken, and then that the election is taken. Use Schedule Y to compute the individual tax.

(Check figure: Aftertax income, Subchapter S election at the $140,000 level = $51,212)

Problem B27-5
Determining the amount of deferred income tax

On January 1, 1985, Clerkenwell Products, Inc., acquired a fleet of autos and light trucks costing a total of $750,000. The company will depreciate the fleet in its entirety over 5 years, but for tax purposes will use the Accelerated Cost Recovery System. For the years 1985 through 1989, the company estimates that income before taxes and depreciation will amount to $250,000 each year.

Required   1. Assuming a 40% tax rate, prepare a schedule computing net income in accordance with generally accepted accounting principles.
2. Prepare a schedule that will compute the amount of income taxes that must be paid each year.

(Check figure: Taxes payable, 1987 = − $11,000)

3. Prepare general journal entries that will show the amount of the deferred income taxes at the end of each of the 5 years.

Problem B27-6
Determining the balance in the deferred tax account

Artful Dodger Enterprises is an expanding business. The company started operations on January 1, 1982, and acquired $225,000 of depreciable assets classified as 3-year assets under the Accelerated Cost Recovery System. The company will depreciate these assets (no residual value) over 5 years on the books. In 1983 the company acquires another group of similar assets costing $225,000. And in 1984, 1985, and 1986 the company again acquires $225,000 of similar assets for each of those years.

Required   Prepare a schedule computing the balance in the Deferred Income Tax account as of December 31, 1986, assuming a 40% tax rate.

(Check figure: Deferred income taxes, 1986 = $79,200)

Index

Index

DATE DUE

Demco

KEY CONCEPTS IN MANAGERIAL ACCOUNTING

Cost Behavior Graphs

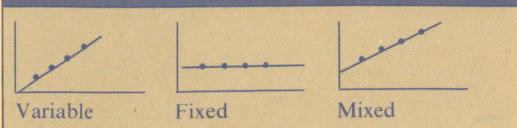

Variable   Fixed   Mixed

Different Formats for Net Income

Traditional	Contribution
Sales	Sales
— cost of goods sold	— total variable costs
= gross profit	= total contribution
— selling and	margin
administrative	— fixed costs
= net income	= net income

Key Terms Used in C-V-P Analysis

$$VC\% = \frac{\text{total costs}}{\text{total sales}} \text{ or } \frac{VCU}{\text{sales price}} \text{ or } 1\text{-}CM\%$$

$$CMU = \text{sales price} - VCU \text{ or } \frac{TCM}{\text{unit sales}}$$

$$CM\% = \frac{TCM}{\text{total sales}} \text{ or } \frac{CMU}{\text{sales price}} \text{ or } 1\text{-}VC\%$$

C-V-P Formulas
(X_1 = unit sales and X_2 = dollar sales)

Contribution Margin Technique:

$$X_1 = \frac{\text{fixed costs} + \text{net income}}{CMU}$$

or

$$X_2 = \frac{\text{fixed costs} + \text{net income}}{CM\%}$$

Income Equation Technique:

$$\text{Sales price } (X_1) - VCU (X_1) - \text{fixed costs} = \text{net income}$$

or

$$X_2 - VC\%(X_2) - \text{fixed costs} = \text{net income}$$

Evaluation of a Mixed Cost

Equation of a mixed cost:

$$Y = a + bX.$$

Determining the variable cost rate:

$$\text{Variable cost rate} = \frac{\text{difference in total costs}}{\text{difference in activity}}$$

Determining the fixed cost:

$$\text{Fixed cost} = \text{total mixed cost} - (\text{variable cost rate} \times \text{activity})$$

A Comparison of Direct and Absorption Costing

	Direct	Absorption
Product costs:	DM	DM
	DL	DL
	VFO	VFO
	—	FFO
Period costs:	FFO	—
	VS&A	VS&A
	FS&A	FS&A
Income higher when:	$Q_s > Q_p$	$Q_p > Q_s$

Variances from Variable Standard Costs:
Price Variance (PV) and Quantity Variance (QV)

Direct Materials:

PV = difference in actual and standard price per input $\times$ actual quantity purchased

QV = difference in actual quantity used and standard quantity allowed $\times$ standard price per input

Direct Labor and Variable Overhead:

PV = difference in actual and standard rate per hour $\times$ actual hours worked

QV = difference in actual hours worked and standard hours allowed $\times$ standard rate per hour